CASES — TEXT — MATERIALS

SCHLESINGER'S
COMPARATIVE LAW

SEVENTH EDITION

by

UGO A. MATTEI

Alfred and Hanna Fromm Professor of
International and Comparative Law,
University of California, Hastings College of Law
Professore Ordinario di Diritto Civile,
Universita' di Torino
Academic Coordinator, The International University College

TEEMU RUSKOLA

Professor of Law, Emory University School of Law

ANTONIO GIDI

Assistant Professor of Law, University of Houston Law Center

FOUNDATION PRESS
2009

THOMSON REUTERS™

© 1950, 1959, 1970, 1980, 1988, 1998 FOUNDATION PRESS

© 2009 By THOMSON REUTERS/FOUNDATION PRESS

      195 Broadway, 9th Floor

      New York, NY 10007

      Phone Toll Free 1–877–888–1330

      Fax (212) 367–6799

      foundation–press.com

Printed in the United States of America

ISBN 978–1–58778–591–7

To the memory of
RUDOLF BERTHOLD SCHLESINGER
1909–1996

*

PREFACE

It is with a profound sense of both humility and pride that we write this preface to the seventh edition of R.B. Schlesinger's Comparative Law. This was not only the first and leading casebook on the subject in the United States for the past sixty years, but it is also known and cited worldwide more than any other American casebook in any field and more than any other comparative law book published anywhere. Indeed, "the Schlesinger" is the almost casual product of a towering twentieth-century intellectual, a man of a stupendous range of knowledge, humanity, and brilliance who, like many others before World War II, came to the United States to escape Nazi brutality.

Schlesinger left Germany in 1933 as a fully formed German lawyer and legal scholar. Upon arriving in the United States, he taught himself English, obtained a new U.S. legal education at Columbia law School (where he was the first and quite likely the only non-native Editor in Chief of the *Columbia Law Review*), and (after the usual U.S. practicing *cursus honorum*) he accepted a teaching job at Cornell Law School. The first edition of this book, published in 1950, consisted of the teaching materials of the young German comparative law professor. One of Schlesinger's colleagues had given them to an editor at Foundation Press who was visiting at Cornell when Schlesinger happened to be out of town. In fact, Schlesinger came to know of the book only when, to his surprise, he received the proofs in the mail.[1] Schlesinger attended alone to several subsequent editions, which were published roughly every ten years. For the fifth edition (1988), he was joined by a distinguished team of co-authors: Hans Baade (Texas), Mirjan Damaška (Yale), and Peter Herzog (Syracuse). For the sixth edition (1998), Damaška left the team and was substituted by Edward Wise (Wayne State), while Schlesinger himself still remained an active lead author. Unfortunately, he never saw the final edition, because in 1996 he left this world together with his beloved lifetime companion, Puti.

The honor and responsibility to keep the book alive was bestowed by Schlesinger himself on Ugo Mattei, a former student and successor to the Chair of Comparative Law that Schlesinger held at the Hastings College of the Law at the time of his death. The project for this edition was initiated under the leadership of Hans Baade, early in 2000. Meanwhile, Ed Wise died prematurely and Baade and Herzog decided not to be involved in the project any more. Subsequently, Teemu Ruskola and Antonio Gidi (who took care of civil procedure) joined the team. Through a process of accre-

---

1. The story is told in the posthumously published R.B. Schlesinger, *Memoir* (Ugo Mattei & Andrea Pradi eds.2000).

tion, the Schlesinger has grown considerably over time, incorporating new work with each edition. The new team owes their first and greatest debt to their predecessors. Without their work, this book could never have been kept alive.

The philosophy of this seventh edition is best described as an apparently radical departure that belies a deeper intellectual continuity. The world and the scholarly community have changed enormously not only from 1950, which is obvious, but also in the intervening years since the publication of the sixth edition, which have witnessed unprecedented historical and intellectual transformations worldwide. (The fifth edition was published one year before the fall of the Berlin Wall). When the sixth edition was written, self-congratulatory Western "rule of law" rhetoric was at its peak. The Cold War, the onset of which had coincided with the publication of the first edition, was finally over, and the category of "socialist law" was fast disappearing from comparative legal scholarship. Questions regarding the convergence versus divergence of civil law and common law again occupied the center stage. Fortunately, the Schlesinger did not go as far in this direction as other dominant books in the field (e.g. Zweigert & Kötz), yet it too reflected the intellectual climate in which it was produced. During this same period, there emerged a younger cohort of scholars with interests beyond the traditional comparison between continental Europe and the United States. Again, it might have been because of the economic rise of Asia and the relative decline of Europe, but there was an increasing sense of urgency that a broader perspective is needed and that non-Western legal knowledge needs to be integrated with the mainstream study of comparative law, rather than segregating it in Area Studies or under the notion of "radically different cultures."

At the same time, with accelerating globalization the state was losing its centrality as the main producer and repository of law, and the structural linkage between law, sovereignty, and statehood was questioned even within the mainstream legal scholarship. Comparative lawyers were well aware of both supranational and subnational producers of law and of the need to incorporate them in a comparative framework. Meanwhile, post–9/11 legal transformations in the United States, Europe and the Middle East put tremendous stress on the rule of law in the West, yet they also provoked greater scholarly interest in understanding Islam and the legal experiences of the global South.

Some important conferences have been convened, and some important articles, monographs and even a few textbooks have been published that seek to take account of these various developments and their significance for the mainstream of comparative law. But the new editions of various comparative law casebooks, which remain crucial as the first introduction for most U.S. students to the subject, have remained largely unchanged as far as their basic organization and orientation are concerned. This is simply no longer tenable. In adapting the Schlesinger to the new circumstances of the twenty-first century, we have sought to return to the book's original philosophy. Given that from its inception the book has tended to focus on comparing the legal systems of various Western states, this may sound somewhat paradoxical.

The first edition of the Schlesinger was an extraordinary reflection of the state of the world at the time. Most fundamentally, it was motivated by a desire to re-open a vital dialogue between Europe and the United States, in order to re-establish a notion of international legality in the aftermath of the catastrophe of World War II. It also provided comparative law with an important first interpretation of legal realism, the most advanced scholarly paradigm of the time which gave the United States a considerable world-wide advantage. In this edition we went back to the principles of the original book. How would R.B Schlesinger have written his casebook today? His work always arose out of teaching which in turn focused on key legal transformations. Today, this means paying considerable attention to the East and the South as well to the changing sources of the law. Insofar as Schlesinger sought to open a dialogue where it was most urgent, today that means turning toward China and the Islamic world, most notably. And honoring Schlesinger's desire to incorporate cutting edge scholarship and new methods translates today to the adoption of a multi-disciplinary perspective that goes beyond the old state-centered paradigm.

We have sought to accomplish all of this, even though our intellectual capacities fall far short of those of R.B. Schlesinger. We have adopted the original three part structure of the first edition, with its first part devoted to method, its second part to sources and its third to in-depth study of specific issues. We have re-envisioned and "globalized" the first and the second parts of the book as much as possible. The third part now includes the dialogue on procedure with Comparovich (not included in the first edition) adapted by Professor Gidi. It now reflects more faithfully the early evolution of the case book, with some new materials on China and Islamic law.

In the ten-plus years during which the lead author has collected materials to set up the team and follow new developments, many generations of Hastings students have been involved directly or indirectly in this project. The lead author was a student at Hastings when the fifth edition first came out and he has taught for fifteen years from the fifth and sixth editions, even as they were growing increasingly obsolete. Thanks to students and their feedback, various organizational issues became evident. Important contributions came from Claire Harvey, Vanina Shakutrukul, Boris Mamlyuk, Cosmos Eubani, Saki Bailey, Avi Singh, Jacob Linetsky, Brian Walsh, Regina Burch, and many others.

When the final drafting took place, a team of Hastings students provided crucial assistance. Leah Price, Yuan Feng, Dong Ho Yoo, Joshua Horowitz, Wendy Yang, James Dallal, Candice Hyton, Matthew Haluk, and Mattew Watts all provided us with hours and hours of volunteer help. Without their help and friendship this edition would not have been possible.

Various scholars and friends were also kind enough to read portions of the manuscript as well as to provide suggestions, updates, and other help (without of course bearing responsibility for the inevitable flaws of the final product). Among them we thank especially Abdullahi An-na'im, David Bederman, Luisa Antoniolli, Mauro Bussani, David L. Eng, Ahmed Feiz, Martha Fineman, Francesca Fiorentini, Elisabetta Grande, Michele Graziadei, Marta Infantino, Luca Pes, Mathias Reimann, Kim Lane Scheppele, and Tibor Varady. We have discussed the project with Ralph Michaels and Franz Werro whom we also wish to thank.

Antonio Gidi has edited and adapted the entire part related to civil procedure: Chapter 6 (sections 3 and 4); Chapter 7 (section 8); Chapter 8 (sections 1, 2, 3). He wishes to thank Professor Stefaan Voet for his invaluable suggestions. He also wishes to thank Sebastien Chain, Florian Zweifel, and Charlotte Simon.

Ugo Mattei and Teemu Ruskola share responsibility for the rest.

UGO MATTEI &
TEEMU RUSKOLA

Airali, (Turin)
January 26, 2009

ANTONIO GIDI

Houston
January 28, 2009

INSTRUCTOR'S NOTE

A MESSAGE TO PROSPECTIVE TEACHERS
USING THE SCHLESINGER

Because comparative law is a subject in rapid transformation and because it has no objective canon or subject matter we need to spend a few words on the fundamental logic of the Shlesinger. We kept this logic that provides a framework within which every teacher should be able to interpret the discipline according to her own disposition.

The book is divided in three parts.

The first has two main purposes: a) setting the scene of the "legal world" that the student of comparative law has to explore in her own historical time; b) offering a reliable professional toolkit that the tradition of comparative law has produced in order to offer her a way to begin the "understanding" of such legal world. The first chapter is devoted to the first task and should allow the instructor to offer to the students a map of the current challenges that a non-formalistic and non-parochial approach to the law must meet. The second chapter keeps insisting on the first aim but also begins the exploration of our professional toolkit. The student will take home a sense of complexity and relativism but also a feeling that some fundamental understanding based on problems and questions asked is possible. The third chapter again offers a picture of how the law is in the interconnected world and explores some special methodological developments that should give to the comparative lawyer an "advantage" in approaching complexity.

The second part starts from the assumption that comparative law is the best approach to handle fundamental institutional settings, those that are not going to be changed with the strike of a legislator's pen. It thus has two main purposes: a) offering to the student a deep sense of continuity through time and space of that fundamental human experience called "the law"; b) making him familiar with the sources of law seen as a deeply rooted and culturally specific depository of knowledge that legal systems accumulate in the unfolding of their experience. This is why the chapters are devoted to the history (Chapter 4) and to the two most fundamental sources of the professional legal experience: legislation (Chapter 5) and case law (Chapter 6). The instructor should lead the student in a fascinating intellectual journey through time and space allowing her both to experience the uniqueness of her own system and the fundamental cultural and intellectual debt that her system has contracted with "the other".

Also the third part that is devoted to topics has a foundational ambition. In picking the organization of the legal profession (Chapter 7), procedure (Chapter 8) and a selection of fundamental private law issues

(Chapter 9), it approaches areas that could not be more central to the very way in which lawyers think and thus contribute to developing their own professional culture. All the topics are approached with a historical and comparative method and the main purpose is, again as it was in the first edition of this book, to give to the student that modicum of understanding of the technical peculiarities of the foreign legal experience (and of consciousness of her own) that will allow her to intelligently communicate with colleagues that have been trained outside of the United States.

No course of comparative law can possibly cover this entire book. A usual three-unit course on comparative law can reasonably cover with appropriate discussion approximately two-thirds of it. According to their personal sensibilities, teachers can easily choose any two of the three parts, each of which consists of three chapters (as in the original). For example, more traditionally inclined colleagues may wish to skip Part I and devote their efforts to Parts II and III (in whole or in part). Others might approach Parts I and II. But any combination should work. All chapters are self-contained and can be assigned separately in whatever order the teacher prefers to proceed. Only Chapter 6 (Sections 3 and 4) and 7 (Section 8) should be assigned before Chapter 8 for colleagues that are keen on putting procedure at the center of the stage.

SUMMARY OF CONTENTS

*

TABLE OF CONTENTS

*

TABLE OF CASES

Principal cases are in bold type. Non-principal cases are in roman type. References are to Pages.

TABLE OF AUTHORS

*

CASES — TEXT — MATERIALS

SCHLESINGER'S

COMPARATIVE LAW

*

PART ONE

THE NATURE OF GLOBAL LEGAL PROBLEMS

CHAPTER 1

BASIC TRANSFORMATIONS OF THE GLOBAL LEGAL CONTEXT

1. COMPARATIVE LAW AND GLOBALIZATION PROCESSES

In the last twenty years humankind has experienced a major phenomenon of economic and social transformation that has been labeled, using a neologism, "globalization," This phenomenon has produced an unprecedented degree of communication (and competition) among human beings located in different areas of the world.[1] Many behavioral patterns have consequently become more common than they used to be and a thick layer of dominant western culture has been imposed practically everywhere. To be sure, cultural differences have not disappeared, and they are still much more significant and deeply rooted than similarities. Nevertheless, they have been pushed somewhat in the shadow by the impressive extent of similarities that scholars in different disciplines relentlessly observe.

Law crystallizes patterns of behavior and reflects culture, so that "globalization" could not leave the law unaffected. There are practically no areas of the law that remain unchanged by the increased interaction among human beings located far away from each other. Contract law has to cope with an increasing number of trans-border transactions. Tort law has to deal with the potentially catastrophic impact of the global enterprise in order to secure accountability worldwide for major damage to the environment. Family law is affected by phenomena of immigration, and different labor laws, responsible for major human exploitation, determine largely the location of transnational economic production. In public law the partial surrender of state sovereignty to international institutions (G8, WTO, UN, IMF) is creating new and unprecedented problems producing a veritable revolution in the traditional hierarchy of the sources of law, still taught in law schools worldwide. Examples could be multiplied.

There is one law school discipline that more than any other is affected by these recent transformations. This discipline, the subject matter of this casebook, is comparative law. And in fact, in the last few years, comparative law has undergone unprecedented change, as an academic discipline and as a practical endeavor.[2]

---

1. For a comprehensive multidisciplinary discussion see David Held, The Global Transformations Reader: An Introduction to the Globalization Debate (2000).

2. The relationship between comparative law and globalization has produced a quite broad debate. A recent book length

Ugo Mattei, An Opportunity not to be Missed. The Future of Comparative Law in the United States

46 Amer. J. Comp. Law 709, 709 (1998)
(materials have been partially updated and some additions introduced).

In recent years it has become fashionable to talk about globalization of the law. A number of important law schools—New York University leading the group—have stressed their commitment to a global law program. A number of writings have been devoted to this topic.[1] A large number of conferences in the field of international and comparative law have been organized.... The question consequently arises: what is the future of comparative law in the global law school?[2]

The answer that one would find natural is that comparative law will have a brilliant future in this new institutional environment. After all, comparative law scholars—since the birth of their discipline early in our century—have been claiming that the legal system does not end at the borders of the national State. Moreover, they have been the only ones that have invested in preparing for the moment in which the nation state would collapse and in which we would revert to a period when, like at the time of the *ius commune* in Europe, (see materials *infra* Chapter 4, Section 7 at 351) the nationality of a lawyer would not matter and the law would have its force not *ratione imperii* (because of the political force behind it) but, once again, *imperio rationis* (because of its force of persuasion backed by the rationality of its rules). Rather than stemming from the State, the authority of law would stem from its intrinsic character, no matter which jurisdiction produced the law.[3] Scholars from varied social sciences have now declared that the nation state, if not dead, is at least in great decline. In an important book, for example, international political scientist Susan Strange has argued that the power in the world is now diffused and that if one only looks at the nation state one will overlook most of the places in which legal decision making occurs.[4] Moreover, for a few years now anthropologist Laura Nader has made a similar point when looking (among other things) at the structure of the multinational corporation in order to detect the relationships of power that really matter in the production of law worldwide today.[5] A few lawyers in the United States have arrived at

treatment is in William Twining, Globalization and Legal Theory (2001).

1. See Symposium on Globalization, 46 J. Legal Educ. 301 (1996).

2. See most recently the Symposium issue on "Transnational Legal Education" in 56 J. of Legal Educ. 161 (2006) with thorough discussion of the specially advanced model developed at McGill law school in Montreal.

3. See Jareborg, Nils (Ed.), Towards Universal Law: Trends in National, European and International Lawmaking (1995) with writings stressing this point by such leaders

in the field as Hein Kötz, James Gordley, Mireille Delmas–Marty, Arthur Hartkamp, etc.

4. See S. Strange, "The Retreat of the State: the Diffusion of Power in the World Economy" (1996).

5. See, most recently, Laura Nader, "The Phantom Factor: Impact of the Cold War on Anthropology," in "The Cold War & The University: Toward an Intellectual History of the Postwar Years" (1997); Laura Nader & Elisabetta Grande, "Current Illusions and Delusions About Conflict Management," in I. W. Zart (Ed.) African Traditional Conflict Medicine (1998).

similar conclusion and a number of paper writers have dedicated a *de profundis* prayer to the State, the most successful and powerful form of political organization that humankind has invented in its long path to civilization.[6]

If the enemy of comparative law scholars was the nation State, and legal nationalism and chauvinism produced by its centrality in legal thinking, its decline should present a great opportunity for our discipline. We will finally stop occupying marginal positions in the legal curriculum, and our discipline will be able to seize a central role everywhere, not just in a few law schools in this country. As a consequence, there will be many job openings in the academic and professional market and a large number of young, ambitious and bright potential legal scholars and practitioners will devote their energies to becoming comparative lawyers in order to occupy those attractive openings. In a few years comparative law will occupy the mainstream in teaching and research. As with law and economics, critical legal studies, legal feminism, critical race theory etc., comparative law will finally become "cutting edge stuff" in the legal academia. Everybody in this country will read the American Journal of Comparative Law at least as much as it is read in Europe. The generation of post-world war II German refugees, such as Rudolf B. Schlesinger, the initiator of this casebook, will be finally replaced.

This wonderland is in the distant future. There is no rising star in the American legal academic profession that is a comparative lawyer by training. Most tenured comparative law professors of the younger generation are still foreigners. As far as I know, even at NYU, despite their global law school, there is no core comparative law course offered every year taught by a "full time" professional comparativist. The same is true at Stanford, Columbia, the University of Chicago, and many other less well known institutions.

The question that arises is: why? The answers may vary. To begin with, it might be that my analysis is wrong. That what I regard as a professional full time comparative law person is indeed itself an obsolete figure in the global world. That people such as the refugee scholars were not replaced simply because there was no more need for the kind of work they were proposing. Perhaps American law absorbed the minimum amount of civil law learning that was necessary to survive and to develop, and now domestic developments are self-sufficient, actually robust enough to guarantee to parochial U.S. lawyers global hegemony.

Another possibility is that American legal culture is desperately in need of replacing such towering figures, but this does not happen for one of the following reasons: a) it is difficult to do so or b) curricular needs do not really require this to happen because some other disciplines more familiar or easy for lawyers work as good substitutes for comparative law. I think that the first possibility (that there is no need to replace the post war

---

6. See Symposium, "The Decline of the Nation State and Its Effect on Constitutional and International Economic Law", 18 Cardozo L.R. 903 (1996).

refugee comparative law scholars) is simply absurd. If American law faculties were packed with experts on African Law, Chinese Law, Japanese Law, Latin American Law, etc., the argument that post war refugees' learning (grounded as it was in the opposition between civil law and common law) is obsolete could have some ground.[7] But, as far as I know, this is by no means the case. Considering as obsolete the function of cross-fertilization—even limited as it was between the United States and Western Europe—that comparative scholarship has carried on in the United States means to have no grasp of the pathetic episodes of reinvention of the wheel in which so many modern American Legal theorists fall. Even more important, the lack of professional, general comparative law scholars means that in those schools a general introduction to comparative law is not ordinarily offered. This shortcoming is very serious. A general introduction to comparative law is where students might develop the methodological awareness of the "parochial" nature of the legal education they are receiving. Without this awareness there are no incentives to overcome the domestic phase of legal consciousness, to give up the imperialist hubris of US legal education and to "prepare for a global world" in a civilized fashion.

I think that both of the other explanations have more merit. It is still difficult to replace academic comparative lawyers with American trained scholars because of the language gap and of the very high sunk investments that are needed to engage in comparative law in a competitive academic environment such as the U.S. Moreover, due to the provincial attitude widespread in American legal academy, whatever disciplines dealing with legal problems abroad are considered to be equal among themselves. Consequently, disciplines such as International Law, International Human Rights, International Business Transactions, International Organizations etc. are considered good curricular substitutes for comparative law particularly because their methodology, based as it is on a body of *real* (positive) law is much more palatable and understandable for a domestic lawyer. . . .

Nor is the situation likely to improve because of the globalization of the economy, assuming that it will continue in the next decades. Indeed, it is easy to observe that the *only* significant meaning of globalization in the law today is Americanization. American Law has become hegemonic in the world at the scholarly level.[8] However, this is true also at the teaching level. International LLM programs in the U.S., on top of being fat milk cows for law schools budgets, are nothing more than one year introductory courses to American Law for foreigners. The customers of these programs come to the States to study American Law. They do not care about having someone teaching them comparative law, so a number of law schools are able to offer International LLM programs without having comparative law

7. Indeed one could argue that in the global world scholarship should mostly be devoted to radically different legal cultures. See J. Van Der Linden, Comparer le Droit (1995) and Rodolfo Sacco, 48 Rev. Int'l Droit Comp. 659 (1996). See H. Patrick Glenn, Legal Traditions of the World (2004).

8. See U. Mattei, "Why the Wind Changed: Intellectual Leadership in Western Law," 42 Am. J. Comp. Law 195 (1994).

experts on the faculty. And even theoretically, if globalization means a uniform worldwide conception of the law based on the U.S. notion of the *Rule of Law*, it is easy to observe that there seems to be not much need to know alternative ideas of law and order, or alternative institutional arrangements in the global world. After all, the job of the comparative law scholar is to explore differences, analogies, analogies hidden behind apparent differences or differences hidden behind apparent analogies. If differences disappear the main focus of our discipline disappears as well. . . .

Of course, if this is the picture, there is not much to be optimistic about. Things however, as usual, are neither this simple nor this dark. In the history of our discipline, there was already one moment in which one major object of observation has disappeared. I'm referring, of course, to the fall of the Soviet legal order in Central–Eastern Europe and Russia. Nevertheless, not many are so arrogant as to say that there is no more interesting work to be done for comparative law types in the post-socialist world, and indeed what has been called "transitional jurisprudence" in Central and Eastern Europe, is probably today one of the most interesting objects of observation for anybody interested in legal and social change.[9]

I suspect that if comparative lawyers have not played an important role in those developments, it is because the methodology that they were able to offer was uninteresting and obsolete. In transition, there is no need of black letter analysis or even of descriptive approaches such as those in which comparative law scholars worldwide have done most of their work. There is a need for institutional engineering based on informed guesses and informed choices between alternative institutional arrangements.[10] Such choices must be done considering the social and economic impact of them and should be compatible with a complex formal and informal institutional background.[11] This is why a certain brand of comparative law people would be of tremendous help in transitional contexts. These observations are by no means limited to the context of transition and development. If there is one meaning of the term globalization, it must be connected with the idea of change: a global institutional change affecting altogether most of the legal systems in the world. Globalization can be seen as a general flux of the law, a general transition towards a more integrated legal order following the demise of the State and the development of alternative international centers of power. Nevertheless, cultural differences will never completely disappear. In a way, globalization is to general comparative law what the fall of the Berlin wall was for Soviet legal studies. Globalization is a revolutionary moment which makes a great opportunity for comparative law.

9. See Ruti G. Teitel, "Transitional Jurisprudence: The Role of Law in Political Transformation," 106 Yale L. J. 2009 (1997).

10. See generally, U. Mattei, Comparative Law and Economics (1997).

11. See Douglass C. North, Institutions, Institutional Change and Economic Performance, Cambridge Univ. Press (1991).

QUESTION

This piece was written at the end of the last century. How does it reflect its historical moment? What major global changes have occurred since the fall of the Berlin Wall that might affect the comparative study of law?

2. COMPARATIVE LAW AND NEIGHBORING DISCIPLINES: THEORY AND PRACTICE

Unlike most other subjects in the law school curriculum, comparative law is not a body of rules and principles limited by a jurisdictional scope. It is not part of the "positive law", governing a particular territory or geographic area. To clarify, talking about California, German or Peruvian contract law, tort law, criminal law or labor law, conveys the sense of a body of rules and principles *as applied* in those geographic areas. To talk about California or German or Peruvian comparative law does not convey the same meaning. If anything at all, German comparative law means only the way in which some lawyers in Germany do comparative legal work as scholars, teachers or practitioners.[1] Much more frequently, a geographic attribute is not attached nor makes sense referred to the label comparative law. Comparative law is a cosmopolitan discipline, with the very same subject matter, if taught in Bangalore, New York, Paris or Brazzaville.

Comparative law is a body of potentially "universal" knowledge about the law, acquired by observing the legal phenomenon as it appears in a variety of social and geographic contexts. It is an approach to legal institutions or to entire legal systems that study them in comparison with other institutions or legal systems as they exist elsewhere. In this sense comparative law allows us to study *the law* as a phenomenon of social organization that, as language, fashion, culture or religion, shows differences, sometimes very acute, or analogies, sometimes striking, in different geographic settings. In this respect, the term comparative law is a misnomer. It would be more accurate to speak of Comparison of Laws and Legal Systems. However, by the force of tradition, the term comparative law has become the accepted title of our subject.[2]

1. See the Oxford Handbook of Comparative Law, Zimmermann & Reimann, Eds. (2006), containing entries on national traditions of comparative law. For example, Benedicté Fauvarque–Cosson, "Development of Comparative Law in France," Ingeborg Schwenzer, "Development of Comparative Law in Germany, Switzerland, and Austria," Elisabetta Grande, "Development of Comparative Law in Italy," John W. Cairns, "Development of Comparative Law in Great Britain," etc.

2. Its counterpart in French is droit comparé ("law compared"); in German, Rechtsvergleichung ("comparison of laws"). The German term has been criticized as too exclusively method-oriented; likewise, the statement that comparative law is primarily a method or way of looking at law has been criticized as implying that comparative law lacks meaningful substantive content. But "comparison" would seem to denote both the process, or method, of comparing laws and legal systems and the body of insights and knowledge acquired through that process.

(a) Comparative Law, Conflict of Laws, and International Law

In today's close-knit world, the practicing lawyer finds to an ever-increasing extent that local as well as foreign clients are faced with problems that cut across national boundaries and the legal systems of more than one country. In metropolitan centers, matters of this kind have long been "part of the daily legal fare."[1] What may be less generally appreciated is the fact that, through the American operations of foreign concerns and the increasing involvement in international trade of medium-and small-sized American firms located in every part of the country, outlandish problems are carried into the offices of countless practitioners far from the big cities. Similarly, in dealing with the estates and domestic relations of foreign-born individuals and of United States citizens permanently residing abroad, practitioners in every community encounter problems of foreign and international law.[2] International travel by millions of Americans further adds to the growing volume of such transnational legal problems.

In handling these problems, a lawyer must, first of all, know the internal law of his or her own state or country. In addition, the lawyer will have to have some familiarity with the more specialized, internationally oriented subjects. Traditionally, these subjects are grouped under four headings: international Law, conflict of laws,[3] foreign law and comparative law.[4] From a functional point of view, it might be argued that all of these subjects should be considered together.[5] But merging them would create a unit much too large to be convenient for the teacher or textbook writer; hence, as a rule, they continue to be presented separately.[6] In order to

---

1.   Arthur H. Dean, "The Role of International Law in a Metropolitan Practice," 103 Univ. Pa. L. Rev. 886, 888 (1955).

2.   See Schlesinger, Book Review, 41 Cornell L.Q. 527 (1956).

3.   In the present context, the emphasis is on international rather than interstate conflicts. The term conflict of laws thus is used in the sense in which the civilians speak of private international law and international law of procedure.

4.   From the standpoint of an American practitioner faced with legal problems arising from international transactions, the term comparative law, as used in the text, may be defined as the body of knowledge and techniques that one has to assimilate in order to deal successfully with the foreign law elements of such problems.

For some purposes it may be proper and indeed necessary to distinguish between comparative law and foreign law. But from the point of view of one who aims to handle actual legal problems presenting foreign aspects, the distinction has little utility: comparative law, or the comparative method, can

be learned and practiced only by dealing with foreign legal materials; while learning and understanding foreign law inevitably involves drawing comparisons with the law with which one already is familiar.

5.   The term "International Legal Studies" has been used to designate integrated programs of research and instruction which cover or cut across all three traditional subjects. See J. B. Howard, International Legal Studies, 26 U. Chi. L. Rev. 577 (1959).

6.   Needless to say, each of the three traditional subjects can be subdivided in various ways. Moreover, books and courses intended to perform more specialized functions increasingly combine selected elements of all three subjects in exploring such areas as international and regional organizations, international business transactions, or the legal aspects of development. See, e.g. M. Katz, "The International Education Act of 1966: The Place of Law and the Law Schools", 20 J. Legal Educ. 201, 204–5 (1967). See also Horatia Muir Watt—in Reimann and Zimmermann, eds., Oxford Handbook of Comparative Law, Oxford University Press (2006)

understand the organization of law school curricula, library collections, and the pertinent literature, it becomes necessary, therefore, to know approximately where the lines of demarcation are drawn between international law, conflict of laws, foreign law and comparative law.

In theory comparative law is clearly distinguishable from other branches of the law that make an international curriculum. Comparative law is different from public international law, since international law is the body of *positive law* (customary or based on treatises) governing the relationship between sovereign states or international organizations (which today are much more numerous than the roughly 200 currently existing states). Comparative law is different from private international law, (also known as conflict of laws, or choice of law), again for the *positive* nature of this body of law. Indeed, you can compare Private international law—a body of domestic law dealing with fact situations with some of their elements located abroad—as it is in France or in England as much as you can compare English or French property or criminal law. Nor should comparative law be confused with foreign law. A law review article written by an American author dealing with the law of intellectual property in China is not a piece of comparative law since it does not compare two or more entities on equal footing, but only describes a foreign system at most "translating" it into a language and into legal categories understandable domestically. These distinctions should not be taken rigidly however.

One thing that the student should learn by comparing the law is a high degree of cultural relativism, a very deep skepticism towards legal dogmatism, and a humble inquisitive attitude aimed at understanding by keeping a distance from his object of observation. Law schools usually frame the brain of students to communicate as national lawyers with other lawyers with the same training. The result is that for a lawyer trained in one legal system the conceptual difference between a "trust" and "agency" that between "contract" and "tort" or between "felony" and "misdemeanor", is as natural and real as that between a dog and a television set. By comparative study one sees how these notions are contingent, local and culturally constructed. A gift, for example, is not a contract for lack of consideration in the common law, while it is a *contrat* in French law. Marriage is a *contrat* in France but it is not a *contratto* in Italy and so on.[7] The same conceptual skepticism should be applied also when one differentiates comparative law from neighboring disciplines.

---

7. The definition of contract offered by the Italian Civil Code is the following: Art. 1321 "Contract is an agreement between two or more parties to establish regulate or extinguish between them a patrimonial legal relationship." (emphasis added). Because the essence of a marriage is not considered "patrimonial" in Italian law, marriage is consequently not a contract. See Alberto Musy and Alberto Monti, The Law of Contracts, in Jeffrey Lena & Ugo Mattei (Eds.), An Introduction to Italian Law (2001).

Mathias Reimann, Beyond National Systems: A Comparative Law for the International Age

75 Tulane L. Rev. 1103, 1103–1108 (2001).

Meeting for the centennial of the Paris Congress of 1900, widely considered the birth hour of modern comparative law, is a welcome occasion to celebrate our discipline's past accomplishments as well as its current revival in many parts of the world.[1] More importantly, however, it provides an opportunity to reflect upon the difficulties and problems that beset the field. The most widespread concern is, perhaps, that in most places in the world, comparative law does not play nearly as prominent a role in legal academia and practice as befits our age of globalization (real or perceived). Comparative law should occupy a central place in an environment in which trans-boundary issues have become routine. However, all too often, our discipline "fail[s] to excite the imagination of students and practicing lawyers."[2]

. . .

In order to understand how our discipline has come to lag behind twentieth-century developments, we must recall some of its history.[3] Comparative law was not, of course, invented at the Paris Congress. It had existed for hundreds of years, although it was not called comparative law (droit comparé, Rechtsvergleichung, diritto comparato, or the like) before the nineteenth century. At least since the Middle Ages, jurists had compared an extraordinary variety of legal rules and systems: Roman and canon law, droit ecrit and droit coutumier, tribal and feudal regimes, biblical commands and natural law precepts, among others. To this, the late nineteenth century added an ethnic dimension by comparing whole legal cultures from a historical and worldwide perspective.[4]

In contrast to this richness, the concept of comparative law that the Paris Congress bequeathed to the twentieth century was extremely narrow. Its lodestar was the science of a "droit commun legislatif."[5] This meant, essentially, the comparison of the private law codes and statutes of continental European countries with the purpose of legal harmonization and

1. Comparative law has recently become prominent in Western Europe in the context of the Europeanization of private law. The discipline has also experienced somewhat of a revival in the United States as demonstrated by the proliferation of teaching materials, specialized journals, and other literature about the field. Of course, comparative studies are well established in many other parts of the world, such as Japan, Korea, Israel, and South Africa.

2. Basil Markesinis, "Comparative Law—A Subject in Search of an Audience", 53 Mod. L. Rev. 1, 1 (1990).

3. For an overview of the developments until the nineteenth century, see Walther Hug, The History of Comparative Law, 45 Harv. L. Rev. 1027 (1932). More recently, Mathias Reimann & Reinhard Zimmermann, eds. The Oxford Handbook of Comparative Law, Oxford University Press (2006).

4. See K. Zweigert & H. Kötz, An Introduction to Comparative Law 1–12 (Tony Weir trans., 2d ed. 1987; one-volume paperbound ed. 1992) at 57–58.

5. See id. at 61.

unification.[6] Most importantly in our present context, it meant reducing the discipline to the comparison of national legal systems.

At the time, this seemed obvious and was quite appropriate. After all, there simply were no other legal regimes that seemed to matter (anymore). Feudal and tribal rules were legal history. Roman law and indigenous customs had just been rendered obsolete by the great codifications. Canon law had lost most of its force in the modern secular state. Distant religious or customary regimes were far beyond the orbit of the dominant Eurocentric approach.[7] Public international law operated somewhere at the outer margins of the legal universe and played a very limited role in practice. In short, in the age of the modern state with its monopoly on lawmaking and enforcement, the law of the civilized world consisted exclusively of the laws of sovereign nations, such as France, Germany, or Italy. At the time, this seemed almost too obvious to mention.[8] Thus was born the traditional concept of twentieth-century comparative law: it meant the study of national legal systems, their laws, and virtually nothing else. . . .

Needless to say, the legal universe changed in the twentieth century, especially in its last few decades.

In the second half of the twentieth century, we witnessed the rise of numerous legal systems outside of, and above, the national ones. Since the founding of the United Nations, international law has developed into a complex legal regime with rulemaking bodies, a multitude of written provisions, a court, and enforcement mechanisms, however effective or ineffective. Several international trade regimes were created. On a global level, the General Agreement on Tariffs and Trade (GATT) and the WTO were formed; on a regional level, the European Economic Community (now the EU) and the North American Free Trade Agreement (NAFTA) were established; others, like the Common Market of the South (MERCOSUR), are now emerging. In the area of private law and litigation, international conventions of all sorts have proliferated under the auspices of the Hague Conference of Private International Law, the United Nations Commission on International Trade Law (UNCITRAL), or the European Community and pertain, inter alia, to the sale of goods, choice of law, procedural matters—such as service of process, taking of evidence, and jurisdiction and judgments—and arbitration. Human rights systems have also developed, again, in both a worldwide and a regional, especially European, context. In addition, there are several unofficial codifications of substantive law in the international sphere that have lately enjoyed much attention, especially the

---

6. We must not forget, however, that the intellectual horizon of the major participants was by no means so narrow. Édouard Lambert displayed a very broad and highly sophisticated view of comparative law and all its then-current ramifications. See Congrès International de Droit Comparé, Procès-Verbaux des Séances et Documents 26–61 (1st ed. 1905).

7. All participants in the Paris Congress were Europeans. See 2 Congrès International de Droit Comparé, Procès-Verbaux des Séances et Documents 609–21 (2d ed. 1907).

8. The whole proceedings are imbued with the understanding that the law to be compared has to be the positive law of modern nation-states.

UNIDROIT Principles[9] and the Principles of European Contract Law.[10] Perhaps the most striking of all these developments is that the countries of Western Europe have recently formed a political union with standardized passports, common policies, a common currency, and other common elements. More than any of the other changes, the EU demonstrates that, today, national legal systems are no longer alone in the legal universe. They coexist with regimes operating on the supra- or international level.

Through these transnational regimes, national legal systems have become interconnected in manifold ways. They are subject to, and modified by, international treaties and conventions, trade regulations, and European directives. Some countries harmonize their laws or promise to recognize each other's judgments. Others cooperate in antitrust enforcement and coordinate their fiscal policies. Consequently, countries have suffered a curtailment of sovereignty, ranging from mild, as in the case of the United States, to severe, as in the case of the members of the European Union. It is true that the nation-state has survived and that the news of its death is greatly exaggerated. But it is also true that the nation-states' legal systems are no longer nearly as separate and independent as they were in 1900.[11]

In addition, the internationalization of the economy has entailed the growth of large-scale legal practice on the international level. This was fueled by, but would probably have occurred even without, the rise of transnational law regimes. Today, there are innumerable firms, clients, transactions, and disputes that are international in the sense that their geographic location hardly matters anymore. As a result, there is a world of commercial law practice, i.e., of counseling, negotiating, drafting, and arbitration, that is operating on its own terms and becoming increasingly independent from national systems.

Of course, not nearly all law and legal practice has developed in this direction. In fact, vast areas have remained untouched by internationalizing trends. But in the trans-boundary context, the very area with which comparative law is concerned, these trends are broad and strong, and they continue to gather momentum. . . .

How is comparative law dealing with these developments as we meet in New Orleans in the year 2000? The short answer is, so far, not well. Its mainstream still clings to the nationalistic concept underlying the Paris Congress. . . .

---

9. Int'l Inst. for the Unification of Private Law, Principles of International Commercial Contracts (1994). For an explanation, see Michael Joachim Bonell, "The UNIDROIT Principles of International Commercial Contracts: Why? What? How?" 69 Tul. L. Rev. 1121, 1121–47 (1995).

10. Ole Lando & Hugh Beale eds., Comm'n of European Contract Law, Principles of European Contract Law: Parts I and II (2000).

11. For example, in France, more than half of the legislative measures taken in 1991 (1564 out of 2981) emanated from Brussels, and in The Netherlands, roughly thirty percent of all recent legislation serves to implement European Community directives. See G. Federico Mancini, "Europe: The Case for Statehood", 4 Eur. L. J. 29, 40 (1998).

Serious efforts to integrate transnational law fully into our discipline are nowhere in sight, at least as far as I can see.[12] Even where international regimes are considered, they are normally treated merely as an addendum to the well-known materials about nation-states and legal families. In summary, transnational law is out there, somewhere on the periphery of our vision. We cast it an occasional glance, but we do not consider its study a necessary part of our job.

(b) Comparative Law and Economics: the so-called Washington Consensus[1]

While for a long time more cosmopolitan legal scholars could complain that the dominant approach to the law was insular or parochial, this is not any more the case in the current phase of trans-national capitalism. State sovereignty, which has traditionally been the intellectual cage of the western lawyer's thinking and that made the law a genuinely local political and cultural artifact (politicians are called "legislators" in the US) has progressively yielded to an idea of law as a "technology", a form of social engineering that works as a separate backbone of any economic organization, thus radically inverting the Marxist perspective of law as a "super-structure" of the economic system. While many western professional lawyers were used to think to law an almost "naturally" local matter with significant variations from place to place according to who is the sovereign (thus the need to compare different state regimes), today we tend to look at it as a stylized, technological and quite politically neutral "rule of law" that may be present or may "lack" in different geographical areas but that, when "lacking", is in need of being introduced or "reconstructed" (such as after the socialist parenthesis in Central and Eastern Europe) typically with the generous help of western "donor" countries.

This vision thus transforms comparative law into the study of what is lacking in other societies to make them more similar to western capitalist settings. It is a vision shared by the International Financial Institutions organized in 1944 at the Bretton Woods Conference (World Bank, International Monetary Fund) and by a variety of other powerful agencies engaged in international legal aid, including USAID, the American Bar Association and many other "donor" countries in the West. Supported by quite a few leading legal scholars in this country, this approach is the legal translation of the so called "Washington Consensus" the triumphant political and economic doctrine of the 1990's.

A former executive of the Pepsi Cola Corporation recently summarized it for the sake of discussion in a top level conference organized by the American Bar Association. His comment is perhaps well intentioned, but it

---

12. Because I have not looked at every book and article on comparative law recently published in the world, I may be overlooking something. If so, I would be glad to be proven (at least partially) wrong in my description of the current situation. I recognize that outside the traditional comparative law camp there are some efforts at integrating transnational material into specific comparative studies.

1. See U. Mattei, Comparative Law and Economics (1997). See also F. Faust, "Comparative Law and Economic Analysis of Law" in The Oxford Handbook of Comparative Law, pp. 837–868 (2006).

nevertheless indicates an almost incredible degree of intellectual hubris, as it evidently implies that the rule of law could be lacking only abroad:[2]

> We live in a world plagued by serious gaps in the rule of law—the legal doctrines and institutions that help ensure basic human security and the just and efficient functioning of society. In a globalized world, we cannot afford to and indeed we may not be able to isolate ourselves from the effects of rule of law deficits abroad. Because so much of the world economy is intertwined—a significant and growing percentage of the GDP of the U.S. is generated overseas—the lack of rule of law, even in faraway countries, can strip the world's economies of the predictability and stability they need to thrive. Furthermore, in purely human terms, gaps in the rule of law cause terrible suffering. In a shrinking, globalized world this poses tangible risks to our prosperity and security at home. The need for rule of law is clear.

While presented in the neutral and objectively scientific language of the economic science, the "consensus", progressively questioned in these very recent years, displays a powerful desire to transform local settings of non-western or "less advanced" systems profoundly affecting the political and cultural specificities of the law of many countries. Thus it becomes a powerful transformative force of the law, a de facto "private" source of law determining a global political and constitutional order "open for business" mostly mirroring the United States. (Of course the degree of its success in making this "Golden Arch" law uniform or harmonized worldwide is still to be seen.) While the more recent misfortunes of financial capitalism might have reduced the degree of celebratory optimism of the years since the fall of the Berlin Wall, a few fundamental political and economic assumptions of the Washington consensus and of the recently launched movement for the rule of law are however still very present in the mainstream legal consciousness.[3]

In the words of an American comparative law professor, that has done field-work in Niger, a good pupil of the consensus:

> Consensus holds that economic and social development (the theory assumes that the latter inevitably follows the former) are possible only if poor countries privilege the market as the locus of economic decision making. Accordingly, it calls for reducing social spending and reallocating resources to the private sector, budgetary austerity, trade liberalization and privatization, and privatization of agricultural land. The Consensus also requires developing countries to reform their legal systems as a means of spurring economic development. Under the rubric of "good governance," it insists upon the transparency, consis-

2. D. Andrews, "International Rule of Law Symposium Introductory Essay", 25 Berk. J. Int'l Law 2007.

3. See the 2007 Symposium issue of Berkeley International Law Journal with remarkably bi-partisan interventions among Senator Hillary Clinton, Secretary of State Condoleezza Rice, Justices Breyer, O'Connor and others. The responsibility to outline the results of that powerful gathering has been significantly given to a Comparative Law Professor from Columbia University, Professor Katharina Pistor.

tency, and predictability of laws to provide would-be investors with a stable and inviting governmental and legal framework in which to do business.

The Bretton Woods organizations, along with other multilateral institutions and bilateral donor countries, encourage this strong economic and legal medicine by making "policy based loans" that contain "conditionalities." These conditionalities—we might resort to plain English and call them "conditions"—provide money to poor countries only if their governments comply fully with the reform packages developed by western experts.... [4]

The following materials show the technically neutral language, almost a user's manual, that the World Bank has used to prescribe worldwide adjustments to legal systems:

The World Development Report 2002, Chapter 6. The Judicial System[5]

Courts develop gradually, reflecting a society's own development. When society is a small, close-knit collection of kin, informal means of intervention suffice to resolve conflicts. But as economic activity becomes more complex and commerce expands, group ties weaken, and the demand for more formal means of intervention grows. This pattern is exemplified by the rapid growth of commercial litigation in modern China. In 1979 China embarked on a path of economic reform that spurred new enterprise creation, increased interprovincial trade, and allowed the entry of foreign investors. The expansion of business was followed by an increase in the number of cases filed in commercial courts. In 1979–82 the average number of commercial disputes filed in the courts was around 14,000 a year; by 1997, 1.5 million new cases were filed—more than a 100–fold increase. At the same time, the number of commercial disputes arbitrated by community committees, the traditional mediation mechanism, hardly increased. As the number of entrepreneurs grew, the enforcement capacity of informal dispute resolution mechanisms weakened....

Comparison of legal and judicial systems

Legal and judicial systems vary substantially across countries in terms of their output. In Latin America the average duration of commercial cases is two years, and it is not uncommon for complex commercial cases to take more than five years. In Ecuador the average case takes almost eight years to reach a verdict. In contrast, it takes less than a year to reach a verdict in Colombia, France, Germany, Peru, Singapore, Ukraine, and the United States for similar cases.

4. See Thomas A. Kelley III, "Cell Phones and Oracles: Legal Globalization Meets the Marabout's Mystical Justice in the West African Republic of Niger", American Journal of Comparative Law (forthcoming).

5. The World Development Report is a yearly product of he World Bank. Each year it covers different development issues. It is highly circulated and easily available on the Internet.

Reform of the legal and judicial system depends critically on a sound understanding of its existing structure and level of efficiency. Description of the key characteristics of the system and measurement of the speed and cost of judicial decisions are crucial. However, it is only in rare cases that governments have developed indicators to track the development of the judiciary. There is very little systematic evidence on the structure and performance of the judiciary and on the determinants of its performance. Recently, there have been some attempts to fill this gap.[6] Legal scholars have focused their efforts on documenting the inputs into the judicial systems (number of judges, budget of the judiciary branch, number of administrative support staff), access to justice, and the workload of judges (measured by the number of cases filed and resolved within a given period). The output these studies measure is the number of resolved cases. Examples include studies on eight European countries and a World Bank study on seven Latin American countries.

There are significant problems in making meaningful comparisons between the ways that different judicial systems function. Difficulties are encountered even in defining the concept of a "judge." In one country a legal dispute might be dealt with by a professional judge in a formal courtroom, while in another country a similar dispute might be handled by a public official who is not a judge or a lawyer. In other cases the same dispute might be resolved by an unpaid volunteer lacking any legal qualifications.

The studies show large differences in the number of legal professionals, even across advanced European countries. In some countries lay judges staff labor tribunals and small claims courts. Austrian judges have the most support staff (117 per 100,000 inhabitants). Adjudication services are also organized differently across industrial countries. Ecuador and Peru have one judge per 100,000 people. This is an order of magnitude smaller than the number of judges in Western European countries. Not all countries with efficient judicial systems have many judges, however. Singapore and the United States have fewer than one judge per 100,000 people.

6. Box 6.3

Surveys on judicial performance

The most popular method for assessing judicial performance relies on surveys based on public perceptions of the weaknesses of the judicial system. Some surveys depend on in-house legal experts who summarize the relevant literature for each country but do not have first-hand knowledge of the judicial system, while others survey business executives.

However, people's perceptions are colored by their expectations. Coverage also depends on the availability of information, which is generally better in richer countries. Despite weaknesses with these surveys, they do convey some information. Richer countries have less corrupt judicial systems, which in turn helps their business community and supports economic growth. Other data show that the public's perception of corruption in the judiciary is very highly correlated with its perception of corruption in government.

New evidence on two aspects of judicial efficiency: speed and cost

This Report uses a detailed survey of practicing lawyers to benchmark the relative efficiency of judicial systems and the access to civil justice in 109 countries.[7] The survey focuses on the complexity of litigation, that is, on how difficult it is for a layperson to pursue a legal procedure in defense of his interests. Elements investigated include the various steps in the litigation process, the difficulty in notification procedures, the complexity of the complaint, and the possibility of suspension of enforcement because of appeal.[8]

7. Box 6.4

Comparing judicial efficiency

A survey developed for this Report analyzes particular aspects of judicial systems. It does so through detailed questions addressed to lawyers. The data systematically compare the pace of litigation by means of a standardized survey delivered to private law firms in 109 countries. The survey presents two hypothetical cases that represent typical situations of default of an everyday contract: (a) the eviction of a tenant; and (b) the collection of debt (a returned check or an invoice in countries where checks are not popular).

These two cases proxy for all types of commercial disputes that enter the courts. Two quite different cases are chosen in order to check whether the findings can be generalized to all civil litigation. The questions cover the step-by-step evolution of these cases before local courts in the country's largest city. Importantly, the survey studies both the structure of the judicial system—that is, where the plaintiff would seek redress in specific cases—and the efficiency with which judicial decisions are made.

The survey chooses cases in which the facts are undisputed by the parties but where the defendant still does not want to pay. The judge consistently rules in favor of the plaintiff. In this way the survey controls for fairness across countries, as judges follow the letter of the law. We assume that no post-judgment motions can be filed. Should any opposition to the complaint arise, the judge always decides in favor of the plaintiff. The data consist of the number of steps required in the judicial process, the time

it takes to accomplish each step, and the cost to the plaintiff. The last provides a comparable measure of access to the judicial system, while all three address the issue of judicial efficiency. The questionnaire makes a distinction between what is required by law and what happens in practice.

The following are examples of questions asked: What is the most commonly used mechanism for collecting overdue debt in your country? Does this mechanism differ if the debt amount is small, equal to 5 percent of GNP per capita, or large, equal to 50 percent of GNP per capita? What types of court will this mechanism be applied through? Would the judgment in the debt collection case be an oral representation of the general conclusions, an oral argument on specific facts and applicable laws, or a written argument on specific facts and applicable laws?

Source: Lex Mundi, Harvard University, and World Bank. *World Development Report 2002* background project.

8. Box 6.5

Index of the complexity of litigation

This index measures how complex judicial litigation of simple commercial disputes is, and therefore how difficult it is for a layperson to pursue a legal procedure by herself in defense of her interests. The index ranks from 0 to 1, where 1 means that litigation is very complex, while 0 means that it is not. The index is formed by adding five equally weighted variables:

Legal language or justification. This describes how much legal language or

For the countries in which the procedures are complex, the adjudication process is perceived to be less efficient even after adjusting for the level of income (figure 6.1a). The data indicate that the complexity of litigation does not decrease uniformly as national income per capita declines (figure 6.1b). This shows that the developing countries with the fewest resources and weaker judicial capacity also have complex procedures. One explanation is that the judicial system in these countries is more prone to failure and that the complexity of litigation ensures the availability of checks and balances on the way to the final judicial decision. Alternatively, procedures may be put into place to limit access to the judicial system and favor more privileged individuals or firms. Some developing countries, however, have simpler procedures, and several countries have undertaken reforms of judicial processes. Among the industrial countries, while some may have more complex procedures, the superior enforcement capacity and presence of complementary institutions and higher levels of human capital counteract the negative effects of complexity (figure 6.1c). Complementary institutions include rules affecting judge's incentives, rules promoting greater transparency, rules affecting other litigants' incentives, and clearer substantive rules.

Countries differ significantly in terms of the duration of simple civil litigation related to commercial disputes.[9] It takes less than three months

legal justification is required in different stages of the process.

Notification procedure. This describes the level of complexity involved in the process of notification of the complaint (service of process) and the notification of final judgment.

Legal representation. This describes whether for the case provided, the legal assistance of a licensed attorney would be required by law or by practice.

Complexity of complaint. This evaluates the level of complexity for preparing and presenting a complaint for the case.

Suspension of enforcement because of appeal. This describes whether the enforcement of final judgment would normally be suspended when the losing party files an appeal until the appeal is finally decided, or if judgment is generally enforceable.

Source: Lex Mundi, Harvard University, and World Bank. World Development Report 2002 background project.

9.   Figure 6.1

(a) Procedural complexity reduces efficiency

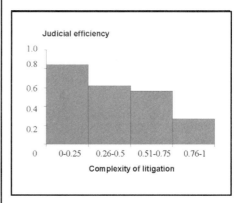

to reach a judgment on small debt collection, equivalent to 5 percent of GNP per capita, in Denmark, Japan, New Zealand, Singapore, and the United States. In contrast, it takes more than two years to reach a judgment in Colombia, the Czech Republic, Kuwait, Malta, Mozambique, and the United Arab Emirates.

Enforcement of judgment differs significantly between countries. In the richest quartile of countries it takes on average 64 days to enforce a judgment on small debt collection once the judge has produced an opinion. The countries in the poorest quartile fare worse. On average, it takes 192 days—a long time, particularly for small businesses with little access to credit—to collect debts once a judgment is rendered.

The survey underscores how countries vary greatly in the details of the law as well as the enforcement of the law. And these difficulties can affect efficiency. First, the speed with which the same case is adjudicated in different countries varies enormously. For example, it can take anywhere from 35 days (Singapore) to four years (Slovenia) to solve a commercial dispute that involves a returned check. Second, a large part of this difference can be explained by the procedural structure of the judicial system. This includes the prevalence of oral versus written procedures; the existence of specialized courts, including small claims courts; the possibility for appeal during or after the trial; and the allowed number of appeals. Third, some characteristics of the judicial system are much more likely to be associated with superior judicial performance. For example, the existence of oral procedures and continuous court cases (the court meets on

(b) Rich countries also have complex regulations, but . . .

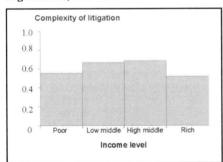

(c) . . . they have more efficient systems because of complementary institutions and capacity

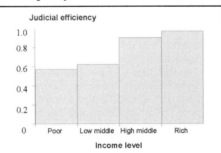

Note: Higher values indicate greater efficiency (figures 6.1a and 6.1c) or greater complexity (figure 6.1b).
Source: Lex Mundi, Harvard University and World Bank. *World Development Report 2002* background project.

continuous days until the case is resolved) explains much of the variation in the length of commercial dispute resolution.[10]

The study also indicates that 90 percent of procedures for Costa Rica, Ecuador, Guatemala, Morocco, and Senegal, and 100 percent for Argentina, Honduras, Spain, and Venezuela, are written. Not surprisingly, the judicial process of collecting debt lasts on average 180 days in Honduras, 300 days in Argentina, and 432 days in Senegal. The predominance of written procedures is evident in some of the industrial countries as well. For example, in both Norway and Japan 80 percent of all judicial procedures in the debt recovery case studied require written documents. Yet the duration of cases is reasonably short: 90 and 60 days on average, respectively. This evidence suggests that complicated procedures are especially problematic in poorer countries, where they may facilitate corruption or be unsuitable given the existing levels of administrative capacity. Also, they frequently serve as barriers to entry for poor people.

When building effective judicial institutions, policymakers aim to establish courts that decide cases cheaply, quickly, and fairly, while maximizing access. These variables are not independent of one another. However, the evidence indicates that tradeoffs among them exist only at the margin. For example, when judicial performance is very slow, improvements in speed can be made without compromising fairness. A recent study from Argentina suggests that policymakers are not always bound by such tradeoffs; it demonstrates that to be fair, the justice system need not be slow, but many policymakers use the existence of a tradeoff as an excuse for maintaining the status quo.

Access to the judicial system, partly by the poorer members of society, can be limited by factors such as procedural complexity, whether legal

---

10. Box 6.6
Debt recovery in Tunisia

In Tunisia the recovery of overdue small debts is normally achieved by means of a special procedure called injunction de payer before a general-jurisdiction judge. Provided that the debt has been proven and established, the judge grants the injunction to pay. The debtor cannot oppose the order. Therefore, the civil lawsuit excludes the usual stages of service of process, opposition, hearing, and gathering of evidence. On average, the entire procedure from filing until payment takes less than a month.

This simplified procedure does not mandate legal representation. Legal costs are very low, approximately $54 when represented by a lawyer, and zero if the plaintiff represents herself. There are no court fees for the injunction, and the plaintiff only pays bailiff fees, of around $20, for the actual collection. In contrast, many countries at a similar level of economic development have a considerably lengthier and more costly process for small debt recovery. Recovering small debt in Venezuela, for example, involves a complicated process. The parties to the case and the adjudicators must go through 31 independent procedural actions from filing of the lawsuit to payment of the debt. The average duration of the process is about one year, and legal representation of parties is mandatory, as is the case in most other Latin American countries. Small debt recovery in Venezuela is also associated with markedly high legal costs. Average attorney fees are approximately $2,000, while court fees reach $2,500.

Source: Lex Mundi, Harvard University, and World Bank. World Development Report 2002 background project.

representation is required, and high financial costs. For example, where most procedures are in written form rather than oral, access is limited.[11]

The types of cases a nation's courts tackle represent policy choices. The procedure for resolving a dispute must be proportionate to the value, importance, and complexity of the dispute. Low-value or simple disputes might be assigned to simpler and faster procedures consuming fewer court resources. For example, disputes over small amounts of money should be handled by small claims courts. The World Bank has been involved in establishing this system in the Dominican Republic, where it was discovered that more than 80 percent of commercial cases involved trivial amounts of money.

Policy choices should also be dictated by public preferences. For example, recent empirical work suggests that disputants value the chance to describe their version of the story to an impartial adjudicator; that is, oral procedures in front of a judge are perceived as particularly "fair." In fact, this "day in court" factor outweighs every other variable tested, including the actual outcome of the dispute.

Judicial reform efforts

Attempts to improve judicial efficiency have varied widely across industrial and developing countries. However, three key themes run through the successful initiatives to improve judicial efficiency.

Increased accountability of judges. For public sector employees, ensuring accountability is the mirror image of private sector contracting. The judge is contracted to provide efficient adjudication. However institutional features of the judicial system and the presence of complementary institutions (such as the media) affect the incentives of judges to provide such adjudication. The provision of information on judicial performance and monitoring play a key role in affecting judges' incentives and accountability. Accountability can also be increased through pressure from civil society.

Simplification. Simplification of legal procedures can lead to more efficient outcomes. Simplification may result from replacing written hearings by oral ones or by creating specialized courts. An excessive emphasis

11. Figure 6.2
Excessive written procedures limit access to justice

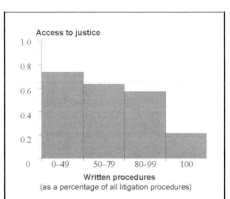

Written procedures
(as a percentage of all litigation procedures)

Note: Equal number of countries in each category. Higher values indicate greater access. Access to justice is defined as the extent to which citizens are "equal under the law, have access to an independent, nondiscriminatory judiciary, and are respected by the security forces. Scale from 0 to 10. The higher the rating, the greater the degree of equality under the law" (Freedom House 2000).

Source: Access to justice: Freedom House 2000; written procedures: Lex Mundi, Harvard University, and World Bank, *World Development Report 2002* background project.

on procedure may undermine fairness, but so may excessive informality. As explained earlier, however, the evidence shows that judicial systems in developing countries which suffer from capacity constraints also suffer from an excess of formality and complexity of procedure.

Increased resources. In some countries the judiciary seriously lacks resources. In such cases, additional resources have been found to improve judicial efficiency. But in most cases, increased resources for the judiciary enhance efficiency only if they complement more fundamental reforms, such as eliminating all easily identifiable redundancies and inefficiencies in the judicial system. Recently, the Philippine Supreme Court asked for a large increase in public funding. However, a report by the Center for Public Resource Management, a Philippine NGO, has identified a large number of duplicative units and functions within the office of the clerk of court and the office of the court administrator. There are also 11 separate records divisions in the various offices of the Supreme Court. These units are not electronically or manually networked. Each maintains its own records processing, filing, and archiving functions. It is estimated that if these redundancies were eliminated from the judicial system, resources equivalent to 8 percent of its budget would be freed for other uses. . . .

Simplification and structural reform

Simplification of procedures and enforcement has been found to improve judicial efficiency. Three main types of simplification or structural reform are considered in this section: the creation of specialized courts, alternative dispute resolution mechanisms, and the simplification of legal procedures.

Specialized courts. The structure of adjudication can be changed by creating specialized courts. These courts may be specialized around the subject matter (such as bankruptcy and commercial courts) or around the size of the claim. Creating or extending small claims courts are among the most successful of all judicial reforms. There are many examples. In Brazil, for example, small claims courts have halved times to disposition and expanded access to justice. In Hong Kong, China, it takes only four weeks from filing a case to its first hearing in the Small Claims Tribunal.

Specialized courts with a particular subject-matter jurisdiction can also increase efficiency. Such courts have been set up for streamlined debt collection in several countries, including Germany, Japan, and the Netherlands. Labor tribunals in Ecuador have been associated with reduced times to disposition. Many of these specialized courts emphasize arbitration and conciliation, so some of the positive results for specialized courts may be the result of their emphasis on alternative dispute resolution methods. Specialized courts also introduce simplified steps if they cut some of the general civil court procedures. For example, the recently established specialized commercial court in Tanzania cut the average time to disposition from 22 months to 3 months. The creation of the Tanzanian commercial court was the result of the combined efforts of the government, private business, and international donors.[12]

Alternative dispute resolution. In developing countries where judicial systems are ineffective, alternative dispute resolution (ADR) mechanisms can substitute for ineffective formal legal procedures. ADR mechanisms range from informal norm-based mediation to formal arbitration courts based on a simplified legal process. These systems may be run by communities or by the state. As formal systems develop, use of formal courts increases, so proportionately more disputes are resolved in these courts. Finally, as courts become very efficient and their judgments sufficiently predictable, the use of out-of-court settlements may increase relative to the number of court filings.

The experience on ADR mechanisms is generally positive. Many successful specialized courts and indigenous justice courts incorporate a strong element of arbitration and conciliation—including the Dutch *kort geding,* Ecuadorian labor mediation, justices of the peace in Peru, mediation centers in Latin America, Indian *lok adalats,* and the Russian *treteiskie* courts.

The presence of alternative dispute resolution may reduce opportunities for corruption in developing economies. A judicial system in competition with other institutions is less able to extract rents from litigants. The poorest members of society and firms unaffiliated with large business groups are most likely to be affected adversely by inaccessible, corrupt, or inefficient courts. The experience with establishing a mediation facility in Bangladesh illustrates that transparent, swift, and accessible adjudication

---

12. Box 6.7

The creation of a specialized commercial court in Tanzania

Tanzania's Commercial Court was established in 1999 as a specialized division of the country's High Court. It was launched at a time when the government of Tanzania had committed to embracing a market system and wanted to accelerate the process of building a legal and judicial system to support market reforms.

The Commercial Court has jurisdiction over cases involving amounts greater than Tsh10 million (about $12,500). It has a higher fee structure than the general division of the High Court. The filing fee is about 3 percent of the amount in dispute in the Commercial Court, while in the general division fees are capped at Tsh120,000 (about $150). The high fees discourage many litigants; these litigants use the High Court. Appeals of the Commercial Court's preliminary or interlocutory orders, a common source of delay in the Tanzanian system, are barred by rule until the case is finished.

The Commercial Court may keep filing fees until it has covered its annual operating budget. The general division must remit all fees collected to the Treasury. This means that the Commercial Court has a more stable and timely funding source. Cases filed with the court from September 1999 to November 2000 have an average value of about Tsh 52 million ($65,000). About half involve debt recovery, a quarter involve other contract disputes, and the rest involve tort, trademark, property, company law, insurance, or tax claims. Banks and financial institutions are the heaviest users of the Commercial Court. About 80 percent of cases that go to the court are settled out of court through mediation or settlement negotiations.

Source: Finnegan 2001.

is possible with a relatively low budget.[13] The evidence indicates that enforcement works best when all parties understand how the decisions are reached. The legitimacy of mediation depends in large part on incentives for agents to abide by the decisions of the forum. In most countries, this incentive is provided by societal norms, the prospect of repeat dealings, or the threat of court actions. As the Bangladeshi example shows, transparency in the mediation process is important.

The main criticism of alternative dispute resolution methods, voluntary or otherwise, is that such mechanisms generally work better when the courts are efficient. In other words, parties to a dispute have incentives to settle when they know what court judgments they will get; courts complement ADR systems. However this is clearly not the case in many developing countries, where ADR systems function as substitutes. But to function in this manner, they need to effectively represent the community for whom they adjudicate. The *lok adalat*s in India, for example, are not very popular since they do not offer adequate compensation for victims, who face high costs in the courts to enforce their rights. These are more likely to be the poor people.

While few question the value of voluntary ADR mechanisms, mandatory systems have a mixed record and may have unintended consequences. This is partly due to the fact that litigants are bound by arbitration decisions. For example, they may go to the courts after mandatory arbitration. Voluntary arbitration systems may be set up by private parties or the government. In the United States, for example, the courts with the most intensive civil settlement efforts tend to have the slowest disposition times. Neither processing time nor judicial productivity is improved by extensive settlement programs. Referring cases to mandatory arbitration has no major effect on time to disposition, lawyer work hours, or lawyer satisfaction and has an inconclusive effect on attorneys' views of fairness. In some

---

13. Box 6.8

Alternative dispute resolution in Bangladesh

The Maduripur Legal Aid Association (MLAA), a Bangladeshi NGO, has set up a mediation structure in rural areas to deliver dispute settlement services for women. The local MLAA mediation committees meet twice a month to hear village disputes, free of charge. More than 5,000 disputes are mediated each year, of which two-thirds are resolved. The mediation program builds on the traditional shalish system of community dispute resolution and is not part of the court system. The MLAA staff is composed of only 120 people, since the mediation committees are made up of volunteers. The annual budget is small: only $80,000. The evidence suggests that a large majority of the settlements are respected because they are reached in full view of the community. Information on the process has helped strengthen legitimacy of the association. Approximately 60 percent of disputes involve family matters, 15 percent deal with property and land disputes, and the remainder mostly deal with disputes between neighbors. Plaintiffs prefer the mediation system since it is locally administered, free of charge, and relatively quick to render judgment; a decision is made within 45 days of the filing. In contrast, a court case will cost 250 taka in initial fees, and a minimum of 700 taka in lawyer's fees for a simple case. It will, on average, take three years to reach judgment.

Source: USAID 1998.

mediation programs—for instance in Japan and in some countries in Latin America—the mediator is also the judge. This situation may be procedurally unfair, as the judge may pressure the parties into a settlement. Parties will fear being frank before the same official who will pass judgment on them later.

Procedural law. Case studies also show that simplifying procedural law can increase judicial efficiency. A factor commonly associated with inefficiency in civil law countries is the predominance of written over oral procedures. This is particularly important in Latin America. A move toward oral procedures has produced positive results in Italy, Paraguay, and Uruguay. In the Netherlands the *kort geding*—technically, the procedure for a preliminary injunction—has developed informally into a type of summary proceeding on matters of substantive law. A *kort geding* rarely requires more than one oral hearing. Each party presents its case and replies immediately. The president of the court indicates the parties' chances of success in a full action, and the oral hearing often ends in settlement. On average, *kort geding* cases take six weeks. Oral procedures are a dominant characteristic of small claims courts and specialized tribunals.

Simplification of procedures tends to have a positive impact on efficiency because greater procedural complexity reduces transparency and accountability, increasing corrupt officials' ability to obtain bribes. Procedural simplification tends to decrease time and costs and increase litigant satisfaction (for instance, the streamlined procedure of British small claims courts, or justices of the peace in Peru). The efficiency of small claims courts seems to be driven by the simplicity of procedures. Indeed, English small claims courts are not a separate institution. County court procedures have merely been modified over the years to accommodate small claims.

The overall impact of procedural simplification depends on how burdensome the procedures were previously. Reforms in clogged systems may bring about a large increase in filings in the short run but in the long run will be associated with improved service, greater litigant satisfaction, and improvements in access.

Streamlining the system by which judicial procedure itself is determined can be beneficial. If every procedural change must go through the legislature, experimentation and innovation become difficult. Powers of the legislature to determine the organization and procedural rules of courts could be partially delegated to the judiciary; such a step has proved beneficial in Uruguay. Or the legislature could partially delegate these powers to individual courts to encourage more flexibility, as has been done in the United Kingdom, where small claims judges have the ability to adopt any procedure they believe will be just and efficient. Many procedures have been adopted because they were believed to serve fairness, protect the accused, and improve access of the poor. But the judiciary itself needs checks and balances. Such authority is best devolved to judges when there are also measures established to enhance accountability.

Another constraint on the ability of procedural reform to deliver greater judicial efficiency is the law itself. When the substantive rules are unclear and other institutions are weak, there may be a limit as to how much judicial efficiency can be improved through procedural reform. For instance, when most land is untitled, land tenure is insecure because no one is sure how courts will rule on a contested claim. A land-titling program, as Peru's experience shows, may increase judicial efficiency. In the Dominican Republic substantive changes in family and commercial law—reducing gender bias in custody cases, modernizing the commercial code, and implementing more effective sanctions against debtors—were necessary conditions for successful judicial reform. Substantive simplicity may also be behind the efficiency gains associated with the small claims court studies.

Fairness

Good governance requires impartial and fair legal institutions. This means guaranteeing the independence of judicial decision-making against political interference. A judiciary independent from both government intervention and influence by the parties in a dispute provides the single greatest institutional support for the rule of law. If the law or the courts are perceived as partisan or arbitrary in their application, the effectiveness of the judicial system in providing social order will be reduced. As discussed in previous sections, fairness also requires institutions that make judges accountable for their actions. Judicial independence needs to be coupled with a system of accountability in the judicial system. Civil society organizations and the media play a key role in monitoring judicial performance. The absence of checks on the judicial system can create arbitrariness.

Guarantees of judicial independence from the state

Judicial reform that aims to improve the quality and integrity of judicial decisions is best focused on creating politically independent, difficult-to-intimidate judges. Creating a system of checks and balances also improves fairness and integrity. For this, judicial independence needs to be coupled with a system of social accountability. . . .

A study commissioned for this Report collected data from the constitutions of 71 countries, examining three factors that guarantee judicial independence: the duration of appointment of supreme and administrative court judges; the extent to which administrative review of government acts is possible; and the role of legal precedent in determining how disputes are resolved. The same study shows how judicial independence strengthens enforcement of property rights in countries.[14]

Duration of appointment. When judges have lifelong tenure, they are both less susceptible to direct political pressure and less likely to have been appointed by the politicians currently in office. Independence is particularly important when judges are adjudicating disputes between citizens and the state (for example, freedom of speech issues and contract disputes). Therefore, the study focuses on the tenure of two different sets of judges: those in the highest ordinary courts (the supreme courts), and those in administrative courts, which have jurisdiction over cases where the state or a government agency is a party to litigation. Countries in which judges are independent from the influence of the state also tend to be countries where the judiciary is free from interference by private parties. The tenure of judges matters in both cases. Peru is frequently rated as the country with the least judicial independence. Former President Fujimori kept more than half of judges on temporary appointments from 1992 to 2000.

Administrative review. In some countries citizens can challenge administrative acts of the government only in administrative courts, which are part of the executive branch. In other countries, citizens can seek redress against administrative acts directly through ordinary courts, or they can request the supreme court to review decisions made by administrative courts. Arbitrary government actions, including those that limit the role of the judiciary, are less likely when the judiciary can review administrative acts.

The role of legal precedent. In some countries the role of courts is merely to interpret laws. In other countries courts have "lawmaking" powers because jurisprudence is a source of law. Judges have greater independence when their decisions are a source of law. Indeed, many legal scholars consider that the existence of case law as a legitimate source of law is the clearest measure of judicial independence. In some countries case law exists de facto although not de jure. For example, the French Revolution stripped all legislative power (and power over administrative acts) from the judicial system. However, judges in many civil law countries such as France and Germany do pay attention to precedent.

14. Figure 6.3
The independence of the judiciary enhances property rights

Note: Higher values indicate better enforcement and more independence.

Source: La Porta and others, 2001, World Development Report 2002 background paper.

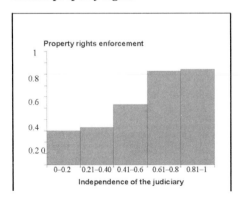

Property rights enforcement

Independence of the judiciary

In 53 out of the 71 countries in the sample, supreme court judges are appointed for life. This diverse group of countries includes, for example, Argentina and Ethiopia, Iran and Indonesia. Supreme court judges are appointed for terms of more than six years, but less than life, in nine countries, including Haiti, Japan, Mexico, Panama and Switzerland. Supreme court judges are appointed for less than six years in China, Cuba, Honduras, and Vietnam. The results for the tenure of administrative court judges follow a similar pattern.

The next indicator measures the independence of courts in ruling on the disputes between the government and its citizens. There are two aspects to this measure: which courts have the ultimate power over administrative disputes, and the tenure of judges in these courts. Administrative judges adjudicate many key disputes in this area. However, whereas in 17 countries, including France and Italy, the rulings of administrative judges are final, in 50 countries, including Bangladesh, Kenya, Mozambique, the United Kingdom, and the United States, these rulings can be appealed to judges in ordinary courts. A key implication of the ability to appeal administrative sentences in ordinary courts is that, as a result, the supreme court has ultimate jurisdiction over rulings of the administrative courts.

Supreme court control over administrative cases is possible in countries of any legal origin, but it tends to happen more in common law countries. Whereas the supreme court has ultimate control over administrative cases in 90 percent of the English legal origin countries, it has final authority only in 67 percent of the countries of French and German legal origin. But the ability of the supreme court to review sentences by administrative courts is a meaningful restraint on the power of the executive only when coupled with independent, tenured judges. Administrative review is conducted by judges with lifelong tenure and subject to supreme court review in 90 percent of English origin countries and 80 percent of Scandinavian countries, but only 37.5 percent of French origin countries and 16.7 percent of German origin countries.

Jurisprudence is a source of law in all English origin countries. However, jurisprudence is also a source of law in all Scandinavian origin countries and in 80 percent of German origin countries, including Germany, Japan, Korea, and Switzerland. French origin countries occupy an intermediate position. Jurisprudence is a source of law in 36 percent of these cases, including in France and in many Latin American countries that modeled their constitutions after that of the United States. These differences in case law across legal origins are magnified by the tenure of supreme court judges, the judges who ultimately interpret the law. For example, not only do supreme court judges have law-making power in English and Scandinavian origin countries but they also have lifelong tenure.

The data indicate that independence of judges from the state can be built into any legal system. The main constraint is not the nature of the legal system, but rather political factors, which determine the degree of independence of the judicial system. Restraint of arbitrary state action and accountability of the state is a critical development that needs to accompany overall judicial system development. In many developing countries, judicial independence could be enhanced by giving judges lifelong tenure, by giving them lawmaking powers, and by allowing supreme court review over administrative cases.

There are several other ways to enhance judicial independence in addition to the three just listed. First, the budget of the judicial system can be set as a fixed percentage of the total government budget by law. In this way, it will not be possible to deny resources to the judiciary. In most courts, as the example of the Tanzania commercial court illustrates, court fees can go toward the court budget. Only after this budget is replenished will money go toward the government budget. Second, transfers in judicial appointments can be made subject to the written approval of judges. This rule was instituted in France in 1976 and is necessary in countries like Kazakhstan, where the media recently reported cases of judges being reassigned after deciding cases against government agencies. Third, transparent criteria for career advancement are also likely to determine the degree of political independence. In most countries around the world, the executive or legislative branch decides on appointments to higher positions in the courts. This process creates opportunities for bargaining between politicians and judges in countries with high levels of corruption.

Conclusions

The judicial system plays an important role in the development of market economies. It does so in many ways: by resolving disputes between private parties, by resolving disputes between private and public parties, by providing a backdrop for the way that individuals and organizations behave outside the formal system, and by affecting the evolution of society and its norms while being affected by them. These changes bring law and order and promote the development of markets, economic growth, and poverty reduction. Judicial systems need to balance the need to provide swift and affordable—that is, accessible—resolution with fair resolution; these are the elements of judicial efficiency.

Judicial reform, like other institutional reforms, is often politically difficult. When considering institutional reform in this area, recognizing the complementarities among different institutional elements is key. Many elements affect judicial performance—for example, the institutional process for setting wages and promotions, procedural law, substantive law, the capacity of lawyers and judges, and the perceived relevance of the courts by people. Not all the elements that affect judicial performance are equally difficult politically. This is important: institutions work as systems. An improvement in one part can affect the efficiency of the whole system; that is, policymakers may complement various small reforms to improve efficiency while building momentum for larger reforms.

The success of judicial reforms depends on increasing the accountability of judges; that is, providing them with incentives to perform effectively, simplifying procedures, and targeting resource increases. One of the most important elements affecting judicial accountability is transparency, or the provision of information that makes it easy to monitor judicial performance and affect judges' reputations—for example, judicial databases that make cases easy to track and hard to manipulate or misplace.

Simplifying legal procedures tends to increase judicial efficiency. For example, for judicial systems that rely excessively on written procedures, a shift toward oral hearings tends to make trials simpler, faster, and cheaper, with little loss of accuracy. Reforms of this sort have improved efficiency and access in countries with diverse legal traditions. Small-claims courts and justices of the peace are widely popular because of their lay language and pared-down procedures. Simplification is particularly important in countries where complementary institutions are weak, and other types of reforms may be more difficult in the short run. Simplified procedures may also benefit the poorer members of society and increase their access to the judicial system. Alternative dispute resolution systems—based on social norms or on simplified legal procedures—can also enhance access of the disadvantaged to legal services. Partially delegating the "nuts and bolts" of procedural reform to the judicial branch can speed the process of innovation and experimentation.

Judicial reform that aims to improve the quality and integrity of judicial decisions is best focused on creating politically independent, difficult-to-intimidate judges. Creating a system of checks and balances also improves fairness and integrity. For this, judicial independence needs to be coupled with a system of social accountability. The channels for such accountability can be the free media and civil society organizations, or accountability can be built into the judicial system itself.

NOTES AND QUESTIONS

(1) The World Development report is perhaps the most influential policy paper prepared by the World Bank. Widely circulated, it produces tremendous informal pressure for "assisted" countries to comply with its general directives. The report is based on comparative data offered by bank sponsored projects such as the "Lex Mundi," comparing a very large number of countries (190). At the end of his comparative law course, the student will have tools to evaluate the value of policy recommendations based on such kind of comparative work.

For the time being it suffices to say that none of those in charge of preparing such comparative law based policy papers are jurists, let alone comparative legal scholars. Do you think it is responsible on the part of the World Bank to base its policy recommendations on how the law should be changed without employing comparative lawyers? What are the most visible biases that you can observe in the materials discussed above? Do you think it is a reasonable assumption that the same policy should guide transformations of so many different countries? Can a "one size fits all" approach work in the law? Can you think about some disturbing legitimacy implications of such an approach?

(2) Particularly revealing of the shortcomings of the WB comparative methodology is the discussion on ADR. In many non-industrial countries, mediation of disputes, with social peace as the most important prize, is the main "group centered" form of dispute resolution. It is not a new professionalized process (such as mediation or arbitration) developed for "efficiency reasons" as an alternative to formal rights based adjudication in a court of law. Thus, western style ADR, as that introduced in countless standard contracts, becomes, outside of the West, an even more powerful disempowering device. Indeed, participants to such mediations are stripped outside of the group protection and also outside of the fundamental western idea (or ideology) that individual rights of the weaker party are entitled to the same protection of those of the stronger. For a critical discussion of the social implications of ADR see Laura Nader, *Harmony Ideology: justice and control in a Zapotec mountain village* (1990) and, with a focus on the "group centered" nature of many non-western legal systems, an aspect completely neglected by the World Development Report, Laura Nader & Elisabetta Grande, "Current Illusions and Delusions about Conflict Management—In Africa and Elsewhere," 22 Law and Social Inquiry 3, 567 (2002).

(3) One of the most notable examples of economic growth in the last few decades is the People's Republic of China. The country is still widely considered to be "in transition" to the rule of law. See, for example, Stanley Lubman, *Bird in a Cage: Legal Reform in China After Mao* (2002), and Randall Peerenboom, *China's Long March toward Rule of Law* (2002). According to the rule of law orthodoxy that reigns among development economists as well as lawyers, the existence of clearly settled property rights is a pre-condition for stable economic growth. Remarkably, China did not even have a property law until 2007—a fact that seems to question the prescriptions offered by the World Bank Report. For a critique of simplistic invocations of rule law, see Frank Upham, *Myth-Making in the Rule of Law Orthodoxy*, Carnegie Paper No. 30, September 2002. For an analysis of China's "failure" to conform to the norms of the rule of law orthodoxy, see Donald C. Clarke, "Economic Development and the Rights Hypothesis: The China Problem," 51 Am. J. Comp. L. 89 (2003).

3.   W.T.O. AND LEGAL REFORMS: THE CASE OF CHINA

The W.T.O. plays a major role in the globalization of legal reforms, and its role has been especially central in the case of China. China became a member of the World Trade Organization on December 11, 2001, after a protracted negotiation process. The way to China's entry was paved by the bilateral U.S.-China trade agreement on November 15, 1999, which signified United States' support for China's admission. China's accession to the WTO has obviously been of great political, economic, and social interest. From a legal perspective, some of the most difficult issues have involved integrating non-market based aspects of China's legal regime with WTO's market based principles. (For a critical analysis of such issues, see Julia Ya Qin, "WTO Regulation of Subsidies to State–Owned Enterprises (SOEs): A Critical Appraisal," 7 J. Int'l Econ. L. 863 (2004).) Pointedly—and as expected—some commentators have complained of a general lack of rule of law in China, while others have expressed enthusiasm at the prospect of China's final alignment with the norms of liberal Western states.

Donald C. Clarke, China's Legal System and the WTO: Prospects for Compliance

2 Wash. U. Global Stud. L. Rev. 97, 104–116 (2003).

In assessing China's ability to fulfill its commitments respecting its legal system and to comply with WTO procedures . . . , we need both to look forward and to look back. Looking back, one cannot fail to be impressed with the amount of work that has been done by the government so far in identifying and revising—or abolishing where necessary—laws and regulations inconsistent with China's WTO obligations. This work began, of course, long before China's formal accession in November 2001. The scope of the effort can be appreciated by seeing what the Ministry of Foreign Trade and Economic Cooperation (MOFTEC) is reported to have achieved by the end of 2000 in anticipation of WTO membership: the review of over 1400 laws, regulations, and similar documents, including six statutes (of which five were revised), 164 State Council regulations (of which 114 were to be repealed and 25 amended), 887 of its own ministry regulations (of which 459 were to be repealed and 95 amended), 191 bilateral trade agreements, 72 bilateral investment treaties, and 93 tax treaties. In the first two months of 2001, the various ministries and commissions of the State Council reportedly reviewed some 2300 laws and regulations, of which 830 were identified as in need of repeal and 325 as in need of revision.

Needless to say, the process of trying to identify inconsistent regulations in the abstract is bound to miss many problem areas. Identifying inconsistency is sometimes easy, but at other times takes a high level of expertise and a full hearing by a dispute settlement panel in the context of a particular set of facts. Thus, we should not be surprised if many inconsistencies remain despite the government's efforts. Nevertheless, the government has so far shown a great deal of energy in addressing problems of legislative inconsistency.

A great deal of activity has also occurred outside of the field of legislative revision. In a relatively short period of time both before and after China's accession to the WTO, the government promulgated a flood of new regulations designed to implement China's commitments. Chinese officials have participated in countless training sessions, many with foreign financial support. The government has begun restructuring to facilitate the satisfaction of WTO requirements. For example, MOFTEC has established a Department of WTO Affairs to handle implementation and litigation, and a China WTO Notification and Enquiry Center in order to help implement its transparency commitments. MOFTEC has also established a Fair Trade Bureau for Import and Export to handle issues relating to unfair trade practices. The courts, for their part, have also undertaken training and other activities, such as review for WTO-compatibility of existing Supreme People's Court interpretations and other directives, designed to meet the requirements of WTO accession.

While much work remains to be done, there can be little doubt of the energy and commitment shown so far by the Chinese government. And this is to say nothing of the enthusiasm for knowledge about the WTO displayed outside of government. Almost any lecture or presentation mentioning the WTO is guaranteed to draw a large audience, and indeed among urban Chinese the English abbreviation is probably as common as, if not more common than, the original (and shorter) Chinese abbreviation (shi mao).

Looking forward, there is reason to be generally sanguine about the prospect of China's compliance with its commitments and its willingness and ability to modify its rules if it loses a WTO dispute settlement proceeding. But there will be disappointments, and it is necessary to understand and anticipate them in order to put them in proper perspective and distinguish real and pressing problems from temporary and minor ones.

As noted earlier, China undertook in the Working Party Report to meet its WTO commitments "through revising its existing laws and enacting new ones fully in compliance with the WTO Agreement." The extent to which China revises its existing laws and promulgates new ones is something that can be monitored with relative ease. But clearly it is not enough simply to promulgate new regulations. They must be applied and enforced. Here, there are at least two major issues worthy of discussion.

The first is the extent to which local governments will engage in WTO-inconsistent practices that the central government is unable or unwilling to stop. One issue is clear: there is no question that, as a legal matter under China's constitutional system, local governments must follow directives from the central government. Because the central government has the legal capacity to require local governments to conform to WTO obligations, it has the obligation to do so.

Some members of the WTO Working Party on China's accession were reported to have expressed concern that sub-national governments in China might take measures inconsistent with China's WTO obligations, and that the central government would not or could not remove such measures. China's representative assured them that local governments had no autonomous authority over trade-related matters, and that the central government would "ensure" (not merely take the "reasonable measures" called for by Article XXIV:12 of the General Agreement on Tariffs and Trade (GATT) 1994) that local government regulations conformed to China's WTO obligations. This assurance is one of China's formal commitments. Article XXIV: 12 of the GATT 1994, which presupposes a degree of independence on the part of local governments, simply does not apply.

Obviously, however, the real question is not quite as simple as the legal question. Sub-national governments in China can enjoy considerable de facto autonomy from Beijing; this is a fact, not simply a convenient excuse for inaction cooked up by the Chinese central government. China suffers from numerous internal trade barriers that the central government is continually struggling, often unsuccessfully, to remove. We should not be surprised if, even with good intentions, it has at least as much difficulty removing barriers to foreign goods and services.

The phenomenon of local protectionism is one that has attracted the attention and concern of academics and policymakers in China for some time. Internal trade barriers are just one aspect of it; favoritism to local parties in courts is another. But it is important to understand that it is not just foreigners who want to get rid of local protectionism. It is generally in the interest of the central government to expand its sphere of actual authority and to reduce such local protectionism. Practical considerations, more than ideological ones, have stood in the way of progress in this area. Academics and others have proposed for years, for example, that judges in local courts should be appointed and salaried by the central government instead of the local government. So far, however, the central government has not been willing to expend the political and financial resources necessary to put this reform into practice. But pressure for such reform is building. A recent article in Jingji Yaocan (Economic Reference), the internal (non-public) journal of the State Council's think tank on development issues, advocated precisely such a reform.[a]

The main factor behind local economic protectionism is the dependence of local government upon local enterprises for revenues. To the extent a government collects revenues, whether in the form of taxes or profits from an enterprise, it is similar to an owner and has an interest in protecting those revenues. When the owner of an enterprise can control the conditions under which that enterprise competes, the results are utterly predictable. With the further progress of economic reform in China, one might expect to see a widening of the tax base along with a reduction in the dependence of local governments upon specific enterprises for revenues. Needless to say, however, the influence of powerful local businesses seeking protection will not disappear in China any more than it has disappeared in China's trading partners.

The second issue is that of the capacity of China's courts to handle a substantial workload of reasonably complex cases. Here the news is neither especially good nor especially news, since it has been widely known for some time that China's courts are weak and its judges, on the whole, poorly qualified. China's courts will continue to present difficulties in the years ahead. On the other hand, as in many other areas of Chinese legal and political life, reform is most likely where there is a solid domestic constituency for it, and court reform is undoubtedly one of those areas. The key issues in court reform, from the standpoint of China's fellow WTO members, are the qualifications of judges, the willingness and capacity of courts to render fair judgments free of corruption and pressure from local government, and the ability of courts to execute those judgments once rendered.

The low qualifications of China's judges are no secret and indeed are a regular subject of discussion by high government officials, including the President of the Supreme People's Court. As of 1995, for example, only five percent of China's judges nationwide had a four-year college degree in any subject (let alone in law), and it is currently estimated that about ten percent of judges have a four-year college degree in law. A 1998 study of nine basic-level courts (the lowest level) in a major provincial city revealed that only three percent of the judges had a bachelor's degree in law. The "great majority" had held other types of jobs in the court administration such as bailiff, clerk, or driver before being promoted to the rank of judge.

a. See Wang Xu, Tuijin Sifa Tizhi Gaige, Ezhi Sifaquan Difanghua Qingxiang [Push Forward Reform of the Judicial System, Block the Trend Toward Localization of Judicial Power], Jingji Yaocan [Economic Reference], Nov. 31, 2001, at 11.

The frequency with which situations such as this are reported suggests strongly that there is no political difficulty with advocating reform and that such advocacy is supported in important sectors of the central government. China has in fact recently taken solid steps toward improving the qualifications of judges. In March of 2002, for example, China held the first administration of a new unified judicial examination for lawyers, prosecutors, and judges. Although sitting judges will not be required to take or pass the examination, to require this of judges going forward is already a surprisingly far-reaching reform at this stage of China's legal development. Indeed, one wonders whether the pool of those who pass and are willing to serve as judges will be big enough to serve the needs of the court system. In any case, however, this reform—and the political difficulties that must have been overcome to affect it—is solid evidence of the potential for significant reform to occur where there is a domestic constituency for it. Fortunately, there is a domestic constituency for significant further reforms in the judicial system.

In addition to the problem of the quality of judges, China's courts are at present not fully reliable as enforcers of statutorily guaranteed rights. This is true for a number of reasons. First, while statutes are superior to regulations issued by government ministries in China's formal constitutional structure, both government officials and court officials will generally consider a ministry regulation that is directly on point to be the applicable rule. This is simply a matter of what might be called customary legal culture; it has been both noted and criticized in China as well as abroad and many critics viewed WTO accession as a helpful spur to change. Nevertheless, change will not come quickly. Second, there is the well known problem of corruption in the judiciary. This problem is not of course unique to China. Third, Chinese courts often have difficulty enforcing their judgments. Fourth, and less well known, is the tendency of Chinese courts not to aggressively seek jurisdiction over cases, but on the contrary to fear it and often to go to great lengths to avoid taking difficult or sensitive cases. Courts in China have the choice of accepting or declining a case. This power is somewhat akin to the institution of summary judgment in its gate-keeping function, but quite unlike it in that it is not governed by any consistent set of principles other than the court's general sense of whether the case seems meritorious and deserving of further proceedings. Courts can use this power simply to decline to hear, and thus avoid ruling on the merits of, cases that look troublesome and likely to offend powerful interests no matter how the court decides. . . .

Because of China's relative lack of experience with a market economy, it is inevitable that despite the government's efforts to identify and weed out WTO-inconsistent legislation, some inconsistent rules and practices will remain, and new ones will crop up. It is in fact likely that many such inconsistent rules will be discovered over time. The government has already devoted considerable energy to making Chinese laws and regulations consistent with its WTO obligations. As in any country, there may be rules the government wishes to retain that its trading partners view as questionable under WTO principles, such as the E.U. rules on bananas or the U.S. rules on Foreign Sales Corporations. There may also be rules that displease China's trading partners that do not in fact run afoul of the WTO agreements. But there is no reason to doubt that the Chinese government is in principle genuinely committed to getting rid of many of the old rules that shackled the economy and has seized WTO accession as an opportune moment to do it. There is no reason to think that the Chinese government is committed to defending every WTO-inconsistent rule to the bitter end.

NOTE

Much attention has been paid on what joining WTO means for China's legal system and the status of rule of law in China. However, Julia Ya Qin has posed also the question of what China's access to WTO means for the WTO legal system.[1] Unlike its predecessor, the General Agreement on Tariffs and Trade, the WTO provides uniform rules of conduct for all its member states, replacing the fragmented GATT regime under which different contracting parties could have different obligations—an issue of concern to a comparative lawyer who wants to understand the interaction among different legal systems, whether those systems are national or international. As Professor Qin points out, however, when China acceded to WTO, its Accession Protocol prescribed a series of extensive obligations specific to China that go far beyond the ordinary requirements of the WTO, or what she calls "WTO-plus" obligations. For example, unlike any other WTO member, China is obligated to translate all laws and regulations related to trade into at least one of the official language of the WTO, and it has to do so within no later than 90 days of their implementation or enforcement. Unlike any other post-socialist "transition economy," China has been obligated to make commitments about its domestic economy structure and investment liberalization that go beyond simple compliance with WTO rules, and its economy is subjected to a much stricter discipline than any other WTO member. Although the WTO has not articulate any rationale for the extraordinary China-specific rules, Professor Qin speculates they are motivated by concerns about the sheer size of the Chinese economy. Yet whatever the rationale, she observes that such singling out of a single member-state for differential treatment goes against one of the most basic principles underlying the entire WTO regime: the principle of non-discrimination. The China Accession Protocol goes against the general rule-of-law notion that rules ought to be generally applicable. Effectively, it signals the creation of separate classes of WTO members. As Professor Qin puts it, the China Accession Protocol highlights a tension between "a generally rule-based WTO system" for existing members and a "power-based" regime based on *ad hoc* bargaining for those seeking accession.

4.   DEMOCRACY AND "RULE OF LAW" INITIATIVES

As the previous materials have made clear, since the end of the Cold War the promotion of democracy and, concomitantly, of rule of law around

---

1. Julia Ya Qin, "WTO–Plus: Obligations and Their Implications for the World Trade Organization Legal System: An Appraisal of the China Accession Protocol", 37 Journal of World Trade 483 (2003).

the globe has become a major preoccupation of western governments as well as non-governmental organizations. In his review of Thomas Carothers' influential book, *Aiding Democracy Abroad* (1999), William Alford sounds a few cautionary notes about the risks and limitations that are inherent in such enterprises.

William P. Alford, Exporting the Pursuit of Happiness

113 Harv. L. Rev. 1677, 1695–1711 (2000).

Why Democracy Promotion?

... The question of motivation [in democracy promotion] is more complex than it might at first seem. One could imagine a number of different and perhaps simultaneous purposes at play in the American impulse to promote democracy abroad. For example, such efforts could result from a genuinely altruistic desire to share what we believe is best about our society; from a belief in the promise of a more peaceful world (premised on the Kantian notion that democracy restrains governments from going to war, save against tyrants); or from a conviction that democracy is more conducive than any other political system to sustained economic growth. Alternatively, American efforts may be more attributable to an unwitting hegemonism; to a need to vindicate our ideals (or the ways in which we aspire to realize them) by having others adopt them; or to the waging of domestic academic and ideological debates on foreign terrain. Or perhaps the explanation owes more to realpolitik—as borne out in the solution democracy promotion may provide to practical political battles; in its potential for legitimating measures taken for American security, economic, and other interests; or in the capture by some self-interested subset of actors (such as aid bureaucracies, consultants, developing country elites, etc.) of a policy in which most Americans have little direct stake. What is the mix at any given point of these and other factors? How are tensions between them to be resolved? After all, it is conceivable that the goal of empowering others to elect governments that may better represent their views might simultaneously be at odds with the goal of using democracy promotion programs to advance specific American national interests (as, for example, when the Senate of the post-Marcos Republic of the Philippines voted to terminate the U.S. lease on Clark Air Base and the Subic Bay Naval Station that the ancien régime had been only too happy to allow the United States to hold)....

What Are We Measuring and How?

... How are we to attribute success or failure to a particular democracy promotion effort, given that few foreign actors (beyond the aid community) experience such projects directly and that the more general impact of these programs is likely to be inextricably linked with a host of other influences? For example, it seems reasonable to think that factors such as the expectations of a populace that has long suffered under nondemocratic regimes, the collapse of the Soviet Union (as the chief provider of financial and ideological support for certain nondemocratic regimes), the behavior of neighboring states, and multilateral assistance or private philanthropy of the type represented by George Soros, would be more likely to explain moves toward democracy than a modestly funded, fairly bureaucratized U.S. governmental undertaking. Indeed, it could be that such factors might even be strong enough to overcome an ill-conceived or poorly executed democracy promotion program; or perhaps that American and other bilateral assistance is more likely to flow to projects with a good possibility of success, rather than those with limited prospects, no matter how worthy the latter may be relative to the former. Conversely, one could imagine a well-designed, competently executed program of democracy assistance failing for a myriad of reasons, including local ethnic tensions, distrust of the United States resulting from support of the previous (or current) authoritarian regime, the unwillingness of other important democratic states to support a principled American call for sanctions, and the sheer frustration of a newly liberated populace with the adjustments and delay occasioned by any serious effort at democratization. Moreover, there is the important question of the appropriate time frame for judging the effectiveness of the democracy promotion program in question. Although Brian Tamanaha may well have been correct in chastising Trubek and Galanter for their impatience in writing off earlier rule of law programs as a failure after less than a decade,[a] we might nonetheless be reluctant to adopt the perspective attributed to the late Chinese premier Zhou Enlai (1899–1976) who purportedly replied to a question about the significance of the French Revolution with the answer that "it is too early to say." . . .

Efforts at measuring democracy promotion programs also require recognizing that even the best delivered message will not necessarily ensure comparable results in different settings. Notwithstanding Nebraska Senator Kenneth Wherry's famous declaration that "[w]ith God's help, we will lift Shanghai up and ever up until it is just like Kansas City," the jazz band at Shanghai's Heping Hotel still leaves a good deal to be desired even before we get to the question of barbecue. To make this point is not to lose sight of the good in search of the perfect. As Alan Watson has nicely chronicled, for centuries we legal types have been lifting ideas from our foreign compatriots, often benefiting from such legal transplantation even in the face of imperfect understanding, incomplete replication, and inapt application.[b]

Consider, for example, the case of the People's Republic of China (PRC), although one could just as well substitute that of Russia, Indonesia, or several African or Eastern European states. Since the end of the Great Proletarian Cultural Revolution in the mid–1970s, the PRC has been

a. See Brian Z. Tamanaha, Lessons of Law-and-Development Studies, 89 Am. J. Int'l. L. 470, 473 (1995) (reviewing Law and Crisis in the Third World (Sammy Adelman & Abdul Paliwala eds., 1992); and Law and Development (Anthony Carty ed., 1993)).

b. See Alan Watson, Legal Transplants: An Approach to Comparative Law (2d ed. 1993).

engaged in the most concerted effort in world history to construct a legal system, with assistance from the U.S. government and a veritable cavalcade of other governments, multilateral bodies, foundations, universities, and individuals. Thousands of laws and other legal measures have been enacted; the court system has been revamped; a host of new regulatory bodies has been established; and a bar that numbered 3000 in 1979 has already multiplied more than fifty-fold (with plans to expand to 300,000 over the next decade), facilitating citizen use of the legal system in unprecedented numbers.

The conventional wisdom portrays such developments as bearing out the PRC's convergence, importantly influenced by the United States, toward the rule of law. Such accounts, however, fail adequately to heed the ways in which these very developments may arguably be impeding, as well as advancing, liberal legality. The Chinese state, for example, is increasingly invoking the law to justify both at home and abroad its harsh treatment of dissidents and autonomous spiritual groups. Corruption has mushroomed, facilitated by opportunities for rent seeking made possible by the bevy of new regulatory and licensing measures. And evidence suggests that some among the PRC's burgeoning corps of legal professionals, far from serving as a vanguard of legal and political reform, have much to gain from an economy that remains perched between plan and market, subject to the discipline of neither.

To acknowledge the underside of legal reform is neither to be dismissive of the way in which Chinese legal development may be empowering the citizenry, irrespective of the Communist Party's intentions, nor to make a blanket argument against foreign efforts to assist that development. Rather, it is to contend that serious attempts to assess democracy promotion must account for unintended and undesired consequences far more than they have. In the case of law, such an accounting would require that those shaping and executing democracy promotion programs embrace a more nuanced appreciation of the uses to which law may be put. Law has, in recent years, come to occupy an increasing role in democracy assistance because some proponents see it as promoting liberal values (at least in the minimal sense of fostering regularity, predictability, and constraints on the arbitrary exercise of state power). Paradoxically, however, a considerable number of democracy promotion advocates also tend to portray law as neutral and hence capable of being effectively deployed by a range of different regimes to achieve a broad spectrum of developmental ends. This inconsistency may in part be due to the awkwardness of raising certain sensitive issues, or to the formal prohibition in the charters of some multilateral bodies on dealing in the political realm, but it also, I suggest, is indicative of a serious and largely unacknowledged tension in our thinking regarding democracy promotion. We are, in effect, extolling law as distinguishable from politics in that it rises above the instrumental at the same time that we are proclaiming its utility as an instrument for development (through promotion efforts that themselves might be described by some as highly instrumental). Perhaps we ought, therefore, not be surprised that political figures facing fundamental issues of power and state building, if not survival itself, would utilize law in ways other than those we might have hoped or envisioned.

What Are the Ethical Implications of Democracy Promotion?

As the foregoing suggests, embedded in democracy promotion are difficult ethical questions. . . . For example, how does one weigh the introduction of what may be useful new notions of democracy to a people living under a repressive regime against the possible perpetuation of that regime by virtue of legitimating its rule and providing it with instruments that it might employ toward a repressive end? Without romanticizing the past, what are the implications, in terms of "traditional" social arrangements, of the introduction of a more rights-focused, marketized approach to life? Are we proposing legal solutions to problems that might be better addressed through politics or other means? Is our faith in highly rational, carefully sequenced evolutionary change ultimately so illusory as to be misleading, particularly for societies emerging from and needing to cope with searing national trauma? What degree of disclosure of our aspirations for the programs we promote do we owe to recipient regimes or their broader populace? Before or while engaging in democracy promotion programs, what responsibility do we have to address other American governmental or private activities that may be impeding democratic development abroad? What responsibility do we have concurrently to address serious impediments to the fuller realization of our ideals at home? And, ultimately, no matter how much we cherish that which we impart, what do we believe entitles us to interject ourselves into the lives of others, especially if we are far more willing to provide advice than funding for basic needs? These and many other questions that one might raise defy ready answers, but their difficulty arguably makes it all the more crucial that they feature more prominently in the debate over democracy promotion.

The need for more open discussion of the ethical implications of democracy promotion is important, of course, not only because of the considerable effect such programs may have on those on the receiving end, but also because of their influence on those providing the assistance. One major illustration of the hubris that infuses the democracy promotion effort has been the near absence of serious scrutiny of what such undertakings mean for those on the transmitting end.

History suggests that the experience of endeavoring to shape others inevitably shapes us, both with respect to our thinking about our own society, the complexity of legal reform, and law more generally, and with respect to our reaction to exercising the quite considerable power these efforts frequently bestow. To take one cogent example from American legal academe, it is no exaggeration to say that the critical legal studies movement emerged in part from the disillusionment of David Trubek and others who, in attempting to utilize American models of liberal legality to transform Brazil while under contract to USAID, became profoundly skeptical about the claims of those models, even on their home terrain. But the impact might well be felt in very different ways, as borne out, for instance, by Roscoe Pound who, after serving as a key advisor on legal reform to the government of the Republic of China during the Chinese civil war of the late 1940s, reacted to the failure of the measures he proposed to take hold in China by embracing the fervent anti-communism of Senator Joseph McCarthy following his return home. And as recent attempts by foreign actors to influence our presidential elections suggest, some lessons, intended or otherwise, of our democracy promotion programs may have been absorbed only too well. . . .

NOTES AND QUESTIONS

(1) The World Development Report 2002, while dealing with law uses as its most visible inspirational value "efficiency" and "judicial performance". Other extremely significant social values, which we will discuss in this book, are thus completely erased. For example, judicial decision making might have a strong identity structuring function. In many occasions it has a pedagogical value to bring the knowledge of law to the people. Comparativists have been talking about "legal cultures" as extremely delicate and deeply grounded aspects of social organization. The law has been studied in analogy with language. It would be reductive for a linguist to discuss its subject matter with in mind only the "communicative" performance of language. Language serves indeed many other purposes (such as writing beautiful, civilizing, prose or poetry) even if one looks at it within a purely functionalist approach. It seems that the focus on efficiency driven reform equates law to a technology rather than to a cultural or political artifact of social organization. While this trend seems the rule in the United States, within a dominant utilitarian and economically driven paradigm, it is questionable to assume that efficiency driven reforms would make all societies per se better off. Comparative law should resist this approach. Its vision of the law is broad, richly textured and highly contextualized in the social and political setting is has to govern. Perhaps a more diffused study of comparative law would make U.S. lawyers more sensitive to the many legitimate alternative functions and visions of law.

(2) According to increasing numbers of scientists and now a majority of ecologists, global transformations have enormously accelerated a pattern of unsustainable economic development. From the eighties of last century the heavy demands imposed on mother earth have largely overcome the replacement rates. Oil extraction is reaching the "tipping point" after which a very fast exhaustion of the world reserves is predictable. Water extraction from deep in the earth is also far beyond sustainability. Global warming is producing melting of glaciers with consequent rising of the sea levels (with grim prediction of millions of coastal refugees); transformation of major rivers (such as among many others the Ganges and the Yellow River) into seasonal water flows with devastating prospects for agriculture; increase of the frequency and the strengths of metrological catastrophes such as Hurricane Katrina. Deforestation, highly accelerated by the need of clear land (mostly for bio-diesel production) and by the construction demands for sheltering some seventy million new human beings a year in what is already an overpopulated world (6.7 billion humans) is itself contributing to a foreseeable disaster that might endanger human civilization.

Short term individual economically driven motivations are behind this state of affairs. The law has long been the instrument by which collective decision making can be imposed on individual behaviors. There is today a need of more global law rather than less to tackle this millennium emergency. But global law cannot stem from the ideological agenda of more or less authoritative policy makers, looking into abstract economic theory to tackle a far too complex reality, artificially simplified (see the World Development Report) or even caricaturized. There is at least a need to have available a catalogue of historically tested "best legal practices", of local success stories around which to build from the bottom up a new legal civilization. For the production of such a catalogue, which is needed sooner rather than later, comparative law is uniquely located. In the historical Chapter we will discuss the rich Chinese legal tradition that is simply erased by focusing only on the last thirty years of state-capitalist developments.

(3) Professor Alford's discussion on "democracy promotion" opens the issue of hubris and of double standards, too often deployed by western and especially U.S. observers of a foreign reality. To the issue of the legitimacy of international intervention comparative law has much to offer. We will discuss this issue further but, for the time being, the student might want to start thinking on the following experience he/she might have felt. Most often, if we travel in Africa or in South America and we see social realities we dislike (e.g. lower rates of literacy for girls ad opposed to boys) we feel an urgency to "intervene", to do something, to "help out" in solving the problem. Interestingly we may not feel the same urge when we travel in different settings such as northern Europe or North America. We probably do not feel morally compelled to open an NGO or "to do something" on the issue of alcoholism or of women abuse, say, in Sweden. Why?

5.   A CAVEAT ON LEGAL ORIENTALISM

After having read the previous materials, it is worth pausing to consider one of the most fundamental problems of comparison which tends not even to arise so long as our analyses focus primarily on the differences and similarities between professionalized civil law and common law systems (like in the "legal origins" metaphor deployed by the World Development Report). That is, the moment we move beyond the metropolitan West, it is no longer self-evident just what constitutes "law" and whether there is even a "there" for us to compare. For example, some cultures such as China and Japan have been described as lacking "real" law or "real" rights historically, and some have disputed whether the notion of "socialist law" is a coherent concept. The category of religious law likewise has given rise to much jurisprudential debate.[1]

---

1. To be sure, as we will see when we discuss legal pluralism, *infra* at pp. 131–44 and 248–58, the notion of law is in fact far more complicated even in the contemporary United States than we might think at first blush: determining what is "law" and what is culture will arise in analyzing the "cultural" defense, "gypsy law," and the micro-legal system of queuing, for example. See *infra*.

(a) Problem of Legal Orientalism: Rites or Rights?

Teemu Ruskola, Legal Orientalism

101 Mich. L. Rev. 179 (2002).

That the Chinese legal tradition is lacking is an observation as clichéd as the solicitude that is routinely expressed toward comparative law.... But just what does it mean to claim that China suffers from a (relative or absolute) lack of "law"? After all, only the most negligent observer could miss the fact that imperial China boasted dynastic legal codes going back to the Tang dynasty, and earlier. The point is usually a subtler one: whatever law China has known is a form that falls short of "real" law. This view is implicit in the oft-stated claim that Chinese law has been historically exclusively penal and associated with criminal sanctions. Especially in continental systems, civil law stands at the heart of jurisprudence, and its absence thus signifies a gaping hole at the center of the Chinese legal system. Sometimes, the implicit yardstick for "real" law is formal legal rationality in the Weberian sense, while at other times it is a liberal legal order that constrains the state in a particular way—a configuration often referred to as "the rule of law." Legal historian Thomas Stephens has recently argued that Chinese law is not even worthy of the term "jurisprudence." As a more descriptive term for the study of Chinese non-law, Stephens offers the neologism "obsequiiprudence,"[1] presumably signifying the scholarly study of obsequious submission to authority and hierarchy. Whatever the merits of Stephens' thesis may be, in the view of nineteenth-century international lawyers, Chinese law was so "uncivilized" as to exclude China from the "Family of Nations," which in turn served as a justification for reducing the country to a semi-colonial status under a regime of Western extraterritorial privileges.[2]

The goal of this Article is not to defend Chinese law, whether past, present or future. Ultimately, the answer to the question whether or not there is law in China is always embedded in the premises of the questioner: it necessarily depends on the observer's definition of law. Hence, my aim here is not to "prove" that there is in fact such a thing as a tradition of Chinese "law." Indeed, there already exists a considerable scholarly literature on Chinese law (however defined), and among students of Chinese law the idea of China's inherent lawlessness—at least in the crude form of the thesis—is a discredited notion.

However, outside of the academic study of Chinese law, ideas of China's lawlessness continue to abound. Indeed, one of the primary obstacles to a serious discussion of Chinese law is the blank stares with which one is frequently met upon confessing an interest in the subject: "What

---

1. Thomas B. Stephens, Order and Discipline in China: The Shanghai Mixed Court 1911–27, at 115 (1992). While one can in good faith argue about the possibility of comparative law across cultures and times, Stephens coinage is gratuitously offensive.

2. *See generally* Gerrit W. Gong, The Standard of 'Civilization' in International Society 130–63 (1984).

Chinese 'law'? There is no law in China!'' (Sometimes followed by a more tentative, ''Is there law in China?'') Unlike the more traditional comparativist who studies French or German law, for example, the student of Chinese law frequently needs to convince her audience that the subject matter exists in the first place.... Why, despite vigorous efforts to debunk it, does the view of China's lawlessness continue to prevail—not only in the popular opinion and among policy-makers, but even among legal scholars who do not specialize in China as well as China scholars who do not specialize in law? Chinese civil law, for example, has been discovered and re-discovered periodically in the West. What preconceptions make it possible for it to be discovered and forgotten again so quickly, leaving it to wait for yet another round of ''discovery''?

There are, no doubt, multiple answers to this complex of questions. This Article directs the inquiry into a certain historiographic tradition it calls ''Legal Orientalism.'' It starts from the premise that, in many ways, ''history does not belong to us; we belong to it.''[3] Inevitably, ''[o]ur historical consciousness is always filled with a variety of voices in which the echo of the past is heard.''[4] The Orientalist history of comparative law constitutes one important tradition from which the work of today's comparative lawyers emerges, and whether we consciously reject or embrace that tradition, it still provides the context against which that work is written, read, understood, and misunderstood. As David Halperin describes the marvelous efficiency with which prejudice relies on unstated ''truths'' in communication, ''if the message is already waiting at the receiver's end, it doesn't even need to be sent; it just needs to be activated.''[5] Whatever our own ''prejudices'' about Chinese law may be—and they may be either positive or negative—in our writings we are likely to be activating messages of which we are not even aware. By elaborating a genealogy of legal Orientalism, I hope to analyze some prevailing cultural prejudices that inform the interpretation of comparative scholarship on Chinese Law....

I begin the account of Chinese legal subjectivity, or its absence, by outlining Hegel's vision of China in his *Philosophy of History*. I do so without any implication that Hegel ''invented'' Orientalism or is somehow singularly responsible for it. Uninterested in either accusing or excusing its author, I use the *Philosophy of History* simply as a textual case study, for it happens to provide a truly classic statement of many Orientalist ideas that continue to structure the perception of Chinese law even today.

According to Hegel, ''The history of the world travels from East to West, for Europe is absolutely the end of History, Asia the beginning.''[6] In Hegel's dual ontology, Oriental states ''belong to mere space,'' or ''unhistorical history,'' while the West exists in the ''form of time.''[7] According to Hegel,

---

3. Hans-Georg Gadamer, Truth and Method 276 (Joel Weinsheimer & Donald G. Marshall eds., Crossroad 2d rev. ed. 1989) (1960).

4. *Id*. at 284.

5. David M. Halperin, St. Foucault: Towards a Gay Hagiography 13 (1995).

6. Georg Wilhelm Hegel, The Philosophy of History 103 (J. Sibree trans., 1956).

7. *Id*. at 105–06.

With the Empire of China, history has to begin, for it is the oldest, as far as history gives us any information, and its principle has such substantiality, that for the empire in question it is at once the oldest and the newest. Early do we see China advancing to the condition in which it is found at this day, for as the contrast between objective existence and subjective freedom of movement within it is still wanting, every change is excluded, and the fixedness of character which recurs perpetually takes the place of what we should call, the truly historical.[8]

Hegel's statement of China's extraordinary stability is no doubt extreme, yet it has many historical variations. In Marx's scathing metaphor, China "vegetates in the teeth of time,"[9] while Weber saw in Confucianism a religion that worshipped the status quo and thus radically impeded China's passage into modernity.

In Hegel's particular teleological view, History's end goal is the accomplishment of freedom, which coincidentally culminates in the political system of Prussia. In contrast, China, standing at the threshold of History, is the paradigmatic example of "Oriental Despotism." Despotism is in fact the natural form of government for the Chinese, for the simple reason that they do not exist as individual subjects. In Hegel's words, in China "all that we call subjectivity is concentrated in the supreme Head of the State,"[10] while "individuals remain mere accidents."[11] This despotism results in part from a confusion between family and state: "The Chinese regard themselves as belonging to the family, and at the same time as children of the state."[12] By implication, the Chinese also lack a proper distinction between law and morality: moral dicta are expressed in the form of laws, but lacking subjectivity, the Chinese obey these laws merely as external forces, like children who fear parental punishment.

Analyzed as an Orientalist discourse, Hegel's account accomplishes several things. First, the purported fact that China is timeless and static implies that the West is not. Second, imputing to the Chinese a lack of subjectivity and moral character suggests that Westerners do not lack those progressive qualities. Third, observing that the Chinese are confused about the real nature of "law" establishes the European legal ordering as proper. The Orientalist implications are not difficult to grasp: China is an anti-model and stands for everything that we would not wish to be—or admit to

---

8. *Id.* at 116.

9. Karl Marx on Colonialism and Modernization 323 (Shlomo Avineri ed., 1968); *see also* Marx on China, 1853–1860: Articles from the New York Daily Tribune (Dona Torr ed., 1951). For an elaboration of the theoretical place of China in Marx's thought, see Donald M. Lowe, The Function of "China" in Marx, Lenin, and Mao (1966).

10. Hegel, *supra* note 6, at 113.

11. *Id.* at 105. For a twentieth-century version of the enduring idea of Oriental Despotism, updated for the needs of the Cold War, *see* Karl A. Wittfogel, Oriental Despotism: A Comparative Study of Total Power (1957).

12. Hegel, *supra* note 6, at 121.

being. This is an entirely negative definition: China is basically just a "glimpse of what it, itself, is not," viz., we, the Occident.[13]

Hegel, Marx, and Weber are classical European Orientalists whose work ultimately affirms the superiority of Western civilization and law. However, they do not exhaust the universe of legal Orientalisms, which vary by historical and cultural context. The anti-immigrant Orientalism of nineteenth-century United States provides an example of a peculiarly American form of Orientalism. As one historian of Chinese immigration observes, nineteenth-century Americans viewed almost every aspect of Chinese life as an illustration of their backwardness: "wearing white for mourning, purchasing a coffin while still alive, dressing women in pants and men in skirts, shaking hands with oneself in greeting a friend, writing up and down the page, eating sweets first and soup last, etc."[14]

The usefulness of this particular Orientalist discourse lay in its role in justifying the legal exclusion of Chinese immigrants at that historical moment. Indeed, the text of an 1878 report by the California State Senate Committee on Chinese Immigration sounds as though it had been excerpted directly from Hegel's Philosophy of History:

> The Chinese are ... able to underbid the whites in every kind of labor. They can be hired in masses; they can be managed and controlled like unthinking slaves. But our laborer has an individual life, cannot be controlled as a slave by brutal masters, and this individuality has been required by the genius of our institutions, and upon these elements of character the State depends for defense and growth.[15]

Such sentiments may have very much a nineteenth-century flavor, but consider also the following analysis of the Chinese immigration exclusion, made by a federal judge in the 1920s:

> The yellow or brown racial color is the hallmark of Oriental despotisms, or was at the time the original naturalization law was enacted. It was deemed that the subjects of these despotisms, with their fixed and ingrained pride in the type of their civilization, which works for its welfare by subordinating the individual to the personal authority of the sovereign, as the embodiment of the state, were not fitted and suited to

---

13. Haun Saussy, Hegel's Chinese Imagination, in The Problem of a Chinese Aesthetic 161 (1993).

14. Stuart Creighton Miller, The Unwelcome Immigrant: The American Image of the Chinese 1785–1885, at 27–28 (1969).

15. State of California, Senate Special Committe on Chinese Immigration, *quoted in* Thomas Almaguer, Racial Fault Lines: The Historical Origins of White Supremacy in California 174 (1994). These conclusions were foreshadowed by a joint special committee of the U.S. Congress: "To admit these vast numbers of aliens to citizenship and the ballot would practically destroy republican institutions on the Pacific coast, for the Chinese have no comprehension of any form of government but despotism, and have not the words in their own language to describe intelligibly the principles of our representative system." Report of Joint Special Committee to Investigate Chinese Immigration, S. Rep. No. 689, 44th Cong., 2nd Sess. (1877), *quoted in* Leti Volpp, Obnoxious to Their Very Nature: Asian Americans and Constitutional Citizenship, 5 Citizenship Stud. 57, 63 (2001).

make for the success of a republican form of Government. Hence they were denied citizenship.[16]

To the judge, it was thus self-evident that Congress's exclusion of the Chinese from immigration was not based on "color" but cultural disqualification for citizenship.[17] That is, the Chinese were so radically "un-legal" that they were simply not capable of the kind of self-governance that was required by America's "republican form of Government."

(b) Note on the "Ritual of Rights"

In a study entitled The Ritual of Rights in Japan: Law, Society, and Health Policy (2000), Eric Feldman challenges the oft-made claim that the Japanese do not assert their "rights" because to do so goes against Japanese legal, political, and social norms. Feldman argues that because of their almost exclusive focus on litigation rates, both Japanese and Western scholars have not understood properly what he calls "the ritual of rights" in Japan. In his book, Feldman gives examples of just how rights are in fact being asserted, but in different ways and in different contexts, such as negotiation rather than formal litigation, for example.

> To better understand the contours of the alleged contrast between the United States and Japan, it is critical to distinguish between jurisprudential rights, cultural myths about rights, and the strategic assertion of rights .... Rights in Japan do matter, but they exhibit differences from, and matter in different ways than, rights in the United States. Living in Japan and in daily contact with the Japanese, one is aware of how rarely the word *kenri* (right) is used in daily conversation, even when there is an overt dispute that from an American perspective seems to involve rights. When individuals are angry, or feel cheated, or abused, they are likely to walk away, or to change the subject, or to act extraordinarily polite, rather than to claim that their rights have been aggrieved. Such behavior is not an indication that the parties fail to understand rights, but that rights are not an acceptable tool of one-on-one argument. It is a bad strategy to start talking about rights, because the other party will recoil, the relationship will be severely damaged, and the possibility of a fast or advantageous solution will vanish. Thus the public, aggressive assertion of rights is reserved for particular types of conflicts, generally those in which the hope of continuing a superficially harmonious relationship between the parties has been abandoned, and the possibility for informal agreement is stalled. (pp. 4, 5)

---

16. Terrace v. Thompson, 274 F. 841, 849 (W.D. Wash. 1921), *aff'd*, 263 U.S. 197 (1923).

17. *Id.* ("It is obvious that the objection on the part of Congress is not due to color, *as color*, but only to color as an evidence of a type of civilization which it characterizes.") (emphasis added).

6. THE COMPARATIVE METHOD AS AN APPROACH TO LEGAL SCHOLARSHIP

Comparative law used to be labeled as a method or sometimes as a science. The debate, started early in the twentieth century, shortly after the already mentioned Paris conference of 1900, conventionally known as the "founding moment" of our discipline.[1] It unfolded at a time in which the Western legal scholarship in general and the European one in particular, were successfully claiming a scientific status. It is just natural that comparative law, eager to be recognized as a prestigious academic discipline, would make similar claims. At this very early moment in its childhood, comparative law had developed what some critical observers call a *Cinderella Complex*.[2] On the one hand, its adepts felt that their approach was more worldly and sophisticated than that of their "municipal" or "parochial" law school colleagues. Therefore, they developed a sense of pride and belonging to a community that was early-endowed with its academic institutions like the prestigious International Academy of Comparative Law founded in The Hague, in Holland in 1924, which has ever since presided over the organization of a major event every four years. On the other hand, comparative law experts have always been quite marginal in law schools, regarded as a strange type of jurists compelling them to justify their very existence. In most U.S. law schools, even today the comparative law professor is often known by his peers as the colleague with the funny accent. . . .

Early methodological debates on the nature and functions of comparative law, therefore, abound on law review articles and introductory chapters of books, producing a large amount of highly technical literature that certainly has not helped in enhancing the reputation of our discipline.[3] Recently, a leading comparative lawyer, participating in a new wave of critical methodological discussion, has gone as far as arguing for the end of comparative law as an autonomous discipline.[4]

Today, we know that the early debates on comparative law as a science or a method are pedantic and rather pointless. There is no one method of comparative law but a large variety of methods to compare laws, fitting the different objects of a given comparative project. For example, if we wish to compare the land law of Mali with the land law of Afghanistan, two legal cultures in which a thick component of the legal system is neither written

---

1. *See* Anna di Robilant & Ugo Mattei, "The Art and Science of Critical Scholarship: Postmodernism and International Style in the Legal Architecture of Europe," 75 Tulane Law Review 1053–1092 (2001).

2. *See* Günther Frankenberg, Critical Comparisons: Re-thinking Comparative Law, 26 Harvard International Law Journal 411, 412 (1985).

3. *See* L.J. Costantinesco, Traité de droit comparé Tome II, Lgdj, Paris, 1972, pp. 81ff.

4. *See* Mathias Reimann, The End of Comparative Law as an Autonomous Subject, 11 Tulane European & Civil Law Forum 49 (1996).

nor dominated by a formalized legal profession as in Germany or the U.S., we might find useful or even unavoidable to use an *ethnographic or an anthropological method* in the study of comparative law.[5] However, if we wish to compare corporate governance in Switzerland with corporate governance in the United States, an approach known as *Comparative Law & Economics* might be in order.[6] Moreover, to compare the *styles* of judicial legal decisions in different legal systems, we might find useful a comparative study using literary criticism as its central method.[7]

As to comparative law as a "science," today, we are generally skeptical (at least in the United States) about such claims when it comes to the nature of law. We can, however, accept that law, as a social phenomenon, can be approached with a *scientific method* of inquiry by advancing hypotheses concerning its nature and by testing them empirically. Comparative data about the behavior of law in different contexts and conditions are certainly a crucial component of any scientific testing of a proposition about the nature of law.[8] To be sure, one should also consider and take into account the critical position that denies any possibility of objective "scientific knowledge" in the social sciences. For such critics then, comparison, rather than being a scientific exercise should be considered an experience of participatory observation, discounting the inevitable political and cultural biases of the observer.[9]

In more critical vein, comparative law has been described as a narrative hiding behind a façade of scientific neutrality—a conservative political agenda.[10] Without belaboring too much on a scholarly dispute, interesting as it might be, we might want to sum up the most recent developments by mentioning that "ethnocentrism" and "orientalism" are broadly pointed out as the two main enemies of serious comparative inquiry in the domain of the law.[11] Any student approaching for the first time our discipline must be prepared to get rid of all assumptions about the very nature of the law, including those that he or she might consider more natural. Comparativists should always display an attitude of learning rather than of teaching, of

---

5. *See* Keita, Amadou (2003) "Au Detour des Pratiques Foncieres a Bancoumana: Quelques Observations sur le Droit Malien," Global Jurist Frontiers: Vol. 3, Iss. 1, Article 4. Available at: http://www.bepress.com/gj/frontiers/vol3/iss1/art4.

6. *See generally* on this method, Ugo Mattei, Comparative Law and Economics, (1997). Of course, the ethnographic and historical method can be usefully applied even in the case of "economic" subject matter. *See e.g.,* Ellen Hertz, The Trading Crowd: An Ethnography of the Shanghai Stock Market (1998), and Teemu Ruskola, Conceptualizing Corporations and Kinship: Comparative Law and Development Theory in a Chinese Perspective, 23 Stan. L. Rev. 1599 (2000).

7. *See* Mitchell de S.O.l'E. Lasser, Judicial (Self-) Portraits: Judicial Disclosure in

the French Legal System, 104 Yale Law Journal 1325, 1332 (1995).

8. *See* R. Sacco, Legal Formants: a Dynamic Approach to Comparative Law, 39 American Journal of Comparative Law, 1–34 (Part I); 343–401 (Part II) (1991).

9. *See* Günther Frankenberg, Critical Comparisons: Re-thinking Comparative Law, 26 Harvard International Law Journal 411, 412 (1985).

10. David W. Kennedy, The Politics and Methods of Comparative Law in Pierre Legrand (ed.) Comparative Legal Studies: Traditions and Transitions (2003).

11. *See* Teemu Ruskola, Legal Orientalism, 101 Michigan Law Review 179 (2002).

listening rather than of talking. They should never be judgmental but only try to understand. They should be humble and ready to be surprised about others, but also about themselves. In Gunther Frankenberg's image, the comparative lawyer should be like a traveler, experiencing the marvel of discoveries.

By the use of comparison, it then should become possible to make observations and to gain insights that would be denied to one whose study is limited to the law of a single country.[12] Of course, the mental attitude of the enterprise, whether we look for analogies or for differences, in a word whether we consider the glass "half empty" or "half full" might make all the difference. Most times however, because we belong to history, this does not mean that the endeavor of comparing is completely subjective. On this issue, it might be worth reading an excerpt from the last published piece, a true intellectual testament, of a great master of our discipline and the first author of this casebook.

R.B. Schlesinger, The Past and Future of Comparative Law

43 American Journal of Comparative Law 477 (1995).

Let me begin with the obvious: To compare means to observe and to explain similarities as well as differences. In comparing legal systems and institutions, depending on the purpose of the undertaking at hand, the emphasis is sometimes on differences, and at other times on similarities. In Europe, where endeavors directed at legal comparisons have a long and venerable history, periods of contrastive comparison (with emphasis on differences) have alternated with periods of what we might call integrative comparison, i.e., comparison placing the main accents on similarities.

Any discussion, however summary, of the past history of comparative law has to include a careful look at the period that elapsed from the days when Irnerius began to teach at Bologna until the more recent era marked by codification of private law in most civil-law countries. During those

---

12. For an extensive discussion of "the concept of comparative law," *see* K. Zweigert & H. Kötz, An Introduction to Comparative Law 1–12 (Tony Weir trans., 2d ed. 1987; one-volume paperbound ed. 1992). A new German edition (K. Zweigert & H. Kötz, Einführung in die Rechtsvergleichung (3d ed. 1996)) has since been published. Other general texts on the subject include Michael Bogdan, Comparative Law (1994); L.–J. Constantinesco, Rechtsvergleichung (3 vols., 1971–1983); *id.*, Traité de Droit Comparé (3 vols., 1972–1983); René David & John E. C. Brierley, Major Legal Systems in the World Today (3d ed. 1985); H. G. Gutteridge, Comparative Law (2d ed. 1949); M. Rheinstein, Einführung in die Rechtsvergleichung (R. von Borries ed., 2d ed. 1987); Rodolfo Sacco, Introduzione al Diritto Comparato (1990), most of which has been translated as R. Sacco, Legal Formants: A Dynamic Approach to Comparative Law (pts. 1 & 2), 39 Am.J.Comp.L. 1, 343 (1991). More recently, Patrick Glenn, Legal Traditions of the World. Sustainable Diversity in Law (2000); Esin Orucu & David Nelken, Comparative Law. A Handbook (2007); Werner Menski, Comparative Law in the Global Context (2006).

seven centuries, there emerged what we call the *ius commune* of continental Europe....[1]

Comparison of laws and legal materials across political frontiers became a standard technique of lawyers and judges during the era of the *ius commune*. To make the point more concrete, let me assume for a moment that as a practicing lawyer or a judge in, say, 17th century Brussels I have to struggle with a difficult question of law not answered by any local statute or ordinance. What sources will I consult in my search for convincing arguments leading to a solution? Unless the text of the Corpus Juris provides unambiguous guidance, I shall of course look at the writings of the recognized sages. Some of those scholars, like Azo and Bartolus, lived and taught in Italy; the nationality or university affiliation of other legal authors may have been French, German, Spanish, Portuguese or Dutch. A court sitting in Brussels would measure the authority to be accorded to each of those scholars by his reputation and by the strength of his exposition of the relevant points, but certainly not by the number of kilometers or of political frontiers separating Brussels from that particular scholar's birthplace or from the situs of his university ... reported judicial opinions also formed part of the legal materials and authorities that were consulted at that time by anyone seeking to ascertain the principles and rules of the *ius commune*. But here again, as in the case of scholarly writings, the judicial decisions to be consulted by a Brussels jurist might have been rendered by a court sitting in Italy or Germany, or indeed anywhere in continental Europe.... It is important to note, however, that when they studied, and often relied upon, materials and authorities emanating from other parts of the continent, they did not treat such materials and authorities as belonging to a foreign legal system. On the contrary, they studied those out-of-state materials as part of their routine endeavor to ascertain and to concretize the ius commune, i.e., their own law. Quite naturally, therefore, the process of comparison tended to be *integrative* rather than *contrastive*.

All of this changed during the age of codification that commenced in the second half of the 18th century. The new codes that were adopted in virtually all countries on the European continent were national codes, thus, largely unifying the law within each of the nation states. Each code was written in its own national language. The common language of previous legal learning—Latin—was abandoned; and because each of the codes in its text and its application reflected a good deal of national individuality, formidable new intellectual barriers were erected between the legal systems of the several nations. Lawyers and legal scholars working within any of the newly codified systems now had to treat other similarly codified systems—even those on the European continent—as truly foreign law, with which the great majority of judges and practicing lawyers, and even most law professors teaching at national law schools, were totally unfamiliar.

Under these changed circumstances, comparative law became a specialized branch of legal studies, with a different emphasis. Legislators, who

---

1. *See infra.*

desired to learn from the good or bad example of foreign laws, began to seek help from comparative law specialists who were familiar with those laws. And in legal practice, whenever the foreign elements of a case required resort to foreign law, again it was the same specialists who were called upon to ascertain and explain, and if necessary to prove, the applicable foreign law. With all this dominant focus on "foreign law," those engaged in the study and practice of comparative law were compelled to emphasize differences rather than similarities, i.e., to take a contrastive approach that was radically different from the integrative approach of the previous period.

The contrastive approach continued to prevail well into the second half of the 20th century. In the last two or three decades, however, the pendulum has again begun to swing the other way. Under the impact of a dramatic world-wide intensification of the trans-national exchange and movement of persons, goods, services and capital, the work of all branches of the legal profession tends to become globalized. . . .

QUESTION

Do you agree that globalization carries with it "integrative" approaches to comparative law? Within which political, cultural and geographic limits?

7. COMPARATIVE LAW IN DOMESTIC LEGAL PRACTICE

Often, comparative law is perceived as a merely theoretical effort, an exquisite example of a rich and cosmopolitan tradition in the study of institutions. Indeed, many towering intellectuals that have defined western civilization both in the antiquity and in modern times have resorted to more or less sophisticated observations of the way in which foreign people dealt with the organization of their society. Plato in his *Dialogue on Laws* or Aristotle in his *Politica* are noticeable examples. More recently, Montesquieu or Tocqueville among others, have been claimed among the founding fathers of the western discipline of comparative law. On top of this highly prestigious academic pedigree, comparative law is very often a practical necessity for professional lawyers that use it for a variety of purposes.

"When counsel, admitted to the Bar of this State, are retained in a matter involving foreign law, they are responsible to the client for the proper conduct of the matter, and may not claim that they are not required to know the law of the foreign State."[1]

This judicial pronouncement makes it clear that whenever American lawyers encounter a foreign-law problem in litigation or in counseling, they are duty-bound either to familiarize themselves with the relevant aspects of

1. In re Roel, 3 N.Y.2d 224, 232, 165 N.Y.S.2d 31, 37, 144 N.E.2d 24, 28 (1957).

the foreign law, or to obtain proper advice from a person who has the requisite expertise.[2]

There are various ways in which foreign law can become an important element in (actual or potential) domestic litigation. Foreign law may govern the case at hand for the reason that the conflict of laws rule of the domestic forum points to the internal law of a foreign country. Contracts made or performable (or otherwise having their center of gravity) abroad, marriages entered into abroad, torts committed abroad, estates of foreign domiciliaries leaving assets in this country—all are examples of the countless matters arising in domestic legal practice which, according to our own conflict of laws rules, may be wholly or partly governed by foreign law.

Foreign law may have to be consulted, moreover, even in cases which are wholly "governed" by domestic law. There are numerous situations, for example, in which a foreign law, although not controlling in a conflict of laws sense, is invoked as a *de facto* excuse for non-performance of a contract[3] or for non-compliance with the discovery order of an American court.[4] The relevance of foreign law in domestic litigation is similarly illustrated by a case in which it was held that a witness in an American court can invoke the privilege against self-incrimination if it can be shown that the answer to a particular question might give rise to a substantial risk of prosecution under the law of a foreign country.[5]

Or suppose P, a citizen and domiciliary of Mali, has furnished goods to the United States government under a contract which expressly stipulates that it shall be governed exclusively by the law of the United States. A dispute arises, and P sues the United States in the court of claims. Clearly, all substantive issues in this case are "governed" by U.S. law. Nevertheless, the outcome of the litigation may be crucially affected by the law of Mali because citizens or subjects of a foreign government can bring such an action against the United States only if their government "accords to citizens of the United States the right to prosecute claims against [such] government in its courts."[6] A similar reciprocity rule applies in cases in which an alien sues the United States for damages caused by a public vessel, or for compensation for towage or salvage services.[7] These examples of reciprocity statutes (which can be found in state as well as federal legislation) could be multiplied without difficulty.[8] They provide a point of

---

2. *See generally* M. W. Janis, The Lawyer's Responsibility for Foreign Law and Foreign Lawyers, 16 Int'l Law. 693 (1982).

3. *See* 11 R. Lord, Williston on Contracts Section(s) 1:2, p. 11 (4th ed. 2004).

4. *See infra* at Chapter 8, Section 3(i) at 809 (Discovery and Gathering Evidence Abroad).

5. In re Cardassi, 351 F.Supp. 1080 (D.Conn.1972).

6. *See* 28 U.S.C. § 2502(a). Reciprocal treatment sometimes is accorded by a bilateral Treaty of Friendship, Commerce and Navi-

gation. *See* Zalcmanis v. United States, 146 Ct.Cl. 254, 173 F.Supp. 355 (1959), cert. denied, 362 U.S. 917, 80 S.Ct. 668 (1960).

7. *See* 46 U.S.C. § 785.

8. *See* Lenhoff, Reciprocity in Function: A Problem of Conflict of Laws, Constitutional Law and International Law, 15 U.Pitt.L.Rev. 44 (1953); *id.,* Reciprocity: The Legal Aspect of a Perennial Idea, 49 Nw.U.L.Rev. 619, 752 (1954–55); *id.,* Reciprocity and the Law of Foreign Judgments: A Historical—Critical Analysis, 16 La.L.Rev. 465 (1956), Louisa B. Childs, Shaky Foundations: Criticism of Reciprocity and the Distinction Between Public

entry through which massive doses of foreign law penetrate into domestic legal practice.

Other domestic statutes, without referring to foreign law as such, may implicate foreign institutions which must be viewed, in turn, in the light of a foreign legal system. For instance, an individual or corporate citizen of the United States may, for purposes of the federal income tax, be entitled to a credit for "income taxes" paid abroad. What is meant by the term "income tax" in this context is a matter of the construction of our own statute; but can the term, however clearly we understand its statutory meaning, be applied to a foreign tax unless we know (a) the position which the particular foreign tax occupies in the tax system of the country involved, and (b) the basis on which it is levied and computed?[9]

Many examples of statutory references to foreign institutions and conditions are provided by the immigration laws. The admission of a would-be immigrant may depend on whether under the law of his country of origin he is the "legitimate" child of a United States citizen or a resident alien. Thus, that country's law must be consulted with respect to its definition of legitimacy.[10] An otherwise deportable alien may not be deported to a particular country if the Attorney General determines that "such alien's life or freedom would be threatened in such country on account of race, religion, nationality, membership in a particular social group, or political opinion."[11] In discharging her duty under this provision, the Attorney General has to consider whether in fact, as well as in form, the legal system of the country in question protects the individual's life and freedom against such persecution.[12] Similarly, an understanding of foreign legal processes is needed if an event which occurred abroad is to be classified as a "conviction" or an "offense" within the meaning of exclusionary provisions of the immigration laws.[13]

Or suppose a criminal defendant who has been found guilty by a jury and is due to be sentenced is shown to have a record of previous "convictions" in a foreign country. Is the defendant, for this reason, to be treated as a multiple offender? Many of the pertinent recidivist statutes provide in terms that all previous judgments of conviction should be counted, regard-

and Private International Law, 38 N.Y.U. J. Int'l L. & Pol. 221 (2006).

9.   This issue was developed in the sixth edition of this book, Chapter IX, Section 2 at 979.

10.   *See* Lau v. Kiley, 563 F.2d 543 (2d Cir.1977) (involving the law of the People's Republic of China).

11.   *See* 8 U.S.C. § 1253(h), as amended in 1981.

12.   *See* Berdo v. Immigration & Naturalization Service, 432 F.2d 824 (6th Cir. 1970); Coriolan v. Immigration & Naturalization Service, 559 F.2d 993 (5th Cir.1977).

13.   8 U.S.C. § 1182(a)(9) & (10), commented on by Professor Schlesinger in 2 Am. J.Comp.L. 392, 397–8 (1953).

The fact that the foreign court's procedure was different from ours is irrelevant, provided that no uncivilized methods were used to obtain the conviction. *See* Brice v. Pickett, 515 F.2d 153 (9th Cir.1975); Pasquini v. United States Immigration & Naturalization Serv., 557 F.2d 536 (5th Cir.1977). But U.S. authorities and U.S. courts cannot invoke a foreign "conviction" if it was procured by procedures "repugnant to the moral sense" of our community. *Cf.* Cooley v. Weinberger, 518 F.2d 1151, 1155 (10th Cir.1975).

less of whether they were rendered in the forum or in another state or country.[14] As a matter of due process, however, it is clear that a foreign conviction, although proved by proper documentary evidence, may not be used as a basis for multiple offender treatment if it resulted from proceedings which failed to meet certain minimum standards of fairness.[15] Thus it becomes necessary for the sentencing court to inquire into the standards, which as a matter of law and of actual practice were observed in the earlier foreign proceedings.

The Foreign Corrupt Practices Act of 1977[16] criminalizes certain "corrupt" payments to foreign public officials. The question of whether a given recipient is a public official can only be determined with reference to foreign law. Moreover, the further question of whether the payment was improper quite often cannot be answered intelligently without some knowledge of the law and culture of the country involved.

In these and countless other instances U.S. laws must deal with conditions and events shaped by foreign institutions.[17] As the world has become as small and close-knit as it is today, it should be no surprise that in myriad and often complex ways, the U.S. legal system interacts with the legal systems of other countries.[18] A large body of U.S. "domestic" law

14. For references and an interesting discussion, *see* Pye, The Effect of Foreign Criminal Judgments in the United States, 32 UMKC L.Rev. 114, 127–30 (1964), reprinted in International Criminal Law 479 (G.O.W. Mueller & E.M. Wise eds., 1965).

15. *See, e.g.,* United States ex rel. Dennis v. Murphy, 265 F.2d 57 (2d Cir.1959), upon remand 184 F.Supp. 384 (N.D.N.Y. 1959); United States ex rel. Foreman v. Fay, 184 F.Supp. 535 (S.D.N.Y.1960). For further references and a fine analysis of this and related problems, *see* Note, 90 Harv.L.Rev. 1500, especially at 1504–10 (1977). *See also* I. P. Stotzky & A. C. Swan, Due Process Methodology and Prisoner Exchange Treaties: Confronting an Uncertain Calculus, 62 Minn. L.Rev. 733 (1978).

16. Pub. L. 95–213, 91 Stat. 1494. The act is codified, for the most part, at 15 U.S.C. §§ 78dd–1, 78dd–2, 78ff. & 78m. It was amended by the Omnibus Trade and Competitiveness Act of 1988 to impose liability only if the defendant knows (rather than "has reason to know") that the payment will be passed directly or indirectly to a foreign official for an improper purpose. The 1988 amendments also allow for an affirmative defense on the ground that the payment was "lawful under the written laws and regulations" of the foreign official's country. On these amendments, *see* Adam Fremantle & Sherman Katz, The Foreign Corrupt Practice

Act Amendments of 1988, 23 Int'l Law. 755 (1989); on the act in general, *see* 2 Kathleen F. Brickey, Corporate Criminal Liability §§ 9.01–9.27, at 250–87 (2d ed. 1993); Don Zarin, Doing Business Under the Foreign Corrupt Practices Act (1995).

17. Recognizing that they have to deal with conditions and events shaped by foreign institutions, our legislators sometimes explicitly direct that a comparative study of those institutions be undertaken. An example is provided by sec. 6 of the Federal Water Pollution Act of 1972, Pub.L. 92–500, 86 Stat. 898, 33 U.S.C.A. § 1251 Note, which ordered the Secretary of Commerce to study the pollution laws of foreign countries in order to determine whether by virtue of differing standards of pollution control U.S. manufacturers are unduly disadvantaged vis-à-vis their foreign competitors.

18. When extraterritorial application of the laws of country A affects individuals and business concerns in country B, it often happens that the latter country will enact countermeasures; such countermeasures, in turn, may have an impact felt by citizens and residents of country A. For a dramatic example, *see* the French "blocking" statute discussed *infra* in Chapter 8, pp. 814–817. *See also* Extraterritorial Application of Laws and Responses Thereto (C. Olmstead ed., 1984), re-

reflects such interactions. One of the tasks of comparative law is to promote comprehension and proper application of this important part of U.S. law.[19]

As a result of the accelerated transnational mobility of (some) persons and goods which characterizes our age, it more and more frequently occurs that American corporations and individuals become parties to legal actions brought in the courts of other countries.[20] Every day, as a matter of routine, American corporations enter into transactions which, *in case* of a dispute, *may* lead to litigation abroad, and which therefore, have to be negotiated and concluded with that possibility in mind.

A party who is faced with the prospect of litigation in, say, Colombia, or who enters into an agreement which in case of a breach may have to be enforced in the courts of Colombia, will require the assistance of Colombian counsel.[21] To select such counsel, to make the proper arrangements concerning his compensation, and to instruct him in terms which can be understood by a lawyer brought up in the civil law, is a task which ordinarily will fall to the client's American counsel. Since the Colombian agreement (or lawsuit) probably will have effects in this country as well, it may be necessary, at the same time, to familiarize Colombian counsel with certain points of our law and to establish with Colombian counsel the kind of give-and-take communication which is necessary for a truly cooperative handling of the matter. Such cooperation, at its best, can yield highly gratifying results; but it requires, on the part of each participant, a measure of familiarity with the sources, the classificatory system, the procedure, and the basic substantive concepts to which the mind of the foreign colleague is attuned. True, today many foreign lawyers come to the United States to complete their legal education, so that the U.S. lawyer will more easily find a colleague in any corner of the world that is acquainted with the U.S. system. This advantage however might cut two ways. The usual complete ignorance by the U.S. attorney of the foreign legal system might create an unbalance of power (knowledge asymmetry) between the

---

viewed by B. Zagaris in 20 Int'l Law. 1105 (1986).

19. When the applicable law is embodied in a treaty, comparative studies may become necessary for the additional reason that the treaty employs technical terms deriving their meaning from the legal systems of other signatories. For instance, some of the crucial terms of the Warsaw Convention (the official text of which is in French) can be correctly understood only in the light of their civil-law background. *See* Eastern Airlines, Inc. v. Floyd, 499 U.S. 530, 111 S.Ct. 1489 (1991); Air France v. Saks, 470 U.S. 392, 105 S.Ct. 1338 (1985); Palagonia v. T.W.A., 110 Misc.2d 478, 442 N.Y.S.2d 670 (Sup.Ct.1978). *Cf.* Zicherman v. Korean Air Lines Co., Ltd., 516 U.S. 217, 116 S.Ct. 629 (1996).

20. The overwhelming majority of such actions are civil proceedings; but the additional danger of criminal prosecution (often used to reinforce civil claims) is far from negligible for those venturing into foreign markets and cultural environments. In 1983, "more than 5,000 Americans were reported to have been arrested or detained abroad." R. D. Atkins & R. L. Pisani, How to Get Arrested Doing Business Abroad, 22(6) Across the Board (The Conference Board Magazine) 57, 58 (June 1985).

21. The consequences of a failure to make timely inquiry concerning foreign law can be drastic. For examples, see J. Wolff, Trademark Protection of American Firms in Argentina, 16 Geo.Wash.L.Rev. 342 (1948).

two colleagues that might put the U.S. attorney at the complete mercy of his foreign counterpart.

The recent case of *Roper v. Simmons* has produced quite an intense academic and political debate on the legitimacy of the use of comparative law in domestic practice. Most discussed cases have been those in which the U.S. Supreme Court has aligned itself to standards of international decency in issues of anti-sodomy law, of racial segregation and, especially, by rejecting death penalty when applied to individuals that were minors at the moment of committing the crime. We reproduce here the important parts of the holding that used comparative arguments in the death penalty issue.

Roper v. Simmons

Supreme Court of the United States, 2005.
543 U.S. 551, 125 S.Ct. 1183.

■ JUSTICE STEVENS writing for the majority.

Our determination that the death penalty is disproportionate punishment for offenders under 18 finds confirmation in the stark reality that the United States is the only country in the world that continues to give official sanction to the juvenile death penalty. This reality does not become controlling, for the task of interpreting the Eighth Amendment remains our responsibility. Yet, at least from the time of the Court's decision in *Trop,* the Court has referred to the laws of other countries and to international authorities as instructive for its interpretation of the Eighth Amendment's prohibition of "cruel and unusual punishments." 356 U.S., at 102–103, 78 S.Ct. 590 (plurality opinion) ("The civilized nations of the world are in virtual unanimity that statelessness is not to be imposed as punishment for crime"); *see also Atkins,* 122 S.Ct. 2242 (recognizing that "within the world community, the imposition of the death penalty for crimes committed by mentally retarded offenders is overwhelmingly disapproved"); *Thompson,* 108 S.Ct. 2687 (plurality opinion) (noting the abolition of the juvenile death penalty "by other nations that share our Anglo–American heritage, and by the leading members of the Western European community," and observing that "[w]e have previously recognized the relevance of the views of the international community in determining whether a punishment is cruel and unusual"); *Enmund,* 102 S.Ct. 3368 (observing that "the doctrine of felony-murder has been abolished in England and India, severely restricted in Canada and a number of other Commonwealth countries, and is unknown in continental Europe"); *Coker,* 97 S.Ct. 2861 (plurality opinion) ("It is ... not irrelevant here that out of 60 major nations in the world surveyed in 1965, only 3 retained the death penalty for rape where death did not ensue").

As Respondent and a number of *amici* emphasize, Article 37 of the United Nations Convention on the Rights of the Child, which every country in the world has ratified, save for the United States and Somalia, contains an express prohibition on capital punishment for crimes committed by juveniles under 18. United Nations Convention on the Rights of the Child,

Art. 37, Nov. 20, 1989, 1577 U.N.T.S. 3, 28 I.L.M. 1448, 1468–1470 (entered into force Sept. 2, 1990); Brief for Respondent 48; Brief for European Union et al. as *Amici Curiae* 12–13; Brief for President James Earl Carter, Jr., et al. as *Amici Curiae* 9; Brief for Former U.S. Diplomats Morton Abramowitz et al. as *Amici Curiae* 7; Brief for Human Rights Committee of the Bar of England and Wales et al. as *Amici Curiae* 13–14. No ratifying country has entered a reservation to the provision prohibiting the execution of juvenile offenders. Parallel prohibitions are contained in other significant international covenants. See ICCPR, Art. 6(5), 999 U.N.T.S., at 175 (prohibiting capital punishment for anyone under 18 at the time of offense) (signed and ratified by the United States, subject to a reservation regarding Article 6(5), as noted, *supra,* at 1194); American Convention on Human Rights: Pact of San Jose, Costa Rica, Art. 4(5), Nov. 22, 1969, 1144 U.N.T.S. 146 (entered into force July 19, 1978) (same); African Charter on the Rights and Welfare of the Child, Art. 5(3), OAU Doc. CAB/LEG/ 24.9/49 (1990) (entered into force Nov. 29, 1999) (same).

Respondent and his *amici* have submitted, and Petitioner does not contest, that only seven countries other than the United States have executed juvenile offenders since 1990: Iran, Pakistan, Saudi Arabia, Yemen, Nigeria, the Democratic Republic of Congo, and China. Since then, each of these countries has either abolished capital punishment for juveniles or made public disavowal of the practice. In sum, it is fair to say that the United States now stands alone, in a world that has turned its face against the juvenile death penalty.

Though the international covenants prohibiting the juvenile death penalty are of more recent date, it is instructive to note that the United Kingdom abolished the juvenile death penalty before these covenants came into being. The United Kingdom's experience bears particular relevance here in light of the historic ties between our countries and in light of the Eighth Amendment's own origins. The Amendment was modeled on a parallel provision in the English Declaration of Rights of 1689, which provided: "[E]xcessive bail ought not to be required nor excessive fines imposed; nor cruel and unusual punishments inflicted." 1 W. & M., ch. 2, § 10, in 3 Eng. Stat. at Large 441 (1770). As of now, the United Kingdom has abolished the death penalty in its entirety; but, decades before it took this step, it recognized the disproportionate nature of the juvenile death penalty; and it abolished that penalty as a separate matter. In 1930, an official committee recommended that the minimum age for execution be raised to 21. House of Commons Report from the Select Committee on Capital Punishment (1930), 193, p. 44. Parliament then enacted the Children and Young Person's Act of 1933, 23 Geo. 5, Ch. 12, which prevented execution of those aged 18 at the date of the sentence. And in 1948, Parliament enacted the Criminal Justice Act, 11 & 12 Geo. 6, Ch. 58, prohibiting the execution of any person under 18 at the time of the offense. In the 56 years that have passed since the United Kingdom abolished the juvenile death penalty, the weight of authority against it there, and in the international community, has become well established.

It is proper that we acknowledge the overwhelming weight of international opinion against the juvenile death penalty, resting in large part on the understanding that the instability and emotional imbalance of young people may often be a factor in the crime. The opinion of the world community, while not controlling our outcome, does provide respected and significant confirmation for our own conclusions. . . .

It does not lessen our fidelity to the Constitution or our pride in its origins to acknowledge that the express affirmation of certain fundamental rights by other nations and peoples simply underscores the centrality of those same rights within our own heritage of freedom.

* * *

The Eighth and Fourteenth Amendments forbid imposition of the death penalty on offenders who were under the age of 18 when their crimes were committed. The judgment of the Missouri Supreme Court, setting aside the sentence of death imposed upon Christopher Simmons, is affirmed.

It is so ordered.

■ JUSTICE O'CONNOR, dissenting

. . . I turn, finally, to the Court's discussion of foreign and international law. Without question, there has been a global trend in recent years towards abolishing capital punishment for under–18 offenders. Very few, if any, countries other than the United States now permit this practice in law or in fact. While acknowledging that the actions and views of other countries do not dictate the outcome of our Eighth Amendment inquiry, the Court asserts that "the overwhelming weight of international opinion against the juvenile death penalty . . . does provide respected and significant confirmation for [its] own conclusions." Because I do not believe that a genuine *national* consensus against the juvenile death penalty has yet developed, and because I do not believe the Court's moral proportionality argument justifies a categorical, age-based constitutional rule, I can assign no such *confirmatory* role to the international consensus described by the Court. In short, the evidence of an international consensus does not alter my determination that the Eighth Amendment does not, at this time, forbid capital punishment of 17–year-old murderers in all cases.

Nevertheless, I disagree with Justice Scalia's contention, that foreign and international law have no place in our Eighth Amendment jurisprudence. Over the course of nearly half a century, the Court has consistently referred to foreign and international law as relevant to its assessment of evolving standards of decency. This inquiry reflects the special character of the Eighth Amendment, which, as the Court has long held, draws its meaning directly from the maturing values of civilized society. Obviously, American law is distinctive in many respects, not least where the specific provisions of our Constitution and the history of its exposition so dictate. But, this Nation's evolving understanding of human dignity certainly is neither wholly isolated from, nor inherently at odds with, the values prevailing in other countries. On the contrary, we should not be surprised to find congruence between domestic and international values, especially where the international community has reached clear agreement—expressed in international law or in the domestic laws of individual countries—that a particular form of punishment is inconsistent with fundamental human rights. At least, the existence of an international consensus of this nature can serve to confirm the reasonableness of a consonant and genuine American consensus. The instant case presents no such domestic consensus, however, and the recent emergence of an otherwise global consensus does not alter that basic fact.

■ JUSTICE SCALIA, dissenting (THOMAS and REHNQUIST joining)

. . . Though the views of our own citizens are essentially irrelevant to the Court's decision today, the views of other countries and the so-called international community take center stage.

The Court begins by noting that "Article 37 of the United Nations Convention on the Rights of the Child, [1577 U.N.T.S. 3, 28 I.L.M. 1448, 1468–1470, entered into force Sept. 2, 1990,] which every country in the world has ratified *save for the United States* and Somalia, contains an express prohibition on capital punishment for crimes committed by juveniles under 18." The Court also discusses the International Covenant on Civil and Political Rights (ICCPR), December 19, 1966, 999 U.N.T.S. 175, *ante,* at 1194, 1199, which the Senate ratified only subject to a reservation that reads:

> "The United States reserves the right, subject to its Constitutional constraints, to impose capital punishment on any person (other than a pregnant woman) duly convicted under existing or future laws permitting the imposition of capital punishment, including such punishment for crimes committed by persons below 18 years of age."

Unless the Court has added to its arsenal the power to join and ratify treaties on behalf of the United States, I cannot see how this evidence favors, rather than refutes, its position. That the Senate and the President, those actors our Constitution empowers to enter into treaties, have declined to join and ratify treaties prohibiting execution of under–18 offenders can only suggest that *our country* has either not reached a national consensus on the question, or has reached a consensus contrary to what the Court announces. That the reservation to the ICCPR was made in 1992 does not suggest otherwise, since the reservation still remains in place today. It is also worth noting that, in addition to barring the execution of under–18 offenders, the United Nations Convention on the Rights of the Child prohibits punishing them with life in prison without the possibility of release. If we are truly going to get in line with the international community, then the Court's reassurance that the death penalty is really not needed, since "the punishment of life imprisonment without the possibility of parole is itself a severe sanction," gives little comfort.

It is interesting that whereas the Court is not content to accept what the States of our Federal Union *say,* but insists on inquiring into what they *do* (specifically, whether they in fact *apply* the juvenile death penalty that their laws allow), the Court is quite willing to believe that every foreign nation—of whatever tyrannical political makeup and with however subservient or incompetent a court system—in fact *adheres* to a rule of no death penalty for offenders under 18. Nor does the Court inquire into how many of the countries that have the death penalty, but have forsworn (on paper at least) imposing that penalty on offenders under 18, have what no State of this country can constitutionally have: a *mandatory* death penalty for certain crimes, with no possibility of mitigation by the sentencing authority, for youth or any other reason. I suspect it is most of them. *See, e.g.,* R. Simon & D. Blaskovich, A Comparative Analysis of Capital Punishment: Statutes, Policies, Frequencies, and Public Attitudes the World Over 25, 26, 29 (2002). To forbid the death penalty for juveniles under such a system may be a good idea, but it says nothing about our system, in which the sentencing authority, typically a jury, always can, and almost always does, withhold the death penalty from an under–18 offender except, after considering all the circumstances, in the rare cases where it is warranted. The foreign authorities, in other words, do not even speak to the issue before us here.

More fundamentally, however, the basic premise of the Court's argument—that American law should conform to the laws of the rest of the world—ought to be rejected out of hand. In fact the Court itself does not believe it. In many significant respects the laws of most other countries differ from U.S. law, including not only such explicit provisions of our Constitution as the right to jury trial and grand jury indictment, but even many interpretations of the Constitution prescribed by this Court itself. The Court's pronounced exclusionary rule, for example, is distinctively American. When we adopted that rule in *Mapp v. Ohio,* 367 U.S. 643, 655, 81 S.Ct. 1684, 6 L.Ed.2d 1081 (1961), it was "unique to American jurisprudence." *Bivens v. Six Unknown Fed. Narcotics Agents,* 403 U.S. 388, 415, 91 S.Ct. 1999, 29 L.Ed.2d 619 (1971) (Burger, C. J., dissenting). Since then a categorical exclusionary rule has been "universally rejected" by other countries, including those with rules prohibiting illegal searches and police misconduct, despite the fact that none of these countries "appears to have any alternative form of discipline for police that is effective in preventing search violations." Bradley, Mapp Goes Abroad, 52 Case W. Res. L.Rev. 375, 399–400 (2001). England, for example, rarely excludes evidence found during an illegal search or seizure and has only recently begun excluding evidence from illegally obtained confessions. *See* C. Slobogin, Criminal Procedure: Regulation of Police Investigation 550 (3d ed.2002). Canada rarely excludes evidence and will only do so if admission will "bring the administration of justice into disrepute." *Id.,* at 550–551 (internal quotation marks omitted). The European Court of Human Rights has held that introduction of illegally seized evidence does not violate the "fair trial" requirement in Article 6, § 1, of the European Convention on Human Rights.

The Court has been oblivious to the views of other countries when deciding how to interpret our Constitution's requirement that "Congress shall make no law respecting an establishment of religion...." Amdt. 1.

Most other countries, including those committed to religious neutrality, do not insist on the degree of separation between church and state that this Court requires. For example, whereas "we have recognized special Establishment Clause dangers where the government makes direct money payments to sectarian institutions," (citing cases), countries such as the Netherlands, Germany, and Australia allow direct government funding of religious schools on the ground that "the state can only be truly neutral between secular and religious perspectives if it does not dominate the provision of so key a service as education, and makes it possible for people to exercise their right of religious expression within the context of public funding." S. Monsma & J. Soper, The Challenge of Pluralism: Church and State in Five Democracies 207 (1997); *see also id.,* at 67, 103, 176. England permits the teaching of religion in state schools. *Id.,* at 142. Even in France, which is considered "America's only rival in strictness of church-state separation," "[t]he practice of contracting for educational services provided by Catholic schools is very widespread." C. Glenn, The Ambiguous Embrace: Government and Faith–Based Schools and Social Agencies 110 (2000).

And let us not forget the Court's abortion jurisprudence, which makes us one of only six countries that allow abortion on demand until the point of viability. *See* Larsen, Importing Constitutional Norms from a Wider Civilization: Lawrence and the Rehnquist Court's Use of Foreign and International Law in Domestic Constitutional Interpretation, 65 Ohio St. L.J. 1283, 1320 (2004); Though the Government and *amici* in cases following *Roe v. Wade,* 410 U.S. 113, 93 S.Ct. 705, 35 L.Ed.2d 147 (1973), urged the Court to follow the international community's lead, these arguments fell on deaf ears. *See* McCrudden, A Part of the Main? The Physician–Assisted Suicide Cases and Comparative Law Methodology in the United States Supreme Court, in Law at the End of Life: The Supreme Court and Assisted Suicide 125, 129–130 (C. Schneider ed. 2000).

The Court's special reliance on the laws of the United Kingdom is perhaps the most indefensible part of its opinion. It is of course true that we share a common history with the United Kingdom, and that we often consult English sources when asked to discern the meaning of a constitutional text written against the backdrop of 18th-century English law and legal thought. If we applied that approach today, our task would be an easy one. As we explained in *Harmelin v. Michigan,* 501 U.S. 957, 973–974, 111 S.Ct. 2680, 115 L.Ed.2d 836 (1991), the "Cruel and Unusual Punishments" provision of the English Declaration of Rights was originally meant to describe those punishments "out of [the Judges'] Power" that is, those punishments that were not authorized by common law or statute, but that were nonetheless administered by the Crown or the Crown's judges. Under that reasoning, the death penalty for under–18 offenders would easily survive this challenge. The Court has, however, I think wrongly, long rejected a purely originalist approach to our Eighth Amendment, and that is certainly not the approach the Court takes today. Instead, the Court undertakes the majestic task of determining (and thereby prescribing) *our* Nation's *current* standards of decency. It is beyond comprehension why we should look, for that purpose, to a country that has developed, in the centuries since the Revolutionary War and with increasing speed since the United Kingdom's recent submission to the jurisprudence of European courts dominated by continental jurists, a legal, political, and social culture quite different from our own. If we took the Court's directive seriously, we would also consider relaxing our double jeopardy prohibition, since the British Law Commission recently published a report that would significantly extend the rights of the prosecution to appeal cases where an acquittal was the result of a judge's ruling that was legally incorrect. *See* Law Commission, Double Jeopardy and Prosecution Appeals, LAW COM No. 267, Cm 5048, p. 6, ¶ 1.19 (Mar.2001); J. Spencer, The English System in European Criminal Procedures 142, 204, and n. 239 (M. Delmas–Marty & J. Spencer eds.2002). We would also curtail our right to jury trial in criminal cases since, despite the jury system's deep roots in our shared common law, England now permits all but the most serious offenders to be tried by magistrates without a jury. *See* D. Feldman, England and Wales, in Criminal Procedure: A Worldwide Study 91, 114–115 (C. Bradley ed. 1999).

The Court should either profess its willingness to reconsider all these matters in light of the views of foreigners, or else it should cease putting forth foreigners' views as part of the *reasoned basis* of its decisions. To invoke alien law when it agrees with one's own thinking, and ignore it otherwise, is not reasoned decision-making, but sophistry.

NOTES AND QUESTIONS

(1) This Supreme Court decision, and in particular the strong reaction of dissenters, shows the compelling power that a comparative argument can exercise when it comes to issues of "decency" and "civilization." Of course, the strengths of such arguments might be much milder when it comes to more technical aspects of the domestic legal systems, such as a variety of those invoked by Justice Scalia in his dissent. There are indeed aspects of the law that are more deeply grounded in the structure and the fabric of one legal system. We will see many such examples, like the function and role of the notary in civilian countries, where deeply rooted technical structures are much more important than moral or decency values in explaining divergence between legal systems. In the light of this, do you agree with Justice Scalia that selective borrowing is just sophistry?

Justice Scalia introduces an interesting distinction between what the law "says" and what the law "does", thus opposing, in the best legal realist tradition, the law in the books to the law in action. This approach is fundamental in comparative law, where an old black letter tradition known as *Legislation Compare'* (Comparative Legislation) dominant through the first half of the past century, has been abandoned in favor of an approach that stresses the need to take into particular consideration the "context" of the legal rules.

(2) American constitutional law has been perhaps, especially insular and inward-looking.[1] Professor Langbein captures this idea vividly when he states

1. *See* Mary Ann Glendon, Rights Talk: The Impoverishment of Political Discourse   145–70 (1991). *See also* The Plea for Less Parochialism in the Teaching of Constitution-

that U.S. courts have been struggling to find some principles in abortion cases as if pregnancy were a phenomenon unique to the United States.[2] Yet, there have been cases in which counsel, seeking to uphold the *constitutionality of a statute* which has been attacked as violating due process, has made effective use of the fact that a number of other "civilized" countries have statutes similar to the one under attack. The famous, almost legendary brief with which Louis Brandeis, as counsel for the State of Oregon, won the landmark case of *Muller v. State of Oregon*[3] contained many references to foreign legislation concerning the working hours of women. In its opinion, the Court repeated some of these references and intimated that a statute which has counterparts in most countries of the "civilized" world cannot easily be struck down as unreasonable, arbitrary and capricious.[4] Of course, as we will better see, the very notion of a "civilized" country has a long and sad colonialist pedigree. "Civilization" has long been a western political construction most often showing complete lack of respect for cultural practices of what have been called the "people without history".[5]

Similarly, in *Palko v. Connecticut*,[6] upholding the constitutionality of a statute permitting appeals by the state in criminal proceedings, Justice Cardozo called attention to the practice of civil-law countries where the prosecutor generally has the right to appeal from an acquittal, or even from a judgment of conviction if he regards the sentence as too mild.[7] *Palko* has been overruled by the subsequent determination that the double jeopardy clause of the Fifth Amendment applies to the states[8] and therefore restricts prosecutorial appeals in state as well as federal cases.[9] But *Palko*'s fundamental holding—that to permit prosecution appeals in criminal proceedings is not necessarily a shocking violation of due process—is still intact and continues to be of practical importance both in domestic cases[10] and in situations involving U.S. recognition of foreign criminal judgments.[11] In any event, whatever the present status of the *Palko* holding, it would seem that *the method* used in that case—the

al Law in David Weissbrodt, Globalization of Constitutional Law and Civil Rights, 43 J.Legal Educ. 261 (1993).

2. *See* J. Langbein, Cultural Chauvinism in Comparative Law, 5 Cardozo Journal of International & Comparative Law 41 (1997).

3. 208 U.S. 412, 28 S.Ct. 324 (1908).

4. *Id.* at 419–20, 28 S.Ct. at 325–26. More recently, the same kind of reasoning was employed by Judge Sneed in upholding the constitutionality of the California Resale Royalties Act (Cal.C.C. § 986) against a due process attack. Morseburg v. Balyon, 621 F.2d 972, 979 (9th Cir.1980).

5. *See* Eric Wolf, Europe and the People Without History, (1982).

6. 302 U.S. 319, 58 S.Ct. 149 (1937).

7. *See* Kepner v. United States, 195 U.S. 100, 120–21, 24 S.Ct. 797, 801 (1904) (discussion of Spanish law). For a survey of state statutes similar to that upheld in Palko, *see* Note, 35 U.Cin.L.Rev. 501 (1966).

8. Benton v. Maryland, 395 U.S. 784, 89 S.Ct. 2056 (1969).

9. The limits which the double jeopardy clause, as construed in ever-shifting Supreme Court opinions, imposes on prosecutorial appeals have been staked out in United States v. Scott, 437 U.S. 82, 98 S.Ct. 2187 (1978).

10. *See, e.g.,* Swisher v. Brady, 438 U.S. 204, 98 S.Ct. 2699 (1978).

11. *See* United States ex rel. Bloomfield v. Gengler, 507 F.2d 925, 929 (2d Cir.1974); Houle v. United States, 493 F.2d 915 (5th Cir.1974).

method of looking beyond national borders to gain perspective in deciding whether a given procedure is civilized[12]—is still a viable one.[13]

As demonstrated by *Roper v. Simmons* not only in seeking to uphold, but also in attacking the constitutionality of a statute, counsel can make effective use of foreign laws and the experience gained under them. Comparison with foreign law may show, for instance, that a domestic statute providing for a certain type of punishment falls below "standards of decency more or less universally accepted."[14] Unfortunately, this cosmopolitan line of reasoning has not been widely accepted by the American judiciary whose degree of parochialism is still very high. For example, despite wide criticism, raging from the U.N. Human Right Commission, to the European Union, to human rights organizations such as Human Rights Watch, the United States remains the only system within "first" world nations to continue to judicially uphold the death penalty. Such punishment, though very recently rejected for juveniles and the retarded, still puts at high risk many innocent defendants, especially coming from racial minorities (data offered by the New York-based Innocence Project are appalling). The death penalty is considered barbaric and a violation of international standards of decency by most "civilized" countries[15] but it is apparently supported by a large segment of the U.S. public opinion.

Do you agree with Justice O' Connor's argument that the Supreme Court should yield to the "national consensus," or, especially because of how public opinion is influenced and thus created, do you believe that Courts of law should play a "civilizing" role in society?

(3) Students of American legal history have observed that, during the early nineteenth century, a "strong inclination towards French law had grown out of the political situation after the revolution.... It was chiefly in the form of Comparative Law, in the hands of Kent and Story, that French and Dutch authorities could be used to enrich our commercial law and to reinforce a point of common law doctrine, on a theory that [the foreign materials thus found were] declaratory of the law of nature."[16] As a result, we find massive references to civil-law authorities in many of the earlier American cases.[17]

12. The view that a rule traditionally followed in a number of "civilized" legal systems should not easily be struck down as being fundamentally unfair and hence violative of due process has been adopted also by the German Constitutional Court. Bundesverfassungsgericht, June 13, 1952, 1 BVerfGE 332 (1952). *See* Schlesinger, Western Germany: Recognition and Enforcement of Soviet Zone Criminal Judgments, 2 Am. J.Comp.L. 392 (1953).

13. There are cases which indicate, however, that in the area of criminal procedure, all else being equal, the fairness of a given practice has to be examined within the framework of "the *American* scheme of justice" (emphasis supplied). *See* Duncan v. Louisiana, 391 U.S. 145, 149, 88 S.Ct. 1444, 1447 (1968). For comments on this shift from a "civilized" to an "American" standard, *see* Judge Wisdom's opinion in Melancon v.

McKeithen, 345 F.Supp. 1025, at 1038–39 (E.D.La.1972) (3–judge Court), aff'd mem. sub nom. Hill v. McKeithen, 409 U.S. 943, 93 S.Ct. 290 (1972).

14. *See* Francis v. Resweber, 329 U.S. 459, 469, 67 S.Ct. 374, 379 (1947) (Frankfurter, J., concurring). Here too, however, recent cases indicate a more provincial approach. *See e.g.*, the statement in Stanford v. Kentucky, 492 U.S. 361, 369 n. 1, 109 S.Ct. 2969, 2975 n. 1 (1989), that "it is American conceptions of decency that are dispositive, [not] the sentencing practices of other countries." But *see* Roper, *supra* at 57.

15. *See* Louis Henkin, The Age of Rights, (1990), with stress on Human Rights as an "export only" activity in the U.S.

16. Roscoe Pound, The Influence of the Civil Law in America, 1 La.L.Rev. 1, 9 (1938). *See also* Michele Graziadei, in *The Oxford*

Overt judicial reliance on civil-law authorities declined during the second half of the nineteenth century, although, even then, jurisprudential ideas coming from Europe, especially Germany, remained highly influential among legal scholars.[18] By mid-twentieth century, the trend seemed to have turned again in the direction of a more cosmopolitan spirit. This may have been due in part to the country's growing involvement in world affairs, to the increased availability of foreign-law materials in English, and perhaps also to the influence of European-bred legal scholars who came to the United States as refugees from totalitarian oppression.[19]

Ugo Mattei, A Theory of Imperial Law: A Study on U.S. Hegemony and the Latin Resistance

10 Indiana J. Global Legal Studies (2003). (footnotes renumbered and partially re-written).

By the early part of the last century, (a century significantly labeled "the American century"),[1] U.S. law had already received from Europe, and digested in a genuinely original way, the fundamental components of its

Handbook of Comparative Law, edited by Mathias Reimann and Reinhard Zimmermann (2008).

17. *See* O. Schroeder, Comparative Law: A Subject for American Lawyers, 41 A.B.A.J. 928, 929 (1955). One of the most famous examples of such early cases influenced by the civil law is Pierson v. Post, 3 Caines 175, 2 Am.Dec. 264 (N.Y.1805), which has found its way into many first-year Property casebooks.

For further discussion of civil-law influences in the United States before the Civil War, *see* P. Miller, The Life of the Mind in America from the Revolution to the Civil War 164–71 (1965); R. H. Helmholz, Use of the Civil Law in Post–Revolutionary American Jurisprudence, 66 Tul.L.Rev. 1649 (1992); M. H. Hoeflich, John Austin and Joseph Story: Two Nineteenth Century Perspectives on the Utility of the Civil Law for the Common Lawyer, 25 Am.J.Legal Hist. 36 (1985); M. H. Hoeflich, Transatlantic Friendships and the German Influence on American Law in the First Half of the Nineteenth Century, 35 Am.J.Comp.L 599 (1987); M. H. Hoeflich, Roman and Civil Law in American Legal Education and Research Prior to 1930: A Preliminary Survey, 1984 Ill.L.Rev. 719; P. Stein, The Attraction of the Civil Law in Post–Revolutionary America, 52 Va.L.Rev. 403 (1966). *See also* M H. Hoeflich, Roman & Civil Law and the Development of Anglo–

American Jurisprudence in the Nineteenth Century (1997).

18. *See, e.g.,* Mathias Reimann, Historische Schule und Common Law: Die Deutsche Rechtswissenschaft des 19 Jahrhunderts im amerikanischen Rechtsdenken (1993); The Reception of Continental Ideas in the Common Law World 1820–1920 (Mathias Reimann ed., 1993); David S. Clark, Tracing the Roots of American Legal Education: A Nineteenth–Century German Connection, 51 Rabels Z. 313 (1987); and the symposium on Savigny in Modern Comparative Perspective, 37 Am.J.Comp.L. 599 (1987). More recent historical literature and data include H.M. Hoeflich, Translation and the Reception of Foreign Law in Antebellum United States, 50 Am. J. Comp. Law 753 (2002).

19. On the influence of German emigré jurists, *see* the papers (many in English) in Der Einflu EF Deutscher Emigranten auf die Rechtsentwicklung in den USA und in Deutschland (Marcus Lutter, Ernst C. Stiefel & Michael H. Hoeflich eds., 1993). *See also,* K.Graham, The Refugee Jurists and American Law Schools, 50 Am. J. Comp. Law 777 (2002).

1. *See* Olivier Zunz, Perché il secolo americano?, Bologna, Il Mulino (2002); E.J. Hobsbawm, The Age of Extremes: The Short 20th Century, London (1994); Giovanni Arrighi, The Long Twentieth Century, Verso (1994).

legal structure. The English common law tradition has transmitted to the former colony the ideal of judges as oracles of the law and of a strong, independent judiciary as the institutional framework in which judges can perform their role of guardians of individual rights. American law has developed this legacy and expanded it to the point of "inventing" constitutional adjudication, an achievement that was not accomplished in England even by the great Sir Edward Coke. Judges not only are the oracles of the law and the leaders of the professional legal system. They have also the power to declare, in the process of adjudication, political decision making as unconstitutional.[2] Because of such outstanding extension of judicial power within American law, the belief, already noticed by Tocqueville, that any political problem can be, sooner or later, decided by a Court of law, has been carried to its symbolic extreme in the Nuremberg Trial, and possibly to its very limit in *Bush v. Gore*.[3]

The civil law tradition has also transmitted to the United States some fundamental modes of thought that U.S. law has been busy *expanding and exaggerating* through the nineteenth and twentieth century. France has conveyed to the United States the idea of universal individual rights. These "negative" rights of first generation have been enshrined in the U.S. Constitution, influential as they were on the majority of the founding fathers.[4] Not only has the universalistic ideal been carried to the extreme, as witnessed among other things by notions of universal jurisdiction of U.S. courts in the vindication of such rights,[5] but negative rights, in the absence of thick notions of sovereignty and statehood, as developed by the Jacobeans, became a genuine limit to the re-distributive activity of the American State. Notions of freedom from government intrusion were by no means limited to judicial law-making in the Lochner era. A strong limit to any proactive role of government, except in areas such as military and defense, can thus be traced back to French-inspired notions of economic rights.

Also, Germany has transmitted to the U.S. one of its fundamental present day characteristics: the presence of strong, independent academic institutions as another circuit of professional check on the political process.[6]

It was only because the law was considered a science that it was natural to argue for its teaching in University contexts. Otherwise it could well have remained a practical business, as it continued to be in England until well after the Victorian age. American Law Schools, professional schools staffed with faculty that regard themselves as academic scholars, are the only ones in the world that offer basic legal education at the

---

2. *See* Marbury v. Madison, 5 U.S. 137 (1803).

3. On comparative constitutional adjudication, *see infra*, Chapter 6, Section 3(e) at 523.

4. For a recent, fascinating discussion of their credo and ideology, see Ellis Joseph J., Founding Brothers (2002).

5. *See* the discussion, *infra*.

6. For materials on comparative legal education, see *infra*, Chapter 7 at 628.

graduate school level.[7] Consequently, and paradoxically, for a system based on a "professional school," the average American lawyer is exposed to more years of academic training than any other colleague in the world. Moreover, because of this further expansion as compared to academic undergraduate legal education in Europe, American academia can well be seen today as the global lawyer's graduate school, in the sense that ambitious lawyers worldwide do complete in the U.S. their undergraduate legal education.[8]

NOTES AND QUESTIONS

(1) Domestic lawyers have long lost track of the indebtedness of U.S. law to foreign models, sources, ideas or images. Why do some lawyers consider disturbing the notion that law might be foreign born?

(2) Beginning in the last part of the past century, U.S. law has been able to capture world-wide hegemony. History shows that intellectual leadership in the law carries with it phenomena of intensive cultural arrogance. Both French and German lawyers in the years of their respective intellectual hegemony proved highly parochial and very scarcely keen on learning rather than teaching, listening rather than on talking (they would, for example, only cite domestic legal authority). The result of parochial attitudes has always been loss of international intellectual leadership. In a sense, global leadership of a given legal culture carries with it a special degree of responsibility, and especially the need to live up to international expectations.

From your experience in law school, do you believe that the U.S. legal culture is today living up to international expectations? Do you think that post September 11, 2001, legal transformations in U.S. law will imperil its intellectual leadership, based on cultural prestige?

---

7. One should consider the recent changes in Japan as part of a conscious pattern of "americanization of that system." *See infra.*

8. *See* W. Wiegand, The Reception of American Law in Europe, 39 Am. J. Comp. L. 229 (1991).

CHAPTER 2

INTEGRATIVE AND CONTRASTIVE COMPARISON

Part 1. Integrative Comparison: Bridging the Differences Among Legal Systems

As is true for all scholarly disciplines, much of comparative law is about the interpretation of data. A glass can be described as half empty or half full according to the mental disposition of the observer. When emphasis is on differences we can talk about "contrastive" comparative law. When emphasis is on similarities we may talk of "integrative comparative law". However, integrative comparison is not only a theoretical and cultural approach to the law. Sometimes it is also the basis of grandiose political projects of legal integration. The first part of this chapter will approach some of the theoretical and practical issues of integrative comparison. The second part will be devoted to some theoretical and practical issues connected with the opposite approach, that of contrastive comparison.

Comparative law is in essence a sophisticated way to describe and explain legal phenomena on a large scale for a variety of purposes.[1] Thus, to compare means to observe and explain similarities as well as differences. Similarities among legal systems may be due (1) to deliberate and organized efforts, sponsored by international bodies or groups, aimed at the unification or harmonization of different national or supranational laws, or (2) to the play of more complex and less easily pinpointed forces such as, for example, legal transplants. Similarities of the latter kind sometimes are called "accidental," but this is a misnomer. On closer inspection, such "accidental" similarities will be found to result either from the migration of legal ideas (discussed in Chapter 3 *infra*) or from the fact that in resolving a pervasive or perhaps universal problem several legal systems, independently of each other, have reacted in similar fashion and have given legal recognition to the same needs and aspirations. It is worth dwelling a little more here on a variety of deliberate efforts that might have more or less political force and legitimacy.

---

1. *See* R. B. Schlesinger, The Past and Future of Comparative Law, 43 Am. J.Comp.L. 477 (1995); *See* also Gerhard Dannemann, Comparative Law: Study of Similarities or Differences?, in Mathias Reimann & Reinhard Zimmermann, Oxford Handbook of Comparative Law 383 (2006).

1. Global Legal Integration[1]

At the beginning of this century, in part as a reaction against excessive nationalism, there arose a strong movement favoring massive comparative studies and postulating, as the ultimate aim of such studies, the total or at least substantial unification of all "civilized" legal systems.[2] Since then, this unbounded enthusiasm for universal unification has yielded to second thoughts. It has come to be recognized that legal systems reflect the values of diverse cultures; that cultural diversity should not be turned into homogeneity unless there are very strong reasons for doing so; and that there is no strong reason for world-wide, across-the-board unification of all law.[3] There may be good reasons, on the other hand, for unifying the law with respect to certain selected subjects, either on a regional or even on a world-wide scale. On an intercontinental or potentially world-wide scale, a degree of unification or effective coordination of national laws has been accomplished with respect to certain subjects in areas such as international trade, transportation, communications, intellectual property, and arbitration.

Whether the aimed-for harmonization be regional or intercontinental, it often turns out that the participating states cannot agree upon complete unification or even approximation of the legal rules and principles relating to a given subject.[4] Difficulties arising from existing differences among national laws must then be overcome by more subtle and modest tech-

---

1.   The literature on the subject is vast. For extensive discussion and further references, *see* R. David, The International Unification of Private Law, 2 Int'l Ency.Comp.L., ch. 5 (1971); Ferid, Methoden, Möglichkeiten und Grenzen der Privatrechtsvereinheitlichung, 3 Zeitschrift für Rechtsvergleichung 193 (1962); H. Patrick Glenn, Harmonization of Private Law Rules Between Civil and Common Law Jurisdictions, in Rapports Généraux au XIIIe Congrès International de droit comparé—Montréal 1990, at 79 (1992); O. Lando, The Contribution of Comparative Law to Law Reform by International Organizations, 25 Am.J.Comp.L. 641 (1977); Peter H. Pfund, Contributing to the Progressive Development of Private International Law: The International Process and the United States Approach, 249 Hague Academy Recueil des Cours 9–144 (1994–V); George A. Zaphiriou, Harmonization of Private Rules Between Civil and Common Law Jurisdictions, 38 Am. J.Comp.L. 71 (Supp. 1990); Symposium (edited by Baade) on Unification of Law, 30 Law & Contemp.Probs. 231 (1965); Symposium (edited by Hay) on International Unification

of Law, 16 Am.J.Comp.L. 1 (1968). Mathias Reimann, Comparative Law and Private International Law, in Mathias Reimann & Reinhard Zimmermann, Oxford handbook of Comparative Law 1397 (2006).

2.   *See* Zepos, Die Bewegung zur Rechtsvereinheitlichung und das Schicksal der geltenden Zivilgesetzbücher, 19 Rev.Hell. Dr.Int. 14, 17–18 (1966), where attention is called to the proceedings of the First International Congress of Comparative Law held in Paris in 1900.

3.   A Recent Revival of this idea of wordly law can be found in the work of the famous French jurist Delmas Marty

4.   Moreover, even a successful effort to unify the text of the applicable law in the participating countries does not assure uniformity of interpretation of that text. A striking example of nonuniform interpretation of a uniform text is discussed by B. H. Greene, Personal Defenses Under the Geneva Uniform Law on Bills of Exchange and Promissory Notes: A Comparison, 46 Marq.L.Rev. 281 (1962–63).

niques, such as unification of applicable conflict-of-laws rules. Unification of such rules (along with rules of international civil procedure)[5] has been the object of the Hague Conference on Private International Law, established in 1893.[6] Another technique is to limit unification efforts to the law of *international* transactions of a particular kind, leaving local transactions of the same nature to remain governed by diverse national laws. The latter method is exemplified by some of the provisions of the Warsaw Convention on air transportation.[7] Unification of the law of *international trade* has been the object of the United Nations Commission on International Trade (UNCITRAL), established in 1966 as an organ of the U.N. General Assembly, and also, to a large extent, of the International Institute for the Unification of Private Law (UNIDROIT), established in 1926 as an organ of the League of Nations, but now an independent organization with headquarters in Rome.[8] The biggest recent success along these lines is the United Nations Convention on Contracts for the International Sale of Goods, which came into effect in 1988.[9]

While this kind of unification of rules for particular kinds of international transactions is no doubt important from a practical standpoint, it does not, of course, reduce the number of discordant voices promulgating the law; it merely adds one further voice—the one controlling international transactions as defined by the draftsmen—to the chorus of independent national legislators.

Until the 1960s, the United States stood aloof from most organized international unification efforts.[10] At the end of 1963, however, Congress passed a statute authorizing U.S. participation in the work of the Hague Conference on Private International Law and the International Institute for the Unification of Private Law.[11] Since then, U.S. delegates have participated in the work of these bodies.[12]

5. Hazard, Geoffrey; Stürner, Rolf; Taruffo, Michele; Gidi, Antonio; Principles and Rules of Transnational Civil Procedure, NYU Journal of International Law and Politics, vol. 33, number 3, 2001.

6. *See* Kurt Lipstein, *One Hundred Years of Hague Conferences on Private International Law*, 42 Int'l & Comp.L.Q. 553 (1993); Symposium, The Hague Conference on Private International Law, 57(3) Law & Contemp.Probs. 1–331 (1994).

7. 137 L.N.T.S. 11 (1929), 49 Stat. 3000 (1934). The Convention contains (a) a number of uniform rules of tort law applicable to international flights, plus (b) uniform rules relating to jurisdiction, and (c) some uniform rules of choice of law relating to subjects as to which it proved impossible to unify the substance of the applicable law. Several methods of unification and harmonization thus are illustrated in a single treaty.

8. Rouland, Nobert. The Unidroit Principles in Practice (2nd ed., 2006).

9. For the English text of the convention, *see* 19 I.L.M. 668, 671 (1980). There is a large literature. For references in English, *see* Peter Winship, *The U.N. Sales Convention: A Bibliography of English–Language Publications, 28* Int'l Law. 401 (1994); *see* also Peter Winship, *Changing Contract Practices in the Light of the United Nations Sales Convention: A Guide for Practitioners*, 29 Int'l Law. 525 (1995).

10. *See* E. M. Wise, *Legal Tradition as a Limitation on Law Reform*, 26 Am. J.Comp.L. 1, 4–7 (Supp. 1978).

11. 22 U.S.C. § 269g, as amended in 1972.

12. For reports on U.S. participation, *see*, *e.g.*, R. D. Kearney, *The United States and International Cooperation to Unify Private Law*, 5 Cornell Int'l L.J. 1 (1972); P. H.

In the area of commercial law, where differences in national laws have proved particularly irksome, special techniques have been developed to bring about a measure of international uniformity even in the absence of concerted action on the part of national legislators.[13] Under the sponsorship of private or public international organizations, many standard forms and agreed upon articulations of commercial usages have been drawn up.[14] In countless international transactions of a commercial nature, the terms of such uniform usages or forms become "the law" as between the parties, through adoption by contract.

Whether prepared for governmental imposition or for contractual adoption by the parties, the terms of any instrument aiming at international unification or harmonization of legal rules must be fitted into the substantive and procedural law of the participating countries. In consequence, the drafters of such instruments can do their work only on the basis of the most painstaking comparative studies; and experience has shown that unifying or harmonizing efforts, whenever and wherever undertaken, are accompanied by, and indeed wholly dependent on, extensive studies of this kind.

Outside of the domain of private law, the most significant attempt to move in the integrative direction has been the establishment of the International Criminal Court. The treaty establishing the Court, aimed at holding accountable under international law perpetrators of the most serious crimes against humanity (defined after an interesting effort in comparative criminal law), entered into force after ratification by 60 states in 2002. The court suffered a hard blow when the U. S. under the George W. Bush administration withdrew the ratification, originally provided by President Clinton. Moreover, the Court's prestige has suffered because it

Pfund, *United States Participation in International Unification of Private Law*, 19 Int'l Law. 505 (1985); *id., International Unification of Private Law: A Report on U.S. Participation*, 1985–86, 20 Int'l Law. 623 (1986); *id., International Unification of Private Law: A Report on U.S. Participation—1986–88,* 21 Int'l Law. 1245 (1987); *id., International Unification of Private Law: A Report on U.S. Participation—1987–88,* 22 Int'l Law. 1157 (1988). *See also* Pfund, *supra* note 2.

13. *See* David, *supra* note 2, at 56–61; Schmitthoff, The Law of International Trade—Its Growth, Formulation and Operation, in The Sources of the Law of International Trade 3 (Schmitthoff ed., 1964).

14. Among the examples mentioned by Schmitthoff, *supra* note 20, at 18–19, are two documents sponsored by the International Chamber of Commerce and widely accepted in international trade: Incoterms (defining terms such as "f.o.b." and "c.i.f.") and Uniform Customs and Practice for Commercial Documentary Credits. The latter document is expressly referred to in § 5–102(4) of the Uniform Commercial Code as adopted in New York and a few other states. Even in the absence of such a statutory reference, the Uniform Customs are of enormous importance because bank forms relating to letters of credit ordinarily incorporate them into the parties' contract. *See* U.C.C. § 5–101, cmt. 5th para., 2d sent. (1996). *See* Sandeep Gopalan, *New Trends in the Making of International Commercial Law* University of Pittsburgh Journal of Law and Commerce, 23 J.L. & Com. 117 (2004), Ole Lando, *Optional or Mandatory Europeanisation*, 1 EUR. REV. PRIVATE L. 59 (2000), Wagner, Gerhard. The Economics of Harmonization: The Case of Contract Law 39 *Common Market Law Review* 995 (2002).

has become effectively a forum for "victors' justice" in the few cases that have come before it.

Nevertheless, the experiment of the International Criminal Court shows yet another possible model of integration, this time functioning by the unification of a jurisdictional body.[15]

2. REGIONAL INTEGRATION

The prime example of successful regional unification on a small scale is to be found in Scandinavia, where four independent nations (Denmark, Finland, Norway and Sweden) have unified relatively large segments of their legal systems.[1] Similar endeavors by the three Benelux countries (Belgium, Holland and Luxemburg), on the other hand, have yielded only meager results.[2]

On a larger scale, for the whole continent of Europe, unification efforts have been undertaken by the Council of Europe, which was founded in 1949 to promote the unity of western European countries and which now includes forty-seven member states from both western and eastern Europe. These efforts have resulted in a large number of European Conventions on subjects ranging from road traffic and compulsory auto insurance to extradition, terrorism, and torture. The most important of these conventions is the European Convention on Human Rights.[3] All members of the Council of Europe have been required to ratify the European Convention on Human Rights and to accept the jurisdiction of the European Court of Human Rights (which sits at Strasbourg).

Within the 27 member European Community (also making the European Union) an even greater degree of legal coordination, harmonization, and unification has been achieved. Until recently, the term "European Community" was the collective designation for three formally distinct treaty organizations: the European Coal and Steel Community, established in 1952; the European Economic Community (EEC), established in 1958 and known informally until the late 1980s as the Common Market; and the European Atomic Energy Community (Euratom), also established in 1958.[4] Of the three, the EEC had the widest scope and has been the most

---

15. Schabas, William A., An Introduction to the International Criminal Court (2004).

1. *See* R. David, *supra* p. 70 note 2, at 180–88, where further references can be found.

2. Id., at 188–91. Unification efforts have met with even more limited success in Latin America. *See* Alejandro M. Garro, *Unification and Harmonization of Private Law in Latin America*, 40 Am.J.Comp.L. 587 (1992).

3. [European] Convention for the Protection of Human Rights and Fundamental Freedoms, Nov. 4, 1950, 213 U.N.T.S. 221, Eur. T.S. No. 5. For a survey of the effect of the Convention on the domestic law of member states, *see* Jörg Polakiewicz & Valérie Jacob–Foltzer, The European Human Rights Convention in Domestic Law, 12 Hum.Rts. L.J. 65, 125 (1991).

4. The original six members were Belgium, France, Germany, Italy, Luxembourg, and the Netherlands. Britain, Denmark, and Ireland joined in 1973; Greece in 1981; Portugal and Spain in 1986; and Austria, Finland, and Sweden in 1995.

significant. In 1967, the institutions of the three communities were merged into a comprehensive set of institutions designated the "European Community" and having four main branches: the Commission of the European Communities (or European Commission), which (among other things) proposes community legislation; the Council of Ministers, which consists of representatives of national governments and accepts or rejects the Commission's proposals; the European Parliament, which since 1979 has been directly elected but which has limited legislative powers; and the European Court of Justice, which sits at Luxembourg. In 1987, the Single European Act amended the original treaties and made structural changes designed to accelerate the move toward a single internal European market, which was supposed to be achieved by 1992. The Treaty of European Union, which was signed at Maastricht in 1992, and which entered into force on November 1, 1993, established a new entity, the European Union, of which the three Communities now form part.[5] They continue to exist and constitute the so-called "first pillar" of the European Union; provisions for cooperation in foreign and security policy and in police and judicial cooperation in criminal matters (which until the Amsterdam Treaty covered justice and home affairs) constitute, respectively, the second and third "pillars." At the same time, the Maastricht Treaty renamed the EEC the "European Community," so that technically the term now has a narrower connotation than it did before 1993.

(a) European Union Law

The European Court of Justice has played a major role in the creation of a real body of European Law. Its decisions became a major factor of incremental European legal integration. They have taken on an important role as indirect sources of European law aside of the ones directly disciplined by the Treaty.

Sources of EC law are disciplined by art. 249 Treaty European Community (formerly art. 189). According to it: A) a *regulation* is a statutory provision that has general application, binding in its entirety and directly applicable in all Member States. B) A *directive* is a statutory provision that mandates results for each Member State to which is it addressed, leaving to national authorities the choice of form and methods of implementation; under specific circumstances, according to the rules established by the ECJ, it can be directly applicable even in case of lack of or wrongful implementation. C) A *decision* is an individualized act binding in its entirety upon those entities (States, natural or legal persons) to whom it is addressed.

Art. 34 TEU regulates acts under the so-called third pillar, the area of EU law dealing with police and judicial cooperation in criminal matters, which has a more intergovernmental nature than the European Community. According to art. 34(2)(b), framework decisions approximate the laws of the Member States and are binding as to the results to be achieved, but leave to the national authorities the choice of form and methods. They do

---

5. Technically the CECA Treaty expired in 2002 and has not been renewed. Its competences merged in the European Union (first pillar)

not entail direct effect, contrast to EC directives (which they resemble otherwise in their structure).

The following cases are landmarks of this most advanced process of legal integration between sovereign States. Interestingly, this judicial integration has been carried on despite much political resistance towards the making of a European political system.

Flaminio Costa v. E.N.E.L.

Case 6/64, Judgment of 15 July 1964. ECR [1964] 585.

[In this case a lower Italian judge (*giudice conciliatore*) asked the Court of Justice to rule on the compatibility of an Italian statute that nationalized electricity with the rules of the EC Treaty on monopolies, state aid and the so called right of establishment. The Italian government claimed that Italian judges were bound to apply the relevant provisions of Italian law, even in case of contrast with EC rules. The ECJ refused this argument, stating that the Community legal system is integrated in the national legal systems, and as a consequence national judges have a duty to apply relevant EC legal provisions.

The reader should remember that Articles 5 (concerning the duty of loyal cooperation by member States in the fulfillment of Community obligations), 7 (which prohibits any discrimination on the base of nationality), 177 (regulating the preliminary reference procedure, under which a national judge can send a case to the ECJ concerning the interpretation of EC rules) and 189 (which defines the types of EC acts) have been renumbered after the Treaty of Amsterdam and they are now respectively articles 10, 12, 234 and 249 TEC.].

Judgment of the Court of 15 July 1964.

Reference for a preliminary ruling: Giudice conciliatore di Milano—Italy.

Case 6/64.

■ Lecourt, Judge–Rapporteur:

■ Lagrange, Advocate General:

By contrast with ordinary international treaties, the EEC treaty has created its own legal system which, on the entry into force of the treaty, became an integral part of the legal systems of the member states and which their courts are bound to apply.

By creating a community of unlimited duration, having its own institutions, its own personality, its own legal capacity and capacity of representation on the international plan and, more particularly, real powers stemming from a limitation of sovereignty or a transfer of powers from the states to the community, the member states have limited their sovereign rights, albeit within limited fields, and have thus created a body of law which binds both their nationals and themselves.

The integration into the laws of each member state of provisions which derive from the community, and more generally the terms and the spirit of the treaty, make it impossible for the states, as a corollary, to accord precedence to a unilateral and subsequent measure over a legal system accepted by them on a basis of reciprocity. Such a measure cannot therefore be inconsistent with that legal system. the executive force of community law cannot vary from one state to another in deference to subsequent domestic laws, without jeopardizing the attainment of the objectives of the treaty set out in article 5(2) and giving rise to the discrimination prohibited by article 7.

The obligations undertaken under the treaty establishing the community would not be unconditional, but merely contingent, if they could be called in question by subsequent legislative acts of the signatories. Wherever the treaty grants the states the right to act unilaterally, it does this by clear and precise provisions (for example articles 15, 93(3), 223, 224 and 225). applications, by member states for authority to derogate from the treaty are subject to a special authorization procedure (for example articles 8(4), 17(4), 25, 26, 73, the third subparagraph of article 93(2), and 226) which would lose their purpose if the member states could renounce their obligations by means of an ordinary law .

The precedence of community law is confirmed by article 189, whereby a regulation "shall be binding" and "directly applicable in all member states". This provision, which is subject to no reservation, would be quite meaningless if a state could unilaterally nullify its effects by means of a legislative measure which could prevail over community law.

It follows from all these observations that the law stemming from the treaty, an independent source of law, could not, because of its special and original nature, be overridden by domestic legal provisions, however framed, without being deprived of its character as community law and without the legal basis of the community itself being called into question.

The transfer by the states from their domestic legal system to the community legal system of the rights and obligations arising under the treaty carries with it a permanent limitation of their sovereign rights, against which a subsequent unilateral act incompatible with the concept of the community cannot prevail. Consequently article 177 is to be applied regardless of any domestic law, whenever questions relating to the interpretation of the treaty arise. . . .

NV Algemene Transport- en Expeditie Onderneming van Gend & Loos v. Netherlands Inland Revenue Administration

Case 26–62, Judgment of 5 February 1963, ECR [1963] 1.

[This case concerned the import of chemicals from Germany to the Netherlands, which had been charged with an import duty that was alleged to have increased after the entry into force of the EEC Treaty, in contrast to its provisions on customs duties. The national judge (*Tariefcommissie*) asked the ECJ to rule on whether the rule prohibiting customs duties was directly applicable, i.e. it granted individual rights to European citizens that had to be protected by national judges. The Netherlands claimed that the EC Treaty is an international treaty, and therefore its provisions cannot have direct effect: if there is a breach of EC obligations by a member State, this must be eliminated through a centralized infringement procedure against it. The ECJ, in contrast, ruled that the EC is a new legal order which confers both obligations and rights to individuals, and that Art. 12 TEEC, containing a clear, unconditional and negative obligation, is in fact a directly applicable provision conferring individual rights that must be judicially protected.

Arts 12 (prohibiting customs duties on imports and exports), 169 and 170 (regulating enforcement actions against Member States in breach of EC obligations) are now respectively arts 25, 226 and 227 TEC.]

Judgment of the Court of 5 February 1963.

Reference for a preliminary ruling: Tariefcommissie—Pays–Bas.

Case 26–62.

■ Hammes, Judge–Rapporteur:

■ Roemer, Advocate General:

The first question of the *Tariefcommissie* is whether article 12 of the treaty has direct application in national law in the sense that nationals of member states may on the basis of this article lay claim to rights which the national court must protect.

To ascertain whether the provisions of an international treaty extend so far in their effects it is necessary to consider the spirit, the general scheme and the wording of those provisions.

The objective of the EEC treaty, which is to establish a common market, the functioning of which is of direct concern to interested parties in the community, implies that this treaty is more than an agreement which merely creates mutual obligations between the contracting states. This view is confirmed by the preamble to the treaty which refers not only to governments but to peoples. It is also confirmed more specifically by the establishment of institutions endowed with sovereign rights, the exercise of which affects member states and also their citizens. Furthermore, it must be noted that the nationals of the states brought together in the community are called upon to cooperate in the functioning of this community through the intermediary of the European parliament and the economic and social committee.

In addition the task assigned to the court of justice under article 177, the object of which is to secure uniform interpretation of the treaty by national courts and tribunals, confirms that the states have acknowledged that community law has an authority which can be invoked by their nationals before those courts and tribunals. The conclusion to be drawn from this is that the community constitutes a new legal order of international law for the benefit of which the states have limited their sovereign rights, albeit within limited fields, and the subjects of which comprise not only member states but also their nationals. Independently of the legislation of member states, community law therefore not only imposes obligations on individuals but is also intended to confer upon them rights which become part of their legal heritage. These rights arise not only where they are expressly granted by the treaty, but also by reason of obligations which the treaty imposes in a clearly defined way upon individuals as well as upon the member states and upon the institutions of the community.

A restriction of the guarantees against an infringement of article 12 by member states to the procedures under article 169 and 170 would remove all direct legal protection of the individual rights of their nationals. There is the risk that recourse to the procedure under these articles would be ineffective if it were to occur after the implementation of a national decision taken contrary to the provisions of the treaty.

The vigilance of individuals concerned to protect their rights amounts to an effective supervision in addition to the supervision entrusted by articles 169 and 170 to the diligence of the commission and of the member states. . . .

Amministrazione delle Finanze dello Stato v. Simmenthal SpA

Case 106/77, Judgment of 9 March 1978. ECR [1978] 629.

[Beef was imported from France into Italy for which it was charged fees for veterinary inspection when crossing national borders. Simmenthal, a well known company of canned meat, claimed that the fees were in conflict with EC rules on free circulation of goods, and this was also the decision of the ECJ on a preliminary reference. Based on this ruling, a national judge (*Pretore*) ordered repayment of the fees, but the Italian fiscal authorities claimed that in case of conflict between a national rule and EC law the judge could not refuse to apply the national provision, but had instead to submit the case to the Italian Constitutional Court in order to decide whether the rule is unconstitutional due to the conflict with the EEC Treaty (which has been ratified on the basis of the provisions of the Constitution). The *Pretore* consequently referred the case to the ECJ, which declared that a national judge has a duty to set aside national provisions that are in conflict with EC law, in order to guarantee uniform and full application of directly effective EC rules and the supremacy of EC law.]

Judgment of the Court of 6 March 1979.

Common organization of the market in beef and veal.

Case 92/78.

■ Pescatore, Judge–Rapporteur:

■ Reischl, Advocate General:

The main purpose of the first question is to ascertain what consequences flow from the direct applicability of a provision of community law in the event of incompatibility with a subsequent legislative provision of a member state.

Direct applicability in such circumstances means that rules of community law must be fully and uniformly applied in all the member states from the date of their entry into force and for so long as they continue in force.

These provisions are therefore a direct source of rights and duties for all those affected thereby, whether member states or individuals, who are parties to legal relationships under community law.

This consequence also concerns any national court whose task it is as an organ of a member state to protect, in a case within its jurisdiction, the rights conferred upon individuals by community law.

Furthermore, in accordance with the principle of the precedence of community law, the relationship between provisions of the treaty and directly applicable measures of the institutions on the one hand and the national law of the member states on the other is such that those provisions and measures not only by their entry into force render automatically inapplicable any conflicting provision of current national law but—in so far as they are an integral part of, and take precedence in, the legal order applicable in the territory of each of the member states—also preclude the valid adoption of new national legislative measures to the extent to which they would be incompatible with community provisions.

Indeed any recognition that national legislative measures which encroach upon the field within which the community exercises its legislative power or which are otherwise incompatible with the provisions of community law had any legal effect would amount to a corresponding denial of the effectiveness of obligations undertaken unconditionally and irrevocably by member states pursuant to the treaty and would thus imperil the very foundations of the community.

The same conclusion emerges from the structure of article 177 of the treaty which provides that any court or tribunal of a member state is entitled to make a reference to the court whenever it considers that a preliminary ruling on a question of interpretation or validity relating to community law is necessary to enable it to give judgment.

The effectiveness of that provision would be impaired if the national court were prevented from forthwith applying community law in accordance with the decision or the case-law of the court.

It follows from the foregoing that every national court must, in a case within its jurisdiction, apply community law in its entirety and protect rights which the latter confers on individuals and must accordingly set aside any provision of national law which may conflict with it, whether prior or subsequent to the community rule.

Accordingly any provision of a national legal system and any legislative, administrative or judicial practice which might impair the effectiveness of community law by withholding from the national court having jurisdiction to apply such law the power to do everything necessary at the moment of its application to set aside national legislative provisions which might prevent community rules from having full force and effect are incompatible with those requirements which are the very essence of community law.

This would be the case in the event of a conflict between a provision of community law and a subsequent national law if the solution of the conflict were to be reserved for an authority with a discretion of its own, other than the court called upon to apply community law, even if such an impediment to the full effectiveness of community law were only temporary.

The first question should therefore be answered to the effect that a national court which is called upon, within the limits of its jurisdiction, to apply provisions of community law is under a duty to give full effect to those provisions, if necessary refusing of its own motion to apply any conflicting provision of national legislation, even if adopted subsequently, and it is not necessary for the court to request or await the prior setting aside of such provision by legislative or other constitutional means. . . .

Andrea Francovich and Daniela Bonifaci and others v. Italian Republic

Joined Cases C–6/90 and C–9/90, Judgment of 19 November 1991, ECR [1991] I–5357.

[The applicants did not receive their wages due to the insolvency of their employer; according to an EC directive, they would be entitled to a guarantee of payment for unpaid wages, but that directive was not timely implemented by Italy. As a consequence, the applicants brought a case to an Italian court, a *Pretura*, asking for direct application of the relevant EC rules. On a preliminary reference by the *Pretore*, the ECJ ruled that even though the rules of the directive were not directly effective because they were not sufficiently precise, they conferred individual rights which were infringed by Italy's failure to implement them, and as a consequence Italy was liable to pay the damages for this breach.]

Judgment of the Court of 19 November 1991.

References for a preliminary ruling: Pretura di Vicenza and Pretura di Bassano del Grappa—Italy.

Failure to implement a directive—Liability of the Member State.

Joined cases C–6/90 and C–9/90.

THE COURT,

composed of: O. Due, President, Sir Gordon Slynn, R. Joliet, F.A. Schockweiler, F. Grévisse and P.J.G. Kapteyn (Presidents of Chambers), G.F. Mancini, J.C. Moitinho de Almeida, G.C. Rodríguez Iglesias, M. Díez de Velasco and M. Zuleeg, Judges,

■ Rodriguez Iglesias, Judge–Rapporteur:

■ Mischo, Advocate General:

As the court has consistently held, a member state which has not adopted the implementing measures required by a directive within the prescribed period may not, against individuals, plead its own failure to perform the obligations which the directive entails. Thus wherever the provisions of a

directive appear, as far as their subject-matter is concerned, to be unconditional and sufficiently precise, those provisions may, in the absence of
implementing measures adopted within the prescribed period, be relied
upon as against any national provision which is incompatible with the
directive or in so far as the provisions of the directive define rights which
individuals are able to assert against the state *(Judgment in Case 8/81
Becker v Finanzamt Muenster-innenstadt [1982] ECR 53)* ...

Accordingly, even though the provisions of the directive in question are
sufficiently precise and unconditional as regards the determination of the
persons entitled to the guarantee and as regards the content of that
guarantee, those elements are not sufficient to enable individuals to rely on
those provisions before the national courts. Those provisions do not identify
the person liable to provide the guarantee, and the state cannot be
considered liable on the sole ground that it has failed to take transposition
measures within the prescribed period.

The answer to the first part of the first question must therefore be
that the provisions of directive 80/987 which determine the rights of
employees must be interpreted as meaning that the persons concerned
cannot enforce those rights against the state before the national courts
where no implementing measures are adopted within the prescribed period.

That issue must be considered in the light of the general system of the
treaty and its fundamental principles.

(A) The existence of state liability as a matter of principle

It should be borne in mind at the outset that the EEC treaty has
created its own legal system, which is integrated into the legal systems of
the member states and which their courts are bound to apply. The subjects
of that legal system are not only the member states but also their
nationals. Just as it imposes burdens on individuals, community law is also
intended to give rise to rights which become part of their legal patrimony.
Those rights arise not only where they are expressly granted by the treaty
but also by virtue of obligations which the treaty imposes in a clearly
defined manner both on individuals and on the member states and the
community institutions *(See the judgment in case 26/62 Van Gend en Loos
[1963] ECR 1 and case 6/64 Costa v Enel [1964]ECR 585).*

Furthermore, it has been consistently held that the national courts
whose task it is to apply the provisions of community law in areas within
their jurisdiction must ensure that those rules take full effect and must
protect the rights which they confer on individuals *(See in particular the
judgments in case 106/77 Amministrazione Delle Finanze Finanze Dello
Stato v Simmenthal [1978] ECR 629, paragraph 16, and case C–213/89
factortame [1990] ECR I–2433, paragraph 19).*

The full effectiveness of community rules would be impaired and the
protection of the rights which they grant would be weakened if individuals
were unable to obtain redress when their rights are infringed by a breach
of community law for which a member state can be held responsible.

The possibility of obtaining redress from the member state is particularly indispensable where, as in this case, the full effectiveness of communi-

ty rules is subject to prior action on the part of the state and where, consequently, in the absence of such action, individuals cannot enforce before the national courts the rights conferred upon them by community law.

It follows that the principle whereby a state must be liable for loss and damage caused to individuals as a result of breaches of community law for which the state can be held responsible is inherent in the system of the treaty.

A further basis for the obligation of member states to make good such loss and damage is to be found in article 5 of the treaty, under which the member states are required to take all appropriate measures, whether general or particular, to ensure fulfillment of their obligations under community law. Among these is the obligation to nullify the unlawful consequences of a breach of community law *(see, in relation to the analogous provision of article 86 of the ECSC treaty, the judgment in case 6/60 Humblet v. Belgium [1960] ECR 559)*.

It follows from all the foregoing that it is a principle of community law that the member states are obliged to make good loss and damage caused to individuals by breaches of community law for which they can be held responsible. . . .

Criminal Proceedings against Maria Pupino

Case C–105/03, Judgment of the Court (Grand Chamber) of 16 June 2005, ECR [2005] I–5285.

[Pupino was a school teacher charged with a criminal offense for having mistreated children in her care. According to Italian criminal procedure the judicial process is divided in two phases, and evidence is generally taken in the second stage. The Public Prosecutor asked to take evidence from the children in the first phase, because they might in the meantime forget relevant facts that had occurred. The case did not come under the exceptions to the rule envisaged by Italian law, but the need of a specific treatment of vulnerable victims was foreseen by an EU framework decision on the standing and protection of victims in criminal proceedings. On a preliminary reference by the Italian *Tribunale*, the ECJ ruled that even though framework decisions are taken under the third pillar and are therefore outside the scope of EC rules, there is nevertheless a duty to interpret national rules so far as possible in conformity with relevant EU rules. Art. 1 TEU establishes the European Union, founded on the European Communities and other policies; art. 34(2)(b) regulates framework decisions, entailing approximations of national laws but lacking direct effect; art. 35 TEU grants limited jurisdiction to the ECJ to review acts under the third pillar]

JUDGMENT OF THE COURT (Grand Chamber)

16 June 2005

(Police and judicial cooperation in criminal matters—Articles 34 EU and 35 EU–Framework Decision 2001/220/JHA—Standing of victims in criminal proceedings—Protection of vulnerable persons—Hearing of minors as witnesses—Effects of a framework decision)

In Case C–105/03,

REFERENCE for a preliminary ruling under Article 35 EU by the judge in charge of preliminary enquiries at the Tribunale di Firenze (Italy), made by decision of 3 February 2003, received at the Court on 5 March 2003, in criminal proceedings against

THE COURT (Grand Chamber),

composed of V. Skouris, President, P. Jann, C.W.A. Timmermans, A. Rosas, R. Silva de Lapuerta and A. Borg Barthet, Presidents of Chambers, N. Colneric, S. von Bahr, J.N. Cunha Rodrigues (Rapporteur), P. Kūris, E. Juhász, G. Arestis and M. Ilešič, Judges

Advocate General: J. Kokott,

Judgment

(. . .)

On those grounds, the Court (Grand Chamber) hereby rules:

Having regard to the arguments of the French, Italian, Swedish, Netherlands and United Kingdom governments, it has to be examined whether, as the national court presupposes and as the French, Greek and Portuguese governments and the commission maintain, the obligation on the national authorities to interpret their national law as far as possible in the light of the wording and purpose of community directives applies with the same effects and within the same limits where the act concerned is a framework decision taken on the basis of title VI of the treaty on European Union.

If so, it has to be determined whether, as the French, Italian, Swedish and United Kingdom governments have observed, it is obvious that a reply to the question referred cannot have a concrete impact on the solution of the dispute in the main proceedings, given the inherent limits on the obligation of conforming interpretation.

It should be noted at the outset that the wording of article 34(2)(b) EU is very closely inspired by that of the third paragraph of article 249 EC. Article 34(2)(b) EU confers a binding character on framework decisions in the sense that they "bind" the member states "as to the result to be achieved but shall leave to the national authorities the choice of form and methods".

The binding character of framework decisions, formulated in terms identical to those of the third paragraph of article 249 EC, places on national authorities, and particularly national courts, an obligation to interpret national law in conformity.

The fact that, by virtue of article 35 EU, the jurisdiction of the court of justice is less extensive under title VI of the treaty on European Union than it is under the EC treaty, and the fact that there is no complete system of actions and procedures designed to ensure the legality of the acts of the institutions in the context of title VI, does nothing to invalidate that conclusion.

Irrespective of the degree of integration envisaged by the treaty of Amsterdam in the process of creating an ever closer union among the peoples of Europe within the meaning of the second paragraph of article 1 EU, it is perfectly comprehensible that the authors of the treaty on European Union should have considered it useful to make provision, in the context of title VI of that treaty, for recourse to legal instruments with effects similar to those provided for by the EC treaty, in order to contribute effectively to the pursuit of the union's objectives.

That jurisdiction would be deprived of most of its useful effect if individuals were not entitled to invoke framework decisions in order to obtain a conforming interpretation of national law before the courts of the member states.

In support of their position, the Italian and United Kingdom governments argue that, unlike the EC treaty, the treaty on European Union contains no obligation similar to that laid down in article 10 EC, on which the case-law of the court of justice partially relied in order to justify the obligation to interpret national law in conformity with community law.

That argument must be rejected.

The second and third paragraphs of article 1 of the treaty on European Union provide that that treaty marks a new stage in the process of creating an ever closer union among the peoples of Europe and that the task of the union, which is founded on the European communities, supplemented by the policies and forms of cooperation established by that treaty, shall be to organize, in a manner demonstrating consistency and solidarity, relations between the member states and between their peoples.

It would be difficult for the union to carry out its task effectively if the principle of loyal cooperation, requiring in particular that member states take all appropriate measures, whether general or particular, to ensure fulfillment of their obligations under European Union law, were not also binding in the area of police and judicial cooperation in criminal matters, which is moreover entirely based on cooperation between the member states and the institutions, as the advocate general has rightly pointed out in paragraph 26 of her opinion.

In the light of all the above considerations, the court concludes that the principle of conforming interpretation is binding in relation to framework decisions adopted in the context of title vi of the treaty on European Union. When applying national law, the national court that is called upon to interpret it must do so as far as possible in the light of the wording and purpose of the framework decision in order to attain the result which it pursues and thus comply with article 34(2)(b) EU.

It should be noted, however, that the obligation on the national court to refer to the content of a framework decision when interpreting the relevant rules of its national law is limited by general principles of law, particularly those of legal certainty and non-retroactivity.

The obligation on the national court to refer to the content of a framework decision when interpreting the relevant rules of its national law ceases when the latter cannot receive an application which would lead to a result compatible with that envisaged by that framework decision. In other words, the principle of conforming interpretation cannot serve as the basis for an interpretation of national law contra legem. That principle does, however, require that, where necessary, the national court consider the whole of national law in order to assess how far it can be applied in such a way as not to produce a result contrary to that envisaged by the framework decision. (. . .) it is for the national court to determine whether, in this case, a conforming interpretation of national law is possible.

NOTES AND QUESTIONS

(1) Very early at the beginning of the 1960's in *Costa v. Enel* the European Court of Justice asserted the principle of supremacy (or primacy) of EEC law (as it then was, now EC) as a fundamental principle, by developing a systematic interpretation of the EEC Treaty founded on the permanent limitation of sovereignty of Member States and on the integration of the EC with the national legal systems. As a consequence, valid EEC rules (either treaty provisions or secondary acts) take precedence over contrasting national legal provisions, irrespective of their nature (e.g. constitutional provisions) and their timing (i.e. also provisions enacted after the relevant EEC rules).

(2) Roughly at the same time *Van Gend & Loos* dealt with a different but related issue concerning the possibility of granting direct effect to treaty rules, i.e. to give a right to individuals to claim protection of rights deriving from treaty rules before their national courts. The Court of Justice affirmed direct effect starting from the premise that the EEC is a new legal order of international law which not only creates obligations for states, but also confers rights and obligations on individuals. As in *Costa v. Enel* the rule is based on the limitation of sovereignty that member states have accepted by becoming members of the EEC.

(3) A further step deriving from the principle of direct effect of EEC rules was taken by the Court of Justice defining the effects of incompatibility of national legal rules with EEC rules. In the *Simmenthal* case the court established that national courts have a duty to apply EEC rules, setting aside conflicting national provisions, even if they would not have that power according to national law (e.g. in legal systems where the invalidity of a statutory rule must be decided by the constitutional court)

(4) The European court of justice has extended in the 1970's and 1980's the notion of direct effect from treaty rules to rules of unimplemented directives, stating that under certain conditions they can be directly applicable (i.e. they grant individual rights enforceable in national courts), in spite of the fact that according to the letter of the relevant treaty provision directives create individual rights only after transposition, since they are directed at states, rather than individuals. *Francovich* has finally complemented in the 1990's this judge-made law by establishing the fundamental principle of state liability, according to which if states do not timely and duly transpose directives and these are not directly effective, or otherwise breach fundamental EC obligations, they are liable to pay damages to individuals who are affected by that infringement.

(5) *Pupino* is a recent leading case showing the remarkable activism of the European Court of Justice extending its reach beyond European Community law. Here the Court has extended the reach of some of the fundamental principles also to the third pillar, concerning police and judicial cooperation in criminal matters, which is considered an area having an intergovernmental nature, where national interests have a stronger role and consequently community rules and mechanisms only partly apply (e.g. with limitations to the jurisdiction of the court of justice: ART. 35 TEU). In the 2005 Pupino decision the court has imposed a duty to interpret national provisions in accordance with EU law (the so-called principle of conforming interpretation) also in the case of framework decisions (a form of EU act typical of the third pillar, which lacks direct effect: see art. 34(2) TEU). The decision was based on the principle of loyal cooperation, according to which member states must take all measures required to ensure the fulfillment of EU obligations (ART. 10 TEC), and it is clearly linked with the conspicuous case law of the ECJ defining the scope of supremacy of EC/EU law and the limitations that it imposes on national laws.

(6) As we will discuss in Chapter 6 *infra*, case law is a weak source of law in countries belonging to the continental European civil law tradition. Only two of the 27 members of the European Community/Union are common law countries (UK and Ireland). How do you explain the activism of the ECJ? Tensions between the US Supreme Court and the Supreme Courts of the member States emerged in the formative era of American Law before the supremacy of the Federal Constitutional court became finally unchallenged. Do you remember any of such famous leading cases?

(7) As of January 1 2002, a number of European States (16 now belong to the so called "Euro-zone" and 10 other countries use the new currency) have unified their currency, putting the Euro into circulation and giving birth to a Central European Bank sitting in Frankfurt. This remarkable sacrifice of state sovereignty, displaying a genuine desire to give birth to "a more perfect union", going in the direction of some kind of political unification, has not been accomplished by all member States. Some of them were not able to meet the requirements to enter into the "club" of the Euro. Some others, like Great Britain, simply refused to join.

(8) Perhaps under the activist lead of the Court and of the monetary policy authorities (with a remarkable lack of democratic legitimacy) the next step that European countries took was the development of a more integrated foreign policy, perhaps the most crucial aspect of sovereignty. European leaders attempted to meet the organizational and political challenges of the global economy and of the integration of many new States, mostly coming from the former socialist block. A constitution making process, aimed at the ratification of a new Constitutional Treaty was thus set in motion. The new ambitious Treaty, substituting all the previous ones, and containing a Charter of Rights (Treaty of Nice entered into force February 1, 2003 containing a "bill of rights" thus far of mere political rather than legal value) has been signed by all the Member States governments after a very intense process of negotiation on

October 29, 2004 in Rome. Perhaps because of its unsatisfactory, highly technocratic and ultra-complicated content, perhaps because of the resurgence of nationalistic feelings, the Constitutional Treaty has been defeated in the ratification process by popular vote in 2005 in Holland and France.

A new somewhat abridged version, signed in Lisbon on December 13 2007, reproducing many of the provisions (and problems) of the previous one (and still containing a reference that makes the Nice Charter binding law) (ART 6. Poland and UK kept an opt out option in Protocol n. 30), has also been defeated in the ratification process by popular vote in Ireland in June 2008. So that, for the time being Europe remains a quite unique international organization endowed with a powerful bureaucracy (almost 20,000 employees in Brussels) but lacking a political soul.

Nevertheless, while the political integration process is highly perplexing, the process of legal integration is proceeding at full steam under the pressure of legal scholarship, the jurisprudence of the European Court of Justice, and the very abundant legislative and regulatory activity of Brussels. While many observers raise issues of political legitimacy about this scenario, an industry of unifying forces of legal integration is thriving.[1]

(9) The founders of the European Community anticipated that some measure of unification or at least of harmonization and coordination, of the national laws of member states would be necessary if serious distortions of the competitive process within the Community were to be avoided. Accordingly, the Treaty of Rome establishing the EEC contained a number of special provisions for harmonization of legislation in certain fields (e.g., corporation law, indirect taxes, transportation, and social security); in addition, the more general provision of Article 3(h) of the Treaty stated as one of the Community's objectives the "approximation" of the municipal law of member states "to the extent necessary for the orderly functioning of the common market."[2] Initially, European Community law was perceived to be of limited scope, "dealing merely with agricultural subsidies and import duties . . . the shape of tractor seats and the size of cucumbers, and . . . competition among producers of pasta and beer."[3] With respect to the bulk of every-day legal matters, the national legal systems of member states were largely unchanged. Gradually, however, the process of harmonizing or "approximating" the laws of member states has not only intruded into specialized areas of legal practice; it has massively affected (or infected) even basic private law subjects such as tort and contract law,[4] while

---

1. *See* Ugo Mattei & Fernanda Nicola, *A "Social Dimension" in European Private Law? The Call for Setting a Progressive Agenda*, 41 New England Law Review, Vol. 41, pp. 1–66, 2006.

2. How "approximation" is to be accomplished is set out in arts. 100–102. Directives (provided for in art. 100) have been of particular importance. Directives supposedly define the result to be achieved, while leaving form and method to be determined by national law.

3. Reinhard Zimmermann, Civil Code and Civil Law: The "Europeanization" of

Private Law Within the European Community and the Re-emergence of a European Legal Science, 1 Colum.J.Eur.L. 63, 68 (1994–95).

4. *Id. See* also, e.g., P.–Ch. Müller–Graff, Europäisches Gemeinschaftsrecht und Privatrecht, 46 N.J.W. 13 (1993); *id.*, Common Private Law in the European Community, in The Common Law of Europe and the Future of Legal Education 239 (Bruno De Witte & Caroline Forder eds., 1992). Examples will be encountered later in this course. These developments have prompted talk about the emergence of a new "common law of Europe." *See*, e.g., New Perspectives for a

the case law of the European Court of Justice has worked profound changes in the public law of member states. Today in Europe, as we will discuss in a later chapter, (see *infra* Chapter 5) a heated debate, mostly conducted with the tools of comparative law is unfolding on whether legal integration should be supported by a continent wide-codification effort.[5]

(10) The principle of supremacy, which was in its origin and for a very long time a judge-made principle, was finally inserted in the text of the European Constitution Treaty, which was signed in 2004 in Rome:

> Treaty establishing a Constitution for Europe (Official Journal C310 of 16 December 2004)
>
> ARTICLE I–6
>
> "The constitution and the law adopted by the union's institutions in exercising competences conferred on it, shall have primacy over the law of the member states."

After the European Constitution was discarded, because of popular referendum rejections in Holland and France, a new reform treaty was approved in 2007 in Lisbon, which is currently undergoing the ratification process (and again experiencing problems after a negative vote in the referendum held in Ireland in June 2008). The Lisbon treaty contains the vast majority of the amendments and novelties that were part of the European Constitution, but with some differences, among which also the deletion of the provision stating the principle of supremacy of EC/EU law. Reference to the principle is now made in a declaration annexed to the treaty, which nevertheless lacks binding legal effect. This change should not have significant practical effects, since the principle of supremacy remains as a fundamental principle established by the case law of the court of justice and consequently as a cornerstone of the so-called *acquis communautaire*. Yet, the deletion of the rule has a highly symbolic value, showing an attitude of growing mistrust on the part of member states.

> Treaty of Lisbon—consolidated versions of the treaty on European Union and the treaty on the functioning of the European Union—declarations. (*Official Journal C 115, 09/05/2008, P. 1–388*)
>
> **17.   Declaration Concerning Primacy**
>
> "The conference recalls that, in accordance with well settled case law of the court of justice of the European Union, the treaties and the law adopted by the union on the basis of the treaties have primacy over the law of member states, under the conditions laid down by the said case law.
>
> The conference has also decided to attach as an annex to this final act the Opinion of the Council Legal Service on the primacy of EC law as set out in 11197/07 (JUR 260):
>
> **"Opinion of the Council Legal Service of 22 June 2007**
>
> It results from the case-law of the court of justice that primacy of EC law is a cornerstone principle of community law. According to the court, this

---

Common Law of Europe (M. Cappelletti ed. 1978); The Common Law of Europe and the Future of Legal Education, *supra*. This prospect will be further considered. *See infra*.

5. *See* Ugo Mattei, The European Codification Process. Cut and Paste (2003).

principle is inherent to the specific nature of the European community. at the time of the first judgment of this established case law (Costa v. Enel, 15 July 1964, case 6/641 [1] there was no mention of primacy in the treaty. it is still the case today. the fact that the principle of primacy will not be included in the future treaty shall not in any way change the existence of the principle and the existing case-law of the court of justice.

[1] "it follows (...) that the law stemming from the treaty, an independent source of law, could not, because of its special and original nature, be overridden by domestic legal provisions, however framed, without being deprived of its character as community law and without the legal basis of the community itself being called into question."

(11) As the discussed materials show, the process of European integration has thus far been much more judicial than political. What are the main problems of a process of judicial integration unfolding outside or even despite the will of the people involved? Can judicial integration work as a model for other experiences? Is it a desirable task for a more global legal system?

(12) The literature on European law is now very abundant. The following is a short reading list:

P. Craig, G. de Burca, *EU Law–Text, Cases and Materials*, 4th ed., Oxford University Press, 2008

G.A. Bermann, J Goebel, E.N. Fox, W.J. Davey, *Cases and Materials on European Union Law*, 2nd ed., 2004, West.

S. Weatherill, *EU Law–Cases & Materials*, 8th ed., Oxford University Press, 2007.

D. Chalmer et al., *European Union Law: Text and Materials*, Cambridge University Press, 2006

J. Steiner, L. Woods, C. Twigg–Flesner, *EU Law*, 9th ed., Oxford University Press, 2006

T.C. Hartley, *The Foundations of European Community Law*, 6th ed., Oxford University Press, 2007

(b) South America

In addition to Europe, regional integration efforts are carried on elsewhere from Africa to Asia to Latin America. In the following excerpt the state of legal and political affairs in the last mentioned context is discussed.

Samuel A. Arieti, Development: The Role of MERCOSUR as a Vehicle for Latin American Integration

6 Chi. J. Int'l L. 761 (2005–2006).

In March 1991, Argentina, Brazil, Paraguay, and Uruguay acceded to the Treaty Establishing a Common Market between the Argentine Republic, the Federative Republic of Brazil, the Republic of Paraguay, and the Eastern Republic of Uruguay, creating MERCOSUR. Supplemented by the

Additional Protocol to the Treaty of Asuncion on the Institutional Structure of Mercosur, the Treaty of Asuncion states that the goals of MERCOSUR are to eliminate trade barriers, establish a common external tariff, coordinate macroeconomic policies, and develop the harmonization of laws. Initially, MERCOSUR was a resounding success. An economic union of the four nations seemed logical. Linked geographically, these countries already depended upon one another for trade and had little overlap between their respective economies. Economic integration was to be achieved slowly through decisions made by various temporary and ad hoc institutions and by the subsequent ratification of those decisions by the respective legislatures of the member states. The MERCOSUR institutions themselves, including the arbitral panel for dispute resolution, were to exercise little coercive power over the members and were not to be the guiding force behind integration. Instead, member states retained control over economic progress through their representatives sitting on the various MERCOSUR institutional committees. The effect of such retention of control by the member states has been to repeatedly subject the integration process to changes in the political climate of one or more of the member states. Thus, during the recent economic meltdowns of Brazil and later Argentina, MERCOSUR's integration process was stalled.

But despite this sense of reluctance to cede political sovereignty, the history of MERCOSUR's expansion also reflects the desire to gain the benefits of economic integration. Following the successes of the common market's booming early years in the mid-nineties, Chile and Bolivia gained the status of associate states by entering into economic complementation agreements with MERCOSUR in 1996. Peru became MERCOSUR's third associate state through a similar treaty in 2003. The terms of the agreements call for the creation of free trade areas within fixed periods and for increases in various forms of cooperation and investment.

Because neither the Treaty of Asuncion nor the Ouro Preto Protocol contemplated the expansion of MERCOSUR's membership, the common market lacks formal procedures for admitting new members. Therefore, instead of incorporating Bolivia, Chile, and Peru directly into its existing institutions, which would have required a major overhaul of its foundations, MERCOSUR chose to grant its associates indirect relationships through the mechanisms of the Latin American Integration Association ("ALADI").

Practically speaking, the associate states of MERCOSUR are not members of the common market in any real sense. They possess little authority to participate in the decisions and meetings of MERCOSUR's institutional bodies, and they are not bound by those decisions or even by the broad MERCOSUR policies outlined in the Treaty of Asuncion and in the Ouro Preto Protocol. Instead, the associate states' relationships with the common market are governed by commissions representing both parties that work to fulfill the obligations of the respective economic complementation agreements. Because the associate states cede no control to a supranational MERCOSUR entity, they are free to pursue alternative economic arrangements as seem politically expedient. One such example was Chile's decision to enter into a free trade agreement with the United States in June 2003, which effectively blocked the likelihood of its full incorporation into MERCOSUR. Additionally, the agreements signed between MERCOSUR and its associate states are merely bilateral arrangements—nothing ensures the deepening of an economic relationship among the various associate states themselves in a way which might suggest broader regional integration. As it stood before the Puerto Iguazu summit, MERCOSUR's expansion process seemed to be particularly vulnerable to changes in the political climate and was severely clouded by doubts concerning the member states' commitment to expand the economic integration organization beyond its original membership.

The recent entries of Colombia, Ecuador, and Venezuela as the fourth, fifth, and sixth associate states of the common market do little to allay these concerns because those nations also joined MERCOSUR through an ALADI agreement. Nevertheless, recent political conditions in South America favoring regional cooperation have produced the widespread expectation that MERCOSUR nations will lead the way towards total regional integration. Regional unity has become a centerpiece of foreign and domestic agendas for not only the leaders of MERCOSUR—Brazilian President Luis Ignacio Lula da Silva and his Argentine counterpart, President Nestor Kirchner—but also for nearly all the leaders from around the continent. A revived MERCOSUR played the role of a vital bargaining chip in Argentina and Brazil's negotiations with the United States during the Bush Administration's FTAA talks in Cancun and Miami in late 2003, and MERCOSUR has emerged from the Miami summit as a leader of sorts for Latin American nations disillusioned with US policies in the hemisphere ... the genuine expansion of MERCOSUR has become a powerful vision backed across many fronts by popular support, capital resources, and sincere political commitment. Pressures associated with this new reality were clearly behind the CMC's decision to open up MERCOSUR's institutions. . . .

Decision 18/04 marks the beginning of the CMC's efforts to create internal mechanisms capable of admitting states into the group and developing those associate states into full-fledged members of the common market. . . .

In early July 2004, the foreign and economic ministers of the four member states of the Common Market of the Southern Cone ("MERCOSUR") convened in Puerto Iguazu, Argentina, for the twenty-sixth meeting of the economic integration organization's most powerful institutional body, the Council of the Common Market ("CMC"). To a large extent, the exhilarating optimism and flowery rhetoric at the convention seemed characteristically hollow, considering that the common market has yet to achieve its first and most basic goal of establishing a common external tariff and that MERCOSUR's two largest members, Argentina and Brazil, were locked in a bitter trade dispute over the dumping of Brazilian exports. However, in a showing of interest and solidarity that highlights the recent reenergizing and politicization of the integration process in Latin America since the close of the 2003 talks for the Free Trade Area of the Americas ("FTAA"), the summit also drew the attendance of the presidents of MERCOSUR's four member states (Argentina, Brazil, Paraguay, and Uruguay), as well as leaders from MERCOSUR's associate states (Bolivia, Chile, and Peru), the presidents of Mexico and Venezuela, and representatives from other nations in the region and from around the world.

Following its potentially momentous acceptance of Venezuela as the common market's fourth associated state, and with the future expansion of MERCOSUR clearly on its mind, the CMC enacted Decision 18/04 ("Decision 18/04" or "Decision"), which implements a structure whereby associate states can participate in the organizational institutions of MERCOSUR that were formerly accessible only to the four member states. This initiative might dispel criticism that the common market lacks the ability to expand beyond its initial members, and given the incredible enthusiasm for regional interdependence that has swept like-minded, progressive presidents into power across the continent, Decision 18/04 might also reveal that the winds of change might at last be blowing in favor of the full integration of Latin America first envisioned by Simon Bolivar.

Other events also suggest that a MERCOSUR with coherent expansion procedures might be the best mechanism for bringing that revolutionary vision of integration into reality. In mid-October, MERCOSUR and the Andean Community of Nations ("CAN") finalized a free trade agreement which effectively includes Brazil and all of the Spanish-speaking nations in South America except for Chile. Only ten days later, the former Argentine president and current chairman of MERCOSUR's representative council, Eduardo Duhalde, announced the December scheduling of a presidential summit to discuss the political and economic incorporation of MERCOSUR, CAN, and possibly Chile, into a South American Community of Nations ("CSN"). Since those meetings occurred, Ecuador and Colombia have been formally granted status as associate states in MERCOSUR and the bloc has passed other measures that signify that it no longer views itself as a mere four-member customs union.

In this regard, Decision 18/04 shows that the CMC is considering a clear program for advancing associate states' influence within MERCOSUR, and the act is a small but critical step toward the sort of active and participatory role in decision-making that would mark full and legitimate membership in a more politically orientated common market. Nevertheless, Decision 18/04 falls short of representing a wholly new identity for MERCOSUR because it leaves in place the group's original customs union structure. By attempting to balance the member states' economic accomplishments and the region's current political aspirations, Decision 18/04 is perhaps best viewed as a significant, albeit hesitant, first step towards greater regional integration. . . .

The principal goals of Decision 18/04 are to intensify regional integration and to deepen and formalize MERCOSUR's relationships with the nations, or associate states, with which it has signed ALADI agreements.

The CMC seeks to accomplish those goals by "creating conditions for the association of the ALADI states with MERCOSUR and by regulating those states' participation in the meetings of the bodies of MERCOSUR's institutional structure." In Article 1 of Decision 18/04, the CMC confers the formal status of "Estado Asociado" or associate state upon any ALADI nation which has signed a free trade agreement with MERCOSUR. Decision 18/04 then briefly outlines the steps that interested nations should take to apply to the CMC for status as associate states. The key article in Decision 18/04 is Article 4, which grants associate states the right to participate in MERCOSUR's institutions ... the Decision does not guarantee associate states unreserved access to MERCOSUR proceedings. Indeed, Articles 5 and 6 contemplate the limitations to the role that associate states will play in MERCOSUR's internal deliberations. Article 5 states that "the participation of the Associated States in each meeting will be granted by invitation from the appropriate MERCOSUR body or as an answer to a request from the Associated State." Associate states receive unrestricted access only to MERCOSUR's nonbinding consultative group. In order to attend the meetings of more important institutions, such as the CMC, the associate state must first seek approval from the representatives of the four member states. . . .

The limitations imposed on the associate states' access also illustrate that the image of MERCOSUR sketched at Asuncion in 1991 has not yet been rejected in favor of a new common market that would include most other South American nations. Instead, Decision 18/04 shows that the current vision of regional integration will have to coexist alongside the four-nation common market created by earlier treaties. Rather than immediately opening up MERCOSUR's full membership to other nations, the member states have chosen to create a two-tiered system through which other nations seeking admission will first gain status as associate states and then harmonize slowly with the core group at the pace set by an economic complementation agreement. Full integration of an associate state could be achieved on such a bilateral basis, with the individual state eventually coming into line with MERCOSUR's requirements and then being granted status as a full member state. Article 11, however, suggests that the CMC's goal for the next year is to change MERCOSUR's relationship from that of a bilateral partnership with each associate state in favor of a broader, self-sustained relationship with all of its associates. In this regard, the probable approach will be to create a second high-profile organization like the CMC that consists of representatives from all states affiliated with MERCOSUR. Such an organization could prove effective at devising common integration measures, and it would certainly be an improvement over the bilateral commissions that currently monitor the progress of an associate state in terms of its ALADI accord. A better alternative would be for MERCOSUR to follow the European model by creating a supranational entity charged with directing the policies of integration. Given member states' reluctance to cede sovereignty to the group, this option may not seem viable at the moment. Nevertheless, the recent creation of MERCOSUR's second supranational entity, the Permanent Review Tribunal, implies that nations in the region are finally committed to making the tough compromises associated with creating real economic and political union. . . .

NOTES AND QUESTIONS

(1) All Latin American member States involved in the Mercosur, share a fundamentally civil law professional legal background. All of them, with the exception of Brazil where the official language is Portuguese, also share Castillian Spanish as the official language. No such a communality of legal and linguistic background exists in Europe. Do you think such structural similarities of the legal system are relevant in a complex political effort such as integration? In Latin America a large variety of local legal systems and languages are still in place. Such a variety, at least as far as customary law is concerned, is much less in Europe. To what extent do you consider such contextual differences relevant?

(2) Can you see any analogy between the E.U. and the Mercosur experience in integration? What would be the special difficulties in the comparison between E.U. and Mercosur? Would the European institutional experience work as a model? In the affirmative, how? Could the E.U. political experience of post World War II integration be transplanted in Latin America?

(3) In the previous materials we have seen at play a variety of possible actors of legal integration. Which are in your opinion in a better position to produce legal integration? Legislatures? Courts? Legal Scholars? Can you think of advantages or disadvantages in deploying different legal sources in processes of integration?

(4) As the European and Mercosur experience have shown, political integration is quite a difficult task to obtain since sovereignty is very reluctantly ceded. Do you believe that the decline in the strength of state sovereignty, under the forces of economic globalization might allow more legal integration to happen? Do you think economically rather than politically driven integration would be more desirable? What would be the legitimacy of such a world legal order?

(5) While efforts aimed at general integration of legal systems seem to face the formidable resistance of local legal and political structures, more limited, topical efforts have been much more successful. In your opinion are there good reasons to maintain diversity in certain domains of the law while pushing for integration in others? In the affirmative what would be the areas in which diversity is more in need of being respected?

(6) The English language literature on Mercosur is still not abundant. The interested student should consult the following sources:

> Additional Protocol to the Treaty of Asuncion on the Institutional Structure of Mercosur (1994), 34 ILM 1248 (1995) (hereinafter Protocol of Ouro Preto).
>
> Rafael A. Porrata–Doria, Jr., *MERCOSUR: The Common Market of the Twenty–First Century?*, 32 Ga J Intl. & Comp. L. 1, 7–9 (2004).

Mario E. Carranza, *MERCOSUR, The Free Trade Area of the Americas, and the Future of U.S. Hegemony in Latin America*, 27 Fordham Intl. L. J. 1029 (2004).

Jan Kleinheisterkamp, *Legal Certainty in the MERCOSUR: The Uniform Interpretation of Community Law*, 6 NAFTA: Law and Business Review of the Americas 5 (2000).

Alejandro Garro, *Unification and Harmonization of Private Law in Latin America*, 40 Am. J. Comp. Law 584 (1992).

3. FUNCTIONAL INTEGRATION: IS THERE A COMMON CORE OF LEGAL SYSTEMS?

In sections A and b we have looked at different kinds of official top down attempts to reach legal integration. Here, to the contrary we look bottom up at instances where integration might already exist functionally if not formally. Unveiling such functional integration entails both theoretical and practical challenges.

(a) What should we compare?

In order to ascertain the reality of legal integration and uniformity (by a correct process of comparison) one should get rid of a large set of tacit assumptions that we learn in law school. To begin with, that the meaning of law is the same in every legal culture. One must overcome the tacit bias that what we study in law school is "the law" and not just one local limited epiphany of the legal phenomenon.

In fact, there are only a limited number of cultures that have professionalized their law and a large majority of inhabitants of this world live under legal systems that are not professionalized.[1] We should avoid the mistake of considering these systems as "informal", governed by rules that cannot be "recognized" as proper law just because a state organization has not centralized power as it seems to have done in most western settings. We simply cannot exclude the possibility that non professionalized legal systems do (more or less often) reach the same results than professionalized ones. If we fail to take note of fundamentally different legal conceptions, it will be difficult for us to say anything meaningful about legal integration as a global phenomenon. Maintaining that any social organization "lacks" law or that is governed by "informal" law is just an ethnocentric assertion that a comparative lawyer should avoid. Too often lawyers have condescendingly considered "informal" or sometimes even "lacking" legal cultures that are highly formalized, though perhaps not written, just because we have not been able to understand their forms. For example most legal cultures other than the Anglo–American one have traditionally endorsed far less individual-centered perspectives. This is true in continental Europe, where a parent has no power to disinherit his children, given the central legal role of the family, (almost everywhere an ancient doctrine

---

1. Norbert Rouland, Legal Anthropology 155 (Philippe G. Planel trans. 1994).

the *legitima pars bonorum* makes disinhcritancc void). It is certainly true in African legal cultures where the individual does not really exist outside of his group of belonging. The rules of the group in terms of solidarity among the members (which are not necessarily part of the same family like in the case of the Malian *kari* the group of individuals circumcised in the same day) are legally binding as much as for an American is binding the official, professionalized law of torts. Such rules of group responsibility, which make the legal framework of many villages and also urban African economies, are very effectively enforced and applied, and they evolve over time to meet the changing social needs. In most settings, (probably for a vast majority of the individuals living on this earth) such binding legal rules are much more effective than the rules of State law that might formally be considered in force in any given territory. Clearly different conceptions of the individual in society create tremendous difficulties for comparative analysis, but not to the point of claiming "uncomparability" or to assume unbridgeable differences. Many of the sources of law and many of the rituals by which they present themselves might be hidden in inaccessible cultural aspect, so that the frustrated western jurist might pretend that they are "informal" or might deny their being law. Nevertheless, just because a legal culture is very different from ours, that is not a good reason to avoid the effort to understand it and to respectfully try to describe and explain analogies and differences with our own. The task might be very difficult but it is well rewarding both in terms of understanding "the other" and in terms of understanding ourselves.

Because the very meaning of law is highly controversial in a global perspective, and because it is very difficult to grasp the large variety of social, political, philosophical, religious, ritual and economic factors that determine a legal regime, the tradition of comparative law has focused its attention only on the professional aspects of the legal systems. By so doing, it has been able to assume as common a variety of social, political and economic aspects, mostly by comparing western European systems among each other or with the Anglo–American tradition. In such a perspective, comparative observations are thus limited to the structure of lawyer's law, focusing on those aspects of the professional legal toolkits that the different traditions have developed historically. Obviously such an approach, on the one hand makes comparative observation more specific and thus useful for the professional lawyer, but on the other hand it inserts a very strong western-centric and state-centric bias. The traditional approach assumes that the professionalized layer of the national legal systems (how professional judges, attorneys or law professors think and operate) exhausts the legal universe, which is neither true in the West nor, to a stronger extent, in much of the rest.

Nevertheless, many of the tools that have been created by the mainstream comparative legal tradition, limited as they might be, are useful, actually quite unavoidable, and can be upgraded to capture the more nuanced sensitivity of current times. The present discussion and the next chapter are devoted to these traditional tools of comparative inquiry and to the challenges that they have to face today. We will also offer some of the more recent tools that contemporary comparative lawyers are deploying to obtain more realistic visions of the current global legal landscape.

Comparative law has developed its tools in the effort to describe and understand other forms of professional legal cultures. Professional legal cultures (such as the U.S or the western-European) train lawyers as a discrete professional social group, endowed with a form of specialized knowledge that allows them to communicate with other individuals that received the same kind of training. In professional legal cultures the knowledge of lawyers is different from that of the lay person. Lawyers after a few terms of specialized training learn to "think like a lawyer," which means that they observe and interpret the irreproducible reality of each distinct episode of human experience into abstract, reproducible categories such as that of "contract", "tort", "unjust enrichment" etc. Any professional legal culture creates a discrete set of such abstract legal categories that ignore the real life of social interactions (a large number of crucial social and political aspects such as happiness, wealth, power, age etc. simply become irrelevant most of the time: an "owner" is an "owner" both if his estate is limited to a small apartment or if he is a billionaire). Thus, in the mind of professionally trained lawyers such domestic legal categories acquire a structure in their own, becoming objects ontologically different from each other, much like a cat or a television set. Unless a lawyer makes a conscious intellectual effort, he/she believes by training that such legal entities are "natural" and not historically or geographically contingent. Once such contingency and its historical, social, intellectual and economic causes are clear, lawyers may make formidable progress in the understanding of each other's intellectual world (or *mentalité*). The deconstruction of legal ontology allows lawyer's categories to plug into each other often discovering fundamental analogies hidden behind apparently unreconcilable differences. The same achievement is possible (though even more difficult) when comparing professionalized with less professionalized law.

To be sure, formidable economic political and cultural forces are today at work and they might seem to determine some sort of single paradigm within the dominant global legal community (see Chapter 1 *supra* at 322).[2] Nevertheless, local variations, even within the western legal tradition, are still very strong in particular because we are far from the development of a uniform legal language.[3] While the English language might appear today to function as some sort of *lingua franca* (as Latin used to be in a past period of European legal civilization. See *infra* Chapter 4 at 320–323), it is still the case that deep institutional, linguistic and stylistic variations make legal systems appear very different to the point that most of the time a domestic lawyer finds it tremendously difficult to grapple with foreign legal systems. Such differences *in form* make the question of whether difference dominates also the *substance* of the law crucial.

---

2. *See* Horatia Muir Watt, Globalization and Comparative Law in Mathias Reimann & Reinhard Zimmermann, Oxford Handbook of Comparative Law, 579 (2006).

3. *See* Vivian Grosswald Curran, Comparative Law and Language, in Mathias Reimann & Reinhard Zimmermann, Oxford handbook of Comparative Law, 675 (2006).

In nearly all fields of law, even in the absence of organized unification efforts, there appears to exist a *common core* of legal concepts and precepts shared by some or even most of the world's legal systems. To explain this phenomenon in terms of the underlying historical and social causes is a task of considerable complexity; the explanations will differ from subject to subject and region to region.[4] In spite of the difficulty of establishing its etiology, however, the existence and vast extent of this common core of legal systems appears quite obvious if only one thinks for example to the fact that stealing is repressed in all societies no matter the fundamental understanding and extension of property rights.[5]

(b) The Cornell Hypothesis

Beginning in the 1950's of the past century, comparative lawyers deepened their methodological consciousness of the common core phenomenon. In the words of the Late Professor Rudolf B. Schlesinger, the first author of this casebook, reflecting in 1968 on his major project launched at the Cornell Law School more than ten years earlier:

> "Much of the comparative research undertaken by legal scholars in the past was severely limited in at least one of several ways: either the number of legal systems taken into consideration was very small, ordinarily restricted to two; or the topic chosen for comparative exploration was too narrow to permit to discover, within each of the legal systems selected, of the functional and systematic interrelationship among a large number of precepts and concepts. True, there were some previous projects which covered a relatively broad subjects and a considerable number of legal systems; but these projects as a rule were limited to the compilation or juxtaposition of the various solutions found, without proceeding to the further step of comparison. The difference between juxtaposition and true comparison is a crucial one for all those who study legal phenomena observed in more than one legal system . . . the legal scholar if he wishes to engage in comparison rather than in mere juxtaposition, must strive to delineate areas of agreement and disagreement, and to do so in terms of formulated standards, principles, rules, tendencies and factors. Only in this way it is possible to grasp the common core of legal systems considered and

4. *See,* e.g., Rudolf B. Schlesigner, Introduction, in 1 Formation of Contracts—A Study of the Common Core of Legal Systems 1, 41 (Rudolf B. Schlesinger ed., 1968); Sarfatti, *Roman Law and Common Law: Forerunners of a General Unification of Law,* 3 Int'l & Comp.L.Q. 102 (1954).

5. In addition to the material cited *supra* n. 1, *see* M. Gluckman, African Traditional Law in Historical Perspective, 60 Proc. Brit.Acad. 295 (1974). T.W. Bennett, Comparative Law and African Customary Law in Mathias Reimann & Reinhard Zimmermann,

Oxford Handbook of Comparative Law, 641 (2006). Many of the components of a legal system are apt to be of a local or regional nature. *See* E. Wahl, Influences climatiques sur l'évolution du droit en orient et en occident—contribution au régionalisme en droit comparé, 25 Rev.Int.Dr.Comp. 261 (1973). This, however, does not preclude the existence of other components which respond to basic human needs and traits, and thus are bound—at least in their core—to be universal.

clearly to discern the borders beyond which the common core does not extend".[1]

The common core approach, later to become one of the most influential methods in comparative law, was born. The common core seeks to describe commonalities among legal systems hidden below apparent differences. Its hypothesis is that the degree of agreement between legal systems facing the same factual situation is higher than what might appears if one limits the analysis to the black letters of the law. If only the analysis is carried on further in depth, very often legal systems are more similar than it might appear. Of course the hypothesis might be disproved in practice or might even be substituted by the suspicion that behind apparent vague commonalities (such as global commitment to the "rule of law") a lot of actual differences might be hidden. Despite this very realistic possibility the common core remains a highly productive methodology guiding the comparative study of the law.

There is a very important distinction, to be immediately considered between researching the common core of legal systems and engaging in the unification or harmonization projects. This difference can be captured by notions of a bottom up rather than a top down approach. In theory, one can observe the existence or non-existence of a common core among legal systems (no matter whether national or supra-national) only as the result of a painstaking effort to analyze and understand actual analogies and differences between the systems he or she is comparing. After having thoroughly examined what the courts or other decision-makers do (and/or what they say they are doing) in the context of a concrete factual question one can ascertain the existence of a common core. For a very simple example, while looking at enacted law the United States has not ratified the international convention protecting the minors against death penalty, subsequent evolutions culminated in the decision *Roper v Simmons* (discussed and reported *supra* Chapter 1 at 57) may allow us nevertheless to say that *there is a common core* among legal systems of the world banning execution of individuals that were underage when they committed a certain crime no matter how bad and cruel. Of course, it is possible to make such a statement only after a thorough analysis of what all the legal systems in fact do which might require quite a complex factual analysis of systems that might have ratified the Convention banning execution of underage minors but nevertheless doing it in practice (in this sense ironically Justice Scalia made a sophisticated comparative remark in his isolationist dissent in *Roper*). Naturally the vaguer the hypothesis and the more limited the number of systems under consideration the more likely it is to find a common core. (Is there a common core banning insider trading among France, Germany and the U.S.?). Conversely, the more specific the hypoth-

---

1. *See* R.B. Schlesinger, Formation of Contracts. A Study on the Common Core of Legal Systems II Volumes (1968).

esis and the larger the number of systems, the more unlikely it is to find a common core (is there a common core on the amount of compensation paid after a taking of private property in the countries of Asia, Europe and Latin America?). No matter what the practical difficulties and the intellectual limits of common core inquiry, it seems clear that the bottom up approach is something very different from an attempt to reach a common result by a top down act of formal unification or harmonization of the law, such as for example an attempt to ban Female Genital Mutilation after having described it as a human right violation of great severity, or to pass a general moratorium on death penalty as European countries have done at the United Nations.

Today, common core research is carried on systematically in the context of developing a common European legal culture. A large project was launched in Trent, Italy in 1993 and it continues today in Turin at the International University College. It has already produced thousands of pages of empirical data.[2] The methodology is quite simple. Scholars from all of the European jurisdictions are convened to elaborate factual questionnaires. These common factual questionnaires drafted in a way to avoid as much as possible all implicit legal categories and structures, are then circulated and answered by lawyers from many jurisdictions. The answers gathered by questionnaire editors are compared in a way to understand analogies and differences at different semantic levels. When a common core emerges it is pointed out. An example would be interesting.

(c) The Common Core of European Private Law

The Cornell approach has been expanded and applied in the last fifteen years in a major international scholarly project known as The Common Core of European Private Law that involves now about 200 legal scholars. The following excerpt, taken from one of the completed volumes shows some methodological issues.

2. Ten volumes have thus far been published they are: Reinhard Zimmermann and Simon Whittaker, Good Faith in European Contract Law, "The Common Core of European Private Law", Cambridge University Press, James Gordley, The Enforceability of Promises in European Contract Law, "The Common Core of European Private Law", Cambridge University Press, Mauro Bussani and Vernon V. Palmer, Pure Economic Loss in Europe, "The Common Core of European Private Law", Cambridge University Press, Franz Werro and Vernon V. Palmer, The Boundaries of Strict Liability in European Tort Law, "The Common Core of European Private Law", Stämpfli–Carolina Academic Press, Eva–Maria Kieninger, Security Rights in Movable. Property in European Private Law, "The Common Core of European Private Law", Cambridge University Press, Ruth Sefton–Green, Mistake, Fraud and Duties to Inform in European Contract Law, "The Common Core of European Private Law", Cambridge University Press, Michele Graziadei, Ugo Mattei, Lionel Smith, Commercial Trusts in European Private Law, "The Common Core of European Private Law", Cambridge University Press, Barbara Pozzo, Property and Environment, Stämpfli–Carolina Academic Press, Thomas Möllers and Andreas Heinemann, The Enforcement of Competition Law in Europe "The Common Core of European Private Law", Cambridge University Press, Monika Hinteregger, Environmental Liability and Ecological Damage in European Law, "The Common Core of European Private Law", Cambridge University Press, 2008.

M. Bussani & V.V. Palmer, *Pure Economic Losses in Europe*

in M. Bussani U. Mattei (Gen Eds.), *The Common Core of European Private Law Project*, Cambridge University Press 2004.

The general purpose of this study is to inquire to what extent, if any, there exists a common core of principles and rules concerning compensation for pure economic loss within European tort law.

. . . Such a common core seems to us worth revealing in order to obtain at least the main outlines of a reliable geographical map of that specific field in the law of Europe.

For the transnational lawyer indeed, the present European situation is as that of a traveler compelled to use a number of different local maps. Each one could contain misleading information. We wish to eliminate this misleading information. We do not wish to force an actually diverse legal reality into one single map simply for the sake of uniformity.

Our specific enterprise, like the general project from which it stems, seeks to find the common features of the "pure economic loss" law in European national systems, but the goal is not to impose new rules and categories. . . .

The preliminary problem we had to resolve was how to obtain comparable answers to the questions we wished to pose about different legal systems. The answers had to refer to identical questions interpreted as identically as possible by all the respondents. Besides, the answers had to be self-sufficient in two ways. First, they had to be complete answers: additional explanations should not be required. The level of specificity that was to be expected, therefore, was to be on a par with the most detailed rules. Second, they had to be authoritative answers which could be accepted at "face value." The editors would therefore refrain from superimposing their own views upon the scenario depicted by the national contributors.

To obtain consistency, after lengthy discussions within the working group, each hypothetical case was formulated with the view of taking account of any relevant circumstance occurring in any of the legal systems under consideration, so that these circumstances would be considered in— and therefore become comparable with—the analysis of every other system.

In this way another important objective was achieved. Often, the circumstances that operate explicitly and officially in one system are officially ignored and considered to be irrelevant in another system and yet, in that other system, they operate secretly, slipping silently in between the formulation of the rule and its application by the courts. Thus, one of the special features of our work is that it has made jurists think explicitly about the circumstances that matter, by forcing them to answer identically formulated questions, by asking them about the results that would be reached in particular cases, not about a doctrinal system. . . .

[We reproduce here one of the factual hypotheses discussed. For reasons of space we limit the answer to two legal systems. Typically volumes in the Common Core of European Private Law discuss around fifteen such factual questions for about 15 legal systems]

Auditor's Liability

Donna audits the accounts of Caterpillar, Inc. inaccurately. Paul relies on these published accounts to launch a take-over bid. This is successful but Paul then discovers that the accounts overestimated the value of the company and that the price Paul paid per share was twice its actual value.

A) **FRANCE** (Art. 1382: *Any act whatever of man which causes damage to another obliges him by whose fault it occurred to make reparation*. Art. 1383: *Each one is liable for the damage which he causes not only by his own act but also by his negligence or imprudence*) [for more applications of these articles see *infra* Chapter V, pp. 456ff].

I.   Upon showing fault and that the inaccurate audit was the cause of his loss, Paul may recover against Donna if she is the statutory auditor of the company, but he may be denied recovery if she is a specially hired contract auditor.

II.   Donna's liability has a different basis and scope, depending on her status. If she is the statutorily-required auditor of Caterpillar (commissaire-aux-comptes) she has wider civil and penal responsibility, including toward third persons like Paul. If she is instead a specially-hired auditor under contract for a particular purpose, her responsibility is essentially governed by her contract and her liability toward third persons in delict is restricted. Case 17 does not specify Donna's status and therefore both possibilities will be dealt with.

A.   Donna is the statutorily-required auditor of Caterpillar.

The Commissaire-aux comptes's essential mission is to certify that the annual accounts of a French company present "a faithful picture" of the company's operations. The Commissaire-aux-comptes's obligation is not one of result, but one of means, that is, it is an obligation to be diligent and prudent.[1] The Commissaire-aux-comptes's civil liability rests upon the fault principle for this is the basis articulated in the special law of July 24, 1966. Article 234 of that law declares:

> "The Commissioner of accounts (commissaire-aux-comptes) is responsible both toward the company as well as toward third persons for the harmful consequences of the fault or negligence which they have committed in the exercise of their functions."[2]

The Commissaire-aux-comptes is seen as fulfilling a public institutional role to present accurate accounts. The Commissaire-aux-comptes's duties are not only to keep the company and its shareholders properly informed, but to keep company workers, creditors and third persons properly in-

1. Petites Affiches, p. 4.   **2.** Authors' translation.

formed as well. If the Commissaire-aux-comptes deliberately misstates financial information, he may incur penal responsibility by way of a fine or prison term.[3]

Coming back to civil liability toward Paul, the latter would have to establish fault, causation and his damage. In terms of fault, her liability may first depend upon whether the company accounts were certified "with reserve" or "without reserve" or perhaps with "observations" that may qualify or explain the financial information's meaning or warn the reader to be on guard as to its reliability. Assuming, however, that Donna's certification was "without reserve" or that no qualifications or reserves were issued, her fault may be established by showing serious inaccuracies which a competent auditor should have discovered.[4] Given the enormity of the valuation error in Caterpillar's case, it may well be that serious professional mistakes were made. Nevertheless the auditor is not a guarantor of the authenticity of the information he compiles. It has been held by the Tribunal de commerce de Paris that where incomplete and disordered documents were submitted, which included a fraudulent invoice that had no suspicious appearance, fault was not shown because such matters could escape a normally vigilant auditor's attention.[5] On the other hand the Commissaire-aux comptes has been found liable in circumstances where (s)he failed to detect inaccuracies created by the particular billing system used by the company.[6] It should be noted that in France the tribunal will frequently appoint an expert to assist it in the evaluation of the Commissaire-aux comptes's fault.

Even if Donna's fault is established, Paul's claim requires proof that her fault caused his damage. On more than one occasion, however, courts have shown reluctance to allow recovery in favor of third parties, such as Paul, even in the event of fault on the part of the Commissaire aux comptes, by refusing the claim on the ground of causation.[7] The reasons for this restrictive tendency are partly inherent in the nature of the auditor's role. The fault of the Commissaire is usually one of omission rather than positive action, and his fault is never the only cause of the damage suffered by the company or the third person. The "cause" of the loss is usually multiple[8] and lies, at the outset, in the fault or fraud of the administrators, and may even be attributed to plaintiff's subsequent lack of vigilance. The commentators unanimously recognize that proof of causation in this area is

3. *Ibid*. Art. 457.
4. Com. 9 Février 1988, D. 1988. IF. 53; Petites Affiches, 7 Mars 1988, p. 13, Pierre Moretti.
5. Trib. Paris, 12 Juillet 1984, Bull. C.N.C.C., 1985—478 Juris–Data no. 001646.
6. Lyon, 2 Juin 1994, *Ibid*. Petites Affiches.
7. *See* Lara Khoury, "The Liability of Auditors Beyond Their Clients: A Compara-

tive Study," 46 McGill L.J. 413 (2001). Gratitude is expressed to the author for sharing her research prior to publication.

8. The multiplicity of causal conditions is stressed by T. Honoré with respect to all "interpersonal transactions." "Necessary and Sufficient Conditions in Tort Law," in DG Owen (ed.), Philosophical Foundations of Tort Law (Clarendon Press 1995) at pp. 382–383.

somewhat difficult to meet.[9] Thus third-party claims have failed where the evidence showed that the irregularities would not have been discovered even if the Commissaire had exercised reasonable diligence;[10] when the errors did not modify substantially the results of the statements; and when the court considered that the plaintiff would have acted the same way had he known of the errors.

In most cases of refusal, however, the plaintiff is defeated because the evidence shows that, despite the errors of the report, he knew or should have known about the real situation from other sources of information at his disposal. Often when the cession or acquisition of a company takes place, there may be several audits and financial reports other than that of the Commissaire-aux-comptes, and these reports may well reveal the errors and discrepancies of the Commissaire's report. The Tribunal d'Amiens found an absence of causal connection in circumstances where it believed that these reports should have dissuaded an acquirer from taking control.[11]

Since Case 17 furnishes only the sketchiest facts about causation, and in those circumstances it would be hazardous to predict the disposition that a French court might make. While the claim is reparable in principle, awards are in fact rarely made.

Apparently the French judge's control over the causation requirement is one of the means by which the Commissaire's liability toward third person is kept within reasonable bounds.

B. Donna is a contract auditor (auditeur, prestataire de service).

If Donna has been hired by Caterpillar for a particular accounting purpose, her liability toward investors like Paul is more restrained. Her responsibility toward the company basically flows from her contract, while her liability toward third persons must be resolved in terms of general tort law under Civil Code Arts. 1382–83. So long as s(he) accomplishes the contractual mission, the contract auditor is not viewed as an adviser to the shareholders or to outside acquirers and is not obliged to advise them of a problem in the account which may cause them harm.[12]

III. Though the French delictual system takes no particular note of the type of damage which pure economic loss represents, cases such as this one furnish evidence of a subconscious concern with the question of excessive, indeterminate liability toward third persons. Some maintain that the French judges are perfectly aware of these dangers.[13] Their concern,

9. E. du Pontavice, Le commissaire aux comptes. Manuel pratique, t.1 (Ormesson-sur-Marne 1981) A. 15, 209; P. Merle, annotation to Lyon 27 Jan. 1994, Bull CNCC. 1994.271; Y. Guyon & G. Coquereau, Le commissariat aux comptes: aspects juridiques et techniques (Paris: Litec 1971), 399; D. Vidal, annotation to Cass.com, 27 Oct. 1992, Rev. Soc. 1993.86.

10. Aix-en-Provence, 7 Juin 1985, Bull CNCC. 1985.487.

11. Amiens. 20 Juin 1988, Bull. C.N.C.C., n . 71, p. 317, note E. du Pontavice.

12. Com. 15 Juin 1993, Bull. Joly 1993, p. 1130, note Michel Jeantin.

13. B. Markesinis, "La politique juris-prudentielle et la réparation du prejudice

however, is not expressed, in the manner of the English judges, by a careful tailoring of the "duty of care" situation so that liability is contained. In France it is believed that the judges turn to a restrictive application of causal requirements as the limiting device.[14] It is difficult, however, to observe this policy directly, since it is never avowed. Causal determinations by the lower courts lie within the theoretical control and supervision of the Court of Cassation, but the Court has not laid down clear rules on the issue.[15] Thus considerable confusion results from this refusal to take position. Because the notion of causation is a flexible tool that may be used subjectively, case outcomes are not as predictable as in systems that confront such issues openly and employ more precise tools.

B) AUSTRIA (Austrian General Civil Code (ABGB) Art. 1295: *(1) A person is entitled to demand indemnification for the damage from a person causing an injury by his fault; the damage may have been caused either by the violation of a contractual duty or without regard to a contract. (2) A person who intentionally injures another in a manner in violation of public morals, is liable therefor; however, if the injury was caused in the exercise of legal rights, the person causing it shall be liable therefor only when the exercise of this right obviously has the purpose to cause damage to the other.)*

I. Paul has neither a claim in tort against Donna nor a claim based on a contract with protective effects to a third party.

II. 1. Tort Claims.

In recent decisions the OGH has followed the suggestions made by an influential learned scholar[16] and imposed liability on an expert *vis-à-vis* a third party according to art. 1300 ABGB, if such expert has violated objective-legal duties in favour of a third party.[17] The Court saw a "parallel situation" to that of a contract with protective effects to a third party.

However, the facts are different here: Paul relies on "published accounts". Whether Donna had known or had to know that her audit was also addressed to certain third parties, who should be able to rely on its accuracy, does not follow from the hypothetical facts. Therefore, a claim has to be denied.

It has to be mentioned, that the provision of art. 1330 (2) ABGB does not apply in this case, either. Art. 1330 (2) is aimed at the protection of the business reputations (*"wirtschaftlicher Ruf"*) of persons and enterprises

économique en Angleterre: Une approche comparative," 1983 RIDC 31, 44.

14. *See* Lara Khoury, above fn. 7.

15. E.g. it is not clear whether France follows the theory of "equivalence of conditions" or the theory of "adequate causation," *see* G. Viney et P. Jourdain, Traité de droit civil: Les conditions de la responsabilité, No. 350 (LGDJ 2e ed. 1998) ("la Haute jurisdic-

tion a soigneusement évité de poser des règles générales ou même susceptibles de généralization.")

16. *See* Welser, Die Haftung für Rat, Auskunft und Gutachten (1983) 87.

17. Cf. OGH SZ 57/122; SV 1991/2, 22; JBl 1993, 518; see however, OGH ÖBA 1989, 89.

against infringements caused by untrue rumours. In the present case third parties are not within the scope of protection.

2.   Contract with protective effects to third parties.

The same considerations as those on the "infringement of objective-legal duties of care in favour of a third party" ("*Verletzung objektiv-rechtlicher Sorgfaltspflichten zugunsten Dritter*") directed the Court in earlier decisions. These were based on the theory of contractual protective effects in favour of third parties.[18] Courts and scholars requested that it had to be clear to the expert that the person who ordered an expert opinion was also acting in the interest of certain third parties.[19] However, this is not the case here. Therefore the special requirements for recovery of pure economic loss are apparently not fulfilled.

III.   The OGH assumes that an expert opinion is, as a rule, established only in the interest of the person ordering it and that outsiders rely on these accountants at their own peril.

Only if it is beyond doubt that certain third persons, *e.g.* potential buyers of an enterprise, were entitled to rely on the opinion, would protection against economic damage be expanded to such "certain third parties", who would not have to be explicitly named. Thus, measurements (static calculations) are always made in the interest of the constructor and builder, whether or not their names are known to the engineer performing the measurement.[20]

NOTES AND QUESTIONS

(1) The authors use a geographic metaphor to explain the common core project. Do you like it? Is there any other metaphor you think might work?

(2) Is there or is there not a common core between French and Austrian Law in the solution of the hypothetical? Please try to spell it out.

The following is an evaluation of some of the results of the common core project which seems particularly useful in perceiving the kind of knowledge that common core research might offer to comparativists.

Mathias Reimann, Of Products and Process: The First Six Trento Volumes and Their Making

in U. Mattei & M. Bussani (Eds.) Opening Up European Law: *The Common Core Project Towards Eastern and South Eastern Europe*, Stämpfli Publishers Ltd. Carolina Academic Press 2006, pp. 83–100.

At first glance, it seems that the books [of the Common Core project] simply provide half a dozen studies of fairly specific private law topics. If

---

18.   *See* OGH SZ 43/236; RdW 1985, 306.

19.   *See* Wilhelm, Unrichtige Guta-chten—Haftung für Dritte, ecolex 1991, 87.

20.   *See* OGH NZ 1992, 110.

that were all, it would hardly justify the efforts undertaken in the past decade. Fortunately, these works have accomplished much more than that: they have generated highly significant information about fundamental characteristics of European private law, albeit in select areas. If one looks at the volumes as a body of work, they bring home three points. First, analyzed in concrete contexts, European private law displays significant commonalities as well as far-reaching and often fundamental differences. Second, this is true both on the level of actual results and on the level of black letter rules, doctrinal concepts, background principles, and underlying values. Third, these commonalities and differences have little to do with the traditional dichotomy between the civil and the common law....

It may well be true that a purely descriptive view is a dream (or a nightmare, as the case may be); that all activity in the field of European private law is necessarily legislative in a sense;[1] and that some bias in favor of uniformity is inevitable when searching for a *"common core."*[2] ....

Zimmermann's & Whittaker's impressive study of *Good Faith in European Contract Law* already attest to the complexity of the situation. As the premier advocate of a renewed *ius commune* and a member of the Lando–Group, one might consider Reinhard Zimmermann a major suspect for bias in favor of uniformity. Yet, if such bias exists at all, it is not only disavowed by the authors,[3] it also does not preclude them from finding both "[h]armony and dissonance."[4] They conclude that there is a "considerable degree of harmony as to the results reached on the particular facts of many of the cases"[5]—although one may question whether rough identity of outcomes in two thirds of all cases deserves that characterization. Be that as it may, the editors also find that "the notion of good faith (or its equivalents in the various languages used by the legal systems under consideration) actually means different things both within a particular system and between the legal systems."[6] In some instances, the book actually points to "striking contrast."[7]

1. *See* Martin Shapiro, The Common Core: Some Outside Comments, in Mauro Bussani and Ugo Mattei, Making European Law. Essays on the The "Common Core" Project, 123, at 124–125 (2000).

2. *See* George Fletcher, Comparative Law as Subversive Discipline, 46 Am. J.Comp.L. 683, 694; R. Michaels, The Functional Method of Comparative Law, in M. Reimann & R. Zimmerman, The Oxford Handbook of Comparative Law 339, 374 (2006) (" 'common' goes beyond similar" "... something that predates—historically or philosophically—each of these individual legal orders" ... "Core" "signifies that these commonalities are central.... Also, if the commonalities are to form a core, they must somehow cling together, while their periphery of differences could well constitute a clattered multiplicity of scattered single events.")

3. The authors set out "to ascertain the amount of common ground already existing between the national legal systems and to identify discrepancies on the level of specific result, general approach and doctrinal nuance." Zimmermann and Whittaker, *supra* p. 100, note 2 at 12; *see also id.* 62 ("it should be emphasized that while this project forms part of a wider umbrella project entitled 'Common Core of European Private Law', this should not be interpreted as reflecting a particular position on the appropriateness of harmonization or codification of private law in Europe, nor a particular expectation as to the results which were anticipated as the conclusion of the project").

4. *Id.* 653.

5. *Id.* 653.

6. *Id.* 690.

James Gordley is perhaps equally suspect of pro-uniformity bias.[8] Yet, investigating *The Enforceability of Promises in European Contract Law*, he also observes that many cases come out differently in different countries. His wonderfully lucid and subtle analysis shows that may be true even between closely related legal systems, such as France and Belgium, Germany and Austria, and England and Ireland.[9]

Mauro Bussani and Vernon Palmer lay the groundwork for their rich and nuanced analysis of *Pure Economic Loss in Europe* by distinguishing three basic (and different) torts regimes (liberal, pragmatic, and conservative)[10] and find the European picture decidedly mixed in terms of actual outcomes. There is a "limited common core"[11] in that some types of pure economic loss are protected virtually everywhere. Yet, "Europe is also split over the outcomes that should occur in a number of loss situations."[12]

Franz Werro's and Vernon Palmer's study of *The Boundaries of Strict Liability* pursues the question "to what extent the role and understanding of strict liability in European tort systems is governed by the same or similar principles" but find "no hard and fast answer."[13] The editors identify a convergence with regard to several underlying policies and concepts.[14] Yet, practice is often a different matter. As soon as one examines how these concepts are implemented in practice, one notes that, even within a given legal system, there is a much greater variety of solutions than is suggested by the traditional dichotomy between fault and strict liability.[15]

Ruth Sefton–Green's volume on *Mistake, Fraud, and the Duty to Inform in European Contract Law* concludes that the study reveals "significant differences about how contract law works in thirteen European legal systems and, despite the fact that the solutions proposed are often similar, demonstrates what divergent values underlie the legal rules".[16] For example, "whereas some jurisdictions recognize increasing duties to inform in numerous contracts ... other jurisdictions continue to refuse such duties as a general rule or fail to recognize the need to protect one of the parties where there is an imbalance in bargaining power or information."[17]

Finally, Eva Maria Kieninger's hefty tome on *Security Rights in Moveable Property in European Private Law*, perhaps the most practically relevant of all these studies, clearly detects more difference than uniformity. She speaks of "the divergencies with respect to both principle and to the

7. *Id.* 696.

8. *See*, e.g., James Gordley, Common Law und Civil Law: eine überholte Unterscheidung, 93 Zeitschrift für europäisches Privatrecht 498.

9. Gordley, *supra* p. 100, note 2 at 337–391.

10. Bussani and Palmer, *supra* p. 100, note 2 at 120–159.

11. *Id.* 536.

12. *Id.*

13. Palmer and Werro, *supra* p. 100, note 2 at 455.

14. *Id.* 457–458.

15. *Id.* 455.

16. Sefton-Green, *supra* at p. 100, note 2 back cover.

17. *Id.*

practical outcome of cases"[18] and of the "present heterogeneity".[19] She shows how "the jurisdictions favor different legal models"[20] which lead to several "fundamental differences."[21] Her impressive study concludes that there are really only two areas of uniformity (retention of title and leases) and that as to all the rest, there is no common core on which European legislators or codifiers could hope to build.[22]

NOTES AND QUESTIONS

(1) In the light of the sophisticated nuances emerging from the comparison of laws of systems belonging to the same regional organization (the EU), do you consider more or less reliable the comparative data produced in the Lex Mundi project (190 states from all the latitudes and longitudes) and used by the World Bank in the World Development Report discussed in Chapter 1 *supra* at 15?

(2) Some critics consider "common core methodology" as common law-biased due to the fact that "cases" occupy the center of the stage. Do you agree with the critique? How would you address it? Please hold on the answer until you have familiarized yourself with materials in Chapter 6 *infra*

(d) The Common Core in Legal Practice

Shared principles and rules often furnish the only body of law available for the resolution of disputes which cut across national boundaries. For this reason, treaties and other instruments of public international law, as well as private contracts (especially arbitration agreements) among parties in different countries, more and more frequently provide for the application of principles and rules common to legal systems of more than one nation. What follows is an illustration of some technique of utilizing the common core.

Statute of the International Court of Justice*

Article 38.—1. The Court, whose function is to decide in accordance with international law such disputes as are submitted to it, shall apply:

    a. international conventions, whether general or particular, establishing rules expressly recognized by the contesting states;

    b. international custom, as evidence of a general practice accepted as law;

    c. the general principles of law recognized by civilized nations;

    d. subject to the provisions of Article 59,** judicial decisions and the teachings of the most highly qualified publicists of the various nations, as subsidiary means for the determination of rules of law.

---

18. Kieninger, *supra* p. 100, note 2 at 6.
19. *Id.* 9.
20. *Id.* 14.
21. *Id.* 15.
22. *Id.* 664, 672.

* Annexed to the Charter of the United Nations, San Francisco, June 26, 1945; entered into force October 24, 1945.

** Article 59 provides: "The decision of the Court has no binding force except be-

2.   This provision shall not prejudice the power of the Court to decide a case ex aequo et bono, if the parties agree thereto. (emphasis added)

NOTES AND QUESTIONS

(1) "The Court" to which Art. 38 refers is the International Court of Justice which in 1945 succeeded the former Permanent Court of International Justice. The significance of Art. 38 is not limited, however, to the relatively infrequent cases submitted to that Court. Art. 38 defines the sources of international law. These sources must be consulted whenever a dispute involving a question of international law is adjudicated by any international or municipal tribunal. Resort must be had to the same sources in the many instances in which the settlement of such a dispute is sought by negotiation and conciliation rather than by formal adjudication.

The phrase "general principles of law recognized by civilized nations" refers to principles which find expression in the municipal laws of various nations. These principles, therefore, can be ascertained only by the comparative method.[1]

Example: During the Second World War, the Government of Uruguay requisitioned and used two Italian ships. After the war the owners of one of those ships, the *Fausto*, submitted a claim to the Uruguayan courts asking for just compensation. The Government of Uruguay, as defendant, relied on a provision in the Italian Peace Treaty of 1947, expressly waiving claims of this nature "against any of the United Nations which broke off diplomatic relations with Italy, and which took action in cooperation with the Allied and Associated Powers." Uruguay had broken off diplomatic relations with Italy during the war, and the seizure of the *Fausto* had been a measure taken in cooperation with the Allied and Associated Powers. The Government of Uruguay, however, had not declared war on Italy. Therefore, Uruguay was not a party to the Peace Treaty. The Italian claimants argued that for this reason Uruguay could not rely on the waiver stipulated in the Treaty. The Government of Uruguay, on the other hand, contended that it was a third-party-beneficiary of the waiver stipulation, and that the right of a third-party-beneficiary to enforce a stipulation made in its favor is established by "general principles of law" within the meaning of Art. 38. In support of this contention, counsel for the defendant Government proved that many nations, both in the civil-law and the common-law orbit, *in their law of contracts*, recognize the right of a third-party-beneficiary to bring a direct action against the promisor.[2]

tween the parties and in respect of that particular case."

1. *See* Rudolf B. Schlesinger, Introduction to 1 Formation of Contracts—A Study of the Common Core of Legal Systems 1, 7–16 (Rudolf B. Schlesinger ed., 1968). For further references, *see id.* 62–63, and the interesting article by H.–V. von Hülsen, Sinn und Methode der Rechtsvergleichung, insbesondere bei der Ermittlung übernationalen Zivilrechts, 22 J.Z. 629 (1967). *See also* M. Bothe & G. Ress,

The Comparative Method and Public International Law, in International Law in Comparative Perspective 49 (W. E. Butler ed., 1980).

2. *See* E. Jiménez de Aréchaga, Treaty Stipulations in Favor of Third States, 50 Am. J.Int'l L. 338, 346–48, 351–57 (1956), referring to the pertinent code provisions of a number of civil-law countries and also to common-law (especially American) authorities. *See also* Millner, Ius Quaesitum Tertio: Comparison and Synthesis, 16 Int'l & Comp.

The claimants countered by pointing to Art. 1119 of the French Civil Code which provides that "As a general rule,[3] a party to a contract cannot . . . , stipulate in his own name, except for himself." Claimants' counsel argued that the principle of stipulations for the benefit of a third party, although accepted in many countries, cannot be said to be "recognized by civilized nations," since it is rejected by a codification as important and as influential as the Code Napoleon. Counsel for the Government of Uruguay rebutted this argument by demonstrating, on the basis of thorough comparative research, that the enforceability of the rights of a third-party-beneficiary is judicially recognized even in those countries, such as France, in which old code provisions on their face seem to indicate a different result.[4] It follows that today, whatever may have been the situation in Napoleon's time, there is a "general principle" to the effect that the third-party-beneficiary of a consensual stipulation has the right to bring an action for its enforcement.[5] Uruguay, therefore, although not a signatory of the Peace Treaty, may avail itself of Italy's waiver.[6]

The resolution of international disputes, and the formulation of rules of international law, thus may depend on whether court and counsel can find a sufficient core of agreement, concerning the point at issue, among the legal systems of "civilized nations." As is shown by the efforts of counsel in the *Fausto* case, the requisite core of agreement can be proved or disproved only by the comparative method.[7]

L.Q. 446 (1967); and the section on Contracts and Third–Party Rights in German and English Law, in The Gradual Convergence: Foreign Ideas, Foreign Influence, and English Law on the Eve of the 21st Century 65–131 (Basil Markesinis ed., 1994).

3. This general rule is subject to somewhat vaguely formulated exceptions. French Civil Code, art. 1121.

4. French case law on the subject has developed since the middle of the last century, especially in connection with life insurance policies. It permits the third-party-beneficiary, if he is sufficiently identified, to recover from the promisor. Theoretically, it is required that the beneficiary "accept" the benefit provided in the contract between the *promettant* and the *stipulant*; but such acceptance can be tacit, and it is implied in any attempt on the part of the beneficiary to enforce the contract. *See* Jiménez de Aréchaga, *supra* n. 2; 2 Planiol–Ripert, Traité élémentaire de droit civil, English Translation by the Louisiana State Law Institute, §§ 1234, 1251 (1959); Barry Nicholas, The French Law of Contract 181–93 (2d ed. 1992).

5. *See* Millner, *supra* n. 2, where the reader will find, also, a discussion of the somewhat unique position of English law. For further discussion of the problem from the standpoint of English law, *see* A. G. Guest, Anson's Law of Contract 363–81 (26th ed. 1984); P. S. Atiyah, An Introduction to the Law of Contract 355–85 (5th ed. 1995).

6. The claimants in the Fausto case had instituted their action in a court not having admiralty jurisdiction. Holding that the claims were within the exclusive admiralty jurisdiction which the Uruguayan constitution vests in another court, the court of first instance dismissed the case. *See* 1963 Revista de la Facultad de Derecho y Ciencias Sociales de Montevideo (No. 2, April–June) 395 ff. There was no appeal, and apparently no new action was brought in the proper court. The statement in the text thus reflects the authors' opinion rather than a judicial decision, since the merits of the dispute were never reached by the Uruguayan courts.

7. Note that in the Fausto case the defendant Government sought to prove, and the claimants sought to disprove, such a core of agreement. Quaere whether the claimants' lawyers supported their position in the best possible way. They pointed to France as the odd-man-out; but that argument was untenable. *See supra* n. 4. A better argument would have been to point to English law as the dissenting voice. *See supra* n. 5. In the end, however, even this better argument would not have helped the claimants, because art.

(2) Art. 38(1)(c) of the Statute of the International Court of Justice is by no means the only example of a provision pointing to the common core of legal systems as the source of applicable principles and rules.

Anyone drafting a legal instrument of a transnational nature, whether the prospective signatories be private or governmental parties, must provide some machinery for the settlement of possible disputes. In this context, the drafter must face the further question of what body of substantive law will be applied by those called upon to determine such a dispute. Very frequently, it turns out that the only body of law that is acceptable to the parties is the core of norms common to the domestic legal systems of the parties, or to an even larger group of legal systems. Thus the drafter will have to resort to a choice-of-law clause which expressly or by implication refers to that common core.[8]

The disputes which in this way are to be resolved by reference to a multinational common core of principles and rules can be of many kinds. They may be intergovernmental disputes arising under treaties or executive agreements; they may involve the operational or housekeeping transactions of an international organization; they may relate to concession agreements, development contracts, or other transactions between a private party in a highly industrialized country and the government of a developing nation; or they may, and frequently do, result from everyday transactions in international trade. Treaties, contracts, and other legal instruments often provide, in varying language, that such disputes be resolved by reference to legal principles and rules shared by more than one legal system.[9]

38(1)(c) does not require complete unanimity among the world's legal systems concerning the point at issue. *See* R. B. Schlesinger & P. Bonassies, Le fonds commun des systèmes juridiques, 15 Rev.Int.Dr.Comp. 501, 514–16 (1963). A strong majority suffices, and there can be little doubt that the "general principle" invoked by the Government in the Fausto case is supported today by a strong, and indeed overwhelming, majority of the leading legal systems. *See* Millner, *supra* note 2; K. Zweigert & H. Kötz, An Introduction to Comparative Law 488–502 (Tony Weir trans., 2d rev. ed. 1992).

8. For an example of such a choice-of-law clause, *see* art. 46 of the 1954 Agreement between the Iranian Oil Consortium and the Government of Iran, quoted in Noto v. Cia Secula di Armanento, 310 F.Supp. 639, 646 n. 17 (S.D.N.Y.1970). *See* also Giuditta Cordero Moss (2008) "International Arbitration and the Quest for the Applicable Law," Global Jurist: Vol. 8: Iss. 3 (Advances), Article 2.

Available at: http://www.bepress.com/gj/vol8/iss3/art2.

In international commercial arbitration, if the agreement fails to stipulate the applicable law, the arbitrators have leeway to to choose what they regard as the most appropriate rule. It has been suggested (although the suggestion is controversial) that, in such cases, arbitrators are not necessarily bound to apply national law, but may and in fact do base their awards on what they determine to be the rules of the lex mercatoria, a modern version of the old law merchant, which exists apart from systems of national law. In devising such rules, however, they naturally "turn to preexisting rules and institutions for guidance." Friedrich K. Juenger, The Lex Mercatoria and the Conflict of Laws, in Lex Mercatoria and Arbitration: A Discussion of the New Law Merchant 213, 215 (Thomas E. Carbonneau ed., 1998). *See* also F. K. Juenger, American Conflicts Scholarship and the New Law Merchant, 28 Vand.J.Transnat'l L. 487 (1995). In this respect, the notion of a lex mercatoria would seem to be a congener of the "common core."

9. The subject is treated more extensively in Schlesinger, *supra* note 1, at 7–16.

(e) The Common Core in U.S. Litigation

Thus the common core approach is not only a sophisticated and detailed method of scholarly comparison. There are practical implications too. If a rule is recognized as part of a "common core of principles recognized by the civilized nations" it reaches a special status as a "source of international law" which in turn, because of the so called "incorporation theory" of international law, might become part of U.S. Law.

The following excerpt reproduces part of an expert declaration rendered by one co-author of this book in the process of certification of an international class for the purpose of Holocaust related litigation in the United States:

> "I have been asked to express my opinion on the existence of a common issue of international law, prevailing on each class member individual issues for the purpose of class certification in the settlement with Swiss Banks defendants. In my opinion, a variety of such common prevailing fundamental issues characterize this litigation.

The fundamental legal structure of the Nazi Regime makes any cooperation with it a violation of International Law.

Since Hitler seizure of power at the end of January 1933, the Nazi party has rapidly transformed the German Constitutional order into a criminal organization in violation of the most fundamental and minimal requirements of international law.

The most basic assumptions of a civil society ordered according to the rule of law have been formally abolished by the German Law of 23 of march of 1933 (Ermachigungsgesets) which has enacted the so called *Furerprinzip* (principle of the Chief) according to which the unrestrained will of Hitler was recognized as the supreme law of the land. Only a few days later (march 29, 1933) the so called *Lex Van der Lubbe* has established another fundamental principle of Nazi law: retroactivity of the criminal punishment (including capital punishment). In the following few weeks 27 special Courts have been established with the only function of repression of political opposition. A special police force, the *Gestapo*, has been organized in April and granted full immunity in front of the law. A year later, the Court of Justice of the Popular Racial Community, a parody of a Court of Law, constituting just a waiting room of a butchery, was in place.

It would be beyond my task to dwell in any detailed discussions of the appalling escalation in violating international law as recognized at the time that lead to the Expansion of the Third Reich, to the Holocaust, to the Final Solution and eventually to the War. Two points are important however: first, that the international community has early been aware of such an escalation of terror and of such violations of international law, despite the propaganda and the attempts to hide the truth (See, T. Feral, *Justice et Nazisme*, Paris, L' Harmattan, 1997) Second, that the experience of Nazi Germany must be fully recognized as a *per se* violation of international law not only as far as the specific criminal conducts ascertained by the Nurnberg Trial, but also, more generally, in regard to the whole production of a legal facade pronounced in the name of the German People (Im namen des deutschen Volkes) by the institutions of Nazi Justice. In fact, according to the *Restatement Third of Foreign Relation Law*, principles of due process such as the opportunity of defendants to present their cases, or that no one can be a judge in his own case, intrinsically at odds with the idea of Nazi justice are part of international law.

While some of the personal responsibilities for the many fundamental violations of international law have been ascertained by securing some of the perpetrators to criminal punishment, the more general institutional responsibilities that allowed such a catastrophe to happen have largely remained in obscurity. On the civil side, such institutional responsibilities include: those of foreign Governments both belonging to the Axis or secretly cooperating with it in violation of principles of neutrality; those *of major financial institutions, including Banks and Insurance Companies*, both in Germany and abroad, playing a key role in financing the Nazi regime; those of industries both directly involved in the industrial production of artifacts necessary for the perpetration of the international law violations, as well as benefiting from such violations. . . .

Dealing in good faith is a principle of international law recognized by the legal systems of the civilized nations grossly violated by the alleged behavior of defendants.

Short from offering a discussion of comparative law describing the language of a variety of legal texts, my discussion will be limited to a few legal systems that can be seen as paradigmatic of the two major legal traditions of the world (common law and civil law) and of relevant specific provisions that are part of the legal systems that are more directly involved in this issue, i.e. Germany and Switzerland.

In the domain of good faith it should be said at the outset that the very language of the Swiss Constitution offers a clear statement of the importance of this principle. Within article 5 devoted to the Rule of Law, the third paragraph . . . states: "State organs and private persons must act in good faith". Again Art. 9 of the same Constitution carrying title "Protection against arbitrariness and Principle of Good Faith" says that "Every Person has the right to be treated by the State organs without arbitrariness and in good faith".

The same principle enjoys a central position in the Swiss Civil Code (1907). According to Art. 2: "Every person is bound to exercise his rights and to fulfill his obligations according to the principle of Good Faith". Good faith is a key principle in the interpretation of more than half a dozen other specific provisions of the Code of Obligations that would be pedantic here to report.

As to German Law, the provision of § 242 BGB (1900) according to which "The obligor is bound to perform the obligation in such a way as is required by the principles of good faith with due regard to existing usage". Treu und Glauben (translation: fidelity and faith), is so central in the deep structure of German private law and it has captured so many areas of the law that it might well be considered the most important amongst the famous general clauses of German law. The principle can be found in other provisions of the Code too (e.g. § 157: "Contracts shall be interpreted according to the requirements of good faith") but it is the explosive expansion of case law that has applied the principle virtually across the whole legal system.

By 1933, at the beginning of the Nazi era, good faith was already celebrated as "the queen of rules" of German private law. Nazi jurists started to consider it dangerous. Hedemann, for example, later a proponent of substituting the BGB with a People's Code better suited to a national spirit emanating from the community of blood and soil, subtitled a monograph mostly concentrated on Treu und Glauben "Dangers for State and Law" (See Justus Wilhelm Hedemann, *Die Flucht in die Generalklausen: Eine Gefahr für Recht un Staat*, 1933 p. 10). But German Courts never stopped to apply this principle. An opinion rendered by the German Reichtgericht in 1935, for example, witnesses the "dangers" that Hedemann was fearing. The Court made use of the principle of good faith to protect a Jewish defendant against a Nazi plaintiff in a matter of Corporation law. (The decision 2d Civil Division, January 22, 1935, RGZ 146, 385 is translated in English and interestingly discussed in Shlesinger–Baade–Herzog Wise, Comparative Law 6 ed. p. 637).

Most European Civil Codes contain general good faith provisions. Amongst them, Art. 1134 sec. 3 of the French Civil Code, Arts. 1175 and 1375 of the Italian Civil Code, Art. 288 of the Greek Civil Code Art. 762, sec. 2 of the Portuguese Civil Code, Art. 6:2 and 6:248 Dutch Civil Code, Art. 1641 Belgian Civil Code.

A recent study conducted in the last five years within an International Project ... shows in much detail that even in those European systems that do not have a specific Code Provision (this includes Great Britain and Ireland) good faith can be considered "a common core principle" that actually determines the law in action. See R. Zimmermann & S. Whittaker, *Good Faith in European Contract Law*, in *The Common Core of European Private Law Project*, pp. 701, Cambridge University Press 2000 (M. Bussani & U. Mattei Gen. Eds.).

The existence of such common core is acknowledged by the two most important recent collective works in the domain of Uniform Contract Law. The Restatement of European Contract law recently published by the so called Lando Commission as well as the Principles of International Commercial Contracts published by UNIDROIT contain general provisions according to which "in exercising his rights and performing his duties each party must act in accordance with good faith and fair dealing" (see respectively Art. 1–106 Principles of European Contract Law; Art. 1.7 Principles of International Commercial Contracts).

Outside of Europe, the Uniform Commercial Code Sec. 1–203 contains a language similar to the German BGB (According to the most accredited scholarly reconstruction such language was imported from Germany to the U.S. by the work of Karl Llewellyn) and a general principle of good faith in the contract law of the different States is now recognized. (See the classic R.S. Summers, *Good Faith in General Contract Law and the Sale Provisions of the Uniform Commercial Code*, 54 Virginia L.R. 195 (1968).

Just a cursory look to the foreign law collection of the University of California at Berkeley allowed me to locate general provisions on good faith in Venezuela, Honduras, Panama and Argentina amongst the Latin American Countries. In Africa, good faith provisions of general scope can be found among others in both of the most influential Civil Codes those of Egypt and Ethiopia. Amongst the former socialist countries, Hungary as well as in the new Civil Code of the Russian Federation have provisions on the duty to act in good faith.

The principle of good faith has a very long and reputed history. It was recognized by the Roman Law as the stronger device to introduce Equity into the strict form of their contracts. It has been developed in the European *Ius Commune*, by the Canon Law, the Late scholastic and by Natural Law. It has found its way in the common law, through the Court of Chancery which has applied since its beginning basic principles derived from the Canon Law, including good faith. Natural Law, in turn has characterized the idea of international law since its very early developments in the hands of such scholars as Hugo Grotius, Samuel Pufendorf and may other of the founding fathers of international law in the seventeenth century. Its impact on the American Constitution is known to everybody.

Good Faith Is certainly a principle of International Law "recognized by the civilized nations" and arguably even a principle of customary Jus Cogens.

Within this scenario, there is no doubt in my opinion that the principle of good faith qualifies as a "General Principle of Law recognized by civilized nations" which is a source of international law according to art. 38c of the Statute of the International Court of Justice. It might arguably qualify even as a general norm of customary *Jus Cogens* (art. 38b same statute) being recognized as part of international law by so many writers in the field.

In a decision of 1957 the International Court of Justice, has expressly recognized the principle of good faith as a "general principle of law recognized by the civilized nations" 1957 (I.C.J.) 9, 53 France v Norway July 6, 1957. And indeed the same conclusions have been generalized by one of the most important international law scholars of our century, Judge Lauterpacht; "... These 'general principles' are not, as such, principles of moral justice as distinguished from law; they are not rules of 'equity' in the ethical sense; nor are they a speculative law conceived by way of deductive reasoning from legal and moral principles. They are, in the first instance, those principles of law, private and public, which contemplation of the legal experience of civilized nations leads one to regard as obvious maxims of jurisprudence of a general and fundamental character—such as the principle that no one can be judge in his own cause ... *that legal obligations must be fulfilled and rights must be exercised in good faith,* and the like." See 1 Hersh Lauterpacht, International Law (1970) at 68–69 (emphasis added).

According to the scholar that has linked his name more than anybody else to the research by means of comparative law of common core principles of law recognized by civilized nations, such general principles: "Must be consulted whenever a question of international law is adjudicated by any international or municipal tribunal. Resort must be had to the same source in many instances in which the settlement of such a dispute is sought by negotiation and conciliation rather than by formal adjudication. The phrase 'general principles of law recognized by civilized nations' refers to principles which find expression in the municipal laws of various nations". (See Schlesinger, Comp. Law cit. p. 43; 1 Formation of Contracts—A Study of the Common Core of Legal Systems (R.B. Schlesinger Ed.1968) 1–43. See also Burns H. Weston et al., International Law and World Order 118–19 (2d ed. 1990), and Bin Cheng, General Principles of Law as Applied to International Courts and Tribunals 326–57 (1987).

As the United States Supreme Court has long recognized, "the customary law of nations can be ascertained by consulting the work of jurists, writing professionally on public laws or general usages or practices of Nations; or by judicial decisions recognizing and enforcing that law". See United States v. Smith, 5 Wheat. 153 (1820) 160, 161; see also The Paquete Habana, 175 U.S. 677, 20 S.Ct. 290 (1900). It is difficult to object to the fact that many jurists would give to the principle of good faith even the higher status of customary *Ius Cogens* in the ranking of the sources of international law. . . .

In my opinion the alleged behavior of defendants, if proven, constitutes a gross violation of international law both *per se,* as cooperation with an internationally illegal regime, and by the bad faith characteristics of the behavior involved both during and after the fall of the Nazi regime. Making good such gross violation of international law is a primary interest common to the members of the class that certainly prevails to any individual interest of the members to obtain redress.

NOTES AND QUESTIONS

In *Roper v. Simmons* cit. *supra* Chapter 1 at 57 we discussed the strengths and the weaknesses of comparative law arguments as deployed by the U.S. Supreme Court in the matter of a juvenile execution issue. In the Holocaust litigation the argument was that this fundamental common core, as a basic source of international law, becomes part of US domestic law. Can you spell out a difference between the two uses of comparative law for purposes of domestic U.S. litigation?

(f) Common Core and Integrative Approaches in the Critical Training of Lawyers

There are additional reasons why it is important to ascertain and formulate the common core of legal systems. In the face of a dramatic worldwide intensification of the transnational exchange and movement goods, services, and capital (Much more barriers are out there for persons. Why?), the work of all branches of the legal profession is becoming globalized, with the result that it is indispensable for lawyers to be acquainted with at least some elements of the law of several legal systems.

Looking for similarities is also a useful antidote to the tendency on the part of Comparative Law teachers to focus on differences in order to warn students against taking for granted their own law. To combat an uncritical attitude toward one's own law is indeed one of the main objectives of teaching Comparative Law, and this objective often results in more time being spent on differences than on similarities.

We know from the historical experience of anthropological studies that a strong emphasis on perceived differences in unequal power contexts can lead to phenomena that have been described as "orientalism". (See *supra* Chapter 1 at 42.) Due emphasis on analogies and painstaking analysis of the social and political context of norms is essential to avoid such western-centric mistake. Such efforts sometimes can lead to disturbing results but it is nevertheless crucial in going beyond the quite sterile opposition between "cultural relativism" and "universalism". The following article stretches the integrative approach to comparative law to its full potentialities by comparing law as cultural practice.

Elisabetta Grande, *Hegemonic human rights and African Resistance. The Issue of female circumcision in a broader comparative perspective*

Global Jurist Frontiers, 2004
www.bepress.com/gj/frontiers/vol4/iss2/art3/.

The issue of female circumcision (hereinafter F.C.) . . . is a powerful example of the double standard that affects much of the internationally dominant human rights discourse. . . . It also suggests the importance of conducting any work related to human rights from both the perspectives of "we" and the "others", "insiders" and "outsiders", "westerners" and "non-westerners", "helpers" and "helped", in a word from a broad comparative law perspective. . . . A genuinely universal approach to human rights work requests a communication among cultures that can only be achieved following the lesson taught by both anthropologists and comparative law scholars: "participant observation" or "cultural immersion" are the keys for understanding and communicating. In this paper I claim that the international approach against F.C. has not engaged in a "dialogical dialogue", i.e. a dialogue among cultures that give "them" and "us" a third eye, making it possible a critical understanding of each one's attitudes, beliefs and practices; a dialogue that requires us to "look in the mirror from the start". Only a serious and comprehensive approach towards *all modifications of sexual organs*, African and western, "theirs" as well as "ours", using a single, not a double, standard to evaluate all body modifications related to human sexual apparatus, will make the human rights discourse ... less imperialistic, more effective and less assimilating....

This comparative work should offer the opportunity to reflect on the grounds we use to justify the different treatment reserved to F.C. when compared to other modifying practices concerning sexual organs. What makes F.C. a human rights' violation while male circumcision (M.C). and breast augmentation (B.A). are considered acceptable and even respectable cultural practices? ...

In describing the reactions that the legal system of my country (Italy) and that of this country (U.S.) have in front of three different practices that in various ways end up in modifying human sexual organs, let me consider the following three cases:

1) In Italy and in the U.S., M.C. is routinely performed, for no therapeutic reasons, in public hospitals right after the baby is born (in the second mentioned country to the extent of at least 60% of the newborn male population)[1] and it is a practice that the law fully accepts. M.C., as everyone knows, consists of removing the foreskin or prepuce, the natural sheath of skin that covers the penis. In the same two countries, however, F.C., even the less extreme of its forms, the so called *Sunnah circumcision*, is outlawed and criminally sanctioned. Sunnah circumcision, as very few would know, in its mildest expression is a largely symbolic circumcision that entails a small cut in the prepuce (the hood above a girl's clitoris). It removes no tissue and leaves only a small scar. It is far less invasive than M.C. Nevertheless, proposals by doctors at medical centers in the two countries that envisaged to perform this light form of F.C. at parents' request (or even with the girl's informed consent) have produced a major uproar of the anti-F.C. movements and have been deemed unacceptable by the law itself.

2) In Italy and in the U.S., B.A. surgery is a sexual organ modifying practice generously allowed by the legal system *even on minors*, who by giving consent can have their breasts augmented as long as they give consent together with but *one* of their parents. In the same two countries F.C., no matter how mild, performed on a minor is punished as a serious crime. Minors' and their parents' consent is no excuse, nor is it so their belief that the operation is required as a matter of custom, ritual or religion. In Italy, the minor age of the recipient of F.C., no matter how strongly she consents, is an aggravating factor that increases the sentence to be imposed on perpetrators and their accomplices.

3) Finally, in Italy and in some U.S. States, but not at the Federal level (thanks to African immigrant women activists that strongly opposed a situation in which adult immigrant women would have otherwise been treated as legal minors), an adult women, i.e. a woman over 18, cannot validly consent to a F.C. surgery while of course can consent to have her breast augmented.

---

1. Sexual Mutilation: A Human Tragedy 93.

A similar legal framework is nowadays found everywhere in the western world, and consequently is starting its spreading march, as a token paid to civilization, in African legal systems. F.C. in fact, became the object of a massive attack at the international level since 1979, when the WHO (World Health Organization) sponsored the first Seminar on Harmful Traditional Practices Affecting the Health of Women and Children, in Karthoum, Sudan. The efforts in eliminating F.C. (*eradication* is the term employed) earned the support of the international community and F.C. was later framed as a human rights violation and addressed as such in many international settings. As a result many countries, western as well as African, passed criminal legislations specifically addressing F.C. within the mentioned framework.[2]

Yet, despite this "common core of civilized nations" the question remains open: why is F.C. treated differently than other "cutting" practices? What makes only F.C. a human rights violation? On what grounds (other than cultural bias) can we justify the singling-out of F.C. among the different sexual organs modifying procedures practiced in the world?

The first answer that comes to the mind of an unbiased observer attains to health concerns....

Acknowledging that it is with a great approximation that we can address F.C. as a unitary category, it seems that many forms of FC, with the sure exception of infibulation, if performed in the same non-septic, safe and hygienic setting of a good hospital, would not entail greater health risks in terms of short-term and long term complications than M.C. or B.A. Surgery routinely performed in our countries in case of congenital adrenal hyperplasia, Id. cliteridectomy for those newborn who have been called "intersex babies" ..., can prove at least the medical point.

What makes F.C., addressed as a unified concept, a human rights violation seems therefore to be its understanding as a patriarchal practice meant to limit women's sexual fulfillment for the men's sake of controlling women's sexuality. This is why, according to the usual perspective in the international community, F.C. violates women's rights and why, even in the absence of health complications, the practice calls for its eradication....

In an essay on FC, Obioma Nnaemeka recently wrote: "Ultimately, the circumcision debate is about the construction of the African woman as the 'Other'" ...[3]

2. For details on criminal legislations passed in recent times world-wide, *see* FGM, 61 and part II.

Criminal laws addressing FC have generally not recognized circumstances in which a woman is deemed to have capacity to consent to undergoing the procedure. Only Canada, Tanzania and the United States have limited their prohibitions of FC to procedures performed upon a person under the age of 18.

3. Obioma Nnaemeka, If Female Circumcision Did Not Exist, Western Feminist Would Invent It, in Eye to Eye, Women Practicing Development Across Cultures, S. Perry–C. Schenck Eds., Zed Books, London, N.Y., 2001, 179.

In its address of the issue of F.C. however, the international human rights community doesn't seem to have profited from this lesson. The result is a highly distorted image of African people's lives and attitudes, together with the banalization and decontextualization of their practices that ultimately determine a lack of critical understanding of our practices as well. . . .

Female as well as male circumcision practices in Africa are . . . strictly related to a gender construction enterprise, they are imposed by a gender-identity cultural rule, that define the standard for femininity and masculinity and that in turn finds its roots in the legitimization's and organizational needs of the group as a socio-legal structure. . . .

It is often argued that female circumcision maintains good health in women and it is widely believed by women "that these genital alterations improve their bodies and make them more beautiful, more feminine, more civilized, more honorable" and the removal of the clitoris is positively associated with the "attainment of full female identity". Female genitalia, in its natural state, is seen as ugly (as much of course as male genitalia before circumcision) and the clitoris, revolting. Cleanliness and hygiene feature consistently as justification for F.C., because the clitoris is seen as the source of bad odors and secretions. In many societies, an important reason given for F.C. is the belief that it reduces a woman's desire for sex, therefore reducing the chance of sex outside marriage.

Why, among all these various ex post explanations given for F.C., we, the westerners, in order to describe, explain and attack it, picked just the last one? It obviously seemed to us a more plausible explanation compared to the others; it also matches with the reason that made us to clitoridectomize our women until as late as the first half of last century, when erotomania was supposedly cured by it. . . . It seems . . . far from established that the clitoris removal necessarily reduces a woman's desire for sex or entails a sexual fulfillment limitation, since sexual satisfaction seems always to be the result of physiological, psychological and sociological determinants. Experiencing the feeling of being socially integrated, of being beautiful according to the standards of the living community, or of having met the femininity requirements of your own society seems very important, often even more important, for sexual fulfillment than having the anatomical structure intact. . . .

. . . Over-emphasizing the connection between F.C. and the limitation or even the suppression of women's sexuality in the interest of male sexuality, . . . arbitrarily reduces the meaning of FC to a cruel barbarian ritual, carried out against half of the population in the (short-sight) interests of the other half (that would end up sexually dealing with frigid women, which in turn means carrying out a biological suicidal policy). They also clearly mark the contrast with MC and BA, producing a feeling of "positional superiority" that distinguishes civilized from barbaric cutting practices.

In this narrow light, MC appears to be a substantially different practice than FC. And it is so, not because it entails lower health risks than many forms of FC, but because it doesn't amount to a "castration" as FC, but to the contrary, it "enhances man's masculinity". Nor MC carries the social message of subordination that is generally associated with FC, but on the contrary it "affirms manhood with its superior social status and associations to virility". Interestingly enough these arguments never face the medical fact that also male circumcision entails an anatomical reduction of sexual pleasure. . . .

Moreover, framed as women rights' violations, i.e. as practices designed to subjugate women, African FC also appears ontologically different from western BA. To be sure, the difference here does not relate to the sexual fulfillment reduction in anatomical terms: no one would in fact question that BA modifies often even eliminates breast and breast's nipples sensitivity in women, being breasts an intrinsic part of her sexual organs-indeed a very important one for many women. Nor the difference between many forms of FC and BA relates to health concerns. In comparable medical settings BA, indeed quite an invasive form of surgery, would probably appear even more dangerous to women's health than most FC practices.

The difference here holds in the illusion of "free choice" that we get from comparing by contrast "our" practice with "theirs". The image of African women as subjugated by men and as oppressed in their sexuality by them, contrasts so much with the idealized emancipation of western woman that we immediately perceive our practices as profoundly different from theirs. "Our" consent to our cutting practices is a good one (even if given by a minor dreaming about having a big breast like her favorite actress, or having been told that she has "micromastia", i.e. the serious illness of having small breasts), because it is not forced upon us, yet it is given because BA would "improve the individual's self-image" or increase "women's self-esteem". "Their" consent to their cutting practices, on the contrary, cannot possibly be meaningful, because "refusing to undergo FC/FEM may jeopardize a woman's family relations, her social life or her ability to find a spouse". . . .

By putting FC seriously in context, we would have reached different comparative conclusions. By avoiding the confusion between FC narratives and FC function in its political and social context, we could have been able to recognize that all African cutting practices, FC as well as MC, find their purpose in a gender identity rule, deeply rooted in the survival needs of the group as a socio-legal entity. It is this identity rule that sets up femininity and masculinity standards and that imposes itself on every member of the community and controls them all, males and females alike. . . . To stress the inseparability between patriarchy and FC therefore, prevents us to see that FC implies more than patriarchy and that its profound reasons, rooted in *gender identity,* are not different from those of our own practices. . . .

The reasons why African people go through FC or MC are not very different from those that push western women to have their breasts augmented, or make western men have their penis circumcised. In all these cases it is the urgency to meet that masculinity or femininity requirements, determined outside the individual by the gender identity rule that accounts for his or her (or his/her parents') "choice". From this perspective African women's consent to their cutting practices is motivated by the same desire to enhance their self-confidence, personal well-being and social worth that motivates western women to have their breast augmented. It is the feeling of belonging that any-one any-where derives from having met the beauty and femininity (or masculinity) standards of their own society. In both cases the price for refusing the cutting practice can be high in terms of social exclusion, either self-inflicted or produced by others. And of course the greater is the social pressure for undertaking the procedure (as when a medical concept like micromastia is invented in order to convince women to undertake the practice) the higher will be the price of social exclusion in case of refusal.

An observation of African cutting practices profiting from the concept of cultural immersion and requiring "us" to look in the mirror from the start, would allow to find points of convergence and commonalties more than differences between "them" and "us". The opportunity to look at ourselves through "their" eyes would have permitted "us" to gain a critical understanding about "our" practices as well. It would have therefore allowed us to seriously question such concepts as "free choice" when we deal with culture-imposed rules, and also forced us to challenge narratives about our own practices that exclude any control of men over women.... To Africans BA would probably appear as "a form of patriarchal colonization of the female mind and body, an unnatural phenomenon", just as their practices appear to us....

NOTES AND QUESTIONS

(1) Grande concludes her thought provoking plea for "integrative comparison" with the following words: "How we, the westerners, perceive others' treatment of their women-folk has always been a tool in ranking the level of civilization and development of foreign countries in order to decide whether or not to admit them in the family of the civilized nations. A low ranking operated in the past as a justification for colonizing, looting and plunder. Is history repeating itself?" Do you share her worries? Please think about the intense media coverage of *burqua* in the eve of recent U.S. lead intervention in Afghanistan and Somalia in light of the colonial experience. A whole tradition of human sacrifice has been invented in the past to morally justify the destruction of the Inca empire by the Spanish conquistadores.[1]

Often overemphasized differences, particularly when displayed by radically different cultures, might induce the observer to overlook similar practices in our own law or culture. Such apparently irreconcilable differences might be mistaken for "lack of civilization" or can be used in the construction of the inferiority of the "other". Professor Elisabetta Grande has called the attention of the international human rights community to the fact that in the west we

---

1. The point is forcefull made by an African scholar. Abdulmumini A. Oba (2008), "Female Circumcision as Female Genital Mutilation: Human Rights or Cultural Imperial- ism?," Global Jurist: Vol. 8: Iss. 3 (Frontiers), Article 8. Available at: http://www.bepress. com/gj/vol8/iss3/art8.

also engage in sexual cutting, such as in breast augmentation or in male circumcision. The author advocates the use of integrative comparisons in order to avoid ethnocentrism and positional superiority. At stake there is the dramatic tension between cultural relativism and ethnocentric universalism, a tension that goes well beyond the superficial stereotype that comparativists are cultural relativists while international human rights scholars are universalists. Of course the recognition of similarities can also be problematic. Comparative Law should not only warn against universalism. It should also help in putting ourselves in the shoes of "the other" by acknowledging similarities that might be disturbing. This is where "integrative approaches to comparative law" such as the common core might be particularly useful, as it has been pointed out by comparing female circumcision and western cutting practices.

In order to perceive this more advanced use of the common core hypothesis in the study of radically different legal systems such as those in Africa or Asia, one should, however, master a few more tools such as the notion of legal formants and that of legal pluralism to which we will turn in the next chapter.

(2) Many critics of the common core methodology argue that it is falsely neutral, since it cannot help eventually to emphasize analogies over differences and it is thus little respectful of cultural diversities. Do you share this critique? Can you see a difference between the common core as a scholarly method in the hands of comparativists (professionally dealing with differences) or in the hands of international human rights activists (who tend to downplay cultural relativism)?

(3) Most legal systems in the world ban torture as an illegal practice. Torture is banned also by innumerable international conventions on human rights. Nevertheless, we learned with much disappointment, that even in the U.S. and Great Britain, torture is practiced quite routinely under circumstances that are deemed extreme and we know from Amnesty International that in most countries of the world torture is a tragic reality. What would be your common core analysis of torture? Is there a common core of legal systems to ban torture? Is there a common core of legal systems to allow it once we look at the law in action rather than at the law in the books?

(4) Because it is practically impossible to deeply analyze all the legal systems of the world, the common core usually ends up singling out some of them as representative of all. Thus the choice of the significant legal systems is very important and potentially dangerous. It requires a sophisticated taxonomy of the families of legal systems[2] (see also *infra* Chapter 3, Section 7 at 258). It also runs the risk of considering significant for the purpose of common core inquiry the usual suspects i.e. the dominant systems of the western (common law and civil law) legal tradition thus excluding from the inquiry and assuming as participating in the "civilized consensus" other less economically powerful countries. This problem is particularly relevant when the common core becomes a source of international law through its being considered the foundation of the "general principles recognized by the civilized nations" according to Art 38 of the Statute of the International Court of Justice (see *supra* p. 109; and on the colonialist use of such ideas of civilization, *infra* pp. 330ff). The same

2. *See* Patrick Glenn, *Comparative Legal families and Comparative Legal Traditions*, in Mathias Reimann & Reinhard Zimmermann, Oxford Handbook of Comparative Law, 421 (2006).

problem is also relevant, at the European level (where issues of cultural imperialism might appear less significant) where a variety of reform and restatement projects (often sponsored by the European Commission) claim to based on shared elements of European private law by considering only the four or five dominant legal systems out of 27 member countries.

4.   ISSUES OF METHOD: HOW DO YOU ASCERTAIN WHAT LAW IS?

The following section deepens the analysis of the methodological issues already introduced in Section 3(a) *supra*. It attempts to make the student aware of the tremendous mischiefs that might follow a superficial understanding of the laws of the others.

(a) Difficulties of Knowledge

One problem of common core methodology is that of the reliability of the findings of what the foreign law is.[1] In U.S. litigation, for instance, one risk is that of making up the common core for the strategic purposes of litigation, such as when the common core becomes the instrument through which the *lex fori* can be applied (favoring one side) in the instances in which a conflict of law provision would otherwise point at foreign law (favoring the other). In fact most often, if a common core can be demonstrated, US courts would happily apply their local *lex fori* assuming that this would be the same as foreign law pointed at by choice of law rules. Consequently, plaintiff might try to prove the existence of a common core while defendant might try to disprove it.

This is not more of a problem than that created by partisan expert witnesses or even by the very nature of adversary advocacy. A descriptive argument in litigation is invariably more persuasive than an openly normative one. This difficulty in ascertaining what the law is is however present even outside of problems of strategic partisanship and it is particularly devastating for the gathering of data for comparative purposes. Not only the honesty of jurists that try to answer any given factual problem but also their preconceptions might play a role in evaluating if what they describe is actually "the law".

Problems related to ascertaining what the law is are exacerbated when serious comparison attempts to be extended beyond the limit of the professionalized western legal tradition. In such contexts it is almost impossible to know what the law is by simply looking up books and publications.[2] This is not merely a problem of knowledge and consequent

1. *See* Mathias Reimann, Comparative Law and Private International Law, in Mathias Reimann and Reinhard Zimmermann, Oxford Handbook of Comparative Law 1364 (2006) 1381 ff.

2. *See* for example T.W. Bennett, Comparative Law and African Customary Law in Mathias Reimann & Reinhard Zimmermann, Oxford Handbook of Comparative Law, 641 (2006)

poor quality of data gathered. Many times, poor understanding of different legal systems by western lawyers or economists produces tragic results due to flawed policy recommendations following western-centric biases. The following excerpt offers a telling example as well as some interesting materials for comparing property law (see *infra* Chapter 9 at 920ff):

Thomas Kelley, *Unintended Consequences of Legal westernization in Niger: Harming Contemporary Slaves by Reconceptualizing Property*

56 Am. J. Comp. L. 999 (2008).

Slaves living today in the Republic of Niger are being harmed by that country's aggressive program of legal westernization. Nigerien law reformers and their western[1] sponsors have inadvertently disadvantaged the slaves by passing laws that institute private property ownership, a legal concept that had been known to Niger's rural citizens but never fully embraced by them....

Law reformers and international development experts have adopted as a guiding principle the theory that poor countries can rise with the economic tide of globalization and grow their way out of poverty if, and only if, they provide citizens with consistent, predictable, and enforceable rights in private property....

Niger Before Legal Westernization: Demographic Challenges, Customary Land Tenure Rules, and Lingering Slavery Traditions

The Republic of Niger has four major ethnic groups—Hausa (56%), Zarma (22%), Fulani (8.5%), and Tuareg (8%)[2]—each with its own language, history, and set of cultural and legal traditions....

Niger is a large, hot, landlocked, desperately poor country that ranks dead last in the United Nations' Human Development Index. Its population stands at approximately 13 million, while its fertility rate (7.9 children per woman) and its population growth rate (3.3%) are among the highest in the world. This rapidly expanding population must compete for a scant pool of natural resources including a critically short supply of arable land. The vast majority of Niger's citizens are subsistence farmers, which means that if they lose access to agricultural land—something we later will learn is happening to Niger's slaves as a result of legal westernization—they will not be able to feed themselves....

---

1. The "West" refers to European and North American donor countries and the international institutions they control, most notably the United Nations, the World Bank, and the International Monetary Fund. Non–Western countries such as China and Libya also wield power in Niger. However, those countries' agendas have not focused on law reform, leading me to disregard them for purposes of this project.

2. Bureau of African Affairs, U.S Department of State, Background Note: Niger (March 2005), available at http://www.state.gov/r/pa/ei/bgn/5474.htm [hereinafter Niger Background Note 2005].

Traditional Land Tenure in Niger

Traditional land tenure is a shorthand term that refers to a complex and dynamic set of traditions and practices related to land use.[3] One thing that can be said with certainty, however, is that traditional land tenure customs in Niger are not constructed upon the western legal concept of private ownership.

In the not distant past, access to agricultural land in Niger depended almost entirely on a man's stage in life and status within his community. As a child (*zanka*) he would have no control over any land and would be expected to work in the family fields and contribute to the commonweal. As a young bachelor approaching marriageable age (*arwasu*) he would continue to work in the extended family's fields under elder males' direction, but those elder males would set aside a small plot of land (*kurga*) for him, which he would cultivate in the evenings and on rest days to earn money for a bride payment. After marrying and establishing his own family, the elder males of his lineage would expand his *kurga* into a full sized field, or *fari*. He would cultivate that full-sized field, still under the general guidance of his father and other elder males of the lineage, and in so doing, would achieve the status of *alfari*, which means farmer but also connotes a respected, responsible adult. Ultimately, as the man's beard grayed and his own sons matured, he would achieve the status of *dotigi*, or respected elder, and would, in consultation with other *dotigi* of his family lineage, make land available to the next generation of males.

The use rights granted to younger men were generally predictable and stable, but they always were subject to the needs of the larger group. If, for example, a young man absented himself from the village for an extended time, the elder males could limit or extinguish his right to continue cultivating a particular plot.[4] If a plot of land needed to be ceded to a neighboring village to resolve a dispute, the elder males could do so, trumping a younger man's presumptive use right.[5]

Although elder males controlled and mediated access to agricultural land, their power sprang from and was subject to the authority of the *laabu koy*, or land chief,[6] whose role was to ensure that mortals' use of the land would not offend its original inhabitants, the *gangi bi*, or black spirits. If the spirits were offended, they could visit all manner of misfortune on the community: sickness, drought, pestilence, and locusts, to name a few.[7] Thus, under traditional Nigerien land tenure customs, a man received use

3. Christian Lund, Struggles for Land and Political Power: On the Politicization of Land Tenure and Disputes in Niger, 40 J. Legal Pluralism & Unofficial L. 3, 4 (1998).

4. Thomas Kelley, Squeezing Parakeets into Pigeon Holes: The Effects of Globalization and State Legal Reform in Niger on Indigenous Zarma Law, 34 N.Y.U. J. Int'l L. & Pol. 635, 682 n. 176 (Spring 2002).

5. *See id.*

6. Paul Stoller, Fusion of the Worlds: An Ethnography of Possession Among the Songhay of Niger 27 (1989).

7. *See* Nobert Rouland, Legal Anthropology 216 (Philippe G. Planel trans., Stanford Univ. Press 1994) (1988).

rights from the males of the previous generations, but that man could never be said to own the land because his use rights were subject to the needs of the community (including the spirits who were the original owners), as mediated through the offices of the community elders and the *laabu koy*.

In the 1960s, with the growing influence of Islam and French civil law, both of which favor inheritance of land within nuclear families, there began a gradual cultural shift toward farmers viewing themselves as something more than merely the users of agricultural land.[8] Today, most Zarma men presume that the land that has been passed down to them will remain under their control and that they will be free to pass their land on to their sons. Yet, in practice, most farmers still exercise something less than complete ownership over the fields they cultivate. For example, they acknowledge the rights of secondary users of the land, such as women from the community, who may enter without permission to gather herbs or glean unused grain stalks.[9] Further, many state flatly that they do not have the right to alienate the land that they cultivate, implicitly acknowledging that the lineage has an inchoate claim. Consistent with that view, men express distaste at the prospect of formally dividing large tracts of communally held lineage land, saying obliquely that dividing land between brothers is something that nobles simply do not do . . . .[10]

Slavery

For complex political reasons only summarized here, Niger's government did little to combat slavery after the colonizers departed in 1960. At independence the French handed the colonial apparatus over to a class of Nigerien leaders, known as *les evolues* (the evolved ones),[11] who represented a thin slice of the population that had aligned itself as clients of France by attending French schools and adopting the French language and culture. Some of these *evolues* were the sons of traditional chiefs, but others came from the ranks of former slaves, either because they had sought shelter from their masters during the colonial administration, or because their noble masters, when required by the French to send their children to state sponsored schools, had often sent the children of their slaves rather than their own. Although many of the *evolues*, then as now, looked upon rural people and traditional chiefs with disdain,[12] once they had their hands on the reins of power they discovered, just like the French before them, that

---

8. Interview with Group of Villagers, in Fandou Berri, Republic of Niger (June 1, 1996); Interview with Yaye Issa and Issafou Lali, in Fandou Berri, Republic of Niger (May 22, 2000)

9. Interview with Bachirou Djibo and others, in Fandou Berri, Republic of Niger (October 21, 2003).

10. Interview with Yaye Issa, in Fandou Berri, Republic of Niger (May 27, 1996); *see* Interview with Bachirou Djibo, in Niam-

ey, Republic of Niger (May 18, 2000) (discussing continuous joint ownership of land).

11. Robert Charlick, Niger: Personal Rule and Survival in the Sahel 40 (1991).

12. *See* Jean–Pierre Olivier De Sardan, Anthropology and Development: Understanding Contemporary Social Change 205 (Tidjani Alou trans., 2005) (referring to Nigerien civil servants' contempt for peasants);

they could not rule without the chiefs' backing and participation. The upshot was that the post-independence state was under the control of two elite groups: the educated descendants of slaves who generally wished to downplay their servile origins, and traditional chiefs (and some of their educated sons) whose power and wealth depended at least partly on slavery. Neither group had any desire to raise the divisive subject, and slavery in Niger went on as before. . . .

In general, we in the West conceive of one broad category of servile people that we refer to as slaves or, in French, *esclaves*. Nigeriens, on the other hand, think of slavery as a diverse set of servile social positions, each described by a different term.[13] For example, the most encompassing term in the Zarma language for slave is *banya*, which describes any person acquired through capture, trade, purchase or gift, as well as anyone whose ancestors were so obtained. A subcategory of *banya* is *tam*, a newly captured slave who must be watched carefully and, in some cases, chained or hobbled to prevent escape. The *tam* looks much like our western conception of slavery: he is completely at the mercy of his master and may be sold, bartered, pledged, exchanged or killed, and may be required to perform onerous and dangerous labor such as well digging.[14] Among Zarma people, few if any have been enslaved in recent generations, so the numbers of *tam* are diminished even though the category continues to have cultural resonance.[15]

The category of slave that now is most common in Zarma society and that most confounds western preconceptions of slavery is *horso*. A slave who has been assimilated into the master's lineage–usually after his line has been connected to a noble family for three generations–achieves the status of *horso*.[16] The *horso* experiences little of the violence and overt repression that a westerner associates with slavery. He wears no chains, and according to cultural norms may not be beaten, exchanged or sold. He often is raised beside his master's children, and when he grows older is

13. *Id.* at 27.

14. Oral history accounts of the founding of Zarma villages often begin with the patriarch departing on a slave raiding expedition and then requiring the captured slaves to dig the well that becomes the symbolic and practical life spring of the new community. *See, e.g., infra* note 177–78 and accompanying text.

15. There are other important social categories that, in translation, end up being folded into the English word slave. For example, a female can fall into any of the categories thus far described, but if she is taken as a concubine by a noble (most often her master), and if she bears him a child, she becomes wahay. As such, she is no longer a banya, though her origins are never forgotten and she never achieves the status of noble

(koyize) or free person (talaka) within the social group. The son born of a wahay is a wahayize, or child of wahay. A wahayize is considered to have no maternal ancestors. He is invested with his father's nobility and has the right to inherit and to vie for political leadership; however, he carries the stigma of servile blood in a society where status and rights are determined largely by one's ancestry. Many great political leaders and warriors in Zarma history have been wahayize and it is said that they are driven to greatness by a desire to prove themselves and overcome their servile origins.

16. Jean-Pierre Olivier de Sardan, Les Voleurs D'Hommes (Notes Sur L'Histoire Des Kurtey), Etudes Nigeriennnes 29, p. 11 (1969).

addressed with respectful terms such as "father" or "brother."[17] He is free to wander through the community without restraint and may even live in a separate village and simply pay a tax or tithe (*laabu albarka*)[18] to the master at the end of each harvest. . . .

According to the French anthropologist Jean–Pierre Olivier de Sardan, the status of *horso* is most accurately likened to that of a child. Like the child, the *horso* must depend on the elder males of the lineage for food and shelter. Like the child, the *horso* usually works in the collective fields of the extended family, fields controlled by noble elder males. Like the child, the *horso* may be permitted to cultivate a plot of land (*kurga*) for his own account, but only so much and so long as the noble patriarch permits.

However there are vital differences between *horso* and noble children. The noble child progresses through the various culturally determined stages of life that permit him to form a marriage alliance with a noble lineage, become a head of household, participate in political and spiritual leadership of his community, and, most important for our purposes, assume control over lineage land. The *horso*, in contrast, never progresses beyond the status of child. He spends his entire life remitting a percentage of his harvest to his master, never becomes an *alfari* (farmer) or *dotigi* (elder), and therefore never claims control of agricultural land.

Indeed, the ideology of Zarma slavery closely associates *horsos'* servile status with their landlessness. . . .

The *horso* lacks *tubu*, a word that translates to English roughly as "inheritance," but that connotes more than the mere right to receive personal and real property from deceased forbearers and encompasses the spiritual underpinnings of land tenure described above. . . . The vitality of this slavery ideology is maintained over time by the constant repetition of culturally ingrained stereotypes. . . . [I]t is vital to his family's honor that the noble patriarch provide generously for his guests, clients and dependents—including *horso*—especially in times of scarcity. . . .

NOTE

Introduction of a western notion of ownership, implying individual rights and powers rather than collective duties and liabilities might have been well intentioned but has left *horsos* without the social protection provided as a matter of customary law by the nobles. Also, focusing on individualization of property rights has produced incentives to sell land, something very functional to the interests of powerful western investors and very dysfunctional to the need of a subsistence economy. The example of Niger is not alone and points at

17. Olivier de Sardan, *supra,* note 16, at 161.

18. The term laabu albarka, which translates roughly to "land praise," describes annual post-harvest payments that borrowers of land remit to those who control it. In some cases it is nominal and largely symbolic, an acknowledgment that the person farming the land has only temporary rights in it. In other cases it looks more like a rent by which the cultivator turns over an agreed upon percentage of his harvest.

the major risks of legal intervention carried on in severe power unbalance without an understanding of the social context.

After many such examples the question arises: who benefits from this ignorance of local conditions, and can we assume that such ignorance is motivated? How are the two questions linked in contexts of severe power unbalance such as any transaction between a country such as Niger and the International Financial Institutions producing development reports? (See *supra* at 15.)

(b) Law as Culture

Professor Kelley's paper proves the challenges of ascertaining "what the law is" for purposes of comparison. Indeed the law in the books in Niger reflects only a tiny part of the complex legal organization of the country. In these cases, most often conceptual categories, such as "ownership" or "slavery" that the western observer considers "natural" carry very different actual meaning. They can be much more complex than "ours"; they are highly ritualized and formalized in society which is a string indictment of the arrogance of calling non-westernized written law "informal".

In such cases, a serious legal scholar will use cultural immersion,[1] i.e. will try to have access to first-hand information by painstaking direct observation of the way in which laws and institutions work. Knowing the local language will be necessary but often will not be sufficient. Often legal information, much sensitive from the political perspective, is not accessible to the "foreigner" just as a lot of legal knowledge in the West cannot be understood by someone who is not a lawyer by training.

In such cases the comparativist will have to refer to an informant (just like the editor of a common core book which covers many jurisdictions will have to rely to a national reporter). As anthropologists know very well, using informants is very risky. Informants might lie (sometimes even honestly) for one of the following reasons: they usually are in a position of power disparity towards the western scholar that hires them, so they might try to please him or her by guessing what his or her expectations are and simply confirm them. Alternatively informant's lying can be a form of resistance. Too often in the past westerners have pursued knowledge on people they wished to conquer.[2] The history of anthropology is full of these instances, so it is completely predictable that societies wish to maintain delicate information (such as that on slavery or on the structure of local power determined by property law) secret.

Conditions of legal pluralism, such as those prevailing in Niger often result in debates about the relative worth of different cultures. In the United States, this debate has frequently been framed in terms of the validity of "cultural defenses" in law. Unlike France, for example, which

1. *See* Vivian Grosswald Curran, Cultural Immersion, Difference and Categories in U.S. Comparative Law, 46 Am. J. Comp. Law 43 (1998).

2. *See* Ugo Mattei & Laura Nader, Plunder. When the Rule of law is Illegal, (2008).

has a very strong tendency to universalism in its legal categories and in their application (witness the head scarf controversy reported *infra* pp. 248–252), the United States is at least politically, if not always legally, more open to the existence of multiculturalism. However, even for the U.S. legal system, it is often difficult to accommodate culture in the court room.

The following excerpt visits the so called cultural defense in action.

Leti Volpp, *(Mis) Identifying Culture: Asian Women and the "Cultural Defense"*

17 Harv. Women's L.J. 57 (1994).

The "cultural defense" is a legal strategy that defendants use in attempts to excuse criminal behavior or to mitigate culpability based on a lack of requisite mens rea. Defendants may also use "cultural defenses" to present evidence relating to state of mind when arguing self defense or mistake of fact. The theory underlying the defense is that the defendant, usually a recent immigrant to the United States, acted according to the dictates of his or her "culture," and therefore deserves leniency. There is, however, no formal "cultural defense"; individual defense attorneys and judges use their discretion to present or consider cultural factors affecting the mental state or culpability of a defendant. . . .

[The case below] involves an Asian man seeking a "cultural defense" for his violence towards an Asian woman. . . .

Invisible Woman: *The People v. Dong Lu Chen*

In 1989, Brooklyn Supreme Court Justice Edward Pincus sentenced Chinese immigrant Dong Lu Chen to five years probation for using a claw hammer to smash the skull of his wife, Jian Wan Chen. The defense sought to demonstrate that the requisite state of mind was lacking by introducing evidence about Chen's cultural background. After listening to a white anthropologist "expert," Burton Pasternak, provide a "cultural defense" for Dong Lu Chen, Pincus concluded that traditional Chinese values about adultery and loss of manhood drove Chen to kill his wife.

The defense introduced most of the information about Dong Lu Chen's cultural background through Pasternak's expert testimony. Defense Attorney Stewart Orden presented Pasternak with a lengthy hypothetical designed to evoke a response about the "difference" between how an "American" and a "Mainland Chinese individual" might respond to a particular set of events. This hypothetical was in fact a history of Dong Lu Chen and provided the defense's explanation for why he killed Jian Wan Chen.

As Orden set forth in this "hypothetical," Dong Lu Chen was fifty-four years old at the time of trial. Since 1968 Dong Lu Chen believed he was hearing voices around him; doctors told him there was something wrong with his mind.

In September, 1986, the Chen family immigrated to the United States. While Dong Lu Chen worked as a dish washer in Maryland, Jian Wan Chen and the three children stayed in New York. During a visit when Jian Wan Chen refused to have sex with him and "became abusive," Dong Lu Chen became suspicious she was having an affair. He returned to Maryland, burdened with the stress of his wife's assumed infidelity.

In June, 1987, Dong Lu Chen moved to New York. On August 24 he rushed into his wife's bedroom and grabbed her breasts and vaginal area. They felt more developed to him and he took that as a sign she was having affairs. When he confronted her the next day, she said she was seeing another man. On September 7, when he again confronted her and said he wanted to have sex, "she said I won't let you hold me because I have other guys who will do this." His head felt dizzy, and he "pressed her down and asked her for how long had this been going on. She responded, for three months." Confused and dizzy, he picked something up and hit her a couple of times on the head. He passed out.

After presenting the above "facts" as part of his hypothetical, Orden asked Pasternak if this history was consistent with reactions "under normal conditions for people from Mainland China." Pasternak responded:

> Yes. Well, of course, I can't comment on the mental state of this particular person. I am not a psychiatrist. I don't know this particular person. But the events that you have described, the reactions that you have described would not be unusual at all for Chinese in that situation, for a normal Chinese in that situation. Whether this person is normal or not I have no idea.... If it was a normal person, it's not the United States, they would react very violently. They might very well have confusion. It would be very likely to be a chaotic situation. I've witnessed such situations myself.

Orden also asked Pasternak to verify that a "normal Chinese person from Mainland China" would react in a more extreme and much quicker way than an "American" to the history as given in the hypothetical. Pasternak answered:

> In general terms, I think that one could expect a Chinese to react in a much more volatile, violent way to those circumstances than someone from our own society. I think there's no doubt about it.

This initial testimony highlights some important issues. First, the distinction Orden and Pasternak draw between "American," "someone from our own society," and "Chinese" implies that "Chinese" and "American" are two utterly distinct categories: "American" does not encompass immigrant Chinese. This dichotomy rests on the lingering perception of Asians in America as somehow "foreign," as existing in "America" while not being "American." Importantly, the perspective that Chinese living in the United States are not "American" is the very basis for the assertion of the "cultural defense," on the grounds that someone from a distinctly "non-American" culture should not be judged by "American" standards.

Perceiving Chinese living in the United States as American, as part of our polis, significantly affects our responses to Dong Lu Chen. Referring to Dong Lu Chen's identity as a hyphenated identity—Asian American—

recognizes the specific histories of people of color in the United States while emphasizing the existence of a community of other Asian Americans that is best situated to evaluate and judge his actions. . . .

After dichotomizing "American" and "Chinese," Orden and Pasternak's second step in creating a "cultural defense" was to assert that a man considered "normal" in the category "Chinese" would react very differently from someone in the category "American" to the belief that his wife was having an affair. Their third step collapsed the history of a particular person with specific mental problems into the category "normal person from Mainland China." Finally, Orden's and Pasternak's description of Dong Lu Chen's reaction was predicated on the "stress theory" of violence: abuse happened because the batterer experienced stress. This is a theory much criticized by battered women's advocates who note that batterers *choose* to abuse power over their victims and that violence is not an automatic stress-induced response beyond batterers' control. As the prosecuting attorney pointed out, Chen waited from August 25, when he was allegedly informed by his wife that she was having an affair, until September 7 to confront his wife violently.

To bolster Pasternak's assertions about Dong Lu Chen's behavior, Orden asked him to testify about the particularities of family life in China. Pasternak spoke of the "extraordinary" difference between "our own" ability and the ability of "the Chinese" to control the community through social sanctions. He added to the "voices" that Dong Lu Chen heard in his head, earlier presented as a sign of mental difficulties, another set of "voices" controlling Chen. Pasternak testified that his "Chinese friends" often said "there is no wall that the wind cannot penetrate," meaning that the voices of social control "will be heard everywhere." Orden and Pasternak repeated these "voices of the community" throughout the trial to signify that in a tradition-bound society like Mainland China, social control is more strict and unchanging than in the West, and that a "Chinese individual" carries these "voices" of social control wherever he goes.

Continuing his description of Chinese familial life and values, Pasternak asserted that "casual sex, adultery, which is an even more extreme violation, and divorce" are perceived as deviations from these social mores. "In the Chinese context," adultery by a woman was considered a kind of "stain" upon the man, indicating that he had lost "the most minimal standard of control" over her. Pasternak contrasted the condemnation of adultery in China with the United States, "where we take this thing normally in the course of an event." He claimed that the Chinese woman was likely to be "thrown out" and that both parties would have difficulty remarrying.

Pasternak proceeded to delineate the ramifications of a woman's adultery for the Chinese man and Chinese woman in the context of the United States. Pasternak relied on his perception of the prevalence of "yellow fever" among white males and the desexualization of Asian men in America to assert that a Chinese "adulteress" would have no problem establishing a relationship with a white man, while the Chinese male cuckold would have no chance of finding a white woman. The Chinese male would be considered a "pariah" among Chinese women because he would be viewed as having been unable to "maintain the most minimal standard of control" within his family.

Pasternak's bizarre portrayal of divorce and adultery in China in fact had little basis in reality. When Assistant District Attorney Arthur Rigby pressed Pasternak for his sources during cross-examination, Pasternak mentioned fieldwork he did between the 1960s and 1988 (he could not remember the title of his own article), incidents he saw, such as a man chasing a woman with a cleaver, and stories he heard. He admitted he could not recall a *single instance* in which a man in China killed his wife or having ever heard about such an event, yet he suggested that this was accepted in China. Pasternak's description of "Chinese society" thus was neither substantiated by fact nor supported by his own testimony. The description was in fact his own *American* fantasy.

During his cross-examination of Pasternak, Rigby attempted to undermine Chen's "cultural defense" by deconstructing Pasternak's identification of "American," his description of Chinese as insulated from western influence and his depiction of Chinese Americans as completely nonassimilated. Rigby began his questioning by asking, "What would you consider your average American?" Pasternak responded, "I think you are looking at your average American."

With this statement Pasternak situated his own subjective position as the definition of the "average American." In other words, Pasternak defined the "average American" to be a white, professional male. By situating himself as the "average American," Pasternak exposed his subjective identification as the "average American" against whom the "foreigner," Dong Lu Chen, was to be compared. He also demonstrated his identification with masculinity. He thereby abandoned any pretensions towards "objectivity" he might have claimed as an anthropologist and revealed his personal investment in his identity as dominant anthropologist and white male, vis à vis the subordinated Chinese male and female objects of study. . . .

Although Orden attempted to point out some of the flaws inherent in Pasternak's characterizations of Chinese culture and its relationship to Jian Wan Chen's death, Justice Pincus was swayed by the "persuasiveness" of Pasternak's testimony about the "cultural" roots of Dong Lu Chen's actions. He held:

> Were this crime committed by the defendant as someone who was born and raised in America, or born elsewhere but primarily raised in America, even in the Chinese American community, the Court [sic] would have been constrained to find the defendant guilty of manslaughter in the first degree. But, this Court [sic] cannot ignore . . . the very cogent forceful testimony of Doctor Pasternak, who is, perhaps, the greatest expert in America on China and interfamilial relationships.

. . . .

But where was Jian Wan Chen in this story? The defense strategy rendered her invisible. She was most notably present in the testimony as a dead body and as a reputed "adulteress," bringing a "stain" upon her husband. Jian Wan Chen did not exist as a multi-faceted person but was instead flattened into the description "adulteress." ... The defense presented a narrative that relied on her invisibility as an Asian woman for its logical coherence. This invisibility was manifest through the absence of Jian Wan Chen as a subject, a void that was filled only by stereotypes of the sexual relationships of "Chinese women" and an image of her silent physicality.

NOTES AND QUESTIONS

(1) Is "cultural defense" a useful concept? Why (not)? Note that Professor Volpp is not arguing against the notion of cultural defense as such; in fact, in the remainder of her article she provides an example of a court that engages in a nuanced and culturally sensitive analysis of a Chinese female defendant.

(2) Are cultural defenses ever available to "average" Americans? Is it useful to think of the common law's "reasonable person" as a kind of "cultural defense" for white Anglo–Saxon Americans? And if so, are there any defenses that are *not* based on cultural notions? Instead of asking whether culture is an appropriate basis for legal defense, should we be asking *whose* culture ought to be considered legally relevant and why?

(c) Non–State Law in the United States, or Culture as Law

The existence of non-state law and various orders of "customary law" is often viewed as a condition that is typical of postcolonial states and newly constituted states. Taking legal pluralism seriously—the notion that in *every* legal system there are competing normative orders—means acknowledging that even in modern, developed states such as the U.S. there remain "other" legal orders. (For more discussion on the notion of "Legal pluralism" see *infra* Chapter 3, pp. 248–58).

Walter Otto Weyrauch & Maureen Anne Bell, *Autonomous Law–Making: The Case of the "Gypsies"*

103 *Yale L.J.* 323 (1993).

The Article discusses the highly developed internal laws of the Gypsies to illustrate how private lawmaking is central to the everyday workings of society. The Vlax Roma, the largest Gypsy group in the United States, has laws that are generations old, administered by their own courts (kris) and judges (krisnitorya). For centuries, their courts have functioned autonomously virtually without regard for those of the host country. Although these judicial gatherings are not officially recognized and, if noticed, tend to be misunderstood, they effectively impose sanctions within their own communities. . . .

The terminology used by non-Gypsies to describe the Romani people reflects hidden value judgments. The term "Gypsy" as used in scholarly writings and encyclopedias supports misconceptions that all Gypsies are migratory, roam the countryside, and are engaged in questionable or illegal activities, as exemplified by slang terms like "to gyp" (meaning to swindle) and "gyp joints." It is only natural that many Roma, therefore, view the word "Gypsy" as offensive....

Nevertheless, non-Gypsies (gaje) use the term "Gypsy" to describe all Romani people and their descendants, who are believed to have left northern India about a thousand years ago. Despite the generic label "Gypsy," the Romani people actually comprise many different groups bound together by notions of purity and pollution, and by Gypsy law....

Functions of Concepts of Impurity (*Marime*)

... Gypsy society relies heavily on distinctions between behavior that is pure (vujo) and polluted (marime). The marime concept has powerful significance for Gypsies. Marime has a dual meaning: it refers both to a state of pollution as well as to the sentence of expulsion imposed for violation of purity rules or any behavior disruptive to the Gypsy community. Pollution and rejection are thus closely associated with one another. The marime rules minimize and regulate association between Gypsy and non-Gypsy....

According to *romaniya*, or Gypsy law, the human body is both pure and impure. The waist is the equator, or dividing line. The lower body is marime because the genital areas and the feet and legs may cause pollution and defilement. The upper body is fundamentally pure and clean. Any unguarded contact between the lower and upper bodies is marime. Rituals of purification preserve the power attributed to the upper half of the body and the health of the Gypsy concerned. Only the hands may transgress the boundary line between the upper and lower parts of the body.

Notions of purity and impurity follow the life cycle. Gypsies consider children marime for six weeks after birth because the birth canal is a polluting site. After this six-week period, children enjoy a privileged status in society until puberty, when they become subject to marime taboos. Following the onset of puberty, women remain in a latent stage of impurity until they reach menopause. In old age, Gypsies believe that one regains some of the innocence of childhood....

Women may contaminate men in a number of ways. Because of menstruation and childbirth, the Gypsies consider the female genitalia impure. A severe state of marime befalls any man if a woman lifts her skirt and exposes her genitals to him ("skirt-tossing"). A woman must never walk by a seated man because her genitals would be at the same height as his face. A man may not walk under a clothesline where women's clothes are hanging. Women cover their legs when they sit down and, in mixed company, single women keep their legs together when seated....

Sexual mores are rigorously enforced and a wife's complaint of "shameful practices" is ground for annulment as well as a sentence of marime and banishment of the husband. Gypsy law considers oral sex, sodomy, and homosexuality crimes against nature and prohibits them. . . .

In spite of myths of Gypsy immorality, most Roma follow strict rules of sexual behavior. Prostitution and infidelity are unusual. . . .

Complex rules also govern tangible items considered dirty or unhygien-ic. In Romani society, food preparation is replete with ritual. A woman must serve a man from behind and guard against reaching across or in front of him. Gypsies use the dining table exclusively for eating and keep it immaculately clean . . . Gypsies guard their dishes and utensils closely and generally do not share them with their gajikane guests. . . .

Marime taboos extend to animals as well, from the edibility of certain types of meat to pet ownership. For example, dogs and cats, as opposed to horses, are considered polluted because of their unclean living habits . . . .

Socially disruptive behavior may result in legal sanctions, including a sentence of marime. . . . A marime label can be removed by the forgiveness of the offended party, the passage of time or by a Gypsy legal proceeding called kris Romani. Readmission to Gypsy society following a sentence of marime is cause for celebration. . . .

Administration of Justice

Because of the general lack of territorial boundaries, each Gypsy group can determine its own form of adjudication. . . . Each associational unit is involved in the administration of justice, beginning with the smallest, the familia, which informally settles minor disputes, and extending to the larger units with increasing formality. . . .

Gypsies have no kings in the traditional meaning of the term. Every *vitsa* has a *rom baro*, literally meaning "Big Man," commonly referred to as the chief. The chief is elected for life, and the position is not inheritable. If a chief dies or falls into disgrace, another chief is chosen to replace him. The main criteria for chiefdom are intelligence and a sense of fairness. Wealth and large physical stature are not required, although they help. Most chiefs are literate. Elders are considered particularly suited to this role because they have greater knowledge of romaniya and are believed to be less susceptible to the temptations of violating the marime code. The chief chairs the council of elders, generally the patriarchs of the extended families. He is held accountable if he himself violates Gypsy law or ignores the other chiefs. All chiefs have equal authority and decide jointly about when the larger group should migrate.

There is a female counterpart to the chief. Her power is unofficial but substantial. The Vlax call her mami, daki-dei or dadeski-dei. Other Gypsy groups use the term phuri-dae (old mother). She is the guardian of the moral code and helps decide matters involving women and children. In important affairs involving the entire kumpania, she is the spokeswoman for Gypsy women.

The tribal chiefs are not necessarily aware of all the laws; not only are the laws too numerous, but many laws have been lost because they have never been written down. The Gypsies interpret laws according to contemporary custom. Former rationales and interpretations of laws gradually may be revised as the needs of the community evolve. The exclusive reliance on oral transmission has led to a high degree of flexibility. Nevertheless, there is a shared, though not necessarily realistic, feeling that the law is clearly defined. Few ever challenge this notion. This strict adherence to the law in part accounts for the continued cohesion of the Gypsies in spite of their persecution and forced migration. Secrecy surrounds Gypsy law; unauthorized disclosure to the gaje may lead to sanctions.

Each chief handles all day-to-day conflicts within his population. When conflict emerges between Gypsies of different vitsi or kumpaniyi (singular kumpania), a divano may assemble. A divano is an informal proceeding where the chiefs of the various clans try to mediate a dispute. The parties themselves are not required to attend-and they are not technically bound by the chiefs' suggestions. But the contestants sometimes do bow to peer pressure and settle the case. Blatant disregard for the chiefs' recommendations could cost them the respect of the community. . . .

When the Roma cannot settle a controversy amicably in a divano, a kris may become necessary. In former times, the kris usually adjudicated three kinds of cases: property losses, matters of honor, and moral or religious issues, including nonobservance of marime taboos. Brawls, demands by parents for return of their married daughters, defaults in payments of debts, marime violations and personal retribution all required the attention of the kris. In the United States today, the kris calendar is largely occupied by divorce cases and economic disputes.

Divorce cases are complex. Even today, most Gypsy marriages (which may not be legal marriages according to gajikano law) are arranged, and the groom's family pays a bride price. If the marriage ends in divorce, a kris may be called to determine how much, if any, of the bride price should be returned to the groom's family.

Economic cases, on the other hand, cover such issues as who has the right to engage in fortune-telling in a specific territory. Gypsies believe that every Gypsy has the right to work. Accordingly, groups divide territory into economic units. Controversies may result when some Gypsies poach on others' turf, and then a kris is called. A first-time offender may receive a warning by the kris. Repeated violations result in a sentence of marime.

In all cases, it is the aggrieved party who must request the kris, which is then held at a neutral kumpania. If the alleged victim is old, sick, or very young, the victim's nearest male relative brings the case to the kris. If the welfare of the community demands joint action, the entire clan may be a plaintiff.

The elders of the tribes then hold a meeting and select one or more men to act as the krisnitorya (singular krisnitori), or judges. The plaintiff is allowed to choose the judge who will preside over his case, but the defendant has a right to veto that choice. Among the Roma in the United States it is not unusual for more than one judge to preside. The senior judge is surrounded by the members of the kris council, who act as associate judges. Generally, five or more men from both sides, usually the elders, form the council. In the United States, the council may have as many as twenty-five members. . . .

Witnesses may speak freely about the case, for the Gypsies believe there can be no justice without hearing the matter out to its fullest. Exaggerated claims and ornate stories referring to folktales and mythology are common. When members of the audience think the witness is not being truthful or responsive, they hiss or make jokes. In some delicate matters, such as adultery, the public and witnesses can be excluded. At a kris only Romani may be spoken, and participants discourage lapses into English by shouting and hissing. Furthermore, arguments are often presented in a special oratory that differs grammatically from ordinary Romani and re-sembles a legal jargon. When the accused testify on their own behalf they are expected to be truthful. The kris can further insure their honesty by invoking the magic power of the dead with an oath. If the witnesses must swear an oath, an altar of justice consisting of icons of the clans present is erected. In complex situations, the judge may ask for expert opinions from tribal chiefs or the elders. Nonetheless, only the judge decides guilt and punishment.

The judge declares the verdict in public to those who are present. . . . Recent developments suggest the possibility of cooperation between the Romani and American judicial systems. By March 1987, local Roma in Southern California had reportedly established eighteen territorial jurisdic-tions, each with its own judge. The idea was that these kris would receive case referrals from the California state courts of civil and domestic disputes involving only Gypsies. The local kris would then refer nonbinding recom-mendations back to the California courts. In another recent development, over two hundred Roma gathered for an advisory kris in Houston to discuss improving the rights of divorced women under the Romani legal system, to keep pace with developments in American law and to remove the incentive for Gypsy women to appeal to the American legal system for a stronger remedy. These developments could conceivably lead to the establishment of standing Romani courts within each state. But it is unclear how the American legal system would respond to such a system, since it does not recognize Romani law as binding. Gypsies, too, might find it difficult to abandon their traditional distrust of American courts. . . .

The kris imposes punishment according to the seriousness of the offense. . . . Nowadays, the kris relies primarily on such sanctions as fines, corporal punishment, and banishment. The responsibility to pay a kris-imposed fine, called glaba, falls collectively on the wrongdoer's lineage. . . .

A sentence of marime, or banishment, is today considered the most severe punishment. Marime stigmatizes all wrongdoers as polluted and justifies their expulsion from the community. No one will eat with them. If they touch an object it must be destroyed, no matter what the value. Nobody will even attempt to kill them, for fear of contamination. When they die, no one will bury them, and they will not have a funeral. They will soon be forgotten. No marriages are arranged for those stigmatized as marime, and without marriage in Gypsy society one's economic and social life is over. In other words, permanent banishment is the equivalent of social death. Such punishment is rare and used only for serious crimes such as murder.... The kris may impose a form of "community service" and require the marime Rom to work for an indefinite time without pay in order to compensate Gypsy society for violating the taboo of stealing from another Gypsy....

Peer pressure fanned by gossip and communal knowledge of the verdict tend to ensure the wrongdoer's compliance. The Gypsy community may place a curse on the guilty party to insure that he or she accepts the chosen punishment, and it appears that this practice is still effective. Only in rare cases, when the Roma have difficulty enforcing a judgment by the kris, do they turn to the gajikano penal system....

NOTE

Note the opposite uses of the comparative method that are employed in the pieces by Volpp and Bell & Weyrauch. Volpp's analysis suggests that culture is always already in the courtroom and that there are ultimately no legal categories that are *not* defined by culture. It teaches us how to view something that we tend to view as quite legal—defenses available in the courtroom—*as culture*. At the same time, Bell & Weyrauch take up something that seems at first blush to be pure culture—the life of Roma communities—and give us a way to re-interpret it *as law*. Effectively, the two readings allow us to deconstruct the law/culture dichotomy from both ends: reinterpreting what is "legal" as cultural (Volpp) and what is "cultural" as legal (Bell & Weyrauch). Many religious traditions, such as Islamic law or Jewish law, also contain legal rules that the dominant western tradition would not consider "legal," but only norms of good behavior.

Islamic Law, for example, includes rules about how to pray and what to avoid eating (see *infra* Chapter 4 at 362ff). As to sanctions determining "social death" we have seen already some at play also in the customary law of the zama people in Niger. Fascinating common core analysis of what is law could be carried out.

(d) Is There Law Everywhere?

Re-interpreting the cultural norms of a group such as the Roma in terms of law might seem to be the limiting case in adopting an expansive comparative notion of law. However, W. Michael Reisman's analysis of "lining up" stretches the notion of law even further, to the "culture" (or "law") of waiting in lines.

W. Michael Reisman, *Lining Up: The Microlegal System of Queues*

54 *U. Cin. L. Rev.* 417 (1985).

... Like most other social situations, mundane microsituations—even with only two actors and of the shortest duration—have the complex and significant normative components that are characteristic of law in its conventional usage. These components are essentially expectations, which are shared by the people in the situation. The expectations are first, the belief that there is a 'right' way of acting; second, the idea that defections from that 'right' way will lead to a shared subjectivity that the defection was 'wrong'; and third, the consensus that authorizes the injured party to respond in a way that will hurt or sanction the offending actor and at the very least reaffirm the norm that has been violated. It is appropriate to refer to these microsystems as legal systems because, for all of their informality, there is a rule and an attendant set of expectations about proper subjective and objective responses to norm violation, intimating some sort of system for enforcing the norm. Enforcement is significant, for without an expectation of enforcement, alleged microlaw is no more than the mundane 'you oughts' and 'you shoulds' of daily conversation. But enforcement need not be formal control by 'an authority.' The sanction may be embedded in the situation and may be no more than symbolic approval or disapproval....

... Like many other evanescent microlegal systems, queues involve complex normative systems with informal but rather consistently recurring decisionmaking processes for determining lawful exceptions and imposing microsanctions. Without these processes, queues could not operate; indeed, they would not be social organizations. But this does not of itself warrant a policy-oriented study of the phenomenon. In light of the indispensability of queuing to distribution in mass societies, public order requires that queues have *appropriate* microlegal systems. Like other microlegal systems, queues thus must be appraised for their contribution to public order....

A queue is a linear community, with some unique, even peculiar features. Whether the queue is spontaneous or signalled in some fashion, its common characteristic is that it has no manifest decision structure. In many organizations which lack manifest and articulated lawmaking and law-applying procedures, norms are established, modified and changed, characterizations of behavior in terms of the norms are made, and sanctions are meted out without formalities and in some cases without the participants even appreciating that they are making and applying law, indeed, that there is law....

To a rather high degree, the members of the queue community are aware of the rights and duties of group membership and understand the common interests they share with the other community members. But for the most part when queues work, those who participate in them-those who stand-have contacts only with two other sets of members-those in front of them and those behind them. These direct links between himself and those before and after police his own role behavior. These links confirm the existence of the queue and its operation and validate his role in it....

Signals to form a line may be express or implicit, from a sign indicating where the queue should be, to a person with authority indicating that a queue should form, to no more than a rope strung along a hall, or simply some distribution point such as a bus stop or a ticket window. . . .

The queue system self-enforces to the extent that its members believe that they will be better off with the queue than without it. . . . Once the queue has been formed, a number of norms come into play. The primary norm is sequential priority: one holds to one's place and respects the sequential priorities of those in front and those behind. As for those in front, one does not push ahead of them. Ambiguous situations in which two parties are abreast of each other are usually resolved by subtle maneuvering with peripheral observation but without eye contact, unless a queue norm has been violated, at which point the injured party will glare or grumble.

The norm of sequential priority imports respect for the priority sequence behind as well as forward. One does not abuse one's position, for example, by inserting friends before oneself. But every rule has its exceptions and there are a number of exceptions to this aspect of the priority principle. One is what we may call the unit rule. One's priority may be extended to include a belated husband or wife, a companion and, in some cases, two or even three other couples if they came as a group, which is popularly conceived of as a unit. In quantitative terms, there seems to be no limit on the number of children who may join a parent but presumably a busload of couples or of children would excite protest from other queuers further back in the line. If there is some grumbling from those behind, the latecomer may turn and remark to those most immediately behind, "We came here together," "We're together," "I was parking the car," and so on.

Another exception to the rule of sequential priority is the "clarification rule." You may go to the head of the line *momentarily* if it is only to seek clarification, for example, to ask whether it is the right queue or if there are special documents required. But clarification can be abused and other queuers may begin to protest if the person seeking clarification seeks to transact his queue business at the same time. Clarifiers generally demonstrate good faith if they stand away from the server and call out their question, but even then a general uneasiness is sensed in the rest of the line, for the server can always wave the clarifier over and serve him out-of-turn. . . .

An important test of a legal system is whether it can sanction violations. In some spontaneous queues, functional decisionmakers do emerge. We may refer to them as "queue stewards." Their authority derives from their ability (and sometimes their courage) to express the indignation of other queue members over the violation of a basic norm. Often the protest or expression of indignation may be quite cryptic. "This is a line," "I was here first," or, more persuasive because of the absence of self-interest, "He (she) was here first." In many cases, the mere expression of indignation and its confirmation of the normative demands of other queue members will suffice to deter the queue breaker, thereby reinforcing for everyone the basic rules of the queue. Even when it does not, the queue-breaker, while persisting in the violation, may seek to justify himself in ways that confirm the basic norm; for example, he might insist that he was there first. In such cases, where common indignation has failed to shame the queue-breaker back to conformity, the effectiveness of the application of the queue steward to a particular deviation will turn ultimately on his physical size relative to the queue-breaker, his credibility or unpredictability as a threat and perhaps the support of other proximate queue members.

NOTES AND QUESTIONS

(1) Are you persuaded by Reisman's analysis of the norms of "lining up" as *law*? The availability of social sanctions seems to be important to his definition of such norms as "legal"—but are there *any* norms that have *no* social sanctions? If so, is there any distinction between social norms in general versus legal norms? Does it matter?

(2) Reisman is in fact an international lawyer by training, yet paradoxically he has written an entire book on *microlegal* systems: *Law in Brief Encounters* (1999). On the one hand, this is perhaps surprising. On the other hand, as an international lawyer he is already accustomed to thinking about law outside the framework of the state, in the absence of direct sanctions. Indeed, international law is frequently depicted as a "primitive" or decentralized legal system.[1] Despite the differences in scale, Reisman's expertise in studying supra-national legal phenomena is undoubtedly helpful in analyzing sub-national laws as well.

(3) To what extent does Reisman's analysis reflect the specific cultural context of the United States, in its emphasis on law-abiding behavior and the value of time, for example? Would the same analysis apply in Italy, among other places—or in Little Italy or Chinatown?

Part 2.   *Contrastive Comparisons: Contrasting Foreign Solutions to Gain Perspective*

While the integrative approach to comparative law starts from a fundamental presumption of similarity[1] and considers differences as the exception rather than the rule, the contrastive approach to comparative law takes the opposite starting point. Comparative law treats legal systems as complex cultural artifacts, unique in their meaning to the point that analogies and commonalities can at most be seen as exceptional circumstances.[2] Both these approaches come in more or less extreme versions and the dispute *per se* can be quite idle.

In the rest of this chapter we will discuss some of the deep structural differences among legal systems that have to be taken into consideration

---

1. *See*, e.g., Yoram Dinstein, "International Law as a Primitive Legal System," 19 *N.Y.U. J. Int'l L. & Pol.* 1 (1986).

1. *See* Ralf Michaels, The Functional Method of Comparative Law, in Mathias Reimann & Reinhard Zimmermann, The Oxford Handbook of Comparative Law 339 (2006).

2. Some scholars consider such differences as unreconcilable. *See*, for example, Pierre Legrand, The Same and the Different in Pierre Legrand and Roderick Munday, Comparative Legal Studies: Traditions and Transitions, 240 (2003).

for any meaningful comparison. In fact, even in the case of ascertained similar results in the solution of a conflict, certain structures deeply determine the way in which the results are reached. So, for example, the fact that a given legal culture does not write its laws or has not developed a class of professional lawyers, will certainly affect the meaning of any observed similarity with another society displaying written law and a class of attorneys. Even within highly professionalized systems certain differences are rooted in the deep structure of the law. A few examples will help us understand.

1. THE LATIN NOTARY AS A STRUCTURAL DIFFERENCE

At common law, a promise not supported by sufficient consideration could be made binding by affixing a seal to the contract. This ancient rule was enforced by the New York Court of Appeals as late as 1937, to enforce an option to buy certain real and personal property for $115,000 that was gratuitously granted and open for 120 days.[1] This decision reinforced a feeling already widespread among New York lawyers—the seal was an obsolete institution and should be abolished. The legal profession remembered the words of Judge Cardozo:

> In our day, when the perfunctory initials "L.S." have replaced the heraldic devices, the law is conscious of its own absurdity when it preserves the rubric of a vanished era. Judges have made worthy, if shamefaced, efforts, while giving lip service to the rule, to riddle it with exceptions and by distinctions reduce it to a shadow. . . . The law will have cause for gratitude to the deliverer who will strike the fatal blow.[2]

In 1941, the New York Law Revision Commission[3] recommended, and the Legislature adopted, a statute reading as follows:

> Except as otherwise expressly provided by statute, the presence or absence of a seal upon a written instrument hereafter executed shall be without legal effect.[4]

In making this recommendation, the Law Revision Commission naturally examined the broader question of "whether and to what extent a person should be able to bind himself by a promise without consideration." More specifically, the Commission inquired whether it would be possible to substitute the seal for a more modern *formal* device that assures deliberation and recognition by the parties of the legal consequences of their

1. Cochran v. Taylor, 273 N.Y. 172, 7 N.E.2d 89 (1937).

2. Cardozo, The Nature of the Judicial Process 155–56 (1921).

3. Acts, Recommendation and Study Relating to the Seal and to the Enforcement of Certain Written Contracts, 1941 Report of the New York Law Revision Commission 345.

The Study supporting the Recommendation of the Commission was prepared by Professor Paul R. Hays.

4. § 342 of the former New York Civil Practice Act. The substance of this provision now appears in N.Y. Gen. Construction Law § 44–a.

transaction. A Commission's consultant[5] called attention to the rule prevailing in most civil-law countries where the requirement of consideration is unknown[6]—but promises to make a gift, i.e., promises prompted by an *animus donandi*—are void unless made before a notary.

At first blush, this civil-law rule seemed to provide a feasible substitute for the seal. Closer examination revealed, however, that a "notary" in a civil law country is drastically different than one in the United States. A civil law notary is an important official whose legal education included examinations as thorough as that of an attorney or a judge.[7] Ordinarily, the office of notary is a full-time occupation in civil-law countries, and the official conduct of the incumbent is subject to intensive supervision by the Presiding Judge of the local court, by the Department of Justice, and by the Chamber of Notaries. Normally, the notary is not salaried; his clients have to pay substantial fees fixed by a statutory tariff. Thus, the notary is a professional practitioner as well as a public official. The notary may or may not have a monopoly within the district. There is not much competition among notaries because, in most civil-law jurisdictions, the number of notarial offices (notariats) is severely limited.[8] As a result, many notaries achieve considerable affluence, and the Herr Notar or Monsieur le Notaire invariably is a person of high standing in the community.[9]

5. The consultant was the late R.B. Schlesinger first author of this casebook.

6. *See* Lorenzen, *Causa and Consideration in the Law of Contracts*, 28 Yale L.J. 621 (1919). For a penetrating comparative study of the methods by which the actionability of promises is determined in the common law and the civil law, see Gorla, Il Contratto (2 vols., 1954), reviewed by Rheinstein, 4 Am.J.Comp.L. 452 (1955); and John P. Dawson, Gifts and Promises: Continental and American Law Compared (1980). Enforceability of Promises in European Contract Law (James Gordley ed., 2001).

7. *See infra* Chapter 7 at 628, on legal education in civil-law countries.

8. *See* G. F. Margadant, *The Mexican Notariate*, 6 Cal.W.L.Rev. 218, 224 (1970).

9. For a description of French practice and comparison of the French notary with the English solicitor, *see* L. N. Brown, *The Office of the Notary in France*, 2 Int'l & Comp.L.Q. 60 (1953). For further accounts of notaries in different countries, *see* Notariats d'Europe, du Quebec et du Zaire (Léon Rancent ed., 2 vols. 1991). On some interesting recent developments, *see* Jürgen Basedow, Zwischen Amt und Wettbewerb—Perspektiven des Notariats in Europa, 55 Rabels Z. 409 (1991), with an English summary at 434–35.

For surveys tracing the history of the notarial institution from Roman to modern days, see Del Russo, *The Notary Public in the Civil Law of Italy*, 20 Geo.Wash.L.Rev. 524 (1952), and (with an emphasis on Spain and Latin America) Margadant, *supra* n. 165, at 3. See also P. A. Malavet, *Counsel for the Situation: The Latin Notary, A Historical and Comparative Model*, 19 Hastings Int'l & Comp.L.Rev. 389 (1996), which is probably the most thorough treatment of the civil-law notary to date. *See also* Ditlev Tamm, Roman Law and European Legal History (1997); Reinhard Zimmermann, Roman Law, Contemporary Law, European Law: The Civilian Tradition Today (2001); Peter Temin, Financial Intermediation in the Early Roman Empire, 64 J.Econ.Hist. 3 (2004). *See also* Ugo Mattei, Regole Sicure, Analisi Economico–Givridica Comparata per il Notariato (2006).

A version of the civil-law notariat has existed in "socialist" countries. These notaries, however, have been salaried state functionaries with nothing like the prestige of their civil-law counterparts. Problems with the notarial system have been a factor hampering expansion of the private section in former "socialist" countries moving back into the civil law orbit. In Poland, for instance, notaries have been privatized but, at least a few years ago, remained in short supply. Locating a notary was said to be difficult. Ob-

Civil-law countries ordinarily require notarial form not only for gratuitous contracts, but—*inter alia*—for nearly all transactions involving real estate, for marriage settlements and for many corporate acts such as the formation of a corporation and any amendment of its charter.[10] This form requirement is rarely satisfied by mere authentication from the parties' signatures. The document must be executed in the form of a protocol; the original is preserved forever in the notary's office and protected against any insertion or alteration.[11] The parties can obtain certified copies of the document from the notary or his successor in office.

The civil-law notary is under a duty to use the utmost care in examining the legality, and generally the validity, of the transaction. This includes diligent inquiry into the identity and legal capacity of the parties.[12] If the transaction requires approval by a third party or by a public authority, the notary must so inform the parties. Generally, the notary is bound to advise the parties as to the legal significance of the contemplated act, including the tax liabilities arising therefrom. If one of the parties to the transaction appears to be of insufficient experience, he must try to avoid overreaching. Intentional or negligent violation of any of these duties

taining the requisite notarial approval for land and housing transactions, or for the formation of a corporation, was inordinately time-consuming. Part of the problem apparently was the inexperience of notaries with complicated forms, so that articles of association had to be simplified for the notary to understand them. *See* Cheryl W. Gray et al., *The Legal Framework for Private Sector Development in a Transitional Economy: The Case of Poland*, 22 Ga.J.Int'l & Comp.L. 283, 291, 303–04 (1992).

On the role of notaries in the PRC, *see* Chen, *The Chinese Notariat: An Overlooked Cornerstone of the Legal System of China*, 35 Int'l & Comp.L.Q. 63 (1986).

10. Generally, a notarial instrument is necessary in the frequent cases in which the document is to serve as the basis for an entry in one of the public registers that are of great importance in civil-law countries, *e.g.*, the land register, the commercial register, or the matrimonial property register.

The functions of notaries in civil-law countries are not confined to the recording of transactions. As was said in Makofsky v. Cunningham, 576 F.2d 1223, 1228 (5th Cir. 1978): "Among the duties the notary public may perform in civilian legal systems are conveyancing of title, drafting of land title documents, holding of family meetings, mak-

ing of inventories, appraisements and partitions...."

Notaries in civil-law countries also perform functions which we would classify as judicial. In some of those countries, they conduct judicial sales of real property. In other civil-law jurisdictions one finds that letters testamentary and letters of administration can be issued by a notary and that the notary likewise performs other official acts necessary for the processing of a decedent's estate. As a result, in countries adhering to that system, probate matters "reach the courts only if one of the parties is dissatisfied with the notary's ruling." Estate of Chichernea, 66 Cal.2d 83, 99, 57 Cal.Rptr. 135, 424 P.2d 687 (1967).

11. In France, for example, the original is kept in the office of the notary for 125 years; thereafter it may be delivered to the national or district archives.

A notarial protocol constitutes a so-called acte authentique or öffentliche Urkunde; as such, it has special probative force. See French Civil Code, arts. 1317–1319, and German Code of Civil Procedure, secs. 415, 417, 418; see also, *infra* Chapter 8 at 757 and 760.

12. If the notary is not satisfied concerning any of these points, he must refuse his services. See, e.g., the German Beurkundungsgesetz of August 28, 1969 (BGBl I 1513), sec. 4.

may subject the notary to disciplinary proceedings and to civil liability for damages.[13]

When this comparative information concerning the status and functions of notaries had been submitted to the New York Law Revision Commission, they and their consultant realized the following: First, the requirement of a "notarial" document in a civil-law country truly assures informed deliberation to the parties entering into the transaction. In addition, the parties are prevented from acting without legal advice and are compelled to have the document embodying their transaction drawn up by a properly qualified person. Third, the requirement of notarial form protects the public by making it more difficult both for agents without proper authority and for persons lacking legal capacity to create the semblance of a valid legal transaction.

The Commission concluded adopting a notarization requirement would produce none of these beneficial effects in New York. Except for the name—a "notary public" in New York, and generally in the United States—it has little in common with the civil-law notary.[14] The *institution* of the notary, as developed in the civil-law world over the course of many centuries, was found by the Commission to have no counterpart in this country.[15] It is very difficult, if not impossible, to subject the execution of certain types of instruments to formal requirements more effective and more solemn than a simple signed writing. A comparable institution cannot be created by a mere stroke of the legislative pen. From this it followed, in the Commission's view, it would be impracticable for the New York

13. Whenever necessary, the notary performs the function of an escrow agent. Sometimes, moreover, he is responsible for collecting stamp taxes and for assisting in the collection of other taxes which become payable in connection with the transaction recorded by him. In addition to his other functions, he may thus serve as an auxiliary fiscal officer.

Under a totalitarian regime, the requirement of notarial form means in effect that the government must be informed of the transaction. See, e.g., Guins, Soviet Law and Soviet Society 110, 116, 126 (1954).

14. Concerning the qualifications and functions of notaries in the United States, *see* W. Gilmer, Anderson's Manual for Notaries Public (5th ed. 1976, and Cum. Supps.); Michael L. Closen et al., Notary Law & Practice: Cases & Materials (National Notary Ass'n 1997).

Leyser, *Notaries in Australia*, 37 Austl. L.J. 308 (1964), traces the history of notaries in England and other Commonwealth countries and compares their status with that of civil-law notaries. For a brief discussion of

the historical reasons which account for the relatively low status of notaries in common-law countries, *see* 5 Holdsworth, History of English Law 114–15 (1945).

In Louisiana and Quebec, the status of notaries seems to be somewhere between the civil-law and common-law models. *See* D. B. Burke & J. K. Fox, *The Notaire in North America: A Short Study of the Adaptation of a Civil Law Institution*, 50 Tul.L.Rev. 318, 325–32 (1976).

15. Many foreign-born residents of the United States brought up in Mexico or other civil-law countries erroneously believe any person carrying the title of "Notary" is competent to render legal advice. American notaries sometimes have fraudulently exploited this belief. *See, e.g.,* Lawscope, *Unscrupulous Notaries Spur Chicago Probe,* 68 A.B.A.J. 1357 (1982). For a statute seeking to counteract such fraudulent practices and thus taking cognizance of the essential difference between civil-law notaries and their common-law namesakes, *see* Cal.Govt.Code sec. 8219.5, as added in 1974 and amended in 1976 and 1993.

legislator to fashion a satisfactory *formal* requirement as a substitute for the seal.[16]

After seeing the problem in its true perspective, the commission decided making the requirement of consideration applicable to promises generally—making no distinction between sealed and unsealed promises. An express statutory provision recommended that certain written promise cases shall not be unenforceable because of the absence of consideration. This method of dealing with the problem was already employed by the Legislature in the cases of releases and modification agreements.[17]

> The Commission is now prepared to recommend that the requirement of consideration be dispensed with in the case of promises, in writing, expressly based upon a past consideration; in the case of assignments, in writing, of a chose in action; and in the case of an offer, in writing, which expressly states that it shall be irrevocable for a specified time. As experience demonstrates the desirability of further additions to the list of exceptions, they may be made without the necessity of revising the entire law of consideration.[18]

The New York Legislature followed these recommendations and thereby deprived the seal of its ancient effect and modernized an important segment of contract law.[19]

NOTES AND QUESTIONS

(1) In what way did the Law Revision Commission use the comparative method? By way of imitation? By way of simple contrast, i.e., pointing to a horrible example which should not be followed?[1] As a starting point for critical

---

16. The Commission pointed out that the Uniform Written Obligations Act, which was adopted only in Pennsylvania (and temporarily in Utah), cannot be regarded as providing a satisfactory modern substitute for the seal.

Concerning this question of a modern substitute for the seal (or of a functional equivalent of civil-law notarization), see also the Notes and Questions following this Illustration.

17. The Commission referred to § 33(2) of the New York Personal Property Law and § 279(1) of the Real Property Law. The substance of these provisions, which had been enacted prior to 1941, has meanwhile been transferred to N.Y. Gen. Obligations Law § 5–1103.

18. *See* Recommendation to the Legislature, in 1941 Report of the New York Law Revision Commission, *supra* note 3, at 360.

19. The statutory provisions adopted by the legislature pursuant to this recommendation of the Law Revision Commission originally were inserted into the Personal Property Law and the Real Property Law. In 1963, they were transferred to, and they now appear in, N.Y. Gen. Obligations Law § 5–1105 (written promise expressing past consideration), § 5–1107 (written assignment), and § 5–1109 (written irrevocable offer).

1. *Cf.* Eder, A Comparative Survey of Anglo–American and Latin–American Law 157 (1950): "The most valuable contribution that comparative studies can make is perhaps a negative one," in that "comparative law teaches us, by the light of costly experience in other countries, what to avoid." One might add that the costliest experience, in terms of human suffering, is that of countries living under a totalitarian regime. From that experience, we have much to learn. *See, e.g.,* People v. Barber, 289 N.Y. 378, 386, 46 N.E.2d 329, 332 (1943).

analysis of an existing rule (e.g., by showing available alternative solutions)?[2] As a means of discovering possible flaws in a proposal for reform? As an aid in understanding the social function of the rules in question and a vehicle for clarifying the historical and institutional context in which these rules must be developed and applied as part of our legal system?[3]

(2) It will hardly be denied that the New York Law Revision Commission, having taken a look at the functionally comparable civil law solution of the problem at hand, was able to view that problem with a better perspective. It should be recognized, however, that here as in other instances the lessons derived from a comparative study were of a subtle and perhaps debatable character.

Surely the Commission was on solid ground when it concluded New York, like most common-law jurisdictions, did not have a class of officials similar to the civil-law notary, and it would be difficult for the New York Legislature to create a profession comparable to the civil-law notary whose high standing is due, at least in part, to an uninterrupted professional tradition of more than two thousand years.[4] One might, however, question the Commission's assumption that for a legal system lacking the institution of a notary in the civil-law sense, it is wholly impossible to create *a fair equivalent* of a civil-law-style notarial document. For instance, under our system, it is normally the attorney who drafts legal documents and thus performs one of the most important traditional functions of the civil-law notary. Thus the question might be posed whether, e.g., a "written agreement concluded upon the advice of counsel to both parties as evidenced by counsels' signatures thereto"[5] and filed in a public

---

2. *See* Jerome Frank, *Civil Law Influences on the Common Law—Some Reflections on "Comparative" and "Contrastive" Law,* 104 U.Pa.L.Rev. 887, 914–15 (1956).

3. *Cf.* Rheinstein, *Trends in Marriage and Divorce Law of Western Countries,* 18 Law & Contemp.Probs. 3 (1953); Patterson and Schlesinger, Problems of Codification of Commercial Law, N.Y.Leg.Doc. (1955) No. 65(A), 1955 Report of the New York Law Revision Commission 86 (116); H. J. Ault & M. A. Glendon, The Importance of Comparative Law in Legal Education: United States— Goals and Methods of Legal Comparison; Law in the United States of America in Social and Technological Revolution: U.S. Reports to the IX Congress of the International Academy of Comparative Law 67 (J. N. Hazard & W. J. Wagner eds., 1974); Hugh Collins, *Methods and Aims of Comparative Contract Law,* 11 Oxford J.Legal Stud. 396 (1991).

4. This tradition pervades the whole civil-law world and, indeed, constitutes an element of cohesion among civil-law systems. In spite of differences of detail, the age-old essential elements of the notarial institution have remained common to all civil-law coun-

tries, so much so that the notarial governing bodies of those countries have been able to form an international professional organization, the Union Internationale du Notariat Latin (UINL). *See* H.H. & H. Schippel, *Lateinisches Notariat,* 5 Juristen–Jahrbuch 78 (1964–65). The UNIL has been in existence since 1948. Since 1996, it has published (partly in English) an official journal, Notarius International.

5. This type of form requirement is not a product of the authors' fancy. It has been used, for instance, in a Texas statute dealing with arbitration agreements. 1A Vernon's Tex.Rev.Civ.Stat.Ann., art. 224 (1973). For a brief discussion of this statute, with further references, *see* J. M. Perillo, *The Statute of Frauds in the Light of the Functions and Dysfunctions of Form,* 43 Fordham L.Rev. 39, 53 (1974). (Note that a 1979 amendment changed the statutory language quoted in the text, *supra*; but a similar form requirement remains in force for certain types of arbitration agreements).

Compare this to Cal.Code Civ.Proc. § 1132(b) (attorney's certificate required for cognovit note).

office would constitute the fair equivalent of a document prepared by a civil-law notary.[6] There is room for reasonable difference of opinion concerning the answer to this question. Even if the answer is in the affirmative, it is not entirely clear what role such a novel formal requirement could and should play in replacing the ancient seal. The point is raised here in order to show analyzing a problem with the comparative method provides a deeper perspective and the potential for a number of alternative solutions.

(3) Although the Law Revision Commission may have failed to consider all of the possible alternatives, there is agreement among most observers it adopted a sound and progressive solution.[7] On other occasions the Commission also made significant and successful recommendations in the light of foreign experiences that were learned through comparative studies.[8]

6. The question in the text refers to a document prepared for domestic use. Where the document is to be used in a civil-law country, existing New York law purports to give a New York notary the powers of a civil-law notary; but whether the civil-law country will recognize this to be the case depends on what function the notary has performed.

More recently, it has been proposed to create in the United States, for purposes of international transactions, particularly with Latin America, a new type of notary who would have the legal expertise necessary to satisfy civil-law notarial requirements. *See* Steward Baker & Theodore Barassi, *The International Notarial Practitioner*, 24(4) Int'l L.News 1 (ABA Sec. Int'l L. & Prac., Fall 1995).

7. It will be recalled that one of the fruits of the Commission's recommendation was a New York statute (N.Y.Gen.Obligations Law § 5–1109) making certain written offers irrevocable in spite of the absence of consideration. Subsequently, the essential features (though not all of the details) of this innovation were replicated in the famous "firm offer" provision of § 2–205 of the Uniform Commercial Code. It is possible that the latter provision was inspired by § 145 of the German Civil Code, and so furnishes another example of German influence on the UCC.

8. The most momentous task ever undertaken by the Commission was its study of the 1951–52 draft of the Uniform Commercial Code, with a view to advising the Legislature whether the Code should be adopted in New York. It was known at the time that New York's adoption or rejection of the Code might well determine its success or failure on a national scale. Thus the Commission's recommendation to the Legislature was a matter of nationwide significance. When the Commission made its historic recommendation— that, after revision of the 1951–52 draft, the Code be adopted in New York—it relied heavily on arguments derived, *inter alia*, from "the experience of foreign countries as well as American states." *See* 1956 Report of the New York Law Revision Commission, Leg.Doc. (1956) No. 65(A), at 57(67).

As the Commission's consultant, the first author of this book, Professor Schlesinger, had prepared a report on "The Uniform Commercial Code in the Light of Comparative Law". That report suggested, on the basis of the experience of code countries in the civil-law world, that adequate machinery be set up for "constant revision" of the UCC in order to keep it modern and uniform. *See* Schlesinger, *The Uniform Commercial Code in the Light of Comparative Law*, 1 Inter–Am.L.Rev. 11, 33–35 (1959). This suggestion was adopted by the Commission. *See* its 1956 Report, at 58(68). Ultimately, the suggestion led to the establishment, by the American Law Institute and the National Conference of Commissioners on Uniform State Laws, of the Permanent Editorial Board for the Uniform Commercial Code. *See* James J. White & Robert S. Summers, Uniform Commercial Code 5 (3d ed. 1988). The creation of this Board, which today is the most important American law reform agency in the field of commercial law, thus was the direct result of a comparative study undertaken on behalf of the New York Law Revision Commission.

For a recent reappraisal of this study, *see* Peter Winship, *As The World Turns: Revisiting Rudolf Schlesinger's Study of the Uniform Commercial Code "In the Light of Comparative Law"*, 29 Loyola L.Rev. 1143 (1996).

One wonders why other law reforming agencies throughout the United States so often fail to avail themselves of the advantages of the comparative method. A list of missed opportunities of this kind would be boringly long if it were compiled. The provincialism of our reformers is particularly flagrant in the area of criminal procedure.[9] There is no dearth of useful descriptions in English of the laws and practices that guide the criminal process in foreign countries.[10] But our criminal-law reformers—including the U.S. Supreme Court, which at one time assumed such a prominent reformer's role in this area—invariably refuse to benefit from the experience of other countries.[11]

(4) In the last few years, within a cultural climate particularly inclined to exaggerate the virtues of "free competition" and deregulation, the notarial profession has been put under attack by the European Commission and by other international institutions such as the World Bank. The latter has approved a variety of reports called "doing business" that, deploying the same methodology already discussed for the *Lex Mundi*, *see supra* Chapter 1 at 15, dismissed the latin notariat as an inefficient burden for a market friendly legal environment. The European Commission has commissioned the Center for European Law and Politics (ZERP) at the University of Bremen, under the leadership of Professor Christoph Shmid for a comparative legal and economic study on conveyancing services that, completed in December 2007, also concluded for the inefficiency of countries granting a monopoly to the Latin Notariat as compared to such EU countries like Great Britain or Sweden that do not employ notaries in real estate transactions.[12] The study has provoked a reaction from the Council of Notaries of the European Union (CNUE) that in a press release[13] denounced that the study "lacked the necessary technical accuracy and scientific rigour" and failed to demonstrate "the link between the level of regulation and the costs of real estate transactions." The stake of this polemic is certainly the rich real estate transactions market, a business that in the common law world is handled by banks and title insurance companies. These financial actors are attempting, through their access to international (and national) policy-makers, to expand the size of their business to jurisdictions

---

9. The attachment of lawyers to the traditions of their own system seems to be particularly strong in the area of procedure, in which legal rules have the most obvious impact on lawyering activities. In the area of substantive law, including substantive criminal law, there appears to be less reluctance to learn from foreign experience. See, e.g., H.-H. Jescheck, The Significance of Comparative Law for Criminal Law Reform, 5 Hastings Int'l & Comp.L.Rev. 1, 18 (1981).

10. For materials and references on the law of criminal procedure in civil-law countries, *see infra* Chapter 8, Sections 4 and 5 at 828.

11. What might be learned from foreign criminal procedure has been the subject of

lively controversy and will be discussed, *infra* in Chapter 8, Section 4 at 828. For Professor Schlesinger's own views, *see* Rudolf B. Schlesinger, Comparative Criminal Procedure: A Plea for Utilizing Foreign Experience, 26 Buff.L.Rev. 361 (1977), reproduced (in part) in Chapter 8, Section 4.

12. *See* Comp/2006/D3/003 "Summary of the Comparative Legal and Economic study of the EU conveyancing services market" http://ec.europa.eu/competition/sectors/professional_services/studies/csm_standalone_en.pdf.

13. CNUE, Press Release 29/1/2008 http://www.cnue-nouvelles.be/en/000/actualities/cp-zerp-29-01-08-en.pdf.

that use the Latin Notary, as a public official to regulate these transactions. The vehemence of the polemic has been attenuated by recent financial scandals and by the explosion of mortgage fraud in the U.S.[14] (a phenomenon completely absent in countries deploying the latin notary) that has produced much afterthought on the virtues of unregulated markets. Ironically, a leading U.S. financial economist has suggested as a possible remedy the adoption of Latin Notaries in the U.S.

2.   TRANSLATION: THEORETICAL AND PRACTICAL CHALLENGES DUE TO LINGUISTIC DIVERSITY

"Writers often stress the number of traps, snares, and delusions which can hinder the student of comparative law or lead him quite astray. It is impossible to enumerate them all or wholly to avoid them, even by the device of enlisting multinational teams for comparative endeavors. The best advice one can give the novice is Eichendorff's: *'Hüte dich, sei wach und munter'* (Watch out, be brave, and keep alert)." K. Zweigert & H. Kötz, An Introduction to Comparative Law 33 (Tony Weir trans., 2d rev. ed. 1992).

These perils in comparative law are largely a matter of limitations inherent in the wide-ranging nature of the academic study of comparative law: superficiality, lack of proper methodology and the possibility of getting foreign law wrong.[1] In the previous pages we have seen a number of dramatic consequences determined by basing policy on superficial comparison: from the suffering of slaves in Niger, *see supra*, at pp. 126ff, to the financial risks of getting rid of a strong professional gatekeeper such as the latin Notary, *see supra*, at pp. 145ff. Often, as we have discussed, such policies are based on recommendations from scholars (usually American or European academics) with no knowledge whatsoever of the language and of the country targeted for reform. Unfortunately, because in the law "form is substance", first hand knowledge of the language (especially of the legal language) is an unavoidable condition for serious comparative work. This is why projects such as *Lex Mundi* covering hundreds of countries should not be taken seriously.

The following sections tackle issues of language, a fundamental structural difference among legal systems.[2] While there are many theoretical issues involved, we will be more narrowly concerned with the dangers encountered when practical exigencies require transposing the rules of one legal system into language and categories used in another.

---

14. *See* Department of Justice, Federal Bureau of Investigation, Financial Crimes Report to the Public http://www.fbi.gov/publications/financial/fcs_report052005/fcs_report052005.htm#d1

1. For more on "the perils of comparative law," see Alan Watson, Legal Transplants: An Approach to Comparative Law 10–15 (2d ed. 1993). *See also* Bernhard Grossfeld, The Strength and Weakness of Comparative Law 39 (Tony Weir trans., 1990).

2. *See* the masterful discussion by Vivian Grosswald Curran, Comparative Law and Language, in Mathias Reimann & Reinhard Zimmermann, Oxford Handbook of Comparative Law, 675 (2006).

Fritz Moses, International Legal Practice
4 Fordham L. Rev. 244, 248–51 (1935).

"Words are very rascals," says Shakespeare's Clown in "Twelfth Night." ... The flavor of a sentence is apt to change or disappear in a translation; and just this flavor may change the aspect of the case....

The consequences of these difficulties can be seen in many instances....

The German, French and Italian texts of the most carefully prepared Swiss Civil Code are equally authoritative. Yet various discrepancies between the three texts have crept in and courts have had to decide for the one or the other version....

The discrepancies between the English and French texts of the Treaty of Versailles, both "authentic" according to a provision of the Treaty, have become the subject of numerous court decisions. [As an example, Dr. Moses mentions a provision of the Treaty which in the English version speaks of "*debts*," while the French text refers to "*dettes*." Though linguistically of the same origin, the two terms do not have the same meaning. Debt denotes an obligation to pay a sum certain. The French term is much broader and includes any kind of obligation, whether liquidated or not. In interpreting the Treaty, English judges apparently were not even aware of the different meaning of the French text, and limited the term "debt" to claims for a sum certain. French and Belgian judges, equally without recognizing the problem, treated unliquidated claims as "dettes."][a]

While the limelight of international court proceedings brings into strong relief the linguistic mistakes in international treaties, the errors made and misunderstandings arising in the daily intercourse of citizens of different nations are, of course, much more frequent.

There are treacherous words which sound almost alike in two different languages, but have a different meaning. The German word *eventuell*, for instance, does not mean *eventually*, but *perhaps*. The French *transaction* [may mean] *compromise*, while the French *compromis* means *arbitration clause*.[b] Interesting are the terms for *divorce* and *separation* in the various languages. The Romans used the term *divortium* in the sense of the

a. Multilingual texts of national laws as well as international treaties (and "uniform laws" adopted by several nations speaking different languages) frequently engender such difficulties. Many examples are discussed by H. Dölle, Eine Vor–Studie zur Erörterung der Problematik mehrsprachiger Gesetzes- und Vertragstexte, in Twentieth Century Comparative and Conflicts Law—Legal Essays in Honor of Hessel E. Yntema 277 (1961); and K. Lipstein, *Some Practical Comparative Law: The Interpretation of Multi–Lingual Treaties with Special Regard to the EEC Treaties*, 48 Tul.L.Rev. 907, 913–14 (1974). Rodolfo Sacco & Luca Castellani (Eds.) Les Multiples Langues du Droit Europeen Uniforme (1999).

b. Another slippery word, which in the languages and under the legal systems of the civil-law orbit sometimes has a meaning unsuspected by an English-speaking lawyer, is "director." In a foreign country, a person whose title sounds like "director," often is more nearly comparable to an officer than to a director of an American corporation. See Moses, Excerpt at 268–9; Société Internationale v. Clark, 8 F.R.D. 565 (D.D.C.1948).

American term *divorce*, but in Spain and the Latin–American countries the canonical law, opposed to a dissolution of the marriage bond, was applied directly or indirectly to matters relating to marriages, and therefore the word *divorcio* was used in the sense of separation. However, reforms of the family laws have been widespread, and the meaning of the word *divorcio* now differs among these countries, in some cases even within the countries before and after the reform. In some countries it means both divorce and separation. [In a number of countries it means only separation, and in others again it refers only to divorce.] In Germany divorce is *Scheidung* and separation *Trennung*; but in Austria these same German words have just the contrary meaning: *Trennung* corresponds to divorce or *Scheidung* in Germany and *Scheidung* to separation or *Trennung* in Germany;[c] and recently it happened here that, due to the translation of an Austrian decree as if it had been a German decree, an Austrian, although only separated from his wife, received a marriage license in New York. Translation difficulties are a prolific source of confusion in comparative law.

NOTES AND QUESTIONS

(1) Perhaps the most important terms in legal parlance are the words "law" and "right"; a search for equivalents of these terms in foreign languages and foreign legal systems, however, is considerably difficult. In many languages there is only one word for "law" and "right": Latin (ius), French (droit), Italian (diritto), Spanish (derecho) and German (Recht). To avoid ambiguity, legal writers sometimes use this one word solely in the sense of "right," and employ the term denoting a code or statute as synonymous with "law." In a code jurisdiction this usage is satisfactory for the lawyer's everyday work, but it may lead the uninitiated to the inaccurate conclusion that statutory law is the only kind of law known in those countries.[1]

Other legal writers and courts on the continent distinguish between "subjective" *ius* (right) and "objective" *ius* (law); but in the everyday use of the word *ius*, or of its modern equivalents, civilian lawyers do not always spell out whether they have the subjective or the objective ius in mind. Ye comparative lawyers beware!

In dealing with languages and legal systems of non-European origin it is even more important to take nothing for granted.[2] In an obvious sense, the modern Western notion of "rights" did not exist in China and Japan, for example, before the introduction of Western jurisprudence. There were certain-

---

c. In 1938, after Dr. Moses' article was written, Austria adopted the German terminology. See 2A Bergmann, Internationales Ehe-und Kindschaftsrecht, 32–49 (Oesterreich) (1966). But the point raised in the text still has practical significance with respect to pre-1938 decrees.

1. In order to negative this conclusion, the German Civil Code (Art. 2 of the Intro-

ductory Law) expressly provides that throughout the Code the term "Gesetz" means "any legal norm."

2. *See* J. Frank, *Civil Law Influences on the Common Law—Some Reflections on "Comparative" and "Contrastive" Law*, 104 U.Pa.L.Rev. 887, 918–19 (1956).

ly notions of duty and obligation, but not as the opposite of something called a "right" that something the modern West takes for granted.[3]

Similar observations have been made by Professor Macneil with respect to East African law:

> The essence of customary law may be that even litigation is essentially a negotiating process, the goal of which is the wise pacifying of both parties rather than the effectuating of "rights" of an injured party. The aim would therefore be to provide a satisfactory framework for future relations whether or not the "command" of the judge conforms to prior notions (if any) of general rules. And it may follow that there is a large and essential element of "unknowability" about customary law and that an attempt to make it known in the sense that non-customary law is known, is to change its character quite radically.[4]

To speak of "law" and "rights" in reference to such a system of customs surely involves the danger of inaccuracy; yet trying to explain the substance of the customary "law" without ever using those words may be difficult for one trained primarily in the common law or the civil law.

(2) A special difficulty arises with terms such as Notary or Equity that convey very different meanings in different legal traditions. There are striking differences in education and social status between a continental notary and a notary in the United States. These differences have given rise to a classification problem. Professor Nussbaum long ago stated the problem as follows: "Insofar as German provisions require the embodiment of a jural act in a notarial record ... it may become doubtful to what extent a foreign recorder is to be regarded as a 'notary.' This is so especially with respect to Anglo–American 'notaries'."[5]

In struggling with this problem, German courts and legal writers usually start with the observation that there are two kinds of documents executed with the help of a notary under German Law. One kind are "notarially authenticated" documents. These are ordinary signed writings, with respect to which the notary does no more than to authenticate the signature of one or several parties. Where German law requires merely a notarially authenticated document, it is generally recognized that such authentication can be provided by an American notary public.[6] For example, such is the case for communications addressed to the Commercial Register and when providing information concerning registrable facts.[7] Performing the authenticating function does not require any legal training, and thus it would seem the differences between a civil-law notary and an American notary public are irrelevant.

---

3. On the concept of "law" in Japanese culture, *see also* Dan Fenno Henderson, *Comparative Law in Perspective*, 1 Pac.Rim L. & Pol'y J. 1, 4–7 (1992). For a recent sophisticated discussion *see also*, Eric Feldman, The Ritual of Rights in Japan: Law, Society, and Health Policy (2000).

4. I. R. Macneil, *Research in East African Law*, 3 E.Afr.L.J. 47, 67 (1967). *See also* R. E. S. Tanner, *The Codification of Customary Law in Tanzania*, 2 E.Afr.L.J 105 (1966). This point is, of course, connected with some of the observations previously made in that part of the course in which we attempted to classify and survey legal systems. See, *supra* Chapter 3, sec. 3.

5. Nussbaum, Arthur, Deutsches Internationales Privatrecht 95 (1932).

6. *See* U. Drobnig, American–German Private International Law 381 (2d ed. 1972), and authorities there cited.

7. *See* German Commercial Code § 12.

The other kind are "Notarial Documents," i.e., protocols of what the parties declared and transacted in the notary's presence. A document of this kind is necessarily prepared and issued by the notary. The notary retains the original of such a document and issues only certified copies to the parties. Where a true notarial document is required—as in the cases of most real estate transactions, of promises to make a gift and other transactions—it is the prevailing view among German courts and legal authors that a document drawn up by an American notary public does not meet this form requirement.[8] The reason is such a document is not a notarial document as that term is understood in Germany and other civil-law countries, because of the low status of the American notary public.[9]

(3) The question discussed in the preceding paragraphs is of considerable interest to international practitioners. Their clients that own interests in German corporations or other German assets often have to execute documents that require notarial form under German law. Since the fees of a German notary can be very substantial, especially in matters involving large amount,[10] international practitioners often explore the possibility of having the transaction recorded by a non-German notary.

Example: Suppose your client X Corp., a New York corporation, owns shares of Deutsche Luftverwertungs—GmbH, a German limited responsibility company. X desires to assign these shares to its subsidiary, Y Corp., in a way Germany will recognize as valid. As the reader knows, German law requires a notarial document for such assignment (see p. 145). In what form, if at all, can such assignment be effectively executed in New York? Proper analysis discloses that this question is a composite of two sub-questions:

> (a) Would a German court, pursuant to German choice-of-law rules, have New York law govern the assignment, and on that basis dispense with the requirement of a notarial protocol?[11]

8. *See* ibid.

9. Another reason sometimes adduced is that an American notary public under American law lacks power to prepare and execute "notarial documents" within the German meaning of the term. *See ibid.* Quaere, however, whether statutes such as § 135 of the N.Y. Executive Law do not supply such power.

10. In many cases, this remains true, even though a statute of August 20, 1975 (BGBl I 2189) had the effect of reducing the "amount involved" in a number of instances. In contrast to attorneys' fees, the statutory fees of a notary are not subject to agreement.

Inga Markovits poignant account of the twilight of the East German regime includes a description of East Berliners lined up at the courthouse for the "special notaries' hours" which were arranged in order to help people avoid the higher fees that would be charged

by private West German notaries after reunification, *e.g., for certifying that an individual has formally resigned church membership and therefore is not liable to the heavy church taxes imposed by West German law on those who remain church members.* See I. Markovits, Imperfect Justice: An East–West German Diary 8 (1995).

11. A negative answer to this controversial choice-of-law question, which was left open in the Bundsgerichthof decision cited *infra* n. 10, has been suggested by some leading authors. *See* Baumbach–Hueck, GmbH Gesetz, § 2, Anno. 9 (14th ed. 1985); G. Kegel, Internationales Privatrecht 280–81 (4th ed. 1977). Thus, a German court possibly might hold that the formal validity of the assignment is governed by German law rather than by New York law, even though the assignment is executed in New York.

(b) If the requirement is not dispensed with, can it be met by notarization in New York? Is a New York notary a "Notar" within the meaning of the German statute?

Even though New York law purports to give a New York notary public all the powers of a German "notar,"[12] a German court most probably would answer these questions in the negative and would invalidate the assignment notarized in New York. Pursuant to § 17 of the Beurkundungsgesetz (Law Concerning Public Documents), a "notar" is under a duty to advise the parties concerning the legal significance and consequences of the proposed transaction. Only a law-trained person can furnish such advice, and a New York notary public thus seems unable to fill the shoes of a German "Notar."[13]

At one time, some German intermediate appellate courts went further and held even a Swiss notary, whose qualifications are similar to those of German confreres, cannot perform the functions of a German "Notar" with respect to transactions governed by German law. The reason given for these holdings was the legal training a Swiss notary received did not allow them to properly advise the parties on matters of German law.[14] These intermediate appellate court holdings were overruled by a 1981 decision of the court of last resort, wherein it held a document properly executed before a Swiss notary is a "notarial document" within the meaning of a German statute requiring such form for such a transaction.[15] The highest court emphasized, however, that it reached this result only on the ground that in training and status a Swiss notary is on a par with German colleagues. The court therefore appears to have confirmed the above-stated conclusion that an American notary public, who lacks equivalent training and status, is not a "Notar" within the meaning of German statutes requiring a notarial document.[16]

(4) Using translations, especially code translations, without resort to the original text will often lead to inaccurate results. There is one instance where a reputable translator reversed the meaning of a code provision by substituting the word "less" for the word "more."[17] Other illustrations of the maxim of *caveat lector* exist, unfortunately, in abundant numbers.[18]

Good translations are sometimes required by American Law. For example, the Foreign Sovereign Immunity Act grants jurisdiction to U.S. courts against a foreign sovereign or an instrumentality of a foreign sovereign only in exception-

---

12. *See* N.Y. Executive Law § 135.

13. For historical reasons, see *supra* p. 146 note 9.

14. For critical discussions of these holdings, see J. Kropholler, Auslandsbeurkundungen im Gesellschaftsrecht, 140 Zeitschrift für Handelsrecht 394 (1976); H. Bernstein, Erwerb und Rückerwerb von GmbH–Anteilen im deutsch-amerikanischen Rechtsverkehr, id. at 414.

15. Decision of February 16, 1981, BGHZ 80, 76, discussed by Baumbach–Hueck, *supra* note 11. The numerous subsequent comments on this decision, which led to a great outflow of notarial business from

Germany, are cited in Joachim Schervier, Beurkundung GmbH-rechlicher Vorgänge im Ausland, 45 N.J.W. 593 (1992).

16. The question of whether a German court would recognize the validity of an assignment executed in the United States was not, however, authoritatively resolved and remains somewhat controversial. See J. Schervier, *supra* note 15, at 598.

17. *See* the third edition of this book, at 399.

18. See, e.g., Capistrano, Mistakes and Inaccuracies in Fisher's Translation of the Spanish Civil Code, 9 Philippine L.J. 89, 141 (1929).

al circumstances. 28 U.S.C. §§ 1604–1607. To guarantee foreign sovereignty, mostly for reasons of "international comity", the statute requires service on a foreign sovereign to be performed in its *official language* by serving a full translation of the complaint and of the other papers served. Litigation might occur on the appropriateness of the foreign translation to convey *the meaning of the action* to the foreign sovereign. If the translation is of a poor quality, a foreign reader might not understand the actual "legal meaning" of the litigation. This can become a winning argument to be advanced by a foreign sovereign (or instrumentality) willing to avail himself of the foreign immunity only exceptionally limited by the FSIA.

Professional comparativists became particularly aware of these linguistic difficulties in recent years. A variety of international conferences have been held on multilingual law as a result, but also in part because of the tremendous pressure imposed on the legal profession by the process of European integration and because all member states are entitled to maintain their language as an official language.[19]

Sometimes translating is simply not feasible and it is better not to translate. This is particularly true for terms of art existing in one legal tradition and not in another, such as, "trust" or "corporate governance".[20] Sometimes, the only way is to create a neologism to render the term of art that one wishes to translate into another language. This is true, for example, in the case of the German famous term Rechtsgeshaft, translated into English as "Juridical act" or "juristic act" or "jural act" and in Italian as "Negozio Giuridico" all words that do not exist in plain English or Italian. Other times, a plain translation is possible and sufficient, such as for example between English judge, Spanish juez, or Italian giudice. In certain other instances it is better to briefly explain the meaning of the term in the translated text.[21]

The translator should at least have a basic knowledge of the legal system of the language he/she is translating from in order to properly translate at a scholarly level.[22] A particularly funny accident occurred in the Italian translation of the well known book "The Death of Contract" by Grant Gilmore. The idea that "the Restatement was putting American law in *black letters*" was translated into the Restatement putting American law in *forma oscura*, which means "obscure form"! Clearly the translator had no clue of the technical meaning that *black letter law* has assumed in legal English and the closest translation to "black" he found in the dictionary was "obscure".... While the translator might have rendered the inner feeling of the great realist jurisprude Grant Gilmore, who was very critical of the Restatement, the accident shows how the meaning of a phrase can be transformed by a translator lacking adequate comparative training.

---

19. See Sacco–Castellani, Les Multiples langues du Droit Européen Uniforme (1999). The International Academy of Comparative Law has been active in this field too.

20. *See* Commercial trust in European Private Law (Michele Graziadei et al. eds., 2005).

21. *See* Sacco, *Legal Formants a Dynamic Approach To Comparative Law*, 39 Am. J. Comp. Law 1, 11 (1991).

22. For a judicial acknowledgment of "the perils of converting the legal terms and concepts of one system into those of another" (citing the 4th edition of this Casebook), *see* Practical Concepts, Inc. v. Republic of Bolivia, 811 F.2d 1543, 1546 (D.C.Cir.1987).

A translation may be good enough for one purpose and not sufficiently accurate for another. Where the decision of a case hinges on the precise meaning of language used in a foreign statute or code, it may be necessary for the translator to go through at least two stages of reasoning. First, the translator must establish the literal, non-technical meaning of each term. Then he must show a different technical meaning as evidenced by cases, commentaries, textbooks or any other embodiments of foreign law. Most of the older bilingual law dictionaries do not go much beyond the first stage. Among those published during the last few decades, however, there are several which not only *translate* but also *explain* legal terms, thus constituting more useful tools.[23]

The following is a terminological note developed by the Common Core of European Private Law sub-group to handle the many translation difficulties in the domain of trust an institutions that, like the Latin notary in the common law, does not exist in the civil law tradition.

Michele Graziadei, Ugo Mattei and Lionel Smith, A Short Note on Terminology

Commercial Trusts in European Private Law
45–55 (M. Graziadei, U. Mattei & L. Smith gen. eds. 2005).

It did not seem sufficient or appropriate to provide a standard glossary of terms as an appendix to the study. Instead, a note addressing the most pressing terminological issues raised by the reports was prepared to encourage the use of a vocabulary that would be more stable and transparent....

In our experience, serious problems of terminology were mostly related to two topics. The first was the description of the various notions employed in Europe to express the relationships which exists where one person agrees that another person should act on his behalf when entering into legal relations with a third party. The second related to the problems raised by the need to name and discuss in English a number of legal transactions or institutions that are redolent of trust (*eg* "fiducia", "*Treuhand*"), but are governed by Austrian, Italian, German, Spanish law, etc. Could these transactions be described as "trusts", even though the concepts employed to analyse them had nothing or little in common with the building blocks of the law of trusts in common law jurisdictions? Could this choice be justified also in the light of the fact that in many of our cases it appeared, after all, that the proper characterisation of the relationship between the parties under English law, Irish law, Scottish law *was* "trust"?

The questionnaire was *not* designed to elicit answers that would tell readers whether "trusts" were part of the legal system covered by the national reporter or not. It was designed to know what the law on certain facts was in the various jurisdictions covered by our study. Nonetheless, it soon became apparent that on both side of the Channel several of our cases triggered responses evoking institutions redolent of the idea of "trust"

---

23. For a listing of dictionaries, *see* Szladits, Bibliography on Foreign and Comparative Law 30–33 (1953 & Supps.).

(though, to be sure, not across the entire European continent!). The Spanish "fiducia cum amigo," the German and Austrian *Treuhand* that is created for the administration of assets, the Italian *fiducia a scopo di gestione*, etc., are examples of this phenomenon.... The fact that for many purposes words like "fiducia", or "Treuhand", can be translated as "trust"—think of everyday conversations—does not mean, however, that they should be so translated in this study. Readers need to know to what legal institution the country report is referring to in each case. These expressions, therefore, will often be left untranslated, but to speak of "fiduciary contract" or of "fiduciary transfer of ownership" is not inappropriate to refer to any of those institutions. Though the English term, as such, has no settled legal meaning across Europe, it will put readers on the alert as to the context to which it belongs.

NOTE

Interestingly, in the case of *trust* we face two different but related problems. To the already complicated issue of translation, one has to add a strong structural difference. In fact the Anglo–American Trust is rooted in a fundamental institutional distinction, that between *Law* and *Equity*.

The Law/Equity distinction is absent in non common law traditions at the same deep structural level in which the notary is absent in non latin legal systems. In other words, the terms exist (just like notary in England) but do not carry the same deep institutional meaning. While, for the stated reasons, in the Trust volume of the common core a terminological discussion was in order, another group has opted for the production of a basic glossary.

Eva–Maria Kieninger and George L. Gretton, Glossary

Security Rights in Movable Property in European Private Law
150–69 (Eva–Maria Kieninger & George L. Gretton Editors, 2004).

The glossary originated from the necessity to establish some degree of terminological uniformity in the national discussions of the cases. It was felt by all contributors that for a number of key terms such as "security right," "ownership," "execution," "insolvency proceedings" etc. a standardized term (in English) should be used. Given that the approach of English law is quite different from that of the Civil Law systems—a general statement which is especially true in property law—it was thought advisable not to use standard English law terminology but to choose neutral expressions where available, such as for example "enterprise charge" instead of "floating charge." As a consequence of this approach, terms of art in English law which have not at the same time been chosen as overall standard terms appear *italicized* in the discussions of the cases, just as national terms of art in languages other than English.

The glossary which emerged from the work on the reports was first meant to be addressed only to the contributors. However, as we went along, it became apparent that the glossary was not only to be useful for the reader to know, but that knowledge of our terminological decisions would indeed be necessary for a proper understanding of the reports.

The glossary is divided into three parts. In the first column the reader will find the standardized terms used in the reports. Sometimes, related terms (which are not translated) are added in square brackets, which are not translated. For some terms it was felt that a note or definition might be helpful. These can be found in the third column. The second and more important column contains translations of the standard terms into the various languages of the legal systems under consideration. . . .

Standard term	Terms in other languages[1] in the same (final) order as the cases always separated by ";": (Order: Germany; Austria; Greece; France; Belgium; Portugal; Spain; Italy; the Netherlands; England; Ireland; Scotland; South Africa; Denmark; Sweden; Finland)	Selected Notes
Action in court	Klage; Klage; agogi; action en justice, demande en justice; action en justice, demande en justice/ vordering in rechte; acção; demanda judicial; azione, azione in giudizio; rechtsvordering; action in court; action in court; action; action; søgsmål; talan; kanne/talan.	
Ownership (of), title (to)	Eigentum; Eigentum; kyriotita; droit de propriété; propriété/eigendom; propriedade; propriedad, dominio; proprietà, titolarità; eigendom; ownership; ownership; ownership, title; ownership, title; ejendomsret; äganderätt; omistusoikeus/äganderätt.	Both terms are used, though some contributors may prefer to use "ownership" for corporeal things (tangible movables) and "title" as the broader term. The term "property" is not used in the sense of ownership, but only as a general, non-technical expression, in the sense of s.o.'s assets, whatever legal form they have.
Possession	Besitz; Besitz; nomi, katochi; possession; bezit/possession; posse; posesión; possesso, detenzione;[2] feitelijke macht, bezit, houderschap; possession; possession; possession; possession; besiddelse; besittning; hallinta/besittning.	The term does not distinguish whether A possesses for himself or for another person. It is left to the contributors to make such distinctions and to choose appropriate terms.
		The term "direct possession" is used to stress that someone (e.g. the creditor) has to have actual control of the thing, in other words, that a *constitutum possessorium* is not sufficient.

[1] Terms in different languages that are used in one jurisdiction are separated by a "/". Different terms within one language and jurisdiction are separated by a ",".

[2] These two terms are not synonyms under Italian law: the first is used to denote the exercise of a real right, the second the exercise of a personal right.

3. PROBLEMS OF COMMUNICATION AND LANGUAGE INTERPRETATION

It is increasingly common that defendants in American courts do not understand English—a phenomenon that is largely due to immigration. In such cases, knowing the defendant's foreign language attributes someone the ability to "legally" translate. The Courts Interpreters Act of 1978 was intended to stop the court from using any person as an interpreter simply because he/she spoke the language. Some observers state that "[b]efore the Act courts used janitors, family members or people who did not have the competency needed to accurately translate ... [,] but if someone's life or liberty is at stake, you want to have the most accurate translation possible."[1] The Act creates a status of and requires "certified interpreters" to be primarily used when a defendant is not proficient in English. In 2000, President Clinton passed Executive Order 13166. This Order mandated all Federal Agencies to provide meaningful access to service for people with limited English proficiency so as not to discriminate by national origin according to Title VI of the Civil Rights Act of 1964.

A recent example of the kind of problems translations can cause are found in *United States v. Hasan*, a Tenth Circuit case.[2] There, the court held the district court committed plain error in concluding the plaintiff was entitled to an interpreter under the Court Interpreters Act ("CIA") during his trial for perjury without clearly explaining why he had not been entitled to an interpreter at the grand jury hearings that formed the basis for the perjury charges.

Mr. Hassan was a native Somalian that was granted asylum in 1997. He transferred to Oklahoma, and he got a job as a School Bus driver after marrying an American woman. In 2004, a federal immigration agent questioned him regarding statements he had made during his asylum application. The FBI requested this interview for reasons that are not clear in the record. In 2005, Mr. Hassan was called two times by a grand jury that was investigating the truthfulness of statements he made during the 2004 interview. Mr. Hassan was then indicted for perjury for statements made during the grand jury proceedings themselves—not for statements made during the 1997 hearing or the 2004 interview.

---

1. Claire Conrad, Need for court interpreters on rise, The Arizona Daily Star, Dec. 10, 2007, available at http://www.azstarnet.com/sn/printDS/215521. This article also reports that at Pima County Superior Courts in 2007 there were more than 1000 open criminal cases a year requiring court appointed interpreter.

2. United States v. Hasan, 526 F.3d 653 (10th Cir. 2008).

At trial, Mr. Hassan sought an interpreter pursuant to the CIA. He also argued that he had been entitled to an interpreter at the grand jury proceedings under CIA, and the charges against him should thus be dismissed. The district court ultimately found Mr. Hassan was entitled to an interpreter at the trial, but did not consider whether he was entitled to an interpreter during the grand jury proceeding. The Tenth Circuit noted that the CIA does not distinguish between trials and grand jury proceedings, and indeed, was in part designed to avoid perjury prosecutions based on language difficulties. It thus remanded the case to the district court with instructions to explain its apparently contradictory determinations.

The appellate court attached excerpts of the grand jury transcripts. From these it seems clear that the indictments were an unusual exercise of prosecutorial discretion—given that Mr. Hassan was not a native English speaker. Count III was based on a conflict between the following exchanges:

Q: How were you hurt by being beaten?

A: Just break my teeth and I was trying to run away from them.

Q: What injuries did you receive . . .

A: There is no injury, just beating me up. There was beating up and I had some blood in my mouth. . . .

Q: Did they break any teeth?

A: No.

While the misunderstandings above might have been of a factual rather than of a legal nature it is still true that interpreters should be proficient with the language and have a grasp of the legal language to perform their job well.[3] An attorney with some training in comparative law might be in a better position to assist and prepare an interpreter for the defense of his/her client, especially in the cases in which the use of technical terms occurs.

Occasionally problems of linguistic misunderstanding or plain lack of knowledge of a common language apt to communicate happen at the highest level of the international legal profession, that of international arbitration. Recently a fascinating book has been published, by a major international arbitrator and law professor to discuss the very important legal consequences of this fact. *See* Tibor Varady, *Language and Translation in International Commercial Arbitration. From the Constitution of the Arbitral Tribunal through recognition and Enforcement Proceedings,* The Hague, Asser Press, 2006.

---

3. Constance Crooker, The Art of Legal Interpretation: A Guide for Court Interpreters, Portland State University Continuing Education Press (1996). The notion of injury, not understood by Mr. Hassan is indeed freight of factual and legal meaning variable across systems

4. CORRUPTION ANALYZED WITH CONTRASTIVE IDEOLOGY: LAW IN THE BOOKS AND LAW IN ACTION

With its undertones of moral reprobation, corruption is an emotive word. Often American lawyers are quick to see corruption in remote countries and they "contrast" it with the blessing of our own rule of law. We should be cautious using it when discussing the conditions of traditional societies in early stages of modernization.[1] The need for caution diminishes, however, as societies become modernized, and there is even less need for restraint in making value judgments when we turn to the problem of the political perversion of highly developed legal systems. The dangers of essentially contrastive approaches become real here. Excesses in contrastive attitudes, may lead the U.S. observer simply not to see at home issues and practices that would be deemed obviously corrupt if they happen abroad. Very often there is a risk of being blind to morally undesirable practices in our own so called "advanced" societies because, in a display of notable cynicism, they get legalized. Contributions to political campaigns would be an obvious example. A recent article by a leading comparative law professor has produced quite a stir when he empirically demonstrated the outcome of Louisiana Supreme Court decisions systematically favored attorneys that contributed to the justices' electoral campaigns.[2] Similarly, when policy advice of legal scholars that are beneficiaries of corporate grants is adopted, there is a thin line between corruption and more subtle and difficult to detect ways by which powerful corporate interests operate in the legal system. An interesting example can be seen at play in recent U.S. Supreme Court jurisprudence that caps punitive damages or in the decisions on the lengths of copyrights decided on exquisitely partisan lines by the same Court.[3] A balanced approach here requires awareness of the dangers of the

---

1. Legal institutions transplanted from a western legal system to a non-western environment often function in ways that appear anomalous to the western observer. In instances of this kind it is important not to use the word "corruption" when in reality we deal with a transformation caused by cultural differences. The institution of the jury furnishes an apt illustration. In our view, that institution can function only if the jurors are able to exercise independent judgment, basing their decisions exclusively (or at least principally) on the evidence and on the court's instructions. If in a given culture the tribal or family ties of the jurors are so strong as to make the exercise of such independent judgment impossible, then trial by jury "would be impractical and anomalous." King v. Morton, 520 F.2d 1140 (D.C.Cir.1975) (holding that factual findings on cultural conditions are necessary before it can be determined whether jury trials in American Samoa

are feasible). See also the same case upon remand to the District Court, King v. Andrus, 452 F.Supp. 11 (D.D.C.1977).

2. See V.V. Palmer and W. Levendis, The Louisiana Supreme Court in Question: An Empirical and Statisical Study of the Effects of Campaign Money on the Judicial Function, 82 Tul. L. Rev. 1291 (2008).

3. Exxon Shipping Co. v. Baker, 128 S.Ct. 2605 (2008) (punitive damages in a maritime tort case are not warranted in an amount greater than the amount of the compensatory damages award); *See* A. Mitchell Polinsky and Steven Shavell, Punitive Damages: An Economic Analysis, 111 Harvard Law Review 869 (1998). *See also,* Eldred v. Ashcroft, 537 U.S. 186 (2003) (Copyright Term Extension Act provisions extending copyright terms for both existing and future copyrighted works by 20 years was a rational exercise of legislative authority conferred by Copyright Clause).

contrastive comparison. The struggle against "corruption" in developing countries most often is unfortunately a justification for heavily intrusive conditional policy by the World Bank, an organization with its own morally ambiguous records.

Some American lawyers, used to regarding the United States as a model of rule of law, use strategies of "contrast" with "the other" in quite an ideological manner. The following case reflects "lack of rule of law" rhetoric at play during the Cold War.

Carl Zeiss Stiftung v. V. E. B. Carl Zeiss, Jena

United States District Court, Southern District of New York, 1968.
293 F.Supp. 892.

[The parties' dispute relates primarily to the ownership of certain exceedingly valuable U.S. trademarks, which originally belonged to the Abbe Foundation in Jena, Germany. The plaintiff, a foundation existing under German law and having its corporate domicile in West Germany, claims to be the successor, and thus to have acquired all the trademark rights, of the Abbe Foundation. The defendant, a "people-owned enterprise" incorporated in 1951 under the law of Soviet-occupied East Germany, contends that it (the defendant) is the true successor of the Abbe Foundation.

The parties' conflicting claims had given rise to litigation in many countries, including West Germany and East Germany. Some of these cases had been decided prior to the trial of the present action. The defendant relied heavily on some decisions in its favor rendered by East German courts, including a 1961 opinion of the Supreme Court of East Germany.][a]

■ MANSFIELD, DISTRICT JUDGE. . . . The opinions of the courts of East Germany prove to be of little assistance in resolving the issues before us . . . [The court points to the fact that the East German proceeding, which culminated in the 1961 opinion of the Supreme Court of East Germany, was conducted *ex parte*, and that the East German courts did not have before them much of the essential proof relied upon by the court in the present case.]

Quite aside from the fact that the decisions of the courts of East Germany were based on different factual premises, however, it must be recognized in weighing these decisions that East German courts do not speak as an independent judiciary of the type found in the United States or even in West Germany, but orient their judgment according to the wishes of the leaders of the socialist state, which are expressed through two

---

a. The East German decisions, having been rendered in a proceeding in which plaintiff received no notice and no opportunity to be heard, clearly did not have any collateral estoppel effect. It seems that defendant relied on those decisions primarily as evidence of the applicable German law.

coordinated administrative organs, the Ministry of Justice and the Office of the Attorney General. See "The Administration of Justice and the Concept of Legality in East Germany," 68 Yale L.J. 705, 707 (1959).[b] In short, even the East German Supreme Court is made responsible to the highest authorities of the state as a means of insuring "that the content of socialist law and its implementation through the courts are in harmony with the overall state administrative activity during the period of the comprehensive construction of socialism."[c] Law and Legislation in the German Democratic Republic (Comments on 1963 Decree as to Fundamental Tasks and Methods of Work of the Judiciary Organs (East Germany)). Nevertheless, to the extent that they may shed light on the legal issues before this Court, they have been considered.

Such consideration reveals the decisions of the Supreme Court of East Germany to be so completely lacking in any objectivity of approach and so thoroughly saturated with a combination of communist propaganda, diatribes against the "capitalist oriented" decisions of the West German courts, and absence of judicial restraint, that any logical analysis is obfuscated by their obvious political mission. [The court then quoted some selected morsels of propagandistic invective from the East German decisions in the Zeiss matter[d] and turned to other, more reliable evidence of the applicable German law. On the basis of that evidence, plaintiff was held to be the owner of the trademarks in question.][e]

b. The article cited by the court was by Professor Otto Kirchheimer, who was also the author of a comprehensive and instructive book titled Political Justice: The Use of Legal Procedure for Political Ends (1961).

c. Toward this purpose East German judges after being selected by the Ministry of Justice are "instructed" by it and are removable for inefficiency or unreliability arising out of policy differences. The "judge remains a simple party servant," 68 Yale L.J. 707–12, 749 (1959). [Footnote by the Court.]

d. In Zschernig v. Miller, 389 U.S. 429, 88 S.Ct. 664, at 669–71 (1968), the United States Supreme Court took certain American state court judges to task for having displayed, in some of their opinions, foreign policy attitudes relating to the cold war, and for having engaged in "judicial criticism of nations established on a more authoritarian basis than our own." Some of the state court opinions castigated by the Supreme Court were, indeed, somewhat intemperate; but they were mild and judicious compared to the venomous attacks against "capitalist" courts contained in the Zeiss decisions of the East German courts.

e. This decision of the District Court was modified (on a point not relevant here) and, as modified, affirmed, 433 F.2d 686 (2 Cir., 1970), cert. denied, 403 U.S. 905, 91 S.Ct. 2205 (1971). The District Court's findings concerning the attitudes and approach of the East German courts were left undisturbed (433 F.2d at 700–02).

For discussions tracing the history of the world-wide litigious struggle between Zeiss–West and Zeiss–East, see I. Shapiro, Zeiss v. Zeiss—The Cold War in a Microcosm, 7 Int'l Law. 235 (1973); and H. L. Bernstein, Corporate Identity in International Business: The Zeiss Controversy, 20 Am.J.Comp.L. 299 (1972). The latter article, at 305–06, points out that, as to the relative merits of the East German and West German Supreme Court decisions, the House of Lords in a 1967 decision (i.e., a decision antedating the principal case) had taken a view sharply at variance with that expressed by the American courts in the principal case. For comments on the House of Lords decision, see the opinion of the U.S. Court of Appeals, 433 F.2d at 700–02.

NOTES AND QUESTIONS

(1) Typically when lawyers speak of a "corrupt" legal system, they mean, strictly speaking, a substantial portion of governmental and especially of judicial business are disposed of in a manner that is not in accordance with the substantive and procedural rules announced in the law books. To some extent, as legal realism has taught us, some divergence between the printed word and actual practice can be observed in every legal system. This is why the distinction between law in the books and law in action is critical for any understanding of corruption.[1] But there are important differences of degree, ranging all the way from the stifling atmosphere of a Gestapo-ridden dictatorship[2] to the subconscious bias or occasional indiscretion of a judge or other official from which even a decent system is not entirely safe. Sometimes however corruption is deployed in a different sense to indicate any society whose legal system departs from the impartial ideal of the "rule of law".

(2) There are two principal channels through which, singly or in combination, corruption enters the machinery of the law: graft and political influence. The subject of graft is very interesting.[3] Studying this form of corruption presents certain difficulties, since those who are in the best position to observe it are not usually inclined to publish their observations. Still, the pervasiveness and significance of bribery in a given society can be reconstructed from a variety of sources.[4] Sociologists and anthropologists have tried to throw light on the causes and patterns of graft in various parts of the world,[5] and occasional

---

1. In studying the divergence between law in "the books" and law in action, one must keep in mind that "the books," especially when they provide reports of actual cases, often reveal important features of the law in action. But the extent to which "the books" thus reflect reality differs from country to country, because the types of "books" available under one system may be much more revealing than those found in another. *See* K. H. Neumayer, Fremdes Recht aus Büchern, fremde Rechtswirklichkeit und die funktionelle Dimension in den Methoden der Rechtsvergleichung, 34 Rabels Z. 411, 414–17 (1970). A student of the law in action will find it relatively easier to focus attention on countries where there is a great wealth of reported judicial and administrative decisions and where the published reports of such decisions thoroughly recite the underlying facts. Ibid. The reader will recall that in this respect there are significant differences not only between common-law and civil-law countries, but also among the latter. *See infra* "Case Law" in Civil–Law Jurisdictions, Chapter 6, Sections 5 and 6 at 563 and 582.

2. Concerning the Nazi regime, *see* Estate of Leefers, 127 Cal.App.2d 550, 274 P.2d 239 (1954); *In re* Krachler's Estate, 199 Or. 448, 263 P.2d 769 (1953); N. S. Marsh, Some Aspects of the German Legal System under National Socialism, 62 L.Q.Rev. 366 (1946). On the general problem of corruption of the legal order by fascist regimes, *see* A. H. Campbell, *Fascism and Legality*, 62 L.Q.Rev. 141 (1946).

3. For a fascinating, richly detailed history of legal reactions to this form of corruption, from ancient times to the present, *see* John T. Noonan, Jr., Bribes (1984).

4. *See id.* at xiv–xv.

5. *See, e.g.,* the interesting study by Simon Ottenberg, Local Government and Law in Southern Nigeria, in Traditional and Modern Legal Institutions in Asia and Africa 26 (D. C. Buxbaum, 1967), where further references, not limited to African law, can be found. *See also* for a comprehensive overview International Handbook on the Economics of Corruption (Susan Rose–Ackerman ed., 2006). For studies focused on Asia, *see also* Wayne Sandholtz and Rein Taagepera, Corruption, Culture, and Communism, 15 Int'l.Rev.Soc. 109 (2005); Tomas Larsson, Reform, corruption, and growth: Why corruption is more devastating in Russia than in China, 39 Communist & Post–Communist Stud. 265 (2006). *See also* Susan Rose–Ackerman, Corruption: A Study in Political Econo-

nuggets of relevant information can be found in the legal literature, as exemplified by the following quotation:

> A recent empirical study of Rio de Janeiro lawyers found that 80% of those interviewed customarily made grease payments to the clerks.... In some states, payment of both "speed money" and "delay money" is common. Payments to make the entire file disappear are not infrequent in some areas.[6]

International practitioners have a fairly accurate notion, based on experience and gossip, of the countries in which they can expect an impartial determination of litigated issues.[7] They will try to avoid litigation in the courts in certain geographic areas because they are almost intuitively aware of conditions such as these:

> [J]udges, police chiefs, and other local officials in Latin America are notoriously underpaid and provided with inadequate working facilities; judges in smaller cities are usually isolated from each other for months or years at a time—there are no annual conferences or conventions; and finally, their tenure may well depend on maintaining their local political contacts and friendships. Not surprisingly, then, while adequate social and economic legislation (such as labor and water laws) is not difficult to find in Latin America, in many cases it is ignored, inefficiently enforced, or implemented in a manner that unduly favors a given element of society.[8]

Experienced practitioners are also aware of the complexity of the corruption issue, especially with respect to so-called developing countries. Such

my (1978); Rose–Ackerman, Corruption and Government: Causes, Consequences, and Reform (1999); Corrupt Exchanges: Empirical Themes in the Politics and Political Economy of Corruption (Rose–Ackerman et al. eds., 2002). *See also* the following articles Rose–Ackerman, The Political Economy of Corruption, in Corruption and the Global Economy (Kimberly Ann Elliott ed., Institute for International Economics 1997); Rose–Ackerman and Silvia Colazingari, Corruption in a Paternalistic Democracy: Lessons from Italy for Latin America, 113 Pol.Sci.Q. 447 (1998); Rose–Ackerman and Jana Kuniková, Electoral Rules and Constitutional Structure as Constraints on Corruption, 35 Brit.J.Pol.Sci. 573 (2005); Daniel Lederman et al., Accountability and Corruption: Political Institutions Matter, 17 Econ. & Pol. 1 (2005); Reto Foellmi and Manuel Oechslin, Who Gains from Non–Collusive Corruption?, 82 J.Dev.Econ. 95 (2007); Thomas Fitzpatrick, A Taxonomy of Corruption, 2 Studia Universitatis Babes Bolyai 13 (2007); Seung–Hyun Lee & Kyeungrae Kenny Oh, Corruption in Asia: Pervasiveness and Arbitrariness, 24 Asia–Pac. J.Mgmt. 97 (2007); Grant Richardson, The Impact of Economic, Legal and Political Factors on Fiscal Corruption: A Cross–Country

Study, 22 Austl.Tax F. (2007); Yadong Luo and Binjie Han, Graft and Business in Emerging Economies: An Ecological Perspective, Journal of World Business, In Press, Corrected Proof (2008).

6. K. S. Rosenn, Civil Procedure in Brazil, 34 Am.J.Comp.L. 487, at 518 n.205 (1986). See also id., Brazil's Legal Culture: The Jeito Revisited, 1 Fla.Int'l L.J. 1, 36 (1984).

7. Transparency International, which was founded in 1993 to lobby in favor of measures to deter corruption in international business, now publishes an annual "Corruption Perception Index" in which countries are ranked in terms of their relative degree of official honesty and corruption. Such rankings however must be carefully handled. First because they use the slippery idea of "perceived" corruption. And secondly because they display political biases and superficiality issues similar to those encountered with by the World Bank Lex Mundi discussed in *supra* Chapter 1 at 15.

8. J. R. Thome, The Process of Land Reform in Latin America, 1968 Wis.L.Rev. 9, 20–21.

practitioners commonly believe that "in many traditional societies the use of public office or authority for private advantage and gain was often expected and in part sanctioned. The officials of the traditional Chinese bureaucracy were permitted to retain a portion of the taxes they collected, and clerks and runners were permitted numerous 'customary' fees."[9] When modern western political and legal institutions and standards are imposed on traditional societies, these traditional customs can then be qualified by Western observers as corruption.[10]

Similarly, in the principal Case, a typical aspect of "socialist legality" [see the discussion *infra* in Chapter 4 at 306] has been downgraded to propaganda and corruption by an itself biased U.S. Court of law.

(3) The U.S. Congress dealt with the world-wide phenomenon of corruption (abroad only) by enacting the Foreign Corrupt Practices Act of 1977,[11] which makes payments designed to influence the conduct of foreign officials a crime under U.S. law. In mounting this unilateral global attack on corruption, our lawmakers failed to allow for the reality that in countries where (either *de jure* or *de facto*) governmental powers can be arbitrarily exercised, the questionable payment may be the only remedy for protecting the interests of a victim threatened with arbitrary government action.[12] In certain legal systems, such payments thus may serve purposes functionally comparable to what in our system might be accomplished by judicial and other legal remedies or perhaps by special interests investing in lobbying to make a market friendly environment for business.[13]

When first enacted, the Foreign Corrupt Practices Act was widely derided as an example of American puritanism that was likely to put U.S. companies at a competitive disadvantage.[14] International sentiment has shifted in favor of the approach represented by the Foreign Corrupt Practices Act since then for a number of reasons that include the following: a rising tide of scandals in other

---

9. D. C. Buxbaum, Introduction, *supra* note 5, at 3. See also F. G. Dawson & I. L. Head, International Tribunals, National Courts and the Rights of Aliens 106 (1971) (referring to Spanish colonial policy "whereby minor officials, after purchasing their offices, were to receive their remuneration in fees from the public they were serving").

10. *See* Buxbaum, *supra* note 5. For another interesting and ambitious attempt to explain the prevalence of "corruption" in developing countries, *see* C. Clapham, Third World Politics—An Introduction 50–54 (1985).

11. Pub.L. No. 95–213, 91 Stat. 1497 (codified, as amended, at 15 U.S.C. §§ 78m, 78dd–1, & 78dd–2). *See, supra* Chapter 1, Section 7 at 52), and the references there cited. *See also* N. H. Jacoby, P. Nehemekis & R. Eells, Bribery and Extortion in World Business (1978); T. Atkeson, The Foreign Corrupt Practices Act of 1977, 12 Int'l Lawyer 703 (1978); Note, Questionable Payments by Foreign Subsidiaries: The Extraterritorial Jurisdictional Effect of the Foreign Corrupt Practices Act of 1977, 3 Hastings Int'l & Comp.L.Rev. 151 (1979).

12. *See* G. T. McLaughlin, The Criminalization of Questionable Foreign Payments by Corporations: A Comparative Legal Systems Analysis, 46 Fordham L.Rev. 1071, 1095 (1978).

13. *See ibid.*

14. For comparison with earlier European approaches to the problem, *see, e.g.,* R. J. Goebel, Professional Responsibility Issues in International Law Practice, 29 Am. J.Comp.L. 1, 28ff (1981); M. Bogdan, International Trade and the New Swedish Provisions on Corruption, 27 Am.J.Comp.L. 665 (1979); W. Fikentscher & K. Waibl, Ersatz im Ausland gezahlter Bestechungsgelder, 7 IPRax 86 (1987).

countries and at home, greater demands for public accountability, and insistence by the U.S. on a level playing-field.

(4) In the principal case the court based its conclusions regarding the realities of the East German judicial system on a study by a leading scholar in the Yale Law Journal. The use of published materials of this kind is clearly authorized by Rule 44.1 of the Federal Rules of Civil Procedure. Where no such materials are available, it may become necessary for the parties, formally or informally, to introduce expert evidence on the actual practices as well as the book law of the foreign country in question. Experience has shown, however, that evidence of "law in action" can be effectively presented only if the proponent keeps two important points in mind:

(a) The actual working of a legal and political system can be understood only if the system is viewed as a whole. Even though the case at hand seemingly may involve no more than a narrow issue of foreign substantive law, a proper evaluation of the relevant foreign sources always requires an awareness of the actualities of the legislative and judicial process in the particular country. In many situations, moreover, when a case turns on the validity and effect of a judicial or other official act of a foreign government (e.g., a criminal conviction), the true significance of the particular act to be evaluated may well escape one who is not familiar with how the system functions over-all.

(b) "Law in the books" and "law in action" are not neatly separated compartments. A knowledgeable expert will frequently be able to find, in the law books themselves, striking indications of actual corruption of a legal system. For example, Professor Kirchheimer's findings concerning the absence of judicial independence in East Germany—relied upon by the court in the principal case—were based, in large part, on statutory provisions and official pronouncements of communist functionaries in East Germany.

Occasionally, special evidentiary difficulties may be encountered in instances where the legal realities in country X are deliberately concealed. The most reprehensible techniques of totalitarian governments (and not only totalitarian ones, if one thinks about Israel), especially torture and other methods of terror, usually are practiced in secret (this became very well known also in the U.S. as part of the post-september 11, 2001 anti-terrorist measures). Some of the policies of such governments, moreover, may be so complex and shifting that even experts are unable to find tell-tale traces in published materials. In such a case, some courts may be willing, by way of judicial notice, to draw broad inferences from what is known of the general governmental system of X.[15] That failing, it becomes

---

15. *See In re* Volencki's Estate, 35 N.J.Super. 351, 114 A.2d 26 (1955), and other cases cited in Heyman, The Nonresident Alien's Right to Succession Under the "Iron Curtain Rule", 52 Nw.U.L.Rev. 221, 233–34 (1957).

Problems of this kind arise very often in deportation proceedings. By statute, the Attorney General is directed not to deport or return an alien to a particular country "if the Attorney General determines that such alien's life or freedom would be threatened in such country on account of race, religion, nationality, membership in a particular social group, or political opinion." 8 U.S.C. § 1253(h), as amended.

necessary to present evidence, or at least materials for judicial notice, concerning the specific practices in question. This may call for testimony by expert witnesses who have lived in X in the not-too-distant past, or otherwise have the requisite knowledge of actual conditions there.[16]

(5) For the practicing lawyer, exploring the law-in-action within foreign legal system, in order to contrast it with the law at home becomes necessary in a variety of contexts. The litigator is not the only type of legal practitioner needing to conduct such an exploration. Knowledge of the actual practices as well as the written law of a foreign nation may be required, for instance, in order to determine the feasibility and reliability of treaty arrangements with that nation.[17] Similarly, a study of the investment climate in a given country will have to include a thorough look at the social and institutional elements that impact the certainty and enforceability of legal rights.

When we turn to litigated matters, we find that the outcome of innumerable cases has been influenced by proof of foreign law in action. The principal case furnishes an illustration. A few further examples can be given.

(a) Suppose the government of Graustark is interested in an action pending in the United States. Witness W, a resident (and perhaps an official) of Graustark, testifies by deposition or in response written interrogatory. His testimony is favorable to the government of Graustark. In evaluating W's credibility, the court must examine whether W would have had to fear arbitrary reprisals under the conditions actually prevailing in Graustark if W testified differently.[18] The same is true if *W* comes to the U.S. and testifies in open court, but thereafter intends to return to Graustark.[19]

---

16. *See* Canadian Overseas Ores Ltd. v. Compania de Acero Del Pacifico S.A., 528 F.Supp. 1337, 1342–43 (S.D.N.Y.1982), aff'd 727 F.2d 274 (2d Cir.1984); *In re* Wells' Estate, 204 Misc. 975, 126 N.Y.S.2d 441 (Sur.Ct. N.Y.Co.1953).

17. Thorough and searching studies of foreign law have been undertaken for this exceedingly practical purpose. *See, e.g.,* H. J. Berman & P. B. Maggs, Disarmament Inspection Under Soviet Law (1967); Z. L. Zile, R. Sharlet & L. C. Love, The Soviet Legal System and Arms Inspection: A Case Study in Policy Implementation (1972), reviewed by J.N. Hazard in 72 Colum.L.Rev. 1448 (1972), and by G. Ginsburgs in 21 Am.J.Comp.L. 188 (1973).

18. *Cf.* Zwack v. Kraus Bros. & Co., 133 F.Supp. 929, 936–37 (S.D.N.Y.1955), modified on another point, and otherwise aff'd, 237 F.2d 255 (2d Cir.1956); United States v. Kungys, 571 F.Supp. 1104, 1108–33 (D.N.J.1983), rev'd on other grounds, 793 F.2d 516 (3d Cir.1986), rev'd on other grounds, 485 U.S. 759, 108 S.Ct. 1537 (1988). The district court's opinion in the latter case strongly supports the statement in the text; but the court of appeals opinion questions the district court's non-reliance on Soviet depositions, and cites a number of conflicting cases in point.

It has been suggested that W's deposition should not even be taken, and that to do so would be a waste of time, if conditions in Graustark are such that the testimony of the witness is likely to be influenced by fear. The courts, however, have granted motions for the taking of depositions and the issuance of letters rogatory regardless of possible pressure upon the witness, saying that "the evaluation of evidence must wait until it is formally produced" at the trial. *In re* De Lowe's Estate, 143 N.Y.S.2d 270 (Sur.Ct.N.Y.Co. 1955). To the same effect, *see* Bator v. Hungarian Commercial Bank of Pest, 275 App. Div. 826, 90 N.Y.S.2d 35 (1st Dept.1949); Ecco High Frequency Corp. v. Amtorg Trading Corp., 196 Misc. 405, 94 N.Y.S.2d 400 (S.Ct.N.Y.Co.1949), aff'd 276 App.Div. 827, 93 N.Y.S.2d 178 (1st Dept.; Van Voorhis, J., dissenting).

19. *See* Matter of Draganoff, 46 Misc.2d 167, 173, 259 N.Y.S.2d 20 (Sur.Ct.Westchester Co.1965).

(b) A motion for dismissal on grounds of *forum non conveniens* should be denied if the forum defendant seeks is "lacking in due process" in relation to the plaintiff.[20]

In one case where the allegedly more convenient forum was Iran, a federal District Court rejected defendant's *forum non conveniens* motion with a tone (quite arrogant to say the least) similar to that used in the principal case in front of the legal system of Eastern Germany:

> ... I have no confidence whatsoever in the plaintiff's ability to obtain justice at the hands of the courts administered by Iranian mullahs. On the contrary, I consider that if the plaintiffs returned to Iran to prosecute this claim, they would probably be shot.[21]

In another case decided by the same court,[22] a Bermuda corporation (CANOVER) sued a government-owned Chilean corporation (CAP) for payment of goods sold and delivered and for repayment of a loan. CAP moved to dismiss on *forum non conveniens* grounds, arguing that the action could more conveniently be tried in Chile where, after a US-sponsored coup in 1973, a fascist military junta was in power. In denying the motion, the court stated:[23]

> [C]ANOVER has raised serious questions about the independence of the Chilean judiciary vis a vis the military junta currently in power. Having carefully considered the views of eminent experts on both sides, a significant doubt remains whether [CANOVER] could be assured of a fair trial in the Chilean courts in view of the fact that CAP is a state owned corporation. Specifically, the expressed power of the junta to amend or rescind constitutional provisions by decree impugns the continuing independence of the judiciary regardless of the fact that it appears that the constitutional provisions relating to the independence of the judiciary are currently in force. Affidavit of Henry P. DeVries, Professor of Latin American Law at Columbia University School of Law, ¶ 5, citing Executive Decree of September 11, 1973; Executive Decree No. 128 of November 12, 1973; Executive Decree No. 527 of June 17, 1974; Executive Decree No. 788 of December 2, 1974. There is some suggestion that the junta has in fact interceded in a pending case to request reversal of an interlocutory decision where the government was not a party. Id. at n. 6. While we do not hold as a matter of fact that the Chilean judiciary is not independent of the junta or that

20. Gantuz v. Dominican S.S. Line, 22 Misc.2d 567, 198 N.Y.S.2d 421 (Sup.Ct.Bronx Co.1960). To the same effect, see Constructora Ordaz, N.V. v. Orinoco Mining Co., 262 F.Supp. 90 (D.Del.1966); Flota Maritima Browning v. The Ciudad De La Habana, 181 F.Supp. 301 (D.Md.1960).

21. Rasoulzadeh v. Associated Press, 574 F.Supp. 854, 860–61 (S.D.N.Y.1983), aff'd, 767 F.2d 908 (2d Cir.1985). See also Continental Grain Export Corp. v. Ministry of War–Etka Co., 603 F.Supp. 724, 729 (S.D.N.Y.1984), where it is pointed out that Iranian attorneys are unwilling to be retained by U.S. clients because of fear of per-

secution; and Cabiri v. Assasie–Gyimah, 921 F.Supp. 1189, 1198–99 (S.D.N.Y.1996) (adverting to the danger plaintiff would face if torture suit against deputy chief of national security were to be brought in Ghana). But cf. Mercier v. Sheraton International, Inc., 935 F.2d 419, 427 (1st Cir. 1991), where the court rejects the argument that an American *woman* could not obtain justice against a Turkish *man* in the Turkish courts.

22. Canadian Overseas Ores Ltd. v. Compania de Acero Del Pacifico S.A., 528 F.Supp. 1337 (S.D.N.Y.1982), aff'd, 727 F.2d 274 (2d Cir.1984).

23. *Id.* at 1342–43.

CANOVER could not possibly receive a fair trial there, the doubts raised are sufficiently serious to put the burden on CAP, the party asserting the appropriateness of the Chilean forum, to demonstrate its adequacy. Since we are unable to conclude from the differing views expressed by the experts that Chile would be an adequate forum, CAP has failed to carry its burden of persuasion that CANOVER's choice of forum should be disturbed. Accordingly, its motion to dismiss the complaint under the doctrine of forum non conveniens is denied.

By the same token, a contractual forum-selection clause purporting to confer exclusive jurisdiction on the courts of country X will not prevent an action in an American court if it can be shown the parties could not obtain a fair trial in the courts of X under the actual conditions prevailing in X. This has been held in a number of cases with specific reference to the post-revolutionary Islamic courts in Iran.[24]

(c) The judgment of a foreign court will not be recognized or enforced in the U.S. unless it was rendered "upon regular proceedings, after due citation or voluntary appearance ..., and under a system of jurisprudence likely to secure an impartial administration of justice...."[25] Whether the foreign court was impartial, and whether its proceedings were regular, can be determined only after examining the realities as well as the rules of its procedure.[26] This should be kept in mind, in particular, when a question arises whether effect should be given to foreign criminal judgments. Suppose D, a refugee from Graustark, was convicted of some offenses by a Graustark court.[27] Is this a "conviction" which under our immigration laws forever bars D from entering the United States?[28]

---

24. *See, e.g.*, McDonnell Douglas Corp. v. Islamic Republic of Iran, 758 F.2d 341, 345–46 (8th Cir.1985), where numerous other cases to the same effect are cited. *See also, supra* n. 13. But note that where an exclusive forum-selection clause is involved, the burden of proof may be on the party contending that the contractually chosen forum is inadequate.

25. Hilton v. Guyot, 159 U.S. 113, 202, 16 S.Ct. 139, 158 (1895) (this dictum is good law even in those jurisdictions which reject the reciprocity doctrine announced in the same case). *See* Medellin v. Dretke, 544 U.S. 660, 667, 125 S.Ct. 2088 (2005) (Ginsberg, J. Concurring) (reaffirmed the quoted language above from Hilton v. Guyot as the "long-recognized general rule"). *See* Restatement (Second) of Conflict of Laws § 98, cmt. c (1971); W. L. M. Reese, The Status in This Country of Judgments Rendered Abroad, 50 Colum.L.Rev. 783, 795–96 (1950); C. H. Peterson, Foreign Country Judgments and the Second Restatement of Conflict of Laws, 72 Colum.L.Rev. 220, 249–51 (1972).

26. Provided the foreign judgment is regular on its face, it would seem that the burden of alleging and proving any defect of the foreign proceedings is on the party opposing recognition or enforcement of such judgment. *See* Peterson, *supra* note 25. *See also* the recent discussion of this issue in Bank Melli Iran v. Pahlavi, 58 F.3d 1406, 1408–09 (9th Cir.1995), cert. denied, 516 U.S. 989, 116 S.Ct. 519 (1995) (giving summary judgment for the defendant in an action to enforce Iranian judgments against the sister of the former Shah of Iran); Bridgeway Corp. v. Citibank, 45 F. Supp. 2d 276 (S.D.N.Y. 1999) (plaintiff must establish prima facie the judgment was made in regular proceedings conducted under a system that provides impartial tribunals and procedures compatible with due process).

27. Perhaps the conviction was for an "economic crime"; perhaps it was for "tax evasion," the tax law being administered discriminatorily and as an instrument of the "class struggle." *See* the instructive German cases reported by M. M. Schoch in 55 Am. J.Int'l L. 944–97 (1961).

28. *See* R. B. Schlesinger, Comment, 2 Am.J.Comp.L. 392, 397–99 (1953).

Is it a "conviction" within the meaning of our recidivist statutes?[29] Is it a "conviction" even though there is no judicial independence in Graustark and everybody knows that the Graustark Ministry of Justice often gives telephonic instructions to criminal courts, suggesting conviction of the accused and specifying the expected sentence?[30] Would it be necessary to prove that such instructions were given in D's case, or would it suffice to prove the general practice?

(6) Even if not engaged in a legal practice, the comparatist who is faced with questions such as those suggested above cannot afford to ignore the legal realities of our world. Whatever one's purpose for studying foreign institutions, it amounts to self-deception to limit one's work to what Dean Wigmore called "the barren dissection of verbal texts."[31] The danger of such self-deception is acute. Like many of the other pitfalls in comparative law, it stems from the indiscriminate use of domestic experience in dealing with foreign problems. At home, every experienced lawyer is a "practicing anthropologist," to use an expression coined by the late Jerome Frank. By living and practicing in one's own community, a person becomes intuitively aware of the way in which legal institutions actually work;[32] but when one tries to penetrate into a foreign system, no such intuition or experience is available to serve as a guide. The comparative law student who recognizes this handicap is well on the way to overcoming it. One is better able to define one's projects realistically with this realization by asking searching questions and critically evaluating the sources from which valid answers can be obtained.

(7) Do you agree with the statement of Jerome Frank that a domestic lawyer is indeed a "practicing anthropologist"? Isn't the domestic lawyer, particularly in a legal environment such as the U.S. that often engages in ideologically

---

29. Under recidivist statutes, a former felony "conviction" in a foreign country often may lead to enhanced punishment. *See, e.g.,* California Penal Code § 668. Of course, if the former conviction is invalid, it may not be used in sentencing. United States v. Tucker, 404 U.S. 443, 92 S.Ct. 589 (1972). But what criteria should be employed in order to determine whether a foreign-country conviction (assuming it is valid under the law of the foreign country in question) must be treated as invalid by a court in the United States? It has been held that a foreign conviction is not necessarily invalidated by the foreign court's failure to grant the defendant a specific right (the right to counsel) to which he would have been entitled in an American court. *See* Houle v. United States, 493 F.2d 915 (5th Cir.1974). The opinion in that case implicitly recognizes, however, that the foreign conviction would have to be treated as invalid if the foreign system "has failed to provide a fair trial" (id. at 916). In determining whether the foreign conviction was based on a fair trial, the sentencing court will have to look at the foreign country's entire criminal process as it affected the defendant; actual practice as well as the law in the books will have to be considered. *See also,* Alex Glashausser, Note: The Treatment of Foreign Country Convictions as Predicates for Sentence Enhancement under Recidivist Statutes, 44 Duke L.J. 134 (1994).

30. *See* the principal case and the article by Professor Kirchheimer cited by the court. *Cf.* Marsh, *supra* note 2, at 374; International Commission of Jurists, Justice Enslaved: A Collection of Documents on the Abuse of Justice for Political Ends, at 126ff. (1955).

31. Wigmore, More Jottings on Comparative Legal Ideas and Institutions, 6 Tul. L.Rev. 244, 263 (1932).

32. For example, in those American jurisdictions which still adhere to the contributory negligence rule, no local lawyer will be misled by the book-learning concerning that rule. It is known that juries do not always take such learning seriously.

"contrastive" approaches with other legal cultures more at risk of developing less of a critical attitude towards his own legal system? Most often legal opinions as well as the western press convey a self congratulatory attitude of U.S. (and more generally Western) lawyers that deeply identify themselves with the rule of law. These same lawyers often contrast themselves with other systems they assume "lack" the rule of law just because they operate differently. Try to read the materials offered in the previous section as reflective of either the cold war climate (as in case of the GDR) or fears of Islamic jurisprudence (as in the Iran cases). You will then understand some of the limits of less than critical "contrastive" attitude.

Is law in action actually considered by U.S. lawyers when they approach their own legal system? All too often, U.S. criminal procedure casebooks, for example, offer pages and pages of progressive Warren Court rhetoric without discussing the "rule of law" implications of the fact that more than 95% of criminal defendant plea guilty under severe, economically unbalanced prosecutorial pressure. Together with the material here, please re-read the opinion of Justice Scalia in *Roper v. Simmons* (Chapter 1 *supra* at 57 where similarly biased "law in action" arguments are offered).

CHAPTER 3

DIFFUSION OF LAW

The discussion of a common core of legal systems in the previous chapter demonstrates some specialized methodologies that are part of the toolkit developed by comparative lawyers at work. Comparative lawyers have also been attracted to other issues traditionally important to the field and which, in turn, have generated their own methodological tools over time. In other words, comparative law is not dominated by a single canon. At the same time, certain concerns and study methods are commonly discussed in any introductory work on comparative law so that anyone who wishes to approach a legal problem from a comparative perspective can familiarize herself with a certain body of fundamental comparative legal knowledge.

This chapter introduces some of these methodological tools that are part of what has been called a "dynamic approach" to comparative law. These tools are helpful in approaching the issue of legal change and transformation in different geographical settings. The law never simply "is". It is always "becoming". As any other social institution (for example, fashion), it changes, evolves, and transforms under both endogenous and exogenous pressures. This fluidity makes it difficult to know what the law "is" at any point in time. The law does not stand still, waiting to be described, like a mineral's structure analyzed by a geologist. It is constantly changing, and indeed it is the very perspective of the observer that ultimately determines what counts as "change." In fact, the legal scholar, the judge or the practitioner, while describing the law, is participating, though most of the time imperceptibly and very incrementally, in the making of the law.

1. LEGAL SYSTEMS AS OPEN AND COMPLEX AGGREGATES OF LAWS

Domestic lawyers tend to regard each national legal system as a self-contained close aggregate of rules and principles that are valid within the borders of one jurisdiction. They are typically most familiar with legal change over time. Comparative lawyers, in contrast, have long operated on the basis of the fundamental observation that legal systems communicate with each other across space as well as time and that jurisdictional borders are extremely porous when it comes to the transfer and diffusion of ideas, including "legal" ideas. They thus have developed a special sensitivity for the spatial dimension of legal change and variations. From the comparative legal perspective, legal change is often caused by a process of legal diffusion, i.e., the spreading of legal ideas, concepts and rules across jurisdictions. Thus, comparative law merges the approach of the legal historian with that of the legal geographer. The following case from the Philippines will give a sense of the kind of complexities that the student of comparative law must handle.

In re Shoop

Supreme Court of the Philippine Islands, 1920.
41 Phil. 213.

■ ... MALCOLM, J.[a] Application has been made to this court by Max Shoop for admission to practice law in the Philippine Islands under paragraph four of the Rules for the Examination of Candidates for Admission to the Practice of Law, effective July 1, 1920. The supporting papers show that the applicant has been admitted to practice, and has practiced for more than five years, in the highest court of the State of New York.

The Rules

That portion of the rules of this court, in point, is as follows:

> "Applicants for admission who have been admitted to practice in the Supreme Court of the United States or in any circuit court of appeals or district court, therein, or in the highest court of any State or territory of the United States, which State or territory by comity confers the same privilege on attorneys admitted to practice in the Philippine Islands, and who can show by satisfactory affidavits that they have practiced at least five years in any of said courts, may, in the discretion of the court, be admitted without examination."

The above rule requires that New York State by comity confer the privilege of admission without examination under similar circumstances to attorneys admitted to practice in the Philippine Islands. The rule of the New York court permits admission without examination, in the discretion of the Appellate Division, in several cases, among which are the following:

a. Many of the questions presented by this case had been discussed, four years earlier, in an extensive article by Malcolm, Philippine Law, 11 Ill. L. Rev. 331, 387 (1916–17).

A look at the names of the judges who participated in deciding this case is not without interest. It appears that "there was a well-established policy throughout the period of American administration to maintain marginal but majority control [of the Supreme Court] by allocating five seats to Americans and four (including the Chief Justiceship) to Filipinos." A. B. Salmonte, The Philippine Supreme Court: A Study of Judicial Background Characteristics, Attitudes, and Decision–Making, in G. Schubert & D. J. Danelski, Comparative Judicial Behavior 157, 162 (1969). For an interesting discussion of the history of that policy, see *id*. The author quotes a 1909 telegram from the Governor General to the U.S. Secretary of War, reading: "Believe that the appointment of Filipinos to the Supreme Court, making the majority of that body native, would have very disastrous effect upon capital and those proposing to invest here...." *Id*.

"2. Any person admitted to practice and who has practiced five years in another country whose jurisprudence is based on the principles of the English Common Law."[b]

This court is advised informally that under this rule one member of the bar of the Philippine Islands has been admitted to practice, without examination, in the State of New York, and one member of the same bar has been refused such admission, the latter being the more recent case. The rulings of the New York court have not been brought to the attention of this court authoritatively, but assuming that reports of such rulings by the New York court are true, in view of the apparent conflict, it seems proper to enter upon the consideration of whether or not under the New York rule as it exists the principle of comity is established. It must be observed that under the rules of both jurisdictions, admission in any particular case is in the discretion of the court. Refusal to admit in any particular case is not necessarily conclusive as to the general principles established by the rules.

... What is "jurisprudence based on the principles of the English Common Law?" ...

Common Law in the United States

We must assume that the New York court, in using this phrase, considered that the jurisprudence of New York State was based upon the principles of the English Common Law. We should, therefore, consider to what extent the English Common Law principles apply to New York. In a case in 1881 we find the following:

"And the Common Law of England was the law of the colony at that date (April 19, 1775), so far as it was applicable to the circumstances of the Colonists. And it has since continued so to be, when conformable to our institutions, unless it was established by an English statute which has since been abrogated or was rejected in colonial jurisprudence, or has been abolished by our legislation." Cutting v. Cutting, 86 N.Y. 522, 529 (1881).

In Morgan v. King (30 Barber [sic], N.Y., 9), the New York court said that in adopting the English Common Law, New York adopted:

"The written law of England as a constantly improving science rather than as an art; as a system of legal logic, rather than as a code

b. For a summary of the comparable (and largely similar) rules presently in effect, see Pascual v. State Bd. of Law Examiners, 79 A.D.2d 1054, 435 N.Y.S.2d 387, 388 (3d Dep't 1981), motion for leave to appeal denied, 54 N.Y.2d 601, 442 N.Y.S.2d 1027, 425 N.E.2d 901 (1981). New York now requires, additionally, graduation from a law school substantially the equivalent of an "approved" law school in the United States. This requirement is established or denied by the Board with the aid of consultants who are experts in the law of the foreign country in question. As reported in 435 N.Y.S.2d at 388, only two Philippine law schools were at that time considered by the consultants to be the substantial equivalents of "approved" law schools. As reported in Benitez v. Clark, 1987 W.L. 14613 (E.D.Ill.1987), the Illinois Board of Bar Examiners rejected a Philippines attorney of twenty-six years' standing in 1975 "on the ground that the Philippines system of jurisprudence was not based on principles of English common law."

of rules,—that is, that the fundamental principles and modes of reasoning and the substance of the rules of the Common Law are adopted as illustrated by the reasons on which they are based, rather than the mere words in which they are expressed."[c] ...

The above statements of the New York court clearly indicate the scope of the English Common Law in that state. In most of the States, including New York, codification and statute law have come to be a very large proportion of the law of the jurisdiction, the remaining proportion being a system of case law which has its roots, to a large but not an exclusive degree, in the old English cases. In fact, present day commentators refer to American jurisprudence or Anglo–American jurisprudence as distinguished from the English Common Law.

Accordingly, in speaking of a jurisprudence which is "based on the English Common Law," for present purposes at least, it would seem proper to say that the jurisprudence of a particular jurisdiction *is based* upon the principles of that Common Law, if, as a matter of fact, its statute law and its case law to a very large extent includes the science and application of law as laid down by the old English cases, as perpetuated and modified by the American cases.

Common Law Adopted by Decision

The concept of a common law is the concept of a growing and ever-changing system of legal principles and theories, and it must be recognized that due to the modern tendency toward codification (which was the principle of the Roman and Civil Law),[d] there are no jurisdictions today with a pure English Common Law, with the exception of England itself.[e] In the United States the English Common Law is blended with American codification and remnants of the Spanish and French Civil Codes. There a legal metamorphosis has occurred similar to that which is transpiring in this jurisdiction today. Some of the western states, which were carved out of the original Louisiana territory, have adopted the Common Law by decision. [Citations.]

Louisiana has long been recognized as the one State of the Union which retained a portion of the Civil Law. In a case in 1842 in Louisiana, the court considered the question of whether a protest on a promissory note had been made within the required time. The court rejected the straight Civil Code rule, and adopted the custom of New Orleans, which was the law of the sister States, saying:

c. This is a paraphrase rather than an exact quotation of the language used by James, J., in Morgan v. King, 30 Barb. 9, 14–15 (N.Y.Sup.1858), reversed on other grounds, 35 N.Y. 454 (1866).

d. Is this statement correct in respect of classical Roman law? See note on The Code's Break With the Past, *infra* Chapter 5 at 396, notes 37 and 38.

e. Is it correct to assume that in England, "pure English common law" is in force today, or was in force at the time this opinion was written?

"The superior court of the late territory of Orleans very early held that although the laws of Spain were not abrogated by the taking possession of the country by the United States, yet from that event the commercial law of the Union became the commercial law of New Orleans; and this court has frequently recognized the correctness of these early decisions, principally in bills of exchange, promissory notes and insurance." Wagner v. Kenner, 2 Rob. [La.], 120.[f] . . .

Louisiana, by statute, adopted certain common law rules, and with reference to these the court said, in State v. McCoy (8 Rob. [La.], 545):

"We concur with the counsel in believing that the legislature in adopting the Common Law rules of proceeding, method of trial, etc., adopted the system as it existed in 1805, modified, explained and perfected by statutory enactment, so far as those enactments are not found to be inconsistent with the peculiar character and genius of our government and institutions."

From this brief survey of the extent of the English Common Law basis in the States, we may conclude—(1) that the New York Court in referring to a jurisdiction whose jurisprudence is based on the English Common Law, uses the phrase in a general sense; and (2) that such Common Law may become the basis of the jurisprudence by decision of the courts where practical considerations and the effect of sovereignty gives ground for such a decision. If, in the Philippine Islands, a comparatively young jurisdiction, English Common Law principles as embodied in Anglo–American jurisprudence are used and applied by the courts to the extent that such Common Law principles are not in conflict with the local written laws, customs, and institutions as modified by the change of sovereignty and subsequent legislation, and there is no other foreign case law system used to any substantial extent, then it is proper to say in the sense of the New York rule that the "jurisprudence" of the Philippine Islands is based on the English Common Law.

In the Philippine Islands

The extent of the English or the Anglo–American Common Law here has not been definitely decided by this court. But when the subject has been referred to by this court there has been a striking similarity to the quotations from the American decisions above cited with reference to the English Common Law.

In Alzua and Arnalot v. Johnson, 21 Phil., 308, this court, in passing upon an objection of counsel, that while a certain rule was universally recognized and applied in the courts of England and the United States, it was not the law in the Philippine Islands, said:

f. The Custom (*coutume*) of Paris was in effect in French Louisiana until it was replaced by the law of Castile and of the Indies in 1769. There was no such thing as the "custom" (*coutume*) of New Orleans properly speaking. Presumably, the reference is to commercial custom prevailing in New Orleans under United States rule. See R. H. Kilbourne, Jr., Louisiana Commercial Law: The Antebellum Period (1980).

"To this we answer that while it is true that the body of the Common Law as known to Anglo–American jurisprudence is not in force in these Islands, 'nor are the doctrines derived therefrom binding upon our courts, save only in so far as they are founded on sound principles applicable to local conditions, and are not in conflict with existing law' (U.S. v. Cuna, 12 Phil. 241); nevertheless many of the rules, principles, and doctrines of the Common Law have, to all intents and purposes, been imported into this jurisdiction, as a result of the enactment of new laws and the organization and establishment of new institutions by the Congress of the United States or under its authority; for it will be found that many of these laws can only be construed and applied with the aid of the Common Law from which they are derived, and that to breathe the breath of life into many of the institutions introduced in these Islands under American sovereignty recourse must be had to the rules, principles, and doctrines of the Common Law under whose protecting aegis the prototypes of these institutions had their birth." . . .

"And it is safe to say that in every volume of the Philippine Reports numbers of cases might be cited wherein recourse has been had to the rules, principles and doctrines of the Common Law in ascertaining the true meaning and scope of the legislation enacted in and for the Philippine Islands since they passed under American sovereignty." Pp. 331, 333.

And later in speaking of the judicial system of the Philippine Islands (page 333):

"The spirit with which it is informed, and indeed its very language and terminology would be unintelligible without some knowledge of the judicial system of England and the United States. Its manifest purpose and object was to replace the old judicial system, with its incidents and traditions drawn from Spanish sources, with a new system modelled in all its essential characteristics upon the judicial systems of the United States. It cannot be doubted, therefore, that any incident of the former system which conflicts with the essential principles and settled doctrines on which the new system rests must be held to be abrogated by the law organizing the new system."

In U.S. v. De Guzman, 30 Phil. 416, the court spoke as follows:

"We have frequently held that, for the proper construction and application of the terms and provisions of legislative enactments which have been borrowed from or modelled upon Anglo–American precedents, it is proper and ofttimes essential to review the legislative history of such enactments and to find an authoritative guide for their interpretation and application in the decisions of American and English courts of last resort construing and applying similar legislation in those countries. . . ."

In U.S. v. Abiog and Abiog, 37 Phil. 137, this court made this further statement on the subject:

"... What we really have, if we were not too modest to claim it, is a Philippine Common Law influenced by the English and American Common Law, the *derecho comun* of Spain and the customary law of the Islands and builded on a case law of precedents. Into this Philippine Common Law, we can properly refuse to take a rule which would estop other courses of reasoning and which, because of a lack of legal ingenuity would permit men guilty of homicide to escape on a technicality."

At this juncture, three years after the last quoted comment, the influence of English and American jurisprudence can be emphasized even more strongly. A survey of recent cases in the Philippine Reports, and particularly those of the last few years, shows an increasing reliance upon English and American authorities in the formation of what may be termed a Philippine Common Law, as supplemental to the statute law of this jurisdiction.[g] An analysis will show that a great preponderance of the jurisprudence of this jurisdiction is based upon Anglo–American case law precedents—exclusively in applying those statutory laws which have been enacted since the change of sovereignty and which conform more or less to American statutes, and—to a large extent in applying and expanding the remnants of the Spanish codes and written laws.

Philippine Statute Law

Introductory to analyzing what Spanish written laws remain in force to-day, we will consider in a general way those Spanish laws which were in force at the time of the change of sovereignty.

Spanish law became highly codified during the nineteenth century. All of the laws of Spain were, however, not made applicable to the Philippine Islands: only those were effective here which were extended by royal decree. The chief codes of Spain made effective in the Philippines were as follows:

Penal Code 1887
Code of Commerce 1888
Ley Provisional, Code of Criminal Procedure, and Code of Civil
    Procedure 1888
Civil Code . . . . 1889[h]
    (Except portion relating to marriage, thus reviving a portion of
    Marriage Law of 1870)
Marriage Law 1870
Mortgage Law 1889
Railway Laws . . . . 1875 and 1877
Laws of Waters 1866

In addition to these there were certain special laws having limited application: Las Siete Partidas; Las Leyes de Toro; Leyes de las Indias; La

g. Concerning the approach to this problem in Puerto Rico, see *infra* note r.

h. On the history of the Spanish Civil Code, and its roots in the Code Napoleon, see H. W. Baade, Marriage Contracts in French and Spanish Louisiana: A Study in "Notarial" Jurisprudence, 53 Tulane L. Rev. 3, 90–91 (1978).

Novisima Recopilacion; Mining Law; Notarial Law; Spanish Military Code, and the Copyright Law.[i]

The foregoing were written laws which, by change of sovereignty, acquired the force of statute law in the Philippine Islands. There was no properly called Common Law or Case Law of Spain to accompany and amplify these statutes, although there were, of course, the customs of the people of the Islands, which constituted, in a sense, unwritten law. Spanish jurisprudence does not recognize the principle of *stare decisis*; consequently, there could be no Common Law in any sense analogous to the English or American Common Law.[j] Article 6 of the Civil Code provides:

> "When there is no law exactly applicable to the point in controversy, the customs of the place shall be observed, and in the absence thereof, the general principles of law."[k]

In order to determine the general principles of law "judicial decisions cannot be resorted to". (2 Derecho Civil of Sanchez Roman, pp. 79–81; 1 Manresa, p. 80.)[l] A lower court of Spain is at liberty to disregard the decisions of a higher court. This is the general continental rule. (Holland's Jurisprudence, 11th Ed., pp. 68–70.)[m]

> "The Partidas is still the basis of Spanish Common Law, for the more recent compilations are chiefly founded on it and cases which cannot be decided either by these compilations or by the local *fueros* [customary laws] must be decided by the provisions of the Partidas." (IV Dunham, History of Spain, p. 109).[n]

i. As to these sources and their hierarchical relationship (*prelación*), see *infra* note n; Chapter 4, Section 6 at 348 (Law of Castile and the Indies).

j. Pre-codification Castilian law, which supplies most of the substance of the Spanish Civil Code of 1889, is (and was) commonly referred to as *derecho común*. See the terminology in U.S. v. Abiog and Abiog, 37 Phil. 137, quoted in the principal case, *supra*.

k. The new Preliminary Title of the Spanish Civil Code, enacted in 1974, replaced article 6 with a new (but essentially similar) authoritative listing of the sources of Spanish civil law. See translation and discussion *infra*, Chapter 6, Section 2 at 481ff.

l. This is a correct quotation from a respected and influential treatise; but the question has long been highly controversial among legal writers in Spain. See Brown, The Sources of Spanish Civil Law, 5 Int'l & Comp. L. Q. 364, 367–72 (1956).

m. The last two sentences in the text illustrate the danger of over-generalization which is ever-present in comparative law. In many continental countries, such as Germany and France, a lower court is *in theory* free to disregard prior decisions of higher courts, even though in practice the lower courts ordinarily hesitate to invite a reversal by exercising this freedom. So far as Spain is concerned, however, the statement in the text was not even theoretically correct. Article 1692 of the Spanish Code of Civil Procedure then provided that an appeal to the Supreme Court may be based on the lower court's violation of "a law" (written law) or of a *doctrina legal*. The latter term (now changed to *jurisprudencia*) has been defined by the Supreme Court as meaning a doctrine which has been followed and applied by that Court in more than one decision. The question of the extent to which the notions of "general principles of law" and of "*doctrina legal*" overlap and perhaps conflict, has given rise to fascinating academic controversies. Article 1(6) of the Spanish Civil Code now provides that *jurisprudencia* "complements" the legal system.

n. Does this statement indicate that (in the absence of an applicable *doctrina legal*) the Siete Partidas, promulgated by Alfonso X of Castile and Leon in 1265, must be looked to today as one of the important repositories

The Partidas is a code law and cannot in any proper sense be considered as Common Law. It specifically provided, however, for recourse to customs when the written law was silent. The customs to which resort is to be had are the customs of the particular place where the case arises;[o] the customs of one locality in Spain having no effect on the application of law in another place. 1 Manresa, pp. 77, 79; Civil Code, art. 6; Code of Commerce, art. 2. Accordingly, the Spanish customary law could not have any force here. The law or custom cannot be migratory. Manresa does not define what is meant by "general principles of law," but from his discussion under article 6 of the Civil Code it appears how far from a case law system is Spanish jurisprudence. He formulates the rule that courts are governed: first, by written law; second, by the customs of the place; third, by judicial decision; and fourth, by general principles of law. In fact, in urging that resort to judicial decisions should come before resort to general principles of law, Manresa rather implies that the practice of the courts is the contrary.[p]

English Common Law is quite a different conception. While it grew out of the early Anglo–Saxon customs, it came in time to be a case law of

of the "general principles of law"? *Cf.* Geigel v. Mariani, 85 P.R.R. 43, 50 (1962), where a provision of the Siete Partidas was relied upon to answer a question left open in the Code.

In the hierarchy (*prelación*) of sources of pre-codification Spanish ultramarine law, the Siete Partidas ranged last (see *infra* articulated in the principle case). Nevertheless, this text (a legal manual in the form of a code) had a tremendous influence on the development of the law not only in Spain, but also throughout Spanish–America, including the Southwestern part of the United States (*infra* Chapter 3, sec. 2). For an English translation see Scott, Lobingier & Vance, Las Siete Partidas (Commerce Clearing House, 1931). A summary of the contents of the Partidas, with a brief but masterful historical introduction by the late Max Radin, is to be found in Nichols, Las Siete Partidas, 20 Calif.L.Rev. 260 (1932).

o. In Spain, the victory of central Government and unified law over regional customs and privileges was less complete than in Germany and especially in France. Arts. 12 and 13 of the Spanish Civil Code preserve the local laws and customs (the so-called "foral laws") of Aragon, the Balearic Islands, Catalonia, and several other provinces. The foral laws thus preserved are not as comprehensive as a modern civil code; they deal mainly with matters of testate as well as intestate succession, and with matrimonial property

regimes. But as to points covered by it, an applicable foral law prevails over the provisions of the national Civil Code. The latter thus becomes a mere subsidiary source of law in those provinces whose foral laws have been preserved. See Brown, *supra* note l, at 372–377. J. Cadarso Palau & J. W. Fernandez, The Spanish Constitution of 1978: Legislative Competence of the Autonomous Communities in Civil Law Matters, 15 VK. J. Transnat'l L. 47, 48–57 (1982).

It should be noted that the regional *fueros* are written sources of law. They originated as customs, but were reduced to writing long before the age of codification. Spanish lawyers clearly distinguish between (a) the *fueros*, which are a form of written regional law, and (b) *costumbres*, i.e., unwritten customs. The latter, although under certain conditions theoretically recognized as sources of law, play no significant role in Spanish legal practice; but the *fueros*, as pointed out above, are of enormous practical importance in certain parts of Spain. The opinion in the principal case fails to even mention the distinction between *fueros* and *costumbres*.

p. The statement by Manresa to which reference is made in the text undoubtedly is one of that famous author's contributions to solving the controversial problem of the relationship between "general principles of law" and "doctrina legal." For a fuller discussion of Manresa's theory, see Brown, *supra* note l, at 371.

binding force which controlled custom. In fact, it became so binding that it was found necessary, in order to effect justice in particular cases, to establish the Court of Chancery, which became the court of equity. The English Common Law recognizes custom only so far as it does not conflict with the well settled principles of that law. Under the Spanish system, on the other hand, when the written law is silent, before considering precedents in the cases the court is governed by the customs of the locality at the time.

Consequently, by the change of sovereignty there was no body of case law or common law of Spain which could be considered as existing in connection with the written law retained in force in these Islands. The only amplification of that written law was the local customs of the people of the Islands. This is particularly true of Spanish decisions rendered since the change of sovereignty, which do not preclude the local courts from exercising an independent judgment. Cordova v. Rijos, 227 U.S. 375, 33 S.Ct. 350.

Spanish Statute Law

The Spanish statute law, as amplified by Spanish commentaries but without a background of Spanish precedent or case law, was by the change of sovereignty, severed from Spanish jurisprudence and made effective in this jurisdiction to the same extent as if Congress had enacted new laws for the Philippines modelled upon those same Spanish statutes. This retention of the local private law was merely in accordance with the principles of International Law in that regard.[q] However, by the mere fact of the change of sovereignty, all portions of that statute law which might be termed political law were abrogated immediately by the change of sovereignty. Also, all Spanish laws, customs, and rights of property inconsistent with the Constitution and American principles and institutions were thereupon superseded. Sanchez v. United States, 216 U.S. 167, 30 S.Ct. 361.

. . . [The court refers to a great number of Spanish statutes which were repealed and replaced by new enactments.] Even the Spanish Civil Code has been largely modified [Note omitted]. . . .

Cases Under American Derived Statutes

It thus appears that the bulk of present day Statute Law is derivative from Anglo–American sources; derivative within the sense of having been copied, and in the sense of having been enacted by Congress or by virtue of its authority. This court has repeatedly held that in dealing with the cases which arise under such statute law the court will be governed by the Anglo–American cases in construction and application. [Citations.]

q. International law would not have prevented the new Sovereign from subsequently repealing all of the Spanish codes. In fact, however, there was no such wholesale repeal. Compare the methods employed in the Philippines with the laws adopted for the Trust Territory of Saipan, where by one stroke of the legislative pen the common law was substituted for the pre-existing civilian code system. Cf. Caldwell v. Carmar Trading Co., 116 F.Supp. 546 (D.C.Haw.1953).

To illustrate more clearly the scope of the use of Anglo–American cases in this connection, a brief analysis of some of the more recent decisions of this court is advisable. For convenience the cases will be taken up in the note by subjects. [The voluminous Note is omitted.] In all of them, Anglo–American decisions and authorities are used and relied upon to a greater or less degree. Although in many cases the use is by way of dictum, nevertheless, the net result is the building up of a very substantial elaboration of Anglo–American case law.

From the foregoing selection of the more recent and typical cases, it appears how broad is the scope of the use of Anglo–American authorities and precedents in the field of law subjects affected by American derived legislation. In the application of those statutes in the many cases which come before the court, there is bound to be developed a substantial common law. There is no question that this exists. We are merely concerned with its extent and source.

Cases under Spanish Statutes

In addition to the subjects covered above, there is a wide field of use of Anglo–American cases in the interpretation and application of the remnants of the Spanish statutes. Such is of even greater importance in showing the real permanency of the hold which Anglo–American Common Law has fastened upon the jurisprudence of this jurisdiction. . . .

To illustrate the scope of the use of Anglo–American cases in connection with the remaining Spanish statutes, a brief analysis of the more recent cases under a few of the principal subjects, will be appropriate. [Note omitted.] Frequently in these cases reference to Anglo–American precedents is for the purpose of showing that Spanish law and the Anglo–American law is the same, and frequently it is for the purpose of amplifying or extending the Spanish statutes.[r] In most cases it is for the purpose of applying those statutes to the particular case before the court; but whatever the use, the fact remains that through the influence of these cases a broad exposition of American case law is made. . . .

The foregoing two groups of cases in combination, those under the subjects covered by Spanish statutes and those under the subjects covered by American–Philippine legislation and effected by the change of sovereignty, show conclusively that Anglo–American case law has entered practically every one of the leading subjects in the field of law, and in the large majority of such subjects has formed the sole basis for the guidance of this court in developing the local jurisprudence. The practical result is that the past twenty years have developed a Philippine Common Law or case law based almost exclusively, except where conflicting with local customs and

r. The Supreme Court of Puerto Rico now publishes its decisions only in Spanish, and freely refers to post–1898 Spanish authorities and decisions. See, e.g., De Jesus Diaz v. Carrero, 112 D.P.R. 631, 636–38 (1982). The Court has also, at least on occasion, expressed its displeasure at unnecessary references to "continental" (United States) law.

institutions, upon Anglo–American Common Law. The Philippine Common Law supplements and amplifies our statute law.

Collateral Influences

This conclusion is further justified by the practical situation which has surrounded the Bench and Bar of the Philippine Islands for many years and which there is every reason to believe will continue unabated in the future.

This court has, in an increasing degree during the past twenty years, cited and quoted from Anglo–American cases and authorities in its decisions. The following analysis of the citations of the last twenty volumes of the Philippine Reports show this graphically. [Table omitted.]

The American citations are over ten times as numerous as the Spanish citations. (In Vol. 1 there were 63 Spanish to 53 United States.) Add to this the cumulative effect of perpetuating this ratio through the citations of Philippine cases in which American cases have been cited, and it is obvious that Spanish decisions have had comparatively slight effect in the development of our case law.

It is a fact of considerable practical importance that there are no digests of Spanish decisions to aid the study of Bench and Bar. On the other hand, the local libraries contain both digests and reports of the Federal Courts and Supreme Court of the United States, and of most of the State courts, and also many reports of the English courts. Added to this is a liberal supply of English and American text books. The foregoing not only has a natural influence on the results of the work on the Bench, but it has a very decided influence on the development of the present Bar of the Philippine Islands; each year adds to the preponderance of lawyers trained chiefly from a study of Anglo–American case law.[s]

The fact that prolific use of Anglo–American authorities is made in the decisions of this court, combined with the fact that the available sources for study and reference on legal theories are mostly Anglo–American, present a practical situation at this moment from which this court can draw but one conclusion, namely, that there has been developed, and will continue, a common law in the jurisprudence of this jurisdiction (which for purposes of distinction may properly be termed a Philippine Common Law), based upon the English Common Law in its present day form of an Anglo–American

---

s. For an account of the initial phase of that process, see A. L. Garcia Martinez, La Americanizacion de Filipinas—la Justicia—la Imposición del Idioma Inglés en los Tribunales en el Periodo 1898–1906, 45 Rev. Abo. P. R. 143 (1984). Unsurprisingly, its main propelling force was none other than the author of this opinion, who as a "young graduate of the University of Michigan law school," proposed the establishment of a law school in the Philippines in 1910 and became the first permanent dean of the College of Law, University of the Philippines, one year later. I. R. Cortes, Legal Education in the Philippines: The Role of the Philippine Law Journal in the 1990s, 65 Phil. L. J. 1 note 1 (1990). Justice Malcolm served on the Supreme Court of the Philippines from 1917 to 1936. The tenure of other "state-side" judges on that court was usually (but not invariably) much shorter. D. F. Batacan, The Supreme Court in Philippine History, 1901 to 1971, table at 29–36 (1972).

Common Law, which common law is effective in all of the subjects of law in this jurisdiction in so far as it does not conflict with the express language of the written law or with the local customs and institutions.

Conclusions

We may summarize our conclusions as follows:

. . . (2) In interpreting and applying the bulk of the written laws of this jurisdiction, and in rendering its decisions in cases not covered by the letter of the written law, this court relies upon the theories and precedents of Anglo–American cases, subject to the limited exception of those instances where the remnants of the Spanish written law present well-defined civil law theories and of the few cases where such precedents are inconsistent with local customs and institutions.

(3) The jurisprudence of this jurisdiction is based upon the English Common Law in its present day form of Anglo–American Common Law to an almost exclusive extent.

(4) By virtue of the foregoing, the New York rule, given a reasonable interpretation, permits conferring privileges on attorneys admitted to practice in the Philippine Islands similar to those privileges accorded by the rule of this court.

Accordingly, the supporting papers filed by the applicant in this case showing to the satisfaction of the court his qualifications as an attorney-at-law, his petition is hereby granted and he is admitted to the practice of law in the Philippine Islands. Our decision is based upon our interpretation of the New York rule, and it does not establish a precedent which may be controlling on this court with respect to future applications if our interpretation is not borne out by the future enforcement of that rule by the New York court. So ordered.

■ MAPA, C.J., JOHNSON, ARAULLO, STREET, AVANCENA, and VILLAMOR, JJ., concur.

Petition granted.

NOTES

(1) One thing that the reader should immediately notice by observing the In Re Shoop Case is how Justice Malcolm only contemplates one of the following alternatives: the Philippines either have a civil law tradition or a common law tradition, both of which arrived there through colonial occupation. Justice Malcolm effectively erases the presence of quite a significant body of Islamic law that existed in the southern Philippines. (Indeed, the Islamic law of Mindanao not codified until 1978 under Marcos' rule). Furthermore, he also assumed that without colonization there would have been no law in the Philippines. The Orientalist notion of lawlessness, which we have discussed previously, creeps in as an option on how to consider ''law'' in a colonial setting.

(2) In his debate about whether the Philippines are a common law or a civil law jurisdiction, Justice Malcolm uses a variety of criteria. Thus the reader will observe that there is no one single test sufficient to identify to which legal "family" (e.g. civil law, common law, etc.) a legal system "belongs". Rather, the rich variety of the "sources of law" has to be interrogated to find evidence of such "belonging". Justice Malcolm's ideological choice is to include within the realm of the possibilities only the western imported professional sources such as statutes, case law and codes. In fact, he effectively engages in a "preponderance test" analysis between the archetypical aspects of the common law (e.g. hegemony of case law between the sources) and of the civil law tradition (e.g. hegemony of codified law), by means of an historical approach. In the next chapter, the reader will become familiar with historical narratives typical of the comparative law tradition. Justice Malcolm's method is one that follows the different waves of western law "reception" in the Philippines or, as seen from the west, the "diffusion" of western law in the periphery.

Observing the diffusion of the thick "ideological stratum" of professionalized law from the western legal tradition towards the rest of the world, sometimes assuming that the receiving field contains no law or a lesser law, has been perhaps the most important activity demonstrating the comparative law scholar role as a social geographer.

2.   THE COMPARATIVE LAWYER AS A GEOGRAPHER: TENTATIVE AREA-BY-AREA SURVEY

Let us keep following the "diffusion" of Spanish law and look to Latin America. The Spanish and Portuguese conquerors introduced to Latin America legal systems rooted in the civil law. Most of the nineteenth and twentieth century codes, although adopted after emancipation, continued this civil law tradition by following European models.[1] Thus, Latin American legal systems are generally classified as belonging to the civil law orbit. Their fundamental civil law character has been judicially noticed by courts in the United States.[2] Nevertheless, common law ideas (especially the elements of common law entrenched in the U.S. Constitution) have had a considerable impact on Latin American legal systems, primarily in the area of public law.[3] For example, the notions of due process and habeas corpus have been incorporated into the constitutions and statutes of a number of Latin American nations.[4] Even in the field of private law, common law

1. See José Castan Tobeñas, Contemporary Legal Systems of the Western World, 25 Comp. Jurid. Rev. 105 (1988) (discussing the relationships between Latin American codes).

2. See, e.g., Banco De Sonora v. Bankers' Mutual Casualty Co., 124 Iowa 576, 100 N.W. 532, 536 (1904).

3. It is because of the traditional classification's focus on private law that the "civil law" label is pinned with ease on Latin American systems. A comparative study of public law might require a different scheme. See J. A. Jolowicz, Development of Common and Civil Law, Lloyd's Mar. & Com. L. Q. 87, 95 (Feb. 1982).

4. In practice, these borrowed institutions may assume a somewhat different character on Latin American soil. Nevertheless, they remain a genuine link between the legal systems of North and South America. See. e.g., Jaffin, New World Constitutional Harmony, 42 Colum. L. Rev. 523 (1942); B. M. Carl, Erosion of Constitutional Rights of Political Offenders in Brazil, 12 Va. J. Int'l L. 157 (1972); D. S. Clark, Judicial Protection of the Constitution in Latin America, 2 Has-

influences are not lacking, as illustrated by the adoption of the express trust concept in a number of Central and South American countries.[5]

The same legal mixed-character that exists in a large portion of the Western Hemisphere is evident, and perhaps more prominently so, in Puerto Rico, Louisiana and Quebec, a trio often referred to as the civil law enclaves in the common law world or "mixed legal systems".[6] Of the two last-mentioned jurisdictions, perhaps Quebec has better resisted the encroachment of the common law,[7] although much of the province's commercial law, both statute and case law, reflects common law influence.[8] Even

tings Const. L. Q. 405 (1975); D. B. Furnish, The Hierarchy of Peruvian Laws: Context for Law and Development, 19 Am. J. Comp. L. 91 (1971); P. P. Camargo, The Claim of "Amparo" in Mexico: Constitutional Protection of Human Rights, 6 Cal. W. L. Rev. 201 (1970); Note, The Writ of Amparo: A Remedy to Protect Constitutional Rights in Argentina, 31 Ohio St. L.J. 831 (1970).

The impact of political realities upon constitutional safeguards is discussed in A. S. Grebert & S. Y. Nun, Latin American Law and Institutions 69–82 (1982). See also Ugo Mattei, Comparative Law and Economics 246–249 (1997); Maximo Langer, From Legal Transplants to Legal Translations: The Globalization of Plea Bargaining and the Americanization Thesis in Criminal Procedure, 45 Harv. Int'l L.J. 1 (2004); Maximo Langer, Revolution in Latin American Criminal Procedure: Diffusion of Legal Ideas from the Periphery, 55 Am. J. Comp. L. 617 (2007).

In Mexico, since 1994, reforms initiated by President Ernesto Zedillo have aimed at enhancing respect for the rule of law. On one aspect of those reforms, see Jorge A. Vargas, The Reform of the Supreme Court of Mexico: An Appraisal of President Zedillo's Judicial Reform of 1995, 11 Am. U. J. Int'l L. & Pol'y 295 (1996); Note, Liberalismo Contra Democracia: Recent Judicial Reform in Mexico, 108 Harv.L.Rev. 1919 (1995). See also Sergio López-Ayllón, Notes on Mexican Legal Culture, 4 Soc. & Legal Stud. 477 (1995).

5. See Phanor J. Eder, The Impact of the Common Law on Latin America, 4 Miami L. Q. 435, 438–40 (1950). What has been said in note 4, *supra*, applies equally to the transplantation of the trust. See B. Kozolchyk, Fairness in Anglo and Latin American Adjudication, 2 B. C. Int'l & Comp. L. Rev. 219, 225–27 (1979); See also Jan Kleinheisterkamp Development of comparative law in Latin America, in Oxford handbook of Comparative Law (Mathias Reimann & Reinhard Zimmermann eds. 2007).

For references to other common law institutions which have influenced the private law of Latin American countries, see Phanor J. Eder, A Comparative Survey of Anglo–American and Latin–American Law (1950). See also Helen L. Clagett, The Administration of Justice in Latin America (1952); Recasens Siches et al., Latin American Legal Philosophy (1948); Diego Eduardo Lopez Medina, Teoria Impura Del Derecho (2004).

6. See Vernon Palmer, Mixed Jurisdictions Worldwide. The Third Legal Family (2001); see also Ignazio Castellucci, How Mixed Must a Mixed System Be? 12–1 Electronic J. Comp. Law (2008) www.ejcl.org.

7. The persistence of French language, culture and traditions, as well as the greater continuity of Quebec's legal history (as compared to the repeated upheavals in Louisiana), aid in explaining this phenomenon. On the legal system of Quebec, see generally Jean–Gabriel Castel, The Civil Law System of the Province of Quebec (1962); Quebec Civil Law: An Introduction to Quebec Private Law (J. E. C. Brierley & R. MacDonald eds., 1993); H. Patrick Glenn, Quebec: Mixité and Monism, in Studies in Legal Systems: Mixed and Mixing 1 (E. Örücü, E. Attwooll & S. Coyle eds., 1996); Gerald L. Gall, The Canadian Legal System (5th ed. 2004).

On the recent reform of the Civil Code of Quebec, see J. E. C. Brierley, The Renewal of Quebec's Distinct Legal Culture: The New Civil Code of Quebec, 42 U. Toronto L.J. 484 (1992).

8. See Glenn, *supra* note 7, at 6; L. Lilkoff, La circulation du modèle juridique français et le droit commercial québécois, in Droit québécois et droit français: communauté, autonomie, concordance 399 (H. P. Glenn ed., 1993).

Louisiana, laboring under the decadence of the French language and the impact of a federal system, still maintains a civil law flavor in juridical method as well as in legal substance.[9]

Common law influences have been felt, also, in areas which are geographically remote from the United States and Great Britain. These areas are by no means contiguous; to a large extent, their shape and location reflects the crazy-quilt pattern of former British conquests in Africa and Asia.

During the colonial period the British rulers usually adhered to the policy that with respect to matters of family law, marital property, succession upon death, and related questions of land tenure, the personal law of the individuals involved should be applied. Islamic law,[10] Hindu law, and other non-European systems thus continued to be of great importance throughout the British Empire insofar as the personal relations and property interests of indigenous populations were concerned.[11] Even with respect to these matters, however, common law influences made themselves felt because disputes often were decided by British judges[12] (the Privy Council acting as court of last resort). As a rule these judges were empowered by statute or ordinance to interpret—and sometimes even to correct or reject—the parties' personal law in the light of the court's notions of "justice, equity and good conscience."[13] In other fields of law, especially relating to

---

9. However, if the conventional focus were not on private law, one could hardly consider Louisiana an oasis of civil law.

10. The influence of Islamic law has been considerable, not only in the so-called Near East countries and in South and South East Asia, but also in large parts of Africa. See J. N. D. Anderson, Islamic Law in Africa (1954).

11. This included the application of what was supposed to be Chinese customary law to the Chinese population in Malaysia, Singapore, and Hong Kong. See Carol G. S. Tan, The Twilight of Chinese Customary Law Relating to Marriage in Malaysia, 42 Int'l & Comp. L. Q. 147 (1993); D. I. Lewis, A Requiem for Chinese Customary Law in Hong Kong, 32 Int'l & Comp. L. Q. 378 (1983). For a critical treatment of the colonial history of "Chinese customary law" which argues that the very concept is in fact a twentieth-century invention, see Jérôme Bourgôn, "Uncivil Dialogue: Law and Custom did not Merge into Civil Law under the Qing", 23 Late Imperial China 50 (2002).

12. It is true, of course, that the tribal, "native" or local courts, as well as the religious tribunals (especially the Sharia courts administering Islamic law) which function throughout the African and Asian parts of the British Commonwealth, normally are pre-

sided over by judges who are not Europeans and who as a rule are not trained in the common law. In some countries, especially in Africa, where much of the law applied by such courts consists of tribal customary law, local African judges are further insulated from the common law by statutes prohibiting professional counsel from appearing in these courts. It must be remembered, however, that frequently an appeal will lie from the decisions of the local courts to a higher tribunal staffed with "learned" judges. The local court's ruling on a point of customary law is often treated as a finding of fact, not freely reviewable on appeal. See A. Allott, Essays in African Law 87 (1960). But where, by frequent proof in the courts, a particular custom becomes "notorious," it can be judicially noticed and thus becomes "law" for purposes of appellate review. Id. at 88–94. Thus the customary law, even where it is administered in the first instance by chiefs or other indigenous judges, may come under common law influences through the appellate process. See M. B. Hooker, Legal Pluralism: An Introduction to Colonial and Neo–Colonial Laws 137–39 (1975).

13. See Hooker, *supra* note 12, at 58–61, 86–87, 109; Derrett, Justice, Equity and Good Conscience, in Changing Law in Developing Countries 114 (J. N. D. Anderson ed.,

contracts,[14] commercial law, procedure, and evidence, the common law tended to displace non-European systems, either entirely or to a very large extent.[15]

The strong influence of the common law in the African and Asian parts of the British Commonwealth, although originally dating from a period of occupation or colonization, generally has persisted after the end of that period. It appears, indeed, that, on gaining independence, most former colonial countries, trying to modernize their law in order to promote economic development, have swept out some of the customary and religious elements and strengthened the western or western-influenced components of their legal systems.[16] Among other examples,[17] one might cite India's abolition of the caste system and the ambitious attempt made by the same country to modernize and "codify" the customary law pertaining to family relations and family property.[18] The newly independent Commonwealth

1963). It is also true that in matters of family law and successions it was often left to the individuals concerned to decide whether to opt out of the indigenous system and become subject to common law. Moreover, in dealing with cases involving more than one "personal law," the appellate courts, again using common law techniques, developed highly sophisticated conflicts rules.

14. See, e.g., Saxena, Some Comments on the Indian Legal System, with Particular Reference to the Law of Contracts, in 1 Formation of Contracts—A Study of the Common Core of Legal Systems 281–93 (R. B. Schlesinger ed., 1968).

15. Sometimes, when they acquired a territory originally colonized by another European power, the British retained the legal system previously established, i.e., a system the European component of which was derived from the civil law rather than the common law. Examples are Roman–Dutch law in South Africa, Ceylon (now Sri Lanka), and British Guiana (now Guyana), and French law in Quebec. For the peculiar mixture of imported European law in Botswana, see H. Barton, J. Gibbs, V. Li & J. H. Merryman, Law in Radically Different Cultures 81–82 (1983). These instances are, however, exceptional; as a rule, it was the common law which furnished the European component of the legal systems prevailing in African and Asian countries under British control.

16. It is true that almost all newly independent countries established their own supreme court and renounced the jurisdiction of the Privy Council. But law teachers and legal writers tended to be western-trained, as were most of the judges of the higher and

highest courts, even though they might be of non-European descent. As a result, the courts in many of the newly independent nations of the British Commonwealth have strongly adhered to common law techniques, especially to the doctrine of *stare decisis*. Indeed, in some of those countries one can observe that *stare decisis* is more rigidly applied than it has been (since 1966) in the English courts.

17. Such examples can be found in both Africa and Asia. See, e.g., A. Allott, New Essays in African Law 45 (1970); Z. Mustafa, The Common Law in the Sudan 182–228 (1971); Guttmann, The Reception of the Common Law in the Sudan, 6 Int'l & Comp. L. Q. 401 (1957); Buss–Tjen, Malay Law, 7 Am J. Comp. L. 248 (1958); Maung Maung, Lawyers and Legal Education in Burma, 11 Int'l & Comp. L. Q. 285 (1962). Martin Channock, Law, Custom, and Social Order: The Colonial Experience in Malawi and Zambia (1985).

18. The statutes comprising this "codification" were enacted between 1955 and 1961. See Derrett, Introduction to Modern Hindu Law 559–610 (1963); K. S. Sidhu, An Institutional and Historical Study of Property in Land in Relation to Punjab Customary Law 172–82, 224–29, 240 (unpubl. thesis, Cornell Law Library, 1957); Werner Menski, Hindu Law: Beyond Tradition and Modernity (2003). One of the important objectives of this legislation was to get rid of archaic restrictions upon the alienability of real property. See instructive discussion by Derrett, Statutory Amendments of the Personal Law of Hindus Since Indian Independence, 7 Am. J. Comp. L. 380 (1958).

nations, moreover, invariably have faced fundamental problems of constitutional law. Almost all of them adopted written constitutions. The framers of these documents and the judges interpreting them usually have been familiar, not only with British traditions, but also with at least some aspects of American constitutional law. Sometimes, they have had to choose between (the somewhat conflicting) British and American solutions, thus strengthening the basic common law orientation of their public law, whether their preference in the particular case is for Dicey or for Holmes and Brandeis.[19]

Countervailing tendencies should be recognized, however, in a number of former British colonial possessions. Some of these countries incorporated elements of a "socialist" character into their law for a period of time, while others have tried to preserve and adapt indigenous legal institutions.[20] In the Sudan, which earlier went through a "socialist" phase, there was a shift to Islamic law starting in 1983[21] that has been given a rather emphatic twist since President Omar el-Bashir took power in 1989.

Hong Kong is a special case since it did not become independent but rather reverted from British sovereignty to Chinese sovereignty on July 1, 1997. Under British rule, Hong Kong was basically a common law jurisdiction (with an admixture of "Chinese custom").[22] According to the terms of

There are remnants of civil law influence in those small parts of India that were formerly Portuguese or French. See K. M. Sharma, Civil Law in India, 1969 Wash. U. L. Q. 1. It does not seem, however, that these civil law pockets have substantially affected the overall legal development of independent India.

19. See, e.g., Mustafa, *supra* note 17, at 212–13. Concerning India, see Alexandrowicz, Constitutional Developments in India (1957); Pradyumna K. Tripathi, Foreign Precedents and Constitutional Law, 57 Colum. L. Rev. 319, 334–42 (1957). The amalgamation of Islamic and secular (common law) elements in the public law of Pakistan is interestingly discussed by McWhinney, Judicial Review 140–52 (4th ed., 1969). Relevant comparative materials can be found in the casebook by T. M. Franck, Comparative Constitutional Process—Fundamental Rights in the Common Law Nations (1968), and also in the proceedings of the Roundtable on the Rule of Law in Oriental Countries, held in 1957 in Chicago under the auspices of the American Foreign Law Association in cooperation with the International Association of Legal Science, and published in the Annales de la Faculté de Droit d' Istanbul (8e annèe, t. IX), no. 14, 1960; for a brief summary by the General Reporter, see Schlesinger, The Rule of Law in Oriental Countries, 6 Am. J. Comp. L. 520 (1957).

20. See D. N. Smith, Man and Law in Urban Africa, 20 Am. J. Comp. L. 223 (1972); H. Barton, et al., *supra* note 15, at 96–101; D. Weisbrot, Customizing the Common Law: The True Papua New Guinea Experience, 67 A.B.A.J. 727 (1981). Even without effort, "customary law flourishes de facto as soon as the state does not invest enough resources to oppose its operation and offer an alternative option." Ugo Mattei, *supra* note 4, at 245.

21. See C. N. Gordon, The Islamic Legal Revolution: The Case of Sudan, 19 Int'l Law. 793 (1985). Aharon Layish and Gabriel R. Warburg, The Reinstatement of Islamic Law in Sudan under Numayr. An Evaluation of a Legal Experiment in the Light of its Historical Context, Methodology, and Repercussions (2002).

22. See Peter Wesley–Smith, An Introduction to the Hong Kong Legal System (1987). For an ethnographic case study of the continuing, and contested, role of "custom" in Hong Kong in the 1990's, see Sally Merry & Rachel Stern, The Female Inheritance Movement in Hong Kong: Theorizing the Local/Global Interface, 46 Current Anthropology 387–409 (2005). See also Ignazio Castellucci, Rule of Law with Chinese Characteristics,

the Sino–British Joint Declaration of 1984[23] and of the Basic Law for Hong Kong (Hong Kong's "mini-constitution"),[24] Hong Kong is now a Special Administrative Region within the People's Republic of China (PRC). For at least fifty years, it is to be largely self-governing and to retain its capitalist system and "the laws previously in force" (defined to include "the common law, rules of equity, ordinances, subordinate legislation, and customary law," but not British statutes, which were replaced by local legislation in order to ensure that Hong Kong had its own body of statute law). A five-judge Court of Final Appeal has replaced the Judicial Committee of the Privy Council as the court of last resort. At the same time, Hong Kong courts are precluded from reviewing "acts of state," and the determination of whether new laws are consistent with the Basic Law rests with the Standing Committee of the National People's Congress of the PRC in Beijing. There has been much speculation about the future of the Hong Kong legal system.[25] That depends, in large part, on what happens within China itself. One key issue is the use of the English language (which is not the first language of 98% of the population) in courts, and the extent to which the common law (and, more important, the legal sensibilities that underpin the common law) can survive translation into Chinese.[26] Similar problems have arisen in Macau, a former Portuguese colony that also reverted back to China in 1999.[27]

13 Ann. Surv. Int & Comp. L. 35, 75–82 (2007) on Hong Kong, Macau and other Special Zones.

23. 23 I.L.M. 1366 (1984).

24. 29 I.L.M. 1511 (1990).

25. See, e.g., The Future of Law in Hong Kong (Raymond Wacks ed., 1989); Philip W. Baker & Berry Fong–Chung Hsu, Common Law Under Socialist Legal System: The Future of Hong Kong, 7 China L. Rep. 1 (1991); Anna M. Han, Hong Kong's Basic Law: The Path to 1997, Paved with Pitfalls, 16 Hastings Int'l & Comp. L. Rev. 321 (1993); Donna Deese Skeen, Comment, Can Capitalism Survive Under Communist Rule? The Effect of Hong Kong's Reversion to the People's Republic of China, 29 Int'l Law. 175 (1995); Peter Wesley–Smith, Law in Hong Kong and China: The Meshing of Systems, 547 Annals Am. Acad. Pol. & Soc. Sci. 104 (Sept. 1996); Ann D. Jordan, Lost in the Translation: Two Legal Cultures, the Common Law Judiciary and the Basic Law of the Hong Kong Special Administrative Region, 30 Cornell Int'l L.J. 335 (1997).

In Nowak v. Tak How Investment Ltd., 899 F.Supp. 25, 34 (D.Mass.1995), aff'd, 94 F.3d 708 (1st Cir.1996), cert. denied, 520 U.S. 1155, 117 S.Ct. 1333 (1997), "the uncertain future of the Hong Kong legal system" (along with the fact that Hong Kong does not permit contingent fees) was given as a reason for retaining jurisdiction in Massachusetts over a wrongful death action arising out of events in Hong Kong.

26. For an interesting study of the preservation of English as the language of the law in other former British colonies in which it is not the predominant language, and consideration of the possibility of its survival in Hong Kong, see Tomasz Ujejski, The Future of the English Language in Hong Kong Law, in The Future of Law in Hong Kong, *supra* note 25, at 164. For an optimistic view of the possibilities of translation, see Derek Roebuck & King-kui Sin, The Ego and I and Ngo: Theoretical Problems in the Translation of the Common Law into Chinese, in Hong Kong, China and 1997: Essays in Legal Theory 185 (Raymond Wacks ed., 1993).

The Basic Law assumes, however, that Chinese will be primary and provides (in art. 9) that "in addition to Chinese, English may be used."

27. For a recent analysis of the status of Hong Kong, see, e.g, Albert Chen, The Basic Law and the Development of the Political System in Hong Kong, 15 Asia Pac. L.

In a few countries, such as the Philippines, the common law followed the American rather than British flag. The American impact upon the law of the Philippines[28] has been strong and apparently lasting.[29] Japan, traditionally considered a civil law country also demonstrates in many ways the strong American influence of the postwar period, especially in its judicial organization and its constitutional and administrative law.[30] Common law institutions, such as habeas corpus, have also been superimposed on the legal order of South Korea, another civil law country.[31]

On the other side of the globe, we find in Liberia a legal system essentially patterned after that of the United States.[32] Apart from village communities in the interior of the country, which continued to be governed by customary law, the official legal system of Liberia originally derived from American sources and was modernized in the 1960s with the assistance of American consultants. Relatively ancient features of Anglo–American law, such as strict common law pleading, were preserved much longer in Liberia than in the United States. Ultimately, however, Liberian civil procedure was revised in the light of modern developments in the United States,[33] and this was followed by a thorough revision of the entire body of the country's statute law, patterned after the American experience.[34]

Rev. 19–40 (2007). On Macau, see Ignazio Castellucci, *supra* note 6.

28. See Winfred Lee Thompson, The Introduction of American Law in the Philippines and Puerto Rico 1898–1905 (1989).

29. See *supra* In Re Shoop. After World War II, the common law also replaced the civil law in some formerly Japanese islands in the Pacific. See South Pacific Islands Legal Systems (Michael A. Ntumy ed., 1993).

30. A significant shift from civil law to common law institutions is indicated by article 76(2) of the Japanese Constitution, which provides that "no extraordinary tribunal shall be established, nor shall any organ or agency of the Executive be given final judicial power." This has the effect of abolishing continental-style administrative courts. The function of judicial review of administrative acts was transferred to the regular law courts. Severe problems of transition were caused by this shift. See Ichiro Ogawa, Judicial Review of Administrative Actions in Japan, 43 Wash. L. Rev. 1075 (1968). It should be borne in mind, however, that the practical operation of the Japanese system of judicial review of administrative acts is quite different from the American. See M. Schaar, Verwaltungsrecht, in Das japanische Rechtssystem 85, 95–98 (P. Eubel ed., 1980); Hiroshi Oda, Japanese Law (2001).

31. See Sang Hyun Song, Introduction to the Law and Legal System of Korea (1983). For a bibliography, see Chin Kim, Korean Law Study Guide (2d ed. 1995). For a very useful source focusing on the public law in a large variety of Asian countries, see Administrative Law and Governance in Asia: Comparative Perspectives (Tom Ginsburg & Albert H. Chen eds., 2008).

32. See Konvitz & Rosenzweig, Liberia, in Judicial and Legal Systems in Africa 122–25 (Allott ed., 2d ed., 1970).

33. See Konvitz & Rosenzweig, Background and Summary of the New Civil Procedure Law, 1 Liberian L.J. 3 (1965).

34. The Liberian Code of Laws of 1956, prepared by the Liberian Codification Project at Cornell University, was a systematic rearrangement of existing laws. The new Code, on which the Project (under the direction of Professor Konvitz) worked for many years in co-operation with leading Liberian lawyers and officials, must be regarded as a revision rather than a mere rearrangement.

For additional references concerning common law influences in Africa and Asia, see L. E. Trakman, The Need for Legal Training in International, Comparative and Foreign Law: Foreign Lawyers at American Law Schools, 27 J. Legal Educ. 509, 511–12 (1976). See also Werner Menski, Comparative

The common law has worked, also, upon the uncodified civil law systems of Scotland, South Africa, Sri Lanka, and Guyana.[35] Scots law retains much of its original character, particularly in the traditional fields of contracts, torts, property, and inheritance; but centralized legislative and judicial control, combined with the economic integration of the United Kingdom, have had the effect of anglicizing many facets both of substance and procedure.[36] The law of South Africa, likewise, has been influenced by the common law; but, until now, it has preserved its basic Roman–Dutch character.[37] South African law, for a long time plagued by a harsh system of apartheid, was not subject, to the same extent as Scots law, to legislative and judicial controls exercised in Britain, and this fact, coupled with political sentiments of the white dominant minority of Dutch origins, helped to assure the survival of the Roman–Dutch system.[38] In Sri Lanka,[39] and even more in Guyana,[40] on the other hand, the common law widely replaced the former Roman–Dutch system.[41]

Law in the Global Context. The Legal Systems of Africa and Asia (2000);

35. For a more complete listing and an informative discussion of the somewhat exceptional civil law jurisdictions in which a code system of the civilian type has never been adopted, see T. B. Smith, Studies Critical and Comparative at ix–xxxvii (1962).

Attempts to introduce particular common law institutions into such a predominantly civilian system sometimes are made by statute. The difficulties engendered by legislation of this kind are illustrated in the article by T. B. Smith, Exchange or Sale?, 48 Tul. L. Rev. 1029, especially at 1036–41 (1974).

36. English influence has been particularly marked in those areas in which Roman law was defective and failed to provide adequate solutions, e.g., in agency and trust situations. Along with English rules of substantive law, some common law notions of *stare decisis* seem to have infiltrated into Scots law, a development regretted by some Scots lawyers. See T. B. Smith, English Influences on the Law of Scotland, 3 Am. J. Comp. L. 522 (1954); Cooper, The Common Law and the Civil Law—A Scot's View, 63 Harv. L. Rev. 468 (1950); Kennet Reid & Reinhard Zimmermann, A history of private law in Scotland (2000).

37. See Leyser, Some Comments on the South African Legal System, in 1 Formation of Contracts—A Study of the Common Core of Legal Systems 321–3 (R. B. Schlesinger ed., 1968); R. Zimmerman and D. Visser,

Southern Cross: Civil Law and Common Law in South Africa (1996).

South Africa's notorious system of racial legislation was not inherited from traditional Roman–Dutch or common law sources. It was a relatively recent statutory accretion. See E. S. Landis, South African Apartheid Legislation, 71 Yale L.J. 1, 437 (1961–62).

38. With respect to the future, see Albie Sachs, The Future of a Roman Dutch Law in a Non–Racial Democratic South Africa: Some Preliminary Observations, 1 Soc. & Legal Stud. 217 (1992).

39. For a case study of common law influences upon the originally Roman–Dutch system of Ceylon, see L. W. Athulathmudali, The Law of Defamation in Ceylon—A Study of the Inter–Action of English and Roman–Dutch Law, 13 Int'l & Comp. L. Q. 1368 (1964). See also L. J. M. Cooray, The Reception of Roman–Dutch Law in Ceylon, 7 Comp. & Int'l J. S. Afr. 295 (1974); M.H. J. van Den Horst, The Roman Dutch Law in Sri Lanka (1985); J.W. Wessels, History of The Roman Dutch Law (2005).

40. See Demerara Turf Club Ltd. v. Wight, [1918] A.C. 605 (P.C. 1918).

41. For an account of the legal system of Zimbabwe in which, as of a few years ago, Roman–Dutch law was combined with elements not only of common law and African customary law, but also Marxist–Leninist teachings, see R. Zimmermann, Das römisch-holländische Recht in Zimbabwe, 55 Rabels Z. 505 (1991).

A "mixed" legal system of singular complexity prevails in Israel.[42] Matters of personal status, especially of marriage and divorce, are still left to the (frequently exclusive) jurisdiction of Jewish, Moslem, and Christian religious courts; subject to some legislative inroads, these courts apply the traditional law of their respective communities. Otherwise, the legal system is a secular one; but its various parts stem from different cultures and periods. Before it became a British Mandate in the wake of World War I, Palestine was a province of the Ottoman Empire. Some remnants of the law from that period, which itself reflected a mixture of Islamic and French sources, are still in force.[43] During the Mandate era, some areas of the law—especially procedure, evidence, and torts—were thoroughly anglicized, partly by legislation and partly by judicial importation of common law and equity.[44] Since the founding of the State of Israel in 1948, new legislation enacted by the Knesset has unfortunately come to play an ever increasing role in introducing discriminatory elements towards part of the population in various instances, a phenomenon at odds with the otherwise highly-developed existing legal culture.[45] Aiming at the creation of a national and independent legal system, the Israeli government embarked on a program of codification. After some initial discussions, the idea of a single civil code, to be enacted at one stroke, was rejected. Instead, between 1962 and 1981, the codifiers successively tackled various branches of substantive private law. The Law of Succession, enacted in 1965, marked one of the first major steps along this road.[46] It was followed by the codification, in stages, of parts of the law of property and major areas of contract law—to the point where the Israeli legal system is now deemed ready for a comprehensive Code of Private Law.[47] As their sources and models, the codifiers used traditional Jewish law, common law, and the codes of the civil law world.[48]

42. See, e.g., D. Friedmann, The Effect of Foreign Law on the Law of Israel (1975); G. Tedeschi & Y. S. Zemach, Codification and Case Law in Israel, in The Role of Judicial Decisions and Doctrine in Civil Law and in Mixed Jurisdictions 272 (J. Dainow ed., 1974); U. Yadin, Judicial Lawmaking in Israel, in *id.* at 296; Stephen Goldstein, Israel: Creating a New Legal System from Different Sources by Jurists of Different Backgrounds, in Studies in Legal Systems, *supra* note 7, at 147; Yoram Shachar, History and Sources of Israel Law, in Introduction to the Law of Israel 1 (Amos Shapira & Keren C. DeWitt–Arar eds., 1995).

43. See Friedmann, *supra* note 42. The most important enactment of that period was the Ottoman code of civil law, the *Mejelle.* This code, although somewhat French-influenced in its structure and later in its application, was essentially a compilation of rules of Moslem law. In 1984 the *Mejelle* was repealed, but some other remnants of Ottoman law are still in force.

44. See, e.g., H. W. Baade, The Eichmann Trial: Some Legal Aspects, 1961 Duke L.J. 400, 403, where further references can be found. See also *supra* note 42.

45. David Kretzmer & International Center for Peace in the Middle East, The Legal Status of the Arabs in Israel (1990).

46. SeeYadin, The Law of Succession and Other Steps Towards a Civil Code, in Studies in Israeli Legislative Problems 104 (Tedeschi & Yadin eds., 1966).

47. See Aharon Barak, The Codification of Civil Law and the Law of Torts, 24 Israel L. Rev. 628 (1990).

48. See G. Shalev & S. Herman, A Source Study of Israel's Contract Codification, 35 La. L. Rev. 1091 (1975); U. Yadin, The New Statute Law of Contracts, 9 Israel L. Rev. 512 (1974).

It may be worth noting, in this connection, that a number of the Israeli lawyers who played a part in the preparation of the

In interpreting the new enactments, some of which contain an "autarchy clause,"[49] the courts seem to have been somewhat torn between the common law method of falling back on pre-code case law and the civilian approach of treating the code as a new start.[50] There is little doubt, however, that, at least in the area of substantive private law, the ongoing process of codification has weakened the common law ties of Israel's mixed legal system and moved it somewhat closer to the civil law camp.[51]

The civil law, even though its core areas are in continental Europe and Latin America, has spread into many parts of Asia and Africa. Japan,[52] having adopted the main structure of the German code system at the beginning of the twentieth century,[53] subsequently felt a measure of common law influence following World War II.[54] It remains true, nevertheless, that a German-trained member of the legal profession encounters much less difficulty in comprehending Japanese legal materials than a lawyer brought up in the common law; in this sense Japan is still a civil

various codes received their original legal training in civil law countries.

49. Such a clause precluded resort to art. 46 of the Palestine Order-in-Council, 1922, which (until its repeal in 1980) called upon courts to "exercise their jurisdiction in conforming with the substance of the common law and the doctrines of equity in force in England."

50. Among Israeli legal scholars there is much debate on how the codes should be interpreted, and how their gaps should be filled. So far as the courts are concerned, subtle changes in legal method may occur with the advent of a new generation of judges who have been brought up on the codes, and also as codification becomes more comprehensive, encouraging treatment of the codes as an integrated system. On the other hand, with the passage of time, the continental sources that informed the work of the drafters of the several codes have become less accessible to Israeli judges and jurists. Issues of interpretation have been the main interest of the long time Justice of the Supreme Court. See Aharon Barak, Purposive Interpretation in Law (Sari Bashi trans., 2007).

51. In the areas of procedure and evidence, Israeli law thus far has retained its strong common law orientation. The same is true of the field of torts; in dealing with automobile accidents, however, Israel went its own way by enacting a statute which imposes strict liability on the driver and owner but limits the amount of damages recoverable by the victim. "The ambit of the tort of negligence has, thus, been considerably curtailed." Friedmann, *supra* note 42, at 125.

52. For English-language introductions to the Japanese legal system, see e.g., John Haley, The Spirit of Japanese Law (2006); Frank Upham, Law and Social Change in Post–War Japan (1987); Hideo Tanaka & Malcolm D. H. Smith, The Japanese Legal System (1976); Y. Noda, Introduction to Japanese Law (A. H. Angelo trans., 1976); D. F. Henderson, Foreign Enterprise in Japan: Laws and Policies (1973); Hiroshi Oda, Japanese Law (1992). See also Das japanische Rechtssystem, *supra* note 30; C. R. Stevens, Modern Japanese Law as an Instrument of Comparison, 19 Am. J. Comp. L. 665 (1971); L. W. Beer & H. Tomatsu, A Guide to the Study of Japanese Law, 23 Am. J. Comp. L. 284 (1975); M. K. Young, The Japanese Legal System: History and Structure, in 2 Doing Business in Japan, ch. 3 (Z. Kitagawa ed., 1992). For a review of recent books in English and German, see Harold Hohmann, Modern Japanese Law: Legal History and Concept of Law, Public Law and Economic Law of Japan, 44 Am. J. Comp. L. 151 (1996). For the most recent transformations R. Daniel Kelemen & Eric C. Sibbitt, The Americanization of Japanese Law, 23 U. Pa. J. Int'l Econ. L. 269 (Summer 2002).

53. The process by which a predominantly German-inspired Civil Code was adopted in Japan was somewhat akin to the choice of a compromise candidate. For details of the irreconcilable controversy between the English and the French schools, and the eventual adoption of the German Code, see Takayanagi, Contact of the Common Law with the Civil Law in Japan, 4 Am. J. Comp. L. 60 (1955).

54. See *supra*, text at note 30.

law country. The same is true of South Korea.[55] German law also influenced the legal system of pre-communist China,[56] and this German influence remains clearly noticeable in the basic codes of the Republic of China (Taiwan).[57]

Eclectic importation and adaptation of codes stemming from various civil law countries may be said to characterize the Turkish legal system.[58] Turkey virtually copied the Swiss Civil Code and the Swiss Code of Obligations and subsequently adopted a revised Commercial Code which, although largely German-inspired, was carefully integrated into the (Swiss) scheme of the two older codes.[59] The Turkish Penal Code follows the Italian model, while the Code of Criminal Procedure shows German influence and the Code of Civil Procedure is patterned after the procedural code of the Swiss Canton of Neuchatel.[60] The system of administrative courts and of (un-codified) administrative law is distinctly French-influenced.[61]

Similar eclecticism marks the legal systems of some other developing countries which, like Turkey, remained formally free from colonial rule but nevertheless followed western models in modernizing their law.[62] Often, this was a defensive act taken in the hope of offering proof of "civilization" and thereby preventing eventual colonization. This was what motivated the Kingdom of Hawaii, for example.[63] In "semi-civilized" countries, such as

---

55. For a discussion of the 1960 Civil Code, see Sang Hyun Song, *supra* note 31, at 382–84 (1983); Kim Chung Han, The New Civil Code of Korea, 4 The Just. 3 (1960); Kyu–Chang Cho, Koreanisches Buergerliches Gesetzbuch at xviii–xx (1980).

56. See William C. Jones, Trying to Understand the Current Chinese Legal System, in Understanding China Legal System (C. Stephen Hsu ed., 2003).

57. The Civil Code, in particular, is substantially patterned after that of Germany. See H. H. P. Ma, General Features of the Law and Legal System of the Republic of China, in Cosway, Ma & Shattuck, Trade and Investment in Taiwan: The Legal and Economic Environment 8 (1973). See also the second (1985) ed. of the same work, by H. H. P. Ma.

58. See generally T. Ansay & D. Wallace, Introduction to Turkish Law (4th ed. 1996); Vahit Bıçak, Turish Law: A Bibliogrpahy of Turkish Legal Materials in English (2001), available at http://www.geocities.com/vbicak/trlaw.htm.

59. See Hirsch, Der Einfluss des schweizerischen Rechts auf das neue Tuerkische Handelsgesetzbuch, 52 Schweizerische Juristenzeitung 325 (1956); Ansay, Turkey: New Commercial Code, 6 Am. J. Comp. L. 106 (1957).

60. See Karlen & Arsel, Civil Litigation in Turkey 7–8 (1957).

61. See R. Aybay, Administrative Law, in Ansay & Wallace, *supra* note 58.

Some of the problems of adjustment which arose as a result of Turkey's importation of foreign codes are interestingly discussed by Hamson, The Istanbul Conference of 1955, 5 Int'l & Comp.L.Q. 26 (1956), and by Hooker, *supra* note 12, at 364–71. On the whole, however, Turkey is one of a few countries where Western institutions were successfully introduced into a traditional Moslem milieu. This is often attributed to the charismatic influence of Kemal Atatürk. See G. J. Mussell, The Surrogate Proletariat 392 (1974).

62. When a country which has not been under colonial rule independently embarks on a program of modernizing and westernizing its legal system, it has a choice between civil law and common law models. Experience has shown that such countries tend to look to the civil law, probably for the reason that the civil law models present themselves in the conveniently packaged form of codes.

63. See Sally Engle Merry, Colonizing Hawai'i: The Cultural Power of Law (2000); Stuart Banner, Possessing the Pacific: Land, Settlers, and Indigenous People from Australia to Alaska (2007).

China, western powers often insisted on the privilege of extraterritoriali-ty—that is, subjects of western powers were subject only to their own law even when on sovereign Chinese territory. The implied condition for removing the regime of extraterritoriality was again the native system's attainment of the elusive standard of "civilization."[64] Thailand, for exam-ple, sought to rid itself of the system of extraterritoriality by enacting a Penal Code derived from French, Japanese, English, and indigenous sources,[65] while the draftsmen of its Civil Code drew inspiration mainly from the codes of France, Germany, and Switzerland.[66]

As another example, one can mention Ethiopia, where a similarly variegated bouquet of codes, prepared by French, Swiss, and other Europe-an scholars, was adopted during the reign of Emperor Haile Selassie I.[67] Prior to the revolution of 1974, Ethiopian law students seeking to master this essentially civilian code system—which had never become actual living law in much of the country—were instructed at a law school in Addis Ababa whose faculty at the time was largely American and took an American approach to teaching and research.[68] After the overthrow of the Emperor, the new regime passed a series of "basic laws" which expressed the regime's socialist orientation (e.g., nationalization of land and industry) and appointed a legislative commission to consider code reforms in the

64. See, e.g., Teemu Ruskola, Colonial-ism Without Colonies: On the Extraterritori-al Jurisprudence of the U.S. Court for China, 71 Law & Contemp. Probs. 217 (2008), and Teemu Ruskola, Canton Is Not Boston: The Invention of American Imperial Sovereignty, 57 Am. Q. 859 (2005). On the role of the concept of "civilization" in international law, see Gerritt W. Gong, The Standard of "Civili-zation" in International Society (1984).

65. See T. Masao, The New Penal Code of Siam, 18 Yale L.J. 85 (1908); Apirat Petch-siri, Eastern Importation of Western Crimi-nal Law: Thailand as a Case Study (1987).

66. See F. C. Darling, The Evolution of Law in Thailand, 32 Rev.Pol. 197 (1970). The influence of French law was particularly strong, due to the predominance of French advisors during the codification process, and to the large number of Thai lawyers who had received their legal training in France. See also Chin Kim, The Thai Choice-of-Law Rules, 5 Int'l Law. 709 (1971).

67. See J. H. Beckstrom, Transplanta-tion of Legal Systems: An Early Report on the Reception of Western Laws in Ethiopia, 21 Am. J. Comp. L. 557 (1973); N. J. Singer, The Ethiopian Civil Code and the Recogni-tion of Customary Law, 9 Hous. L. Rev. 460 (1972); R. A. Sedler, The Development of

Legal Systems: The Ethiopian Experience, 53 Iowa L. Rev. 962 (1967); J. Vanderlinden, An Introduction to the Sources of Ethiopian Law, 3 J. Eth. L. 227 (1966); R. David, A Civil Code for Ethiopia, 37 Tul. L. Rev. 187 (1963); R. David, Les sources du code civil Éthiopien, 14 Rev.Int.Dr.Comp. 497 (1963); F. F. Russell, The New Ethiopian Civil Code, 29 Brook. L. Rev. 236 (1963); F.F. Russell, The New Ethiopian Penal Code, 10 Am. J. Comp. L. 265 (1961). 'Abarā Ğambaré, An introduction to the legal history of Ethiopia 1434–1974 (2000).

68. See J. C. N. Paul, Fourth Annual Report from the Dean, 4 J.Eth.L. 21 (1967); J. Vanderlinden, Civil Law and Common Law Influences on the Developing Law in Ethio-pia, 16 Buff. L. Rev. 250 (1966). See also R. A. Sedler, Legal Education: Ethiopia, 7(1) Foreign Exch. Bull. 7 (1965), where the fol-lowing observation is made: ". . . teaching in the areas covered by the codes—all private and penal law—calls for a knowledge of con-tinental law. It is very difficult to obtain con-tinental-trained lawyers who can teach in English [the country's second language]; con-sequently there is a great need for American or British lawyers who have training in com-parative law and are bilingual [in the sense that they can work with French or French-derived legal materials]."

spirit of socialist values and policies.[69] American law teachers were replaced by Ethiopians and a sprinkling of East Europeans.[70] The Menghistu regime was overthrown in 1991; and, since the codes adopted during Haile Selassie's reign were still un-repealed, they have continued in force as the law of the new Federal Democratic Republic of Ethiopia.[71]

The Code Napoleon has enjoyed a wide sphere of influence, not limited to the traditional civil law areas of Europe and Latin America.[72] Throughout the vast area of North and West Africa[73] as well as the Near East (except in Turkey and Israel) French influence has been stronger than that of any other western legal system; but the depth of its penetration has varied from period to period and from country to country.[74] Generalizations, even if limited to the predominantly Arab countries of the area, have to be formulated with caution.[75] There are a few nations, such as Saudi

69. See F. Nahum, Socialist Ethiopia's Achievements as Reflected in Its Basic Laws, 11 J. Eth. L. 83–88 (1980).

70. See D. Haile, Annual Report from the Dean, 12 J. Eth. L. 112–13 (1982).

71. Under Ethiopia's new federal constitution, the Penal Code, Commercial Code, and Labor Code, will remain in effect as coming within federal power; the Civil Code only to the extent that the Federal Council deems necessary to maintain a single economic community. See R. A. Sedler, A Return to Ethiopia, 7(2) Mich. Int'l L. 21, 24 (Fall 1995). Ethiopia enacted a new Criminal Code in 2004.

For a stimulating collection of essays (some in English) on the relationship between imported models and indigenous law in Ethiopia and other countries in the Horn of Africa, see Transplants, Innovation and Legal Tradition in the Horn of Africa (Elisabetta Grande ed., 1995). For older (somewhat dated) accounts of remnants of both Italian and British law which were to be found, together with local customary law, in the legal systems of Eritrea and Somalia, see F. F. Russell, Eritrean Customary Law, 3 J. Afr. L. 99 (1959); M. R. Ganzglass, A Common Lawyer Looks at an Uncommon Legal Experience, 53 A.B.A.J. 815 (1967). Present-day Somalia is without central government, and the national legal system is in abeyance; in some areas, Islamic courts have taken over the function of maintaining order.

72. See Limpens, Territorial Expansion of the Code, in The Code Napoleon and the Common Law World 92, especially at 101–02 (B. Schwartz ed., 1956); I. Zajtay, Les desti-

nées du Code Civil, 6 Rev. Int. Dr. Comp. 792 (1954), reprinted in I. Zajtay, Beitrage zur Rechtsvergleichung 109 (1976).

73. For comprehensive bibliographies on the law of all African countries, see Jacques Vanderlinden, Bibliographies internationales de la doctrine juridique africaine (22 vols., 1994). See also Rodolfo Sacco (and others) Il diritto Africano (1995)

74. French influence remained particularly strong in Lebanon and (at least until 1979) in Iran, although the codes of the latter country reflected a measure of eclecticism. See H. J. Liebesny, Stability and Change in Islamic Law, 21 Middle East J. 16, 28, 30 (1967); W. G. Wickersham & M. M. Nsouli, Legal System of Lebanon: Summary and Bibliography, 5 Int'l Law. 300 (1971); The Lebanese Legal System (Antoine Elias El-Gemayel ed., 1986); G. B. Baldwin, The Legal System of Iran, 7 Int'l Law. 492 (1973); W. J. Butler & G. Levasseur, Human Rights and the Legal System of Iran (Int'l Comm'n Jurists 1976). For a comprehensive survey of codifications of private law in Arab states, see F. Castro, La Codificazione del Diritto Privato negli Stati Arabi Contemporanei, 31 Rivista di Diritto Civile 387–447 (1985).

75. Liebesny, *supra* note 74, provides an excellent brief survey covering most of the countries of the area. For thorough treatment and documentation, see S. H. Amin, Middle East Legal Systems (1985); Comparative Law of Israel and the Middle East (N. H. Kittrie ed., 1971); H. J. Liebesny, The Law of the Near and Middle East: Readings, Cases and Materials (1974). Chibli Mallat, From Islamic to Middle Eastern Law. a Restatement of The Field, part 1 , 51 Am. J. Comp.

Arabia and Oman, where the law is still largely based on the Koran and other religious sources.[76] In most of the legal systems of the region, however, one observes a mixed pattern. Some version, often a considerably reformed version, of Islamic law is apt to govern matters of family law, including perhaps certain related problems of property and succession; the jurisdiction of religious courts over such matters has been preserved in some (but not all) of the countries in question.[77] In other fields, especially in the law of obligations and in the area of commercial law, civil law influence, traditionally of the French variety, has been predominant. One must note, however, that law has been at the center of a long-standing and ongoing struggle between European-style modernity and Islamic traditionalism; and that this has resulted (to say the least) in pressures to depart from western law whenever it appears to conflict with basic principles of Islamic law.[78]

Along these lines, the Egyptian Civil Code of 1949,[79] although modern in style and organization, sought to achieve a synthesis between Islamic teachings and western legal institutions. The same is true of other civil codes, based more or less on the Egyptian prototype, which have been enacted in Syria (1949), Iraq (1951, eff. 1953), Libya (1954), Algeria (1975),

Law 699 (2003); part 2, 52 Am. J. Comp. Law, 233 (2004).

76. See G. Baroody, Shari'ah—The Law of Islam, 72 Case and Comment, March–April 1967, at 3; Hart, Application of Hanbalite and Decree Law to Foreigners in Saudi Arabia, 22 Geo. Wash. L. Rev. 165 (1953). Although the basically Islamic character of the Saudi Arabian legal system remains unchanged, the country's oil wealth has led to the enactment of much modern legislation, some of which is based on western models. See N. H. Karam, Business Laws of Saudi-Arabia (1979); J. Asherman, Doing Business in Saudi-Arabia, 16 Int'l Law. 321 (1982); T. M. Hill, The Commercial Legal System of the Sultanate of Oman, 17 Int'l Law. 507 (1983); George N. Sfeir, The Saudi Approach to Law Reform, 36 Am. J. Comp. L. 729 (1988). The Islamic tradition, as modified in part by codes and other statutes, also played a dominant role in the legal system of Afghanistan. See A. S. Sirat, The Modern Legal System of Afghanistan, 16 Am. J. Comp. L. 563 (1968). This might have changed under the Marxist regime in power after 1978. Under the Taliban, who captured Kabul in 1996, an extreme form of Islamic traditionalism has been imposed. For recent developments accounting of dramatic political circumstances, Faiz Ahmed, Shari'a, Custom, and Statutory Law: Comparing State Approaches to Islamic Jurisprudence, Tribal Autonomy, and Legal Development in Afghanistan and Pakistan,7 Global Jurist Advances (2007).

77. See Lynn Welchman, The Development of Islamic Family Law in the Legal System of Jordan, 37 Int'l & Comp. L. Q. 868 (1988).

78. See G. F. Borden, Legal Counseling in the Middle East, 14 Int'l Law. 545, 560 (1980); H. Barton et al., *supra* note 15, at 36. It also has resulted, of course, in mounting pressure to abandon western models entirely and return to a strict application of traditional Islamic law. See H. J. Liebesny, Judicial Systems in the Near and Middle East: Evolutionary Development and Islamic Revival, 37 Middle East J. 202 (1983).

79. This Code went into effect upon abolition of the Mixed Courts, as to which see Brinton, The Mixed Courts of Egypt (rev. ed. 1968). See also G. M. Wilner, The Mixed Courts of Egypt: A Study on the Use of Natural Law and Equity, 5 Ga. J. Int'l & Comp. L. 407 (1975). Until 1949, Egypt had a Civil Code for the Mixed Courts (1875) and a Civil Code for the National Courts (1883), both of which largely followed the Code Napoleon. The 1949 Code thus marks a partial recession of foreign and especially of French influence.

In 1980 the Constitution was amended to make Islamic law the principal source of legislation, and several courts have invalidated contracts with interest provisions on the ground that such provisions violate Islamic law. See H. Barton et al., *supra* note 15, at 36.

Qatar (1976), and Kuwait (1980).[80] To the extent that they have followed western models, modern Near–East legislators (differing in this respect from earlier codifiers who drew their civil law learning exclusively from French sources) have tended to be selective.[81] But, although the Code Napoleon is no longer blindly followed, it is still the most potent source of western influence on private law codes in the Arab world.[82]

The Islamic tradition is also an important factor in Indonesia, another country touched by civil law influence. There, the Dutch introduced the so-called "dualist" system;[83] the majority of the indigenous population lived under their own customary law ("adat" law, varying from region to region), while Europeans, and others who voluntarily accepted European law were governed by Dutch codes.[84] There also was a dual court system. Upon gaining independence, the Indonesian Republic created a substantially unitary court system;[85] but the dualism of the substantive law, although greatly reduced by the enactment of unitary statutes covering certain important areas (especially of business law),[86] has not been completely eliminated.[87]

80.   In addition to the sources cited *supra* note 76, see Gamal Moursi Badr, The New Egyptian Civil Code and the Unification of the Laws of the Arab Countries, 30 Tul. L. Rev. 299, 303–04 (1956); R. Khany, The Legal System of Syria, 1 Comp. L. Yearbook 137 (1977); Jwaideh, The New Civil Code of Iraq, 22 Geo. Wash. L. Rev. 176 (1953); Chibli Mallat, Middle Eastern Law (2007). For a foundational legal anthropological case study investigating the relationship between modern and "traditional" law in the area, see Martha Mundi & Richarda Saumarez Smith, Governing Property, Making the Modern State: Law, Administration and Production in Ottoman Syria (2007).

81.   See F. J. Ziadeh, Law of Property in Egypt: Real Rights, 26 Am. J. Comp. L. 239, 246 (1978).

82.   This is illustrated by the Egyptian Civil Code's provisions on land law, which apparently were inspired by somewhat archaic rules embodied in the Code Napoleon. See *id.*, and D. F. Forte, Egyptian Land Law: An Evaluation, 26 Am. J. Comp. L. 273 (1978).

83.   This phenomenon is not limited, of course, to Indonesia. "Dualism" or "pluralism" (i.e., different law for different groups within a given territory) characterized many colonial regimes and continues to characterize most of the legal systems of the southern hemisphere.

84.   See Ter Haar, Adat Law in Indonesia (1948), with an instructive Introduction by Hoebel and Schiller; Leyser, Legal Developments in Indonesia, 3 Am. J. Comp. L. 399 (1954); Indonesia. Law and society (Tim Lindsey ed., 2d ed. 2008).

The codes for the East Indies were not entirely but very largely identical with the French-influenced codes adopted in Holland in 1838. The Netherlands East Indies Civil Code of 1847, for example, was essentially based on Holland's own Civil Code of 1838, which in turn was a derivative of the Code Napoleon. Subsequent amendments of the Dutch codes were not always incorporated into the East Indies codes.

85.   However, religious courts exercising jurisdiction over Moslems in matters of family law (with the Islamic High Court as appellate court) were preserved. Largely as a result of the Marriage Law of 1974, there was a notable increase in the power and stature of these courts. See J. S. Katz & R. S. Katz, Legislating Social Change in a Developing Country: The New Indonesian Marriage Law Revisited, 26 Am. J. Comp. L. 309, 317 (1978).

86.   See the series of English-language monographs directed by Professors Mochtar Kusumaatmadja and Sudargo Gautama (J. Katz & R. Katz, advisors) which were published by Padjadjaran University Law School under the title Survey of Indonesian Economic Law (1973–74).

87.   See S. Gautama & R. N. Hornick, An Introduction to Indonesian Law: Unity in

A survey of common law and civil law jurisdictions, even a most cursory one, would not be complete without some reference to the special position of the Scandinavian (or, more properly, Nordic) legal systems.[88] Nordic law has many of the characteristics of civil law; it also has features that differentiate it from other civil law systems and make it look like common law (although it is not directly an offshoot of English law).[89] Nordic law is, for instance, pragmatically oriented; it was not influenced by Roman law to the same extent as French and German law; and, while it is largely embodied in systematic statutes, often of fairly broad coverage, these are not comprehensively organized like the codes of typical civil law jurisdictions.[90] There are differences *inter sese* between the various Nordic legal systems; but these countries also have cooperated closely in enacting considerable quantities of uniform legislation[91] and, indeed, for a long while stood as the premier example of legal and legislative cooperation among sovereign states.[92]

Diversity (1974); E. Damian & R. N. Hornick, Indonesia's Formal Legal System, 20 Am. J. Comp. L. 492 (1972) (with bibliography); D. S. Lev, The Lady and the Banyan Tree: Civil Law Change in Indonesia, 14 Am. J. Comp. L. 282 (1965).

88. See generally, Nordic Law: Between Tradition and Dynamism (Jaakko Husa, Kimmo Nuotio & Heikki Pihlajamäki eds., 2007); R. B. Ginsburg, A Selective Survey of English Language Studies on Scandinavian Law (1970). Ole Lando, Northern Countries. A Legal Family? A Diagnosis and a Prognosis, in 1 Global Jurist Advances, Issue 2 Art 5 (2001).

For a birds-eye view of the essential features of the Swedish legal system, see J. B. Board, Jr., Legal Culture and the Environmental Protection Issue: The Swedish Experience, 37 Alb. L. Rev. 603 (1973).

89. Some scholars classify Scandinavian law as a distinct group independent of both common and civil law. See B. Gomard, Civil Law, Common Law and Scandinavian Law, 5 Scandinavian Studies in Law 27 (1961); S. Jorgensen, Les traits principaux de l' évolution des sources du droit Danois, 1971 Rev. Int. Dr. Comp. 65. See also S. Jorgensen, Grundzüge der Entwicklung der skandinavischen Rechtswissenschaft, 25 Juristenzeitung 529 (1970) (emphasizing the independence of Scandinavian legal scholarship).

For others, Scandinavian law is more or less clearly a branch of "continental" civil law. See, e.g., Franz Wieacker, A History of Private Law in Europe 399–400 (Tony Weir trans., 1995); Michael Bogdan, Comparative Law 88–90 (1994); J. W. F. Sundberg, Civil Law, Common Law and the Scandinavians, 13 Scandinavian Studies in Law 179 (1969).

90. Common law as well as civil law characteristics can also be found in the Swedish Code of Civil Procedure. See Ginsburg and Bruzelius, Civil Procedure in Sweden (1965).

The Scandinavian courts' attitude toward precedents has been described as an intermediate one, midway between stare decisis and the corresponding doctrines of the civilians. See von Eyben, Judicial Law Making in Scandinavia, 5 Am. J. Comp. Law 112 (1956).

91. The working methods of legislative co-operation among the Nordic countries are interestingly described in S. Jorgensen, Abbestellungsrecht und nordische Gesetzeszusammenarbeit, 1971 Zeitschrift für Rechtsvergleichung 12.

92. See S. Petrén, Nordic and International Lawmaking, 12 Scandinavian Studies in Law 69 (1968); N. E. Holly, Legal and Legislative Co-operation in the Scandinavian States, 49 A.B.A.J. 1089 (1963).

In assessing the world-wide influence of the civil law, we must also consider the legal systems of those nations which fall or which until recently fell within the communist orbit. We should say a word as well about the common problems of transition faced by "post-socialist" legal systems.

As a distinct type of legal system, "socialist" law, once "the third family of legal systems" survives as a residual element in the legal systems of countries moving to cast off their communist past[93] and, somewhat more robustly, in countries (China, Vietnam, Laos, North Korea, and Cuba) that are still officially "socialist." China, while still adhering to tight one-party rule politically, has been moving away from central economic planning economically. Its standing as a "socialist" is thus a subject of debate.[94] On the other hand, President Chavez plan called "Socialism for the 21st century", much inspired by the resilience of the Cuban experience, has attracted admiration from a variety of other Latin American countries resisting U.S. hegemony. Countries like Bolivia and Ecuador have inserted highly innovative socialist elements in their constitutional systems, have developed important ties with China, and might be the signal of a change of trend after twenty years of post-soviet "single thought". Equally importantly, many of the legal developments in Western Europe and North America during the Cold War can be viewed as partial—often defensive—borrowings from socialist law.

In any event, all "socialist" countries have retained elements of their pre-communist law. They differ widely, however, with regard to the strength of these elements. Although the Republic of China used the German Civil Code as a model and the People's Republic of China referred to the Soviet model, eventually much of the borrowing was lost in the era of Mao's "legal nihilism." After Mao's death in 1976, there was a revival of interest in the legal ordering of society, including a program of national codification.[95] In much of this legislation, one finds the definite influence of civil law concepts. Additional legal reforms have accompanied the accelerating move towards a "socialist market economy." The major task now is the creation of institutions and cultural attitudes for their realization and enforcement.[96]

93. These include not only the core group of countries which comprised (in Soviet terminology) the "world socialist system," but also a number of developing countries, mostly in Africa, on which "socialist" law had a marked influence. Residues remain, but, by and large, with the collapse of communism at the center, "peripheral" regimes (in places such as Angola, Mozambique, and Madagascar) also have embraced multi-party politics and a market economy.

94. For a recent assessment of China's democratic and economic achievements and shortfalls, see Randall Peerenboom, China Modernizes: Threat to the West or Model for the Rest? (2007).

95. This included the important General Principles of Civil Law of the P.R.C., which took effect on Jan. 1, 1987.

96. Donald C. Clarke, Power and Politics in the Chinese Court System: The Enforcement of Civil Judgements, 10 Colum. J. Asian L. 1 (1996); Sarah Biddulph, Legal Reform and Administrative Detention Powers in China (2008).

Elements of pre-Communist civil law have been preserved to a much greater extent in the countries of Eastern and Southeastern Europe which (with the exception of Albania)[97] truly belonged to the civil law world until the 1940s.[98] Under communism, the ideological basis of the legal systems of those countries was radically changed, as were the sectors of the law that reflected the character of the state. But, on the working level, these countries preserved most of the concepts and techniques, and a considerable number of the actual institutions, which had been part of their civil law heritage.[99] Thus, in spite of the chasm that separated the capitalist west from the communist east, a lawyer trained in the civil law would find, at the level of legal form, much that was recognizable in the legal systems of communist countries located to the west and southwest of the Soviet Union.[100]

Without much exaggeration, a similar statement could be made about the legal system of the former Soviet Union itself.[101] Although its historical antecedents were quite different from those of the law in Western and Central Europe, the Russian legal system came under the strong influence of western civilian codes during the half century preceding the October

---

97. In spite of the adoption of some codes influenced by French and Italian models, it seems that Islamic and Ottoman influences were predominant in the pre-communist legal system of Albania. See Kolaj & Pritsch in 1 Rechtsvergleichendes Handwoerterbuch fuer das Zivil- und Handelsrecht des In- und Auslandes 1–5 (1929); Hooker, *supra* note 12, at 410.

98. Except for Hungary, all of the countries in question had adopted code systems modeled on the Austrian or other classical continental patterns. Some countries, notably the Kingdom of Yugoslavia, had preserved enclaves of Islamic law (relating to personal status) for the benefit of their sizable Moslem minorities.

99. See René David & John E. C. Brierley, Major Legal Systems in the World Today 181–84 (3d ed. 1985).

One of the principal legacies of the civil law to the socialist legal systems of Eastern Europe was the technique of codification. See Codification in the Communist World (F. J. M. Feldbrugge ed., 1975). See also Gianmaria Ajani, Il modello post-sociaista (2008).

100. See W. J. Wagner's introductory comments on the Polish legal system and the legal systems of other communist countries, in 1 Formation of Contracts, *supra* note 14, at 213–23, 311–17. See also W. J. Wagner,

Polish Law Throughout the Ages (1970). In large part because of a rejection of rigid central planning, the Yugloslav legal system developed along lines which differentiated it from the legal systems of other socialist countries. Nevertheless, its civil law features also remained quite pronounced. On the civil law features of the 1978 Yugoslav Statute on Obligations, see K. Muscheler, Deutsch–Jugoslawisches Juristentreffen, Mitteilungen der Gesellschaft für Rechtsvergleichung, No. 18 (May 1981), at 320. Americanization is not absent through the area. See Jacques deLisle, Lex Americana?: United States Legal Assistance, American Legal Models, and Legal Change in the Post–Communist World and Beyond, 20 U. Pa. J. Int'l Econ. L. 179 (1999).

101. Generally speaking, the association of "socialist" law with civil law forms was more a matter of historical contingency than intrinsic affinity. The means of production could just as easily have been socialized using common law as civil law property concepts. Much as capitalism has flourished both under common and civil law, so socialism, at least in most of its definitions, appears to be able to function using widely divergent legal techniques. See Zdenek Kuhn, Development of Comparative Law in Central and Eastern Europe, in The Oxford handbook of Comparative Law (Mathias Reimann & Reinhard Zimmermann eds., 2006).

Revolution of 1917.[102] Soviet codes[103] did not make a sharp break with traditional civilian techniques.[104] A lawyer brought up in the civil law might find unfamiliar the ideology that permeated the text or the implementation of those codes[105] but nevertheless would find their structure, terminology, and technique reasonably familiar.[106] By the same token, many of the distinctive features of the common law appeared equally alien both to "socialist" lawyers and to lawyers trained in western civil law systems.

What marked off "socialist" law most notably as a distinct type of law, were not features relating to legal form or technique, but extra-juridical factors. The label "socialist law" refers to the legal systems of those states that have (i) socialized the means of production, (ii) expanded the role of the state or state-affiliated organizations in all spheres of social life, (iii)

102. See S. Kutcherov, Courts, Lawyers and Trials Under the Last Three Tsars (1953); K. Grzybowski, Legal Science During the Last Century: Russia, in Inchieste di Diritto Comparato—La Scienza del Diritto nell' Ultimo Secolo 623–43 (M. Rotondi ed., 1976); H. J. Berman, The Comparison of Soviet and American Law, 34 Ind. L.J. 559, 562–63 (1959).

103. For an English translation of the former RSFSR Civil Code, see W. Gray & R. Stults, The Civil Code of the Russian Soviet Federated Socialist Republic (1965). See also W. E. Butler, Collected Legislation of the USSR & the Constituent Union Republics (1979).

104. See, e.g., the numerous references to "Romanist tradition" in J. N. Hazard, Communists and Their Law (1969).

In matters of technical detail, the civilian tradition appeared at every step. As one of many examples, one might mention the list of transactions requiring the formality of a notarial act. See Hazard, Butler & Maggs, The Soviet Legal System 69–71 (3d ed. 1977). Socialist legal scholars seem to have agreed that "legal forms" in bourgeois and socialist law might be similar. See I. Szabo, The Socialist Conception of the Law, in 2 Int'l Ency. Comp.L. ch. 1, at 59 (1970). Nevertheless, it should be kept in mind that many traditional civilian techniques and institutions underwent a more or less subtle change of purpose when used in the Soviet system: policies pursued in the new context are different. There is little doubt, for example, that in the Soviet system the requirement of a notarial act reflected a stronger degree of state supervision

than would be the case in a western civil law country.

105. On the impact of ideology on the Soviet administration of justice, see W. J. Wagner, The Russian Judiciary Act of 1922 and Some Comments on the Administration of Justice in the Soviet Union, 41 Ind. L.J. 420 (1966).

For a broad-based discussion of the jurisprudential underpinnings of socialist law, see D. A. Funk, Lessons of Soviet Jurisprudence: Law for Social Change Versus Individual Rights, 7 Ind. L. Rev. 449 (1974). See also I. Markovits, Socialist vs. "Bourgeois" Rights, 46 U. Chi. L. Rev. 612 (1978).

106. See, e.g., O. Joffe & P. B. Maggs, Soviet Law in Theory and Practice 1 (1983). Nonetheless, the problem of the comparability of socialist and nonsocialist legal institutions spawned a voluminous literature. Comparatists from socialist countries usually stressed the uniqueness of their system and the limits of comparability. See, e.g., I. Szabo, *supra* note 104, at 59–61; A. A. Tille, Socialisticheskoe Sravnitelnoe Pravovedenie (1975). For Western views, see Hazard, Socialist Laws and the International Encyclopedia, 79 Harv. L. Rev. 278 (1965); Schlesinger, Introduction to 1 Formation of Contracts, *supra* note 14, at 22–29; D. Loeber, Rechtsvergleichung zwischen Ländern mit verschiedener Wirtschaftsordnung, 26 Rabels Z. 201 (1961). See also F. Mádl, A Comparative Law Synthesis Theory v. Private Transnational Law as a New Concept in Private Law, 2 Comp. L. Yearbook 1 (1979); M. Bogdan, Different Economic Systems and Comparative Law, 2 Comp. L. Yearbook 89 (1979).

established a "vanguard party," and (iv) adopted Marxism as their official ideology.[107]

Accordingly, among the main objectives of reform in all countries that have rejected their communist past have been (i) to privatize state-owned enterprise, (ii) to introduce the market into the economy and other spheres of life, (iii) to create some form of multi-party democracy, and (iv) to institute a constitutional system in which law is perceived as independent from a given political platform. Each of these objectives amounts to the negation of one of the characteristic features of a communist party state (although, conceived in positive terms, each still allows for a broad range of economic and political possibilities). There was some movement toward each of these objectives as part of Gorbachev's program of *perestroika* ("restructuring") in the Soviet Union between 1985 and 1991.[108]

The first two objectives are linked. It is possible to raise questions about the exact nature of other relationships between these objectives— about the relationship between a market economy and pluralistic democracy or between democracy and constitutional government.[109] But privatization and the development of a market economy appear to be interdependent. Privatization is not peculiar, of course, to ex-communist regimes and for the last twenty years governments everywhere have been put under pressure to shrink the size of the state by selling off public corporations.[110] However after the recent catastrophic performance of U.S corporate financial capitalism that began in the summer of 2008, the wind might have also changed globally from this "pressure to privatize" perspective. In any event, the privatization trend has been massive in former socialist countries for more than a decade: moving from a planned to a market economy requires taking steps not only (a) to abandon central planning and restrictions on private business activity, but also (b) to dissolve the monopoly position of the state by transferring (at least some) enterprises from state to private ownership, and (c) to create as well the whole web of supporting

---

107. These four interrelated elements were, at least until the late 1980s, the defining characteristics of a "communist party state." See, e.g., Stephen White, Communist Party States, in Oxford Companion to World Politics 167, 168 (Joel Krieger ed., 1993).

108. On legal aspects of reform during this period, see, e.g., The Emancipation of Soviet Law (F. J. M. Feldbrugge ed., Law in Eastern Europe No. 44, 1992); Harold J. Berman, Gorbachev's Law Reforms in Historical Perspective, 5 Emory J. Int'l Aff. 1 (1988); Frances H. Foster, Procedure as a Guarantee of Democracy: The Legacy of the Perestroika Parliament, 26 Vand. J. Transnat'l L. 1 (1993); Hubert Izdebski, Legal Aspects of Economic Reform in Socialist Countries, 37 Am. J. Comp. L. 703 (1989); Paul B. Stephen III, Perestroyka and Property: The Law of

Ownership in the Post–Socialist Soviet Union, 39 Am. J. Comp. L. 35 (1991); Symposium, Legal Reform in the Soviet Union, 28 Colum. J. Transnat'l L. 1 (1990); Symposium, Perestroika in Soviet Legal Institutions, 15 L. & Soc. Inquiry 417 (1990).

109. *Cf.* Jon Elster, Making Sense of Constitution–Making, 1(1) E. Eur. Const. Rev. 15, 16 (Spring 1992).

110. On the problems of privatization in general (especially in less developed countries), see Yacob Haile–Mariam, Privatization of State–Owned Enterprises and the Law: Issues and Problems, 7 Emory Int'l L. Rev. 35 (1993). For a wealth of further references, see also Terence Daintith & Monica Sah, Privatisation and the Economic Neutrality of the Constitution, 1993 Pub. L. 465.

institutions and laws that is taken for granted in western market (or mixed) economies.

Each of these steps involves a complex series of tasks. Some have produced dramatic social costs that we are now in the process of assessing. Some counter-tendencies to re-nationalization are visible as well when unbound corporate capitalism proves unaffordable even to right-wing leaning parties. A major recent example would be Fannie Mae and Freddie Mac during the mortgage crisis in the United States. Closing down inefficient enterprises results in unemployment; not closing them down means state subsidies to keep them afloat, which produces even greater inflation. Questions of sequence and timing have been quite controversial.[111]

The first set of steps have included governments abandoning central planning, freeing prices, remove other state controls, make the currency convertible, and relax trade barriers and restrictions on foreign investment.

The second step has been transferring the ownership of state enterprises to private hands which have produced a massive plunder favoring whoever was in the best position to literally pocket the public wealth.[112] This was a formidable undertaking even in eastern Germany where the country was able to shortcut many other transition problems simply by becoming part of the Federal Republic.[113] Before an enterprise could be

---

111. For objections to the conventional neo-classical economic recipe that called for doing everything quickly, if possible in one "big bang," see, e.g., Stephen S. Cohen & Andrew Schwartz, The Tunnel at the End of the Light: Privatization in Eastern Europe, 7 Transnat'l Law. 7 (1994); Paul H. Brietzke, Designing Legal Frameworks for Markets in Eastern Europe, 7 Transnat'l Law. 35 (1994); Inga Markovits, Exporting Law Reform: But will it Travel?, 37 Cornell Int'l L. Journal 95 (2004).

112. There has been a vast literature on privatization in Eastern Europe particularly in the immediate aftermath of the fall of the Berlin Wall. See, e.g., Roman Frydman, Andrzej Rapaczynski, John S. Earle, The Privatization Process in Central Europe (1993); Roman Frydman , The Privatization Process in Russia, Ukraine and the Baltic States (John S. Earle & Andrzej Rapaczynski eds., 1993); Privatisation in Central and Eastern Europe (Stephen A. Rayner ed., 1992); Vladimir K. Andreev, The Privatization of State Enterprises in Russia, 18 Rev. Cent. & E. Eur. L. 265 (1992); Cheryl W. Gray et al., The Legal Framework for Private Sector Development in a Transitional Economy: The Case of Poland, 22 Ga. J. Int'l & Comp. L. 283 (1992); Vratislov Pechota, Privatization

and Foreign Investment in Czechoslovakia: The Legal Dimension, 24 Vand. J. Transnat'l L. 316 (1991); Symposium, The Privatization of Eastern Europe, 12 N. Y. L. Sch. J. Int'l & Comp. L. 335–62 (1991).

113. Privatization in the former German Democratic Republic was governed largely by the Treuhandgesetz of June 17, 1990, enacted by the East German government before unification. It remained in effect by virtue of art. 25 of the Unification Treaty signed on Aug. 31, 1990 (1990 BGBl I 889). A translation of the treaty appears in 30 I.L.M. 463 (1991).

On privatization and related problems of restitution in eastern Germany, see, e.g., Martin E. Elling, Privatization in Germany: A Model for Legal and Functional Analysis, 25 Vand. J. Transnat'l L. 581 (1992); Michael Gruson, Privatization in the Former German Democratic Republic, 12 N.Y. L. Sch. J. Int'l & Comp. L. 347 (1991); Norbert Horn, The Lawful German Revolution: Privatization and Market Economy in a Re–Unified Germany, 39 Am. J. Comp. L. 725 (1991); Ulrich K. Preuss, Restitution vs. Investment, 1(2) E. Eur. Const. Rev. 22 (Summer 1992); Quint, The Constitutional Law of German Unification, 50 Md. L. Rev. 475, 541–62 (1991); A. Bradley Shingleton, Volker Ahrens & Peter

transferred to private owners, a number of preliminary problems have to be resolved. For instance:

(i) The enterprise has to be defined and disentangled from other components of the state economy and its assets identified.

(ii) It has to be given private law form. Typically, this means converting the enterprise into a company with shares that can be sold and traded. Usually these shares are initially held by the government agency in charge of the privatization process. Under the German Treuhandgesetz, former East German Kombinate (conglomerate enterprises) were converted into stock corporations (AGs); their subsidiary factories and outlets, into close corporations (GmbHs). The Treuhandanstalt ("Trust Agency") in charge of privatization became owner of shares in the AGs; the AGs initially became owners of GmbHs formerly subordinate to them.

(iii) Claims on the part of those with a prior stake in the enterprise have to be settled. There is the question of whether to allow preferential shares (and on what basis) to current managers or workers. There is also the question of whether to recognize claims of former owners from whom the particular property may have been illegally confiscated under the communist regime; and, if so, whether to restore the property or only provide compensation.

The question of restitution to former owners of a business or land is one of a knot of problems that is entangled with the issue of how should the state come to terms with its past.[114] Related problems concern the treatment of informers, former officials,[115] and secret police files. The question of restitution has attracted considerable controversy.[116] Some countries such as the Czech Republic and Germany[117] provided for restoring property to expropriated owners; others have not.

Ries, Property Rights in Eastern Germany: An Overview of the Amended Property Law, 21 Ga. J. Int'l & Comp. L. 345 (1991); D. B. Southern, Restitution or Compensation: The Land Question in East Germany, 42 Int'l & Comp. L. Q. 690 (1993).

114. For the treatment of these problems in reunified Germany, see Quint, The Imperfect Union: Constitutional Structures of German Unification (1997). For a comprehensive study of these problems generally, see Transitional Justice: How Emerging Democracies Reckon With Former Regimes (Neil J. Kritz, ed., 3 vols. 1995).

115. See Symposium: Law and Lustration: Righting the Wrongs of the Past, 20 L. & Soc. Inquiry 1 (1995). On "lustration" in Czechoslovakia in particular, see Vojtech Cepl, Lustration in the CSFR: Ritual Sacrifices, 1(1) E.Eur.Const.Rev. 24 (1993); Jirina Siklova, Lustration or the Czech Way of

Screening, 5(1) E. Eur. Const. Rev. 57 (1996). On the vetting of East German legal professionals, see Inga Markovits, Children of a Lesser God: GDR Lawyers in Post–Socialist Germany, 94 Mich. L. Rev. 2270 (1996).

116. On the issues involved, see Vojtech Cepl, Restitution of Property in Post–Communist Czechoslovakia, in Privatisation in Central and Eastern Europe, *supra* note 118, at 16; Jon Elster, On Doing What One Can, 1(2) E. Eur. Const. Rev. 15 (Summer 1992); Forum on Restitution, 2(3) E. Eur. Const. Rev. 30 (Summer 1993).

117. The German Unification Treaty provided for restitution with respect to property confiscated by the Nazis (1933–1945) or by the East German regime (1949–1990), but excluded the period of Soviet occupation (1945–1949). This exclusion was upheld by the Federal Constitutional Court in its Deci-

Once these preliminary questions are resolved, privatization still requires finding a buyer or else giving the enterprise away. Some countries have relied entirely on sales (public or private) to willing buyers, where they could be found; others (such as the Czech Republic, Russia, and Poland) have adopted voucher schemes by which all citizens are given the opportunity to acquire a stake, directly or indirectly, in the larger privatized companies.[118]

A third set of steps, apart from the abandonment of state controls and privatization, have involved establishing the whole complex of ancillary institutions and rules that seem to be indispensable for the operation of a modern market economy.[119] This includes, for instance, enactment of property laws, intellectual property laws, company laws, bankruptcy laws, accounting rules, securities regulation, banks and banking laws, tax laws, pension and unemployment systems, labor laws, insurance laws, consumer protection and anti-monopoly and competition laws. To bring all of them into being requires a massive amount of legislation, with developments that stretched over decades in the west being squeezed into a few years.[120]

Along with economic transformation, ex-socialist countries have been seeking to institutionalize multiparty-systems and constitutional govern-

sion of April 23, 1991 (BVerfGE 84, 90). Implementing legislation was contained in the Law on Regulation of Open Property Questions of Oct. 3, 1990. Initially, this law prohibited the disposition or transfer of any property as to which a timely claim was pending; but, since this proved an impediment to new investment, subsequent statutes of March 22, 1991 (1991 BGBl I, 766), and July 14, 1992 (1992 BGBl 1257), made it easier to sell such property to third party investors, while preserving the right of the original owners to compensation.

118. The details of "voucher privatization" vary. The Czech scheme involved auctions of shares in state-owned companies, with citizens being allowed to buy (for roughly a week's salary) a book of vouchers useable in these auctions. Vouchers were tradable and could be sold or exchanged for shares in investment funds (many set up by banks) which bid for large blocks of shares. Russia employed a modified version of the Czech system. The Polish scheme involved assigning most of the shares in large companies directly to a limited number of mutual investment funds, with a controlling interest in each company going to a single fund; citizens in turn received certificates that can be exchanged for shares in the investment funds. The idea is to rely on professional fund managers to ensure the efficiency of the companies they control.

119. See, e.g., Thomas W. Waelde & James L. Gunderson, Legislative Reform in Transition Economies: Western Transplants—A Short–Cut to Social Market Economy Status?, 43 Int'l & Comp. L. Q. 347 (1994).

120. For a general picture of recent legal reform in Russia (with much as well on the Russian legal tradition), see Gordon B. Smith, Reforming the Russian Legal System (1996). See also the essays collected in The Revival of Private Law in Central and Eastern Europe: Essays in Honor of F. J. M. Feldbrugge (George Ginsburgs, Donald D. Barry & William B. Simons eds., Law In Eastern Europe No. 46, 1996).

Russia enacted the first two of three parts of a new Civil Code in 1994 and 1995 (as well as a new Criminal Code in 1996). For an excellent English translation, see The Civil Code of the Russian Federation, Parts 1 & 2, with Introductory Commentary by A. L. Makovsky & S. A. Khokhlov (Peter B. Maggs with A. N. Zhiltsov trans., 1997). See also Lane H. Blumenfeld, Russia's New Civil Code: The Legal Foundation for Russia's Emerging Market Economy, 30 Int'l Law. 477 (1996). On the Criminal Code, see Anatolyi V. Naumov, The New Russian Criminal Code as a Reflection of Ongoing Reforms, 8 Crim. L. F. 191 (1997). For a comprehensive introductory discussion William E. Butler, Russian Law (2d ed. 2003).

ment.[121] Like economic reforms, these political objectives have two sides: one involves removing state controls, the other, positive constitutional reconstruction.

One goal articulated practically everywhere is the establishment of a "law governed-state" (or *Rechtsstaat*): a term often rendered into English as "the Rule of Law." The idea of the Rule of Law is not entirely a precise concept;[122] and there has been debate about whether all varieties of Marxist legal theory are necessarily incompatible with the Rule of Law.[123] Nevertheless, in all states which have officially embraced Marxist ideology, law has been treated as subordinate, in principle, to political ends.

Various institutional arrangements serve to foster the Rule of Law, among them provisions ensuring the independence of the judiciary and permitting judges to review the acts of other classes of public officials, including legislators. A notable recent development in Eastern Europe has been the establishment of constitutional courts.[124] Although the competence of these courts varies considerably, they all are based on the "European model" of judicial review which "concentrates" the power to declare legislation unconstitutional in a single court rather than "diffusing" it throughout the judiciary of a given country.[125]

121. On the general problems involved, see, e.g., Constitution Making in Eastern Europe (A. E. Dick Howard ed., 1993); Symposium: Approaching Democracy: A New Legal Order for Eastern Europe, 58 U. Chi. L. Rev. 439 (1991).

122. For suggestive discussions of its various aspects, see George P. Fletcher, Basic Concepts of Legal Thought 11–27 (1996); John Finnis, Natural Law and Natural Rights 270–73 (1980); Joseph Raz, The Authority of Law 210–29 (1979); Brian Z. Tamanaha, Law as a Means to an End: Threat to the Rule of Law (2007); Ugo Mattei & Laura Nader, Plunder. When The Rule of Law is Illegal (2008).

123. See, e.g., Christine Sypnowich, The Concept of Socialist Law (1990); Debate: Marxism and the Rule of Law, 15 L. & Soc. Inquiry 633 (1990).

124. See, e.g., Georg Brunner, Development of a Constitutional Judiciary in Eastern Europe, 18 Rev. Cent. & E. Eur. L. 535 (1992); Mark F. Brzezinski, Toward "Constitutionalism" in Russia: The Russian Constitutional Court, 42 Int'l & Comp. L. Q. 673 (1993); Mark F. Brzezinski, The Emergence of Judicial Review in Eastern Europe: The

Case of Poland, 41 Am. J. Comp. L. 153 (1993); A. Gwidz, The Constitutional Court in Poland, in Supranational and Constitutional Courts in Europe: Functions and Sources 383 (I. Kavass ed., 1992); Herbert Hausmaninger, From Soviet Committee of Constitutional Revision to Russian Constitutional Court, 25 Cornell Int'l L.J. 304 (1992); Herbert Hausmaninger, Towards a "New" Russian Constitutional Court, 28 Cornell Int'l L.J. 349 (1995); Istran Pogany, Constitutional Reform in Central and Eastern Europe: Hungary's Transition to Democracy, 42 Int'l & Comp. L. Q. 332 (1993); Herman Schwartz, The New East European Constitutional Courts, 13 Mich. J. Int'l L. 741 (1992); Symposium: The New Constitutional Courts, 2(2) E. Eur. Const. Rev. 28 (Spring 1993); Roundtable: Redesigning the Russian Court, 3(3–4) E. Eur. Const. Rev. 72 (1994); Feature: Questioning Constitutional Justice, 6(1) E. Eur. Const. Rev. 61 (1997).

125. For further elaboration of the distinction between "concentrated" and "diffuse" judicial review (as well as an excellent comparative account of various systems of judicial review), see Allan R. Brewer–Carías, Judicial Review in Comparative Perspective (1989).

3. Diffusion of Law as Political Ideology

As suggested by the review above, socialist legal systems were long considered a third main grouping of legal systems, in addition to civil law and common law. With the end of the Cold War, the number of at least nominally socialist states has plummeted, and it is indeed an open question what it means for a country like China, for example, to insist that its legal system is both "socialist" as well as oriented toward a "market economy." However, it is noteworthy that the category of socialist law, even in its most developed form, has been the object of much jurisprudential debate. Indeed, whether socialist law is really "law" has been questioned by both liberal as well as Marxian critics.[1] Consider Harold Berman's exposition of some Marxian theories of law.

Harold J. Berman, Justice in the U.S.S.R.: An Interpretation of Soviet Law

20–65 (revised and enlarged ed., 1963).

Classical Marxism ... contents itself with exposing what it conceives to be the ultimate sources of law. In broad terms it states that law is politics, that justice is a cloak for class interests, and that "bourgeois" justice is permeated with conceptions of private property and private contract which exclude the interests of the propertyless masses.... The proletariat is the last class; with its triumph over the bourgeoisie, and with its extermination of the last vestiges of capitalism, a new society without class antagonisms will emerge. The coercive institutions with which ruling classes of the present and past have held class antagonisms in check and thereby preserved their own dominant position will no longer have any reason for being. There will be no need for state and law, since these are merely instruments for maintaining property relations that will have vanished....

It was left to one Soviet writer, E.B. Pashukanis, to develop these notions into a theory of law which had substantial intellectual content. Pashukanis became the leading figure in Soviet legal development and acquired a high reputation in Western Europe as well.

Pashukanis sought to explain not merely the origin of law in class domination but also its particular unique features, which distinguish it from other means of class domination. These he saw as a reflection of the market. The economic traders who trade commodities in the market require a legal system for the enforcement of their transactions; they therefore identify themselves as juristic persons, "right-and-duty-bearing

---

1. For a more detailed study of the relationship between law and Marxism, see Hugh Collins, Marxism and Law (1982).

units", who, primarily through the medium of contracts, create reciprocal legal relations which express their reciprocal economic relations. The cornerstone of law is John Doe, the abstract individual, who by entering into transactions with other individuals creates mutual rights and duties. This John Doe is nothing but the legal version of the economic man. Just as a commodity is viewed as an abstraction expressing the commensurability of all things in the market, so a right is an abstraction expressing the commensurability—or reciprocity—of relations in the law court. Law therefore ultimately rests on the intentional voluntary conduct of individuals dealing with each other on a reciprocal basis.

According to Pashukanis, the agreement of the intention of the parties, which is the foundation of contract law, is at the same time the foundation of all other branches of the legal tree. . . . [E]ven in constitutional law Pashukanis saw the idea of government by consent, "social contract", as underlying a political order based on an alleged harmony of individual expressions of will. Thus all law is, in essence, commercial in character; all law presupposes the reasonable prudent individual who engages in arm-length transactions with other equally abstract legal entities. . . .

Thus law is in its very essence a capitalist, or bourgeois, institution. It may exist in embryonic form in feudal or slave societies, but essentially these societies are religious or military in character. "Law reaches its highest point of development under capitalism", wrote Pashukanis in 1930. To speak of "proletarian law" is therefore incorrect. The proletarian state may use bourgeois law, and must use it insofar as vestiges of the capitalist economy remain; but it cannot develop proletarian law, since law is by its nature based on individualism and contractualism. . . .

In 1936 the original Marxist vision of a classless socialist society in which "the public power will lose its political character" was officially recognized as impossible of achievement in the foreseeable future. . . . [I]nstead of the withering away of state and law, of money and property, of the family, of criminal sanctions, and the rest, there was to be a whole restoration of these institutions on a new "socialist" basis. . . .

The formal reason given for this radical departure from earlier Marxist and Leninist doctrine was the existence of socialism (and eventually communism) in one country; surrounded by capitalist powers, Soviet socialism requires the protection of a state, and the state in turn requires law. But such a reason is theoretically inadequate to explain the fact that the new classless (or class-conflictless) socialist state, supported by classless socialist law, now came to be treated not as a necessary evil but as a positive good. . . . In this new period [starting in 1936], political and legal structures hitherto accepted as temporary concessions to capitalist survivals were given a new "socialist" dignity. . . .

The new party line concerning law was authoritatively laid down in 1938 in a series of articles by Procurator–General (Attorney General) Vyshinsky, who replaced Pashukanis as dean of the Soviet legal profession, and by his book on Soviet public law. . . . Vyshinsky attacked Pashukanis' thesis that law reaches its highest stage of development under capitalism.

In fact, he wrote, "the development of capitalist society goes in the direction of the decay of law and legality" in its imperialist and fascist stages, capitalism leads "not to the strengthening of legality and of the rule of law but the final destruction of the rule of law". "History demonstrates that under socialism, on the contrary, law is raised to the highest level of development." . . .

Yet when it came to the elaboration of a positive theory of law, and not merely to the renunciation of the negative and nihilistic theories of the past, Vyshinsky could scarcely get beyond platitudes. "Our law is the embodiment in statutes of the will of the people," he wrote. "In capitalist society reference to the will of the people serves as a screen which covers the exploitational character of the bourgeois state. In our conditions the matter is in principle otherwise." "Our laws are the expression of the will of our people as it directs and creates history under the leadership of the working class. The will of the working class with us is fused with the will of the whole people." . . .

Having solved the basic economic problem by the elimination of antagonistic classes—so went the theoretical justification—it was possible to concentrate on the moral and legal aspects of social relations. There was no longer an economic excuse for moral or legal deviations. But whatever the justification and whatever the reason, the Soviet state was struggling to legalize its position; it was seeking in law a justification of authority which the original apocalyptic vision no longer provided. The Soviets turned away from the original Marxist question: how can the coercive, formal institutions of politics and law be superseded by a wholly rational social order in which "the free development of each is the condition for the free development of all"? They now asked the questions: How can economic, political, and socio-cultural institutions be integrated through law? How can law change to meet changing conditions and yet provide stability in a society which badly needs stability?

NOTES AND QUESTIONS

(1) What does the (putative) disappearance of the Second World of socialist states mean for the First–Third World relationship? Is this cause for concern in terms of the sustainable diversity of legal systems?[1]

(2) Despite the disappearance of the Soviet Union, an understanding of socialist law is not merely of historical interest. In his study *Soviet Legal Innovation and the Law of the Western World* (2007), John Quigley analyzes the influence that socialist law has had on the development of law in the West. The radical legal reforms of the Soviet Union posed a profound theoretical as well as practical challenge to the organization of society in Europe and North America. Some thought these reforms were worth imitating in their own right. Others saw them as threats to capitalism that were best contained by a partial

---

1. Cf. H. Patrick Glenn, Legal Traditions of the World: Sustainable Diversity in Law (2007).

accommodation of "socialist" features. Quigley illustrates how, over the course of the twentieth century, Western governments transformed their legal systems by amending and enacting an astonishing number of laws that reflected Soviet reforms—from labor law to welfare rights to family law to children rights to criminal law, and more. Observing that the Marxist ideology itself originated in the West, Quigley argues that the dynamic relationship between "Western law and the law promoted by the Bolsheviks reveals a complexity that makes it difficult to speak of them as separate systems and then to discuss whether one affected the other.... Much of what is viewed as 'modern' in the law first appeared, in the form of ideas and in the form of legislated law, in Soviet Russia." (p. 192)

(3) For a study of the role of Cold War in the development of civil rights law in the United States, and especially its role in *Brown v. Board of Education,* see Mary Dudziak, *Desegregation as a Cold War Imperative*, 41 STAN. L. REV. 61 (1988), and Mary Dudziak, Cold War Civil Rights: Race and the Image of American Democracy (2000).

(4) In order to understand legal diffusion through time and space, we need a broad definition of "law." The law is constantly in communication with the social, political, and cultural orders, which are in turn all interconnected, both at the local and at the international level. Therefore, it also plays a major role in identity formation. For example, the Western legal tradition is heavily invested in the idea of the "rule of law." Although the concept is vague, undefined and under-theorized, it would not be useful to deny its general ideological importance (the generalized professional belief in being governed by the rule of law).[2] Indeed, it may be one of the keys to understanding the relentless spread of Western-style legal institutions all around the planet.

Tibor Varady, Notes on Ideological Precepts as Formants of Private Law in Central–East European Countries

in Mauro Bussani & Ugo Mattei, Opening up European Law: The Common Core Project towards Eastern and South Eastern Europe 127 (2007).

In the country I am originally coming from (former Yugoslavia), for decades, the way to win an argument was to show that whatever you are saying *serves the cause of further progress of self-management*. This was somewhat better than the Soviet Union, where the clinching rhetoric punch lines were the *dictatorship of the proletariat* or *the leading role of the Communist Party*. Today, in the same countries people win debates by putting themselves (and their argument) on the side of *"European values"*, and *"market economy"*. The skills which have been needed have remained essentially the same. The argument is given, the punch line is permanent.

---

2. On the key cultural role of the "rule of law" as part of the construction of a contrast between "Western" and Chinese law, see Teemu Ruskola, Law Without Law, or Is "Chinese Law" an Oxymoron?, 11 Wm. & Mary Bill of Rts. J. 655 (2003).

The task is to pull your proposition under the shelter of the uncontestable punch line.

Let me also mention that I am not sure I know what exactly *"European values"* are; just as I never really understood what actually served *"the cause of further progress of self-management"*. All I learned is that it was (and remained) important to recognize the prevailing patterns, precepts, and intonations.

Ideological correctness branded titles of many legislative acts. Often, these titles either mirror the painstaking endeavor to avoid even the appearance of heresy, or they reflect the zeal, which tends to use every pretext to add the heavy imprint of established ideology. Let me give you a few examples. In 1982, Yugoslavia enacted an act on Private International Law. Most drafters wanted to call it "The Private International Law Act". This would have been very simple, but it had no chance. One of the key tenets of the then prevailing Marxist legal theory was that "the dichotomy between private and public law is already on the dumpsite of legal history". "Private law" was a wrong term. Even worse, a reactionary one. And as I said, titles rarely escape the attention of the legislators.[1] But how do you craft the title without the term "private law" (and, of course, without an unconditional acceptance of the Anglo–American "conflict of laws" designation). One had to come up with a really complicated zigzag. Here is the result. The name of the Act was: *"Act on the Resolution of Conflicts of Laws with Prescriptions of Other States in Certain Relations"*. (In 1996 by an act of stylistic mercy—although still not revival—the words "in certain relations" were omitted form the title, although this was the key, the *Ersatz* for "private law".)

In searching for manifestations of affirmative zeal (rather than just avoidance) I found many examples.... Looking through my old Belgrade textbooks that I still have on my shelves, looking at Soviet books in the library, I found quite a few ideology-tainted titles. I found the word "progressive" here and there without much contact with the context–and with a lot of contact with the zeal to use another opportunity to show that we are on the side of progress. With respect to one further example, I did not have to look anywhere, because I remember that the company act in Yugoslavia was called "Act on Associated Labor" in order to give emphasis to the precept that what is quintessential is the pooling of labor rather than of money. In Soviet law I found much more robust examples as well. On November 11, 1917, for example, full-swing revolutionary spirit in Soviet Russia yielded the following title of a legislative act: "On the Struggle with the Bourgeoisie and its Agents who are Sabotaging the Process of Food Supply in the Army, and who are Thwarting the Accomplishment of Peace. Or, to take a somewhat more recent example from the realm of Soviet law, on June 30, 1987, the USSR enacted a law entitled: "On All–National Discussion of Important Issues of State Life." This time, the language is

---

1. Sometimes they do. No system is really watertight. Communism was no exception. In 1979 the Hungarian legislator did pass an act which has in its title the magic words "Private International Law". The issue was not raised.

less aggressive, but it still shows an absolute dominance of ideology, it actually demonstrates an abuse of the space of legal norms.

But communism has had no monopoly on titles shaped by ideological zeal. The Helms–Burton Act[2] which deals with the economic boycott of Cuba[3] has the following title: "The Cuban Liberty and Democratic Solidarity (Libertad) Act"). (This is the act which provides, e.g. that a "[c]orporate officer, principal or shareholder with a controlling interest" of a company which is trading with a nationalized Cuban entity shall be denied a visa and shall be excluded from the U.S.; the same applies to "[a] spouse, minor child or agent" of such persons (§ 6091). The Act also provides that a person buying goods from a Cuban nationalized company may be liable for damages up to the whole value of the nationalized property (§ 6082). This enthusiasm was, however, surpassed by a new act enacted in a boiling atmosphere. One of the legislative reactions to the September 11th 2001 tragedy (and to the agitations which followed this tragedy) was the USA PATRIOT Act. This is actually an acronym which stands for: *Uniting and Strengthening America by Providing Appropriate Tools Required to Intercept and Obstruct Terrorism Act.* Again, the endeavor to fill every space with the messages and slogans of the current agitation prevailed over the logic, style and dignity of the discipline of law.

I am not a fan of the term "transition". During communist times in Central Eastern European countries, it was never said that we were a communist or socialist country. Communism and socialism were supposed to be kept as ideals, and it would have been difficult to maintain the ideal, had it been said that what we see and experience is already *it*. Therefore, it was said and repeated that we were "building socialism/communism", that we were "in transition towards socialism/communism". This was conducive to an attitude of waiting until the real thing comes, rather than to identifying the imperfections, and trying to change them. Now we are saying that what we have is not perfect yet, but this is because this is still not *it*, we are "in transition towards market economy"....

4. LEGAL FORMANTS

If the common core methodology is strictly bound to the name of the late lead author of this book, Rudolf B. Schlesinger, a German émigré scholar to the United States who is unanimously recognized as the "founding father" of American comparative law,[1] then *legal formants*, another

---

2. Enacted in 1996 Pub. L. 104–114, 110 Stat. 785, 22 U.S.C. §§ 6021–6091. See on this Act. Lowenfeld, The Cuban Liberty and Democratic Solidarity (Libertad) Act, 90 Am. J. Int. Law, 419 (1996).

3. Year after year, the economic blockade of Cuba has been condemned in UN resolutions. The 2003 resolution was passed by 179 "yes" votes, 3 votes against (the Unit-

ed States, Israel and the Marshall Islands) and 2 abstentions (Morocco and Micronesia).—See UN A/Res.58.7.

1. His fascinating life is narrated in his memoire published shortly after his death. See Rudolf B. Schlesinger, Memories 199 (Ugo Mattei & Andrea Pradi eds., 2000).

important methodological contribution is similarly linked to the name of Italian jurist Rodolfo Sacco.[2] The two approaches interestingly complement each-other.[3] Professor Sacco has shown that often, in a given legal system, there is no single unvarying rule on a particular point, but rather a series of different (and sometimes conflicting) formulations of the applicable rule, depending on the source consulted. The code may say one thing, the courts another; scholars may state the rule differently; the tacit rule actually followed may again differ from what anyone says it is. These different possible formulations are formants (the term being borrowed from phonetics, the science that studies sounds), formative elements or components of the rule as it obtains in that particular jurisdiction. Understanding a legal system requires attention to the different incidences of its rules at various levels of practice and layers of discourse. An important reason for such differences is that the formants of a rule may derive from different sources. For instance, the legislature's rules may derive from a particular foreign system, while scholars might have established systematized rules by using concepts and principles borrowed from another legal system. This phenomenon is particularly noticeable in the many civil law systems which, like Italy, initially adopted codes based on the French prototype but later fell under the spell of German legal scholarship.

As seen by the materials in Chapter 2, the common core project as applied to European private law does not limit itself to the analysis of the black letter solutions of the Code. In the excerpt below Mauro Bussani and Vernon Palmer, discuss their use of legal formants:

M. Bussani & V.V. Palmer, Preliminary Remarks of Methodology

in Pure Economic Loss in 168–70 (M. Bussani & V.V. Palmer eds., 2004).

A full understanding of what the legal formants are and how they relate to each other allows us to ascertain the factors that affect solutions, making it clear what weight interpretative practices (grounded on scholarly writings, on legal debate aroused by previous judicial decision, etc.) have in molding the actual outcomes. Hence the notion of legal formant is more than an esoteric neologism for the traditional distinction between "Loi", "Jurisprudence" and "Doctrine", i.e. between enacted law, case law and scholarly writings. Within a given legal system, the legal rule is not uniform, not only because one rule may be given by case law, one by scholars and one by statutes. Within each of these sources there are also formants competing with each other. For example, the rule described in the headnotes of a case can be inconsistent with the actual rationale of the

2. See Rodolfo Sacco, Legal Formants: A Dynamic Approach to Comparative Law (pts. 1 & 2), 39 Am. J. Comp. L. 1, 343 (1991).

3. See Ugo Mattei, The Comparative Jurisprudence of R.B. Schlesinger and R. Sacco: A Study in Legal Influence, in Rethinking the Masters of Comparative Law (A. Riles ed., 2001).

decision, or the definition in a code can be inconsistent with the detailed rules contained in the code itself.[1] This complex dynamic may change considerably from one legal system to another as well as from one area of the law to another. In particular, in each legal system certain legal formants are clearly leading in a different way—differences in formants' leadership are particularly clear in the (traditional) distinction between common law and civil law.[2]

Given the factual methodology we have adopted, it should be clear why our research cannot be regarded as a mere collection of decided cases....

As a general guideline, we have drafted our questionnaire with a sufficient degree of specificity so as to require the reporters' answers to address all the factors in his or her system which have practical impact on the operative rules. This is our best guarantee that rules formulated in an identical way (by an identical code provision, for instance) but which may produce different applications, or even different doctrinal rhetoric, were not regarded as identical. This has also allowed us to expose the elements that play an official and declared role in one system, versus those that play a more cryptic, unsystematic and unofficial role in another system—the role of such cryptic elements being of course crucial when drafting the map of the applied law.[3]

As previously mentioned, these considerations were particularly important because the systems within our study belong to the common law as well as to the civil law tradition. The structure of the judicial process and the "style" of the legal system (in the broad sense described by Zweigert & Kötz and John Merryman),[4] could not be neglected if we were to obtain correct results. It is indeed in the structure of the legal process, which municipal lawyers take as given, that most of the differences can be detected, understood and possibly explained.[5]

All this hopefully leads one to understand why we asked every contributor to set her/his answers up on three levels, labeled I. "Operative Rules", II. "Descriptive Formants", and III. "Meta-legal Formants". In the interest of readability we have taken these working titles out of the responses; nevertheless we have left intact the inner structure of each response.... The level dealing with "Operative Rules" is designed to be a concise summary. The reporters were asked to summarize the basic applicable rules and to state the outcome to the case that would be reached under national law. Reporters were also asked to indicate whether the reasoning

1. See R. Sacco, Legal Formants: A Dynamic Approach to Comparative Law, 39 Am. J. Comp. Law 1991, 1, 21–27.

2. As regards to this topic, the state-of-art is delineated by U. Mattei, Comparative Law and Economics 66 (1997).

3. See R. Sacco, Comparazione giuridica e conoscenza del dato giuridico positivo, in L'apporto della comparazione alla scienza giuridica, 241 (R. Sacco ed., 1980).

4. K. Zweigert & H. Kötz, Introduction to Comparative Law 63 ff. (T. Weir trans., 3rd ed. 1985); J. H. Merryman, The Civil Law Tradition: An Introduction to the Legal Systems of Western Europe and Latin America (2d ed., 1985).

5. The participants in our project are comparativists, and as comparativists are asked to deal with the questionnaires also if they have to describe their own law.

and outcome would be considered clear and undisputed or only doubtful and problematic.

The level called "Descriptive Formants" has a twofold goal. On one hand, the aim is to reveal the reasons which lawyers feel obliged to give in support of the "operative rules", and the extent to which the various solutions are consistent either with specific and general legislative provisions, or with general principles (traditional as well as emerging ones). The reporter was therefore obliged to investigate how the hypothetical case has been solved by case law in the given legal system; whether this is or is not the solution given by the other legal formants; whether all these formants are concordant, both from an internal point of view (the source of disaccord may be minority doctrines, including dissenting opinions in leading cases, opposite opinions in scholarly writings, etc.), and from a diachronic point of view (whether the various solutions are recent achievements or were identical in the past); whether the solution is considered to be a question of fact or a question of law. The latter factor may determine not only the degree to which the solution can be enforced by supreme courts against lower courts, but also the impact of judicial precedent on the solution. On the other hand, the goal at this level is to understand whether the solution depends on legal rules and/or institutions outside private law, such as procedural rules (including rules of evidence), administrative or constitutional provisions.

Finally, the level called "Meta-legal Formants" asks for a clear picture of the other elements affecting the operative and descriptive levels, such as policy considerations, economic factors, social context and values, as well as the structure of the legal process (organization of courts, administrative structure, etc.): that kind of data the researcher can never leave out whenever the aim is to understand what the law is.[6]

The following case studies, then, cannot be dissociated from the techniques by which our information and insights have been produced.

NOTES AND QUESTIONS

(1) Common core research thus requires a very careful and skeptical look to what each lawyer knows and says about his or her own legal system. Much of the knowledge that lawyers receive from law school can be considered "tacit" or "mute",[1] i.e. part of those automatic patterns of reasoning that are never questioned. For example, Italians do not know why they do not drink cappuccino after dinner and immediately recognize and poke fun on American tourists for this diffused habit. For Italians to drink Cappuccino after dinner is comparable to inviting your mother to the prom. Should they give it a try once

---

6. As sometimes happens in collective enterprises such as this one, not each and every national reporter has perfectly abided by the guidelines that we established at the outset of the project. Nevertheless there is, we believe, broad enough compliance in most cases to produce the advantages that we had hoped for.

1. Michael Polanyi, Tacit Dimension (1966); Sacco, Mute Law, 43 Am. J. Comp. L. 455 (1995).

after dinner they might discover it is actually good. A tacit knowledge survived for decades (i.e. cappuccino is bad after dinner) might be challenged by the actual empirical knowledge of that form of espresso.

Additional, tacit assumptions are a diffused component of our knowledge. For instance, very few native speakers actually know why they construct a sentence the way they do, or why they choose certain words rather than others of the same meaning in different contexts. There is a deep difference between someone fluent in a language and someone who, as a linguist, knows the deep structure of that language (in which he might not even be fluent).

Do you think that the analogy between someone fluent in a foreign language and a linguist might be similar to that between someone with a very good knowledge of a foreign legal system and a comparativist? Can you think about an example of your own tacit knowledge that you discovered by comparison?

(2) Is the legal formants analysis capable of answering questions and doubts about the legitimacy and biases of common core inquiry?

5.   LEGAL TRANSPLANTS

Within the toolkit of the comparative lawyer, there is one notion that has generated a remarkable amount of knowledge and controversy: the notion of *legal transplants*. This idea, advanced in the mid-nineteen-seventies in a book by the Scottish Roman law scholar Alan Watson,[1] attempts to explain simultaneously the observable data that the *same* law can be found in places with radically different social contexts and advances a theory of legal change that this phenomenon occurs because weaker legal cultures tend to copy stronger ones.

(a) Transplants of Rules and Transplants of Rhetoric

In the early nineties of the last century, as a "peripheral" consequence of the end of the cold war, there was a new wave of constitution-creation in Africa that has involved particularly countries that were previously allied with the Soviet block. Many concepts and ideas developed in the highly advanced U.S. experience of constitutional law found their way, through the scores of lawyers deployed as advisers, as the "supreme law" of radically different lands.

Ugo Mattei, The New Ethiopian Constitution: First Thoughts on Ethnical Federalism and the Reception of Western Institutions

in Transplants Innovation and Legal Tradition in the Horn of Africa 111–126 (Elisabetta Grande ed., 1995).

If you ask a comparative lawyer to take a look to a "new" code or constitution, the answer that you are more likely to get is that there is not

---

1. Alan Watson, Legal Transplants: An Approach to Comparative Law (1974).

much "new" in it. This sort of reaction happens in front of the new Ethiopian Constitution too.

Of course, this is true in general, if you look at the law as a worldwide phenomenon of social organization. The number of truly original laws and institutions (and of constitutions, of course) is very much limited. It has always been easy for comparative lawyers to find a certain number of paradigmatic (or leading) experiences that are followed and/or adapted worldwide.

The new Constitution, to be sure, is a big change in the Ethiopian constitutional tradition. To much regret, however, short from putting Ethiopia as a frontrunner of a new and ripe African Constitutional tradition, it locates it within the mass of countries that, for one reason or another, follow the rhetoric (part of the) structure, and many of the categories of the American model in a more or less conscious attempt to import the strongest version of the western conception of the rule of law.

The new Ethiopian constitution, in my mind, offers to the scholarly community an occasion to ask fundamental questions such as: Is the western rule of law a desirable target for an African Country? What are the fundamental structural and cultural arrangements that a legal system must offer in order to make the rule of law work as a legitimate problem solving device? Can a Constitutional document, although a very sophisticated one, provide, if left alone, the basis for the rule of law? Was it an unrealistic dream to expect from Ethiopia new and original constitutional arrangement able to face ethnic tensions and problems of development outside of a dangerous intellectual dependency from the western concept of the rule of law?

The Ethiopian Constitution of December 8, 1994 is a new wall made of old imported bricks. How solid such a wall in withstanding the tremendous pressure that it will have to face, is a question that it is too early to answer. I argue here that, given the bricks of which it is made, there is not much to be optimistic about.

I will argue that this evolution is just another example of an ethnocentric and a historical episode of cultural imperialism. It is the result of intellectual dependency, the last but not least dangerous, between the power relations in postcolonial Africa. It is likely that the result of this constitutional evolution, inherently foreign to the African structure of power and decision making, will simply result in another piece of unapplied written legislation. . . .

In particular, I see problems arising from an American-patterned rhetoric of rights and of competition, the foundations of an ethnic federalism extremely dangerous in Africa as elsewhere, the institutional weakness, and the unbearable complexity of the constitutional organization.

The political background of the new constitution is too well known to be discussed here. Important to our purposes is only that none of the political and ethnic forces that make the opposition to the Ethiopian People's Revolutionary Democratic Front (EPRDF) had participated in the

Constitutional making process. All opposition parties, most important those representing the Amhara and Oromo groups (38 and 35% respectively), withdrew from the electoral competition. The new Constitution is therefore supported politically and ethnically only by the Tigrynia minority, which accounts for less than 10% of the population.

A good experiment to conduct would be to cancel a few provisions of the Constitution such as those in which the word Ethiopia is contained, or such as Art. 47, which contains the list of the member states of the Federal Democratic Republic of Ethiopia, and then ask what links such a document to the Ethiopian reality. If there were many of such links, this document could not be proposed as a constitution for a different country. Otherwise, changing the word Ethiopia, we could have a model constitution apt to fit all the realities. The treasure hunt for typically Ethiopian (or even only African) provisions gives indeed meager results. Four provisions (Art. 32, 1 and 40, 5; art. 41; art. 44), granting the right of free establishment in any place of the country, are what remains of the cruel practice of Menghistu (but of other dictators too) to relocate the population.

Art. 28 reflects the past tragic experience of the "red terror" by banning the statute of limitation for crimes against humanity. A few provisions such as those on private versus public property (art. 40) do reflect a typical post colonial arrangement, precluding the de plano substitution the word Ethiopia with Norway or with Europe. There is not much uniquely Ethiopian in all of this, however, and such mixed provisions on property rights may be found also today in post-communist Eastern European countries, not to mention other African or Asian countries.

Finally, another couple of Ethiopian Constitutional Articles try to reflect legal pluralism. In particular Art. 34, 5 ("the Constitution shall not preclude the adjudication of personal or family disputes by religious or cultural laws ...") and Art. 78, 5 ("The Council of People's Representatives and State Councils can establish or give official recognition to religious and cultural courts").

These few provisions were all I was able to locate that would make this constitutional draft unsuitable for a European or for a Northern American country. Indeed, the impact of American constitutional rhetoric is staggering. It is not only the rhetoric and the fundamental federal structure of the U.S. Constitution that is reflected here. There would be nothing unusual in this. After all, the U.S. Constitution has always been the most influential constitutional document in the world. What I'm observing is the impact of the rhetoric of American modern law professors which appears rather ridiculously out of context.

A cursory look to the Ethiopian Constitution will give you the flavor of what I'm talking about. Art. 9 tells us that the constitution is "The supreme law of the land". Art. 14 assumes the necessity of a trio of fundamental values: "life, liberty, and property" becomes "Life, liberty, and the security of the person". Art. 19 introduces the Miranda warning made famous by the American movies. The Ethiopian person arrested has "A right to remain silent and to be notified that any statement that they make or evidence they give may be used against them in court". The "right to privacy" is not only generally guaranteed (Art. 26) but also specifically to the accused (Art. 20). "Double Jeopardy" is prohibited (Art. 23). Of course "the equal protection of the law" is granted (Art. 25). . . .

Many other examples of American constitutional language can be found. Talking about fashionable provisions (within the American academia) we will find that the press should not only be free but "diverse" (Art. 29, 4); Women are entitled to "affirmative action" in order to be able to "compete on the basis of equality with men in political economic and social life" (Art. 35,3). The problems that may arise from the competition between men and women should be resolved "in the best interest of the child" (Art. 36, 2). Ethiopians should have a "Right of Access to justice" which, of course, can be effective only with the introduction of class actions lawsuits (Art 37, 2). A right to a "clean and healthy environment" (Art 44) completes the list of the rights formulated with academic rhetoric. Other non-American fashionable ideas find their way into the Constitution as well. Between these finds the Scandinavian idea of the "ombudsman" (Art 55, 15) which in the eighties became a "must" for any proposal claiming to be progressive. The right to "sustainable development", whatever it may mean, found its way in the constitution as well. A very progressive section on social rights is added. It would be difficult for a Scandinavian country to afford its implementation. . . .

As far as the judiciary is concerned, the mixed nature of the systems is even more clear. Following the U.S. example, "The supreme Federal Judiciary authority is vested in the Federal supreme court" (Art 78, 2). The same provision grants the possibility of establishing federal lower Courts. State Courts will adjudicate federal questions if such a lower judiciary is not established. Special Courts are prohibited and tenure of office is guaranteed in order to guarantee the independence of the judiciary.

The American model the dominates today's Ethiopian Constitution is the leading legal system worldwide. Most of its success is due to its effectiveness in protecting individual rights in the course of the two world wars. The rhetoric of individual rights, of individualism and of competition that is produced by the American model could not be more foreign to the African mentalité. A strong and ideological assertiveness of rights can have very destabilizing impact on the Ethiopian society. This is in particular true when such rhetoric touches such crucial problems as self determination and secession. A Somali legal scholar, the late refugee scholar Ahmed Botan, has conveyed with bitterness this idea, with a sad joke which was circulating in Addis Ababa during the early negotiations for the peace in Somalia: "Somalia and I against the world. My clan and I against Somalia. My family and I against my clan. My brother and I against my family. Me against my brother!"

In Africa, right assertiveness is particularly dangerous if it is understood as rights of a clan to be asserted against the others. The traditional decentralized ethnic African society endorsed and endorses a decision making style that could not be more far from the western right assertiveness. It was a culture of mediation, of unanimity, of peacekeeping. . . .

(b) The Treatment of Imported Elements within a Legal System

The problem of imported law has a double aspect. It can be viewed prospectively through the eyes of a lawmaker who in creating new statutory or decisional law consults foreign solutions, and perhaps will adopt them as models or guides. On the other hand, the problem presents itself retrospectively to the lawyer or judge who in applying existing law discovers that the pertinent rule is an imported one, and thus is faced with the question of whether to undertake comparative research in order to ascertain how the rule operates in the country of its origin.

Where local authorities are scanty and the necessary foreign materials are easily accessible, such research probably will be undertaken. Suppose, for instance, that Country A has adopted an essentially French-oriented legal system.[1] So long as Country A has not yet developed a strong legal tradition of its own, and provided French legal materials remain available, it is likely that Country A's lawyers and law students will make ample use of these imported materials.[2] As it has been pointed out, the "context of reception" particularly if located in a less developed country, might have only a limited amount of materials available from the "context of production" so that different strange hybridizations often occur.[3] Very often obsolete authorities from the context of production keep full force and prestige in the context of reception.

Where, on the other hand, the borrowing country itself has a highly developed legal culture and the imported ideas relate only to an isolated problem or to a limited segment of the legal order, the foreign antecedents

1. Country A, substitutes the original Ruritania, the name of an imaginary country, derived from the story, The Prisoner of Zenda (1894), and its sequel, Rupert of Hentzau (1898), by the English author (and barrister) Anthony Hope. In these novels, Ruritania is a small German-speaking kingdom located roughly southeast of Dresden. The name has been applied, by extension, to any small imaginary state. "It could be argued that tales [set in imaginary places] should be called Ruritanian only if they are located somewhere along the mountainous border between Czechoslovakia and Poland, and that tales set in Balkan enclaves should be called Graustarkian, after the otherwise very similar Graustark (1902) by the US writer George Barr McCutcheon (1866–1928); but this would be both pedantic and unproductive." John Clute & Peter Nicholls, The Encyclopedia of Science Fiction 1034 (1995).

2. As time goes on, and local court decisions and other local materials become available, it is possible that the courts and practitioners of Country A will cease to pay attention to the foreign antecedents of their legal system, while Country A's legal scholars and law teachers continue to rely on French or other imported textbooks almost to the exclusion of local authorities. How the rule on a particular point is stated may depend on the kind of source consulted, and the rule actually followed may again be different from what anyone says it is. The outsider studying Country A's law must be attentive to these various (and sometimes conflicting) levels of discourse in order to avoid error and misunderstanding. This aspect of the complexity of legal systems is particularly emphasized in Rodolfo Sacco, Legal Formants: A Dynamic Approach to Comparative Law (pts. 1 & 2), 39 Am. J. Comp. L. 1, 343 (1991).

3. See Lopez Medina, Teoria Impura Del Derecho (2004).

of the borrowed elements may soon be forgotten. In the United States, for instance, not many remember today that the Workers' Compensation Acts, which since 1910 have been adopted in every state, were largely based on a German model.[4]

It even may happen that a legislative draftsman, although in fact borrowing from foreign sources, consciously seeks to keep the future application of the statute free from continuing alien influence.[5] An attempt of this kind was made by the sponsors of the Uniform Commercial Code (hereinafter known as "U.C.C." or "the Code"). The principal architect of the Code, the late Professor Karl N. Llewellyn, had spent considerable time in Germany, and there can be no doubt that some of the Code's important features were inspired by his study of German law, especially by his fascination for the work of nineteenth century commercial law scholar Levin Goldschmidt. An example which readily comes to mind is the separation of the contract aspects of a sales transaction from the title aspects—probably the fundamental innovative idea embodied in Article 2. Equally "German" in style is the famous provision of § 2–302, by which unconscionable contracts and contract clauses are rendered unenforceable. The drafters, however, clearly sought to discourage any future tendency on the part of courts or commentators to look to German authorities in applying these and other German-inspired provisions. They did so by two devices, namely (a) by not flaunting the foreign model,[6] and (b) by an express provision emphasizing that the Code must be read against a common law background.[7] The first of these devices, by itself, would hardly be effective, since legal scholars have been quick to perceive some of the pertinent civil law models and counterparts.[8] In combination, however, the

---

4. See M. L. Perlin, The German and British Roots of American Workers' Compensation Systems, 15 Seton Hall L. Rev. 849, 860 (1985). This migration of the German compensation scheme has been called "a triumph of comparative law." P. W. Schroth, Products Liability, 26 Am. J. Comp. L. 67, 68 (Supp. 1978).

5. Some of the policy considerations which—even in a society not given to blind nationalism—may be cited in support of such "insularity" are pointed out by Summers, American and European Labor Law: The Use and Usefulness of Foreign Experience, 16 Buff. L. Rev. 210 (1966).

Although comparative law has been of obvious importance in the development of European Community law, the European Court of Justice has preferred to treat certain basic concepts used in the EEC Treaty as "autonomous" and independent of the law of the particular member states from which they may have been derived. See Francis Jacobs, The Uses of Comparative Law in the

Law of the European Communities, in Legal History and Comparative Law: Essays in Honour of Albert Kiralfy 99 (Richard Plender ed. 1990). See also Reinhard Zimmermann, Comparative Law and the Europeanization of Private Law in The Oxford Handbook of Comparative Law 539 (Mathias Reimann & Reinhard Zimmermann ed., 2006).

6. Concerning the lack of any published preparatory studies of a comparative nature, see Schlesinger, The Uniform Commercial Code in the Light of Comparative Law, 1 Inter–Am. L. Rev. 11, 27–28 (1959).

For a general (and most enlightening) description of the genesis of the Code, see W. Twining, Karl Llewellyn and the Realist Movement 270 ff. (1973).

7. § 1–103. See also § 1–102.

8. See, e.g., Note, Unconscionable Contract Provisions: A History of Unenforceability from Roman Law to the UCC, 42 Tul. L. Rev. 193 (1967), where further references can be found. For speculation about the precise

two devices seem, at least so far, to have accomplished the drafters' objective of minimizing reliance on foreign authorities.[9]

A related explanation of the success of the strategy of obliterating the German debt of the U.C.C. might be due to the leading position reached by the U.S. legal culture in the aftermath of World War II. It always occurs that legal systems that enjoy an "exporting" posture (contexts of production) tend to develop a higher level of parochialism due to a sense of self-sufficiency. These leading contexts do not care about looking abroad, something that, to the contrary, is unavoidable in weaker legal settings. The typical result of this state of affair is that comparative law is usually more prestigious and well-developed in smaller countries than in bigger, more important ones. Israelis, and Dutch comparative lawyers, for example, are much more influential in their own legal system than their U.S. colleagues. It has been narrated that one day in Chicago, Professor Llewellyn, obviously a very able comparative legal scholar, warned the young German émigré Stefan Riesenfeld, never to mention comparative law in his job search. "It is the Devil's kiss!" he said to the young man who was later to become a leader in the U.S. international and comparative law. One should consider however, that while Llewellyn warning is still relevant in the present U.S. academic job market, parochialism produces the decline of legal cultures.[10]

In "advanced" systems it is thus legal culture that harmonizes imports, sometimes even hiding them, making the local state-based legal system a somewhat coherent order, despite borrowings that many times occur from a variety of contexts of production. For example, Italy is a highly developed legal culture of reception. It has borrowed from France, Germany and recently the United States. Despite tensions between these different sources of legal influence, Italian law can still be considered a relatively coherent system of rules.[11]

Sometimes, the context of reception does not have institutions working as agencies of harmonization of imports with local elements. This happens either because of the weakness of the State incapable of imposing one legal order on the territory, or because of conflicting loyalties by which different

German sources of Llewellyn's ideas, see S. Herman, Llewellyn the Civilian: Speculations on the Contribution of Continental Experience to the Uniform Commercial Code, 56 Tul. L. Rev. 1125 (1982); James Whitman, Commercial Law and the American Volk: A Note on Llewellyn's German Sources for the Uniform Commercial Code, 97 Yale L.J. 156 (1987).

9. See T. B. Smith, The Preservation of the Civilian Tradition in "Mixed Jurisdictions," in Civil Law in the Modern World 3, 8 (A. N. Yiannopoulos ed., 1965): "The Uniform Commercial Code ... has drawn extensively on German solutions, though, perhaps

surprisingly, leading commentators upon it do not seem much interested in comparative material." This seems to remain true today. Of course, there is a growing number of studies comparing the Code's solutions with those of other legal systems; but little is done to utilize its civil law antecedents in the interpretation and application of the Code itself.

10. See Mattei, Rise and Fall of Law and Economics: An Essay for Judge Guido Calabresi, 64 Md. L. Rev. 200 (2005).

11. See Elisabetta Grande, Imitazione e diritto: ipotesi sulla circolazione dei modelli (2000).

subgroups feel bound by and identified with a certain set of rules and not others. Naturally this phenomenon can happen at different degrees of intensity. When this is the case, legal transplants produce phenomena of legal pluralism (see *infra* Chapter 3, Section 6, p. 248).

(c) Legal Transplants and Colonialism

Much of the "diffusion" of law has been coercive and is the direct or indirect result of colonialism. Indeed, it is striking that today the entire world is covered by a single form of political organization—the territorial modern state—which claims monopoly over law-making everywhere, with the (still) controversial exception of international legal norms. The modern state has more or less successfully displaced alternative forms of political organization, or at least their claims to legitimacy over and above the state. Equally strikingly, all modern states can be categorized into a handful of legal families—civil law and common law alone cover most of the world. Obviously, law has not been the primary idiom in which political and social life have been understood in all communities at all times in history. Remarkably, today law as the defining structure of the modern state has conquered essentially the entire planet and displaced the claims to legitimacy of alternative forms of politics, so that "rights talk" has become the uncontested language of justice. At the same time, civil law and common law have increasingly gained a duopoly over modern law itself, with most states seeking to pattern their legal systems on one model or the other, as we saw earlier in this chapter. For one thing, this may give rise to concern over the "sustainable diversity" of legal systems, to use Patrick Glenn evocative metaphor.[1] At the same time, it calls for historical explanation that looks not only at domestic legal systems but also at their hierarchical interrelationships organized by international law.

When comparing different legal systems, it is vital to be aware of their historical origins and of the fact that colonialism itself was a *legal* process, facilitated by the norms of classic international law. As a comparative law student, when reading the following excerpt, consider how the operation of international law has entailed both explicit and implicit comparisons among different legal systems.

Antony Anghie, Finding the Peripheries: Sovereignty and Colonialism

in Nineteenth–Century International Law, 40 Harv. Int'l L.J. 1–2, 49–54 (1999).

International law is universal. It is a body of law that applies to all states regardless of their specific cultures, belief systems, and political organizations. It is a common set of doctrines that all states use to regulate relations with each other. The association between international law and

---

1. H. Patrick Glenn, Legal Traditions of the World: Sustainable Diversity in Law (3d ed. 2007).

universality is so ingrained that pointing to this connection appears tauto-logical. And yet, the universality of international law is a relatively recent development. It was not until the end of the nineteenth century that a set of doctrines was established as applicable to all states, whether these were in Asia, Africa, or Europe.

The universalization of international law was principally a conse-quence of the imperial expansion that took place towards the end of the "long nineteenth century." The conquest of non-European[1] peoples for economic and political advantage was the most prominent feature of this period, which was termed by one eminent historian, Eric Hobsbawm, as the "Age of Empire." By 1914, after numerous colonial wars, virtually all the territories of Asia, Africa, and the Pacific were controlled by the major European states, resulting in the assimilation of all these non-European peoples into a system of law that was fundamentally European in that it derived from European thought and experience.

The late nineteenth century was also the period in which positivism decisively replaced naturalism as the principal jurisprudential technique of the discipline of international law. Positivism was the new analytic appara-tus used by the jurists of the time to account for the events that culminated in the universalization of international law and the formulation of a body of principles that was understood to apply globally as a result of the annex-ation of "unoccupied" territories such as the Australian continent, the conquest of large parts of Asia, and the partitioning of Africa....

In somewhat simplistic terms, non-European peoples could be brought within the realm of international law through four basic, and often interre-lated, techniques. First, treaty making constituted the basic technique for regulating relations between European and non-European peoples. Treaties provided for a broad set of arrangements ranging from agreements govern-ing trading relations between the two entities, to treaties by which the non-European entity ostensibly ceded complete sovereignty to the European entity. Second, non-European peoples were colonized and thus subjected to the control of European sovereignty. Colonization took place by a number of methods including by a treaty of cession, by annexation, or by conquest. Third, independent non-European states such as Japan and Siam could be accepted into international society by meeting the requirements of the standard of civilization and being officially recognized, by European states, as proper members of the family of nations. Fourth, European states, particularly in the late nineteenth century, often acquired control over Asian and African societies by way of a special type of treaty: protectorate agreements. While these four categories are crudely distinct, they are nevertheless far from mutually exclusive: protectorates were established through treaties, for example, and sometimes became colonies....

---

1. By "non-European" I refer to the areas that were the subject of colonial expan-sion in the late 19th century, that is, princi-pally, Asia, Africa, and the Pacific. The im-pact of the Americas on the development of international law gives rise to an important and distinct set of issues, which I do not address here. See Werner Menski, Compara-tive Law in a Global Context: The Legal Systems of Asia and Africa (2d ed. 2006).

Colonization

The problem of the legal personality of non-European peoples could be most simply resolved by the actual act of colonization, which effectively extinguished this personality. Once colonization took place, the colonizing power assumed sovereignty over the non-European territory, and any European state carrying on business with that territory would deal with the colonial power. In this way, legal relations would once again take place between two European powers. The tension that existed between these European states (for example, over access to markets or resources of a colony) was in many respects less jurisprudentially complicated than relations between European and non-European entities were.

Nevertheless, questions of native personality played an important role in determining whether colonization had properly taken place in the first instance. The jurisprudence concerning the issue of how sovereignty was acquired over non-European peoples was controversial and unsettled because, once again, states took very different views depending on their own interests. Broadly, however, discovery, occupation, conquest, and cession were some of the doctrines historically devised to deal with this issue. The conceptual framework offered by private law, particularly property law, played an influential role in the jurisprudence regarding the acquisition of territory. In order to prevent a state from claiming that it had acquired valid title over an entire territory simply by landing there, positivist analysis focused on questions such as what acts were sufficient to show that the European state had acquired control over the territory or that occupation had been "effective."

Conquest generally involved militarily defeating an opponent and thus acquiring sovereignty over the defeated party's territory. Conquest was one of the most ancient ways of acquiring title; within the nineteenth-century framework, it was a completely legal and valid way of expanding territory. Recognition of such a right of conquest is completely contrary to the very concept of law as it legitimizes outcomes dictated by power rather than legal principle. Nevertheless, conquest received legal sanction. Given the military weakness of the non-European states and the absence of any legal limitations on a state's ability to commence a war, it was inevitable that European colonial empires expanded by the conquest of large parts of Asia and Africa. As Korman notes, furthermore, European states quite openly relied on the doctrine of conquest as a basis for their title.[2]

Furthermore, the emphasis on the concept of property and the positivist view that uncivilized peoples were not legal entities contributed towards doctrines such as "occupation" erasing the existence of many non-European peoples. Only such territory can be the object of occupation as is no State's land, whether entirely uninhabited, as e.g. an island, or inhabited by natives whose community is not to be considered as a State. Even civilized individuals may live and have private property on a territory

2. See Sharon Korman, The Right of Conquest: The Acquisition of Territory By   Force in International Law and Practice 66 (1996).

without any union by them into a State proper which exercises sovereignty over such territory. And natives may live on a territory under a tribal organization which need not be considered a State proper.[3]

This meant that the territory of "tribal" peoples could be appropriated simply through occupation by the European state on the basis that tribal organization did not correspond with a "State." Thus, British title to the Australian continent was based on occupation of uninhabited territory, *terra nullius;* it was irrelevant that Aboriginal peoples had occupied the continent for more than forty thousand years and had developed sophisticated forms of political and social organization in this time.

Each of these doctrines relied upon different notions of native personality, as the particular means of asserting title depended on the positivist assessment of the degree of civilization of the peoples occupying the land. Using this scale, the positivists asserted, for example, that in the case of merely tribal peoples occupation itself would suffice. Still, if the natives belonged to what positivists regarded as an uncivilized, but organized, polity, European powers would have to assert title through some other means such as conquest or cession. The issue of cession raised the problems discussed earlier as to treaty relations between European and non-European peoples. The legitimacy of conquest as a mode of acquiring control, together with the positivist argument that resort to force was a valid expression of sovereign will, meant that few restrictions were imposed on imperial expansion. This, coupled with the fact that municipal courts of the colonized countries were precluded from inquiring into sovereign behavior, effectively meant that the attempts made by colonized peoples to question the legality of actions taken by the colonizing state or other entities vested with sovereignty by the colonizing state were bound to fail.

Complying with the Standard of Civilization

States such as Japan and Siam succeeded in retaining their nominal independence. For such states, acceptance into the Family of Nations could only occur if they met the "standard of civilization," which amounted, essentially, to idealized European standards in both their external and, more significantly, internal relations.

These standards presupposed and legitimized colonial intrusion in that a non-European state was deemed to be civilized if it could provide an individual, a European foreigner, with the same treatment that the individual would expect to receive in Europe. The development of this framework appears to correspond with the changing nature of European penetration of the non-European world and the legal regimes that had been devised to promote this. As discussed earlier, the first phase of contact took place through trading companies, which confined their activities principally to trade. As they gradually adopted a more intrusive role in the governance of the non-European state in order to further their trading interests, more demands were made on non-European states, which were compelled under

3. See Lassa Oppenheim, International Law 292 (2d ed., 1912).

threat of military action to make increasing concessions to the interests of the traders. Apart from demonstrating some of the characteristics of an unequal treaty, the Treaty of Nanking suggests how different European practices and policies were gradually introduced into non-European societies and then expanded. Once it had been established by way of treaty that a European had a right to reside and trade in a particular state, it was not altogether surprising that international jurists would use this as a measure of whether a country was civilized or not. Westlake presents the basic test: "When people of European race come into contact with American or African tribes, the prime necessity is a government under the protection of which the former may carry on the complex life to which they have been accustomed in their homes...."[4]

Westlake argued that the "Asian Empires" were capable of meeting this standard, provided that Europeans were subject to the jurisdiction of a European consul rather than subject to the local laws; but even so, this meant only that European international law had merely to "take account" of such Asian societies rather than accept them as members of the Family of Nations. For the European states, the local systems of justice were completely inadequate, and there was no question of submitting one of their citizens to these systems. Thus, non-European states were forced to sign treaties of capitulation that gave European powers extra-territorial jurisdiction over the activities of their own citizens in these non-European states. This derogation from the sovereignty of the non-European state was naturally regarded as a massive humiliation by that state, which sought to terminate all capitulations at the earliest opportunity. Capitulations were an aspect of the unequal treaty regime imposed on these states and usually comprised just one part of these treaties, which also granted rights to trade and to establish residences, for example. Once these treaties allowed for a trading presence, it was almost inevitable that the scope of the rights demanded by the European powers to enable them effectively to carry on their trade expanded.

Both external and internal reform had to be carried out by a state seeking entry into the family of nations. In the external sphere, the state had to be capable of meeting international obligations and maintaining the diplomatic missions and channels necessary to enable and preserve relations with European states. In the internal sphere, the state was required to reform radically its legal and political systems to the extent that they reflected European standards as a whole. Put in another way, this test in effect suggested that the project of meeting the standard of civilization consisted of generalizing the standards embodied in the capitulation system, which was specific to aliens, to the entire country. In the domestic sphere, then, the non-European state was required to guarantee basic rights relating to dignity, property, and freedom of travel, commerce, and religion, and it had to possess a court system that comprised codes,

4. See John Westlake, Chapters on the Principles of International Law 141 (Cambridge Univ. Press 1894).

published laws, and legal guarantees. All these rules compelling domestic reform essentially required profound transformations of non-European societies in ways that negated the principle of territorial sovereignty. Oppenheim states the principle in its fullest form:

> In consequence of its internal independence and territorial supremacy, a State can adopt any Constitution it likes, arrange its administration in a way it thinks fit, make use of legislature as it pleases, organize its forces on land and sea, build and pull down fortresses, adopt any commercial policy it likes and so on.[5]

While positivist jurisprudence insisted that states were formally equal and that states possessed extensive powers over their own territory, a different set of principles applied in the case of non-European states, which significantly compromised their internal sovereignty and their cultural distinctiveness in order to be accepted as legal subjects of the system. It was not open for non-European states to exercise the far ranging freedoms over their internal affairs suggested by Oppenheim, principally because it was only if the non-European states had adopted Western forms of political organization that they were accepted into the system. Essentially the actions that non-European states had to take to enter into the system negated the rights that they were supposed to enjoy formally upon admittance.

(d) Colonialism and Indigenous Groups

Despite all its "successes", colonialism has in fact not been entirely successful in eradicating all earlier political forms: indigenous groups of various sorts remain in many parts of the world. The problems of indigenous rights are notoriously difficult for modern legal systems to deal with, as they do not fit easily within the structure of equal sovereign nation-states. Correspondingly, they have been resolved (or not) in quite different ways in different places. It is easy to forget that even in the United States the history of colonialism isn't in fact yet "history".

Perry Dane, The Maps of Sovereignty: A Meditation

12 Cardozo L. Rev. 959–963 (1991).

A few years ago, some students at my school formed a group to discuss Native American issues. One of their posters featured a multiple-choice question. I do not recall the exact words of either the question or the answers, but a paraphrase will do. The question was, "how many sovereign governments are there in the United States?" The first answer was one. The second answer was fifty-one. The third answer was fifty-two or fifty-three or thereabouts, adding Puerto Rico and such to the list. The fourth answer-the right answer-was a number in the high three digits, or fifty-some plus the number of American Indian tribes. The point was that

---

5.   Oppenheim, *supra* note 3, at 178.

Indian tribes, the first occupants of this land, must be included in the tally of sovereign governments that now share jurisdiction in that land.

This poster bears three morals. The first is that the civics class vision of the American polity is wrong. We are not one nation, born in 1776. We are many nations, most much older than that. The majority of those nations are small and poor. They are victims of centuries of war and plunder. But they are nations. They are not only nations metaphorically, or sociologically. They are nations by law. Like other nations, they legislate and adjudicate, manage public policy, and regulate private order. This is a commonplace to those of use who spend some time studying American Indian law, but it often seems to surprise almost everybody else.

The second moral of the poster is more subtle. Tribal sovereignty does not exist only in the contemplation of Native Americans and their friends. It is recognized by the United States. Court decisions speak of it. United States Indian policy has included expulsion, theft, murder, and forced assimilation. But it has never wholly abandoned the principle of legal recognition.

Actually, the United States does more than admit Indian sovereignty. A body of United States law largely defines the shape of-and the considerable limits on-Indian self-rule. The federal government recognizes about 500 tribal governments. The effective power of these governments depends on a jumble of federal law. Tribes that do not have federal recognition seek it. They realize that sovereignty means little without it. Some scholars argue that even the idea of the tribe as a basic unit of identity and governance, as opposed, say, to the kin group or village, was imposed on Indians from the outside.

Maybe, then, tribal sovereignty is a sham. Maybe tribes are only agents, or subsidiary organs, of the national polity. But this judgment would be too hasty. Federal law speaks to Indian sovereignty. But so do treaties and agreements with the tribes. Indian nations are not creatures of the United States Constitution, and are not bound by it. Historically and legally, they are distinct entities. The tribes' complex tie to the United States limits the exercise of their sovereignty. But the source of that sovereignty is not the United States but themselves. American governance, including for that matter American federalism, is usually explained by way of a general, more or less unified, constitutional vision. Indian sovereignty is an exception to that vision. It would not exist if Indians had not fought for it, and lived it.

And even if Indian sovereignty is partly constructed from the outside, that still does not disqualify it. All claims to sovereignty arise from a union of self-assertion and external perception. Legal communities, much like people, constantly construct each other as they construct themselves.

This brings me to the third message of the poster. Perhaps more remarkable than that the United States recognizes Indian sovereignty is that Native Americans, on the whole, recognize United States sovereignty. After all, they have every reason to see European settlement here as an illicit foreign incursion. Nevertheless, from colonial times, Native Americans saw in the settlers a corporate dignity very different from, say, undocumented aliens. This was in part a pragmatic concession. But not entirely. Singly, Europeans could-and sometimes did-assimilate into Indian society. As a group, however, they were themselves a tribe. Today, that tribe has spread across the continent, and most Native Americans are willing to respect the political map that is the result of that expansion.

To be sure, some Native Americans have denied the legitimacy of the United States. Understandably, many reject the broadest claims of United States authority. Nevertheless, the very importance of the idea of nation-to-nation relations in modern Native American political theory testifies to a willingness to live with, and in, the American nation. More than that, most Indians, while not ceding their own nationhood, accept the rights and obligations of United States citizenship. Moreover, if Indian sovereignty is in part constructed by United States recognition, then maybe United States sovereignty is—in part rounded on Indian willingness to return the favor.

NOTES AND QUESTIONS

(1) Once comparative observations point to some commonality between two legal systems, the next step is to *explain* such commonality. How can one explain the existence of the same legal idea, rule, concept or ideology in jurisdictions that might be geographically very remote and perhaps politically very far from each other? Are similar practical solutions the product of what can be considered a "re-invention" of the wheel, according to which different legal systems reach similar practical results by independent paths, or do legal systems copy from each other? Why does the Ethiopian constitution of 1992 display so much U.S. ideology in its phrasing, including articles on affirmative action and gender equality that seem remote from the sensitivity of the society such Constitution is aimed to serve?

Comparative law has reached an important conclusion in its more recent and sophisticated developments. In most cases, changes in a legal system are due to legal transplants. "The moving of a rule or a system of law from one country to another"[1] has now been shown to be the most fertile source of legal development since "most changes in most systems are the result of borrowing".[2] Comparative lawyers have been prolific in amassing evidence for this somewhat paradoxical conclusion.[3] Indeed, it would be impossible to understand the very idea of a Western legal tradition without acknowledging the enormous variety of legal rules and styles which are common within it, not only within the civil law and the common law orbits, of course, but also across the borders of these legal families.[4] Such analogies are the results of legal transplants, ancient as well as recent.

---

1. This is the definition given by Alan Watson, Legal Transplants: An Approach to Comparative Law (2d ed. 1993).

2. *Id*. at 94.

3. The history of any system of law is said to be "largely a history of borrowings of legal material from other legal systems and of assimilation of materials from outside of the law." Roscoe Pound, The Formative Era of American Law 94 (1938). Nor is the phenomenon limited to law. See, e.g., Gilbert Highet, The Migration of Ideas (1954).

4. To the works of Sacco and Watson just cited we can add Simpson, Innovation in nineteenth century Contract law, 91 L. Q. Rev. (1975); E. Agostini, Droit Compare

Both the Babylonian Code of Hammurabi (17th century B.C.) and the Old Testament contain legal rules which—in form as well as substance—derive from sources elsewhere in the ancient Near East.[5] The laws of Solon were influenced by study of the codes of other Greek or Greek-dominated city-states; Roman tradition had it that similar studies preceded enactment of the Twelve Tables which marked the earliest period of Roman law.[6] The Islamic tradition itself has borrowed from the Hammurabi Code before returning law to Mesopotamia.

In most times and places, legal culture has been transnational in character. This was the case in continental Europe down to the nineteenth century (as will be seen when we come to trace the development of European law in Chapter 4, section 2). We have already described the early receptions that happened in the United States from England, France and Germany. Even English common law, despite its relative insularity, has been subject throughout its history to influences from abroad and never entirely isolated from continental ideas.[7] The notion of hermetically-sealed national legal systems is largely a product of nineteenth-century legal positivism and nationalism combined with a superabundance of local legal building material in those countries, such as France, Germany, England, and the United States, which have been the principal exporters of legal ideas.[8]

(1989); J. Gordley, The Philosophical Origins of Modern Contract Doctrine (1991).

5. See Watson, *supra* note 1. See also Bernard S. Jackson, Evolution and Foreign Influence in Ancient Law, 16 Am. J. Comp. L. 372 (1968).

6. See Zepos, Die Bewegung zur Rechtsvereinheitlichung und das Schicksal der geltenden Zivilgesetzbücher, 19 Rev. Hell. Dr. Int. 14, 17 (1966).

7. See, e.g., Peter Stein, The Character and Influence of the Roman Civil Law: Historical Essays, pt. II, at 151ff. (1988); Bernard Rudden, Comparative Law in England, in Comparative Law and Legal System: Historical and Socio–Legal Perspectives (W. E. Butler & V. N. Kudriavtsev eds. 1985); Gino Gorla & Luigi Moccia, A "Revisiting" of the Comparison between Continental Law and English Law (16th–19th Century), 2 J. Legal Hist. 143 (1981); R. H. Helmholz, Continental and Common Law: Historical Strangers or Companions?, 1990 Duke L.J. 1207; Reinhard Zimmermann, Der Euopäische Charakter des Englischen Rechts—Historische Verbindungen zwischen Civil Law und Common Law, 1 Zeitschrift für Europäisches Privatrecht 4 (1993). Michele Graziadei, Changing Images of the Law in XIX Century English Legal Thought (The Continental Impulse), in The Reception of Continental Ideas in the Common Law World 1820–1920, 115ff. (Mathias Reimann ed., 1993).

In its beginnings, English common law was a precocious offshoot from continental developments. See R. C. Van Caenegem, Judges, Legislators and Professors: Chapters in European Legal History (1987). Even after the common law took shape, borrowing from the continent never quite ceased. For instance, it has been surmised that Edward I of England, the creator of the Statutes of Westminster, De Donis and Quia Emptores, may have become acquainted with the great medieval Spanish Code called *Las Siete Partidas* (1256–1265) when he visited his cousin and brother-in-law, Alfonso X of Castile and Leon, known as the "Wise." See Radin, Introduction to Nichols, Las Siete Partidas, 20 Calif. L. Rev. 260, 261 (1932). On firmer historical ground, we know that the English Statute of Frauds was largely copied from the French Ordonnance de Moulins of 1566. See Rabel, The Statute of Frauds and Comparative Legal History, 63 Law Q. Rev. 174 (1947). In the 19th century, the rule in Hadley v. Baxendale, 156 Eng.Rep. 145 (1854), which limits contract damages to those foreseeable at the time the agreement was concluded, was taken from French sources.

8. See H. Patrick Glenn, Persuasive Authority, 32 McGill L.J. 261 (1987).

(2) Exogenous influence is particularly noticeable in instances in which legislators have resorted to the wholesale importation of foreign law.[9] Most of the codes presently in force in Latin America are the result of extensive comparative study and eclectic choice among European models.[10] Other examples of wholesale reception[11] of foreign laws include adoption of the Swiss Civil Code and of a modified version of the German Commercial Code in Turkey and adoption of the German Civil Code in Japan.[12] Developing countries, in particular, sometimes rely not only on foreign models but also on foreign personnel for the preparation, drafting, and educational and administrative implementation of their new laws.[13]

As we have seen, reception may be voluntary or semi-voluntary, as was the case with Turkey's adoption of the Swiss Civil Code and Japan's original adoption of western laws. It may, on the other hand, be the result of conquest or colonization[14] or of other forms of military or political pressure. The subjection of French settlers in Louisiana to Spanish law after the 1769 victory of the Spaniards under General O'Reilly, the extension of German law into Austria after the Anschluss of 1938, and the Sovietization of law in Eastern Europe after World War II, may be cited as instances of involuntary "reception." The provisional ordinances of Governor Bremer in militarily occupied

9. This has the advantage of utilization of foreign achievements and of foreign experience, but involves the danger that foreign institutions may be copied without sufficient adaptation to local conditions. See, e.g., Hamson, The Istanbul Conference of 1955, 5 Int'l & Comp. L. Q. 26 (1956); P. H. Sand, Die Reform des aethiopischen Erbrechts—Problematik einer synthetischen Rezeption, 33 Rabels Z. 413 (1969). See also Apirat Petchsiri, Eastern Importation of Western Criminal Law: Thailand as a Case Study (1987).

10. See José Castan Tobeñas, Contemporary Legal Systems of the Western World, 25 Comp. Jurid. Rev. 105 (1988).

11. For an interesting general discussion of the phenomenon of reception, see Zajtay, Die Rezeption fremder Rechte und die Rechtsvergleichung, 156 Archiv fuer die Civilistische Praxis 361 (1957); Zajtay, La réception des droits étrangers et le droit comparé, 9 Rev.Int.Dr.Comp. 686 (1957).

12. For further examples, see 1 Schnitzer, Vergleichende Rechtslehre 58 ff. (2d ed. 1961); Lobinger, The Modern Expansion of Roman Law, 6 U. Cin. L. Rev. 152 (1932).

Reception of common or civil laws of European origin, often superimposed on an indigenous system, is typical of most legal systems in Asia and Africa. The resulting crazy-quilt of legal systems is discussed *supra* Chapter 3 sec. 2 (The Comparative Lawyer as

a Geographer: Tentative Area-by-Area Survey).

13. For example: Working in close cooperation with the Government of Liberia, the Liberian Codification Project at Cornell, headed by Professor Milton Konvitz, compiled and subsequently revised that country's Code of Laws, and oversaw publication of the Liberian Law Reports. See P. Copeland, Konvitz Directs Liberian Codification Project, 25(1) Cornell Law Forum 5 (Winter 1973).

For further examples, see E. D. Re, Legal Exchanges and American Foreign Policy, 21 J. Legal Educ. 419 (1969); Hardberger, The Men of the Peace Corps: "Founding Fathers" of a New Order, 52 A.B.A.J. 131 (1966); J. A. Hoskins, United States Technical Assistance for Legal Modernization, 56 A.B.A.J. 1160 (1970). However, for scathing criticism of the premises of the Law and Development movement of the 1960s, see J. A. Gardner, Legal Imperialism: American Lawyers and Foreign Aid in Latin America (1980). In some respects, the current scramble to influence legal developments in former "socialist" countries might be regarded as a new third wave of "legal imperialism." See *infra* p. 242ff.

14. The effects of conquest or colonization upon the legal system of the subdued group are interestingly discussed by R. Rodière, Introduction au droit comparé 12–14 (1979).

Iraq, or the new Code of Criminal procedure manufactured by the Italians for Afghanistan after the Bonn conference of "donor" countries, are other recent and dramatic examples of forced transplants.[15]

It should be noted, however, that foreign laws involuntarily received are not always abrogated when the pressure to adopt them ends. Several of the European countries to which the French code system originally was brought by Napoleon's armies retained that system for a long time after Napoleon had been crushed and they had regained their independence; some essentially adhere to the French system even today. Japan, likewise, has voluntarily retained most of the legal institutions imported from the United States as part of its second reception of foreign legal institutions during the occupation period following World War II.[16] Another example is presented by India which, upon gaining independence, chose to preserve and indeed to strengthen the common law features of its legal system.[17]

To sum up: every legal system contains imported elements. All legal systems are, to some extent, mixed; no legal system has been constructed out of purely indigenous materials.[18]

The traditional theory of legal transplants as developed by Alan Watson places heavy emphasis on the autonomous intellectual history of the law, and minimizes the extent to which that intellectual history may have been affected by social and political events. The controversy his views have attracted involves, in part, the question of whether it is (a) possible and (b) fruitful to treat

15. On Afghanistan, see Faiz Ahmed, Shari'a, a Custom, and Statutory Law: Comparing State Approaches to Islamic Jurisprudence, Tribal Autonomy, and Legal Development in Afghanestan and Pakistan, 7 Global Jurist 1(2007). On Iraq, see Mattei & Nader, Plunder. When the Rule of Law is Illegal (2008).

16. A similar development, although limited to a single area of law, can be observed in Germany where antitrust legislation of distinctly American flavor was first introduced by the occupation authorities. See Loevinger, Antitrust Law in the Modern World, 6(2) Int'l & Comp. L. Bull. 20, 26–27 (ABA Sec. Int'l & Comp.Law, May 1962). On regaining full sovereignty, the German Federal Republic passed a Law Against Restrictive Competitive Practices (BGB1 1957 I 1081 ff.) which, although granting broad discretionary powers to the newly created Federal Cartel Authority, in principle adopted most of the prohibitions of restrictive trade practices which had made their first appearance in the German legal system under the auspices of occupying powers. See D. J. Gerber, The Extraterritorial Application of the German Antitrust Laws, 77 Am. J. Int'l L. 756, 757–58 (1983), where further references can be found. For a fascinating argument to the effect that the German version of antitrust has been more successful than its American model, see J. Maxeiner, Policy and Methods in German and American Antitrust Law (1986).

17. See M. C. Setalvad, The Common Law in India (1960).

18. 1 P. Arminjon, B. Nolde & M. Wolff, Traité de droit comparé 49 (1950). Imported elements are likely, however, to undergo some "assimilatory modification" or "functional shift" in their new environment. But how far this is the case, how far cultural, economic, or political factors are likely to impede successful legal transplants, how far law is bound to be affected by the social environment in which it operates, has been the subject of lively and fascinating controversy. Compare, e.g., Otto Kahn–Freund, On Uses and Misuses of Comparative Law, 37 Mod. L. Rev. 1 (1974) and Alan Watson, Legal Transplants and Law Reform, 92 Law Q. Rev. 79 (1976). See also William Ewald, Comparative Jurisprudence (II): The Logic of Legal Transplants, 43 Am. J. Comp. L. 489 (1995); E.M. Wise, The Transplant of Legal Patterns, 38 Am. J. Comp. L. 1 (Supp. 1990); and Eric Stein, Uses, Misuses—and Nonuses of Comparative Law, 72 Nw. U. L. Rev. 198 (1977).

a legal system as the mere embodiment of an intellectual tradition and, for purposes of scholarly study, to isolate that tradition from the social and political problems to which the law at all times has to respond, and to the solution of which we are trying to direct the law today?

It seems that the enormous quantity of evidence gathered by scholars interested in legal transplants worldwide has not been explained in a satisfactory way for quite a long time. Indeed, the few early attempts to explain legal transplants from one system to another have relied on the empty idea of "prestige".[19] This shortcoming is due to the fact that comparative lawyers who have been working on legal transplants are less interested in a theoretical explanation of why a legal borrowing happens than in observing its occurrence. This concern is the result of their desire to accumulate evidence to challenge the widespread paradigm of contemporary legal theory, "the mirror image", according to which law is the result of the "felt social needs" of a given society.[20] The result of this situation is that "we are still at the stage where even the basic factors of legal change are not understood".[21] Such lack of theoretical explanation, however, makes sometimes the very theory of legal transplants unsatisfactory. In many cases there is no evidence of legal transplants and indeed a convergence occurs. Sometimes a legal change happens because minority views in a country become the rule; and often minority views from another country which never become law there may also be imported.

Watson's theory has been thus discussed and amended in many ways. It has been divided into a hard version and into a soft version.[22] Legal transplants have been deemed "impossible".[23] Notions of "import-export",[24] of "legal translation",[25] of "legal borrowing", of "legal imitation" of "legal migration" and many others have been proposed as better metaphors to capture the nature of the phenomenon. More recently, scholars have focused on the "context of reception" distinguishing it from the "context of production"[26] in order to discuss "patterns of resistance"[27] or of "counter-hegemony" accounting for the fact that most legal transplants "fail", or at least that the legal institutions

19. Sacco, Legal Formants: A Dynamic Approach to Comparative Law, 39 Am. J.Comp.L., at 398: "Usually, reception takes place because of the desire to appropriate the work of others. The desire arises because this work has a quality one can only describe as 'prestige'. This explanation in terms of prestige is tautological, and comparative law has no definition of the word 'prestige' to offer".

20. This so to say deterministic approach can be traced back mainly to Marx and Max Weber. Its classical deep treatment is W. Friedmann, Law in Changing Society (1959). It is of course still in vogue particularly within American academia. For a recent use of such a paradigm in comparative law, M. Damaška, The Faces of Justice and State Authority (1986); for an opposite view A. Watson, The evolution of Law (1985).

21. Watson, Legal Transplants: An Approach to Comparative Law 320 (1974).

22. See W. Ewald, The Logic of Legal Transplants, 43 Am. J. Comp. Law 489 (1995).

23. See Pierre Legrand, The Impossibility of Legal Transplants, 4 Maastricht J. Europ. & Comp. L. 111, 121 (1997).

24. See G. Ajani, By Chance and Prestige: Legal Transplants in Russia and Eastern Europe, 43 Am. J. Comp. L. 93 (1995).

25. See Maximo Langer, From Legal Transplants to Legal Translations: The Globalization of Plea Bargaining and the Americanization Thesis in Criminal Procedure, 45 Harv. Int'l L.J. 1 (2004).

26. See Lopez Medina, Teoria Impura Del Derecho (2004).

27. Elisabetta Grande, Italian Criminal Justice: Borrowing and Resistance, 48 Am.J. Comp.L. 227–259 (2000).

once they reach the "context of reception" fundamentally change their nature and functioning.[28]

Some observers have pointed at "legal imperialism" as a phenomenon largely explaining transplants.[29] Blackmail, or "conditionality", has been suggested as a third explanation in between voluntary reception and coercive transplants.[30] The economic factor has thus been used to explain legal transplants, claiming that the more efficient legal rules and solutions tend to circulate. Alternatively, focusing on power disparity, scholars have exposed legal export as an institutional pre-requisite for exploitive economic relationships between the centre and the periphery of the world. The more recent literature has even attempted some quantitative evaluation of the "transplant factor" in order to make predictions on transnational institutional behaviour.[31] Finally, a wave of scholarship has shown the importance of "images" and appearances in the dynamics of legal transfer.[32] This line of inquiry has shown that what circulates only has to appear more civilized, efficient, advanced or aesthetic because transplants tend to happen at very low level of knowledge both in the context of production and in that of reception.[33]

(3) As it is always the case in the law, legal transplants is not merely a theoretical concern. Legal transplants might be produced by the work of a scholar (such as in the famous case of Llewellyn's doctrine of unconscionability, incorporated in the UCC as a direct transplant from Germany) or by the activity of a Court of law, eager to import from abroad the solution to a case of first impression. It should be considered however that a court is not always free to use foreign materials to solve domestic legal problems. Such freedom exists only in cases which are not plainly governed by local statute or binding domestic precedent. For *legislative draftsmen*, however, resort to comparative materials is not so restricted and thus legislative transplants are much more frequent than judiciary ones.[34]

---

28. See Elisabetta Grande, Imitazione e diritto. Ipotesi sulla circolazione dei modelli (2001).

29. See John Gardner, Legal Imperialism: American Lawyers and Foreign Aid in Latin America (1980).

30. See Sally Falk Moore, An International Legal Regime and the Context of Conditionality, in Transnational Legal Processes: Globalization and Power Disparities (Michael Likoskey ed., 2002).

31. See D. Berkowitz, K. Pistor & J.F. Richard, The Transplant Effect, 51 Am. J. Comp. Law 163 (2003).

32. Elisabetta Grande, Imitazione e diritto: ipotesi sulla circolazione dei modelli (2000); Anna di Robilant, The Aesthetics of Law, 1 Global Jurist (2001).

33. See Grande, *supra* note 32. See also for a general discussion, Michele Graziadei, Comparative Law as the study of Transplants and reception, in The Oxford Handbook of Comparative Law (Mathias Reimann & Reinhard Zimmermann eds., 2006).

34. On the importance of comparative law as an aid to the legislator, see, e.g., Schmitthoff, The Science of Comparative Law, 7 Cambridge L.J. 94, 103–4 (1939). The point was well put by Lepaulle, The Function of Comparative Law, 35 Harv. L. Rev. 838, 858 (1922): "When one is immersed in his own law, in his own country, unable to see things from without, he has a psychologically unavoidable tendency to consider as natural, as necessary, as given by God, things which are simply due to historical accident or temporary social situation.... To see things in their true light, we must see them from a certain distance, as strangers, which is impossible when we study ... phenomena of our own country. That is why comparative law should be one of the necessary elements in the training of all those who are to shape the law for societies...."

In modern times,[35] in the most advanced countries of continental Europe, it has become standard practice to survey pertinent foreign legislation before an important and innovative bill is submitted to parliament.[36] In these countries it has long been recognized that in the legislative development of the law the public interest is not adequately represented by pressure groups.[37] Therefore, responsibility for undertaking or at least co-ordinating the necessary preparatory research and for formulating a draft proposal is assumed by an arm of the government, usually the Ministry of Justice. Calling on the services of expert staff members or consultants, these permanent and well organized government agencies tend, as part of their work in preparing important bills, routinely to resort to comparative research.[38]

Great Britain and most other common law countries have not developed the institution of a Ministry of Justice.[39] But even the part-time and ad hoc committees which until 1965 were chiefly responsible for law reform in the United Kingdom often undertook or sponsored comparative studies.[40] The Law Commissions Act of 1965, which created permanent Law Commissions for England and Scotland, contains an express provision making it the duty of both Commissions "to obtain such information as to the legal systems of other countries as appears to the Commissioners likely to facilitate the performance of any of their functions."[41] Many of the Commissions' Working Papers and Reports show that in accordance with this legislative mandate they have indeed made substantial use of the comparative method.[42]

35. Perhaps the most massive (though by now almost forgotten) comparative studies in preparation of legislative reform were those engaged in by Russian Tsarist drafting commissions charged with overhauling the procedural system. The reform included the transplantation of the jury system and its creative adaptation to Russian conditions. See S. Kucherov, Courts, Lawyers and Trials Under the Last Three Tsars 23–24, 51 ff. (1953). In post-socialist Russia, the jury system has been revived, partly out of nostalgia, partly out of concern with ensuring the autonomy of the trial court in a country in which the judiciary has not been noted for its independence. See Stephen C. Thaman, The Resurrection of Trial by Jury in Russia, 31 Stan. J. Int'l L. 61 (1995). See also, William E. Butler, Russian Law 267 (2d ed. 2003).

36. See, e.g., Dölle, Der Beitrag der Rechtsvergleichung zum deutschen Recht, in 2 Hundert Jahre deutsches Rechtsleben—Festschrift zum hundert-jährigen Bestehen des deutschen Juristentages 19 (1960); Escarra, The Aims of Comparative Law, 7 Temp. L. Q. 296 (1933).

On the use of the comparative method by legislators on the Continent and in Great Britain, and on the relative paucity of similar efforts in the United States, see Stein, *supra* note 18, at 210–212.

37. See P. John Kozyris, Comparative Law for the Twenty–First Century: New Horizons and New Technologies, 69 Tul. L. Rev. 165, 176–78 (1994).

38. Examples and further references can be found in B. Grossfeld, The Strength and Weakness of Comparative Law 15–18 (T. Weir trans., 1990).

39. A continental-type Ministry of Justice exists in New Zealand. Headed by a member of the Government, the New Zealand Department of Justice is responsible for law reform and acts as secretariat for a Law Revision Commission. See J. H. Farrar, Law Reform and the Law Commission 80–89 (1974), where further references can be found. The best-known plea for such an agency in the United States is Benjamin Cardozo, A Ministry of Justice, 35 Harv. L. Rev. 113 (1921).

40. See, e.g., Report of the Royal Commission on Capital Punishment 1949–1953, at 2–3, 411–13, 414–16, 420–28, 432–66, 475–85 (1953).

41. Law Commissions Act of 1965, sec. 3(1)(f).

42. See N.S. Marsh, Law Reform in the United Kingdom: A New Institutional Approach, 13 Wm. & Mary L.Rev. 263 (1971); L.

In the United States, where examination of the laws of fifty-three American jurisdictions imposes a heavy load on the legislative draftsman even without the study of foreign materials, it is still not the routine practice of legislators and those assisting them to study the comparable laws of foreign countries.[43] Nonetheless, in its heyday, the New York Law Revision Commission did try to utilize the experience of other countries,[44] and there is some indication that comparative studies have become more frequent than they once were as a prelude to law reform.[45]

(4) In the United States, apart from the broader civil law influences mentioned above, large parts of the country have a heritage of Spanish and French law derived from early settlers and conquerors.[46] Some of the early session laws of a number of states were published in Spanish, French or German, in addition to English.[47]

Scarman, Inside the English Law Commission, 57 A.B.A.J. 867 (1971); L. N. Brown, A Century of Comparative Law in England, 19 Am. J. Comp.L. 233, 247–49 (1971); J. H. Farrar, *supra* note 39, at 34. For more recent assessments, see Stephen Cretney, The Politics of Law Reform—A View from the Inside, 48 Mod. L. Rev. 493, 507–08 (1985); P. M. North, Law Reform: Processes and Problems, 101 Law Q. Rev. 338, 338–46 (1985); Anthony Ogus, Economics and Law Reform: Thirty Years of Law Commission Endeavour, 111 Law Q. Rev. 407 (1995).

43. See Stein, *supra* note 18; E. M. Wise, Legal Tradition as a Limitation on Law Reform, 26 Am.J.Comp.L. 1, 14–15 (1978). See also, with specific reference to labor law, C. W. Summers, Book Review, 72 Colum.L.Rev. 1119, 1125–26 (1972).

44. See J. W. MacDonald, The New York Law Revision Commission, 28 Mod. L.Rev. 1, 13 (1965). This is borne out by the example discussed *supra* Chapter 2, Part 1, Section 1 at 70.

45. See G. A. Zaphiriou, Use of Comparative Law by the Legislator, 30 Am. J.Comp.L. 71, 78–80 (Supp. 1982); C. J. Whelan, Labor Law and Comparative Law, 63 Tex.L.Rev. 1425, 1450–51 (1985).

46. "There are many parts of Texas law today that came from the Spanish law, notably those relating to ... marital and community rights, and the lack of distinction between law and equity." Markham, The Reception of the Common Law of England in Texas and the Judicial Attitude Toward that Reception, 1840–59, 29 Tex.L.Rev. 904, 909 (1951).

For comprehensive discussions of the subject, see H. W. Baade, The Form of Marriage in Spanish North America, 61 Cornell L.Rev. 1, especially at 1–5 (1975); H.W. Baade, The Formalities of Private Real Estate Transactions in Spanish North America, 38 La.L.Rev. 655 (1978); H.W. Baade, Book Review, 26 Am.J.Comp.L. 647 (1978). The symposium entitled Bicentennial Survey of Civil Law Influences on American Legal Development, 69 L. Lib. J. 610 (1976), contains a useful bibliography. See also K. Knaup, The Transition from Spanish Civil Law to English Common Law in Missouri, 16 St. Louis U. L.J. 218 (1971); Joseph W. McKnight, Spanish Legitum in the United States—Its Survival and Decline, 44 Am.J.Comp.L. 75 (1995).

Most studies of legal history in these parts of the United States tend to assume that the process of "Americanization" was more or less inexorable. For further references, see J. P. Reid, Some Lessons of Western Legal History, 1 W. Legal Hist. 3 (1988). For exceptions emphasizing the clash of legal cultures as it appeared to contemporaries, see G. Dargo, Jefferson's Louisiana: Politics and the Clash of Legal Traditions (1975); D. Langum, Law and Community on the Mexican California Frontier: Anglo–American Expatriates and the Clash of Legal Traditions, 1821–1846 (1987); and (to some extent) M. Arnold, Unequal Laws Unto a Savage Race: European Legal Traditions in Arkansas, 1686–1836 (1985).

47. See J. Fedynskyj, State Session Laws in Non–English Languages, 46 Ind.L.J. 473 (1971).

Nowadays, these remnants of civil law often are hidden under a thick layer of common law;[48] but a lawyer who practices in Florida, Texas, New Mexico, Arizona, or California, or in any of the states which were included in the Louisiana Purchase, cannot afford to overlook these remnants when dealing with problems of land titles,[49] mining law,[50] water rights[51] or matrimonial property.[52]

In no other part of the United States are civil law influences as strong as in Louisiana and Puerto Rico. The French settlers of Louisiana originally lived under French law; but from 1769 to 1803, Spanish law was imposed on them as a result of treaties concluded among European powers, followed by military conquest.[53] In 1803, French authorities again took possession of New Orleans,

48. See R.R. Powell, Compromises of Conflicting Claims: A Century of California Law 1760–1860, especially at 127–32 (1977), and the authorities cited *supra* note 46.

49. See Ainsa v. New Mexico & Arizona R.R., 175 U.S. 76, 79, 20 S.Ct. 28, 29 (1899). For many further references, see the articles cited *supra* note 46, and H. W. Baade, Proving Foreign Law and International Law in Domestic Tribunals, 18 Va. J. Int. L. 619, 620–23 (1978).

In Humble Oil & Refining Co. v. Sun Oil Co., 190 F.2d 191, 194–95 (5th Cir.1951), a question of title to Texas land was decided on the authority of a provision of the Siete Partidas (see *supra* note 7), and the court also relied on quotations from Justinian's *Corpus Juris*.

50. See Swenson, Civil and Common Law Precedents to American Mining Law, in 1 The American Law of Mining, sec. 1.1 (Looseleaf ed.); 1 Snyder, Mines and Mining 38 ff. (1902). Cf. Moore v. Smaw, 17 Cal. 199 (1861).

51. See City of Los Angeles v. San Fernando, 14 Cal.3d 199, 123 Cal.Rptr. 1, 537 P.2d 1250 (1975). In this case, seventy trial days were devoted to presentation of expert testimony and other evidence on the issue of whether plaintiff had a *pueblo* water right under Spanish–Mexican law.

See also McCurdy v. Morgan, 265 S.W.2d 269 (Tex.Civ.App.1954) (holding that the civil law doctrine of sovereign ownership of the beds of watercourses was limited to perennial streams and did not apply to dry creeks. The briefs in that case, written with the assistance of Spanish and Mexican scholars, traced the civil law distinction between perennial and torrential streams to Seneca, Ulpian, and Justinian's *Corpus Juris*); In re Adjudication of Water Rights in Medina River

Watershed of San Antonio River Basin, 670 S.W.2d 250 (Tex.1984); Maricopa County Municipal Water Conservation District No. 1 v. Southwest Cotton Co., 39 Ariz. 65, 4 P.2d 369 (1931). A thorough discussion and many further references can be found in H. W. Baade, The Historical Background of Texas Water Law, 18 St. Mary's L.J. 1 (1986). See also H. W. Baade, Roman Law in the Water, Mineral and Public Land Law of the Southwestern United States, 40 Am.J.Comp.L. 865 (1992).

52. See, e.g., McDonald v. Senn, 53 N.M. 198, 212, 204 P.2d 990, 998 (1949) ("It is the rule in this state that we should look to the Spanish–Mexican law for definitions and interpretations affecting our community property statutes"); Clark, Community Property and the Family in New Mexico 6–7 (1956). For comprehensive information concerning the civil law origin and civil law nature of community property, see Charmatz and Daggett, Comparative Studies in Community Property Law (1955); De Funiak and Vaughn, Principles of Community Property 39–108 (1971).

53. See Batiza, The Influence of Spanish Law in Louisiana, 33 Tul.L.Rev. 29 (1958); Batiza, The Unity of Private Law in Louisiana Under the Spanish Rule, 4 Inter–Am. L. Rev. 139 (1962).

Concerning the nature and sources of the body of Spanish law introduced in Louisiana and other parts of the New World, see the articles by Baade cited *supra* note 46. With respect to the situation in Louisiana, it should be noted that, while from 1769 to 1803, the official law was predominantly Spanish, the law in action, i.e., the legal practices of the inhabitants, largely continued to reflect French traditions. See H. W. Baade, Marriage Contracts in French and Spanish Louisiana: A Study in "Notarial"

but only for three weeks, and merely for the purpose of handing over control to the United States under the terms of the Louisiana Purchase. Shortly thereafter, in 1808, Louisiana's substantive private law was codified; this codification is of present-day significance since large portions of the Civil Code of 1808 were subsequently incorporated into the Civil Codes of 1825 and of 1870, the latter (with extensive revisions enacted piecemeal since 1976) being in effect today.[54]

The draftsmen of the 1808 Code utilized Spanish as well as French sources; the latter included not only the works of famous 17th and 18th century scholars such as Domat and Pothier, but also a draft and the final version of the Code Napoleon, which had been promulgated in 1804. The question of whether the draftsmen relied predominantly on these French texts (as is generally believed), or on the Spanish ones, is hotly controverted and has given rise to a fascinating scholarly debate.[55] Certain it is, however, that the Louisiana Civil Code has its roots in the civil law.[56]

In areas of law not covered by the Civil Code, especially in matters of procedure, commercial law and public law, Louisiana experienced the intrusion of many common law institutions. Even in the interpretation and application of the Civil Code itself, the impact of common law methods was felt, and several decades ago it was a matter of some controversy whether Louisiana had not become, in essence, a common law jurisdiction.[57] Since then, however, deliberate efforts have been made to revitalize the state's civil law tradition. As part of these efforts, the Louisiana State Law Institute, pursuant to legislative mandate,[58] has sponsored English translations of leading French treatises on private law and other publications of a distinctly civilian bent.[59] In any event, it

Jurisprudence, 53 Tul.L.Rev. 3, especially at 73ff. (1978).

54. For concordances among sections of the Codes of 1808, 1825, and 1870, see the 1972 Compiled Edition of the Civil Codes of Louisiana (J. Dainow ed., 1973, & Supps.), which comprises vols. 16 & 17 of West's Louisiana Statutes Annotated. Vol. 17, at 803–10, contains a helpful bibliography. See also, especially on recent revisions, which have produced a substantially new code, A. N. Yiannopoulos, An Introduction to the Louisiana Civil Code, in 1 West's Louisiana Civil Code, at xiii (1993).

Statutes relating to codal subjects enacted after 1870 appear in Title 9 (Civil Code—Ancillaries) of the Louisiana Revised Statutes of 1950, which comprises vols. 3, 3A, & 4 of West's Louisiana Statutes Annotated.

55. See Batiza, The Louisiana Civil Code of 1808: Its Actual Sources and Present Relevance, 46 Tul.L.Rev. 4 (1971); Pascal, Sources of the Digest of 1808: A Reply to Professor Batiza, 46 Tul.L.Rev. 603 (1972); Batiza, Sources of the Civil Code of 1808—Facts and Speculation: A Rejoinder, 46 Tul. L.Rev. 628 (1972); Batiza, The Actual Sources of the Louisiana Projet of 1823: A General Analytical Survey, 47 Tul.L.Rev. 1 (1972).

For a concise, detached, and plausible summing up of the controversy, see A. N. Yiannopoulos, The Early Sources of Louisiana Law: Critical Appraisal of a Controversy, in Louisiana's Legal Heritage 87 (E. F. Haas ed. 1983).

56. For guides to the sources of Louisiana law, including the Roman, Spanish, and French antecedents, see A. N. Yiannopoulos, *supra* note 218; Kate Wallach, Louisiana Legal Research Manual (1972). See also Symposium: The Romanist Tradition in Louisiana: Legislation, Jurisprudence, and Doctrine, 56 La.L.Rev. 249 (1995). The introduction to this symposium by Symeon Symeonides also contains an extensive bibliography (at 249–51).

57. For conflicting answers to this question, compare Ireland, Louisiana's Legal System Reappraised, 11 Tul.L.Rev. 585, 591–2 (1937), and Comment, 7 Tul.L.Rev. 100 (1932), with Daggett, Dainow, Hebert & McMahon, A Reappraisal Appraised: A Brief for the Civil Law of Louisiana, 12 Tul.L.Rev. 12, 17–24 (1937), and Note, 17 Geo. Wash. L. Rev. 186, 192–3 (1949).

58. See Tucker, The Civil Law Objectives of the Louisiana State Law Institute, in Civil Law in the Modern World, at xi–xvi (A. N. Yiannopoulos ed. 1965).

is clear that few questions of substantive private law can be answered by a Louisiana lawyer without resort to the provisions of a code of civil law ancestry. The system, the terminology, and the unarticulated assumptions of such a code cannot be understood by one whose training is limited to the common law.[60]

The Civil Code of Puerto Rico derives from Spain.[61] In interpreting its provisions, the courts of Puerto Rico have considered themselves bound by Spanish decisions rendered prior to October 18, 1898.[62] Other Spanish authorities have persuasive force.[63] By virtue of a 1961 congressional enactment,[64] it is no longer possible to appeal to any federal court from decisions of the Supreme Court of Puerto Rico interpreting the Civil Code or other local laws. Even before 1961, the federal courts were not permitted to inject common law notions into the application of local laws derived from the civil law;[65] and the same rule continues to apply whenever federal courts in the exercise of their ordinary jurisdiction (especially in diversity cases) are called on to apply Puerto Rican law.[66] During the first half of the 20th century, the Supreme Court of Puerto Rico was a leading agent in the "Americanization" of Puerto Rican law; since 1952, when Puerto Rico became a "Commonwealth," the Supreme Court of Puerto Rico has led in trying to halt "Americanization" and has asserted the primacy of civil law elements in the Puerto Rican legal system.[67] It has had to contend, however, with powerful centripetal influences exerted by "continental" law[68] that make legal life in Puerto Rico, in many respects, a constant struggle over communal self-definition.[69]

59. See A. N. Yiannopoulos, Louisiana Civil Law Treatise: Property 15–18 (2d ed. 1980). See also the other volumes in the important series entitled Louisiana Civil Law Treatise.

60. See the instructive article by A. N. Yiannopoulos, Louisiana Civil Law: A Lost Cause?, 54 Tul. L.Rev. 830 (1980). Also see Robert A. Pascal, Louisiana Civil Law and Its Study, 60 La. L. Rev. 1 (1999); William Tetley, Mixed Jurisdictions: Common Law v. Civil Law (Codified and Uncodified), 600 Louisiana L. Rev. 677 (Spring 2000).

61. See 31 Laws of Puerto Rico Ann. sec. 1, Note "History of Civil Code" (1968).

62. Olivieri v. Biaggi, 17 P.R.R. 676 (1911); Marchan v. Eguen, 44 P.R.R. 396 (1933) (construing the term "professor" as used in the Code).

63. See Geigel v. Mariani, 85 P.R.R. 43 (1962), where the court relied not only on a post–1898 decision of the Supreme Court of Spain, but also on a wide range of other civil law authorities.

64. 75 Stat. 417, repealing former 28 U.S.C. § 1293.

65. Bonet v. Texas Co., 308 U.S. 463, 60 S.Ct. 349 (1940); Diaz v. Gonzalez, 261 U.S. 102, 43 S.Ct. 286 (1923).

66. See De Castro v. Board of Commissioners, 322 U.S. 451, 459, 64 S.Ct. 1121, 1125 (1944); First National City Bank v. Gonzalez, 293 F.2d 919 (1st Cir.1961). Cf. Fornaris v. Ridge Tool Co., 400 U.S. 41, 91 S.Ct. 156 (1970); Gual Morales v. Hernandez Vega, 579 F.2d 677, 682 (1st Cir.1978); and also by a former judge of the First Circuit in Stephen Breyer, The Relationship Between the Federal Courts and the Puerto Rico Legal System, 53 Rev. Jur. U. P. R. 307 (1984). See also discussions on Puerto Rico by Former Chief Justice of Puerto Rico Jose Trias Monge, First Worldwide Congress on Mixed Jurisdiction: Salience and Unity in the Mixed Jurisdiction Experience: Traits, Patterns, Culture, Commonalities: Legal Methodologies in Some Mixed Jurisdictions, 78 Tul. L. Rev. 333 (December 2003).

67. This development is discussed in Reyes–Cardona v. J. C. Penney Co., Inc., 694 F.2d 894, 896 (1st Cir.1982). One of the court's most emphatic statements rejecting the use of common law precepts to solve civil law problems appears in Valle v. American Int'l Ins. Co., 108 D.P.R. 692 (P.R.1979).

68. When Puerto Rican lawyers speak of "continental" law, they refer to the legal system of the continental United States. This differs, of course, from the usage which asso-

(5) In the recent literature, more explanations of legal transplants have been advanced. Some attempt to take into consideration the impact of power, particularly its "diffused" form, focusing on the complex phenomena of psychological dependency of subordinated countries.[70] Others have introduced an aesthetical dimension of law including notions of seductiveness and of aesthetics of legal systems capable of explaining their capacity to conquer the imagination of foreign observers.[71] Still others have pointed to the fact that legal systems capable of circulating should be simple and broad enough to be adaptable to the different positive laws of the contexts of reception.[72]

6. LEGAL PLURALISM

Legal transplants, no matter how we wish to explain them, produce observable outcomes in the structure of the law. One possibility is the increase in legal uniformity and the development of a "common core" of principles, rules or actual solutions among different legal systems.[1] If a transplant is not well digested in the receiving country, the outcome will be legal pluralism, a phenomenon, originally observed by legal anthropologists working on remote settings, but more recently deployed by comparative law scholars even in the study of core, highly professionalized legal systems.[2]

Jessica Fourneret, France: Banning Legal Pluralism by Passing a Law

29 Hastings Int'l & Comp. L. Rev. 233–246 (Winter 2006).

On September 2, 2004, the first day of la rentrée in France, an estimated million French Muslim students were forced to either take off their headscarves—or watch their female counterparts do so—upon entering the school buildings. The consequences for failing to comply were temporary suspension, expulsion, or even, prosecution. This is because on

ciates continental law, like continental cuisine, with the continent of Europe.

69. See Liana Fiol–Matta, Civil Law and Common Law in the Legal Method of Puerto Rico, 40 Am. J. Comp. L. 783 (1993); Liana Fiol–Matta Civil Law and Common Law in the Legal Method of Puerto Rico: Anomalies and Contradictions of Legal Discourse, 24 Cap. U. L. Rev. 153 (1995); Liana Fiol–Matta, Common Law and Civil Law in the Legal Method of Puerto Rico: The Transmission of Legal Discourse, 64 Rev. Jur. U. P. R. 501 (1995).

70. See Mattei & Nader, *supra* note 16; Duncan Kennedy, Two Globalizations of Law & Legal Thought: 1850–1968, 36 Suffolk U. L. Rev. 631 (2003).

71. See Heather Hughes, Aesthetics of Commercial Law–Domestic and International Implications, 67 Louisiana L. Rev. 689 (2007).

72. See Alan Watson, The Importance of Nutshells, 42 Am. J. Comp. L. 1 (1994); Ugo Mattei, Why the Wind Changed: Intellectual Leadership in Western Law, 42 Am. J. Comp. L. 195 (1994).

1. See *supra* Chapter 2, Part 1 Section 3 at 95.

2. John Griffiths, What Is Legal Pluralism?, 25 J.Legal Pluralism & Unofficial L. 1 (1986); Sally Engle Merry, Legal Pluralism, 22 Law & Society Review 869–896 (1988).

March 15, 2004, French president Jacques Chirac enacted a law to prohibit public school students from wearing clothing and insignia that "openly manifest a religious affiliation."[1] While the law, on its face, bans "all such symbols," including "large" Catholic crucifixes, Jewish yarmulkes and Sikh turbans, the unstated but clear aim of the law was to prohibit female Muslim students from wearing the hijab,[2] or headscarf.[3] The French parliament voted almost unanimously (494 to 36) to pass the ban.[4] Early polls indicated that the French public understood the motive behind the law in the same way and were overwhelmingly supportive of it....

France has coupled its near open-door policy with a tradition of assimilating immigrants to turn them into "children of France."[5] There is a strong sense of French national identity that is promoted as a unifying force. The compulsory use of the French language is one example. Similarly, the government has recently insisted that Muslim imams receive training in French laws and society.[6] Upon nationalization, immigrants are encouraged to take classes on French culture, including language and culinary education.[7]

1. Projet de Loi Encadrant, en Application du Principe de Laïcité, le Port de Signes ou de Tenues Manifestant une Appartenance Religieuse dans les Ecoles, Collèges et Lycées Publics, No. 253, Assemblée Nationale, Douzième Législature (2004), available at www.assemblee-nat.fr/12/pdf/ta/ta0253.pdf ("Dans les écoles, les collèges et les lycées publics, le port de signes ou tenues par lesquels les élèves manifestant ostensiblement une appartenance religieuse est interdit. Le règlement intérieur rappelle que la mise en oeuvre d'une procédure disciplinaire est précédée d'un dialogue avec l'élève." [It is forbidden to wear symbols or clothing that openly manifests membership to a religion in public elementary, intermediate and high schools. The rules of procedure require that disciplinary proceedings be preceded by a discussion with the pupil.]).

2. The Question Of Hijab: Suppression Or Liberation?, The Institute of Islamic Information and Education, at www.usc.edu/dept/MSA/humanrelations womeninislam/whatishijab.html (visited Mar. 6, 2005) ("The word 'hijab' comes from the Arabic word 'hajaba' meaning to hide from view or conceal. In the present time, the context of hijab is the modest covering of a Muslim woman.").

3. Derek H. Davis, Reacting to France's Ban: Headscarves and Other Religious Attire in American Public Schools, 46 J. Church & State 221 (Spring 2004).

4. Elisa T. Beller, The Headscarf Affair: The Conseil d'Etat on the Role of Religion and Culture in French Society, 39 Tex. Int'l L.J. 581 (2004).

5. Jacques Chirac, Speech at the Elysee Palace (Dec. 17, 2003) [hereinafter Chirac, Elysee Palace Speech], available at elysee.fr/elysee/anglais/speeches_and_documents/2003/speech_by_jacques_chirac_president_of_the_republic_on_respecting_the_principles_of_secularism_in_the_republic-experts.2675.html.

6. *Id.* ("A new milestone will also be reached when French imams can be trained in France, allowing the assertion of the identity of a French-based Islam."); Carol Eisenberg, Standoff Over Head Scarfs, Newsday, Dec. 13, 2004, at A20 ("the French interior minister announced plans to 'strongly encourage' imams to take university classes in French law and society starting next fall").

7. See, e.g., Cynthia DeBula Baines, L'Affaire des Foulards—Discrimination, or the Price of a Secular Public Education System? 29 Vand. J. Transnat'l L. 303, 312–13 (Mar. 1996); Augustin Motilla, Religious Pluralism in Spain: Striking the Balance Between Religious Freedom and Constitutional Rights, 2004 BYU L. Rev. 575, 596 (2004) ("A 1993 law modified the requirements for French citizenship to require applicants to show linguistic and cultural assimilation").

However, many immigrants of the Muslim faith do not have the same idea of secularism as the French and cannot simply separate their "French" selves from their "Muslim" selves. An inherent conflict results when the government tells the young Muslim woman to remove her veil but she feels that wearing it is a religious obligation imposed on her by God.

Nevertheless, on the first day of school, only 639 of an estimated million Muslim students showed up in religious symbols and most were persuaded to remove them voluntarily.[8] As of November 2004, forty such students had been expelled, including thirty-six Muslim girls and four Sikh boys who wore turbans. Lawsuits related to many of these cases have been filed. These paltry numbers suggest this highly controversial law targeting schoolgirls is misplaced. The idea behind it is also flawed. Instead of reaching out to include these young Muslims in mainstream society, the French are forcing them first to conform. Promoting a policy of cultural uniformity can work to increase social tension, eventually favoring the proliferation of cultural ghettos hostile to the dominant society. . . .

Many see the passage of the law as Chirac merely making a tough statement on what it means to be French, and more importantly, what is not French.[9] The Prime Minister of France at the time of the ban's passage, Jean–Pierre Raffarin, insisted the government's vision of laïcité was not hostile to religions. His stated view upon passage of the bill was that everyone has the right to freely express his or her faith on the condition that, while at school, he or she obeys the law. The purpose of the ban is to send a "strong message, fast," he added. The message, however, seems to be that one must not be a Muslim in public (at least while attending French public school), because the presence of Muslims will confuse and fluster the children by creating divisiveness. It is important to note that the law, according to the President, is not meant to ban Catholic crosses on the condition that they are not excessive in size. Most Catholics, when they do wear crosses, generally do not wear ones of an "excessive size." In addition, wearing a cross is usually the result of a personal choice rather than a sense of obligation. The law therefore clearly has a discriminatory effect on the Muslim students. . . .

Although the highest French administrative court (the Conseil d'Etat) had ruled as early as 1989 that French children have the constitutional right to wear religious insignia to school,[10] according to Chirac's conception

---

8.   Eisenberg, *supra* note 6, at A20.

9.   Jane Kramer, Taking the Veil; How France's Public Schools Became the Battleground in a Culture War, The New Yorker, Nov. 22, 2004, at 58. ("Chirac clearly felt that the time had come to make a tough, resoundingly 'French' statement on secularism.")

10.   T. Jeremy Gunn, Under God but Not the Scarf: The Founding Myths of Reli-gious Freedom in the United States and Laïcité in France, 47 J. Church & State 1 (Winter 2004).

The Conseil ruled, on November 27, 1989, that wearing religious symbols to school is permissible as long as those symbols are not so "ostentatious" as to "constitute an act of intimidation, provocation, proselytizing, or propaganda; threaten the dignity and freedom of students or other members of the educational community[;]" or disrupt the

of the laïcité doctrine, the French do not have to accommodate religious groups at all. . . .

Yet to a lot of Europeans, still steeped in memories of the Catholic Church's intellectual repression, religion is an irrational force. So women who cover themselves are foolish at best and dangerous otherwise. The ban on headscarves, to many Europeans is a desirable development as it is a step in the direction of freedom from religion rather than religious freedom. . . .

One reason the external Muslim world is so appalled by the French ban relates to the controversy over whether wearing the hijab is obligatory for female Muslims. There has been a wave of assertions that it is indeed a mandatory element of complying with Qur'anic law and that France is therefore depriving these girls of a fundamental right, a right to religious freedom which is embodied in the Declaration of the Rights of Man and of the Citizen. . . . Others proclaim that to wear the veil is a personal choice, made by the individual woman. It is practically impossible to determine why one wears the headscarf because there is no uniform justification. As one author explains:

> For some girls it may offer a strong sense of identity; for others, an oppressive symbol. The hijab may represent (to both its wearers and viewers) religious faith, extremist politics, gender inequality, cultural identity, and solidarity with other Muslim women, all at the same time. These girls belong to their particular religious and cultural communities and may feel compelled to wear the hijab because of their membership in, and allegiance to, their families and religious faith. . . . Yet "many Muslim feminists maintain that the [Qur'an] does not so much prescribe veils as record that the wives of the Prophet went veiled and in this way were able to recognize one another and to be honored by other women for their distinction."

Many women, however, assert a strong desire to wear the veil. As one self-proclaimed modern Muslim woman explains:

> Religion supplies a set of values, including discipline, that serve as a counterweight to the materialism of life in the West. I could have become a runaway materialist, a robotic mall rat who resorts to retail therapy in pursuit of fulfillment. I didn't. That's because religion introduces competing claims. It injects a tension that compels me to think and allows me to avoid fundamentalisms of my own.

Still others insist there is no choice; that to practice the religion, women of a certain age must wear the hijab. Indeed, one such girl, Cennet Doganay, a 15–year-old French Muslim of Turkish origin, shaved her head in order to avoid making a decision about which "law" to obey. She said, "I will respect both French law and Muslim law by taking off what I have on my head and not showing my hair."

school's normal functioning. *supra* Beller, note 4, at 584.

It is impossible to know what the veil represents to all of the women who are now forbidden to wear it at certain times and in certain places. The infamous Stasi Report (named after its chairman, Bernard Stasi) that Chirac commissioned on the subject of laïcité in France, listed several explanations for why Muslim girls wear headscarves to school. The first was that young men force them to wear asexual clothing and to lower their gaze in order to avoid being stigmatized as whores. Second, the headscarf is imposed on girls by violence and thus wearing it offers protection. Third, they are victims of pressure imposed by the family or community. The report concluded that Muslim girls are pressured to wear religious insignia by both their families and social environments and therefore have no choice of their own. The Commission clearly felt that the overwhelming reason girls wear headscarves is not for personal piety but due to unwanted coercion. The report stamped these girls as oppressed victims of their own communities.

Nevertheless, to many, the headscarf is viewed as an obligatory part of their religious devotion. Consequently, banning this element is extremely disruptive as it presents a difficult choice between their external French laws (their community and its school system, which defines itself as open, liberal, diverse, and committed to individual rights and autonomy) and their internal sense of obligations. The government cannot simply write this duty out of their religious practices by passing a law. All the opining on the question of whether the veil is necessary or not to the definition of a devout Muslim is irrelevant; non-Muslims' understanding of Islam will not change the minds of Muslim girls who believe they must (or who sincerely want to) wear the veil. . . .

France, like the United States, has a system comprised of the government and the individual. The individual must answer to the government while everything else—such as the church—is on the side: We either do not call it law or we outlaw it.

Islamic law is personal and non-geographical.[11] Regardless of where a Muslim finds himself on the globe, he must operate under Islamic law. Similarly, merchants used to internalize the law so that they carried it with them, from port to port.[12] . . . The West, by contrast, bases law on territory instead of on individuals. When those two systems collide, there is an inherent conflict that a Muslim cannot rationalize away; she will either break her country's law or her own religious law that she internalizes and carries with her at all times, regardless of the characterization of the soil under her feet. . . .

---

11. See, e.g., Near/Middle East: Round-up of Friday Sermons, BBC News (Jan. 2, 2004): For the Muslim woman, putting on the hijab is an act of worship and a religious duty. It applies to every Muslim woman from the east to the west of the globe at any time and place in the midst of men. [T]he hijab is clearly sanctioned in the Koranic verse in which God says: "They should draw their veils over their bosoms and not display their beauty."

12. See, e.g., Sosa v. Alvarez–Machain, 542 U.S. 692, 743 (2004).

NOTES AND QUESTIONS

(1) Based on what we have discussed thus far we can see that a legal system consists not only of rules and principles which can be cast in propositional form, but also of higher order understandings, received techniques, constellations of values, ideologies and shared ways of perceiving reality, which are pervasive, often subtle, and themselves deeply layered in complex and important ways.[1] The anthropologist Clifford Geertz uses the term "legal sensibility" to designate this constitutive aspect of a legal system, its distinctive "manner of conceiving decision situations, so that settled rules can be applied to them."[2] Others talk about "style", "mentalité" and so on.[3] Legal sensibilities are peculiarly tenacious. In the contemporary world, Geertz observes, despite the spread of common law and civil law practically everywhere, traditional legal sensibilities formed in earlier times persist: "In every Third World country—in Volta, even Singapore—the tension between established notions of what justice ... *haqq* ... *dharma* ... *adat* ... is and how it gets done and imported ones more reflective of the forms and pressures of modern life animates whatever there is of judicial process."[4]

It is increasingly common to speak of the resulting condition as one of legal pluralism. In its older sense, the term legal pluralism refers to situations in which different bodies of personal law apply to different groups within a single territory: this was a typical feature of colonial regimes in which, despite the importation of European law, the courts were authorized to apply indigenous law in cases involving "natives,"[5] and it often continued into the post-colonial era. Nowadays, a growing body of literature uses the term in an extended sense to refer to all situations in which a body of law interacts with another system of norms, whether or not the latter is officially designated as "law."[6] It therefore

1. See Adam Czarnota & Martin Krygier, Revolutions and the Continuity of European Law, in Revolutions in Law and Legal Thought 91–99 (Zenon Bankowski ed., 1991).

2. Clifford Geertz, Local Knowledge: Fact and Law in Comparative Perspective, in Local Knowledge: Further Essays in Interpretive Anthropology 167, 215 (1983).

3. See Pierre Legrand, John Henry Merryman and Comparative Legal Studies: A Dialogue, 47 Am. J. Comp. L. 3 (1999); Werner Menski, Comparative Law in a Global Context: The Legal Systems of Asia and Africa (2006).

4. Geertz, *supra* note 2.

5. The great classic on legal pluralism in this older sense is M. B. Hooker, Legal Pluralism: An Introduction to Colonial and Neo-colonial Laws (1975).

6. On this "new" legal pluralism—much of which are reprinted in Law and Anthropology (M. Mundy ed., 2002)—see, e.g., People's Law and State Law (Anthony N. Allott & Gordon R. Woodman eds., 1985);

Masaji Chiba, Legal Pluralism: Toward a General Theory through Japanese Legal Culture (1989); Legal Polycentricity: Consequences of Pluralism in Law (Hanne Petersen & Henrik Zahle eds., 1995); Norbert Rouland, Legal Anthropology 46–65, 72–82 (Philippe G. Planel trans., 1994); Marc Galanter, Justice in Many Rooms: Courts, Private Ordering, and Indigenous Law, 19 J. Legal Pluralism & Unofficial L. 1 (1981); Symposium: State Transformation, Legal Pluralism and Community Justice, 1 Soc. & Legal Stud. 131–320 (1992); F. von Benda Beckmann, Who's Afraid of Legal Pluralism?, 47 J. Legal Pluralism & Unofficial L.37–82 (2002); S Merry, Global Human Rights and Local Social Movements in a Legally Plural World, 12(2) Canadian J. L. & Soc'y 247–271(1997); B. Santos, Law of the Oppressed: The Construction and Reproduction of Legality in Pasargada Law, 12 L & Soc'y Rev. 5–126 (1977); B. Santos, Law: A Map of Misreading. Towards a Post–Modern Understanding of Law, 14(3) J. L. & Soc'y 279–302 (1987).

includes all cases in which official norms established by the state are supplemented or modified in practice by unofficial rules or popular notions of justice.[7] Legal pluralism in this sense is a fairly pervasive phenomenon, not necessarily confined to the former third world.[8]

As we have mentioned in the text above, scholarship on legal change and on the related field of legal transplants has already identified a staggering variety of patterns at play. Consider, for example, the reality of legal change in three countries that are participating in the worldwide phenomenon of rebirth of Islamic Jurisprudence (the *Shari'a*). In Pakistan, Islamic Law is receiving a sort of constitutional status, and previously imported non-Islamic legislation is subject to a kind of judicial review of compatibility with Islamic principles. In Indonesia, there are attempts to domesticate and to marginalize the *Shari'a* within an effort of secularisation of the legal system. In Malaysia, the *Sharaitic* legal system, short from being marginalized, is recapturing the centrality of the scene, but it is reformed to accept aspects of the English common law that are themselves dressed up as Islamic. Such a variety in relatively homogeneous and historically similar experiences![9]

Each legal transplant seems thus different from each-other. What happened in the modernization process Hataturk's Turkey is different from what happened in Haile' Selassie's Ethiopia. To be sure, we may assist similar attempts to modernize, but imports are from different legal systems, and different impacts of the reforming attempt are evident because of the different degree of resistance of local legal sensitivity. Further, if one opens the picture to capture legal transplants as a worldwide phenomenon of legal change, meaningful generalizations may seem impossible.[10] This tension between local knowledge and the need to generalize, between universalism and local specificity, is at the core of the comparative lawyers' expertise. The full perception of legal pluralism is as important as that of common core, of legal transplants and of the operating of legal formants. Legal pluralism, easier to observe in less developed countries, is by no means limited to exotic contexts.[11]

7. For the objection that speaking of "legal" rather than "normative pluralism" unnecessarily blurs the distinction between legal and non-legal rules, see Brian Z. Tamanaha, The Folly of the "Social Scientific" Concept of Legal Pluralism, 20 J. Law & Soc'y 192 (1993).

8. See, e.g., Robert C. Ellickson, Order Without Law: How Neighbors Settle Disputes (1991); Sally Engle Merry, Getting Justice and Getting Even: Legal Consciousness Among Working–Class Americans (1990). In particular, for a "normative" version of legal pluralism see Gunther Teubner, "Global Bukowina:" Legal Pluralism in the World Society, in Global Law Without a State (Gunther Teubner ed., Dartmouth, Aldershoot 1997) (and the whole book); Gunther Teubner, "Breaking Frames Economic Globalization and the Emergence of Lex Mercatoria", 5(2) Euro. J. Int'l L. 199–218 (2002); and, for an application to European law, see F. Snyder, "Governing Economic Globalisation: Global Legal Pluralism and European Law", 5(4) Euro L. J. 334–374 (1999).

9. See D. L. Horowitz, The Qur'an and the Common Law: Islamic Law Reform and the Theory of Legal Change, in two parts in 42 Am. J. Comp. L. 233–293, 543–580 (1994).

10. See Alan Watson, Legal Transplants (2d ed. 1993); Rodolfo Sacco, Legal Formants: A Dynamic Approach to Comparative Law, 39 Am. J. Comp. L. 1 (1991); Ugo Mattei, Efficiency in Legal Transplants: An Essay in Comparative Law and Economics, 14 Int'l Rev. L. & Econ. 3 (1994); Horowitz, *supra* note 9.

11. See, e.g. Pure Economic Loss in Europe (Mauro Bussani & Vernon Palmer eds., 2003).

For a more extended discussion of the headscarf controversy in France, see Joan W. Scott, *The Politics of the Veil* (2007).

(2) As examples of legal pluralism, we can look to Congo, Somalia, Ethiopia, and Eritrea, four African countries in which, because the modern State exercises only limited control over the territory (particularly but not only outside of the city), legal pluralism is a very visible phenomenon. One should always consider, when dealing with Africa that the very idea of the State is an imported device of colonial origins so that its boundaries do not coincide at all with national entities. For example, there are significant native Somali communities in Somalia, Djibouti, Kenya, and Ethiopia so that, particularly in front of nomadic people, the very legitimacy of the State territorial entity (where it exists) is at stake. In extremely schematic terms, one can describe the incredibly complicated phenomenon of legal pluralism by using an "archaeological approach" which observes the law as it appears today as an incremental accumulation of different layers still easily discernible from each-other. These layers all produce systems of command that, because of the principle of "personality" of the legal system, or because of the particular power ratio in one place or the other, obtains different loyalties.

A first layer (traditional layer) of the legal system is traditional customary law. With tremendous variations in substance and in process from one area to the other of the world, sometimes changing from one quarter to the other of the same town, customary law is characterized by flexibility and absence of writing. It is by no means immutable in time. In Africa it is usually captured by the notion of being "group-centered" rather than individual-centered, but of course the differences stemming from different traditions and economic activities (nomadic vs. sedentary populations) are so staggering and local to discourage generalizations. Customary law is not necessarily based on blood kinship, although that might have been its historical origin. Its role in everyday problem solving and dispute resolution is extremely important and is growing with the growth of the informal economic sector in Africa.[12] Its fundamentally oral character, it is certainly one of the strongest aspects of African legal sensibility, a structural aspect that is usually beyond the understanding of the "textually educated" western lawyer. Because of its pervasiveness, many contend that it is responsible for the failure of most attempts of modernization.

A second layer (the religious layer) of the legal system—second from the perspective of the historical origins but very important today in the Horn of Africa—is Islamic Law. We will discuss its history and sources in Chapter 4 *infra*. For the time being, it is suffice to say that Islamic Law present in a large number of non-western countries and is usually depicted as immutable, scarcely adaptable to modernity and incapable of accepting differences. Today, the very world *Shari'a* excites in the West's worries about fundamentalism. Highly formalized in substance, it is usually applied in rather informal processes by religious judges known as *Quadis*. Most of the traditional perceptions have been now reconsidered in serious comparative legal scholarship.[13] In the Horn

12. See M. Guadagni, Il Modello Pluralista, in A. Procida Mirabelli di Lauro, Sistemi Giuridici Comparati 83 (1997); Ugo Mattei, Legal Pluralism, Legal Change and Economic Development, in New Law for New States. Politica del Diritto in Eritrea 23–50 (L. Favali, E. Grande, M. Guadagni ed., 1998).

13. See, e.g., Horowitz, *supra* note 9; F. Castro, Diritto musulmano e dei paesi islami-

of Africa, Islamic Law, penetrating through the coast, has played an important role in some contexts and not in others. It has proved adaptable to change. Some of its property law, for example, has incorporated traditional aspects of Somali traditional law, the *Xeer*. Absent in Congo, this layer of law is sometimes substituted by another religious layer such as the Ethiopian Feta Negast.[14]

A third layer (the colonial layer) is the formal legal system that colonial powers have used to rule their colonies. Colonial law, despite the political difference between the British indirect rule and the French direct approach, can be observed as significantly similar to the two contexts as far as its substance is concerned. It is mostly based on command and control written regulations and on the close monitoring of property rights by the State.[15] When it comes to the process, the difference in legal traditions between common law Britain and civil law France may be a little more relevant mostly in what comparativists refer to as the *style* of adjudication. Interestingly, in Africa the French Civil Code and Our Lady the Common Law were not applied to local populations but were limited to conflict involving white people. In the Horn, Ethiopia practically did not experience colonization, despite the clumsy and bloody Italian effort. Somalia suffered French (Djibouti), English (British Somaliland), and Italian colonization. Eritrea experienced Italy with a deep and long lasting colonization and cultural influence similar to that experienced by Congo from the French.

A fourth layer (the formal post-independence law) is the one affected, to a certain extent, by the common law versus civil law distinction. From a phenomenon of cultural dependency, the former French colonies have codified the French model and the former British colonies regarded themselves as belonging to the common law, as all the other members of the Commonwealth. To be sure, the newly independent States maintained all of the colonial property rights structure with the predominant role of the State. The influence of the former colonial legal tradition was maintained because of a number of privileged contacts with the former colonial power, that some call neo-colonialism. Congolese students go to France, Somali students went to Italy. The law school of Brazzaville was organized with French aid and the one in Mogadishu with Italian. Students from former British colonies attend the Inns of Courts and the English Universities. Countries such as Ethiopia which did not experience significant colonization show a remarkably cosmopolitan flavour in their modern legal systems, borrowing freely from common law and civil law experiences including the U.S.

A fifth layer (socialist law) appears in a number of post-independent African countries, mostly (an exception can possibly be Nierere in Tanzania) as a political option opportunistically driven by some of their military leaders to get the most (in USSR aids) from the cold war confrontation. Such experience was followed by Marien Ngouabi in Congo, by Siad Barre in Somalia and by Mengistu in Ethiopia (and Eritrea). While the structure of property rights

---

ci, in Digesto delle discipline privatistiche. Sezione civile, vol VI, Utet, Torino (1990).

14. See Modelli Autoctoni e Modelli d'Importazione nei Sistemi Giuridici del Corno d'Africa (Elisabetta Grande ed., 1995).

15. See Ugo Mattei, Socialist and Non-Socialist approaches to Land Law: Continuity and Change in Somalia and other African States, 16 R. Sol. L. 17–55 (1990).

shows remarkable continuity, with only some cosmetic changes, and a few more nationalizations, socialist law has offered a formal cover and a modern ideological legitimacy to the authoritarian character of African political leadership. The rhetoric of official law has been affected by a number of transplants from the USSR.[16] The layer of colonial law, in combination with the subsequent ones, provides the legal education of the African legal profession, producing, in different combinations, the very eclectic nature of the local legal élite.

Finally, beginning with the fall of the Berlin Wall, another layer, mostly borrowed from U.S. based economic approach to the law, has been imposed by means of "conditional" loans in a variety of "structural adjustment programs" sponsored by the World Bank Group and by the International Monetary Fund. Again, another legal style is archeologically added on to the previous historical legal experience.

What makes legal pluralism easy to perceive is that none of these layers have ever been strong enough to subvert and cancel the other ones. Many Africans still display a much stronger loyalty to their own group-centered legal order than to the state-based one. Many high level local bureaucracies, trained in civil or soviet law, strenuously resist the "Americanization" process typical of the internationally imposed "Structural Adjustment Plans". Because of the relative weakness of the State compared to traditional clan structure, this situation of pluralism leads to a variety of adaptations and compromises. The outcome of the relative power equality between the different legal orders surviving in the same territory is open competition, which makes modern African law a core context of legal pluralism.

Legal pluralism is by no means a phenomenon unique of Africa. The materials above evidence that even in France, there exist a radical conflict between the Islamic legal order, prescribing to women the covering of "their beauty," and the State legal system. The result, as decided by President Chirac and enacted by law, is to ban the use of religious symbols. Because legal pluralism refers to situations where "two or more legal systems coexist in the same social field,"[17] the fact that one or both of those legal systems are not "official," state-based systems is entirely irrelevant. Although Islamic law is obviously not an official, state-based system in France, it is personally binding on individual Muslims and can be sanctioned within the community of the faithful by a variety of institutional actors. As is the case with most statutes, the Islamic provision has been interpreted broadly and narrowly. Under a broad definition it mandates the covering of female "beauty" and thus, the hair and neck. Using this broad interpretation, it clearly conflicts with Article 141–5–1, thereby creating a situation of legal pluralism. In other words, when a law of Islam conflicts with a law of the State, "a conflict of laws is born".[18] When State law is strong enough to enforce its denial of other legal sensitivities the clash can be violent and involve innocent victims.

(3) Historically, in a number of non-western countries, attempts to induce change and modernization were carried on by colonial powers or by local elites.

---

16. See Mattei, *supra* note 15.

17. Sally Engel Merry, Legal Pluralism, 22 L. & Soc'y Rev. 869, 870 (1988).

18. See Jessica Fourneret, France: Banning Legal Pluralism by Passing a Law, 29

Hastings Int'l & Comp. L. Rev. 233 (Winter 2006).

Today, international governmental or non-governmental institutions such as the World Bank, the International Monetary Fund, U.S.AID, etc. are engaged in similar ambitious modernization projects. All attempts of modernization heavily use the technique of "importing" law. Can and should law reform be induced from outside, by transplanting Western ideas (and ideals) of law?

(4) If the law is "path dependent", imbedded in traditional, cultural, and political realities, one may be tempted to conclude with a rather sceptical approach towards theorizing about legal change and law reform. All observations may only be local; any approach to law reform should be grounded in the reality of a given country and sometimes even in different internal realities within the country. Field research is the only solution to acquire the kind of "thick" knowledge that we need for legal reform. No comparative knowledge is possible. There is no space for arm chair work. Do you agree with this strongly sceptical vision of the possibility of foreign aid in the domain of the law?

(5) Whatever your answer to the previous question, it is a fact that the World Bank, and the other Western agencies of "development" are not satisfied by this context-specific approach, because they seek to target the entire less developed world and they desire to invest as little as possible in acquiring local knowledge. How is it possible to do so? Is it legitimate or useful to consider "poor countries" a family of legal systems for purposes of Comparative Law? The reading of the following materials should help in answering this crucial question.

7.   THE COMPARATIVE LAWYER AS A ZOOLOGIST: THE PROBLEM OF CLASSIFYING LEGAL SYSTEMS

Scholars interested in comparative law have expended considerable time and effort in trying to arrive at a systematic classification of the world's legal systems. To date, these endeavors have produced little standardization and much controversy. One reason for this situation is that classification is never an end in itself: when we classify legal systems, we do so for a specific purpose, and it cannot be taken for granted that a classificatory scheme that is suitable for one purpose will prove equally useful in other contexts. Another reason is that the systems to be classified undergo continual change: the legal map of the world today is not what it was in 1798, or in 1898, or even in 1989, and it no doubt will continue to change in the future. Still another reason is that we can attempt to compare particular segments of legal systems (e.g., private or public law) or legal systems as a whole, and classificatory schemes will differ depending on precisely what it is that is being compared. Yet another reason is that, even granted the same purpose, objects, and scope of comparison, there is disagreement concerning the threshold problem of the criteria to be used. Thus, in classifying legal systems as a whole, some schemes are based on "genetic" relationships or historical development, while others are analytic or "typological" and disregard derivation and pedigree; some schemes use extra-juridical criteria, such as type of civilization or political ideology, while others rely on criteria related to forms of law and on considerations peculiar to legal scholarship.

Older classifications tended to use a single criterion of differentiation;[1] more recent efforts propose that either a composite criterion, such as the "style" of legal systems,[2] or a combination of several criteria,[3] be used. But while these recent efforts may have yielded more satisfactory results in some respects, they have generated new controversies. For example, the choice of the elements of composite criteria and the mutual relationship among those elements, have become new bones of contention.[4]

Classification involves relating one object to others and specifying how those objects are similar and how they differ. In a sense, classification is

---

1. Among earlier efforts, some of the better-known classifications are those by cultures (Schnitzer), by races and languages (Esmein and Sauser–Hall), by historical origins (Glasson and Sarfatti), and by legislative families (Lévy–Ullman). See 1 P. Arminjon, B. Nolde & M. Wolff, Traité de Droit Comparé 42–47 (1950); 1 A. F. Schnitzer, Vergleichende Rechtslehre 133–42 (2d ed. 1961). For a critique of these classificatory attempts, see 3 L.–J. Constantinesco, Traité de Droit Comparé 80–105 (1983). See also T. P. van Reenen, Major Theoretical Problems of Modern Comparative Methodology (3): The Criteria Employed for the Classification of Legal Systems, 29 Comp. & Int'l L.J. S. Afr. 71 (1996); Åke Malmström, The System of Legal Systems: Notes on a Problem of Classification in Comparative Law, 13 Scandinavian Studies in Law 127 (1969); Werner Menski, Comparative Law in a Global Context: The Legal Systems of Asia and Africa (Cambridge Univ. Press 2006); Ugo Mattei, Three Patterns of Law: Taxonomy and Change in World's Legal Systems, 45 Am. J. Comp. L. 5–44 (1997).

2. See K. Zweigert & H. Kötz, An Introduction to Comparative Law 63–75 (Tony Weir trans., 2d rev. ed. 1992). According to these authors, the elements determining the style of a legal system are (1) historical background and development; (2) method of legal reasoning; (3) distinctive legal institutions; (4) nature and treatment of sources of law; and (5) ideological factors. Another composite criterion is that of "legal tradition." See, e.g., John H. Merryman, Rogelio Pérez–Perdomo, The Civil Law Tradition 1–5 (3d ed. 2008); Mary Ann Glendon, Paolo G. Carozza, Colin B. Picker, Comparative Legal Traditions: Text, Materials and Cases on Western Law (3d ed. 2006); David S. Clark, The Idea of the Civil Law Tradition, in Comparative and Pri-

vate International Law: Essays in Honor of John Henry Merryman 11 (D. S. Clark ed., 1990).

3. See René David & John E. C. Brierley, Major Legal Systems in the World Today 20 (3d ed. 1985), where it is suggested that two independent criteria be used: (a) legal method and (b) the philosophical, political and economic fundamentals of the legal order. It will be noted that there is relatively little difference between this view and that of Professors Zweigert and Kötz (*supra* note 2), except that the latter, in the first four determinants of "style," subdivide the concept of legal method into several component elements.

4. It has thus been argued that historical development may explain characteristics of a legal "style," but cannot be regarded as a stylistic element. See, e.g., Constantinesco, *supra* note 1, especially at 128.

Legal anthropologists and sociologists have faulted most of these classifications for focusing too much on legal doctrine. See, e.g., G. Gurwitch, Sociology of Law, ch. 4 (1962); A. Podgorecki, C. J. Whelan & D. Khosla, Legal Systems and Social Systems (1985); Sally Falk Moore, Legal Systems of the World: An Introductory Guide to Classifications, Typological Interpretation, and Bibliographical Resources, in Law and the Social Sciences 11 (L. Lipson & S. Wheeler eds., 1986).

For general criticism of "an all-absorbing preoccupation with doctrine" in comparative law, see I. Markovits, Hedgehogs or Foxes, 34 Am. J. Comp. L. 113, 128, 132–35 (1986). See also Lawrence M. Friedman, Some Thoughts on Comparative Legal Culture, in Comparative and Private International Law, *supra* note 270, at 49.

the ultimate purpose of any kind of comparative scholarship: comparison implies a statement about the relationship between particular objects of study, their resemblances and their differences. Much of the controversy about classification in Comparative Law has to do with the failure of all schemes of classification so far proposed to capture anything like the full complexity of the relationships between contemporary legal systems.

In another sense, however, classification is a beginning rather than an end, a preliminary step designed "to facilitate study of otherwise unwieldy bodies of information."[5] It is a prerequisite to thinking and speaking about the underlying differences and similarities among various objects. Classification in this sense is a matter of applying loose identifying labels which are subject to complication and qualification as one goes into the details and into deviations from the norms that such labels imply. For classification in this sense, rough and ready methods are often sufficient.

One such rough tentative starting point, that we have already at least implicitly used in the previous pages, is the division of legal systems into two groups: common law and civil law. Almost every legal system presently in existence has at least some of its professional characteristics, more or less closely, with one or the other (and sometimes both) of these two groups. The features that define particular legal systems as falling within one group or the other are of European origin; and emphasizing the common law or civil law affiliations of almost every legal system in the world therefore smacks of Eurocentrism. But, in fact, one lasting consequence of the great expansion of the political hegemony of European states across the rest of the globe that took place between the late fifteenth and early twentieth centuries is a situation in which practically every contemporary legal system has acquired features that definitely mark it, at least in some respects, as a common law or a civil law system. Of course, this approach is highly problematic in post-colonial settings. Indeed, it sets the "origins of law" in every country that has been colonized at the origins of colonization when it entered in contact with either the civil law or the common law. This complete erasure of the existence of any "law" before colonization has in-fact been a strong ideological justification of the colonial violence. The frontier challenge of comparative law today is how to rid the discipline of a whole pedigree of Western-centric biases assuming a "lack" wherever the law looks different from the Western, professionalized style.[6]

It should be said at once (and the point will recur throughout our discussion) that the simple dichotomy between common law and civil law, although useful as a starting point, does not exhaust the rich variety of legal systems to be found in the modern world or the fine nuances of the differences between them. It treats as crucial a distinction which it is becoming fashionable to downplay on the ground that a "gradual convergence" is taking place among common law and civil law systems, at least in Europe.[7] It disregards what are perhaps equally significant differences in

---

5. John N. Hazard, Book Review, 38 Am. J. Comp. L. 191, 192 (1990).

6. See Mattei & Nader, Plunder. When the Rule of Law is Illegal (2008).

7. See, e.g., The Gradual Convergence: Foreign Ideas, Foreign Influences, and English Law on the Eve of the 21st Century

the extent to which formal legal rules, whether of common or civil law origin, actually operate to influence and constrain social and political behavior in particular countries. It ignores the fact that, especially in Africa and Asia, many legal systems, notwithstanding common law or civil law affiliations, also have retained large elements of non-European law,[8] and these seem to be becoming more rather than less important, most notably in Islamic countries. Yet, for all its drawbacks, the dichotomy between common law and civil law probably provides as useful a categorical framework as any from which at least to start mapping the legal systems of the world.

Until recently, instead of the dichotomy between common and civil law, most western comparatists employed a trichotomy that distinguished three large groups of legal systems: common law, civil law, and socialist law.[9] As we have seen, in the wake of the breakup of the Soviet empire and of the Soviet Union itself, socialist law is being abandoned by most of the countries in which it formerly prevailed. Even during the period when socialist law was dominant, the countries of Eastern Europe, as well as the Soviet Union, retained important elements of their pre-communist civil law;[10] the survival of these elements made possible interminable dispute as to whether socialist law really was a distinct legal genus or rather a species of civil law.[11] In the case of one country, East Germany, absorption into the

(Basil Markesinis ed., 1994). For a critical discussion, see Ugo Mattei & Luca Pes, Civil Law and Common Law. Towards Convergence?, in Oxford Handbook of Law and Politics 267–280 (Keith E. Whittington, R. Daniel Keleman & Gregory A. Caldeira eds., 2008).

8. See, e.g., European Expansion and Law: The Encounter of European and Indigenous Law in 19th-and 20th-Century Africa and Asia (W. J. Mommsen & J. A. de Moor eds., 1992); Asian Indigenous Law in Interaction with Received Law (Masaji Chiba ed., 1986).T.W. Bennett, Comparative law and African Customary Law, in Oxford Handbook of Comparative Law 641 (Mathias Reimann & Reinhard Zimermann eds., 2006).

9. Comparatists from "socialist" countries tended to treat the distinction between socialist and capitalist law as basic. For an interesting discussion from the "socialist" point of view, see G. Eörsi, Comparative Civil (Private) Law: Law Types, Law Groups, The Roads of Legal Development (1979). It was occasionally suggested, however, that a further subdivision of capitalist systems into common law and civil law systems might make sense. See V. A. Tumanov, On Comparing Various Types of Legal Systems, in Comparative Law and Legal System: Historical and Socio–Legal Perspectives 69, 76 (W. E. Butler & V. N. Kudriavtsev eds., 1985). In

effect, this position coincided with the standard western trichotomy.

In the west, too, it was sometimes suggested that socialist law be contrasted with a type of law encompassing both common and civil law jurisdictions of western pluralist countries. See C. M. Lawson, The Family Affinity of Common Law and Civil Law Systems, 6 Hastings Int'l & Comp.L.Rev. 85 (1982); M. Ancel, La Confrontation des Droits Socialistes et des Droits Occidentaux, in Legal Theory, Comparative Law 13–24 (Z. Peteri ed., 1984). For a thoughtful treatment of this theme, see I. Markovits, Socialist v. Bourgeois Rights, 46 U. Chi. L. Rev. 612 (1978). On the other hand, some common lawyers tended to lump Eastern and Western European continental countries together in the same classificatory niche. See, e.g., R. J. Aldisert, Rambling through Continental Legal Systems, 43 U. Pitt. L. Rev. 935, 961–81 (1982).

10. See, e.g., R. Sacco, The Romanist Substratum in the Civil Law of Socialist Countries, 14 Rev. Socialist L. 65 (1988).

11. For the argument favoring grouping with the civil law, see John Quigley, Socialist Law and the Civil Law Tradition, 37 Am. J. Comp. L. 781 (1989); John Quigley,

West German state has brought it completely back into the civil law orbit.[12] Elsewhere in Eastern Europe and in successor states of the Soviet Union, the situation is more complicated. Each of these countries is constructing a new legal system which, in the end, may well be classifiable, purely and simply, as civil law (except in those republics of Central Asia where Islamic law is likely to play a significant role). For the moment, however, these countries perhaps still form a distinct group, differentiated by the common problems they face.[13]

Should this distinct group be treated as *sui generis*, or should it be regarded as a species of civil law?[14]

NOTES

(1) In the first place, the dichotomy between common law and civil law clearly ignores the convergences taking place between the two groups, prompted in part, and especially in Europe, by the growing importance of supranational institutions and international human rights norms.[1] It also rather obviously ignores the heterogeneity that exists within each of these two groups, particularly within the very diverse civil law group, where among other things there is no common language like in the common law where all the countries of the family express themselves in English.

(2) The classification of legal systems, even on a provisional basis, is enormously complicated by the fact that "legal systems are not monolithic institutions but very dynamic entities composed of a plurality of layers,"[2] each of which may have a different relationship to other legal systems. The division of all legal systems into two groups ("common law" or "civil law") only represents a first cut; further qualification will be required if our categories are to be tolerably accurate. But even this first cut (as well as any discussion of the necessary qualifications) is bound to be complicated by the "layered complexity"[3] of legal systems. If it is sought to classify a legal system by the use of a

The Romanist Character of Soviet Law, in The Emancipation of Soviet Law 27 (F. J. M. Feldbrugge ed., Law in Eastern Europe No. 44, 1992).

12. See Daniel J. Meador, Transition in the German Legal Order: East Back to West, 1990–91, 15 B. C. Int'l & Comp. L. Rev. 283 (1992); Peter E. Quint, The Constitutional Law of German Unification, 50 Md. L. Rev. 475 (1991); and the fuller account in Peter E. Quint, The Imperfect Union: Constitutional Structures of German Unification (1997). For a fascinating account of the transition, in part from the point of view of judges and lawyers in East Germany, see Inga Markovits, Imperfect Justice: An East–West German Diary (1995).

13. See Victor Knapp, Comparative Law and the Fall of Communism, 2 Parker Sch. J. E. Eur. L. 525 (1995).

14. Insofar as common law and civil law are supposed to be re-converging into an undifferentiated "neo-western" family, it might be argued that former "socialist" systems in Russia and Eastern Europe are becoming "western" rather than civilian. For this argument, see Gianmaria Ajani, By Chance and Prestige: Legal Transplants in Russia and Eastern Europe, 43 Am. J. Comp. L. 93 (1995).

1. See *supra* Chapter 2, Part 1, Section 2 at 73.

2. Ugo Mattei, Comparative Law and Economics 225 (1997).

3. The term comes from Adam Czarnota & Martin Krygier, Revolutions and the Continuity of European Law, in Revolutions in Law and Legal Thought 90 (Zenon Bankowski ed., 1991).

single label, that label often will describe only some of the many layers of which every legal system consists. Each of these layers may stand in a somewhat different relation than others to particular foreign systems and, as a result, no single label can adequately begin to characterize the system as a whole. Moreover, where a legal system is caught in a competition between plural legal sensibilities, how it should be classified may well be contested not only by outsiders but even more vigorously by those within the system itself for whom the question of affiliation is a matter of self-identity. Calling the system by one name or another can have treacherous implications.

(3) Finally, it should be noted that most accounts of the affiliations of particular legal systems turn mainly on differences and similarities in the field of private law. Indeed, most of the classificatory schemes which have been produced in the past, while purporting to classify legal systems as a whole, have tended to treat this one branch of the law as a synecdoche for the whole. They are therefore apt to convey less information, and to be especially misleading, regarding the character of a country's public law.

(4) It is possible to develop groupings based on a variety of criteria other than the binary opposition between common and civil law. Experience shows that such other groupings are frequently useful and, for certain purposes, indispensable as supplemental tools of categorization. Let us consider some of these alternative criteria. For some purposes, the legal systems of countries having a federal structure can and should be viewed synoptically and distinguished from unitary systems. Important scholarly studies have been made possible by the use of this grouping;[4] and all experienced international practitioners realize that one cannot even begin to conduct research on a question arising under the law of Country A unless one knows whether Country A has a federal or a unitary structure.[5] But the categories "federal" and "unitary" cut across the basic dichotomy between common law and civil law countries: there are both federal and unitary systems on both sides of the divide.

(5) For other purposes, it has been found useful to group together those legal systems that provide for judicial review of legislative acts and to contrast them with systems lacking such review.[6] Needless to say, such a classification again cuts across the basic dichotomy.[7]

4. See, e.g., the 1970 Colloque of the International Association of Legal Science entitled "Federalism and Development of Legal Systems" (publ. 1971, with a Foreword and Summary by J. N. Hazard, and national reports from West Germany, Canada, U.S.A., India, Czechoslovakia, U.S.S.R., and Yugoslavia); E. McWhinney, Federalism and Supreme Courts and the Integration of Legal Systems (1973).

5. An illustration from the civil law world is presented by the Swiss case of Haass v. Wyler, 1st Civil Division, July 3 1915, BGE 41 II 474. The federal system of West Germany is ably discussed by P. M. Blair, Federalism and Judicial Behaviour in West Germany (1981).

6. See, e.g., R. David, Sources of Law, 2 Int'l Ency.Comp.L., ch. 3, secs. 64–84 (1984); M. Cappelletti & W. Cohen, Comparative Constitutional Law: Cases and Materials (1979); Constitutional Judicial Review of Legislation: A Comparative Law Symposium, 56 Temple L. Q. 287–438 (1983).

7. In the European heartland of the civil law, systems of judicial review spread following World War II (e.g., Italy, West Germany). A further expansion took place on the Iberian peninsula three to four decades later. On the spread of judicial review in Latin America, see D. S. Clark, Judicial Protection of the Constitution in Latin America, 2 Hastings Const. L. Q. 405 (1975); on its spread in

More broadly, one could classify legal systems according to the relative influence which various branches of government have on the development of the law. The relative influence of the legislature and the courts is one of the criteria often used to differentiate between common and civil law.[8] But, in many legal systems, the executive branch also has important law-making functions. This is true, to a greater or lesser extent, even in Western countries; it is true to a very large extent, for example, in France under the Fifth Republic or even in the United States in the post-September 11, 2001 legal evolution.[9] Thus, legal systems might for certain purposes be classified according to the relative strength of *executive* (as well as legislative and judicial) influence on the development of the law.[10]

(6) For different purposes, it is undoubtedly useful to lump together all legal systems which are strongly influenced by a particular religion and to distinguish them from secular legal systems. The prime example of such a category (although not the only one) is "Islamic law." There are very few countries where traditional Islamic notions dominate all fields of law; but in many African and Asian legal systems the Islamic component is of great importance for some areas of law, especially for matters involving the family. Moreover, there is great pressure in many of these countries to enlarge the Islamic component of the legal system. International practitioners and scholars engaged in comparative legal studies thus would find their discourse severely hampered if they could not utilize the category of "Islamic law."

This category, based on a religious criterion, supplements the basic dichotomy; and, to some extent cuts across it, because there are both civil law and common law countries whose legal systems contain an Islamic component.

(7) For other purposes, one might want to treat all pluralistic legal systems as a distinct category,[11] to be distinguished from "unitary" systems.[12]

It is important to be clear here about how the term pluralism is being used. There is a sense, as we saw above, in which normative or legal pluralism is an attribute of all legal systems.[13] In that sense, it is such a ubiquitous phenome-

former socialist countries, see the sources cited *supra* p. 213, note 124.

8. In this connection, the reader will recall the reasoning of Malcolm, J., in the *Shoop* case, *supra* at 178.

9. See, e.g., B. Nicholas, Loi, Reglement and Judicial Review in the Fifth Republic, 1970 Pub. L. 251; G. Bermann, French Treaties and French Courts: Two Problems in Supremacy, 28 Int'l & Comp.L.Q. 458, 481 (1979).

10. Following the German sociologist Max Weber, legal scholars have also attempted to classify legal systems according to the role played in their development by "key groups" such as judges or academic jurists. See, e.g., H. Bernstein, Rechtsstile und Rechtshonoratioren; Ein Beitrag zur Methode der Rechtsvergleichung, 34 Rabels Z. 343 (1970); J. P. Dawson, The Oracles of the Law

(1968). See also Mirjan Damaška, Faces of Justice and State Authority (1986).

11. See F. Reyntjens, Note sur l'utilité d'introduire un système juridique "pluraliste" dans la macro-comparison des droits, 43 Rev. Int.Dr.Comp. 41 (1991).

12. The term "unitary" has more than one meaning. It may also be used to characterize the legal system of a country not having a federal structure. See *supra* under (4). In the present context, however, "unitary" is the opposite of "pluralistic."

13. See text *supra* at p. 261. For examples of normative legal pluralism, see Gunther Teubner, Global Bukowina:Legal Pluralism in the World Society. Gunther Teubner, Global Law Without A State, Dartsmouth (1996); Gunther Teubner, Breaking Frames Economic Globalization and the Emergence of Lex Mercatoria, 5(2) Euro. J. Soc. Theory 199–218 (2002). For an application to the European law, see F. Synder, Governing Eco-

non that there are no entirely unitary legal systems; or, at best, the distinction between "pluralistic" and "unitary" systems is a matter of degree depending on the extent to which the rules of an imported system of law have penetrated into everyday life. We will come back to these kinds of differences under (8) below.

In its more conventional sense, as the reader will recall, the term pluralism means that, even within the official legal system of a given country, different groups of people are to some extent subject to different bodies of law, with the result that interpersonal (as distinguished from inter-territorial) conflict-of-laws problems arise in many situations. "Pluralism" in this sense is typical of the legal systems of a large part of Africa and Asia, and also cuts across the dichotomy between common and civil law.

In many countries, especially Islamic ones, the roots of such pluralism reach far back into history. Like their Germanic predecessors, the Arab conquerors of the middle ages recognized that everyone, conqueror and conquered alike, should live under their own personal law. Applying this principle, they ordained that the law applicable to a person (and the jurisdiction of religious courts over him) should be determined by that person's religion.[14] In Islamic countries, and especially in the Ottoman Empire, the tradition of pluralism thus established was continued into the twentieth century.[15]

During the nineteenth century and the first half of the twentieth century, colonialism became the principal force behind the spread and preservation of pluralistic legal systems throughout the southern hemisphere. "Natives" and "Europeans" became subject to different laws.[16] A common feature of most African legal systems, even today, is the coexistence of imported law and the customary and religious law of the various groups within a society.

Because it was partly (although not entirely)[17] a creation of the colonial era, legal pluralism has been severely criticized in newly independent countries. But, in spite of such criticism, it seems that complete internal unification of the legal system is a long way off in most African and many Asian nations.

At the same time, various other factors are at work, which have the effect of diminishing the significance and impact of pluralism. In the first place, in

nomic Globalisation: Global Legal Pluralism and European Law, 5(4) Euro. L.J. 334–374 (1999).

14. See H. J. Liebesny, Comparative Legal History: Its Role in the Analysis of Islamic and Modern Near Eastern Legal Institutions, 20 Am. J. Comp. L. 38, 39–41 (1972). Harold G. Berman, Comparative Law and Religion in Oxford Handbook of Comparative Law 739 (Mathias Reimann & Reinhard Zimmermann eds., 2006).

15. See W. Yale, The Near East—A Modern History 19 (1958).

16. In substance, this was true in all of the colonial empires, although colonial policy was not the same everywhere. For a detailed treatment of the impact of British, French, and Dutch colonial policy on the legal systems of former colonies, see Hooker, Legal Pluralism: An Introduction to Colonial and Neo–Colonial Laws (1975).

17. The discussion in the text above has shown that pluralistic legal systems have existed in pre-colonial and non-colonial environments. See also Rheinstein, Problems of Law in the New Nations of Africa, in Old Societies and New States 220, 222–25 (Geertz ed., 1963).

the formulation of internal conflicts rules, the emphasis gradually is shifting from affiliation with racial or tribal groups to "objective" criteria such as geographic situs and the actual or presumed intention of the parties.[18] Second, as we have seen, many countries have restricted pluralism to matters of family law and closely related subjects. In other areas, especially in the law of obligations and commercial transactions, we usually find that modern law patterned after European models, whether of the civil law or the common law variety, is applied as the law of the land, regardless of the parties' group affiliations.[19] Thirdly, through codification, restatement of rules of customary law, and similar techniques, even indigenous law may become western in form. In the process, its nature or substance is frequently changed.[20] Finally, on top of the indigenous and imported sectors, most countries with pluralistic legal systems have superimposed a third sector of legal ordering: statutes and regulations concerned with political processes and economic planning[21] (which, at one time, were often "socialist" in character).[22] Such statutes and regulations, which belong to the sphere of public law, ordinarily are of nation-wide application.[23] Whether these "internationally inspired" national rules have the effect of further reducing the relative significance of the vestiges of pluralism that persist in private law or in-fact just add another stratum in legal complexity is an open question.[24]

18.   To some extent, this is true even with respect to matters traditionally governed by personal status. See Rheinstein, *supra* note 17, at 235: "Clear-cut rules will be necessary in all parts [of Africa] to render it possible for an individual to change his subjection to the law of one group to that of another. The African who moves from the bush into the city and adopts the urban, modern way of life cannot for all times remain subject to the tribal customs of marriage, succession, or land tenure."

19.   See, e.g., Farnsworth, Law Reform in a Developing Country: A New Code of Obligations for Senegal, 8 J. Afr. L. 6 (1964).

20.   See, e.g., Macneil, Research in East African Law, 3 East Afr. L.J. 47, 67 (1967); Tanner, The Codification of Customary Law in Tanzania, 2 E. Afr. L.J. 105 (1966); M. Galanter, The Aborted Restoration of "Indigenous" Law in India, 14 Comp. Stud. Soc'y & Hist. 53 (1972). See also *supra* at p. 192–93.

21.   See Seidman, Law and Economic Development in Independent, English–Speaking, Sub–Saharan Africa, 1966 Wis. L. Rev. 999.

22.   For an early (and short-lived) instance, see John Hazard, Mali's Socialism and the Soviet Legal Model, 77 Yale L.J. 28 (1967). See also Mattei, Socialist and Non–Socialist Approaches to Land Law: Continui-

ty and Change in Somalia and Other African States, 16 R. Sol. L. 17 (1990).

In recent years, "third world" countries as well as former "socialist" countries have turned to neoclassical economic solutions; these are often a condition of IMF and other development aid. But (as our look at the problems of transition in ex-socialist countries indicated) massive state action, involving an enormous quantity of legislation, is also required to reduce the role of the state in the economy and to establish an adequate legal foundation for capitalism. See *supra* P. 209FF.

23.   The fact that these laws are of nationwide application does not always assure their effectiveness. The difference between book law and living law must be kept in mind. For an interesting discussion of the role of corruption and of its impact on the implementation of economic planning, see S. Ottenberg, Local Government and the Law in Southern Nigeria, in Traditional and Modern Legal Institutions in Asia and Africa 26 (D. C. Buxbaum ed., 1967).

24.   Scholars whose attention is focused exclusively on the private law of a given country thus are apt to overemphasize the pluralist and to underestimate the nationally unified elements in that country's legal system.

(8) In discussions of problems of "law and development,"[25] countries are labeled "developed" or "less developed" according to their place on a notional scale of economic or socio-economic achievement. The labels thus applied cut across the dichotomy between common law and civil law (and across most other schemes for classifying legal systems).

One reason for treating "less developed countries" as a group has been to arrive at generalizations that are valid for all of them in order to help clarify the role of law in the "development process." The task is rendered extremely difficult, however, in part by the fact that any study relating to all such countries—in Africa, Asia, and Latin–America—necessarily has to deal with a forbidding array of political, social, and cultural variables. This lesson is systematically ignored by studies such as the World Bank's *Lex Mundi* or the economist's "legal origins" literature discussed in Chapter 1 *supra*.[26]

(9) Another (in some respects related) way of classifying systems turns on the insight that the importance of law as an ordering device, "the weight of law as a social force,"[27] is not the same everywhere. Sentiments about professionalized law and the law's impact on social life are not invariables. The ways of thinking about law and litigation prevalent in the west do not necessarily obtain in the legal systems that have "received" some version of western law. Thus, another criterion for distinguishing between legal systems may be the extent to which they share the underlying, working conceptions of law typical of legal systems in the "west."

Among the features of law generally taken for granted, to a greater or less extent, in the west, but not necessarily found in all systems of law, are the following:

(a) The supposition that law constitutes an autonomous body of rules, independent and separate from (although not uninfluenced by) religion, morality, and other social norms. In most traditional systems of law outside the west, not only the religious ones, this feature is absent; and the idea of the autonomy of law also is incompatible with most versions of Marxist legal theory.

(b) The idea that law exists to regulate the conduct not only of individuals but of the state as well: that rulers as well as the ruled are subject to law. This is a difficult idea to realize in many societies that prefer to give to the law a "human face" rather than assuming it as an objective and neutral autonomous entity.[28]

25. See, e.g., the International Legal Center reports on Law and Development (1974) and on Legal Education in a Changing World (1975).

26. See Rafael La Porta, Florencio Lopez-de-Silanes, Andrei Shleifer, and Robert Vishny, Law and Finance, 106 J. Pol. Econ. 1113–1155 (1998); Edward Glaeser and Andrei Shleifer, Legal Origins, 117 Q. J. Econ. 1193–1229 (2002); Simeon Djankov, Rafael La Porta, Florencio Lopez-de-Silanes, and Andrei Shleifer, Courts: the Lex Mundi Project, 118 Q. J. of Econ. 342–387 (2003); and

Simeon Djankov, Caralee McLiesh, and Andrei Shleifer, Remedies in Credit Markets, Working Paper, Department of Economics, Harvard University, Cambridge, Mass. (2003).

27. Markovits, Hedgehogs or Foxes, 34 Am.J.Comp.L. 113, 134 (1986)

28. Cf. Inga Markovits, Law and Glasnost': Some Thoughts About the Future of Judicial Review Under Socialism, 23 L. & Soc'y Rev. 399 (1989); Inga Markovits, Socialism and the Rule of Law: Some Speculations and Predictions, in Comparative and Private

(c) A view of dispute settlement as involving the application of pre-existing, general, abstract, depersonalized rules so that only a narrowly-defined class of facts, falling within the confines of the applicable rules, are considered material to the resolution of the dispute. All other events and circumstances, all the intricacies of the relationship between the parties, the personal side-issues which complicate their controversy, are considered immaterial and are to be ignored.

(d) A view of dispute settlement as a zero-sum game, a contest calling for a decision by which one party will win and the other lose. The object is to determine right and wrong and to see the right prevail, rather than to reconcile or restore harmony among the parties or to promote their future cooperation.[29]

To the extent that these features are found in all "western" legal systems, they amount to a body of shared convictions about law that transcends the divide between common and civil law[30] and that differentiates "western" from "non-western" law. The western legal tradition is highly professionalized and the profession of the "lawyer" is socially distinct from that of the "politician" or of the "priest".

In the same vein, it has been suggested that contemporary legal systems can be triangulated by distinguishing between (1) western systems (whether of common or civil law) in which the idea of autonomous law predominates; (2) the legal systems of both developing and ex-socialist countries where the idea of autonomous law has not fully taken hold and politics tend to be stronger than law; and (3) legal systems in which, again despite the importation of the rules and institutions of western law, the predominant legal sensibility is rooted in a non-western tradition.[31]

One wants to be careful, however, not to exaggerate the extent to which it is cultural differences that account for differences in the way legal systems operate.[32] A good illustration of the need for caution in this regard is provided by the problem of explaining Japanese non-litigiousness.

As we have seen Japan is often cited as an example of a society with a legal system patterned after western models which nevertheless functions to a large extent on the basis of traditional non-legal restraints and conventions, and in which, because of the cultural conviction that resort to law is shameful,

International Law: Essays in Honor of John Henry Merryman on His Seventieth Birthday (David S. Clark ed., 1990).

29. On these last two features, and on alternative styles of dispute settlement, see Richard Lempert & Joseph Sanders, An Invitation to Law and Social Science 196–241 (1986).

30. Western or "European-style legal systems" are said to "all share certain fundamental convictions about law" and the importance of the rule of law "which have never been abandoned even in the fearful crises and ideological schisms of this century." F. Wieacker, A History of Private Law in Europe 392 (Tony Weir Trans., 1995). On the

"peculiar legalism" of European legal culture, see also Franz Wieacker, Foundations of European Legal Culture, 38 Am. J. Comp. L. 11 (1990). On the key place of the idea of law throughout the history of western thought, see Donald R. Kelley, The Human Measure: Social Thought in the Western Legal Tradition (1990).

31. See Ugo Mattei, Three Patterns of Law: Taxonomy and Change in the World's Legal Systems, 45 Am. J. Comp. L. 5 (1997).

32. See Roger Coterrell, Comparative law and legal Culture, in The Oxford Handbook of Comparative law 709 (Mathias Reimann & Reinhard Zimmermann eds. 2006).

recourse to the legal process occurs only as a last resort. One piece of evidence for this assertion is said to be the low volume of litigation in Japan[33] (which, in turn, means less need for lawyers' services and hence far fewer lawyers in proportion to population than are found in other countries).[34]

To some extent, however, Japanese non-litigiousness can also be explained in terms of (economic) constraints on opportunity rather than (cultural) constraints on preference.[35] Various institutional factors, among them the scarcity of lawyers, make litigation expensive in Japan, while the availably of low-cost procedures for conciliation and mediation makes alternative methods of dispute resolution quite attractive. The small number of lawyers may therefore be a cause rather than a consequence of the small volume of litigation. At the same time, it is possible that the institutional factors which discourage litigation are themselves, to some degree, the result and expression of traditional cultural convictions on the part of the Japanese people and their policy-setting authorities. At any rate, the relationship between cultural, economic, political, and institutional factors is complex and problematic; it should not be assumed that one particular kind of factor is inevitably primary.

33. Not only private law litigation, but also public law litigation (including attempts to have administrative action reviewed by the courts) is less frequent in Japan than in other highly industrialized countries. See M. K. Young, Judicial Review of Administrative Guidance: Governmentally Encouraged Consensual Dispute Resolution in Japan, 84 Colum. L. Rev. 923, 951–53 (1984).

34. See *supra* Chapter 1, Section 5(b) at 47.

Tens of thousands of Japanese law school graduates however work in legal capacities but are not considered "lawyers" (*bengoshi*: a term closely equivalent to, and apparently derived from, the English "barrister"). On the derivation of *bengoshi* from barrister, see John Owen Haley, Authority Without Power: Law and the Japanese Paradox 100 (1991).

More generally, on legal professions in the two countries, see Masanobu Kato, The Role of Law and Lawyers in Japan and the United States, 1987 BYU L.Rev. 627; Richard S. Miller, Apples vs. Persimmons: The Legal Profession in Japan and the United States, 39 J.Legal Educ. 27 (1989). On the numerous licensed specialists other than "lawyers" who are available to the Japanese public for legal advice and drafting of documents in non-litigated matters, see also T. Hattori & D. F. Henderson, Civil Procedure in Japan § 2.09 (1983). On the training of Japanese "law-yers," see Edward I. Chen, The National Law Examination of Japan, 39 J.Legal Educ. 1 (1989); Edward I. Chen, The Legal Training and Research Institute of Japan, 22 U.Tol. L. Rev. 975 (1991). For a broad discussion in context, see Eric Feldman, The Ritual of Rights in Japan (2000).

35. Recent writing has tended, in fact, if not to reject the cultural explanation for Japanese non-litigiousness, at least to treat it as a question rather than a given. See, e.g., Haley, *supra* note 34, at 83–119; H. Oda, Japanese Law 3–10, 83–88 (1992); Koichiro Fujikura, Administering Justice in a Consensus–Based Society, 91 Mich. L. Rev. 1529, 1538–42 (1993); Setsuo Miyazawa, Taking Kawashima Seriously: A Review of Japanese Research on Japanese Legal Consciousness and Disputing Behavior, 21 L. & Soc'y Rev. 219 (1987); Mark Ramseyer & Minoru Nakazato, The Rational Litigant: Settlement Amounts and Verdict Rates in Japan, 18 J. Legal Stud. 263 (1989). See also Frank K. Upham, Law and Social Change in Post–War Japan (1987); V. Lee Hamilton & Joseph Sanders, Everyday Justice: Responsibility and the Individual in Japan and the United States (1992).

For general criticism of "cultural determinism" in explaining differences in the way law operates in western and East Asian countries, see Dae–Kyu Yoon, Law and Political Authority in Korea (1990).

Moreover, it is important to avoid portraying cultural attitudes towards law as monolithic and impervious to change. Cultures are sites of conflict and they can and do change.[36]

(10) Another possible approach to comparative law which gives up attempts to broader generalizations is to use an area studies approach. Divide up the world into different areas (more or less specific) and assume that in those contexts one will find similar legal characteristics due to similarities in history, culture, politics, etc. This is a traditional approach in social sciences: in many universities we find departments of Latin American Studies, Middle Eastern Studies, African Studies, Eastern European Studies, etc.

The problem is that geographical proximity and even cultural or religious proximity may mean very little when we come to approach the law. A few examples may clarify this point. There is no doubt that Holland and England are in a geographic and cultural proximity that would allow one to deal with them within one Area. They have similar climate, similar religion, similar entrepreneurial spirit, similar ethnic composition, similar cuisine, and even similar timing in their history of expansion. In contrast, the geographic and cultural distance between Holland and Spain is huge. They differ in climate, in religion, outlook, cuisine, and more generally, we would say, in "culture". Nevertheless as far as the law is concerned, the legal systems of Spain and Holland, both at the heart of the civil law tradition, are much closer than that of Holland and England, the crib of the common law.

Similar examples of irrelevant geographical proximity in the domain of the law abound everywhere in the world. Malaysia, in its effort to reform the law, has not looked at Indonesia and the Philippines.[37] Chile and Argentina simply ignore each-other even in closely common, and indeed local, problems, such as the legal regime of water.[38]

Yet certain scholarly traditions in the field of the law have segregated themselves from the mainstream Comparative Law. For example legal sinologists, sovietologists, Islamists or scholars of Japanese law, have tended to communicate more with sociologists historians and other students of their area rather than with comparative lawyers. This is unfortunate because comparative law has much to gain in its theoretical strengths from appreciating and understanding "radical" differences. And this is why we have tried to integrate this casebook with non-western materials, in an attempt to keep it up to the transformations in the political geography of the world.

8. LAW AND DEVELOPMENT

Perhaps the notion most at risk of transforming economic technological and military superiority into self-serving and self-congratulatory rhetoric is that of "development". Western observers and policy makers, as we have seen in Chapter 1, when discussing the World Bank's *World Development Report*, usually blame "lack" of development to shortcomings of the legal systems of the so-called less developed countries. This is a very

---

36. *Cf.* William P. Alford, To Steal a Book is an Elegant Offense: Intellectual Property Law in Chinese Civilization (1995).

37. See Horowitz, The Qur'an and the Common Law: Islamic Law Reform and the Theory of Legal Change 42 Am.J.Comp.L. 233 and 543 (1994).

38. See Karl Bauer, Against the Current in Chile: Property, the Market and the State in Water Rights, 1979–1995 (1998).

delicate area in which the value skepticism and the experience of comparative law could be a precious asset particularly since, in more recent times, this field has been colonized by economists and political scientists.

Amy L. Chua, Markets, Democracy, And Ethnicity: Toward a New Paradigm for Law and Development

108(1) Yale L.J. 11–20 (1998).

The Early Law and Development Movement

The law and development movement was born in the mid–1960s at leading American law schools such as Harvard, Stanford, Wisconsin, and Yale. The movement adhered to the basic premise of modernization theory "that development was an inevitable, evolutionary process of increasing societal differentiation that would ultimately produce economic, political, and social institutions similar to those in the West." Emphasizing the importance of law in the development of a market economy and democratic values, law and development scholars attempted to assist developing countries in establishing Western-style legal institutions. In so doing, the law and development movement self-consciously sought to supplant Third World "localism," "irregularity, and particularism" with the "unity, uniformity, and universality" of the modern Western state. Ethnic identity and ethnic conflict were aspects of traditionalism or "pre-modernity" that in the course of development "were ultimately supposed to disappear."[1] The ultimate goal of the development process was to be the creation of a free-market system (which in turn would bring economic growth), liberal democratic government institutions, and the rule of law.

By the mid–1970s, barely a decade after its inception, the law and development movement had fallen into open crisis. In a well-known piece entitled Scholars in Self–Estrangement: Some Reflections on the Crisis in Law and Development Studies in the United States,[2] Professors Trubek and Galanter criticized the paradigm of "liberal legalism," which they had previously championed, as being "ethnocentric and naive." Liberal legalism, they argued, ignored the severe "social stratification and class cleavage" in developing societies and failed to recognize that "in much of the Third World the grip of tribe, clan, and local community is far stronger than that of the nation-state."[3] More radically, Trubek and Galanter challenged the institution of law itself, suggesting that even in countries such as the United States the legal system reinforces "domination by elite groups" and legitimates "arbitrary actions by government."[4]

1. Björn Hettne, Ethnicity and Development: An Elusive Relationship, in Ethnicity and Development: Geographical Perspectives 15, 15 (Denis Dwyer & David Drakakis–Smith eds., 1996) (discussing modernization theory).

2. David M. Trubek & Marc Galanter, Scholars in Self–Estrangement: Some Reflections on the Crisis in Law and Development Studies in the United States, 1974 Wis. L. Rev. 1062.

3. Id. at 1080.

4. Id. at 1083.

Not long after the publication of Scholars in Self–Estrangement, "the law and development movement in the United States all but expired. Money stopped flowing from foundations. Various institutes and programs dedicated to the subject were scaled back or terminated. The scholars involved moved on to other pursuits."[5] Since that time, numerous scholars have pondered the "death" of the law and development field. A few have even written "memoirs." As I will suggest, however, the epitaph remains to be written.

Law and Development Today

Despite the demise of the early law and development movement, American lawyers and legal scholars today are helping to shape the fundamental economic and political institutions of the developing world to an extent unprecedented since decolonization. Much has changed about the law and development field. Today, many of the lawyers most centrally involved in the developing world are law and economics luminaries, constitutional designers, and Wall Street practitioners. With some exceptions, legal work on development is more sophisticated than ever. Moreover, the disintegration of the former Communist bloc has raised a host of challenging legal issues of first impression.

Nevertheless, the thrust of international development policy today remains essentially what it was in the sixties and seventies: to export markets, democracy, and the rule of law to the developing world. In this Section, I will first survey the current literature relating to law in the developing world. This literature is highly interdisciplinary, including political scientists and economists among its leading contributors. I will limit my discussion here to work directed at the legal community or relating specifically to legal institutions. I will then discuss international development policy and practice.

The Current Literature

Today's law and development literature can be divided into two broad categories. First, a relatively small number of scholars who consciously identify themselves with law and development have generally picked up where the movement of the 1960s and 1970s left off. Often associated with "leftist" causes, these scholars continue in their writings to struggle with a host of difficult and profound issues, such as law's impotence or "epiphenomenality"; its disingenuous claims to neutrality; its ethnocentricity; and its "infamy" in contributing to the oppression of the disempowered.

In terms of sheer volume and actual influence, however, by far the more massive contribution to the law and development literature has been made by lawyers who probably do not think of themselves as law and development "types." This second category includes practitioner-written pieces as well as a much more theoretical academic literature.

5. See Richard Bilder & Brian Z. Tamanaha, The Lessons of Law-and-Development Studies, 89 Am. J. Int'l L. 474 (1995) (reviewing Law and Development (Anthony Carty ed., 1992)).

In the last five years, there have been hundreds of articles written by legal practitioners involved in the developing world. In Professor Mark Sidel's words, "[t]his output is almost entirely descriptive and oriented in a wholly instrumental fashion to the requirements of trade and investment."[6] Typical topics include trade and foreign investment regulation, taxation and tax policy, banking law, concession law, dispute resolution, and technology transfer. Professor Sidel is correct in cautioning that "[w]e should not impose an entirely scholarly lens on materials written, primarily, for practical, utilitarian reasons."[7] Still, it is noteworthy that the overwhelming thrust of this massive body of legal commentary is to urge the rapid and full-blown liberalization and marketization of developing world economies (hardly surprising when one considers the financial interests involved).

Alongside this practitioner-oriented work, there is also a large academic literature relating to today's developing world transformations. Most of this literature too can be characterized as addressing either marketization or democratization. As to marketization, a significant part of the literature addresses, from a variety of perspectives, the transitions from command to market economies in the countries of the former Soviet bloc. The more halting market-oriented reforms of Cambodia, China, Vietnam, and other nominally Communist countries also have generated a proliferating body of commentary. More generally, there have been dozens of recent law review articles seeking to assist developing countries in their economic liberalizations. As with marketization, the work on democratization in the developing world varies considerably in scope and quality. Besides the massive political science literature on this subject, there is also a growing body of work by lawyers and legal academics struggling with the issue of the transplantability of Western-style democratic and rule-of-law institutions in countries with vastly different histories and social structures. This work ranges from highly abstract treatments; to region-or country-specific studies of democracy's preconditions, optimal institutions, or effects; to "on-the-ground," village-to-village analyses of local governmental processes.

Consistent with the vast part of the law and development literature, the ideology of free-market democracy forms the theoretical core of today's international development policy and practice. This ideology is propagated by the two institutions wielding by far the greatest influence on the developing world—the World Bank and the International Monetary Fund—as well as by the United States Agency for International Development (USAID), the Asian Development Bank, the Ford Foundation, the Soros Foundation, the United Nations Development Programme, the American Bar Association's Central and East European Law Initiative, and a host of new private or quasi-private organizations with names like "The Institute for Public–Private Partnerships" or "The Democracy Development Initia-

---

6. Mark Sidel, New Directions in the Study of Vietnamese Law, 17 Mich. J. Int'l. l. 705, 713 (1996) (reviewing Vietnam and the Rule of Law (Carlye A. Thayer & David G. Marr eds., 1993)).

7. Id. at 714.

tive." Moreover, many academics involved in the developing world are working in some capacity to promote markets or democracy. Even law students are marketizing: The government of Estonia recently asked six Georgetown law students and their professors "to help determine what types of laws are required to start a free-market system."[8]

Additionally, unlike in the 1960s and 1970s, the field of law and development today is shaped significantly by legal practitioners. There is no question that practitioner-structured market interventions such as privatization (frequently of telecommunications enterprises or major utilities), cross-border offerings, or international mergers and joint ventures[9] are having a tremendous impact on the economic landscape of many developing and transitional countries. Indeed, because international business transactions often mean potential profits in the order of hundreds of millions of dollars—often much more than multilateral lending institutions can offer—practicing lawyers wield decisive influence over developing governments.

The Problem in the Current Paradigm

Despite frequent claims of "new paradigms"[10] and "lessons learned,"[11] prevailing law and development orthodoxy recapitulates a basic and potentially fatal error of the earlier movement. It ignores ethnicity and ethnic conflict in the developing world. To be sure, ethnic conflict figures prominently in the human rights area, particularly in the context of war crimes. But the distinctive, structural relationship between ethnicity and today's marketization and democratization efforts has been almost completely overlooked by all lawyers and legal scholars involved in the developing world, including those in the human rights area.

Why this has been so is itself fascinating. Practitioners probably view ethnic tensions as lying far beyond the scope of their responsibility. Law and economics scholars involved in marketization also tend to treat ethnic conflict as beyond the scope of their analyses; although all behavior can be described as preference-maximizing in a tautological sense, the "preferences" and behaviors associated with ethnic hatred escape the kind of rationality assumed in most economic models. Moreover, Western discomfort with potentially invidious ethnic generalizations may go a long way toward explaining the neglect of the ethnic dimensions of markets and democracy in the developing world.

---

8. Brooke A. Masters, GU Legal Eagles Flying to Estonia's Aid, Wash. Post, June 18, 1992, at D3.

9. See, e.g., John J. McKenna, North American Firms Compete for Latin American Investments, Oil & Gas J., Feb. 23, 1998, at 26, 26–27 (describing the recent wave of joint-venture and merger-and-acquisition activity in the Latin American energy sector).

10. See, e.g., The World Bank Group, Learning From the Past, Embracing the Future 10 (1994) (stating that "[a] new development paradigm has emerged, one that emphasizes market friendly approaches and stresses the importance of private sector development").

11. See, e.g., Mary M. Shirley, The What, Why, and How of Privatization: A World Bank Perspective, 60 Fordham L. Rev. S23, S31–S32 (1992) ("The present interest in privatization is no fad.... Lessons have been learned ... and today's strategies reflect these lessons.").

For whatever reason, today's dominant law and development orthodoxy regards ethnic conflict as just another aspect of underdevelopment, which the universal prescription of markets and democracy is supposed to cure.

Carol V. Rose, The "New" Law and Development Movement in the Post–Cold War Era: A Vietnam Case Study

32 Law & Soc'y Rev. 93, 122–24 (1998).

The intellectual origins of LDM [Law and Development Movement] reflected a uniquely U.S. orientation toward legal scholarship:

> Rather than asking himself what he could learn (about law, about development, about some other aspect of either, about the relationship between them) from the study of some aspect of law in one or more developing societies, the lawyer was mostly interested in bringing about development-in engineering social progress through law reform.

David Trubek, an early participant and later critic of LDM, described the "core conception" of the LDM as a misguided reading of Max Weber's work, in which development was equated with a "gradual evolution in the direction of the advanced, industrial nations of the West" and "modern law" was equated with the "legal structures and cultures of the West".…

Gardner outlined a four-part framework that the early practitioners in the movement sought to carry to developing countries: (1) methodological, specifically, exporting the American case law and Socratic method of teaching law; (2) educational, as U.S. legal scholars attempted to replicate the U.S. legal education system in other countries; (3) the model of the lawyer as a professional or social engineer; and (4) jurisprudential, which Gardner describes as an "anti-formal, 'rule skeptical' and 'instrumental' vision of law drawn largely from American realism."

Despite variances in the descriptions of the particular ideological underpinnings of LDM, the legal assistance projects that arose from LDM consistently reflected American conceptions of law and lawyers. This ethnocentric, often parochial, approach to legal assistance fostered a critique of LDM that culminated in its collapse.…

Attacks on the LDM movement were launched primarily by scholars from within the movement who voiced concern that the movement was doing more harm than good in many countries.

Critics of LDM also published case studies showing that, rather than leading to economic and political modernization, the transfer of U.S. legal methods and knowledge often reinforced and legitimized existing authoritarian power structures. Some critics traced this phenomenon to preexisting social, economic, and political structures within developing countries, many of which were characterized by class cleavages and authoritarian or totalitarian political regimes.[1] . . .

Critics also charged that the early LDM strengthened the central power of authoritarian states by emphasizing court-centered formal legal systems while ignoring customary law and informal methods of conflict resolution. The resulting bias against traditional, decentralized methods of dispute settlement shifted power to the state from individuals and indigenous communities.

Others attacked the assumption that developing countries were merely "behind" in their development, needing only tools of modernization to "catch up." This critique paralleled the rise of the so-called Dependency Theory of development, which suggested that developing countries were kept poor and marginalized (and developed countries remained rich) as a result of structural forces inherent in the world political economy. . . .

LDM critics also chided U.S. lawyers for their lack of scholarship and their failure to better understand the cultures in which they were working. American legal assistance often was characterized as "inept, culturally unaware, and sociologically uninformed. [I]t was also ethnocentric, perceiving and assisting the Third World in its own self-image." Merryman attacked LDM as a "parochial expression of the American legal style". . . .

The danger that U.S. lawyers were doing more harm than good led critics to conclude that LDM should discontinue its activities until such time as a workable theory of legal assistance was developed: "at least for Americans, Third World law and development *action* is premature. Until we have tested, reliable theory (i.e. tested and reliable vis-a-vis the target society), we will be more responsible and productive if we limit ourselves to Third World law and development inquiry."

NOTES AND QUESTIONS

(1) Based on Professor Chua's description, what is—or should be—the relationship between comparative law and Law and Development discourse? For example, is the relationship merely instrumental (comparative law providing help in structuring "modern" legal institutions so as to promote development projects), or does comparative law also provide a potential basis for critiquing Law and Development projects?

(2) As Professor Chua points out, the term Law and Development is not necessarily even used in connection with contemporary legal reform projects, largely because of its historical baggage. Rather, today's reform enterprises tend to travel under the rubric of "rule of law" and similar phrases, whether they are sponsored by Western nation-states (such as the United States) or

---

1. Trubek, for example, noted that Weber's analysis that European law was conducive to capitalism had been misinterpreted by the Law and Development Movement. He noted, instead: "To the extent . . . that economic development in the Third World is not based on free markets Weber's work cannot support any inference that modern law as defined by the [Movement's] core conception will cause or contribute to economic development . . . [or] will enhance the efficacy of the regime" (Trubek 1972:53–54).

multilateral organizations (such as the World Bank). Yet what unites the "old" and "new" Law and Development movements is their shared faith in modernization theory in general and law's fundamental role in modernization in particular. The excerpt by Rose sets out in greater detail some of the main criticisms of the early Law and Development movement. To what extent could the same criticisms be directed to the "new" Law and Development movement as well?

(3) Common core research, legal transplants, legal formants, and legal pluralism are the methodological tools that should shield the skilled comparative lawyers from becoming neither simple minded (such as much work in law and Development, old and new) nor nihilistic, such as some post-modern trends would like lawyers and reformers to become. These methodological tools should be employed to approach the daunting task of understanding the law as a global phenomenon.

What is in your opinion the main lesson that Comparative Law should learn from Area Studies? What lesson can it teach? What lesson can Comparative Law learn from law and Development? What lesson can it teach?

(4) The Law and Development movement may overestimate the power of law to lead economic and social change. Its power to do so varies. The obstacles are not everywhere the same. In some instances, there may be flaws in what is formally proclaimed as "law";[1] in others, a law which on its face seems perfectly sound to the outside observer may fail to accomplish its purpose because of lack of implementation.[2] Lack of implementation, in turn, may be due to a variety of causes. Perhaps the formally enacted laws have not been effectively communicated to the citizenry, or even to the judges and other officials expected to enforce them.[3] Or perhaps they are so unresponsive to the particular social needs of the country that it becomes customary to circumvent them.[4] Or, again, the role of official legal rules in the particular society may be eclipsed, to a greater or less extent, by other cultural forces and competing normative systems.[5] At the same time, an unqualified statement to the effect

1. The formally established law of land tenure may stand in the way of obtaining agricultural credit, or in other ways inhibit the efficient use of land; or the rules of commercial law may be unsuited as a basis for a modern credit system. See B. Kozolchyk, Toward a Theory on Law in Economic Development: The Costa Rican USAID–ROCAP Law Reform Project, 1971 L. & Soc. Order (Ariz.St.L.J.) 681; B. Kozolchyk, Commercial Law Recodification and Economic Development in Latin America, 4(2) Law. of the Am. 1 (1972); L. M. Hager, The Role of Lawyers in Developing Countries, 58 A.B.A.J. 33 (1972).

2. For examples, see the sources cited *supra* note 1. See also B. Kozolchyk, Law and the Credit Structure in Latin America, 7 Va. J.Int'l L. 1 (1967).

The problems that arise when actual practice diverges from the law in the books are of course not limited to developing countries. But experience suggests that they tend to be particularly acute there. See Hager, *supra* note 1, at 35, where further references can be found.

3. See J. H. Beckstrom, Transplantation of Legal Systems: An Early Report on the Reception of Western Laws in Ethiopia, 21 Am. J. Comp. L. 557 (1973); J.H. Beckstrom, Handicaps of Legal–Social Engineering in a Developing Nation, 22 Am. J. Comp. L. 697 (1974).

4. See, e.g., K. S. Rosenn, The Jeito—Brazil's Institutional Bypass of the Formal Legal System and Its Development Implications, 19 Am. J. Comp. L. 514 (1971).

5. See the discussion *supra* p. 125ff.

that law is impotent as an instrument of modernization would also be an unwarranted generalization. Even in societies which are not completely attuned to western-style law, desirable social change can be brought about by legislation provided the legislator uses whenever possible respected existing institutions as agencies of reform and recognizes that legislation often is most effective when it operates obliquely.[6]

* * *

Summing up, comparing legal phenomena among themselves is a complex exercise that should include at least the following activities.[7] First, it has to gather and describe analogies and differences. This approach begins with "thick descriptions", capable of appreciating the many structural variations of law (e.g. written or oral) due to pluralism. Thick descriptions of a plurality of systems might bring as a result the discovery of a common core. Second, it has to put the objects of observation in a relationship to each other to se whether the commonalities are due to legal transplants rather than to reinvention of the wheel in different geographical places. Third, it has to develop a theory to explain the observations. Finally, it might contain some normative lessons out of the process of observation and explanation.

The quality of each one of these processes can be evaluated from scholarly or practical perspectives. The more the data gathering is based on primary sources the more valuable it is. The more evidence of a process of contamination by means of thorough historical inquiry, the more convincing will be the "transplant hypothesis". The broader and farther reaching the theory that one is able to develop to explain his data, the more valuable and interesting the contribution will be. The more the policy advocated looks convincing, the more it would have been worthwhile to have spelled it out. This basic recipe is of course compatible with the idea that the questions that we ask determine the range of the answers that we might get and that, as a consequence, the very choice of the objects to compare is

---

6. Indonesian's National Marriage Act of 1974 provides an interesting illustration. See J. S. Katz & R. S. Katz, The New Indonesian Marriage Law: A Mirror of Indonesia's Political, Cultural and Legal System, 23 Am. J.Comp. L. 653 (1975); J. S. Katz & R. S. Katz, Legislating Social Change in a Developing Country: The New Indonesian Marriage Law Revisited, 26 Am. J. Comp. L. 309 (1978). The second of these two studies concluded that the act had been directly successful in achieving its objectives—e.g., in reducing the frequency of child marriage—and was indeed a model for reform in traditional societies. A more recent study suggests that the decline in early marriage had other causes as well, and that the state can influence behavior only through a complex and dynamic process of interaction and struggle between formal law and competing authority systems. See Mark Cammack, Lawrence A. Young & Tim Heaton, Legislating Social Change in an Islamic Society—Indonesia's Marriage Law, 44 Am. J. Comp.L. 45 (1996). For a classic collection of data, see Laura Nader (ed.) Law in Culture and Society (1969).

7. A recent attempt for a modern normative theory of comparative law is J.C. Reitz, How to do Comparative Law, 46 Am. J. Comp. Law 617 (1998).

not in itself a neutral exercise. This should effectively rebut of some of the most verbose critiques to comparative law.[8]

8. See David Kennedy, The Politics and Methods of Comparative Law, in The Common Core of European Private Law: Essays on the Project 131–207 (Mauro Bussani & Ugo Mattei ed., 2003).

*

PART TWO

COMPARISON OF HISTORY AND SOURCES

CHAPTER 4

COMPARISON INVOLVES HISTORY
The Roots of Contemporary Legal Structures

1. AN EARLY LEGAL TRADITION AND ITS DEVELOPMENTS: CHINA

China is a major example of a legal tradition that is often excluded from mainstream comparative legal scholarship. The Chinese legal tradition is obviously important in its own right, both historically (going back at least as far back as the western legal tradition) and in terms of China global importance today. At the same time, its influence has also reached beyond its borders, into surrounding civilizations. It would be an exaggeration to identify a single, homogeneous East Asian legal tradition, but Korea, Vietnam, and Japan, for example, have been influenced by the Chinese model to various degrees.[1]

(a) On the Rule of Man: *Li* versus *Fa*

As suggested by the materials later in this Chapter, some of the key features that distinguish the Islamic legal tradition from both the civil law and common law tradition are its status as divine revelation and the fact that it was not administered by a centralized state. In these two regards, the Chinese legal tradition seems remarkably modern: it was indeed administered by a centralized state bureaucracy (in fact long before European states reached a similar level of organization) and this law was in principle strictly imperial rather than divine. However, as we have seen, China has nevertheless at times been seen as lacking law in various respects.[1] This perception has to do with the fact that while codified law certainly has existed in China at least since the Tang dynasty (618–907 A.D.), law itself has not been viewed as a separate activity from administration more generally, or in today parlance, there was no formal separation between judicial and executive roles. Moreover, Confucianism as the official state ideology accorded law (*fa*) a relatively low social value. Instead, the official ideal was governance through virtuous example, by reliance on the power of ritual observance (*li*). This did not mean that law did not in fact play an important role in the governance of the Chinese empire—surely no empire has ever submitted to moral suasion alone—but it did mean that

---

1. See, e.g., Alexander Woodside, Vietnam and the Chinese Model: A Comparative Study of the Nguyen and Ch'ing Civil Government in the First Half of the Nineteenth Century (1971); Paul H. Ch'en, The Formation of the Early Meiji Legal Order (2002).

1. See *infra* Chapter 1, Section 5, at 42, on Legal Orientalism.

the official *ideal* was not the "rule of law" but its very opposite: the rule of men—namely, men of great Confucian virtue.

Benjamin Schwartz, On Attitudes toward Law in China

in Milton Katz, *Government under Law and the Individual* (1957), pp. 27–39.

No attempt will be made in this paper to account for all attitudes toward law which can be met in the millennial history of China. Our attention will rather be focused on what might be called the main line of Confucian development. While the attitudes discussed are typical they are by no means universal and do not even represent the views of all those in Chinese history who have called themselves Confucianist. The same holds true of our brief survey of the modern scene.

What might be called the typical Confucian attitude revolves about a basic dichotomy—the dichotomy between the concept of *li* and the concept of *fa*. The importance of this dichotomy can hardly be exaggerated. Not only does it have extremely ancient roots but it is linked with certain central events in Chinese history. This historic association lends the antithesis a resonance it would not have if it were merely based on a conceptual distinction derived in abstracto. *Li* is associated with the great figure of Confucius himself while *fa* is associated with the harshly despotic Ch'in dynasty which united the Chinese world under the control of a centralized bureaucratic empire in the third century B.C.

Now we have available certain conventional English equivalents of these two terms. *Li* has been translated as "propriety" while *fa* has been translated as "law." On the basis of these translations, one might assume that any discussion of law in China would revolve about the concept of *fa*.

Unfortunately the actual situation is much more complex.... Thus, instead of attempting to find single-word definitions of these terms, it would perhaps be better to attempt to describe in as brief a compass as possible (with all the risks of error involved) some of the major associations with them.

In the background of the concept *li* there lurk certain assumptions which resemble some of the assumptions underlying Western conceptions of natural law. One is the assumption of the existence of an eternal "natural" order underlying both the human and the nonhuman world *(tao)*. As far as human society is concerned, this *tao* is normative—it tells us what human society ought to be or what it "really" is in a Platonic sense. As in Western conceptions of natural law, we are constantly confronted with the problem of how actuality is related to the normative order. In the view of Confucius, his own period was marked by a tragic falling away of actuality from the *tao*. In the past—particularly during the early Chou dynasty—the *tao* had actually been realized in actuality. Thus in studying the institutions of the historic past one was, in effect, recovering the pattern of the *tao*.

So far, we are strongly reminded of some of the basic assumptions underlying concepts of natural law in the West. However, when we come to examine more closely the concrete vision of this "natural" order, we immediately note a marked difference of focus. The basic units of this order in the Confucian case are human beings enacting *certain fundamental social roles*. As in some modern schools of sociology, social role is the key term in the Confucian definition of social structure: the structure of society is basically a network of relations of persons enacting certain social roles. Social roles do not merely place individuals in certain social locations but also bear within themselves normative prescriptions of how people ought to act within these roles. The notion "father" does not refer to a social status but prescribes a certain pattern of right behavior. It is this, of course, which has led many to speak of the importance of personal relations in China. Actually, there is something very impersonal about these personal relations since they are always relations of persons acting according to norms prescribed by social roles. Later Confucianism reduces these relations to the "five relations"—relations between father and child, husband and wife, elder and younger brother, ruler and subject, and friend and friend (the latter being the most "personal"). These categories are presumed to embrace all fundamental relationships. Actually the "ruler-subject" relationship involved a tremendous variety of patterns of behavior based on one's position in an elaborate hierarchy.

Now within this structure *li* refers to the rules of conduct involved in these basic relationships. They are the rules governing the behavior of the individual in his own social role and governing his behavior toward others in their social roles. Actually *li* has a wider range of meaning. The character is derived from the name of an ancient sacrificial vessel and many of the prescriptions of *li* involving sacrifices to ancestors and gods' festive rites, etc. belong to the category of religious ritual. This, indeed, may have been the original sense of the term. *Li* are thus rules of conduct governing the relations between men (in their proper social roles) and the gods and ancestors, as well as relations among men. However, leaving aside the much debated question of Confucius' religious attitude, there can be no doubt that the purely human aspect of *li* has become of central importance with him even though the religious rites continue to form an integral part of the whole order of *tao*.

Another basic aspect of *li* is its association with moral force rather than with the sanction of physical force. Confucian thought is marked by an extremely strong feeling for the antithesis between moral force or spiritual force and physical coercion. So strong is this feeling, that moral force is practically equated with the good while anything associated with the sanction of physical coercion is tainted with evil. Granet has gone so far as to maintain that moral force was regarded as a magical potency by the Chinese. A man in whom moral force has won the ascendancy will naturally live up to the ethical demands of his social role. He will submit to *li* without hesitancy. Furthermore, the moral force which the noble man manifests in his behavior and in his attitudes acts as a radiating force, as it were, bringing others into its field of radiation. Hence the tremendous emphasis on the power of example as well as on proper education. Furthermore, while the prevalence of *li* depends on the prevalence of this moral force, moral perfection of the individual can only manifest itself in outward behavior as *li*. There are, to be sure, many schools of thought within Confucianism concerning the actual relationship between moral perfection in the individual and *li*. Some maintain that is merely a manifestation of the moral perfection of individuals. Others maintain that it is *li* itself which, through education, brings about the moral improvement of men. Others maintain that only the ancient sages possessed moral perfection innately, while mankind as a whole must acquire it through the training in *li*. In all cases, however, the moral force which works within men and the *li* which manifests itself in external conduct are inseparable.

Within the *ideal* Confucian order, the institution of government would play a peculiarly restricted role. The good ruler and his ministers would, on the one hand, provide the people with an example of proper behavior according to *li* (it should be noted that many of the duties of *li* are confined to the ruling classes), and on the other hand would educate the people in *li*. Within the ideal system, the ruling class becomes a sort of focal point of this moral force. Presumably the foundation of such a state would rest wholly on moral force rather than on physical coercion.

When we come to examine some of the concrete prescriptions which come under the heading of *li,* we find that many of them concern matters of proper ritual, etiquette, manners, gestures, and mien. There are points at which rules of *li* impinge upon matters which would come under the heading of civil or private law in the West—marriage, divorce, support of parents, burial responsibilities, disposition of property within the family, the status of concubines, etc. Taken as a whole, however, *li* as a body of rules, does not touch vast areas of experience which fall within the scope of Western law.

It is important to remember here that *li* is not a body of rules designed to take care of every circumstance. *Li* is an instrument for training character, and nourishing moral force. In a society where *li* prevails, unbridled self-interest is placed under effective control from within, as it were. Men may continue to have individual interests, and these interests are legitimate up to a point; but in a society where men are governed by *li,* conflicts of interest can be easily resolved. Both sides will be ready to make concessions, to yield *(jang),* and the necessity for litigation will be avoided. In such a society any highly explicit system of civil law would be unnecessary.

It is at this point, by the way, that the Confucian conception of *li* becomes linked to the Confucian attitude toward the whole realm of what we call "individual rights." Individuals have legitimate interests, to be sure, and in the good society these interests will be taken care of (in accordance with requirements of the individual's social status). To sur-round these interests with an aura of sanctity and to call them "rights," to elevate the defense of these individual interests to the plane of a moral virtue, to "insist on one's rights" is to run entirely counter to the spirit of *li*. The proper predisposition with regard to one's interests is the predisposition to yield rather than the predisposition to insist. A man who has led a life conforming to *li* will know how to behave properly when his interests are involved.

These, it seems to me, are some of the main characteristics of *li* and the question remains—are we here dealing with a variety of law? According to some Western definitions of law, the roles of *li* would definitely fall under the category of law. Stammler maintains that law includes any rule of conduct considered to be inviolable, universal, and independent of the wishes of the individual, whether such rule is supported by political sanction or not. However, if *li* is law, it is law within a restricted framework. Presumably, in most Western conceptions of law the primary focus is on human behavior in various given circumstances. The subjects of law are only of interest to the extent that they are involved in the legal action. In *li* the primary focus is on the relations of social roles, and the rules of conduct are significant because they are concerned with these relations.

Now in discussing *li* so far we have been describing the ideal social order. Both Confucius and his followers were only too acutely aware that actuality falls short of the ideal. Confucianism recognizes that there are elements in human society impervious to the influence of *li,* and that there are whole periods when *li* cannot be made to prevail. There is even the notion that in periods of deep economic distress the masses cannot be led by *li*. The economic distress itself, of course, is generally attributed to the ruling class's failure to conform to the demands of *li*. In all areas where *li* cannot be made to apply, *fa* must be employed to maintain order. *Fa* is enacted law designed to keep order by the appeal to the fear of punishment. It is thus based directly on the sanction of force. So closely is *fa* associated with punishment, that the word has become a synonym of the word punishment. *Fa* thus represents the sanction of force in a very direct and literal sense and its first and primary meaning is penal law. Where *li* is ineffective in maintaining public order, *fa* must take over. Where the ruling class must place heavy reliance on *fa,* it is a symptom of its own inability to rule by *li*.

However, since Confucianism recognizes that there are always elements in human society which must be controlled by *fa*—that human reality almost inevitably embodies this element of defect—*fa* still occupies a legitimate, albeit regrettable, place in the general nature of things. It is recognized as a necessity but deprecated. "If the people be led by laws," states Confucius, "and uniformity sought to be given them by punishments, they will try to avoid punishments but have no sense of shame. If they be led by virtue and uniformity sought to be given them by *li,* they will have a sense of shame and, moreover, will become good." *Li* and *fa* produce as it were their own corresponding psychologies. Where government does not rely on *li, li* cannot exercise its educative effect—it cannot become a transmission belt for transmitting virtue to the people and the people will not be curbed by an inner moral force. *Fa* makes its appeal to the bare interest in avoiding pain. It works with a simple hedonistic pleasure-pain psychology. Not only does it lead men to think in terms of self-interest in avoiding punishment, but makes them litigious—makes them skilled in the ways of manipulating laws to suit their own interests. In a society dominated by *fa,* the people as a whole will all develop the peculiar talents of the shyster lawyer and the sense of shame will suffer.

In one of the Confucian classics we find a fierce diatribe against a minister who has publicized a penal code (by having it engraved on bronze vessels). There is a double offense here—the heavy reliance on *fa* and its publicization. This act, it is contended, will inevitably lead to a litigious spirit on the part of the people. They will no longer look to their superiors for an example of moral behavior but "appeal to the letter of the text hoping that, by chance, they may succeed in their argumentation.... They will reject *li* and appeal to your text." Here we note that the psychology which underlies the litigious spirit has nothing to do with the psychology which underlies *li.* There is another significant point made in this passage which reflects an important facet of the whole Confucian attitude toward law. "The ancient kings," states our author, "deliberated on circumstances in deciding (concerning the punishment of crime)." The Confucian view that where men are guided by *li,* conflicts are easily resolved, has made it possible for Confucianists to develop an acute feeling for the uniqueness of every human situation—for the fact that "no two cases are alike" and a corresponding skepticism toward all attempts to subsume all possible circumstances under certain generalized legal categories. As a result, the judge—whom we may presume to be a man guided by *li*—will (within limits) simply think of the legal code as providing certain guidelines but in his judgment will rely very heavily on the unique features of the circumstances of the case. He may even base his judgment on some situation described in the classics rather that on the provisions of the code. Hence, as one Chinese author states, "it is the judgment and not the law which makes justice."

These, it seems to me, are some of the major characteristics of the Confucian concept of *fa,* as it developed in the centuries immediately following the Master's death. However, as we know, the Confucian gospel by no means found immediate acceptance in the stormy period which followed his death. It is interesting to note, however, that many of the basic antitheses established by Confucianism (which undoubtedly rested on a much older substratum of thought) furnish the frame of reference within which later thought operates. Thus in the fourth and third centuries B.C. we have the emergence of a group of political philosophers known as the "school of *fa*" or "Legalists" in current Western literature. Their view of the nature of *fa* is strikingly similar to that of Confucius. *Fa* is penal law directly based on the sanction by force. It presupposes that the people can be led only by an appeal to the pleasure-pain principle. However, not only do the legalists accept these definitions, but they frankly and boldly assert that social order can be maintained only by *fa.* Contemporary events led them to a radical disbelief in *li* and moral force as ordering principles of society.

However, their thought is not only characterized by a revaluation of *fa* but by what might be called its heavily statist orientation. Living in an environment where great powers were contending for domination of the Chinese world, they offered themselves to the rulers of this world as experts in the science of power. By relying on *fa,* the ruler would be able to establish a Draconian order within his borders. However, this was not the final end. By making the people a pliable instrument of his will, the ruler would be able to use them in increasing the economic, political, and military power potential of the state and thus make possible ultimate victory in the international struggles of this period of "contending states." Beyond their addiction to harsh penal law, the legalists thus became the advocates of what Max Weber would call the "rationalization" (within the limits of the period) of the social order from the point of view of enhancing the power of the state. They were advocates of the bureaucratic principle, of something like a conscript army, of sweeping economic reforms, etc. Thus, *fa* became with them not only penal law but all forms of state-initiated institutional change.

We know, of course, that the Ch'in dynasty, which finally united the Chinese world during the third century B.C. into a centralized bureaucratic empire, actually operated within the framework of a legalist philosophy. It not only established a harsh and detailed system of penal law but, by the very nature of bureaucratic government, brought about an enormous extension in what might be called administrative law. It also initiated all sorts of institutional changes by government enactment.

While the dynasty was short-lived, this historic experience strongly conditioned the whole subsequent orthodox Confucian attitude toward *fa chih* (which, ironically, must be translated as "rule of law"). Harsh despotism, heavy reliance on brute force, oppressive demands on the people by an interventionist state—all these are the orthodox associations with *fa chih.* Furthermore, all attempts to improve society by heavy reliance on institutional change initiated by state enactment have also been associated with *fa* as a result of this experience. Presumably, the common denominator between this meaning of *fa* and its meaning as "penal law" are the facts that (1) the sanction of force lies behind both, (2) they both try to reform men "externally" by using incentives of reward and fear, (3) in both, the reliance on *li* is neglected.

While the Ch'in dynasty disappeared, while Confucianism subsequently became the official state philosophy, the basic structure of the centralized bureaucratic state created by the Ch'in remained. To the extent that the Chinese state has had to rely on the machinery of compulsion and rules based on the sanction of force (and it has probably had to do so to the same extent as any other state) it has relied on a machinery whose basic skeletal structure was created by the Ch'in legalists.

NOTE ON MODERN "RITUAL"

Is *li* something that is relevant only to China and Confucianism? What role does ritual play in modern life? The contemporary philosopher Herbert Fingarette suggests that we should not dismiss the Confucian notion of *li* as either empty formalism or a faith in some kind of primitive "magic".

Herbert Fingarette, Human Community as Holy Rite

in *Confucius: The Secular as Sacred* (1972), pp. 9–14.

[According to Confucius,] there are two contrasting kinds of failure in carrying out *li*: the ceremony may be awkwardly performed for lack of learning and skill; or the ceremony may have a surface slickness but yet be dull, mechanical for lack of serious purpose and commitment. Beautiful and effective ceremony requires the personal "presence" to be fused with learned ceremonial skill. This ideal fusion is true *li* as sacred rite....

Having considered holy ceremony in itself, we are now prepared to turn to more everyday aspects of life. This is in effect what Confucius invites us to do; it is the foundation for his perspective on man.

I see you in the street; I smile, walk toward you, put out my hand to shake yours. And behold—without any command, stratagem, force, special tricks or tools, without any effort on my part to make you do so, you spontaneously turn toward me, return my smile, raise your hand toward mine. We shake hands—not by my pulling your hand up and down or your pulling mine but by spontaneous and perfect cooperative action. Normally we do not notice the subtlety and amazing complexity of this coordinated "ritual" act. This subtlety and complexity become very evident, however, if one has had to learn the ceremony only from a book of instructions, or if one is a foreigner from a non-handshaking culture.

Nor do we normally notice that the "ritual" has "life" in it, that we are "present" to each other, at least to some minimal extent. As Confucius said, there are always the general and fundamental requirements of reciprocal good faith and respect. This mutual respect is not the same as conscious feeling of mutual respect; when I am *aware* of a respect for you, I am more likely to be piously fatuous or perhaps self-consciously embarrassed; and no doubt our little "ceremony" will reveal this little awkwardness. (I put out my hand too soon and am left with it hanging in midair.) No, the authenticity of mutual respect does not require that I consciously feel respect or focus my attention on my respect for you; it is fully expressed in the correct "live" and spontaneous performance of the *act*. Just as an aerial acrobat must, at least for the purpose at hand, possess (but not think about his) complete trust in his partner if the trick is to come off, so we who shake hands, though the stakes are less, must have (but not think about) respect and trust. Otherwise, we find ourselves fumbling awkwardly or performing in a lifeless fashion, which easily conveys its meaningless to the other.

Clearly it is not necessary that our reciprocal respect and good faith go very far in order for us to accomplish a reasonably successful handshake and greeting. Yet even here, the sensitive person can often plumb the depths of another's attitude from a handshake. This depth of human relationship expressible in a "ceremonial" gesture is in good part possible because of the remarkable specificity of the ceremony. For example, if I am your former teacher, you will spontaneously be rather obvious in walking toward me rather than waiting for me to walk toward you. You will allow a certain subtle reserve in your handshake, even though it will be warm. You will not slap me in the back, though conceivably I might grasp you by the shoulder with my free hand. There are indescribably many subtleties in the distinctions, nuances and minute but meaningful variations in gesture. If we do try to describe these subtle variations and their rules, we immediately sound like Book 10 of the [Confucian] *Analects*, whose ceremonial recipes initially seem to the modern American the quintessence of quaint and extreme traditionalism. It is in just such ways that social activity is coordinated in civilized society, without effort or planning, but simply spontaneously initiating the appropriate ritual gesture in an appropriate setting. This power of *li*, Confucius says, depends upon prior learning. It is not inborn. . . .

Looking at these "ceremonies" through the image of *li*, we realize that an explicitly sacred rite can be seen as an emphatic, intensified and sharply elaborated extension of everyday *civilized* intercourse.

The notion that we can use speech only to talk *about* action or indirectly to *evoke* action has dominated modern Western thought. Yet contemporary "linguistic" analysis in philosophy has revealed increasingly how much the ritual word is itself the critical act rather than a report of, or stimulus to, action. The late professor J.L. Austin was one of those who brought the reality and pervasiveness of this phenomenon to a focus in his analyses of what he called the "performative utterance." These are the innumerable statements we make which function somewhat like the "operative" clause in a legal instrument. They are statements, but they are not statements *about* some act or inviting some action; instead, they are the very execution of the act itself.

"I give and bequeath my watch to my brother," duly said or written is not a report of what I have already done but is the very act of bequeathal itself. In a marriage ceremony, the "I do" is not a report of an inner mental act of acceptance; it is itself the act which seals my part of the bargain. "I promise. . ." is not a report of what I have done a moment before inside my head, nor is it indeed a report of anything at all; the uttering of the words is itself the act of promising. It is by words, and by the ceremony of which the words form a part, that I bind myself in a way which . . . is more powerful, more inescapable than strategies or force. Confucius truly tells us that the man who uses the power of *li* can influence those above him—but not the man who has only physical force at his command.

There is no power of *li* if there is no learned and accepted convention, or if we utter the words and invoke the power of the convention in an inappropriate setting, of if the ceremony is not fully carried out, or if the persons carrying out the ceremonial roles are not those properly authorized ("authorization"—again a ceremony). In short, the peculiarly moral yet binding power of ceremonial gesture and word cannot be abstracted from or used in isolation from ceremony. It is not a distinct power we happen to use in ceremony; it is the power *of* ceremony. I cannot effectively go through the ceremony of bequeathing my servant to someone if, in our society, there is no accepted convention of slavery; I cannot bet two dollars if no one completes the bet by accepting; I cannot legally plead "Guilty" to a crime while eating dinner at home. Thus the power of *li* cannot be used except as the *li* is truly respected. . . .

Indeed, the central lesson of these new philosophical insights is not so much a lesson about language as it is about ceremony. What we have come to see, in our own way, is how vast is the area of human existence in which the substance of that existence *is* the ceremony. Promises, commitments, excuses, pleas, compliments, pacts—these and so much more are ceremonies or they are nothing. It is thus in the medium of ceremony that the peculiarly human part of our life is lived. . . .

NOTE

Notice that many of Fingarette's examples of ritual, or "ceremonial," acts are in fact *legal* acts—entering into marriage, bequeathing property, pleading guilty, making a contract. In this light, "law" is not necessarily the opposite of "ritual" but rather a particular kind, or class, of ritual.

(b) Imperial Chinese Law

The process whereby the Chinese state developed an increasingly sophisticated legal system combining aspects of both *li* and *fa* has often been called the "Confucianization of law" (although it could just as well be called the "legalization of Confucianism"). Below, William Jones describes some key aspects of that legal system as it developed over time.[1]

William C. Jones, Trying to Understand the Current Chinese Legal System

in C. Stephen Hsu, ed., *Understanding China's Legal System* (2003), pp. 7–21.

The Imperial and Republican Background

Chinese law is very easy to misunderstand. It is not at all certain that anyone—Chinese or foreign—understands it. The reason for this is that when we think about law, we think about a formal legal system of the western type. We look at China and expect to find such things as a law of

---

1. For a fuller exposition of the role and substance of late imperial law, and of the Code in particular, see William C. Jones, "In-troduction," in The Great Qing Code (William C. Jones trans.).

contracts, a bench and bar, and all the other paraphernalia that we associate with law. At present, one can find such institutions in China, but they *are* modern imports. Until recently, they did not exist. What one found instead—and still finds—quite easily, are a vast number of statements by China's most prominent thinkers, notably including Confucius, that show great hostility to what we think of as law. As Confucius supposedly said: "In hearing cases I am as good as anyone else, but what is really needed is to bring about that there are no cases." More recently a Hong Kong barrister of Chinese descent remarked to Professor Jerome A. Cohen, when the latter was beginning his researches into Chinese law:

> The trouble with you Westerners, is that you've never got beyond that primitive stage you call the "rule of law": You're all preoccupied with the "rule of law." China has always known that law is not enough to govern a society. She knew it twenty-five hundred years ago, and she knows it today. [1]

It was possible to conclude from all this—and in the early days of Sino–European relations many people, both Chinese and foreign, did conclude—that China did not have a legal system. This was quite untrue, but it is easy to see why the belief arose. Nor has the situation changed all that much. Although on paper modern China has all of the apparatus of a western legal system, it is a country that is still heavily influenced by tradition, and any study of Chinese law that concentrates solely on the statutes and institutions copied from the West is bound to come to wrong conclusions. There still has to be a search for the elements of a legal system quite unlike ours.

Probably the most important aspect of Chinese traditional law that has to be understood is the fact that during the dynastic era it was a system that was totally uninfluenced by the West. During that period China always had a land mass and a population that were as large as or larger than those of western Europe. Moreover, the bulk of the area that we call China was united into one highly centralized political unit in the third century B.C., by the first emperor, Qin Shi Huang-di. It never suffered the kind of permanent disintegration that occurred in Europe after the fall of Rome. It remains today, in terms of internal and external boundaries, language, and, to a certain extent, governmental organization, very much the China of 2,000 years ago. By and large, it was a self-contained society that influenced its neighbors, such as Japan and Korea, and absorbed and sinicized its conquerors, such as the Mongols and Manchus. It was difficult for outside institutions to penetrate. Thus at the time when contacts with the West became extensive in the eighteenth century, China was a very ancient and highly advanced society that had developed pretty much on its own. It had its own system of law which had developed along with the other aspects of Chinese society, and seemed to work well enough. That is a very hard thing for westerners to take in. They are used to the cultural dominance of western institutions. Just as western missionaries took it

---

1. Cohen, The Criminal Process in the People's Republic of China 4 (1968).

upon themselves to correct the defective Chinese system of religion, western jurists have felt impelled to show the Chinese what a proper legal system is like. Initially, the Chinese themselves were, on the whole, ungrateful for all this help. They eventually succumbed to western arguments—backed, as they were, by western arms—and established a new European style legal *system,* but they have never been entirely convinced. Traces of the legal system perfected in the Tang dynasty (618–906 A.D.)—unlike anything we think of as a system of law—are very much with us.

If one turns to the institutions of this system, the most striking aspect is its intimate connection with the administrative system of the central government. The system of government that developed in China after its unification in the third century B.C. consisted of a strong central government headed by the Emperor, who ruled through a highly centralized bureaucracy, mostly selected, in the later dynasties, by competitive examinations. This continued to be its structure until the end of the Empire in 1911. The Emperor's power was, in theory, absolute. There could be no doctrine of separation of powers. The lowest ranking officials who represented the central government at the bottom level—the district magistrates—were, in effect, the Emperor in little. Each of them exercised all of the power of the state in collecting taxes, providing for defense, carrying on public works, conducting religious ceremonies and supervising the local examination system for entry into the civil service, deciding lawsuits, etc. Of course these actions were subject to review, and the magistrates were subject to strict rules in the exercise of their powers. Nevertheless as will be discussed in somewhat more detail below, deciding cases was simply one administrative task among many. It was, indeed, an aspect of the magistrate's general charge to keep order. The magistrate adjudicated cases, but he was not a judge as we understand the term. He was the official who carried out all governmental functions at the local level, and adjudication was one of them.

From the Chinese point of view, the central element of their legal system was a body of rules promulgated by the Emperor. The title of this collection is usually translated by the word "code." Each dynasty had its own code which would be called the Great Ming Code, Qing Code, or whatever, according to the name of the dynasty. Since the formal legal system was an integral part of the governing apparatus of the Empire, when the Empire collapsed in the early part of this century, the legal system disappeared along with everything else. Prior to that, there is clear continuity from the Tang dynasty to the end of the Qing (1911), and there is every reason to suppose that the tradition stretches back many centuries—possibly many millennia—before the Tang. During most of the period for which there is a clear documented tradition (653–1911) the Chinese legal system governed a territory and a population that was as large or larger than that governed by Roman law, either when it was the law of the Roman Empire or when it became the dominant law of medieval and modern Europe. In addition to governing China itself, China's legal system formed the basis of the formal legal systems of those nations which were subject to its influence: Korea, Japan, and Vietnam. It was only when

Roman law spread out beyond Europe and the Mediterranean that it began to exceed Chinese law in importance.

Thus the importance of Chinese law is clear. The difficulty is finding out how to study it. The materials available for its study are vast. In addition to the codes themselves, there were annotations to the codes, and many other collections of statutes and regulations are still extant. There are also thousands of decisions in cases that arose under the codes, in addition to some studies of customary law in which elements of what we would call family and commercial law can be found. Finding a way through the material is a daunting task. There are no systematic legal treatises as we understand the term. The Chinese had commentaries and what are sometimes called treatises, but these do not help one to understand their system. As a nineteenth century French student of the system observed:

> [N]one of the these collections [treatises], to my knowledge at least, contains an analysis of the whole of Chinese law or has tried to deduce from it any theory whatsoever. Each commentator picks over the law, phrase by phrase, and tries to bring out some comparison, to find some unforeseen circumstance, and most of all, to justify the provision of the law. Alongside certain remarks which show a great exactitude in criticism, there are often platitudes and wretched inanities.[2]

One possible solution to the problem is to regard the code itself as a treatise of sorts. If one considers the Qing Code, the final code in the tradition, then it is clear that its structure is the product of a great deal of thought. It is tightly arranged. The rules themselves show much refinement. There are many cross references, for example. Hence it comes close to constituting a scientific analysis of what the Chinese regarded as law. To be sure, it is, in part, a collection of rules that deal with particular fact situations, sometimes in great detail. Nevertheless, it is not just a compendium of rules, and the rules themselves have been refined and harmonized to a considerable degree. General principles have been factored out. It is, in other words, a true code, and as such can be taken to represent the considered view of some of China's leading jurists as to the ways to think about law, to think about what law is. It showed the way to analyze legal problems and provided methods for applying legal rules to them.

In some ways, that seems to have been the function of the Code. At least by the end of the dynasty, it was not the direct or immediate basis of decision for most cases (although it has, as indicated, some fairly detailed rules). Rather, the cited authority would more than likely be a *li*, a word usually translated as "sub-statute," though "codified precedent" might be better.[3] The *li* were detailed rules that were normally based on decisions or interpretations by officials at the highest level of the central government, and were printed following the article of the Code to which they referred.

---

2. Philastre, Le Code Annamite 4 (1909).

3. The term *li* here is different from the homonymous term *li* which refers to "rit-ual" (in opposition to "law" as a form of social control). [Eds.]

If there was an applicable sub-statute, it would be applied instead of the statute. There were, in addition, as indicated above, a number of statutes and regulations outside the Code. But in this the situation is not so different from that in western law. The French Civil Code is probably the direct authority in only a small number of present-day cases (despite the technique of decision-writing of the Court of Cassation, which might lead one to think it was [the authority in most cases][4]). Precedent plays an enormous role, as do the opinions of eminent authorities and, on occasion, other statutes and regulations. Nevertheless, the Code remains at the heart of the system, and serves as the basis for organizing instruction in the civil law. It seems reasonable to make a similar claim for the Chinese codes like the Great Qing Code.

The Conceptual Scheme of the Code Compared to Those of the West

One of the principal difficulties in studying the Code is learning how to look at it as the Chinese did, or at least not to look at it with expectations formed by exposure to western ideas about law. To avoid this problem, it is necessary to know something about the legal system of which the Code was a part, for the system is so different from what we are accustomed to that it is sometimes hard to realize that it is a legal system. One of the aspects that especially strikes the western observer is that the Code and hence the law are not much concerned with the disputes of private individuals, nor with the notion of "rights." We are accustomed to think that a legal system is primarily a social institution within which "persons"—private individuals, or groups of such individuals, or even the state—can make claims against other "persons" and have these resolved by a neutral trier of fact and law—the court. Normally the persons or parties will be represented by lawyers. We also tend to think that the laws applied by the courts will deal to a very considerable extent with private law, with torts, contracts, property, and the like. An organized bar, judicial independence, separation of powers, and some judicial review of administrative acts are also institutions that we expect to see.

These are all aspects of the legal systems we are familiar with. To a certain extent, they reflect the point of view of our law, and it is well to remember what that is. It seems safe to say that it was formed by Roman law, and Roman law arose, after all, in a very small and predominantly agricultural community with a weak government. As Professor W. Kunkel points out, by the beginning of the fourth century B.C., when Roman law was developing, Rome was about half the size of modern Luxembourg. As a consequence, the legal problems that Roman law dealt with in the formative period were what one would expect: the resolution of disputes between private individuals that arose out of torts, simple contracts, and succession. In addition, there were problems of status, both because different groups of Roman society were sharply divided—patricians, plebeians, and slaves, for instance—and because Romans distinguished themselves from the citizens of other Latin states, to say nothing of those from farther away. Although

---

4. See the discussion in *infra* Chapter 5, Section 9.

Roman society soon changed radically, the focus or point of view of Roman law had been set. Thus Gaius, writing in the period of the Antonines (c. 161 A.D.), said, "The whole of the law observed by us relates either to persons or to things or to actions." Yet the Rome of that time was of enormous size and was headed by an emperor whose status and power, despite the republican forms that still survived, approached, if it did not surpass, those of the autocratic Chinese emperors. Gaius' analysis was continued by the draftsmen of the *Corpus Juris* of Justinian, whose power and system of government were in every way comparable to those of his Chinese counterparts. Nevertheless, the basic law of the Empire—civil law—continued to look at society from the point of view of individuals and its basic concerns were those of individuals. Of course Rome had many statutes that dealt with governmental matters such as control of the bureaucracy, but civil law was the heart of the system.

This approach has been maintained in western law down to the present. Modern civil codes cover the same material as the Institutes of Gaius, more or less, and follow his scheme of analysis. Civil law is at the heart of western law, and the influence of the approach is pervasive. Western jurists use a model of the universe composed of discrete entities—persons—who create legal obligations by the exercise of their individual wills. They also assume that these persons can get their disputes resolved, if they wish to, by professionally trained judges. These "persons" are no longer human beings, but the central abstractions or figures of the legal system. They are sometimes called "rights-bearers," and it is an accurate description. Even the state can appear as a "person" in a domestic lawsuit, and states are, in effect, the "persons" of public international law, whose terminology and structure are based on Roman private law.

The situation in China was radically different. By the time the legal system was formalized, the polity of China consisted of a highly centralized government headed by an absolute ruler who ruled by means of a bureaucracy. The primary obligation of every Chinese was to fulfill the duties assigned him by the Emperor. All human activities had to be carried on so as to fit into his scheme for directing society. Consequently the imperial law took note of human activity only as it was perceived to affect imperial policies. It was natural that the primary focus of attention would be the activities of bureaucrats in the performance of their duties, not the activities of ordinary human beings in their private lives. As one of the Tang emperors, Li Shimin, is supposed to have remarked, "The wise emperor governs his officials, he does not govern the people." In China the subject matter of Roman civil law was considered only when it affected the interests of the Emperor.

Thus many aspects of marriage were dealt with, since marriage and the family system were basic to the polity. An institution that was similar to the English mortgage, the *dian,* was given considerable space, presumably because it was important to know who owned land so that the government could collect the taxes on it (the provisions are included in the section on land taxes). Very little attention is paid to private matters.

There is almost no treatment of contracts, for instance. This does not mean that the Chinese did not use contracts, or even that the magistrates did not deal with them, but such matters were of no concern to the Code, and hence were not "law" as the Chinese understood the term. The matters which we deal with by means of civil law, especially contracts, property, and succession, were dealt with in a variety of ways in China. One was settlement by village mediation committees or guilds, depending on what was involved. It was even possible to bring an action on an obligation in a situation not covered by the Code before the magistrate. But none of this was "law" or part of the "legal" system. The actions in private matters before the magistrate were not "legal" because they did not involve enforcement of the Code. "Law" was concerned with the enforcement of government policy. Thus over half the Code is devoted to the regulation of the official activities of government officials. For example, exceeding the number of employees allotted to a particular office; failing to forward documents promptly: "or for a stable-keeper in the Imperial Stud to fail to have his herd produce enough young."

Such matters are dealt with in the West by internal regulations of government offices. For example, in the United States, within the Navy Department, there are regulations that govern the transfer of goods and funds within the Department as well as the assignment of personnel and the way instructions are transmitted. But they are not regarded as being part of the American legal system except on the rare occasions when they are relevant to some action that is being brought in the regular courts, such as a wrongful discharge.

One consequence of the difference in points of view is that the categories of western law are meaningless in China. One cannot speak of civil law or criminal law. Civil law as the law which deals with the private concerns of citizens from the point of view of those citizens did not exist. There were no "citizens" for one thing, only subjects. More importantly, the law dealt with all matters from the point of view of the ruler. How did a matter concern him? The Code has often been described as a penal code. If by that it is meant that each article imposes a penalty, the statement is correct. But does the term "penal code" connote a body of law that deals with such matters as breach of promise of marriage and the quality of goods produced and sold? So also for "administrative law" or the public–private law distinction, which are important categories we use to arrange legal rules. The entire system of law can be regarded as governing internal administrative matters, so that it was entirely administrative law. Since there was no other system of law, however, what would it mean to say that a rule is administrative? We can say administrative law as opposed to civil law, for instance. But in China there was simply law. In the same way, all Chinese law was, in a sense, public, and yet it dealt, on occasion, with private matters. The distinction we make between the two areas did not exist. Actually, it could not exist.

The point is that Chinese law has to be examined on its own terms. Categories of western law do not work. There was simply one body of "law." The only categorization was the grouping of articles under the name of a board or ministry of the central government—Officials, Revenue, Rites, War, Punishments, and Works—to whose work they seemed most closely connected. It makes no more sense to talk about Chinese civil or criminal law than it would to talk about U.S. Agriculture Department law when referring to the UCC (Uniform Commercial Code), even though a number of UCC provisions are related to agriculture and some of these are also dealt with by government regulation. But that would be a natural way for someone trained in traditional Chinese law to think about our law. He would start with the administrative categories of the U.S. Code as the tools for analyzing law. In other words, the categories of Chinese law are meaningless in the United States.

Rather than try to fit Chinese law into western patterns, it would seem wise to try to approach Chinese law in the way the Chinese did if we can. Otherwise there is the temptation to concentrate on matters that we recognize as similar to our own ideas. There are many such areas in the Code, especially in criminal law and torts. Not only do they cover much the same ground (homicide, theft, battery, rape, trespass, etc.), the substantive elements of the offenses are often almost the same. Homicide, for instance, is divided into plotting a killing, killing intentionally but without previous planning (as, for example, killing during an affray), and killing by mistake. The asportation required for theft is similar to that required by our law. There are many others. But that is not where the Chinese began their own analysis. The Code, which seems to have been at the center of the Chinese legal system, was, in form, a directive to the district magistrate to tell him when to punish and precisely what punishment to inflict in any circumstances that were perceived by the state to be legally significant. That is, as injurious to the Emperor. The primary concern of the Code, therefore, was to make it clear to the magistrate what activities he was required to punish, and precisely what penalties he was to impose.

Moreover, as mentioned above, the majority of the provisions were not only part of a code addressed to magistrates to enforce as part of their administrative duties. They also concerned the behavior of officials on the job. Thus while there are provisions that deal with the private concerns of individuals such as a wife cursing her husband's relatives, or mortgagees refusing to allow redemption, and the like, there are far more that deal with such matters as the conduct of the great sacrifices by officials or their failure to discover the theft of grain from government warehouses. The feature that seems to be common to all of the activities that the Code dealt with is that they were significant to the activities of the government or Emperor.

Our law has grown outward, as it were, from the concerns of individuals or "persons." It fulfills large social purposes, but it does so indirectly by dealing with the affairs of individuals, largely from their points of view. It can be argued that the stability of contract relations and the enforceability of contracts are essential for a society's economic development. Indeed, such arguments are often made. Contract law is, nevertheless, primarily concerned with providing a way for persons to ensure that their decisions regarding matters that interest them will be enforced. As the interests of individuals are served, societal interests get an indirect benefit.

In China, precisely the reverse was the case. The state promulgated laws to make sure its interests were advanced. As this was done, the interests of private individuals or groups of such persons were often protected as an indirect result. This difference was indicated not only by the content of the substantive law, but by the nature of the legal proceeding. There were no parties in our sense. There might be an accuser, and there was certainly an accused, but the magistrate was in immediate and total control, and he was concerned with protecting and advancing the interests of the state. Moreover, he was at the very bottom level of a bureaucratic pyramid. The cases he could decide on his own were very few. In any significant case, he could only propose decisions which could be (and often were) revised or reversed by superiors. Thus he was not a judge in our sense. He was the means through which the Emperor governed at the lowest level, and he exercised all of the powers of the state at that level. As one noted authority has written:

> He was the judge, the tax collector, and the general administrator. He had charge of the postal service, salt administration, *pao-chia*, police, public works, granaries, social welfare, education, and religious and ceremonial functions. His over-all duty is summed up in the *Ch'ing shih kao* (Draft history of the Ch'ing dynasty):
>
> > A magistrate takes charge of the government of a district. He settles legal cases, metes out punishment, encourages agriculture, extends charity to the poor, wipes out the wicked and the unlawful, promotes livelihood, and fosters education. All such matters as recommending scholars [to the court], reading and elucidating the law and imperial edicts [to the public], caring for the aged, and offering sacrifices to the gods, are his concern.
>
> A magistrate, although a civil official, also had to defend the city in an uprising or a foreign invasion. Failure to do so would incur dismissal and physical punishment. [5]

Deciding legal cases or what we call lawsuits or prosecutions was one of his two most important tasks (the other being the collection of taxes), but that is all. It was just one administrative task among many. Neither he nor the superiors who reviewed his work were legally trained in a formal sense since there was no formal legal training to be had, although they might, of course, have picked up a good deal of legal knowledge on the job. They were, for the most part, career civil servants who were selected by competitive examinations based on the Chinese classics—essentially philosophy and literature. Law was not normally one of the subjects tested.

Obviously, in such a system the proceeding was not left up to the initiative of private parties. The adversary trial which we regard as stan-

---

5. Chu, Local Government under the Ch'ing 16 (1969).

dard did not really exist in connection with enforcing the Code. Instead, when the magistrate took jurisdiction over a case, he called in all interested parties and interrogated them. If there was significant, real, non-testimonial evidence, such as a corpse, he went out to examine it. Finding the facts was regarded as much more difficult and important than finding the law—something that the magistrate tended anyway to leave to his clerk. There were, in theory, no lawyers to perform the functions of either barristers or solicitors. The magistrate made a preliminary decision, and it was reviewed in exactly the same way that superior officials would have reviewed a decision to reduce the area's tax assessment because of natural disasters. That is, the review was simply a part of the system of bureaucratic control. Did the magistrate follow the proper procedures and guidelines? Did he report in the proper way and give adequate reasons for his decision? Was this the right decision under the circumstances? The Chinese had elaborate rules for all administrative tasks, not just for those we call adjudication.

The proceeding could be quite dreadful for everyone, including the complainant. Persons concerned, including witnesses, were usually imprisoned under appalling conditions pending final conclusion of the matter. The innocent word translated "interrogate" often involved torture. The lightest punishment—beating—could be crippling or even fatal. Despite this, the system seemed to function in a way the government found fairly satisfactory for its purposes, and it was not so unbearable as to cause the populace to revolt. With minor changes, it survived for many centuries. Despite its horrors, it was a system that worked.

If we are to understand the law of imperial China, these are all matters that have to be kept in mind. Its centerpiece—the Code—was a body of law promulgated by a bureaucracy that was primarily interested in regulating the affairs of its own officials. It concerned itself with other matters only when they affected imperial designs. It was administered by the same civil servants who, at the same time, administered all of the other activities of government, from collecting taxes to supervising examinations for the civil service. There were no facilities for training jurists and no lawyers to represent parties at the trial. The system was not based on the idea of rights and their enforcement. It was entirely within the control of the magistrates. And yet it constituted a legal system that was comparable in its breadth and organization to western ideas of law as shown in the German Civil Code, for while it did not deal with much that would be covered in one of our civil codes, it also dealt with areas that we do not address.

The Informal Legal System of Traditional China

This was the formal legal system of imperial China. Of course, there was much more to what we would call the legal system of China than the formal system embedded in the Code. For example, though the Code did not deal much with contracts or other commercial matters, the Chinese had an active and sophisticated commerce. They had developed devices similar to negotiable instruments and had a number of business arrangements such as agencies and partnerships of a sort. It was apparently possible to get disputes over these matters resolved by magistrates, but the thrust seems to have been to use other dispute-settling devices such as mediation by village elders and guild procedures. There were even persons who performed many of the functions of our lawyers such as the drafting of complaints and appeals. There was an elaborate body of what we would call customary law that dealt with such matters as *tenancy,* debts, family law, etc. The Chinese would not have thought of such matters as legal, but they are, of course, the sort of thing western law concerns itself with.

Thus the traditional legal culture of China consisted of a formal legal system that was an integral part of the system of government, different from ours in every way, and an informal legal system that dealt with many other matters including much of what we call civil and commercial law. This culture was destroyed by China's contacts with the West in the nineteenth century. Initially the Chinese government refused to let Europeans enter China or do business with it except in an extremely narrow area adjacent to Canton. The Europeans insisted on being permitted to trade inside China and carried on a series of wars to achieve their aims. The most important was the group of wars called the Opium Wars between Britain and China of 1839–1842 (so called because much of what Britain wished to trade was opium). As a result, China was forced to permit foreigners to enter and trade—and to teach the Gospel, since Christian missionaries benefited from the opening. Once they got in, the Europeans did not wish to be subject to Chinese law since they regarded it as barbarous. Accordingly they forced the Chinese to let them have their own courts both for criminal and civil matters. This was the principle called extra-territoriality.

There were, in addition, certain areas in important Chinese cities, notably Shanghai, that were, in effect, self-governing foreign enclaves in China. This meant that in parts of China foreign legal systems were functioning in place of the Chinese. As a result of these events, there was a movement to establish a western legal system in China. The motives were mixed. In part this was perceived as a way of getting rid of extra-territoriality. In part, however, it was the result of the belief by some Chinese intellectuals that European legal systems was superior to their own—that they were modern whereas the Chinese system was backward. Elements of that attitude persist to the present day.

During the last years of the Qing dynasty, there were efforts to draft law codes that reflected a western influence. Chinese began to go abroad to study western law, not only in Europe and America, as might have been expected, but also in Japan, where western-style faculties of law were well established and western codes had been adopted. Western style law schools began to develop in China, and of course western law was applied in the special courts used by foreigners. This process accelerated after 1911.

In that year a combination of forces that had been developing for many years erupted in a revolution which was led by Sun Yat-sen. This destroyed the Empire and established a republic. The apparatus of the governmental system of the Empire did not disappear immediately, any more than the

Emperor himself did. He remained in the Palace for several years. Similarly, the Code continued to be enforced by the magistrates in those areas where they still functioned. But the imperial system crumbled away quite rapidly as the central government ceased to have much power. After a great deal of disorder and civil war, the Kuomintang (KMT), the Chinese National Party, under the leadership of Chiang Kai-shek established nominal control despite the persistence of Japanese incursions, warlords, and an active Communist movement.

The new government presented a curious picture. The governmental institutions and constitution were essentially modeled on those of the United States, modified by Sun Yat-sen to reflect his sense of China's needs and traditions, as well as by his perception of American progressivism of the turn of the century (the initiative, referendum, and recall are embedded in his scheme). The government was run, on the other hand, by a party that was modeled on the Leninist version of a communist party, although it did not share the Marxist ideology of such a party. It was, indeed, engaged in a bitter struggle with the Chinese Communist Party.

As the Republican or Nanking government grew stronger, it attempted to establish a western style legal system, in part to get rid of extraterritoriality. In addition to establishing a system of courts, it also enacted a series of western style codes. These are the so-called Six Laws—the Constitution, the Civil Code, the Criminal Code, the Codes of Civil and Criminal Procedure, and administrative law. These Six Laws served as subject-matter headings under which other laws could be placed. For example, the company law (corporation code) was placed under the heading Civil Code. Like much of western law adopted by China, this idea was taken from Japan. In both countries the compendium of the nation's laws has been called the Six Laws (China following Japan).

These codes were all much influenced by western law. Indeed, they were, for the most part, merely copies of Japanese laws, which in turn were pretty much copies of western codes, usually those of Germany. Legal education was also organized after the European model. Both in the law departments of state universities, such as Nanking Central University, and in private universities (usually western missionary institutions), the western style codes were explicated in the European manner—though sometimes according to the American case method. It is very hard to say what the effect of all this legal activity was. It seems certain that it had no effect on the lives of the vast majority of Chinese who were peasants (over 80 percent), and who were, for the most part, illiterate. That is, they lived the lives that had always been theirs. Mostly concerned with survival, they arranged their family affairs as they always had, made arrangements with or punished local criminals, and tried to avoid the government and its tax collectors as well as the anti-government forces, whether Japanese or domestic, Since many urban Chinese had got used to a western legal system because of their dealings with westerners, and in some cases because they lived under it in the foreign concessions, there was some use of the new western system in civil as well as criminal matters. However, the Nationalist government was never in control of all of China, and in 1937, when the Japanese invaded China, they lost many of the areas and cities that had been theirs. When the war with the Japanese was over in 1945, the civil war between the Nationalists and the Communists, which had never really ceased, broke out in full force. The re-establishment and strengthening of the pre-war legal system was obviously not a very high priority although a new constitution was promulgated. The war was won by the Communists relatively quickly in 1949 and one of the first acts of their new government—the People's Republic of China—was to repeal all the laws of the old Nationalist government.

NOTES AND QUESTIONS

(1) Why does Jones insist that only rules included in the imperial code count as "law"—unlike, say, customary rules regarding contract or property? Do you agree with his distinction? Why (not)?

(2) Jones argues that "the categories of western law are meaningless in China." If this is true, is it even meaningful to insist on definition of what is "law" (as Jones himself does)?

(3) Jones' methodological prescription is that "Chinese law has to be examined on its own terms." What does this mean? Is it possible for an outside observer to comprehend Chinese law "on its own terms"? Why (not)?

(c) From Republican to Maoist Law

Albert H.Y. Chen, *Introduction to the Legal System of the People Republic of China*

(3d ed., 2004), pp. 25–33.

[T]he KMT [Kuomintang, or Nationalist Party] government never established control over the whole of China because of the dual factors of domestic strife between the KMT and the Chinese communists and of military aggression on the part of Japan. (One writer points out that after two decades of KMT rule, basic-level courts had been established in fewer than one-fourth of all counties in China.) The Communist Party of China (hereinafter called the "CPC") was founded in 1921 and had co-operated with the Kuomintang in the "First Revolutionary Civil War" (1923–1927), until [KMT leader] Chiang Kai-shek turned against and persecuted the communists in 1927. Since 1927, the Communist Party had tried to develop its own system of government and law in the rural "revolutionary bases" under its control. For example, in 1931, they formed the Chinese Soviet Republic and promulgated a constitutional outline as well as some laws, largely modeled on enactments in the Soviet Union. A system of "people's courts" was also established. Thus in works by mainland Chinese scholars on modern Chinese legal history, it is generally stated that the "people's democratic legal system" had already been developing for a period of 22 years before the People's Republic of China was established in 1949. This period, which these scholars call the "New Democratic Revolution," included the Second Revolutionary Civil War (1927–1937), the War of Resistance

Against Japan (1937–1945), and the Third Revolutionary Civil War (1945–1949).

The laws introduced in these periods in the revolutionary bases were described in Chinese texts as "anti-imperialist" and "anti-feudal" in nature. Many were directed towards the overthrow of the "feudal landlord class" in the rural areas. Different approaches were adopted in accordance with changing circumstances. At some stages the law provided for the reduction of land rent and interest so as to protect the peasants. At other stages, landlords' land was confiscated and given to the peasants.

The following are examples of some of the most significant laws promulgated in the period of the New Democratic Revolution: Constitutional Outline of the Chinese Soviet Republic, Resolution on Economic Policy, Provisional Establishment Law of the Red Army of Chinese Workers and Peasants, Land Law, Labour Law, Marriage Law, and Regulations for the Punishment of Counter-revolutionaries (these were introduced during the period of the Second Revolutionary Civil War); Constitutional Principles of the Shaanxi–Gansu–Ningxia Border Regions, Regulations on Human Rights and Rights of Property (these belonged to the period of the War of Resistance Against Japan); Declaration of the Chinese People's Liberation Army, Outline of Chinese Land Law, and laws relating to the confiscation of "bureaucratic capital" and the protection of national industry and commerce (these were introduced during the period of the Third Revolutionary Civil War, also known as the War of Liberation). These laws and regulations are said to have provided a foundation for the development of socialist law in China after 1949.

Observers have pointed out that many features of the post–1949 legal system of the People's Republic of China (hereinafter called the "PRC") can be traced back to this pre–1949 period. Examples are differential treatment according to a person's "class background," the use of violence and terror and the arousing of "class hatred" in dealing with "enemies," "reactionaries" or "counter-revolutionaries," the practice of "mass trials" *(gongshen),* the systems of people's assessors, procurators, and adjudicative committees within courts, and the use of conciliation and mediation to settle disputes. Some post–1949 laws also had their origins in the pre-Liberation period. Examples are laws relating to land reform, marriage, labour and the organisation of courts and mediation committees.

We now turn to the history of the formal construction of a new legal system after the establishment of the PRC in October 1949. Looking back at these 54 years, a commonly expressed assessment by mainland Chinese scholars is that while significant achievements have been made, painful mistakes have also been committed at some stages; the journey has not been an easy and straightforward one. An outline of major developments is provided below.

The first step in the construction of the new legal system was the abolition of the existing one which was considered to have supported "semi-feudal and semi-colonial rule." The Instructions on the Abolition of the Collection of the Six Laws of the Kuomintang and the Confirmation of the

Judicial Principles of the Liberated Areas, issued by the Central Committee of the Communist Party of China in February 1949, declared the abolition of all existing laws of the Kuomintang regime. This approach towards existing laws was confirmed by the Common Programme adopted by the Chinese People's Political Consultative Conference in September 1949. The document was jointly produced by the CPC and the "democratic parties" and served as the provisional constitution of the country until 1954.

The period 1949–1953 was regarded by mainland scholars as the first stage in the "transition from New Democracy to Socialism." It was characterised by several mass movements initiated by the Party. Such mass campaigns were conceived at the level of the top Party leadership and involved mobilisation of "the masses" (the people) to act in accordance with particular Party policies. They were considered necessary to enhance the "political awakening" of the masses, to break down the old social order, and to establish in its place a new revolutionary order. During the campaigns, ad hoc "people's tribunals," a kind of revolutionary court, were set up, and "mass trials" were held all over the country. In these trials, the accused were subjected to verbal and physical attacks and cruel and inhuman treatment; they had no right to defend themselves. Feelings of hatred on the part of the assembled crowds were stirred up; they often called for the death penalty and for no mercy for the accused. The number of "class enemies" executed in this way ranged from 800,000 by Mao Zedong's own admission in 1957 to several million as estimated by scholars. Many more were sentenced to long terms of "reform through labour." The practice of mass campaigns and mass accusation and struggle meetings was to become a common feature of Chinese political life until the death of Mao in 1976.

The mass campaigns of the early 1950s included the Land Reform Movement of 1949–1951 to attack the classes of landlords and rich peasants, the 1950 Movement to Suppress Counter-revolutionaries, and the 1952 Movement Against the Three Evils (sanfan) and Movement Against the Five Evils (wufan). The "Three Evils" were corruption, waste and bureaucratism in Party and government organs and in state enterprises. The "Five Evils" were bribery, tax evasion, theft of state property, cheating on government contracts and stealing state economic information, all of which were supposed to be widespread at the time among private industrial and commercial enterprises. Wufan was therefore mainly directed towards the "national bourgeoisie" who at that time were still in control of some industrial and commercial enterprises. In 1952–1953, there was a movement on a smaller scale, known as the Judicial Reform Movement, during which about 80% of judges formerly appointed by the Kuomintang government were removed.

The mass movements were guided in their initial stages by Party policies rather than by any formal legal instruments. However, some of the policies were later codified into law. Important laws introduced before 1954 included the Land Reform Law, the Regulations on the Punishment of Counterrevoluntionaries, the Regulations on the Punishment for Corruption, the Marriage Law, the Trade Union Law, and the Outline for Regional National Autonomy. Other laws and decrees were also issued relating to matters such as state institutions, finance and banking, taxes, trade, industry, labour protection, communications, transport, and culture, though many of the legal rules were of a provisional nature.

The period 1953–1956 was described by Chinese scholars as the second stage in China's transition from "New Democracy" to "Socialism." For legal system building, this was a period of planned development and rapid growth. One foreign observer even described it as, relatively speaking, a "golden age" of law in the PRC. Just as the Soviet economic model was adopted for the PRC's economy, it was also decided to develop a Soviet-style legal system. It should be noted in this regard that in the 1950s, the principle of "socialist legality" was already fairly well-established in the Soviet Union and Eastern Europe, despite the traditional Marxist theory that law would wither away in the ideal communist society. In Soviet legal history, there were indeed periods in which legal ideas were disregarded or even disgraced. For example, in the first half (1928–1936) of the Stalinist period, law was de-emphasized and "the rule of the plan" advocated instead. It was said that what was needed was "proletarian politics," not "proletarian law." The major turning point in modern Soviet legal history came in 1936 when Stalin, in his speech on the new draft constitution of the USSR, called for the stability of laws and emphasized the constitution as the cornerstone of "socialist legality." Vyshinsky's theory was used to legitimise and rehabilitate law, and to confer on it dignity and authority. The previously prevailing view, represented mainly by Pashukanis's theories, was attacked for being a negative and nihilistic theory of law. According to the new orthodoxy, although law represented decay in capitalist societies, law and "revolutionary legality" in the socialist state was the most highly developed form of law and represented the will of the people. Law was therefore a creative force and had a positive role to play in the construction of a socialist society.[1]

A highly significant step in the development of the legal system of the young Chinese republic was the promulgation by the new National People's Congress in 1954 of the first Constitution of the PRC.... When the Constitution Drafting Committee worked on the draft, it used as reference materials the earlier and later constitutions of the Soviet Union and the constitutions of other people's democracies ...

The same first session of the first National People's Congress passed five basic laws relating to the structure of the state: the Organic Laws of the National People's Congress, the State Council, the People's Courts, and the People's Procuratorates, and the Organic Law of Local People's Congresses and Local People's Councils. The framework of the PRC's constitutional and legal system was thus established.

Shortly after the adoption of the Constitution, a climax was reached in what was known as the "socialist transformation" of agriculture, handi-

---

1. See discussion of socialist law and legal theory *supra* at 214–17.

crafts, and capitalist industry and commerce. Rules and regulations relating to these matters were therefore introduced. Other laws and decrees in the economic field were enacted in connection with the implementation of the First Five–Year Plan (1953–1957). In the field of criminal procedure, the Regulations on Arrest and Detention were introduced in 1954. Work on the drafting of basic laws such as the codes of criminal law, civil law and criminal procedure was also begun.

Much progress in legal system building was made in this period, not only in the field of law-making but also in the construction of legal institutions and the development of legal professional practice. The judicial and procuratorial systems were consolidated; basic principles were established such as the equality of citizens before the law, the independent exercise of judicial and procuratorial powers, and handling cases in accordance with the facts and the law; institutions such as public trials, the use of people's assessors in trying cases, the participation of defence lawyers in criminal proceedings and the review of death sentences were developed. At the same time, law schools were set up and legal publications multiplied; lawyers began to practise; legal educational propaganda was promoted among the masses.

Yet it cannot be said that the period 1954–1956 was one of complete peace and unity. In 1955–1956 a second movement against ''counterrevolutionaries'' was launched—the campaign against the ''Hu Feng counter-revolutionary clique,'' which was accompanied by a general campaign against alleged counter-revolutionaries in various sectors. Hu Feng was a poet and literary theorist; he was purged after he presented a report to the Central Committee of the Party criticising the rigid standards imposed by the Party on literary creation and demanding greater literary and artistic freedom. The campaign against Hu marked the beginning of a series of large-scale persecutions of intellectuals in the next two decades.

The Party policy of strengthening the socialist legal system, also called ''the people's democratic legal system,'' was confirmed at the Eighth National Congress of the CPC in September 1956. The Congress took the view that socialism had now been basically established in China, and the main contradiction existing in Chinese society was no longer that between the proletariat and the capitalists, but rather between the people's need for rapid economic and cultural development and the failure of the existing economic and cultural conditions to fulfill that need. The main task ahead was therefore the development of the productive forces of society.

Regarding the legal system, Dong Biwu, President of the Supreme People's Court, admitted in his speech that the existing legal system was weak, and discussed the possible causes for such weakness—the traditional feudal-imperial heritage, the fact that the Chinese communist movement was historically a revolutionary movement with the CPC being an organisation outlawed under the legal system of the KMT regime, and the fact that many cadres in the legal and judicial fields of the PRC were new and inexperienced. The Congress therefore declared that one of the most pressing tasks of the country was to codify the laws systematically, so as to develop a more complete and orderly legal system and to safeguard the democratic rights of the people; every person in the country must understand that as long as he or she did not violate the law, his or her rights as a citizen would be protected; all government agencies and organs must strictly abide by the law, and the public security organs, procuratorates and courts must thoroughly carry out the division of responsibility and mutual restraint called for by the principle of legality. Mainland Chinese scholars now believe that the Eighth Party Congress correctly determined the direction of socialist construction and legal system development.

The year 1957 marked another turning point in PRC history. Earlier, in 1956, the Party had announced the new policy of "letting a hundred flowers bloom and a hundred schools contend," and encouraged all people to help "rectify" the Party by expressing their opinions freely and offering criticisms on matters such as Party policy. This "Hundred Flowers Movement" evoked strong criticisms from intellectuals of the Party's bureaucratic practices and repressive policies, the excesses and abuses in the previous mass campaigns, the defects of the existing legal system, and violations of legality. The Party responded by launching the Anti–Rightist Campaign to purge its critics both inside and outside Party ranks. Hundreds of thousands of people were designated as "rightists" and sent to "rehabilitation" farms for "re-education through labour" without recourse to any formal court procedure.

Many jurists, lawyers and judges, who had been among the more outspoken critics of the regime during the Hundred Flowers Movement, were the victims of the Anti–Rightist Campaign. They were, for example, accused of "using the law to oppose the Party," or attempting to reject Party leadership by stressing the independent administration of justice. After 1957, the prestige of legal institutions such as the courts and the procuratorates fell sharply. Lawyers ceased to practise, the publication of legal materials declined, the law schools switched to teach politics rather than law.Ë Many courts, particularly those at lower levels, were merged with the corresponding public security organs and procuratorates. In 1959, the Ministry of Justice and the organs of judicial administration under it were abolished. All the following principles or practices were denounced as bourgeois and reactionary: judicial independence, procuratorial independence and the role of the procuratorates in legal supervision, equality before the law, the emphasis on procedural regularity, the system of defense lawyers in criminal trials, the principles of no criminal punishment without a violation of a specific law *(nulla poena sine lege),* correspondence or proportionality between a crime and the punishment for it, socialist humanism in penal policy, the heritability of bourgeois legal ideas, the presumption of innocence on the part of the accused, and the idea of human rights. The system of public trial virtually came to an end.

In the early 1960s, however, there appeared to be a slight abatement of the extreme leftist thinking and practices of the late 1950s in the legal as well as economic arenas. For example, in March 1962, Mao Zedong himself declared that there was a need to enact both criminal and civil laws. In

1962–1963, drafting work on the codes of criminal law and criminal procedure, already begun in the 1950s, was recommenced. There were also relative increases in the numbers of legal educational institutions and law students in the country.

The next stage in PRC political and legal history began in 1966 when Mao Zedong launched the "Great Proletarian Cultural Revolution" to purge all "counter-revolutionaries," including the "revisionists" and "capitalist roaders in the Party." Although the precise causes leading to the Cultural Revolution are complex and obscure, a widely held view is that it stemmed from the power struggle at the high echelons of the Party between the "pragmatists" led by Liu Shaoqi, who wanted to modernise China by methods of rational management with emphasis on technical and administrative skills, and the "radicals" led by Mao himself, who stressed the primacy of ideological commitment and revolutionary zeal, and advocated continuous revolution and unending class struggles to achieve the utopian goal of the classless society. By relying on his personality cult and appealing to the anti-bureaucratic instinct of the masses, Mao was able to mobilise millions of Red Guards—mainly students and youths—all over the country to support his cause. The result was three years of civil anarchy and a reign of terror in which, according to some estimates, nearly a 100 million people were subject to persecution or victimisation in one way or another. (According to the official materials published in connection with the subsequent trial of the "Gang of Four," 720,000 persons were directly persecuted during the Cultural Revolution, and 34,000 among them lost their lives.)

During the Cultural Revolution, local Party committees and administrative organs were partly dismantled. Ad hoc groups were set up to carry out Mao's instructions. Many cadres and officials, including those at high levels, were accused of being revisionists or reactionaries, "dragged out" and "struggled against" by the Red Guards. An uncountable number of people were randomly branded as counter-revolutionaries and also "struggled against"; their family members were subject to severe discrimination. And rival factions of Red Guards, each claiming ideological purity and questioning that of others, fought savagely among themselves.

The "struggles" of the Cultural Revolution took the forms of "struggle meetings," arrest, detention, interrogation, torture, imprisonment, exile to labour reform, or execution. The "struggle meetings" were inhuman and cruel; the accused persons would be shouted at, denounced, insulted, and beaten to death or until they confessed that they were counter-revolutionaries. They were often forced to wear dunces' caps and other signs or labels describing their "reactionary crimes"; after the struggle sessions they were usually paraded and further humiliated in the streets. The psychological maltreatment was therefore as severe as the physical; gross violations of the human body and of human dignity occurred at the same time. Many victims could not endure this maltreatment and committed suicide or became insane. Apart from attacking persons, the Red Guards also ransacked homes for evidence of counter-revolutionary activities, confiscated property, and destroyed most books or paintings they found as objects of decadent, bourgeois or feudal culture.

2. AT THE ROOTS OF THE WESTERN LEGAL TRADITION

Aspects either of the common law or of the civil law tradition can be seen at play in the professionalized layer of practically all of today's legal systems in the World. In fact the western legal tradition, understood as foundation of both common law and civil law, displays a highly professionalized style where the lawyer (in his different capacities as a private professional, a judge, and a professor) performs a social role distinct that of the politician or of the priest, for example.

In his indirect participation in the production of social rules, the lawyer is not legitimized by his political power (as the politician is), nor by his religious authority (as the priest is). Rather, he is legitimized by a technical professional knowledge that he or she acquires by the study of the law.

Professional figures like lawyers were absent in ancient Greece. In the western legal tradition they made their first appearance in forums comparable to the modern ones in the context of Roman law, over the period from fifth century B.C. to fifth century A.D. These professional ancestors of ours emerged almost by chance, as a by-product of the procedural needs of the old so-called formulary procedure developed during the "classical" period of Roman Law (roughly from first century BC to through first century AD). Very roughly speaking, private professional lawyers emerged as advisors to a politician (the *Praetor*) in his effort to prepare the instructions (*formula*) to a one man jury (the *iudex*).

The next excerpt illustrates how this legacy survives in a contemporary legal system, that of South Africa. In reading the case you should know that Roman law made a fundamental distinction between the *ius civilis* (considered an immutable structure, strictly formalistic, *ius strictum*, contained in the most ancient sources of the law such as the fifth century BC twelve tables) and the *ius praetorium* or *ius honorarium* (originating in the political platform of an elected politician, much more flexible and adapted to the concrete circumstances). In principle the *ius civilis* needed to be supplemented by the *ius praetorium*. Thus the early jurists were acquainted with both the *ius civilis* and the *ius praetorium* (contained in the enactments (*edicta*) of the different subsequent praetors). Their role was mainly to work out *formulae* capable of presenting the complexities of each different case as a set of clear, spelled-out alternatives, to serve as the basis for a decision by the *iudex*. In the absence of an adversary pleading to reach the issue, such as that later developed in the common law, this exercise required considerable knowledge of the law. For hundreds of years the written and collected opinions of such private citizens, the jurists, accumulated in tremendous numbers. They organized themselves in schools divided on almost any issue. Finally in 533 AD the Emperor Justinian attempted, through a commission led by his aid Tribonianus, a general binding "restatement" of these scholarly opinions including some of them (and discarding many others) in the Digest, the most important part of the *Corpus Iuris civilis*. Justinan's compilation (much cited in the following opinion) can be considered with no doubt the foundational document of the entire western legal tradition , and not only the civil law.

Bank of Lisbon and South Africa Ltd. v. De Ornelas and Another

Supreme Court of South Africa, Appellate Division, 1988.
[1988] 3 S.A. L.R. 580 (AD).

[In 1981, the Bank of Lisbon extended a line of credit ("overdraft facilities") to the Ornelas Fishing Company. This line of credit was secured by deeds of suretyship and mortgage bond which, although given solely to secure the "overdraft," were worded so as to cover other obligations "from what(so)ever source arising." In 1984, the company requested an increase of the line of credit, and the bank refused. The company thereupon discharged its entire indebtedness and closed its account with the bank. It requested cancellation of the deeds of suretyship and the mortgage bonds. The bank refused, relying on a contingent liability of the company based on an entirely different transaction which was the subject of a separate dispute between the parties. The company (respondents herein) then sought cancellation or return of the securities, contending that since it had discharged its principal indebtedness to the appellant, the appellant's conduct in retaining these securities amounted to *dolus generalis*. This is an appeal from a decision in favor of the company.]

* * *

■ JOUBERT J.: This appeal is concerned with the applicability of the *exceptio doli generalis* to written contracts. In our law uncertainty surrounds its very existence as well as the scope of its application. It is therefore necessary to investigate its origin, development, scope and applicability.

Let us commence our investigation with Roman law. Under the *ius civile* as a *ius strictum* liability for fraud was unknown. Nor could liability under *negotia stricti iuris* (formal contracts) be resisted on the ground of fraud. These shortcomings of the *ius civile* were ameliorated and remedied by the praetorian law (*ius honorarium*). In 66 BC Gallus Aquilius, Cicero's colleague in the praetorship, provided in his *edictum praetoris* for two praetorian remedies, viz the *actio doli mali* and the *exceptio doli mali* but in the *Corpus Juris Civilis* they are usually referred to as the *actio doli* and the *exceptio doli*. In *D* 4.3.1.2 *Ulpian*, one of the most eminent Roman jurists who was unfortunately murdered in AD 228, for purposes of the *actio doli* adopted *Labeo's* definition of *dolus malus*. Our interest centres on the *exceptio doli* which became the most important of all exceptions in Roman Law. Since its inception the *exceptio doli* was available in the sphere of contracts (in the Roman sense of *contractus*) to be pleaded by a

defendant in defence to a claim based on a *negotium stricti iuris* such as
stipulation (*stipulatio*) or loan (*mutuum*). [In the Roman Ius *civilis* there
was no general figure of contract but only a variety of contractual figures to
be interpreted strictly] Because the *stipulatio* was the chief contract of
Roman law with widespread use by *cives Romani* throughout the Roman
world it stands to reason that the use of the *exceptio doli* acquired great
importance in mitigating the harshness and inflexibility of the *ius civile* as
a *ius strictum*.

How did a defendant raise the *exceptio doli* as a defence? The answer is
to be sought in the Roman law of civil procedure. In 149 BC the *Lex
Aebutia*, followed by two *leges Juliae*, legitimated the practice of using the
formulary procedure (*per forumulas agere*) which largely superseded the
formal *per legis actionem* procedure. In AD 294 the formulary procedure in
turn made way for the extraordinary procedure (*extraordinaria cognitio*). It
is very noticeable how closely the lifespan of the formulary procedure
coincided with the period of classical Roman law (150 BC to AD 250). To
understand the application of the *exceptio doli*, as expounded in the texts of
Roman jurists from the classical period which have been included in the
Corpus Juris Civilis, I shall very briefly investigate the nature of the
formula as pleading with the *exceptio* as one of its clauses.

The formulary procedure comprised two important stages after the
plaintiff sued the defendant to appear before the praetor (*in ius vacatio*) for
the purpose of obtaining a written *formula*. The first stage took place
before the praetor (*in iure*) with the object of determining the issues
between the parties which were to be embodied in a very rudimentary
manner in the *formula*. The praetor's share in "settling" the *formula* is
fully described by Moyle *Imperatoris Justiniani Institutionum Libri Quatt-
uor* 5th ed. at 643. A *formula* could consist of various clauses such as:
demonstratio (*Gaius* IV 40), *intentio* (*Gaius* IV 41), *adjudicatio* (*Gaius* IV
42), *exceptio* (*Gaius* IV 119) and *condemnatio* (*Gaius* IV 43). In the *intentio*
the plaintiff circumscribed his claim by stating the right or the facts on
which he relied in hypothetical form: "*Si paret* ... 'The plaintiff was
referred to as Aulus Agerius [From *agere* to act the acting part] and the
defendant as Numerius Negidius [from *negare;* the denying part] As to the
vital function of the *intentio* consult Buckland *A Text Book of Roman Law
from Augustus to Justinian* 2nd ed. at 651–2. If the defendant wanted to
rely on a defence other than a bare denial of the plaintiff's claim it was his
duty to disclose the nature of his defence by way of an *exceptio*.'

> The *exceptio* did not deny the *intentio*, but raised a counter-hypothesis,
> "unless something else is true." It was negative in form, introduced by
> *nisi, si non, si nihil* or the like, and thus directed the *iudex* not to
> condemn if the *exceptio* was proved. In the *exceptio* the defendant was
> *in loco actoris* [in the place of the actor] and the burden of proof was
> on him.

(*Buckland* (*op. cit.* at 655).) See also Thomas *The Institutes of Justinian*
(1975) at 316:

An *exceptio* was unnecessary if the defendant intended a direct denial of the claim; it was utilised when he admitted the existence of the claim but wished to adduce further points which would preclude enforcement of the claim. In the parlance of English pleading, an *exceptio* was needed when the defendant wished to confess and avoid.

The plaintiff could meet the *exceptio* by the insertion in the formula of a *replicatio* based on countervailing facts (*Gaius* IV 126). The *condemnatio* was the final clause of the *formula*, instructing the *iudex* to condemn the defendant if the conditions therefor were satisfied, and if not, to absolve him. The *exceptio* was placed between the *intentio* and the *condemnatio*. The entire *formula*, including the *exceptio*, required the praetor's approval. The next step was the appointment of a *iudex*. This done, the praetor reduced the *formula* to writing. On completion of the *formula* the proceedings *in iure* before the praetor terminated. *Litis contestatio* was reached. [and it is in the preparation of the formula in the more complicated cases that the Praetor, a non lawyer, needed the help of the jurists].

The second stage of the formulary procedure then took place before the *iudex* (*in iudicio*), who at the conclusion of the hearing was to pronounce his judgment in accordance with the *condemnatio* of the *formula*. His judgment would be a *iudicium strictum* or a *iudicium bonae fidei* depending on whether the action was *stricti iuris* or *bonae fidei*. Suffice it to say that in a *iudicium stricti iuris* the power of the *iudex* was limited by the strict and literal meaning of the words employed in the *stipulatio* or *mutuum* in question. He was also confined to the *formula* of the parties. He could not consider anything that was not included in the *formula*. The defendant's duty was to ensure that his collateral defences were expressly stated in the *exceptio* clause of the *formula*, otherwise they could not be considered by the *iudex*.

To revert to the *exceptio doli* which a defendant could plead *in iure* as a defence to a claim based on a *negotium stricti iuris*. According to *Gaius* IV 119 the wording of the *exceptio doli* for purposes of the formulary procedure was: *Si in ea re nihil dolo malo Auli Agerii factum sit neque fiat.* (If in that matter nothing has been done or is being done by fraud on the part of Aulus Agerius, i.e. the plaintiff.) . . .

According to the formulary procedure the *exceptio doli generalis* was in substance a briefly-worded plea which, without specifying the factual basis of the defence, enabled the defendant *in iudicio* to rely on facts upon proof of which the plaintiff's claim would be ousted. The facts proved *in iudicio* by the defendant could, for instance, relate to a *pactum de non petendo* [pact not to require payment] entered into between the parties after the conclusion of the *negotium stricti iuris* on which the plaintiff relied as the basis of his claim. The true basis of the defence was not the plaintiff's *dolus generalis* but rather the existence of the *pactum de non petendo* which gave rise to either the *exceptio doli generalis* or the *exceptio pacti conventi* as appears from *D* 44.4.2.4 (*Ulpian*):

> The question also arises whether the defense of fraud avails if someone has unconditionally stipulated for a definite sum because this was so

arranged, but after the stipulation was completed he entered into a pact that the money is not to be claimed for the time being until a specified day. And, indeed, there must be no doubt that the defense of agreed pact can in any event be brought, but also if he wishes to make use of the present defense, nonetheless, he will be able to do so; for it cannot be denied that one who claims contrary to what was agreed is acting with fraud.

(*Watson's* translation.)

The object of the *exceptio doli generalis* was equitable, viz to ameliorate the harshness of a plaintiff's claim based on a *negotium stricti iuris* such as a *stipulatio* or a *mutuum*. *D* 44.4.1.1 (*Paul*). (*Watson's* translation: "The praetor established this defense to the end that a person's fraud should not benefit him through the medium of the civil law but contrary to natural equity"). See also *D* 44.4.12 (*Papinian*): *Qui aequitate defensionis infringere potest, doli exceptione tutus est.* (*Watson's* translation: "A person who can impede an action by the equity of a defense is protected by the defense of fraud.") The *ratio decidendi* of the *iudex* was, however, not based on equity as a yardstick or criterion but on the facts proved by the defendant in the circumstances of the case....

Let us take an example of a *formula*, based on *Gaius* IV 41, 43, 119 and *D* 44.4.2.4, where the plaintiff claimed that the defendant in terms of a *stipulatio* was obliged to pay him 10,000 *sestertii*, whereas the defendant's defence was that the plaintiff subsequently agreed by means of a *pactum* to allow him a year within which to pay the debt and that the year had not yet elapsed. The whole *formula* for an *actio certae creditae pecuniae* with an *exceptio doli clause* as a defence would then read as follows:

Lucius Octavius iudex esto [Will be iudex Mr. Lucius Octavius]

(*Intentio*)

Si paret Numerium Negidium Aulo Agerio sestertium X milia dare oportere [If you believe that Defendant Numerium Negidium owes $ten thousand to plaintiff Aulus Agerius]

(*Exceptio doli*)

Si in ea re nihil dolo malo Auli Agerii factum sit neque fiat

[If in that matter nothing has been done or is being done by fraud on the part of plaintiff Aulus Agerius]

(*Condemnatio*)

Iudex Numerium Negidium Aulo Agerio sestertium X milia condemnato, si non paret absolvito. [Then Iudex you will condemn defendant Numerium Negidium to pay plaintiff Aulus Agerius $10.000, if you do not believe so you shall absolve defendant]

* * *

When the formulary procedure was superseded by the extraordinary procedure at the end of the third century AD the *formula* disappeared with it since there was no *formula* in the *extraordinaria cognitio*. The *excep-*

tiones of classical Roman law were superseded by post-classical *praescriptiones* or objections.... The heading of *Cod* 8.35 is: *De Exceptionibus sive Praescriptionibus*. The *exceptio doli generalis* in post-classical Roman law ceased to function as a praetorian procedural remedy. The word *formula* was extirpated from all texts of the *Digest* with the exception of *D* 47.2.42 pr. The compilers of the *Corpus Juris Civilis*, however, retained the *exceptio*. *Inst* 4 tit 13 substantially preserved the texts of *Gaius* IV 115–24 on the *exceptiones* while extensive use was made in the *Digest* (see for instance some of the titles of *Digest* book 44) of excerpts from the writings of Roman jurists dating from the classical period. This method has been responsible for great confusion. See Van Warmelo *Die Oorsprong en Betekenis van die Romeinse Reg* 2nd ed. para. 105(*e*) and *Buckland* (*op cit* at 666–7):

> "Much of the old terminology remained. We still hear of *exceptio*, *replicatio*, *litis contestatio*, interdict, but the terms have changed significance. When Justinian said that an *exceptio doli* was available he meant that *dolus* might be pleaded and would (in general) bar the claim; he did not mean that it was pleaded in the old way."

A defendant, desirous of raising the *exceptio doli generalis* as a defence, would in his plea (*libellus contradictionis*) by way of confession and avoidance on the one hand admit the existence of the plaintiff's right of action as set out in the latter's *libellus conventionis* but he would on the other hand plead the facts on which he claimed to have a countervailing right of defence.... Obviously, the *ratio decidendi* of the judgment of the *iudex* was not based on equity but on whether or not the defendant established the facts of his case as pleaded. There was no room in the extraordinary procedure for the praetor's formulation of the *exceptio doli* as pleaded in the formulary procedure. Moreover, until the time of Emperor Diocletian (AD 284–305) the *ius honorarium* and the *ius civile* continued to exist side by side but thereafter they were blended into one system. Justinian united them but unfortunately traces of their different origins still appear in the *Corpus Juris Civilis*....

In concluding my investigation of Roman law I feel compelled to emphasise the importance of the fact that the disappearance of the formulary procedure also entailed the termination of the use of the *formula* of the *exceptio doli* (which comprises both the *exceptio specialis* and the *exceptio doli generalis*) as a technical term of pleading. The great significance of the extraordinary procedure was that it marked the first stage in the development of our modern system of pleading in actions.... A defendant, desirous of relying on what amounted to an *exceptio doli generalis* as a defence, had, as I explained *supra*, to mention specifically in his plea the facts on which he relied to resist the plaintiff's claim, e.g. reliance on the existence of a *pactum de non petendo*.... Where a defendant, for instance, relied on the existence of a *pactum de non petendo*, that was the real basis of his defence and not the *exceptio doli generalis*.... If his defence was upheld he really established that the plaintiff had not established a cause of action....

[The author then engages in a highly scholarly discussion of the history and changing nature of the *exceptio doli generalis* through the history of medieval and early modern law and concludes that while the terminology survived it does not no longer serves a general supplemental function while being instead incorporated in the general principles and terminology of civilian private law]

The conclusion is inevitable. The *exceptio doli generalis*, in my judgment, was never part of Roman–Dutch law. . . . Nor can I find any evidence of the existence of a general substantive defence based on equity. This is not surprising inasmuch as the Dutch Courts, unlike the English Courts until the Judicature Act 1873 became operative in 1875, did not administer a system of equity as distinct from a system of law. Roman–Dutch law is itself inherently an equitable legal system. In administering the law the Dutch Courts paid due regard to considerations of equity but only where equity was not inconsistent with the principles of law. Equity could not override a clear rule of law. That is also the position of our Courts as regards their equitable jurisdiction. * * * Moreover, I cannot find any support in Roman–Dutch law for the proposition that in the law of contract an equitable exception or defence, similar in effect to the *exceptio doli generalis*, was utilised under the aegis of *bona fides*. . . .

All things considered, the time has now arrived, in my judgment, once and for all, to bury the *exceptio doli generalis* as a superfluous, defunct anachronism. *Requiescat in pace*. . . .

It follows that the appeal should succeed. * * *

Rabie, ACJ, Hefer, JA and Grosskopf, JA concurred in the judgment of Joubert, JA.

■ JANSEN, JA. * * * The roots of the *exceptio* in its modern guise must be found in the treatment of the subject in the *Digest* title *De Doli Mali et Metus Exceptione* (*D* 44.4), where *inter alia* the following is found (at *D* 44.4.1.1): "The praetor established this defence to the end that a person's fraud should not benefit him through the medium of the civil law but contrary to natural equity" (*The Digest of Justinian* (Mommsen and Krueger ed.), *Watson's* translation vol. 4 at 631). Seen as a substantive defence the *exceptio* would imply that in appropriate circumstances a Court could grant relief where the strict law would have an effect *contra naturalem aequitatem*, and in so doing it would modify the law. Broadly speaking this is what happened in Rome and in the course of time new defences developed as a result (e.g. *exceptio non numeratae pecuniae* etc.). Critics of the survival of the *exceptio* would have one believe that the defences so developed constituted a *numerus clausus* to this day. This would deny the possibility of the law being adapted according to the exigencies of the times and in the light of the changing mores and concepts of fairness and proper conduct. It must be emphasised that seen as a substantive defence the *exceptio* is no longer a procedural device, as it once was in the hands of the praetor to enable the objective standard of *bona fides* to be applied to *negotia* which would otherwise have given rise to *judicia stricti* juris.

It is said that the recognition of the *exceptio doli* in this sense would be an infraction of the freedom of contract and of the principle that *pacta servanda sunt*—that it would lead to legal uncertainty. Freedom of contract, the principles of *pacta servanda sunt* and certainty are not however absolute values. They did not prevent the modification in England of the common law by equity, which *inter alia* gives relief against "unconscionable" bargains. . . . In the United States a somewhat similar development has taken place. The Uniform Commercial Code contains provision against "unconscionable" contracts (UCC para 2.302) and this has, according to Calamari and Perillo *Contracts* 2d 1970 para 9–39 "entered the general law of contracts." They cite the *Restatement of the Law of Contract* 2d (1979) vol. 2, para 208:

> If a contract or term thereof is unconscionable at the time the contract is made a court may refuse to enforce the contract, or may enforce the remainder of the contract without the unconscionable term, or may so limit the application of any unconscionable term as to avoid any unconscionable result.

The authors in para 9–40 point out:

> "Unconscionable" is a word that defies lawyerlike definition. It is a term borrowed from moral philosophy and ethics. As close to a definition as we are likely to get is "that which affronts the sense of decency."

They also say in para 9–37 that the legislative purpose of the section (viz of the UCC) is illuminated by the following language in the official comment:

> This section is intended to make it possible for the courts to police explicitly against contracts or clauses which they find to be unconscionable. In the past such policing has been accomplished by adverse construction of language, by manipulation of the rules of offer and acceptance or by determinations that the clause is contrary to public policy or to the dominant purpose of the contract.

* * * [Under South African law] the Court may reduce a stipulated penalty "to such an extent as it may consider equitable in the circumstances" (Act 15 of 1962, s 3—reinstating the common law). Not only contracts against public interest or public policy are subject to control by the Court, but also those offending the *boni mores*. In this field reference must be made to the sense of justice ("regsgevoel") of the community, as is the case in delict, where it is now recognised that there is no *numerus clausus* of actionable wrongs.

Perforce our Courts must in a variety of cases work with the prevailing *mores* and the sense of justice of the community as a norm. In principle there can be no real objection in the case of the *exceptio* to determine an objective standard of *aequitas* along similar lines.

In discussing the *exceptio* reference is sometimes made to its fate in German law. It is said that at the time of the introduction of the BGB it was a dead letter. However, the true position seems to be that it was considered obsolete because its underlying principles were absorbed into the requirement of *bona fides* (cf BGB art 242).[1] . . .

The existence of the *exceptio doli* as a defence based on equity is demonstrated by the decisions of this Court; moreover, our lower courts have overwhelmingly assumed for many years such a defence to be available. Although the underlying principle is to be traced back to the *Digest* it seems, in view of the aforegoing, to be of no crucial import whether the *leges* dealing with the exceptio were received in Holland or fell into disuse. However, it is significant that Groenewegen in his *De Legibus Abrogatis*, where he deals with D 44.4, does not state the relevant *leges* to be inapplicable. Nor does Voet (*ad Pandectas*) do so under this title, although he is careful to state where the modern law differs in other instances. . . .

The *exceptio doli generalis* constitutes a substantive defence, based on the sense of justice of the community. As such it is closely related to the defences based on public policy (interest) or *boni mores* (cf *Ismail v. Ismail* 1983 (1) SA 1006 (A) at 1025F–1026C). Conceivably they may overlap: to enforce a grossly unreasonable contract may in appropriate circumstances be considered as against public policy or *boni mores*. By the nature of things no general definition can be given of what would constitute *dolus*. In *Zuurbekom Ltd v. Union Corporation Ltd* 1947 (1) SA 514 (A) an example is to be found: where the enforcement of a "remedy by the plaintiff would cause some great inequity and would amount to unconscionable conduct on his part" (*per* Tindall JA at 537). However, each case must be judged on its own facts in the light of the sense of justice of the community.

The facts in the present case present a number of salient features: the respondents were suppliants for an overdraft (or its increase); they had not equal bargaining power with the Bank; standard forms with standard terms were used by the Bank; the Bank stipulated for security far beyond its needs; the respondents never actually contemplated that the security would cover anything but the overdraft. These facts go beyond mere unreasonableness of the contract *per se* (cf. *Paddock Motors v. Igesund* 1976 (3) SA 16 (A)). In my view it would offend the sense of justice of the community to allow the Bank to use the strict wording of the documents to retain the securities after payment of the overdraft. I find support for this in the views expressed by Botha J in *Rand Bank Ltd. v. Rubenstein* (*supra*) and that of the Judge *a quo* in the present matter.

I would dismiss the appeal.

---

3. Early Professionalism in the Western Legal Tradition. The Legacy of Justinian

The previous decision shows how notions and concepts developed by the first known class of professional jurists, those employed to advise the Praetor in his "setting in action" the formulary procedure, have survived

---

1. A translation of the German Civil Code (BGB) § 242 appears *infra* p. 571, note 20.

well beyond the decline of the Roman formulary procedure. Similarly, it has survived well beyond the final fall of the Roman Empire. The idea that reducing the complexities of the life into relatively simple reproducible legal concepts is a highly professionalized business to be carried on by learned professionals.

But who were these early ancestors of western lawyers?

Classical Rome knew no professional judges. Its leading lawyers were the jurists whose writings shaped the civil law and are preserved in Justinian's Digest, and the orators [eloquently attempting to persuade the Iudex] whose forensic performances survive mainly through Cicero's detailed accounts of his own forensic efforts. Cicero's *Brutus* is mainly a sketch of the leading forensic orators; Pomponius offers a thumbnail sketch of the leading jurists.[1] These lists are almost mutually exclusive, for in the classical period, jurists mainly disdained forensic oratory. Nor, apparently, did they have a high opinion of the legal knowledge of forensic orators. *Nihil hoc ad ius: ad Ciceronem*, [nothing of that should go to the law. It should rather go to Cicero] is what Cicero reports his friend Aquilius Gallus (a jurist) as saying when someone brought him a question of fact. (Cicero, in turn, belittled the competence of eminent jurists as compared to that of persons with "continued practice and application" in specialized fields of public importance.)[2]

Students should keep in mind that this internecine rivalry occurred at the top of the legal profession. Both jurists and orators belonged to the senatorial or (latterly) also the equestrian classes of society. Litigants could be represented in court by any honest man,[3] including a freedman, acting as a *procurator* (hence "proctor" in admiralty and in ecclesiastical courts more than a millennium later). Notaries were as yet simply the scriveners who wrote instruments known as *tabellae*. As *tabelliones*, they were to mature into a separate profession—although not, in Roman days, to one enjoying *ex officio* the numerous "privileges and immunities" to which advocates were entitled.

About 250 AD, Roman jurists stopped writing authoritative texts on the civil law—perhaps, as has been suggested recently, because everything that could be said on that subject had already been said.[4] In any event, the late Empire saw the emergence of an organized bar at major imperial courts, called *consortia* of *advocati* or *togati*, limited in number and protected by imperial privilege—including, incidentally, preferred admission of sons of advocates into what had become a closed profession. Admission to a *consortium* of advocates at an imperial court had to be

---

1. Cicero, Brutus; Dig. 1, 2, 35–53 (Pomponius). References to Roman-law sources are given and explained in editors' note e to Demerara Turf Club v. Wight, *infra* at 323.

2. Cicero, Pro Balbo 45.

3. Women could not postulate (appear in court or before public officials) on behalf of others: Dig. 3, 1, 1, 5 (Ulpian). As there narrated, this disability went back to "a shameless woman called Carfania who by brazenly making applications and annoying the magistrate gave rise to (its incorporation into the Praetorian) edict."

4. A. Watson, The End of Roman Juristic Writing, 29 Israel L. Rev. 228 (1995).

earned nevertheless by demonstration of professional qualification as well. This included, by 460 AD at the latest, successful demonstration that the candidate was instructed in the professional knowledge of the law—*peritia iuris instructus*.[5]

Where, then, was such knowledge obtained? Once again, caution is indicated by the sparsity of sources, but it seems reasonably clear that by the fifth century at the latest, professional instruction in law was obtainable at law schools in Rome, Constantinople and (for a time most prominently) at Beryt (Beyrouth). Unlike the jurists of the classical period, those teaching at the law schools of the late Empire do not appear to have been creative legal authors and authorities, but they were authorities, nevertheless. For one thing, as *iuris periti* [knowledgeable in the law] or *doctores*, they passed on the professional qualifications of advocates. Secondly (but perhaps not secondarily) some of them ranked at the pinnacle of official society. A highly influential civil law tradition in much more recent times is traceable to the few surviving records relating to fifth-century advocates and professors, most of which have just been cited. Advocates become members of the legal profession only upon demonstrating sufficient legal knowledge, acquired from professors at law schools (now law faculties). Both advocates and professors are members of a learned profession, but professors (who teach and examine prospective advocates) are more learned, and they claim (and they usually are accorded) a much higher rank in the social and official hierarchy. The fifth-century vicar presided over a diocese, as does the bishop whose title when sitting judicially is *ordinarius*—as is that of the German full professor (and, as "Ordinary," of Scottish Court of Session judges of first instance).

One direct consequence of the privileged status of Latin and of law school-taught learned lawyers at a few administrative centers was the entrenchment of the division of the forensic legal profession into a "higher" and a "lower" branch: advocates at the imperial courts, and procurators at the lower ones. The procurators (originally the personal agents or representatives of an absent litigant) became pleaders in lower courts, and their inferior status was reinforced by their need to consult advocates learned in the (Roman) law (and fluent in Latin) in complicated cases. On the non-litigious side, changes in the law of evidence and in the formal requirements for important transactions (especially donations) combined with the need for documentation by a largely illiterate and monolingual population to enhance the importance of the *tabellio*, who turned from a scrivener into a notary. Although the notarial profession as such was not organized into a guild until the Byzantine period, Justinian enacted no less than three *novellae constitutiones* to regulate the notaries' art of passing public instruments in the appropriate form and manner. His other main contribution to the development of the legal profession (which was to bear fruit much later) was the minute regulation of the law school curriculum, divided into five one-year segments with specific texts assigned to each.

---

5. Cod. 2, 7, 11 (460).

Most of the concepts produced and utilized by these early professionals, transformed and adapted through time and space by their successors, have survived to our days and make up the toolkit of the western lawyer both in the civil law and in the common law tradition.

Occasionally, when the spontaneous aggregation of opinions developed by jurists and the inevitable interpretive contradictions thus produced reach unmanageable limits, the political power attempts to re-capture control of the legal order. This happened a first time in the thirties of the sixth century AD when a Christian Roman Emperor, holding Court in Constantinople, (modern-day Istanbul) charged a committee with the high task of producing a general codification of the civil law as accumulated up to his day. In the record time of three years the "Body of the Civil Law" was offered to the Emperor.

Justinian's *Corpus Juris Civilis,* the most influential legislative pronouncement of all time, is divided into four parts:

(a) The *Institutiones,* four books written in textbook style, but given the force of law. This part reproduced with some changes a study aid produced by Gaius, a quite mysterious classic era law teacher (possibly a slave), whose "nutshell" enacted as a preliminary part of the *Corpus Iuris,* not only framed the mind of early Roman students of law but also makes up the fundamental framework of much of the following legal developments in the West and, through legal transplants, much beyond.

(b) The *Digesta* or *Pandecta,* the longest and most important part of the whole work, arranged in 50 books and constituting a compilation of excerpts (edited and sometimes revised by Justinian's commission) from the opinions and writings of the 38 most famous Roman jurists of prior centuries, especially Ulpianus, Paulus, Papinianus, Gaius and Modestinus.

(c) The *Codex,* a compilation of prior imperial decrees in twelve books, again edited and in part revised by Justinian's commission under the chairmanship of Tribonianus.

(d) The *Novellae,* a collection of decrees and revisions issued by Justinian after 534 AD, i.e., after the three original parts of the work were completed.

Note that a "book" corresponded to a papyrus roll capable of being handled conveniently by the reader—at most about fifty pages in modern print. In the 1954 reprint of the Krueger–Mommsen edition of the *Corpus Iuris Civilis,* the four books of the Institutes come to 56 pages, and the fifty books of the Digest to 926 in small double-column print.[6] Keep in mind that

---

6. Standard texts with English translations currently in use are P. Birks & G. McLeod, Justinian's Institutes (1987), and Alan Watson ed., The Digest of Justinian (4 vols., 1985). For a recent account, see D. Pugsley, On Compiling Justinian's Digest, 11 Oxford Legal Stud. 325 (1991), 13 J.Legal Hist. 209 (1992), 14 J.Legal Hist. 94 (1993), and 20 Syracuse J.Int'l L. & Comm. 161

the codex (or bound book) replaced the papyrus scroll in the third century AD, and that what then became known as the *Corpus Iuris Civilis* did not appear in print until the sixteenth.

It is important to note that the continuous importance of Justinian's codification of Roman law has been quite remarkably disconnected from the actual force of law of the *Corpus Iuris*. Its official force kept declining as the Eastern Roman Empire eroded from the East and from the West due to mighty competitors. Because both the German Tribes and the Arab (and later Turkish) Muslims opted for the principle of personality and not of territoriality, the *Corpus Iuris* was incrementally transformed into a form of vulgar law, possibly being applied here and there during the high middle ages. Nevertheless, as a single Latin language document, it disappeared for centuries during the "Dark Ages" when throughout the once highly-developed space of the Roman Empire, woods, forests and wild beasts recaptured much of the lost ground. For centuries in Europe (while Arab populations where thriving and offered, among other things, remarkably sophisticated legal work) it was only the humble activity of monks busy in their remote convents to copy the sacred scriptures that prevented western culture from final illiteracy.

The "rediscovery" of the manuscript in Pisa coincided with the early European renaissance of the early eleventh century when a highly superstitious culture woke up after realization that the biblical prediction of the year 1000 as the date of the end of the World has not been accurate. And it was a scholarly tradition, certainly not the might of a political authority (in most places absent), that has guaranteed the continuous influence of Justinian's legal masterpiece. Students should be aware that shortly after Justinian's codification (533–563 AD) knowledge of learned Roman law based on familiarity with the teachings of classical Roman lawyers became extinct in the Western Empire (mainly today's Italy, France, and Spain). Roman legal forms and the Latin language survived in Italian municipal administration, notarial practice, and especially the Church—to what extent is still debated.[7] The "second life" of Roman law, starting with the rediscovery of the Digest in the late eleventh century and law teaching at Italian universities in the twelfth found the notarial profession in place. Law teachers at the universities quickly identified with the Roman jurists, emulating the *responsa* of the latter with *consulta*, or learned opinions, to counsel in litigated cases as well.[8] The "learned" lawyers acquired their legal knowledge, in Latin, in multi-year university courses following Justinian's curriculum but now including Canon law. It was this latter legal

(1994). Cf. C. H. Roberts & T. C. Seat, The Birth of the Codex (1983).

7. See especially Ugo Gualazzini, L'Insegnamento del Diritto in Italia durante l'Alto Medievo, in Ius Romanum Medii Aevi Part I5ba a (1974); Paolo Frezza, L'Influsso del Diritto Romano Giustinianeo nelle Formule e nella Prassi in Italia, *id.* I, 2, c e e (1974) (with discussion of notaries at 99–108); and most recently Charles M. Radding, The Origins of Medieval Jurisprudence, Pavia and Bologna 850–1150 (1988).

8. Heinrich Gehrke, Die privatrechtliche Entscheidungsliteratur Deutschlands 167–213 (1975), lists well over one hundred collections of consilia by professors at German universities alone.

system which provided the first coherent scheme of hierarchical juridical organization and legal procedure. A recent study places the emergence of a practicing profession of university-trained advocates in ecclesiastical courts in the latter part of the thirteenth century, with emphasis on the year 1274, which also is the date of enactment of the first French Royal ordinance relating to advocates.[9]

It is likely that this profession, and ecclesiastical court practice generally, provided the prevailing model for civil lawyers. Surprisingly at least to the uninitiated, it did so even in England, where admiralty lawyers were divided, well into the nineteenth century, into advocates educated in the civil law at Oxford or Cambridge and proctors (a contraction of procurators) or pleaders of a more humble practical background. This parallel should not be stretched too far, however, because the English notary (although clearly of canon or civil law progeny) was not a major factor in this scheme (or, for that matter, in English law generally).[10]

Demerara Turf Club, Ltd. v. Wight

Judicial Committee of the Privy Council, 1918.
[1918] A.C. 605.

[Roman–Dutch law is usually defined as the system of law which prevailed in The Netherlands (or, more precisely, in the province of Holland) from the middle of the fifteenth century until the age of codification. The substantive private law of The Netherlands was codified in 1838. In those overseas territories, however, which the Dutch had lost prior to 1838 (including the former Dutch possessions in South Africa, Ceylon and British Guiana), these nineteenth century Dutch codes were never introduced; to the extent that the new Sovereign retained the prior law in those territories, it was preserved in the form of uncodified Roman–Dutch law. The three Dutch settlements later united as British Guiana were captured in 1803 and ceded to Britain in 1814. The then existing system of law (i.e. Roman–Dutch law) was retained for over a century; but in 1916, after the commencement of the present action, the civil law of British Guiana Ordinance abrogated most of the Roman–Dutch law, except that relating to real property and intestate succession.]

9. James A. Brundage, The Rise of Professional Canonists and the Development of the Ius Commune, 112 ZZS Kan. 26, 42–43 (1995). In 1274, the Second Council of Lyon adopted an oath of office for advocates and procurators in ecclesiastical tribunals. See also, by the same author, The Medieval Advocate's Profession, 6 Law & Hist. Rev. 493 (1988), and The Profits of the Law: Legal Fees for University–Trained Advocates, 32 Am. J. Legal Hist. 1 (1988), and for further medieval canon law background, James J. Hogan, Judicial Advocates and Procurators, An Historical Synopsis and Commentary 32–51 (Catholic University of America, Canon Law Studies No. 133, 1941). For France, see Jean Pierre Royer, Histoire de la Justice en France 145–53 (1995).

10. For full discussion, see C. W. Brooks, R. H. Helmholz & P. G. Stein, Notaries Public in England Since the Reformation (1991).

The judgment of their Lordships was delivered by

■ Sir Walter Phillimore. The plaintiff in this case, the present respondent [Wight], brought an action to enforce specific performance of an alleged contract of sale whereby he contended that he became the purchaser of certain real estate in the Colony of British Guiana which was the property of the defendant company.

The Chief Justice of British Guiana, Sir Charles Major, gave judgment for the defendant company, dismissing the action with costs. On appeal the Supreme Court, Berkeley and Hill JJ., reversed the decision of the Chief Justice, and ordered the defendant company to transport and deliver to the plaintiff the property in dispute on payment of the sum of 16,005 dollars and one-half the costs of transport,[1] and ordered the defendant company to pay the plaintiff's costs in both Courts. The company appeals from this decision.

The story is a short one. Some matters were controverted in the evidence; but the facts as found by the Chief Justice, and not disputed in the Court of Appeal or before their Lordships, are as follows: The company was in liquidation, and one Cannon, the liquidator, who was also a licensed auctioneer, obtained leave from the Court to sell the real property of the company, 55 acres of land known as Bel Air Park with the buildings thereon. Cannon was to be the auctioneer, making no charge for his services.

The sale was advertised as a sale at public auction by the liquidator in the grand stand of the club. On the appointed day, December 4, 1914, the auctioneer began the proceedings by reading out the conditions of sale, which were as follows:—

"Conditions on which the undersigned will offer for sale at public auction on Friday, the 4th December, 1914, at 1 o'clock P.M., on the premises (in the grand stand), by order of Mr. N. Cannon (as liquidator of the Demerara Turf Club, Limited), 55 acres of land known as Bel Air Park, with all the buildings, erections, fixtures, and fittings thereon:— Article 1: The purchaser or purchasers shall provide good and sufficient securities to the satisfaction of the auctioneer, who shall sign these conditions of sale along with the said purchaser or purchasers, and shall be bound as they do hereby bind and oblige themselves jointly and severally with such purchaser or purchasers to pay the purchase-money. Article 2: Payment of the purchase-money shall be paid to the auctioneer as follows: 10 per cent. in cash on the knock of the hammer, and the balance on the passing of the transport. Article 3: The purchaser or purchasers shall pay to the auctioneer in cash on the knock of the hammer the church and poor money payable on the sale. Article 4: Possession will be given on the passing of the transport, the cost, including the revenue stamp, to be divided between the seller and the purchaser. Article 5: Two or more persons bidding at the same

---

1. To "transport" means to convey the property. It is a literal translation of overdracht (Dutch) = Übertragung (German), usually translated as "transfer." See also R. W. Lee, An Introduction to Roman–Dutch Law 139 (1953). In New York, the term "transport" was used in a similar sense during the Dutch period.

time, or any dispute arising, the auctioneer reserves to himself the right of deciding and settling the same in such manner as he may think fit.''

A bid of 15,000 dollars was made, and a second bid of 15,005 dollars. Then came a third bid of 16,000 dollars, and then the plaintiff bid 16,005 dollars. No further bid was made. Cannon then said, ''I am sorry, gentlemen, but I cannot sell at that price.'' The plaintiff says that he said, ''The Turf Club is mine,'' using consciously or unconsciously a phrase common at Dutch auctions by way of a descending scale. If he did say so Cannon did not hear him; and without more being said the company dispersed. There was some correspondence afterwards, and then the plaintiff brought his action on March 23, 1915.

It is to be noted that there was, on the one hand, no intimation either beforehand or at the auction that there was a reserved price, or that the vendor reserved the right to bid; nor, on the other hand, was there any intimation that the sale was to be without reserve, or that the property would be knocked down to the highest bidder.

In these circumstances their Lordships have to determine what was the nature of the business which was entered upon when this property was put up for sale.

It is contended on behalf of the plaintiff that this matter is concluded by law; that by the Roman–Dutch law[2] which rules, or at the time ruled, in British Guiana,[3] the auctioneer who puts up property for sale thereby makes an offer, that each bidder is an acceptor, that by each bid a provisional contract is made, one liable to be displaced or superseded by a higher bid, but forming unless so displaced or superseded a contract binding on both parties. Alternatively the contention is expressed in this way: that the auctioneer when he puts up property for auction tacitly promises to accept the highest bid, and is bound to accept it, and that his verbal or physical acceptance is a mere formality which he is bound to give. Hill J. apparently decided for the plaintiff on both grounds; Berkeley J. probably on the second only.

It is to be observed that this is not an action for damages for not accepting a bid or for withdrawing the property from sale. It is an action which proceeds upon the assumption that there was a sale. For the plaintiff, therefore, to succeed, either the bidder must be an acceptor, or the auctioneer's acceptance of the last bid must be a mere formality.

It is contended on behalf of the defendant company that there is no settled rule of Roman–Dutch law to the effect asserted by the plaintiff, and

---

2. See R. W. Lee, An Introduction to Roman–Dutch Law 2 (1953); R. Feenstra & R. Zimmermann, eds., Das holländisch-römische Recht, Fortschritte des Zivilrechts im 17. und 18. Jahrlundert (1992).

3. See M. Shahabuddeen, The Legal System of Guyana 202–203 (1973). As to post-independence developments in the legal system of this former British colony, see *id.*, passim, and J. N. Hazard, Guyana's Alternative to Socialist and Capitalist Legal Models, 16 Am.J.Comp.L. 507 (1968).

no rules of Roman–Dutch law which apply to such auctions as this was, and that in any case, this being a voluntary sale, the auctioneer could make his own arrangements, and that the nature of the business for which he was arranging was sufficiently indicated by the use of the phrase "knock of the hammer" in the second and third of the conditions of sale, which showed that the bidder was to be deemed the offerer and the auctioneer, if he so willed, the acceptor. It is no doubt true that the auctioneer could make his own terms on which he proposed to conduct the sale; but it is also true that if there was a silence as to any term or a doubt what the term was, it is material to know what is the underlying law, or the law which would prevail in the absence of any special term.

Their Lordships therefore proceed to examine whether there is any rule of Roman–Dutch law applying to auctions of this nature, and if so what its effect is. All the judges in the Courts below seem to have thought that there is a rule of Roman–Dutch law upon this point, but they have differed in their view of its effect. There are no decided cases which can be quoted as authorities and there is no Code, Statute, or Ordinance. The law has to be extracted from the works of writers of authority. These start by referring to the Roman law.

In the Roman law itself, though sales by auction and the letting of tolls by auction were well known, there is no direct guidance to be found. There are references to auctions, but no rules of law, to be found in the Digest. In the Code there are two passages (lib. 10, tit. 3, s. 4; lib. 11, tit. 31, s. 1); but these relate to necessary or judicial sales, and, moreover, have no bearing on the point in question.

The writers on Roman–Dutch law endeavour to help themselves out by the analogy of the Roman law as to sales by *addictio in diem*.[4] This analogy is noticed in the judgments of the judges in the Court below; but as it was agreed at the Bar before their Lordships, is a misleading analogy. It is unnecessary, as there was this agreement, to explain at length why no assistance can be got from the analogy, and why, indeed, confusion will arise if it is attempted to bring sales by auction under the law as to sales by *addictio in diem*. The writers on Roman–Dutch law also avail themselves of the writings of commentators of other European nations, such as Bartolus, who was an Italian, and Choppinus, who was a Frenchman from Anjou. How far they can be used as authorities on Roman–Dutch law may be doubted.[5] They, too, found themselves on the law as to sales by *addictio in diem*.

---

4. "An agreement between buyer and seller giving the latter the right to declare the sale annulled, if, within a certain time, he received an offer of a higher price (adiectio) for the object sold. In such a case the first buyer had the possibility to increase his bid and to keep the thing.—D. 18.2." A. Berger, Encyclopedic Dictionary of Roman Law, in Transactions of the American Philosophical Society, N.S., Vol. 43, Part 2, at 348 (1953).

5. Is this doubt well-founded? See the debate between Justices Joubert and Jansen in the Bank of Lisbon case, *supra* at 311, and the excerpt from R. Zimmermann's article on Roman–Dutch Jurisprudence following that case.

The authority principally relied upon in the Courts below and before their Lordships is Matthaeus, an author of much learning and repute, and quoted as an authority by later writers who are accepted authorities on Roman–Dutch law. He wrote a treatise on auctions. His book De Auctionibus was published at Utrecht in 1653. His work is founded on the Roman law and the European commentators upon it from Bartolus onwards. He also makes frequent reference to local Ordinances as precedents.

Unfortunately, however, for its value as a guide in the present case, the principal scope of the work is to treat of public (so called) or necessary sales; that is, sales made under the authority of a Court of justice, either of confiscated property or of property taken in execution of a civil judgment. Private or voluntary sales are matters of subsidiary treatment only. This is stated on the title page, and in bk. i, chapter 4, ad finem. And there is another reason. Voluntary sales by auction, using the word "auction" for a sale by increasing bids and "reduction" (as it will be convenient to do) for sales by decreasing bids, were, and apparently still are, unknown in Holland, except as tentative or provisional transactions. Two classes of competitive sales are known in Holland. Necessary sales are in the ordinary form of auction sales, but at the close of the day no contract binding the vendor is created between him and the highest bidder; for all the authorities, including Matthaeus, are agreed that further offers may be, and, indeed, must be, taken till the last moment when the decree of the Court is made, till the seal of the Court has been lifted from the wax, as it is picturesquely expressed.

As to voluntary sales, those at any rate of land, they take two days. The first day there is an auction, and the highest bidder receives a "treckgelt" or "strijckgelt," "premium quod datur augenti pretium," as Matthaeus calls it (lib. 1, chapter 1, s. 6, and chapter 9, s. 11). In consideration of this "premium" [presumably a modest sum of money] the bidder is provisionally bound, but the vendor is not bound. On the second day the vendor makes a starting price, usually one-third higher than the highest bid of the previous day, and then descends (the process being called "afstach") till some bidder calls out "Mine" (see "Matthaeus," lib. 1, chapter 12, s. 1). This process is so prevalent that a verb has been coined, "mijnen" "to mine," meaning to bid, and bidders of all sorts are called "mijnders" (lib. 2, chapter 2, s. 5). Hence, too, comes the English phrase a "Dutch auction." The vendor is apparently not bound to keep reducing, but can withdraw at any stage. If, however, he chooses, he can descend to the level reached by the highest bid at the first day's sale, and if no one else bids, compel the bidder of the first day to complete his bargain.

Though Matthaeus refers but slightly and allusively to this practice, he certainly knew of it. But the difficulty is to fit those observations of his, on which the plaintiff and the judges in the Supreme Court rely, to either form of competitive sale. Necessary sales are by way of auction, but it is clear that the highest bidder at the auction cannot claim to have bought the property, though he may be bound to complete his purchase. In voluntary sales the first step is by way of auction, but the highest bidder cannot claim to have bought the property, though he may in a certain event be bound to complete his purchase. During the second stage of reduction it may be that the vendor offers the property at every price which he names. If the observations of Matthaeus on which reliance is placed are intended for a sale by reduction, they have no application to the case before their Lordships. If they contemplate a sale by auction, they are theoretical merely.

These observations of Matthaeus are to be found in bk. 1, chapter 10, De Licitationibus,[6] ss. 44–48. In s. 40 he is drawing the distinction between necessary and voluntary sales, and insisting as against other authorities that in necessary sales there is no concluded bargain till the seal of the Court has been attached.

Contrariwise in voluntary sales, the matter is completed, "simul augendi seu adjiciendi facultas praecisa sit."[7] But this passage leaves it an open question when the "facultas" is "praecisa." It may be by the last bid, or it may be by acceptance of the last bid. In s. 41 he appears to admit of the prolongation of the auction from day to day till the vendor is satisfied. In s. 43 he discusses the question whether a bidder can withdraw his bid, and concludes, in contradiction to other authorities, which he quotes, that he cannot. But whether this means that he cannot withdraw when once the words are out of his mouth, or that he cannot withdraw when his bid has been accepted, or has been taken as a bid so that a further bid is made upon it, does not appear.

Lastly, in s. 48 he puts the question whether, after bids have been made, but there has been no acceptance by the vendor, "post licitationes facta ante tamen addictionem,"[8] the vendor can withdraw. He states, and states correctly, that the authority of Bartolus and of Damhouder is against him; but he concludes, and this is the passage mainly relied upon, that the vendor cannot withdraw. His reasons are that it would be absurd that the bidder should be bound and not the vendor, and that he who proclaims that he is going to hold a sale by auction tacitly promises that the property shall be sold to the winning bidder "ei qui vicerit licitatione."[9] As to the first reason, it may be observed that there are cases where it will happen that the bidder is bound while the vendor is not: as to the second reason, that, pushed to its logical conclusion, it would extend to prevent the vendor from withdrawing the property before any bid was made, as it would disappoint the company, or from announcing that there is a reserve, or from stating any conditions of sale which he has not previously advertised, unless indeed they be in common form.

It is further to be noticed, as the Chief Justice points out in his judgment, that Matthaeus does not take the view that the auctioneer offers

---

6. Licitatio means bid.

7. As soon as the power to make a higher bid or to knock down [the property] has been cut off.

8. The word "facta" probably should read "factas." The phrase means "after the bids have been made but before the knocking down."

9. Literally, "to the one who shall have won out in bidding."

and the bidder accepts. There are Continental writers on jurisprudence who take this view; for instance, Puchta, Pandekten (6th ed., by Rudolph, Leipzig, 1852, s. 252). Voet also is claimed for it;[10] and it is certainly the view of his translator and editor, Berwick; and it is the view to which Hill J. expressly gives his assent. But it is not that of Matthaeus. He takes the more common view that the bidder offers and the auctioneer accepts; but he thinks, for the reason which he gives, that the auctioneer has tacitly promised to accept.

Remembering that there were in the Dutch usage of his time no conclusive auctions with rising bids, their Lordships think that Matthaeus, if he was writing of such auctions, was writing as a professor of jurisprudence and not as a witness bearing testimony to the existing Roman–Dutch law.[11]

As to other writers, Bartolus, so far as he is an authority to be quoted on Roman–Dutch law, takes, as Matthaeus admits, the contrary view. So does Damhouder, a practising lawyer and writer in Holland. Grotius is quoted on other points by Matthaeus, but has made, apparently, no statement on this point. Voet, it is suggested, favours Matthaeus's view; but it is not clear that he does, and he has very much involved himself with addictio in diem. Van Leeuwen and Van der Linden[12] are apparently silent on the point. Sir Andries Maasdorp in his Institutes of Cape Law (vol. 3, p. 130) certainly expresses himself to the effect that the sale is not completed till the fall of the hammer. On the other hand, Burge in his Foreign and Colonial Law (vol. 2, p. 576) and Nathan in his Common Law of South Africa (vol. 2, p. 718) translate and accept Matthaeus.

The industry of counsel has furnished their Lordships with quotations from several other writers not mentioned in the judgments of the Courts below; but they are chiefly interesting for their full statements as to Dutch usage and for their silence on the point in question.

One modern author, S. J. Fockema Andreae, in a work published at Haarlem in 1896, speaking of the usage of lighting a candle for the period of the auction, says that the last bidder before the candle burnt out is the purchaser, if his offer be accepted.

10.   Johannes Voet (1647–1713) was one of the most famous Dutch jurists. His Commentarius ad Pandectas, to this day one of the principal authorities on Roman–Dutch law, has been translated into several modern languages. The most recent English translation by Judge Percival Gane (8 vols., 1955–58) contains explanatory annotations and references to South African cases which are kept up to date by supplements. For a list of the other famous seventeenth and eighteenth century Dutch authors on Roman–Dutch law, see R. W. Lee, An Introduction to Roman–Dutch Law 15–18 (1953). See also R. Feenstra & C. J. D. Waal, Seventeenth Century Leyden Law Professors and Their Influence on the Development of the Civil Law: A Study of Bronchorst, Vinnius and Voet (1975), and G. F. Margadant, La Secunda Vida del Derecho Romano 253–63 (1986).

11.   See the Joubert–Jonsssen debate in the Bank of Lisbon case, *infra*.

12.   J. Van der Linden (1756–1835) was regarded as a pre-eminent authority on Roman–Dutch law in South Africa. See G. T. Moris, trans., Van der Linden's Institutes of the Laws of Holland (2d ed. 1922). The Transvaal Constitution of 1859 declared his treatise to be "the Legal Code (wetboek) of this State" (article 52, sec. 1).

On the whole, their Lordships are of opinion that there is no rule of Roman–Dutch law which prescribes that at sales by auction the bidder is the acceptor. In sales by reduction it may be otherwise. Neither is there any rule that the highest bidder can insist that the property shall not be withdrawn from sale and claim to have bought it. This being so, the matter is governed by the provisions in the conditions of sale, and they indicate with sufficient clearness that the offer will come from the bidder, and that there is no bargain till it has been accepted by the auctioneer, and they do not indicate that the auctioneer is bound to accept the highest bid.

Their Lordships will therefore humbly advise His Majesty that this appeal should be allowed, that the judgment of the Supreme Court should be reversed and that of the Chief Justice restored, and that the appellant company should have its costs in the Court below and of this appeal.

NOTE

The reader will have noted that in the principal case a court sitting in London in 1918, passing on a matter which had occurred a few years earlier in the Caribbean region, used as its principal authorities (a) a compilation of laws promulgated in the year 533 AD by a Byzantine emperor holding court in Constantinople, and (b) the writings of a Dutch author who lived in the seventeenth century. The case thus furnishes a dramatic—though by no means unique—illustration of the hardy persistence and world-wide extension of Roman-inspired civil law.

"Roman Law" as used in this case means Justinian's *Corpus Juris*. To the modern mind, this may seem a startlingly narrow definition, in view of the fact that the *Corpus Juris* was itself the culmination of an unbroken historical development spanning the preceding ten centuries—a development that can be traced back at least to the Twelve Tables (451 BC). By incorporating the writings of older jurists in the Digest, the *Corpus Juris* on its face reveals its indebtedness to the work of jurists who lived several centuries before Justinian's day. Nevertheless, it was only during a relatively brief spell of sixteenth century humanism, and then again in the last 150 years, that substantial and sustained scholarly efforts were devoted to the pre-Justinian history of Roman law. During most of the period from the eleventh to the nineteenth century, the *Corpus Juris* was regarded as a book of authority, a tool for lawyers rather than an object of the historian's study and research.

After modern codifications deprived the *Corpus Juris* of its authoritative stature in most civil law systems, Roman law scholarship assumed a predominantly historical bent. The efforts of students of "Roman law" shifted mainly to aspects previously neglected: pre-Justinian developments, including Greek and other "foreign" influences, and detailed study of (a) changes made in the older texts by Tribonianus and his colleagues (interpolations) as well as (b) changes in original older texts which—already prior to Justinian's day—had been made by commentators of the intermediate period (glossemes). It is clear, however, that the Privy Council does not use the term "Roman law" in this modern, academic sense, but rather as more or less synonymous with the *Corpus Juris*.

Lest the reader jump to exaggerated conclusions, it should be pointed out right away that today there are very few countries in which Justinian's *Corpus Juris*, or the writings of civilian authors who lived in centuries long past, would still be recognized as primary sources of present-day law. Scotland, South Africa, Sri Lanka and Andorra are countries which have preserved essentially civilian and yet uncodified systems of law. In the overwhelming majority of civil law countries, however, relatively modern codes enacted during the last two centuries have replaced the older sources of law. These codes, as will be explained below (sec. 2B), to some extent marked a conscious break with the past. Nevertheless, they did not—Athena-like—spring from the head of Zeus. Each of the codes was drafted by lawyers—practitioners or professors—and these members of the legal profession, though acting as draftsmen for reform-minded rulers or legislatures, invariably had acquired their training and experience under the older system and thus were steeped in traditional learning.

Demarara offers a very interesting example of how a system of law could work (and indeed has worked for centuries) using scholarly opinions (either of the early jurists who "made it" to the *Corpus Iuris* or of the subsequent continental writers active from the eleventh to the eighteenth century AD). As we will see, only after another seven centuries of independent legal production by jurists did the resulting amount of pluralism prove (as for Justinian before) quite unbearable so that most Continental systems attempted, through codification, a break with the past.

H. Coing, The Roman Law as Ius Commune on the Continent

89 L.Q.Rev. 505 (1973).

... The question ... is "What developments gave Roman Law such outstanding significance in the Europe of modern times?"

I.

One might imagine that the role Roman Law played in European history was a direct consequence of the fact that the Romans once dominated many parts of Europe. This was certainly not the case. When the Roman armies had left Britain, Western and Southern Germany and finally France at the end of Antiquity, new barbarian states were organized on the former Roman territory. The influence of Roman legislation did not cease completely but during the centuries which followed slowly withered away. We cannot follow here the different stages of this process nor state in which regions and to what extent there remained certain survivals of Roman Law. But there is one fact of great historical importance. In the sixth century, the East Roman Emperor Justinian brought about the great summary of antique Roman Law which is called the *Corpus Iuris Civilis*—the law-book which is the main source of our knowledge of ancient Roman Law. But this great piece of legislation could not at the time be introduced into the Latin West, since Justinian's Empire was restricted mainly to the eastern half of the ancient Roman Empire and included, as far as the West was concerned, only [a part of] Italy. Although Justinian greatly widened the frontiers of his Empire, he never ruled in Northern France, Germany or Great Britain.

It is necessary therefore to turn to other factors and times to explain the historical influence Roman Law had on modern European legal development. And here we have to take into consideration a period of the later Middle Ages and, in this period, three developments in particular. The first is the development in education: the history of the law schools in the universities of medieval Europe. The second is concerned with the development of State and administration in the same period. Thirdly we have to look at the development of ideas about law in this period.

II.

The first subject to be considered is the origin of the medieval universities.

It is well known that universities as a social institution in education owe their existence to medieval civilisation. There is quite a difference between the character of a modern university and a university of the thirteenth or fourteenth century. The modern university unites research with teaching. The main task of the medieval university was to introduce the student to traditional knowledge as laid down in a certain number of books of authority. It is characteristic of the medieval university that the knowledge it had to impart to its students and the books of authority it used for this purpose, were taken from a civilisation which had long since passed away and which, nevertheless, was considered as the origin and model of all spiritual culture: Greco–Roman antiquity. In the medieval university, philosophy was at first taught on the basis of platonic tradition and, from the thirteenth century, on that of the writings of Aristotle, mainly known by translations from the Arabic countries. The same author, Aristotle, together with texts of Galenus, was used in the courses on medicine. In the Divinity Schools one used a compilation of the Fathers of the Church, the *Sententiae* of Lombardus. It is true that with the progress of time, medieval science itself produced a vast literature, *e.g.* the great *Summa Theologica* of Thomas Aquinas, but even these writings were the fruit of the discussion the medieval mind conducted with the authors of Antiquity.

It is in harmony with this general feature of the medieval universities that legal education, which began in the twelfth century, was based on the greatest collection of legal materials Antiquity had left to posterity, the *Corpus Iuris* of Justinian. Modern research has shown that there may also have been political considerations which led the legists of Bologna to turn to the *Corpus Iuris Civilis*, since the medieval emperors considered themselves the successors of the Roman *imperatores*, and their partisans welcomed arguments drawn from the *Corpus Iuris* in the great struggle against the Papacy. But it is the great authority of ancient civilisation in general that is the most convincing explanation for the attitude the medieval law schools took.

The first medieval universities were not founded by act of State or church but slowly grew out of groups of students gathering around and entering into contract with individual professors. These first universities were generally restricted to one or two main subjects. They did not aim at comprehensive scientific education as most modern universities do. Theology and philosophy were taught at Paris, medicine at Salerno and Montpellier. For law, it was an Italian university which took the lead: Bologna. Here, law courses began at the end of the eleventh century, and an organized curriculum including examinations for different degrees developed during the following century. The subject taught was at first only the *Corpus Iuris* of Justinian[a]. . . . Canon Law, that is the law of the medieval Roman Catholic Church, was added in the twelfth century; about 1140 the Bolognese monk Gratianus completed the great collection of Canon Law materials called the *Decretum*. To this, several official collections of Papal Decretals were added in later times. Thus Bologna had two law faculties, one devoted to Roman Law (the Legists), the other to Canon Law (the Canonists). The totality of the legal material taught at Bologna was described by the term *ius utrumque*, i.e. both laws, Roman Law and Canon Law.

The educational system worked out in Bologna became the model for all legal instruction given at universities in Europe during the Middle Ages. It is most important to understand this fact if we wish to comprehend the significance Roman Law acquired on the European continent.

Already in the twelfth century Bologna had developed into an international centre of legal studies. This can be seen in the fact that the emperor Friedrich Barbarossa in 1158 gave by the so-called Authentica "Habita" very important privileges to the students of Bologna. The Emperor promises the students protection during their journey from their home country to Bologna. He grants them exemption from the city jurisdiction of Bologna, giving them a choice between the jurisdiction of the Bishop and of their own professors. Furthermore, he lays down that no reprisals can be taken against a member of a student community. This last privilege calls for a few words of explanation. The Middle Ages considered it lawful that a citizen of one community, let us say the city of Cologne, should be held responsible in a foreign city for the debts any citizen of Cologne had incurred to a citizen of that foreign city. So a student from Cologne or Montpellier coming to Bologna had to run the risk that the city judges of Bologna would compel him to pay for the debts any of his countrymen had incurred in the city of Bologna. The imperial privilege abolished this institution of reprisals as far as students were concerned. Now, if the emperor found it necessary to provide for the students of Bologna by such

---

a. During the centuries of intellectual decline and "vulgarized" Roman law (see supra), much of what later became known as the Corpus Juris (certainly most of the Digest) was unknown in Western Europe. Lawyers of that period would not have been equipped to understand its finer points. But toward the end of the 11th century—the beginning of an intellectual renaissance—the Digest was discovered when an ancient manuscript containing its text came to light in a library at Pisa. See H. J. Berman, The Religious Foundations of Western Law, 24 Cath.U.L.Rev. 490, 492 (1975)

specific legislation, there must have been at the time a considerable number of foreign students in Bologna.

In fact, modern research, undertaken especially by the Swiss historian Stelling–Michaud, had shown that in 1269 more than a thousand foreign students were present at Bologna.[1] That would be a considerable number even for a modern law school. But Bologna was not only a great international centre of legal studies. It also became the model for all the law schools which were organised at medieval universities.

As has already been mentioned, a number of medieval universities grew up during the twelfth and thirteenth centuries, some of them out of former educational institutions like cathedral schools. The latter is for example true for the great French Universités de loi, Orléans and Angers. In part they came into existence by migrations of doctors and students from one place to another. That for example is true for Cambridge (1209) and Padua (1224). But most later medieval universities were founded by a planned act of the political powers of the time, by princes or cities. The first of this type of university is Naples, founded in 1224 by the famous emperor Frederick II. Other examples are provided by Salamanca (ca. 1220), Cologne (foundation of the city 1388), Prague (1356), Cracow (1383). These planned and organised universities mostly had the four classical faculties: arts or philosophy, divinity, medicine and law. In total, up to 1500 about seventy new universities were organised.

Now the important fact for legal history is that as far as their law schools were concerned, all these universities more or less followed the model worked out by Bologna. In some cases, this was decided by the universities themselves. This is for example true for the Aragonese university of Lerida (founded 1300). On others it was imposed by papal legislation. Thus, for example, it was laid down for the university of Perugia in 1318 that the law curriculum and examinations in law should follow the example of Bologna. Moreover, in statutes of new universities reference is made to the university of Bologna. This is for example the case for the university of Toulouse, founded in 1229, although it is not yet completely clear what such references really meant for the university in question. Whatever may have been the legal basis, what interests the legal historian is the fact that all these law schools—this applies also to medieval Oxford and Cambridge—did follow the model of Bologna and taught Roman and Canon Law to the exclusion of local or territorial law. The result was that all over Europe a new professional group came into existence: the lawyers, the *juristae*. They all had had the same training, the *ius utrumque*;[b] they all used the same method, the method of scholastic legal interpretation, and they all had at their disposal the same international literature on Roman and Canon Law.

1. Stelling–Michaud, L'Université de Bologna, Geneva 1955.

b. J.U.D. stands for juris utriusque doctor = doctor of both laws. The two laws were civil law and canon law.

It is the social function of this new group to which we have now to turn to understand the influence it exerted on late medieval culture.

III.

It is at this point that the development of state administration comes in. We can start with the simple question: where did the members of the new profession look for a place in society? The answer to this question will lead us to answer the sociological question—what social function did the new profession exercise in medieval society?

There is no doubt that in the later centuries of the Middle Ages, quite a few of the universities founded in this period were created because princes or cities wished to have a place where lawyers could be trained to help in their administration. This is true for example for the university of Cologne (1388) as well as for Rostock and Greifswald. It also applies to many universities founded in this time by princes in order to develop their territory. This demand for lawyers is to be explained by the fact that in these centuries the church as well as the different medieval states were changing and widening their administrative and judicial systems. It is in this period that origins of the modern administrative state are to be found. Slowly and step by step, medieval feudalism is replaced by a centralised administrative system handled by civil servants at the centre as well as on the level of the local administration, and it was in these new or transformed judicial and administrative bodies that the new profession of lawyers found its place in society.

The first great organisation which called in the lawyers was the Roman Catholic Church. Modern research seems to have established that the number of lawyers holding church offices grows steadily during the fourteenth and fifteenth century. This has been shown especially for England in the two ecclesiastical provinces of Canterbury and York. More important was the fact that from the second half of the twelfth century the church began to reorganize its judicial system. This reorganization was a long process. It ended only in the middle of the fourteenth century. The aim of this reform was to introduce the "learned law" into the procedure as well as the substantive rules of the ecclesiastical courts, and this, of course, meant that university-trained lawyers had to fill the role of judges as well as advocates. It is well known how extensive was the jurisdiction of ecclesiastical courts in the later Middle Ages. Their jurisdiction was by no means restricted to purely ecclesiastical questions in the modern sense of the word. It not only extended to all matters of marriage and divorce and consequently of "status," but covered also all questions concerning wills and many cases of general contracts. This powerful organization, then, was the first stronghold of the new legal profession in Europe.[c]

But states and cities followed. We first find the lawyers as general counselors. This applies as well to kings and princes as to free cities. A

---

c. For a comprehensive account, see H. J. Berman, Law and Revolution, The Formation of the Western legal tradition, pt. I: The Papal Revolution and the Canon Law (1983).

famous example is the fact that King Edward I of England hired the services of the son of the famous glossator, Accursius; for a decade he served as a general counsel. But the same phenomenon more or less is to be observed at all the great courts of Europe. Even the emperors of the Holy Roman Empire, backward as their administrative system was, had some lawyers in their council from the thirteenth century onwards.

As the administrative organisation of the medieval state developed, lawyers began to fill places in the new administrative organisation and especially in the Central Courts which were set up. In many instances, they replaced the noblemen who in feudal times had been members of these courts. This too was a slow development and there were quite big differences in space and time if we compare the individual European states. We find that by about 1180 some Italian city-states had university-trained lawyers as judges in their courts.... In Germany, it was not until the fifteenth century that the same development took place at the central courts as well as the territorial ones. This development was confirmed when in 1495 it was laid down for the newly organised central court, the *Reichskammergericht*, that half of the judges had to be university-trained lawyers, the other half being taken from the nobility....

IV.

The lawyers, thus firmly established in the new civil service, began in the exercise of their new [administrative and judicial] functions to apply the law they had learned at the university, that is the Roman Canon Law. This is easily to be explained as far as church administration and ecclesiastical courts are concerned. It was quite natural that ecclesiastical courts applied Canon Law, and Canon Law itself was based on Roman Law. But things were different for the lawyers in the service of states and free cities. All the states, territories and cities had, of course, their own law laid down in statutes or customs. Here then the question arises how a judge or administrator could apply the Roman Canon Law instead of restricting himself to the local norms.

To explain this phenomenon, we have to turn to the ideas of law prevailing in this period. The theories developed by Austinians[d] are of no assistance in understanding the attitude of the lawyer of the fourteenth or fifteenth century towards the sources of law. According to those theories legal rules are norms laid down by the sovereign for the subjects, for the citizens of the state. There is according to this view no law except what is contained in the orders of the sovereign. Consequently, no judge and no administrator is entitled to apply a rule which is not recognised by the sovereign, and the legal system is strictly territorial, strictly tied to the boundaries of the individual state. Although Austin and his school have

---

d. The reference is to legal positivism, as set forth in J. Austin, The Province of Jurisprudence Determined (1st ed. 1832). For representative recent works in this tradition, see H. L. A. Hart, The Concept of Law (1963); J. Raz, The Concept of a Legal System (1980); N. MacCormick & O. Weinberger, An Institutional Theory of Law: New Approaches to Legal Positivism (1986).

presented this theory as a general theory of law, the historian must admit that it expresses only the attitude lawyers adopted in the nineteenth century and especially since the French Revolution when the idea of national sovereignty began to gain strength. The ideas of the Middle Ages and even of the Ancien Régime, of the time before the French Revolution, were quite different. Views prevailing then can be described by the term "Pluralism" as applied to legal sources. Pluralism means first that unity of law in the modern sense is absent. There are different rules for different cities and territories and different rules for the individual professional groups like merchants, nobility, peasants, etc. But Pluralism of legal sources also means that a judge who has to decide a specific case, has to look for rules not only in the orders of the sovereign, but can apply rules which he finds in any book of authority, whether this has been expressly recognised by the sovereign or not. It is more important for him to find an appropriate rule than to be sure to confine himself to following the orders the sovereign has given.

It was this basic attitude of the medieval period which made it possible for the *juristae* to apply the law they had learned at the university, the Roman Canon Law, in daily practice. The Italian law professors elaborated a convenient theory of sources of law. Broadly speaking, this theory was that a judge must first apply local customs and statutes, but whenever he could not find an appropriate rule to decide the case before him in this legal material, he could turn to Roman Canon Law and fill the gaps found in territorial or local law by the rules of Roman Law. He also was entitled according to this theory to construe local customs and statutes within the framework of Roman Law. This, of course, was a quite natural intellectual attitude for a time which did not look on Antiquity as a historical period long gone but rather as a model to be applied immediately to the present day. There were different opinions as to what the basis of the authority of Roman Law was. Most widely accepted was the idea that Roman Law was to be considered as *ratio scripta* (written reason) and as such applied in every country. In the medieval empire, there was a legend that one of the medieval emperors, Lotharius, had expressly introduced Roman Law.

Later on, with the beginning of historical criticisms at the Renaissance, this theory was replaced by the idea that Roman Law was received by the custom of the courts. But whatever argument was used, the practical outcome was that Roman Law was generally considered as a subsidiary to which one could turn if local law failed to answer a problem. As the famous medievalist, Kantorowicz, has said, Roman Law was a kind of treasure-house where everybody could enter and find what he needed to solve a legal problem.[2] An event which took place in the second half of the thirteenth century in Northern Germany will illustrate this. The city of Lübeck asked the city of Hamburg what rules were applied in Hamburg to a certain question of maritime law. The head of the Chancery of the City of Hamburg could not find any specific rules in the Hamburg statute book or custom. But as he was a learned lawyer, he translated certain passages of

---

2. Kantorowicz, Bractonian Problems, p. 126.

the Digest of Justinian into German and in his answer to the citizens of Lübeck stated it as the law of Hamburg. The latter from that time on followed the rule of the Digest.[3] The general result of this process was that the lawyers on the Continent applied a mixed legal system whose components were on one hand local statutes and customs and on the other hand the law books of Justinian and the Canon Law.

V.

On the whole, this result was reached by the end of the Middle Ages. It led on the Continent of Europe first to the *juristae*, the university-trained lawyers, a uniform professional group having the same scientific background. Furthermore, it led to a unified legal literature based on Roman Canon Law and allowing scientific discussion of common problems all over the Continent. In the library of the Canon Law College of the university of Coimbra in Portugal are the writings of a German legal author, Carpzow, with handwritten notes of a Portuguese judge who evidently used the book in his own practice. It is again well known that German bankruptcy law has its historical origin in the writings of a Castilian judge of the seventeenth century, Salgado de Samoza. Also, decisions of the Court of Appeal of Hanover dating from the eighteenth century show that the judges used the works of Argentré, a famous French commentator on local custom of the sixteenth century, to decide cases about the inheritance of Hanoverian peasants.[4]

There were, of course, within the framework of this Common Law on the Continent developments and changes, notably the influence of the enlightenment and of the so-called Natural Law Movement in the eighteenth century. Yet on the whole the system of *Ius Commune* on the Continent lasted up to the eighteenth century and was finally changed only by the modern national codifications, especially by the influence of the legal ideas of the French Revolution whose outcome on the Continent was the modern national state. Since then, the law on the Continent has been split up into a series of national systems. Still, one cannot deny the common background all these systems have, and modern writers on Comparative Law rightly speak of the Continental legal systems as a family of laws which can be opposed as a unit to the great systems of the English-speaking nations, the English Common Law. In this sense we can still say today that Roman Law on the Continent is a kind of *ratio scripta*. It has given to Continental lawyers their underlying basic notions and Roman legal expressions still are the *lingua franca* of Continental lawyers.

Finally, what of the position of England in this whole development of Roman Law since the Middle Ages? It would certainly be wrong to say that England was never touched by these developments in legal ideas and

---

3. See Reincke, "Frühe Spuren Römischen Rechts in Nieder–Sachsen." Festschrift Haff, pp. 174–184.

4. The Court of Appeals at Celle started its eighteenth-century library collection with an appropriation of 140 Thalers. A glossed edition of the Corpus Juris Civilis cost 40 Thalers at that time. Baade, Book Review, 14 Int'l J. Legal Inf. 264, 265 (1986).

practice. It has been clear since Maitland's writings[5] that ecclesiastical courts in medieval England followed the Roman Canon Law. It is also clear that the medieval law-schools in Oxford and Cambridge taught Canon and Roman Law. What is more, in the twelfth and thirteenth century there were English judges having a broad background of knowledge of the Roman Canon Law.[6]

Bracton's famous book *De Legibus Angliae* is proof enough. We also know that up to the end of the eighteenth century there were courts in England which not only followed Roman Canon procedure but also based their judgment, as far as substantive law is concerned, on *Ius Commune*. This is true for the High Court of Admiralty and the Curia Militaris, the Court of the Constable and Marshal.

Despite all this, the fact remains that the English Common Law developed independently and is a legal system of its own, not based on Roman Canon Law. Where are we to look for the explanation of this specifically English development? Modern research is inclined to see the answer in the fact that the English Monarchy after the Norman conquest was the most centralised and powerful state in Europe and, in a certain sense, had the most progressive administrative and judicial organisation.[7] At the time when the Roman Canon Law began to expand over the Continent—the critical period being the beginning of the thirteenth century—when the Church had begun to reorganize its court system, the English Monarchy, and the English Monarchy alone, had organised a permanent system of central courts at Westminster whose judges used to apply English statutes and feudal customs and to follow their own precedents. As a result, Roman Law, as Van Caeneghem has put it, in a sense came to England too late. When the other European countries adopted Roman Law as *ratio scripta* or as imperial law, the English Monarchy already had a system of central courts with traditions of its own. So, even in terms of the theory of legal sources of the Continental lawyers there was not much room for Roman Canon Law, the main ground being covered by legal rules developed in England itself.

There is a second factor to be considered. We have seen that the Continental rulers in the course of the thirteenth, fourteenth and fifteenth centuries began to appoint university-trained lawyers to their courts. The same, perhaps, could have happened in England too. But here we encounter one of the accidents which again and again we find in history and in the last resort cannot explain. Edward I organised a training for the judges of his courts which was independent of the law schools of Oxford and Cambridge. The English lawyer, consequently, was not a lawyer trained at universities; he was educated at the inns of court and the court itself.

5. Maitland, Canon Law in the Church of England.

6. For a case study in point, see R. Helmholz, Support Orders, Church Courts, and the Rule of Filius Nullius: A Reassessment of the Common Law, 63 Va.L.Rev. 431 (1977). See generally R. H. Helmholz, Marriage Litigation in Medieval England (1974); R. H. Helmholz, Canon Law and the Law of England (1988).

7. See especially Van Caeneghem, Royal Writs in England from the Conquest to Glanville (publ. Seld.Soc. LXXVII).

English lawyers as a professional group were separated from the *juristae* of the universities and developed their professional knowledge on different lines. Nevertheless, the English Common Law has never been completely separated from legal development on the Continent. There has always in the course of centuries been give and take from [England] to the Continent and vice versa. . . . [8]

NOTES

(1) *Later Developments in the Eastern Empire.* In the Eastern Empire, Justinian's codification had the force of law. During subsequent centuries, Greek translations of the (originally Latin) *Corpus Juris*, increasingly reduced to summaries (*epitomes*), remained the basis of the Byzantine legal system. The last of these summaries was the *Hexabiblos,* written in 1345 by Judge Harmenopoulos in Thessaloniki. Byzantine law, administered by indigenous local authorities and the Greek Orthodox Church, survived as the personal law of the Greek community under Ottoman law, and in 1835, shortly after Greek independence (1821), "a Royal Decree of 1835 declared that 'the civil laws of the Byzantine emperors contained in the *Hexabiblos* of Harmenopoulos shall remain in force till the promulgation of the civil code whose drafting we have already ordered' and that 'customs, sanctioned by long and uninterrupted use or by judicial decisions, shall have the force of law wherever they prevail.' " A. N. Yiannopoulos, Historical Development, in K. D. Kerameus & P. J. Kozyris, eds., Introduction to Greek Law 1, 9 (2d ed. 1993).

See also *id.* 7: "Of extraordinary significance in this regard are the codes of the Danube principalities that were governed by Greek envoys of the Sultan. All such codes were written in the Greek language and reproduced Byzantine law *par excellence*. The Constitution of Alexander Ypsilantis (1780), the Code of Wallachia of John Caratzas (1818), the Code of Moldavia of Callimachis (1817), and the Syntagma of Michael Photinopoulos (1765), a summary of the Basilica in Modern Creek, are among the first codifications in western Europe."

(2) *Remnants of Roman Law in western Europe.* In spite of temporary military victories, Justinian and his successors ultimately failed in their attempt to "reconquer" the Western Empire from the Germanic tribes which had swarmed over western Europe and had captured Rome itself in 476 AD The Germanic rulers of western Europe (not unlike the Arab conquerors a few centuries later) believed in the principle of "personal law," which meant that within each territory the Germanic subjects lived under their own inherited laws and customs, while the indigenous population continued to live under Roman law. A remnant of Roman law thus survived in the West, but how much remains controversial. The classic account is still E. Levy, West Roman Vulgar Law: The Law of Property (1951). For a recent update, see Hermann Lange, Die Anfänge der modernen Rechtswissenschaft, Bologna und das frühe Mittelalter (1993).

During the centuries of intellectual decline and "vulgarized" Roman law, much of what later became known as the *Corpus Juris* (certainly most of the

8. This last point was further developed by the same author in a more recent paper. See H. Coing, European Common Law: Historical Foundations, in New Perspectives for a Common Law of Europe 31 (M. Cappelletti ed., 1978).

Digest) was unknown in western Europe. Lawyers of that period would not have been equipped to understand its finer points. But toward the end of the eleventh century—the beginning of an intellectual renaissance—the Digest was discovered when an ancient manuscript containing its text came to light in a library at Pisa. See H. J. Berman, The Religious Foundations of Western Law, 24 Cath.U.L.Rev. 490, 492 (1975).

(3) *Civilian influence on the common law.* Professor Coing's enumeration of the successive waves of civil law influences upon the law of England is not meant to be exhaustive. See also L. Moccia, English Law Attitudes to the "Civil Law," 2 J.Legal Hist. 157 (1981).

One must also remember that in the formative years of the equity courts the Chancellors, who at that time tended to be clerics, adopted a Romano-canonistic form of procedure as well as a number of substantive principles derived from canon law. See E. Re, The Roman Contribution to the Common Law, 29 Fordham L.Rev. 447, especially at 479–83 (1961); J. Barton, Roman Law in England 50–53 (1971). The absorption of the law merchant into the common law should be considered in this context. And one should not forget Blackstone's heavy reliance on civil law authorities. See B. Nicholas, Rules and Terms—Civil Law and Common Law, 48 Tul.L.Rev. 946 (1974). Finally, during the nineteenth century the Code Napoleon and other civilian codes not only inspired Bentham and his followers but also directly influenced decisions handed down by English courts on numerous occasions. For instance, the key sentence in Hadley v. Baxendale, 9 Ex. 341, 156 Eng.Rep. 145 (1854) (a classic in the development of the modern approach to damages for breach of contract) is a paraphrase of art. 1150 of the French Civil Code.

The student of American legal history should keep in mind that, in addition, both Roman and modern civilian ideas were imported into the United States during the first half-century of the Republic, and in more limited measure again in recent times, e.g., in connection with the Uniform Commercial Code.

4. ROMAN LAW AS A COMMON WESTERN HERITAGE

As Professor Coing mentions in his masterful reconstruction, Roman Law ideas, concepts and terminology had actually a quite important role in the early foundation of the English common law tradition. In fact, the practice of any court of law, without some fundamental principles behind it, declines into mere casuistry and expediency. Thus while accidents of local political history (the battle between the Monarchy and the Parliament) explain the birth of the common law/equity distinction and of other purely insular developments of English law, Roman law learning played a significant role in many crucial phases of the development of the common law tradition. Suffice to think about the Roman law roots of the natural law thinking of which Sir William Blackstone's *Commentaries* were imbued. Thus the first general systematic explanation of the English Law, perhaps the most influential law book in the history of American Law, and thus a milestone in the making of a common law tradition was organized around an exquisitely Roman law framework reminiscent of the Institutes of Gaius.

The end of the eleventh century was a crucial point in the development of the western legal tradition. England was unified under the Norman Reign of William the Conqueror after the Battle of Hastings in 1066. William early established a centralized Court, which soon became staffed with locally trained lawyers at Westminster Hall in central London, developed its own parochial practice and professional culture, prevailed over the Roman law taught at Oxford and Cambridge in declaring the law and custom of land (though we know not in complete insulation from Roman Law influences). In the Continent, beginning at that same time, and for centuries thereafter, successive generations of influential scholars fashioned a modernized Roman law, a *jus commune*, [common law. The term is left in Latin not to be confused with the thick meaning of its English language translation] which became one of the strongest elements of a common European culture. In referring to the accomplishments of these scholars, one usually distinguishes between three schools:

(i) The *glossators* were law teachers of the eleventh, twelfth and thirteenth centuries. Irnerius, the founder, and the other most important representatives of this school taught at Bologna, where thousands of students from every part of Europe sat at their feet.[1] Many of the Italian law teachers referred to as glossators, and not a few of their former student, also taught at other Universities throughout continental Europe and in England.[2] The principal scholarly accomplishment of the glossators consisted of *glossae*, or annotations appended to the text of the *Corpus Juris*. Accursius (1182–1259) combined several previous glossae into the famous *Glossa Ordinaria*. It was in this annotated form that the *Corpus Juris* was used in practice for several centuries thereafter.[3]

(ii) The fourteenth and fifteenth century *commentators* (formerly also referred to as post-glossators) like their predecessors were largely centered in Italy; but their influence, again as in the case of the glossators, reached to the far corners of the Christian world. Bartolus da Sassoferrato (1314–1357) was the greatest representative of this school. While the glossators had not ventured beyond mere exegesis and systematization of the Roman texts, the commentators' approach was primarily a practical one. They sought to adjust the law to the needs of their own time, often by taking great liberties in interpreting the *Corpus Juris* and in reconciling conflicting (or seemingly conflicting) passages of the original Justinian compilation, canon law texts, as well as the glossae. In their effort to modernize the law, the commentators also took note of legal materials outside the *Corpus Juris*, such as statutes and local and commercial customs.

---

1. See H. Rashdall, The Universities of Europe in the Middle Ages 87–267 (2d ed. F. M. Powicke and A. B. Emden, 1936).

2. In the middle of the twelfth century the Italian Glossator Vacarius founded the law school at Oxford.

3. The scholastic method employed by the glossators also left a lasting imprint on the civil law. See H. J. Berman, The Origins of Western Legal Science, 90 Harv.L.Rev. 894, 908–30 (1977).

The commentators' influence on legal practice throughout Europe was strong and sustained. A Spanish statute of 1449, for example, directed the courts to follow the views of Bartolus and his pupil Baldus in any case not governed by the terms of a written law. Even in the absence of such a statutory direction, the writings of Bartolus and Baldus were similarly authoritative in other countries, especially in sixteenth century Germany.

(iii) The *humanists*, whose principal seat of learning was the French University of Bourges, during the sixteenth and seventeenth centuries sought to cleanse the Roman texts of the glossators' and commentators' incrustations, and by going back to the sources of the classical period of Roman law (100 BC to 250 AD) even to uncover the interpolations of Tribonianus and his commission. The humanists, who were excellent classical scholars, poked fun at the commentators' ignorance of Greek and the inelegance of their Latin. Some of the harsh criticisms which the humanists directed against the commentators, have been enshrined in world literature by Rabelais. But since the endeavors of many of the humanists, in spite of their unquestionable scholarly merit, were antiquarian rather than practice-oriented, their *mos gallicus* (French style) gained less influence in most parts of Europe than the *mos italicus* (Italian Style) of the commentators. Significantly, the *mos gallicus* was the prevailing style in English Universities. Lawyers at Oxford and Cambridge had less of a need to take into consideration the "practical aspects" of the law, being those taken care by the common lawyers at Westminster Hall.

When we speak of the more modern era, especially of the seventeenth century, it becomes increasingly difficult to label each of the important scholars as a member of a particular school. Some of the great Dutch law teachers, for instance, who were to become the outstanding oracles of Roman–Dutch law, combined the classical learning postulated by the *mos gallicus* with the practical methods and objectives of the *mos italicus*.[4] To varying degrees, moreover, they began to exhibit a critical attitude toward traditional Roman Law learning, under the influence of the new "school" of natural law.[5]

Reinhard, Zimmermann, Roman Dutch Jurisprudence and its Contribution to European Private Law

66 Tulane L. Rev. 1685, 1711–18 (1992).

When the seventeenth century unfolded, there were two main traditions in which the study of Roman law presented itself: the more practice-

4. See Zimmerman, Roman–Dutch Jurisprudence, *infra*.

5. Conversely, Calvinist theology appears to have helped them in emancipating Roman law-based rules of commercial law from Thomist natural law. J. Q. Whitman, The Moral Menace of Roman Law and the Making of Commerce: Some Dutch Evidence, 105 Yale L.J. 1841 (1996).

oriented approach adopted, above all, by Bartolus and the other commentators (*mos italicus*); and the "elegant" jurisprudence of, particularly, the French humanists (*mos gallicus*), who were concerned more with the Roman law of the antiquity than with contemporary legal practice. In a way, the Roman–Dutch lawyers, by combining these two mainstreams of tradition, succeeded in rejuvenating the *ius commune* at a time when the *mos italicus* had become fossilized and the *mos gallicus* had reached a state of purely antiquarian over-refinement that was, more often than not, devoid of any practical significance. In other words, the Roman–Dutch jurists reinvigorated the *mos italicus* on the basis and level of the humanistic learning provided by the *mos gallicus*. They thus brought about a modernization of Roman law that ensured its survival in Germany until the end of the nineteenth century and in South Africa until today.[1] I submit that five factors were essential for this process of modernization...

The first, and possibly most important aspect was the practice-orientation of most of the jurists responsible for the blossoming of legal science in the Netherlands of the seventeenth and early eighteenth centuries. Roman–Dutch law was not a typically "professorial" law characterized by impractical abstractions, deductive reasoning, and concept-jurisprudence; to a large extent it was judicial law ("*jurisprudentia forensis*") developing through lawyers' interpretation and judicial opinions and leading towards an authoritative "*communis opinio totius orbis, secundum quem usum semper interpretatio fieri debet* [the common opinion of all the world according to which interpretation must always be done]." Protagonists of this "law in action" were academically trained practitioners as well as professors who had usually spent at least a part of their career as an advocate or judge.... [among the great masters of Dutch natural law that never had an academic chair one finds Grotius whose work enormously influenced Blackstone].

It can safely be maintained that the Dutch, in their capacity as humanists, were mere successors of the French. They adopted their great research programs and thus gained new individual insights; but they did not open up new perspectives. Had their jurisprudence been merely "elegant," it hardly deserved to be remembered as a particularly fruitful era of the *ius commune*. The high level of Roman legal learning was of specific significance in that it enabled contemporary lawyers to appreciate in what areas, and how far, the *mores hodierni* [contemporary customs] had moved away from Roman law. This facilitated a rational discussion of these *mores hodierni* and their integration into the systematic framework of the Roman–Canon common law.

A third important factor was the continuity of development. In spite of the fact that for almost eighty years a war was waged between Spain and the Northern Netherlands, the Dutch jurists did not attempt a radical new departure that would have set them free from their intellectual indebted-

---

1. On the South African usus modernus of Roman–Dutch law, see Reinhard Zimmermann, Das Römisch-Holländische Recht in Südafrika 1 (1983); Reinhard Zimmermann, Synthesis in South African Private Law: Civil Law, Common Law and Usus Hodiernus Pandectarum, 103 S.Afr.L.J. 259 (1986).

ness to their (Spanish) past.... an important intellectual connection to late Medieval Spanish jurisprudence was retained.[2]

The fourth consideration one has to mention is the urbanity and intellectual liberality that characterized the Northern Netherlands in the seventeenth century. Men of the calibre of Descartes and John Locke did not accidentally live and publish in Holland; the Jewish community of Amsterdam produced thinkers like Spinoza and Manasseh ben Israel. As far as legal science is concerned, we see that many Dutch jurists brought back lasting impressions from their *peregrinatio academica* [academic wandering]....

More important was the policy adopted by the Dutch universities when it came to filling vacant chairs.... great efforts were made to attract foreigners to fill arising vacancies, among them, most notably, the French humanist Donellus who was persuaded to come to Leyden ... During the seventeenth and the first half of the eighteenth century, German scholars were appointed at all faculties in the Netherlands. * * * Between 1636 and 1815 nearly thirty percent of the law professors teaching at the University of Utrecht were Germans.

Of even greater importance for the influence of Dutch jurisprudence in Europe was the fact that the universities of the United Netherlands also attracted great numbers of foreign students. Leyden, of course, was the most popular. No less than 15,000 of a total of 35,000 students enrolled in Leyden during the seventeenth century came from beyond the borders of the Netherlands. Particularly during the Thirty Years' War, many German students, for obvious reasons, preferred Holland to their home universities; between 1616 and 1650, 2,966 of 5,718 foreign students were Germans. The number of lawyers among them was considerable.[3] A second, particularly important "nation" among the foreign students were the Scots ...; between 1676 and 1725, 422 were law students. * * * Thus, it is hardly surprising that among the 663 advocates admitted to the Faculty of Advocates in Edinburgh between 1661 and 1750, no less than 275 had studied in the Netherlands. * * *

In view of such a cosmopolitan atmosphere, it is not surprising that the great Dutch scholars drew not only from the local literature of their province, but also made ample use of, and received their inspiration from the works of the writers of the other provinces in addition to German, French, Italian, and Spanish legal literature....

The United Netherlands of the seventeenth century constituted a focal point for all the different strands of that had over the centuries shaped the

---

2. See, e.g., [James Gordley], The Philosophical Origins of Modern Contract Doctrine passim (1991); James Gordley, Natural Law Origins of the Common Law of Contract, in Towards a General Law of Contract 367 (John Barton ed., 1990); Antonio T. Serra, Grotius dans ses rapports avec les classiques espagnols du droit des gens, 4 Recueil des Cours 431 (Académie de Droit International, 1983); D. P. Visser, Die invloede op Hugo de Groot, 46 THRHR 136 (1983).

3. For details, see Robert Feenstra, Scottish–Dutch Legal Relations in the Seventeenth and Eighteenth Centuries, in Scotland and Europe 128 (T.C. Smout ed., 1986).

ius commune. One of them, and this is the fifth point, was the idea of a natural law that (in a secularized version) was about to experience a spectacular revival. It was, of course, Hugo Grotius, the "father of Roman–Dutch law," whose *De jure belli ac pacis* provided the foundations for this renaissance. Grotius's exposition of Roman–Dutch law could not remain completely unaffected by the new way of thinking. * * *

5. NOTE ON NATURAL LAW AND ITS EXPANSION

The birth of natural law thinking, perhaps the most significant intellectual common development in the western, deserves some thoughts. Natural law, quite like the idea of international human rights today, assumed the existence of a body of fundamental legal principles, rights and rules that are universal and that should guide the law at all times. An earlier version of the idea emerged in the work of fifteenth and sixteenth century Jesuit jurists active in Spain (mostly Salamanca). These Jurists believed that the Christian God was the source of natural law that and that it was a duty of the Christian civilized nations to enforce it worldwide. In a different more secular version, mostly developed in Holland, natural law imagined the source of such universal rights not so much in God but in human reason. Indeed, beginning in the 1500s, and coming to a climax in the seventeenth and eighteenth centuries, increasingly rationalistic and secularized versions of *natural law thinking* exerted a powerful influence on law-teaching and legal institutions.[1] Insofar as private law was concerned, this influence made itself felt in two ways:

First, with respect to the substance of legal rules, the authority of the *Corpus Juris* was challenged. Medieval scholars, when seeking to adjust Roman law to the conditions of their own time, had done so by interpretation, even bold interpretation, of the ancient texts; but they had not questioned the authoritative nature of those texts. Now a different attitude emerged. The legal scholars of the "natural law" era, which in part coincided with the period of the broad intellectual movement known as humanism [seeking the roots of civilization in a mythological vision of ancient Greece and Rome], were conversant with Roman law, and they made ample use of the rich casuistry of the Roman texts as indicative of the practical legal problems to be resolved. In many instances, they even adopted the Roman solution; but they no longer felt bound to do so. In their view, the *Corpus Juris* had ceased to govern *ratione imperii* (by reason of force) Whatever persuasive force it retained—and that force was still considerable—it had to exercise *imperio rationis* (by force of reason), by virtue of the rational superiority of a particular rule or principle announced by the Roman jurists. On many points, such as the question of the enforceability of a *nudum pactum* [naked pact: an agreement entered into outside of the typically enforceable forms of the Roman contract law]

---

1. See Bodenheimer, Jurisprudence 31–59 (rev. ed. 1974).

the Roman formalistic solution was regarded as unreasonable and was, therefore, rejected by the followers of the new school.

Even before the advent of the great national codifications, this attitude of the natural law thinkers not only influenced the jus commune, but also had a strong impact on legislation. For instance, in Portugal (and Brazil), where an older statute had given the force of law to the opinions of Accursius and Bartolus, the Law of Sound Reason, enacted in 1769, provided that gaps in the written law should in the future be filled by resort to reason rather than by invoking the Roman law learning of the medieval Doctores. [2]

Secondly, and perhaps even more importantly, the legal thinkers of the natural law period revolutionized the methods of systematization. Prior to the seventeenth century, the civil law had been far less systematic than is commonly believed. The spirit of classical Roman law was pragmatic and casuistic, and even the sophisticated compilers of the *Corpus Juris* excelled more in practical wisdom than in system-building.[3] The medieval scholars, especially the commentators, improved the systematic treatment of certain subjects; but like the Roman jurists, they thought primarily in terms of specific problems or topics rather than in terms of an overall system. It was not until the natural law era that scholars began to build coherent and comprehensive systems of private law. The method of system-building used during the seventeenth and eighteenth centuries was deductive. Employing a small number of very general concepts and precepts as his starting point, the system-builder of that period deductively developed successive ranges of less and less general abstractions, categories and principles until finally, on the lowest level of abstraction, he laid out the specific rules governing concrete fact situations. The influence of this method upon the legal thinking of the immediate pre-codification period, and on the structure and spirit of some of the modern civilian codes, has been profound. Later in this course, especially when we study the structure of the German Civil Code, we shall have occasion to trace its continuing present-day effect.

In admiring the intellectual elegance of natural law theory, and before recommending its revival in the form of universal International Human Rights one should not forget its profound western-centrism and its less than admirable historical pedigree. Natural law theories have been behind the dispossession and genocide of indigenous populations in the Americas and elsewhere. The Spanish *conquistadores* (always traveling with a notary along to formalize the taking of possession) were legitimized by the idea that the *terra nullius* [owned by nobody] could be occupied through

---

2. See Orlando Gomes, Historical and Sociological Roots of the Brazilian Civil Code, 1 Inter–American L.Rev. 331, 332–33 (1959).

3. The Institutiones, serving primarily an educational function, were organized in a simple but understandable manner. In dealing with private law, they followed the Institutiones of the great classical jurist Gaius (about 160 AD) by focusing, successively, on persons, property, wills, intestate succession, and obligations. The "system" or organizing principle of the more important Digest, on the other hand, generally follows the much less systematic Praetorian Edict, authoritatively reconstructed by E. Lenel, Edictum Perpetuum (3d ed. 1927).

acquiring original title. Indigenous populations not recognizing the "natural" idea of private property were regarded as savages whose systems of tenure would not count as law. Later on, the English colonists in North America would similarly legitimize their take by theories (such as that of John Locke) grounded in the same vein of natural law thinking. Both the *conquistadores* and Anglo–Saxon settlers regarded the indigenous peoples' failure to recognize *individual property rights on land* as a sign of barbarism which in turn served to justify the introduction of "civilization" and Christianity by force.[4] These early expansions of western legal ideology based on individual property right—a legacy of the Roman law idea of *dominium* ("the sole and despotic dominion" known to U.S. students as Blackstone's definition of ownership)—played an important role in the production of genocidal violence.[5] These brutal consequences indeed produced some troubles in the holy conscience of the catholic Queen Isabel of Castile and of many Spanish jurists at the time. Quite an extensive scholarly debate has been produced. Well-known and quite fascinating is that on the human nature of savages having as protagonists De Las Casas, and Sepulveda.

6.   Note on the "Law of Castile and the Indies"

The term "Indies" refers to the ultramarine possessions of the Spanish Crown, including those in the Americas and the Philippines but excluding some islands. Constitutionally, these ultramarine possessions were part of the Crown of Castile,[1] and their legal orders were derived from Castilian law to the exclusion of other Peninsular *fueros*, or systems of law of local applicability.[2]

Nevertheless, Spanish ultramarine law, the law of the Indies, was not at any given time necessarily identical with Castilian law. Substantial identity of norms of general applicability can be assumed until 1614, but pursuant to a royal *cédula* (decree) dated December 15 of that year,[3] Peninsular legislation thereafter became effective overseas only if enacted (or reenacted) by the Council of the Indies. This *cédula* is but one manifestation of the geographical division of governmental, judicial, and legislative powers between the Councils of Castile and of the Indies which eventually led to the development of a special corpus of "Indian" law that was peninsular (metropolitan) in origin but applicable only overseas.

---

4. See Aldo Andrea Cassi, Ultramar (2007), Ugo Mattei & Laura Nader, Plunder. When the Rule of Law is Illegal (2008).

5. For a more detailed analysis of colonizers' land policies, see Stuart Banner, How the Indians Lost Their Land: Law and Power on the Frontier (2005) and Stuart Banner, Possessing the Pacific: Land, Settlers, and Indigenous People from Australia to Alaska (2007).

1. Bull of Donation of May 4, 1493. Recopilación de Leyes de los Reinos de las Indias (R.I.) Book 3, Title 1, Law 1 (1681 ed.).

2. The 1493 cession was made specifically to the Castilian Crown. See R.I. Book 3, Title 1, Law 1. Thus, only Castilian law applied. See R.I. Book 2, Title 15, Law 66.

3. See Decree of December 15, 1614. R.I. Book 2, Title 1, Laws 39–40.

The chief repository of this "law of the Indies" is the *Recopilación de Leyes de los Reynos de las Indias* (R.I.), a selective and systematic rearrangement of the major relevant texts up to 1680. The R.I. contains some 6,385 provisions, representing a composite edition of about twice as many enactments, and these, in turn, were selected from over 400,000 *cédulas* or other legislative instruments pertaining to the Indies.[4] It is frequently possible to reconstruct the "legislative history" of a *recopilada*, *i.e.*, of an enactment incorporated into the R.I. and hence effective throughout the Indies, by tracing its legislative antecedents.

The R.I. is divided into nine books, and covers mainly what would now be considered public law. Various titles of the fourth book, dealing with population settlements, land grants, and public places, are of continuing importance in disputes over historical land and water rights, as is the sixth book, which relates to Indians. More fundamentally, however, the R.I. also contains a key provision designating the sources of law to be resorted to for the resolution of disputes and, incidentally, the relation of these sources to each other. These are, in the order of precedence, the *Recopilación* of the Indies, prior "Indian" legislation not repealed, and the laws of the kingdom of Castile in conformity with the *Leyes de Toro*. Subsequent legislation takes precedence over the R.I. whenever pertinent.[5]

The reference to the *Leyes de Toro* establishes, again by indirection, the sources and the precedence of pre–1680 Castilian private law so far as applicable in the Indies. These are, again in the order of precedence, the *Leyes de Toro* themselves, the *Ordenamiento de Alcalá*, the *Fueros Municipales y Reales*, and, finally, the *Siete Partidas*. As a practical matter, however, the reference to legislation not repealed by the *Recopilación* of the Indies included the *Nueva Recopilación* of the kingdom of Castile, which was adopted in 1567 and thus needed no separate approval by the Council of the Indies.[6] Without sacrifice of accuracy, these ground rules can be summarized in two basic propositions: the law of the Indies prevailed over Castilian law in Spanish America, and later law prevailed over earlier law but usually did so without express repeal.

Justinian's codification of the Roman law, the *Corpus Iuris Civilis* of 533 AD, was not a formal source of the law of the Indies, either directly or by reference to Castilian law. The reason for this is in part historical: In 533 AD, the Western Empire had been lost, and the *Corpus Iuris Civilis* could not be formally enacted in the Iberian Peninsula. Nevertheless, Roman law is reflected in many rules of Castilian law, including, e.g., some key provisions of the *Siete Partidas* relating to the ownership of beds of public streams.[7]

4. See C. Garcia Gallo, La Legislación Indiana de 1636 a 1680 y La Recopilación de 1680, 9 Boletin Mexicano de Derecho Comparado 297, 298–99 (1976).

5. See R.I. Book 2, Title 1, Laws 1–3; *id.* Book 2, Title 15, Law 66.

6. See G. Margadant, Introducción a la Historia del Derecho Mexicano 18 (1971).

7. See R.I. Book 3, Title 28, Law 31. This provision is almost literally copied from Justinian's Institutes (J. Inst. 2,1,23).

Even more importantly, until about the middle of the eighteenth century, Latin was the language, and Roman law the substance, of civil law instruction at the Spanish and ultramarine universities. Justinian's codification furnished the text, and the professor occasionally referred to the *derecho real*, i.e., the Royal law sanctioned by the King of Spain (also called *derecho patrio*, or law of the country), by way of illustration. The standard book of instruction in use in Peninsular law faculties was *Institutionum Imperialium Commentarius*, by A. Vinnius, a four-volume commentary on Justinian's Institutions written by a Netherlands scholar.[8]

All this changed in the latter half of the eighteenth century. At a transitory stage, commentaries of Justinian's *Institutes* were expanded through the inclusion of references to the *derecho real* (or *patrio*), which in Peninsular editions did not include the legislation of the Indies. An exception in this respect is *Elucidationes ad Quatuor Libros Institutionum Imperatoris Justiniani Opportune Locupletatae Legibus Decisionibusque Juris Hispani* by J. Magro, posthumously completed by E. Bentura Belaña and published in Mexico in 1787 with some annotations to the law of the Indies which, however, their author judged to be insufficient.[9]

By the end of the eighteenth century, Royal insistence on teaching in the *derecho patrio* had brought about a fundamental change. The order of instruction was almost exactly reversed, with the *derecho patrio* (in Castilian) furnishing the text, and Roman law supplying the occasional examples. A Castilian-language work, Juan Sala's *Ilustración del Derecho Real de España*, which first appeared in 1803, became the standard book of instruction as well as one of the leading sources for practitioners. After setting forth the relation of Mexican, "Indian," and Castilian law as outlined above, the 1845 edition of the "Sala Mexicano" states, with respect to Roman law:

> The Roman laws are not, and may not be called, laws in Spain. They are learned opinions, which may only be followed where there is a gap in the law, and to the extent that they are inspired by natural law and follow the Royal law (*derecho real*). The latter, not Roman law, is the *derecho comun*, and neither the laws of the Romans nor those of other foreigners are to be used and observed.[10]

For the practical consequences of all this, see H. W. Baade, Roman Law in the Water, Mineral, and Public Land Law of the Southwestern United States, 40 Am.J.Comp.L. 865 (1992).

---

8. See M. Perset Reig, Derecho Romano y Derecho Patrio en Las Universidades del Siglo SVIII, 45 Anuario de Historia del Derecho Español 273, 317 (1975).

9. See 1 J. Magro, Elucidationes ad Quatuor Libros Institutionum Imperatoris Justiniani Opportune Locupletatae Legibus, Decionibusque Juris Hispani x (1787).

10. 1 Sala Mexicano 159 (1845) (footnote omitted).

7.   SOME NATIONAL DEVELOPMENTS

Deák and Rheinstein, The Development of French and German Law

24 Geo.L.J. 551, 553–56, 568–71 (1936).

I.   The Development of the Law of France

Although France achieved political unity, under a comparatively strong central authority, several centuries before the various German states were consolidated into the Reich, uniformity of law was not accomplished until the beginning of the nineteenth century. German legal uniformity followed closely on the heels of political consolidation. On the other hand, mediaeval France, although a "nation," in the modern sense of the word, for several centuries before codification, presents to the legal historian a kaleidoscope of various legal systems existing contemporaneously, yet independently in the various provinces and districts.

Pre-revolutionary France, living under what French legal historians designate as the period of "ancient law" (*l'ancien droit*),[1] may be divided into two geographical zones. In the south (the *Midi*), Roman law was paramount and that section is therefore designated by French legal historians as the country of written law (*pays de droit écrit*). In the various provinces of the north, local customs were in force and this area has been termed the country of customary law (*pays de coutume*). This geographical division should not be regarded as a complete cleavage; like every generalization, it is subject to qualifications. The *pays de droit écrit* had some customary law (e.g., the *coutume de Bordeaux*), though it was strictly local and considerably less elaborate than in the northern provinces. On the other hand, the *pays de coutume* recognized at least the persuasive authority of Roman law, especially when customary law was silent. Roman law, furthermore, was to a large extent the common background of legal learning and of law teaching in the Universities, even in the North of France.

The customs were numerous and varied. Some called *coutume générale*, of which there were about sixty, were in force in an entire province, or in a large district (e.g., *coutume de Paris, coutume de Normandie, coutume d'Orléans*). It may be noted that the influence of the *coutume de Paris* was extended beyond the geographical limits of its actual authority. Others were in force only in a city or a village; these are called *coutumes locales*, of which there were some 300. In view of their number, and in view of the fact that the customs were originally not reduced to writing, there must have been considerable confusion and uncertainty. To remedy the situation,

---

1. Ancien régime and ancien droit are commonly used as references to French government and law before the Revolution of 1789. "Ancient law" is, even today, not an entirely accurate translation of ancien droit, i.e., pre-revolutionary French law.

Charles VII, in his ordinance of Montils-les-Tours, 1453, ordered the official compilation of all customs. More than a century was necessary to accomplish this task; but by the end of the sixteenth century the bulk of French "customary" law was, in fact, reduced to written law.

An additional factor, still further emphasizing the particularism of ancient French law, was the power of the *Parlement* of Paris and the thirteen provincial *Parlements*—in the exercise of their judicial functions—to resolve moot questions. In exercising this power, they often adopted conflicting views. These decisions, called *arrêts de règlement*, were not rendered in actual litigation, but declared the position the *Parlement* would take in the future in similar cases. This was, of course, a form of judicial legislation, although it was limited both in substance (i.e., the *Parlements* had no power to modify the existing law) and in extent (i.e., within the jurisdiction of the respective *Parlements*).

Despite the existence of numerous customs, the royal ordinances issued in exercise of the King's legislative power had a certain unifying force. These ordinances were, as a rule, in force throughout the kingdom. Their unifying effect was somewhat impaired by the occasional refusal of some of the provincial *Parlements* to execute them by "registration" within their respective jurisdictions; their reluctance was, however, usually overcome by the pressure of royal authority....

To complete this picture, mention should be made of the canon law which also exerted profound influence on some branches of French law, especially in the field of family law.

The advent of the Revolution marks the end of the period of "ancient" law and, at the same time, the beginning of the transitional period commonly called the period of "intermediary" law (*droit intermédiaire*). Revolutionary legislation aimed chiefly at reform in the field of public law and of political institutions. Its main accomplishments were the abolition of ancient privileges, the establishment of equality before the law, the guarantee of individual liberty, and the protection of private property....

II. The Development of the Law of Germany

The law of mediaeval Germany consisted mostly, as did mediaeval law generally, of customs and tradition. Although originating in common Germanic ideas, they were locally developed in each part of the vast territories of Central Europe which made up the "Holy Roman Empire of the Germanic Nation." Many of these customs prevailed over large stretches of territory, others were confined to a single city, village, or manor, or to a special group of persons. Many were privately collected and expanded in law books, some of which, in the course of time, attained quasi-statutory force similar to the English books of authority.[2]

---

2. The most influential of these books was Eike von Repgow's Mirror of Saxon Law (Sachsenspiegel) about 1225.

While in mediaeval England the customs and rules which were applied by the royal courts at Westminster gradually supplanted all local customs and became the Common Law of the Realm, the central power in the Empire did not attempt such an undertaking until the law of Rome (i.e., Justinian's *Corpus Juris*), had so effectively encroached upon the native Germanic laws that it had come to be regarded as the Common Law of the Empire. With this infiltration virtually an accomplished fact, the period of Roman law dominance, from the fifteenth to the end of the nineteenth century, began. When, in 1495, a central imperial court, the *Reichskammergericht*, was established, its judges were ordered to decide the cases coming before them "according to the Common Law of the Empire," i.e., according to Roman law.

However, the Roman law did not completely supplant the local laws. The *Usus Modernus Pandectarum* [modern use of the digest] was rather an amalgamation of Roman law with the old local customs, in which Roman law, being more comprehensive and elaborate, was the dominating element. The result of this amalgamation was different in the various parts of the country. The differences among the local customs and precedents were increased through territorial legislation, which assumed considerable importance with the growing independence of the territorial rulers. Natural law philosophy, the merging of various smaller states into larger political units, and the rise of absolute monarchy led to more or less comprehensive territorial codifications which, however, partly preserved the pre-existing law as a "subsidiary" source to be applied in the absence of statute. When the Empire was formally dissolved in 1806, state legislation had been supreme for a considerable time, and when, in 1871, the new *Reich* was created, the country was governed by a multitude of laws, much as prerevolutionary France had its multitude of customs.

. . . All these different laws were linked together by a common jurisprudence, developed by the universities, which taught the common features and foundations rather than the details of the various local laws. This policy of the universities resulted in some measure of uniformity of German law, despite all the actual differences, so that there was a *German* legal profession, with a universal legal terminology and system, based mostly on "Romanist" learning.[3]

This academic molding process was assisted by legislation after the middle of the nineteenth century, first by the adoption of uniform statutes in the various German states, then, after 1866, by federal legislation. . . .

The most important step in the process of unification was the enactment, on August 1, 1896, of the Civil Code (*Bürgerliches Gesetzbuch, BGB*). The Code, covering almost the entire field of private law, abolished all the various local laws and replaced them with a uniform legal system. It came into force on January 1, 1900, accompanied by an Introductory Law. . . .

---

3. See J. Q. Whitman, The Legacy of Roman Law in the German Romantic Era: Historical Vision and Legal Change (1990).

As in France the Civil Code of 1804 marks the beginning of the period of modern French law, so in Germany, the adoption of the *Bürgerliches Gesetzbuch (BGB)* almost a century later meant a fresh start for German law. It should be noted, however, that the break in evolution in Germany was less violent than in France. Codification in Germany was a molding process following political unification; it was not blended with antagonism toward an old order, the institutions of which were swept abruptly away by revolution....

(a) Note on Provincial Parlements and Napoleonic Reform

The *Parlement* of Paris, which emerged as the judicial branch from the King's court (*curia regis*) and which became independent toward the end of the thirteenth century, and the various provincial *Parlements* established between 1443 and 1775 (Toulouse, Grenoble, Bordeaux, Burgundy, Brittany, Normandy, Aix, Trévoux, Bearn, Metz, Besançon, Douai, and Nancy) were chiefly courts of justice. At the same time they exercised legislative as well as administrative powers. Concerning the history and functions of these *Parlements*, see Brissaud, History of French Public Law [Continental Legal History Series, vol. 9] (1915) §§ 403–419, and for the more recent past, D. A. Bell, Lawyers and Citizens, The Making of a Political Elite in Old Regime France (1994).

It may be noted that this power of the provincial *Parlements*, or rather its abuse, became a fertile source of discontent. Thus may be explained, in good part, the hostility to judicial legislation in the revolutionary and Napoleonic era, and the disregard of precedent as a source of law until very recent times. See in this connection Art. 5 of the French Civil Code, which requires courts to decide only the actual case before them and enjoins them from rendering decisions laying down general principles. (See the discussion *infra* in 594ff).

The philosophical roots of "intermediary" revolutionary legislation are traced in an essay by C. J. Friedrich, The Ideological and Philosophical Background, in The Code Napoleon and the Common–Law World 1–18 (B. Schwartz ed., 1956). The same essay interestingly discusses the subsequent process of consolidation, moderation and compromise by which Napoleon, working with a small team of lawyers—men of great professional competence but reared in traditional, pre-revolutionary legal learning—transformed the laws of the Revolution into a workable system of codes.

(b) Note on the Development of the Common Law of England

The English legal experience is characterized by the early creation by William the Conqueror and the other Norman Kings of a powerful centralized bureaucracy which soon gave rise to the development of a centralized system of courts of law. While it is not clear whether the first stable Court in the heart of London has been the Court of Common Pleas, the King's Bench or the Exchequer, the fact is that the first English Constitutional document, the *Magna Charta* (1215), guarantees the presence of a static Court in Westminster Hall (a location abandoned only in 1882) and abolished the personal jurisdiction of the sovereign (later re-established in a variety of occasions).

From the Magna Charta onward we find in England a judicial organization produced mostly by the accident of history and by the struggle for power and for jurisdiction between the Feudal Barons, the King, the Parliament (representing the landed peers) and the different Courts of law both at the center and in the periphery. For many centuries, until the reforms of the late nineteenth century, the competition between the different superior common law Courts, has been carried on by means of a complex variety of technical expedients in the hands of a self-trained bench and bar that in competing for patronage and social prestige has created by means of "an invisible hand" one of the two great families of the western legal tradition.

In the feudal organization, property in land (always retained as a concession from the King in the well-known structure of the feudal chain) carried with it jurisdictional power. Because justice has never been free, such power was a source of income for the large landlords (so called Tenants-in-Chief) similar to what would be generated by charging for the use of a bridge, a mill or a street. Consequently, the centralization of justice would subtract a source of income from the barons. It would be resented like a taking of property, a very delicate thing to do in circumstances in which the King depended on the military and economic services of the Barons. The "miracle" of the common law is that of a centralized legal system early established by the Monarchy that has been able to unfold within the interstices of particular laws as a subsidiary system, a true common law of the realm. This system proved powerful because, by its formalism and its strength in the protection of property rights, it has been able to emancipate itself even from the King, establishing a powerful alliance with the very barons whose jurisdiction it was curtailing. By displaying this appearance of technical impartiality, in the hands of very skilled jurists trained in its technicalities, the common law system has survived showing relatively little discontinuity through revolutions, civil wars and tremendous historical strains to reach our day with still a high degree of social prestige.

Early on the King would not claim jurisdiction other than that belonging to him from the very structure of feudalism. It could address the so called Pleas of the Crown, those serious issues that would directly affect the King or the dignity of the Crown. But by elaborating a notion of breach of the King's peace, the common law Courts have been able to capture all criminal jurisdiction, at the time not well separated from the law of torts. The King, even in feudal theory, was recognized as the Lord of all Lords. He could consequently exercise some supervision over the activity of local courts by offering justice to litigants that otherwise would remain unsatisfied because of the poor quality or the lack of access to local justice: *propter defectum justitie* [because of lack of justice]. Finally, his Courts had jurisdiction over direct conflicts between his Tenants-in-Chief (the Barons). In carrying on this recognized jurisdiction, the common law Courts would claim they were applying the common customary law of the land, something that very soon became undistinguishable from their own technical practice. Thus the common law lawyers sitting and practicing in Westminster Hall and teaching the Laws to each-other in the Inns of Court, legitimized their own professional practice and project as the supreme law of the land.

The tremendous care necessary for success in their incremental expansion of jurisdiction (and hence of power), and the tension with the political authorities whose power they would curtail in so doing, generated a sharp increase in the formalism practiced in dispensing the writs that set the judicial process in motion. Because of the increasing instances where formalism caused a denial of justice (for example: only damages were available in torts; no action would lie against an unfaithful administrator to whom property had been transferred in order to take care of the wife and the minors during a crusade), by early fifteenth century the King began entertaining an extraordinary justice of prerogative to supplement or substitute the too formalistic common law courts. Such *equity* justice, transferred to the King's Chancellor (most often a clergyman trained in canon law) soon became a complete alternative system that has survived until our day as a unique feature of the common law as a family of legal systems.

Some of the other jurisdictions competing with the common law courts did not have the same success as the Court of Equity. For example, the Admiralty Court, staffed with a highly cosmopolitan Roman-law-trained bench and bar with significant ties to the high centers of learning of Oxford and Cambridge (the so called Doctor's Commons) has been literally put out of business by the common law courts that, under the lead of the Scottish jurist Lord Mansfield, successfully claimed exclusive jurisdiction over commercial law matters.

While courts of law have certainly been the protagonists of English legal developments, the judges rather than the professors being oracles of the law in England, one should not rush to the conclusion that scholarly writings were absent in the unfolding of the pre-contemporary era common law system. From Bracton to Glanville, from Coke to Blackstone, the highly influential legal literature was not absent and always played a crucial role in keeping the common law system from being entirely consumed by unprincipled technicality and casuistry. With the exception of Blackstone, the latest common law jurist writing before "the age of statutes," none of these great writers were academics. They were nevertheless men of high learning often participating in the European intellectual debate of their times.

(c) Notes on Additional Complexities at the Roots of the Western Legal Tradition

At this point, the reader may feel that an image of pre-modern western legal tradition is emerging. One should, however, be aware of the dangers inherent in all generalizations. In speaking of "pre-code civil law," for example, we refer to a galaxy of legal systems which, although sharing a common European tradition, were widely separated from each other in time and space.

(1) That there are important *differences from country to country* has been shown by the preceding materials, especially the excerpts from the article by Deák and Rheinstein. These differences relate, inter alia, to the depth of Roman law influence; the time when the "reception" of Roman law occurred; the relative strength of central and territorial political power; the predominance of one or the other of the doctrinal schools (see *infra*); the revolutionary or evolutionary nature of change; and the earlier or later date of modern codification on a national scale.

(2) When we speak of the history of civil law prior to the age of modern codifications, we have in mind a period which lasted from 534 AD until the nineteenth century. When we talk about a history of the western legal tradition before its nineteenth century modernization we talk of a period of eight hundred years. Indeed, as we shall see, modernization in Continental Europe took the form of a general codification effort while in the common law it took the form of judicial reform (English Judicature Acts 1873–1876). It may be a truism (but it is important to remember) that, although the pace of change was slower than in our day, *the law did not stand still during that period*.

A comprehensive description of the development of legal institutions in continental Europe during those 13 centuries would fill many volumes.[1] No attempt is made here to present such an encyclopedic history. Our endeavor is merely (a) to emphasize those successive developments in the teaching of Roman or Roman-influenced law which have left a permanent imprint on civil law methods while only in very limited part altering the common law method of reasoning, and (b) to remind the reader that modern civil law was shaped not only by the Roman law tradition but also by forces that were more or less independent of that tradition, and sometimes openly opposed to it.

(3) Not all of the crucial stimuli of legal development (during the pre-codification era of civil law) came from the Roman heritage. Only a brief listing of the non-Roman impulses is possible here. The following appear to be particularly important:

(a) In northern Europe, *local and regional customs of Germanic origin* played a significant role until the age of codification, as explained in the above excerpts from the article by Deák and Rheinstein. The Langobards and Visigoths, moreover, carried some of their customs into parts of Italy and Spain.

(b) Both in public law and in the law of real property, the *feudal epoch* gave rise to social and legal institutions unknown to antiquity. It was only by a dazzling display of ingenuity, and indeed a bit of legerdemain, that the commentators were able to fit some of these

---

1. For ample documentation, see Cappelletti, Merryman & Perillo, The Italian Legal System 4–41 (1967); S. L. Sass, Medieval Roman Law: Sources and Literature, 58 L.Lib.J. 130 (1965); G. Margadant, La Secunda Vida del Derecho Romano (1986).

institutions into their Romanist system and into the terminology of the *Corpus Juris.*

In England the feudal organization brought in by William the Conqueror was staunchly defended by means of Parliamentary resistance of Barons against the modernization efforts of the Tudor Crown in the early sixteenth century. The powerful alliance between the Parliament and the common law Courts preserved the feudal structure, defeated legal modernization and produced the birth of Equity as an alternative competitive system whose open struggle with the common law was settled only in late seventeenth century. The legendary hero of this struggle to preserve the feudal property structure has been Sir Edward Coke, Chief Justice of the Court of Common Pleas (the most important common law court at the time) that in 1608 baldly communicated to the King, in the name of the "rule of law" that not being trained as a common lawyer he could not participate in the decision making of the common law courts, dispensing justice in his name. The feudal origins of English Law are particularly visible in the Law of Property, restated by Sir Edward Coke himself in the famous book *Coke on Littleton* which also played a major role in the making of early North American law. Both England and most of the United States eventually reformed their property law getting rid of most of its feudal incrustation and many of the complexities of the theory of estates (fee simples, fee tails, reversions etc.). Paradoxically, however, some U.S. states, like for example West Virginia, never reformed their English-imported property law so that today, they still show the traces of the feudal structure, while never having experienced feudalism as a form of political organization!

(c) The law of the Church, the *jus canonicum*, was an independent system, co-existing with the *jus civile* taught by the glossators and commentators—the "legists" as distinguished from the "canonists." The law faculties, however, included both the former and the latter, and the standard first academic law degree achieved after five years' study could be taken either as a magister (or licenciate) of *leges* or of *canones* without prejudice to future career as a secular or ecclesiastical lawyer. Students necessarily studied both secular and ecclesiastic law; the highest academic degree was called appropriately Juris Utriusque Doctor—doctor of both laws. No love was lost between canonists and theologians, but in the law faculties, professors of *leges* and *canones* competed for students, not for ultimate authority.

Canon law was, however, sharply distinct from (revived) Roman law in two respects. First, as to sources: Enacted Roman law was textually complete, and in need of scholarly exposition and systematization. Justinian's codification ended with the last of his *novellae constitutiones* in 556 AD. Canon law, on the other hand, drew its very texts from papal decrees successively reduced to systematic compilations until 1502. The six "masses" of the *Corpus Iuris Canonici* are Gratian's Decree (ca. 1140), the Decretals of Gregory IX (1234; the so-called Liber Extra = X), the Liber Sextus of Boniface VIII (1298) (the Liber Extra has five books; hence Liber Sextus for its successor), the "Clementines" of Clement V (1317), the Extravagantes of John XXII, and the Extravagantes Communes (1499–1502). In contradistinction to the five subsequent "masses," Gratian's Decree, as such, did not have the force of (ecclesiastical) law. [2]

Secondly, as to method: As early as the year 1200, the Pope reminded the canon law scholars at Bologna that *interpretatio* flowed from the same source as legislation,[3] and by the end of that century, the Holy See had vindicated its claim to supreme legislative and judicial authority [which it maintains as of today in the Vatican City State and on matters of Canon law regulating the priesthood world-wide].[4] Canon law scholarship developed, therefore, within a strictly hierarchical system, and against the ever-present possibility that scholarly interpretation of papal decrees might be overturned summarily by an act of authentic interpretation: *Roma locuta, causa finita.* ["Rome has spoken; the case is closed."] In the secular realm, on the other hand, royal and princely power over legal interpretation could be asserted successfully only by absolute rulers, and then only as to texts not requiring the assent of municipal councils or feudal estates.[5]

It has been argued that after the Reformation, at least, there was no such thing as "Romano–Canon" law in Protestant realms.[6] Whether this was so seems mainly a terminological question. In England, for instance, the canon law of the Anglican Church was taught at Oxford and Cambridge as part of "civil law" after Henry the Eighth had prohibited the teaching of canon law;[7] elsewhere as well, canon law authority on procedural law was followed for the simple reason that it was the only one available initially for secular tribunals staffed by learned judges and following written proceedings in hierarchical order.[8] In any case, as a glance even at Blackstone's Commentaries shows, books of authority in Protestant lands after the Reformation routinely referred to the *Corpus Juris Canonici* along with the *Corpus Juris Civilis* of Justinian.[9]

2. For brief description, see T. Bouscaren et al., Canon Law 2–3, 11 (4th ed. 1966).

3. C. 31 X de sententia excommunicationis 5, 39.

4. For a thoroughly documented discussion of this process, see Sten Gagnér, Studien zur Ideengeschichte der Gesetzgebung 121–288 (1960).

5. Philippe Godding, L'Interprétation de la "Loi" dans le Droit Savant Médiéval et dans le Droit des Pays–Bas Méridionaux, in L'Interprétation en Droit, Approche Pluridis-

ciplinaire 446, 460–62 (Michel Van de Kerchove ed., 1978).

6. H. J. Berman & C. J. Reid, Roman Law in Europe and the Jus Commune: A Historical Overview with Emphasis on the New Legal Science of the Sixteenth Century, 20 Syracuse J.Int'l L & Comm. 1, 9–10 (1994).

7. See generally R. H. Helmholz, ed., Canon Law in Protestant Lands (1992).

8. E. J. H. Schrage, Ultrumque Ius 83–86 (1992).

9. E.g., 1 Bl. Comm. *424 note k.

The views of the Church were, of course, paramount with respect to those subjects of which the ecclesiastical courts had jurisdiction, such as matrimonial and testamentary matters. Beyond that, ecclesiastical jurisdiction often could be founded on the allegation that defendant's conduct, e.g., his non-performance of a promise, constituted a sin. On this jurisdictional basis, Bartolus reports, the ecclesiastical tribunals of his time "daily" enforced promises for the breach of which there would have been no remedy, or no adequate remedy, in the secular courts.[10] As a rule, such decrees of ecclesiastical courts were obeyed; a recalcitrant party would have faced excommunication, with its secular as well as spiritual consequences. Canon law, as enforced by ecclesiastical tribunals, thus significantly supplemented, and in effect changed, the Roman-derived law of contracts.[11]

In many areas of law, the views of the Church, as reflected in the *jus canonicum*, also had a strong impact on the jus civile itself. Again, the law of contracts furnishes an apt illustration. Under the Roman system of contract law, the details of which need not be restated here,[12] only certain categories of contracts were enforceable. An executory contract which did not fit into any of these categories was called *nudum pactum* and was not actionable (although it could be pleaded by way of defense). Under the influence of canon law, the glossators and commentators attempted to liberalize this somewhat rigid Roman system, and to bring it closer to the expansive canon law interpretation of *pacta sunt servanda* [agreements have to be respected]. As one might expect, however, these attempts to reconcile two irreconcilable approaches led to much refinement, controversy and confusion, with the result that concerning this particular subject the *jus civile* was, and for several centuries remained, in a very unsatisfactory state. The modern civil law solution to the problem emerged from two other sources, i.e., the *law merchant* and the teachings of the "Natural Law" school, that we know has been substantially a conceptual refinement of Roman law categories legitimized either by the authority of God (Spanish version) or by that of reason (Dutch version).

(d) The *law merchant*, the history and present-day significance of which are discussed *infra* Chapter 5, Section 1 at 385, was another independent system co-existing with the Roman-derived jus civile and with the English common law. In many instances the rules of the law merchant were superior to those taught by the Romanists. Thus, in transactions among merchants, there was never much doubt concerning the enforceability of executory contracts, even non-typical ones. In time, it became clear that—in this instance as in others—the solution

10. See H. Coing, English Equity and the Denunciatio Evangelica of the Canon Law, 71 L.Q.Rev. 223, 231 (1955).

11. There is a notable parallel between this continental development and the subsequent growth of English equity. See Coing, *ibid.* See also H. J. Berman, Law and Revolution, The Formation of the Western Legal Tradition 245–50 (1983).

12. See R. W. Lee, Elements of Roman Law 290–344 (1956).

adopted by the law merchant was the most desirable one, and that solution was then gradually taken over into the general law.

(e) At the beginning of the nineteenth century, to be sure, the historical school revolted against the allegedly lifeless rationalism of the preceding period (in particular of natural law). Even in Germany, however, where under Savigny's leadership this revolt was particularly strong, it did not lead to antiquarian reconstruction of ancient Roman or Germanic law. The commanding academic voices who developed and in some measure unified German law during the nineteenth century (see Deák & Rheinstein *supra*, at 351, postulated greater respect for grown legal institutions than had been shown by the rationalists; Savigny's idea was that the law had to reflect "the spirit of the people", thus being local rather than universal. But the rationalist's method of systematization was used and indeed perfected by Savigny and the other representatives of the German *Pandektenwissenschaft* [pandectist schools also known as legal Romanticism]. It is to this systematicity—never surpassed or equalled anywhere—that the nineteenth century German legal scholars owed the world-wide influence of their writings, and of the BGB which was the ultimate embodiment of their teaching.

(4) The relative strength of Roman and non-Roman influences upon the development of the civil law during the pre-code era varied not only from country to country and from period to period, but also *from subject to subject*. We have seen, for instance, that in the seventeenth and certainly in the eighteenth century the Roman rule against affirmative enforceability of the *nudum pactum* had been abandoned by most of the leading authorities. At the same time, the essence of the Roman doctrine of *negotiorum gestio* [literally, management of someone else's business, a form of unjustified enrichment] was preserved intact by the great French jurist Pothier and other influential writers, with the ultimate result that it was written into the modern codes.

Note on additional materials. The student who seeks extensive information on European legal history from Justinian to the present will find that in the past many of the best-known works were written in terms of national (e.g. French or German or Spanish) legal history, thus making it relatively difficult for the reader to gain an overview of European trends and developments. Valuable recent works dealing with European rather than national legal history are P. Koschaker, Europa und das römische Recht (1953), F. Wieacker, A History of Private Law in Europe (T. Weir trans., 1995), and H. Coing, ed., Handbuch der Quellen und Literatur der neueren europaeischen Rechtsgeschichte (8 vols. to date, 1973–88). Paolo Grossi, L'Europa del diritto (2008). The Max Planck Institut at Frankfurt, founded by Professor Helmut Coing, is devoted to research on *European* (not merely German) legal History. See R. A. Riegert, The Max Planck Institute for European Legal History, 22 Southwestern L.J. 397 (1968). The Institute publishes a series of monographs entitled Ius Commune. Over one hundred volumes have appeared in this series between 1967 and 1996. Another invaluable source, mainly but not entirely in English, is the

Comparative Studies in Continental and Anglo–American Legal History series, edited by Professors Coing and K. W. Nörr.

8.   ISLAMIC LAW

(a) Early Foundations of Islamic Law

As the previous materials suggest, when we think of law as something that emanates from a modern nation-state, we are dealing with a western concept. Although the style of political organization to which it refers has spread all over the globe—most notably through western colonialism—it is important to note that the concept, as we use today, is indeed of western origin. Hence, when we are comparing, say, the common law and civil law traditions, it seems self-evident that both traditions are *legal* traditions and the very concept of law itself requires little elaboration. However, as soon as we step outside the metropolitan West and turn to "other" societies, it is no longer so clear whether or not those societies have law (properly so-called). Ultimately, the answer to the question obviously depends on our definition of law. We can define it broadly and take *ubi societas, ibi jus* as our axiom "where there is society, there is law"—in which case *all* societies at all times have had (some kind of) law, or we can define it narrowly as just the way in which modern nation-states are organized, in which case *no* other form of social organization can lay a claim to "real" law.

Given the history of the concept, the focus of this book is primarily on the way in which law organizes modern societies structured on the originally European but now globalized the model of the nation-state.[1] Yet at the same time, it is vital to keep in mind that even with the triumph of the modern centralized state, the notions of civil law and common law hardly exhaust the legal universe: other legal systems and other legal cultures remain, albeit usually—indeed necessarily—in some type of accommodation with the fact of the modern state and its law. It is obviously impossible to canvass all of the world legal traditions within the confines of this book. However, it is also not possible to appreciate the historical contingency and particularity of the western-style legal tradition (even its globalized form) without at least some consideration of "other" legal systems. We have already considered some aspects of Chinese law above. Here we take up Islamic law. Obviously both of these traditions are historically important, but in no way are they offered here as somehow exemplary or more worthy of study than many others. Rather, their value in this context is above all heuristic: trying to give us a way to try and see the western legal tradition from another perspective. An oft-mentioned pedagogical purpose of comparative law is to make what is familiar seem foreign, and what is foreign seem familiar.

---

1. For a comparative law text focusing primarily on non-Western law, see, e.g., Werner Menski, Comparative Law in a Global Context: The Legal Systems of Asia and Africa (2d ed., 2006).

Islamic law is, above all, a form of religious law. Of the three great monotheistic religions of the Middle East, Islam is the youngest. After Muhammad's death in 632 A.D., armies drawn from inhabitants of Arabia conquered surrounding territories in Islam's name and founded a new empire. The religion spread rapidly along the northern coast of Africa to Spain, and through Persia to Central Asia. By the tenth century, an entire "Islamic world" had emerged, bridging the Mediterranean and the Indian Ocean.[2] By 1453, the Ottoman dynasty conquered Constantinople and Islam became established in southeastern Europe as well. Before the English colonized India, the Moghul dynasty controlled much of the sub-continent, and indeed Islamic law remains the "personal law" of the significant Muslim minority in India today. When Pakistan split from India after World War II, it became a majority Muslim state, and Islam remains a major religion also in Southeast Asia. Millions of Muslim immigrants and their descendants also live as increasingly significant minorities in Europe and North Africa, sometimes employing Islamic jurisprudence to resolve private legal matters pertaining to, e.g., inheritance, marriage, and family law. Our discussion here, however, will focus on the operation of Islamic law in Muslim-majority societies.

Below is a brief account of the nature and sources of *shari'a*, the body of Islamic religious law.

S.G. Vesey–Fitzgerald, Nature and Sources of the Shari'a

in *Law in the Middle East*, Majid Khadduri & Herbert J. Liebesny eds. (1955), pp. 85–112.

Islam is not only a religion, it is a political system, and though in modern times devout Muslims have endeavored to separate the two aspects, Islam's whole classical literature is based upon the assumption that they are inseparable. Most legal systems have at one time or another in their history been intimately connected with religion; but the two great Semitic systems, the Jewish and the Islamic, are probably unique in the thoroughness with which they identify law with the personal command of a single Almighty God. This is the more remarkable in that Islam has never recognized a priesthood, and in the Jewish system the priesthood became extinct at an early stage in the elaboration of the law.

To the Westerner, law is a system of commands enforced by the sanction of the state. This concept is wholly alien to Islamic theory. On the one hand, the state has from time to time enforced much which could not be called law; on the other hand, the law of God remains the law of God even though there is no one to enforce it, and even though in many of its details it is quite incapable of enforcement. Indeed, the law is revered for its divine character even by people who do not profess to obey it; and so we

---

2. Albert Hourani, A History of Arab Peoples 54 (1991).

find communities living according to customs completely at variance with the divine command, yet on occasion imbued with religious fanaticism.

Law, then, in any sense in which a Western lawyer would recognize the term, is but a part of the whole Islamic *system,* or rather, it is not even a part but one of several inextricably combined elements thereof. **Sharī'a**, the Islamic term which is commonly rendered in English by "law" is, rather, the "Whole Duty of Man." Moral and pastoral theology and ethics; high spiritual aspiration and the detailed ritualistic and formal observance which to some minds is a vehicle for such aspiration and to others a substitute for it; all aspects of law; public and private hygiene; and even courtesy and good manners are all part and parcel of the Sharī'a, a system which sometimes appears to be rigid and inflexible; at others to be imbued with that dislike of extremes, that spirit of reasonable compromise which was part of the Prophet own character. The word Sharī'a originally meant the path or track by which camels were taken to water, and so by transfer the path ordained of God by which men may achieve salvation. This conception of a path or way of life is very common in early Islam. It occurs again in the word *sunna* (see below) and in the name of the earliest Maliki law book, the *Muwatta'* of Malik himself.

The scientific study and elucidation of the Sharī'a is called fiqh, a word which today is commonly and aptly translated "dogma", but which in its origin means ratiocination, *the* use of the human reason, as opposed to 'ilm, knowledge based solely on revelation or intuition. But this early distinction has long since been obscured so that it is not uncommon to speak of 'ilm al-fiqh, the science of jurisprudence or dogma, having become a general word for all knowledge. Fiqh is divided into two branches, 'usūl al-fiqh or the bases or roots of jurisprudence, and furū', the branches or the detailed applications.

One further observation of a general character must be made here. Sharī'a, being the whole duty of man, played an important role in the Islamic educational system. When a heroine of the *Arabian Nights,* reciting a list of her charms, says that she knows the rules of inheritance according to all the four schools, she is not claiming to be a professional lawyer but merely to have had the best university education available. It follows that the teachers of the law developed problems which in practice could never occur, merely for their educational value as exercises in logic, dialectics, and even arithmetic. The same phenomenon is also observable to some extent in other systems which *have* been developed in a scholastic atmosphere, notably in the Talmudic stage of Jewish law and among the later medieval Hindu lawyers. It is also worth emphasizing again that, as in Rabbinical law, the lawyers are theologians and the theologians lawyers. For example, the two most famous Islamic philosophers and theologians, al-Ghazzālī and Averroes, wrote legal treatises of first-class importance.

The Roots of Jurisprudence

Islamic orthodoxy conceives of the Sharī'a as having sprung from four principal roots, or, to use English legal terminology, sources. These are: (1)

the Qur'ān (the Word of God); (2) the sunna (the Practice of the Prophet); (3) ijmā' (consensus); and (4) qiyās (analogy).

There are also certain minor sources to be considered later, but these four should be discussed first.

The Qur'ān

Every word of the Qur'ān is regarded as the utterance of the Almighty communicated in His actual words by the angel Gabriel, the Holy Spirit, to the Prophet. The correct method of introducing a quotation from the Qur'ān is not (as in the case of the Old Testament) "It is written" but "God (be He exalted) said." The Qur'ān is not and does not profess to be a code of law or even a law book, nor was Muhammad a lawgiver in any Western sense. The Qur'ān is an eloquent appeal (to Muslim ears, "a miracle of eloquence") . . . to obey the law of God which, it is (in the main) implied, has already been revealed or is capable of being discovered. Nevertheless, it would be a grave mistake to overlook the influence of the Qur'ān in the creation of the Islamic legal system. That influence has been exercised in four different ways.

First, in the last years of his career the Prophet, as a ruling sovereign, was faced with a number of legal problems on which he sought divine guidance, and the answers which he uttered in trance form a definite legal element in the Qur'ān. There are commonly said to be five hundred such [verses], but most of these deal with the ritual law, and there are no more than about eighty which deal with subjects which Western lawyers would regard as legal material. These eighty texts have been construed, by a method of statutory interpretation which Anglo–American lawyers might well find congenial, so as to extract the utmost ounce of meaning from them. . . .

Second, non-legal texts in the Qur'ān, moral exhortations, and even divine promises have been construed by analogy to afford legal rules. Thus the texts, "Surely they say, usury is like sale. But God has made sale lawful and usury unlawful" (Q. II 276–277), and "They will ask thee concerning wine and gambling. Say, in both is sin and advantage to men. But the sin thereof is greater than the advantage" (Q. V. 216), have had an all pervading influence on the whole doctrine of contract and those unilateral acts (e.g., kafāla, iqrār) which in Islamic law resemble contract. The lawfulness of such acts is estimated in terms of their resemblance to sale, and the only appreciation of or attempt to define contract in general terms is normally to be found in discussions of sale. Usury, the taking of a "use" for money, and gambling (the idea being extended to cover almost any transaction which involved the transference of a risk) are regarded as the opposite types.

It cannot be doubted that among a wealthy mercantile community such as that of Mecca these puritanical doctrines were a complete innovation; and it is equally beyond doubt that in spite of the abiding strength of devout Muslim sentiment against usury and gambling, these prohibitions have been consistently evaded throughout the history of Islam. Otherwise, commerce and finance, particularly the financing of agriculture, would have been brought to a standstill. Similarly, it has been argued with considerable plausibility that Qur'ānic texts proclaiming that God will not punish any man save for his own sins have been applied to the debts which he leaves unpaid at his death with far-reaching results in the law of administration of assets . . .

Third, it is explicitly stated in numerous texts of the Qur'ān that the law of God has been previously revealed to Jews and Christians, and in one text (Q. X. 94) the pious Muslim (or the Prophet himself) is expressly bidden if he have any doubt to consult those to whom the Scriptures have been revealed before him. Therefore, although as the gulf between Islam and the previous "peoples of the Book" grew wider, and the doctrine arose that preceding revelations had been corrupted and were unreliable, the founders of the Islamic legal system could hardly be blamed if they turned to proselytes from the earlier religions for assistance. So far as Christians were concerned there was at that date no body of Christian civil law claiming to derive its authority from revelation. Any influence which Roman law may have had on Islamic jurisprudence was not by the channels of direct or conscious borrowing and may for our present purpose be ruled out. But the case was otherwise with Rabbinical law. Here, at any rate, was a system of law akin at many points to Arabian custom, founded on the same monotheistic principles and imbued with the same spirit as Islam. In other fields than law the impact of Rabbinical learning on Islam is well established, In law, the influences are still obscure; but 'Umar's instructions to the qādi, if genuine, are by far the oldest Islamic legal documents outside the Qur'ān which we have, and even if not genuine they are interesting as early evidence of how Islamic lawyers believed their system to have been developed. Of those instructions it has been well said that the man who delivered them had a Jewish lawyer at his elbow. There is reason also to suppose (a point which will be discussed further in dealing with qiyās) that the logical and dialectical methods of Islamic lawyers owe something to the Rabbinical schools.

Finally and above all, the Qur'ān converted the heathen Arabs (whose pre-Islamic law had consisted entirely of ancestral and mercantile customs and apparently had had little or no connection with what passed for religion among them) to the idea that law is the direct command of God; and since it is the cardinal tenet of Islam that God is One, it follows that His law must be a single whole. For that whole the devout builders of the Islamic system were bound to search.

All three of the other principal sources of law, but more particularly sunna and ijmā, are a necessary deduction from the Qur'ānic axiom of the unity of God's law.

The Sunna

The most obvious source of information concerning the law of God to which enquirers could turn was the path or practice of the Prophet himself, and of his companions so far as their practice could be taken as evidence of what he approved. Just as the Common Law is to be culled from the decisions of the judges recorded in the year books and law reports, so the sunna, the Common Law of Islam, is to be culled from the traditions which are for this purpose the Law Reports of early Islam. We may add that just as in fact the Common Law is older than the Law Reports, so also the sunna is older than the traditions. Here we come to a curious point. The normal course of intellectual development in the humanities and the social sciences is that practice comes first and theory afterwards by a process of generalization from observed facts: logical thought comes before logic and society before the social sciences. Similarly religion, any great religion, is older than its theology, and law *(Recht)* is older than jurisprudence *(Rechtswissenschaft)*. Yet according to orthodox Islamic exposition, which was in the main apparently accepted even by such great scholars as Sachau and Snouck Hurgronje, the theory came first and the practice was built upon it. This is certainly not true; much of the law is pre-Islamic and all of it had a history before being cast into the theoretical mold. Nevertheless, the theory profoundly influenced the whole structure of the law and is still a vital force. To put the same thing in other words: professors of law do not initiate law, but they classify, clarify, amplify, and sometimes correct it. This was the real function of the mujtahids or professors of legal science. Of the process by which ijtihād (independent reasoning) became atrophied we shall speak below.

From the very earliest days of Islam and throughout its history there has been a cleavage between the umarā' (amirs, military leaders, and civil governors) and the fuqahā' or lawyers. One may compare, omitting the hereditary aspect, the *noblesse de l'epee* and the *noblesse de la robe* of aristocratic France. The cleavage, like every other important fact in Islamic history, is consecrated by a forecast traditionally ascribed to the Prophet. It is as dangerously easy to exaggerate the importance of this cleavage as it is to ignore it. The lawyers on the one hand were bound by the Qur'ān itself to acknowledge the unity of the Islamic state and consequently the necessity for a head of the state, however distasteful an individual occupant of that office might be to them. The rulers on the other hand, however lightly religion may have sat on their consciences, were bound to make some outward deference to it, for it was to the religion of Islam that they owed their position. Nevertheless, the cleavage is there.

Islamic tradition is apt to emphasize the splendor of Islam by painting pre-Islamic Arabia in unduly gloomy colors. That the civilization of Mecca before Muhammad was harsh and crude, degenerate in some respects and undeveloped in others, is probable. Nevertheless, it was a civilization: the complicated life of a great city, wealthy, prosperous, and with business connections of very long standing extending into the Roman Empire in one direction and in the other to Abyssinia, Arabia Felix, and directly or indirectly into India and perhaps beyond. Such a civilization could not have existed without a legal system, particularly since there was no strong central authority. The use of the words qadā (judgment) and fatwa (legal opinion) in the Qur'ān shows that there was not only a body of substantive law but a system of courts and lawyers not unlike that which has since become familiar in Islam; and at least one famous rule of procedure

("Evidence is for him who claims, the oath is on him who denies") has been traced to a pre-Islamic source.

This pre-existing legal system of Mecca and the probably somewhat more primitive law of Medina are, as Goldziher has shown, the main material of the sunna of Islam, [although] the caliphs and their judges continued to administer the existing law except insofar as it had been clearly abrogated by the Qur'ān. The Qur'ān readers in the mosques who developed into the jurists (fuqahā') could not but deal with this same legal material subjecting it to the religious test: did the Prophet (who was born, brought up, and lived nearly all his life under this system) approve of this or that rule, or condemn it? But the fuqahā' were not working in a vacuum; they were testing and according to their lights refining an existing system.

Here, a suggestion may be very tentatively put forward. When the schools of law become definite, we find the school of Abū Hanīfa described as ahl al-ra'y, the people of opinion, and that of Mālik as ahl al-hadīth, the people of tradition. It is difficult, however, to fit these labels to the facts. Mālik frequently decided questions on the basis of his own personal opinion; on the other hand, the *Kitāb al-Kharāj* of Abū Yūsuf, the oldest Hanafī law text extant, is very definitely an attempt to build up law on a basis of tradition, though largely traditions of the Companions and their successors. May it not be that the term ahl al-ra'y was originally applied by the orthodox casuists (the puritans of their day) to the caliph's judges and lawyers and later used to describe Abū Hanīfa and his school when they allied themselves with the 'Abbāsid regime? The two jāmi's (collections) of Muhammad al-Shaybānī, the third great Hanafī doctor who has been described by Sachau as the real founder of the Hanafī school, breathe an entirely different spirit. They rarely quote either Qur'ān or Tradition, and are concerned with the dialectical elaboration of a known and settled system.

The sunna is to be found in traditions, according to the accepted classification, traditions of what the Prophet said, did, or by his silence approved. Another possible division is into ahadīth qudsiyya, traditions claiming to contain direct divine inspiration; traditions of the Prophet himself; and traditions which embody legal decisions of the first four caliphs or of other Companions of the Prophet....

That there has been wholesale fabrication of traditions is universally admitted by Muslim and Western scholars alike. Indeed, the existence and the danger of such fabrication was well known from almost the earliest period of Islam. [However,] Snouck Hurgronje, in reference primarily to the great mass of nonlegal tradition, held that the skepticism of Western scholars had perhaps been carried too far. On the other hand, devout Muslim scholars from a very early date recognized that there was an immense amount of falsification, some of it deliberate, going on. They set about, therefore, to sift the traditions with such critical apparatus as they possessed.

The Qur'ān and the sunna are sometimes spoken of as the roots of the bases (usūl al-usūl), a phrase which implies that the other foundations of the law are merely subordinate to and dependent on them. There are, however, as we shall show, some independent elements in the other sources.

Ijmā or Consensus

It was a reasonable deduction from Qur'ānic teaching, duly consecrated by a *hadith*, that God would not permit His people universally to be in error. *Quod semper, quod ubique, quod ab omnibus fidelibus*[1] is no less a Muslim than it is a Catholic doctrine. Such consensus was reckoned to be of two kinds, ijm al-umma, consensus of the whole community of Islam, and ijmā' al-'a'imma, consensus of the imāms, or leaders of the people, which for this purpose means the great law teachers. Examples of the first sort are to be found in the details of the ritual of the Mecca pilgrimage, universally practiced by all pilgrims though it would be hard to find authority for them in any early legal text. In modern times the authors of the Ottoman Family Law of 1917 . . . cited the universal and longstanding practice of all respectable Muslims throughout the world, among other reasons, in support of their proposal to make the registration of Muslim marriages compulsory, although in fact no such provision will be found in any authoritative law book. Of the second sort of ijmā' we may distinguish two kinds. The first is agreement on the interpretation of a Qur'ānic text or tradition, such as for instance that Q. IV, 12 refers to the uterine, and Q. IV, 177 to the agnate, brothers and sisters, or that the payment of debts comes before the distribution of legacies though the Qur'ān three times over mentions them in the reverse order. Of this class of ijmā' one can only say that, quite apart from reverence for authority, any careful student would almost inevitably reach the same conclusion. They are in fact instances of universal qiyās. The second and more remarkable class consists of a number of pithy statements of legal principle which do not profess to be based on anything in the Qur'ān or in the Prophet's own practice, but which are, nonetheless, universally accepted as authoritative. Of these a striking instance is the rule that "the will of the wāqif (founder of a waqf)[2] [a sort of Islamic law foundation or trust] is as an express text of the lawgiver" (irādat al-wāqif ka nass al-shāri'); i.e., the founder of a waqf, creating, as he does, a perpetuity, may legislate for the devolution of the enjoyment of the waqf in perpetuity, probably a wider privilege than any other system of law concedes to the individual, and this within a system which in theory, at least, confines the legislative power of the State within the narrowest possible limits!

Nass and Qiyās

Authoritative texts of the Qur'ān, authoritative traditions, and the pithy statements of consensus above mentioned are commonly called nass, a word implying the highest degree of textual authority. They are contrasted with qiyās or reasoning by analogy, a source of less authority. It is said,

---

1. "What has been held always, everywhere, by everyone." [Eds.]

2. A sort of Islamic law foundation or trust. [Eds.]

for instance, that "custom can override a qiyās, it cannot override a nass." Qiyās is probably older, though of less authority, than ijmā'.

It is frequently said that the doctrine of qiyās is an importation of Rabbinical methods of legal exegesis into Islam, and it has been suggested that the word qiyās itself is of the same origin as its Rabbinical counterpart, *ha kasha* and that the latter is merely a rendering into Hebrew of the Greek *symballein*. Such identifications have their dangers. All rational beings reason by analogy even if they are unconscious of it, just as Monsieur Jourdain spoke prose *sans le savoir*. There is nothing extraordinary or even noteworthy in the fact that the reasoning processes of two different communities are the same. It becomes remarkable when we find not only that they reason in the same way but that they consciously classify their own mental processes in similar categories....

The Shī'ī Schools

A somewhat different view of the usul al-fiqh is taken by the Shī'ī schools.... It is here sufficient to note that, while the Shī'a vie with the Sunnis in devotion both to the Qur'ān and (subject to a divergence in criteria of hadīth) to the sunna, there is strictly speaking no room for ijmā', qiyās, istihsān, or istislāh so long as a Shī'ī sect has a living and accessible imām to whom all legal questions can be referred as a final authority and who (in theory at least) possesses considerable power of legislation. Such an imām is the Agha Khan, the head of the Nizāris. But where the imām recognized by the sect has disappeared from worldly ken as in the case of the Ithna 'Asharī sect and of the Bohoras, reference to universal agreement (ijmā') and of intellect ('aql) to tackle new problems becomes inevitable and is openly acknowledged. It appears, however, that the dā'ī of the Daudi Bohoras claims and exercises some part of the pontifical powers of the occult imām whose representative he is. In Iran, legislation by the Parliament is expressed as being provisional pending the "return of the Lord of the Hour."

At this point, and before proceeding to the minor sources of law, it may be well to survey the system which has been built up on the foundations which have been discussed thus far. Dīn (religion) is held to consist of two parts, imān or faith and Islam or obedience, each of these being based on a list of pillars or essentials with which we are not here concerned. The word "islam" means literally absolute surrender, i.e., to the will of God; and the will of God is that men should pursue husn (beauty) and avoid qubh (ugliness) of life and character. The ultimate guide to the will of God is, of course, revelation, from which alone one can discover what is right or wrong. The law being concerned first and last with the relation between God and the human soul, it follows that the individual is the paramount consideration; the law is strongly individualist and is primarily subjective in form. Men are to consider the value of each action in the sight of God; its earthly consequences are incidental. The Shāfi'ī jurist al-Nawawī, in the Preface of his work, *Minhāj al-Talibīn,* well sums up the spirit of the system when he says that "the best way to manifest obedience to God and to make right use of precious time is assuredly to devote oneself to the study of the law."

The Five Values

All human acts are, therefore, classified in five categories according to their value in the sight of God: (1) fard or wājib, expressly commanded either in the Qur'ān or in the Traditions, or by ijmā'; (2) sunna, masnūn, mandūb, or mustahabb, recommended or desirable; (3) jā'iz or mubāh, permitted or indifferent; (4) makrūh, reprobated; (5) harām, absolutely forbidden and abominable.

The first category is normally divided into fard 'ala al-'ayn, commands which are absolutely binding on every individual Muslim, and fard 'ala al-kifāya, those which are binding on the Islamic community as a whole but are sufficiently discharged so long as some portion of the community is obeying them. The outstanding instance of the latter is the jihād or holy war. This is binding on the Islamic community but not on individual Muslims save in a grave emergency in which the existence of Islam is threatened. Some Muslim moralists, however, distinguish between al-jihād alkabīr, the greater warfare, i.e., the warfare of the human soul against the forces of evil which is fard 'ala al-'ayn (for which purpose the martial texts of the Qur'ān are construed in an allegorical sense) and al-jihād al-saghīr, the lesser warfare, which is fag' 'ala al-kifāya.

It should be noted that even the absolute commands, fard, and prohibitions, harām, of the sacred law do not necessarily imply the sanction of the state. Thus, it is an absolute command based upon well-authenticated tradition that a bridegroom should give a marriage feast according to his means, and that the guests whom he invites should not refuse to attend without lawful excuse. But though absolutely binding in conscience these rules do not look to the state for enforcement, nor will their infraction affect the validity of the marriage.

While the absolute commands and prohibitions are not always matters of strict law, it is hardly too much to say that recommendation and disapproval (masnūn and makrūh) are never so. They belong rather to the spheres of morality, good manners, and pious zeal. As an instance of good manners, one may cite the rule that parties to a bargain should not separate without some interchange of courtesies, though by remaining together each of them, according to Shāf'i doctrine, exposes himself to the possibility of the other calling off the contract. Additional fasting (in the month of Muharram) and additional prayers (besides the daily five) are similarly recommended. And the Prophet ... is reputed to have said that divorce is "in the sight of God the most detestable of all permitted things"—a tradition which, whether genuine or not, has proved totally powerless to limit capricious divorce.

Of the five values by which human acts are judged, the norm is ibāha, or permission. All human acts are permitted, or indifferent, unless and until some authority can be discovered in the sources of the law which either raises them to a higher or degrades them to a lower class. Permissible acts are of two classes, those for which express permission is to be found in an authoritative text (nass), e.g., permission to a free Muslim to have in his discretion as many as four wives, and those the permissibility of which is inferred from the fact that they are mentioned in legal sources. But whether express or implied, the doctrine of permissibility has been a protection (albeit flimsy at times) for the individual Muslim against irresponsible despotism and has also contributed to the immutability of the law. Who is the merely human ruler that he should dare to take away or to modify a liberty which is granted by God Himself? The individual Muslim need not avail himself of the divine permission; that is a matter which God has left to his discretion. But it would be presumptuous for him to endeavor to contract himself *altogether* out of a liberty which God has allowed. Nevertheless, on occasions in Islamic history, powerful rulers, or in recent years, legislative assemblies with public opinion behind them, have from time to time been able to amend the law; and devices by which a man may restrict his liberty (e.g., of polygamy), even though he cannot completely abrogate it, were early invented by the lawyers.

(b) The Institutional Structure of Islamic Legal Systems

In contrast to the elaborate nature of Islamic jurisprudence, its institutional structures were much less definite. The key figure was the *qadi*, or judge, who did possess an officially recognized position. However, as one observer of comparative legal traditions emphasizes, beyond the *qadi*, Islamic law has historically been sustained by the religious community: "There is no Islamic legislator (though there are now state legislators in Islamic jurisdictions), no appeal or supreme courts (they came with the state) ... and no institutionalized, hierarchical church.... Those learned in Islamic law are not authorized or licensed in any way; they simply become learned and become known as such. So legal authority is in a very real sense vested in the private, or religious, community and not in any political ruler." Although early on there was a movement to reign in the increasingly plural interpretations of *shari'a* through legislation, the movement did not succeed and, indeed, "there have been conceptual problems with the idea of an Islamic state forever after."[1]

As to the role of the *qadi,* and another key figure, the *mufti*, they had distinct roles in the process of adjudication:

> Once reached, the decision of the *qadi* is simply given, with no written reasons and often with no explicit reasons of any kind. By this point the partners, [who have played an active role as] partners in the process, are expected to understand what is going on, and why. Absent reasons, there is no system of case-reporting. Absent case-reports, there is no operative notion of precedent, still less of any strict concept of stare decisis ...
>
> As an adjudicator, the *qadi* neither contributes to the development of the law nor stands among those most learned. So, as in the civil law, there is a large place for expertise outside the courts. Here the *mufti*,

---

1. H. Patrick Glenn, Legal Traditions of the World 179 (2d ed. 2004).

or jurisconsult, appears to play a role remarkably similar to that of the Roman jurist or contemporary European law professor (in providing *Gutachten* or opinions to courts). Free of formal responsibility, yet posssessed of immensely useful knowledge and great analytical ability, the *mufti* comes to be the most effective means of bringing vast amounts of law to bear on highly particular cases. The opinion of the *mufti*, the *fatwa*, is often filed in court as a means of assisting deliberation.[2]

A. Quraishi, Interpreting the Qur'an and the Constitution: Similarities in the Use of Text, Tradition and Reason in Islamic and American Jurisprudence
28 Cardozo Law R. 67, 69–75 (2006).

The fundamental text in Islam is the Qur'an, believed by Muslims to be the word of God revealed to the Prophet Muhammad in the seventh century AD. The Qur'an commands Muslims to follow the way of the Prophet himself, and therefore his life example, the *sunna*, is also normative "text" for Muslims. A documented record of his life was not compiled, however, until well after his death. The enterprise involved the complicated task of sifting through fabricated stories and corroborating chains of narration. It ultimately gave rise to a distinct field of scholarship dedicated to the verification and preservation of *"hadith,"* the textual record of the Prophet's *sunna*.

Parallel to *hadith* scholarship grew the scholarly community of jurists who answered legal questions presented by the growing Muslim community. This happened primarily in the realm of private scholarship, with individual scholars contemplating the source texts and teaching their understandings to students and laypeople seeking legal advice. Over time, the legal methods and conclusions of the most influential scholars evolved into distinct schools of thought. Because Muslims never created a formal church, Islamic legal orthodoxy formed around those private scholars who distinguished themselves by education, dialectical skill, and popularity with students and the public who consulted them. Over the years, many schools of law emerged as students collected the lectures and legal opinions of influential jurists and eventually wrote commentaries upon them. With a sufficient number of disciples preserving and expanding the work of a particular jurist (and especially when accompanied by popular and other external support), that jurist's corpus of opinions and accompanying legal methodology became known as a *"madhhab"* (literally, "path," or "road to go")—a school of Islamic law. These *madhhabs* (which eventually shrunk in number from hundreds to just a few major schools surviving to today) were the means by which the *fiqh* [legal knowledge] was produced, preserved and transmitted in Muslim societies. The body of Islamic legal doctrine, simply put, is these *madhhabs*. Moreover, and especially relevant

2. *Ibid.*

to our present study, each *madhhab* has a characteristic legal methodology, reflecting its particular preferences for how to use text, tradition and reason in the search for God's Law. It is the interpretive methods of these developed *madhhabs* that form much of the material for the present comparative study.

In undertaking the job of interpreting God's Law from the source texts, Muslim jurists operated with an awareness of their own human fallibility. Their work of legal interpretation is called *ijtihad*, a word derived from the root *"jahada,"* meaning "to strive" or "struggle." The product of *ijtihad* is an exhaustive effort to understand God's Law, but ultimately constitutes only a probable articulation of that Law and thus cannot be treated as a certainty. This epistemological foundation is reflected in the terminology used in classical Islamic legal literature. Muslim jurists referred to the collective body of their *ijtihad* conclusions as *"fiqh,"* derived from the Arabic word *"faqaha,"* meaning "to understand." The word "shari'a," on the other hand (which is today often translated into English as "Islamic law") denotes the ultimate Law of God which the jurists' *fiqh* understanding always strives to achieve, but which remains ultimately unknowable in this world.

Significantly, though there is no way for a Muslim jurist to be sure in this lifetime if her *ijtihad* opinions have successfully articulated the true Law of God, this nevertheless does not detract from the legal authority of those opinions. As a reported saying (*"hadith"*) of the Prophet Muhammad puts it: "The one who performs *ijtihad* and reaches the right answer will receive two rewards [from God], and the one who performs *ijtihad* and reaches the wrong answer will receive one reward [from God]." Thus, the promise of heavenly reward for even wrong *ijtihad* conclusions means that there is nevertheless some value in an *ijtihad* conclusion separate from its ultimate rightness or wrongness: a jurist has fulfilled her duty to God simply by performing the *ijtihad* effort itself. Ultimate success in hitting the target is an added bonus. Moreover, what becomes immediately relevant to the inter-relationship of jurists to each other is the reality that there is no way to know in this lifetime which *ijtihad* conclusions are deserving of one reward and which of two. Therefore, Muslim jurists must all operate on the assumption that an opposing legal conclusion might in fact turn out to be correct. That reality leads to the practical result that any *ijtihad* conclusion carries legitimacy as a potentially true articulation of God's Law. The overall result is a built-in acceptance of uncertainty as part of the Islamic lawmaking enterprise, as well as significant Islamic legal pluralism. Because all *ijtihad*-generated legal opinions are equally probable, there quickly grew a great diversity of conclusions about the meaning of the source texts, disagreeing with each other both in interpretive approach and specific legal conclusions, yet all existing simultaneously as valid Islamic law.

But before we can explore how these interpretive methods parallel those in American jurisprudence, we must first acknowledge the significantly different institutional structure of law and government in Muslim societies as compared with that familiar to American lawyers. The first important feature of classical Muslim legal systems is that legal authority was not located exclusively in the sovereign state power (such as the caliph, sultan, or king). Rather, the articulation of the Law of God through *fiqh* was virtually the exclusive domain of private jurist scholars. It is for this reason that the above description of the evolution of the *madhhabs* does not mention any particular role for state authority, for it was not a necessary part of this enterprise. Nevertheless, state authority did exist in classical Muslim societies. Caliphs and sultans did issue orders, collected taxes, and prosecuted crimes, all with a real life impact upon the people. . . .

One way to explain the relationship between the two realms of ruler and scholar is to emphasize the notion of separate but complementary aspects to Muslim legal authority, both applying God's Law (shari'a), but manifested in two distinct forms: *fiqh* and *Siyasa* (literally, "administration, policy, management"). The *fiqh* realm is, as we have just described, that of the private jurists undertaking the job of interpreting the divine texts to provide doctrinal legal answers for society. *Siyasa*, on the other hand, covers all those laws and ordinances and innumerable other legal actions promulgated by the ruler, who has the responsibility to keep public order and administer justice. This responsibility is a Qur'anically-recognized function, and thus is part of the shari'a, the Law of God. In carrying out this responsibility, various Muslim rulers created a host of different institutions and appointed a variety of officials throughout history. Included in these institutions were courts responsible for adjudicating cases based on the *fiqh*. The judges appointed to these courts—*qadis*—were therefore drawn from the *fiqh* community of legal scholars, creating the first of many instances of the overlapping and interconnection of the two realms of *fiqh* and *Siyasa*. Nevertheless, these two worlds maintained distinct identities with characteristic features that help to explain the complicated interactions between their members throughout Islamic history.

To further understand the difference in types of Islamic legal authority represented by *fiqh* and *Siyasa*, consider that *Siyasa* rules need not be derived directly from divine texts through scholarly interpretive effort, but rather could be ostensibly justified in terms of service of the public welfare. It was enforced with real-life consequences by sovereign rulers, whom the people must obey, but not because it was necessarily a manifestation of God's ultimate truth. *Fiqh*, not *Siyasa*, had that sort of prestige and permanence over the long term. *Siyasa* was temporal, based only on the particular needs of a given society; its only necessary connection to revelation was its fulfillment of a general principle of maintaining justice and public good and avoiding basic conflict with shari'a. *Fiqh*, on the other hand, was a complicated elaboration of specific divine directives and—even though it was made up of many different interpretations of those directives—wore a mantle of permanence and long-term authority in every Muslim society.

In sum, Islamic legal systems as a whole were comprised of two separate but generally complementary spheres: (1) the *fiqh*, consisting of various interpretations of divine texts (eventually collected into schools of law, the *madhhabs*) that lasted over time, and (2) the *Siyasa*, composed of the particular governing rules of a given Muslim society, issued by a temporal ruler. Where enforcement was necessary, both types of laws relied upon the sovereign power, and thus some creative choices could be made by the ruler to affect legal outcomes without controlling the substantive law, for example, through judicial appointments favoring or disfavoring a particular *madhhab*. But the doctrinal substance of the *fiqh* remained within the control of the private jurist class.

This separation of laws and lawmaking powers illustrates a unique aspect of the constitutional structure of classical Muslim governments. The articulation of the Law of God (*fiqh*) is found not in the legislative enactments of rulers, but rather in the work of private legal scholars, and *Siyasa* takes a secondary role in substantive prestige, but a primary role in terms of temporal obedience. It is important to note that this is not a "religious-secular" divide, as many western observers have understood the picture. Better understood, *Siyasa* is the realm of mutable law, and *fiqh* is the immutable. The separation is a constructive concept representing the realization that the rules governing a Muslim state—all ultimately beholden to God's Law (shari'a)—will be a combination of immutable, divinely-derived legal standards and mutable decisions whose validity needs to rest on political judgments of what constitutes the best rule given a particular set of temporal circumstances.

[O]ne might wonder whether there was any mechanism to check the temporal rulers by God's Law, so that if a given *Siyasa* law violated the shari'a, there was a way to stop it. This question demands too complicated an answer for this short survey, given the vast diversity of governmental structures implemented over Islamic history. The closest short answer is "it depends." That is, it depends upon the relative power of the *Siyasa* authorities vis a vis the *fiqh* authorities at a given time and place. Generally speaking, in Islamic history, where *fiqh* scholars had a significant amount of social and political influence, they could operate in this "checking" fashion. But where the *Siyasa* authority was paramount, there was very little checking of sovereign power, at least not in the name of shari'a wielded by the *fiqh* scholars. Some Muslim governments have experimented with institutionalization of *fiqh* authorities in the *Siyasa* apparatus, operating as somewhat of an internal check built into the overall *Siyasa* system, or vice versa, as a *Siyasa*-generated check on the *fiqh* authorities. But these experiments each have their own unique characteristics and historical paradigms, and do not provide a sufficiently relevant template for governmental institutions across all Muslim societies in all generations. They are therefore not useful for the present comparative study.

NOTES

(1) *Terminology: "Shari'a" and "Islamic Law."* The word "Shari'a," in early usages, referred to the path by which camels were taken to water, to the source of life. In later and current times, it refers to "the way" or "the path" whereby a Muslim is to conduct his or her life, in every aspect of life. Thus, the Shari'a is comprised of and embodies religion, ethics, morality and behavioral admonitions as well as requirements that are more customarily recognized as legal in nature. Muslim law is in a sense broader and in a sense narrower than the corresponding western idea. Islamic law prescribes behavior that in the West we consider of non legal nature, such as when and how to wash oneself or how and what to eat. On the other hand, the domain that we might consider of public law and government is part of the *Siyasa*. Thus it is not strictly speaking "Islamic law."

Shari'a as a body of divine law that has developed over 1400 years is mature and comprehensive. It is not limited in its jurisdictional reach. For example, the Shari'a, being comprehensively applicable to all aspects of human existence and endeavor, extends to every aspect of commercial and financial matters, giving rise to highly relevant developments in Islamic finance. Thus, it addresses sales (*bay'*), leasing (*ija-ra*), options, suretyship, agency (*waka-lah*), transfer of obligations (*hawala*), mortgages and pledges (*rahn*), deposits for safekeeping (*emanet*), loans, gifts (*hiba*), joint ownership and joint ventures (*sharika-t, mush raka and muda-raba*), guarantees, and virtually every other aspect of what we consider private law in the West. Like any other mature body of law, application of the principles and precepts is detailed and complex and subject to variations in interpretation, particularly as among the different schools of law (*madhahib*).

(2) *Schools of Islamic Jurisprudence.* The schools of Islamic jurisprudence take the name from their founders, ancient scholars of much global prestige comparable to that of Bartolus or Baldus, whose dates of death we report in parentheses: The surviving schools are the Hanafi, (767), Malik, (795), Shafi (820), Hambali (855). Although these schools displayed important differences in their doctrinal preferences and interpretive styles, they often overlapped in time and space, much like the competing schools of glossators, commentators, humanists, and natural lawyers in the western tradition.

(a) *The Hanafi School.* The oldest and still most diffused, the Hanafi developed in Iraq sustained by the Abbasidic dynasty and later became the official school of the Ottoman Empire (which fell in 1918). Today it remains the most territorially diffused. The school emphasized the importance of analogical reasoning and the individual reasoning of the jurist in teaching an understanding of the Book.

(b) *The Maliki School.* The Maliki school developed in Medina and its founder authored the first comprehensive compilation of Islamic law. This school emphasizes the *Sunna*, the teaching and customs of the Prophet and of the early communities, as the main source of interpretation of the book. The Maliki school survives today in the Maghreb, in Egypt and in a few sub-Saharan African countries.

(c) *The Shafi School.* The Shafi school, named after a pupil of Malik, has offered the first comprehensive rationalization of the system of the sources of Islamic law, an innovation which makes Al Shafi the true founder of the "science" of *fiqh*. In his systematization the *Sunna* of the Prophet Muhammad prevails absolutely over all the subsequent ones. The Shafi School rejects the idea of independent reasoning on the text. Today it is followed in Bahrain, Yemen, India, Indonesia, Eastern Africa and Egypt.

(d) *The Hambali School*. The Hambali school was founded by a student of al Shafi in Iraq, who was even more committed than his mentor to traditionalism and the denial of analogical reasoning. His school enjoyed enormous prestige before the advent of the Ottomans when it became marginalized. Today it survives in some areas of the Persian Gulf and, significantly, it remains the officially recognized Islamic law of Saudi Arabia.

(3) *Some extended applications*. While family law has been a key concern of Islamic law, it has regulated other areas of what is known in the western tradition as private law, including property relations. Indeed, there is also a body of what could be called Islamic "international law" as well. See Majid Khadduri, *The Islamic Law of Nations: Shaybani's Siyar* (1966); Majid Khadduri, *War and Peace in the Law of Islam* (1955).

(c) Islamic Law and The Modern State

The Islamic legal tradition did not develop in the context of the modern centralized state. Hence, it is a controversial matter whether, or to what extent, Islamic law is in fact compatible with the existence of a modern state. In the post–9/11 world, Islam has become increasingly politicized, and the status of Islamic law has become increasingly contested as well.[1] Abdullahi An-na'im, for one, insists vigorously on the primarily religious nature of shari'a law. To the extent that modern Arab states make claims to be applying "Islamic law," he insists that "claiming to enforce Shari'a principles as state law is a logical contradiction that cannot be rectified through repeated efforts under any conditions."[2] He explains,

> The notion of an Islamic state is in fact a postcolonial innovation based on a European model of the state and a totalitarian view of law and public policy as instruments of social engineering by the ruling elites. Although the states that historically ruled over Muslims did seek Islamic legitimacy in a variety of ways, they were not claimed to be "Islamic states." The proponents of a so-called Islamic state in the modern context seek to use the institutions and powers of the state, as constituted by European colonialism and continued after independence, to regulate individual behavior and social relations in ways selected by the ruling elites.[3]

In particular, An-na'im objects to the codification of Islamic law by modern postcolonial states because of the way in which codification necessarily turns a dynamic and pluralistic tradition into a static and rigid one: "Since

---

1. See, e.g., Jeffrey A. Redding, "Constitutionalizing Islam: Theory and Pakistan," 44 Va. J. Int'l L. 759 (2004); Jennifer E. Cohen, "Islamic Law in Iran: Can It Protect the International Legal Right of Freedom of Religion and Belief?", 9 Chi. J. Int'l L. 247 (2008); Ann Elizabeth Mayer, "Conundrums in Constitutionalism: Islamic Monarchies in an Era of Transition," 1 UCLA J. Islamic & Near E. L. 183 (2002).

2. Abdullahi An-na'im, Islam and the Secular State: Negotiating the Future of Shari'a 2 (2008).

3. *Ibid*. at p. 7.

modern states can operate only on officially established principles of law of general application, Shari'a principles cannot be enacted or enforced as the positive law of any country without being subjected to a selection among competing interpretations, which are all deemed to be legitimate by the traditional Shari'a doctrine."[4] That is, An-na'im continues, "the enforcement of Shari'a as state law is inconsistent with its nature, because enactment requires the selection of some views over others, whereas that choice is the right and responsibility of each Muslim as a matter of religious conviction. That is why the founding scholars of Shari'a objected to the adoption of their views by the state and did not claim exclusive authority to determine the Shari'a ruling on any issue for all Muslims."[5]

In short, An-na'im emphasizes the historic incompatibility between Shari'a as it existed in "the traditional 'minimal' imperial state of the past" and the existence of positive Islamic law in "the centralized, hierarchical, bureaucratic state of today."[6] Indeed, he argues that historically there existed a distinction—if not a strict separation—between religious and state institutions. Although many kinds of rulers have in fact claimed authority in the name of Islam, An-na'im observes that "rulers needed to balance their control of religious leaders by conceding their autonomy from the state, which is the source of the ability of religious leaders to legitimize the authority of the rulers"—an arrangement that ultimately constituted a "deep and complex paradox."[7]

NOTES AND QUESTIONS

(1) *"Islamic Law" as a concept.* When we discuss "Islamic law" or the "Islamic legal tradition," what exactly are we referring to? Many, and perhaps most, Islamic law courses have tended to focus on Islamic law as a *historical* tradition, describing primarily the way in which it functioned in the pre-colonial Islamic world. It is important to note that even as a historical tradition, it is difficult to uncover a "pure" Islamic legal tradition: like all legal traditions, Islamic law, grows out of multiple sources.[1] Chibli Mallat, for example, has proposed an alternative analytic category, "Middle Eastern law," to take into account more fully various regional elements in all their complexity.[2]

Today, in any event, Islamic law exists in a world of modern post-colonial states, as we have observed. Apart from the question whether the idea of positively legislated Islamic law is indeed a contradiction (as suggested by An-

---

4. *Ibid.* at p. 18.

5. *Ibid.* at p. 285.

6. *Ibid.* at p. 46.

7. *Ibid.* at p. 52.

1. As Albert Hourani observes, "The articulation of Islam into a body of religious sciences and practice took place largely in Iraq in the Abbasid period, and in a sense it was a continuation of movements of thought which had begun long before the appearance

of Islam, although this is not to imply that Islam did not give new directions to it." A History of Arab Peoples, at 59.

2. Chibli Mallat, "From Islamic Law to Middle Eastern Law: A Restatement of the Field (Part I)," 51 Am. J. Comp. L. 699 (2003); Chibli Mallat, "From Islamic Law to Middle Eastern Law: A Restatement of the Field (Part II)," 52 Am. J. Comp. L. 209 (2003).

na'im, for example), it is certainly the case that there are no "pure" Islamic legal systems in existence today (just as perhaps there is no longer a pure common civil law tradition of ius commune separate from its different national epiphanies): they are all, in various degrees, post-colonial hybrids. Lama Abu–Odeh explicates the meanings of "Islamic law" as follows:

> The term *Islamic law* encompasses two meanings. The first identifies Islamic law as the law derived from religious sources by Muslim jurists, sources defined as the Quran and prophetic traditions; rules derived through analogy to rules identified in these sources; and rules selected through consensus by the same jurists. In this first meaning, Islamic law refers to a largely historic system that had emerged roughly in the ninth century A.D., was highly formalized around the eleventh and twelfth centuries, but largely came to an end as a legal system effectively applicable to Muslims in the nineteenth century.
>
> The second meaning of Islamic law is the law of the Islamic world. In this second meaning, Islamic law is the law applied to Muslims living in the Islamic world today. It includes the codes, statutes, and regulations that have accompanied the emergence of the modern state in the Islamic world following the collapse of the last Islamic caliphate, the Ottoman Empire, in 1914. The origins of these laws lie in the European legal transplants introduced by the colonial powers to the Islamic world in the nineteenth and first half of the twentieth centuries. Such transplants took on a life of their own in the new localities—so much so that their descendants, the contemporary positive laws of the Islamic world, constitute the bulk of the contemporary legal system of this world. Islamic law in the first sense exists in the contemporary system in a rudimentary form and is mostly embedded in the rules on the family.[3]

Abu–Odeh considers the prevalent emphasis on the study of a no-longer extant legal tradition a distortion: "We need to stop approaching the Islamic world through the prism of religion, culture, and history and start approaching it as a modern product of the colonial experience, with all its complexity ... No more articles on 'Democracy,' 'Constitutionalism,' and 'Jihad' under Islamic law, with the endless mining of medieval sources to prove that the Islamic law is good and liberal, and more 'how do the rules on property in the Jordanian civil code affect the distribution of wealth in that country'?" In essence, Abu–Odeh calls for the replacement of course of "Islamic Law" with courses on "Laws of the Islamic World."

(2) *Western perspectives.* There is a long tradition of western Orientalist scholarship that caricatures Islamic Law. Max Weber, most notably, offered a simplistic vision of the Qadi (an actor of Syasa and not of Shari'a) as dispensing justice sitting under a tree to imply its lack of formalization and thus of legal knowledge. Today at least most scholars analyze the Islamic legal tradition with a greater degree of sophistication. Indeed Islamic Universities (and law schools) were thriving at the time of the University of Bologna even in places as remote from Mecca and Medina as Timbuktu in modern days Mali. Most scholars have finally learned to distinguish a system of Islamic law from the secular law of an

3. Lama Abu–Odeh, "Commentary on John Makdisi's 'Survery of AALS Law Schools Teaching Islamic Law,'" 55 J. Legal Educ. 589 (2005).

Islamic country. Indeed through time and space the variable dialectic between *Shari'a* (province of the scholar, Ulama or Fiqh) and the *Siyasa* (province of the state institutions) has produced much variation.

In a sense this exclusion of "public law" and government from the mainstream part of the law is true also in the western legal tradition where public law only relatively recently emerged as a separate field in the common law, and whose development in continental Europe has been intellectually marginalized until the first academic chairs have been established well into the eighteenth century. To the contrary, in China, as we have seen, it is "private law" that has historically been excluded from the notion of *fa* within a legal system that from the earliest times privileged the power of the state. Thus the formalization of the dialectic between the individual and the authority, highly variable among different societies across time and space, plays a key role in defining "what is the law".

In ancient Rome the great Jurist Ulpian (d. 223 AD), identified two "positions" or perspectives of legal study: public and private. Public law, according to him, was *quod ad statum rei Romanae spectat*, [what belongs to the Roman State] while private law related *ad singulorum utilitatem* [utility of individuals] some matters being of public, others of private interest. Ulpian expressly stated that public law covered religious affairs, the priesthood, and the magistracy. He did not give examples of matters of public interest, utility, or concern.

Ulpian's definition figures prominently in Justinian's *Corpus Iuris*.[4] It does not, however, reflect the fundamental division of Roman legal science into private law and public law components. No separate body of Roman public-law doctrine or literature existed; rather, Roman legal science centered on private law, and public law issues were discussed, where appropriate within the framework of private law analysis. The private/public law distinction of Ulpian can interestingly be compared with that between Fiqh and Siyasa, two entirely different domains in the Islamic legal conception with the latter explored wherever necessary with no scientific claim . .

In the initial phases of its "second life,"[5] Roman law became an academic discipline taught at university law faculties. Reflecting the fundamental division of jurisdiction and authority then prevalent, legal instruction and literature were divided into two basic components: ecclesiastical (canon) and secular (civil). Public law was not expounded as a separate discipline.

Public law as a discrete subject essentially evolved as the twin product of the early-modern territorial state and the Reformation.[6] Printed text editions of

4. Dig. 1.1.1.2 (Ulpian). For a more detailed historical account, see Charles Szladits, The Civil Law System, in 2 Int'l Ency. Comp. L. § 25; see also *id.* at 15. See generally Max Kaser, 'Ius publicum' und 'ius privatum,' 103 Zeitschrift der Savigny–Stiftung für Rechtsgeschichte [Z.S.S.R.] 1 (1986).

5. Roman law once again gained preeminence between 1077 and 1600 AD. See generally Guillermo F. Margadant, La Segunda Vida del Derecho Romano 85–247 (1986)

and H. Coing, The Roman Law as Ius Commune on the Continent, 89 L.Q.Rev. 505 (1973), reproduced *supra* at 331.

6. See generally Die Rolle der Juristen bei der Enstehung des Modernen Staates (Roman Schnur ed., 1986); Dieter Wyduckel, Ius Publicum: Grundlagen und Entwicklungen des Öffentlichen Rechts und der Deutschen Staatsrechtswissenschaft (1984); Hans K. Gross, Empire and Sovereignty: A History of the Public Law Literature in the Holy

fundamental laws (the essential precondition for a non-arcane discipline of public law) started appearing, along with public law monographs and treatises, in the Thirty Years' War (1618–48). Chairs of public law at universities date from the eighteenth century.

The public-law profession developed mainly in response to the need of the rulers, estates, and free cities for skilled counsel as well as effective public advocacy of their causes. With no prospect of secure university employment, and totally dependent on sovereign or quasi-sovereign employers locked in mortal combat, public lawyers acquired the occupational characteristics of political journalists. (The ambiguity of "Publizistik" and of "publicist" continues to evidence this built-in professional tension.)

While Roman law continued to furnish the basic vocabulary and some key notions, early modern public lawyers based their craft mainly on neo-Aristotelian "politics," natural-law theory, Machiavellian or anti-Machiavellian literature on statecraft and Staatsraison, and more immediately, the actual texts of charters, privileges, capitulations, pacts, and enactments.[7] As the European state-system moved away from imperial and papal supremacy to the sovereign equality of independent territorial states interconnected by treaty and diplomatic relations, public lawyers became active as diplomats and as authorities on public international law.[8] Several of the initial chairs of public law created in the eighteenth century (e.g., Edinburgh 1708) encompassed the "law of nature and of nations" in addition to public law generally.[9]

By the nineteenth century, public international law had distinguished itself as a distinct academic specialty.[10] The practice of adopting formal instruments of government called "constitutions," which the United States initiated in 1787 and which generally caught on in nineteenth-century Europe and Latin America, gave rise to national constitutional law as a separate discipline, with its own professorships, treatises, and doctrinal systems. Reflecting the need for systematizations of increasingly complex governmental operations affecting individual and group rights and interests, administrative law came into its own later that century.[11]

While in the civil law tradition the public law developed as a science of the state different from the fundamental body of private law, the same is not true in the common law.

Roman Empire 1599–1804 (1973); Jean Portemer, Recherches sur l'enseignement du droit public au XVIIIe siècle, 33 Revue Historique de Droit Français et Étranger 341 (1959).

7. See, e.g., Michael Stolleis, Arcana Imperii und Ratio Status (1980); R. Hoke, Die Emanzipation der deutschen Staatsrechtswissenschaft von der Zivilistik um 17. Jahrhundert, 15 Der Staat 211, 215–24 (1976); I.P.F. van der Graef, Syntagma Iuris Publici (1645).

8. The classic text is Hugo Grotius, De Iure Belli Ac Pacis (1625). Stolleis, *supra* note 7, at 31.

9. Portemer, *supra* note 6, at 348–49, and documentation at 382–95.

10. The leading treatises are listed in Hans U. Scupin, History of the Law of Nations: 1815 to World War I, in 7 Encyclopedia of Public International Law 179, 203–04 (1984).

11. See Gerald Stourzh, Constitution: Changing Meanings of the Term from the Early Seventeenth to the Late Eighteenth Century, in Conceptual Change and the Constitution 35 (Terence Ball & John G.A. Pocock eds., 1988), and the country-by-country historical survey in Jürgen Schwarze, European Administrative Law 100–205 (1992).

This fundamental difference in attitudes has been attributed, in larger part, to the work of one scholar. Albert V. Dicey (1835–1922) was the leading British authority of his time on constitutional law and the conflict of laws. His influence in both fields was pervasive and continued throughout the British Empire and later the Commonwealth. Dicey regarded himself primarily as a constitutional lawyer.[12] In his seminal treatise on the British Constitution, Dicey maintained that the "rule of law" precluded the adjudication of administrative law disputes and of claims against public officials by specialized tribunals applying a discrete body of law. Accordingly, he rejected French-style *droit administratif* as unconstitutional in the United Kingdom.[13]

This quite extreme position has incrementally lost influence and meaning in practice. Current comparative law scholarship is pointing at the unfolding of a doctrine of public law in the Anglo–American world as an important issue of "convergence" with the civil law tradition. A global approach rooted in history and broad in geographical scope seems necessary to understand deep issues such as the relationship between the private and the public sphere which are at the roots of the very term "law."

12. "Why should I even have become involved in this conflict of laws," he wrote to Bryce on July 24, 1896, after having received an advance copy of his Digest. Robert S. Rait, Memorials of Albert Venn Dicey 139, 140 (1925). None of the more recent monographs discussing his teachings deal even tangentially with private international law.

13. Albert V. Dicey, Introduction to the Study of the Law of the Constitution 241–42 (8th ed., 1915). See the contributions to the All Souls Public Law Seminar: Dicey and the Constitution, 1985 Pub. L. 583–723, especially R. Errera, Dicey and French Administrative Law, A Missed Encounter?, *id.* at 695–707.

CHAPTER 5

CODIFICATION OF THE LAW

In the previous Chapter we learned that understanding legal differences requires exploring their deep historical roots. We saw that political power-holders sometimes seek to simplify, restate or even completely change the entire law of a given place through comprehensive reforms.

Beginning near the end of the eighteenth century, such comprehensive efforts of radical change have been more frequent both in contexts characterized by a revolutionary experience, such as the United States (1776), France (1789), Russia (1918) and China (1911, and again in 1949), and in those where fundamental political continuity has been maintained, such as Germany and England.

This Chapter will explore the sense and meaning of "codification", a typically civil law attitude that nevertheless spread far beyond its point of origin. We will start with a discussion of the most successful codification, implemented by Napoleon in an ambitious attempt to contain the entire law of post-revolutionary France in five discrete, relatively short documents. While Napoleon was not the first to attempt a general codification of law, his experience was a formative event in the development of the civil law tradition.

A key observation sets the scene for the following materials. The Code, today's dominant source of civil law, breaks with the long cosmopolitan tradition of the *ius commune* where legal scholarship was the dominant source of professional law. Like Justinian's *Digest* earlier, it takes the form of statutory provisions in an attempt to enact a break with the past. However, and again like the *Digest*, the Code is a piece of legislation *sui generis*, an exquisite product of juristic learning with the force of law. Because of this general force of law, the Code does not require to be interpreted within the framework of previous legal material which it seeks to substitute. To the contrary, the Code must be interpreted with a forward looking attitude seeking to complete, by means of interpretation, the details of the grand scheme out of which it grows. Codification and statutes are not absent in common law countries. Nevertheless they are interpreted as part of the larger fabric of case law, which has been historically the dominant source of law. Statutory interpretation is therefore itself looking backwards, concentrating on the general scheme of the common law, and attempting to understand the problem that a particular statutory provision seeks to amend. As a rule, the techniques of interpretation of a civilian Code are broad, extensive and analogical. Those of a common law statute (which may also well be called a code) is narrow, generally trying to understand any given text as an exception to the rules and principles contained in the common law.

---

1. THE NATIONAL CODIFICATIONS: THE CODES' BREAK WITH THE PAST

French Law of March 21, 1804

[During 1803 and the early part of 1804, the various parts of the French Civil Code had been enacted by way of thirty six separate statutes. The law of March 21, 1804 re-promulgated the Code as a whole.[1]]

Article 7. From the day when these laws [constituting the Code] become effective, the Roman laws, the ordinances, the general and local customs, the charters and the regulations all cease to have the force either of general or of special law concerning the subjects covered by the present code.

H. C. Gutteridge: Comparative Law*

2d Ed. 1949, p. 77.

When called on to deal with foreign law an English lawyer passes from an environment of case law into a "world governed by codes." His first step must, therefore, be to examine the relevant provisions of the codified law, and it will be necessary for him to remember that there are certain differences between the continental codes and English codifying statutes such as the Sale of Goods Act, 1893. A continental code is intended to lay down new rules and is not conceived as resting on a pre-existing body of law.** The history of a rule of continental law is, consequently, not a

---

1. In 2004 for the two hundred years of the French civil code have been celebrated with countless high profile scholarly conferences through the world. These conferences generated many proceedings thus enriching to a great extent the already abundant literature on codification. See R. Batiza, Origins of Modern Codification of the Civil law: The French Experience and its Implications for Louisiana Law, 56 Tul.L.Rev. 477, 478–578 (1982).

* By permission of Cambridge University Press.

** "So strong was this feeling that the Code must be treated as *res nova* that one of the early commentators, Bugnet, said, 'I know nothing of civil law; I only teach the Code Napoleon.' This fear lest the past should slink back again by a side-door explains Napoleon's remark *mon code est perdu* when he heard of the publication of the first

commentary." S. Amos, The Code Napoleon and the Modern World, 10 J.Comp.Legis. & Int'l L. (3d ser.) 222, 224 (1928). More recent studies properly emphasize the break with the past and the reshaping of French legal, administrative, and educational institutions starting with the abolition of feudalism and of the parlements in the "Night of August Fourth" (1789). Dates of significance are the dissolution of the Paris Order of Advocates in 1790, the closing of university law faculties in 1793, and the suppression of academic legal education until after 1800. For a detailed account, see M. P. Fitzsimmons, The Parisian Order of Barristers and the French Revolution (1987). When university legal education returned almost simultaneously with the Civil Code in1804, its central purpose—stated by law and specified in detail by administrative regulation—was the textual exposition of the new French statutory law, centering on the

matter of very great importance save in exceptional cases. "Whereas an English lawyer seeking to interpret a legal principle will look first to its pedigree, a continental lawyer will search for its policy."[1]

THE CODES' BREAK WITH THE PAST

For many years legal scholars have engaged in lively and sometimes controversial discussions about the extent to which the codes have turned the modern civil law systems away from their past. It would seem, however, that unhelpful generalities can be avoided only if the issue is broken down into two related but distinct questions:

(1) What models and sources *inspired the draftsmen* when they prepared the codes?

(2) How much influence did the pre-code sources—as such—retain *after the adoption of the codes*?

(1) The draftsmen invariably were men who had attained prominence by teaching or practicing under the pre-code system or systems, with which they were intimately familiar. On the other hand, their mandate in each instance was to bring about revision as well as national unification of diverse local laws. Thus, subject to whatever political controls were operative at the time, they were authorized and indeed directed to use independent judgment.[2]

The statement just made requires one important qualification. Into many of the civil law countries, the civil code or the whole code system of

Civil Code. A. Bürge, Das französische Privatrecht im 19. Jahrhundert 496–520 (1991). For a different opinion J. Gordley, Myths of the French Civil Code, 42 Am.J.Comp.L. 439 (1994).

1. Walton and Amos, Introduction to French Law, p. 4. (1st ed. 1935).

2. The statement in the text is true not only with respect to draftsmen commissioned by an absolute ruler (as in the case of the Code Napoleon and the Austrian General Civil Code of 1811), but also regarding draftsmen operating within the framework of a representative constitutional system (as in the case of the German as well as the Swiss Civil Code).

Napoleon commissioned a group of four eminent lawyers, the most influential of whom was Portalis, to prepare a draft of the French Civil Code. Although subsequently the draft was debated and somewhat modified in the course of sessions of the Council of State presided over by Napoleon himself, it is clear that the draftsmen's approach, and the sources used by them, remain a subject of great interest. It is, therefore, fortunate that the brilliant and highly informative statement made by Portalis concerning the nature and sources of the Code is now available in English translation. See M. S. Herman, Excerpts from a Discourse on the Code Napoleon by Portalis, 18 Loyola L.Rev. 23 (1972); and A. Levasseur, Code Napoleon or Code Portalis?, 43 Tul.L.Rev. 762, 767–74 (1969).

For interesting details concerning the manner in which the Austrian, German, and Swiss codes were prepared, see W. Lorenz, Some Comments on the Austrian, German and Swiss Legal Systems, with Particular Reference to the Law of Contracts, in 1 Formation of Contracts—A Study of the Common Core of Legal Systems 251–59 (Schlesinger ed., 1968). See also Schlesinger, The Uniform Commercial Code in the Light of Comparative Law, 1 Inter–Am. L.Rev. 11, 28–31 (1959).

another nation was imported as a result either of military conquest or of cultural influence. In this way, as we shall see, so-called "code families" have come into existence (see *infra*). Thus, when we speak of the codifiers' exercise of independent judgment, we must limit our statement to the seminal codes.

The draftsmen of the various seminal codes, in exercising their independent judgment, very often reached different conclusions regarding the same point. In part, this can be explained by differences in national circumstances and by the fact that some codes were passed much later than others. This, however, is only a partial explanation. To a considerable degree, the differences between the various codes must be ascribed to deliberate choices made by the codifiers—choices that often were personal and accidental in the sense that they were not necessitated by national circumstances or the spirit of the time. In any event, whatever the reasons, the fact is that as a result of codification the differences inter sese among civil law systems have become much more pronounced than they were in pre code days.

(a) The various codes are significantly different in their systematic structure. In this connection, it is instructive to compare the tables of organization of the civil codes which appear *infra*. While the Napoleonic Code, in spite of some refinements,[3] still clings rather strongly to the simple Roman system embodied in Justinian's Institutions, the organization of the German Civil Code shows much less dependence on the somewhat primitive structural thinking of the Romans. Not only its General Part, with its highly abstract, pervasive concepts and precepts, but the whole structure is imbued with the systematic, speculative thinking of the 18th and 19th century scholars of whom we have spoken above.

(b) Similarly, the style and diction of each of the leading codes reflect intellectual and political forces having at least some of their roots in the past, i.e., in the era preceding the particular codification. The Napoleonic Code, still strongly influenced by 18th century rationalism, displayed an optimistic faith in human Reason by being written in elegant and simple language, which was expected to be fully understood by the citizens. The draftsmen of the German B.G.B., on the other hand, doubtless were influenced by 19th century admiration of scientific method. Clearly, they addressed the legal profession rather than the ordinary citizen when they employed the many highly abstract, technical terms and the countless system-wide cross references for which their Code is famous. The Swiss Civil Code, although prepared only a short time after the German and influenced by the latter, again reverted to simple and predominantly non-technical language, in an attempt—inspired by democratic ideals—to bring justice closer to the people. Unlike the Napoleonic Code or the B.G.B., it is

3. The refinements, especially in subdividing the area of Obligations, largely reflect the systematic thinking of Pothier (1699– 1772). See S. Jorgensen, Vertrag und Recht 67–68 (1968), where further references can be found.

substantially the work of a single draftsman, Professor Eugen Huber, then of the University of Basel.[4]

(c) In fashioning specific principles and rules, the codifiers were free to choose among many models and other sources of inspiration. Even a superficial and schematic list of such sources would have to include the following:

(i) Roman law, both in its classical form and as developed through the centuries.

(ii) The non-Roman elements of pre-code civil law, which have been discussed above: Customs of Germanic or feudal origin; canon law; the law merchant; and the scholarly writings originating from the school of natural law and the Pandektenwissenschaft.

(iii) Codes or compilations previously adopted in parts of the national territory.[5]

(iv) Comparative studies of foreign systems, especially of the leading codes previously adopted in other countries.

(v) Original solutions devised by the draftsmen, either by way of free, non-imitative invention, or by fashioning a novel combination of elements borrowed from several older sources.

Even if one focuses on a single code, any attempt to generalize concerning the relative strength of these various sources of inspiration is difficult and often hazardous.[6] In order to get the "feel" of the sources drawn upon by the codifiers, one must select specific problems and examine the historical background of the treatment which these problems have received in particular codes. This is the purpose of the illustrations which follow.

Illustration 1 (Formation of Contracts)[7]

On the eve of the age of codification, the recognized oracles of the civil law had reached a measure of agreement concerning the question of the

---

4. Professor Huber had previously abandoned a distinguished career as a journalist because he disagreed with the anti-labor editorial policy of his employer, a leading Swiss daily.

5. Local codes previously enacted in some of the German kingdoms and principalities constituted a particularly important source for the draftsmen of the German Civil Code. In this connection, it must be remembered that throughout most of the 19th century some major regions of Germany lived under a code system modeled on the French. Originally that system may have owed its adoption, at least in part, to Napoleon's armed might; but in Baden, and some other parts of Germany not far from the French border, it was voluntarily retained after Na-

poleon's downfall. The draftsmen of the German Civil Code thus had to consider a version of the Code Napoleon as the "local" law then existing in some German provinces, and not merely as a foreign system to be examined by way of comparative studies.

6. An example is provided by the Civil Code of Louisiana. There has been a heated scholarly controversy concerning the question whether the draftsmen of the predecessor of the present Code were predominantly inspired by Spanish or by French sources.

7. Now indispensable for historical background: Towards a General Law of Contract (John Barton ed., 1990). See also James Gordley, The Philosophical Origins of Modern Contract Doctrine (1991).

enforceability of non-typical as well as typical contracts. As we have seen above, the classical Roman view (that only certain types of contracts should be enforced) had been rejected. Under the influence of canon law, the law merchant and natural law, it had become recognized that in principle any agreement of two parties, voluntarily entered into and meant to create legal obligations, should be enforced as a contract, regardless of the presence or absence of what a lawyer brought up in the common law would call "consideration."[8]

In view of this state of the authorities of the immediate pre-codification period, it is not surprising to find that the same general principle—often referred to as the principle of freedom of contract, although it deals with only one aspect of such freedom—was taken over into all of the codes.[9]

The adoption of this principle, which made the parties' *consensus* the central and decisive element of the law of contracts, rendered it necessary to deal with the often difficult question of the manner in which such consensus comes about. The Roman jurists, who had never developed a unitary contract theory,[10] left this question unanswered. Even in post-Roman days, so long as most consensual transactions were concluded inter *praesentes* [between bystanders], legal scholars did not feel called upon to devote much deep and systematic thought to the subject of formation of contracts. But when, with expanding trade and travel, contracts inter *absentes* [parties being far away] became a matter of routine, the need for legal rules concerning the mechanics of formation made itself felt. In response to this need, Grotius (1583–1645) developed the modern doctrine of offer and acceptance. From his works, and those of other natural law authors, the doctrine found its way into most of the great codes.[11]

8. Thus, long before the great codifications, the civil law had come to recognize the validity and enforceability of a contractual promise to make a gift (a type of promise in which the Church had always shown a considerable interest), subject to the requirement of notarial or other form, e.g., registration. J. P. Dawson, Gifts and Promises (1980); Baade, Donations Reconsidered, 59 Tex.L.Rev. 179, 181 (1980). For a recent broad comparative treatment within the Common Core of European Private Law project see James Gordley, Enforceability of promises in European Private Law, Cambridge, Cambridge University Press, 2002.

9. The doctrine of consideration is peculiar to the common law and is not recognized in the civil law systems. See A. G. Chloros, The Doctrine of Consideration and the Reform of the Law of Contract, 17 Int'l & Comp.L.Q. 137 (1968); Lorenzen, Causa and Consideration in the Law of Contracts, 28 Yale L.J. 621 (1919); Mason, The Utility of Consideration, 41 Colum.L.Rev. 825 (1941).

For an American decision enforcing a promise to make a gift, where the promise was made in notarial form (see *supra* Chapter 2, Part 2, Section 1 at 145) and was governed by German law, see In re Estate of Danz, 444 Pa. 411, 283 A.2d 282 (1971).

10. See F. Schulz, Classical Roman Law 465–68 (1951); R. W. Lee, Elements of Roman Law 345 (1956); 1 Kaser, Das Römische Privatrecht 229 (2d ed. 1971). Regarding the complexities and confusion that arose during the post-classical period, see 2 Kaser, *Id.* 362ff (2d ed. 1975). See also the *Bank of Lisbon* case, *supra* at 311.

11. The one big exception is the French Civil Code, which—strange to relate—contains virtually no provisions on the subject of offer and acceptance. The reason for this omission seems to be that Domat and Pothier, the two authors on whose works the French codifiers relied most strongly, had been somewhat neglectful in treating this particular subject. See Bonassies, Some Com-

This, however, was not yet the end of the story. Grotius had favored the rule that normally an offer should be revocable until accepted.[12] Some of the earlier codes adopted this rule, along with other aspects of the doctrine of offer and acceptance which Grotius had developed as a matter of natural law. In France, also, the natural law view favoring revocability of offers exerted some influence, even though the Code Napoleon was silent on the point.[13] As a result, some civil law systems still adhere to the view that, in principle at least, an offer is revocable until accepted.

In Germany, however, somewhat different influences made themselves felt. The civil codes of Prussia (1794) and of Saxony (1863) made the offer irrevocable in cases where the offeror had set a time limit for acceptance.[14] The Commercial Code of 1861, going a step further, extended the rule of irrevocability to all offers regardless of whether or not they specified such a time limit;[15] where no time limit was specified, the offer was to remain irrevocable for a reasonable time. This, in essence, was the rule later embodied in the German Civil Code.[16]

The foregoing sketch, though oversimplified, shows that in fashioning the modern rules of offer and acceptance,[17] the codifiers drew on almost all of the types of sources enumerated above. Roman law did not play a significant role in this instance; yet it furnished some of the basic terms and concepts, especially the all-important notion of consensus.[18]

Illustration 2 (A Problem of Strict Liability in Tort)[19]

Article 170 of the Louisiana Civil Code of 1870 (repealed in 1990) made the "master" liable "for the damage caused to individuals or to the community in general by whatever is thrown out of his house into the street or public road." This liability did not depend on proof of negligence. In a case not covered by the language of Art. 177, but arguably coming within its spirit,[20] the Court of Appeals for the Fifth Circuit delved deeply

---

ments on the French Legal System, with Particular Reference to the Law of Contracts, in 1 Formation of Contracts—A Study of the Common Core of Legal Systems 243 (Schlesinger ed., 1968).

12. See Franz Wieacker, A History of Private Law in Europe 233 (T. Weir trans., 1995).

13. See the report by Professor Bonassies in 1 Formation of Contracts, *supra* note 11 at 769ff, especially at 770.

14. See Lorenz, *supra* note 2 at 254.

15. *Id.* at 255.

16. See §§ 145–149; see also *infra* Chapter 9, Section 1(a) at 872.

17. For a comparative and more detailed discussion of the pertinent modern rules, see 1 Formation of Contracts, *supra* note 11 at 109–11, 745–91.

18. See Kreller, Römisches Recht—Grundlehren des Gemeinen Rechts 269 (1950).

19. This illustration is based on Williams v. Employers Liability Assurance Corp., 296 F.2d 569 (5th Cir.1961), cert. denied, 371 U.S. 844, 83 S.Ct. 76 (1962). Judge Wisdom's scholarly opinion in that case contains a wealth of references. A rich comparative discussion is now available within the Common core of European Private Law Project, see Vernon Palmer & Franz Werro, The Boundaries of Strict Liability in European tort Law, Stamphli, Berne (2004).

20. The facts of Williams v. Employers Liability Assurance Corp., 296 F.2d 569 (5th Cir.1961) cert. denied, 371 U.S. 844 (1962), were simple and tragic. The plaintiff, a widow 43 years of age, who worked in a large office building owned and operated by defendant, was brutally assaulted and sexually abused by a young hoodlum who had followed her into the ladies' room. As a result, she suffered physical injuries and severe nervous

into the historical antecedents.[21] On the basis of this research, the Court concluded that the rule of Art. 177 is of Roman origin.[22] It can be found, in terms substantially similar to those of the Louisiana Code, in Justinian's Digest as well as in the Institutiones. From there, through the *Siete Partidas* (see *supra* sec. 1, at note n) and the writings, among others, of the 17th century French author Domat, it found its way not only into the Louisiana codes of 1808, 1825 and 1870, but also into the Civil Codes of Spain and some other civil law countries, especially in Latin America.[23]

As generally understood, this Roman-derived rule makes the person in possession of the house (not necessarily the owner) absolutely or at least presumptively liable for any injury or damage caused by an object thrown or poured from the house, even though the victim may be unable to show whether the physical act was committed by the defendant himself, a member of his family, a servant, a tenant or sub-tenant, or a stranger. Typically Roman in its casuistic and practical approach to a rather specific problem, at first blush the rule seems basically sound. We find, however, that the French Civil Code, and following it a majority of the modern codes, rejected the rule, thus allowing recovery only if the victim can prove negligence on the part of the defendant or of a person for whose conduct the defendant is vicariously liable.

A preliminary draft of the Code Napoleon, used by the Louisiana codifiers as a source for the Code of 1808, did attempt to codify the law [i.e. the Roman law] relating to things thrown from houses. The Conseil d'État rejected the proposed provisions. The Code Napoleon, a code to reform the law, perhaps influenced by contemporary philosophical interest in individualism, free will, and moral responsibility, takes the approach that the liability of a master for things thrown out of a house must be based on culpability within the general principle of no liability without fault.[24]

disorders. Alleging that defendant, in operating the building, had taken insufficient precautions against intrusions by hoodlums, plaintiff sought damages from defendant. The trial court submitted the issue of negligence to the jury (which found no negligence on defendant's part), but refused to charge that Art. 177, directly or analogously applied, would impose liability on the defendant even if its conduct were not proved negligent. Whether this refusal to charge constituted error was the main issue on appeal.

21. At the end of its historical excursion, the Court affirmed the District Court's judgment for defendant, on the ground that the rule embodied in Art. 177 was never intended to protect a person inside the building.

22. Seemingly disagreeing with Judge Wisdom's conclusion, Professor Batiza has stated that Art. 177 was almost verbatim lifted from Blackstone. See R. Batiza, The

Louisiana Civil Code of 1808: Its Actual Sources and Present Relevance, 46 Tul. L.Rev. 4, at 28, 51 & 137 (1971).

23. The history of the rule in pre-code civil law is interestingly traced by Stein, The Actio de Effusis vel Dejectis and the Concept of Quasi–Delict in Scots Law, 4 Int'l & Comp. L.Q. 356 (1955), commenting on a 1954 case which turned on the question whether the rule mentioned in the text had been received into Scots law. Gray v. Dunlop, 1954 S.L.T. (Sh.Ct.) 75. What result, and why?

24. 296 F.2d, at 575–76. In addition to the philosophical reasons suggested by the Court, the codifiers may have had more specific practical grounds for abolishing the Roman rule. In the age of firearms, a rule imposing absolute or quasi-absolute liability on the owner of the building can lead to rather harsh results, e.g., in the case of a sniper hiding out in the building and killing

The Court does not intimate that concerning the specific point in question the French codifiers were influenced by 17th or 18th century legal authors. On the contrary, the opinion demonstrates by apt quotations that Domat, perhaps the most original and influential of the pre-code French authors, had emphatically and approvingly restated the Roman rule. Thus, if we accept the results of the Court's painstaking historical research, we must conclude that the French codifiers broke with tradition in passing on this issue. Whatever their philosophical or other reasons may have been, they fashioned a novel solution, reversing whatever precedent could be found in the pre-code sources.

The upshot, again, is that the modern civil law codes, in spite of basic similarities in methods and concepts, reached divergent results concerning the specific point at issue. Some of them, probably a minority, have adhered to the essence and almost to the very words of the rule stated by Justinian. In the other codes, the opposite rule has been adopted, following a re-examination in which policy considerations prevailed over tradition.

Illustration 3 (The Fate of the Bona Fide Purchaser of Chattels)[25]

Every developed legal system must resolve the conflict between two innocent parties which occurs in the typical "bona fide purchaser" situation. In the discussion which follows, the original owner will be referred to as *A*. The bailee or thief who, acting as if he had title, purports to transfer such title and delivers possession of the chattel to a third person, will be called *B*. The third person, i.e. the purchaser, will be named *C*.

The civil law systems began very early to face up to the problem. Again, the trail begins in ancient Rome. Roman law clearly resolved the issue in favor of *A*; he had the right to recover his chattel from *C*, even though the latter had paid value and had acted in good faith. In case *C* had possession of the chattel for at least a year prior to the commencement of *A*'s action, he might try to defend on the ground of *usucapio* (comparable to adverse possession); but a person in the position of *C* could successfully invoke this defense only in exceptional fact situations, because *usucapio* did not apply to a chattel which the owner had lost through larceny, and a bailee's embezzlement was regarded as an instance of larceny. Thus *C* could defend on grounds of *usucapio* only in the rare case in which *B* was neither a thief nor an embezzler (e.g., when *B* had made an honest mistake in disposing of the chattel). Even in such a rare case, *C* could prevail only if he had had possession of the chattel for at least a year, and if he had acted bona fide. In the light of later developments, it is important to note that in

or injuring people in the street. For further discussion, see A. Watson, Failures of the Legal Imagination, chapter 1: The Law of Delict and Quasi–Delict in the French *Code Civil* (1988).

25.   A recent comparative discussion attempting to look at the different economic incentives stemming from the different alternative rules can be found in Ugo Mattei, Basic Principles of Property Law. A Comparative Law and Economic Introduction, Greenwood Press (2000).

this way, through the *usucapio* doctrine, Roman law injected the notion of bona fides into the handling of our problem.

The rule prevailing in Germanic customary laws—first reliably reported in the 12th century, but probably of much older origin—was more favorable to *C*. Under this rule, a basic distinction was drawn depending on whether *A* had lost possession of his chattel against his will (e.g., by theft), or whether he had entrusted it to a bailee of his choice. In the former situation, *A* ordinarily prevailed over *C*, even under Germanic law. But where *A* had entrusted his chattel to bailee *B*, he had a cause of action only against *B*, and never against *C*. The theory was that *A*, who had voluntarily parted with his chattel, should not be able to recover it from anyone other than the person in whom he had put his trust. Thus *C* could keep the chattel, and *A* was relegated to an action against bailee *B*. Under Germanic law, this was so regardless of whether *C* had acted in good or bad faith. Nor did the length of the period of *C*'s possession make any difference. The operation of the rule protecting *C* did not depend on the passage of time; *C* prevailed even if he was sued by *A* the day after he (*C*) had obtained the chattel from *B*.

From the 15th to the 19th century, the Roman view and the Germanic rule competed for predominance in Germany, the Netherlands and Northern France. Occasionally, there were attempts to work out a compromise solution with special attention to the protection, developed in the law merchant, of purchases in an open market—in English legal parlance, the market overt.[26]

Most of the draftsmen of modern codes were familiar with the conflict between the two rules, and their tendency was to combine the best features of both. A few countries, including Spain and some of the Latin American republics, essentially adopted the Roman approach, subject to relatively minor exceptions.[27] In the majority of civil law countries, however, a careful weighing of policy considerations[28] led to a different solution. Although far from identical in their details,[29] all of the codes of the majority group—

---

26. See B. Kozolchyk, Transfer of Personal Property by a Nonowner: Its Future in Light of its Past, 61 Tul.L.Rev. 1453, 1484–86 (1987). On the market overt in the City of London, see the authorities collected in Reid v. Commissioner of Police of the Metropolis, [1973] 1 Q.B. 551 (C.A.). The market overt in England and Wales was abolished by the Sale of Goods (Amendment) Act 1994 (U.K.).

27. In the Spanish Civil Code, the relevant provisions are derived in part from the Code Napoleon, and in part from the Siete Partidas, with the result that these provisions are not free from ambiguity. See Comment, Sales of Another's Movables—History, Comparative Law and Bona Fide Purchasers, 29 La.L.Rev. 329, 335–37 (1969).

28. For interesting discussions of these policy considerations, see Zweigert, Rechtsvergleichend–Kritisches zum gutgläubigen Mobiliarerwerb, 23 Rabels Z. 1 (1958); Wolff–Raiser, Sachenrecht 247–50 (1957); F. Baur, Lehrbuch des Sachenrechts 466–67 (15th ed. 1989).

29. For instance, the various codes of the majority group differ among each other concerning the time limitation to which *A*'s action against *C* (provided such action is otherwise well-founded under the facts of the case) will be subjected. See J. G. Sauveplanne, The Protection of the Bona Fide Purchaser of Corporeal Movables in Comparative Law, 29 Rabels Z. 651, 680 (1965).

which includes France,[30] Germany,[31] and Switzerland[32]—contain the following essential features:

(i) In accordance with the Germanic approach, a basic distinction is drawn depending on whether *A* voluntarily parted with possession. If he did not, i.e. if the chattel was stolen from him or lost by him, then *A* prevails over *C*; this, at least, is the ordinary rule, subject to varying exceptions. The most important exceptions are the following: Even though the chattel was stolen from A or lost by him, most of the codes protect C if he has acquired the chattel in a public auction. But the manner in which C is protected in such a case differs from country to country. Under German and Austrian law, C acquires good title if he is a bona fide purchaser; the French and Swiss codes, on the other hand, while compelling C to surrender the chattel to A if the latter brings a timely action, provide that in such a situation the surrender be conditioned upon C receiving from A the amount which C in good faith paid for the chattel. On the other hand, if *A* entrusted his chattel to *B*, and the latter without authority transferred and delivered it to *C*, in that event *A* normally cannot recover the chattel from *C*. Thus, in essence, the old Germanic rule is followed.

(ii) Invariably, however, the qualification is added that even in the case where *A* had entrusted his chattel to *B*, no protection is accorded to *C* if he acted in bad faith. This qualification, which was not recognized under the Germanic rule, was derived from the above-mentioned Roman doctrine of *usucapio*.

One may fairly say, therefore, that in this instance the majority of the codifiers relied on traditional principles, largely of Germanic and to a lesser extent of Roman origin. If, however, one takes a closer look at the pertinent rules as they appear today in the various codes belonging to this group, one finds that in important details they differ from each other. These differences are particularly noticeable in judicial responses to trade in art objects illegally removed or stolen from other countries.[33] The Institute for the Unification of Private Law (UNIDROIT) has studied this subject for several decades, and under its auspices, a Convention on Stolen or Illegally Exported Cultural Objects was proposed for adoption by a diplomatic conference on June 24, 1995. The Convention entered into force on the first

30. For an exposition of the relevant French rules, see C. S. P. Harding & M. S. Rowell, Protection of Property Versus Protection of Commercial Transactions in French and English Law, 26 Int'l & Comp.L.Q. 354, 356–63 (1977).

31. See German Civil Code, §§ 932–35 and German Commercial Code, §§ 366–67, discussed by E. J. Cohn, Manual of German Law, § 362 (2d ed. 1968), and in Kunstsammlungen zu Weimar v. Elicofon, 536 F.Supp. 829, 839–43 (E.D.N.Y.1981), aff'd 678 F.2d 1150 (2d Cir.1982).

32. An English translation of the relevant Swiss provisions appears in the sixth edition of this book, p. 910, note 83. Swiss law in point is discussed in Autocephalous Greek–Orthodox Church v. Goldberg, 717 F.Supp. 1374, 1400 (S.D.Ind.1989), aff'd, 917 F.2d 278 (7th Cir.1990), cert. denied, 502 U.S. 941 (1991).

33. The literature is vast, and growing exponentially. A superb survey, extensively documented, is K. Siehr, International Art Trade and the Law, 243 Académie de Droit International, Recueil des Cours 9 (1993–VI).

of July of 1998 after five signatures. As of today it has been ratified by 29 countries.

Despite the fact that many "art-poor, money-rich" countries including the United States have not ratified the Convention,[34] one result of scholarly and diplomatic efforts in this area, is the steadily expanding awareness of art dealers, the acquisition officers of museums and ultimately the general public, of the phenomenon of "stolen" art and the importance of establishing provenance. Even if temporal and/or geographic islands tolerating the bona fide acquisition of stolen art objects should survive, therefore, it is increasingly unlikely that reputable purchasers will be able to meet the ever increasing prerequisites of good faith. For example, Article 4(4) of the UNIDROIT Convention, states that in determining whether the acquirer acted in good faith, "regard shall be had to all the circumstances of the acquisition, including the character of the parties, the price paid, whether the possessor consulted any reasonably accessible register of stolen cultural objects, and any other relevant information and documentation which it could reasonably have obtained, and whether the possessor consulted accessible agencies or took any other step that a reasonable person would have taken in the circumstances."

Why should there be significant and sometimes crucial differences between the civil codes of major European countries on bona fide purchase of movables, in spite of the fact that in dealing with that topic the draftsmen of all these codes were utilizing the same sources? The answer, clearly, must be that in fashioning a new principle by a combination of Germanic and Roman elements, and in devising the specifics necessary to make the new principle work, the draftsmen of each of the new codes had to resolve numerous questions of policy and of drafting technique. By the time each group of draftsmen had independently and creatively developed its own answers to these questions, it had—while making considerable use of ancient building blocks—constructed an essentially new building, a building somewhat similar to, and yet distinct from, the edifices created by the code architects of other nations.[35]

* * *

Having studied these illustrations, which may be taken as typical, the reader can form his own judgment concerning the relative strength of the traditional and the innovating thoughts which interacted in the minds of the codifiers. On one point, however, there can be no reasonable difference of opinion: The old adage, all too frequently repeated, that the civilian codes presently in force are merely a modernized version of Roman law, is simply nonsense. In many respects, the solutions adopted by the codifiers

34. See John Henry Merryman, ed., Imperialism, Art and Restitution, Cambridge University Press (2006).

35. The draftsmen of the Italian Civil Code of 1942, one of the more recent civilian codes, went further and discarded all of the traditional approaches. They fashioned an original solution (Arts. 1153–57), according to which the bona fide purchaser (C) acquires good title regardless of whether A's loss of possession was voluntary or involuntary. For application, see Winkworth v. Christie Manson and Woods, Ltd. (1980), chapter 496.

were not traditional; and of the traditional ones, many were not Roman.[36] Professor Reginald Parker was probably right when he said: "I seriously believe it would not be difficult to establish, if such a thing could be statistically approached, that the majority of legal institutes, even within the confines of private law, of a given civil law country are not necessarily of Roman origin."[37]

It should be remembered, moreover, that classical Roman law "was never codified in a modern sense, and is, therefore, in many respects more similar to common law sources than to a civil code."[38] Indeed, it has been shown by an imposing array of evidence that in its basic law-making methods, and also in many particulars, classical Roman law is closer to the common law than to the modern civilian codes.[39]

Some of the institutions of Roman law which were eliminated from the civil law by the codifiers have survived in the Anglo–American system, especially on the equity side. Our pretrial discovery, for instance, is directly traceable to Roman and especially to Canon law. Corresponding devices in modern continental systems of procedure are much weaker. Every international practitioner knows that the existence, under U.S. law, of potent devices for the extraction of factual information from an unwilling opponent, and the non-existence or weakness of such devices in civil law countries, constitutes one of the significant facts of life in international litigation. Where choice is possible between a civil law and a common law forum, this procedural difference will loom large in the parties' strategic planning. The difference exists because the influence of the Roman *interrogatio* and the canonical *positio* remained unbroken through centuries of discovery practice in chancery and admiralty,[40] while the draftsmen of the classical continental codes, seeking to protect individual privacy, consciously abolished or weakened the older devices for discovery. Only most recently, and with considerable caution, have civil law legislators taken steps to strengthen their discovery devices.

On the other hand, the civil law has remained more Roman than the common law in its terminology and in its techniques of conceptualization and classification. Without Roman terms and concepts, and without the wealth of illustrative material found in the practical solutions devised by

36. In addition to the examples already given, the following have been mentioned as institutions found in the modern codes but non-existent or only primitively developed in Roman law: assignability of claims; negotiability of instruments; and the law of agency. See Parker, Book Review, 42 Cornell L.Q. 448–49 (1957).

37. Parker, *Ibid.*

38. Ehrenzweig, A Common Language of World Jurisprudence, 12 U.Chi.L.Rev. 285, 289 (1945).

39. See Pringsheim, The Inner Relationship Between English and Roman Law, 5 Cambridge L.J. 347 (1935); Moses, International Legal Practice, 4 Fordham L.Rev. 244, 253–55 (1935); W.W. Bukland & Arnold D. McNair, Roman Law and Common Law (1965).

40. The civil law origin of discovery was stressed by Story, J., in Sherwood v. Hall, 3 Sumn. 127, Fed.Cas. No. 12,777 (1837), and again by Jackson, J., concurring in Hickman v. Taylor, 329 U.S. 495, 515, 67 S.Ct. 385, 396 (1947). See also Millar, Civil Procedure of the Trial Court in Historical Perspective 201–02 (1952).

the Roman jurists, the progressive systematization of the civil law at the hands of glossators, commentators, humanists, natural law scholars and pandectists would not have been possible. It is the continental *jus commune* thus developed over the centuries, and its influence upon the codes, together with the method of codification itself, which has preserved the "civil law systems" as an identifiable group, a group which (except in the case of some mixed systems) is clearly set apart from the common law family.

(2) Up to this point, we have attempted to assess the role which traditional and non-traditional elements played in the thinking of the codifiers. Now we turn to the related but distinct question of the extent to which the single, dramatic event of codification marked a break with the pre-code past for the generations of lawyers who in the various civil law countries have practiced, and are still practicing, under the codes.

The answer to this latter question is relatively simple. In each of the countries of the seminal codes, codification meant not only national unification, comprehensive revision, and intensive restructuring of the whole body of private, criminal and procedural law,[41] but also the enactment of a new and authoritative text.[42] In order to accomplish all of these objectives of codification, it was imperative, in applying the codes, to treat their provisions as the exclusive source of binding authority, subject only to legislative amendment, and not to let the old law slink back under any pretense.

In some of the early attempts at codification, especially the Prussian Code (*Preussisches allgemeines Landrecht*) of 1794, the draftsmen tried to provide specific rules for every conceivable fact situation, and expressly prohibited the courts from amplifying those rules by "interpretation." Although the Prussian Code was a document of excessive length, containing many thousands of sections, it turned out soon after its enactment that there were fact situations which had not been foreseen by the draftsmen and which, consequently, were not covered by the provisions of the Code. Thus the primitive method by which the Prussian draftsmen had sought to secure their Code's status as the exclusive source of law clearly failed.

---

41. The public law of the civil law countries, and especially their administrative law, developed in a different manner. It has never been comprehensively codified. The French system of administrative law has been created essentially by case law, while in Germany the subject was first systematized by legal scholars. Over the years, there has been a tremendous increase in the number of statutes dealing with administrative law; in some countries, especially in Germany, these statutes tend to become more and more systematic. Nevertheless, it remains true that private law, criminal law, and civil as well as criminal procedure are truly codified in civil law countries but that public law (except for constitutional law) is not.

42. The last-mentioned aspect of codification is not a mere technical matter of legal method. Civilians are apt to regard complete codification of the law as an important bulwark against official (especially judicial) arbitrariness. See Schlesinger, The Uniform Commercial Code in the Light of Comparative Law, 1 Inter–Am.L.Rev. 11, 19–21 (1959). This attitude is particularly strong in France, where the pre-revolutionary judiciary had been accused not only of arbitrariness but also of usurpation and abuse of law-making powers. See F. Deák & M. Rheinstein, The Development of French and German Law, 24 Ge. L. J. 551 (1936).

The methods by which 19th century codifiers sought to accomplish the same purpose were less direct but more sophisticated. Many of the 19th century civil codes contain explicit directions enumerating the subsidiary sources of law (e.g., analogy, customs, natural law) to be used in cases not covered by the substantive provisions of the Code. In theory at least, it can be maintained that the courts resort to these other sources only by virtue of the Code's own mandate, and that within the scope of its subject matter the Code governs the disposition of a case even when its substantive provisions are silent. Moreover—and this is of still greater significance— modern codes seek to cover a wide range of unforeseen fact situations by way of substantive provisions of utmost generality and flexibility. These so-called "general clauses" of the codes may provide, for example, that all immoral transactions are void, or that every obligation must be performed in good faith. Thus, even when faced with a novel and unforeseen case, and fashioning what in effect may be a new solution, a civil law court as a rule purports merely to "interpret" and "apply" a provision—though perhaps a broadly worded one—of the Code.

This theoretical adherence to the ideal of a comprehensive Code, supposedly constituting the exclusive source of law in a broadly defined area of the legal order, did not prevent the courts in civil law countries from developing decisional law. Nor today it is anymore the unanimous or in certain countries even the majority opinion of civilian lawyers. It is however true that in contrast to pre-code days judicial law-making as well as scholarly exposition almost invariably are presented as mere "interpretation" of a text of unquestionable authority, and are fitted into the structural framework of the Code.

In every civil law country, codification had a profound effect on legal education and legal literature. The curricula of the law faculties had to be reshaped and new textbooks and treatises had to be prepared, in order to adjust them to the systematic arrangement and the substantive innovations of the codes. Gradually, as it was replaced by more current tools, the pre-code legal literature thus lost its practical value for lawyers and law students.

Practitioners in code countries are thoroughly familiar with the arrangement of their codes, and thus find it convenient to use tools which closely follow that arrangement. In some parts of the civil law world, especially in Germany and German influenced countries, the most popular research tool of lawyers and judges is the code "commentary." The leading commentaries are not merely annotated text editions, but constitute elaborate treatises which offer thorough discussion as well as massive references with the relevant code provisions. This type of legal exposition is readily traced to the Commentators of fourteenth-century Italy who in turn followed the style of classical Roman jurists' commentaries on the Praetorian edict.

There was also a steep decline in the courts' reliance on pre-code authorities. It is true that in some code countries this decline was less abrupt than might have been expected. So long as members of the generation learned and experienced in pre-code law wielded controlling influence on Bench and Bar, judicial decisions continued to refer to pre-code authorities, sometimes in open defiance of code provisions specifying the sources of law which should, or should not, be resorted to.[43]

In France, this was facilitated by the publication, immediately after codification, of code editions which in effect were concordances of code provisions and pre-existing law (Roman law, customs, statutes etc.). Legal tools of this kind soon became obsolete, and were replaced by treatises and other literary aids wholly based on the Code itself, and reflecting *its* interpretation by scholars and courts. But, as the post-code generations of law students, brought up on code oriented lectures and teaching tools, moved into the judicial and other branches of the profession, pre-code authorities were virtually forgotten.[44] Even in scholarly writings, insofar as they dealt with existing law,[45] references to pre-code developments became less and less frequent.

It is in this sense that we can speak of the code systems' break with the past. This break occurred in virtually every country that experienced civilian-like codification, including those outside of the western legal tradition. Depending on political circumstances, however, there were considerable differences from nation to nation regarding the timing, and the degree of abruptness, of the change. In France, the five basic codes were enacted in rapid succession at the beginning of the 19th century. In Germany, codification on a national scale took place during the latter part of the 19th century, and in a much more gradual manner. The first of the basic codes, adopted by the great majority of the German states during the 1860s before the advent of political unification of the Reich, was the Commercial Code.[46] It was followed in the 1870s by the Penal Code and the two procedural codes; but the Civil Code, although preparatory work on it started in 1874, was not enacted until 1896, and went into effect January 1, 1900.[47]

2.   THE MEANING OF CODIFICATION IN THE CIVIL LAW TRADITION

It was stated above that codification, and the consequent break with the past, occurred in virtually every civil law country. There are a few—

43. See, e.g., H. J. B. Dard, Code Napoléon, avec des notes indicatives des Lois Romaines, Coutumes, Ordonnances, Édits et Déclarations qui ont rapport à chaque article (1808).

44. Legal authors occasionally report an instance in which a modern court referred to a pre-code authority. See, e.g., David and DeVries, The French Legal System 93 (1958). The rare and exceptional nature of such instances, however, confirms the fact that resort to pre-code authorities is not a routine technique in civil law countries.

45. Legal history, of course, remained a subject of academic teaching and research in civil law countries even after codification. But in the late 19th and early 20th century the work of the legal historians, though on a high level of scholarship, became an academic specialty totally removed from legal practice. See *infra* at 404

46. See Lorenz. Some comments on the Austrian, German and Swiss Legal Systems, with particular reference to the Law of Contracts, in 1 Formation of Contracts—A Study of the Common Core of Legal Systems 251–59.

47. For details and further references, see Lorenz, *Ibid.*

very few—exceptions.[1] Scotland[2] preserved its civil law system in un-codified form.[3] The Roman–Dutch law of South Africa,[4] Sri Lanka (formerly Ceylon),[5] and British Guiana[6] equally resisted the trend toward Codification. As a result we find that a case coming up in a Scottish or South–African court today may turn on the interpretation of a passage from Justinian's Corpus Juris,[7] or from the works of an authoritative 17th century writer.[8]

1. The substantive law of pre-communist *Hungary* was only partly codified, and the gaps in the written law were filled by customary law and by judicial decisions; the opinions of the highest court sitting en banc were binding on all courts. See Zajtay, Introduction à l'étude du droit Hongrois (1953); A. Csizmadia, Hungarian Customary Law Before the Bourgeois Rebellion of 1848, 4 J. Legal Hist. 3 (1983); von Szladits, "Ungarn", in 1 Rechtsvergleichendes Handwoerterbuch fuer das Zivil- und Handelsrecht des In- und Auslandes 276–86 (1929). Mainly due to the towering influence of Professor Guido (Gad) Tedeschi, *Israel* combines civil law-inspired partial codifications of secular law with a common law background. See A. M. Rabello, Ed., European Traditions in Israel (1994), Part D: Israel Law. See also *supra* at 195ff.

2. For information on the Scottish legal system see, e.g., T. B. Smith, Scotland: The Development of Its Laws and Constitution (1962); A. Watson, Legal Transplants—An Approach to Comparative Law 44–56 (1974). The most convenient and authoritative source of ready reference is the Stair Memorial Encyclopedia of the Laws of Scotland, 25 vols. 1986ff, edited by T. B. Smith from 1981 to 1988 and thereafter by Professor Robert Black.

3. In varying degrees, both Roman–Dutch law and Scots law have been subjected to an infiltration of common law rules and English common law techniques. See T. B. Smith, Scotland: The Development of Its Laws and Constitution (1962); A. Watson, Legal Transplants—An Approach to Comparative Law 44–56 (1974). The most convenient and authoritative source of ready reference is the Stair Memorial Encyclopedia of the Laws of Scotland, 25 vols. 1986ff, edited by T. B. Smith from 1981 to 1988 and thereafter by Professor Robert Black. See also Beinart, Roman Law in South Africa Practice, 69 So.Afr. L.J. 145, 151 (1952); T.P. van Reenen, The Relevance of Roman (Dutch) Law for Legal Interpretation in South Africa, 112 So.Afr. L.J. 276 (1995). Note (not so incidentally)

that both Scots law and South African law, to the extent that they are the products of judicial precedent, are also called "common law" in those countries. The root of this usage is the term *jus commune*, also reflected in "gemeines Recht" in nineteenth-century Germany.

4. In 1952, the Professor of Roman Law at the University of Cape Town noted that the law of South Africa "still breathes the spirit" of the reception of Roman law. Beinart, Roman Law in South African Practice, 69 So.Afr.L.J. 145, 151 (1952). See, e.g., the *Bank of Lisbon* case, *supra* at 311. Professor Beinart's successor, Reinhard Zimmermann, kept that spirit very much alive with his classic work, The Law of Obligations, Roman Foundations of the Civilian Tradition (1990). See also most recently T. P. van Reenen, The Relevance of the Roman (Dutch) Law for Legal Interpretation in South Africa, 112 So. Afr.L.J. 276 (1995).

5. See Jennings & Tambiah, The Dominion of Ceylon—The Development of Its Laws and Constitution 179ff (1952); T. B. Smith, Studies Critical and Comparative xxix–xxxii (1962); 1 Weeramantry, The Law of Contracts 23–68 (1967); T. Nadaraja, The Legal System of Ceylon in Its Historical Setting (1972); L. M. J. Cooray, The Reception of Roman–Dutch Law in Ceylon, 7 Comp. & Int'l J.So.Afr. 295 (1974).

6. See Demerara Turf Club v. Wight, *supra* at 323. On various civil law (not only Roman–Dutch) influences persisting in the area, see also Patchett, Some Aspects of Marriage and Divorce in the West Indies, 8 Int'l & Comp.L.Q. 632, 633 (1959).

7. See, e.g., Cantiere San Rocco S.A. v. The Clyde Shipbuilding & Engineering Co., Ltd. (1923), S.C. (H.L.) 105, as well as the delightful case of Mustard v. Patterson (1923), Sess.Cas. 142, and recently Stirling v. Bartlett, 1993 S.L.T. 763, 767 (0), quoting Inst. 2.1.20.

8. See, e.g., Glazer v. Glazer, 1963(4) S.A.L.R. 694.

The principality of Andorra is another jurisdiction—this one in continental Europe—where un-codified civil law has remained in force to this day.[9] In the decisions (including recent decisions) of the courts of Andorra, many references to Roman law and Canon law can be found. A similar phenomenon can be observed in the tiny and independent Republic of San Marino not far from Bologna in Italy. In some respects, the law of Andorra is similar to that of neighboring Catalonia. In this connection, the reader will know (see editors' note to *In re Shoop*, p. 178ff) that Catalonia is one of those Spanish regions where pre-code customs (*fueros*) have been preserved as the primary source of law in those areas not governed by the national Civil Code.

In the vast majority of civil law countries, the bulk of private, penal and procedural law is enshrined in codes. For the historical reasons explained on previous pages, the codes were intended to be authoritative, systematic *and comprehensive* statements of the law on each of these subjects.

The feature of comprehensiveness is particularly striking in the procedural codes. In the area of substantive private law, the codifiers provided for flexibility and future growth by incorporating a certain number of broad, elastic formulations into the codes themselves. The procedural codes, however, are meant to be essentially all inclusive statements of judicial powers, remedies and procedural devices significantly reducing the discretionary power of adjudicators.

In common law jurisdictions procedure is generally "codified."[10] But, the continued influence of the unwritten law is preserved by statutory safety valves such as § 140–b of the New York Judiciary Law which provides that "The general jurisdiction in law and equity which the supreme court [of the state] possesses under the provisions of the constitution includes all the jurisdiction which was possessed and exercised by the supreme court of the colony of New York at any time, and by the court of chancery in England on the 4th day of July, 1776. . . ." Such reference to the powers which in bygone days the courts possessed by virtue of their own pronouncements at law and in equity makes us feel that at least some of such powers are "inherent" and quite independent of any statute.[11]

---

9. See J. Anglada Vilardebo, Andorra, in 1 Int.Ency.Comp.L. at A29–32 (1970); A. H. Angelo, Andorra: Introduction to a Customary Legal System, 14 Am.J.Leg.Hist. 95 (1970).

10. In the United States, the codification movement is a nineteenth-century phenomenon, heavily influenced by Bentham. David Dudley Field was the most important protagonist of that movement, but not its originator. See D. Van Ee, David Dudley Field and the Reconstruction of the Law (1986); C. M. Cook, The American Codification Movement: A Study in Antebellum Legal Reform (1981).

11. See R. Dale Vliet, The Inherent Power of Oklahoma Courts and Judges, 6 Okla.L.Rev. 257 (1953). The list of inherent powers presented in that article would make a civilian rub his eyes in disbelief. For other examples, see, e.g., Ochs v. Washington Heights Federal Savings & Loan Ass'n, 17

For the continental lawyer it is hard to understand that judicial powers and remedies can exist without an express basis in the written law. This becomes apparent, for example, in cases in which civilian courts are asked to enforce American judgments.[12] Many countries, including a number of civil law jurisdictions, enforce foreign judgments only on condition of reciprocity. Therefore, if a New York judgment is sought to be enforced in a civil law country, the civilian court probably will examine the question whether a New York court in the converse case would enforce its judgment. Actually, the answer to this latter question has long been in the affirmative, because for more than half a century New York has recognized foreign-country judgments as ordinarily conclusive.[13] This liberal New York rule, however, originally was a creature of decisional law, and until 1970 was not embodied in the CPLR (Civil Practice Law and Rules) or any other statute.[14] Thus prior to 1970 it could happen, and in practice it did happen,[15] that the court in a civil law jurisdiction, having carefully examined the pertinent New York "code," inferred from its silence that New York had made *no* provision for the enforcement of foreign judgments.[16] The result of such a mistaken inference was that prior to 1970 New York judgments were refused enforcement in a civil law jurisdiction under its reciprocity rule,[17] although as a matter of fact Civil law judgments were routinely enforced in New York.

To remedy this situation, the Commissioners on Uniform State Laws proposed, and New York as well as a number of other states enacted, the Uniform Foreign Money–Judgments Recognition Act.[18] As the Commission-

N.Y.2d 82, 268 N.Y.S.2d 294, 215 N.E.2d 485 (1966); Matter of Steinway, 159 N.Y. 250, 53 N.E. 1103 (1899); Cf. Petition of Petrol Shipping Corp., 360 F.2d 103 (2d Cir.1966), cert. denied, 385 U.S. 931, 87 S.Ct. 291 (1966).

12. See Kulzer, The Uniform Foreign Money–Judgments Recognition Act, in the Thirteenth Annual Report of the Judicial Conference of the State of New York, Leg. Doc. (1968) No. 90, at 194 ff.; Nadelmann, Non–Recognition of American Money Judgments Abroad and What to Do About It, 42 Iowa L.Rev. 236 (1957); *Id.*, Reprisals Against American Judgments?, 65 Harv.L.Rev. 1184 (1952); *Id.*, The United States of America and Agreements on Reciprocal Enforcement of Foreign Judgments, 1 Nederlands Tijdschrift voor International Recht 156, 158–9 (1954).

13. Johnston v. Compagnie Generale Transatlantique, 242 N.Y. 381, 152 N.E. 121 (1926); Cowans v. Ticonderoga Pulp & Paper Co., 219 App.Div. 120, 219 N.Y.S. 284 (3d Dep't 1927), aff'd on opinion below, 246 N.Y. 603, 159 N.E. 669 (1927).

14. In 1970, New York adopted the Uniform Foreign Money–Judgments Recogni-

tion Act (see *infra* note 18) as Art. 53 of its CPLR.

15. See Nadelmann, *supra* note 12; J. T. Clare, Enforcement of Foreign Judgments in Spain, 9 Int'l Law. 509, 514 (1975).

16. The more sophisticated courts in civil law countries seem to understand that in a common law jurisdiction a foreign judgment may be enforceable although the "code" is silent on the point. See the September 30, 1964, decision of the German BGH reported in NJW 1964, 2350. Proof of reciprocity in the absence of statute may, however, be prohibitively expensive if, e.g., the pertinent decisional materials have to be formally certified in translation.

17. See Nadelmann, *supra* note 12.

18. 13 ULA 261 (1986). In addition to New York, twenty-four other states (including California, Illinois, Michigan, and Texas) and the Virgin Islands have adopted the Act. See Fairchild, Arabatzis & Smith v. Prometco (Prod. & Metals), 470 F.Supp. 610 (S.D.N.Y. 1979).

ers pointed out in their Prefatory Note, the Act merely "states rules that have long been applied by the majority of courts in this country."[19] The purpose of the Act is simply to ease the burden of a litigant who, in seeking enforcement abroad of an American judgment, may have to inform the foreign court of the rules which would be applied here in a converse case.[20] The Act, in other words, owes its very existence to the sponsors' recognition of the fact that courts in civil law countries find it difficult to comprehend the notion of procedural common law rules surviving the enactment of a "code" of procedure.

As the example shows, the very meaning of the word "code" depends on whether it is used by civilians or by lawyers brought up in the common law tradition. In the eyes of the latter a code is supplemental to the unwritten law, and in construing its provisions and filling its gaps, resort must be had to the common law.[21] Though gradually changing, this attitude is still strong in the common law world.[22] To the civilian, on the other hand, a code is a comprehensive, and in the area of procedure often an all inclusive, statement of the law. In its interpretation, the court is always conscious of the interrelation of all the provisions contained in the whole code, and indeed in the entire code system. The intention of the legislator, where it can be ascertained, will not be disregarded. Primarily, however, code construction is grammatical, logical and teleological;[23] in any event, it

19. *Ibid.*

20. See Prefatory Note, *Ibid.* The Florida, Idaho, North Carolina, Massachusetts and Texas variants of the Act contain the requirement of reciprocity, but in Texas, the judgment debtor has the burden of showing the *lack* of reciprocity. Hunt v. BP Exploration Co. (Libya) Ltd. (II), 580 F.Supp. 304 (N.D.Tex.1984). The formulation of the reciprocity requirement in the Texas variant was chosen in order to allay doubt abroad as to the readiness of Texas to recognize foreign-country decisions. The draftsman failed in his attempt to persuade the Legislature to exclude the reciprocity requirement entirely.

21. For an instructive discussion of codification in common law jurisdictions, see Patterson, The Codification of Commercial Law in the Light of Jurisprudence, 1955 Report of the New York Law Revision Commission at 41, 67–74, N.Y.Leg.Doc. (1955) No. 65–A, at 11, 37–44. Professor Patterson calls attention to § 5 of the California Civil Code, which expressly provides: "The provisions of this code, so far as they are substantially the same as existing statutes or the common law, must be construed as continuations thereof, and not as new enactments." Concerning the supplementary nature of the California Civil Code, see also Harrison, The First Half–Century of the California Civil Code, 10 Cal-

if.L.Rev. 185 (1922); Van Alstyne, The California Civil Code, in West's Anno.California Codes, Civil Code, Sections 1 to 192, pp. 1 ff. (1954). See generally E. Bodenheimer, Is Codification an Outmoded Form of Legislation? 30 Am.J.Comp.L. 15, 16–18 (Supp. 1982).

22. In the United Kingdom, there was a period in the late 1960s when the English and Scottish Law Commissions appeared to pull in the direction of civilian-style codification of the law of contracts. See Chloros, Principle, Reason and Policy in the Development of European Law, 17 Int'l & Comp.L.Q. 849, especially at 863–64 (1968). More recently, however, much of the momentum towards such codification has been lost, even though the meaning of the term "code" continues to be debated. See J. H. Farrar, Law Reform and the Law Commission 37–39, 57–62 (1974).

23. The volume of scholarly writings on methods of code interpretation in civil law systems is colossal. A classic account—indeed "the" classic account according to some scholars—is François Gény's Méthode d' interprétation et sources en droit privé positif (2d ed. 1919). See also Jaro Mayda, François Gény and Modern Jurisprudence (1978). For a brief discussion of French and German methods of statutory interpretation, see W.

is relatively free from historical reminiscences reaching back into the period prior to the preparation of the code.[24]

It stands to reason, therefore, that for the bread-and-butter purposes of the legal practitioner in a modern civil law country, familiarity with the older history of his legal system is hardly necessary—certainly less necessary than for his common law colleague who even today may win cases with esoteric citations.[25]

Thus, it may strike us as paradoxical that in many civil law countries a law student has to take courses on Roman Law and other historical subjects, while the great majority of his American colleagues, whose legal system has never undergone a sharp break with the past, is very likely to graduate from law school in the darkest ignorance of her own Legal History. It should be noted, however, that a student of the common law, reading through cases and other materials often stemming from former periods, gains a certain amount of historical perspective even though this is a very poor substitute of a course labeled "Legal History."[26] The civilian, whose courses and textbooks on present day law are code-centered and do not contain many references to pre-code developments, would find himself in a complete historical vacuum if he did not have the benefit of courses especially devoted to legal history.[27] On the other hand, within the professional and quite un-intellectual attitude of current U.S. law schools, it seems the student, more than an awareness of history, will only become able to go pretty far back in the often mechanical (and today almost entirely computerized) research of a precedent fitting his case.

From the foregoing discussion, the reader may have concluded that historical studies are of limited "practical" value to a lawyer faced with problems arising under a modern civil law system. History, however, provides important clues to an understanding of the differences between legal traditions and certainly makes the law less of a technical enterprise in "social engineering" and more of a civilizing experience.

3.   SYSTEM AND ORGANIZATION OF THE CODES

In studying the following materials, the reader should keep in mind that in each of the countries that we will discuss the enactment of the

---

Dale, Legislative Drafting: A New Approach, at 298–303, 306–08 (1977).

24. See M. Franklin, The Historic Function of the American Law Institute: Restatement as Transitional to Codification, 47 Harv.L.Rev. 1367, 1377 (1934), quoted by the court in Shelp v. National Surety Corp., 333 F.2d 431, 435 (5th Cir.1964); Patterson, *supra* n. 69, N.Y.Leg.Doc. (1955) No. 65–A, at 31.

25. See, e.g., Murphy v. Extraordinary Special and Trial Term of the Supreme Court, 294 N.Y. 440, 63 N.E.2d 49 (1945).

26. Whatever its title, a course dealing, e.g., with estates in land or with the law-equity dichotomy necessarily must reach back into centuries long past. It should, however, always be kept in mind that undue reliance on legal history as stated in judicial decisions is a pernicious side effect, to be guarded against.

27. See Gorla, Book Review, 6 Rivista di Diritto Civile I 558, 561 (1960).

codes constituted (a) the culmination of a long historical evolution, and (b) the starting point of new, code-oriented developments in the national legal system. Thus it goes without saying that the materials which follow must be placed into the historical context.

In particular a quite harsh and very famous scholarly controversy has occupied German scholarship in the first half of the nineteenth century about whether it was a good idea at all to codify the law like the French and Austrians have just done. After the fall of the Holy Roman Empire in 1806 Germany was divided in 39 independent states and the only strong agency of legal unification and of construction of a German legal identity was legal academia. As early as 1814 the dominant jurist of the time, the famous Pandectist scholar Friedrich Karl Von Savigny, the founder of the historical school (also known as legal romanticism) was contrary to codification. His idea was that German legal scholars, the true interpreters of the German Volksgeist (the spirit of the people), were not ready for the enterprise. Codification in general would stifle legal development, and if carried on too early, it would produce a mere import of the French Civil Code. His colleague Anton Friedrich Justus Thibaut opposed his views. He advocated codification of the private law as a particularly important necessity for Germany. He hoped that Germany would remain politically organized in a variety of smaller State entities (that he considered less oppressive for the individuals than bigger State entities). These entities nevertheless were to share a common codified legal system. Although it was delayed for almost 30 years after the German reunification (1871), the final victory belonged to Thibaut, and the German Civil Code was finally enacted on January 1, 1900. In comparing the table of contents of the French and German Codes the reader will judge the impact of almost one hundred years of scholarly belaboring of notions and concepts. A very similar polemic, on the desirability and the scope of a European civil code is unfolding in contemporary Europe and will be discussed later.[1]

French Civil Code—Table of Contents

Preliminary Title: Publication, Effects and Application of Laws in General

Book I. Persons

Title I: Civil Rights[2]

      Chapter 1. Civil Rights

      Chapter 2. Respect for the Human Body

      Chapter 3. Genetic Studies of the Characteristics of Individuals and Their Identification by Genetic Means

Title I (bis): French Nationality[3]

      (Division into Chapters omitted)

---

1. See Ugo Mattei, The European Codification Process: Cut & Paste (2003).

2. In French legal terminology, the expression "civil rights" (*droits civils*) does not have the same connotation as it has in American legal usage; "rights of citizens in their private relationships" might come somewhat closer.

3. Title I of the Civil Code, as originally enacted, contained rules as to the acquisition

Title II: Records of Civil Status

> (Division into Chapters omitted)

Title III: Domicile

Title IV: Absent (Missing) Persons

> (Division into Chapters omitted)

Title V: Marriage

Title VI: Divorce

Title VII: Filiation

> Chapter 1. Common Rules Relating to Legitimate and Illegitimate Children
>
> Chapter 2. Legitimate Children
>
> Chapter 3. Illegitimate Children

Title VIII: Adoption

> Chapter 1. Plenary Adoption
>
> Chapter 2. Simple Adoption

Title IX: Parental Authority

> (Division into Chapters omitted)

Title X: Minority, Guardianship and Emancipation

> (Division into Chapters omitted)

Title XI: Majority and Legal Protection of Adults[4]

> Chapter 1. General Rules
>
> Chapter 2. Adults Under Court Protection
>
> Chapter 3. Adults Under Guardianship
>
> Chapter 4. Adults Under Curatorship

Book II. Property and Different Kinds of Property Rights

Title I: Distinctions Among Types of Property

> Chapter 1. Immovables
>
> Chapter 2. Movables
>
> Chapter 3. Property and its Relation to those Possessing it

Title II: Ownership

> (Division into Chapters omitted)

---

and loss of French nationality. These rules were later incorporated in a special, frequently modified statute, called the Code of French Nationality (*Code de la Nationalité française*). The modern tendency in civil law countries is to treat citizenship as a public-law subject, not to be covered in a civil code.

4. In line with modern thinking, this title provides not only for the situation of persons totally unable to act for themselves, on whose behalf a guardian must act, but also for individuals capable to act, but needing some supervision to avoid harm to their interests.

Title III: Usufruct, Use and Habitation

>Chapter 1. Usufruct[5]

>Chapter 2. Use and Habitation[6]

Title IV: Servitudes or Easements

>(Division into Chapters omitted)

Book III. The Different Ways By Which One Acquires Property

General Provisions

Title I: Successions

>Chapter 1. "Opening" of the Succession; the Heirs' Right of "Seizin"

>Chapter 2. Conditions Required for Inheriting

>Chapter 3. The Different Classes of Persons Entitled to Inherit

>Chapter 4. Rights of the State

>Chapter 5. Acceptance and Rejection of the Inheritance

>Chapter 6. Partition

Title II: Gifts Inter Vivos and Wills

>Chapter 1. General Provisions

>Chapter 2. Capacity to Make Gifts or Bequests and to Receive Property by Gift or Bequest

>Chapter 3. Property Available for Bequests; Their Reduction[7]

>Chapter 4. Gifts

>Chapter 5. Wills

>Chapter 6. Provisions Permitted in Favor of the Donor or Testator's Grandchildren and Children of Brothers or Sisters

>Chapter 7. Partition by Ascendants

>Chapter 8. Gifts Made to Spouses by Ante Nuptial Agreement

>Chapter 9. Gifts and Bequests Between Spouses by Ante Nuptial Agreement or Otherwise

---

5. Usufruct involves the right for life, or for a fixed term less than life, to use and enjoy the proceeds of property. It thus resembles more or less a legal life estate, but the "usufructuary" (analogous to the life tenant) and the owner of the "naked title" (analogous to remainderman) are considered as having concurrent, not successive rights in the property.

6. Use resembles usufruct, but involves only the right to use the property, not to enjoy any proceeds; habitation is the right to live in a place for life or a term.

7. This Chapter contains the provisions relating to what is sometimes called the *légitime* which prohibits an individual from bequeathing or giving by gift inter vivos more than a specified portion of the estate if the individual has children or other descendants and, in some cases, ascendants. In France if there is one child, it is entitled to half, if there are two or more children, they are entitled to two thirds of the estate. This has an obvious impact on what we would call estate planning.

Title III: Contracts or Obligations due to Agreement in General

 Chapter 1. General Provisions

 Chapter 2. Essential Conditions for the Validity of Agreements[8]

 Chapter 3. Effect of Obligations

 Chapter 4. Different Kinds of Obligations[9]

 Chapter 5. Extinction of Obligations

 Chapter 6. Proof of Obligations, and of Payment

Title IV: Obligations Which Arise Without Contract

 Chapter 1. Quasi–Contracts

 Chapter 2. Torts

Title V: Ante-nuptial Contracts and Matrimonial Regimes

 (Division into Chapters omitted)

Title VI: Sales

 (Division into Chapters omitted)

Chapter VII: Exchanges

Chapter VIII: Contracts of Hiring[10]

 Chapter 1. General Provisions

 Chapter 2. Lease of Things

 Chapter 3. Hiring of Labor and of Work

 Chapter 4. Loan of [Farm] Animals

Title VIII (bis): Real Estate Development Contracts

Title IX: Companies

 Chapter 1. General Rules[11]

 Chapter 2. [Registered] Partnership Under Civil Law[12]

 Chapter 3. Unregistered Partnerships

Title IX(bis): Agreements Concerning the Exercise of Rights in Undivided Property

 (Division into Chapters omitted)

---

8. This Chapter deals with issues such as consent, capacity to contract, etc.

9. This Chapter deals with obligations subject to conditions and similar matters.

10. In civil law systems, a lease (even of immovable property) generally is treated as a type of *contract* rather than as an estate in land. This accounts for the fact that leases (treated as a species of hiring) are dealt with in Book III, and not in Book II, of the French Civil Code.

11. The provisions of this Chapter apply to all types of companies, whatever their form, unless specific rules applicable to a certain type of company provide otherwise.

12. This Chapter concerns companies under civil rather than commercial law, such as partnerships for the exercise of a profession, or the ownership of real estate.

13. This Title deals with bailments other than those mentioned in Chapter 1 of the preceding Title (loans for use) and with escrow type arrangements made, e.g., in connection with interpleader actions, some other judicial proceedings, etc.

14. Civil Code Art. 1964 defines "aleatory" contracts as contracts where an essential element depends on an uncertain event. The article includes among such contracts, wagering agreements, insurance policies, and annuities.

15. The Code provisions deal essentially only with the relationship between principal and agent, not with the extent of the agent's power to bind the principal.

Chapter 3. Reasons Which Prevent the Running of Limitation Periods

Chapter 4. Reasons Which Interrupt or Toll the Limitation Periods

Chapter 5. Time Periods Needed for Prescription to Operate[16]

Chapter 6. The Protection of Possession

NOTES AND QUESTIONS

(1) The organizational scheme of the French Civil Code is similar to that of Gaius' *Institutiones*. See *supra* p. 347, note 3. Whether this similarity is accidental or due to the Roman law learning of the Code's draftsmen is somewhat controversial.

(2) Compare the organization of the French Civil Code of 1804 with that (a) of the Spanish Code of 1889, (*supra*), and (b) of the German Civil Code, reproduced below. Do you find, in the French and Spanish Codes, anything resembling the German Code's "General Part"? Who, among the several possible participants in the original drafting process (legal practitioners, judges, government bureaucrats, and legal scholars) appear to have been dominant in the preparation of the French Code? Of the German Code? Are there external (non-legal) factors that may have affected some of the differences between the two codes?

German Civil Code—Detailed Synopsis[1]

[Enacted in 1896 and effective as of January 1, 1900, this Civil Code (as amended) is still the law of the German Federal Republic. In the former German Democratic Republic the bulk of the provisions of the 1896 Code, except for those on family law, remained in force until 1975. On June 19, 1975, that State adopted a new socialist Civil Code, which in style and organization as well as in substance differed from the capitalist Code of 1896. According to the Unification Treaty of August 31, 1991, BGBl 1991.II.889, Art. 8, the laws of the German Federal Republic became the law of the former German Democratic Republic, whose (former) territory is now generally referred to as the "New *Länder* (States)"; the former East German legislation was abrogated, except for a number of provisions listed in the Unification Treaty (mainly by way of Annex). The reestablishment of the pre–1945 legal rules (as amended in the interim), has created certain difficulties, in part because the former régime had transferred all ownership of land to the State, leaving to firms and individuals only a right to use, and had, in addition, ceased all entries in the land records.[2]]

---

16. The rules on limitation periods have repeatedly been changed. As to torts generally, the normally applicable thirty year limitation period (which also applies to most contracts) was reduced to ten years by the statute which instituted a compensation system for automobile accidents, Law No. 85–677 of July 5, 1985.

1. By permission of the publisher, Fred B. Rothman & Co., this translation is repro-

duced from I.S. Forrester, S.L. Goren & H.M. Ilgen, The German Civil Code, at v–ix (1975); subsequent legislative modifications reflected in this outline have been translated by one of the editors of this volume. Minor amendments have not been indicated in the notes.

2. For more extensive treatment of the subject, See J. Zekoll & M. Reimann, Introduction to German Law (2d ed. 2005).

Book One: General Part §§ 1–240

Section 1: Persons §§ 1–89

    Title 1: Natural Persons §§ 1–12

    Title 2: Juristic Persons §§ 21–89³

        I.   Associations §§ 21–79

            1. General Provisions §§ 21–54

            2. Registered Associations §§ 55–79

        II.   Foundations §§ 80–88

        III. Juristic Persons under Public Law § 89

Section II: Things, Animals §§ 90–103

Section III: Legal Transactions §§ 104–185

    Title 1: Competency to Enter Legal Transactions §§ 104–115⁴

    Title 2: Declaration of Intention §§ 116–144⁵

    Title 3: Contract §§ 145–147

    Title 4: Condition. Determination of Time §§ 158–163

    Title 5: Agency. Power of Attorney §§ 164–181

    Title 6: Approval. Ratification §§ 182–185

Section IV: Periods of Time. Time Limits §§ 186–193⁶

Section V: Prescription §§ 194–225

Section VI: Exercise of Rights. Self–Defense. Self–Help §§ 226–231

Section VII: Giving of Security §§ 232–240

Book Two: Law of Obligations §§ 241–853⁷

Section I: Content of Obligations §§ 241–304

    Title 1: Obligation to Perform §§ 241–292

3. The Civil Code deals only with Associations and Foundations as legal entities; special statutes regulate other forms of legal entities, such as the (more or less) closed corporation, the larger corporation, etc.

4. German law distinguishes between two types of legal capacity, the abstract capacity to enjoy rights (*Rechtsfähigkeit*) and the capacity to actually engage in legal transactions without the intervention of a third person such as a guardian(*Geschäftsfähigkeit*).

5. Roughly speaking, the German term *Willenserklärung*, literally "declaration of will," covers any declaration of a party which is intended to be transactional. The relationship between the two terms, *Rechtsgeschäft* and *Willenserklärung*, is explained by a leading commentator as follows: "A legal transaction (*Rechtsgeschäft*) consists of one or several declarations of intention (*Willenserklärungen*), which by themselves or in conjunction with other elements [e.g., a necessary governmental authorization] produce an intended legal effect." Palandt, Bürgerliches Gesetzbuch, Introduction preceding § 104 (54th ed., 1995).

6. These provisions deal not with limitation periods (covered by the following title) but with the manner in which time periods mentioned in the law must be calculated (effect of weekends, etc.).

7. A major revision of the German Law of Obligations entered into force on January 1, 2002, the so-called Act on the Moderniza-

---

tion of the Law of Obligations. See *infra* at 418.

8. A "deposit" of this kind is somewhat comparable to our institution of payment into court. Such a deposit is the equivalent of proper performance if the person entitled to performance has impeded actual performance.

I. Contract for Work

II. Travel Contract

Title 8: Broker's Contract §§ 652–656

Title 9: Reward §§ 657–661

Title 10: Mandate §§ 662–676[9]

Title 11: Management without Mandate §§ 677–687

Title 12: Deposit §§ 688–700

Title 13: Delivery of Things to Innkeepers §§ 701–704

Title 14: Partnership §§ 705–740[10]

Title 15: Joint Ownership §§ 741–758

Title 16: Annuity §§ 759–761

Title 17: Gaming. Betting §§ 762–764

Title 18: Guaranty [Suretyship] §§ 765–778

Title 19: Compromise § 779

Title 20: Promise of Debt. Acknowledgement of Debt §§ 780–782

Title 21: Order §§ 783–792

Title 22: Bearer Bonds §§ 793–808a

Title 23: Production of Things §§ 809–811[11]

Title 24: Unjust Enrichment §§ 812–822

Title 25: Delicts §§ 823–853[12]

Book Three: Law of Property §§ 854–1296

Section I: Possession §§ 854–872

Section II: General Provisions Regarding Rights over Land §§ 873–902

Section III: Ownership §§ 903–1011

Title 1: Substance of Ownership §§ 903–924

Title 2: Acquisition and Loss of Ownership of Land §§ 925–928

---

9. These provisions regulate essentially the relationship between principal and agent.

10. The provisions on partnership of the civil code concern only the partnership under civil law (*Gesellschaft des bürgerlichen Rechts*); the partnership of "merchants" (*Offene Handelsgesellschaft: OHG*) is regulated by the Commercial Code.

11. This Title deals with duties to "produce," i.e., to exhibit or to permit inspection of a document or other thing. Under German law there can be no discovery of a document

or other thing in the custody of the opponent or of a third party unless it can be shown that the person from whom discovery is sought is under a substantive-law duty to produce such document or other thing. Whether or not such a substantive-law duty exists is usually determined by §§ 809 to 811 of the Civil Code.

12. This Title contains the tort provisions of the Civil Code. They are supplemented by a large amount of auxiliary (supplemental) legislation.

Title 3: Acquisition and Loss of Ownership of Moveable Property § 929–984

    I.   Transfer §§ 929–936

    II.   Adverse Possession §§ 937–945

    III. Connection, Mingling, Processing §§ 946–952

    IV. Acquisition of Products and Other Components of a Thing §§ 953–957

    V.   Appropriation §§ 958–964

    VI. Finding §§ 965–984

Title 4: Claims arising out of Ownership §§ 985–1007

Title 5: Co-ownership §§ 1008–1011

Section IV: Hereditary Building Rights §§ 1012–1017

Section V: Servitudes §§ 1018–1093

Title 1: Real [Property] Servitudes §§ 1018–1029

Title 2: Usufruct §§ 1030–1089

    I.   Usufruct in Things §§ 1030–1067

    II.   Usufruct in Rights §§ 1068–1084

    III. Usufruct in Personal Wealth §§ 1085–1089

Title 3: Restricted Personal Servitudes §§ 1090–1093

Section VI: Right of Preemption §§ 1094–1104

Section VII: Realty Charges §§ 1105–1112

Section VIII: Mortgage. Land Charge, Annuity Charge §§ 1113–1203

Title 1: Mortgage §§ 1113–1190

Title 2: Land Charge. Annuity Charge §§ 1191–1203[13]

    I.   Land Charge §§ 1191–1198

    II.   Annuity Charge §§ 1199–1203

Section IX: Rights of Pledge in Moveable Things and in Rights §§ 1204–1296

Title 1: Right of Pledge in Moveable Things §§ 1204–1258

Title 2: Right of Pledge in Rights §§ 1273–1296

Book Four: Family Law §§ 1297–1921[14]

Section I: Civil Marriage §§ 1297–1588

Title 1: Engagement §§ 1297–1302

---

13. The "Land Charge" resembles a mortgage, but involves the repayment of a specified sum at a certain time, not gradually; the annuity charge involves the payment of a certain sum each year, without repay- ment of a capital amount (but cancellation by payment of a capital is possible).

    14. All provisions which were inconsistent with the constitutional principle that "Men and women shall have equal rights"

Title 2: Entry into Marriage §§ 1303–1322 [Repealed][15]

Title 3: Voidness and Voidability of Marriage §§ 1323–1347 [Repealed]

Title 4: Remarriage in Case of Declaration of Death §§ 1348–1352 [Repealed]

Title 5: Effects of Marriage in General §§ 1353–1362

Title 6: Marital Property Rights §§ 1363–1563

    I.   Statutory Property Rights §§ 1363–1390

    II.   Contractual Property Rights §§ 1408–1518

        1.   General Provisions §§ 1408–1413

        2.   Separation of Property § 1414

        3.   Community of Property §§ 1415–1518

           (Further subdivisions omitted; §§ 1519–1557 abrogated)

    III. Register of Marital Property §§ 1558–1563

Title 7: Divorce §§ 1564–1587

Title 8: Religious Obligations § 1588

Section II: Relationship [Family Relationships] §§ 1589–1772

Title 1: General Provisions §§ 1589, 1590

Title 2: Descent §§ 1591–1600[16]

    I.   Legitimate Descent §§ 1591–1600

    II.   Illegitimate Descent §§ 1600a–1600o

Title 3: Duty of Maintenance §§ 1601–1615o

    I.   General Provisions §§ 1601–1615

    II. Special Provisions for the Illegitimate Child and Its Mother §§ 1615–1615

Title 4: Legal Relationship between Parents and Child in General §§ 1616–1625

Title 5: Parental Care for Legitimate Children §§ 1626–1698b

Title 6: Parental Care for Illegitimate Children §§ 1705–1712

Title 7: Legitimation of Illegitimate Children §§ 1719–1740g

became ineffective on March 31, 1953. See Basic Law of the German Federal Republic, Arts. 3 & 117.

15. The Second, Third, Fourth, and Seventh Titles were repealed by the Marriage Law of 1938 (based on Nazi racial principles), which in turn was replaced by the Marriage Law of 1946, enacted by the Allied Control Council.

16. The rules on illegitimate children were modified by a Law of August 19, 1969, BGBl 1969 I. 1243, to provide greater equality with legitimate children. Nevertheless, decisions of the Constitutional Court in 1989 and 1994 have declared parts of several provisions of the current law unconstitutional.

---

17. The heading originally referred to the "guardianship" of adults; the title was changed by a Law September 12, 1990, BGBl I. 2002, replacing the "guardian" of mentally incompetent adults by a "protector" (*Betreuer*) whose powers are established by the appointing court and vary so as to deprive the individual protected of only as much of normal legal capacity as is necessary for the preservation of his interests.

18. This Title refers to a series of somewhat unrelated situations where a special curator is to be appointed, e.g., to replace the normal guardian as to a matter where the latter would have a conflict of interest, to take care of the interests of a person who is absent, etc.

Introductory Act

[Promulgated together with the Civil Code]

First Division—General Provisions

Chapter I: Effective Date, Reservation for Laws of the Länder, Definition of "Statute"

Arts. 1–2

19. This is in essence an agreement by which two people, such as spouses, make related testamentary dispositions.

20. The term "compulsory portion" or "obligatory portion" (*Pflichtteil*) refers to that portion of the decedent's estate which, by mandatory provisions of the Code, is set aside for the benefit of his surviving spouse and children.

Chapter II: Private International Law [conflict of laws]

Arts. 3–38[21]

[The Second to Sixth Divisions (here omitted) deal, respectively, with the relation of the Civil Code to the other laws of the Empire (now Federal Republic), the relation of the Civil Code to the Statutes of the States (*Länder*), the original transitional period, transitional periods for some post-World War II statutes, and finally, transitional provisions concerning the application of the laws of the Federal Republic in the new *Länder* (i.e., the old East Germany).

A major revision of the German Law of Obligations entered into force on January 1, 2002, the so-called Act on the Modernization of the Law of Obligations. This Act has dramatically changed Book 2 of the German Civil Code introducing an entirely new law of remedies which includes remedies for:

(1) Compensation

    a. In lieu of performance

    b. For delay

    c. Other damages

(2) Termination

(3) Other possible remedies, e.g.,

    a. Removal of a defect

    b. Price reduction

    c. Delivery of new goods free from defects]

* * *

German Commercial Code—Table of Contents

Book I: Commercial Status[22]

    1. Merchants §§ 1–7

    2. Commercial Register §§ 8–16[23]

    3. Firm Name §§ 17–37

    4. Commercial Books of Account (abrogated; now covered in Book III)

    5. Agents' Power to Act for a Commercial Firm §§ 48–58

21. The conflict of laws provisions of the Introductory Act were substantially revised by a statute of July 25, 1986. For a discussion, see the 6th edition of this book, Chapter VIII.

22. *The German expression is Handels-stand. Another possible translation might be "Merchant Class."*

23. Note that the various *Länder* governments may provide for the commercial register to be kept in the form of an automated data base accessible to some extent by interested parties (see new §§ 8a, 9a). Some further amendments were due to the European Community rules on corporations, mentioned.

6. Commercial Clerks and Apprentices §§ 59–83

7. Commercial Agents [traveling salesmen and other independent agents] §§ 84–92c[24]

8. Commercial Brokers §§ 93–104

Book II: Commercial Companies and "Silent" Companies

[Subheadings omitted. The second Book deals essentially with partnerships and limited partnerships. Formerly, it also dealt with stock corporations.[25]]

Book III: Commercial Bookkeeping

[Subheadings omitted. Book III, inserted by a Law of December 19, 1985 (BGBl 1985 I. 2355) in implementation of European Community rules, deals with the books and records to be kept by merchants and further covers the rules, including the publicity rules, governing the balance sheets and profit and loss statements of corporations. Special rules for banks and insurance companies were added by a Law of November 30, 1990 and a Law of June 24, 1994.]

Book IV: Commercial Transactions

1. General Provisions §§ 343–372

2. Commercial Sales §§ 373–382

3. Commission Merchants §§ 383–406

4. Forwarding Agency §§ 407–415

5. Warehousing §§ 416–424

6. Carriers [of goods] §§ 425–452

7. Railroad Transportation of Goods and Persons §§ 453–460

Book V: Maritime Commerce

[Subheadings omitted. The provisions of Book V (§§ 474–905) deal with the subject of maritime law. By several amendments, and by a partial revision carried out in 1937 and 1940, German maritime law was largely adapted to Anglo–American ideas in this field, especially to those which are reflected in the Hague Rules.[26]]

* * *

NOTES AND QUESTIONS

(1) *Variants in the Civil–Law World.* As the reader will have observed, the Civil Codes of France and Germany—the two most influential seminal Codes of the civil law world—differ from each other in their basic organization. But there is agreement between the French and German systems, and among the

---

24. Substantially changed by the Law for the Implementation of the European Community Directive on Commercial Agents of October 23, 1989 (BGBl 1989 I.1910).

25. See the 6th edition of this book, Chapter VII.

26. See 2 E. J. Cohn, Manual of German Law 3, 44 (2d ed. 1971); Mathias Reiman & Joachim Zekoll, Introduction to German Law (2d ed. 2005).

many followers of both, on a very important point: that the total area of substantive private law should be divided into (a) non-commercial ("civil") law and (b) commercial law, and that this division should be reflected in the enactment of two separate codes, a Civil Code and a Commercial Code.

In the course of the present century, this traditional dualist system of private law codification has come under attack, and a unitary system of private law (and especially of the law of obligations) has been advocated by a number of scholars.[1] Among other points, it has been argued by the unitarists that in a highly developed modern society, with adequate education available to all, there is no longer any need for a separate body of law governing the transactions of the more sophisticated class, i.e., of the merchants. It has been said, moreover, that in a democracy there should be no class legislation, and that for this reason, also, no separate commercial code (or merchants' code) should be enacted.[2]

Responding to these arguments, the Swiss legislature chose a scheme of code organization quite different from the French and German ones. Private law in Switzerland originally was cantonal law. The Swiss legislature first unified the law of obligations, broadly conceived, by adopting a *Code of Obligations*. That Code covers both the law of contracts as found in France or Germany in the civil code and most of those subjects which in other civil law countries (such as Germany, see *supra*) are treated in the commercial code, but also topics, such as the law of corporations, now governed by a separate statute in both France and Germany. The Swiss legislature thus dealt with commercial and non-commercial contracts in the same Code, abolishing, at least on the face of the codes, the traditional civilian dichotomy between "civil" and commercial law. A few years later, the Swiss legislature adopted a Civil Code which deals with those parts of private law (family law, succession, etc.) not already included in the Code of Obligations.[3] A similar trend away from the dualism of "civil" and commercial law can be observed in some (thus far a distinct minority) of the other civil law countries. One example is the Italian Civil Code

---

1. The controversy between the dualists and the unitarists is reflected in the excellent collection of essays appearing in M. Rotondi (ed.), The Unity of the Law of Obligations (1974). For policy arguments in favor of the dualist approach, interestingly presented by an American observer, see J. M. Steadman, Book Review, 120 U.Pa.L.Rev. 1013, 1015 (1972).

2. In the civil law world, a Commercial Code generally is regarded as establishing separate and special rules for the transactions of merchants. This is true regardless of definitional details (see Chapter 5, Section 6 at 433). The concept of our own Uniform Commercial Code is quite different. The coverage of the UCC (which is not as broad as that of a civilian Commercial Code) is based

on the nature of the transaction, and not on the merchant status of the participants. Only relatively few provisions of the UCC turn on such status. See R. B. Schlesinger, The Uniform Commercial Code in the Light of Comparative Law, 1 Inter–Am.L.Rev. 11, 42–44, 48–51 (1959); B. H. Greene, Commercial Law in the United States, in Rotondi, *supra* note 1 at 159; W. Gray, Civil and Commercial Law in the United States, *Id.* at 151. See also UCC § 2–104, Official Comment 2.

3. Substantial revisions of the Swiss Civil Code in the fields of family and inheritance law went into effect in 1988; substantial revisions of the Code of Obligations relating to corporations went into effect in 1992. See R. Tschäni & A. von Planta, Highlights of the Amended Swiss Company Law, 20 Int'l Bus. Lawyer 254 (1992).

of 1942.[4] Likewise, the Revised Dutch Civil Code includes rules concerning commercial matters, including also those on commercial companies; the Dutch Commercial Code is thus still in existence only to the very limited extent that the new Code is not yet fully in effect.[5]

(2) *The Two Great Debates among Modern Civilian Codifiers.* Modern legal systems that undertake to codify their country's substantive private law face two basic problems of code organization:

(a) Whether, in addition to the Civil Code, there should be a separate Commercial Code; and

(b) Whether the Civil Code, following the German example (and in contrast to the French model), should contain a "General Part," i.e., a separate division which serves as a reservoir of rules and principles of such abstractness and generality that they pervade all of the—functionally quite diverse—areas of law covered by the Code.[6]

In part (1) of this Note, some comments have been offered on the first of these great debates. We now turn to the second, the one involving the desirability of a "General Part."

To insert into a code some abstract and pervasive provisions, which are potentially applicable to all of its subdivisions, has some obvious advantages: It promotes economy of words and gives the courts a tool for the resolution of problems not foreseen by the code's drafters. But abstractness and pervasiveness also create complications, as shown in the following examples:

(a) Section 164 of the German Civil Code clearly implies that *any* "declaration of intent" of a person may come into existence either by that person's own declaration or by a declaration of a duly authorized agent. Its authors, however, were aware that the broad rule permitting any such act to be done by an agent had to be qualified by exceptions; some are of such a personal nature that action directly by the principal should be required. The execution of a testament comes to mind as an obvious example, and the German Civil Code in § 2064 indeed requires, by way of a specific exception engrafted upon the general rule, that a testament be personally executed by the testator. In Book IV and Book V of the German Code (dealing with family law and decedents' estates) one finds more than a dozen other provisions which, by way of similar exceptions, require personal declarations and thus preclude the use of an agent for the specified types of acts.[7] It follows that the broad and pervasive rule announced in the General Part, while elegant in its abstractness,[8] can be used with confi-

---

4. Different in this respect from its 19th century predecessor, it contains both civil and commercial law (including rules on business entities). The separate Commercial Code was abolished at the same time. See J. Lena & U. Mattei, An Introduction to Italian Law, Kluwer (2002).

5. For a brief introduction to the new Code, see, e.g., H.J. Cornelis & A.J.P. Tillema, Major Revisions in Netherlands Law: Adoption of New Civil Code and Implementa-

tion of EEC Directives, 26 Int'l Lawyer 1075 (1992).

6. An example is provided by the famous Section 138 of the German Civil Code, invalidating every *Rechtsgeschäft* ("legal transaction" or "jural act") that is immoral.

7. See Palandt, Bürgerliches Gesetzbuch, Introduction preceding § 164 (54th ed. 1995).

8. Compare the unsystematic and unhelpful provision of Restatement (Second),

dence only after one has familiarized oneself with the exceptions that are dispersed through various parts of the Code.

(b) German Civil Code § 158 indicates that any "juridical act" (*Rechtsgeschäft*—also translated here occasionally as "legal transaction") can be subjected to conditions precedent or conditions subsequent. In many instances this is a salutary rule, permitting flexibility in transactional dealings. But with respect to some types of transactions, certainty is more important than flexibility, and where this is so, conditions perhaps should not be tolerated. The draftsmen of the German Civil Code recognized that, and—by way of specific exceptions to the rule of § 158—provided that certain juridical acts cannot be subjected to conditions. Perhaps the best-known examples are marriage (Marriage Law § 13) and transferring real property inter vivos (Civil Code § 925). So far, the legal researcher does not face any great difficulty, but must merely be aware (i) of the rule stated in the General Part of the Code and (ii) of the explicit statutory exceptions appearing in subsequent parts of the Code itself and in other statutes.

What is more troublesome is that German courts and legal writers have found certain types of juridical acts to be resistant to conditions and hence exempt from the rule of § 158, even though the written law does not grant such an exemption. Thus it has been held that the juridical act of rescinding or terminating a contract is valid only if the rescission or termination is unconditionally declared. In cases of this kind, a mere reading of the Code and other statutory materials would mislead the researcher. The reason for this somewhat unsatisfying effect of a supposedly comprehensive Code lies in the enormous breadth and generality of provisions such as § 158. Its authors apparently realized that there were some juridical acts as to which the rule of § 158 had to be qualified by specific exceptions; but understandably they were unable to think of all instances of this kind.

It is not surprising, therefore, that in the civil law world matters of code technique have given rise to "great debates." These debates, as we have seen, focus on the desirability of (i) a separate Commercial Code, and (ii) a German-style general part. In the Netherlands, where a complete overhaul of private law codes has been substantially completed, both of these problems were thoroughly studied and resolved. Concerning the first problem, the traditional dualist approach was discarded. The "General Part" problem was resolved by the draftsmen of the new Dutch Code in an interesting and innovative way. They decided to include a "General Part" in their Code, but to limit its effect to those areas of the law which deal with "patrimony," i.e., with rights having a money value.[9] Thus, purely personal rights, especially in the area of family law,

Agency, § 20 & comment (d), which seems to be aimed at the same problem.

9. For a translation of parts of the new Code (those not dealing with family law and related matters), see P. P. C. Haanappel & E. Mackaay, New Netherlands Civil Code—Patrimonial Law (1992) (with a valuable introduction by Dr. A.S. Hartkamp). See also J. M.

C. Chorus, P. H. M. Gerver & A. K. Koekkoek, Introduction to Dutch Law for Foreign Lawyers (2d ed. 1993). See further H. J. Cornelis & A.J.P. Tillema, *supra* note 5. For some older materials, see A.S. Hartkamp, Civil Code Revision in the Netherlands: A Survey of Its System and Contents, and Its Influence on Dutch Legal Practice, 35 La. L.Rev. 1059 (1975).

are not affected by the rules and principles stated in the General Part of the new Netherlands Code.

In socialist countries, legal systems, in spite of their different ideology, were greatly influenced by the civil law insofar as terminology, code structure, and other legal techniques. But there were also significant differences. Separate commercial codes were frequently eliminated, but often separate statutes were adopted governing relations between state enterprises. For example, special boards rather than the courts settled disputes because the judicial emphasis was on the fulfillment of state planning objectives rather than the rights of the parties. Some countries (such as the former German Democratic Republic) also had special rules for foreign trade. These peculiarities were not immediately eliminated after the end of the rule of the Communist parties but a revision of their legislation is currently underway and some new codification has taken place. Cuba, endowed with a highly sophisticated socialist legal culture rooted in the civil law tradition, has recently enacted a new civil code that is notable for the breath, flexibility and conciseness of its provisions.

(3) *Note on Code Families.* In Chapter 1, Section 7 at 52 and Chapter 4 at 282 we discussed at lengths the general processes of migration and reception of legal ideas. Code law, it seems, is particularly suitable for export from one country to another, because of its systematic, compact and almost package-like form. Such export may be the result of military conquest, of a conscious effort to establish cultural links, or simply of the inspiration which radiates from a great intellectual accomplishment.

Although the worldwide picture of these criss-crossing influences is complex, one can discern a pattern. There is almost no private-law-code in force in any civilian country today which is not substantially copied from, or in its structure or some of its provisions directly or indirectly influenced by, the codes of France, Germany, or Switzerland.[10] The German Civil Code of 1896 (effective date Jan. 1, 1900) was in turn somewhat, although not too strongly, influenced by provisions of the French Code; and the Swiss Code of 1907, while largely based on existing local institutions and on original thinking of its distinguished draftsman, Professor Eugen Huber, did not escape the influence of the German and French codes.

Two interesting examples of how Civil Codes, despite the strong foreign professional influences reflect changing political, cultural, social and historical circumstances are the recent examples of Peru and Brazil. The Peruvian Civil Code of 1984 still reflects the classical model of Latin American Civil Codification, the Chilean Code produced, with a strong French flavor by Andres Bello in 1857. This code, reflecting liberal bourgeois ideology in the law of property and of obligations, but leaving to the canon law of the powerful Catholic Church the

---

10. The sweeping statement in the text requires one (and perhaps only one) qualification: the Austrian General Civil Code of 1811 was a work of great originality. It exercised considerable influence throughout the countries of Eastern and Southeastern Europe; but outside of Austria itself this influence was greatly reduced, when, as a result of the expansion, after World War II, of the communist orbit these countries created new codes, now themselves in the process of revision. The influence of the Austrian Code of Civil Procedure has been more widespread and

whole family law, worked as an early prestigious model through Latin America.[11] The most recent Civil Code entered into force in Brazil in 2003, to the contrary, maintains a loyal alliance to the German idea of a "general part" but merges the civil and commercial law of obligations (following from this point of view the Swiss path).

Both the Peruvian and the Brazilian Codes nevertheless radically break with the free market inspiration of the continental nineteenth century tradition. Being historically located respectively at the dusk and dawn of the twenty years of globalization of neo-liberal ideology, they adopt a social model rooted into ideals of welfare state and attempt to introduce it within the very core of the (professionalized) private law. Clearly both these Codes, important as they are, are introduced into a system of remarkably competitive legal pluralism thus suffering competition both from the bottom up (from customary law of a large part of the population still unaffected by legal modernization) and from the top down from the layer of "business friendly" law introduced by the global private law makers.[12]

Depending on the predominance of French, German, or Swiss influence, it is possible to divide the civil law countries into "code families." Many of the principal members of these "families" have been identified in our earlier discussion. But it should be kept in mind that the code drafters often prefer not to follow a single pattern but to skim what they consider the best features from all existing codes.[13] Moreover, a given country may follow one example in its civil law and other examples in its commercial, criminal, or procedural law. Turkey, for instance, adopted this eclectic method, and so did many, if not most, Latin American countries.

Even if a given code of Nation X has been literally copied by Nation Y, the two codes may not in all respects be uniformly interpreted by the courts of both countries. We have seen an example in the interpretation of identical provisions of French and Austrian tort law in Chapter 2 *supra* in the matter of pure economic losses. This is particularly true when the two nations are at different stages of economic development.[14]

more lasting, as pointed out *infra* in Chapter 8 at 707.

11. See Matthew Campbell Mirow, Individual Experience in Legal Change: Exploring a Neglected Factor in Nineteenth–Century Latin American Codification, 11 Sw. J.L. & Trade Am. 301 (2005).

12. See Ugo Mattei, The Peruvian Civil Code, Property and Plunder. Time For a Latin American Alliance to Resist the Neo Liberal Order (2005).

13. The Greek Civil Code of 1946 is one of the outstanding examples of a code based on painstaking comparative research. While its structure largely follows the German pattern, various other sources (including the Swiss and French models) have contributed to shaping the method and the substance of the Greek Code. See P.J. Zepos, Greek Law 72, 77 ff. (1949); Ugo Mattei, The Peruvian Civil Code, Property and Plunder. Time For a Latin American Alliance to Resist the Neo Liberal Order (2005), The Historical and Comparative Background of the Greek Civil Code, 3 Inter–Am.L.Rev. 285 (1961).

14. For a general discussion, see K. H. Neumayer, Fremdes Recht aus Büchern, fremde Rechtswirklichkeit und die funktionelle Dimension in den Methoden der Rechtsvergleichung, 34 Rabels Z. 411, 418–19 (1970).

4.   THE ISSUE OF THE EUROPEAN CIVIL CODE

Most of the theoretical issues behind codification have recently re-emerged at the European level. We know that Europe is not a sovereign State but the process of legal integration has been carried quite far. Virtually all the significant reforms to the Codes (not only civil) of European member states have been triggered by European legislation. The recent Reform of the German Law of Obligations is a powerful example having affected even the *General Part*, the most prestigious and culturally loaded part of German Law.

Beginning in the early nineteen eighties the question has emerged of whether after almost two centuries of nationalism in private law Europe is reversing towards the pre-national codification days of European cosmopolitanism. Is there such a thing as European private law? The answer was found in the facts. Legislative, judicial and scholarly developments at the European level have characterized even the core areas of private law. Consent on the *existence* of a subject matter called European private law, which involves all member states and thus both civil law and common law countries is now practically unanimous.[1]

European private lawyers have also been remarkably quick in reaching consent on claiming a professional monopoly on the construction of the legal framework for the common market. Early in the nineties a true academic "jihad" has been launched against Brussels bureaucrats claiming that the "Europeanization" of private law should be in the hands of jurists.[2]

Naturally, some divisions were bound to happen when it comes to the question of who are the members of the professional groups involved in the project. Two factions seem to have emerged: *the elitists* against *the democrats*. Both the elitists and the democrats share English as a sort of *lingua franca*.[3] The fact that the debate on European private law is happening mostly in English has dramatically changed the hierarchies of academic prestige in Europe and certainly has granted a quite privileged role to the common law camp, still quite uneasy with the idea that in the not so far future a European civil code might be produced. Jurists active in the

---

1. See the essays in M. Bussani & U. Mattei (Eds.), Making European Law. Essays on the Common Core Project (2001).

2. See, for example, R. Zimmermann, R., Civil Code and Civil law: The Europeanization of Private Law Within the European Community and the re-Emergence of a European Legal Science, 1 Columbia J. European. Law, 63 (1994). See H. Kotz, A Common Private Law for Europe: Perspectives for the Reform of European Legal Education, in B. De Witte–C.Forder (Eds.), The Common Law

of Europe and the Future of Legal Education (1992).

3. Zeup, a scholarly periodical devoted to European Private Law, is published mostly in German. There are also two Italian periodicals Europa e Diritto Privato and Contratto e Impresa Europa that are expressly devoted to the subject matter. Neither Zeup nor these Italian journals however significantly overcome local readership or specialized circles.

European private law movement tend to be a younger generation of academics that, while fluent in English, are neither the mainstream nor the leading jurists within the national legal systems. Of course, there are exceptions, but this sociological delineation seems to be quite clear. Within this common background, nevertheless, there are major differences. "Elitists" tends to refer to self-selected small groups of well-connected and well-known scholars that tend to be male members of the leading European jurisdictions, grounding their prestige on a more or less open claim of law as science.[4] More democratic projects tend to involve a younger generation of academics, with more equal gender and jurisdictional based constituency. "Democrats" are usually more open in the political nature of the projects in which they find themselves involved and, in particular, more open to the idea that some dialogue with the European legislator is unavoidable.[5] But how should the community of involved jurists (however selected) operate in carrying on the project?

The divisions on the issue of the *how* have been polarized around a few basic questions. Should European private law be codified?[6] Should it be restated? Should it be left to legal science within a revival known as *usus hodiernus pandectarum* [contemporary use of the digest]?[7] Should it be developed around some "core" special statutes such as those guaranteeing consumers' protection? Should merchants and consumers be governed by bodies of special law? Should there be attempts to bridge the distinction between common law and civil law by efforts of harmonization, or should this "cultural" difference be preserved?[8] Should such European legislation be in the form of directives (letting leeway to state jurisdictions in the

---

4. See, for example, H. Kotz, Comparative Legal Research and its Function in the Development of Harmonized Law. The European Perspective, in De Lege, Towards Universal Law, Uppsala (1995). An interesting discussion of the roots of such approach with particular attention to the legacy of E. Rabel can be found in D. Gerber, Sculpting the agenda of Comparative Law. Ernst Rabel and the Façade of Language, in A. Riles (Ed.) Rethinking the Masters of Comparative Law (2001). Leading elitist projects is the so called Lando Commission. See O. Lando–H. Beale (Eds.) Principles of European Contract Law, Parts I and II (2000). For a discussion see M. Hesselink, The Principles of European Contract Law. Some Choices made by the Lando Commission, in 1 Global Jurist Frontiers, 2001 www.bepress.com.

5. See in U. Mattei, The Issue of European Codification and Legal Scholarship. Biases, Strategies and Perspectives 21 Hartings Int. & Comp. Law Rev. 883 (1998); see also D. Caruso, The Missing View of the Cathe-

dral: The Private Law Paradigm of European Legal Integration, 3 European Law Journal 3 (1997), and C. Joerges & O. Gernstenberg, Private Governance, Democratic Constitutionalism and Supranationalism (1998). A Democratic Project is, in the intention of its Editors, the Common Core of European Private Law. See M. Bussani & U. Mattei, The Common Core Approach to European Private Law, 3 Col.J.Eur. Law 339 (1997).

6. See M.J. Bonell, The Need and Possibilities of a Codified European Contract Law, 5 ERPL 505 (1997); B. Markesinis, Why a Code is Not the Best Way to Advance the Cause of European Unity, 5 Eur. Rev. Priv. Law 519 (1997).

7. See R. Zimmermann, Roman Law, Contemporary Law, European Law. The Civilian Tradition Today (2001).

8. See for example, H. Collins, European Private Law and the Cultural Identity of States 3 Eur.Rev.Priv. Law 353 (1995).

domain of implementation), or should it be in the form of directly binding regulation?[9] Should codification be comprehensive or piecemeal?[10]

In general since 1989, when the Strasbourg Parliament, the only democratically representative institution of the European Union, has for the first time recommended action in the domain of civil codification, the scholarly reaction has been lukewarm. Someone has suspected an attempt of the "Brussels bureaucrats" to claim an even larger role in the making of private law. Some others have dismissed the recommendations as the action of a weak political actor, not to be taken too seriously. Yet others have denied that the EU would have any jurisdiction on a civil code.

True, some proposals have been advanced by self-appointed groups of scholars, and some of this activity (such as that of the "Lando Commission" from the name of its chairman, the Danish Scholar Ole Lando) has been indeed successful in seizing the stage of European private law.[11] Nevertheless, the issue of legitimacy quickly arose and even such self-appointed groups, lacking any political legitimacy whatsoever, have made it clear that their product had little in common with the traditional idea of codification as a politically supported attempt to break with a previous legal order.[12]

The traditional idea of civilian codification, which is the product of nineteenth century modernist *grand style* and is supported by a transcendent idea of sovereignty vested in the State, is a comprehensive, territorial, systematic body of private law rules claiming quasi-constitutional status in the making of the private legal order. Codes were hard legislative documents, abolishing all previous law, applied and enforced by other, subordinate institutions of the legal order.

Present day codification proposals are much more cautious, less ambitious and limited in scope. They are presented—borrowing from U.S. style even in such a traditionally civilian area of expertise—as "model codes" or "restatements." Notions such as "soft law," "creeping codification," "open texture," and "bottom up" are used.[13] Such proposals are to be, "interpreted," "discussed," "considered," and "harmonized" by a variety of other sources of law.

Perhaps the European civil code discussion is another step in the direction of convergence in a western legal tradition capable of overcoming

---

9. See, for recent collection of essays, M. Van Hoecke & F. Ost, The Harmonization of European Private Law (2000) and V. Heiskanen & K. Kulovesi, Function and Future of European Law (1999).

10. See T. Wilhelmsson, Private Law in the E.U: Harmonised or Fragmented Europeanisation?, 10 Eur. Rev. Priv. Law 77–94 (2002).

11. See O. Lando–H. Beale (Eds.) Principles of European Contract Law, Parts I and II (2000).

12. See for example O. Lando & Beale, Principles of European Contract Law, cit. See also, for the views of another of such groups, G. Gandolfi, Pur un Code Europeen des contrats, Rev. Trim. Droit. Civ. 707 (1991). The first significant Results of the Pavia Group is in G. Gandolfi (Ed.) Code Europeen des Contrats—Avant Project (2001).

13. See Christoph U. Schmid, "Bottom-up" Harmonisation of European Private Law: Ius Commune and Restatement, in Heiskanen and Kulovesi (eds.) Function and Future of European Law, Helsinki (1999).

the great divide between common law and civil law. Whether some kind of continent wide codification of private law will eventually appear is an open question. Currently, within a highly complex scenario of competitive scholarly projects, it would already be a significant result if European scholars were agreeing on producing, as strongly sponsored by the European Union, some common frame of reference. This minimal idea, that according to some observers is not so minimal after all, aims at a first conceptual and linguistic harmonization of contract law in view of future further steps towards harmonization or even unification of private law.[14]

---

5.   CHANGE AND GROWTH OF THE LAW IN A CODE SYSTEM

(a) *Revision of Codes.* Some of the codes of the civil law orbit have proved quite resistant to large scale revision. The task of rewriting a comprehensive code is so staggering and the number of issues, affected groups and interests is so great, that complete overall revision often yields to the more pressing daily demands upon the legislatures' time. Even violent upheavals, such as war, revolution, or political dismemberment of a nation, do not always lead to comprehensive changes in the text of established codes. A good example is the German Civil Code which, until the very recent European driven reform of the Law of Obligation, except in the area of family law, has received only relatively limited amendments.[1]

Not surprisingly, during the period of the Second World War, no major code revisions were undertaken in Europe, with one exception: Italy established a new Civil Code in 1942.[2] As noted above, it also includes matters found in France and in Germany in the commercial codes and some special statutes. In its organization, it substantially departs from its French influenced 1865 predecessor.[3] The Code's somewhat unusual subdivisions are: Book 1: Persons and Family; Book 2: Succession; Book 3: Property; Book 4: Obligations; Book 5: Work (this Book covers both rules on the employment relationship and rules on various types of business organiza-

---

14. For a recent critical discussion see Ugo Mattei & Fernanda Nicola A Social Dimension in European Private Law? The Call for Setting a Progressive Agenda, 41 New Eng. L. Rev. 1–66 (2006) For a collection of articles on the newly published Draft Common Frame of Reference See 4 European Review of Contract Law 3 (2008).

1. The more significant of these changes have been mentioned in the notes concerning the outline of the German Civil Code *supra.* It may be dangerous, however, to draw too general a conclusion from the German experience. The Mexican revolutionary movements, which began in 1910, did result—even though somewhat belatedly—in a new Civil Code for the Federal District which

went into effect in 1932, and has since been adopted, with little or no change, by the majority of the 31 States of the Mexican Union.

2. Purged of its fascist and racist elements, it is still—with some modifications, especially in the area of family law—in effect to-day. On changes effected by the statute (Law No. 218 of 1995) for the revision of the Italian system of private international law, see the sixth edition of this book, Chapter VIII at 933.

3. Mattei and Robilant, Les Longs Adieux: La Codification Italienne et le Code Napoléon dans le Déclin du Positivisme Etatique, 56 Revue internationale de droit comparé 847–864 (2004).

tions, such as partnerships, corporations, etc.); Book 6: Protection of rights (this heading includes the rules on land and other public records, on evidence, on liens and mortgages, on the levying of execution and on limitation periods). The Italian Civil Code, signed by a fascist minister of Justice went through a cosmetic "de-fascistization" in the aftermath of World War II. Subsequently, a general reform of family law was accomplished in 1975, and a variety of piecemeal reforms have been attempted particularly to put it up to date with European normative production. Particularly important are the changes to Book 5, relating to Company Law. In 2007, a committee chaired by the leading property law scholar Stefano Rodotá was appointed to redraft and update Book 3 particularly on its obsolete rules about public property. The Second World War did not stop attempts to re-codify in Latin America.[4]

In the immediate aftermath of the Second World War, within a global intellectual movement aimed at emphasizing social and relational aspects in the domain of private law, by continuing a path initiated in Switzerland and Italy, an important Civil Code has been produced in Egypt (1949) and following its lead in Iraq (1953). The Egyptian code, a quite impressive brainchild of the learned jurist Al Shanhuri, strives to mediate between Islamic values of solidarity and western bourgeois liberal values. The Code, has affected almost all of the subsequent codifications in the Middle East and Northern Africa.

Two great revision projects were launched in Western Europe shortly after the Second World War. They were aimed at the French Civil Code of 1804, and its descendant, the Netherlands Code of 1838. The Netherlands project, on which work had been in progress since 1947, has been completed in 1994.

In France, a Civil Code Reform Commission appointed at that time produced valuable scholarly studies, which contribute to our understanding of the technique of code revision and of the basic substantive issues involved in codifying or re-codifying the private law of a modern nation. The Commission also found, and called attention to, a number of specific and particularly disturbing defects in the existing law, and some of these findings led to the enactment of amendments. But the plan of a total revision of the Civil and Commercial Codes was not successful and was abandoned in the 1950s. The idea of Code reform was revived a decade later, although on a more modest scale. By that time, many of France's more pressing post-World War II problems had been solved and greater governmental support was forthcoming for the project. Furthermore, portions of the Code, particularly in the family law area, were now even less in tune with changes in social attitudes and in the economy than had been true during the post–1945 reform attempts. This time, however, the changes were not to be effectuated all at once, but by groups of Code provisions. Drastic changes were made in the rules concerning the relations

4. In Brazil in 1942. Later, Paraguay, which had used the Argentine Civil Code, adopted a "national" Code.

of spouses, divorce, adoption, illegitimacy, minority, guardianship, etc., leading to an almost complete revision of Book I of the Code dealing with family law. In addition, the provisions on matrimonial property regimes, contained in Book 3, were also completely changed. Two parts of the Code not related to family law received major revisions, the provisions on partnerships (companies-*sociétés*) and those on proof of legal instruments. There were, moreover, numerous changes in individual articles, often on the occasion of the enactment of a statute dealing with a different but related matter. A subsequent period of change occurred in 1993 and 1994, brought about mainly by concern about the impact of some modern scientific developments in the fields of medicine and biology. Under pressure from the perceived risk of being marginalized in the process of European Codification, a committee chaired by the leading Civil law scholar Pierre Catala has recently produced an *Avant Proget* of reform of the law of obligation that has attracted quite significant international attention.[5] The very idea of the Code itself has been deeply discussed in France in the celebration of its two-hundred years.[6]

One significant recent civil code revision occurred in Quebec. An Office of Civil Code Revision was created in 1955 to revise what was then officially called the Civil Code of Lower Canada. Professor Crépeau became the chief draftsman for the project. A draft of a proposed "Civil Code of Quebec" was presented to the Quebec legislature in 1978, but only Book 2 of the draft, dealing with family law, was in fact, enacted in 1980. Further changes were made in 1987 and a complete new Code, incorporating with some changes the earlier texts, was adopted in 1991. It went into effect on January 1, 1994.

The new Code exists in official English and French versions. It uses French-inspired terminology, but its organization is quite different from that of the French Civil Code. Its major divisions (in the English version) are: Book I (Persons, including "legal persons"), Book II (Family), Book III (Succession), Book IV (Property), Book V (Obligations), Book VI (Prior Claims and Hypothecs), Book VII (Evidence), Book VIII (Prescription), Book IX (Publication of Rights), Book X (Conflict of Laws). The new Code starts with an interesting "Preliminary Provision" which should be kept in mind in connection with the discussion *infra* of the interpretation of statutes, and which reads as follows:

The Civil Code of Québec, in harmony with the Charter of human rights and freedoms and the general principles of law, governs persons, relations between persons, and property.

The Civil Code comprises a body of rules which, in all matters within the letter, spirit or object of its provisions, lays down the *ius commune*[7]

5. See Ruth Sefton Green, The DCFR, the *Avant-Projet Catala* and French Legal Scholars: A Story of Cat and Mouse?, 12 Edimburgh Law Review 351 (2008).

6. See Le Code Civil 1804–2004, Livre du Bicentenaire, Dalloz Litec Paris 2004 containing articles from all French leading scholars and a message from President Chirac.

7. The Latin expression *ius commune* was presumably chosen in the English ver-

expressly or by implication. In these matters, the Code is the foundation of all other laws, although other laws may complement the Code or make exceptions to it.

In Louisiana, a project for reform of the Civil Code was undertaken about the same time as in Quebec; in fact there was some consultation between the bodies charged with code reform in the two jurisdictions, given their common problem of reforming a civil code in a common law environment. The project resulted in a step by step revision of the Code between 1976 and 1991, which included the addition of a Book 4, the Louisiana Conflict of Laws statute.[8]

The Swiss Civil Code and Code of Obligations, in spite of their relative newness, have also been subjected to a number of amendments. Revisions of the Civil Code provisions on family law and the law of succession took effect in 1988; substantial changes in the rules relating to corporations were adopted in 1991 and went into effect in July, 1992.

Too long a delay in the overall rejuvenation of a code will, of course, generate pressures for piecemeal amendments. Many recent limited, "piecemeal" amendments have modified here and there all of the civil law codes but have not affected their structure. In most civil law countries, however, the great codes are regarded as national symbols; they are venerable texts, and there is a certain reluctance to tamper with their language. When particular provisions or omissions of a code, reflecting the views of a past generation, become obnoxious to an influential group, the situation is sometimes remedied by the adoption of "auxiliary" statutes remaining outside the Code (see *infra*). In many instances, also, reform is brought about by decisional law which reinterprets or supersedes outmoded provisions of the code. Because of such important changes and developments, the text of the code often no longer reflects the latest state of the law and may mislead the uninitiated.

(b) *Auxiliary Statutes.* From the tables of contents of typical civilian codes, which are reprinted above, the reader will have gathered that the coverage of such codes is exceedingly broad. Carrying the civilian concept of codification to its logical extreme, one might imagine a code system in which the civil code and the commercial code (or the civil code alone, if there is no separate commercial code), cover the whole area of substantive private law. In actuality, however, such all embracing integration has not been achieved anywhere. In every civil law country, there exist, so-called auxiliary statutes (*Nebengesetze*), or special statutes i.e., statutes which, although pertaining to the general subject matter of a code, have been separately enacted and have not been incorporated into the code itself.

sion of the Code because of a fear the literal translation of the French expression *droit commun*, viz. common law, might be misunderstood to be a reference to the (English-derived) "common law."

8. For a further discussion of the revision of the Louisiana Civil Code, see A. N. Yiannopoulos, An Introduction to the Louisiana Civil Code, in West's Louisiana Civil Code xxix, xli (1996).

Such a statute may antedate the code; the codifiers may have decided for some reason to leave the older enactment intact and not to incorporate its provisions into the code. The German Law Concerning Damages For Deaths and Personal Injuries Caused in the Operation of Railroads, Mines and Similar Enterprises of June 7, 1871, for example, which imposes on such enterprises a tort liability not dependent on proof of negligence or other culpability, could have been made a part of the last Title of the Second Book of the Civil Code, dealing with tort law; but this was not done, and the Law of 1871, as amended, is still in force as a separate statute.

More frequently, auxiliary statutes come into existence subsequent to codification, in response to new social or technological developments not anticipated by the codifiers. Land use reform is an example of a social problem usually tackled by way of special enactments outside the framework of the traditional codes. The interaction between the Civil Code and the reform legislation may, however, cause thorny problems in practice. As in the case of the German statute concerning liability for automobile accidents, sometimes the law can be updated without any change in the language of the code through by creating a new cause of action unknown to the Code. On other occasions, legislators have abrogated a segment of a code, and substituted a separate statute for the repealed provisions.

In the area of commercial law, auxiliary statutes are particularly prevalent. By examining the table of contents of the German Commercial Code, for instance, the reader will have found that the Code fails to cover a number of subjects traditionally treated as commercial in the civilian world: e.g., negotiable instruments, limited responsibility companies, and stock corporations. All of these subjects are treated in separate statutes.

The trend to replace provisions of the Commercial Code with separate statutes has been particularly strong in France, where, as a result of a gradual process of what one might call decodification, most "commercial" matters are now covered by separate statutes. It has been said that, as a result, the French Commercial Code, enacted in 1808 and that has just celebrated its two-hundred years,[9] today is not much more than an "empty shell." In 1993, the French government submitted proposals for the adoption of a revised Commercial Code to the legislature. The proposal was severely criticized on the ground that codification required a certain point of stability in the development of the law, a point that had not yet been reached given the rapid changes due to the internationalization of commercial transactions, the interaction between "civil" and "commercial" law, etc.; it was finally withdrawn. When the number of "auxiliary" statutes becomes quite substantial, one of the main purposes of codification, to make the law easily accessible, is in obvious danger of being lost. Several remedies have been developed. Private publishers of existing codes frequently print relevant auxiliary statutes in an appendix or as notes to the provisions to which they pertain. On an official level, some countries

9. For an important recent historical and comparative discussion see Carlo Angelici–Mario Caravale–Laura Moscati–Ugo Petronio–Paolo Spada, Negozianti e imprenditori. 200 anni dal Code de Commerce (2008).

publish "consolidated" versions of their statutes, arranged in some logical order, and with amendments inserted in their proper place. In France, on the other hand, there has been a tendency, when the amount of separate legislation on a topic has become massive, to republish that legislation in the form of a "Code." These new "Codes" are, however, merely publications of existing law, arranged logically and with amendments inserted, not attempts to restate a field in a comprehensive, innovative manner. The earlier of these "consolidating" codifications were mere "administrative" codifications, enacted by decree; in 1989, a Codification Commission (*Commission supérieure de la codification*) was created and new Codifications tend to be enacted by the legislature (though without an intentional effort to change, and not just to consolidate, the law). Thus, in addition to the basic old codes, one finds in France a Labor Code, a Social Security Code, a General Tax Code, a Code of Tax Procedures, an Insurance Code, a Code of Court Organization, a Consumer Code, an Intellectual Property Code, etc.; and an Environmental Code is in the course of preparation.

It follows that for purposes of research on questions arising under a civil law system, it is not sufficient to peruse the basic codes. Just as the student of U.S. law must be on the lookout for statutes that may change a common law rule or supplant the common law's silence, the civilian has to search for auxiliary enactments which may have a comparable impact upon the provisions, or the silence, of the codes.

The relationship which in a civil law country exists between basic codes and auxiliary enactments may generally be compared with the interaction, familiar to us, of common law and statutes.[10] Quantitatively, the growth of auxiliary enactments in civil law countries, and of statutory law in most common law jurisdictions, has been enormous—a fact never to be forgotten by one undertaking research on a concrete point of law. Nevertheless, the basic codes remain to the civilian, as the common law remains to the common law lawyer, the very core of the legal order, containing not only rules but also the general principles which give life and systematic direction to every positive norm, and to which we must turn, in particular, when we are faced with a novel or doubtful case.

Three different direct methods are available to adjust the law to changed conditions in a code system: An over-all revision of the code, piecemeal amendments, and auxiliary statutes. As we will see in the next Chapter none of these "political" methods (i.e. carried on by legislative and executive branches) are sufficient and case law plays a role as well.

6. CIVIL AND COMMERCIAL CODES

(a) *Civil law and Commercial Law.* The word "civil" has different meanings in different contexts. We speak of civil law countries, as distinguished from common law jurisdictions and other legal systems. "Civil"

10. See Guido Calabresi, A Common Law For the Age of Statutes (1982).

also may connote the opposite of "criminal," as in the context of the term civil procedure, in contrast to criminal procedure. In yet other contexts, the system of "civil" law may be contrasted to that of canon law or of military law. Occasionally, and perhaps not too accurately, the term "civil" is used as synonymous with "private," i.e., as opposed to "public." The civilians, finally, often speak of "civil law" as opposed to commercial law. In this latter sense, "civil law" may be defined as comprising the whole area of substantive private law which remains if one excludes commercial law.

A historically driven dichotomy which is of the greatest practical importance for civilian lawyers, being reflected in the very structure of codification is that between "civil" and commercial law. Historically, this division reaches back into the middle ages. Roman law, as developed and perhaps corrupted in medieval times, became unsuitable as a basis for business transactions. This was due to several features of that system of law, such as irksome interference with freedom of contract; restrictions on assignments and powers of attorney; usury laws which sharply limited and often prohibited the taking of interest; over-indulgent protection of debtors; failure to recognize the mercantile concept of negotiability; and, above all, a cumbersome, expensive and irritatingly slow procedure. In order to avoid these fetters of an inadequate general law, the guilds and corporations of merchants developed a customary law of their own; in time secular and ecclesiastic authorities grudgingly recognized the principle that customary merchant law should prevail over general law in the commercial sphere. According to medieval views the guild or corporation had the power to codify its corporate customs and these codifications became known as *statuta mercatorum*. Confirmation of the *statuta* by the sovereign was frequently sought and granted; but it was the prevailing view that the *statuta* had the force of law even in the absence of such confirmation.

The *statutum* conferred on the individual member of the guild a status which he took with him wherever he traveled and which, at least in principle, had to be respected by any court before which he might appear (personality principle). This liberal rule of conflict of laws made it incumbent upon the courts dealing with commercial matters to familiarize themselves with the *statuta* of many trades and countries, with the result that by this practical use of "comparative law" the commercial customs and laws of the western and Mediterranean world (thus including significant portions of Islamic commercial laws) became more and more unified. The most influential *statuta* were those adopted by the merchants' guilds in the great Italian centers of commerce during the 14th and 15th centuries.

The guilds also had the power to elect their own judges. The jurisdiction of these special courts, originally limited to internal affairs of the guild, was later broadened to include all cases involving commercial disputes between merchants. The procedure of the merchants' courts was fair, rational and expeditious. It was in sharp contrast both to the primitive forms of trial (battle, ordeal, or wager of law) which until the reception of Roman law prevailed in Germanic countries, and to the delays and subtleties of canonistic procedure which in non-commercial matters dominated procedural thinking on the continent from the middle ages until the 19th century.

In addition to these guild courts, whose jurisdiction (over their members) originally had a *personal* basis, there existed many a merchants' court having territorial jurisdiction over a market place, a fair or a port. Those courts which sat in port towns are part of the ancestry of modern admiralty courts. But the guild courts (exercising personal jurisdiction over members, and later over all merchants) must be regarded as the most important forerunners of modern commercial courts in civil law countries.

The main characteristics of the substantive law, which was created by the commercial courts, were emphases on freedom of contract and on freedom of alienability of movable property, both tangible and intangible; abrogation of legal technicalities; and, most importantly, a tendency to decide cases *ex aequo et bono* rather than by abstract scholastic deductions from Roman texts. It is therefore not surprising that commercial law was a highly successful institution. Cosmopolitan in nature and inherently superior to the general law, the law merchant by the end of the medieval period had become the very foundation of an expanding commerce throughout the world.

Commercial law as a separate branch of private substantive law, coupled with the special jurisdiction and procedure of commercial courts, thus was well established before the time of the great codifications. In Napoleon's code system, and in most of the later codifications, the dichotomy between "civil" and commercial law was preserved by the enactment of separate commercial codes, and by provisions (either in the code of commerce or in the procedural codes) perpetuating the separate commercial courts.[1]

In England, the law merchant was absorbed into the common law during the 17th and 18th centuries by means of a thorough jurisdictional and cultural assault on a different legal culture that was located at the Doctor's Commons.[2] This lawyers' guild, made of civilian graduates from Oxford and Cambridge, had incrementally acquired a monopoly over the most important issues of international commerce and became more lucrative and prestigious for its members. The guild's prosperity triggered the jealousy of the Common lawyers. The common law courts, always jealous of competing judicial bodies, proved powerful enough to displace the special commercial courts. In the process, many of the merchants' substantive rules and customs, especially those dealing with negotiable instruments, were transformed into common law rules. This incorporation of commercial law into the fabric of the common law was facilitated by the fact that an inductive, pragmatic method was common to both systems and by the towering figure of a legendary Scottish (civilian) Chief Justice, Lord Mans-

---

1. See Schlesinger, The Uniform Commercial Code in the Light of Comparative Law, 1 Inter–Am.L.Rev. 11, 36ff (1959).

2. *Id.*

field.[3] For the same reason, the merchants' resistance to the process of absorption was not too strenuous. On the continent, on the other hand, where at that time the general law was still largely dominated by scholastic thinking and by canonistic procedure, and where the courts of general jurisdiction were much weaker and less respected, the merchant class successfully resisted the merger of "civil" and commercial law.

(b) *Divergences between the Civil Code and the Commercial Code.* Every Commercial Code enacted in a civilian country contains numerous provisions which are at odds with the provisions of the same country's Civil Code. Generally speaking, commercial law favors the easy and informal conclusion of transactions as well as their speedy consummation and rigorous enforcement. The Civil Code, on the other hand, may place a lesser value on speed and efficiency than on the protection (e.g., by form requirements) of the weak, the ignorant, and the imprudent. An important example of this difference in attitude is offered by the German and French Civil Codes (and consumer protection rules) that subject guarantees to a form requirement, but that under the Commercial Codes of both nations the oral guarantee of a merchant is valid and enforceable. The following are further examples, all taken from German law, of tough provisions embodied in the Commercial Code which are at variance with what the Civil Code provides:

(a) Contractual penalties are valid, but ordinarily may be reduced by the court (Civil Code § 343); there can be no such reduction, however, if the promisor is a merchant (Commercial Code § 348).

(b) The rate of legal interest is higher in "commercial" than in "civil" matters. Compare Civil Code § 246 and Commercial Code § 352.

(c) In a commercial sales transaction the buyer is deemed to have waived his right to complain of any discoverable defects of the goods unless he examines them immediately upon arrival, and promptly notifies the seller of the defect (Commercial Code § 377). There is no such requirement in the case of a "civil" sale governed exclusively by the Civil Code.

(d) Among merchants, silence is more easily construed as acceptance of an offer than in non-commercial transactions.

(e) Only a merchant can issue a promissory note as a negotiable one (Commercial Code §§ 363–365). If the issuer is not a merchant, then the note, even though purporting to be payable to the payee's order can be transferred only by way of an ordinary assignment, with

3. More recently, a specialized Bar and Bench (now formally organized in the Commercial Court) has kept England's judicially developed commercial law responsive to commercial needs, as has the concentration of much of international commercial arbitration in London. The fascinating and not very well known story of the civilian bar at London's Doctors Commons is narrated in Daniel R. Coquillette, The Civilian Writers of Doctors' Commons, London: Three Centuries of Juristic Innovation in Comparative, Commercial and International Law (1988).

the result that defenses which would defeat the assignor are equally available as against the assignee.

Suppose a consumer C, who has purchased goods from seller S, has issued a promissory note, or a series of such notes, for the purchase price. Suppose further that these notes are in negotiable form. If S endorses these notes to finance company F, and the law recognizes the negotiability of the notes, C is apt to find himself in a most unenviable position. Although the goods are defective, C may have no defense when he is sued on the notes by F, because F is likely to be regarded as a "holder in due course." Thus F will recover from C, and whether C can ever enforce his claim against S (who may have absconded or gone bankrupt) is most uncertain. Under German law, however, a non-merchant's promissory note cannot be made negotiable. Thus, regardless of the terms of the notes, F cannot acquire the status of a holder in due course; he is a mere assignee, and as such he is exposed to all defenses which C could interpose if he were sued by the assignor, i.e., by S. Attempts to avoid that consumer friendly result by using, instead of promissory notes, drafter predated checks will also fail since their use as a credit instrument is prohibited in consumer transactions by provisions in the Consumer Credit Law (§§ 10 II 1, 2).

Contrast the simplicity and effectiveness of the German solution with the complexities which have been created in U.S. law by the manifold attempts of state courts, state legislatures, and finally the Federal Trade Commission to overcome the "holder in due course" racket. [4]

These German examples could easily be multiplied, and similar examples could be given under the law of most other civil law countries. A further example from French law is provided by French Civil Code art. 1843 under which persons who have acted in the name of a company in the process of being formed are liable for the obligations thus created in a joint and several manner if the company has been formed under commercial law, but only ratably if the company has been formed under civil law. This is in line with the general proposition that "commercial" obligations are normally joint and several but that "civil" obligations are not. More generally, somewhat different rules apply in countries which have separate commercial codes to "civil" and to "commercial" partnerships, though more recently some countries have created forms of "civil" partnerships that have many of the advantages of "commercial" partnerships, such as the generally available *Erwerbsgesellschaft* of Austrian law or the special types of partnerships available for the learned professions under French or German law.

(c) *Which of the Two Codes Applies?* Suppose a French or German lawyer is asked to draft a contract of sale, of bailment, of carriage, or of guarantee; or to deal with a problem involving a partnership or an agency relationship. Will he find the applicable rules in the Civil Code or in the Commercial Code? The answer is seemingly simple: If the matter at hand is not commercial, the Civil Code alone (perhaps in conjunction with some

4. See J.J. White & R.S. Summers, Uniform Commercial Code § 14–9 (4th ed. 1995).

auxiliary statute) will govern, and there is no need for consulting the Commercial Code. If the matter is commercial, then the Civil Code controls only with respect to points not covered by provisions of the Commercial Code, the latter provisions being treated as *lex specialis*.

It follows that in the countless instances in which the positive provisions of the two codes differ from each other, the Civil Code provision must be applied if the matter is "civil" (i.e., non-commercial), while the Commercial Code prevails in commercial matters. The outcome of many cases thus turns on whether the transaction in question is classified as "commercial." In addition, many civil law countries provide that "commercial" actions be brought before special commercial courts, or before commercial divisions of courts of general jurisdiction. Procedure in "commercial" matters usually is simpler and speedier than in ordinary "civil" litigation.

Separate commercial courts (or commercial divisions) may exist even in countries which in their substantive law do not have a separate Commercial Code. This is the case in about four of the Swiss cantons. Jurisdiction and procedure are largely cantonal matters, while substantive private law is essentially covered by federal law, i.e., the Civil Code and the Code of Obligations.[5] Thus, although the structure of the Swiss code system deemphasizes the distinction between civil and commercial matters in the area of substantive law, a Swiss lawyer still may have to struggle with the distinction in order to choose the proper court. In a small minority of civil law jurisdictions, including Italy and the Netherlands, commercial courts have been completely abolished.

Demarcation of what is "commercial" thus becomes a matter of central importance in most civilian systems. Some types of transactions, such as contracts made in the ordinary course of the banking or insurance business, and dealings which involve negotiable instruments, often are regarded as commercial *per se*. Many other transactions, however, of which contracts of sale, bailment, and carriage as well as partnership agreements, may be mentioned as examples are sometimes "civil" and sometimes "commercial." Criteria are sought to be derived either from the parties' status as "merchants," or from the nature of the transaction as a "mercantile act."

Some civil law jurisdictions, especially the German speaking ones, stress the *subjective* element, i.e., the quality of the parties as "merchants" or "mercantile enterprises." The definition of "merchant" may be predicated on (a) the nature and object of the activities carried on,[6] or (b) the

---

5. See H.U. Walder, Civil Procedure, in F. Dessemontet & T. Ansay, Introduction to Swiss Law 257, 268 (2d rev. ed. 1995). In 2009 a national procedural code will displace the cantonal codes.

6. Some codes stress the *nature* of the activities (e.g., buying and selling), while in other codes the profit-making *object* of the activities is made the primary touchstone. Extractive and even agricultural activities may become "commercial" under a code emphasizing the latter point, especially if the enterprise is of such size as to require a commercial organization.

Doubts may arise, also, with respect to the "merchant" status of non-profit-making organizations engaged in large-scale activities which by their nature (as distinguished from their object) could be considered commercial.

existence of a permanent business organization, or (c) the legal form of the organization (some jurisdictions provide that a business corporation is *per se* a merchant), or (d) certain formalities, such as registration in the *Register of Commerce*, or (e) a combination of these factors.

In other countries, especially in those influenced by French legal culture, the *objective* criterion of the "mercantile act" is emphasized. Code definitions of "mercantile acts" usually consist of lengthy and unsystematic enumerations. Even within the French influenced family of codes, there are vast differences with respect to inclusion or exclusion of manufacturing, mining and agricultural activities.

The two concepts, "merchant" and "mercantile act," are interrelated in complex ways. A person's status as "merchant" may depend on whether he makes it his business to engage in mercantile acts. The nature of a transaction as a "mercantile act," on the other hand, may be predicated on whether the parties entering into it are business enterprises permanently engaged in, and organized for, a business involving transactions of the same kind. The resulting confusion is confounded by the circumstance that occasionally a transaction is treated as "commercial" for jurisdictional and procedural but not for substantive purposes.

Both legislative and doctrinal attempts to establish a demarcation line between "commercial" and "civil" transactions have led to obscurity and excessive refinement. The draftsmen of most of the European and Latin–American commercial codes have attempted to blend the subjective and the objective criteria. The resulting mixed systems, however, differ greatly from each other. Even within a single jurisdiction, one often finds controversies among text writers and conflicting judicial decisions, as an examination of standard commentaries shows.

The practical difficulties arising from these doubts, however, are greatly reduced by an institution founded on old tradition and anchored in the commercial codes and statutes of almost all civil law countries: *the Commercial Register.*[7] This Register, operated by a judicial or other public officer, usually is open to public inspection. It facilitates the demarcation between merchants and non-merchants. As has been mentioned before, entry in the Register, or the lack of it, is one of the factors determining a

---

7. The original name "commercial register" (*Régistre du commerce, Handelsregister*) has been modified in some countries to reflect the fact that, now, some "civil" type partnerships must or may also be registered. Thus in Austria, the register is now called the *Firmenregister*, in Italy *Registro delle imprese* (meaning Register of firms), and in France, *Régistre du commerce et des sociétés* (commercial and companies register). The original name has been preserved in Germany, but a separate register (*Partnerschaftsregister*) has been created for the new "civil" partnerships of members of the learned professions. The Commercial Register exists even in countries which do not have a separate Commercial Code. See, e.g., Swiss Code of Obligations Arts. 927–943.

The reader should note, also, that the Commercial Register can be found in many of the countries (e.g., Islamic countries) which have adopted only some features of the civil law. See, e.g., T.W. Hill, The Commercial Legal System of the Sultanate of Oman, 17 Int. Lawyer 507, 516 (1983); F. Swain, Bahrain, in National Association of Credit Management, Inc., Digest of Commercial Laws of the World (L. Nelson, ed., looseleaf, 1990–).

person's status as a merchant. Some codes go further and provide that an individual, partnership, or corporation listed in the Register is deemed to be a merchant, at least for the benefit of other persons dealing with him, who in good faith have relied on the entry in the Register. Moreover, if a person or firm is in fact a merchant under the definition prevailing in his country, the official in charge of the Register normally has the power to compel registration. In practice, therefore, the Register as a rule will furnish reliable information as to whether a given person or organization may be regarded as a "merchant." Indirectly, the Register will be helpful, also, in determining whether (in a jurisdiction adhering to the objective theory) a given transaction is a "mercantile act," because, as we have seen, the latter issue may largely depend on whether the contracting parties are merchants.

(d) *Unilateral Commercial Transactions.* Special difficulties arise in cases of "mixed" transactions, i.e., of transactions which are "commercial" for one party but not for the other. The opera singer who buys securities from or through a brokerage house is a favorite classroom example. More importantly, most retail sales are "mixed," because ordinarily the seller is a merchant for whom the sale is a mercantile transaction, while the consumer is normally neither a merchant nor engaged in a mercantile act.

The Commercial Codes of some countries contain reasonably clear provisions concerning the treatment of "mixed" transactions. The German Commercial Code, for instance in § 345 lays down the rule that: "except as otherwise provided, the provisions concerning commercial transactions apply to a transaction which is commercial for either of the parties." The clause "except as otherwise provided" is of great significance. To avoid hardship, many exceptions to the general rule of § 345 have been spelled out in other Code provisions; e.g., § 350 of the Commercial Code, repeatedly mentioned above, provides that a guarantee is exempt from the Civil Code's requirement of a writing only if *the guarantor* is a merchant. In addition, consumer protection legislation in many countries specifically addresses the problems of contracts between consumers and merchants. In the Member States of the European Union, the adoption of such legislation has been mandated by Council Directive 93/13 on Unfair Terms in Consumer Contracts.[8]

The abundant legislation ostensibly protecting consumers and the development of consumer law as an academic subject matter has produced the birth of a new dichotomy that needs to be approached before knowing what law applies to any given transaction: That between "consumers" and "non consumers." Even where, like in Italy, civil and commercial law have been unified in a single Code and in single Courts, the trend to create "special rites" (now often in the form of ADR) based on personal status is still present.[9]

---

8. Directive 93/13 of April 5, 1993, 1993 O.J. No, L95, p. 29. See generally, Commission of the European Communities, European Consumer Guide to the Single Market, esp. at 73–79 (1995).

9. See Ugo Mattei, Efficiency and Equal Protection in the New European Contract

There are other countries, however, especially in Latin America, where the Commercial Code, by provisions that are either unwarrantedly broad or lacking in clarity, extends its coverage so as to bring too many of the "mixed" transactions within its sweep. Article 7 of the Argentine Code of Commerce reads: "When a transaction is commercial for one of the parties, all parties involved shall be subject to commercial law." In contrast to German law, the law of Argentina does not modify the broad sweep of this rule by proper exceptions. The situation seems to be similar in many, if not most, of the other Latin American countries. Often this results in frustrating the protective purpose of a Civil Code provision, and in oppression of the weaker party.

7. SURVIVING TRACES OF PRE-CODIFICATION LAW IN THE CIVIL LAW WORLD

Summing up, before the age of the great codifications, continental law had three principal characteristics:

(a) In most countries of the continent, it was still strongly Roman influenced;

(b) It was University taught law;

(c) It was based on a largely Roman University tradition which transcended regional and national frontiers,[1] and it was to a considerable extent a *jus commune* prevailing throughout most of the European countries and their overseas possessions.[2]

The first of these characteristics has become greatly attenuated in modern, codified civil law that deprived the *Corpus Juris* of whatever authoritative status it previously possessed. Looking at the historical antecedents of present day civil law systems, we have found that Roman law is just one of a number of strands which are intricately interwoven in those systems.

It remains to explore the question to what extent the two other characteristics of pre-code civil law, its professorial and its transnational nature, have survived the surgical process of codification.

Law. mandatory, Default and Enforcement Rules, 39 Virginia J. International Law 537 (1999).

1. It was only in the late 17th and 18th centuries that a few University chairs for the teaching of local law slowly began to be created in France, Germany and Spain. Until then, the law faculties taught exclusively Roman law and Canon law, with the result that both students and teachers could move freely from one European University to another without changing their intellectual habitat.

2. Of course, there were countless local statutes and ordinances of considerable diversity, as well as local customs reduced to writing. In cases not clearly covered by these local enactments, however, the *jus commune* controlled.

There were occasional attempts, especially during the 17th and 18th centuries, by local statutory provisions to establish a hierarchy of authoritative oracles of the *jus commune*, and thus to bring local influences to bear on the application of the *jus commune* itself; but these provisions (called Laws of Citation), although they led to some local variations of legal method, did not destroy the cosmopolitan quality of the *jus commune*.

(1) *The survival of the professorial nature of civil law.* Prior to the Age of Reason, the law faculties had long held a position of leadership in the development of the law. This was natural during a period when the most important sources of the law were enshrined in Latin texts and writings accessible only to the well trained scholar. During the 17th and 18th centuries, however, the traditional methods and sources were questioned with increasing vigor. The movement toward codification itself arose from this critical attitude; it was aimed at changing the traditional legal method which, in the eyes of the critics, and it relied too heavily on the accumulated cobwebs of centuries of professorial learning.

This new spirit, not surprisingly, tended to diminish the law faculties' position of leadership in the development of the law. In some countries, such as France, academic lawyers (then barely re-emerging from secular excommunication) were not even asked to participate in the drafting of the codes. Elsewhere, e.g., in Germany and Switzerland, law professors did help to prepare the codes, either as single draftsmen or as members of a drafting team; but their proposals required the approval of legislative committees and of the legislature itself. The days when the professors literally were making law *ex cathedra* were gone.

Academic influence on the law, to be sure, was by no means broken. The codes needed interpretation, and the authors of the majority of influential commentaries, treatises and monographs were members of law faculties. So long as a code is relatively new, the opinions of academic commentators (*la doctrine*, as the French expression goes) may constitute the only available guide in the application of the code and in filling its gaps. Even later, when most of the important controversial questions arising under the code have been settled by court decisions (as the French would call it, by *la jurisprudence*), the commentator's role in collecting, explaining, systematizing and often criticizing the judicial decisions remains a significant one. There is little doubt that to this day the authority of leading textbooks and commentaries in civil law countries is considerably stronger than in the common law world. Indeed, the unflattering term "secondary authority" is unknown in the civil law orbit. We shall come back to this point in connection with the question of the persuasive force of judicial and non-judicial authorities (*infra* Chapter 6 at 477).

Another surviving trace of the formerly dominant position of the law faculties may be found in the fact that the young civilian, unlike his counterpart in some common law countries, simply cannot become a lawyer without having passed a course of University study. He cannot enter the profession by "reading law." Even in countries under communist rule, where this University monopoly was temporarily broken, the tendency was toward restoring it once the "revolutionary phase" of the regime was past.

(2) *The survival of the transnational nature of civil law.* Of all of the characteristics of pre-code civil law, its transnational nature was the one most radically changed by codification. The important codes enacted in the civil law world during the 19th and 20th centuries were national codes. *Within* the enacting nation state, codification usually meant unification of

diverse laws. But *as between* one nation state and another, the national codifications had the effect of impeding the interchange of legal thought and experience. Judges, practitioners and academicians in each country began to concentrate their efforts on the interpretation and development of their own code system, without paying much attention to the similarly isolated developments in other countries living under different codes.[3] Linguistic and conceptual barriers between the lawyers of various civil law countries thus were bound to grow, with the result that the civil law orbit has lost its former coherence to a much greater degree than has been the case in the common law world. Only rarely can we speak today of "the civil law rule" on a given point, and the experience of international practitioners shows that the differences *inter sese* among civil law systems are even more pronounced than those among common law jurisdictions. Comparative studies concerning a controversial point often show that there are both civil law and common law jurisdictions in each camp.

The intellectual isolation of each national legal system which resulted from the codifications was somewhat mitigated by the fact that some outstanding codes were used as models by legislatures in other countries. During the 19th century, when all developed legal systems had to struggle with new problems created by the industrial revolution, it became customary for European legislators and their advisers, as part of their work in preparing national legislation, to conduct comparative studies of other countries' legislative experience.[4]

As between two civilian codes which do not share the same ancestor, differences in positive rules and principles, and even in the system of the codes, are apt to be marked. If, nevertheless, judges and legal writers continue to use the generic term "civil law," they must feel that in spite of the differences between the various codes there is a common approach or way of thinking, perhaps a common method and terminology, which binds all civilians together and sets them apart from those who practice under different systems. In studying the materials presented in the following parts of this book, the reader should attempt to identify the mental processes which in this sense may be attributed to the "civil law" rather than to the legal system of an individual civilian nation. It may be found that the features common to all civil law systems can be divided into two categories. Some arise from the very nature of a codified system of law. Others are surviving (and *re*viving) traces of the transnational, professorial, Romanistic law of pre-code days.

This revival proceeds against the background of the increasingly complete unification of European business law, private international law,

---

3. Leading 19th century scholars were quick to recognize that the differences among the various codes call for comparative studies, and that the intellectual isolation of national legal systems brought about by national codification would become complete without "comparative jurisprudence."

4. See H. Coing, European Common Law: Historical Foundations, in New Perspectives for a Common Law of Europe 31, 38–42 (M. Cappelletti ed., 1978).

administrative law, and human rights law under the auspices of the European Community (now Union) and the Council of Europe and more particularly, the European Court of Human Rights.[5] Much of this process has been concentrated on public-law and commercial-law subjects, but there have also been inroads into core matters of private law such as products liability and contract terms. Agreement seems in sight, moreover, on general principles of contract law.[6]

Agreement on principles of contract law reflects not only impulses received from the integrative but specialized European organizations, but also a new transnational consensus by lawyers brought up in different legal traditions currently making a new transnational legal elite. That leaves us with the question whether this consensus can be expanded and consolidated by a return to the transnational "legal style" of the European jus commune or an even broader new *lex mercatoria*. Both the feasibility and the desirability of such a development have become the subject of heated debate[7]—a reasonably sure sign that a major reorientation of European civil law thinking is in the making.

8.   CODIFICATION: A WORLDWIDE PHENOMENON?

The Code, even in its strictly civilian meaning of an attempt to obtain a general, comprehensive and systematic exposition of a full large branch of the law, is not a unique peculiarity of the civil law tradition. In the United States for example the UCC can certainly be considered a "codification" in the Civilian style and indeed the legal culture inspiring its "inventor" and main drafter, Professor Llewellyn, is the German one. However, by express provision, the UCC does not claim to be the only official source of law in its domain of application. Rather it has to be interpreted in harmony with its common law background. In the next chapter we will see the dialectic between Codes and case law at play in the civil law tradition, but some legal systems have maintained a stronger sense that through codification a real modernization and rationalization of law was possible. Because of colonial influence, and in particular because of the status of the legal profession which has always allowed some of its members to extensively travel and study abroad, the equation between codification and modernization/rationalization of law affected many non-western countries. The most important example of an effort of codification within the Islamic legal

---

5. See The European System for the Protection of Human Rights (R. St.J. Macdonald, F. Matscher & H. Petzold, eds., 1993), with numerous contributions.

6. See Principles of European Contract Law, Part I: Performance, Non-performance and Remedies, Prepared by the Commission on European Contract Law (O. Lando & H. Beale, eds., 1995); M. J. Bonnell, An Interna-

tional Restatement of Contract Law, The UNIDROIT Principles of International Commercial Contracts (1994). See also the recent DCFR mentioned *supra* p. 430, note 5.

7. For a programmatic statement in support, see R. Zimmermann, Civil Code or Civil Law?—Towards a New European Private Law, 20 Syracuse J. Int'l L. & Com. 217 (1994).

culture, later to become a model through North Africa and the Middle East is the Egyptian Civil Code.

(a) Egypt

Egyptian Civil Code

English Translation by Perrot, Fanner & Sims Marshall

Le Journal du Commerce et de la Marine, 1952

Preliminary Chapter: General Provisions

Section I: Laws and Their Application

    1. Laws and Their Rights.

    2. The Application of Laws

        a. Conflicts as to Time

        b. Conflicts as to Place

Section II: Persons

    1. Individuals

    2. Juristic Persons

        a. Associations

        b. Foundations

        c. General Provisions Applicable Both to Associations and to Foundations

Section III: The Classification of Things and Property

First Part: Obligations or Personal Rights

Book I: Obligations Generally

Chapter 1: The Sources of Obligations

Section I: Contracts

    1. Elements of Contracts

        a. Consent

        b. Object

        c. Consideration

        d. Nullity

    2. The Effects of a Contract

    3. Dissolution of a Contract

Section II: Unilateral Undertakings

Section III: Unlawful Acts

    1. Liability Arising from Personal Acts

    2. Liability Arising from the Acts of Another

    3. Liability Arising from Things

Section III: Mandate

    1. The Elements of Mandate

    2. The Effects of a Mandate

    3. The End of the Mandate

Section IV: Deposit

    1. The Obligations of the Depository

    2. The Obligations of the Depositor

    3. Certain Kinds of Deposits

Section V: Judicial Custody

Chapter 5: Suretyship

Section I: The Elements of Suretyship

Section II: The Effects of Suretyship

    1. The Relationship Between the Surety and the Creditor

    2. The Relationship Between the Surety and the Debtor

<u>Second Part: Real Rights</u>

Book III: The Principal Real Rights

Chapter 1: The Right of Ownership in General

Section I: The Right of Ownership in General

    1. Limits and Sanctions

    2. Restrictions on the Right of Ownership

    3. Joint Ownership

        a. Provisions Relating to Joint Ownership

        b. The Cessation of Joint Ownership

        c. Obligatory Joint Ownership

        d. Family Joint Ownership

        e. Ownership of Storeys in Buildings

        f. Syndicates of Owners of Stroreys of a Single Building

Section II: Acquisition of Ownership

    1. Acquisition by Appropriation

        a. The Appropriation of Movables Without an Owner

        b. The Appropriation of Immovables Which Have No Owner

    2. Acquisition by Inheritance and Winding Up of an Estate

        a. The Appointment of an Administrator

        b. Inventory of the Estate

        c. Discharge of the Debts of the Estate

        d. Delivery and Division of the Property of the Estate

e.   Rules Applicable to the Estates That Have Not Been Wound Up

3.   Acquisition by Will

4.   Acquisition by Accession

a.   The Right of Accession in Respect of Immovable Property

b.   The right of Accession in Respect of Movable Property

5.   Acquisition by Contract

6.   Acquisition by Pre-emption

a.   Conditions for the Exercise of the Right of Preemption

b.   The Procedure for Pre-emption

c.   The Effects of Pre-emption

d.   Forfeiture of the Right of Pre-emption

7.   Possession

a.   Acquisition, Transfer and Loss of Possession

b.   Protection of Possession (the Three Possessory Actions)

c.   Effects of Possession—Acquisitive Prescription

d.   The Acquisition of Movables by Prescription

e.   The Acquisition of the Fruits by Possession

f.   Recovery of Expenses

g.   Liability in the Event of Loss

Chapter 2: Rights Derived from the Right of Ownership

Section I: The Right to Usufruct, the Right of the User and the Right of Occupation

1.   Usufruct

2.   The Right of User and Occupation

Section II: The Right of Hekr

1.   Some Kinds of Hekr

Section III: Servitudes

Book IV: Accessory Real Rights or Real Securities

Chapter 1: Mortgages

Section I: The Constitution of Mortgages

Section II: The Effects of a Mortgage

1.   The Effects of a Mortgage as Between Parties

a.   As Regards the Mortgagor

b.   As Regards the Mortgagee

Section III: Extinguishment of the Mortgage

Chapter 2: Judgment Charges Upon Immovable Property

Section I: The Constitution of a Judgment Charge

Section II: The Effects of a Judgment Charge, Its Reduction and Extinguishment

Chapter 3: Rights Derived from the Right of Ownership Pledge

Section I: Elements of a Pledge

Section II: The Effects of a Pledge

    1. Between the Contract Parties

        a. Obligations of the Pledgor

        b. Obligations of the Pledge

    2. As Regards Third Parties

Section III: Extinguishment of a Pledge

Section IV: Certain Kinds of Pledge

    1. Pledge of an Immovable (Antichresis)

    2. Pledge of a Movable

    3. Pledge of Debts

Chapter 4: Privileged Rights

Section I: General Provisions

Section II: Kinds of Privileges

    1. General Privileges and Special Privileges Over Movables

    2. Special Privileges Over Immovables

* * *

Nabil Saleh, Civil Codes of Arab Countries: The Sanhuri Codes

Arab Law Quarterly, Vol. 8, No. 2 (1993) 161–67.

Egypt's Civil Code was enacted in 1948, not by any autocratic ruler, but by the people's representatives and following original guidelines conceived by its chief architect, Abd al-Razzaq al-Sanhuri, ordinary politician and outstanding lawyer....

The *Majalla* (the Ottoman Code of Obligations enacted in 1286) was never implemented in Egypt. Instead, the European powers of the nineteenth century secured the creation of "Mixed Courts" which began operation in 1876, using a civil code-and other codes-patterned on their French counterparts....

In 1936, an Anglo–Egyptian Treaty gave Egypt a limited independence. In the course of the same year a Committee for the revision of the Egyptian Civil Codes was formed and Sanhuri was appointed one of its members. Neither this Committee, nor a second one, were successful. Finally, it was

Sanhuri and Lambert, a French Professor of Law, who produced in 1942 a draft Civil Code presented for comments for a lapse of three years and then submitted to the legislature in a revised version.

The draftsman Sanhuri was faithful to his early vision, for Article 1 of the Civil Code of the 1948 enjoins judges to issue their judgments in accordance with the letter and spirit of the provisions of the Code itself, failing that, in accordance with custom, and in the absence of custom, in accordance with the principles of Islamic *Shari'a*. In the absence of the latter, judges will apply principles of natural law and rules of equity, as also instructed by Article 1.

For probably the first time in the modern legal history of the Arab Middle East, the *Shari'a* was officially to back up an important piece of secular legislation. *Shari'a* principles were to fill lacunae found in the statutory provisions and in custom.

The extent of the *Shari'a* back-up role was controversial from the outset and still not exactly delineated or necessarily compiled with. The multiplicity of sources from which judges were invited to draw rules of law developed in practice an ambiguous and unsettled situation, for such sources are not completely related one to the other, and one of these sources, despite being deemed of divine origin, was given a subsidiary (some might say honorary) role compared to the other secular and foreign sources.

The other function that the draftsmen of the Egyptian Civil Code of 1948 intended for the *Shari'a* was to blend a certain number of *Shari'a* principles with the western legal concepts forming the bulk of the Code...[1]

Arab Civil Codes are not carbon copies of the 1948 Civil Code of Egypt .. Beside the Egyptian code, Sanhuri had a direct hand in the drafting of the Iraqi Civil Code [1951] and of Kuwait's 1961 Code of Commerce which includes a substantial treatment of "Obligations."

While Sanhuri approved of the Libyan Civil Code [1954] he was not directly involved in the preparation of Syria's Civil Code [1949], although it faithfully follows his own. In fact, Sanhuri had in mind for Syria a Code in the line of the Iraqi one which was then under preparation. Sanhuri was certainly not involved in the drafting of Qatar's Civil and Commercial Law of 1971 which, however, is a mere adoption of Book Two of the old Kuwaiti Commercial Law with some additions and few adjustments deemed necessary to give the part separated from a whole some consistency.

None of the codes drafted by Sanhuri is a blind reproduction of a prototype: Sanhuri remained faithful to his drafting method. At all times he took into account existing legal background and social environment. Whenever the *Majalla* was in effect, he felt it necessary to draw from its provisions. He did so for Iraq. In Kuwait he went a step further and

---

1. J. N. D. Anderson, "The Shari'a and Civil law" in Islamic Quarterly, 1954, pp. 29–46; Y Linant de Bellefonds, "Le Droit Musul-man et le Nouveau Code Civil Egyptien" in Annales Juridiques, Politiques, Economiques et Sociales, 1965, 4, pp. 223–235.

confined his handling of "Obligations" to commercial matters as opposed to civil matters which remained governed by the *Majalla* until 1980.

Jordan's 1976 Civil Code is a different case; it has distinctive Islamic features which are not found in Arab Codes enacted earlier.

One example will illustrate the point: the Jordanian Civil Code orders the debtor of a contractual obligation specific performance.[2] If specific performance is not possible or too onerous for the debtor, then that debtor has to pay damages. If not pre-agreed nor fixed by law, the court will assess them "on the basis of the damage actually sustained at the time it has occurred."[3] Nothing is said about compensating the victim of a breach for lost profit or for moral prejudice-both considered as conjectural and non-tangible and therefore contrary to *Shari'a* teaching.

That is not the case for the Sanhuri Codes. Egypt,[4] Libya,[5] Syria[6] and Iraq[7] all make room in their statutes for loss suffered and lost profit as well as for compensation for moral prejudice.[8]

(b) People's Republic of China

Legal theorists have debated to what extent the legal system of the People's Republic of China remains a socialist legal system, given the ways in which has changed since the beginning of the economic reforms in 1978. As we have seen, even socialist legal systems were historically based on the template of the civil law tradition, at least insofar as they did not recognize the legitimacy of judge-made law. However, China has not adopted a single (putatively) all-inclusive code, but has proceeded relatively piecemeal in its legislation. It was not until 1986 that China enacted something called The General Provisions of Civil law, which in some ways corresponds to the General Part of a typical civil law code, but has not been followed by the other substantive parts of a code.

William C. Jones, Some General Questions Regarding the Significance of the General Provisions of Civil law of the People's Republic of China

28 Harv. Int'l L. J. 309–310 (1987).

In 1949, the new Chinese government repealed all of the laws of the Nationalists, including the civil code. Ever since then, it has been trying to draft a replacement. In 1982, the government abandoned the idea of publishing a comprehensive code, and decided to draft a general collection of basic principles. This general part, the General Provisions of Civil law of the People's Republic of China (General Provisions), was enacted in April 1986, and went into effect in January 1987. Despite the fanfare with which

2. Article 355.
3. Article 363.
4. Article 221.
5. Article 224.
6. Article 222.

7. Article 207.

8. Article 222 Egypt; Article 225 Libya; Article 205 Iraq; and Article 223 Syria.

the General Provisions was passed, it is written in such broad abstract terms that it cannot be used directly to resolve any legal problems, except perhaps for the appointment of a guardian for an infant or a person of limited mental capacity and a few similar matters. Thus, the General Provisions may not be the "milestone in Chinese legal history" some have thought it to be. . . .

General Provisions of Civil law of the People's Republic of China

13 Rev. Socialist L. 357, at 361 (1987). William C. Jones trans.

(Table of Contents)

Article I: Basic Principles

Article II: Citizens (Natural Persons)

Part 1: The Capacity to Enjoy Civil law Rights. The Capacity to Engage in Civil law Acts

Part 2: Guardians

Part 3: Declaration that [a Person] Is Missing or Dead

Part 4: Individual Industrial and Commercial Households; Rural Contract Management Households

Part 5: Partnerships of Individuals

Article III : Juristic Persons

Part 1: General Rules

Part 2: Enterprise Juristic Persons

Part 3: Organizations, Institutions and Social Groups that are Juristic Persons

Part 4: Joint Ventures

Article IV: Civil law Juristic Acts and Representation

Part 1: Civil law Juristic Acts

Part 2: Representation

Article V: Civil law Rights

Part 1: The Ownership of Property and Rights that are Related to Ownership

Part 2: Obligation Rights

Part 3: Intellectual Property Rights

Part 4: Personal Rights

Article VI: Civil Responsibility

Part 1: General Rules

Part 2: Civil Responsibility for Breach of Contract

Part 3: Civil Responsibility for Trespass [Delia]

Part 4: Methods of Bearing Civil Responsibility

Article VII: Prescription of Actions

Article VIII: The Application of Law to Civil law Relations with Foreign Aspects

Article IX: Related Provisions

---

9.   An Example of the Adaptation of a Code-Based System to Technological and Economic Change: Tort Law and the Shift from Fault to Strict Liability

The following pages are intended to raise in more concrete fashion issues of legal change in a Code based system. In addition, this section will serve as a brief introduction to some aspects of tort law, a field that has become increasingly significant in international legal relations,[1] and will provide some comparative perspective to the discussions about tort reform in the United States. The reader should bear in mind that, as the outlines of the French and German Civil Codes reproduced have shown, tort law is not considered in civil law countries as a free standing field of law, but as part of a broader concept, that of obligations, which also includes contracts. Claims for personal injury or property damage can thus sometimes be based on contract principles, not only in the area of products liability, but in other areas as well.[2]

1.   Note in this context that tort law—and private law in general—represents but one way in which the victim of an accident or other wrong may obtain compensation. The intensity with which private-law remedies are pursued will be obviously less if automatic compensation for all or part of the loss, such as medical expenses and loss of earnings, is provided by social security schemes or similar official programs. For a general discussion, see W. Pfennigstorf & D. G. Gifford, A Comparative Study of Liability Law and Compensation Schemes in Ten Countries and the United States (1991). Cf. J. Reske, Study: Quayle was Right ... and Wrong: Entitlement Programs in Western Europe Help Accident Victims Avoid Court, 78 A.B.A.J. (June 1992) at 42; U. Magnus (ed.), The Impact of Social Security Law on Tort Law (2003); A.J. Sebok, What's Law Got to Do with It? Designing Compensation Schemes in the Shadow of the Tort System, Brooklyn Law School, Public Law Research Paper n. 3, available at SSRN: http://ssrn.com/abstract=508744; W.H. van Boom, M. Fauré (eds.), Shifts in Compensation between Private and Public Systems (2007).

In connection with the following tort-related materials, the reader should also be aware that it is possible to provide compensation for accident victims through a system that abandons tort concepts, as was done in New Zealand. See R. Mahoney, New Zealand's Accident Compensation Scheme: A Reassessment, 40 Am.J.Comp.L. 149 (1992); E.K. Solender, New Zealand Accident Compensation Law has some Unintended Consequences: A Caution to U.S. Reformers, 27 Int'l Lawyer 91 (1993); S. Todd, Privatization of Accident Compensation: Policy and Politics in New Zealand, 39 Washburn L. J. 404 (2000); W. Pfennigstorf, Accident Compensation in New Zealand: How Does It Work?, 6.4 Law & Social Inquiry 1153 (2006).

2.   Liability of various kinds of professionals is an example. Here courts have sometimes implied an "obligation of safety" (to persons and things) in the contract between the parties. On the "obligation of safe-

(a) The Basic Code Provisions

France

Article 1382. Every act of a person which causes damage to another obliges the person through whose fault the damage has occurred to provide reparation.

Article 1383. Everyone is responsible for the damage he has caused not only by his [intentional] act but also by his negligence or lack of prudence.

Article 1384. One is responsible not only for the damage one caused by one's own act but also for the damage that is caused by the persons for whose acts one must answer or by the things one has under one's control.... [1]

Father and mother, to the extent they have custody, are jointly liable for the harm caused by minor children living with them.

Masters and principals are liable for the damage caused by their employees and servants within the scope of the functions for which they have been employed.... [2]

[The only other provisions concerning torts in the French Civil Code are Article 1385, which provides for liability for animals under one's control or who have escaped, Article 1386, which provides for liability for harm caused by buildings due to defective construction or improper maintenance, and Articles 1386–1 to 1386–18 added to the list in 1998 to implement the European Directive on Product Liability. By the 1980s, there had been a limited amount of auxiliary legislation, dealing, e.g., with the liability for harm caused by ski lifts, airplanes, and nuclear installations, but nothing on automobiles. The following Civil Code provisions are also relevant, however as added in 2008]

Article 2224. A prescription period of five years applies in matters related to movable property and obligations, starting as of the date the plaintiff knew or should have known of the facts giving rise to the claim.

ty" (originally imposed on carriers), see Y. Lambert–Faivre, Fondement et régime de l'obligation de sécurité, 1994 D. Chr. 81.

1. The omitted lines deal with liability in the case of fire in a building.

2. Further paragraphs omitted; they specify that teachers and artisans are liable in a way similar to parents while the young persons concerned are under their control, but a 1937 amendment provides generally that parents and artisans are not liable if they can show they were unable to prevent the harm and, for teachers, liability exists only if the plaintiff can show some fault by them.

It had generally been assumed that the liability of the master did not exclude that of the servant; but see SA Parfums Rochas v. Mme Duchesne et autre, Cass.com., 12 Oct. 1993, 1994 D.J. 124 (with a note by G. Viney, indicating that decision changes the prior case law, though there were some indications this might happen). The case holds that the servant is liable only for "personal" fault, not when the servant remains strictly within the scope of the duties assigned.

Article 2225. Tort actions for legal malpractice including those due to destruction or damage of property entrusted to the representative are prescribed in five years from the end of the representation.

Article 2226. Tort actions initiated by the direct or indirect victim of an event that has created a phisical damage are prescribed in then years from the moment in which the initial damage has been realized or has worsened. Nevertheless whenever the damage has been produced by torture or barbarial acts or by sexual violence and aggression against a minor the tort action is prescribed in twenty years.

Germany[3]

§ 249. (1) A person who is liable in damages must restore the position that would exist if the circumstance obliging him to pay damages had not occurred.

(2) Where damages are payable for injury to a person or damage to a thing, the obligee may demand the required monetary amount in lieu of restoration. When a thing is damaged, the monetary amount required under sentence 1 only includes value-added tax if and to the extent that it is actually incurred.

§ 253. (1) Money may be demanded in compensation for any damage that is not pecuniary loss only in the cases stipulated by law.

(2) If damages are to be paid for an injury to body, health, freedom or sexual self-determination, reasonable compensation in money may also be demanded for any damage that is not pecuniary loss.

§ 254. (1) Where fault on the part of the injured person contributes to the occurrence of the damage, liability in damages as well as the extent of compensation to be paid depends on the circumstances, in particular to what extent the damage is caused mainly by one or the other party.

(2) This also applies if the fault of the injured person is limited to failing to draw the attention of the obligor to the danger of unusually extensive damage, where the obligor neither was nor ought to have been aware of the danger, or to failing to avert or reduce the damage. The provision of section 278 applies with the necessary modifications.

§ 276. (1) The obligor is responsible for intention and negligence, if a higher or lower degree of liability is neither laid down nor to be inferred from the other subject matter of the obligation, including but not limited to the giving of a guarantee or the assumption of a procurement risk. The provisions of sections 827 and 828 apply with the necessary modifications.

3. For a description of German tort law, see B.S. Markesinis, H. Unberath, The German Law of Torts. A Comparative Treatise (4th ed. 2002). For a general comparative description of the development of tort law, see C. van Dam, European Tort Law (2006), esp. 61–79; G. Brüggemeier, Common Principles of Tort Law. A Pre–Statement of Law (2004); Ch. von Bar, The Common European Law of Torts, I (1998), 25–27, 39 f., 58 f., 124 f.; F.H. Lawson & B.S. Markesinis, Tortious Liability for Unintentional Harm in the Common Law and the Civil law (1982).

(2) A person acts negligently if he fails to exercise reasonable care.

(3) The obligor may not be released in advance from liability for intention.

§ 823. (1) A person who, intentionally or negligently, unlawfully injures the life, body, health, freedom, property or another right of another person is liable to make compensation to the other party for the damage arising from this.

(2) The same duty is held by a person who commits a breach of a statute that is intended to protect another person. If, according to the contents of the statute, it may also be breached without fault, then liability to compensation only exists in the case of fault.

§ 826.[4] A person who, in a manner contrary to public policy, intentionally inflicts damage on another person is liable to the other person to make compensation for the damage.

§ 831.[5] A person who uses another person to perform a task is liable to make compensation for the damage that the other unlawfully inflicts on a third party when carrying out the task. Liability in damages does not apply if the principal exercises reasonable care when selecting the person deployed and, to the extent that he is to procure devices or equipment or to manage the business activity, in the procurement or management, or if the damage would have occurred even if this care had been exercised. [Paragraph (2) omitted]

The following provisions concern the liability of persons in charge of minors or mental incompetents (§ 832), liability for damage caused by animals (§§ 833, 834), liability in case of collapse of a building (§§ 836–838; § 835 has been abrogated), liability of public officials (§§ 839, 839a, 841), joint and several liability (§ 840), calculation of damages and wrongful death (§§ 842–846).

The following provisions (§§ 848–851) concern rates of interest to be used in calculating damages for loss of or damage to a thing and related matters concerning harm to property.

§ 852: If by a tort the person liable to pay compensation obtains something at the cost of the injured person, then even after the claim to compensation for the damage arising from a tort is statute-barred he is obliged to make restitution under the provisions on the return of unjust enrichment. This claim is statute-barred ten years after it arises, or, notwithstanding the date on which it arises, thirty years after the date on which the act causing the injury was committed or after the other event that triggered the loss. [§ 853 omitted]

---

4. The omitted § 824 deals with liability for spreading material that harms the credit or other economic interests of another and the omitted § 825 with liability for obtaining sexual intercourse with a person by fraud, the exploitation of a situation of dependency, or threats.

5. The omitted provisions deal respectively: §§ 827–829 with the liability of mental incompetents, minors and persons who are deaf and dumb; § 830 with the liability of a plurality of wrongdoers.

As to the time limits by which the law suit can be filed: (New Provisions)

§ 195. The standard limitation period is three years.

§ 199. (1) The standard limitation period commences at the end of the year in which:

— The claim arose, and

— The obligee obtains knowledge of the circumstances giving rise to the claim and of the identity of the obligor, or would have obtained such knowledge if he had not shown gross negligence.

(2) Claims for damages based on injury to life, body, health or liberty, notwithstanding the manner in which they arose and notwithstanding knowledge or a grossly negligent lack of knowledge, are statute-barred thirty years from the date on which the act, breach of duty or other event that caused the damage occurred. [Paragraphs (3), (4) and (5) omitted].

QUESTIONS

The provisions mentioned above are full translations or, where noted, at least summaries of the tort related provisions of the French and German Civil Codes. What may account for the difference in length of the two sets of provisions? Which of the two Codes would, on its face, appear to be more capable of adaptation to changed conditions? Which one would appear to be friendlier towards the victims of torts? Do any of the provisions cited appear to give an answer to some of the issues mentioned in the context of the U.S. debates on "tort reform"?

(b) Automobile Accidents

France

Articles 1382 and 1383 of the French Civil Code imply that liability in tort is based on fault, that is, intentional or negligent conduct. Article 1384 contains a number of limited exceptions to that principle in its paragraphs 2 and following, and so do Articles 1385 and 1386. The first paragraph of Article 1384 appears, on a cursory examination, to be merely an introduction to the provisions that follow, but without independent legal effect. Victims of automobile accidents, which had become fairly frequent by the 1920s in France, thus had to prove the wrongdoer's fault, a task more burdensome than in the United States given the absence of effective discovery devices. In the 1890s, the *Cour de cassation* had, however, given paragraph 1 of Article 1384 some independent significance by holding that a worker injured in an unexplained boiler explosion could obtain damages from the owner without showing fault on the basis of the first paragraph of Article 1384 since the owner was technically in control of the "thing," i.e., the boiler, but nobody had done anything to the boiler at the time of the accident;[1] it was thus quite generally assumed that the principle enunciated in the case could not be applied when something (such as an automobile)

---

1. Guissez v. Teffaine, Cass.civ. June 16, 1896, 1897 D. I. 433.

actually operated by a human being had caused an accident. The situation was radically changed by one of the most famous cases in the French *Cour de cassation*'s history:

Jand'heur v. Les Galeries Belfortaises

Cass.ch.réun., February 13, 1930, 1930 D.P.I. 57.

Facts: Plaintiff's daughter had been hit and badly injured by a truck belonging to defendant while crossing a street. Plaintiff sued and the trial court held that, pursuant to the first paragraph of Article 1384, the person in control of a thing was responsible for the harm caused by it without a need to show fault. The intermediate appellate court reversed on the ground that the first paragraph of Article 1384 could not be applied since the truck had been operated by a human agent and thus plaintiff's only remedy was to show fault under Article 1382. The *Cour de cassation*'s civil panel agreed with the court of first instance and remanded to an intermediate appellate court, which, in line with the then prevailing opinion insisted that Article 1384 could not be applicable in a case like this. There was thus a new appeal to the *Cour de cassation*. Under the then prevailing procedure,[1] the case was referred to the full bench (*Chambres réunies*) which rendered this opinion:

THE COURT: Whereas the presumption of liability established by the first paragraph of Article 1384 of the Civil Code against the person having an inanimate object that has caused harm to another under his control can be rebutted only by proof of an unavoidable and unforeseeable event [*cas fortuit*] or of an Act of God or of an external event for which the person in control is not responsible and whereas it is not sufficient [for the person in control of the thing] to show that he has committed no fault or that the cause of the harm-causing incident has remained unknown;

Whereas on April 22, 1925, a truck belonging to the Galeries Belfortaises company hit and injured the minor Lise Jand'heur; and whereas the decision under review has refused to apply the above-mentioned provision on the ground that the fact that the accident was caused by an automobile but that was in motion, steered and operated by a human being did not, since there was no evidence that it was due to a defect of the automobile, amount to damage done by a thing within the meaning of Article 1384, paragraph 1, so that the victim, in order to obtain compensation, had to show some fault on the part of the driver;

But whereas for the applicability of the presumption [of fault] which it provides, the law [i.e., Article 1384, Par. 1] does not make any distinction depending on whether the thing that caused the damage was or was not operated by a human being; whereas it is not necessary that the thing suffer from an inherent defect likely to cause the harm as Article 1384 bases liability on the control of the thing and not on the thing as such;

1. See *infra*, Chapter 6, Section 3(d), esp. p. 512, note 29.

Whence it follows that in ruling as it did, the decision under review has reversed the burden of proof and violated the statutory provision mentioned above;

For these reasons, reverses ... and remands....

NOTES AND QUESTIONS

The *Jand'heur* case was an obvious boon to traffic victims, so much so that it was not until fifty-five years later that it was found necessary to provide a statutory scheme for traffic victim compensation (see below). Even that legislation has only reduced, but by no means eliminated, its significance. Article 1384, paragraph 1, refers to "things," not to automobiles (not heard of until some ninety years after its enactment); the case here translated is thus relevant for all sorts of harm caused by a thing, and it is hard to imagine any kind of personal injury or property damage in which a "thing" is not involved. Cases applying the principle set down in *Jand'heur* are thus still an everyday event in the French courts.[1]

In spite of its beneficial effects for traffic (and other) accident victims, the case did raise several questions. Reread the case and French Civil Code Articles 1382–1384, *supra*, and try to decide whether the opinion, in conjunction with these articles, answers questions, such as these: 1) The plaintiff obviously does not have to prove fault on the part of the defendant, but does this mean that the burden of proof has simply been reversed, so that the defendant can escape liability by showing freedom from fault, or must the defendant prove more than that? 2) Little Lise Jand'heur was hit by a moving truck; would it have made a difference to the result if she had been injured while going to school on her bicycle and had bumped into the truck, parked while making a delivery? 3) There is nothing in the case to suggest that Lise Jand'heur was anything but careful at the time she was hit by the truck; but assume her own negligence had contributed to the accident, would the result have been the same? 4) Suppose, the driver of the truck, who was a relative, saw her hurrying to school on a rainy day and gave her a ride since his route passed by the school, but had an accident, in which she was hurt; could she recover without proof of fault? As can be imagined, these problems resulted in a considerable number of cases. Unfortunately, the *Cour de cassation* seemed to be swayed sometimes by arguments looking at these problems from the plaintiff's, sometimes by arguments looking at these issues from the defendant's side (can you think of some,

---

1. For a more recent, somewhat unusual, example, see Marché usines Samu Auchan v. Siegler, Cass.civ.2d, June 5, 1991, 1992 D.J. 409, where a store was held liable for the embarrassment to a customer when, because of a malfunction, the security device by the exit rang though plaintiff had no unpaid merchandise. The matter was cleared up quickly, but the *Cour de cassation* ruled the lower court had properly held defendant liable without a showing of fault since it had found that a "thing" (the security device) had been the cause of the problem. For a general discussion, see C. van Dam, European Tort Law (2006), 49–54; F. Werro, V.V. Palmer (eds.), The Boundaries of Strict Liability in European Tort Law (2004), 419–421; Ch. von Bar, U. Drobnig, The Interaction of Contract Law and Tort and Property Law in Europe. A Comparative Study (2004), 37–38; E. Tomlinson, Tort Liability in France for the Act of Things: A Study of Judicial Lawmaking, 48 La.L.Rev. 1299 (1988).

based on either the provisions of the Code, or on the language of the *Jand'heur* case, or on policy? Does the court mention any of these arguments?)

The resulting uncertainties increased the court's already excessive case load.[2] In addition, they made it much more uncertain whether traffic (and other) accident victims actually could obtain a recovery without proving fault.

A number of scholars reacted to that situation, mainly from the early 1960s on, by proposing legislation that would provide for some kind of no-fault system for traffic accident victims.[3] These proposals initially encountered some fairly strong opposition, especially from the bar, though they eventually had the support of the Minister of Justice in office in the early 1980s.[4] It was a decision of the *Cour de cassation* involving one of the issues mentioned in the questions above that appears to have finally encouraged legislation.

The *Cour de cassation* had traditionally held that, even in instances in which liability was based on Article 1384, not on Article 1382, the plaintiff's contributory fault led to reduced damages. The following case (known as *Desmares*) was a surprise.

La Mutualité Industrielle v. Epoux Charles

Cass.civ.2d, July 21, 1982, 1982 D.J. 449.

[Mr. and Mrs. Charles were hit by Mr. Desmares' automobile while crossing a street; in the resulting action, the first instance court divided the damages on the ground of plaintiffs' contributory negligence; the intermediate appellate court reversed and held defendant solely responsible.[1] On further appeal, the defendant argued for reversal on the ground the intermediate appellate court had failed to take plaintiff's contributory negligence into consideration. The Court first held that the intermediate appellate court's findings, from which a conclusion of no contributory fault could be drawn, did not suffer from any reversible error. It then noted the other argument of defendants, namely, that the intermediate appellate

2. See R. Rodière, annotation to Cozette v. Régnier, Cass.civ.2d, April 23, 1971, 1972 D.J. 613, where Prof. Rodière indicates that, at that time, France's highest court had about 2000 new tort cases annually. The author felt that in deciding these cases, the Court performed a kind of high-wire act, being pulled in one direction by the fault principle and in the other by strict liability.

3. Foremost among these was Prof. André Tunc, who coincidentally had provided a study of the French system of compensating traffic victims for the volume Comparative Studies in Automobile Accident Compensation (1970) of the U.S. Department of Transportation's massive Automobile Insurance and Compensation Study which was to furnish a basis for deciding whether federal legislation on the matter might be appropriate. See, e.g., for some of the English-language writings: A. Tunc, Traffic Accident Compensation in France: The Present Law and a Controversial Proposal, 73 Harv.L.Rev. 1409 (1966); A. Tunc, Traffic Accidents, Fault or Risk, 15 Seton Hall L.Rev. 831 (1985); A. Tunc, The French Law of Traffic Victim Compensation: The Present and the Possible, 31 Am.J.Comp.L. 489 (1983).

4. This was Mr. R. Badinter, subsequently also a President of the French Constitutional Council. When the traffic accident compensation statute was eventually adopted, it became, because of Mr. Badinter's support, known as the "Badinter Law."

1. The name of the case would seem to indicate that, because of the French "direct action" statute, the main defendant was actually Desmares' insurer.

court did not deal with the defendant's argument that the plaintiffs had been guilty of additional negligent conduct not covered in the intermediate appellate court's findings. On that argument, the Court said:]

But whereas only an Act of God frees the person in control of the thing which has been the instrument of the harm of the liability imposed by Article 1384, paragraph 1; accordingly, the victim's conduct cannot remove that liability or lessen it even in part, unless the victim's conduct was unforeseeable and totally unavoidable; and whereas the decision under review finds that the accident occurred at a time of heavy traffic on a four-lane highway, with the street lighting functioning normally when the plaintiffs crossed the highway from right to left while defendant was driving in the left most lane ... and whereas the findings show, that even supposing plaintiffs' fault was established, it did not, for Desmares, have the character of an unforeseeable and totally unavoidable event, so that the intermediate appellate court had, in any event, no duty to look into plaintiffs' possible contributory fault for the purpose of dealing with any division of damages, from which it follows that the intermediate appellate court has justified its holding;

For these reasons, [the Court] dismisses the appeal....

* * *

As noted, the *Desmares* was considered as somewhat of a shocker. By July 1985, a law on the compensation of traffic accident victims had been adopted.[2] The new law did not, of course, render the interpretation the *Cour de cassation* had given in that case of Article 1384 irrelevant in instances where automobiles were not involved. But less than two years after the adoption of the law, and within five years of its decision in *Desmares*, the same panel of the Court reverted to its original holding favoring a division of damages in the case of plaintiff's negligence contributing to the harm due a "thing."[3]

The 1985 law was intended to operate in conjunction with earlier legislation providing for compulsory insurance for automobiles and for a

2. Law No. 85–677 of July 5, 1985, concerning the improvement of the condition of traffic accident victims and the acceleration of the procedures for their indemnification, 1985 J.O. 7584, 1985 D.L. 371.

3. Mettetal v. Mme. Waeterinckx (and another case), Cass.civ.2d, April 6, 1987, 1988 D.J. 32. The court did not explain this double change of position within a period of five years, but in H. Capitant, Les grands arrêts de la jurisprudence civile (10th ed. by F. Terré & Y. Lequette, 1994) at 560–61, the editors add this comment to their reprint of the case:

How can one explain that a high judicial body reverses a venerable case law in order to come back to its original solution only five years later? What may appear [to the reader] as merely a regrettable lack of consistency can actually be understood only if one takes some distance and examines these decisions not by themselves but in relation to the statute. Far from being an aberration, they then appear as the expression of a deliberate policy: wanting to achieve a legislative change, the court set out to bring it about by what has been called a "decision meant to be a provocation" [citation omitted]. Once the result desired had been achieved, the court came back to its original solution. Clearly, one cannot find a better example of the interactions that operate sometimes between legislation and court decisions.

"Guarantee Fund" for victims of accidents unable to obtain compensation through insurance as well as direct actions against insurance companies.[4] The 1985 French statute in essence replaces, when it applies, the liability provided in the Civil Code;[5] nor does it limit the amount of damages, though such limitations were contained in the earlier proposals mentioned. The liability it imposes is, in some ways, similar to that based on Article 1384(1), but it eliminates most defenses available under the former case law concerning that provision. In particular, victims of motor vehicle accidents, other than drivers, may recover for personal injuries even if the accident was due to an act of God or of a third party, or the fault of the victim, unless the fault of the victim was inexcusable and the sole cause of the accident.[6] That exclusion too is inapplicable to minors under 16 years, the aged over 70 years, and the severely handicapped. The fault of the driver reduces the driver's recovery, or excludes it (if the sole cause of the accident), but drivers too can recover from the person "in control" of a vehicle if the accident was caused by an act of God or the act of a third

4. See Insurance Code Arts. L124–3, L124–4, L211–1, L421–1. Compulsory insurance for automobiles was made mandatory in the Member States of the European Community by a Council Directive of April 24, 1972, 1972 O.J. No. L 103, p. 1, since amended on a number of occasions. This Directive operates in conjunction with a Convention sponsored by the Council of Europe concerning the mutual recognition of insurance certificates and cooperation among automobile insurance carriers under which the victim of an accident due to a car from another country can obtain compensation by making a claim locally (against a local insurance association, if defendant's insurer has no local branch). How this scheme works is exemplified, e.g., in Bureau Central Français v. Fonds de Garantie Automobile, Case No. 64/83, February 9, 1984, 1984 E.C.R. 689.

5. M.-P. Camproux, La loi du 5 juillet 1985 et son caractère exclusif, 1994 D.Chr. 109 (thus the plaintiff cannot, instead of using the law, rely on defendant's fault under Civil Code Art. 1382). But in some regards, the point is not entirely free from doubt.

6. On that point (which does not apply to the driver, however), the *Cour de cassation* has held that the fault must be voluntary, unusually serious, and expose a person without valid reason to a harm of which he should have been aware; on the question whether a drunk pedestrian crossing a road qualifies, see the following case: on October 1986, L, fairly inebriated, went into the middle of a rural street in the hope of being picked up by a passing motorist, almost was hit by one, and then hit by another one who tried to stop abruptly but was hit from behind; the court of first instance held for defendant in 1988, saying the accident was plaintiff's own fault; the intermediate appellate court affirmed in 1990; the *Cour de cassation* reversed on June 5, 1991, apparently on the ground the victim's fault was not shown to be inexcusable; on remand, the court ruled (Cts. Larher v. Sté Harscoat, Cour Paris, March 16, 1994, 1994 D.J.277) that the decision of the court of first instance should be confirmed, the four elements of inexcusable fault were present: plaintiff entered a highway at night not inadvertently but to make a car stop, was aware of the risk since he almost got hit and put himself and others into danger; that he was drunk did not prevent him from knowing the risk as two weeks later he gave police a coherent report on what had happened. There was a new appeal to the *Cour de cassation*. In their brief opinion, the court's *assemblée plénière* restated the findings of the Paris appeals court but reversed, saying these findings did not indicate inexcusable fault. Cts. Larher v. Sté Harscoat, Cass.ass. plén., Nov. 10, 1995, 1995 D.J. 633 (with the "report" of the "Reporting Judge," Y. Chartier, analyzing in detail the previous cases and much of the commentary). The case (especially by the massive citations in judge Chartier's report) is a good example of some uncertainties left by the law—and of the delays caused by the French system of "cassation."

party. Persons who have brought harm upon themselves intentionally are excluded from recovery.[7] At the same time, the rules on compulsory insurance were amended to require that motor vehicle liability insurance cover also the liability of persons whose control of the vehicle was not authorized. When no other insurance is applicable, coverage must be provided by the uninsured motorist fund.[8] The liability insurer of the vehicle implicated in the accident must offer to settle claims made by victims no later than eight months after the accident. If the offer of settlement is not timely, interest is payable at double the legal rate. In the event litigation ensues, the judge may impose a penalty on the insurance company, payable into the uninsured motorist fund, and award additional damages and interest to the plaintiff, if he finds that the settlement offered was "manifestly insufficient."[9] In line with previous French practice, victims cannot recover for medical expenses which have, in fact, been paid by a health insurance organization under the French laws on social security, nor for wages which their employers have paid during their absence from work. But these organizations and employers have subrogation rights.[10] The new law has been criticized as inconsistent because it has not completely adopted no-fault principles, while at the same time not fully maintaining a system based on fault.[11]

In spite of the uncertainties inherent in the 1985 French statute, it has been imitated, but in a manner somewhat less favorable to victims, in Belgium.[12] A no-fault scheme for the indemnification of automobile acci-

---

7. Law No. 85–677, *supra* note 2, arts. 1–6. The statute also appears to resolve another problem which arose formerly under article 1384(1), namely, whether the article could be used when the object under the "control" of the defendant played a purely passive role in the accident, as when the operator of a motorcycle, who had made a turn too rapidly, was precipitated against a lawfully parked automobile. Under article 1 of the new law, liability is to be imposed whenever a motor vehicle is "implicated" in an accident. This would not seem to require an "active" role of the object. That construction appears in line with legislative history and had been adopted by early cases, but later ones seem to have taken a more restrictive view, but which the court relaxed again. See R. Raffi, Implication et causalité dans la loi du 5 juillet 1985, 1994 D.J. 158. Cf. Cass. civ.2d., March 23, 1994, 1994 D.J. 299.

8. Law No. 85–677, *supra* note 2, arts. 7–11.

9. Law No. 85–667, *supra* note 2, arts. 12–27.

10. Law No. 85–677, *supra* note 2, arts. 28–34. At times, insurers governed by the social security laws may also have a direct

claim (not based on subrogation) against persons having caused injuries to their insured. Association générale des institutions de retraite des cadres v. Cie Le Lloyd Continental, Cass.ass.plén., May 23, 1986, 1986 D.J. 341. Compare the rule mentioned in the text with variations on the "collateral source" rule in the United States. Does this say anything about policy preferences for lower health insurance or lower automobile insurance costs?

11. There were numerous comments on the new law soon after its adoption, e.g., Ph. Bihr, La grande illusion, 1985 D.Chr. 63; Ch. Larroumet, L'indemnisation des victimes d'accidents de la circulation: amalgame de la responsabilité civile et de l'indemnisation automatique, 1985 D.Chr. 237. For a book-length treatment on the basis the first ten years of its operation, see F. Chabas, Les accidents de la circulation (1995), reviewed by A. Tunc, 48 Rev.int.dr.comp. 221 (1996), noting Chabas' finding that the 1985 law has resulted in a substantial reduction in the amount of automobile accident litigation, in spite of ambiguities such as the one mentioned *supra* n. 20.

12. On March 30, 1994, Belgium adopted a law on automobile accidents some-

dent victims exists also in Québec; though it has some features resembling those of the French law, it is older. Originally based, like the French system, on private insurance, it is now administered through a governmental fund.[13]

Germany

Developments in Germany were rather different. Very quickly after the founding of the German Empire the rapid development of German industry seemed to make it desirable to provide protection to the victims of these new endeavors in a manner that was uniform throughout the country. The result was the Law Concerning Damages for Death and Personal Injuries Caused in the Operation of Railroads, Mines, and Similar Enterprises of June 7, 1871. It imposed on such enterprises a tort liability not dependent on proof of negligence. At the time of the adoption of the German Civil Code, which, as noted, went into effect on January 1, 1900, that legislation could have been incorporated into its the tort provisions, reproduced above, but this was not done; the law, although amended, is still in force as a separate statute.[14]

As applied to automobile accidents, § 823 clearly makes the defendant's liability dependent on proof of negligence, while § 826 does not cover such cases at all. In 1896, when the Code was promulgated, the automobile was still a *rara avis*, and the draftsmen of the above provisions surely did not anticipate the social and legal problems arising from widespread use of the automobile and the resultant slaughter on the highways. But within a decade after the date when the Code went into effect, the frequency of motor vehicle accidents in Germany increased quite dramatically, and it became apparent that the Code's tort provisions, embodying the fault principle, were not adequate to deal with the new problem. Indeed, one of the German Code's tort provisions created a problem for the plaintiff the French provisions did not: if an accident was caused by an agent or servant, then the principal was not automatically liable, for under

what modelled on the French law, but apparently inspired by a desire to reduce the cost to the social security system of medical expenses of automobile accident victims by imposing a greater burden on the car insurers. An amendment of April 13, 1995, included passengers in the coverage of the law. See B. Dubuisson (ed.), L'indemnisation automatique de certaines victimes d'accidents de la circulation. Loi du 30 mars 1994 (Brussels 1995), reviewed by A. Tunc in 47 Rev.int.dr. comp. 1047 (1995).

13. In 1961, Quebec adopted a statute providing for strict liability in automobile accident cases, but without a limitation of damages. S.Q. 1960–61, c. 65. That system was eventually abandoned in favor of a scheme under which automobile accident vic-

tims receive their compensation directly from an official insurance agency (*Régie*). Quebec Automobile Insurance Act, Quebec Revised Statutes 1977, ch. A–25 (effective 1978). The legislation putting the new Quebec Civil Code into effect made some conforming amendments. S.Q. 1992, c. 57, §§ 433, 434. Article 1465 of the new Quebec Civil Code has a provision similar to that of Article 1384 of the French Code concerning liability for things, but adds that defendant can avoid liability by proving that defendant is not at fault.

14. Re-enacted in somewhat revised form in 1978 (and amended in 2002), this auxiliary statute is now known under the shortened and simplified title of *Haftpflichtgesetz* (Liability Law).

§ 831, quoted above, the principal could avoid such liability by showing the servant had been carefully chosen and received adequate tools and appliances. Nor were there juries in Germany to informally "amend" the harsher aspects of the law. But the 1871 law was an indication of how a satisfactory system of strict liability could be created by a separate statute remaining outside the Code and thus not interfering with its internal consistency based on the fault principle.

In a relatively quick response to new problem of automobile accidents, the German legislature thus followed the existing statutory precedent and enacted an auxiliary statute dealing with liability for motor vehicle accidents.[15] The statute makes *the driver* liable for deaths, personal injuries, and property damage unless he proves that he was not at fault. At the same time, the statute imposes an even more stringent liability upon the "*Halter*," i.e., the person (usually the owner) who at the time of the accident was entitled to the use and control of the vehicle.[16] The latter can avoid liability only by proving that the injury or damage was due to an unavoidable event which was not connected with any defect in the condition of the vehicle or a failure of its mechanical parts. This heavy burden of proof can be met by the "*Halter*" only in exceptional cases, e.g., when he can show that the accident was caused *exclusively* by the victim,[17] by a third party, or by an animal, and that both "*Halter*" and driver used every reasonably possible precaution to avoid the accident.

Where the vehicle has been used without the "*Halter's*" consent, e.g., by a thief, the statute provides that in principle the former is not liable, unless by failure to remove the ignition key or by similar negligence he facilitated the unauthorized use of the car. There is, however, an important exception to this principle of non-liability for unauthorized trips. Pursuant to a 1939 amendment of the statute, the "*Halter*" is responsible for every accident caused by an employee to whom he has entrusted the custody of the vehicle. This responsibility exists even though the particular trip, in the course of which the accident occurred, was totally unauthorized and not within the scope of employment (e.g., a drunken joyride of the employee and his girlfriend).

Liability *under the statute* is restricted. The statute covers only personal injury, death and physical harm to property. In case of personal injury, equitable compensation can be claimed also for non-pecuniary losses. In case of death, the defendant is liable to pay damages to the third party

15. Motor Vehicle Traffic Act of 1909 (re-enacted in 1952 and 2003 under the title of Road Traffic Act), as amended in 2008. In 1922, a similar auxiliary statute extended the principle of liability without proof of negligence to the operation of aircraft. See Air Traffic Law of 1922 (re-enacted in 1968).

16. As a practical matter, every person "to whose house or business the car belongs," is apt to be treated as a "Halter." See

1 E.J. Cohn, Manual of German Law 165 (2d ed. 1968).

17. In cases where the victim's negligence is a contributing but not the exclusive cause of the accident, the amount of his recovery may be reduced, under the "comparative causation" principle (somewhat similar to our comparative negligence statutes) embodied in § 254 of the German Civil Code, quoted above.

towards whom the victim had a duty of maintenance. Liability *under the statute*, moreover, is limited in amount. The aggregate of claims arising from deaths and personal injuries caused by a single accident may not exceed a statutory maximum.[18] The amount of that maximum has been raised periodically since the original enactment of the statute.[19]

It should be kept in mind, however, that the statute does not preclude the victim from pursuing a cause of action under the general tort provisions of the Civil Code, pursuant to which an unlimited amount of damages, including an adequate compensation for pain and suffering, can be recovered if the plaintiff proves that his injury (or the death of his provider) was caused by the negligence of the defendant or of a person for whose fault the defendant is liable under the Code's general principles of vicarious liability.[20]

Where the victim is a passenger who gratuitously was given a ride in the vehicle, the liability provisions of the 1909 statute do not apply at all. Such a victim thus can recover solely on the basis of the Civil Code, i.e., only if he can prove negligence.[21]

By way of additional auxiliary enactments—again outside of the Civil Code—Germany has adopted a system of compulsory liability insurance and a direct action statute.[22]

(c) Products Liability

France

The absence of effective discovery devices makes the proof of fault particularly difficult in products liability cases even when, as in France, the liability of the master for the wrongs of the servant is not restricted. As in the United States before the impact of Section 402A of the Restatement of Torts, the courts developed a remedy on the basis of sales law, not tort law, however. Thus French Civil Code Arts. 1641, 1643 and 1645 provide:

18. It is interesting to note that the original German statute embodying this scheme was enacted in 1909, more than 50 years before the idea of no-fault liability was born (or reborn) in the United States.

19. The maximum amounts for property damage are considerably lower than those for personal injury or death.

20. With respect to automobile accidents, the German courts have mitigated the restrictive liability imposed on masters and principals under § 831, quoted above, by requiring proof of a high degree of diligence in selecting and supervising any employee entrusted with the operation of a potentially murderous machine such as an automobile. See Palandt, Bürgerliches Gesetzbuch § 831 (54th ed. 1995).

21. For a more extensive discussion of the German scheme, see Van Gerven, J.

Lever, P. Larouche, Tort Law (2000), 583–587. Another helpful description of the German scheme can be found in the report by W. Pfennigstorf which appears in U.S. Department of Transportation (Automobile Insurance and Compensation Study), Comparative Studies in Automobile Accident Compensation 33 (1970). For a discussion of a series of German auxiliary statutes providing for strict liability in certain situations, see C. van Dam, European Tort Law (2006), 77–78; Ch. von Bar, The Common European Law of Torts, II (2000), 368–373; M. Will, Quellen erhöhter Gefahr 2–39 (1980).

22. See Pflichtversicherungsgesetz (Compulsory Insurance Law) of 1939, re-enacted in 1965, as amended in 2007. The direct action provision appears in § 115 Versicherungsvertragsgesetz (Insurance Contract Act) of 2007.

Article 1641. The seller must warrant against hidden defects in the thing sold which render it improper for the use for which it is intended, or which reduce that use to such an extent that the buyer would not have bought it, or would have bought it only for a lesser price.

Article 1643. The seller is liable for hidden defects even if he did not know them, unless it had been agreed that there would be no warranty.

Article 1645. If the seller was aware of the defects of the thing, he is liable to the purchaser not only for a return of the purchase price, but for all damages.

The provisions quoted appear, on their face, to permit compensation for personal injury or property damage only in rather limited instances. In the first place, only the "purchaser" seems covered, but the French courts have extended coverage to any subsequent owner.[1] Furthermore, Article 1645 implies (and then Article 1646 states specifically) that only return of purchase price and repayment of expenses caused by the sale is required if the seller was not aware of the defect. This might have eliminated consequential damages, such as those for bodily injury, death, or property damage, but the French courts eventually came to hold that a seller in the business of selling goods of the kind involved in the case *must* know all defects and hence is always liable for consequential damages.[2] The plaintiff must show that the defect was in the product at the time it left the defendant's premises. If the person harmed due to a defective product is neither a direct nor a remote purchaser, the warranty for hidden defects may not be used as a basis for liability. Instead, liability must then be predicated on the fault-based Article. 1382. However, the courts have consistently held that a manufacturer is under a duty to know the problems inherent in his products and is consequently at fault if he puts a defective product on the market. Whether liability is based on Article 1641 or on Article 1382, there is not much difference in result.[3] Because of the requirement of control, Article 1384 has been used relatively rarely in products liability cases, except when it could be said that control had been retained by the manufacturer to some extent.[4]

---

1. See B. S. Markesinis, The Not so Dissimilar Tort and Delict, 93 L.Q.Rev. 78 (1977).

2. The rule was reinforced by Article L221–1 of the Consumer Code, providing that under conditions of normal or foreseeable use, products and services must have the qualities of safety one can legitimately expect and may not impair the health of human beings. Furthermore, the Annex to Article L132–1 of the Consumer Code, which voids "abusive" (unconscionable) clauses in contracts with consumers, includes, among presumptively "abusive" clauses, clauses which exclude or limit the legal liability of the (commercial) seller in case of death or personal injury.

3. There is, however, a difference between Articles 1382 and 1641 as far as limitation periods are concerned: under Art. 1648, liability based on Art. 1641 must be asserted within two years after discovery of the defect; for actions under Article 1382 the tort limitation period is now of five or, in case of personal injuries, ten years: Articles 2224 and 2226.

4. At times, courts have drawn a distinction between control over the thing itself (which the purchaser would obviously have)

Germany

Under German law, an injured consumer having no direct link with the manufacturer can sue the latter only in tort, that is, on the basis of § 823 of the Civil Code, which clearly requires fault and, as repeatedly noted, this is difficult because of the absence of effective discovery devices and because of the restrictive rules on *respondeat superior* of Civil Code § 831. In the 1960s, some younger German scholars, who had become familiar with American notions of products liability during stays in the United States, appear to have been particularly active in pointing out how unsatisfactory it thus was to adhere to the fault principle in this type of situation.[5] This time, however, change came from the courts, not through a special statute.[6] In the famous "Chicken Pest" case,[7] the *Bundesgerichtshof* held that once the plaintiff has proved that the defect which caused the damage arose within the manufacturer's sphere of interest,

> ... then the manufacturer is closer to the facts and he must clarify them.... He knows the circumstances of production, he determines and organizes the manufacturing process and the inspections when the finished products are delivered. The size of the plant, complexities in the organization caused by division of labor, and complicated technical, chemical or biological processes often render it impossible for the victim to find the cause of the defect which resulted in damage. He is therefore not able to explain the facts to the court in such a way that a court can judge whether the management should be blamed for an omission.... [Consequently,] if somebody uses an industrial product in accordance with the expected use and suffers damage with respect to one of the interests specified in § 823 par. 1, ... it is for the manufacturer to elucidate the events which caused the defect in the goods and to prove that they did not involve fault on his part.

The case thus reversed the burden of proof and required the manufacturer to show he was *not* at fault. Subsequent cases show that this burden is difficult to carry. Thus, liability has been imposed, e.g., on the manufacturer of a carbonated beverage when the bottle exploded, but also on the manufacturer of a beverage for babies sold in a special bottle capable of

and control over the thing's "behavior." See the note by Ch. Larroumet appended to Guilbert v. Dame Sekierzak, Cass.civ.2d, Dec. 15, 1986, 1987 D.J. 221. The courts have applied this principle at times when a thing had "its own internal dynamic," as in the case of bottles containing carbonated beverages which explode.

5. M. Will, Asides on the Nonharmonization of Products Liability Laws in Europe, in Harmonization of Laws in the European Communities: Products Liability, Conflict of Laws and Corporation Law 28–29 (Peter Herzog, ed., 1983)

6. See W. Lorenz, Some Comparative Aspects of the European Unification of the Law of Products Liability, 60 Cornell L.Rev. 1005, 1011–12 (1975).

7. Decision of November 26, 1968, 51 BGHZ 91; 22 N.J.W. 269 (1969). Interestingly, in a part of the opinion not translated here, the court uses the expression "strict liability" *in English*—some indication of American influence on the development of German products liability law.

being sucked for long periods of time, because of the resulting tooth decay.[8] While that liability is still formally based on fault, it thus comes close to strict liability.[9]

European Community Law

At times, changes in a codified (or other) legal system are due to factors other than internal developments (whether based exclusively on local ideas or on outside influences). Treaties or other rules of international organizations may also have that effect. In the area of private law, products liability is a good example. In a number of European countries, products liability was less favorable to consumers than in France and Germany. In Italy, for instance, a Code provision reversing the burden of proof in the event of harm caused by dangerous activities[10] has, in spite of some scholarly opinion favoring its use in products liability cases, generally not been applied in that context.[11] Fault had been the basis for liability in a number of other countries as well. Variations in European law were thus substantial. Feeling that this state of affairs impeded the free flow of goods across national borders and distorted conditions of competition by giving manufacturers in low liability countries an unfair advantage, the Commission of the European Communities proposed a Directive in 1976 for the harmonization of product liability law among the Member States.[12] The original proposal provided for strict liability for personal and property damage, subject to certain maximum limitations. Even harm not foresee-

8. On the "selters bottle" case, see BGH, June 7, 1988, 41 N.J.W. 2611 (1988); on the baby drink cases, BGH, Jan. 31, 1995, 48 N.J.W. 1286 (1995); and BGH, Dec. 12, 2000, 54 N.J.W. 964 (2001). The Court ruled in the latter case that, as the burden of proof was reversed, the plaintiff did not have to show the manufacturer knew about the possibility of tooth decay.

9. W. Lorenz, *supra* note 6. Cf. G. Brueggemeier, Perspectives on the Law of "Contorts": A Discussion of the Dominant Trends in West German Tort Law, 6 Hastings Int'l & Comp.L.Rev. 221 (1983). Additionally, liability may be based on the violation of a protective statute, for instance requiring manufacturers to produce only safe machinery for use at work. The Drug Law (*Arzneimittelgesetz*) of August 24, 1976, 1976 BGB*l* 2445, amended by a law of February 24, 1983, 1983 BGB*l* 169, imposes, in its section 84, strict liability on the manufacturers of drugs. Liability is limited to an amount of 500,000 German Marks per person, with total liability arising out of incidents concerning the same drug limited to 200 Million Marks. Japanese courts, operating under a Code provision akin to § 823 of the German Civil Code, similarly

have shifted the burden of proof. D.F. Henderson, Japanese Regulation of Recombinant DNA Activities, 12 U.Tol.L.Rev. 891, 899 (1981). For a brief comparative discussion of products liability law, see also Mr. Justice Marshall's opinion in Piper Aircraft Co. v. Reyno, 454 U.S. 235 at 252 n. 19 (1981).

10. Italian Civil Code Art. 2050. Exculpation requires a showing that everything possible to avoid the harm had been done.

11. M. Will, *supra* note 5 at 189; E. Rajneri, Interaction between the European Directive on Product Liability and the former liability regime in Italy, in D. Fairgrieve (ed.), Product Liability in Comparative Perspective (2005), 67 ff.; S. Biglieri, A. Pupeschi, C. Di Mauro, The Italian Product Liability Experience, in D. Campbell, S. Woodley (eds.), Liability for Products in a Global Economy (2005), 13 ff.; Ch. von Bar, U. Drobnig (eds.), The Interaction of Contract Law and Tort and Property Law in Europe. A Comparative Study, 207 (2004).

12. For the original proposal, see 1976 O.J. No. C 241, p. 9; 1976 E.C.Bull.Supp. No. 11.

able by the manufacturer at the time of manufacture (called by the Europeans the manufacturer's "development risk") would have been included. The proposal produced extensive comments; its provision for limitations on liability led to objections from consumer groups, the inclusion of "development risks" to objections by industry. Craftsmen and farmers wished to be completely excluded.[13] The Directive, when finally enacted in 1985,[14] maintained the principle of strict liability for product defects causing personal injury, or death, or property damage to non-commercially used property. It puts the burden on the manufacturer to show that the defect which caused the harm occurred after the product had left its premises. Non-commercial sales are not covered, nor are sales of unprocessed agricultural goods. The Directive does not mandate liability for "development risks," but the Member States may impose such liability. It does not contain a maximum limit of recovery for individual plaintiffs, nor any global limitation; but Member States are authorized to impose a global limitation of 70 Million Euro for personal injuries and death due to the same defect in the same kind of product. Property damage (to the extent covered at all) is compensable only if it exceeds 500 Euro. Suits must be brought within three years of discovery of harm and cause, subject to a ten year statute of repose.[15]

"Development risk" is an acceptable defense everywhere except in Luxembourg and, for medical products, in Germany and for medical and food products, in Spain. In most Member States, including Austria, Denmark, Finland, Germany, and Italy, the threshold of 500 Euro set forth by Art. 9 is treated as a "deductible", in that the amount of damages awarded to a successful claimant (for property damage) is reduced by the specified amount. In some other Member States, such as the Netherlands and United Kingdom, the threshold is treated as a minimum amount, such that, provided the claim exceeds that minimum, the full amount of damages is

---

13. Some of these criticisms are reflected in the opinions of the Community's Economic and Social Committee, 1979 O.J. No. C 114, p. 15, and of the European Parliament, 1979 O.J. No. C 127, p. 61, and were partially reflected in an amended proposal by the Commission at 1979 O.J. No. C 271, p. 3, which did not, however, eliminate the liability for "development risks."

14. Directive 85/374 of the Council on the approximation of the legislative, regulatory and administrative provisions of the Member States concerning liability for defective products, 1985 O.J. No. L 210, p. 29. The official English text of the Directive, together with translations, in whole or part, of the statutes of the Member States, which had, by 1993 implemented it, appears at 32 I.L.M. 1352, with (at 1347) an introductory note by S. Hurd & F. Zollers containing many references to legal periodical articles.

15. For comments on the Directive, in addition to the references cited by S. Hurd & F. Zollers, *supra* note 4, see J. R. Maddox, Products Liability Law in Europe: Towards a Régime of Strict Liability, 19 J. World Tr.L. 508 (1985); K. M. Nilles, Defining the Limits of Liability: A Legal and Political Analysis of the European Community Products Liability Directive, 25 Va. J. Int'l L. 729 (1985); J. J. Coe, Products Liability in the European Community, An Introduction to the 1985 Council Directive, 10 J.Prod.Liab. 197 (1987); P. Thieffry, Ph. Van Doorn & S. Lowe, Strict Products Liability in the EEC: Implementation, Practice and Impact on U.S. Manufacturers of Directive 85/374, 25 Tort & Ins.L.J. 65 (1985); D. G. Smith, The European Directive on Product Liability: A Comparative Study of its Implementation in the UK, France and West Germany (1990), 2 Leg.Iss. Eur.Int. 101.

recoverable. In Spain, the above amount of money is stated in the implementing legislation as a deductible but in practice the courts treat it as a threshold, such that the amount has never actually been deducted from any award.[16] Since the enactment of the Directive, the European Court of Justice has ruled several times on its interpretation, in order to clarify the meaning of notions such as 'damage' or 'put into circulation' and to judge the appropriateness of the national measures of transposition.[17] To decide whether to start a full-blown review of the functioning of the Directive, the Commission continuously reviews the efficiency of the product liability framework.[18] National rules (such as the German ones on the reversal of the burden of proof) concerning matters not covered by the Directive remain in effect.

NOTES AND QUESTIONS

(1) Does the information set forth above lead to any conclusions concerning the relative merits of code revision, auxiliary statutes, and case law as vehicles of reform?[1]

In some respects the French case law regarding the "custodian's" presumptive liability for motor vehicle accidents is strikingly similar to the rules laid down in the German auxiliary statute.[2] But the French courts, which until 1985 lacked the aid of the legislator, did not adopt (and clearly were unable to adopt by decisional law) the most refined feature of the German solution: unlimited recovery of all damages from the defendant when negligence can be proven; and amount-limitation as well as restriction to pecuniary damages in those cases in which the judgment against the defendant is based exclusively on the more modern doctrine of quasi-absolute liability for the risks created by the operation of the vehicle. Similarly, given the broad language of Article 1384, the French courts could hardly have developed a special system of quasi-strict

16. Report from the Commission to the Council, the European Parliament and the European Economic and Social Committee—Third report on the application of Council Directive on the approximation of laws, regulations and administrative provisions of the Member States concerning liability for defective products (85/374/EEC of 25 July 1985, amended by Directive 1999/34/EC of the European Parliament and of the Council of 10 May 1999), COM/2006/0496 final, 4.

17. *Ibidem*, 3, 5.

18. See R. Rice, A Question of Safety, Financial Times, Jan. 16, 1996, at 13.

1. As demonstrated by the above materials, it is clear that in many countries, especially those belonging to the European Economic Community, measures of law reform today are sometimes sparked by supra-national agreements and institutions. It is only for the sake of focusing the discussion on our present topic (structure and evolution of code systems) that the question formulated in the text has been limited to methods of change within the context of national systems only. But supranational or international legislation, when not directly applicable without any transformation into national law (as is true, e.g., of European Community Regulations, but not of Directives) raises the related issue whether such transformation should occur through special statute or through Civil Code amendment. Germany implemented the Products Liability Directive by special statute, a European Community Directive on equal treatment of men and women in employment by Code amendment (new Civil Code §§ 611 a, 611 b).

2. Cf. A. Tunc, Traffic Accident Compensation: Law and Proposals, 11 Int'l Ency. Comp.L. (Torts), chapter 14 (1983).

liability for motor vehicles only, excluding other accidents due to arguably less dangerous objects. Being based on a broadly-worded Code provision referring to "things" generally, rather than on a special statute, the judge-made rule of quasi-strict liability logically had to be applied to all things, of whatever nature, in defendant's custody. The German auxiliary statute, on the other hand, is clearly limited to motor vehicle accidents. The German statute thus contains a number of qualifications and limitations which could not easily be duplicated in a judge-made rule.

Even the brief outline of the relevant French case law which has been presented above demonstrates that the unsteady and vacillating course of the courts' decisions had an adverse effect on certainty and predictability of French law in this area. One may wonder whether this complexity and uncertainty is an inherent feature of decisional law, or is to some extent due to peculiarities of French legal method, especially the non-communicative way in which the *Cour de cassation* writes its opinions, of which two have been presented above, or to still some other reason.[3]

(2) As to problems concerning narrow fact situations, auxiliary statutes are, generally, the preferred tool. Thus it is not surprising that automobile accidents eventually became the subject of such statutes in both countries.[4] That the French statute was adopted so much later than the German one may have been due to both historical and political factors. When automobile accidents began to become a significant problem, the German Civil Code was still quite new. Its language had been carefully drafted and its tort provisions were clearly based on the fault principle. The previous significant departure from that principle, the Liability Law of 1871, had not even been incorporated into the Code.[5] Consequently, it would have been difficult for the German courts to impose strict liability for motor vehicle accidents by an audacious interpretation of the Code, and the enactment of a special statute seemed a plausible solution especially given the precedent of the Liability Law.[6] In France, on the other hand, the Code was over one hundred years old at that time. Article 1384 had already received an expansive interpretation and its extension to automobile accidents in the *Jand'heur* case, while a significant departure, was not an extraordinary feat of judicial activism. Besides, the broader nature of its tort rules obviously left more room for judicial activism than the much more detailed German ones. Following *Jand'heur*, there seemed to be no great social

3. Prof. Rodière appears to suggest that the reason in connection with Article 1384 may be that the Court was pulled by two opposing policy considerations: a) to insure compensation to accident victims, but b) also to leave part of the fault principle (which after all involves "moral" considerations too) intact. See R. Rodine, Annotation to Cozette v. Régnier, Cass.Civ.2d, April 23, 1971, 1972 D.J. 613.

4. The Italian Civil Code, in art. 2054, has a specific provision dealing with motor vehicle accidents, but the provision has been part of that relatively recent Code since its enactment in 1942.

5. See the discussion and materials on auxiliary statutes *supra* this section.

6. At about the same time the German statute was enacted, similar statutes were adopted in Austria and in the Scandinavian countries. See A. Tunc, Limitation on Codification—A Separate Law of Traffic Accidents, 44 Tul.L.Rev. 757, 759 (1970). The Austrian statute was reenacted in 1959 as the Railroad and Motor Vehicle Liability Law of January 1, 1959, 1959 [Austrian] BGBl 48, since repeatedly amended. Unlike the German law, it permits recovery for pain and suffering, but like the German law has a "cap," currently, for automobile accidents, about $200,000.

need for the enactment of special legislation dealing with automobile accidents. Indeed, legislation along German lines, with its limitations on liability, might have been perceived as regressive. On the other hand, the volume of automobile litigation in France was, as already noted, quite high.[7] This type of litigation was thus a substantial source of income for the Bar, and the Bar reacted on the whole unfavorably when the enactment of no fault legislation was proposed. Reform legislation thus had a chance for enactment only after the socialist electoral victory of 1981 put a person with a substantial interest in law reform in that particular area at the head of the Ministry of Justice. Moreover, confusion due to the refusal of many lower courts to follow the *Desmares* case had resulted in widespread dissatisfaction with the relevant case law. Even so, the French legislation was only a limited modification of existing law, especially if one compares it with a much more radical statute enacted in Quebec in 1977 against a quite similar Code background. That the long delayed and relatively modest character of French law reform in the automobile accident area has been due to factors other than opposition to strict liability based on legal principle may also be seen from the fact that in certain areas, such as the liability of aircraft operators, operators of cable cars and of nuclear installations, statutes providing for strict liability were enacted.[8] But the volume of actual litigation in all these areas was relatively small.

As to products liability, on the other hand, the problem began to be regarded as requiring special solutions only during the third quarter of this century, after European scholars had studied strict liability rules developed in the United States. The problem was not difficult for the French courts, which had become used to interpret many provisions of their (by then quite old) Code with great liberality. They solved it by imposing a rather far reaching liability on manufacturers, in part on a contractual basis, in part on a tort basis. Furthermore, by that time—more than fifty years after the enactment of their Civil Code—the German courts also had become bolder in interpreting the Code, and probably more receptive to the idea of using the law of torts as a risk spreading device. Thus the courts, acting on the basis of § 823 of the Code, were able to devise a reasonable solution of the problem of products liability, and to do so rather promptly once the social significance of the problem was recognized. This made it unnecessary for the legislature to tackle the politically sensitive task of formulating a broad rule of products liability applicable to all industrial processes until it was required by European Community enactments to do so.

Some subsequent developments in both France and Germany suggest an additional conclusion. Inertia also plays a certain role. Once a particular way of law reform has been adopted and has become familiar, subsequent problems are likely to be handled in a somewhat similar way. In France, AIDS tainted blood and blood products administered in particular to hemophiliacs had resulted in numerous illnesses and deaths, and a major political controversy as well. To provide compensation to victims, France adopted statutory provisions creating

7. See *supra* p. 462, note 2 and accompanying text.

8. See B. Starck, the Foundation of Delictual Liability in Contemporary French Law:

An Evaluation and a Proposal, 48 Tul.L.Rev. 1043, 1046–47 (1974).

a special Indemnification Fund to pay compensation to these victims.[9] As the tainted blood was supplied essentially through public or quasi public bodies, the Fund is financed by government contributions, so that insurance is not directly involved. Otherwise, however, there are substantial similarities to the 1985 automobile compensation scheme. In particular, no proof of negligence or other fault is required and there is no "cap" on damages. Suits by victims are not excluded, but somewhat like health insurance carriers in the automobile liability statute, the Fund then normally has subrogation rights. Conversely, when the environmental movement in Germany led to the adoption of several statutes creating liability for environmental harm, the statutes generally imposed strict liability, but with a "cap" on damages, while leaving open the possibility of a suit based on the Civil Code rules requiring proof of fault.[10]

One further generalization may be ventured. Whatever technique is used to adjust the private law of a codified legal system to changed conditions, the pertinent provisions of the Code always remain the all important point of departure. When decisional law is used as the vehicle of reform, it can be developed only by way of interpreting the language of the Code. And when reform is accomplished by way of an auxiliary statute, the statute must be fitted into the system of the Code; for the statute to work well, close attention must be paid to the interaction between the Code and the auxiliary statute.

9. See now Code de la Santé Publique, Articles L3122–1 ff. Although the Fund is, as noted, financed essentially by contributions from the State budget, its decisions are reviewable by the Paris intermediate court of appeals, not by the administrative courts, with further review possible by the *Cour de cassation*.

10. The principal statute is the *Umwelthaftungsgesetz* (Environmental Liability Law) of December 10, 1990 (as amended in 2007), effective January 1, 1991, 1990 BGBl I. 26343. See also the *Umweltschadensgesetz* (Environmental Damage Act) of May 14, 2007, effective November 10, 2007, 2007 BGBl I. 19 (allowing claims—without any cap on damages—for damage to "common" environmental resources (such as animals, plants, water, soil)). See generally, Scherer, Liability for Environmental Damage in Germany, 19 Int'l Bus.L. 309 (1991); M. Hinteregger (ed.), Environmental Liability and Ecological Damage in European Law (2008), 474–478.

CHAPTER 6

CASE LAW

1. THE HISTORICAL DIVERGENCE IN THE WESTERN LEGAL TRADITION

In his *History of the English Speaking Peoples*, Winston Churchill again and again drives home an important point: the focal role which the common law played in the process by which England was welded into a nation. It was the common law which brought about national unification of England's legal system. Neither a reception of a professorial "Roman" law nor a subsequent codification was needed in England to unify the law on a national scale.

The historical processes by which the leading continental countries attained nationally unified law differ in at least two respects from those to be observed in English history:

(a) In England, unification was accomplished by the Bench and the Bar of powerful central courts which succeeded in gaining the respect of the other centers of power, the Barons (the Parliament) and the King. Although they represented the central Government and wielded the tremendous power of judicial lawmaking which was the very source of the common law, the royal judges did not succumb to limit judicial arbitrariness, at least when adjudicating among the few that could afford to litigate at Westminster Hall.[1] Despite their formal role as representatives of the central government, their perceived independence from the Crown helped the common law and the equity judges to survive the regicide and the interregnum that eliminated the other royal prerogative courts such as the Star Chamber in criminal matters.

During the critical revolutionary period in English history, the Bench and the Bar of the common law courts successfully defended the law—their law, as they had created it and they were its institutional representatives—against attempts at modernization and the encroachments of the Tudors and Stuart Kings. "The law," which was a matrix of the writs of habeas corpus, certiorari, and mandamus, was perceived to favor the liberties of the subject, and was allied with the powerful landed interests represented in the Parliament during the constitutional crisis of the early seventeenth century.[2] In the eighteenth and nineteenth centuries, the common law

---

1. See Tunc, The Grand Outlines of the Code Napoleon, 29 Tul.L.Rev. 431 (1955).

2. Those courts, on the other hand, which did not follow the common law but operated without a jury and under the inquisitorial procedure imported from the continent (e.g., the Star Chamber) became the very symbols of oppression. English civil law-courts were able to align themselves with the forces which transformed England from a feudal agricultural society into a commercial and industrial nation. Thus the rule of law in England has always been on the winning side in great social transformations. England's legal institutions, still centered on a powerful and respected judiciary,[3] thus entered the modern age almost entirely without a violent break in continuity.[4]

By way of contrast, continental courts were unable to create nationally unified law. These courts could not attain the stature of the English Curia Regis due to the divisive struggles between ecclesiastic and secular power, and between overlord sovereignty and local or regional independence which characterize the medieval period in continental history.[5] In the absence of authoritative precedents set by a powerful central court, lawyers and judges had to turn to other sources of authority. Roman law was favored as such a source not only by the Church, which had absorbed much of the Roman system into its Canon Law, but also by the Emperor who under the theory of "Continuous Empire" claimed to be the legitimate heir of Justinian's imperial power and who could but benefit from the Byzantine doctrine: that only a written text approved by the Ruler was "the law." Nor were the other kings and princes of Europe, as much as their claims to power competed with those of the Emperor, averse to the absolutist implications of this doctrine, believed to be enshrined in the *Corpus Juris.*

The seat of Roman law learning was in the Universities. While in England the Bench and the Bar of the common law courts provided for the professional training of young lawyers practicing before the secular tribunals,[6] the continental rulers had to turn to the law faculties to supply them with men trained to become judges, lawyers and administrators. The Universities, in exchange for generous charters and privileges, willingly complied, and turned out large numbers of *doctores* who were well versed in Latin and in both Roman and Canon law. Thus it came about, as we

yers were tarred with the same brush. D. R. Coquillette, Legal Ideology and Incorporation I: The English Civilian Writers, 1523–1607, 61 B.U.L.Rev. 1, 77–86 (1981).

3. To this day, continental writers marvel at what many of them call the *Richterkoenigtum* (king-like stature of judges) prevailing in Anglo–American countries. See 2 W. Fikentscher, Methoden des Rechts 4–5 (1975). For an excellent comparative study, seeking to make the English system of administration of justice understandable to a continental audience, see E. J. Cohn, Richter, Staat und Gesellschaft in England (Schriftenreihe der Juristichen Studiengesellschaft Karlsruhe No. 37/38, 1958).

4. Even the Commonwealth was less disruptive in this respect than might be thought. S. F. Black, The Courts and Judges of Westminster Hall During the Great Rebellion, 1640–1660, 7 J. Legal Hist. 23 (1986).

5. True, there were similar struggles in medieval England; but relatively soon after the Norman Conquest, and several centuries before the emergence of a strong and stable national government in any continental country, the English kings gained the upper hand in their political and military battles against the centrifugal forces. See A. R. Hogue, Origins of the Common Law 19, 57–64 (1966). Thus, almost from its beginning, the English Curia Regis had a political power base far stronger than that of any court on the continent.

6. See Radcliffe & Cross, The English Legal System 387–90 (6th ed. by Hand & Bentley, 1977); Chroust, The Legal Profession During the Middle Ages: The Emergence of the English Lawyer Prior to 1400, 31 Notre Dame L.Rev. 537, especially at 579–81 (1956).

have seen before,[7] that a Roman-influenced, university-taught and university-developed *jus commune* became dominant (although perhaps in varying degrees) in almost every part of the continent. This domination (the exact period of which, again, varies from country to country) lasted for several centuries, from the middle ages to the late 18th and early 19th century.

During this whole period, continental courts failed to play a leading role in the development and the national unification of the law. True enough, when sufficiently supported by the political power of the local potentate, certain courts were able, for limited periods of time, to attract eminent men to the judiciary and under their leadership to assert real influence.[8] But this influence, while perhaps not strictly confined to the court's own territory, always remained relatively short-lived. The university still retained the monopoly of instructing the fledgling lawyers, and in their lectures and writings the professors paid scant attention to the decisions of contemporary courts. When they needed practical examples to illustrate their points, they generally preferred the rich casuistry of classical Roman law—i.e., disputes the facts of which had occurred about a thousand years earlier—over the cases decided in their own time.

Continental courts, moreover, never gained the prestige necessary for sustained leadership in the development of the law. By their Roman-canonistic, inquisitorial procedure,[9] by their failure to fashion legal remedies against official oppression,[10] and by their frequent obstruction to reforms desired by their own governments,[11] they lost popular support and respect.[12] In France, in particular, they became identified with the hated *ancien régime*, and with it, they were swept away during the French Revolution. The Revolution, at the same time, released strong feelings of nationalism. New national law and new democratic (or at least non-feudal) courts had to be created.[13] They were created *by legislation*. Not a court,

7. See *supra* Chapter 4.

8. As an example one might mention the Supreme Court, also called Senate, of Piedmont and Savoy during part of the 17th and 18th centuries. See the fascinating studies by Gorla, I "Grandi Tribunali" italiani fra i secoli XVI–XIX: un capitolo incompiuto della storia politico-giuridica d'Italia, published in Quaderni del Foro Italiano (1969), and Die Bedeutung der Präzedenzentscheidungen der Senate von Piemont und Savoyen im 18. Jahrhundert, in Ius Privatum Gentium—Festschrift für Max Rheinstein 103 (1969). See also G. Gorla & L. Moccia, A "Revisiting" of the Comparison Between "Continental Law" and "English Law" (16th–19th Century), 2 J. Legal Hist. 143 (1981).

9. See *infra* Chapter 8.

10. Frequently, the courts themselves were agents of the feudal system, and thus viewed as instruments of oppression. See,

e.g., Deák & Rheinstein, reproduced *supra* at 351.

11. See Riesenfeld, The French System of Administrative Justice, 18 B.U.L.Rev. 48, at 56 (1938), where further references can be found.

12. In Germany, the "Doctores" and their Latin jurisprudence always were felt to be a foreign-imported, non-German element. The importance of this factor is a matter of scholarly controversy. Probably it was the academic flavor of Pandectist law, and its inadequate procedure, rather than its foreign origin, which made it objectionable.

13. In other European countries, outside of France, the development was less violent and less abrupt (see Deák & Rheinstein, reproduced *supra* at 351); but the direction was the same. It must be remembered, moreover, that Napoleon's armies carried much of the spirit of the Napoleonic legal system across vast stretches of the continent.

but a code became the instrument and symbol of the national unification of law in continental countries. Historically, therefore, it is true, though perhaps an over-simplified truth, that the English common law postulates a law created by the courts, while to the civilian the court is merely a creature of legislated law.[14]

The common law had grown into a system at a time when men's ideas about law were still encased within rigid formulas. The eternal need for flexibility had to be met, at least in part, outside of "the law"; and this function was taken over by the Court of Chancery. The latter Court also served a political purpose by becoming a seat of countervailing power, used by the King as an antidote to the power of the common law courts. Thus originated the division between law and equity which is still one of the outstanding features of Anglo–American law.

On the continent, there was no central court possessing such independent power and prestige as to provoke the creation of another central court intended to constitute an antidotal or countervailing instrument of judicial power. Furthermore, we must again remember that modern civil law, i.e., code law, is essentially a product of the last two centuries, a period sufficiently free from ancient formalism so that the draftsmen of the codes have been able to combine both strict rules of law and broad equitable principles in a single unified structure.[15] Thus, there seemed to have been no need for a separate system of equity courts and of equity jurisprudence. The result is that the law-equity division is unknown in modern civil law.[16]

(b) Another significant difference between the English and the continental way of attaining nationally unified legal systems becomes apparent if we consider the time element.

The growth of the English common law has been a slow, gradual process which has continued from the time of William the Conqueror to this day. Therefore, the institutions of the common law bear the imprint of many different ages. On the other hand, each of the modern continental legal systems was shaped into a nationally unified structure at one stroke, by a more or less revolutionary act of codification.[17] Each code, consequently, breathes the spirit of the particular age in which it was born.

---

14. Viewed from a purely logical standpoint, this may sound like the story of the chicken and the egg. But logical or not, these historically conditioned attitudes are very real forces in a society. They produce important practical effects, of which the relatively modest social standing and the low rate of compensation of judges in many civil law countries may be mentioned as examples.

15. The broad, general provisions, inserted into the codes in order to assure flexibility and to provide for unforeseen and unforeseeable situations (see *infra* Chapter 9, Section 3 at 938, constitute the modern civil law counterpart of many of our "equitable" doctrines.

16. In classical Roman law there coexisted two bodies of law and of institutions which bore a striking resemblance to English "law" and "equity." See Pringsheim, The Inner Relationship Between English and Roman Law, 5 Cambridge L.J. 347, 357 (1935). See also, for a collection of interesting comparative essays on this matter Alfredo Rabello (ed.) Aequitas and Equity (1998).

17. Even in countries such as Prussia and Austria, where codification was not preceded by political revolution in the ordinary sense of the word, the codes of the late 18th and early 19th century were the result of a "revolution at the top," i.e., a revolution in

The influential codes of France (1804) and of Austria (1811) were products of the age of enlightenment and of rationalism. That was an era which extolled reason over tradition. The draftsmen of the codes sought reasonable rather than traditional solutions. True, the draftsmen were learned in and greatly influenced by, the laws and legal writings of the pre-code period; but traditional solutions which did not stand the test of reason, as seen in the light of the political and social views prevailing at the time, were eliminated without regret. The codes which thus emerged, were no mere restatements, but important vehicles of innovation.

The very idea of codification rests on the sanguine 18th century belief that the human mind could use reason to project the solution of future controversies in a systematic and comprehensive manner. The great legal compilations of older periods, including Justinian's *Corpus Juris*, the *Siete Partidas*, and the German *Sachsenspiegel*, had been restatements rather than codes. It remained for rulers and lawyers who understood the philosophy of rationalism, the teachings of the French Revolution and the practical needs of the 19th century to develop the technique of a true code, i.e., of a systematic, authoritative and direction-giving statute of broad coverage, breathing the spirit of reform and marking a new start in the legal life of an entire nation. This *technique* is still part of the civilian mentality, even in those civil-law countries in which the codes' *positive provisions*, adopted or revised at a later date, reflect philosophies of more recent vintage.

2.   CODE PROVISIONS RELATING TO SOURCES OF LAW

Austrian General Civil Code (1811)

Sec. 7: Where a case cannot be decided either according to the literal text or the plain meaning of a statute, regard shall be had to the statutory provisions concerning similar cases and to the principles which underlie other laws regarding similar matters. If the case is still doubtful, it shall be decided according to the principles of natural justice, after careful research and consideration of all the individual circumstances.[1]

the thinking of the rulers. See Thieme, Das Naturrecht und die europaeische Privatrechtsgeschichte, especially 17–18, 38–43 (2d ed. 1954), where the influence of natural-law philosophy upon the great continental codifications is traced and discussed. For a more general discussion of the intellectual and political forces responsible for the emergence and continuing importance of codes in many legal systems, see M. Damaška, On Circumstances Favoring Codification, 52 Rev. Jur.U.P.R. 355 (1983).

1. This provision must be read together with Sec. 12 of the same Code, which expressly states that a decision is not the source of law, and that its effect is not suitable for being extended to other cases. See Lenhoff, On Interpretative Theories: A Comparative Study in Legislation, 27 Tex.L.Rev. 312, 321 (1949).

Spanish Civil Code (1889)

PRELIMINARY TITLE: LEGAL NORMS, THEIR APPLICATION
AND EFFECT[2]

Article 1.

(1) The sources of the Spanish legal system are legislation (*ley*),
custom and the general principles of law (*derecho*).[3]

(2) Any norm that contravenes another norm of a higher order shall be
void.

(3) Custom[4] shall govern in the absence of applicable legislation,
provided it is not contrary to morals or to the public order, and
provided it is proved. . . .

(4) The general principles of law shall apply in the absence of legislation or custom, without prejudice to their informative function[5] in the
legal system.

(5) Legal norms contained in international treaties shall have no direct
application in Spain until they have become part of the domestic legal
system by being published in the Official Gazette.

(6) Judicial decisions shall complement the legal order with such
doctrine (*doctrina*) as the Supreme Court shall repeatedly establish in
interpreting and applying the written law, custom, and the general
principles of law.[6]

2. As the reader will recall from our
discussion of the *Shoop* case, *supra* at 178,
the preliminary title of the Spanish Civil
Code was revised in 1974. The present Art. 1,
reproduced in the text, *supra*, is the new
version of former Art. 6, quoted by the court
in the *Shoop* case. The new version is more
elaborate, but does not substantially change
the hierarchy of sources of law established in
old Art. 6.

3. While the Austrian Code speaks of
"principles of natural justice," the Spanish
Code uses the expression "general principles
of law." The two phrases are not synonymous. During the 19th century, the disciples
of positivism and of the historical school insisted that "general principles of law" could
be derived only from the *positive* norms of a
given *national* system, thus sharply differen-
tiating the "general principles" from natural
law. It was only in the relatively recent past
that a broader view of the notion of "general
principles of law" became predominant, partly in consequence of the fact that the same
notion has been used in Art. 38 of the Statute
of the International Court of Justice. See
Schlesinger, The Nature of General Principles of Law, in Rapports Généraux au VIe

Congrès international de droit comparé 235,
269 (Belgian Centre Interuniversitaire de
Droit Comparé 1964).

4. The Spanish word is *costumbre*. As
explained in the *Shoop* case, *supra*, *costumbre*
must be distinguished from *fueros*, which today are written sources of law in certain
regions of Spain.

5. Where there is an applicable written
law, general principles of law cannot be invoked as sources of law; but such principles
might still provide "information" (guidance?)
concerning the meaning as well as the structure of the written law (*ley*).

6. This provision appears to be an attempt to fit the notion of what was known
until 1984 as *doctrina legal* and is now called
jurisprudencia into the system of sources of
law. Whatever its precise nature may be, a
doctrina legal (jurisprudencia) in theory does
not have the same rank as the three
"sources" enumerated in subd. (1) of Art. 1,
and subd. (7) exhorts the judges to keep that
in mind. For biting criticism of this verbal
camouflage of the "most important" source
of Spanish law, see Serra Dominguez, in Valentin Cortes, Ed., Comentarios a la reforma
de la Fey de Enduiciamiento Civil (1985).

(7) In resolving the matters submitted to them, judges and courts always have the absolute duty to abide by the established system of sources.

Louisiana Civil Code

CHAPTER 1: GENERAL PRINCIPLES[7]

Art. 1: Sources of Law

The sources of law are legislation and custom.

Art. 2: Legislation

Legislation is a solemn expression of legislative will.

Art. 3: Custom

Custom results from practice repeated for a long time and generally accepted as having acquired the force of law.[8] Custom may not abrogate legislation.[9]

Art. 4: Absence of legislation or custom

When no rule for a particular situation can be derived from legislation or custom, the court is bound to proceed according to equity. To decide equitably, resort is made to justice, reason, and prevailing usages.

Code of Canon Law (1983)

Can. 19—Unless it is a penal matter, if an express prescription of universal or particular law or a custom is lacking in some particular matter, the case is to be decided in light of laws passed in similar circumstances, the general principles of law observed with canonical equity, the jurisprudence and praxis of the Roman Curia, and the common and constant opinion of learned persons.

Can. 26—Unless it has been specifically approved by the competent legislator, a custom contrary to the current canon law (*vigenti iuris canonici contraria*) or one which is beyond enacted canon law (*praeter legem canonicam*) obtains the force of law only when it has been legitimately observed for thirty continuous and complete years; only a centenary or immemorial custom can prevail over a canon which contains a clause forbidding future customs.

Can. 27—Custom is the best interpreter of laws.

Civil Code of Quebec (1994)

Preliminary Provision

The Civil Code comprises a body of rules which, in all matters within the letter, spirit or object of its provisions, lays down the *jus commune*,

---

7. This Chapter of the Preliminary Title was revised in 1987, effective January 1, 1988.

8. As stated in Revision Comments—1987, Comment (b) to this article: "According to civilian theory,the two elements of custom are a long practice (*longa consuetudo*) and the conviction that the practice has the force of law (*opinion necessitatis or opinio juris*).

The definition of custom in Article 3 reflects these two elements."

9. As stated in Comment (d): "Legislation and custom are primary sources of law. Article 1, *supra*. However as in all codified systems, legislation is the superior source of law in Louisiana." Do you agree with the reference to *all* codified systems?

expressly or by implication. In these matters, the Code is the foundation of all other laws, although other laws may complement the Code or make exceptions to it.

Swiss Civil Code (1907)

Art. 1: The Code governs all questions of law which come within the letter or the spirit of any of its provisions.

If the Code does not furnish an applicable provision, the judge shall decide in accordance with customary law, and failing that, according to the rule which he would establish as legislator.

In this he shall be guided by approved legal doctrine (Fr: *doctrine*) and judicial tradition (Fr: *jurisprudence*).[10]

Civil Code of Iraq (1951, Eff. 1953)

Article I

Section 1. The code governs all questions of law which come within the letter or spirit of any of its provisions.

Section 2. If the Code does not furnish an applicable provision, the court shall decide in accordance with customary law, and failing that, in accordance with those principles of Muslim law (Shari'a) which are most in keeping with the provisions of this Code, without being bound by any particular school of jurisprudence, and failing that, in accordance with the principles of equity.

Section 3. In all of this, the Court shall be guided by judicial decisions and by the principles of jurisprudence in Iraq and in foreign countries whose laws are similar to those of Iraq.[11]

Usatorre v. The Victoria

United States Court of Appeals, Second Circuit, 1949.
172 F.2d 434.

[The Victoria was an Argentine tank vessel, flying the Argentine flag, and owned by the appellant, an Argentine corporation. Five of the crew

---

10. Concerning the doctrinal antecedents of this famous article of the Swiss Code, see J. Mayda, Gény's Méthode After 60 Years (Introduction to the English translation of Gény, Method of Interpretation and Sources of Private Positive Law (2d ed. 1963) passim, especially at xlii ff).

The Swiss courts have shown restraint in using the broad powers conferred upon them by Art. 1. See A. E. von Overbeck, Some Observations on the Role of the Judge Under the Swiss Civil Code, 37 La.L.Rev. 681 (1977). The classic study remains Arthur Meier–Hayoz, Der Richter als Gesetzgeber (1951).

11. The "foreign countries whose laws are similar to those of Iraq" are said to be Syria, Egypt, and France. Jwaideh, The New Civil Code of Iraq, 22 Geo.Wash.L.Rev. 176, 181 (1953).

were Spaniards, three Portuguese and the others Argentineans. They all signed articles at Buenos Aires for a voyage to Edgewater, New Jersey, and the return. At about 6:50 P.M. on April 17, 1942, when 360 miles from New York and 300 miles off the coast, the Victoria was struck by a torpedo which tore a hole about 25 feet in width and 25 feet in height under the water line on her port side near the bow, opening up tanks 1 and 2. The captain ordered the life-boats to be made ready for use and ordered the chief officer and some members of the crew to board life-boat No. 1, which was launched and made fast to the Victoria.

At about 8 P.M. she was struck again by a second torpedo, which tore another hole about 25 feet wide and 25 feet high under her water line near her stern, opening up tanks No. 6 and No. 7. The captain thereupon ordered the ship to be abandoned and he and the seventeen remaining members of the crew left in life-boat No. 2.

Thereafter the life-boats were rowed or sailed away until they lost sight of the vessel and each other. Shortly after 2 A.M., April 18, 1942, the United States destroyer Owl sighted the Victoria. At about 8 A.M. she went alongside the drifting derelict and placed aboard eight men who got her under way for a short distance. At about 7 A.M. April 19, the Owl picked up life-boat No. 1, transferred the crew to the Victoria and returned the eight men to the Owl, leaving the Victoria in command of her chief officer. At about 11 A.M., the Victoria, escorted by the Owl, got under way for New York under her own power. At 6 P.M., April 19, the U.S. destroyer Nicholson picked up life-boat No. 2 and transferred her crew to the Victoria. At about 10 A.M., April 20, the Owl was relieved by the Navy tug, Sagamore, which continued to escort the Victoria until port was reached.

Some of the crew libeled the Victoria for salvage claims, and the action was tried in the District Court for the Southern District of New York, where the libellants were successful.[1] The trial court held that the jus gentium applied, and not the law of Argentina, and that under the jus gentium the bona fide abandonment of the ship by the master and crew without any hope or intention of returning terminated the voyage and the contractual services of the seamen. The court reasoned that, although ordinarily seamen are not entitled to salvage awards for saving their own ship, because that service is part of their duty, yet they do become entitled thereto when their ship has been abandoned in good faith without any hope of recovery.[2] The court awarded each crew member $500. The shipowner appeals.]

Before L. HAND, CHIEF JUDGE, and CHASE and FRANK, CIRCUIT JUDGES.

■ FRANK, CIRCUIT JUDGE.[3] 1. If, as the trial judge held, the jus gentium applies, then, regarding the decisions of our courts as reflecting it, libellants would seem clearly to be salvors. According to those decisions,

---

1. The prior history of this litigation is discussed in Note, 28 Cornell L.Q. 69 (1942).

2. On the question of salvage by the vessel's own crew, see Robinson on Admiralty

724 (1939); Gilmore & Black, The Law of Admiralty 541–43 (2d ed. 1975).

3. The Court's footnotes are omitted.

abandonment by the master, in the face of what he deems a disaster, without expectation of returning, severs the crew's employment contract even if, subsequently, the vessel turns out to be safe and the crew then returns. That rule would apply here.

. . . .

2.   But while the district court had discretion to take jurisdiction, and that discretion has been said to be justified "because salvage is a question arising under the jus gentium and does not ordinarily depend on the municipal laws of particular countries," we think that whether on the facts as found, the crew were "released from any obligation to exert themselves for the benefit of the vessel," must be determined as a matter of the "internal economy" of the ship, by the Argentine law, the "law of the flag."

3.   For us, Argentine law is a fact. With respect to that fact, defendant introduced the testimony of an expert witness.[4] He is an American and a member of the New York Bar, and of the Bars of Cuba and Puerto–Rico. He studied civil law for forty years. He has a degree of Doctor of Civil Laws from the University of Havana. He was a judge in Puerto Rico for seven years, and a member for two years of a commission that drafted new legislation for Cuba. He has studied Argentine law, and is the author of a digest of that law appearing in the Martindale–Hubbell Law Directory. He has not practiced admiralty or maritime law anywhere, but has "occasionally given advice on maritime law" in Latin–American countries. He is authorized to practice in no Latin–American countries except Cuba, but can give advice in other such countries.

He testified that Article 929 of the Argentine Code of Commerce reads: "A captain is forbidden to abandon his ship, whatever may be the danger, except in case of shipwreck." He also said that the pertinent portions of the Code relating to termination of the employment contract between seamen and their ship are contained in Articles which provide that the contract is terminated in the case of "any disaster happening to the vessel which absolutely renders it incapable of navigation." According to the expert witness, this means that the captain's judgment that the vessel is in such condition is not conclusive, but that the sole test is the actual objective fact as to the ship's condition. ("The final decision is the fact of whether the vessel remained fitted for navigation.") It was the witness' opinion that, on the facts here, under Argentine law the libellants' contract was not ended when the captain ordered them to abandon the ship, although the men were obliged to obey that order.

According to this witness, Latin–American courts pay little attention to court decisions as precedents. He had found "practically nothing" by way of decisions of the Supreme Court of the Argentine bearing on the Code provisions in question, in part because of the difficulty of finding such

4. Otto Schoenrich, among other things, the translator of the Mexican Civil Code.

decisions since they are "badly indexed" or "digested."[5] He relied, as, he said, Argentine lawyers do, on the "commentators," especially including the French commentators because, he said, the Argentine Code of Commerce is based on the French law. Where there was a difference of opinion between commentators, he had made a choice. In his testimony, he cited no commentators, but merely gave his interpretation of united commentators' interpretations of the Code.

The judge is not bound to accept the testimony of a witness concerning the meaning of the laws of a foreign country, especially when, as here, the witness had never practiced in that country. Moreover, as defendant says in its brief, this witness "relied strictly upon the Code provisions." As already noted, he gave little or no attention to Argentine decisional material. We have no knowledge of Argentine "law," nor more than a vague acquaintance with the judicial methods there prevailing. But casual readings of readily available material clearly indicate that, in all civil-law countries, despite conventional protestations to the contrary, much law is judge-made, and the courts are by no means unaffected by judicial precedents or "case law" (which the civilians call "jurisprudence," as distinguished from the interpretation of text-writers or commentators, called "doctrine"). Recaséns Siches, a widely respected professor of law in Spain for many years, now in Mexico, recently wrote: "Now jurisprudence, that is, the decisions of the courts, has had the part of greatest protagonist in the formation of the law; and, although in much less volume, it continues today of great importance." "Both the slavish obedience of [civilian] judges to codes, and their freedom from precedent are largely a myth," writes Friedmann. "In truth, while there is greater freedom towards the provisions of codes, there is also much greater respect for judicial authority than imagined by most Anglo–American lawyers." A recent treatise by Cossio, a distinguished Argentine lawyer, shows that this attitude prevails in the Argentine.

The expert witness' adherence to the literal words of the code may have caused the trial judge to question his conclusions. For, we are told, the civilians, influenced by an interpretative theory which derives from Aristotle (and which has affected Anglo–American practice as well) are accustomed to interpret their statutory enactments "equitably," i.e., to fill in gaps, arising necessarily from the generalized terms of many statutes, by asking how the legislature would have dealt with the "unprovided case." In civil-law countries, "there are countless examples of judicial interpretation of statutes ... which gave the statutory interpretation a meaning either not foreseen by or openly antagonistic to the opinions prevailing at the time of the Code, but in accordance with modern social developments or trends of public opinion. This attitude finds expression in Art. I of the Swiss Civil

---

5. A scholar familiar with the law of Argentina recently remarked: "Of all the Hispano–American countries, Argentina has the best developed system of reporting, publishing and indexing case decisions." R. C. Casad, Unjust Enrichment in Argentina: Common Law in a Civil Law System, 22 Am.J.Comp.L. 757, at 783 (1974). This observation perhaps throws doubt on some of the statements made by the expert in the principal case; but note that Professor Casad's article was written in 1974, while the principal case was litigated in the 1940s.

Code [of 1907] which directs the judge to decide as if he were a legislator, when he finds himself faced with a definite gap in the statute."[6]

In a colloquy which occurred after the judge had filed his opinion, he expressed himself as in disagreement with the witness' interpretation of the Code. But doubtless because the judge thought the jus gentium governed, he did not make a finding as to Argentine law. We must therefore reverse and remand for such a finding. Perhaps it can be made without further testimony on the subject. It may be that, if he considers it desirable, some arrangement will be agreed upon which will enable the judge to summon an expert of his own choosing.[7]

. . . .

Reversed and remanded.[8]

NOTES AND QUESTIONS

(1) Do you share the District Court's and the appellate court's skepticism concerning the correctness of the expert's opinion? If so, does your skepticism spring from the same reasons as Judge Frank's? Consider the following: In Yone Suzuki v. Central Argentine Ry., 27 F.2d 795 (2d Cir.1928), the defendant railway, relying on Argentinian law, had actually produced an Argentinian Court of Appeals decision in another case ("the Moncalieri case") which it claimed to be controlling. Although Argentinian law was in the end not held applicable, the Court had this to say:

> The decree in the Moncalieri Case stands alone in contradiction to the settled maritime law elsewhere. It is not a decision of a court whose opinions express in any controlling way the law of Argentine, for there are a number of divisional courts there of equal weight, all of which administer the civil law, and none of which is in any sense bound by judicial precedent. The mere fact that they naturally may be influenced by former decisions and may finally accept them, when their logic becomes persuasive, is not a reason for regarding a single decision that goes counter to universal maritime law as authoritative as to the law of Argentine, or as binding on other courts. No Circuit Court of Appeals in this country of precedents would feel obliged to follow another circuit in similar circumstances, or to follow the decision of a state court that was not supreme in interpreting state law.

(2) Concerning the reasons which Judge Frank gives for his doubts as to the expert's testimony, the following questions, among others, suggest themselves:

---

6. Quotation from Friedmann, Legal Theory 294 (1944). In the 5th (1967) edition of Friedmann's book the relevant material appears at 533–35.

7. Concerning court-appointed experts, see also *infra* Chapter 8, Section 3(h) at 795.

8. It seems that following this reversal and remand the libellants discontinued the action. See Nussbaum, Proving the Law of Foreign Countries, 3 Am.J.Comp.L. 60, 64 (1954). Perhaps they had received discouraging advice from an expert on Argentine law. More likely, they gave up because of their financial inability to procure the necessary trial testimony of such an expert.

(a) Is it permissible to cite Art. 1 of the Swiss Civil Code as indicative of the spirit permeating a Latin–American code largely modeled upon the French? Even though the court was unwilling (and at that time perhaps powerless) to take judicial notice of specific rules of Argentine law, should it not have noticed that the Argentine Civil Code contains general directions relating to methods and sources of law,[1] and that these directions are quite inconsistent with Art. 1 of the much more modern Swiss Code?

(b) Should civil-law theories of interpretation which grew up principally in connection with the codes' "general clauses" and with gaps in the written law, be resorted to in applying code provisions as specific as those involved in the Usatorre case?

3.   THE MODERN ORGANIZATION OF JUSTICE: THE INSTITUTIONAL SETTING OF CASE LAW

The modern age necessity to rationalize the legal system affected England as well as the Continent. Through the 18th century the degree of discontent for the archaic functioning of the *writ* system of procedure and for the complexities created by the excessive number of courts became a serious political problem. Jeremy Bentham, who, at age fourteen, had been a student in the first English law course offered by Blackstone at Oxford, had been particularly vocal in his critique of the common law and in his crusade for French style codification. Although Bentham was not successful in his own country, codification inspired by him has been successfully adopted in India, and, in the US, the Field Codes (rejected in NY but adopted in California) were certainly inspired by the great utilitarian philosopher. In any event, thanks to Bentham, reform successfully entered the English agenda. While in the continental academic tradition it was just natural to attempt rationalization by tackling substantive law, in the common law tradition, any successful attempt had to begin with the organization of justice, because the procedurally driven common law tradition had its most important legal formant in the judiciary.

In 1873, the liberal government of the time attempted a new hierarchical organization of the common law, equity, and residual civilian courts (Probate, Admiralty etc.), whose jurisdictional relationship had been randomly settled by the accidents of centuries-old competition for jurisdiction. Within this rationalization effort, culminating in the so-called Judicature Acts of 1873–1875, the Government also attempted to introduce some degree of separation of power by taking away the jurisdictional capacity that the (hereditary) House of Lords had been able to seize centuries before by offering a sort of final extraordinary justice.

Justice was thus organized into one single *Supreme Court of Judicature* divided into two layers: a *High Court* of general jurisdiction divided

---

1. See Ireland, Precedents' Place in Latin Law, 40 W.Va.L.Q. 115, 130–34 (1934); A. P. Blaustein, Legislative Interpretation and the Foreign Codes, 16 J.Legal Educ. 317, 318 (1964).

into three branches: *King's bench division* for the common law; *Chancery division* for Equity and *Probate Divorce and Admiralty Division* (re-named *Family division* in 1970) for all the residual civilian jurisdictional matter. At the top a single *Court of Appeals* would entertain appeals. This blunt re-organization only lasted three years because, regaining power in 1876, the Conservative government granted jurisdiction back to the House of Lords setting it at the top of the judicial pyramid. However, the Appellate Jurisdiction Act of 1876 did not grant back the jurisdiction to the entire hereditary Branch of Parliament, but, to the contrary, restricted it to high profile common law lawyers, the *Lords of Appeals in Ordinary*, elevated to peerage because of legal excellence. This three tier hierarchy (though the House of Lords has recently been renamed *Supreme Court*),[1] is the current arrangement, within which the strict hierarchical theory of *stare decisis* unfolded as a relatively recent development of the common law tradition.

Modern civil-law systems, like their English counterpart, have centralized jurisdiction and have organized themselves on one or more court hierarchies. Thus, some knowledge on such organization might be particularly useful in approaching materials on the rather important role of case law in civil-law practice.

In civil law countries, there are generally at least two hierarchies of courts: one dealing with ordinary civil and criminal cases and another with public law disputes, such as governmental licenses, tax matters, and other such cases. Some countries have more. The boundaries between the hierarchies are not the same in every country, making a comparative analysis extremely complex.[2] Public law matters have nowhere been "codified" in the sense of the term with which we are now familiar. Developments in public law have been produced either by "special statutes" or, most importantly, by case law evolution. This is a point to keep in mind when attempting to generalize the fundamental differences between the common and civil law. Too often, comparative law scholarship, in emphasizing differences, has neglected this "other half of the moon" (that of the public law) in its study of the respective role of codes and of "judge made law" in the common and civil-law systems.

(a) Courts of First Instance

Some civil-law countries have special courts for handling smaller criminal and civil cases. For example, in France, the *tribunal d'instance* has subject matter jurisdiction in cases involving up to 10,000 euro, and, in

---

1. Ministry of Justice, http://www.justice.gov.uk/whatwedo/supremecourt.htm (last visited January 13, 2009).

2. Because social security schemes are often not directly administered by a governmental agency but by semi-public bodies with employer and employee representation, the, usually fairly voluminous, litigation concerning such matters frequently goes not to the courts for administrative matters, but, as in Germany, to a wholly separate system of courts or, as in France, to specialized tribunals in the first instance, with subsequent review in the regular courts. Some further variations can only be explained by historical factors. In spite of the eminently public law nature of tax law, in France, income tax matters go to the administrative courts, while matters concerning indirect taxes and customs duties go to the regular courts.

Germany, the Local Court (*Amtsgericht*) has subject matter jurisdiction in cases involving up to 5,000 euro.[1] With the caseloads of the higher courts increasing, there has been a tendency to increase the monetary jurisdiction of this lowest level of courts.

In order to bring the courts closer to the people, a 2006 French statute created an even lower level of courts dealing with cases below 4,000 Euro and with cases involving minor criminal offenses. The *juridiction de proximité* is composed of one non-professional judge recruited from civil society who, in addition to some age requirements, must have experience of at least 25 years in a private or public legal service. The appointment is for a non-renewable term of 7 years. There is one such court in the jurisdiction of every court of appeals. If the non-professional judge encounters a difficult legal issue with respect to the application of a legal rule or the interpretation of a disputed contract, he or she can refer the case to the *tribunal d'instance*.[2]

Cases beyond the jurisdiction of the lower court (10,000 euro in France and 5,000 euro in Germany) are adjudicated by a court of first instance of general jurisdiction, unless the subject matter is assigned to specialized courts (such as commercial, labor, or other courts that may exist in some countries).[3] In many countries, that court also hears appeals from the court of limited jurisdiction. The court of general jurisdiction is called Regional Court (*Landgericht* in Germany and *Landesgericht* in Austria) and *tribunal de grande instance* in France. In France, appeals from the lower level courts go directly to the intermediate appellate courts and not to the courts of first instance of general jurisdiction, but the possibility of making exceptions to that rule by decree remains open.[4] There is usually one court in each judicial district of a country, which may or may not be coterminous with one of the country's administrative subdivisions.

While these countries typically have courts fixed in one place, the French Code of Judicial Organization provides for a particular exception. As a function of the local necessities, all courts can hold *audiences foraines*, or sessions elsewhere than at their formal seat. The first president of the court of appeals (and after the advice of the *procureur general*) fixes the place, date, and nature of this audience.[5]

Traditionally and particularly in Europe, these courts sit in panels of three judges, usually referred to in English somewhat confusingly as "chambers." The number of panels will vary from court to court, depend-

1. See the French Code of Judicial Organization (*Code de l'organisation judiciaire*), art. L221–4 and the German Law on Court Organization (*Gerichtsverfassungsgesetz*) § 23.1. See P. Murray & R. Stürner, *German Civil Justice* 48 (2004).

2. See the French Code of Judicial Organization (arts. L231–1—L232–3).

3. In Belgium, for example, all cases dealing with traffic accidents are adjudicated by the police courts, regardless of the amount of the claim. See Belgian Code of Civil Procedure (art. 601bis).

4. See French Code of Judicial Organization (art. L311–1).

5. See the French Code of Judicial Organization, arts. L124–2 (the general provision), R232–3 (*juridiction de proximité*) and R532–3 (*tribunal de première instance*).

ing on caseloads. The tradition of a collegiate panel of three judges in civil-law countries has its advantages and disadvantages. In principle, it increases the impartiality of the court and the quality of judgments. Not only will a group be able to provide a more thoughtful legal analysis, but it may also avoid the prejudices of a single judge. It also contributes to secure the independence of the judge, because the responsibility for a judgment is allocated amongst a group of judges that may not issue dissenting opinions.[6] On the other hand, the single-judge court gives an appearance of accessibility to the parties and a sense of individual responsibility to the judge. It is also much cheaper.[7] There is a clear trend towards a single-judge court in those European civil-law countries that still adopt a collegiate court.

The three judges are almost always career officials, and, in civil cases, there is usually no lay participation. In some countries, one may find lay participation in commercial or labor cases[8] but never a jury.

The full-blown civil jury (as opposed to a system where a small number of lay assessors may sit with a professional judge) is practically unknown outside the common-law orbit, and even there it is becoming rare. It has practically disappeared in England. Interestingly, in Scotland, to some extent a country of the "civil law" tradition, many personal injury cases are tried before a jury.[9] Lay participation in criminal trial is quite common in some civil law countries but it is only reserved for the most serious offenses, such as murder.[10]

The judiciary is a career service (except for the constitutional courts to be discussed later). Soon after finishing their legal education, its members will start as judges in one of the lower courts, following a training period (in several countries, such as France and the Netherlands, there is a special training institute for that purpose). They spend their lives in that career (except in those countries where it is possible to switch between judicial and prosecutorial functions, a switch, however, not often made even where permissible), advancing gradually into the higher or geographically more desirable courts. This obviously makes for a somewhat different outlook than in the common law tradition, where, at least in principle, judges are normally experienced lawyers. The relatively large number of judges (there

6. Regarding the possibility of dissenting opinions in the civil-law tradition, see *infra* Chapter 6, Section 4(d) at 505.

7. See L. Cadiet, Droit Judiciaire Privé 80 (2000).

8. In some countries, one may even find lay judges in the Court of Appeals. See Belgian Code of Civil Procedure (art. 103–104) (providing for lay assessors in the Labor Court of Appeals). In 1999, Brazil abolished a decade-long expensive tradition of lay asses-sors in the first, second and third instance of labor courts. See Brazilian Constitutional Amendment 24, 1999.

9. See Hardin, An American Lawyer Looks at Civil Jury Trial in Scotland, 111 U.Pa.L.Rev. 739 (1963).

10. See, e.g., the French and Belgian *Cour d'assises*. See the Codes of Criminal Procedure of France (art. 254–67), Belgium (art. 123), Brazil (art. 74.1 and 406–97). See also Brazilian Constitution (art. 5, XXXVIII).

were 17,000 judges in Germany before unification and more than 20,000 in 2008) also contributes to a somewhat different outlook.[11]

Constitutional provisions in civil law countries protect the independence of the judiciary,[12] and there are usually institutions (such as, in France, the *Conseil Supérieur de la Magistrature* and the High Council for the Judiciary in Belgium) intended to remove matters of appointment, promotion, and discipline from political influence. This does not always eliminate claims of "politics" in sensitive cases, such as those involving bribery of public officials or violations of campaign financing laws. However, it is safe to say that, in general, party politics are not even an issue in civil-law countries to the extent they are in the US.

Although this is the general scheme, there are nevertheless significant variations. The system may be more complex in countries with a federal structure. A few countries with a federal political structure still have a unitary court system in which all courts are "federal" institutions (e.g., Austria and Belgium). In other federal countries (e.g., Germany or Switzerland), the first instance courts and intermediate appellate courts are technically "state" courts, and the highest courts are technically "federal" courts [hence the court at the top of the hierarchy of "regular" German courts is simply called *Bundesgerichtshof*: "Federal Court"], but there may also be specialized lower "federal" courts for certain matters such as patents or the like. Completely duplicative and overlapping systems of federal and state courts do not exist outside the United States.

In developing countries, as a matter of economizing scarce resources, the courts of general jurisdiction frequently sit with only one judge, who may have lay assessors. In the former Soviet Union and other countries within its bloc, the court structure resembled to some extent the court structure in Western Europe, but often with some peculiar variants, such as the existence of special boards to handle disputes between state-owned enterprises, more lay participation on judicial panels, etc. Not all of these peculiarities have completely disappeared.[13] In addition, single-judge courts of first instance have been the tradition in Latin America, and although the People's Republic of China generally requires panels of several judges (or assessors), single judges may decide civil cases of first instance when summary procedure is being employed.

11. See J.–P. Lay & Ch. Bigaut, Loi organique n. 94–100 du 5 février sur le Conseil supérieur de la magistrature: la mise en oeuvre de la réforme constitutionnelle du 27 juillet 1993, 1994 D. Chr. 129 (giving also some comparative data).

12. See the Constitutions of France (Arts. 64 and 65), Italy (arts. 104–107) and Belgium (art. 151.1). See also the European Convention of Human Rights (art. 6.1).

13. See, for a recent comment on this rapidly-changing area, W.W. Schwarzer, Civil and Human Rights and the Courts under the New Constitution of the Russian Federation, 18 Int'l Lawyer 825 (1994).

Furthermore, in Western Europe, the increasing volume of litigation (and budgetary constraints) has led to a rethinking of the three-judge system for courts of first instance. In Germany, a single-judge "Family Court" was created, technically annexed to the court of limited jurisdiction, but appeals from it go to the regular intermediate appellate courts, which sit in panels. In the courts of general jurisdiction, certain preliminary matters could always be handled by a single judge, but now, the panel before which a case is pending may refer the case for decision to a single judge for decision, unless it is of peculiar difficulty or of importance beyond the immediate parties. The decision is also subject to review by the intermediate appellate courts.

A somewhat similar situation prevails in France. Family law cases are normally heard by a single judge of the court of first instance with general jurisdiction, known as the judge on family matters (*juge aux affaires familiales*), though that judge can remand a case to a collegiate panel.[14] There are some other matters normally handled by a single judge that are also subject to remand to the panel. In the *tribunal de grande instance*, there is a *juge de l'exécution* (*normally the president of the tribunal*) who deals with issues and disputes on the enforcement of judgments. In some cases, the judge can remand the case to the panel.[15] Traffic accidents—a significant portion of the total case load—are also dealt with by a single judge at the *tribunal de police* (police court).[16] In most other cases, the presiding judge or the judge delegated for that purpose by the presiding judge may assign the matter to a single judge for decision, but, in these cases, it must be transferred to a panel if one of the parties so requests, even without stating any reasons.[17]

In any event, the trend towards single-judge courts is inevitable, as demonstrated by the recent reforms in Italy, Belgium, and Germany, which switched rather dramatically from a three-judge system to a one-judge system.[18]

(b) Commercial Courts and Commercial Panels

In civil-law terminology, civil matters must be distinguished not only from criminal and administrative cases, but also from commercial ones. There are three different systems, each of which has a substantial following in the civil-law world. Under the German system, a court of first instance has three types of chambers: criminal, civil, and commercial. The civil (and criminal) chambers are composed exclusively of professional judges, but a commercial chamber consists of a legally trained, professional judge as

14. See French Code of Judicial Organization (arts. L213–3 and 213–4).

15. See French Code of Judicial Organization (arts. L213–5—L213–6).

16. See French Code of Judicial Organization (arts. L221–10).

17. See French Code of Judicial Organization (art. 212–2).

18. See "la riforma del giudice unico" [the single-judge law reform], from the late 1990s. See Codes of Civil Procedure of Italy (art. 50*ter*, providing the single-judge court as the general rule and art. 50*bis*, listing the exceptional cases to be decided by a panel of three judges), Belgium (art. 91.1, providing the single-judge court as the general rule, and 91.8, providing that at the request of one of the parties, the case be decided by a panel of judges). See P. Murray & R. Stürner, German Civil Justice 53–54 and 210–212 (2004).

Presiding Judge and two merchants as honorary associate judges.[1] The procedure before a commercial chamber is essentially the same as before a civil chamber, regulated by the Code of Civil Procedure, and appeals from its decisions are heard by the same courts (sitting without lay judges) that determine appeals from judgments of a civil chamber. The two merchant judges are judges, not jurors, and factual and legal issues are determined by a majority of the three judges. Their decisions are announced *per curiam* even though as a practical matter they are always prepared by the presiding judge.[2] The commercial panels are not immune to the trend in civil-law countries to abandon the three-judge tradition. Therefore, some preliminary decisions, as well as the final judgment, may be shifted to the presiding judge.

Under the French system, the Commercial Court is a separate court and not a mere chamber of the ordinary tribunal of first instance. It is entirely composed of merchant judges, elected—indirectly—by their fellow merchants.[3] Its procedure is simpler and speedier than that of the ordinary courts.[4] A variant of the French system exists in Belgium where there is a separate Commercial Court, but it is composed of professional and non-professional judges (commonly called "judges in commercial affairs").[5] However, on the appellate level, the French system is much like the German in that the court of appeals and the Court of Cassation are composed exclusively of professional judges, even when they hear appeals from the Commercial Court,

In Russia and countries influenced by its legal system, like Belarus, there is a separate commercial court dealing with "economic disputes" and other affairs related to the performance of entrepreneurial and other economic activities (administrative and civil cases in business). Because these commercial courts are called *Arbitrazh* Courts in Russian, they are frequently translated as "Arbitration Courts".[6] This mistake may lead to serious misunderstandings. The *Arbitrazh* courts are generally composed of professional judges. However, on the motion of the party, two commercial

1. German Law on Court Organization (*Gerichtsverfassungsgesetz*) § 105. The merchant judges are appointed upon recommendation of local or regional Chambers of Commerce and Industry. Cf. Ibid. § 109. Where no commercial courts have been established, the civil panels act in their stead. Ibid. §§ 93, 94.

2. See German Law on Court Organization (§ 105(2)).

3. See the French Commercial Code, title II of book VIII (arts. L721–1—L724–7).

4. For some special procedural rules concerning the commercial courts, see French Code of Civil Procedure Arts. 853–878. Significantly, before a commercial court, the parties may represent themselves or be represented or advised by any person; the use of an *avocat* is thus not required. In places where there are courts of general jurisdiction, but no commercial courts, commercial litigation is handled by the courts of general jurisdiction. The caseload in the French commercial courts is substantial. A significant part of their load, especially when economic conditions are poor, constitutes bankruptcy matters.

5. See Belgian Code of Civil Procedure (arts. 73, 84–85 and 86–100).

6. See, e.g., the website of the Russian *Arbitrazh* Court, http://www.arbitr.ru/eng/ (last visited May 17, 2009).

court assessors from the list of experienced and qualified merchants can be invited to decide a case.

There is also a third system—of which Italy is typical—under which separate commercial courts and commercial chambers have been abolished, with the result that commercial as well as civil cases come before the civil chambers of the ordinary tribunals of first instance. The idea behind this minority system is that the separate treatment of commercial matters, although deeply rooted in the civilian tradition and in existence since the Middle Ages is no longer necessary or even desirable in this age. A variant of the Italian system exists in Austria where the sole commercial court sits in Vienna, which is by far the largest and commercially most important city in that country.

Of course, the basic problem—whether the separate system of rules for commercial transactions should be continued—arises with respect to substantive law as well as with respect to jurisdiction and procedure. It has given rise to much debate throughout the civil-law world.

(c) Intermediate Court of Appeals

Appeals from the first instance court of general jurisdiction (and in some countries also from the first instance court of limited jurisdiction) are heard by an intermediate appellate court (Court of Appeals). Contrary to the rule in common law countries, the court of second instance in civil law countries may review issues of law as well as issues of fact.[1] Further review (but usually restricted to questions of law only) is then normally possible by a court of last resort (Supreme Court).[2] These courts normally sit in panels consisting of a presiding judge and an even number of associate judges. Since the judiciary in most civil-law countries is a career long service, these judges obviously belong to the higher or highest levels of the hierarchy.

A scheme may be the following:

1. Further details *infra*.

2. See also *infra* Chapter 6, Section 3(d) at 505.

Structure of the Courts of France[3]

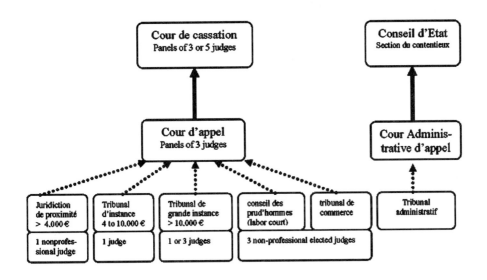

••••••••▶ Appeal on fact and law
━━━━━▶ Appeal on issues of law only

3. This chart does not include criminal and administrative courts.

Structure of the Courts of Germany[4]

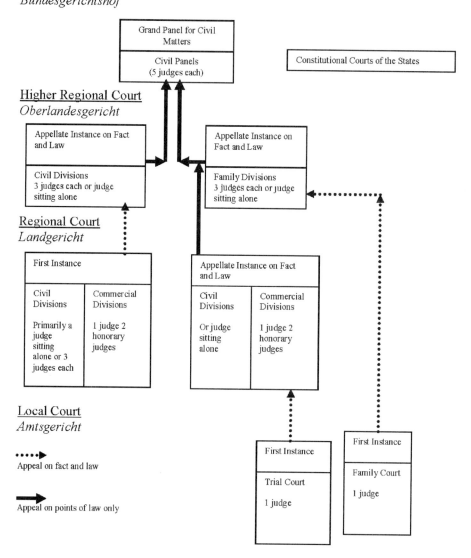

Federal Court of Justice
Bundesgerichtshof

Higher Regional Court
Oberlandesgericht

Regional Court
Landgericht

Local Court
Amtsgericht

4. Due to the complexity of the structure of German courts, this diagram does not include criminal ordinary courts or the courts of specialized jurisdiction (administrative, Patent, Labor, Fiscal, Social). A complete structure can be found on the website of the European Commission, European Judicial Network in Civil and Commercial Matters), http://ec.europa.eu/civiljustice (last visited Jan. 21, 2009).

Structure of the People's Courts of the PRC[5]

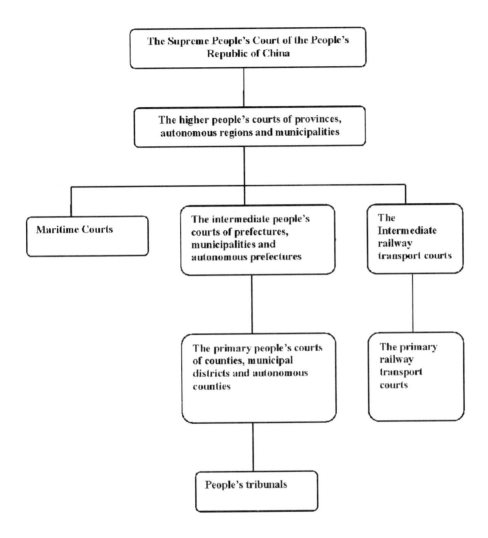

In the U.S., the first appeal (to the intermediate court of appeals) is limited to issues of law. Findings of fact will only be reviewed if they are "clearly erroneous", but courts exercise this possibility with restraint, especially in cases tried by a jury. Although this rule is a corollary of the constitutional right to jury trial, it was blindly extended to non jury cases as well.

Other common-law countries do not have jury trials in civil litigation, except in rare cases (if at all). In those common law countries, the dichotomy is not between issues of fact and issues of law, but, rather,

5. Adapted from R. C. Brown, Understanding Chinese Courts and Legal Process (1997).

between oral evidence and other evidence. For example, English courts will not disturb a judge's evaluation of the credibility of witness' statements because the court of first instance has had the opportunity to analyze the demeanor of the witness. Whenever the findings of fact are not based on the demeanor or credibility of a witness but instead on inferences from facts or documentary evidence, it is presumed the court of appeals can do just as good a job and therefore owes no deference to the court of first instance.[6]

Australian courts are, in principle, authorized to review issues of fact and do not display a blind reliance on "demeanor evidence." However, in practice, they usually defer to the courts of first instance's decisions on credibility, except in cases of clear error. There is no deference to the courts of first instance on drawing inferences.[7]

The U.S. Supreme Court specifically rejected that standard in Anderson v. City of Bressemer City, stating the courts of appeal must defer to the findings of fact of the court of first instance "even when the district court's findings do not rest on credibility determinations, but are based on physical or documentary evidence or inferences from other facts".[8] In that same year, the Federal Rules of Civil Procedure were amended to make explicit that, in an action tried without a jury, findings of fact, "whether based on oral or other evidence", must not be set aside unless clearly erroneous, but kept unchanged the old language to the effect that "the reviewing court must give due regard to the trial court's opportunity to judge the witnesses' credibility."[9]

Although this has become the unquestioned standard in U.S. Civil Procedure, there is nothing necessary about it. Americans tend to forget that, for several decades, U.S. courts of appeals would also give no deference to the first instance court findings of fact based on documentary materials. The rationale was the same as adopted in other common-law countries: the court of appeals could do as good a job of interpreting documents and facts as the court of first instance. The court of appeals would simply ignore the findings of the first instance court and substitute its own, even when written evidence would discredit witnesses statements that the trial court considered convincing.

After citing several decisions on both sides, the Advisory Committee Note to the 1985 Amendment to Rule 52(a) stated its objective was to "avoid continued confusion and conflicts among the circuits as to the standard of appellate review of findings of fact." The Advisory Committee did not deny the traditional common-law rationale, but considered this argument to be "outweighed by the public interest in the stability and judicial economy that would be promoted by recognizing that the trial court, not the appellate tribunal, should be the finder of the facts. To permit courts of appeal to share more actively in the fact-finding function

---

6. See N. Andrews, English Civil Procedure 906–10 (2003) (also stating that a jury finding of fact is traditionally treated as "sacrosanct"); P. Loughlin & S. Gerlis, Civil Procedure 595–96 (2004).

7. B. Cairns, Australian Civil Procedure 554–57 (2005). The rule in New Zealand is rather similar. See A. Beck, Principles of Civil Procedure 267 (2001).

8. See Anderson v. City of Bessemer City, 470 U.S. 564, 105 S.Ct. 1504 (1985).

9. See FRCP 52(a)(6), as amended in 1985.

would tend to undermine the legitimacy of the district courts in the eyes of litigants, multiply appeals by encouraging appellate retrial of some factual issues, and needlessly reallocate judicial authority." It is clear it was a strictly political decision, moved by economic considerations and more specifically to avoid appeals.

Common-law lawyers are usually startled by the fact that in most civil-law countries the first appeal is a *de novo* review of the law and facts. The full record of the court of first instance is sent to the appellate court, which determines factual issues on the basis of that record and of such additional evidence as it orders to be taken.

The second instance is, in effect, a new opportunity to argue the case; it is a re-trial or a continuation of the trial. No deference is due to findings of facts of the court of first instance, although, in practice, it is expected for the courts of appeal to not gratuitously reverse a judgment. Different judges, different countries, different times, and different situations may lead to slightly different practices.

The French model may be the most liberal in this regard. One could even say that the appeal is a new beginning, a full re-trial. The French court of appeals (*cour d'appel*) will not even decide on the record created in the first instance. There will be a completely new proceeding, in which the parties will again bring the evidence (even new evidence), will again exchange briefs, make new claims, and the court can order production of other evidence. Paradigmatic is art. 561 of the French Code of Civil Procedure, stating that the matter is completely re-submitted to the court of appeals so that it may decide anew in its issues of fact and law. This is called "*effet dévolutif de l'appel*."[10]

Other civil-law countries that adopt the French model have a much more restricted view of the definition of such "*dévolutif*" effect and limit the scope of review to the record created in first instance, unless some exceptional situation makes it imperative to accept production of evidence not produced below.

In Germany, since the 2001 reforms, the appellate court must accept issues of fact determined in the first instance "insofar as there is no clear indication of doubt of the correctness or completeness of the fact determinations material to the decision and therefore indication for a new fact determination."[11] There is still a question of whether this new rule restricted the previous scope of fact review, increased it, or merely clarified the prior practice.[12] The courts of appeal will make a determination on the merits and dismiss the case, substituting the first instance decision for its own, without remanding the case to the court below. However, if for some reason a new decision is not possible, due, for example to a wrong

10. See the Codes of Civil Procedure of France (arts. 561–63) and Belgium (art. 1068).

11. See German Code of Civil Procedure, §§ 513(1) and 529(1)(1).

12. *Compare* P. Murray & R. Stürner, German Civil Justice 373–74 and 381–83 (2004) *with* G. Walter, The German Civil Procedure Reform Act 2002: Much Ado About Nothing?, in N. Trocker & V. Varano, The Reforms of Civil Procedure in Comparative Perspective 66, 84 (2005).

procedural decision in the early stages of the proceeding, it may also void the judgment and resend the proceeding to the court below with instructions on how to proceed.[13]

In Italy, since the 1990 reforms, with some limited exceptions, the parties cannot raise new claims, new defenses, or new evidence in appeal.[14]

In sharp contrast with common-law practice, the parties in most civil-law systems routinely appeal an unfavorable decision.

In Louisiana, this traditional civil-law approach has had a strong impact on the practice of the courts, even in jury cases. Although Louisiana courts of appeal pretend to reverse only "manifestly erroneous" findings of fact, it is no secret that jury verdicts in tort cases often are overturned on appeal for no reason other than the appellate court weighs the evidence differently. The constitutionality of this practice, which finds more favor with insurance companies than with plaintiffs, was upheld, against an attack based on the U.S. Constitution.[15] This reality is in sharp contrast with the U.S. common-law tradition.

In the common-law tradition, the second instance is considered neither a continuation of the first instance trial nor a new trial, but merely a review of issues of law. Even a wrong decision of procedure or law will not lead to a reversal if the error was harmless and did not affect the final judgment.[16] This rule considerably limits the possibility of reversal. No trial will ever be free from mistakes, but many errors are ultimately harmless, either because the person prevailed in spite of it, or because the person lost the case for other reasons. A perfect proceeding is neither possible nor necessary; it is widely accepted that one fair and impartial opportunity to present one's case is sufficient. The result is that only a small portion of appealed cases are actually reversed. Therefore, parties usually do not appeal.

There are some voices in the civil-law world suggesting strongly limiting appeals. However, the prevailing view is that a second instance is necessary, and, for some, a constitutional guarantee.

The idea that a court of second instance can take new evidence or re-take evidence previously presented at trial is unfamiliar to the common law

---

13. See Codes of Civil Procedure of Japan (art. 305–08); Germany (§ 538), Italy (353–55), Greece (art. 535); P. Yessiou–Faltsi, Civil Procedure in Hellas 270 (1995).

14. See Italian Code of Civil Procedure (art. 345, as amended in 1990). See V. Varano, Machinery of Justice, in J. S. Lena & U. Mattei, Introduction to Italian Law 99, 107 (2002); F. Carpi & M. Taruffo, Commentario Breve al Codice di Procedura Civile 1036–46 (2002).

15. See Melancon v. McKeithen, 345 F.Supp. 1025 (three-judge court) (E.D.La. 1972), aff'd mem. sub nom. Hill v. McKeith-en, 409 U.S. 943, 93 S.Ct. 290 (1972) (stating that "jury trials in civil cases, and the absolute prohibition of judicial reexamination of jury findings in civil cases, are not so fundamental to the American system of justice as to be required of the state courts by due process, and assuming that the right to a civil jury trial is required by due process, Louisiana scheme providing for review of civil appeals on both the law and the facts does not destroy that right, but modifies it in accordance with fair procedures.")

16. See FRCP 61 and 28 USC § 2111 (on harmless error).

tradition. Traditionally, civil-law countries accept the taking of additional evidence on appeal, particularly documentary, but also oral evidence.[17] The tendency, however, is to restrict it to evidence not previously available, or to facts that occurred after the decision, or to evidence not taken in the first instance for a reason not attributable to the party, such as judicial error.[18] In any event, this power is sparingly exercised depending on the country and the court.

The ALI/Unidroit Principles and Rules of Transnational Civil Procedure also adopt a restrictive approach, providing that the appellate court may consider new facts and evidence "in the interest of justice." The comment suggests that a court may consider additional evidence in "exceptional circumstances," such as evidence discovered after the final decision.[19]

In any event, the idea of a second instance court taking evidence may not be as unfamiliar as it might seem at first blush. In some states, there are explicit statutory provisions granting appellate courts, in non-jury cases, the power to allow the introduction of new evidence on appeal, but this power is sparingly, if ever, exercised.[20]

However, when an offer of proof is made for the first time on appeal, the appellate court has the power to reject such offer if it appears the party making the offer was dilatory. How much this power is used varies from country to country, but it seems the trend is to exercise it more than in years past. For example in Germany the tough preclusion rules introduced by a 1976 reform are carried over into the procedure of the intermediate appellate court (Higher Regional Court—*Oberlandesgericht*).[21] In most civil-law countries, the power to accept evidence on appeal is sparingly used.

Studies have shown that this "repeat performance" of the first instance procedure in general produces delays; in some countries it takes

---

17. See the Codes of Civil Procedure of France (art. 563), Greece (art. 529); C. Goodman, Justice and Civil Procedure in Japan 429–30 (2004); P. Yessiou–Faltsi, Civil Procedure in Hellas 270 (1995).

18. See the Codes of Civil Procedure of Germany, § 531(2); Italy, art. 345(2); Spain, art. 460 and 461(3); Portugal 693b and 524; Ibero–American Model Code of Civil Procedure (art. 223.2); P. Murray & R. Stürner, German Civil Justice 377 and 382–82 (2004); F. Carpi & M. Taruffo, Commentario Breve al Codice di Procedura Civile 1043–46 (2002); M. Ortells Ramos, Derecho Procesal Civil 513–16 (2005).

19. See ALI/UNIDROIT, Principles of Transnational Civil Procedure (2006), Principle 27, Rule 33.4, and Comment R–33F.

20. See, e.g., Cal.Code Civ.Proc., § 909; R. W. Millar, New Allegation and Proof on Appeal in Anglo–American Civil Procedure, 47 Nw.U.L.Rev. 427 (1952).

21. See German Code of Civil Procedure (§§ 527 and 528). A reexamination of witnesses may be necessary on appeal if the appellate court considers the testimony in the file incredible or if the appellate court is not sure exactly what the witness meant to convey. See Decision of December 6, 1990 of the German Supreme Court, 44 N.J.W. 1183 (1991); N. Pantle, Die Pflicht des Berufungsgerichts zur Wiederholung einer erstinstanzlich durchgeführten Beweisaufnahme, 40 N.J.W. 3160 (1987). The power to preclude is limited by constitutional constraints. The German Constitutional Court has ruled that under some circumstances, the appellate court is obliged to hear newly proffered evidence, at least if this would not lead to unduly delaying the decision. Cf. J. Würfel, Verspätete Beweisaufname in der Berufungsinstanz, 45 N.J.W. 543 (1992).

longer for a case to go through the first appeal than it takes in the first instance. A French study undertaken in the beginning of the nineties as a basis for the adoption of a law providing basic guidelines for the funding of justice-related activities noted that a case took, on the average, nine months in the first instance court of general jurisdiction but fourteen months in the intermediate appellate courts.[22] The situation only got worse with time. Several European countries are frequently convicted by the European Court of Human Rights for the violation of art. 6 of the European Convention on Human Rights, which establishes the right to a fair proceeding, for failing to deal with a case within a reasonable amount of time. Usually, these are criminal proceedings. The country must pay damages to the party as a sanction.

However, a second full examination of the facts is often considered an essential ingredient of a good fact-finding mechanism, particularly in a system in which first instance judges are generally young civil servants, as opposed to experienced practitioners (as is the ideal in the common-law tradition). Indeed, the mentality of European attorneys is that they do not have to put so much energy in the first instance because the case will be thoroughly analyzed again in the court of appeals.

In Germany, an argument has been made that a thorough appellate review is necessary because the first instance is more cursory, providing a quick and inexpensive decision. The full review will then provide a more careful analysis of the nuances of fact and law in the minority of cases in which the party on appeal alleges that the expeditious first determination was not correct.[23] On the other hand, judges' professional internal evaluations and their career in the judiciary depend on the number of decisions that are appealed and reversed. Therefore, it is in the judge's own personal interest to deliver well-drafted thoughtful decisions that will either not be appealed or, if appealed, will be sustained.

The problem is compounded by the fact that, as we have seen, in some civil-law countries, appeals are taken against a majority of judgments. Appeals may even be considered a constitutional guarantee in some civil-law countries. However, several legal systems are trying to deal with a crushing increase on litigation, including appeals. The problem of abusive or dilatory appeals is extremely serious in civil-law systems.

Some countries may impose limitations on the right to appeal. In Germany, for example, appeals are limited to cases above 600 euro. Cases below this amount may still be appealed with court permission if it raises an issue of general significance. The law also provides for expedited screening and dismissal of frivolous or unfounded appeals, and the use of a

---

22. See the report annexed to Law No. 95–9 of January 6, 1995, 1995 J.O. 381, 1995 D.L. 62. See also generally on the problems of the courts in France and proposed measures taken to deal with them, A. Chenin, La jus-tice est dotée pour la première fois d'une loi-programme, Le Monde, May 21, 1994, at 11.

23. See P. Murray & R. Stürner, German Civil Justice 368–69 (2004).

single-judge (instead of a panel) in some cases.[24] Similar provisions exist in France and Belgium.[25]

There is also a strong trend in civil-law countries to shift a significant amount of power to the presiding judge of the appellate panel to deal with certain matters and dispose of the case without submitting the case to the full panel. Therefore, while the general rule for the first instance is one judge and the exception is three judges, in appeals it is the opposite: the general rule is three judges and the exception is one judge.

In some countries, the appellant will be fined if the appeal is considered abusive or dilatory.[26] In other countries, whether dilatory or not, an appeal means more costs, not only in terms of an extra filing fee, but also an increased amount of attorney fees in case of failure.[27] In the US, the panel can deny oral arguments if, after an examination of briefs and record, it unanimously considers that the appeal is frivolous, that the legal issue is not controversial, or that the oral argument would not significantly help the decisional process.[28]

(d) Supreme Courts

The fact/law distinction is itself not cast in stone but variable across systems. For example, is the passage of time required by adverse possession a legal or a factual requirement? In any event, such distinction emerges in somewhat clearer lines when a case is further appealed to the court of last resort. The very term, "court of last resort," may require some explanation because of the many different court levels in civil law countries, particularly the administrative courts and the Constitutional Court.

In countries that follow the Austrian model, such as Germany, Austria, Belgium, Spain, and Italy, in addition to the court at the apex of the hierarchy of ordinary courts, there exists a separate Constitutional Court, a political body, situated outside the judicial system, that gives the last word on issues of constitutional law. Therefore, such countries have two courts of last resort, each with a different jurisdiction: one in charge of constitutional law and the other in charge of infra-constitutional law.[1]

A problem arises when a law may have two different interpretations: one that is constitutional and one that is not. A conflict may occur when the Supreme Court considers the correct interpretation to be one the Constitutional Court might find unconstitutional. The Constitutional Court must consider the constitutionality of a law exactly as the law was inter-

---

24. See German Code of Civil Procedure (art. 511); P. Murray & R. Stürner, German Civil Justice 58 and 374–84 (2004); G. Walter, The German Civil Procedure Reform Act 2002: Much Ado About Nothing?, in N. Trocker & V. Varano, The Reforms of Civil Procedure in Comparative Perspective 66, 80–88 (2005).

25. The French Code of Judicial Organization (art. R221–4) limits appeal to cases above 4,000 euro. The Belgian Code of Civil Procedure (art. 617) limits appeals to cases above 1,860 or 1,240 euro, depending on the type of case. A Belgian statute of 19 July 1985 introduced—as an exception—the singe judge in the appellate courts.

26. See Codes of Civil Procedure of France (art. 559 and 581, providing fines up to 1,500 Euro in addition to damages), Japan (art. 303, providing fines up to ten times the filing fee), Belgium (art. 780bis).

27. See *infra* Chapter 7, Section 8(b) at 691 (attorney fee shifting).

28. See Fed R. App. P. 34(a)(2).

1. See *infra* Chapter 6, Section 3(e) at 523 (Constitutional Courts).

preted by the regular courts. However, when the Constitutional Court upholds the constitutionality of a statute but simultaneously requires a particular construction of the statute in order to make it constitutional, the question arises of whether the ordinary courts are then bound to adopt that construction.[2] The balance of power between these courts is very complex and varies from country to country. It is very difficult to find a common thread. In France, however, there is no Constitutional Court and the Constitutional Council can decide a question of constitutionality only before the enactment of a statute.[3]

One must also mention the Council of State (*Conseil d'État* or *Consiglio di Stato*), the highest court of the Administrative Justice in countries that follow the French model. The Administrative Justice sits in three instances, like the regular civil and criminal courts, and resolves, *inter alia*, conflicts between private citizens and the state (*contentieux administratif*).

To make matters even more complicated, in some countries, the names to designate such courts may differ. In the US, the Supreme Court has jurisdiction over both constitutional and non-constitutional matters, while in other countries, the Supreme Court has jurisdiction only over constitutional matters. In others, the Supreme Court has jurisdiction over non-constitutional matters. The confusion is widespread even among comparatists.[4]

In addition, a party's right to what we call "due process" occasionally may receive not only constitutional but also international protection. This is true especially in Europe. When matters involving the interpretation of either the treaties establishing any of the European Communities or the validity of measures adopted by a Community body are at issue before a national court, that court may, and, if it is the highest court, must, stay its proceedings and refer the question to the Court of Justice of the European Communities for a determination, which is binding on the national court. The objective is to ensure the uniform application of community legislation.[5]

One of the most significant developments in procedural law at the European Level is the European Convention on Human Rights, sponsored by the Council of Europe, which currently has 47 member states. After all internal remedies have been exhausted and within six months from the final decision (usually of the Supreme Court), a party can lodge a complaint before the European Court of Human Rights alleging that a contracting state breached one of the convention's human rights. Art. 6 of the European Convention establishes the right for a fair proceeding and is the most

2. See J. H. Merryman & V. Vigoriti, When Courts Collide: Constitution and Cassation in Italy, 15 Am.J.Comp.L. 665 (1966–67).

3. See *infra* Chapter 6, Section 3(e) at 523 (Constitutional Courts).

4. See P. Yessiou–Faltsi, The Role of the Supreme Courts at the National and International Level (1998) (in which some National and Regional Reports analyzed the constitutional courts, others analyzed the courts of cassation and revision, while others included the administrative courts as well).

5. See Treaty establishing the European Community (art. 177).

commonly used in civil procedure. The provision is complex and involves issues of due process, reasonable duration of proceedings, publicity, and independence and impartiality of courts, etc. The European Court of Human Rights is not really a fourth instance because it cannot reverse the judgment issued by the national court. However, if the state is found in violation of the convention, it must pay damages and will eventually change their domestic legislation to comply with the convention.

The significance of such constitutional and international guarantees is greater in administrative and criminal proceedings than in civil proceedings. But even in civil actions, it can happen that the highest court in the ordinary court system will not actually have the last word.

For the purposes of our analysis here, the terms "Supreme Court," "court of last resort," or "highest court" refer to the court at the summit of the hierarchy of ordinary courts, i.e., the court which hears appeals from the decisions of the courts of appeal in civil and criminal cases. In the great majority of cases (i.e., in all cases not involving constitutionally or internationally protected rights) that court does indeed have the last word. We will not refer here to the Constitutional Courts, the *Conseil d'État*, or other international courts.[6]

An interesting peculiarity of some civil-law countries is that, if both parties agree, they may bypass the Court of Appeals and appeal a case directly to the Supreme Court.[7]

In one respect the civilians' treatment of appeals to the court of last resort[8] is similar to U.S. law: such appeals are exclusively limited to issues of law and cannot raise issues of fact.[9] But on several significant points of appellate practice the rules governing the highest courts in civil-law systems (or at least in some of them) differ sharply from those familiar to a common-law lawyer. The main differences relate to the following four issues:

(i) Can an appeal to the court of last resort be taken as of right, or merely by permission, such as a grant of certiorari?

6. On the Constitutional Courts, see *infra.*

7. See Codes of Civil Procedure of Japan (art. 311.2), Germany (§ 566), Italy (art. 360.2), Peru (art. 389). See P. Murray & R. Stürner, German Civil Justice 398–399 (2004); Y. Taniguchi, P. Reich & H. Miyake, Civil Procedure in Japan 3–23 (2008).

8. For an excellent, but by now somewhat dated, comparative symposium on the structure and procedure of courts of last resort in a number of leading civil-law and common-law countries, see A. Tunc (ed.), La Cour Judiciaire Suprême: Une Enquête Comparative, 30 Revue Internationale de Droit Comparé 1 ff. (1978). See also Lasser, Judicial Deliberations (2005).

9. There are minor exceptions to this rule when the Supreme Court must decide as the court of first instance. For example, in some countries, judges or ministers must be tried exclusively by the Supreme Court, and, therefore, the Court decides issues of fact and law. This is not different from the "original jurisdiction" of the U.S. Supreme Court (controversies between two or more States, or between the United States and a State, or when ambassadors or consuls of foreign states are parties). See 28 U.S.C. § 1251.

(ii) What disposition can the highest court make of the case, if it concludes the decision below rests on reversible error?

(iii) Since the highest court of a civil-law country, like the lower courts, normally sits in panels or divisions, the further question arises: how can the decisions of various panels avoid inconsistencies and contradictions?

(iv) What role may the government have on the Supreme Court?

(i) Appeals as a Matter of Right and Discretionary Appeals

The issue of discretionary appeals to the Supreme Court does not involve a mere technicality but is of greatest significance for the development of the law in a given jurisdiction. The principle of "selectivity" is adopted in most common law countries although with significant variations. While in the United States the Supreme Court has full control of its docket, in England it is the Court of Appeals which makes the selection for the House of Lords (now Supreme Court), sending up only a few cases. The idea is that a court of last resort which does not have some form of control over the calendar, is in danger of becoming so flooded with enormous numbers of small and unimportant cases that it can devote only insufficient time and energy to the truly novel and important issues of law coming before it.[10] In this perspective, the real mission of the highest court—to keep the law up to date and uniform—can hardly be accomplished if the system does not have the power to select the cases it considers worthy of thorough review.

In sharp contrast with the tradition in common-law countries, however, the traditional civil-law ideology is that the function of the Supreme Court is not only to maintain uniformity of legal interpretation throughout the country, but also to fix mistakes of the courts of appeal and ultimately to do justice between the parties.[11] Therefore, the party who lost in the Court of Appeals has a right to seek a further (limited) review to the Supreme Court. This traditional ideology has been abandoned in several countries in favor of a system that ignores the immediate interest of the parties and individual justice.

---

10. For data on the caseload of French Supreme Court see http://www.courdecassation.fr/ (last visited January 21, 2009). In the period from 2005 to 2008, the influx of new cases was relatively steady (about 18,500). However, the number of cases pending at the end of each year has decreased dramatically (from 33,880 in 1999, 23,661 in 2004 to 18,890 in 2008), and the number of cases decided every year has decreased the last couple of years (from 24,776 in 2005 to 18,684 in 2008). A case lasts about 16 months in the French Supreme Court.

The Italian Supreme Court receives 25,000 cases every year and decides "only" 20,000. The backlog is 50,000 cases. A case lasts about 3 years in the Italian Supreme Court. See N. Trocker & V. Varano, Concluding Remarks, in N. Trocker & V. Varano, The Reforms of Civil Procedure in Comparative Perspective 264–65 (2005).

11. The view that the correction of errors of the lower courts is a fundamental right is held strongly in France and widely shared in other countries. See Boré, La Cour de Cassation de l'an 2000, 1995 D.Chr. 133; L. Comoglio, C. Ferri & M. Taruffo, Lezioni sul Processo Civile 713 (1995). The same is not true in many other civil-law countries, such as Germany. See P. Murray & R. Stürner, German Civil Justice 386 (2004).

The argument in favor of selectivity is somewhat weakened, moreover, by the fact that civil-law Supreme Courts (like in France, Germany, and Italy) are composed by more than one hundred judges, and can distribute the workload among a larger group of judges, who sit in small panels. Since their decisions do not have binding effect as precedents, in order to have a meaningful impact in the legal system, the Supreme Court needs to take as many cases as possible. It seems natural that the possibility of being selective comes hand in hand with the common law tradition of *stare decisis*.

Nevertheless, civilian scholars have criticized the traditional civil-law rule of non-selectivity on policy grounds similar to those typical of the U.S. model.[12] Under pressure from the significant increase in the workload of courts in the last few decades, a few civil-law countries have indeed modified the traditional system. The trend is clearly towards adopting a discretionary selection, somewhat similar to the "writ of certiorari" of the U.S. Supreme Court[13] or the "leave" of the English Supreme Court (former House of Lords). These courts hear less than 100 cases every year.

In some civil-law countries, appeals to the Supreme Courts now are limited to cases that raise issues of general significance, i.e., issues that go beyond the immediate interest of the parties. This means that, at least in principle, the Supreme Court will only take cases that will contribute to the uniform interpretation and improvement of the law. This is a rather recent trend in civil-law countries and is specifically conceived to deal with the serious problem of overcrowded dockets, but some scholars and practitioners were not pleased with losing the opportunity of correcting the decisions of courts of appeal.

Argentina, Austria, the Netherlands, Japan, and Brazil adopted the U.S. standard: the Supreme Court is master of its own docket and has discretion to decide which cases to take. Germany adopted the English standard: the court of appeals may also grant leave to appeal and the Supreme Court must take the case.[14] Even though these civil-law countries adopt the common law standard, the result is noticeably different: appeals to the Supreme Courts in civil-law countries run in the thousands. Spain rejected the discretionary selection and instead adopted an objective criteri-

12. See M. Cappelletti, The Doctrine of *Stare decisis* and the Civil Law: A Fundamental Difference—or No Difference at All?, in H. Bernstein, U. Drobnig & H. Koetz, Festschrift für Konrad Zweigert 381, 385–87 (1981), and authorities there cited.

13. See 28 U.S.C. §§ 1254(1) and 1257.

14. In principle, a U.S. Court of Appeals may also "certify" a question of law "as to which instructions are desired" from the U.S. Supreme Court. See 28 U.S.C. § 1254(2) and Rules of the Supreme Court of the United States (Rule 19). However, in practice, this is rarely invoked because the Supreme Court has discretion to take the case, despite the clear language of the statute. See C. A. Wright & M. K. Kane, Law of Federal Courts 780–82 (2002) (arguing that it is not for the courts of appeals "to decide what matters are of enough importance to require decision of the Supreme Court" and that "the control of that Court's docket should rest exclusively in its own hands").

on of conflicting case law. In Spain and Japan, there are also appeals as of right to the Supreme Court.[15]

There is no such restriction in France or Italy. However, in order to cope with the Supreme Court's excessive caseload, in France the case will initially be assigned to a small group of only three judges, who could decide the case, whenever the appeal is not admissible or not based on arguable grounds. Otherwise, the case must be heard by a bench consisting of at least five voting members.[16]

Some methods commonly used to discourage the filing of frivolous or abusive appeals to the Supreme Court is to impose fines and damages,[17] to prohibit such appeal whenever the courts of appeal confirm the decision of first instance,[18] to award costs,[19] or to allow the immediate enforcement of the decision appealed.

In France and Belgium, in order to have access to the Court of Cassation, the party needs to hire a special attorney, the *Avocat au Conseil d'état et à la Cour de cassation* or *Avocat à la Cour de cassation*.[20] In France there are only 98 attorneys so qualified and in Belgium, 19. Although each has a team of lawyers working for them, this is a rather limited number. The preliminary advice of these lawyers is considered to be an honest and objective filter to the Supreme Court. Moreover, this special Bar, used as it is in the business of separating the fact from the law, functions (like the jury) as an institutional keeper of this distinction, relevant as it is for the development of a system of case law.

France also adopted a fairly original procedure intended to lighten the load of the *Cour de cassation* at least in the long run. First introduced for the Supreme Administrative Court (the *Conseil d'Etat*) in 1988 and adopted

---

15. See Codes of Civil Procedure of Germany (§ 543, as amended in 2001), Austria (art. 502, as amended in 2002), Argentina (art. 280, as amended in 1990); Japan (art. 318.1, as enacted in 1996), Spain (art. 477, enacted in 2000), Dutch Judicial Organization Statute (art. 81), Brazilian Constitution (art. 102.3, as amended in 2004, reinstating a rule in force from 1977 to 1988). The Brazilian Supreme Court, however, is more akin to a Constitutional Court than to a Supreme Court, as defined in this chapter.

See P. Murray & R. Stürner, *German Civil Justice* 386–88 (2004); G. Walter, The German Civil Procedure Reform Act 2002: Much Ado About Nothing?; E. Barjons, Civil Procedure for Austria Revisited. An Outline of Recent Austrian Civil Procedure Reforms; N. Trocker & V. Varano, Concluding Remarks, all published in N. Trocker & V. Varano, The Reforms of Civil Procedure in Comparative Perspective 66, 82 and 86–88, 125–26, 265 (2005); J. O'Hare & K. Browne, Civil Litigation 645–47 (2005); White Book, Vol. 2,

Section 4A, 1.1; Y. Taniguchi, P. Reich & H. Miyake, Civil Procedure in Japan 3–28, 8–22, 8–29—8–30 (2008); C. Goodman, Justice and Civil Procedure in Japan 442–51 (2004); M. Ortells Ramos, Derecho Procesal Civil 529–53 (2005); R. Arazi, II Derecho Procesal Civil y Comercial 92–93 (2004); O. A. Gozaíni, Código Procesal Civil y Comercial de la Nación Comentado y Anotado 121–122 (2006).

16. See the French Code of Judicial Organization (art. L431–1). See also the Belgian Code of Civil Procedure (art. 1105bis).

17. See Codes of Civil Procedure of France (art. 628) (providing a maximum of 6,000 Euro), Italy (art. 385.4).

18. See Code of Civil Procedure of Uruguay (art. 268).

19. See Code of Civil Procedure of France (art. 700).

20. See Codes of Civil Procedure of France (art. 973) and Belgium (art. 478).

for the *Cour de cassation* in 1991, this procedure authorizes any French court on its own initiative to stay a case that involves a novel and difficult question of law, which appears to arise in numerous instances and to refer the question to the *Cour de cassation* for advice. The decision to refer the question to the Court of Cassation is *non appealable*, but the court must hear the parties before making a decision. The Court of Cassation will answer through a special panel within three months.[21] The procedure was evidently designed to provide a quick answer to the lower courts in instances which might lead to numerous—obviously slow—appeals to the *Cour de cassation*, for instance when a new statute creates a difficult problem of interpretation. It is, however, evidence of the strong French feeling against anything that resembles judicial lawmaking (at least outside the legal profession) that, somewhat counterproductively, the Court's answer is not binding on the lower court which asked for it.[22] But it was obviously intended that the opinion of the Court, though technically only advisory, would be followed not only by the court to which it was addressed, but by courts generally.[23] Although the use of this procedure is extremely rare,[24] there is an ongoing debate to introduce it in the Netherlands and Belgium (where it already exists in competition cases).

(ii) *Cassation and Revision*

Civil-law countries are divided over the issue regarding the Supreme Court's disposition of the case upon reversal. Some follow the German system of revision, while others have adopted the French system of cassation.[25]

Under the German system, if the Supreme Court finds reversible error in the judgment appealed, it may either (1) reverse and remand to the intermediate appellate court for a judgment consistent with its decision, or (2) reverse or modify the judgment below and itself enter such judgment as corresponds to its view of the case. This system is not substantially different from the common law tradition.

The system of cassation, typical of French inspired legal systems, is quite different, despite changes that occurred in France. Some countries that adopt the system of cassation name their Supreme Court with a

---

21. See French Code of Judicial Organization (arts. L441–1—L441–4) and French Code of Civil Procedure (arts. 1031–1—1031–7).

22. See Code of Judicial Organization, art. L441–3.

23. See French Code of Civil Procedure art. 1031–6 (stating the Court may provide that its ruling shall be published in the French Official Journal where all new French laws, decrees, and other official materials are published).

24. The number of *avis* rendered is quite limited: 17 in 2007, 14 in 2006, 11 in 2005, 4 in 2004, 2 in 2003, 8 in 2002, 8 in 2001, 16 in 2000, 14 in 1999, 20 in 1998, 16 in 1997 and 11 in 1996 (see Rapport de la Cour de Cassation 2007 available at http://www.courdecassation.fr/).

25. See F. Ferrand, Cassation française et révision allemande (1993). The appeal to the Court of Justice of the European Communities seems to have been influenced by both models. See J. Nieva, El Recurso de Casación ante el Tribunal de Justicia de las Comunidades Europeas 135–41 (1998).

corresponding name, such as France and Belgium (*Cour de Cassation*) or Italy (*Corte Suprema de Cassazione*). However, this is not the case in all countries and may create some confusion. For example, the Supreme Court in Greece is called *Areios Pagos* for historical reasons. In Spain, it is called *Tribunal Supremo* and in the Netherlands *Hoge Raad* (High Council). In Italy, it is common to refer to the *Corte di Cassazione* simply as *Corte Suprema*.

Under the system of cassation originated in revolutionary France, the highest court traditionally has only the power to *casser,* i.e., to break, quash, or nullify the judgment below. It may not substitute the judgment below by its own final judgment, but instead must remand the case to the court of appeals for a decision on the merits.

An interesting peculiarity of the cassation model even for civil-law countries is that, although a decision of the Court of Cassation has strong persuasive authority, it is not binding whatsoever on the court of appeals that issued the appealed decision.[26] Therefore, in reversing a decision, the Court of Cassation remands the case to a different court of appeals (usually in a neighboring city). In Italy, France, and Belgium, however, the Court may elect to remand the case to either a different court of appeals or to a different panel comprised of different judges of the same court of appeals.[27]

The decision issued by the first court of appeals is void, and the second court of appeals (the one to which the case is remanded to) must decide—possibly within the limits shaped by the Court of Cassation—the issues of law and fact anew. The second Court of Appeals is free to take new evidence and the parties are free to make new claims.[28] There may be a completely new trial, similar to the trials in the court of first instance and in the first court of appeals.

As a rule, the second court of appeals will then decide the case in accordance with the legal views expressed by the highest court, and the case will be over. But upon such remand, it may happen that the court of appeals refuses to follow the opinion of the Court of Cassation. Of course, if the court of appeals issues a judgment defying the view previously expressed by the highest court in the same case, the losing party most likely will appeal again to the Court of Cassation. This time, the appeal is heard in France by the *assemblée plénière*, a super-panel of the Supreme Court consisting of 19 judges. This super panel includes the presiding judge of the court, the presiding judges and the most senior judges of all panels, and one additional judge from each panel.[29] If this large judicial body takes the same

---

26. Some countries that follow the French model have departed from that traditional rule. Since 1942, in Italy, the Court of Appeals is bound by the legal principles established by the Court of Cassation's opinion. See Italian Code of Civil Procedure (art. 384). See also the Statute of the Court of Justice of the European Communities (art. 61.2).

27. See the Codes of Civil Procedure of France (art. 626), Italy (art. 383).

28. See French Code of Civil Procedure (arts. 632–633).

29. See Code of Judicial Organization (arts. L431–6 and L421–5). Before this super-panel was instituted in 1967, cases of this kind had to be decided by the so-called *chambres réunies*, a body which consisted of an

view of the case as the much smaller panel (chamber), which previously entered the Court of Cassation's first judgment of reversal and remand, there will be a second reversal. This time, however, the *assemblée plénière* remands the case to a third court of appeals, which is bound to follow the legal views expressed in the judgment of reversal. This third Court of Appeals, however, is still not bound by the findings of fact of the court of first instance or the previous two courts of appeal. Therefore, in some cases there may be a fourth retrial of the case.

If a case involves a question of principle, it may be referred to the super panel even when initially reaching the *Cour de Cassation*. A reference to the super-panel would be appropriate in cases involving intrinsically important matters as well as in cases where there are conflicts among the courts of appeal or between those courts and the *Cour de Cassation*. Such decisions are binding on remand. While the use of the super-panel is mandatory on a second appeal, it is only discretionary on the first appeal.[30]

There is no adversarial process and the loser who appeals will have a unilateral relationship with the Court of Cassation. Of course, the winner may intervene and make his or her case for maintaining the decision below. However, such a proceeding is expensive because it requires hiring a special attorney (*avoué*) authorized to litigate in the Court of Cassation.[31] Since the decision is not binding, even if the loser prevails on cassation, the winner will have a second opportunity to plead his or her case before the second court of appeals. Therefore, in practice, in most cases, the winner at the court of appeals will not participate in the proceedings before the Court of Cassation.

The danger of such complexities and uncertainties is real although relatively small. On average, the *assemblée plénière* has to be called together a few times a year to deal with such situations. When a conflict occurs, however, the time until a final decision is reached is indeed long.

The complex procedure does, however, also have a function in the legal system. In the absence of dissenting opinions,[32] repeated refusals by several intermediate appellate courts to follow rulings of the *Cour de Cassation* involving the same general principle, may show some change in judicial thinking. As discussed above, this may lead to the assignment of a case to the *assemblée plénière* composed of 19 judges rather than to the regular panel of five judges, thus increasing the likelihood of a modification of the *Cour de cassation*'s position. In Belgium, when the *Cour de Cassation*, in *assemblée plénière*, quashes a decision for the second time, the Ministry of Justice and the Parliament will be notified.[33]

---

even larger number of judges and resembled a true en banc sitting of the then approximately one hundred members of the court. See P. Herzog, Civil Procedure in France 163 (1967).

30. See Code of Judicial Organization (art. L431–6).

31. See *supra* at 510.

32. See *infra* Chapter 6, Section 4(d) at 556 (Dissenting Opinions).

33. See Belgian Code of Civil Procedure (art. 1121).

One has to understand the historical reasons for this excessive complexity of the French system of "cassation." Created in 1790 revolutionary France, it was originally a political body composed of politicians (not judges) and connected to the legislative branch. Based on a strict ideology of separation of powers, its objective was to control the Judiciary's correct application of the law as created (and interpreted) by the legislature. The fact that it was not a jurisdictional body explains why the appeal was limited to issues of law, why it could not decide the conflict between the parties, and why it had to remand the case to the court of appeals. The separation of powers explains why its judgments were not binding on the court of appeals. With time, however, its jurisdictional character prevailed, and the Council of State was transformed into a traditional court with independent judges, yet its fundamental characteristics persisted, particularly the requirement to quash decisions and remand them to the court of appeals. Because of judicial abuses committed by the *Parliements* during the *ancien régime*, post-revolutionary France was unwilling to entrust the country's highest court with much power. As time went on and the practical problems created by the non-finality of decisions of the Court of Cassation became intolerable, the legislator gradually accorded binding effect to some decisions of that Court but only to those rendered by a super-panel.

In a later attempt to lighten the load of the Court, a somewhat limited effort was made to modify the classical system of pure cassation. The Court of Cassation, in its discretion, may reverse the judgment without remand if further proceedings are unnecessary (e.g., if the Court reverses on the ground that no court in France had jurisdiction to deal with the case) or if the Court can apply the correct rule to the facts of the case, as found by the court of appeals and without there being a need for any further factual inquiry. In that last case, the Court of Cassation substitutes the judgment of the court of appeals with its own and renders the appropriate final judgment. This is called "cassation without remand" (*cassation sans renvoi*).[34]

This seems to confer upon the Court of Cassation, albeit with limitations, the same kind of power that is possessed by an American or German Supreme Court, i.e., in case of a reversal, to choose between remand the case to the court of appeals or to issue a final decision where remand is not necessary to resolve new factual questions.

---

34. See the French Code of Civil Procedure art. 627, as amended in 1979 and the Code of Judicial Organization, art. L411–3. Before 1967, this power did not exist at all in France, and all judgments that were reversed were necessarily remanded. In 1967, power was given in a more limited fashion only to the *assemblée plénière*. In 1979, this power was extended to the Court's regular panels as well. See also the Codes of Civil Procedure of Italy (art. 384, as amended in 1990), Uruguay (art. 277.1), Peru (art. 396.1), Venezuela (art. 375). See also the Statute of the Court of Justice of the European Communities (art. 61.1) and the Ibero–American Model Code of Civil Procedure (art. 247.1). See C. Consolo, F. Luiso & B. Sassani, Commentario alla Riforma del Processo Civile 457–80 (1996). The Greek Court of Cassation had this power from 1957 to 1993, but now a remand is mandatory in all cases. See P. Yessiou–Faltsi, Civil Procedure in Hellas 272 and 280 (1995).

This innovation is quite significant because it represents a major departure from the traditional cassation model to the point that the difference between cassation and revision is now almost meaningless, and is simply a matter of degree, perspective, or mindset.

However, the traditional cassation ideology lives on and should not be underestimated. Because of its traditions, the Court of Cassation appears to make a somewhat limited use of its power to reverse without remand.[35] Some civil-law scholars still consider the power to reverse without remand an exception.[36] Other scholars still say first that the Court of Cassation "cannot substitute the decision" of the Court of Appeals, only to make a clarification a few lines below that the traditional formula was changed by the 1979 legislation and a more nuanced language would be more accurate.[37]

Although not negligible, the cassation without remand (*cassation sans renvoi*) is still an uncommon occurrence in practice. According to the statistics of the French Court of Cassation, in 2008, 24% of the requests for cassation in civil litigation were rejected on the merits, 19% were quashed with remand, and in only 3% of the cases was cassation without remand ordered. The remaining 54% of the cases were dismissed for various grounds (inadmissibility, settlement, etc.).[38]

The technique of reversing a judgment without remand, however, is not provided as an exception in the Codes; the law simply says that the Court may substitute the judgment whenever a judgment is possible and may not do so whenever further activity in the second instance is necessary. Whenever possible, the Court of Cassation has complete discretion to substitute the decision below or remand.

The traditional rule of mandatory remand may have made sense in the first decades after the French Revolution, when the Court of Cassation was a semi-legislative body, in charge of quashing decisions from the judiciary branch that would violate the "official interpretation" of the law, as declared by the legislature. However, the persistence of this tradition makes little sense in a Court within the judiciary branch.

Therefore, although clearly different in several aspects, in essence, there is no fundamental difference between the modern system of cassation, the German revision, or common-law Supreme Court.[39] The system of

---

35. See R. Lindon, De certaines récentes modifications de la procédure devant la Cour de Cassation, 1980 J.C.P. I 2967; P. Hébraud, "Aggiornamento" de la Cour de Cassation, 1979 D.Chr. 205, 210–12.

36. See L. Cadiet & E. Jeuland, Droit Judiciaire Privé 644 (2006); C. Mandrioli, Corso di Diritto Processuale Civile 275 (2006).

37. See S. Guinchard, F. Ferrand & C. Chainais, Procédure Civile. Droit interne et droit communautaire 1251 (2008). See also C.

Mandrioli, Corso di Diritto Processuale Civile 274 and note 1 (2006).

38. See www.courdecassation.fr (last visited January 21, 2009).

39. In general, whenever necessary, a U.S. Supreme Court decision must remand the case to the Court below for proceedings according to the opinion rendered. However, the Supreme Court may substitute the Court of Appeals decision for the decision of the court of first instance and end the case.

cassation, for example, is not fundamentally different from a system of courts of appeal limited to issues of law, i.e., cannot make findings of fact, as is the rule in common-law countries. The legal issues decided by these courts may be of legal or constitutional nature, and the decision may be binding or not, depending on the peculiarities of the legal systems.

The ideology of cassation is very strong, almost a source of pride and identity for those countries that adopt such a system. The technique of cassation has almost mythical stature and is considered different from the American and German models. One has to master it to understand it, or so we are told. To stress the point that a cassation is intrinsically different from an appeal, the word "appeal" is not even used: technically, there is no *appel en cassation*, but a *pourvoi en cassation*. In Italy, the expressions used are *appello* for appeals to the Court of Appeals and *ricorso per cassazione* for "appeals" to the Supreme Court.

However, there are breaches in the levee. From an outsider's perspective, and being respectful, but not bound by the local's self-perception, as a comparatist must do, regardless of how peculiar they perceive their own cassation technique, and regardless of the power of tradition, the fact is that the differences between them are now secondary and will not hold a careful analysis. In practice, the difference will probably last for a few more decades. Progress in the area of cassation without remand will probably come painfully slow, but is inevitable. It is true though that in legal systems that still adopt the pure system of cassation, like in Greece, the difference between cassation and revision is still relevant, but this is not the case anymore in most other countries, like France, Spain, Italy, and Belgium, for example.

The traditional method of cassation is not even as peculiar as one might think. The U.S. Supreme Court ordinarily reverses judgments and remands them to the court below for proceedings "not inconsistent" with the opinion rendered. The only difference from the traditional cassation model is that the opinion is binding. In the rare cases in which the court below is recalcitrant or evasive in following the Supreme Court's mandate, the party will again appeal to the Supreme Court, who could then enter a judgment with award of execution or remand again with direction to enter a specific judgment. It is still unsettled whether the judge below may be held in contempt of court.[40]

Another example of miscommunication is that civil law scholars consider that the Court of Cassation is not a third instance *because* the Court does not decide issues of fact. So goes the myth: there are two instances (first instance and court of appeals) plus the Court of Cassation.

This observation is misplaced on several levels, at least for the purpose of a comparative analysis. First of all, in common-law countries, the appeal to the court of appeals is also limited to issues of law, and no one doubts

---

40. See R. Fallon, D. Meltzer & D. Shapiro, Hart and Wechsler's, The Federal Courts and the Federal System 481–83 (2003); C. A. Wright & M. K. Kane, Law of Federal Courts 805–06 (2002).

that it is a "second instance". To accept the civil-law logic, one has to say that in the common-law tradition there is only one instance, which does not make much sense.

Second, nowhere in the concept of "instance" does it say there must be a decision on issues of fact. "Instance" for the purposes of this comment, is merely a court level. A definition of "instance" that limits it to issues of fact is too artificial and formalistic to have any usefulness. The word "instance" or "appeal" should mean nothing more than that a case is submitted for consideration to a higher court.

Another reason why the cassation is not considered a third instance under the traditional civil-law theory is because the Court of Cassation remands the case to the court of appeals and does not substitute its decision. As we have seen, the German revision as well as the common-law Supreme Courts may also remand the case to the court of appeals with instruction on how to proceed, and no one doubts it is a "third instance" Moreover, as we have seen, modern courts of cassation have the power to substitute the court of appeal decision whenever possible. It does not make sense to say, as some civil-law scholars do, that, when the court of cassation substitutes the judgment, it is a true "third instance", but not when it remands the case to the court of appeals.

A civil-law attorney should have some difficulty to explain to a client that an "appeal" to the court of cassation is not "technically" an "appeal" or a "third instance." Intuitively, to a client, this looks very similar to an appeal, especially because it may last longer and cost more than the previous ones. Moreover, the client would most likely be indifferent to whether this is technically a third instance limited to issues of law or a "cassation". Indeed, this does not seem to be a useful classification but merely a peculiarity of those countries with a system of cassation. As a matter of fact, several civil-law countries consider their Supreme Courts to indeed be a third instance.

Putting aside mere technicalities, civil-law countries have three levels of courts (or instances) exactly like common-law countries. There are some differences between them, but the main difference is that common-law countries restrict the second and third instances to issues of law while civil-law countries restrict only the third instance to issues of law.

One must admit that the nomenclature used is merely a matter of mindset or perception. Whether there are "two instances plus cassation" or "three instances" does not change the fact that there are three court levels and two appeals.

In the civil-law tradition, a case can only be fully enforced after it reaches the Court of Cassation. The common-law tradition, however, is much more liberal: a judgment is immediately enforceable the moment it is entered, even if a first appeal is pending. In most civil-law countries, judgments appealed to the Supreme Court may be immediately enforced, even if not yet res judicata.[41] A judgment appealed to the court of appeals is

---

41. See Codes of Civil Procedure of France (art. 579), Italy (art. 373), Belgium (art. 1397). See also the Statute of the Court of Justice of the European Communities (art. 60).

not enforceable, but, in some countries, the first instance judge may declare it enforceable on request of one of the parties.[42]

If the judgment is reversed in the Court of Cassation, the defendant has a right to restitution of the amount paid, and, in some countries, damages as well (if one can prove them). This "temporary enforcement" of the judgment includes the seizure and expropriation of the defendant's property and the transfer of money to the plaintiff.

The plaintiff may indeed enforce the judgment while a cassation appeal is pending and risk the unnecessary expense and embarrassment in case it is reversed. However, plaintiffs usually will not enforce the judgment before it is res judicata. If a plaintiff insists on enforcement, the defendant may request the court to suspend enforcement of the judgment, whenever there is a risk of irreparable damage to the defendant. The court may also order the defendant to post a bond. In some civil-law countries, the defendant may also deposit the payment into a government or private account in order to avoid the transfer to the plaintiff.

Due to problems of delay, there seems to be a trend in civil-law countries to adopt the common-law rule and allow provisional enforcement of first instance judgments, unless the court determines otherwise. This has been the rule in Italy since 1990.[43]

(iii) Internal Contradictions in Supreme Court Decisions

Let us now turn to the question dealing with the internal functioning of a Supreme Court. As mentioned before, civil-law Supreme Courts have dozens or hundreds of judges who sit in panels. Some of these panels deal with civil cases, and others with criminal matters. In the German *Bundesgerichtshof*, a case is heard by five judges. In the French *Cour de cassation*, where formerly a quorum of seven judges was required to hear a case, the number is now also reduced to five;[44] as noted, non-criminal cases will now go initially to a reduced panel of three members of the court, which may decide them if the decision appears obvious.[45] Each panel of the Supreme Court is called a *Senat* in Germany, a *Chambre* in France, a *Sezione* in Italy. The panel consists of more than five members but only five judges will hear a given case (sometimes also called the quorum).

Although all cases relating to a given field of the law (e.g., divorce, or corporations) normally are referred to the same panel,[46] it is inevitable that

42. See Codes of Civil Procedure of France (arts. 515 and 539) and Belgium (arts. 1397 and 1398).

43. See Italian Code of Civil Procedure (arts. 282 and 283); C. Consolo, F. Luiso & B. Sassani, Commentario alla Riforma del Processo Civile 255–82 (1996).

44. See French Code of Judicial Organization (art. L131–6–1).

45. See J. Boré, La Loi du 6 août 1981 et la réforme de la Cour de Cassation, 1981 D.Chr. 299.

46. This system of specialization is particularly refined in Germany. For a detailed description, see D. J. Meador, Appellate Subject Matter Organization: The German Design from an American Perspective, 5 Hastings Int'l & Comp. L.Rev. 27 (1981).

occasional conflicts arise between the decisions of various panels, especially in connection with general problems that cut across diverse areas of law. This problem is rather common in the practice of the United States Courts of Appeals, which ordinarily sits in panels.[47] The problem in the U.S., however, is not quite as serious as it is in the civil-law countries because the U.S. Courts of Appeals are not courts of last resort. If a conflict develops between two panels of a court of appeals,[48] and such conflict is not resolved by that court sitting *en banc*,[49] the Supreme Court ultimately may determine the disputed question. Moreover, when confronted with an intra-circuit conflict, the Supreme Court may remand a case, suggesting—and in effect directing—an *en banc* hearing before the judges of the court of appeals.[50]

The problem is more acute in countries where the Supreme Court has dozens of judges who sit in several panels rather than having a reasonable amount of judges and deciding all the cases *en banc*, like the U.S. Supreme Court.[51] The Germans sought to solve the problem by providing that any panel wishing to deviate from a prior decision of another panel had to submit the question to a plenary session. If both panels involved were civil panels, the plenary session would be attended by all the judges of the civil panels; but if a civil panel wanted to deviate from a previous decision of a criminal panel, the plenary session would become a true *plenum*, and would consist of at least two-thirds of all of the members of the court, i.e., in the case of the former German *Reichsgericht*, the predecessor of the *Bundesgerichtshof*, about fifty persons.[52] Understandably, the judges were reluctant

---

47. 28 U.S.C.A. § 46; Fed.R.App.P. 35. Cf. E. M. Wise, The Legal Culture of Troglodytes: Conflicts between Panels of the Court of Appeals, 37 Wayne L.Rev. 313 (1991).

48. According to a large body of authority, a panel of a U.S. Court of Appeals is bound to follow a precedential decision previously handed down by another panel of the same court, at least until the matter is reconsidered *en banc*. See, e.g., United States v. Olivares–Vega, 495 F.2d 827 (2d Cir.1974); United States v. Hernandez, 580 F.2d 188 (5th Cir.1978). See also Anno., 37 A.L.R.Fed. 274 (1978). Nevertheless, experience shows that intra-circuit conflicts are quite frequent. See Joseph N. Akrotirianakis, Jerry—Building the Road to the Future: An Evaluation of the White Commission Report on Structural Alternatives for the Federal Courts of Appeals, 36 San Diego L. Rev. 356 (1999); A. B. Rubin, Views from the Lower Court, 23 UCLA L.Rev. 448, 452 (1976).

49. See Fed.R.App.P. 35. It is interesting to note that pursuant to 28 U.S.C.A. § 46, as amended in 1978 and 1982, the larger circuits are permitted to hold "en

banc" hearings attended by less than all of the circuit judges. Thus the super-panel, so beloved by the civilians, came to the U.S. as well.

50. See United States ex rel. Robinson v. Johnston, 316 U.S. 649, 62 S.Ct. 1301 (1942).

51. The problem is connected with the broader question of the force of precedents, which will be discussed *infra* in Chapter 6, Section 6 at 582. At this point, the reader should provisionally assume that a "court" (including the highest "court") in a civilian country is not bound by a stringent rule of *stare decisis*, and has the power to overrule its own prior decisions. But there remains the question of whether a single panel may speak for the "court," in a matter as grave as overruling a precedent and whether Panel A may overrule a previous decision by Panel B. The discussion in the text is directed to these procedural issues.

52. For details and for interesting comparative observations, see E. J. Cohn, Precedents in Continental Law, 5 Camb.L.J. 366 (1935).

to employ this cumbersome procedure. Therefore, they developed an attitude known in Germany as *horror pleni*, making strenuous and often ingenious efforts to distinguish previous decisions in order to avoid the open admission of a conflict which would necessitate submission of the case to the *plenum*.

This unwieldy system was modified by the creation of super-panels. These super panels consist of at least nine judges if the conflict is between two civil panels and at least seventeen judges if the conflict is between a civil and criminal panel. To further reduce the need for resort to such a super-panel, an informal practice had developed in the court whereby a panel wishing to depart from a prior ruling of another panel would first ask that panel whether it wished to hold to its views. If it stated it did not, then there was no reference. That practice was made mandatory by legislation adopted in 1990.[53] The super-panels now wield the powers formerly exercised by plenary sessions.[54] The size of the group of judges who must assemble in order to resolve a conflict between panels has been reduced by this reform; and although it seems that the *horror pleni*, i.e., the reluctance of individual panels to invoke the conflict-resolving procedure, has not been entirely eliminated, the revised system is a workable one.

Until 1947, the French had no similar machinery for avoiding conflicts among panels of the Court of Cassation. This was explained as reflecting the strength of "French opinion opposed to the theory of the binding force of judicial decisions."[55] But when in 1947 the Court of Cassation was reorganized, and the number of civil panels increased, the French adopted the German system of a plenary session for the prevention of intra-court conflicts. Furthermore (again following the German example) they replaced that plenary session with a super-panel called *chambre mixte*, consisting of a number of judges varying between 13 and 25 depending on the number of panels involved. A case may be referred to a *chambre mixte*, if it involves a matter within the normal jurisdiction of more than one panel. This includes some tort matters, because claims for damages caused by a tort that is also a crime can be asserted by the private plaintiff in the criminal prosecution[56] and also includes issues already or likely to be resolved in different ways by different panels. A resort to the *chambre mixte* is mandatory if the panel dealing with the case is evenly divided.[57]

French law thus provides for two different types of super-panels of the Court of Cassation. The *assemblée plénière* determines essentially conflicts

---

53. See Gerichtsverfassungsgesetz (Law Concerning the Organization of Courts), § 132 amended in 1990; see 1990 BGBl I 2847, effective January 1, 1992.

54. Even in the absence of an intra-court conflict, any panel of the Court can refer a case of "fundamental importance" to a super-panel if, in the panel's opinion, this is necessary for the development of the law or to insure uniformity in the case law.

Gerichtsverfassungsgesetz § 132(4). It remains true, nevertheless, that the main function of the super-panels is to resolve conflicts among several panels of the Court.

55. See Cohn, *supra* note 52.

56. See *infra* Chapter 8, Section 5 at 855 (concurrent criminal and civil liability).

57. See French Code of Judicial Organization (art. L431–5—431–6).

between the Court of Cassation and the Courts of Appeals, while the *chambre mixte* resolves conflicts among panels of the Supreme Court itself.[58] Both the *chambre mixte* and the *assemblé plénière* must decide all cases referred to them even if they believe the referral was erroneous. There is no litigation over that issue.

(iv) Government Intervention

Another peculiar feature of Court of Cassation practice is that arguments are presented to the Court not only by counsel for the parties but also by the Government. The government thus serves like an *amicus curiae* even in purely private disputes. This role is performed by the *ministére public*, an expression one could translate as the "public function" or less literally the public counsel.

In France and a number of other civil-law countries (not including Germany and Japan, for example), this group of hierarchically organized government attorneys subject ultimately to the Ministry of Justice serve a dual function:

(1) They prosecute criminal proceedings and act as the government's attorneys in some other types of actions to which the Government is a party. In many countries, these hierarchically organized officials have a career pattern that parallels that of the judiciary. This ensures that the officials at the level of the court of first instance of general jurisdiction will be at essentially the same salary as the judges at that court, and likewise for the corresponding officials at the intermediate appellate courts and at the highest regular court. Their offices and collectively the officials attached to a particular court are sometimes referred to as *parquet*. Because of the similarity of their career patterns with that of the judges, these officials and the judges have a common generic name in France, that of *magistrat*. This practice is also found in some other countries. The French word *magistrat* and its equivalent in other languages therefore does not necessarily refer to a judge, a distinction not always correctly noticed in English-language news reports about judicial proceedings in the countries where that terminology is used. It might be noted that while in France they represent the governmental interest in certain civil proceedings, a different body of officials handles most litigation in which the government acts more or less like an ordinary party to a civil suit. In Germany, these government attorneys (*Staatsanwälte*) act essentially only as prosecutors.

(2) They can intervene in *any* litigation to represent the public interest.[59] This power exists even though the Government is not a party to the

58. On the *assemblée plénière* see *supra* at 512ff.

59. By considering this function of the *Parquet* in civil proceedings, we are led to a broader question: Who does, and who should, represent the public interest in civil litigation? While in the U.S. this is done by a class member or a "private attorney general," in civil-law countries this role tends to be performed either by the *ministére public* or by private associations (such as those in protection of consumers or the environment). Maybe a combination of the three models is the best approach. For thought-provoking comparative discussions, see M. Cappelletti, Governmental and Private Advocates for the

particular case and may have no financial interest in its outcome. In the lower civil courts, the power is limited and used sparingly.[60] Because every case reaching the Supreme Court affects the public interest so strongly with regards to the sound development of the law, the views of the government attorneys must be presented.[61] These views do not bind the court in any way, but because of their often brilliant quality, they may prove highly persuasive.[62]

In fact, some countries feel so strongly that a representation of the public interest is useful in the Supreme Court that they have provided for it in other situations as well. In France, for example, an official known as the *Commissaire du gouvernement* makes submission in all cases before the highest administrative court (the Council of State or *Conseil d'État*). The name of the official, government commissioner, is actually misleading. The official does not represent the interests of the government before the Council (if it is a party, it is represented by its own attorney), but the public interest and the correct legal view in general. A similar institution exists before the Court of Justice of the European Communities where an official called Advocate General, usually a highly prestigious jurist of a member state serving for a few years in that job, makes submissions in every case. The Advocate General represents only the law and the Community interest in general and not the views of any of the Community's institutions, who rely on their own lawyers. Its role is highly significant in

Public Interest in Civil Litigation, 75 Mich. L.Rev. 794 (1975); M. Cappelletti & B. Garth, The Worldwide Movement To Make Rights Effective: A General Report, in 1 Cappelletti (ed.), Access to Justice 3, at 35–48 (1978); W. B. Fisch, European Analogues to the Class Action: Group Action in France and Germany, 27 Am. J. Comp. L. 51 (1979); R. B. Cappalli & C. Consolo, Class Actions for Continental Europe? A Preliminary Inquiry, 6 Temple Int'l & Comp. L.J. 217 (1993); A. Gidi, Class Actions in Brazil: A Model for Civil Law Countries, 51 Am. J. Comp. L. 311 (2003).

60. In the lower French courts, there is an optional right to intervene in any case. See French Code of Civil Procedure Art. 425–27. This right is sparingly exercised. In certain matters, such as paternity, guardianship, committees for incompetents, financial liability of company officers, and certain bankruptcy matters, the party must inform the *ministère public* of the pendency of the proceedings so that it may give its opinion to the court. But when the public interest and the interests of the party needing special protection (minor, incompetent, etc.) seem adequately protected by counsel for the parties, the opinion may just be a brief statement of confidence in a correct decision by the court. On the other hand, in some instances in which public policy is particularly involved, the *ministère public* may actually start a civil action. This is true in cases involving the question of whether a person is a French national. See French Civil Code (art. 29–3). (If the action is started by another person the *ministère public* must be made a party.)

61. See French Code of Judicial Organization (arts. L132–1—L132–4; R132–1—R132–3), Italian Code of Civil Procedure (arts. 70.2 and 379.3); Deák & Rheinstein, The Machinery of Law Administration in France and Germany, 84 U.Pa.L.Rev. 846, 857–58 (1936).

Under U.S. practice, the Attorney General has the power to present amicus curiae briefs to the courts, and especially to the highest courts. See Fed. R. App. P. 29, and Sup. Ct. R. 36.4. But, in contrast to the French practice described in the text, *supra*, that power is sparingly exercised in the United States.

62. For a thorough comparative discussion on the impact of this institution on the style of the civil law tradition as compared to U.S. law, see M. Lasser, Judicial Deliberations (2005).

understanding the peculiarities of the unfolding European judicial process.[63]

In a few countries following the former French model, the representative of the *ministère public* can be present during the court's secret deliberations from which private parties and their counsel are rigorously excluded. This practice seems rather objectionable, especially in criminal cases where the government is not merely a defender of the public interest but a party to the proceeding. The European Court of Human Rights eventually objected to it and also held that where the representative of the *ministère public* is the last one to make submissions to the court, the defendant must be given a right to reply.[64]

In some civil-law countries that follow the French model, it is possible for the chief member of the *ministére public*, the Procurator General, to file an appeal, in a private lawsuit to the Supreme Court "in the interest of the law", whenever the court of appeals decision violates the law or represents an abuse of discretion. The *ministére public* may appeal only after the time for the parties' appeal has expired, and it is no longer reviewable. If the Court of Cassation reverses the judgment, such reversal has only "virtual value" because it does not affect the rights of the parties, who remain bound by the decision below. The original decision is res judicata between the parties and cannot be changed, but the wrong decision will eventually be overturned, and the correct legal interpretation will prevail. It is, in effect, merely a "platonic" appeal.[65] This type of appeal is rarely exercised because the judgment will never have the same precedential effect as the common law *stare decisis*.[66]

(e) Constitutional Courts and Judicial Review[1]

Outside of this general picture of the court structure, one should consider constitutional adjudication. Civil law countries—as well as common law countries—are divided on the issue. Some countries have accepted such constitutional review, some have accepted only a partial review, and

63. See the highly instructive study of M. Lasser, *supra* note 62.

64. See Borgers v. Belgium, 30 Oct. 1991, Dec. of the Eur. Ct. Hum. Rights Ser. A, No. 214–A (criminal case). By two decisions rendered on February 20, 1996, the Court extended the ruling of the *Borgers* case to civil matters.

65. See Codes of Civil Procedure of France (art. 618–1), Belgium (arts. 1088–91), Italy (art. 363), Spain (arts. 490–93), Greece (art. 557). See also the Statute of the Court of Justice of the European Communities (art. 62). See L. Cadiet & E. Jeuland, Droit judiciaire privé, 546–47 (2006) (citing Croze & Morel, for the argument that the decision is merely platonic); S. Guinchard, F. Ferrand & C. Chainais, Procédure Civile. Droit interne

et droit communautaire 1258–59 (2008); P. Yessiou–Faltsi, Civil Procedure in Hellas 280 (1995).

66. In Spain, however, such a judgment will be binding. See Spanish Code of Civil Procedure (art. 493, enacted in 2000).

1. Judicial review is a major topic in comparative law, because different countries have a different perspective on the issue of separation of powers. It is divided in three main issues: (a) the control by the judiciary of the legality of administrative acts, (b) the judicial control of the constitutionality of legislative acts, and (c) judicial review of the legality of judicial acts. In this subchapter, we are only concerned with the judicial review of the constitutionality of legislative acts.

others have not accepted it at all.[2] The true boom of constitutional adjudication happened in the aftermath of World War II under pressure from American authorities engaged in a first effort of exporting the rule of law. The trash of legality under Nazi law had persuaded the Americans that civil-law courts were not strong enough to guarantee a democratic form of government. Thus, constitutional adjudication was literally forced on Japan by General McArthur and today is vested in the ordinary Supreme Court. Nevertheless, other defeated countries with a professional tradition deeply rooted in the civil-law, like Germany or Italy, would not entrust the ordinary Courts, staffed with a career judiciary of civil servants, with the formidable political power of second-guessing, on constitutional grounds, the politically legitimized decision making of Parliaments and Governments.

Thus, many post-War constitutions have introduced special courts, comprised of the very elite of the legal profession and appointed for long terms of years by a variety of high state organs (the President, Parliaments, Prime Ministers etc.). Austria, which introduced a limited form of judicial review after World War I, served as a model. Germany and Italy introduced (or, in the case of Austria, reintroduced) judicial review after World War II.[3] Portugal and Spain included judicial review in their democratic constitutions, as did the majority of the countries in the former Soviet bloc, occasionally and to a limited extent even before the bloc's final collapse.[4] A constitutional court has been established for the Croat–Bosnian Federation established as a result of the Dayton accords. Interestingly, for an initial period of five years, it had three international members, legal scholars from Belgium, Nigeria and Syria.[5] Judicial review has also been

2. There is a large amount of writing on the topic of judicial review on comparative perspective. See, e.g., M. Cappelletti, Judicial Review in the Contemporary World (1971); A. R. Brewer–Carias, Judicial Review in Contemporary Law (1989); I. I. Kavass (ed.), Supranational and Constitutional Courts in Europe: Functions and Sources (1992); H. J. Abraham, The Judicial Process: An Introductory Analysis of the Courts of the United States, England and France 289–98 (1993).

3. On the Austrian Constitutional Court, in some ways a forerunner of the others, see K. Heller, Outline of Austrian Constitutional Law 17–31 (1989). On the German Constitutional Court, see, e.g., E. Benda, Constitutional Jurisdiction in West Germany, 19 Colum.J.Transn.L. 1 (1981); D.P. Kommers, The Constitutional Jurisprudence of the Federal Republic of Germany (2d ed. 1997); P. Kirchhof and D.P. Kommers (eds.), Germany and its Basic Law (1993); J. M. McLaughlin, The Unification of Germany: What Would Jhering Say?, 17 Fordham Int'l L.J. 277, 285–87 (1994). On the Italian Con-

stitutional Court, see T. Ritterspach, Constitutional Review in Italy, 4 Human Rights L.J. 179 (1983); A. Pizzorusso, V. Vigoriti & G.L. Certoma, The Constitutional Review of Legislation in Italy, 56 Temple L.Q. 503 (1983).

4. On the Polish Constitutional Tribunal, created as early as 1982, see M. F. Brzezinski, The Emergence of Judicial Review in Eastern Europe, The Case of Poland, 41 Am. J.Comp.L. 153 (1993). See also, E. Stein, International Law in Internal Law: Toward Internationalization of Central–Eastern European Constitutions? 88 Am.J.Comp.L. 427 (1994) (discussion of constitutional courts' roles in connection with international law); G. M. Danilenko, The New Russian Constitution and International Law, 88 Am.J.Int'l L. 451 (1994). W. W. Schwarzer, Civil and Human Rights and the Courts under the New Constitution of the Russian Federation, 18 Int'l Lawyer 825 (1994).

5. See G.A. Hengstler, Out of the Rubble, 82 A.B.A.J. March, 1996, p. 52.

accepted by some countries in the Middle and Far East with a civil-law influence[6] and by a number of members of the Commonwealth. Interestingly, as already mentioned, the presence of a written constitution and of a Court (or Courts) with power of constitutional adjudication in the hands of a professionalized judiciary has become the very idea of Western legality, exported globally with multi-party elections (most recent examples being Afghanistan and Iraq).

The *method* of judicial review adopted by most civil-law countries, however, differs from that in the United States. While in the U.S. any court may declare a statute unconstitutional, in civil-law countries, the power to declare statutes unconstitutional is traditionally entrusted to a special Constitutional Court which stands outside and, in a sense, above the ordinary court system.[7] The judges of the Constitutional Court are subject to special appointment rules so that it is not, or at least not entirely, composed of career judges.[8]

Germany is a fairly typical example on how a case reaches the Constitutional Court. There are three basic ways (we will ignore fine details) of challenging the constitutionality of a statute before the Constitutional Court.

The first way in which the issue of (un)constitutionality may reach the Constitutional Court is through a political initiative. The Court must determine the constitutionality of a statute upon the request of the federal government (i.e., the Chancellor and his cabinet), of a state government, or of a specified number of legislators. The Germans refer to this as the "abstract" review of norms. In some countries, it must be used within specified time limits following the enactment of legislation (or official publication). It is not used very often, but, when used, it is generally by a parliamentary minority party or a state government that has strong objections to a new statute involving a fundamental choice of public policy. It thus provides a fast way by which the validity of legislation that encounters strong opposition and presents constitutional problems can be settled with general binding effect. The constitutionality of the statute is decided "in abstract", not as part of the decision of a concrete case, so it occurs without a "case or controversy" as in the American sense. This model, therefore, would not be constitutionally acceptable in the U.S.

---

6. See, e.g., A. el-Morr, The Supreme Constitutional Court of Egypt and the Protection of Human and Political Rights, in Ch. Mallat (ed.), Islam and Public Law 229–60 (1993); cf., critically and noting the strains between Western and Islamic Ideas, B. Botiveau, Contemporary Reinterpretations of Islamic Law: The Case of Egypt, ibid., 261; L. W. Beer (ed.), Constitutional Systems in Late Twentieth Century Asia (1992); Kun Yang, Judicial Review and Social Change in the Korean Democratizing Process, 49 Am. J.Comp.L. 1 (1993).

7. Some civil-law countries like Japan, under U.S. influence, also allow regular judges to declare the unconstitutionality of statutes. Although extremely interesting from a comparative perspective, they will not be discussed here.

8. The Council of Europe has collected a list of most Constitutional Courts and equivalent bodies. See http://www.venice.coe.int/site/dynamics/N_court_links_ef.asp (last visited on Jan. 21, 2009).

The second way is by judicial referral. When a question of the constitutionality of a statute is raised before an ordinary court (other than the Constitutional Court), judges may have different options. They may apply the statute if convinced it is constitutional. If the court has doubts about that issue, however, it may not declare the statute unconstitutional but must refer the matter to the Constitutional Court, which will decide the issue of constitutionality and then remand the case. Meanwhile, the proceeding is stayed.

This typical model to raise a fundamental question of interpretation has been reproduced in the European Union (Art. 234 of the Treaty establishing the European Community) as the most typical way of bringing an issue of European Law in front of the Court of Justice of the European Communities in Luxembourg. Should a national court believe there is an issue of interpretation of European law that is relevant to its decision and that requires an authoritative decision by the European Court of Justice, it will stay the proceeding and transfer the issue to Luxembourg.[9]

This device is not entirely unknown in the United States either. In principle, a U.S. Court of Appeals may "certify" a question of law "as to which instructions are desired" from the U.S. Supreme Court. However, in practice, this is rarely invoked because the Supreme Court has discretion to take the case, despite the clear language of the statute.[10] In addition, about half the states allow a "certification" procedure by which federal courts may submit an unsettled question of state law arising before them to the appropriate state Supreme Court for guidance.

The third way of bringing a constitutional issue before the Court is by way of Constitutional Complaint (*Verfassungsbeschwerde*). Any person or corporation who feels that some judicial (or administrative) action has violated the person's constitutional rights (e.g., by enforcing an unconstitutional statute) may file such a complaint, but only after having exhausted all judicial remedies. Constitutional complaints constitute over 90% of the Constitutional Court's caseload. The Court has therefore instituted a screening procedure to quickly weed out proceedings that are clearly unauthorized or without merits.[11] In some jurisdictions, such as Italy, this

9. See http://curia.europa.eu/en/instit/presentationfr/index_cje.htm (last visited on Jan. 21, 2009).

10. See 28 U.S.C. § 1254(2) and Rules of the Supreme Court of the United States (Rule 19). See C. A. Wright & M. K. Kane. Law of Federal Courts 780–82 (2002) (arguing against the use of this device because they bring to the Court "abstract questions of law, divorced from a complete factual setting in which they may be explored more carefully").

11. The already heavy caseload of the Court increased after the reunification of Germany. Some members of the Court apparently favored the introduction of a system giving the Court discretion whether to hear cases, as with the *certiorari* procedure before the United States Supreme Court; others favored the establishment of "constitutional advocates," along the lines of the "advocates general" before the Court of Justice of the European Communities, who assist that court by making in each case an impartial presentation as to the applicable law and its relation to the facts. In the end, both ideas were rejected in favor of a tightening of the screening procedure. See R. Herzog and R. Gerhardt, Verfassungsanwälte als "Filter" vor dem BVerfG, 24 Zeitschr.f. Rechtspolitik

method is not available. In other countries, like in Belgium, it is embedded in the first way of abstract review.

Whatever method used, in practice, a litigant must go through four levels of courts to have a statute declared unconstitutional. If a party claims a statute to be applied against it is unconstitutional, it will have to use the Constitutional Complaint only if it fails to convince the lower court that the matter should be referred to the Constitutional Court. The primary way to challenge the constitutionality of a statute is the referral method; the constitutional complaint is subsidiary. If a statute is challenged as incompatible with the federal Constitution in U.S. state courts, there will be four levels of courts as well: state trial court, state court of appeals, state supreme court and U.S. Supreme Court. Because the issue of time can be very sensitive in constitutional matters, the Constitutional Court of South Africa is entrusted with the power to entertain constitutional complaints outside of the exhaustion requirement.[12]

The Constitutional Complaint is not limited to claims of the unconstitutionality of a statute. It can be used whenever any judicial or administrative action is unconstitutional, for instance if a constitutional statute is applied in an unconstitutional manner. It seems that complexity may be the cost for singling out a particularly important issue and submitting it to a court specifically created to deal with it. The German system, followed in other civil-law countries, avoids inconsistent decisions on constitutional issues and submits these issues, which are usually of great political as well as economic and legal importance, to a body particularly well equipped, through the way its members are chosen, to deal with it.[13]

No similar mechanism of judicial control of the constitutionality of legislative acts existed in France and in countries that have followed the French model. From the time of the French Revolution until 1958, France had always been cited as the classical example of a civil-law country that, like Great Britain within the common law orbit, lacked judicial review. Historical reasons (indeed questionable if one considers the parallel British experience), namely the abuses by the pre-revolutionary courts called (somewhat confusingly) *Parlements*,[14] are usually offered as an explanation. The revolutionary but long-surviving notion that the legislature represented "national sovereignty" and was therefore only subject to political constraints, made the French traditionally feel that separation of powers means, in particular, that the judiciary may not interfere with the legislative or executive branches of government.

The 1958 Constitution, however, discarded the dogma of the strong legislature in favor of a strong executive and simultaneously created a

28 (1991); E. Klein, Konzentration durch Entlastung? Das Fünfte Gesetz zur Änderung des Gesetzes über das Bundesverfassungsgericht, 46 N.J.W. 2073 (1993).

12. http://www.constitutionalcourt.org.za/site/home.htm.

13. On these points, see, e.g., F.L. Morton, Judicial Review in France: A Comparative Analysis, 36 Am.J.Comp.L. 89, 109 (1988).

14. See the article by Deák & Rheinstein, *infra* at 351.

Constitutional Council.[15] The Council is composed of nine members, three appointed by the President of the Republic and three each by the presiding officers of the Parliamentary Assemblies (Senate and National Assembly). In addition, former Presidents of the Republic are *de jure* life members of the Council. When a statute has been passed by the French legislature, certain public officials, i.e., the President, the Prime Minister, the presiding officers of the Senate and the National Assembly, or sixty deputies or sixty senators may, before the statute is promulgated,[16] submit it to the Constitutional Council for a review of its constitutionality. If the Council declares the statute unconstitutional, it may not be promulgated. If held unconstitutional in part, only the constitutional provisions that are severable may be promulgated. Some particularly important measures, especially so-called organic laws, which regulate the basic functioning of the main governmental bodies, must automatically be submitted to the Council. Until 2008, the constitutionality of legislation, could not be attacked once the time to bring the challenge before the Council has passed, and no action had been taken.

To summarize, until 2008 in France, the constitutionality of a statute could only be attacked before its promulgation and only by political groups or political leaders.[17] Such attacks are relatively more likely when a parliamentary majority adopts laws to which a minority strongly objects, especially when they involve matters of high visibility.[18] Since the President's and the legislature's terms of office do not coincide, it happens that the majority party in Parliament can be of a different political hue than the President (usually resulting in *cohabitation*). Because the French president has no veto power (he or she may only demand that Parliament reconsider a law), the power to go to the Constitutional Council would then be of use

15. See the French Constitution (Title VII, Arts. 56 to 63). As originally set up, only the President of France, the Prime Minister and the presiding officers of the two houses of the legislature could bring statutes before the Council. Two developments subsequently increased the significance of the Council. A 1974 amendment to the French Constitution added the sixty members of either house to the list of persons entitled to do so. Also, a little earlier, the Council had held that, in assessing the constitutionality of a statute, it could rely not only on the text of the 1958 Constitution (which contains no formal bill of rights, only isolated provisions on that topic), but also on two documents referred to in its Preamble, namely the 1789 Declaration of the Rights of Man and of the Citizen and the Preamble of the 1946 Constitution, which contains numerous, very extensive, but rather vague statements on human rights, including what are sometimes known as "social and economic rights." On that topic, see G. D. Haimbaugh, Jr., Was it France's Marbury v. Madison?, 35 Ohio St.L.J. 910 (1974); A. Stone, The Birth of Judicial Politics in France: The Constitutional Council in Comparative Perspective (1992); J. Bell, French Constitutional Law 9–56 (1992), with a selection of Constitutional Council decisions in English translation at 272ff.

16. Or ratification or approval of an international agreement or entry into force of the rules of procedure of the assemblies.

17. However, any interested party can, at any time, seek judicial review of the constitutionality of a decree enacted by the executive.

18. Thus, the new conservative majority elected in March 1993, had, by August 1993, passed laws on identity checks, education, immigration, and on a revision of the Code of Criminal Procedure, all of which had some civil rights implications. By August 1993, they had all been submitted to the Constitutional Council by members of the legislature belonging to the—then out of power—left.

to the President. The Constitutional Council has a number of functions (including certain electoral or referendum disputes) in addition to those mentioned here. The French Constitutional review, therefore, has traditionally been mainly a political device.

In any event, attacks on the constitutionality of statutes in France are much rarer than in Germany or the United States. The former French President Mitterand recognized there was room for improvement in this area and proposed a constitutional revision under which the courts generally could have referred questions regarding the constitutionality of a statute to the Constitutional Council, but the proposal failed, an indication of the strength the idea of parliamentary supremacy still retains in France.[19]

Finally, in 2008, breaking two centuries of tradition, the French Constitution was amended. The newly enacted art. 61-1 provides that whenever, during a proceeding, a party claims that a legislative provision infringes the rights and freedoms guaranteed by the Constitution, the matter may be referred to the Constitutional Council by the Council of State or by the Court of Cassation. A party still cannot challenge the constitutionality of a statute directly in a proceeding; rather, the party must request the Council of State or by the Court of Cassation to refer the question to the Constitutional Court. A statute shall determine the conditions for the application of this provision, including the period by which the Constitutional Court must issue a decision.

Under the French Constitution of 1958, the legislative power is actually divided between the legislature and the executive. Article 34 of the Constitution lists all those matters on which Parliament can legislate. For some matters, Parliament is authorized to enact the "fundamental principles," while the details are to be filled in by presidential decree. The power of the executive to fill in such details or to legislate freely on subjects not reserved for Parliament is not a delegated power, but derived from the Constitution. It cannot be taken away by Parliament, and any contrary legislation, when submitted to the Constitutional Council, will be declared void. Indeed, the drafters of the Constitution intended this to be one of the Council's main functions. Furthermore, the Constitution authorizes Parliament to delegate, under some limitations, legislative powers to the executive even on matters normally reserved for it. Article 37 grants the executive branch the exclusive power to legislate by decree in the areas not covered by Article 34. This has an impact on judicial review. The constitu-

---

19. See F. Luchaire, Le contrôle de la loi sur renvoi des juridictions, une réforme constitutionnnelle différée, 106 Rev.dr.pub. & sci.pol. 1625 (1990). Several other proposals for reform have been put forward from time to time, including the introduction of review at the instigation of members of the public.

In Chile, there is a system of judicial review somewhat similar to that in France, but a citizen whose rights have been affected by an unconstitutional statute may attack it after its promulgation provided there has been no preenactment decision as to its constitutionality. See R.B. Cappalli, Comparative South American Civil Procedure: A Chilean Perspective, 21 U. Miami Inter-Am.L.Rev. 239, 293–301 (1989–90).

As part of a turn towards a truly democratic system, one country in Francophone Africa, Benin, has created a Constitutional Court. See Int'l Herald Tribune, March 4, 1996, at 2.

tionality of statutes is subject to the very limited review just discussed, but, according to French legal tradition, any interested party can have the legality of an administrative act reviewed by the administrative courts and ultimately by the highest administrative tribunal, the *Conseil d'Etat* (Council of State). Included in this review is the constitutionality of decrees adopted by the executive under Article 37. For example, the French Code of Civil Procedure was adopted by decree. It included a provision interpreted to mean that a court could decide a case on a legal theory not discussed by the parties and not mentioned by the court before its decision. In a proceeding brought by several bar associations (the *Conseil* is liberal as to standing), that provision was declared unconstitutional. A new provision was eventually added to the Code stating that whenever a court wishes to decide a case on a theory not put forward by the parties, it must so inform them and give them an opportunity to argue the point.[20]

A variety of interconnected courts exists in the civil law. An ordinary or administrative case might be stayed at any moment and referred to a special court, such as a Constitutional Court or the European Court of Justice, to decide matters on which ordinary or administrative judges do not have jurisdiction.

(f) Administrative Courts and Judicial Review

(i) The Civil–Law Dichotomy Between Private–Law and Public–Law Litigation

So far, we have discussed the courts dedicated to the resolution of private disputes.[1] In some civil-law countries, in addition to the "ordinary" courts (which deal with the resolution of conflicts between private parties) and "criminal courts", there are also specialized courts and proceedings for "public-law litigation".[2]

A controversy involving the validity or propriety of an administrative act involves issues of public law and, under the civil-law system, will be determined by a separate hierarchy of administrative tribunals.[3] The subject-matter jurisdiction of ordinary and administrative courts depends on whether the dispute belongs to the realm of private law or that of public law (administrative law). Therefore, the distinction between private and public law is of much greater practical significance in civil-law systems than

20. See the Council of State Decision of October 12, 1979, 1979 D.J. 606, voiding former paragraph 3 of art. 12 of the Code of Civil Procedure. The new provision mentioned is paragraph 3 of art. 16.

1. Concerning the historical reasons for the sharp distinction between "private law" and "public law" in continental countries, see *supra* at 381ff and infra 864.

2. As we will see below, the meaning of "public-law litigation" in the civil-law tradition has nothing to do with "public-law litiga-tion" or "public interest litigation" as these expressions are commonly used in the U.S. See A. Chayes, The Role of the Judge in Public Law Litigation, 89 Harv. L. Rev. 1281 (1976).

3. For a comprehensive comparative treatment of the subject, see Max–Planck–Institut fur auslandisches offentliches Recht und Volkerrecht, Judicial Protection against the Executive (H. Mosler, Ed. 1971), especially Vol. 3. See also R. Stürner, Suing the Sovereign in Europe and Germany, 34 Geo. Wash. Int'l L. Rev. 663 (2003).

under the common law (where both types of disputes are resolved in the same courts).

The jurisdiction of administrative courts as well as what constitutes "public-law litigation" (or "administrative proceedings") varies from country to country. Examples include disputes over administrative decisions, tax, appointment to public office, and public authorities revoking or refusing to issue business or construction licenses.

These courts deal with *judicial* remedies available to a party who feels aggrieved by an act of governmental bureaucracy (judicial review of administrative acts). In many countries there are less formal, non-judicial channels through which a citizen can seek redress against alleged government arbitrariness.[4]

In the US, cases in which the government is a party are handled by ordinary courts under writs of *certiorari*, *mandamus* or *prohibition*, or some statutory version of these ancient writs. However, there are certain courts which only deal with specific issues, such as the U.S. Court of Federal Claims (with jurisdiction to hear claims against the U.S.) and the U.S. Tax Court (with jurisdiction to hear federal tax matters).

This difference between the civil law and the common law, however, should not be exaggerated. Common-law countries also assign practical importance to the distinction between "private" and "public rights" disputes, although for a more limited purpose. The legislative branch of the U.S. federal government has the power (not infrequently exercised) to have cases involving public rights—i.e., cases ordinarily involving a dispute between the Government and a non-governmental party—adjudicated by special legislative courts or by administrative agencies. The latter's decision may be subject to review by ordinary courts, but such review can be limited to issues of law, in much the same manner as the reviewing court's scope of review is limited in jury cases. Congress has no similar power to assign cases involving purely private rights to legislative courts or administrative agencies.[5]

(ii) German and French Models

An advantage of the civil-law administrative courts is that their judges have a high degree of expertise in administrative matters: they are well-versed in administrative law and understand how the Public Administration works. This segregation becomes also a self-fulfilling prophecy: since

---

4. See P. Birkinshaw, Grievances Remedies and the State (1994). The most important non-judicial channel is that of a (governmental) *ombudsman*. See, e.g., M. Seneviratne, Ombudsmen: Public Services and Administrative Justice (2003); M. C. Allen and the European Parliament, European Ombudsman and National Ombudsmen or Similar Bodies: Comparative Tables (2001); K. Heede, European Ombudsman: Redress and Control at Union Level (2000).

5. See, e.g., Northern Pipeline Construction Co. v. Marathon Pipe Line Co., 458 U.S. 50, 67, 69, 102 S.Ct. 2858, 2869, 2870 (1982). Nor can Congress, when dealing with actions at law that involve *private* disputes, take the fact-finding function away from the jury. See Atlas Roofing Co., Inc. v. Occupational Safety and Health Review Commission, 430 U.S. 442, 450, 97 S.Ct. 1261 (1977).

administrative and private disputes are always decided by separate courts, there is a tendency to generate different sets of substantive and procedural principles and rules, which in turn require increasing specialized knowledge. Some scholars have raised doubts as to whether the advantages of judicial specialization outweigh the disadvantages of a complex system of courts, especially since the reasons for the creation of specialized administrative courts (i.e. the French revolutionaries' fear and distrust of judges) no longer exist.[6]

The symbolism of the government creating its own specialized court system (in essence selecting its own judge) does not go unnoticed to foreign observers and even to the general public, which may display a natural distrust of such courts. However, at least in the most developed countries, like Germany and France, administrative courts are independent of the Executive and of the administrators over whose acts they judge.[7] They are "judges" in every sense of the word, especially with respect to their independence and impartiality. Their activity is truly jurisdictional in character, not administrative.

This dual court structure differs from the unified common-law court system because in the civil law the administrative and ordinary hierarchies have their own independent supreme court.[8] As aptly illustrated by a commentator, "[i]f the typical common law judicial system can be represented as a pyramid, the typical civil law judicial system must be visualized as a set of two or more distinct structures".[9]

There are some significant differences between the French and German administrative courts. The most fundamental is that, in France, the administrative and ordinary courts are completely independent "jurisdictional orbits" (i.e., the administrative courts are not part of the Judicial branch of government). In Germany, however, both courts belong to the same "jurisdictional orbit" (i.e., the Judiciary).

In Germany, where a high value is placed on specialized judicial expertise, there are two separate hierarchies of tribunals dealing with private-law disputes and three dealing with public-law disputes. In addition to the regular courts (which deal with civil and criminal matters) and the Labor Courts (*Arbeitsgerichte*), there are general Administrative Courts (*Verwaltungsgerichte*) and courts of special administrative jurisdiction, such as Financial Courts (*Finanzgerichte*) and Social Welfare Courts (*Sozialgerichte*). The general administrative courts deal with all public-law disputes not involving tax or social security matters.[10]

---

6. See R. Stürner, Suing the Sovereign in Europe and Germany, 34 Geo. Wash. Int'l L. Rev. 666 (2003); Y. Gaudemet, 1 Traité de droit administratif 341–43 (2001).

7. See R. Perrot, Institutions Judiciaires 35 (2004); J. Vincent, S. Guinchard, G. Montagnier and A. Varinard, Institutions Judiciaires 82–84 (1999); Y. Gaudemet, 1 Traité de droit administratif 341–43 (2001); R. Drago, Some Recent reforms of the French Conseil d'Etat, 13 Int'l. & Comp. L. Q. 1282, 1287 (1964).

8. See *supra* Chapter 6, Section 3(d) at 505 (Supreme Court).

9. See J. H. Merryman and R. Pérez-Perdomo, The Civil Law Tradition 86 (2007).

10. Due to the complexity of the structure of German courts, the diagram reproduced *supra*, p. 498 does not include such

Each of these hierarchies includes tribunals of first instance, intermediate appellate courts (reviewing issues of fact and law) and a court of last resort (reviewing only issues of law). For example, the general Administrative Courts (*Verwaltungsgerichte*) are composed of the Administrative Courts of first instance (composed of different chambers with three professional judges and two lay judges),[11] the Appellate Administrative Courts (*Oberverwaltungsgericht*) (composed of different "senates" with three professional judges and additional lay judges), and the Federal Administrative Supreme Court (*Bundesverwaltungsgericht*) (composed of "senates" with five professional judges). The latter is federally organized, whereas the first two are established by the States.[12] In addition, there is the Federal Constitutional Court (*Bundesverfassungsgericht*) that reviews all legislative, executive and judicial actions. It is the only court in the country with the power to declare a law unconstitutional.[13]

Each of these five court systems has its own independent supreme court at the federal level and lower instances at the local and regional level. Each court system has also its own procedural code, which is a federal statute. Since the procedural code is federal in nature, each Supreme Court may control the uniformity of procedure within its structure, even when dispensed by state courts.[14]

The two procedural codes of private litigation (civil and labor disputes) are very similar, as are the codes of public-law litigation (administrative, social, and tax disputes). However, the principles of private litigation depart from the principles of public-law litigation in some very significant ways. For example, while private procedure is essentially "adversarial" ("because the judge is not permitted to base his decision on facts not asserted by the parties to the litigation"), public-law procedure is inquisitorial ("because the [administrative] judge has full responsibility to determine the correct and true factual basis of the case"). However, one may resist the temptation to exaggerate the differences between them because the administrative court cannot determine the facts without the cooperation of the parties.[15]

specialized courts. A complete structure can be found on the website of the European Commission, European Judicial Network in Civil and Commercial Matters, http://ec.europa.eu/civiljustice (last visited Jan. 21, 2009).

11. In most cases, the law requires the plaintiff to first file a formal objection with the Administration, before filing a lawsuit in the Administrative Court. See P. Murray and R. Stürner, German Civil Justice 44–45 (2004).

12. Appeals to the German Federal Administrative Supreme Court are conditioned to a previous permission from the Appellate Administrative Court or the Supreme Federal Administrative Court itself. This is not sub-

stantially different from the rule about appeals to the German Supreme Court in ordinary procedure, as discussed *infra* Chapter 6, Section 3(d)(i) at 508. See P. Murray and R. Stürner, German Civil Justice 44–45 (2004).

13. See *supra* Chapter 6, Section 3(e) at 523 (discussing the judicial review of the constitutionality of legislative acts).

14. See R. Stürner, Suing the Sovereign in Europe and Germany, 34 Geo. Wash. Int'l L. Rev. 669–70 (2003).

15. See R. Stürner, Suing the Sovereign in Europe and Germany, 34 Geo. Wash. Int'l L. Rev. 669–70 (2003). See also P. Théry, Droit Public et Droit Privé: L'Evolution du Droit Processuel, in J. B. Auby and M. Freed-

In France, historically, the regular courts of the Judiciary branch could not interfere with the activities of the Executive. This policy was strongly influenced by the ideology of the French Revolution and a rather strict doctrine of separation of power. The French Revolution simply reacted to a historical distrust of judges: not only were they opposed to the Revolution, they had also proved to be obstructionists of the *ancien régime*. In light of these ideological and historical circumstances, the judicial review of administrative acts is not politically acceptable in France. The attitude was the same that prohibited the judicial review of the constitutionality of legislative acts.[16] The original objective was essentially to free the Public Administration from any form of judicial oversight, allowing it to make its own determinations. In 1790, the Constituent Assembly determined that judges who interfered with the execution of the laws of the Nation by public officials were guilty of a criminal offense, and that is still the law today.[17]

This reality was in sharp contrast to the situation in England, where the courts had the powers of *mandamus* (to compel an official to perform a duty) and *quo warranto* (to question the legality of an act performed by a public official).[18]

However, since the public authority was bound to follow the law emanated by the legislative, it was essential to provide a forum where private parties could challenge the legality or excesses of the acts of the Administration. Since neither the Judiciary nor the Legislative could interfere with the Executive, the administrative courts in France started as a branch of the Executive: the Administration was simultaneously the judge and a party. When initially created by Napoleon, the administrative courts served only an advisory function: the Council of State (*Conseil d'Etat*), as its name aptly suggests, merely recommended to the head of state specific resolutions for particular complaints. Over the course of a century, however, it slowly emerged as a second set of independent jurisdictional courts, deciding with binding authority controversies between private parties and the Administration over the legality of administrative actions.[19]

The French legal system therefore has two sets of courts: the "administrative jurisdiction" (*ordre administratif*), in charge of the judicial review of administrative acts (conflicts between private parties and the Public

---

land (eds.), La Distinction du Droit Public et du Droit Privé: Regards Français et Britanniques 46–55 (2006).

16. See *supra* Chapter 6, Section 3(e) at 523 (discussing the judicial review of the constitutionality of legislative acts).

17. See Law of August 16–24, 1790 (art. 13): "The judicial functions are distinct and will always remain separate from administrative functions. It is a criminal offense for the judges of the ordinary courts to interfere in any manner whatsoever with the operation of the administration, nor shall they call administrators to account before them in re-

spect to the exercise of their official functions".

18. See J. H. Merryman and R. Pérez-Perdomo, The Civil Law Tradition 88 (2007).

19. See R. Chapus, 1 Droit Administratif Général 747–56 (2001); J. Vincent, S. Guinchard, G. Montagnier and A. Varinard, Institutions Judiciaires 79–84 and 467–69 (1999); Y. Gaudemet, 1 Traité de droit administratif 327–31 (2001); R. Perrot, Institutions Judiciaires 205–07 (2004); L. N. Brown, J. Bell and J.M. Galabert, French Administrative Law 45–50 (1998).

Administration) and the "judicial jurisdiction" (*ordre judiciaire*), in charge of resolving private conflicts between private parties.

The administrative jurisdiction (*jurisdiction administrative*) is composed of 38 administrative courts of first instance (*tribunaux administratifs*), 8 administrative appellate courts (*cours administratifs d'appel*) (reviewing issues of fact and law), and 1 administrative court of last resort or administrative supreme court (*Conseil d'Etat*) at the apex of the administrative hierarchy (reviewing only issues of law).[20] Is judges are drawn mainly from the members of the Public Administration, from those who studied at the *École nationale d'administration (ENA)* as well as from other sources.[21]

For 150 years, the Council of State (*Conseil d'Etat*) was the only administrative court in France (as we have seen above, for almost a century it was not even a "court", but merely a glorified advisory board). However, the increasing caseload led to the creation of the administrative courts of first instance in 1953 and, later, to the creation of the intermediate administrative courts of appeal in 1987. There now is a full-fledged three-tier judicial hierarchy of French administrative courts, paralleling that of the ordinary courts. In Belgium, there still is no hierarchy of administrative courts: after having challenged the administrative decision before the administrative agency that rendered it, the only recourse possible is before the *Conseil d'Etat* (there are no administrative courts of first or second instance).

Ordinarily, the Administrative Courts of Appeals hear appeals from the courts of first instance. The *Conseil d'Etat* has at least three functions. It may serve as court of first (and final) instance or as court of appeals of second instance. It may also serve as a "court of cassation", a function similar to the *Cour de cassation*. It will typically not substitute the decision from the Administrative Court of Appeals over the merits of the appeal; instead, it will simply nullify the decision and remand the case to another Administrative Court of Appeals with instructions on how to proceed.[22]

The administrative jurisdiction over public-law disputes (*contentieux administrative*) is less fragmented in France than in Germany. In particular, there is no separate hierarchy of tax courts, resulting in tax controversies normally coming before the administrative tribunals.[23] The advantages of judicial specialization that we have seen in the German model, however, are not necessarily lost under the French system. The *Conseil d'Etat* normally sits in panels, called *sous-sections*, and matters requiring special-

---

20. See a diagram of the structure of the French courts, portraying the administrative jurisdiction as an independent court structure separate from the ordinary jurisdiction, *supra*, p. 497.

21. See R. Perrot, Institutions Judiciaires 291–96 (2004); J. Vincent, S. Guinchard, G. Montagnier and A. Varinard, Institutions Judiciaires 574–78 (1999).

22. See *supra* Chapter 6, Section 3(d)(ii) at 511 (discussing the method of cassation).

23. The statement in the text should be understood as referring to direct taxes. There are some peculiarities with respect to indirect taxes. See *Code de l'organisation judiciaire* (art. L311–3).

ized knowledge, such as tax cases, are referred to such specialized panels. Moreover, there are numerous administrative courts with jurisdiction to hear specialized disputes (*jurisdictions administratives à compétence spéciale*).[24]

Not all of the business of the *Conseil d'Etat* is judicial. Of all its sections, only one, the "litigation section" (*section du contentieux*), has the judicial function of deciding administrative disputes with binding authority. It is this function that is being discussed here. The other sections play the much less publicized role of legal consultant to the French government and its Ministers. The other specialized sections are: *section des finances* (e.g. taxes), *section social* (e.g. social security cases), *section des travaux publics* (public works), *section de l'administration*, and *section de l'intérieur*.[25]

The French ideology of limited judicial review (of legislative and administrative acts) had profound influence in the civil-law tradition, including Germany, regardless of the fact that other countries had not experienced the same historical circumstances.

Some developing countries, though otherwise influenced by French legal thinking, declined to adopt or retain this dual hierarchy system. Because of a dearth of trained judicial resources, it would be undesirable to maintain several hierarchies of tribunals. After its 1960 independence from France, the Republic of Senegal adopted an unitary system in which private and public-law disputes were decided by the ordinary courts.[26]

The attitude of Latin–American countries toward the jurisdictional separation of "private law" and "public law" disputes varies. These countries belong to the civil-law orbit with respect to their private law, but, in the area of public law, the U.S. model exercised considerable influence at the time of their independence from Portugal and Spain.[27] It is not surprising, therefore, to find that Latin American legal systems are almost evenly divided on the issue of whether public-law disputes should be determined by the ordinary courts, as in the U.S., or by administrative tribunals of the continental type.[28]

Subject to these observations concerning some of the developing nations and Latin America, in the overwhelming majority of civil-law coun-

---

24. See R. Perrot, Institutions Judiciaires 234–44 (2004); J. Vincent, S. Guinchard, G. Montagnier and A. Varinard, Institutions Judiciaires 498–516 (1999); L. N. Brown, J. Bell and J.M. Galabert, French Administrative Law 58–61 (1998).

25. For literature on the *Conseil d'Etat*, see e.g. R. Chapus, Droit du Contentieux Administrative (2006) and E. Arnoult, F. Monnier, Le Conseil d'État. Juger, Conseiller, Server (1999).

26. E.A. Farnsworth, Law Reform in a Developing Country: A New Code of Obligations for Senegal, 8 J. Afr. L. 6, 1, (1964).

27. See *supra* Chapter 3, Section 2 at 190.

28. See F. García Pullés, Tratado de lo Contencioso Administrativo, 2 vols. (2004); C. García, Derecho Procesal Administrativo (2001); A Gordillo, 4 Tratado de Derecho Administrativo. El Procedimiento Administrativo (2004); J. C. Cassagne (ed.), Derecho Procesal Administrativo, 2 vols. (2004); J. Gonzáles Pérez and J.L. Vázquez Alfaro, Derecho Procesal Administrativo Mexicano, 2 vols. (2005); Héctor Fix–Zamudio and E. Ferrer Mac–Gregor, El Derecho de Amparo en el Mundo (2006). See also H. Clagett, Administration of Justice in Latin America 61 ff. (1952).

tries the administrative courts form a judicial hierarchy separate and distinct from that of the ordinary courts. This can be regarded as one of the key distinguishing features between the civil and common-law systems.[29]

The two systems of administrative law and administrative courts which have been most influential throughout the civil-law world are the French[30] and, to a lesser degree, the German. There is a considerable amount of English-language literature on the main features of the French[31] and German[32] administrative systems. Several comprehensive comparative analyses have also been published.[33]

Almost every civil-law system presents some unique features in its administrative law, with considerable diversity as to many points of jurisdiction, procedure, and substantive law. Nevertheless, most civil-law countries have a very similar approach to the subject and readily understand each other's systems. This is clearly demonstrated by the experience of the European Union.

It is important to point out some significant similarities between the French and German models:

(1) In France and Germany, virtually *every* administrative act is subject to review by the administrative courts, and may be annulled in case of unlawfulness or abuse of discretion. If the challenged act is a

29. For a suggestion that the civil-law approach be adopted in the U.S., see C. H. Fulda, A Proposed "Administrative Court" for Ohio, 22 Ohio St .L. J. 734 (1961).

30. The French system of administrative courts and administrative law is said to have served as a model in The Netherlands, Belgium, Luxembourg, Spain, Italy, Turkey, Egypt, and a number of other civil-law countries.

31. E.g., L. N. Brown, J. Bell and J. M. Galabert, French Administrative Law 44–174 (1998); H. J. Abraham, The Judicial Process 282–98 (1998); Kahn–Freund, Lévy, Rudden, Bernard Rudden, A Source–Book on French Law 153ss (1991); J. Bell, Reflections on the Procedure of the *Conseil d'Etat*, in Droit Sans Frontières: Essays in Honour of L. Neville Brown 221 (1991); J. W. F. Allison, A Continental Distinction in the Common Law. A Historical and Comparative Perspective on English Public Law (1996). Two British law journals are particularly important: Public Law and European Public Law Journal. Older works are: C. E. Freedeman, The Conseil d'Etat in Modern France (1961); B. Schwartz, French Administrative Law and the Common Law World (1954); C. J. Hamson, Executive Discretion and judicial Control (1954); Leterneur and Drago, The Rule of Law as Understood in France, 7 Am. J. Comp. L. 147

(1958); M. J. Remington, The Tribunaux Adminstratifs: Protectors of French Citizens, 51 Tul. L. Rev 33 (1976); P. Herzog, Civil procedure in France 112–18 (1967). For a masterful brief description of the workings of the *Conseil d'Etat*, written by an insider but containing some brief comparative references to similar institutions in other counties, see M. Lagrange, The French Council of State, 43 Tul. L. Rev. 46 (1968). For a brief description of the Italian administrative courts, see M. Cappelletti and J. M. Perillo, Civil Procedure in Italy 111–15 (1965).

32. See J. S. Oster, The Scope of Judicial Review in the German and U.S. Administrative Legal System, 9 German L. J. 1267 (2008); M. Künnecke, Tradition and Change in Administrative Law. An Anglo–German Comparison (2007); M. P. Singh German administrative law in common law perspective (2001).

33. See R. J. G. H. Seerden (ed.), Administrative Law of the European Union, its Member States and the United States. A comparative Analysis (2007) (overview of administrative law in Belgium, France, Germany, the Netherlands, the United Kingdom, the European Union, and the United States) P. Birkinshaw, European Public Law (2003) (comparing German and French with English and EU administrative law).

negative one (e.g., a refusal to issue a license or a passport), its annulment may in effect amount to an affirmative command, not unlike an order of *mandamus*.

(2) In both countries, the administrative courts ordinarily have power to annul the administrator's action for errors of fact as well as law.

(3) The administrative courts in both countries have a high reputation for impartiality and efficiency, and their operation is regarded as essential to the maintenance of the rule of law.

(4) Both French and German lawyers are plagued by the difficulty of defining the line of demarcation between the jurisdictions of the ordinary and administrative courts.

(5) Attached to the Administrative Supreme Courts of both countries, there are "state attorneys" or "public attorneys" (*Oberbundesanwalt* in Germany and *commissaire du gouvernement* in France), who intervene in the litigation to protect the public interests, understood not as the interest of the administration, but as the general interest of the society in upholding the legality.

(6) The procedure of the administrative courts is informal, inexpensive, and largely inquisitorial. The court can direct the administrator to submit the entire *dossier* (record) relating to the matter at hand. In addition, parties are given an opportunity to introduce or suggest the taking of new evidence that was not before the administrative agency. Counsel's arguments usually are presented in writing and again orally in open court.

(7) Neither German nor French administrative law has been systematically codified. In both countries there are relevant statutes, especially regarding procedure,[34] but the bulk of the rules determining the legality and propriety of administrative acts is judge-made. This is especially true of France, where a single central institution, the *Conseil d'Etat* has *created* a modern body of administrative law during the last two centuries in much the same way that the common-law courts have created English law. In Germany, the situation is somewhat different. Administrative law is partly state law. Moreover, it was only after World War II that a federal administrative court of last resort was created. Until then, no appeal to a federal court could be taken from the decisions of the various states' highest administrative tribunals.

---

34. The German rules on administrative procedure are laid down in an elaborate and systematic federal statute, the *Verwaltungsgerichtsordnung* (VwGO). In its organization and terminology, the statute is patterned after the Code of Civil Procedure, which is applicable in the absence of a specialized rule. This makes the procedure before the administrative courts comparable and in some respect similar, to ordinary court procedure. But the greater simplicity of administrative court procedure has been preserved. The practice of administrative agencies themselves is governed by another statute, the *Verwaltungsverfahrensgesetz des Bundes* (VwVfG). The States have their own statutes (*Verwaltungsverfahrensgesetze der Länder*). The practice of the administrative agencies likewise is regulated by a separate statute.

Thus, no single court was able to acquire a position of nation-wide importance and prestige comparable to that of the French *Conseil d'Etat*. Therefore, academic influence on German administrative law has been much stronger than in France. When one speaks of the civil-law orbit as a world of codes, we must always remember that the statement requires qualifications with respect to public law.

(iii) Conflicts of Jurisdiction

Although in the vast majority of cases the precise line of demarcation between the jurisdiction of the administrative and ordinary courts is simple,[35] in certain cases, both the French and German legal systems experience serious difficulties. Any legal system that creates several separate judicial hierarchies must provide some method by which jurisdictional conflicts can be avoided or resolved; yet these countries deal with that inevitable difficulty in very different ways. Not only do they draw the line in different places, they use different procedures for resolving conflicts of jurisdiction.

In France, when the jurisdiction of the administrative and ordinary courts is disputed (*conflits d'attribution*), the conflict is submitted to a special jurisdictional court (*Tribunal des conflits*) presided over by the Minister of Justice and composed of four judges from the *Cour de cassation* and four from the *Conseil d'Etat*.[36] Each serves for a renewable term of three years. Other important members are the *commissaires du gouvernement*, one from the *Cour de cassation* and another from the *Conseil d'Etat*. In order to preserve equal representation in each and every case, whenever the presiding judge (reporter) of a certain proceeding is from the *Cour de cassation*, the *commissaire du gouvernement* will be from the *Conseil d'Etat* and vice versa.

Some scholars have criticized the participation of the Minister of Justice in the *Tribunal des conflits* for two reasons. First, as a member of the government subject to political pressure and without the constitutional guaranties of judges, he or she may favor the jurisdiction of the administrative courts. It is true that the Minister of Justice only votes when a tiebreaker is needed (i.e. a 4–4 vote), which is a rare occurrence; it happened in less than a dozen cases in more than a century. However, these happen to be exactly the most important or controversial cases. Second, as a politician with no legal training, he or she may not have the sophisticated knowledge to decide the most complex issues that the courts themselves proved unable to. It is true that such preference for the administrative courts has not manifested itself in practice, but it is undeniable that the conflict of interest is latent and can become viable at any time.[37]

35. See J. Rivero and J. Waline, Droit Administratif 459 (2004).

36. See *Code de justice administrative* (arts. R. 771–1 and R. 771–2).

37. See Y. Gaudemet, 1 Traité de droit administratif 430–31 (2001); R. Chapus, 1 Droit Administratif Général 990 (2001); J. Rivero and J. Waline, Droit Administratif 459–60 (2004).

There are two kinds of conflicts: a "positive conflict" (when both the ordinary and the administrative courts *claim* jurisdiction and consider themselves competent for the same case) and a "negative conflict" (when both *decline* jurisdiction and consider that the other system is competent for the case, resulting in a denial of justice). In either situation, the French *Tribunal des conflits* will render final judgment on which system is competent (*i.e.* has jurisdiction to hear the matter) with binding effect limited to the case at hand, but with strong persuasive authority for the resolution of future cases.

Under the German system, however, both the ordinary and the administrative courts can determine their own jurisdiction. If an ordinary or administrative court, in a decision no longer subject to appeal, has affirmed or denied its own jurisdiction, such decision is binding in all subsequent proceedings that may be brought concerning the same matter in the same or any other court (even if the other court belongs to a different judicial hierarchy).[38] A court which considers itself incompetent (lacking jurisdiction) on the ground that the case should have been brought before a court belonging to a different judicial hierarchy, may, upon plaintiff's motion, transfer the case to the latter court. The decision to transfer, unless it is reversed on appeal, is binding on the transferee court.

It was once possible to say that the German method aimed to *avoid* head-on conflicts between ordinary and administrative courts, while the French provided a mechanism to *resolve* such conflicts. However, although such generalization captures the traditional spirit of the two methods, it is no longer quite accurate because of developments in both legal systems. A German statute authorizes the states to create special tribunals similar to the French Tribunal of Conflicts.[39] The French Tribunal of Conflicts can also issue a preliminary ruling on where the action should be brought, effectively *avoiding* the conflict between an ordinary and an administrative court.[40]

There is still a third method of resolution of jurisdictional conflicts between the administrative and ordinary courts. Some countries, such as Belgium and Italy, bestow this attribution to the Court of Cassation. This places the Court of Cassation somewhat at a higher level than the Council of State.

From a policy point of view, good arguments exist for and against these methods. However, by creating a super-court composed of an equal number

---

38. See *Gerichtsverfassungsgesetz* (§ 17); *Verwaltungsgerichtsordnung* (§§ 40 and 41). Similar problems of conflicts of jurisdiction can arise in U.S. law, e.g., between a Work Compensation Board and an ordinary court. The U.S. solution appears to be similar to the German's: each set of tribunals has the power to determine its own jurisdiction, and such determination, once final, is binding on the parties, with the result that the judgment, even if erroneous on the jurisdictional point, cannot be collaterally attacked on the ground of lack of subject-matter jurisdiction.

39. See *Gerichtsverfassungsgesetz* (§ 17a4).

40. See *décret du 25 juillet 1960*; J. Rivero and J. Waline, Droit Administratif 460–61 (2004); R. Chapus, 1 Droit Administratif Général 1007–08 (2001).

of members of both jurisdictions, the French system seems to be more conducive of a systematic resolution of these conflicts. One could argue that the creation of yet another court to decide the satellite issue of jurisdiction is too complicated and inefficient, but when viewed in light of the fact that the number of cases decided by the Tribunal of Conflicts is very small (about 50 a year), this argument fails because their workload is not overwhelming and decisions are promptly issued.

(iv) Ordinary and Administrative Jurisdiction

There is a great deal of disagreement among civil-law countries on the criteria by which they seek to distinguish between private and public disputes. Relatively little difficulty arises in cases in which the plaintiff seeks to have an administrative act annulled. Really tough problems of demarcation, however, are encountered in the innumerable cases—of contracts, of torts, and of eminent domain—in which the redress sought by the individual is a money judgment against the State or of one of its subdivisions. Are such disputes private or public? Which court is competent to adjudicate such disputes: administrative or ordinary? Are they governed by substantive administrative or private law? On these points, the French and German legal systems differ.

Such problems are frequent in the practice of law of any civil-law country. Imagine a lawsuit to recover property damages in a one-vehicle accident caused by bumps and potholes that were the result of negligent maintenance of public roads. The French government would be sued in the administrative courts, while in Germany such an action must be brought before the Civil Chamber of the ordinary court of first instance.[41]

Determining the reason for this difference leads to an interesting exercise in comparative law. The French tried to draw a distinction along functional lines. If the damage is caused by some malfunctioning of the public service (including human failure of the State's agents, high or low), the State is liable and must be sued in the administrative courts. If the official or employee who caused the damage is personally at fault, he or she is liable as an individual, and his liability can be enforced in the ordinary

---

41. Frequently these jurisdictional problems are treated incidentally in books and articles primarily dealing with the substantive aspects of tort liability for the acts of public officials and employees. See J. Bell and A. W. Bradley (Eds.), Governmental Liability. A Comparative Study (1991); Y. Zhang and T. Fuke (Eds.), Comparative Studies on Governmental Liability in East and Southeast Asia (1999); X., Governmental Liability in Tort, 6 Nat'l J. Const. L. 85 (1996). See also H. Street, Governmental Liability. A Comparative Study (1953) and the 1964 Colloquium on "Liability of the State for Illegal Conduct of Its Organs" (1967).

Under German law (as in the United States under the Federal Tort Claims Act), the substantive aspects of the State's tort liability are essentially governed by general tort law principles, i.e., by private law. In France, on the other hand, it was held that the provisions of the Civil Code are not applicable to governmental liability, which is governed by principles peculiar to public law. This divergence of the relevant sources also leads to substantive differences between French and German law with respect to governmental tort liability.

courts. Such personal fault will be found where an official has maliciously caused defendant's injury or loss. The notion of personal fault (upon which the jurisdiction of the ordinary court as well as the official's personal liability is bottomed) is not limited to cases of malice. A policeman who, in arresting a person, commits hideous and unnecessary acts of brutality, can be personally sued in the ordinary courts, regardless of whether he was motivated by personal hatred of his victim or by an excess of zeal in the performance of his duties. Even a non-intentional but grossly negligent act can constitute personal fault.[42]

Under the old doctrine, which prevailed until the beginning of the 19th century, the situations in which the State was liable, and those in which the official was individually liable for intentional or negligent wrongdoing, were mutually exclusive. But, since then, and with ever growing liberality, the French courts have recognized that there are countless situations in which the State's servant is sufficiently blameworthy to be subjected to personal liability, and in which, at the same time, the damage is so closely connected with the public service that the State should also be held liable.

This is similar to the U.S. doctrine of *respondeat superior*, under which it is possible to sue the servant *and* the master. However, with respect to governmental liability, the French have gone further. "Cumulative liability" of the official and of the Government often exists in French law even though the wrongdoing official has not acted within the scope of his or her employment.[43] As examples, one can cite a number of cases in which the plaintiff's injury or loss was caused solely[44] by what one would call a "frolic" of the official. In one such case, a high official, while inspecting a police station, had engaged in target practice and negligently wounded a person who happened to pass by. Although it was clear that the shooting exercise had been purely for fun and had nothing to do with the wrongdoer's official duties, this was held to be a case of cumulative liability on the ground that the official had acted on the occasion of his inspection visit and had used one of the service guns kept at the police station.[45]

---

42. Some of the cases so holding involved careless use of firearms by soldiers or policemen. See A. Laubadère, Traité de droit administratif, Secs. 1193–94 (1980).

43. See J. Rivero and J. Waline, Droit Administratif 434–36 (2004).

44. In cases where the damage is caused (a) by the wrongdoing official's personal fault *and* (b) by some malfunctioning of the public service that is separable from the conduct of the primary wrongdoer (e.g., failure of higher officials properly to supervise the malefactor), it was even less difficult for the French courts to justify the imposition of cumulative liability.

45. See M. Waline, Droit Administratif, Sec. 1458 (1963); J. Rivero and J. Waline,

Droit Administratif 434–36 (2004) (with references to relevant cases).

In Germany, where governmental tort liability is controlled by private law (see *supra*), a more restricted rule has been adopted. Under relevant principles of private law, which in this respect are somewhat similar to the U.S. notion of "scope of employment", the German courts have declined to hold the State liable in situations where, as in the French case mentioned in the text, the accident was caused by a "frolic" involving misuse of firearms kept for official purposes. See RGZ 105, 230 (1922). The fact that the frolicking functionary acted on the occasion of an official activity, and that he used a service gun or other State-owned instrumentality, in the German view, is insufficient to support

In cases of "cumulative liability", the public authority must be sued in the administrative courts, while an action against the individual is within the jurisdiction of the ordinary courts. Even though it is the plaintiff's choice, in practice, plaintiffs prefer to sue the public authority out of fear that the individual tortfeasor may be judgment-proof, even though the administrative courts have the reputation of being conservative in determining the amount of damages to be awarded.

Changing the traditional French rule, the *Conseil d'Etat* held in 1951 that, having satisfied the judgment of the administrative court, the public authority can recover indemnity or contribution from the negligent functionary (*action récursoire*).[46] However, in practice, the state rarely exercises such prerogative, relieving the official that was guilty of "personal fault" of any civil responsibility.[47] By the same token, if the functionary is sued and has satisfied the judgment, he or she may bring an *action récursoire* to recover from the public authority its share of liability.[48] In either case, the indemnity claim (from the functionary or from the administration) must be filed in the administrative courts.

In the past, these French rules caused grave difficulties in automobile accident cases when one of the vehicles involved was owned by the State or one of its subdivisions. In such cases, it followed from the rules just discussed that the plaintiff was unable to join the driver and the owner of the government vehicle as defendants in the same action. Moreover, in cases of collisions between private cars and government vehicles, when multiple parties assert crossclaims based on tort, indemnity, contribution, and subrogation, the resulting jurisdictional problems were staggering. However, in 1957 the legislator came to the rescue. The statute addressing this specific problem provides that, regardless of the involvement of the government or some other public authority, all actions seeking recovery for injury or damage caused by "a vehicle" shall be governed by principles of private law and must be brought in the ordinary courts.[49] The statute

---

governmental liability in such cases. See Palandt, Bürgerliches Gesetzbuch, § 839, Anno. 2Ac(bb) (1984), and cases there cited. The aim of the present discussion, however, is not to discuss details of the French and German doctrines of governmental tort liability, but merely to throw some light on the jurisdictional demarcation lines between the business of the ordinary and of the administrative courts.

46. See *Laruelle* and *Deville*, July 28, 1951. *Compare* United States v. Gilman, 347 U.S. 507, 74 S.Ct. 695 (1954). It is interesting to observe that in dealing with this important question the French *Conseil d' Etat* and the U.S Supreme Court, both acting at about the same time, effected radical changes *in opposite directions*.

47. See M. Waline, Droit Administratif, Sec. 1615 (1963); J. Rivero and J. Waline, Droit Administratif 397–98 and 436–37 (2004).

48. J. Rivero and J. Waline, Droit Administratif 436 (2004); R. Chapus, 1 Droit Administratif Général 1398–1403 (2001).

49. See Loi n. 57–1424 du 31 décembre 1957 (giving jurisdiction to the ordinary courts to decide cases of liability for damages caused by any vehicle against the public administration). For the text of the 1957 statute, and an instructive discussion of its provisions, see Auby and Drago, 1 Traité de Contentieux Administratif, Sec. 563–65 (1984). The statute applies regardless of whether the "vehicle" travels on land, in the water, or in the air. Nor does it make any difference whether the vehicle serves military

further contains a provision, comparable to a section of the U.S. Federal Tort Claims Act,[50] which in effect deprives the victim of any cause of action against the driver of the vehicle, thus rendering the public authority exclusively liable in cases of this kind.

This rule does not create an exception to the general French rule that the public authority, having satisfied the injured person's claim, can obtain reimbursement from the derelict functionary. The statute renders the public authority's liability exclusive only insofar as the victim is concerned. With respect to the guilty functionary's duty to reimburse the public authority, the vehicular accident cases are governed by the general rule. Thus, if it so chooses, the public authority can obtain total or partial reimbursement from the negligent driver.[51] In determining the amount of such reimbursement, the court takes into account the extent to which the victim's damage has been caused by the driver's "personal fault" and/or by some malfunctioning of the public service not attributable to the driver personally.

The German solution is not radically different from the French, but may be a little simpler. The Germans also distinguish acts that are purely personal wrongs of the employee (e.g., the driver of a mail truck intentionally runs down a bicyclist for personal reasons), and those acts for which the State should be liable. However, according to the German view, liability of the State, where it exists, completely supplants the liability of the individual official or employee.[52] The victim of the tort brings his or her action against the individual in the ordinary civil courts. Contrary to the French rule, moreover, express provisions of the German Constitution and of the German Civil Code confer upon the ordinary courts jurisdiction over tort actions against the State or its subdivisions.[53]

In addition to the other difficulties previously mentioned, the French system produces very doubtful results whenever a public servant commits a tort (such as assault and battery) that has only a slight or problematic

or civilian purposes. If the vehicle is used by a public servant, the statute applies even though the public servant rather than the State or its subdivision owns the vehicle. Tribunal of Conflicts, November 20, 1961. D. 1962, 265.

50.   See 28 U.S.C. § 2679(b) and the removal provision in § 2679(d). Prior to the enactment of these statutory provisions, the driver of a U.S. Government vehicle could be sued in a state court, and sometimes only in a state court, while the Government could be sued only in a federal court. This created difficulties somewhat similar to those experienced by the French before 1957. See, e.g., Falk v. United States, 264 F.2d 238 (6 Cir. 1959).

51.   See Auby and Drago, 1 Traité de Contentieux Administratif, Sec. 564 (1984).

52.   This is a general rule, not limited to vehicular accident cases. The existence of governmental liability constitutes a complete defense in an action by the victim against the individual official or employee. The government, having satisfied a claim for damages, may recover indemnity from the official or employee who caused the damage intentionally or by gross negligence. As in France, however, it cannot be taken for granted that in practice such indemnity will always be collected. For a comparative discussion, see G. A. Bermann, Integrating Governmental and Officer Tort Liability, 77 Colum. L. Rev. 1175 (1977).

53.   See German Constitution (art. 34) and German Civil Code (art. 839).

connection with his official duties.[54] The plaintiff may have to choose at his peril, not only between possible defendants, but also between two different tribunals, unless, as a matter of precaution, he or she brings two actions in two different courts. An enormous amount of lawyers' time and clients' money is spent to resolve such doubts. Dichotomies in the law always lead to such wasted effort. The U.S. dichotomy between law and equity illustrates the same point.

The German system seems to avoid some of these difficulties. However, if the aggrieved individual desires to annul the administrative act *and* wishes to recover damages in tort, it requires two actions: one in the administrative and one in the ordinary court.[55] In France, he or she can get both kinds of relief in one proceeding before the administrative court, which is much more efficient.

People involved in international business have many contracts with foreign governments.[56] Both in France and Germany, contracts between a private party and a public authority are sometimes enforceable in the administrative courts, and sometimes in the ordinary courts, depending on the public or private nature of the particular contract. The French distinguish between "administrative contracts" and *contrats de droit commun*. The Germans use terms such as "public-law contract" and "private-law contract".

However, the criteria used to attribute a contract to the public or the private sphere are different in France and Germany. In general, one can say that the French extend the jurisdiction of the administrative courts over a much wider range of contracts than the Germans do. In searching for a workable basis of distinction, the French avowedly use a flexible and somewhat casuistic method, while the Germans have tried to develop a single abstract criterion.

The German theory is predicated on the essential nature of the legal relationship between the parties. If that relationship is one which could

54. Under the German system, too, these borderline cases may produce doubts as to whether the State or the wrongdoing official is liable. Since both the State and the individual tortfeasor can be sued in the same court, the plaintiff can join them both as defendants, even though his action will be successful only against one or the other.

55. An analogous problem often troubled American courts in the past: Could the petitioner in a *certiorari* or *mandamus* proceeding, or in a statutory proceeding of similar nature, obtain damages as well as an order directing the doing or undoing of an administrative act? The cases, reflecting a quaint common law rule as well as a variety of pertinent statutes, were numerous and disharmonious. See Anno., 73 A.L.R.2d 903 (1960). See Weinstein–Korn–Miller, New York Civil Practice ¶ 7806.01 (1967 and Supp.). It showed that jurisdictional and pro-

cedural difficulties, comparable to those encountered in some of the continental countries, also exist in U.S. law, but that often these difficulties are overshadowed by the obscurity of U.S. substantive rules regarding governmental liability for official wrongdoing.

56. For comparative treatments of British, United States and French law dealing with government contracts see Street, Governmental Liability 81 ff. (1953, repr. 1975) and Mitchell, The Contracts of Public Authorities (1954), reviewed by Pasley, 41 Cornell L.Q. 342 (1956). A good comparative survey of administrative (or public law) contracts in various countries of Western Europe can be found in C. C. Turpin, Public Contract, Vol. VII (Contracts in General), International Encyclopedia of Comparative Law, Chapter 4, pp. 27–31 (1982).

equally well exist between private individuals or corporations, then any dispute resulting from it is "private". Applying this principle to contractual relationships, the German courts have found that some contracts involve the enforcement or distribution of public burdens, or relate to some other subject with which private parties, by themselves, could not deal with under any circumstances.[57] Contracts of this kind are "public" and therefore must be adjudicated by the administrative courts. Most contracts between the Government and a private party, however, involve transactions which in the abstract (and the German criterion emphasizes the abstract nature and the typical features of the relationship more than the particular facts of the case at hand) could equally well be concluded among private parties. Contracts for the sale or purchase of goods, or involving sales or leases of real property, are classical examples. Such contracts are private and hence enforceable in the ordinary courts, even though one of the contracting parties is the Government.

Although its precise formulation as well as its application to borderline situations remains somewhat controversial,[58] this German theory seems to provide a reasonably clear line of demarcation.[59] In virtually all cases of what in the U.S. would be called "government contract disputes", the effect of the German doctrine is to bring such disputes before the ordinary courts.

The French system, in distinguishing between administrative and private contracts, uses an approach more flexible than the German. They have adopted a pragmatic approach, according to which the nature of a contract as administrative or private may be determined by statute,[60] by decisional law,[61] or, to a certain extent, by the terms of the contract.

---

57. E.g., the owner of a city plot, who desires to build an apartment house, but pursuant to the provisions of a statute can get a building permit only on condition of providing a certain number of parking spaces, enters into a contract with the city. Under the terms of the contract, the city will issue the permit unconditionally and will itself provide the parking spaces, while the owner will pay the city a specified sum of money. This was held to be a "public law contract", enforceable only in the administrative courts. BGHZ 32, 214 (1960).

58. There is some doubt, e.g., concerning contracts which publicly-owned suppliers of water, gas, or electricity conclude with their customers. See E. Eyermann and L. Fröhler, Verwaltungsgerichtsordnung, Sec. 40, Annos. 50–53 (1980).

59. The theory seems to work even in complex situations, e.g., where a statute, as part of a subsidy program, authorizes the Government to make loans to private persons for the construction of low-rent housing or for similar social purposes. When an application for such a loan has been denied, it is clear that judicial review of the denial must be sought in the administrative court. But once a contractor has obtained such a loan, the relationship between him or her and the Government is the ordinary one of debtor and creditor, with the result that the Government's action for repayment of the loan must be brought in the ordinary court. In spite of doubts expressed by some authors, this rule has been generally recognized in judicial practice. See the cases cited by E. Eyermann and L. Fröhler, Verwaltungsgerichtsordnung, Sec. 40, Anno. 46 (1980).

60. A statute, for instance, provides that contracts for public works are administrative. But a seller who merely furnishes paving stones to a public authority, without participating in the work of paving, can sue in the ordinary courts. So can the financier whose loan enables a municipality to carry out such a project. A. Laubadére, F. Moderne and P. Devolvé, 1 Traité des Contrats Administratifs 126–28 and 265–66 (1984).

61. The rules have grown in casuistic fashion, and the distinctions are as subtle as

The parties, of course, do not have the power to stipulate in their contract whether the administrative or ordinary courts shall have jurisdiction over any dispute. This stipulation, as such, would have no effect because the parties do not have the power to change the jurisdictional rules. Such rules belong to the public order (*ordre public*) and cannot be contracted around or waived, much like subject-matter jurisdiction in the U.S. (between federal and state courts) cannot be contracted or waived by the parties, and the issue may be raised *sua sponte* by the courts at any time. However, the entire contract will be scrutinized for indications of so-called "exorbitant clauses" (*clauses exorbitantes*), i.e., terms which are unusual or inconsistent with the nature of a contract between private parties. In this connection, an express stipulation providing for jurisdiction of the administrative court may assume some significance. Much more frequently, however, a *clause exorbitante* will be found in contract terms that give the public authority far-reaching powers of supervision, direction and unilateral cancellation.[62] The presence of such a clause will, as a rule, mark the contract as an administrative one, while its absence (in cases not governed by a special statute) is at least a strong indication of the private nature of the agreement.[63]

This is not substantially different from the old U.S. distinction between governmental and proprietary functions of the state.[64] A comparable

---

any to be found in the common law. Sales of movables to a municipal or other local authority are "private" unless the contract contains an "exorbitant" element (as will be seen below). In the case of the sale of movables to the central government, however, the opposite presumption applies: such a contract is administrative unless its terms or certain circumstances external to the contract show that the government intended to subject itself to the principles of private law. See A. Laubadére, F. Moderne and P. Devolvé, 1 Traité des Contrats Administratifs 148 and 270–71 (1984). For example, the presumption would be overcome by the absence of a *clause exorbitante*, or other exorbitant elements, and by the business-like manner in which the transaction was concluded and carried out.

62. The criteria of what constitutes a *clause exorbitante* are not wholly clear and in part controversial. See A. Laubadére, F. Moderne and P. Devolvé, 1 Traité des Contrats Administratifs 213–29 (1984). However, the practical significance of the clause seems to be declining. The distinction between public and private contracts turns less on "exorbitant" elements introduced into the contract

by the parties, than on elements external to the contract that render contractual relationships "exorbitant" (e.g., the impact of governmental regulations). Id., at 131. On the evolving distinction between the *régime exorbitant* and the *clause exorbitante* within the larger notion of *éléments exorbitants*, see id., at 159, 183, 229–35.

63. For examples and discussion, see Auby and Drago, 1 Traité de Contentieux Administratif, Sec. 466–69 and 590–93 (1984); A. Laubadère, Traité de droit administratif, Sec. 576 (1980). There is a further and somewhat controversial refinement. In spite of the absence of a "clause exorbitante", the contract may be treated as an administrative one where the State has delegated the performance of inherently governmental functions or duties to the private party (e.g., to provide food for refugees confined by the Government in a "repatriation center"). See the cases cited by A. Laubadère, Traité élémentaire de droit administrative, Sec. 527 (1967).

64. See Langrod, Administrative Contracts—A comparative Study, 4 Am. J. Comp. L. 325, 328 (1955).

distinction—between acts *jure gestionis* and acts *jure imperii*—is used by courts of many countries in applying the international law doctrine of sovereign immunity.[65]

(v) Inter–Hierarchy Conflicts

In countries in which there are two separate judicial hierarchies (as in France), or more (as in Germany, where there are five), each with its own court of last resort, it frequently happens that on some point of law the several courts of last resort take conflicting positions. When that occurs, there must be a way to determine what the (correct or prevailing) law is.

It is true that, when the *Cour de cassation* and the *Conseil d'Etat* deal with what seems to be the same problem, their respective solutions sometimes can differ from each other without actually being in conflict. For example, in connection with administrative as well as private contracts the question may arise whether a radical and unforeseeable change of circumstances, which has occurred after the formation but before the complete performance of the contract and which has rendered such performance unduly burdensome for one party, gives such party a right to demand cancellation or modification of the contract. Over the last century, the *Conseil d'Etat* has developed an elaborate body of rules (the so-called doctrine of *imprévision*) pursuant to which the administrative court has broad powers[66] to adjust the parties' rights and duties under an administrative contract in such a case.[67] The *Cour de cassation*, in dealing with private contracts, has declined to follow this doctrine. By and large, it has adhered to the view that, unless performance has become literally impossible, the contract should be enforced no matter how painfully the parties' expectations have been frustrated by virtue of a change circumstances.[68]

Thus, on this important point of contract law, the position of the *Cour de cassation* differs drastically from that of the *Conseil d'Etat*. Yet, it would be misleading to call this a "conflict". It merely means that there is one rule for private contracts, and a very different one for administrative contracts. It is not difficult to present policy arguments supporting this

---

65. See 28 U.S.C. §§ 1602 to 1605.

66. In observing the resourcefulness with which the *Conseil d'Etat* has fashioned remedies in cases of this kind, a lawyer brought up in the common law is strongly reminded of the powers and the practice of courts of equity.

67. See R. Chapus, 1 Droit Administratif Général 1211–15 (2001); P. L. Frier, Précis de Droit Administratif 350–51 (2004).

68. See J. Ghestin, C. Jamin, M. Billiau, Les Effets du Contrat 356–416 (2001); Y. M. Laithier, Étude Comparative des Sanctions de l'Inexécution du Contrat 322–37 (2004). See also J. Bell, S. Boyron, S. Whittaker, Principles of French Law 341–49 (2008); K. Zweigert and H. Kötz, An Introduction to Comparative Law 524–27 (1998); B. Nicholas, French Law of Contracts 193–204 (1982); Amos and Walton's Introduction to French Law 165 (3d ed. by F.H. Lawson, A.E. Anton and L.N. Brown, 1967); P. Hay, Frustration and its Solution in German Law, 10 Am.J.Comp.L. 345, especially at 346–56 (1961). With respect to private contracts, the French position on this point is more conservative than that of most other legal systems in the civil-law as well as the common-law tradition. The rigidity of the French law, however, is softened by the widespread practice of drafting contracts with clauses specifically providing for relief in cases of unexpected changes in circumstances.

difference in the treatment of the two types of contracts, and, regardless of what one may think of the strength of these arguments, it is clear that we deal here with an attempted distinction rather that an outright conflict.

There are cases, however, in which the several courts of last resort take truly conflicting positions, creating what is called "inter-hierarchy conflicts".[69] Theoretically such a conflict could arise, first of all, with respect to a question of constitutional law. It appears, however, that in the great majority of those civil-law countries that provide for a judicial review of the constitutionality of statutes, such review is entrusted to a separate Constitutional Court, which stands outside of and in a sense above the top courts of the several judicial hierarchies. If the power of the constitutional review were not concentrated in a single court, it might easily happen in a civil–law country that the same statute is upheld by the highest administrative court but declared invalid by the ordinary court of last resort (or vice versa). The necessity of obviating this kind of inter-hierarchy conflict was one of the most potent reasons for the creation—by Austria, Germany, Italy, and other civil-law countries—of a single separate super-court dealing with the constitutional matters. By adopting that system, they have avoided such conflicts with respect to the most fundamental issues: those of constitutional law.[70]

Outside of the constitutional area, true conflicts can arise when the top courts of several judicial hierarchies take inconsistent positions on the same issue of substantive law. A French case, which at the time caused some flurry in the daily press, may serve as an example.[71] The mayor of Lyon had issued an ordinance that reserved certain parking spaces, near the city's Produce Market, for the trucks of vegetable vendors. A driver not belonging to the privileged class, who had parked in one of the reserved spaces, was criminally prosecuted and fined for violating the ordinance. The offender carried his case all the way to the *Cour de cassation*, where his conviction was reversed on the ground that there was no proper statutory authority for the mayor's ordinance. In another case, the *Conseil d'Etat* refused to nullify the mayor's ordinance (the very same ordinance involved in the case before the *Cour de cassation*), holding that it was valid and duly supported by an authorizing statute.

Here we observe a direct clash of conflicting decisions. In France, this conflict cannot be resolved by the Tribunal of Conflicts, which resolves only jurisdictional conflicts. The Tribunal of Conflicts does not deal with cases where the *Cour de cassation* and the *Conseil d'Etat*, each clearly acting within its jurisdiction, reach inconsistent results on a point of substantive

---

69. For a general discussion of the interaction of administrative decisions and decisions of the ordinary courts in France, see L. H. Levinson, Enforcement of Administrative Decisions in the United States and in France, 23 Emory L. J. 11, at 47–79, 102 (1974).

70. See *supra* Chapter 6, Section 3(e) at 523 (Constitutional Courts and Judicial Review).

71. Le Monde, Dec. 6, 1962, p. 14. Additional examples can be found in G. A. Bermann, French Treaties and French Courts: Two Problems in Supremacy, 28 Int'l. & Comp. L. Q. 458, 477 (1979).

---

law. So, in practice, there is no mechanism for the resolution of such conflicts, unless the legislator acts to resolve the disputed question.[72]

The practical consequence of this unresolved situation is interesting. As a practical matter, it would seem that the ordinary court's view would prevail in the end. It is true that the mayor has won his case in the highest administrative court: nobody can force him to withdraw his ordinance or to discontinue his attempts to enforce it. Yet everybody who has heard of the—probably much-publicized—decision of the *Cour de cassation*, will merrily park in the reserved spaces. Prosecuting violators would be a hopeless undertaking, since the lower criminal courts know that no conviction would survive an ultimate appeal to the *Cour de cassation*. On the other hand, if the mayor orders the police to erect a physical barrier preventing access to the reserved spaces, and to lift the barrier only to admit vegetable trucks, the public authority may have the last laugh. Any legal action challenging the use of the barrier would have to be brought in the administrative court, with predictable results.

The German legal system deals with this problem in an entirely different way. Parliament, implementing a constitutional mandate,[73] has enacted a statute setting up a mechanism for the resolution of conflicts between courts of last resort.[74] The statute is based on the idea that conflicts among the top courts of the several judicial hierarchies should be treated in a similar manner as conflicts between several panels of a single court of last resort.[75] Both types of conflicts are to be resolved by a super-panel of judges. The only difference is that in the case of an inter-hierarchy conflict, the super-panel is composed of judges representing all five hierarchies, i.e., the presidents of the five supreme courts plus four additional judges (two from each of the hierarchies involved in the particular dispute). If a case like the Lyon parking imbroglio occurred in Germany, and the administrative supreme court found itself unable to agree with the position taken by the ordinary supreme court, it would have to refer the controversial question of law to the super-panel.

72. In a pre–1957 automobile accident case the victim of a collision between a private and a government vehicle was denied relief in the civil courts on the ground that the accident had been caused by the governmental car. The administrative courts also denied relief, holding that the driver of the private vehicle was to blame for the accident. In this instance the legislator intervened, conferring power on the Tribunal of Conflicts to resolve a conflict of this kind (even though the conflict is a substantive rather that a jurisdictional one). But this statute has lost much of its significance due to the enactment of the 1957 statute mentioned *supra* note 49. See P. Herzog, Civil procedure in France 117–18 (1967).

73. Basic Law (art. 95, par. 3), as amended in 1968: "A joint Chamber of the courts specified in paragraph (1) of this Article [the Federal Court of Justice, the Federal Administrative Court, the Federal Finance Court, the Federal Labour Court, and the Federal Social Court] shall be established to preserve the uniformity of decisions. Details shall be regulated by a federal law."

74. Law of June 19, 1968, BGBl I 661. The provisions of the statute are reproduced and discussed in Baumbach–Lauterbach–Albers–Hartmann, Zivilprozessordnung, Appendix following § 140 GVG (1987).

75. See *supra* Chapter 6, Section 3(d)(iii) at 518 (discussing the internal contradictions in Supreme Court decisions).

It should be noted, moreover, that in Germany the same mechanism can be utilized to resolve inter-hierarchy conflicts on questions of jurisdiction. As we have seen, in Germany the resolution of inter-hierarchy jurisdictional conflicts as a rule is not entrusted to a Tribunal of Conflicts as in France. Generally, the jurisdictional question can be determined, in binding fashion, by the court of whatever hierarchy in which the action has been brought. But the binding effect of the jurisdictional determination thus made is limited to the case at hand. For example, if in case *A* the administrative supreme court affirms the jurisdiction of its hierarchy, that is the end of the matter insofar as case *A* is concerned. If subsequently case *B*, involving identical facts and issues is instituted by another party in an ordinary court, the decision rendered in case *A* is not binding on the latter court. Thus the jurisdictional question may again be litigated up to the highest court—this time the ordinary supreme court. If that court, in dealing with case *B*, wishes to deviate from the position taken in case *A* by the administrative supreme court, it must submit the question to the super-panel.

It is interesting to observe that the French created a super-panel to resolve conflicts of jurisdiction but the Germans did not do so and that the Germans created a super-panel to resolve inter-hierarchy conflicts but the French did not do so.

(vi) The Importance of the Dichotomy in the International Context

Common-law observers may consider that the aforementioned institutions and approaches are rather strange, and that in the area of public law disputes in particular, there appears to be a real "chasm" between civil law and common law. However, if one views these differences in a broader perspective, one may find that the differences reflected in this "chasm", although they are remarkable and of great significance in legal practice, relate only to matters of technique.

The fundamental social problem to be resolved is the same everywhere: to strike a balance between the interests of individuals and voluntary associations, on the one hand, and those of the community, on the other; and to do so in an era of accelerating industrialization and urbanization, necessarily accompanied by the constant growth and proliferation of the tentacles by which various public authorities reach into our lives. The responses to the problem of "judicial review" of administrative acts that have been fashioned by civil-law and common-law systems, do not seem to be basically dissimilar. In both types of systems, it has been recognized that strengthened judicial protection of the individual against an increasingly powerful and ubiquitous government plays a central role in the required balancing of interests and in the promotion of the rule of law.

To the extent that there existed a measure of disagreement on this fundamental point, the dissenters were to be found in some of the former socialist systems rather than in the civil-law or common-law orbit. The civilian tradition of separate administrative courts was seldom followed in the former socialist countries of Eastern Europe. In some (USSR, Czecho-

slovakia, East Germany), there was virtually no judicial review of administrative acts. In others (Bulgaria, Hungary, Romania, Yugoslavia), a more or
less wide range of administrative acts were reviewable in ordinary courts or
in special sections of supreme courts. In 1980, Poland reintroduced a
special administrative court with broad jurisdiction to set aside administrative acts that violate the law; but certain acts, such as the expulsion of an
alien or denial of a passport, were exempted from the court's jurisdiction.[76]

In principle, there are strong similarities between how the civil law and
common law deal with claims against the public administration. However,
on a technical level, it seems unavoidable that the difference between civil
law and common law as to the nature and treatment of "public-law
disputes" will lead to endless misunderstandings and difficulties. For
instance, when one speaks of a "civil" action in the U.S., one includes in
that category all judicial proceedings other than criminal ones. Thus in the
U.S. view, a proceeding to enforce or to set aside an administrative
determination is a civil proceeding, to be brought in an ordinary court and
governed by the procedural rules applied in civil litigation. But civil-law
countries would not classify such a proceeding as a civil one. This is a
perennial source of misunderstandings among lawyers from different countries seeking to communicate with each other. Such misunderstandings
have indeed occurred on a large scale, but sophisticated international
practitioners are well aware of them.

The international practitioner may encounter several practical difficulties caused by the different ways in which various countries draw the line
between private and public law litigation. The issue has practical importance because the most important international conventions related to
procedure, such as the Hague Convention on the Service Abroad of Judicial
and Extrajudicial Documents,[77] the Hague Convention on the Take of
Evidence Abroad,[78] or the Brussels Regime of international jurisdiction and
recognition of judgments in the European Union[79] apply only in "civil and
commercial matters." While in common-law countries all cases that are not
criminal are considered "civil or commercial", in civil-law countries there is
also, as we have seen, the category of "administrative procedure" or
"public-law litigation", which differs sharply from "civil procedure" or
"private litigation". In those cases, the aforementioned conventions on
judicial cooperation are not applicable.

Since the definition of "civil" is not the same in all of the signatory
countries of such international conventions, there must be a clear-cut rule
(somewhat in the nature of a choice-of-law rule) determining the question
of *whose* definition should prevail in a given case. One solution would be to

76. For a survey of the former socialist
Eastern European systems, see M. Wierzbow-
sky and S.C. McCaffrey, Judicial Control of
Administrative Authorities: A New Development in Eastern Europe, 18 Int. Lawyer 645
(1984). See also the broad-based comparative
study by V. Bolgár, The Public Interest, 12 J.
Pub. L. 13 (1963).

77. See *infra* Chapter 8, Section 3(b) at
736 (discussing service of process abroad).

78. See *infra* Chapter 8, Section 3(i) at
809 (discussing the taking of evidence
abroad).

79. See *infra* Chapter 8, Section 3(a) at
716 (discussing personal jurisdiction).

apply the definition of the country where the proceeding is pending and where the request for co-operation originates (not the definition of the country that must comply with the request). The French, while not admitting that this was a binding rule, have indicated that, as a matter of courtesy, they would cooperate in cases that are classified as "civil" in the requesting country (though not in France).[80] This rule, however, puts countries that have narrower definition of "civil litigation" at a disadvantage over those with a more expansive definition. Civil-law countries therefore will have to comply with certain requests from common-law countries that they themselves would not be able to make. This illustrates the doubts and difficulties arising from the fact that the civil-law treatment of public-law disputes is so fundamentally different from the common-law tradition.[81]

The issue may prove difficult even among civil-law countries. A telling example is provided by the decision of the Court of Justice of the European Communities, where the Dutch Ministry of Transport sued a German shipowner in an ordinary court at The Hague.[82] The action sought reimbursement for the cost of removing the wreckage of defendant's ship, which had sunk in waters belonging to Germany but administered by Dutch authorities. A reimbursement claim of this kind is treated as private under Dutch law, while the other original members of the Common Market would regard it as a public-law dispute. The European Court, applying its own independent criteria, held that this was not a "civil or commercial" matter, and that consequently the Dutch court's jurisdiction was not governed by the Brussels Convention of 1968. At first blush, this may look like a victory of the Dutch Ministry of Transport, which may now pursue the case in a Dutch court under Dutch rules of jurisdiction (permitting an action against a non-resident to be brought at the domicile of the plaintiff). But, because the case is not covered by the Convention, it is disputed whether the German courts (which regard the matter as "public") would enforce the judgment of the Dutch court.

QUESTIONS

(1) At what level of the legal system (legal formant) could you place the residual meaning of the cassation/revision distinction? Do you agree that

---

80. See the Hague Conference Reports in 17 Int. Legal Materials at 315–16, 320–21, 1417–19, 1426–27 (1978). In tax cases, however, the attitude of the civil-law signatories of the Convention is somewhat less accommodating. Id., at 1419. Concerning French, German, and British practice in cases where the request emanates from an administrative agency or tribunal (or a party to a proceeding before such agency or tribunal) in the U.S., see also Restatement (Revised), Foreign Relations Law, § 481, com. f, and § 483, com. c (T.D. 1984).

81. For other illustrations, and further references, see H. Koch, Zur Praxis der Rechtshilfe im amerikanisch—deutschen Prozessrecht—Ergebnisse einer Umfrage zu den Haager Zustellungs—und Beweisuebereinkommen, 5 IPRax 245, at 246–47 (1985).

82. See The Netherlands v. Rüffer, Dec. 16, 1989, RS 814/79, 1982 Common Market Reporter, Transfer Binder § 8702, p. 8388.

common law and civil law systems have now converged in this previously crucial comparative opposition?

(2) Please consider the different models of constitutional adjudication from the perspective of their effectiveness. How would you rank France, Germany, and the United States from this perspective?

---

4.   The Style of Judicial Opinions: Cultural Setting of Case Law

With regard to the length and style of judicial opinions crafted by the various Courts, there is no uniformity in the civil-law world.[1] Nevertheless, a comparative study of the style of judicial decisions shows there are some points on which the civil-law systems, with virtual unanimity, have adopted a practice differing from the common law.

(a) Who prepares

Civil-law courts combine judgment and opinion in a single document and the whole document is prepared by the court and never by counsel. Under prevailing American practice, the court's opinion (if one is filed) must be issued by the court, but counsel commonly is expected to prepare orders and judgments for the court's signature.[1]

(b) Judgment limited by claims

Second, the court will decide the controversy within the strict limits established by the parties in their claims and counterclaims. The court cannot grant a different remedy or award a different object or higher amount than what was prayed for in the parties' pleadings. In some civil-law countries, this limitation is moderated by the possibility of amending the pleadings, but not all countries have flexible amendment rules.[1]

The prohibition of *extra petita* and *ultra petita* judgments (i.e. judgments that will award what was not requested or more than what was requested) is the general rule in civil law countries and is a corollary to the

---

1. The practice of appellate as well as trial courts differs from country to country as can be seen by comparing the opinions of the various foreign courts reprinted in this book. See also J.G. Wetter, The Styles of Appellate Judicial Opinions (1960). For an enlightening discussion of the traditional German technique of preparing and formulating judicial decisions, see W. O. Weyrauch, The Art of Drafting Judgments: A Modified German Case Method, 9 J.Legal Educ. 311 (1956), with a sample opinion at 330–31. For Austrian practice, see Appendix D in F. R. Lacy, "Civilizing" Nonjury Trials, 19 Vand.L.Rev. 73, 121–28 (1965).

1. See Chicopee Mfg. Corp. v. Kendall Co., 288 F.2d 719, 724–25 (4th Cir.1961),

cert. denied, 368 U.S. 825, 82 S.Ct. 44 (1961). Cf. Westside Property Owners v. Schlesinger, 597 F.2d 1214, 1216 (9th Cir.1979). As to the proper authorship of findings of fact and conclusions of law, see the interesting opinion of Judge Wisdom in Railex Corp. v. Speed Check Co., 457 F.2d 1040, 1041–42 (5th Cir.1972), cert. denied, 409 U.S. 876, 93 S.Ct. 125 (1972).

1. The U.S. has a very flexible amendment rule: A party may amend its pleadings once as a matter of course before a response. After that, a party may amend only with the opposing party's written consent or court's leave, but the court should freely give leave when justice so requires. See FRCP 15(a).

adversarial principle that the parties, not the court, must control the subject matter of the proceeding.[2]

This rule is unknown in U.S. procedure. Except in cases of default judgment, a U.S. court "should grant the relief to which each party is entitled, even if the party has not demanded that relief in its pleading".[3]

(c) Reasoned decisions

Third, and most importantly, civil-law countries generally adhere to the rule that every final judgment *must* be accompanied by a reasoned opinion detailing the position of the court on every major issue of fact and law.[1] The court must give a public account of why it reached a certain decision, and explain its reasoning on how it weighted the evidence presented by the parties, and how it reached the legal conclusion. An ambiguous, incomplete, or contradictory reasoning is reversible error. This requirement maintains the appearance of propriety for the losing party, as well as for the public as a whole, and allows for meaningful appellate review. Therefore, it is considered an essential safeguard against judicial arbitrariness. The European Court of Human Rights considered that art. 6 of the European Convention on Human Rights, establishing the right to a fair proceeding, "obliges courts to give reasons for their decisions, but cannot be understood as requiring a detailed answer to every argument."[2] In some civil-law countries, the rule is a constitutional guaranty and an unreasoned or improperly reasoned decision is void.[3] The level of detail required of judges varies from case to case, from country to country, from time to time.

This rule has a direct consequence on congested courts and limited budgets. From time to time, legal systems may try to limit the rule in certain cases. For example in Germany, it was once severely limited in cases involving small amounts of money, but it was argued to be unconstitutional because even in the smallest cases a reasoned opinion is a fundamental guaranty of fairness. The rule does not exist anymore, but in cases involving small amounts of money, it is not possible to appeal.[4]

---

2. See the Codes of Civil Procedure of Brazil (arts. 460 and 128), Germany (§ 308.1), France (art. 4, 5 and 480), Belgium (art. 1138), Italy (art. 112), Portugal (arts. 660.2, 661.1, and 668.1.e), Spain (art. 216 and 218), Japan (art. 246). This traditional rule has a Roman Law pedigree. See L. Wenger, Institutes of the Roman Law of Civil Procedure 207 (1986).

3. See FRCP 54(d).

1. See the Codes of Civil Procedure of Italy (132.4 and 360.5), Brazil (art. 458, II), Germany (art. 313) (allowing the parties to waive this right in most cases), France (art. 455), Portugal (arts. 158 and 659–2), Spain (art. 218), Japan (art. 253), Argentina (art. 163.4), Uruguay (art. 197), Colombia (art. 304), Belgium (art. 780.3), the Netherlands (art. 230.1.e). See also the Ibero–American

Model Code of Civil Procedure (art. 184); ALI/Unidroit, Principles and Rules of Transnational Civil Procedure, Principle 23 and Rule 31.2. See T. Sauvel, Histoire du jugement motivé, 61 Revue du Droit Public et de la Science Politique 5 (1955); M. Taruffo, La Motivazione della Sentenza Civile (1975).

2. See Case of Van de hurk v. The Netherlands, April 19, 1994. See Boré, La motivation des décisions de justice et la Convention européenne des droits de l'homme, JCP G 2002, I, 104.

3. See the Constitutions of Italy (art. 111.6), Brazil (art. 93, IX), Portugal (art. 205–1), Belgium (art. 149).

4. See German Code of Civil Procedure, art. 495a, as amended in 1990. See F. Stollmann, Zur Verfassungsmässigkeit des neuen § 495a ZPO, 44 N.J.W. 1719 (1991).

In some countries, this principle is applicable not only to the final judgment but also to every interlocutory decision.

Furthermore, this rule has important consequences for international litigation, especially when a judgment from a common-law country needs to be enforced in a country that considers a motivated judgment a constitutional guaranty. In the past, civil-law countries would reject enforcement of a common-law judgment not fully motivated. The trend is to enforce them as recognition of the differences between legal systems. However, some countries still might not.

If the party expects a common-law judgment to be enforced abroad, it would be advisable to request the court to issue a reasoned written decision. In non-jury proceedings, federal judges must state findings of fact and findings of law.[5] The problem is compounded in cases of jury verdicts because they have no written justification.[6] In the case of a jury trial, the solution may be to ask the court to issue a statement justifying the grounds for the decision on legal issues and to request the jury to issue a "special verdict" (in which the jury answers questions about the facts) or a "general verdict with interrogatories" (with questions to test whether the jury really understood the case and whether they followed court instructions).[7]

Curiously, this difference has the opposite effect in the decisions of the supreme courts. The traditional civil-law courts of cassation are notorious for their short, ambiguous, and uninformative opinions.[8] U.S. Supreme Court opinions, however, usually have dozens of pages of carefully motivated reasoning.

(d) Dissenting Opinions

A fourth point deals with the possibility of judges writing dissenting opinions. Generally speaking, opinions do not show the name of the judge who authored them, but the practice of the various civil-law countries is not quite uniform in this respect. In France, Italy, and Germany, and in a large number of jurisdictions following their example, every collegiate opinion is decided by majority but issued *per curiam*; this is true even of the opinions of most of the Supreme Courts. The deliberations among the judges (when more than one) are secret.[1] The judgment is signed by every judge who participated in the deliberation, but, as a corollary of the principle of secrecy, the judge who actually wrote the decision is not identified, and no dissenting or concurring opinion is allowed. The parties do not even know whether the decision was rendered by a majority or was

---

5. See FRCO 52(a).

6. According to the European Court of Human Rights, the unmotivated jury trial decision of the Belgian *Cour d'Assises* (criminal proceeding) is not consistent with art. 6 of the European Convention of Human Rights, establishing the right to a fair proceeding. See Taxquet v. Belgium, January 13, 2009.

7. See FRCP 49(a) and (b)

8. See M. de S.-O.-L.'E. Lasser, Judicial Deliberations: A Comparative Analysis of Judicial Transparency and Legitimacy (2005).

1. See, e.g., the Codes of Civil Procedure of Italy (art. 276), France (art. 448). See also the Statute of the Court of Justice of the European Communities (arts. 2, 10, 13, 35).

unanimous, because this would violate the principle of secrecy. The same rule exists in Italy, the Netherlands, and Belgium.[2]

The deliberations of the Supreme Courts in Switzerland, Brazil, and Norway are conducted in public. In this small minority of civil-law countries, therefore, the public is informed of the position taken by each member of the court, regardless of whether formal dissenting opinions are written and published. Since the Supreme Court Justices in Japan are confirmed in general elections and re-confirmed every ten years, their opinions must be expressed in writing in each case. This is another reminder of the American Occupation following World War II.[3]

As we have seen, nowadays most of the decisions in the first instance are made by a single judge.[4] Therefore, much of the importance of "dissenting opinions" is limited to appeals, although, even on second instance, many decisions are now made by a single judge.[5]

Perhaps the civil-law system reflects the status and attitude of a civil service judiciary, but this explanation would not hold for Constitutional Courts. A German sociologist has intimated that his compatriots' traditional resistance to the publication of judicial dissents can be ascribed to a general tendency to suppress conflicts and to a yearning for painless synthesis.[6] However, this theory cannot explain why the publication of dissents is prohibited in France, a country whose citizens can hardly be characterized as conformists and are known to cultivate a tradition of contentiousness and healthy skepticism.

Perhaps an interesting comparative law question is to determine why the majority of common-law systems authorize the publication of dissenting opinions while the majority of civil-law systems do not.

The reality is there is no strict connection between the secrecy of the deliberation and the possibility of dissenting opinions. It is understandable that the deliberations themselves must be in private. Court deliberations are secret in the U.S. as well, but judges may issue dissenting opinions. There is no incompatibility between preserving the secrecy of deliberations

2. The subject of dissenting opinions has given rise to a voluminous literature of a comparative nature. See, e.g., K.H. Nadelmann, The Judicial Dissent—Publication vs. Secrecy, 8 Am.J.Comp.L. 415 (1959); J. Federer, Die Bekanntgabe der abweichenden Meinung des überstimmten Richters, 23 JZ 511 (1968), where many of the other relevant writings are cited. See also K. H. Nadelmann, Non–Disclosure of Dissents in Constitutional Courts: Italy and West Germany, 13 Am. J.Comp.L. 268 (1964); Anand, The Role of Individual and Dissenting Opinions in International Adjudication, 14 Int'l & Comp.L.Q. 788 (1965); A. Tunc, La Cour Suprême Idéale (concluding part of a comparative symposium on Courts of Last Resort), 30 Revue Internationale de Droit Comparé 433, 456–59 (1978). On the importance of dissent, see C. Sunstein, *Why Societies Need Dissent* (2003).

3. See Y. Taniguchi, P. Reich & H. Miyake, *Civil Procedure in Japan* 3–21—3–25 and 3–38—3–39 (2008); C. Goodman, *Justice and Civil Procedure in Japan* 451 (2004).

4. The topic is further developed *supra* Chapter 6, Section 3(a) at 490 (Courts of First Instance).

5. The topic is further developed *supra* Chapter 6, Section 3(c) at 496 (Courts of Appeals).

6. See R. Dahrendorf, Gesellschaft und Demokratie in Deutschland 234–42, 268–71 (1965).

and permitting dissenting opinions, with or without identification of the dissenting judges.

Some civil-law countries allow the publication of dissenting votes or even dissenting opinions. Apparently, it was through Romano–Canonistic procedure that the principle of judicial anonymity—a principle opposed to the Germanic tradition—was brought to the continental legal systems. Nevertheless, historical research has shown that even in the centuries immediately following the reception of Roman law and of Romano–Canonistic procedure, some continental systems permitted the publication of dissenting opinions.[7]

Those who disfavor dissent in civil-law countries do not always make it clear whether their reasoning is intended to militate against (i) the publication of the fact of a split vote, or (ii) the publication of dissenting opinions, or (iii) merely against identifying the dissenters.

This is an issue of policy, and, once civil-law countries face it, it would not take long to recognize that the "unanimity" of their *per curiam* decisions is artificial, and the enforced anonymity of judicial decisions destroys transparency and the judges' sense of individual responsibility.

There is occasionally discourse in civil law in favor of dissent. Where this possibility exists, it seems judges are happy about it. The late Judge Wiltraut Rupp-von Brünneck, the "great dissenter" of the German Federal Constitutional Court, once said, "it is of the very essence of a pluralistic democracy that nobody may claim to have a lease on the absolute truth or correctness of his views."[8] Published dissents constantly remind the public that the members of the court's majority are not infallible, and such a reminder may be an important contribution to the openness of society.

Nevertheless, in countries where the judges are career civil servants, and where respect for the judiciary is not as deeply ingrained as it is in the U.S., some counter-points may be raised. For instance, it is claimed that in such countries the anonymity of the *per curiam* decision may be necessary to protect the individual judges from improper pressures (from the parties as well as from the government), and to add more dignity and moral force to their judgments by keeping judicial disagreements from the eyes of the public. After all, if the public would see the courts disagree on legal matters, it could give a (correct) impression that law is something to be debated and argued, not a given. This would lead to more frustration for the losing party.

Moreover, some dissenting opinions in the U.S. demonstrate that judges may get personal and use a tenor that is not completely civil to each other. They may even make serious accusations. Sometimes the reasons for issuing dissenting opinions may be more personal than the advancement of the legal system.

---

7. G. Gorla & L. Moccia, A "Revisiting" of the Comparison Between "Continental Law" and "English Law" (16th–19th Century), 2 J.Leg.Hist. 143, 151 (1981).

8. Quoted in the interesting article by W. Hill, Die Stimme der Minderheit, 18 Zeitschrift für Rechtspolitik 15, 17 (1985).

It is also arguable that the need for dissenting opinions is greater in common-law than in civil-law systems. In common-law jurisdictions, dissents often mark the controversial and developing areas of the law. Today's dissent frequently foreshadows tomorrow's majority position. By reminding the profession of the possibility of future change, the dissent becomes an element of flexibility that tends to mitigate whatever rigidity may still be inherent in the principle of *stare decisis*. It might be argued that the civil-law systems, which have not adopted that principle, correspondingly have less need for the mitigating device.

From a functional point of view, however, one can see at least three civil-law analogues of the common-law dissent. The first is the possibility of lower courts to deviate from, and even to disregard, a precedent set by the court of appeals or the Supreme Court in a previous case.[9] True, this power is sparingly exercised, but "it is no accident that those parts of the private law in which the lower courts of France and the USSR most frequently diverge from the decisions of the Supreme Courts (...) are precisely those in which the House of Lords is likely to be divided 3–2."[10]

The two other civil law equivalents of the dissenting opinion are found in countries and European Courts that adopt the French model of cassation. First is the power of the court of appeals to disregard the Supreme Court's decision when the case is remanded for further proceedings.[11] Second is the opinion of the *Ministére Public* in some cases and in particular, those cases reaching the Supreme Court. In the French *Cour de Cassation*, a member of the *Ministére Public* will offer "advisory opinions" on how to best apply the law in the concrete case.[12] These advisory opinions are mostly published and have a significant importance as to understand the decision of the Court, especially when the Court disagrees.

Even in Germany, where the law generally reflects the civilians' traditional anti-dissent attitude, special legislation permits the publication of dissenting opinions in the only court whose decisions have a binding effect in future cases: the Constitutional Court. Although allowed, however, dissenting opinions are rare. The German example was followed in Spain for the constitutional court, and, in 1985, all Spanish courts were authorized to issue dissenting opinions.[13]

During the 1960s, the German legal profession engaged in a great debate concerning whether and to what extent the traditional system should be modified.[14] The status quo was left undisturbed with respect to

9. See *infra* Chapter 6, Section 6 at 582.

10. See B. Rudden, Courts and Codes in England, France and Soviet Russia, 48 Tul. L.Rev. 1010, 1016 (1974).

11. See Chapter 6, Section 3(d)(ii) at 511 (Cassation and Revision).

12. See *supra* Chapter 6, Section 3(d)(iv) at 521 (Discussing the Role of Government on Supreme Courts).

13. See art. 260 of the Organic Law of the Judiciary.

14. See, e.g., M. Heidenhain, Der 47. Deutsche Juristentag, 23 JZ 755, 757 (1968).

all courts other than the Constitutional Court. Concerning the practice in the Federal Constitutional Court, the great debate resulted in statutory change;[15] but even in that Court the old principle of anonymity was not completely eradicated. The reader of a decision of the Federal Constitutional Court is always told whether the decision was unanimous and, if not, how many judges voted for and against it. Moreover, if dissenting opinions have been written by one or more of the dissenting judges, those opinions are published together with the majority opinion. Nevertheless, there remain many cases in which the identity of majority and minority judges is not revealed and the names of the actual authors of the various opinions normally remain undisclosed.

Only the judges who join in a dissenting *opinion* are identified by name. Thus, if all of the judges who voted against the majority decision join in a dissenting opinion, the reader in effect knows the identity of all of the judges who voted for as well as against the decision. If the decision is not unanimous, but no dissenting opinion is written, the names of the dissenters are not published. Even when a dissenting opinion is written and published, it may happen that one or several of the judges who voted against the majority, and thus in effect dissented, refused to join in the dissenting opinion. But their names are not revealed, and, as a result, the names of the judges who voted for the decision also remain in doubt. Thus every majority opinion in effect is rendered "Per Curiam," and a dissenting opinion, if concurred in by more than one judge, must be taken as the expression of a group position rather than the voice of an individual judge.

The civilian tradition of not allowing publication of dissent is followed by the Court of Justice of the European Communities. There was, apparently, some vigorous discussion about this when the Court of Justice was first created as The Court of Justice of the European Coal and Steel Community in 1951, but the principle has not been questioned since.[16] The European Court of Human Rights, on the other hand, does publish dissenting and concurring opinions.

(e) The Reporting of Decisions

One noteworthy point, on which there is lack of uniformity among civil-law systems, relates to the important question of whether the names of the parties should be disclosed. In some countries (e.g., Germany), official as well as unofficial reports of judicial decisions omit the names of the parties or give only initials. Such a practice protects the privacy of the parties, but it has the disadvantage that cases cannot be remembered or cited by name and must be referred to, somewhat awkwardly, by date or volume and page number (some very important cases are often referred to by a particularly significant fact or even word mentioned in the opinion). In other civil-law countries, such as France and Switzerland, the names of the

15. See § 30 of the Law Concerning the Federal Constitutional Court (Bundesverfassungsgerichtsgesetz), as amended in 1971. Even before this change in the federal law, the constitutional courts of some of the *Län-* *der* were authorized to, and did, publish dissenting opinions.

16. See G. Isaac, Droit communautaire général 232 (4th ed. 1994).

parties normally are indicated in reported decisions. This practice (like the U.S. practice) of course raises privacy issues. The well-known French law journal, *La Gazette du Palais*, once was sued for having published the name of a respondent in a provincial divorce action.[1] In domestic relations and other cases raising privacy concerns, French reports now substitute X and Y for the names of the parties.

With regards to the reporting of judicial decisions, there is no uniformity among civil-law systems.[2] Decisions of courts of appeal, as a rule, are not officially reported. Even with respect to the decisions of Supreme Courts, many countries leave the reporter's task wholly or partly to private enterprise; where official reports do exist, they may be selective or limited to abstract summaries of the court's legal reasoning. A number of countries publish full official reports; in others, especially in Italy, only summaries tend to be published.[3] It would appear that, in 1994, the French *Cour de cassation* rendered about 24,000 decisions, of which only about 2,100 were officially published.[4]

The consequence is that in many civil-law countries the function of bringing judicial decisions to the attention of the profession must to some extent be performed by legal periodicals. They publish the text of selected important decisions, either in full or in excerpt.[5] An annotation prepared by an expert frequently follows the decision itself. The author of the annotation may have looked at the record or at unpublished parts of the decision and thus may be in a position not only to comment on the legal points involved, but also to enhance the reader's understanding of the facts and the procedural history of the case.

Decisions published in legal periodicals, plus the annotations thereto, thus constitute indispensable sources for anyone engaged in legal research concerning the law of civilian countries. Research is facilitated by the existence, alongside of more general periodicals, of those devoted to special topics such as international law, family law, civil and criminal procedure, etc. However, the absence of a system of complete reporting of all decisions at least of the highest courts does create a fairness problem. Lawyers specializing in certain matters (e.g. in representing insurance companies) may, over time, accumulate a substantial file of unreported cases that their opponents with a more general practice may not have.

---

1. See Le Monde of November 12, 1971, at 19.

2. For details, see C. Szladits & C. M. Germain, Guide to Foreign Legal Materials: French (1985) and the other volumes published in the same series under the auspices of the Parker School of Foreign and Comparative Law.

3. See, e.g., G. Gorla, Some Comments on the Italian Legal System, in 1 Formation of Contracts—A Study of the Common Core of Legal Systems 297, 298 (Schlesinger ed., 1968).

4. See the Rapport de la Cour de Cassation 1994, at 31 (La Documentation Française Paris 1995).

5. Where the decision is still subject to a further appeal, an editorial note ordinarily will so inform the reader. In many civil law countries, legal periodicals are thus important not only because of the commentary they provide, but also as a source of information on recent cases, particularly of the Supreme Courts.

In Austria, the Constitutional Court has ruled that the mere selective publication of decisions by the Austrian Supreme Court violates the Constitution.[6] Similar concerns have led to the creation of a database of all decisions of the highest French courts, the *Cour de cassation* and the *Conseil d'Etat*, available on Legifrance. More recently, there has been a proliferation of official (such as CELEX for Court of Justice of the European Communities and Court of First Instance and HUDOC for the European Court of Human Rights) and unofficial databases, some of which can also be accessed through Westlaw or LEXIS.

The internet is indeed completely changing this reality because now all decisions are easily available on line on the courts' websites. This is particularly true regarding the Supreme Courts, but, in some countries, decisions of the courts of appeal and even of the first instance are available on the internet. Although this publication is mostly for the convenience of the parties, this broad access to precedents may have a long-term impact on the traditional rules denying their precedential effect.

Even when decisions of the courts of appeal are published, their value as precedents is not that great. Since these courts decide on issues of fact as well as law, it is clear that much of what they say deals with factual matters and thus is of no general interest for purposes of legal research.[7]

This problem can arise in any legal system where intermediate appellate courts have the power to review factual findings,[8] but it is of particular importance in civil-law systems. In some types of cases, especially negligence cases, it may often be difficult to determine, in reading the opinion of a court which has power to pass on factual as well as legal issues, whether the court announced a rule of law or merely resolved an issue of fact.[9] Nevertheless, it is generally assumed in the civil-law world that, when an opinion of an intermediate appellate court is cited as an alleged precedent, it is both necessary and possible by careful analysis of the opinion to separate its legal reasoning (which may have some precedential value) from the discussion of factual issues (which has no such value).[10]

In the U.S., the problem simply does not arise in jury cases. Even in non-jury cases, the problem may lose some of its poignancy as a result of statutory provisions, which require the court to specify whether its determination is based on law or facts.[11] Such provisions reflect the attitude of lawyers brought up in the U.S. jury system to whom it has become second

---

6. See Decision of June 28, 1990, Die Presse, September 19, 1990, at 20, col. 1.

7. Regarding the general question of the force of judicial precedents in a civil-law system, see *infra*, Chapter 6, Section 6 at 582.

8. See D. W. Robertson, The Precedent Value of Conclusions of Fact in Civil Cases in England and Louisiana, 29 La.L.Rev. 78 (1968).

9. See Robertson, *supra* note 8.

10. See Employers' Liability Assur. Corp. v. Madden, 219 F.2d 205 (5th Cir. 1955); Wright v. Paramount–Richards Theatres, 198 F.2d 303 (5th Cir.1952); Gillen v. Phoenix Indemnity Co., 198 F.2d 147 (5th Cir.1952).

11. See, e.g., FRCP 52(a)(1) and NYCPLR § 5712(c).

nature, even when dealing with a non-jury case, to keep the law-fact dichotomy constantly present before their eyes.

Not infrequently, American courts are faced with this problem in foreign-law cases. Suppose a tort action governed by French law is brought in New York. The French law expert for one of the parties relies on a decision—squarely on point—in which a French court of appeals held certain conduct to be negligent. In order not to be overly impressed by this decision, the New York court will have to keep in mind that a French *Cour d'appel* examines questions of fact as well as law. Only careful analysis of the French court's decision, based on sufficient background knowledge of French law, can show to what extent that court's finding of negligence in the case before it expressed or necessarily implied a particular view of the law, and to what extent it was a mere factual finding that would not be reviewable by the French Supreme Court. Insofar as it is shown to constitute a factual finding, it has no precedential value—no more than a jury verdict rendered in a common-law court.

5. BETWEEN CODES AND CASE LAW IN THE CIVIL LAW TRADITION—INTERPRETATION, ANALOGY, AND RELATED MATTERS

The previous discussion shows a variety of structural aspects of legal systems that are highly relevant on how a case law system can work. To begin with, some hierarchy of courts is necessary (which we find in almost all modern professional legal systems), for you need "lower" courts to follow "higher courts" precedents in order to develop an idea of "case law." Moreover, highly relevant to the possibility and functioning of a case law system are all aspects related to the way in which cases are (or are not) reported. Without a publication system or with a system very fragmented or too concise, a case law system can hardly develop. The question thus arises: How, to what extent and limitations, does case law develop in jurisdictions that are reluctant to openly recognize this as a "source of law"? Most of the following cases have been in this case book since its first edition in 1950. They are by now "classics," fully representative of the way in which lawyers trained in the respective jurisdictions and within their institutional settings operate. The functioning of case law is a deep cultural and institutional aspect of a legal system that cannot be change with the strike of a legislator's pen or with one court decision. In studying such aspects one can consequently use classic cases, exactly as it happens when studying Marbury v. Madison in a U.S. constitutional law course.

Opinion of the German Reichsgericht in the Matter of S. S. v. M. E. Corp.

2d Civil Division, January 22, 1935, RGZ 146, 385.

[Defendant corporation has a capital of one million Reichsmarks, divided into 1000 bearer shares, each with a par value of RM 1000. Plaintiff has been a substantial minority shareholder since 1919. The majority of the shares are held by one M. W. and members of his family. M. W. has been an officer and shareholder since the corporation was organized. At a shareholders' meeting on Nov. 30, 1932, a vote was taken on a resolution approving the conduct of the corporation's affairs by the management during the fiscal year 1931–32. The vote was 498 for approval and 416 against, a total of 914 votes. Of the 498 approving votes, 486 were cast by J. W., the son of the officer, M. W. The 416 votes against approval were cast by plaintiff and his attorney. Plaintiff then sued to set aside the resolution approving the management's conduct, on the ground that J. W. was only the ostensible holder of the shares voted by him, and that the real owner was M. W. who was disqualified from voting. By a judgment of the Landgericht München, dated May 7, 1933, the resolution was set aside, on the theory that the voting prohibition contained in the Commercial Code, § 252, subdiv. 3, had been violated. This section in substance provides that no shareholder may vote on the question of approval of his own acts as officer or director of the corporation.[1] No appeal was taken from this judgment of May 7, 1933.

Meanwhile, on Dec. 17, 1932, defendant corporation had called a new shareholders' meeting for Jan. 10, 1933. The public notice of this meeting stated that the agenda would include the question of rescinding the Nov. 30 resolution and of adopting a new resolution approving the acts of the management. Any shareholder desiring to vote in the Jan. 10 meeting had to deposit[2] his shares no later than Jan. 6, 1933.]

By notarial document of Jan. 5, 1933, M. W. and J. W. and their wives set up a limited liability company (Gesellschaft mit beschränkter Haftung, GmbH)[3] with a capital of RM 500,000, designating as the object of the new

---

1. The reader will remember that the rules on corporations of the Commercial Code were subsequently replaced by a separate statute. In Germany and in many other countries it is customary (and often prescribed by law) that the stockholders at their regular annual meeting vote on the question whether to grant *Entlastung* (in French, *décharge*; meaning release from responsibility, or approval of management conduct) to the members of the management group. [This applies occasionally to a public body as well; see Treaty establishing the European Community, art. 206.] At the time of the principal case, such a vote of approval, unless set aside by the court, had the effect of releasing any cause of action for mismanagement which the corporation might otherwise have against the officers in question. The Corporation Laws of 1937 and 1965 somewhat weakened the effect of a resolution granting *Entlastung*. See B. von Falkenhausen & E.C. Steefel, Shareholders' Rights in German Corporations, 10 Am.

J. Comp. L. 407, 415 (1961). But it is still an important corporate act, for the reason, among others, that a resolution refusing *Entlastung* to a particular officer would be a vote of no-confidence, which ordinarily would constitute "cause" for the dismissal of that officer. See § 84, subs. 3, of the present Corporation Law.

2. This is necessary when shares are in bearer form in order to establish who has a right to vote.

3. For present purposes, it is sufficient to note that a German GmbH is a close corporation. It must be distinguished from a stock corporation (Aktiengesellschaft, abbr. AG), such as the M. E. Corporation in the principal case, which may issue shares to the public. The GmbH form of organization is suitable for many purposes, including—as the principal case shows—that of a family holding company. The issue was discussed in the

company the investment of its funds in industrial and other enterprises of every description. Of the capital, M. W. subscribed RM 300,000, his wife 100,000, J. W. 70,000 and his wife 30,000; the subscribers paid up their subscriptions by transferring their shares of stock of the defendant corporation to the new company. M. W. was given the right during his life to appoint and remove the officers of the new company, and as the first officers he appointed himself and J. W. . . . On the same day on which it was set up, the new company was registered in the register of commerce. On Jan. 6, it deposited shares of stock of the defendant corporation having a par value of RM 528,000 and announced that it would participate in the Jan. 10 shareholders' meeting with 528 votes.

In the meeting of Jan. 10, 1933, shares of a total par value of RM 953,000 were represented by four shareholders or representatives of shareholders. The plaintiff and his attorney, Dr. E., represented shares of a par value of RM 416,000, with 416 votes. The B.V. Bank represented shares of RM 9,000 par value with 9 votes and the new GmbH, for which Justizrat D. (an attorney) appeared on the basis of a proxy executed by J. W., represented shares of a par value of RM 528,000 with 528 votes.

[Prior to the voting Dr. E. moved in his own name and in the name of the plaintiff to have the conduct of the management examined by auditors. There was no objection to the addition of this point to the agenda.]

The meeting resolved with 537 votes, that is the 528 votes of the GmbH and the 9 votes of the Bank, against the 416 votes of the plaintiff and of Dr. E., to approve the officers' conduct of the corporate affairs. By the same ratio of votes the motion to appoint auditors was voted down. The notarial protocol shows that plaintiff and Dr. E. promptly declared their opposition to both resolutions.

On Jan. 11, 1933, J. W. was registered in the register of commerce as an additional officer of defendant.

[Plaintiff promptly brought this action to set aside the two resolutions of the meeting of Jan. 10, 1933.] Plaintiff contends that both resolutions are void because of the violation, by the participation of the GmbH in the voting, of the voting prohibitions of the Commercial Code . . . and because of the immoral purpose of such participation, such invalidity allegedly flowing from §§ 134 and 138 of the Civil Code.[4] In any event, plaintiff contends, the resolutions are subject to being set aside pursuant to Sec. 271 of the Commercial Code.[5]

6th Edition of this book, Chapter VII, Section 3 at 921.

4. Civil Code, Sec. 134: "A jural act which is contrary to a statutory prohibition is void, unless a contrary intention appears from the statute."

Sec. 138: "A jural act which is contra bonos mores (violative of the commands of morality) is void. . . ."

5. Commercial Code, Sec. 271: "A resolution of a shareholders' meeting may be attacked by an action to set it aside if it violates the law or the articles of association. Such action must be brought within a month. Every shareholder who has been present at the meeting may bring the action provided he has entered his opposition in the protocol . . . ." The substance of this provision is now to be found in §§ 243–46 of the Corporation Law of 1965.

The Landgericht declared the said two resolutions of the meeting of Jan. 10, 1933, to be invalid. The Oberlandesgericht reversed and dismissed the complaint. The further appeal of the plaintiff [to the Reichsgericht] leads to reversal and remand.

Reasons: 1. The intermediate appellate court is correct in holding that on the basis of plaintiff's allegations the case involves no question of the absolute invalidity of the resolutions of Jan. 10, 1933, but only a question of setting them aside, because judged by their contents the resolutions are not contra bonos mores: the alleged violation of the standards of boni mores is based only on the manner in which the said resolutions came about [citing cases supporting the proposition that only those resolutions are absolutely invalid the terms or contents of which are contra bonos mores.] Therefore, this court reviews only the question whether the action to set aside (Commercial Code, Sec. 271) was properly decided....[6]

. . . .

2. ... One whose managerial conduct is to be approved by a shareholders' resolution is deprived of the right to vote on such resolution by virtue of Section 252, subdiv. 3 of the Commercial Code; nor may he in such case exercise the right to vote for another shareholder.[7] Section 266, subdiv. 1, second sentence, of the Commercial Code, as amended ... provides that where the subject of a shareholders' resolution is the appointment of auditors for the examination of certain events connected with the organization or management of the corporation, those shareholders who are directors or officers may not vote, if the examination is to extend to events which have a bearing on the approval of such directors' or officers' conduct of the management, or on the question of the institution by the corporation of an action against such directors or officers.[8]

The voting prohibitions in Sections 252 and 266 of the Commercial Code thus affect the shares of a member of the management if such

---

The action to set aside a stockholders' resolution, while relatively infrequent here, is by no means unknown in our law. Statutes in many states provide for a summary proceeding to set aside an election. See N.Y. Bus. Corp. L. Section 619. Resolutions other than elections can be attacked, on procedural or substantive grounds, by way of a plenary suit in equity. Cf. Goldfield Corp. v. General Host Corp., 29 N.Y.2d 264, 267–68, 327 N.Y.S.2d 330, 332–33, 277 N.E.2d 387, 389–390 (1971).

6. In the principal case it makes no practical difference to the plaintiff whether the resolutions are declared to be "void" pursuant to Sections 134 and 138 of the Civil Code, or whether they are "set aside" pursuant to Section 271 of the Commercial Code. But in a case in which for some reason (e.g., because he failed to bring the action within a month) the plaintiff cannot successfully sue under the latter provision, it becomes crucial for him to know whether he can nevertheless attack the resolution of the stockholders as a "jural act" which is contra bonos mores and hence absolutely void under the broad terms of the above-mentioned sections of the Civil Code.

The criterion by which the court distinguishes void and voidable resolutions, originally was developed by case law. Today, the same criterion appears in §§ 60 and 61 of the Corporation Law of 2004.

7. The corresponding provision of the German Corporation Law of 2004 is to be found in § 47.

8. The German Corporation Law of 2004 contains a similar provision in §§ 47 and 48.

member's conduct is to be approved or the appointment of auditors for the examination of his conduct is in question. Therefore, the prohibition applies only if the member in question is a shareholder of the corporation. . . .

There is no doubt that as an officer of defendant, M. W., if he himself had been a shareholder, would have had no right to participate in the vote on the two resolutions which have been attacked in this action. However, at the time of the resolutions he was no longer a shareholder. The shares with which Justizrat D. exercised the voting rights . . . had at that time been validly transferred to a properly organized family corporation, and had thus become the property of the latter. The mere fact that its officer M. W. was also an officer of the defendant corporation and that the approval or examination of his managerial conduct was the subject of the resolutions, would not have deprived the GmbH of its right to vote. The GmbH being a separate legal entity with independent juristic personality, such extensive interpretation of the voting prohibitions is out of the question. These prohibitions are directed solely against a shareholder; but the officer of a GmbH, that is, of a separate legal entity, cannot be regarded as the owner of shares belonging to the GmbH.

This Division of the Court, overruling prior decisions,[9] has decided in the opinion reported on p. 71 of this volume [of its reports] that the voting prohibition of Section 266, subdiv. 1, second sentence, of the Commercial Code extends to shares owned by a *partnership*, if a member of the management of the corporation is one of the partners of the partnership, and if the resolution [to be voted on by the shareholders' meeting] involves the question whether a damage action for improper conduct of the corporate affairs should be brought by the corporation against the members of its management. This holding, however, was based on the view that according to the prevailing opinion the assets of a partnership are jointly owned by the partners, that shares belonging to a partnership constitute part of these [jointly owned] partnership assets and that the partners are thus "shareholders" within the meaning of the said provisions of law. A general analogous extension of these principles to the GmbH is, however, impossible inasmuch as the shareholders of a GmbH are not co-owners of the GmbH's assets.

3. Nevertheless, under the special circumstances of this case, the exercise of the voting right with respect to the shares belonging to the GmbH was prohibited by Sections 252, 266 . . . of the Commercial Code. This conclusion follows directly from the rationale and purpose of the said provisions. Rationale and purpose are these: If the resolution of the shareholders' meeting involves approval of the acts of a member of the management, or the appointment of auditors for the examination of such acts with the aim of instituting damages actions against such member on the basis of the audit, then the members of the management shall not be

---

9. The prior decisions had been rendered by the same Division, or panel, of the Court. Therefore, as the reader knows, the panel was able to overrule these prior decisions without submitting the issue to a super-panel.

the judges in their own cases, which they would be if they participated in the formation of the corporate will relating to these matters.[10] They would be their own judges if they voted with their own shares; and the same would be true if a vote were carried by shares which are legally controlled by a member of the management, because in the latter case, too, a free and independent exercise of the voting right solely in the best interest of the corporation is not assured, in view of the conflicting interests of the officer or director in question. . . . The officer or director who controls the shareholdings of a juristic person and determines the latter's exercise of its voting right must be treated like a shareholder within the meaning of the said provisions of law. Such identification of a juristic person with the individual behind it, who legally is in complete control of its doings, has been recognized in prior decisions of this Court dealing with other fact situations [citing cases].

Such identification of the corporate owner of shares with the individual who by law and charter dominates it will be unavoidable especially in the case of a one-man GmbH, that is, of a company whose every legal act depends upon the will of this one individual. The case at bar presents a situation of this kind, in view of the way in which according to the factual findings of the court below the new GmbH (to which the W. family transferred its shares) was organized.

[The court then discusses the facts found below, and comes to the conclusion that as matter of law the GmbH was completely controlled by M. W., and that the proxy used in the shareholders' meeting of Jan. 10, 1933, although formally executed by J. W. as an officer of the GmbH, must nevertheless, like every other jural act of the GmbH, be considered a jural act of M. W.]

The courts below discussed the question, answered affirmatively by the Landgericht and negatively by the intermediate appellate court, whether because of the purpose of *evading* the statutory voting prohibitions the formation of, and the transfer of the shares to, the GmbH was contra bonos mores and void;[11] but this is not the decisive question. The said voting prohibitions were here *directly* applicable, because the GmbH was merely the form in which M. W. exercised the voting rights with respect to the shares which the W. family had transferred to the GmbH.[12]

---

10. This statement has been cited many times. See K. Schmidt, Rechtsschutz des Minderheitsgesellschafters gegen rechtswidrige ablehnende Beschlüsse, 39 N.J.W. 2018, 2019 (1986). It is now recognized that voting prohibitions come into play (a) in case of self-dealing and (b) in situations in which a shareholder, were he permitted to vote, would be a judge in his own cause. Id.

11. Plaintiff made two distinct arguments, both based on Sections 134 and 138 of the Civil Code, quoted *supra*: (a) that the *resolutions* adopted at the meeting of Jan. 10,

1933 were absolutely void (this argument was rejected in part "1" of the court's reasons), and (b) that the *transfer* of the shares from M. W. to the family holding company was void. At this point, the court deals with the latter argument.

12. In part 3 of its opinion the German court obviously applies the doctrine of "disregarding the corporate entity" or "piercing the corporate veil." For an interesting comparative discussion of that doctrine, which in essence seems to be almost universally recognized, see Justice O'Connor's majority opin-

4. The foregoing, however, has to be qualified: The voting prohibition was not in all respects applicable to the resolution by which the motion for appointment of auditors was voted down.

[The Court then points out that pursuant to Section 266 of the Commercial Code the shareholders' meeting has power to direct an auditors' examination of certain "events" in the corporate management, but that, according to the prevailing view,[13] the shareholders' meeting has no power to order an audit of "the whole conduct of the corporate affairs." The motion which plaintiff's attorney had made in the meeting of Jan. 10, 1933, was in two parts. The first part demanded a general audit of corporate affairs, whereas the second specified certain "events" to be examined by the auditors. The Court holds that the first part of this motion proposed a general audit which as a matter of law the shareholders' meeting was unauthorized to direct, and that, since this proposal had to be rejected as unauthorized, it was immaterial whether the resolution embodying such rejection had been adopted in a proper manner. As to the second part of plaintiff's motion, the Court holds that further factual clarification is necessary before it can determine whether in this part of the motion the "events" to be examined were sufficiently specified. For the purpose of such clarification the Court remands the matter to the intermediate appellate court.

The Reichsgericht then turns to the question whether, in the event that the second part of plaintiff's motion should be found to have been sufficiently specific, and the resolution rejecting that part of the motion should correspondingly be found invalid, such invalidity would affect that part of the resolution which rejected the first (unauthorized) part of plaintiff's motion.]

. . . In this respect it is material whether this was a so-called composite resolution which pursuant to the will of the shareholders' meeting was to form a united whole, and whether, consequently, by way of at least analogous application of Section 139 of the Civil Code[14] invalidity of a part of the resolution made the whole resolution invalid (see Hueck, Voidable and Void Resolutions of Corporate Stockholders, pp. 221, 222); or whether in the instant case a different rule should prevail in view of the fact that with respect to that part of the resolution which is not in itself invalid the opposite resolution—adoption instead of rejection of the motion—could not have been made because of the lack of legal authorization [that is, because

ion in First National City Bank v. Banco Para El Comercio Exterior De Cuba, 462 U.S. 611, 103 S.Ct. 2591, at 2601–02 (1983).

13. As evidence of the "prevailing view," the court cites two older decisions of intermediate appellate courts, one monograph and one well-known commentary.

14. "If part of a jural act is void, the whole jural act shall be void, unless it ap-

pears that it would have come into being even without the void part."

This section, like the above-quoted sections 134 and 138, is contained in the First Book (General Part) of the German Civil Code. Note that the applicability of the three sections is not limited to contracts, not even to obligations; they apply to all "jural acts."

the shareholders' meeting has no power to order a general audit of corporate affairs without specification of the "events" to be investigated.].[15]

5. According to the above, at least some of the resolutions ... were adopted in violation of the voting prohibitions of §§ 252, 266 ... of the Commercial Code. Nevertheless, the Court is not yet in a position to make a final disposition of this part of the case by setting aside the resolutions to the extent indicated, because no sufficient consideration has yet been given to defendant's contention that under the special circumstances of this case plaintiff's action to set aside constituted an improper exercise of rights, an abuse of rights.

Defendant had alleged and offered to prove that the plaintiff, who had been active in other stock corporations as a professional oppositionist bent on obtaining personal rather than corporate benefits, was here engaged in the same kind of practice; that ever since he failed of reelection as a director in the shareholders' meeting of Nov. 15, 1926, he carried on obstruction solely for the purpose of acquiring the shares of the W. family at a cheap price and to compel either his election as a director or the distribution of a higher dividend; and that the present action, again, was to serve plaintiff's own selfish rather than corporate purposes. The legal relevance of these allegations should not have been denied.

True, according to the decisions of this Court which we reaffirm, it is recognized that the right of action conferred upon a shareholder by § 271 of the Commercial Code does not depend upon a special need for legal protection within the meaning of § 256 of the Code of Civil Procedure;[16] the statutory scheme shows that the shareholder's special need for legal protection results from the sole fact of his membership in the corporation, of his ownership of a share of the capital, by virtue of which, for the preservation of order in corporate affairs, he is given the right to attack those resolutions of the corporation which are inconsistent with law or charter, even though they may cause no detriment to him personally. [Citing a case.] But this right has its limits where it conflicts with the duty of faithfulness which the shareholder owes the corporation and which

---

15. Even if all parts of the resolution (including the rejection of the motion for a general audit) are invalid, it is clear that a new resolution ordering a *general* audit could not effectively be adopted. What, then, is the practical importance of the discussion in this paragraph of the opinion? Consider in this connection that in Germany, as in most other civil-law jurisdictions, the victorious party is entitled to recover costs and attorneys' fees from the loser (see *supra infra* Chapter 7, Section 8(b) at 691), but that this right may be curtailed or defeated if the victory is a partial one only (German Code of Civil Procedure, Sections 91, 92).

16. Section 256 of the German Code of Civil Procedure deals with declaratory judg-

ment actions, and permits such actions only if the plaintiff "has a legal interest in having the legal relation ... immediately determined by judicial decision." See Borchard, Declaratory Judgments 101–03 (1941). An action to set aside a shareholders' resolution is not an action for a declaratory judgment. Nevertheless, some legal writers and lower courts took the position that the general principle announced in Section 256 of the Code of Civil Procedure (i.e., the requirement of a special need for legal protection) should be analogously applied to actions brought under Section 271 of the Commercial Code. The Reichsgericht, as shown by the statement in the text, rejected that position.

permeates all rules of corporation law....[17] In all steps he takes, the shareholder has to consider himself a member of the collective body to which he belongs, and he is bound to make this duty of faithfulness the supreme standard of his actions. If a shareholder exercises the right of action conferred upon him by Section 271 of the Commercial Code for such purposes as here alleged and offered to be proved, that is for the purpose of selfishly and extortionately subjugating the corporation to his will rather than for corporate purposes, then he violates the duty of faithfulness so grossly that the exercise of his right becomes an *abuse* which cannot be tolerated by the legal order. The idea of the impropriety of an abuse of rights has found statutory recognition in the prohibition, contained in Section 226 of the Civil Code,[18] of a purely spiteful exercise of legal rights. Beyond the confines of that provision, however, the same principle must apply whenever the exercise of a right constitutes a gross violation of the maxim dominating the entire field of private law, the maxim of bona fides. This thought has repeatedly been recognized in court decisions; see, for instance, the doctrine of laches in the field of revaluation.[19] In legal literature the same thought has recently been elaborated in the monograph by Siebert, Laches and Abuse of Rights, especially pp. 60 et seq. Decisions of this Court have repeatedly recognized that the principle of bona fides contained in Section 242 of the Civil Code[20] constitutes a general limitation

17. By way of criticism of the principal case, it has been argued that the right to bring an action to set aside a stockholder's resolution (as distinguished from other rights of a stockholder, such as the right to vote) may be exercised not only for corporate but also for individual and even selfish purposes. See Fischer, Die Grenzen bei der Ausübung gesellschaftlicher Mitgliedschaftsrechte, 7 N.J.W. 777, 779 (1954). Do the code provisions set forth in the opinion and in the footnotes, *supra*, support this classification of stockholders' rights? Even if certain rights are given to a minority stockholder for his own rather than the corporation's benefit, does it follow that the exercise of such rights is subject to no restraint whatever? Concerning the latter question, the reader may wish to suspend judgment until the important doctrine of *abuse of rights*, invoked by the court in the principal case, is taken up in more detail.

18. "The exercise of a right is improper if it cannot have any purpose other than that of harming another."

19. In the process of the disastrous inflation following the First World War, old "Marks" became completely worthless. In November, 1923, the new "Rentenmark" or "Reichsmark" (abbr. RM) was created. The subject of "revaluation" covers the statutory and decisional rules by which it was attempted to find a fair basis for the conversion of old "Mark" obligations into RM. For details, see the excellent study by Dawson, Effects of Inflation on Private Contracts: Germany, 1914–1924, 33 Mich.L.Rev. 171 (1934), and also Rashba, Debts in Collapsed Foreign Currencies, 54 Yale L.J. 1, 9–14 (1944). The 1948 currency reform in Western Germany, which in turn abolished the RM currency and substituted a new "Deutsche Mark" (DM) currency, raised similar problems. See Eisner v. United States, 127 Ct.Cl. 323, 117 F.Supp. 197 (1954). This time, however, the problems were met by comprehensive legislation which left little room for decisional law applying the general principles of bona fides and abuse of rights. See Enneccerus–Lehmann, Recht der Schuldverhältnisse 48–51 (1958).

20. "The obligor is bound to perform the obligation in such a way as is required by the principles of bona fides with due regard to existing usage."

Note the similarity between Section 242 of the German Civil Code and UCC Section 1–203. Quaere, however, whether an American court would, by way of analogical application of Section 1–203, declare a plaintiff unfit to bring a stockholders' suit. If it wished to reach such a result, an American court probably would employ different reasoning.

upon the exercise of rights also in the law of stock corporations and of limited liability companies. [Citing several Reichsgericht cases and the comment upon one of them by Hachenburg, at that time the leading German authority on the law of limited liability companies, as well as another article in a legal periodical]....

Of course, in each case in which abuse or improper exercise of rights is alleged, particular caution will be indicated. Ordinarily it can be assumed that the shareholder upon whom the law confers the right to sue for cancellation of a resolution is entitled to make use of such right. The burden of proving that in the particular case the exercise of this right constitutes an abuse is fully upon the defendant; he has to prove beyond doubt that the exercise of the right under the given circumstances amounts to a gross violation of the principles of bona fides, of the duty of faithfulness incumbent upon the shareholder. In the case at bar such gross violation would exist if defendant succeeded in proving that plaintiff uses the remedy for the purpose of selfishly imposing his will upon the corporation rather than for the purpose of protecting the real interests of the corporation.[21] But the question whether in fact there was no real justification for bringing the action will have to be examined with particular care. In this connection consideration will have to be given to the contention of the plaintiff ... that the resolutions were not justified by the real interest of the corporation, and that they came about by the majority, contra bonos mores, beating down the minority.... From the standpoint of substantive law, the discussion of this contention of the plaintiff by the court below is not free from error, in that the court below limits the examination of the real justification [reasonableness] of the attacked resolutions to the question whether the officers, especially M. W., *intentionally* violated their duties as such officers. It has been overlooked that pursuant to Section 241 of the Commercial Code[22] the officers of a stock corporation are liable also for the damage the corporation incurs as a result of their *negligence*. If the possibility cannot be excluded that plaintiff at least believed that the officers became liable to the corporation for a violation, even if only a negligent violation, of their duties as such officers, then it will be hardly possible for the defendant to meet its burden of proving that the action was exclusively brought for noncorporate purposes, and that it therefore constitutes an abuse of legal rights.

21. In Matter of Ochs v. Washington Heights Federal Savings & Loan Association, 17 N.Y.2d 82, 268 N.Y.S.2d 294, 215 N.E.2d 485 (1966), where the plaintiff sought an order permitting him to inspect defendant's membership list, the Court said, at 88: "... the desire of a stockholder to become a member of the board of directors does not constitute bad faith.... We need not even conjecture here whether a design to remove a director motivated by personal malice would preclude the exercise of a right to inspection. However, it is clear that the institution of such a proceeding as this for the sole purpose of harassment, not motivated by any interest in the association but rather by personal gain completely apart from any benefit to the association, would constitute *mala fides* which the courts of this State are loath to protect. Our case law has uniformly and without hesitation required a bona fide intention on the part of him who seeks such common-law relief."

22. Sec. 93 of the German Corporation Law of 1965 is to the same effect.

NOTES AND QUESTIONS

Especially by comparison with the two French decisions reproduced above in Chapter 5 (the *Jand'heur* and *Desmares* cases), what conclusions can be drawn from the principal case regarding a German court's use of authorities? Regarding its methods of reasoning and of developing the law?[1] Regarding the differences between a code and an isolated statute? What does the opinion show regarding the interdependence of the civil, commercial, and procedural codes in the German legal system?[2]

Can a code provision express a *principle* as well as a *rule*? The notes which follow contain some observations bearing on this question.

————

THE USE OF ANALOGY: NOTES AND ILLUSTRATIONS

(1) *Filling Gaps in the Codes.* The problem of the *casus omissus* (literally case left behind)—a fact situation not anticipated by the legislator, and hence not covered in the Code or other written law—is a troublesome one for the civilians. According to their traditional theory, only the written law is authoritative, and there exists no common law.[1] How then, can a court reach a decision when faced with a case not provided for in the written law?

Two principal techniques have been developed by civilian codifiers to meet this difficulty:

(a) Most of the 19th and 20th century codes contain some provisions of enormous breadth and generality. As each of the "general clauses" covers a wide variety of fact situations, including fact situations which perhaps were not in the minds of the Code's draftsmen, it is clear that by the use of this technique the codifiers can reduce the number of instances in which the written law is found to be silent.

(b) To deal with those cases in which neither a specific provision of the Code nor one of its "general clauses" is applicable, civilian codifiers

1. In this connection, consider the difference between the German conception of a code and the use made of "codes" in common-law jurisdictions (e.g., California).

2. A much later case in the Bundesgerichtshof, the successor of the Reichsgericht (May 22, 1989, 42 N.J.W. 2689), liberalizes the rule on abusive corporate litigation by holding that a suit to set aside a corporate resolution would be considered as "abusive" if brought principally for the kind of purpose which we would label as "greenmail," even if the suit might be beneficial to the corporation to some extent. The principal case held that the action would be abusive only if not beneficial to the corporation. The more recent ruling is obviously of great practical importance in instances of "greenmail."

1. To a somewhat uncertain degree, traditional civilian theory makes allowance for customary law; but the practical importance of ancient customary law is insignificant in most of the continental legal systems. Concerning a new type of "customary law," which in reality is decisional law, see *infra* Section 6 at 582.

In the course of the present century, the traditional theory referred to in the text, *supra*, has been somewhat liberalized. Yet it still remains true that at least in the areas of private law, criminal law, and procedural law the civilians think of non-legislated sources of law as something highly exceptional. Cf. D.P. Kirchhof, Richterliche Rechtsfindung gebunden an Gesetz und Recht, 39 N.J.W. 2275 (1986).

developed the further technique of inserting so-called directory provisions into their codes. These provisions, although their terms differ from code to code,[2] invariably express a command addressed to the courts, telling the courts what methods and sources to use (or not to use) when they encounter an ambiguity or a gap in the written law. Since such a directory provision is contained in the Code itself, it is possible to maintain, at least in theory, that a court using the (possibly extra-code) methods and sources thus prescribed is following the Code's own command, and hence is staying within the confines of the written law.

(2) *Analogy as a Gap–Filling Technique.* As we have seen in studying the *Shoop* case, the Spanish Civil Code contains a directory provision which, inter alia, refers a court to the "general principles of law," i.e., the principles which by the use of analogy can be distilled from positive provisions of the Code itself and of other written laws.

A somewhat comparable directory provision was proposed by the draftsmen of the German Civil Code. The first draft of that Code contained the following Section 1:

> Questions for which the Code contains no provision are to be answered by analogous application of the provisions referring to legally similar questions. In the absence of such provisions, the principles derived from the spirit of the legal order shall be determinative.

In later drafts of the German Code this provision was deleted as unnecessary.[3] It was felt that even in the absence of such a code provision the courts could not help but to resort to analogy, when faced with a gap in the written law, This expectation turned out to be well-founded. A study, based in part on quantitative analysis, has shown that since the enactment of the Code the German courts have used analogical reasoning in a very large number of decisions, including many important decisions of the court of last resort.[4]

The above-quoted provision in the first draft of the German Civil Code appears to draw a distinction between two kinds of analogy. The first sentence of the draft provision refers to so-called "statutory analogy," (*analogia legis*) i.e., the derivation of a principle from a single provision, or a group of closely connected provisions, to be found in the Code or some other statute. The second sentence of the draft provision speaks of an even bolder use of analogical reasoning, to which German legal writers refer as "analogy of law (*analogia iuris*)." It means the distillation of a principle from several, and not necessarily inter-connected, provisions of written law, which may be contained in a number of diverse codes and statutes.[5] In practice, the distinction between these two kinds of analogy has not proved to be of great significance.

---

2. In previous parts of this book, we have already encountered several examples of such directory provisions. See art. 6 of the old Spanish Civil Code, quoted in *Shoop, supra* at 178. For further examples and explanations, see *infra* Section 6.

3. See Staudinger–Riezler, Commentary on the German Civil Code, vol. I, Introduction, pp. 34–35 (10th ed., 1936). Due to the deletion of § 1 of the first Draft, the German Civil Code (in contrast to the great majority of comparable civilian codes) contains no express directory provisions.

4. See E. Bund, Die Analogie als Begründungsmethode im deutschen Recht der Gegenwart, 77 Z. für Vergleichende Rechtswissenschaft 115 (1978).

5. See Staudinger–Riezler, *supra* note 3.

The distinction between interpretation and analogy, on the other hand, is important in practice as well as in theory. In a codified legal system, no case can be decided without interpreting and applying one or several provisions of the Code or other statutes. On the other hand, it is clear that resort to analogy, although not infrequent, is justified only in the exceptional cases in which the written law furnishes no answer to the issue at hand.[6] Interpretation, however bold and extensive, "means that the judge applies a norm to the facts because the norm still covers such facts; by way of analogy, he applies the norm to the facts although he finds that the norm does not cover the facts."[7]

Suppose that fact situations A, B, and C are covered by one or several Code provisions, establishing the same rule for all three of these situations. If a court, confronted by fact situation D, holds that the language of these Code provisions, though not explicit on the point, can be stretched to cover D, the court uses the method of extensive interpretation. But if the court, while admitting that the rule expressed in the code provisions cannot be stretched to cover D, finds that these provisions reflect a principle broader than the explicitly stated rule, and if the court then uses that broader principle to determine case D, the decision is made by way of analogical reasoning.

Obviously the very option leaves open discretionary ground to the Court. For Example the already encountered Art 1384 of the French Code Civil States: "Father and mother, to the extent they have custody, are jointly liable for the harm caused by minor children living with them."

Suppose that such a provision has to be applied to a gay couple or to another extended family relationship, so common today and so uncommon when the Code was drafted. Would Art. 1384 make jointly liable the gay partner of one of the parents? Would it apply to damages produced by the son of a single mother living with her own father?

An extensive interpretation would possibly make the partner liable considering him/her as "parent" of the child. However it would not be possible to extensively interpret the Code provision to include "grandparents," a socially and biologically different category that that of "parents" that the Code has not covered. Thus in the latter case analogy would be required according to the maxim: "where there is the same reason for a law there should be the same legal provision."

The use of such reasoning, however, requires caution. The Code provisions dealing with the expressly defined and enumerated fact situations A, B, and C may imply that *only* those fact situations are intended to be covered by the rule, and that other fact situations (including D) thus are to be treated differently. This latter kind of argumentation is known as *argumentum a contrario*. There is no rule of thumb telling the courts of a civil-law country how to choose between the two conflicting approaches of analogical reasoning and *argumentum a contrario*. Whenever such a conflict arises, the court will have to be guided by legislative history as well as policy considerations.[8]

---

6. In the area of criminal law, moreover, the meting out of punishment for an offense not previously defined by the written law is proscribed by constitutional or statutory provisions in most civilized countries.

7. Staudinger–Riezler, *supra* note 3.

8. See Palandt, Bürgerliches Gesetzbuch, Introduction preceding § 1, Anno. VI 3 (54th ed. 1995).

(3) *The Limits of Analogy.* It has been suggested by German legal authors that occasionally the courts are confronted with problems to the solution of which the written law has contributed absolutely nothing, not even a starting point for analogical reasoning.[9] In such a case, these authors propose, a German court should act as if Art. 1 of the Swiss Civil Code[10] were in force in Germany; i.e., after examining potentially helpful ideas developed in other legal systems, the judge should creatively fashion a solution as if he were the legislator. As an example of a solution which the courts, unaided by written law, thus have independently developed, the said authors cite the 1953 decision of the German Supreme Court discussed in Note 4 below.[11] *Quaere*, however, whether that was not a classical case of analogy, i.e., a case in which the written law did furnish the guiding appraisal of values or policies, even though such appraisal may have been expressed in provisions which in terms did not cover the case at hand.

(4) *Decision of the German Bundesgerichtshof* of February 19, 1953, BGHZ 9, 83: Plaintiff, who was vaccinated as a child pursuant to a compulsory vaccination statute, suffered permanent injuries to her health as a result of post-vaccinal encephalitis. The vaccination statute then in force contained no provision for the payment of damages or compensation in such a case. Plaintiff was unable to prove that the vaccination had been negligently performed. She sued the State on the theory that in submitting to the public duty created by the compulsory vaccination statute, she had been compelled to sacrifice her health in the public interest, and that for this loss she should receive adequate compensation from the community.

Both plaintiff and defendant found some support in previous decisions. Plaintiff relied on a line of cases in which the former Reichsgericht, on the basis of statutes providing for just compensation in certain well-defined instances of expropriation (eminent domain), had evolved the general principle that even in the absence of an applicable compensation statute an individual is entitled to damages if he has to sacrifice a private right in the public interest, and that this claim for damages comes into existence regardless of whether or not the detriment suffered by him is due to negligence or any other fault of an official. The defendant, on the other hand, pointed to a 1937 decision rendered by a super-panel of the former Reichsgericht (RGZ 156, 305), holding that this so-called theory of sacrifice should be limited to cases of property losses, and denying recovery in a fact situation indistinguishable from that of the principal case.

In its 1953 decision the Bundesgerichtshof overruled the last-mentioned case[12] and permitted the plaintiff to recover. The court referred to the principle

In later parts of this book, the reader will find several cases in which a (civilian) court was required to make a reasoned choice between analogy and *argumentum e contrario*.

9. See Staudinger–Brändl-Coing, Commentary on the German Civil Code, vol. I, Introduction, p. 41 (11th ed., 1957).

Concerning the jurisprudential roots of these suggestions, see E. Bodenheimer, Significant Developments in German Legal Phi-

losophy Since 1945, 3 Am. J. Comp. L. 379 (1954).

10. See *infra* Section 6 at 582.

11. Other—and perhaps better—examples of cases in which German courts engaged in creative law-making without the aid of analogical reasoning will be found in sec. 2 of this chapter. See also Palandt, Bürgerliches Gesetzbuch, Introduction preceding § 1 (54th ed. 1995).

recognized in the Basic Law of the German Federal Republic, which provides compensation for an individual whose property is expropriated and who thus has to sacrifice his property for the common good. *A fortiori*, the court reasoned, the community owes compensation to one who was forced to make a special sacrifice—i.e., a sacrifice not exacted from other persons in the same class—involving loss of life or health.

The specific holding of the court, allowing recovery in cases of disease caused by compulsory vaccination, subsequently has been confirmed by a statute, which also regulates the amount of compensation in some detail.[13] But the general principle recognized and broadened in the 1953 case retains its great significance; it is, of course, applicable to many fact situations which do not involve vaccination and thus are not covered by the new statute.[14]

A similarly broad principle of compensation for special sacrifices exacted from an individual in the public interest has been developed by the French administrative courts. As in Germany, a plaintiff may recover on this theory even though he can show no fault on the part of a public official.[15] One of the cases in which the French courts allowed recovery on this theory was factually identical with the German vaccination case of 1953.[16]

(5) *Some Comparative Observations.* Reasoning by analogy—i.e., the application "in consimili casu" of a general principle which is derived from rules developed in a different factual context—is a tool employed by judges in the common-law as well as the civil-law orbit.[17] There is, however, a perceptible difference in the way the tool is put to work.

---

12. It was not necessary for the court again to refer the question to a super-panel, because technically the new Bundesgerichtshof, created in the German Federal Republic after World War II and having its seat at Karlsruhe, is not identical with the former Reichsgericht, which was physically and institutionally obliterated when Leipzig, the seat of that court, was conquered by the Soviet Army in 1945.

13. Bundesseuchengesetz (Federal Law Concerning Infectious Diseases) of July 18, 1961, §§ 51 ff. With the German statute, compare the National Vaccine Injury Act, 42 U.S.C. § 300aa–1, an example of a situation where somewhat similar statutes have different purposes; the German statute was principally designed to codify the rules providing for compensation to victims of compulsory vaccination; the American Act, although it provides for compensation, had as it main purpose to forestall a refusal by vaccine manufacturers to produce vaccine out of a fear of excessive liability.

14. The principle has been applied, e.g., to the case of an innocent bystander who was injured when the police (lawfully) opened fire to prevent a felon from fleeing. The plaintiff was permitted to recover from the State without having to prove negligence on the part of the police officers. See Palandt, Bürgerliches Gesetzbuch, Introduction preceding § 903 (54th ed., 1995), where many additional judicial decisions applying the same principle are cited.

15. See the decision of the Conseil d'État of November 6, 1968 in the case of Minister of National Education v. Dame Saulze, reported in the article by L.G. Weeramantry, Judicial Application of the Rule of Law, 1 Rev. Int'l Comm'n Jurists 43 (1969). In that case, the State was held liable to pay compensation to a school teacher whose child suffered from a birth defect caused by German measles which the plaintiff, then pregnant, had contracted when performing her teaching duties.

16. Decision of the Administrative Tribunal of Lyon, reported in La Dépèche du Midi of July 26, 1965, p. 2. For a comparative discussion of the "doctrine of sacrifice" (covering French, German and U.S. law), see Comment, 24 U.Chi.L.Rev. 513 (1957).

17. See J. Stone, Legal System and Lawyers' Reasonings 312–16 (1964); E. H. Levi, An Introduction to Legal Reasoning, 15

The usual starting point for the civilian's reasoning by analogy or by induction will be a provision, or a number of provisions, of the code or codes. The German case involving a stockholder's action, *supra*, furnishes an illustration. As was said by Wisdom, J., in Shelp v. National Surety Corp., 333 F.2d 431, at 435 (5th Cir.1964):

> ... in Louisiana, as in all civilian jurisdictions, the Civil Code is more than an ordinary legislative act. The Code, doctrinally, constitutes the whole body of private law. A statute, on the other hand, is small in scope, narrow in its objective and ... is intended to deal with a specific mischief or a specific need. The relation between a code and a statute in the field of private law may be analogized to the relation between the common law and a statute in derogation of the common law.

Quoting from a law review article,[18] the opinion continues:

> The very nature of a code requires that analogies be drawn from its express provisions in deciding cases for which no exact rule can be found in the code ...

Under our system, a general principle ordinarily will be extracted from case law.[19] Even where a "code" exists, our judges traditionally fill the gaps in the written law by falling back on the common law, rather than by extending or analogizing from the provisions of the "code."[20] But this tradition is becoming weaker; in the United States there is a growing modern trend toward using a statute, or a complex of statutes, as a basis for analogical reasoning.[21] With respect to the Uniform Commercial Code, one of the draftsmen's own comments to § 1–102 invites the use of Code provisions as starting points for such reasoning.[22] Our mental processes thus become more similar to those of the civilians.[23]

U.Chi.L.Rev. 501 (1948); B.H. Levy, Cardozo and the Frontiers of Legal Thinking 51, 56 (rev. ed. 1969).

18. G. Dreyfous, Partial Defacement of Olographic Wills, 15 Tul.L.Rev. 272 (1941).

19. See H.W. Goldschmidt, English Law from the Foreign Standpoint 32–33 (1937).

20. Cf. Los Angeles v. Anderson, 206 Cal. 662 (1929); Strand Imp. Co. v. Long Beach, 173 Cal. 765, 161 P. 975 (1916).

21. See National City Bank v. Republic of China, 348 U.S. 356, 360, 75 S.Ct. 423, 426, 427 (1955); United States v. American Trucking Associations, Inc., 310 U.S. 534, 542–5, 60 S.Ct. 1059 (1940); South & Central American Commercial Co., Inc. v. Panama R.R. Co., 237 N.Y. 287, 142 N.E. 666 (1923); H.F. Stone, The Common Law in the United States, 50 Harv.L.Rev. 4, 13–16 (1936); R.J. Traynor, Statutes Revolving in Common–Law Orbits, 17 Cath.U.L.Rev. 401 (1968).

22. See I.R. Macneil & R.B. Schlesinger, Some Comments on the Legal System of the United States, With Particular Reference to the Law of Contracts, in 1 Schlesinger (Gen.Ed.), Formation of Contracts—A Study of the Common Core of Legal Systems 194–95 (1968), where further references can be found.

It should be noted, however, that our courts have been somewhat slow in responding to this invitation of the UCC draftsmen. In 1978, it was observed by an American scholar that while the UCC occasionally has been used by analogy, "this is a technique generally undeveloped in American law." J. Sweet, Book Review, 26 Am.J.Comp.L. 482, 492 (1978).

23. See J. Frank, Civil Law Influences on the Common Law, 104 U.Pa.L.Rev. 887, 890 (1956).

English courts are said to be more reluctant to treat a statute "as a source of public policy in cases not within its expressed terms." D. Lloyd, Public Policy 8 (1953). See also Lord Lloyd of Hampstead & M. D. A. Freeman, Lloyd's Introduction to Jurispru-

Yet this convergence of civil-law and common-law approaches has gone only part of the way. The very language, e.g., of § 1–103 of the UCC makes it clear that lawyers brought up in the common-law tradition still do not treat a "code" the way the civilians do. That section provides that,

> "Unless displaced by the particular provisions of this Act, the principles of law and equity, including the law merchant and the law relative to capacity to contract, principal and agent, estoppel, fraud, misrepresentation, duress, coercion, mistake, bankruptcy, or other validating or invalidating cause shall supplement its provisions." In a civilian code system, in which each code is intended to constitute a complete statement of authoritative rules and to displace all of the pre-existing law on the subject, such a reference to the supplemental role of "principles of law and equity" would be unthinkable.

Note in this connection the conclusion by two authors who combine expertise in legal philosophy and interpretation of commercial law, based on their comparative study of methods of statutory interpretation involving nine countries (Argentina, Germany, Finland, France, Italy, Poland, Sweden, United Kingdom, and United States).[24] The authors identify eleven basic types of argument employed in statutory interpretation, ranging from ordinary meaning to subjective legislative intent, which they found to be reducible to three main categories: linguistic, systemic, and teleological-evaluative.[25] They conclude that, in the U.K. and the U.S.A., if a statute is not by its terms applicable, courts frequently assume that any prior law continues to control, or that the matter is left for common-law decision-making, and refuse to apply the statute by analogy; in the civil-law countries surveyed by them, on the other hand, arguments from statutory analogy were widely applied.[26]

When is reasoning by analogy legitimate? The following case gives some indications.

Opinion of the German Federal Constitutional Court Concerning the Constitutional Complaint of Building Cooperative "X"

First Panel, April 3, 1990, BVerfGE 82, 6.

[The judicial decision here challenged had accorded the surviving live-in male companion of a deceased tenant the right to continue to live in her apartment under a lease with the complainant, though § 569a of the German Civil Code gives that right only to the surviving "spouse." The court, however, sustained this judicial extrapolation from the statute:]

dence 1143 (5th ed., 1985). But see R. Cross, Precedent in English Law 168–70 (3rd ed. 1977), where it is asserted that English courts do reason from statutes by analogy.

24. D. N. MacCormick & R. S. Summers (eds.), Interpreting Statutes: A Comparative Study (1991).

25. Id. at 512–15.

26. Id. at 471. But see, for a case of analogical reasoning in the United States, e.g., Moragne v. States Marine Lines, 398 U.S. 375, 90 S.Ct. 1772 (1970). Cf. C.R. Sunstein, On Analogical Reasoning, 106 Harv. L.Rev. 741 (1993).

1.a. The interpretation of statutory law, including the choice of the method to be applied for this purpose, is a matter left to the appropriate tribunal, and basically not subject to examination for correctness by the Federal Constitutional Court. If the appropriate tribunal employs traditional methods of interpretation in that connection, that raises no constitutional concerns.

b. The application of statutory provisions by analogy as well is basically unobjectionable constitutionally. Nevertheless, constitutional limitations follow from the primacy of statutory law mandated by article 20(3) of the Basic Law [Constitution], which here, in conjunction with article 14(1) [guarantee of property rights], furnishes the standard for the determination of constitutionality....

As an element of the principle of the Rule of Law, [article 20(3)] at the same time guarantees the degree of legal certainty which is indispensable in the interest of rights of liberty. The citizen must be able to arrange his conduct pursuant to the contents of the legal order and to act accordingly. If the legislature has made an unequivocal decision, the judge may not change [that decision] in accordance with his own views of legal policy and replace it with a solution that was not attainable in Parliament [citations.]

Factual or legal developments, however, can render a previously unequivocal and complete regulation incomplete, needy of supplementation and at the same time capable of being supplemented. The constitutional permissibility of the search for and the closing of gaps finds one of its justification in the exposure of statutes to the aging process. They are surrounded by social conditions and social policy perspectives, the change of which can alter the contents of legal provisions as well [citations.] To the extent that gaps in the legislative scheme come into existence to such changes, the statute loses its ability of furnishing a just solution for all cases within the ambit of its regulatory scheme. The courts are therefore entitled *and obliged* [emphasis added] to examine what is "Law" (*Recht*) within the meaning of article 20(3) [of the Constitution] under changed circumstances.

c. The method of analogy fulfills these constitutional requirements. It is true that by extending the sphere of application of a statutory provision to a case not covered by its wording, [analogy] exceeds interpretation in the narrower sense of the term. This further development of the law, however, is accomplished within the constitutional framework described. It does not constitute the manifestation of illicit judicial arbitrariness by which the recognizable intent of the legislature is pushed aside and replaced by an autonomous judicial balancing of interests. Quite the contrary, the scheme of values of the statute is used to ascertain whether there is a gap, and how it is to be closed.[1]

---

1. It is a comment on the change in social conditions that the provision equivalent to German Civil Code § 569a in France, Article 14 of Law No. 89–462 of July 6, 1989, expressly gives a right to continue the lease to the surviving "concubine" (of more than one years "concubinage").

NOTES AND QUESTIONS

(1) How far does this opinion sanction, how far does it mandate, "judicial activism"?

(2) Does the general reluctance of common-law courts to use statutory analogy also apply to the rules in the Uniform Commercial Code, a comprehensive regulation of commercial transactions and thus closer to civil-law codes? On the UCC, one commentator said, "As to analogy, the drafters of the UCC expressly favored its use, and academic commentators swiftly adopted a similar line. In a steadily growing number of decisions, courts have been willing to extend the UCC by analogy, thereby abandoning older doctrines on narrow construction of statutes."[1]

By now, you have probably studied a considerable number of provisions of the UCC and of cases interpreting them. Is the above passage correct in fact? Is analogy appropriate in that context?

(3) There are constitutional limits to the use of analogy. German Penal Code § 131 prohibits the depiction of cruel and inhuman acts of violence against human beings. A video depicting the killing of "humanoid monsters" was confiscated on the basis of the provision cited. In a Constitutional Complaint by the manufacturers of the video, the Constitutional Court ruled that in the context of § 131 of the Penal Law, "human beings" clearly referred to actual human persons, not wholly imaginary creatures. An extension by analogy to these would violate the constitutional provision (Art. 103II of the Constitution) against retroactive penal legislation. See Decision of October 20, 1992, BVerfGE 87, 209.

(4) In every legal system the courts must face up to the question whether and under what circumstances the interpretation of a written norm may deviate from its literal meaning. In civilian codes, one often finds an explicit directory provision intended to guide the courts in answering this question. But the German Civil Code, as the reader knows, differs from the majority of civil-law codes in that it contains no directory provisions. The German courts, nevertheless, found some helpful guidance in the Code itself. Among the provisions of the First Book which deal with "jural acts" and "declarations of intention" one encounters § 133, which reads as follows: In interpreting a declaration of intention the true intention shall be explored, and the literal meaning of the expression [by which such intention has been declared] is not necessarily determinative.

In terms, this provision governs the interpretation of contracts, deeds, corporate resolutions and other jural acts, but not of codes and statutes. German courts and legal writers, however, are virtually unanimous in recognizing that § 133 should be analogously applied in interpreting the written law.[2] It follows, as the principal case demonstrates, that legislative history and considerations of policy can be resorted to, not only to resolve a doubt arising from an ambiguity in the written law, but even to create a doubt concerning the true

---

1. B.W. Frier, Interpreting Codes, 89 Mich.L.Rev. 2201, 2211 (1991) (citations omitted); See also Aharon Barak, Purposive Interpretation in Law, Princeton University Press 2007.

2. See Palandt, Bürgerliches Gesetzbuch Introduction preceding § 1 (54th ed. 1995).

meaning of a statute or code provision which, if taken literally, would be clear and unambiguous.

In other civil-law countries, directory provisions of the Civil Code are to the effect that legislative history and other interpretive aids can be used only to resolve a doubt, but not to create one. Without further study, however, it cannot be taken for granted that such directory provisions will always be obeyed by the courts.

6.   JUDICIAL INTERPRETATION OF CODES—THE FORCE OF PRECEDENTS IN A CODE SYSTEM

Dorothy Hebert Ardoin et al. v. Hartford Accident and Indemnity Co. et al.

Supreme Court of Louisiana, 1978.
360 So.2d 1331.
Rehearing Denied July 26, 1978.

■ DENNIS, JUSTICE. In this case we are called upon to decide if Louisiana courts are governed by the "locality rule" in determining whether an act of a medical specialist that causes damage to his patient constitutes fault which obliges the physician to repair it.

On July 9, 1976, Lorrie Ardoin died during a "coronary artery by-pass" operation which was being performed by Dr. James Bozeman, a cardiovascular surgeon, at Our Lady of Lourdes Hospital in Lafayette, Louisiana. This type of operation requires that the patient's heart be stopped and that his vital functions be maintained by a "heart-lung" machine throughout the surgery. The apparatus consists of a pump with tubes which are used to suction blood from the patient's body and return it to his arteries after the blood has been oxygenated. This process is known as cardiopulmonary perfusion and the hospital attendants who operate the heart-lung machine are called perfusionists. Coincidentally with Ardoin's operation the hospital initiated the use of new tubing manufactured by Bentley Laboratories, Inc. in its cardiopulmonary perfusion. Because the hospital previously used another medical supplier's tubing, Bentley Laboratories' district manager, Travis Bohannon, was present during the operation for the purpose of assisting Darrell Gregory and Ronald DeBlanc, the hospital perfusionists, in attaching the new tubing to the heart-lung machine. After the cardiopulmonary apparatus had been assembled and the surgery was underway, Dr. Bozeman attached one of the tubes to the ventricle of the patient's heart for the purpose of pumping blood from the patient into the oxygenator. Instead of suctioning blood as it should have, however, the tube pumped air into Ardoin's heart. Death followed instantaneously when a massive air embolism reached the patient's brain.

The decedent's wife and nine children brought a wrongful death action alleging various acts of negligence on the part of the following defendants: Dr. James Bozeman, the cardiovascular surgeon; Darrell E. Gregory, perfusionist; Ronald DeBlanc, perfusionist; Our Lady of Lourdes Hospital; Travis Bohannon, district manager for Bentley Laboratories, Inc.; and Bentley Laboratories, Inc. Numerous third party demands were filed by the defendants and their insurers. Our review is limited to the third party action filed by Travis Bohannon, Bentley Laboratories, Inc. and its insurers against Dr. Bozeman.

At the time of the operation there were four physicians in Lafayette holding themselves out as specialists in cardiovascular surgery, viz., Dr. Bozeman, Dr. Leslie Guidry, Bozeman's expert witness, and Dr. Guidry's two partners. During a trial by jury Dr. Bozeman testified that in Lafayette the customary practice during a by-pass operation did not require a cardiovascular surgeon to test a perfusion tube to determine if it was properly working before inserting it into a patient's heart. Dr. Bozeman admitted that the direction of air flow in such a tube can be tested easily by dipping it in a sterile solution or in the blood draining into the patient's chest cavity. However, the surgeon stated that he did not perform this test but only looked at the line to see if it was the correct one. Dr. Bozeman testified that he depended on the perfusionists to check the heart-lung machinery for proper directional flow of air in the lines because his attention must be directed to other matters of importance during the operation. Testimony given by Dr. Guidry as to the customary practice in Lafayette was in accordance with that of Dr. Bozeman.

In an effort to prove negligence on the part of Dr. Bozeman in not testing the tube before inserting it into Ardoin's heart the third party plaintiffs sought to introduce the testimony of Dr. Prentiss Smith, a cardiovascular surgeon. Because Dr. Smith practiced in Baton Rouge and was not familiar with the care or skill of cardiovascular surgeons in Lafayette the trial judge ruled that Dr. Smith was not a competent witness. A proffer by statement was made which indicated that Dr. Smith would have testified that the degree of skill possessed and care ordinarily exercised by physicians within his specialty in the performance of a coronary artery by-pass operation requires a surgeon to test a perfusion tube by dipping it in either blood or a sterile solution before inserting it into a patient's heart.

Upon conclusion of the trial, the jury found negligence on the part of Gregory, one of the perfusionists, and Bohannon, the district manager of Bentley Laboratories. No negligence was found by the jury on the part of Dr. Bozeman. The demands of the plaintiffs and third parties against Dr. Bozeman were dismissed and judgments totaling $405,000 were rendered in behalf of the plaintiffs against Gregory, Bohannon and their employers and insurers. Appeals were perfected by defendants Gregory and Bohannon, their employers and their insurers. Plaintiffs answered the appeals asking for an increase in the amount of damages awarded.

On appeal the court of appeal refused to vacate or modify the awards made to the plaintiffs and affirmed the dismissal of the third party demands against Dr. Bozeman. In rejecting the third party plaintiffs' assertions that the trial court erred in precluding the testimony of Dr.

Prentiss Smith, the Baton Rouge specialist, the intermediate court relied primarily on this Court's opinion in Meyer v. St. Paul–Mercury Indemnity Co. In that case this Court stated that a physician, surgeon or dentist has a duty to exercise the degree of skill ordinarily employed, under similar circumstances, by the members of his profession in good standing in the same community or locality, and to use reasonable care and diligence, along with his best judgment in the application of his skill to the case. Since Dr. Smith was not qualified to testify as to the degree of skill ordinarily employed by specialists performing cardiovascular surgery in Lafayette, the court of appeal concluded that his testimony was correctly excluded. Secondarily, the intermediate court held that no modifications in the law favorable to medical patients had been effected by La.R.S. 9:2794 and that the trial court's ruling was therefore consistent with this statute.

We granted writs on behalf of third party plaintiff Bohannon, his employer and their insurers, to review the questions of law raised by the exclusion of Dr. Smith's testimony, viz., whether the interpretation of the law as to a physician's duty to his patient was correctly set forth in Meyer v. St. Paul–Mercury Indemnity Co.; whether the law in this regard was altered by La.R.S. 9:2794; and, if so, whether the legislation applies to quasi-offenses occurring before its effective date.

The standard of conduct required of persons in Louisiana in their relationships with one another is stated in simple, general terms set forth in Article 2315 of the Louisiana Civil Code of 1870: "Every act whatever of man that causes damage to another, obliges him by whose fault it happened to repair it. . . ."

This single article forms the basis of all tort liability in Louisiana. The remaining articles of the Civil Code's chapter of legal principles regulating offenses and quasi-offenses, Articles 2316 through 2324, contain amplifications as to what constitutes "fault" and under what circumstances a defendant may be held liable for his act or that of a person or thing for which he is responsible.

Under the civilian tradition of our state the courts have been given a broad, general principle of legislative will from which they are required to determine when the interest of society is best served by requiring one who harms another to respond in damages for the injury caused. In deciding whether the conduct in a specific case falls below that in which a person can engage without becoming responsible for resultant damage, a court must refer first to the fountainhead of responsibility, Article 2315, and next in applying the article to the many other articles in our code which deal with the responsibility of certain persons or that which arises due to certain types of activity. After searching through the code itself a jurist should refer in turn to the acts of the legislature, local governments, and other legislative and administrative bodies. Then, having explored the legislative and administrative sources of standards of proper conduct, a court should turn next to the experience of the judiciary in the interpretation and application of these standards to actual situations.

In deciding the issue before us the lower courts did not follow the process of referring first to the code and other legislative sources but treated language from a judicial opinion as the primary source of law. This is an indication that the position of the decided case as an illustration of past experience and the theory of the individualization of decision have not been properly understood by our jurists in many instances. Therefore, it is important that we plainly state that, particularly in the changing field of delictual responsibility, the notion of *stare decisis*, derived as it is from the common law, should not be thought controlling in this state. The case law is invaluable as previous interpretation of the broad standard of Article 2315, but it is nevertheless secondary information.

Starting first with the keystone for tort responsibility in Louisiana, Article 2315, we notice that it places no geographical or occupational limitations on the notion of "fault." Likewise, Article 2316 speaks very broadly of every person's responsibility for the damage he shall occasion "not merely by his act, but by his negligence, his imprudence, or his want of skill." Under these articles a medical specialist who injures a patient through his negligence, imprudence or want of skill must respond in damages. The code does not in any of its articles condition recovery by an injured patient upon proof of the physician's fault in relation to the medical standard of care or skill within a particular community or locality. Accordingly, the code itself does not provide for special or localized definitions of negligence, imprudence or want of skill by doctors.

By Act 807 of 1975, which became La.R.S. 9:2794, however, the legislature enacted legislation apparently intended to have an effect of this sort upon the proof of fault by physicians and dentists not engaged in a specialized practice. The statute expressly states that a patient who has been damaged by the act or omission of a physician or dentist must prove the degree of knowledge or skill possessed or the degree of care ordinarily exercised by physicians or dentists practicing in the same community or locality in which the defendant practices. The statute further requires that in order to recover a patient must also prove that he suffered injuries proximately caused by the defendant's lack of knowledge or skill or the failure to use reasonable care and diligence, along with his best judgment.

In contrast with the standard of conduct and burden of proof affecting practitioners not engaged in a specialty, the statute further provides that where the defendant practices in a particular specialty and where the alleged acts of medical negligence raise issues peculiar to the particular medical specialty involved, then the plaintiff "has the burden of proving the degree of care ordinarily practiced by physicians or dentists within the involved medical specialty." Thus, the legislature has provided guidance in applying the Civil Code's general principle of fault to the acts of a particular medical specialist by directing that they be measured by the degree of care ordinarily practiced by others involved in the same specialty. Unlike the statute's standard of care for practitioners not engaged in a specialty, the specialist's duty is not governed by the professional standard within a particular locality or community.

The court of appeal read the statute differently and concluded that it impliedly provides localized definitions of negligence, imprudence and want of skill by medical specialists. This erroneous interpretation resulted from a misapprehension of the civilian nature of our delictual responsibility laws as well as a disregard of the rules for their interpretation set forth in Articles 13–20 of the Civil Code.

Instead of beginning with the keystone of responsibility, Article 2315, and reading La.R.S. 9:2794 in the light of it and other pertinent articles, the intermediate court approached the problem as one of deciding the extent, if any, to which the jurisprudence had been amended by the legislative act. Thus, rather than reading La.R.S. 9:2794 as the lawmakers' indication of how the basic principle of Article 2315, as amplified by Article 2316, should be applied in a particular class of cases, the appeals court measured the enactment solely against language contained in a judicial opinion. The basic error in this method of interpretation is that it not only ignores the first principles of our law but it also assumes that jurisprudence is equivalent to legislation instead of treating it as judicial interpretation which may or may not adequately reflect the meaning of the laws for contemporary purposes.

On the other hand, adherence to civilian theory requires a jurist to begin with the broad principle of Article 2315 that everyone must repair the damage caused by his fault, and with the amplification of Article 2316 that fault includes everyone's negligence, imprudence or want of skill as measured against a general standard of conduct. Due notice next should be taken of our constitution's virtual prohibition of local legislation and the lack of any geographical differentiation between physicians licensed in Louisiana under the medical practice act. A comparison should be made of the laws prescribing uniform standards of competence or conduct for other professions or classes of occupations. At this point a tenet of our legal philosophy becomes apparent, i.e., that civil and criminal sanctions imposed for socially unacceptable conduct should be applied equally throughout the state to all citizens within the same class or set of circumstances. Therefore, one must conclude that, if the legislature were to act contrary to this policy by establishing a different definition of negligence, imprudence or want of skill by a medical specialist within each locality, the lawmaking body would express its intention explicitly. Since La.R.S. 9:2794 contains no such expression pertaining to medical specialists, the statute should not be given the effect of Balkanizing those representing themselves as having superior skill or knowledge beyond that common to the medical profession by the application of varying geographic standards of fault.

Furthermore, an application of the Civil Code rules of statutory construction leads to the same conclusion. As the court of appeal opinion plainly reflects, words must be added by the court to the portion of the statute pertaining to medical specialists in order to tie the standard of conduct prescribed therein to the locality rule. Such an interpretation tends to disregard the expression of the legislative will. Courts must give to the words used by the legislature the meaning they are ordinarily understood to have, and when the law is clear and free from any ambiguity, the letter of it must not be disregarded under the pretext of pursuing its spirit.

Since the meaning of the law is not dubious, it is unnecessary to consider the reason and spirit of it, but a survey of the possible considerations underlying its enactment confirms our interpretation.

By refusing to adopt a standard tied to locality for specialists, the legislature simply may have chosen to recognize the realities of medical life. The various medical specialties have established uniform requirements for certification. The national boards dictate the length of residency training, subjects to be covered, and the examinations given to the candidates for certification. Thus the medical profession itself recognizes national standards for specialists that are not determined by geography. Indeed, whatever may have justified a locality rule for physicians fifty or a hundred years ago cannot be reconciled with the actualities of medical practice today. The quality of medical school training has improved dramatically. With modern transportation and communication systems, new techniques and discoveries are available to all doctors within a short period of time through seminars, medical journals, closed circuit television presentations, special radio networks for doctors, tape recorded digests of medical literature, and current correspondence courses.

It is generally recognized that a rule of law which restricts proof of medical negligence to a standard of care within a locality tends to promote three evils: (1) It may effectively immunize from liability any doctor who happens to be the sole practitioner in his community. "He could be treating bone fractures by the application of wet grape leaves and yet remain beyond the criticism of more enlightened practitioners from other communities;" (2) The practitioners in a community are able to establish the standard of care which could, perhaps, be an inferior one; (3) A "conspiracy of silence" in the plaintiff's locality could effectively preclude any possibility of obtaining expert medical testimony. Because fewer specialists than generalists are likely to be found in most communities, the potential for these detrimental effects would only be exacerbated by extending the locality rule to specialists.

In recognition of the locality rule's possible harsh consequences and the fact that the practice of medicine by certified specialists within most medical specialties is similar throughout the country, many jurisdictions have abandoned entirely the locality rules as to specialists. This is consistent with the position advocated by the American Law Institute.

Moreover, only a distinct minority of states still adhere to the strict locality rule. A plurality of states now apply the "similar locality" rule, whereas some courts have extended geographic boundaries to include those centers readily accessible for appropriate treatment.

Although as noted by the court of appeal, La.R.S. 9:2794 was enacted as part of a legislative campaign to provide the medical profession with additional protection from occupational litigation, there is no justification for assuming that every sentence in this body of laws must be construed against its obvious meaning and in favor of the interest group which it generally benefits. Casual observation tells us that all legislation is founded on the principle of mutual concession. To interpret a statute in a totally one-sided manner simply because it was introduced and passed at the behest of one class of citizens may in effect read out of the law compromises which were crucial to its enactment. There is no logical reason why the legislature could not have intended to afford various protections to the medical profession and at the same time reject the idea of localized standards of conduct as to specialists. It is evident, in fact, that a locality rule for specialists would not be rooted in reality.

If La.R.S. 9:2794 does not adopt a standard tied to locality for specialists, counsel for respondent Dr. Bozeman alternatively contends that the statute can have no application to the instant case. Although the statute was in effect before the trial, he argues that because it was enacted subsequent to Ardoin's death it cannot be applied retrospectively to the wrongful death action resulting therefrom.

The general principle of non-retroactivity of laws is stated in Article 8 of the Civil Code, which provides: "A law can prescribe only for the future; it can have no retrospective operation, nor can it impair the obligation of contracts."

According to civilian theory, however, the principle of non-retroactivity of existing legislation admits three exceptions: laws that suppress or lessen penalties, laws that are merely interpretive of existing legislation, and those that the legislature has expressly or impliedly declared to be retroactive.

The exception relating to interpretive laws has been explained by Professor Yiannopoulos as follows: ". . . The exception . . . is justified on the ground that these laws do not establish new rules; they merely determine the meaning of existing laws and may thus be applied to facts occurring prior to their promulgation. In these circumstances, there is an apparent rather than real retroactivity, because it is the original rather than the interpretive law that establishes rights and duties. . . ."

This Court has recognized that interpretive legislation cannot properly be said to divest vested rights, because, under civilian theory, such legislation does not violate the principle of non-retroactivity of laws. The interpretive legislation does not create new rules, but merely establishes the meaning that the interpreted statute had from the time of its enactment. It is the original statute, not the interpretive one that establishes rights and duties.

According to this Court's consistent interpretation, Article 8 of the Civil Code contemplates substantive laws as distinguished from merely procedural or remedial laws which will be given retroactive effect in the absence of language showing a contrary intention.

Applying these principles to La.R.S. 9:2794, we conclude that the statute should be given retrospective effect. To the extent that the statute establishes a burden of proof in malpractice actions, it clearly should be characterized as procedural and therefore applied to pre-existing facts and relations. Insofar as the statute describes a standard of conduct, it merely determines more precisely the meaning of certain kinds of fault by certain classes of defendants, i.e., professional negligence, imprudence and want of skill by medical generalists and specialists, who were originally responsible for the damage occasioned by such fault under Articles 2315 and 2316. Accordingly, La.R.S. 9:2794 is an interpretive statute which does not establish new rights and duties but merely determines the meaning of existing laws and may thus be applied to facts occurring prior to its promulgation.

Having consulted the pertinent legislative sources for standards of proper conduct, we turn next to the experience of the judiciary in search of assistance in the interpretation and application of these standards to the actual situation at hand. Unfortunately, there does not appear to be any previous case in which a court has actually utilized either the civil code or La.R.S. 9:2794 in determining a physician's standard of conduct. Before the enactment of La.R.S. 9:2794 this Court had several opportunities to refer to Articles 2315 and 2316 in suits based on medical negligence, imprudence or want of skill, but in each case it either failed to disclose the legal basis of its decision or chose to rely on the jurisprudence of other states. Consequently, there does not appear to be any authoritative judicial interpretation of Louisiana statutory law pertinent to a physician's duty toward his patient. Moreover, the extant court opinions based on foreign authorities are inconsistent in the articulation of a standard of medical care and in the application of the varying standards to the facts of each case.

In one of the earliest cases on the subject, this Court, without citing any authority, declared in its syllabus that an oculist "must exercise ... the care and skill usually exercised by oculists in good standing ... [and] may be rendered liable for his gross mistakes." No mention of geographical limits appeared in the jurisprudence until Roark v. Peters in which a common law cyclopedia was relied upon to announce that physicians would be held to the standard of skill and learning in "similar localities." Twenty-eight years later this Court again relied on common law authorities in narrowing the similar locality rule to a "strict" or "same locality" rule in Meyer v. St. Paul–Mercury Indemnity Co. Although the rule was proclaimed once more in 1966 by the opinion of Uter v. Bone and Joint Clinic, the Court ignored it in discussing with seeming approval the testimony of a New Orleans specialist in the trial of the defendant Baton Rouge doctor. In view of the lack of coherence in this Court's decisions it is not surprising that the courts of appeal have also been inconsistent.

From our review of these cases, we conclude that in this field this Court and the intermediate courts have failed to base their decisions on applicable civil code articles and statutes. Instead, the courts uncritically adopted from common law cyclopedias malpractice rules which no longer represent either the prevailing or the emerging view in the nation. The past decisions by Louisiana appellate courts demonstrate the danger of forsaking the first principles of our own law for the momentary consensus of the law in other states. Insofar as Meyer v. St. Paul–Mercury Indemnity Co. and our jurisprudence are in conflict with the views expressed in this opinion, they are expressly overruled.

Conclusion

For the foregoing reasons, we hold that a medical specialist is required by La.Civil Code Articles 2315 and 2316, and La.R.S. 9:2794, to exercise the degree of care and possess the degree of knowledge or skill ordinarily exercised and possessed by physicians within his medical specialty; that the plaintiff seeking to prove that a medical specialist failed to adhere to these standards of care or skill is not limited to expert medical testimony by witnesses practicing or familiar with the standards of care and skill within the defendant specialist's community or locality; and that, accordingly, the lower courts fell into error in the instant case by ruling that testimony pertaining to the standard of care or skill within the involved medical specialty could not be presented because of a locality rule.

Accordingly, testimony of qualified experts, regardless of whether practicing within or familiar with the defendant doctor's locality is admissible to prove the degree of care ordinarily exercised and the degree of skill or knowledge ordinarily possessed by physicians within the involved medical specialty. However, evidence of the local facilities and resources available, as well as evidence of other pertinent local conditions, is also admissible and should be considered by the trier of fact in determining whether a physician exhibiting the care, knowledge and skill ordinarily exhibited by physicians within the involved medical specialty would have acted or failed to act in the manner of the defendant doctor at the time in question.

The judgment of the court of appeal is reversed and the third party demand of Bohannon, his employer and their insurers against Dr. Bozeman is remanded to the trial court for a new trial in accordance with the views expressed herein. Costs in this Court are assessed to the third party defendants.

NOTES AND QUESTIONS

(1) This Chapter attempts to show how a large aggregate of cultural and institutional factor affects the way in which precedents can work as a source of law. The *Ardoin* case is thus particularly important for comparative purposes. Being a case from Louisiana, a civil law jurisdiction fully integrated within the U.S. institutional and cultural system, *Ardoin* shows *stare decisis* at play in almost ideal "laboratory conditions." The reader will thus notice how *having followed a precedent* has been considered a reversible error by the Louisiana Supreme Court. The *absence of stare decisis* is thus an obligation for the judge to independently interpret the provision of a statute rather than bureaucratically following what another judge has done in front of the same provision.

(2) *Decision of Landgericht Braunschweig, dated Nov. 28, 1984, reported in 1985 N.J.W. 1171:* By a notarial act, P and two other individuals formed a close corporation (GmbH). Under German law, such a corporation does not come into existence until it is registered in the Commercial Register. Before this particular corporation was so registered, P on the corporation's behalf entered into a contract with X. Under the terms of the contract, X leased a piece of machinery to the corporation, at a monthly rental of about $400.00. Subsequently, the corporation was registered and used the leased machine for several months; but no payments were ever made to X, and after some time the corporation went bankrupt. X then sued P for the accrued rental installments. P retained lawyer D to represent him in the action brought by X. In the court of first instance, X prevailed; in September 1981 he obtained a judgment against P for the full amount of the accrued rental installments, plus interest and costs (including the fees of X's attorneys). No appeal was taken from that judgment.

In the present action, P sues D for malpractice, asserting that D was negligent in failing to recommend an appeal from the judgment obtained by X. Under the German statute relating to this type of corporation (GmbH Gesetz, § 11, subs. 2), it is clear that incorporators who on the corporation's behalf— but prior to its registration in the Commercial Register—enter into a contract with another party become personally liable to such party. The statute, however, is silent on the question whether this personal liability of the incorporators continues after the corporation has been registered and thus has become a legal entity. The judgment obtained by X against P was obviously based on the assumption that the correct answer to this question is in the affirmative. Such an assumption might have been reasonable in the light of pre–1981 German authorities. But in three cases decided during 1981 and 1982, Germany's highest court in civil and criminal matters, the *Bundesgerichtshof* (BGH) decided that:

> (a) at the time of its becoming registered, the corporation automatically acquires all rights and assumes all obligations flowing from a contract which prior to such registration was concluded by the incorporators on behalf of the corporation, and that

> (b) the personal liability of the incorporators arising from such a contract ceases at the time when the corporation itself assumes the liability, i.e., at the time the corporation is registered.

Under the rule established by these decisions of the highest court, the judgment obtained by X against P was clearly incorrect.

In P's malpractice action against D, the court found that the time for an appeal from the judgment obtained by X ran out in October 1981. The last of the above-mentioned three decisions of the BGH was handed down in 1982; thus D could not possibly be familiar with that decision when in September/October 1981 he had to determine whether he should advise his client to appeal. But the situation was different with respect to the first two BGH decisions. The first one, which already spelled out the holding summarized above, was rendered on March 9, 1981, and on June 16, 1981, was reported in an issue of *Neue Juristische Wochenschrift* (NJW), a well-known and widely circulated legal periodical that is published under Bar Association auspices. The second decision, which repeated the same holding, was rendered on March 16, 1981, and similarly reported in the June 30, 1981, issue of NJW.

Clearly, if D had been familiar with these decisions, he would have recommended an appeal from the judgment obtained by X. In the malpractice action, the court held that inasmuch as two of the relevant BGH decisions were rendered in March 1981 and reported in June 1981, D was negligent not to have familiarized himself with the decisions before the time when (in September/October 1981) he had to consider the advisability of an appeal to be taken by his client. Hence D was held to be liable for the full amount of the incorrect—but by now unappealable—judgment obtained by X.

(3) As the reader will recall from our discussion of the *Shoop* case, the Spanish Code of Civil Procedure as construed by the Supreme Court of Spain provides that a repeated holding of that court is regarded as a *doctrina legal* (now *jurisprudencia*), and that by ignoring or disregarding such a line of judicial authority a lower court commits reversible error. This provision of the Code of Civil Procedure, which in effect makes repeated holdings of the Supreme Court binding on the lower courts, is of great importance in practice. Spanish legal scholars, however, have always found it difficult to reconcile the *doctrina legal* (now *jurisprudencia*) with the Civil Code's general theory of sources of law. As originally enacted, the Civil Code in Art. 6 (quoted in the *Shoop* case), recognized only three sources of "law:" written law (*ley*), custom,[1] and general principles of law. Judicial decisions were not included in this enumeration. In 1974, the entire Preliminary Title of the Civil Code was revised, and the wording of old Art. 6, now renumbered as Art. 1, was considerably amplified. The new version, an English translation of which appears *infra* this sec., does mention *doctrina* ("the doctrine which the Supreme Court establishes in a reiterated manner"), but does not recognize it as one of the sources of law.

The precise nature and status of the *doctrina legal* (now *jurisprudencia* in the Code of Civil Procedure and *doctrina* in the Civil Code) thus remains in doubt. The Spanish legislator, although fashioning a sound practical solution, apparently was still too steeped in the civilian tradition to admit openly that judges make law.[2]

(4) In France, it is generally taught that a custom may supplement but not abrogate a rule of written law.[3] But the line between supplementation and

---

1. The Spanish word is *costumbre*. A party who invokes a *costumbre* bears the burden of proving an actual usage (either local or general) that is inveterate, reasonable and recognized as binding. To meet this burden is extremely difficult, and in practice *costumbre* is not often used as a source of law. In contrast to their German colleagues, Spanish judges have not claimed the power to create a *costumbre* by judicial decisions alone.

Costumbre must be distinguished from *fueros* (see *In re Shoop, supra* at 178). The latter originated in medieval customary law, usually of a local or regional nature; from the 15th century on, these local and regional customs were everywhere reduced to writing and thus became a species of local or regional *written law*. While other European countries generally repealed those local and regional

laws when they enacted national codes, Spain preserved a number of the regional *fueros*, which continue to play an important role in the Spanish legal system. See id. The reader should keep in mind, however, that whatever their historical origin may be, these regional *fueros* today do not constitute customary law; they are *written* regional law, in effect statutes of regional applicability.

2. See note to the *Shoop* case, and Art. 1 of the Spanish Civil Code (1889).

3. See, e.g., Loussouarn, The Relative Importance of Legislation, Custom, Doctrine, and Precedent in French Law, 18 La.L.Rev. 235, 250–54 (1958). A comparative discussion of French and other civil-law theories regarding judge-made "customary law" can be found in J. P. Dawson, The Oracles of the Law 416–31, 498–99 (1968).

abrogation sometimes is a shadowy one. For example, Art. 1202 of the Code Civil prescribes that as a rule each of several co-obligors is presumed to be liable only for his ratable share, and not jointly and severally. Under ordinary principles, this rule would govern commercial as well as civil contracts since the Code de Commerce contains no relevant provision. But, in reliance on "usage," the courts have held that Art. 1202 does not apply to commercial obligations, and that the latter, contrary to the plain language of the Code, are presumed to create a "solidary" (i.e., joint and several) liability on the part of the co-obligors.[4] It is true, of course, that Art. 1202 is a *loi supplétive*, i.e., a provision which permits the parties to agree otherwise. In the cases just referred to, however, no actual intention of the parties was shown, nor an actual trade usage which could be read into the agreement of the parties. The rule was created by judicial rather than commercial "usage."

Instances such as this, in which French courts may be said to have *changed* a rule of code law by a judge-made "custom," are quite rare. But judge-made customary law *supplementing* the written law, which French authors often lump together with case law of the nonbinding, merely persuasive kind, is of great importance in France. The French refer to it as *jurisprudence*. A leading textbook defined that term as follows:

> Jurisprudence is the aggregate of the decisions rendered by the courts, from which one can extract general rules enabling him to foresee the solution of future similar disputes. Each decision determines only *a particular case*, but the *repetition of similar decisions* permits the conclusion that the courts recognize the existence of a rule governing the solution and will follow it in the future. Hence it becomes necessary to take that rule into account in the conduct of one's affairs.[5]

Instances of rules and indeed of whole institutions which owe their existence to judicial "repetition of similar decisions" (*jurisprudence constante*) are without number in French law. The reader already is familiar with some pertinent data: that French administrative law is in large measure the creation of the Conseil d'Etat, and that the rules relating to tort liability for automobile accidents until recently were fashioned, on the basis of code provisions of almost meaningless generality, by the *jurisprudence* of the *Cour de cassation*.[6]

The French codes deal with some subjects in specific detail, while other matters (e.g., the whole law of torts) are covered by broad provisions which merely announce a general principle.[7]

---

4. Françoise Dekeuwer–Défossez, Droit Commercial 120 (4th ed. 1995), with citations, where this line of decisions is characterized as a "rare example of custom *contra legem* recognized by *jurisprudence*."

5. Planiol–Ripert, Traité Elémentaire de Droit Civil de Planiol. Tome 1: Principes Generaux 50–52 (1949).

6. See the reports and summaries in Association Henri Capitant, La Réaction de la Doctrine à la Création de Droit par les Juges (vol. 31, 1980).

7. The reader, who has seen an English translation of the French Civil Code's principal tort provisions (*supra* Chapter 5), is fa-

Roscoe Pound: The Spirit of the Common Law

170–181 (1921)*

... As a critic has put it, the theory of the codes in Continental Europe in the last century made of the court a sort of judicial slot machine. The necessary machinery had been provided in advance by legislation or by received legal principles and one had but to put in the facts above and take out the decision below. True, this critic says, the facts do not always fit the machinery, and hence we may have to thump and joggle the machinery a bit in order to get anything out. But even in extreme cases of this departure from the purely automatic, the decision is attributed, not at all to the thumping and joggling process, but solely to the machine....

A conception of the judicial office arose on the Continent which persisted after permanent courts learned in the law had been set up,[1] since it appeared to accord with the theory of the separation of powers and was in line with the political theory which developed in the seventeenth and eighteenth centuries. It was in line also with the eighteenth-century doctrine of a complete code deduced from the principles of natural law. Through the influence of the latter doctrine it became a favorite notion of legislators that the finding of law for the purposes of judicial decision might be reduced to a simple matter of genuine interpretation; that a body of enacted rules might be made so complete and so perfect that the judge would have only to select the one made in advance for the case in hand, find what the law giver intended thereby through application of fixed canons of genuine interpretation and proceed to apply it....

All the nineteenth-century codes in Continental Europe, except the German Civil Code of 1896, go upon the theory that judicial decisions shall have no authority beyond the cases in which they are rendered and that there can be no authoritative interpretation by anyone except the legislature itself. If the codes left anything open, the judges were directed[2] where to turn in order to decide the case. But the next judge was not to look upon the decision of his predecessor as establishing anything. He was to repeat the process independently. An excellent example may be found in *Article 5 of the French Civil Code*. That article reads as follows: *"Judges are forbidden, when giving judgment in the cases which are brought before them, to lay down general rules of conduct...."*[3] [Italics added.] Its purpose

miliar with the broad sweep of those provisions.

* Reprinted by permission of Marshall Jones Company, Francestown, N.H.

1. Recent research has shown that at least in some parts of 17th and 18th century Europe the decisions of the courts were of somewhat greater importance for the development of the law than Dean Pound appears to have assumed.

2. I.e., directed by a provision of the code itself. Dean Pound is alluding to the express provisions contained in most civil codes (but not in the German Code) which deal with the sources of law to which a court should turn in case the written law is silent. We have previously encountered some examples of such directory provisions.

3. A judge who violates this prohibition was, theoretically, guilty of a criminal offense under French Penal Code, Art. 127 (repealed 1994). According to the intention of its draftsmen, the prohibition meant that a court may not decide a case by holding it is

was, as we are told by an authoritative commentator, to prevent the judges from forming a body of case law which should govern the courts and to prevent them from "correcting by judicial interpretations the mistakes made in the [enacted] law." Before fifty years had passed legislation was required to compel the lower courts to follow the solemn decision of the highest court of France[4] and now, after a century of experience, French jurists are conceding that the article in question has failed of effect. Today elementary books from which law is taught to the French students, in the face of the code and of the received Roman tradition, do not hesitate to say that the course of judicial decision is a form of law. . . .

NOTES AND QUESTIONS

(1) Did Art. 5 of the French Civil Code express the true intention of the draftsmen, or did its language present a mere political gesture which the draftsmen themselves did not expect to have any lasting effect?

The reader will recall (see *supra* Chapter 5) that Napoleon commissioned four eminent lawyers to prepare a draft of the Code, and that Portalis was the most influential member of that group. Thus it is rewarding to study the pertinent statements made by Portalis, the most famous of which is his Discourse Préliminaire. Fortunately, excerpts from it have been translated into English.[1]

In perusing Portalis' own comments, the reader will find that he castigated the foolishness of the idea of depriving the courts of the power to *interpret* ambiguous or obscure code provisions. He said: "A Code, however complete it may seem, is hardly finished before a thousand unexpected issues come to face the judge." At the same time, Portalis rejected the notion of *authoritative* judicial interpretation. But his position on this point was less clear, because almost in the same breath he stressed the necessity of case law, which by utilizing experience would "gradually . . . fill up the gaps we leave." On the vital point of the precedential force of judicial decisions, one can find certain contradictions in Portalis' elegant formulations. Perhaps he had to pay lip service to the revolutionary postulate rejecting all *règlements* and *dispositions générales*,[2] while at the same time he also wished to express his personal opinion that as a practical matter it was necessary for the courts to develop, and ultimately to be guided by, a stable case law based on experience.

governed by a previous decision; by so holding the court would convert the previous decision into a "general rule of conduct."

Concerning the historical reasons for French hostility against judicial lawmaking, see Deák & Rheinstein, reproduced *infra* at 351.

4. Dean Pound apparently refers to the Law of April, 1837 (meanwhile repeatedly amended and re-enacted). That Law first introduced the system, described in detail *supra* Chapter 4, sec. 1L, under which the second reversal pronounced in the same case by

the Cour de Cassation (this time sitting en banc or as a super-panel) is binding on the intermediate appellate court to which the case is remanded. The latter court, however, is "bound" only in the case at hand, and not in future cases presenting the same question of law.

1. A. Levasseur, Code Napoleon or Code Portalis?, 43 Tul.L.Rev. 762, 767–74 (1969) (translation by Shael Herman).

2. I.e., the kinds of usurpation of lawmaking power for which certain pre-revolutionary French courts were strongly criticized by the revolutionaries and their successors.

(2) In a civil-law country where the principle of separation of powers is anchored in the Constitution, and where the constitutionality of statutes and other legal norms is subject to judicial review, one can expect a great deal of debate concerning the question whether and under what circumstances *the Constitution* permits the creation of judge-made law. Such a debate is not always academic. The case which follows will demonstrate that substantial rights and obligations of real-life parties may hinge on the outcome of that debate.

Opinion of the German Federal Constitutional Court in the Proceeding Concerning the Constitutional Complaint of Publishing Company "Die Welt" and Mr. K.–H. V.

So called Princess Soraya Case.
First Panel,* February 14, 1973.
BVerfGE 34, 269, also reported in NJW 1973, 1221.

[The plaintiff is Princess Soraya, the ex-wife of the Shah of Iran. At the time in question, after her divorce from the Shah, the plaintiff resided in Germany. The defendants are the publisher and chief-editor of an illustrated weekly paper which is distributed throughout Germany and known to specialize in sensational society stories.

In April 1961, defendants' paper carried a front-page story purporting to be the transcript of an interview with the plaintiff. The interview, which appeared to reveal much of plaintiff's private and very private life, was wholly fictitious, i.e., it was totally and freely invented by its author, a free-lance journalist. Defendants published the story without investigating whether the interview had actually taken place. In July, 1961, defendants' paper carried another story dealing with Princess Soraya, and as a part of that new story the defendants published a brief statement by the Princess to the effect that the alleged April interview had not taken place.

In the present action, plaintiff seeks damages for "violation of her personality rights." The Landgericht as court of first instance awarded her D.M. 15,000. The Oberlandesgericht (intermediate appellate court) and the Bundesgerichtshof (court of last resort in civil and criminal matters, abbr. BGH) affirmed, and the defendants brought the case before the Federal Constitutional Court by way of a constitutional complaint.[a]

In order to understand the thrust of defendants' constitutional arguments, we must take a brief look at the development and present status of the rules of substantive law which the plaintiff successfully invoked in the courts below.

---

* A case coming before the Federal Constitutional Court, unless summarily disposed of (see *supra* Chapter 6, Section 3(e) at 523), is heard by one of the two eight-judge panels.

[a] For an explanation of this procedure, see *supra* Chapter 6, Section 3(e) at 523 (Constitutional Courts and Judicial Review).

Apart from a section protecting a person's right to his name, the German Civil Code contains no specific provisions concerning the subjects which we would label as defamation or invasion of privacy. In Germany, as in France, defamation traditionally has been thought of as a crime rather than a tort.[b] Under this traditional view, defamation actions normally have to be brought in the criminal courts, even though such an action ordinarily has to be prosecuted by the victim rather than the public prosecutor.[c] If the defendant is convicted in such a criminal proceeding, he will be fined, or (in a very serious case) subjected to a jail sentence; but the victim cannot recover substantial damages in that proceeding.[d]

Until after World War II, attempts to bring *civil* actions for defamation or invasion of privacy found little favor with the German courts. The first paragraph of § 823 of the Civil Code[e] authorizes tort recovery only if the plaintiff can show injury to his "life, body, health, freedom, property, or some other (similar) right." In order to bring cases of defamation or invasion of privacy within the ambit of this code provision, plaintiffs often argued that a person's interest in his reputation and privacy should be regarded as his "personality right" and should be protected as one of the "other rights" mentioned in § 823. But throughout the periods of the Empire, the Weimar Republic and the Third Reich, the courts essentially rejected that argument.[f]

A different judicial approach to the problem emerged after World War II, and after the adoption of the new West German Constitution, which contains the following provisions:

Art. 1.   The dignity of man is inviolable. Every state authority is duty-bound to respect and protect it. . . .

b. See B. S. Markesinis, The Not So Dissimilar Tort and Delict, 93 L.Q.Rev. 78, 103–05 (1977); J. F. Murphy, An International Convention on Invasion of Privacy, 8 N.Y.U.J.Int'l L. & Pol. 387, 422–23 (1976).

c. See German Code of Criminal Procedure, §§ 374, 376. The public prosecutor brings such an action only if this is required in the public interest.

German law generally vests the prosecutor with little or no discretion, and requires prosecution whenever there is reasonable cause to believe that the defendant has committed a crime. This general rule, however, is subject to exceptions in the case of certain relatively minor offenses, such as defamation. See *infra* Chapter 8, Section 4 at 828.

d. Apart from other difficulties, German law until recently imposed a relatively low ceiling on the amount which the victim can recover in a criminal proceeding. See *infra* Chapter 8, Section 5 at 855.

e. For a translation of that provision, see *supra* at 458.

f. For details, see Markesinis, *supra* note b, at 105–06.

It is interesting to note that in France the courts began much earlier than in Germany to employ tort remedies for the protection of privacy interests. The reason may be that Art. 1382 of the French Civil Code, in contrast to German § 823, is of such generality that a French court, when granting a tort recovery, could always claim to act on the authority of that Code provision. See W. J. Wagner, The Development of the Theory of the Right to Privacy in France, 1971 Wash. U.L.Q. 45, 49ff. Since 1970, moreover, tort remedies for invasion of privacy are explicitly authorized by the French Civil Code, Art. 9 (added by Law No. 70–643 of July 17, 1970). See also article 1916 (new) of the Civil Code of the Federal District of Mexico, and parallel revisions in the civil codes of many (but not all) Mexican States.

Art. 2.   Everyone is entitled to the free development of his personality insofar as he does not violate the rights of others or offend the constitutional order or the rules of morality. . . .

During the 1950s the BGH, explicitly invoking these constitutional provisions, gave up the former narrow interpretation of § 823 of the Civil Code and repeatedly held that a plaintiff's "personality right" is one of the "other rights" which are protected by § 823 against intentional or negligent infringement. This was an important development. It meant that—in contrast to prior law—the German courts now were treating injuries to a person's reputation or privacy as actionable torts.[g]

Even after this judicial breakthrough, however, a difficult issue remained to be resolved regarding the kind of damages for which recovery could be allowed under German law in cases of injury to the plaintiff's "personality right." The difficulty was caused by one of the Civil Code's provisions dealing with damages. These provisions, insofar as they are relevant to the present discussion, read as follows:

§ 249.   A person who is liable to make compensation, has to bring about the condition which would exist if the circumstances making him liable had not occurred.[h] If the liability exists for injury to a person or damage to tangible property, then the obligee [at his election] may demand, instead of restitution in kind, the sum of money necessary to effect such restitution.

§ 251.   Insofar as restitution in kind is impossible or is insufficient to compensate the obligee, the obligor has to compensate the obligee by the payment of money damages. . . .

§ 253.   *For an injury which is not an injury to patrimony [i.e., to interests having a pecuniary value], compensation in money can be demanded only in the cases provided by (written) law.*[i] (emphasis added).

There are a few limited and narrowly defined cases in which an express provision of written law (within the meaning of § 253) permits the victim of a tort to recover money damages for an injury to non-pecuniary interests; the prime example is the case of personal injury, with respect to which § 847 of the German Civil Code explicitly authorizes the recovery of money damages for pain and suffering. The draftsmen of the Civil Code clearly regarded this provision of § 847 as an exception to the general rule laid

g. For a full account, see Harry D. Krause, The Right to Privacy in Germany—Pointers for American Legislation? 1965 Duke L.J. 481, and most recently Karl–Nikolaus Peifer, Persönlichkeitsschaden and Geldersatz, 96 Zeitschrift für vergleichende Rechtswissenschaft 74 (1997), also discussing parallel developments in Italy at 76–82.

h. This means that as a rule, subject to the exceptions listed in the second sentence of § 249 and in the subsequent sections, the obligor is bound to make restitution in kind rather than to pay money damages.

i. The German text makes it clear that a victim whose non-pecuniary interests have been injured can demand money damages only in the cases provided by "*Gesetz.*" As distinguished from *Recht*, which in its objective sense means law (regardless of its source), the word "*Gesetz*" denotes a statute or other written law. See *supra* this section.

down in § 253, that no money damages can be recovered for an injury to non-pecuniary interests.[j]

Neither the Civil Code nor any auxiliary statute provides for the recovery of non-pecuniary damages by a person whose "right of personality" has been injured. Thus when the tort of injury to a person's "personality right" was first developed by the German courts, it was initially thought that a plaintiff, while perhaps entitled to the publication of a retraction or to similar non-monetary relief under § 249, could not recover money damages without proof of what we would call "special damages," i.e., loss of his job, loss of customers, or the like.[k] The plain language of § 253 indeed appears to preclude the plaintiff in such a case from recovering "general" damages for his soiled reputation and injured feelings.

In 1958, however, the German courts broke away from this restriction seemingly imposed by § 253. The occasion was the so-called *Herrenreiter* case (the case of the gentleman horse-back rider).[l] That case involved a picture of the plaintiff, a well-known equestrian, elegantly positioned on horse-back while jumping over a hurdle. Without plaintiff's authorization, the picture was publicly and widely disseminated by the defendant as part of an advertisement promoting a sexual stimulant. The plaintiff's "personality right" was seriously injured by this advertisement, not only because it conveyed the impression that the plaintiff had sought to commercialize his great reputation as a sportsman, but also because it implied that he needed and used sexual stimulants.

The lower courts awarded the plaintiff a substantial sum of money as damages for the injury to his reputation and feelings. The BGH affirmed, essentially on the ground that § 847 of the Civil Code should be extended by analogy to cover the case at hand. This analogy argument was questionable, because the word "only" in § 253 explicitly prohibits an analogical extension of provisions, such as § 847, which engraft exceptions upon the general rule of § 253. Recognizing this, the BGH subsequently abandoned the analogy argument; but the result reached in the *Herrenreiter* case was reaffirmed in later cases, on the ground that in many situations the tort of injury to a person's "personality right"—a tort developed in response to value judgments expressed in the Constitution—would be without an adequate remedy if the victim of such a tort could not recover money damages for the violation of his non-monetary interests.

The BGH limited the breadth of these rulings by further holding that such a cause of action for money damages should be recognized only if (a) the injury to the plaintiff's "personality right" is substantial, and (b) the defendant's act is sufficiently culpable to justify the rendition of a money judgment in a sizeable amount. According to the BGH, both conditions, (a)

---

j. See Palandt, Bürgerliches Gesetzbuch, § 847, Anno. 1a (53rd ed., 1994). Some additional exceptions are provided for in auxiliary statutes. See id.

k. See Markesinis, *supra* note b, at 105–07.

l. Decision of February 14, 1958, BGHZ 26, 349, translated into English in Basil S. Markesinis, A Comparative Introduction to the German Law of Torts 380–86 (3d ed. 1994).

and (b), are clearly satisfied in a case in which a defendant, by way of large-scale promotion of his own commercial interests, has wantonly violated the plaintiff's "personality right." The repetition of such intolerable conduct, the BGH held, should be prevented by announcing a rule of tort law which makes it clear to would-be violators that such conduct is costly for them.

In the decisions dealing with this question, the BGH also pointed to the drastic technological and social changes that have taken place since the enactment of the Civil Code. The development of mass media, hardly predictable in 1900, makes the protection of an individual's personality right more important and more difficult in our day. Therefore, the BGH held, a court which takes the value system of the Constitution seriously can no longer feel bound by § 253 of the Civil Code insofar as that provision denies recovery for non-pecuniary damages even in cases of grave injuries to an individual's personality right.

The lower courts, after some initial reluctance on the part of some of them, generally followed these holdings of the BGH, which were approved, also, by the majority of the commentators. In the instant case, both the lower courts and the BGH itself based their decision on those previous holdings.

The defendants' constitutional complaint was based mainly on the following provisions of the German Federal Constitution:

> Art. 5.... Freedom of the press and freedom of reporting by broadcast and film are guaranteed....
>
> These rights are limited by the provisions of general (written) laws,[m] by statutory measures for the protection of juveniles, and by the right of personal honor....
>
> Art. 20....
>
> All of the State's power originates with the People. Such power can be exercised by the People through elections and ballots, and by special organs of the legislative, executive and judicial branches of the government.
>
> The legislature is bound by the constitutional order. The executive and the judiciary are bound by statute and law.[n]

In particular, the defendants argued that the substantive rule pursuant to which the lower courts ordered them to pay money damages to the plaintiff had been created by the courts in violation of the principle of separation of powers laid down in Art. 20 of the Constitution. The BGH, they argued, had acted *contra legem* when it developed the right to money

---

m. The German term is "*allgemeine Gesetze.*" As to the meaning of the word "*Gesetz,*" see *supra* n. i.

n. The German term is "*Gesetz und Recht.*" The words "*Gesetz*" and "*Recht*" are not synonymous. See *supra* n. i.

Literally, this provision of the Constitution means that the executive and the judiciary are bound by written law and by other law.

damages for violation of an individual's "personality right." This, it was contended, was usurpation by the courts of legislative power.

The defendants did not question the constitutionality of the view that the personality right of a person is one of the "other rights" mentioned in the first paragraph of § 823 of the Civil Code. Their attack was directed only against the decisional rule which—contrary to the language of § 253 of the Civil Code—permits a plaintiff whose personality right has been gravely injured to recover a money judgment for non-monetary damages.

The defendants did not deny that the recognition of plaintiff's personality right as one of the "other rights" protected by § 823 of the Civil Code was in part dictated by Arts. 1 and 2 of the Constitution. But they argued that the rights derived from Arts. 1 and 2, like other human rights protected by the Constitution, are essentially defensive in nature. For this reason, the defendants contended, it is not possible to treat those constitutional provisions as the direct foundation of a cause of action for money damages.

In addition, the defendants argued, the money judgment rendered by the courts below violated the constitutional principle of freedom of the press. In the defendants' view, the money damage rule developed by the courts and applied in this case did not constitute the kind of "general (written) law" which pursuant to Art. 5 of the Constitution may be used by the law-giver to limit the freedom of the press.]

The constitutional complaint is unfounded.

I

The litigation which gave rise to the judgment under attack was a civil proceeding, to be determined in accordance with the principles and rules of private law. The Federal Constitutional Court does not review the interpretation and application of private law as such. However, the value system reflected in the Constitution's guarantees of fundamental rights has an impact upon all areas of law, including that of private law. To make sure that this "radiation effect" of the Constitution be properly observed is one of the functions of the Constitutional Court. Our Court, therefore, must examine whether the decisions of the civil courts are based on a basically incorrect view of the scope and effect of a fundamental constitutional right, or whether the result of such a decision itself violates fundamental constitutional rights of one of the parties [citations.]

In the instant case the complainants [i.e., the defendants, who have filed the constitutional complaint] not only oppose the result reached by the civil courts; they object above all to the manner in which those courts have reached such result. The complainants argue that an ordinary court is bound to obey the written law, and hence is not permitted to award monetary damages in cases of this kind. This argument compels us to reflect upon the nature and limits of the judicial function as outlined in the Constitution. We must examine the question whether decisions such as those rendered by the courts below can be arrived at by way of judicial application of the law. A judge may not proceed in an arbitrary manner when he seeks to implement the value concepts of the Constitution in his decisions. He would likewise violate the Constitution if he reached a result in accord with the value concepts of the Constitution but did so by employing a method exceeding or disregarding the constitutional limits imposed upon the exercise of the judicial function. The Federal Constitutional Court would have to review, and object to, a decision thus reached.

The plaintiff's claim in the present action was based on the first paragraph of § 823 of the Civil Code. The BGH includes the "general right of personality" among the rights protected by that provision, citing a line of earlier decisions [going back to the early 1950s]. The BGH regards the conduct of the defendants in the instant case as violating that right. It is not the task of the Federal Constitutional Court to examine the "correctness" of this line of decisions so long as their reasoning and development remain within the area of private law. Suffice it to state that the general right of personality—which at the time of the enactment of the Civil Code was still rejected by the codifiers—has successfully asserted itself in the course of scholarly discussions extending over several decades, and, following its recognition by the BGH [in the early 1950s], has now become a formally recognized part of the system of private law [citing several leading textbooks and commentaries].

The Federal Constitutional Court sees no reason why this line of decisions of the BGH should be questioned on constitutional grounds. The personality and dignity of an individual, to be freely enjoyed and developed within a societal and communal framework, stand at the very center of the value system reflected in the fundamental rights protected by the Constitution. Thus, an individual's interest in his personality and dignity must be respected, and must be protected by all organs of the State (see Arts. 1 and 2 of the Constitution). Such protection should be extended, above all, to a person's private sphere, i.e., the sphere in which he desires to be left alone, to make (and to be responsible for) his own decisions, and to remain free from any outside interference. Within the area of private law, such protection is provided, inter alia, by the legal rules relating to the general right of personality.... The Federal Constitutional Court has never questioned the recognition by the civil courts of a general right of personality.

The first paragraph of § 823 of the Civil Code is a "general written law" within the meaning of Art. 5 of the Constitution. [The Court then points out that under the terms of Art. 5 the freedom of the press can be limited by an "allgemeines Gesetz," or "general written law." As the protection of a person's personality right is derived from § 823 of the Civil Code (clearly a "general written law"), it is plain that the courts did not violate Art. 5 when they recognized that injury to a person's personality right may constitute a tort.]

. . . .

II

When a "general written law" potentially limits the freedom of the press, the question arises how such limitation is to be made effective; this question must be answered exclusively in accordance with the terms of such written law. If follows that only the sanctions authorized by such written law may be used against the press to limit its freedom. This is where the argument of the complainants comes in: they contend that there is no "general written law" authorizing a money judgment to compensate for non-monetary damages suffered as a result of injury to the plaintiff's personality right. Section 253 of the Civil Code, they argue, explicitly precludes such a money judgment. Complainants further assert that by granting such money judgments the courts have exceeded the boundaries within which they are permitted by the Constitution to limit the freedom of the press. . . .

The Federal Constitutional Court can examine only the constitutional aspects of these decisions [i.e., of the decisions which permitted recovery for money damages in cases of injury to a plaintiff's personality right]. From the standpoint of constitutional law, there are two questions: first, whether the substantive result brought about by that line of decisions violates the fundamental right of freedom of the press; and secondly, whether it is consistent with the Constitution to reach that result through judicial decisions in spite of the lack of an unequivocal basis in the written law. . . .

III

[In this part of the opinion, the Court addresses the first of the two questions just formulated. It calls attention, first of all, to the fact that money judgments for violation of a plaintiff's personality right can be entered, and have been entered, not only against the press, but against other defendants as well. The line of decisions in question thus does not in any way discriminate against the press.

The Court further refers to the fact that the imposition of monetary damages for injury to non-monetary interests is not a sanction alien to the German legal system. This is shown by § 847 of the Civil Code. A substantive rule extending this sanction to cases of injury to the plaintiff's "personality right" is not unconstitutional, provided the rule is subject to proper safeguards. The rule developed by the BGH does contain the necessary safeguards. It applies only where remedies other than a money judgment (e.g., an injunction or a judgment ordering the defendant to publish a retraction), are impossible or inadequate. Furthermore, the rule developed by the BGH subjects the defendant to a duty to pay money damages only in cases where the injury to plaintiff's reputation and feelings is a grave one, and where the defendants' conduct can be characterized as seriously culpable. For these reasons, the Court concludes that the limitations which the BGH decisions (in allowing money damages for injuries to plaintiff's reputation and feelings) have imposed upon the freedom of the press, must be regarded as reasonable.

The opinion contains a hint to the effect that Art. 5 of the Constitution might be violated if in cases of this kind the courts permitted the recovery of excessively large amounts of damages. There is, however, no indication that the German courts are excessively generous in assessing such damages. In the instant case, in any event, the amount awarded to the plaintiff is distinctly modest.

The second of the two questions formulated by the Court at the end of Part II of its opinion relates not only to Art. 5 of the Constitution (freedom of the press), but equally to Art. 20 (separation of powers). The Court turns to that question—the crucial question in the case—in Part IV of its opinion.]

IV

The judge is traditionally bound by the *Gesetz* (written law). This is an inherent element of the principle of separation of powers, and thus of the rule of law. Our Constitution, however, in Art. 20 has somewhat changed the traditional formulation by providing that the judge is bound by *"Gesetz und Recht"* [i.e., written law and (other) law]. According to the generally prevailing view, this implies the rejection of a narrow positivistic approach predicated solely upon the written law. The formulation chosen in Art. 20 keeps us aware of the fact that although *Gesetz* and *Recht* in general are co-extensive, this is not necessarily always the case. The legal order is not identical with the aggregate of the written laws. Under certain circumstances there can be law beyond the positive norms enacted by the State—law which has its source in the constitutional legal order as a meaningful, all-embracing system, and which functions as a corrective of the written norms. To find this law, and to make it a reality through their decisions, is the task of the courts. The Constitution does not confine the judge to the function of applying the language of legislative mandates to the particular case before him. Such a concept [of the judicial function] would presuppose that there are no gaps in the positive [written] legal order—a condition which in the interest of legal certainty might be postulated as desirable, but which in practice is unattainable. The judge's task is not confined to the ascertainment and implementation of decisions made by the legislator; he may be called upon, through an act in the nature of a value judgment (an act which necessarily has volitional elements), to bring to light and to realize in his decisions those value concepts which are immanent in the constitutional legal order, but which are not, or not adequately, expressed in the language of the written laws. In performing this task, the judge must guard against arbitrariness; his decision must be based upon rational argumentation. He must make it clear that the written law fails to perform its function of providing a just solution for the legal problem at hand. Where this is so, the gap thus found is filled by the judge's decision in accordance with practical reason and "the community's established general concepts of justice".

In principle, this duty and power of the judge to render "creative decisions" has never been questioned since the adoption of our present Constitution. The courts at the apex of our judicial hierarchies have claimed such power from the beginning. It has always been recognized by the Federal Constitutional Court. The legislator himself bestowed upon the highest courts [i.e., the courts at the apex of each of the five judicial hierarchies] the task of "further development of the law" (see § 137 of the Law on the Organization of Courts).º In some areas of the law, such as labor law, this task has become particularly important, because legislation has not kept up with the rapid flow of social development.

There remains only the question of the limits which have to be imposed upon such creative [judicial] decision-making, keeping in mind the principle that the judge is bound by the written law, a principle that cannot be abandoned if the rule of law is to be maintained. Those limits cannot be capsulized in a formula equally applicable to all areas of the law and to all legal relationships created or controlled by the law within those areas.

For purposes of the present decision, the question just posed can be confined to the area of private law. In that area, the judge confronts a great codification, the Civil Code, which has been in force for over 70 years. This has a dual significance: in the first place, the freedom of the judge creatively to develop the law surely grows with the "aging of codifications", with the increased distance in time between the enactment of the legislative mandate and the judge's decision of an individual case. The interpretation of a written norm cannot always, for an unlimited period of time, remain tied to the meaning which the norm has been given at the time of its enactment. One has to explore what reasonable function such norm might have at the time of its application. The norm remains always in the context of the social conditions and of the socio-political views with which it is intended to interact; as these conditions and views change, the thrust of the norm can, and under certain circumstances must, be adjusted to such change. This is true especially when between the time of the enactment of a written law and the time of its application the conditions of life and peoples' views on matters of law have changed as radically as they have in the present century. The judge cannot, by simply pointing to the unchanged language of the written law, avoid the conflict that has arisen between the norm [as written] and the substantive notions of justice of a changed society. If he is not to be derelict in his duty to hand down decisions based on "law," he is forced to manipulate the legal norms more freely. Secondly, as experience demonstrates, legislative reforms encounter particularly great difficulties and obstacles when they are intended to revise a great codification, such as the Civil Code covering our private law, which has put its stamp on the system and character of the whole legal order.ᴾ

o. The Court here refers to the functions of the super-panels of the BGH and the other highest courts. The super-panels can be called upon to decide a case (a) when there is a conflict or potential conflict between two regular panels (see *supra* Chapter 6, Section 3(d) at 505 (Supreme Courts), or (b) when the regular panel (to which the case has been assigned) concludes that, because of the fundamental importance of the issue presented, a super-panel decision is required in the interest of "the further development of the law." See § 137 of the German law on the Organization of Courts.

p. The Court here emphasizes the special difficulty of *legislative* revision of a comprehensive, integrated code. The reader is familiar with this point. See *supra* Chapter 5 at 384. The implication is, of course, that when reform becomes necessary, and *legislative* revision cannot be brought about, the

The question dealt with by the decisions presently under attack [i.e., the question of recoverability of money damages for injury to a non-monetary interest] was controversial already at the time when the preparatory work on the draft of the Civil Code was in progress. The solution chosen by the legislator immediately ran into criticism—criticism which at that time did not yet involve any constitutional arguments. That criticism has never ceased. The critics were able to point to the development of the law in other countries of the Western world, where a more liberal approach has been taken toward the possibility of recovering money damages for injuries to non-monetary interests. [The Court here cites extensive comparative studies]. It was pointed out that only in Germany, and nowhere else in the Western world, could one observe large numbers of cases in which an unlawful act—causing "merely" non-monetary damages—remained without any civil sanction. The rule which permits the recovery of money damages for injury to non-monetary interests only in a few enumerated special cases—which special cases, moreover, were selected without much logic—was characterized as a "legislative failure". Criticism became even sharper after the courts, under the influence of "the Constitution's force of shaping private law," had taken the step of recognizing the general right of personality. The gap that existed in the remedies available for a violation of that right thus became visible. This problem, the importance of which could not be perceived at the time when the Civil Code was drafted, now urgently demanded a solution responsive to a changed awareness of legal rights and to the value concepts of a new Constitution. Such a solution could not be deduced from the enumeration requirement of § 253.[q]

The courts were faced with the question whether to close this gap by the methods at their disposal, or whether to wait for the intervention of the legislator. When the courts chose the first alternative, they were able to refer to the writings of influential legal authors who previously had advocated that course. From the beginning, the relevant [innovative] decisions of the BGH and of other courts were widely approved by legal scholars. This shows that these decisions were in accord with generally recognized concepts of justice, and were not regarded as intolerable restrictions upon freedom of opinion or freedom of the press. . . . Insofar as there was criticism of these decisions, such criticism was directed less against the result reached by the BGH than against the methodological and doctrinal considerations invoked by the courts to justify the new approach. To the extent that this involves methodological questions in the area of private law it is not within the province of the Federal Constitutional Court to determine the validity of the objections raised by the critics. But it should not be overlooked that the majority of the authors who are specialists in

---

need for *judicial* development of the law increases.

q. The expression "enumeration requirement" may call for some explanation. Section 253 of the Civil Code does not itself enumerate the instances in which a money judgment for injury to non-monetary interests is recoverable. But, using a method which might be described as enumeration by reference, that section provides that such a money judgment can be recovered only in the cases provided for (or enumerated) in other code sections or statutes. German courts and legal writers, therefore, often speak of the "enumeration requirement" or "enumeration principle" embodied in § 253.

the area of private law apparently regard the reasoning of the courts as dogmatically unobjectionable. Moreover, the discussions of the Private Law Section of the Society for Comparative Law, at its 1971 meeting in Mannheim, demonstrate that the position which the BGH has taken concerning this question is largely in harmony with the course of the law in other countries. From the standpoint of the Constitution, one cannot object to a result which was reached in a manner at least arguably acceptable in the private law area, and which does not (or at least not obviously) run counter to the rules of interpretation developed in that area; this is particularly true when, as here, that result serves to implement and effectively to protect an interest which the Constitution itself regards as central to its value system. Such a result is "law" in the sense of Art. 20 of the Constitution. It does not contradict, but supplements and develops, the written law.

The other alternative, to wait for legislative regulation, under the circumstance cannot be regarded as constitutionally mandated. It is true that the Federal Government has tried twice to bring about a legislative solution of the problem of private law protection of an individual's personality right. But the bills drafted in 1959 and 1967 died early in the legislative process, even though there was no indication of any legislative intention to perpetuate the status quo. The judge, who is compelled to decide every case submitted to him, thus cannot be blamed if he becomes convinced that he should not, in reliance upon a wholly uncertain future intervention of the legislator, adhere to the literal meaning of the existing written law in a case in which such adherence would to a large extent sacrifice justice.

The method by which the BGH reached the decisions in question is constitutionally unobjectionable also for a further reason: this method deviated from the written law only to the extent that such deviation was absolutely necessary in order to resolve the legal problem presented by the concrete case at hand. The BGH has not regarded § 253 in its entirety as no longer binding. Nor has it treated that provision as unconstitutional.... The BGH has left intact the principle of enumeration[r] expressed in § 253, and has merely added one situation to the legislator's own enumeration of situations in which money damages can be recovered for injury to non-monetary interests; this one addition appeared to the BGH to be compellingly justified by the evolution of social conditions, and also by a new law of higher rank, to wit, Arts. 1 and 2 of the Constitution. The BGH and other courts which followed its holdings thus have not abandoned the system of the legal order, and have not exhibited an intention to go their own way in making policy; they have merely taken a further step in developing and concretizing basic ideas that are inherent in the legal order molded by the Constitution, and they have done so by means which remain within the system. The legal rule thus found is, therefore, a legitimate part of the legal order; and as a "general Gesetz" within the meaning of Art. 5

---

r.   See *supra* note q.

of the Constitution it limits the freedom of the press.[s] The purpose of that rule is to fashion and guarantee, by the methods of private law, an effective protection of the individual's personality and dignity—i.e., of interests that stand at the center of the constitutional ordering of values—and thus, within a particular area of the law, to strengthen the effect of constitutionally protected fundamental rights. For these reasons, the constitutional arguments of the complainants must fail. . . .

NOTES AND QUESTIONS ON "CUSTOMARY LAW" AND "JURISPRUDENCE"

(1) In decisions antedating the case of Princess Soraya, German courts of last resort had claimed the power to give binding effect to a line of decisions—even to a line of decisions in conflict with a code provision or other statute—by calling it "customary law." Calling "customary law" its own practice has been the strategy used by common law courts since the early centralization of justice at Westminster Hall. And the reader will recall that the great German Jurist Savigny claimed that "Jurists" were the interpreters of the "Volksgeist," the people's spirit reflected into local laws and customs. Recent critical literature has shown how often "traditions" are "invented" for purposes of legitimization.[1]

In any event, the use which the *Reichsgericht* (the predecessor of the *Bundesgerichtshof*) has made of "customary law," and the evolution discussed in the Soraya case may appear rather startling to one who has been taught that there is no decisional law in civil-law countries and that in any event decisional law could never abrogate a provision of the written law. The use of "customary law" in quotation marks indicates some judicial unease especially in this latter respect. For analytical purposes, it seems useful to distinguish between three different levels of intensity of customary law in terms of their relation to enacted law. These are known by well-known Latin tags:

> (a) customary law *secundum legem* (following the statute): the interpretive patina formed around any permanent statute by its practical application, reflected in judicial decisions;

> (b) customary law *praeter legem* (beyond the statute): legally binding rules inspired (but not compelled) by enacted law, and not incompatible with it; and finally

> (c) customary law *contra legem* (against the statute): legally binding rules "repealing" rules of statutory law.

It may be asked how "law" can ever be *contra legem*. The (not only) semantic answer is that seemingly all now-known major legal systems with the

---

s. Concerning the meaning of the word "*Gesetz*," see *supra* note i. Does the Court explain why it treats a judge-made rule as a "*Gesetz*" within the meaning of Art. 5?

Note that such a difficulty does not arise with respect to Art. 20 of the Constitution, which speaks of "*Gesetz und Recht*." But the wording of Art. 5 presents a tougher nut to crack. Did the Court successfully crack it?

1. Eric Hobsbawm & Terence Ranger, The Invention of Tradition, Cambridge University Press, 1983.

exception of the English-language ones distinguish between the generic term for law as such and the specific term designating enacted law:

Language	Law as Such	Enacted Law
Latin	Ius	Lex
Spanish	Derecho	Ley
Italian	Diritto	Legge
French	Droit	Loi
German	Recht	Gesetz
Russian	Pravo	Zakon
Turkish	Hukuk	Kanun

This distinction is not only semantic because the specific term is usually value-neutral whereas the generic one reflects two interrelated ultimate values: justice and right (the latter in the dual sense of accurate and appropriate). It is conceivable, therefore, that the judicially-articulated notion of right and justice may trump "mere" statute. On the other hand, statutes give effect to the will of the sovereign, and provide (or should ideally provide) clear-cut legal solutions for specific problems. The resulting dilemma dates back to pre-Justinian Roman law. Julian, who codified the praetorian edict in the second century A.D., was of the view that where there was no written law, resort should be had to long-established custom, and that statutes could be abrogated not only by legislation but also by non-use (desuetude) reflecting general tacit consent. Less than two centuries thereafter, the Emperor Constantine decreed that enacted law could not be abrogated by custom. In 533, Justinian incorporated both Julian's opinion and Constantine's decree into his codification, thus giving them equal authority as enacted law. Civil lawyers (and Canon lawyers) have had to deal with this conundrum ever since—or at least since the late Middle Ages.

For the sake of proper perspective, the following points should also be kept in mind:

(a) Even in the German-speaking countries, the instances of "customary law" *praeter* or *contra legem* are few and far between. Normally, the broad general clauses of the codes themselves enable the judges to avoid undesirable results which might seem to flow from the more specific provisions applicable to a given case; and it is only in exceptional cases, in which no amount of "interpreting" the Code will suffice to reach a desired result, that resort will be had the open announcement of "creation of law" by the courts.

(b) There is thus a sharp distinction between (i) the countless instances, exemplified by almost every German case in this book, of highly persuasive but not formally binding decisions, most of which interpret, or analogize from, one or several provisions of the written law, and (ii) the rare and exceptional instances in which a line of judicial decisions, by being labeled "customary law," has been declared—sometimes in the teeth of a contrary code provision—to be the source of formally binding "law."[2]

(c) In recent years, constitutional attacks have been launched against the notion that courts can create binding "customary law" and especially against the constitutionality much more questionable notion of their power to modify or repeal provisions of written law. As a result of these attacks (which we shall soon survey in detail, see *infra* this sec.), the courts' power to create such "customary law" has been restricted.

Was that power to create "customary law" enlarged or diminished by the Constitutional Court's holding and reasoning in the *Soraya* case? The more recent case which follows makes the answer completely clear.

Opinion of the German Federal Constitutional Court Concerning the Constitutional Complaints of Two Trustees in Bankruptcy

Second Panel, October 18, 1983.

BVerfGE 65, 182, also reported in NJW 1984, 475.

[On the basis of statutory provisions contained in the *Betriebsverfassungsgesetz* (Enterprise Organization Law), employees who lose their jobs because of the closing of a business or plant frequently acquire claims for severance pay. That statute was silent on the important and much-litigated question of the priority (if any) that should be accorded to such claims in the employer's bankruptcy. The issue of priorities, i.e., of the rank order in which claims are to be satisfied, is, however, explicitly and comprehensively addressed in Section 61 of the German Bankruptcy Law. Stated in somewhat simplified form, the rank order established by Section 61 in effect at the time was as follows:

Class I: Claims of employees for wages earned during the last year before bankruptcy.

Class II: Tax claims of enumerated government units.

Class III: Claims of School Districts and other public institutions not enumerated in Class II.

Class IV: Claims of physicians and hospitals for services rendered during the last year.

Class V: Claims of the bankrupt's children and wards that arise out of the management (by the bankrupt) of claimants' property.

Class VI: All other claims.[a]

---

2. A comprehensive survey (already in need of supplementation) is Karl Doehring (ed.), Richterliche Rechtsfortbildung, Erscheinungsformen, Auftrag und Grenzen (Festschrift der Juristischen Fakultät zur 600–Jahr–Feier der Ruprecht–Karls–Universität Heidelberg, 1986)—with no less than thirty contributions to the subject.

a. The comparable provision of our own Bankruptcy Act appears in 11 U.S.C.A. § 507 (2005).

The statutory claims of employees for severance pay were not claims for wages earned during the last year and hence do not come within Class I.[b] Section 61 of the German Bankruptcy Law as then in effect thus relegated claims for severance pay to Class VI.[c] Whether as a matter of social policy this should be regarded as a desirable result, became a hotly debated question. In numerous cases coming before the labor courts, employees and their lawyers developed various legal theories that were aimed at taking severance pay claims out of Class VI and giving them a higher priority. After much conflict and turmoil, the court at the apex of the labor court hierarchy, the *Bundesarbeitsgericht* (BAG) by way of a super-panel decision finally held in 1978 that claims for severance pay were entitled to a rank ahead of all classes of claims described in Section 61, i.e., ahead of Class I.[d] To justify this holding, the BAG invoked reasons of social policy and a provision of the German Constitution stating that the Federal Republic of Germany is a "democratic and social federal State" (article 20(1)). Although the holding was in conflict with the scheme of Section 61 of the Bankruptcy Law, it was consistently followed in subsequent decisions of the BAG.

In the instant case the Labor Court as court of first instance, following the said decisions of the BAG, held that the employees' claims for severance pay ranked ahead of Class I. Affirming that holding on appeal, the intermediate appellate court and the BAG equally accorded super-priority to those claims. The Constitutional Court *reversed*.

The Constitutional Court pointed out that the subject of bankruptcy priorities is regulated by Section 61 of the Bankruptcy Law, which sets forth a clear and exhaustive scheme of classification and rank order. In view of its "breadth and indefiniteness," the constitutional principle of social justice contained, "as a rule, no immediate directions for action which the courts can transform into binding law *without statutory authority*."[e]]

In contrast to the so-called *Soraya* case ... the present case does not involve the protection of the general right of personality, which in view of Articles 1 and 2 of the Basic Law occupies a central place in the value

---

b. In our law, claims for severance pay are equated with wage claims for purposes of bankruptcy priority. See subdiv. (a)(3)(A) of § 507, *supra* note a.

c. Experience shows that Class VI creditors in most cases receive nothing or very little.

d. BAG (Super–Panel), Decision of Dec. 13, 1978, 1979 NJW 774.

e. 65 BVerfGE at 193 (emphasis supplied). In applying general clauses such as Sections 138 or 242 of the Civil Code which supply the necessary "statutory authority," however, courts are not only authorized but also bound to give due consideration to the principle of social justice. 93 BVerfGE 89, 214 (1993). As to the legal effects of that constitutional mandate, see generally Michael Sachs, Grundgesetz, Kommentar 629–30 (1996). The Court, while affirming the duty of Parliament to give effect to the principle of social justice, has accepted a substantial measure of legislative discretion in that regard. 82 BVerfGE 60, 81 (1990); 84 BVerfGE 90, 125 (1991). In any event, Parliament promptly enacted legislation outside of the Bankruptcy Law which gave first priority along with wage claims etc. (but not super-priority). Act of February 20, 1985, § 4, 1985 I BGBl 369.

system of our basic rights. In *Soraya* the BGH dealt with cases of grave violations of an absolute right already recognized by the legal order, and merely added a further sanction, i.e., the awarding of monetary damages for non-physical injuries. The decisions of the BAG, on the other hand, which interfere with the statutory order of bankruptcy priorities in favor of one group of creditors, gravely disadvantage all other groups of creditors. . . . Unlike the BGH in the *Soraya* case, the BAG could, finally, not assert that its judge-made rule is supported by a generally prevailing legal opinion. . . . This is shown by the divided reception which its ruling has encountered in the [legal] literature.

NOTES AND QUESTIONS

(1) Neither of the two preceding opinions of the German Federal Constitutional Court throws any doubt on the proposition that, even in a legal system heavily emphasizing the primacy of the written law, the courts may and indeed must play a creative law-making role (a) in deriving concrete results from code provisions of utmost generality, and (b) in dealing with gaps in the written law. The two opinions focus on a relatively narrow problem: whether and under what conditions an unambiguous mandate of the written law may be modified or bent by judge-made "customary" law or by some other form of decisional law.

(2) In the *Soraya* case, the Constitutional Court put its stamp of approval on a rule of judge-made law although that rule was concededly *contra legem*. In the bankruptcy case, the same Court struck down a rule of decisional law modifying a statutory scheme. It is obvious, therefore, that the Court is trying to draw a line. The courts of the various judicial hierarchies will be permitted to create judge-made law *contra legem* on one side of the line, but not on the other.

(3) German legal writers have criticized the Constitutional Court for not etching that line with sufficient clarity.[1] A truly careful reading of the *Soraya* opinion, however, shows that in that case the Constitutional Court upheld the judge-made rule fashioned by the BGH only because it met all of the following conditions:

> (a) According to the overwhelmingly prevailing view of German judges, lawyers and legal authors—a view strongly fortified by comparative research—a provision contained in an old Code had become unbearable in the light of social developments and changed attitudes.

> (b) The old Code provision, if literally applied, would come into conflict with value judgments *clearly* expressed in the Constitution.

> (c) Over a long period of time it had turned out that legislative reform could not be expected.

> (d) The judicially imposed reform did not go further than absolutely necessary.

1. See, e.g., J. H. Bauer & C. Moench, Sozialplanabfindungen im Konkurs, 1984 NJW 468, 469.

In the bankruptcy case, on the other hand, it would have been absurd to argue that the BAG's rule of decisional law met all of these conditions. Thus it should not be difficult to see the distinction between the two cases.[2]

(4) It should be noted that while the *Soraya* case involved freedom of the press as well as separation of powers, the Constitutional Court's decision in the bankruptcy case rested exclusively on the separation of powers provision of the Basic Law.

The Constitutional Court has also invoked the Equal Protection clause of the German Basic Law in order to strike down judge-made rules improperly modifying provisions of written law. A recent case of this kind involved a provision of the German Income Tax Law which grants the benefit of a reduced tax rate to a certain group of taxpayers. Without any basis in the statute, the *Bundesfinanzhof* (BFH), the highest court in tax matters, in a line of decisions, had excluded a particular sub-group of that group from the benefit of the said provision. The Constitutional Court disapproved that line of decisions, holding that the courts violate the Equal Protection clause of the Basic Law by according unequal treatment to different members of a group all of whom are treated equally by the written law.[3] *Quaere* whether this holding, if pressed to its ultimate logical consequences, will not convert an undue number of issues of statutory construction into constitutional issues?[4]

7. CONCLUDING OBSERVATIONS ON *STARE DECISIS*

(a) *Civilian Theory and Civilian Practice.* The (supposedly) "classical" civilian doctrine, that the judge can never create law, has broken down in practice. This fact is recognized by everybody, even though the text-writers have found it difficult to fit the actual existence of case law into the framework of civilian theory.[1]

2. A further reason for striking down the judge-made rule in the bankruptcy case may have been that the complexity and multiplicity of the interests involved in that case required a balanced and fine-tuned solution of the kind the courts are ill-equipped to fashion. See T. Raiser, Richterrecht heute, Zeitschrift fuer Rechtspolitik 1985, pp. 111 ff., especially at 117.

3. Federal Constitutional Court, Decision of January 14, 1986, reported in 1986 NJW 2242. To the same effect see BVerfGE 66,331, also reported in 1984 NJW 2346. In the income tax case the Constitutional Court apparently assumed that *the Legislature*, without violating the Equal Protection clause of the Basic Law, could have deprived the sub-group of the benefits bestowed on other members of the group. But *the courts* were held to have violated the Equal Protection clause by disregarding the statutory command to treat all members of the entire group alike. Would the U.S. Supreme Court, in dealing with a state statute, go to similar lengths?

4. The query posed in the text, *supra*, is by no means academic. The reader will recall that under German law, if an issue is thus "constitutionalized," the jurisdiction of the Constitutional Court is brought into play. The reports of the Supreme Court of Mexico are full of *amparo* cases adjudicating the "correctness" of State statutory interpretation, held to be within the ambit of the "due process" guarantee of the Federal Constitution (Article 14(2)).

1. The difficulty stems in part from the impossibility of drawing a sharp line between "making" and "applying" law, and from a wide-spread failure to recognize that the two functions are not only complementary but interrelated and interacting in exceedingly

What has caused the breakdown of the classic doctrine (also known as Byzantine doctrine because incorporated in the Digest)? The reasons, no doubt, are numerous and complex; but some factors can be identified:

(i) It has been said that "a principle of mental economy leads judges to follow the opinions of their predecessors rather than to develop their own views, untrammeled by authority."[2]

(ii) Certainty and predictability of the law, a strong legitimating device of professional legal culture allegedly functional to the proper functioning of a complex modern economy, surely would suffer if judges were in the habit of disregarding their prior pronouncements.

(iii) Equality, perhaps the most basic element of justice, would give way to arbitrariness if, without compelling reasons justifying an exception, unequal decisions were made upon identical facts.

(iv) A subordinate court, moreover, will follow the decisions of a higher court for the simple reason that judges do not like to be reversed. This seems to be a world-wide phenomenon; but the fear of reversal is, of course, particularly strong in countries in which the judge is a civil servant whose promotion may be adversely affected if too many of his decisions are reversed.[3] In civil-law countries, most of which have a civil service judiciary, this may create a special pressure for lower court conformance with precedents—a pressure which occasionally may be as strong as the impact of the doctrine of *stare decisis* upon lower judges of the common-law world.

This enumeration of factors, though far from exhaustive, may serve to explain and to emphasize the undeniable fact that decisional law is playing an ever-growing role in the civil-law world. If we further consider that in the common-law orbit, and especially in the United States, the doctrine of *stare decisis* has lost much of its seeming rigidity, the conclusion is clear

---

complex ways. For a thorough comparative study of this problem, with emphasis on its jurisprudential aspects, see Esser, Grundsatz und Norm in der richterlichen Fortbildung des Privatrechts (1956).

2. K. Lipstein, The Doctrine of Precedent in Continental Law with Special Reference to French and German Law, 28 J.Comp. Leg. & Int'l L. (3d Ser.) 34, at 36 (1946).

From the standpoint of a judge, especially one who does not suffer from illusions of infallibility, there are additional considerations pointing in the same direction as that mentioned in the text, *supra*. Modesty and self-restraint will lead judges everywhere to the "humbling assumption, often true, that no particular court as it is then constituted possesses a wisdom surpassing that of its predecessors." People v. Hobson, 39 N.Y.2d 479, 488, 384 N.Y.S.2d 419, 425, 348 N.E.2d 894, 900 (Breitel, C.J., 1976). See also Baden v. Staples, 45 N.Y.2d 889, 892, 410 N.Y.S.2d 808, 809, 383 N.E.2d 110, 111 (1978).

3. In some civil-law countries, every affirmance or reversal of a lower court opinion is reported to the Ministry of Justice and noted in the personnel file of the judge who wrote the opinion below. See, e.g., Karlen and Arsel, Civil Litigation in Turkey 76 (1957).

In Peru, the performance of all lower court judges is periodically reviewed by the members of the highest court sitting as a "jury." Substantial numbers of lower court judges are discharged as a result of such review. This procedure tends to increase the respect of lower courts for the decisions of the court of last resort. See D. B. Furnish, The Hierarchy of Peruvian Laws: Context for Law and Development, 19 Am.J.Comp.L. 91, 101–02 (1971).

that civil-law and common-law attitudes toward the judicial function are slowly converging.[4]

(b) In a common-law system, judicial decisions constitute part of "the law." Therefore, without a doctrine of *stare decisis*, that part of "the law" which is judicially-developed (judge-made) would be uncertain.[5] In a code system, codes and auxiliary statutes are the main body of "the law." In theory, the courts merely "apply" and "interpret" the law. As the written law is thought to provide the necessary element of certainty, judicial decisions need not, and at least in theory might not, have binding force under such a system.[6]

As a general proposition, therefore, and as a convenient starting point for discussion, it is correct to state that in common-law jurisdictions judicial decisions are binding on subordinate courts, and in some measure on co-ordinate courts and on the deciding court itself, while the civil-law world does not regard judicial pronouncements as binding in subsequent cases.[7] But the statement needs to be qualified. First of all, we must allow for the great variations which exist within the common-law world. We know, for instance, that in this country the doctrine of *stare decisis* is applied less rigidly than in England.[8] Secondly, to the broad assertion that in the whole civil-law world the courts are never bound by precedents, we must hasten to add at least the following qualifications:

(i) Under German and French procedure, which we have studied earlier (*supra*), an *en banc* or super-panel decision is required in certain cases in which a division of the highest court desires to deviate from a prior ruling of the court.

(ii) Some civil-law countries, especially in the Spanish speaking world, have constitutional or statutory provisions to the effect that a

---

4. See Esser, *supra*, note 1 especially at 221 ff.; A. F. M. Plötzgen, Präjudizienrecht im angelsächsischen Rechtskreis 11 (1979).

5. Once the doctrine is established, common-law courts tend to apply it, also, to precedents which merely interpret a statute. See H. C. Gutteridge, A Comparative View of the Interpretation of Statute Law, 8 Tul. L.Rev. 1, 16 (1933). This may not be too logical, but a contrary view would lead to practical difficulties in the many instances in which a single decision is based partly on statutes and partly on common law.

6. Resorting to exaggeration in order to drive home the point, one might say that, in a common-law system, the case law, made binding by the doctrine of *stare decisis*, represents an element of stability, and that change is brought about mainly by statutory law. In the civil law, on the other hand, the codes provide some certainty (at least verbal cer-

tainty) and structural stability, while judicial "interpretation," unfettered by a formal rule of *stare decisis*, constitutes an element of flexibility.

7. Until reading all of the materials in this chapter, the reader should suspend judgment as to what practical difference it makes whether judicial precedents are formally binding or not. At this point, attention should be focused on the basic difference between common-law and civil-law theory. The reader already is familiar with some of the historical reasons for this difference .. For further light on the historical and doctrinal roots of this difference, see John P. Dawson, The Oracles of the Law (1968).

8. See P. S. Atiyah & Robert S. Summers, Form and Substance in Anglo–American Law: A Comparative Study of Legal Reasoning, Legal Theory, and Legal Institutions (1987), especially at 115–56.

certain number of successive decisions, all of which express the same view on the same point of law, shall have the force of a controlling precedent. In Mexico, for instance, five uninterrupted decisions of chambers of the Supreme Court by majority of at least four votes, as well as plenary decisions of that court resolving differences between the decisional law of two of its Chambers and supported by fourteen votes, constitute *jurisprudencia* and are binding on all inferior tribunals, whether federal or State.[9] The Spanish rules concerning what was called until recently *"doctrina legal"*, now *jurispridencia*, although not themselves specifying the required number of successive decisions, have a similar effect.[10]

In Brazil, the official headnotes of certain appellate decisions— either rendered en banc or sufficiently repetitive to reflect the weight of authority—can be inscribed in a collection called the *Súmula*; they then acquire a "de facto *stare decisis*" effect.[11]

(iii) In Germany and Italy, and also in other civil-law countries which have a separate Constitutional Court, certain decisions of that Court shall have the force of law. This is routinely the case where that Court holds a statute (or part of a statute) unconstitutional, but in at least some countries (Germany, now also Spain) binding effect extends to the *ratio decidendi*.[12]

---

9. Ley de Amparo, article 192, implementing Constitution, article 107. Since the word *jurisprudencia* appears in the latter document as well, it is common ground in Mexico today that the *jurisprudencia* of the Supreme Court as defined in the Ley de Amparo is a source of law. See, e.g., Genaro Góngora Pimentel, Introducción al Estudio de Amparo 413–31 (3d ed. 1990), citing cases. Richard D. Baker, Judicial Review in Mexico, A Study of the *Amparo* Suit (1971) is still useful for background.

10. The history of these rules is not without interest. A Royal Decree of 1838 permitted annulation appeals to the Supreme Court of Spain not only for violations of statute law but also of *doctrina legal*, redefined as *"doctrina* established by the Tribunals" in the 1855 Code of Civil Procedure. The Supreme Court interpreted these terms to mean rules laid down by two separate decisions of that Court, but not of inferior tribunals. Since Spanish civil law was not codified until 1889, this double coup d'état was accepted gratefully by the legal system as supplying a means of legal certainty not obtainable from the Legislature. Antonio Serrano, Die "Doctrina legal" des spanischen "Tribunal Supremo" in der rechtshistorischen Analyse des Justizbegriffs, 16 Ius Commune 219, 219–20 & 241 (1989). The 1984 revision of the Code of Civil Procedure substituted *jurisprudencia* for *doctrina legal* as a ground for appeal to the Supreme Court (article 1692(5)). This displacement of a "genuinely Spanish term" has been deplored by a commentator. Manuel Serra Dominguez, in Valentin Cortes, ed., Comentarios a la Reforma de la ley de Enduiciamiento Civil 828, 852 (1985). As there acknowledged, however, *jurisprudencia* (French: *jurisprudence*) is currently a more appropriate term for judicially-developed rules than *doctrina* (French: *doctrine)* which in Romance-language legal terminology stands for taught law.

11. K. S. Rosenn, Civil Procedure in Brazil, 34 Am. J. Comp. L. 487, 513–14 (1986).

12. Section 31(1) of the (German) Federal Constitutional Law Statute, implementing article 94(2) of the Basic Law (Constitution), provides: "The decisions of the Federal Constitutional Court bind the constitutional organs of the Federation and of the States as well as all courts and government agencies." It is well established now that his "binding" effect includes the *rationes decidendi*. Klaus Stern, 2 Das Staatsrecht der Bundesrepublik Deutschland 1037–39 (1980) with citations.

(iv) Like other socialist legal systems, China's legal system too is based on a modified version of civil law. At the same time, the influence of the common law—both in its substantive and institutional aspects—has grown considerably over the last few decades, as Chinese lawyers have come into increasing contact with U.S. lawyers in China and more and more Chinese lawyers have obtained degrees in law schools in the United States. However, one continuing aspect of the civil law heritage is that judicial decisions do not have formal precedential value. Needless to say, in the People's Republic of China, as in conventional civil law jurisdictions, adjudicated cases do nevertheless generate many kinds of norms, some of which are more binding than others. Yet at the outset perhaps the most noteworthy aspect in this regard is the fact that, constitutionally, the power to interpret laws is a *legislative* function that belongs to the National People's Congress, to be exercised by its Standing Committee (NPC–SC). As a socialist legal system, the PRC is not based on the notion of separation of powers. From this perspective, the legislature is regarded as being in the best, and proper, position to interpret the laws it has enacted. In fact, however, it is difficult—indeed impossible—for the NPC–SC to provide sufficient interpretation in order for courts to fulfill their functions. In practice, these "legislative interpretations" (effectively, legislative amendments) have been relatively rare. Besides, even such legislative interpretations ultimately require judicial interpretation when applied in the context of specific adjudications.

It is therefore not surprising that even in China there exists something like "the functional equivalent of case law in other jurisdictions."[13] China's highest court, the Supreme People's Court (SPC), has in fact considerable powers which are judicial, legislative, as well as administrative in nature. Although cases are not published systematically in China, the SPC in fact publishes some of its decisions in its legal publication, the Gazette. For lower courts, these cases provide what has been called—somewhat oxymoronically—"binding guidance,"[14] a kind of *de facto* system of precedent. In addition to this type of garden-variety judicial interpretation, the SPC also issues other types of guidance to lower courts. Some of them are replies to specific legal questions submitted by lower courts, others are quasi-legislative general "opinions" regarding particular laws, yet others are rules that are administrative in nature. When the President of the SPC was asked some time ago whether the PRC legal system was closer to the civil law or the common law model, he responded, with a great deal of common sense, "Neither, it is Chinese law with Chinese characteristics."[15]

13. Albert Chen, An Introduction to the Legal System of the People's Republic of China 118 (Butterworths Asia 3d ed. 2004).

14. Ronald C. Brown, Understanding Chinese Courts and Legal Process 81 (Kluwer Law International 1997).

15. Ibid. at 82.

(v) Most civil-law systems recognize "customary law" as a subsidiary source of law, i.e., a source that can be used to fill gaps in the written law. In general, the practical importance of this source of law tends to be limited. There are occasional instances, however, in which a particular line of decisions of the highest court is said to have created a rule of "customary law." See the German cases *infra* this section. Needless to say, by thus being converted into "customary law," certain judicial decisions are given the force of law and acquire the status of binding precedents.

Although subject (at least) to these exceptions and qualifications, it remains true that the civilians are reluctant to accord formally binding force to judicial precedents. Earlier this century, when that attitude was particularly strong, some prominent scholars believed that, at least in theory, this created a gulf between civilian thinking and ours.[16] Much has been written on the subject, under the heading of Jurisprudence as well as Comparative Law. Some writers go so far as to regard a given jurisdiction's attitude toward *stare decisis* as the principal touchstone determining whether it is a common-law or a civil-law jurisdiction. The treatment of precedents by Louisiana courts, for instance, has played a major part in the scholarly controversy concerning the question whether that State is still a civil-law jurisdiction.[17]

(3) A judicial decision rendered in a civil-law country, and not constituting a binding precedent in such country, may become binding elsewhere by a strange process of transplantation. In Puerto Rico, for instance, it was held that the Insular Legislature, when it reenacted a Civil Code almost entirely copied from that of Spain, adopted not only the provisions of the Code but also the interpretations previously placed upon them by the highest court of Spain. See Olivieri v. Biaggi, 17 P.R.R. 676 (1911); Marchan v. Eguen, 44 P.R.R. 396 (1933). Spanish decisions, which under the civil-law doctrine may have had no binding force in Spain, and which were not binding in Puerto Rico when it was a Spanish possession, thus became binding precedents under American rule. Is this the necessary result of reenactment of a civil-law-inspired statute or code? Or is the well-known rule that, by reenacting a statute the legislature presumably adopts prior judicial interpretations of the statutory language, itself an outgrowth of common-law thinking? If so, is it sound to apply this rule of statutory interpretation to a civilian code, reenacted by legislators who were probably not thinking in common-law terms, without asking whether that rule of statutory interpretation was also part of the pertinent civil-law tradition at the time material?

16. See, e.g., Pound, The Theory of Judicial Decision, 36 Harv.L.Rev. 641, 645–49 (1923).

17. This question is debated at least once every generation. One such debate was between Ireland, Louisiana's Legal System Reappraised, 11 Tul.L.Rev. 585, 591–2 (1937) (answer: No), and Daggett, Dainow, Hebert & McMahon, A Reappraisal Appraised: A Brief for the Civil Law of Louisiana, 12 Tul.L.Rev. 12, 17–24 (1937) (answer: Yes).

(4) Finally, consider the following: In recent years, legal historians have embarked on detailed studies of the publication of judicial decisions from the late Middle Ages to the present. Prominent among such studies is *Judicial Records, Law Reports, and the Growth of Case Law*, edited by Professor John H. Baker in 1989. The 11th British Legal History Conference held at the University of Exeter in July, 1993, was devoted entirely to the history of law report.[18]

One probable result of such studies is that *stare decisis* and, more particularly, a well-established theory of judicial precedent are of much more recent origin in English law than is ordinarily supposed.[19] Another, even more remarkable insight is that *stare decisis* is readily traced to medieval canon law or, more particularly, to the jurisprudence of the *Rota Romana*. Thus not only are there "common-law" or "civil-law" attitudes, but also significant variations from time to time and place to place within the families.

(5) *Civilian Practice and Common–Law Practice.* Not all differences between common-law and civilian methods in the treatment of precedents have disappeared. Some of the remaining differences are clearly observable; others are more elusive and controversial.

(a) Clearly, the two systems differ concerning the question of the relative weight to be accorded to judicial authority and to the authority of legal writers. The very term "secondary authority," by which we deprecate the scholar's interpretation of the law, as distinguished from "the law" laid down by the judges, does not exist in the civilians' vocabulary.

Civilian text-writers are much bolder in their criticism of judicial opinions, while courts in civil-law countries show more respect for the scholar's view than is customary in the common-law world.[20] Overwhelming disapproval of a rule of case law by the academic commentators often induces a civil-law court to reexamine its holding.

As an experienced observer of both systems remarked some time ago, the average practitioner in a civil-law country

> "can quickly obtain information in a systematic form on any subject of the law through monographs and commentaries, large or little; and this refers also to new important statutes, on which commentaries appear often immediately after their enactment and before the courts have had occasion to interpret them.[21]

18. John H. Baker (ed.), Judicial Records, Law Reports, and the Growth of Case Law (1989); Chantal Stebbins (ed.), Law Reporting in England (1995).

19. Cf. E. M. Wise, The Doctrine of *Stare decisis*, 21 Wayne L.Rev. 1043, 1047–51 (1975).

20. Concerning the historical reasons for this attitude, see Angelesco, La technique législative en matière de codification civile 445 ff. (1930). A much-cited but dated history of code interpretation by French textwriters is Gaudemet, L'Interprétation du code civil en France (1935).

21. As there are generally no citators or similar mechanical tools in civil-law countries, a commentary, textbook, or register of decisions keyed to statutes also will serve as the practitioner's efficient and time-saving guide to the cases in point. (This might change some due to the expanding possibility of automatic electronic retrieval.)

"With this literature the lawyer must be familiar. For lawyers, when working on a case, first reach for the commentaries, not for the reports; and in briefs the literature is quoted at least as often as court decisions. When a lawyer in a "civil-law" country has a legal problem which is not definitely settled by statute he may be satisfied to solve it without reference to decisions, but never without the literature."[22]

No wonder, then, that doctrinal influence on the development of the law is strong in civil-law countries.[23] Some of the modern codes, especially the Swiss Civil Code recognize this influence by expressly reminding the judges that in deciding novel or doubtful questions they should consult "approved legal doctrine" (Fr. *doctrine*) as well as "judicial tradition" (Fr. *jurisprudence*).[24]

In common-law countries, the trend seems to be in the same direction; but there is still a discernible difference of degree.

(b) In some civil-law countries, the courts are reluctant to rely on a single precedent, even though it may be on point, and instead are much more easily persuaded by a line of decisions.[25] This is in direct contrast to the English doctrine of *stare decisis*,[26] while in the United States the courts

22. Moses, International Legal Practice, 4 Fordham L.Rev. 244, 266 (1935). To the same effect, see Razi, Guided Tour in a Civil Law Library, 56 Mich.L.Rev. 375 (1958).

23. Occasionally this influence transcends national frontiers. In Latin America, especially, textbooks of French, Italian, and occasionally German origin are much in use, sometimes in the form of Spanish translations. It may be expected, however, that this foreign influence will decline as a result of the growing productiveness of scholars in Latin America.

24. In those civil-law countries whose law has remained uncodified, the influence of certain authors is even greater. In Scotland, for instance, "there is no doubt that opinions expressed in works of certain authors referred to as the 'institutional writers' enjoy a special authority—an authority which Lord Normand set as just inferior to that of a House of Lords decision." T. B. Smith, Authors and Authority, 12 (N.S.) J.Soc.Pub.T. of L. 3, 7–8 (1972). Concerning the similar situation in South Africa, see Reinhard Zimmermann, Roman Law in a Mixed Legal System—The South African Legal Experience, in Robin Evans–Jones (ed.), The Civil Law Tradition in Scotland 41, especially at 55–58 (Stair Society 1995), with further references including statistics. See also id. at 63: "It is writers like Voet and Grotius, Van Leeuwen and Groenewegen, Vinnius and Van der Keessel who carry specific weight. If they agree on a particular question, their view is binding for a modern South African court."

25. In the most advanced civil-law countries, however, this attitude is changing. In France, for instance, there used to be a well-known saying that "The student weighs the precedents; the practitioner counts them." 1 Planiol–Ripert, Traité élémentaire de droit civil 56 (1948). This reflected the view that in practice only a "*jurisprudence constante*" could fix the state of the law. More recently, however, this view has been called obsolete and erroneous by Professor Tunc, who asserts that, at least so far as decisions of the Cour de Cassation are concerned, a single precedent in point "pratiquement" establishes the law. See A. & S. Tunc, Le droit des États–Unis d'Amérique—sources et techniques 179–81 (1955). It must be remembered, moreover, that in France and Germany a panel of the court of last resort may not deviate from a decision—even a single decision—of another panel without submitting the matter to a super-panel.

The reader should keep in mind that the statement in the text refers only to some (probably the more old-fashioned) of the civil-law systems.

26. See Goodhart, Precedent in English and Continental Law, 50 L.Q.Rev. 40 (1934).

occasionally indicate that there may be a difference of degree between the binding force of a single precedent and that of a line of cases.[27]

(c) Civilians as a rule seem to be disinclined to draw fine distinctions between holding and dictum. Occasionally, however, a German court of last resort, when driven by its *horror pleni* (see *supra* at 520), will excuse its disregard of a rule announced in a prior case by explaining that the result reached in the former case did not "rest upon" such rule.

A civilian often displays a lack of interest in the precise facts of the former case on which he relies—an attitude shocking to the common-law mind. The abstract proposition which can be distilled from a precedent or a line of precedents is more likely to impress itself on a civilian's memory than the factual setting in which that proposition was applied.[28] This attitude of course is determined to a great extent by the less clear-cut institutional distinction between what is "the fact" (belonging to the jury) and what is "the law" (belonging to the judge) within procedural traditions developed without jury trial. The very fact that non-common law traditions appeal on the facts as well as on the law bears an impact on the actual working of a case-law system.

(d) In a common-law system, where judges openly avow that they are making and not merely "discovering" law,[29] little theoretical difficulty is encountered in holding that the courts, like legislators, in principle have the power to give a newly announced rule of case law either prospective or retroactive effect.[30] But where, as in the civil-law systems, the law-making power of the judiciary is in theory denied, or recognized only in exceptional circumstances, it becomes much harder to justify a judicial decision laying down a new rule for the future only, i.e., a decision which admits that the law *was* otherwise but *is being changed by the court.* If it is assumed that the court does not make law but only finds what always has been the law, it is difficult to escape the conclusion that today's holding, although perhaps overruling prior decisions, merely "finds" a rule which (at least in a non-existential and rather transcendental form) has been in force since the enactment of the code section or statute which the court purports to "interpret." It is probably due to these conceptual difficulties that most civil-law courts thus far have failed to avail themselves of the technique of prospective overruling of prior decisions. Even in Germany, where the

---

27. See, e.g., Kimball v. Grantsville City, 19 Utah 368, 57 P. 1 (1899); St. Germain v. Lapp, 72 R.I. 42, 48 A.2d 181 (1946).

28. In some of the civil-law countries, this way of looking at judicial decisions is reflected in, and in turn reinforced by, the form of the law reports, which may fail to contain an accurate statement of the facts, or even (as in Italy) be limited to what we would call headnotes.

29. See U.S. ex rel. Durocher v. LaVallee, 330 F.2d 303, 312 (2d Cir.1964), cert.

denied, 377 U.S. 998, 84 S.Ct. 1921 (1964), and authorities there cited.

30. The Supreme Court of the United States has even developed rules for the intertemporal application of constitutional precedent, distinguishing between non-criminal and criminal cases and, within the latter category, the subcategories of incremental and "new" precedents. See Hans W. Baade, Time and Meaning Notes on the Intertemporal Law of Statutory Construction and Constitutional Interpretation, 43 Am.J.Comp.L. 319, 331–36 (1995).

Bundesgerichtshof in recent years has discussed and occasionally used the technique,[31] the court found it necessary to justify this step by resort to complex and unrealistic notions of changes in "customary law."[32]

(e) From the theoretical premise that judges do not make law, it also follows that (subject to exceptions and qualifications we have previously noted) judicial decisions are not binding in other similar cases that may subsequently arise. The judges before whom these other cases are brought, in civil-law theory are free from any constraint of *stare decisis*. In practice, this freedom is seldom used; but occasionally it is asserted (very clear in *Hardoin v. Hartford, supra*), with the result that even lower courts sometimes display a rather independent attitude, especially where controversial issues or borderline questions are involved.[33] Particularly in instances in which decisions of the highest court have been subjected to criticism by the more prominent legal writers, such independence of intermediate or lower courts may assert itself rather forcefully.[34]

It must be remembered, in this connection, that one of the principal reasons for the lower courts' adherence to precedent is fear of reversal. In the many cases which cannot be appealed to the highest court,[35] the lower courts make ample use of their freedom from binding precedents.

(f) Precedents affect only the "law" to be applied to a case, and not the "facts." Therefore, in a comparative appraisal of the effect of precedents, we must ask ourselves whether civil law and common law are in agreement as to where to draw the line between "law" and "facts." The answer is in the negative. In the law of torts, in particular, the civilians treat many issues as factual which to us are issues of law.[36] This, of course, tends to

31. See C. H. Fulda, Prospective Overruling of Court Decisions in Germany and the United States, 13 Am.J.Comp.L. 438 (1964). The Court of Justice of the European Communities also has on occasion made its decisions applicable prospectively.

32. See the decisions of July 8, 1955, BGHZ 18, 81, and especially of June 19, 1962, BGHZ 37, 219.

Quaere whether the theory of these decisions should now be modified in the light of the opinion of the Federal Constitutional Court in the *Soraya* case, *supra* at 596.

33. See Goodhart, *supra* note 26. For a fascinating example (involving the lower courts' refusal to go along with the Cour de Cassation when the latter court permitted the enforcement of outrageous contractual penalty clauses), see J. Beardsley, Compelling Contract Performance in France, 1 Hastings Int'l & Comp.L.Rev. 93, 104–07 (1977).

34. It has been remarked above, in pt. 2(a) of these Notes, that vigorous criticism by leading scholars, directed at a decision or line of decisions of the highest court, may induce that court to re-examine its position. A fortiori, a re-examination may be forced upon the court of last resort in instances where a number of intermediate appellate courts and other lower courts—perhaps influenced by scholarly writings—refuse to accept the view previously expressed by the highest court. For an interesting example, see E. Wahl & H. Soell, Ersatzansprüche wegen Unfruchtbarmachung auf Grund unrichtiger Entscheidung des Erbgesundheitsgerichts, 167 Arch.Civ.Pr. 1, at 28 (1967).

35. E.g., actions originally brought in an inferior court. Ordinarily, an appeal can be taken from the inferior court's judgment to the lowest or the intermediate layer of the hierarchy of courts of general jurisdiction; but many legal systems do not permit a further appeal to the highest court in such a case.

36. See *supra* Chapter 6, Section 3(c) at 496 (discussing issues of Law and Facts on Appeals) and Chapter 9 at 863. In the law of contracts, also, some civil-law systems (especially the French) tend to treat as factual, and governed by "the intention of the parties," many questions which in our view are

increase, in the civil-law orbit, the lower courts' area of freedom from precedents.

(6) *The Mortal Danger of Generalization.* Much that has been written on the subject (including, perhaps, some of the preceding remarks) suffers from the defects which necessarily attend the use of too wide a brush.

We have seen that the significance of case law, and the method of its use, vary *from time to time*. It is no less important to remember that such variations can be observed also (a) *from subject to subject* and (b) *from country to country*.

(a) It has been pointed out above, but the point bears repeating, that the substantive codes and auxiliary statutes which were passed by civilian legislators during the 19th and 20th centuries embody provisions of two different kinds:

(i) With respect to certain subject matters, the legislator consciously refrained from laying down any detailed rules and limited himself to the formulation of a broad and sweeping principle. The greater part of the German law of unfair competition, for example, is governed by the sole provision that any competitive act which is contra bonos mores is illegal. (Section 1 of the German Law Against Unfair Competition). Such "blank norms" have been construed as express legislative authorization for the creation of decisional law, and in the fields governed by norms of this type the courts have consciously set about to build up a body of case law which has almost all the earmarks of a "common law."

Similar developments occur whenever political or economic upheavals make existing law unbearably obsolete, and the legislative machinery proves too slow to keep pace with events. The collapse of the German currency in the early twenties resulted in such an upheaval. Legislation afforded only belated and partial relief. In this situation, the courts, taking the general clauses of the Civil Code as their verbal starting point, sought to master the ensuing problems by creating a body of decisional "revaluation" law which any American or English lawyer would recognize as case law in every sense of the word.[37]

Working in such an area of the law, where he is fettered neither by explicit code provisions nor by "binding" precedents, the civil-law judge may well have more creative freedom than his common-law colleague.

questions of law. In these civil-law systems, an intermediate appellate court's finding concerning such a question is (a) not reviewable by the court of last resort, and (b) of no precedential value. See 1 Formation of Contracts—A Study of the Common Core of Legal Systems 56 (Schlesinger ed., 1968).

37. See note 19 to Opinion of the German Reichsgericht in the Matter of S. S. v.

M. E. Corp., *supra* at 571. Inflation has given rise to similar developments in other civil-law countries as well. The example of Argentina is discussed in the article by G. R. Carrió, Judge Made Law Under a Civil Code, 41 La.L.Rev. 993 (1981).

(ii) Other subject matters, however, such as mortgages, the matrimonial property regimes, wills and intestate succession, negotiable instruments, corporation law, and many others, usually are treated in the codes in specific detail. Doubts and ambiguities may occur even in those areas, but only with respect to the more extraordinary situations; the bulk of positive rules is found in the written law itself.[38]

In their criminal law, non-totalitarian countries adhere to the principle *nulla poena sine lege*. This means that nobody may be subjected to punishment except for an act which at the time it was committed was declared criminal by a *lex*, i.e., a rule of *statutory law*.[39] Thus the power of U.S. city councils to enact ordinances making certain behaviors a crime (recent anti-poor legislation banning panhandling might be a dramatic example) would be considered highly uncivilized and in violation of fundamental constitutional guarantees as to the "sources" of criminal law, by a civil-law lawyer.

Procedure is another area in which, as the reader will remember, the more modern civilian codes are so complete and, on the whole, so specific as to leave relatively little scope for the development of case law. Code provisions, of course, may require interpretation; but decisional law fashioning new procedural devices and remedies, without the aid of specific code provisions, is rarely encountered in civil-law countries today.[40]

(b) From a practical point of view, it seems obvious that decisional law, in the sense in which we know it, is most likely to develop in a jurisdiction where opinions, especially appellate opinions, are reported fully, that is with a full statement of the facts as well as the reasons and authorities relied on. Such full reports of appellate opinions are available in some but not all of the civil-law countries.[41]

---

38. Not infrequently, we find that specific provisions and general clauses interact (see, e.g., the Opinion of the German Reichsgericht in the Matter of S. S. v. M. E. Corp., *supra* at 563) in much the same way in which law and equity interact under our system. In such instances, the specific code rules play the same role as our "law," while case law based on the broad doctrines of boni mores, bona fides, and abuse of rights develops "equitable" causes of action and defenses. By such case law, the civilians usually reach results very similar to those encountered in our courts of equity. See, e.g., the examples of civilian counterparts of estoppel and laches discussed in the material on abus de droit, *infra* Chapter 9, Section 3 at 938. But note that the civilians' ability to match the accomplishments of equity seems to be limited to the area of substantive law; the flexibility of equity in fashioning procedural remedies has no parallel in the civil law.

39. See Edward M. Wise, General Rules of Criminal Law, 25 Denver J. Int'l L. & Pol'y 313 (1997).

40. There is one celebrated example of a procedural device originally fashioned by case law: the French *astreinte*. This example has been played up by writers on comparative law, for the very reason that innovative judicial law-making in the area of procedural devices and remedies is exceptional in civil-law systems. Recently, however, the *astreinte* has been given a statutory basis. See Arts. 5–8 of Law 72–626 of July 5, 1972, as amended by Law 75–596 of July 9, 1975.

41. For an extensive comparative study of the style of reported opinions, see J. G. Wetter, The Styles of Appellate Judicial Opinions (1960). See also F. Schmidt, The Ratio Decidendi—A Comparative Study of a French, a German and an American Supreme Court Decision (vol. 6, Acta Instituti Upsal-

All of the German-speaking countries have such reports, as is shown by the many examples of German and Swiss cases in this book.

The opinions of the French *Cour de Cassation*,[42] on the other hand, are of utmost brevity. Trying to describe them in American terms, one might say that they are comparable to one-paragraph *per curiam* opinions of American appellate courts.[43] Where this system of opinion-writing and of reporting prevails, those who have access only to the reports of opinions of the Court in official publications or commercial publications are unable to use a precedent in the typical common-law manner; if the facts of the former case are not fully reported, then the judge deciding a later case cannot determine whether the two cases are "on all fours," and he cannot apply the familiar common-law technique of probing for factual differences which may form the possible basis for a distinction. The difficulty of discerning the precise holding in a decision of the *Cour de Cassation* is further increased by the fact that the court's opinions do not cite any previous cases. Often this makes it impossible for those who only have access to the published opinion accurately to reconstruct the grounds on which the holdings of prior cases have been extended or distinguished by the court.

This is, however, only an outsider's view of the matter. The Court formulates its decision without citing its prior decisions because its appellate jurisdiction extends only to violation of enacted law, not *jurisprudence*, and because it seeks to avoid the impression of laying down general rules in violation of Article 5 of the Civil Code. But it decides after receiving a report of the *rapporteur* (the judge to whom the case has been assigned), and that report will contain a full account of pertinent prior case law as well as academic authority.[44] Moreover the *amicus briefs* produced by the *Parquet* intervening in the case keeps open a hidden dialogue with all possible legal authority. Sometimes, these reports are published. Sometimes, they leak into case notes by the *arrêtistes*, who are keen at identifying the crucial change in theretofore boilerplate passages in what are, after all, the mass products of a grossly overworked court.[45]

iensis Iurisprudentiae Comparativae, 1965). See also Lasser, Judicial Deliberations (2005).

42. For examples, see Chapter 9, Section 3 at 938; F. Schmidt, *supra* note 41, and Mitchel de S.-O.-l'E. Lasser, Judicial (Self) Portraits: Judicial Discourse in the French Legal System, 104 Yale L.J. 1325, 1337 & 1340–41 (1995).

43. For the reasons, largely historical, which explain this style of opinion-writing, see T. Sauvel, Histoire du jugement motivé, 61 Revue du Droit Public 5 (1955); I. Zajtay, Begriff, System and Präjudiz in den kontinentalen Rechten und im Common Law, 165 Arch.Civ.Pr. 97, 105 (1965); M. Lupoi, Cenni storici introduttivi allo studio delle fonti del diritto francese, 1968 Rivista Trimestrale di Diritto e Procedura Civile 1253; J. L. Goutal, Characteristics of Judicial Style in France, Britain and the U.S.A., 24 Am.J.Comp.L. 43, 60–65 (1976).

44. For illustrations and discussion, see Lasser, *supra* note 42, at 1355–1410. The author calls the published decisions of the French Supreme Court the "official portrait" of the French judicial system, and the internal *rapports* its "unofficial" one. This study should be required reading for those who have access to the French legal system only through the English language—and perhaps not only for them.

45. The Civil Chambers of the Court (three civil, one social) adjudicated over 18,-000 matters per annum from 1989 (19,255) to

In other countries, again, the technique of opinion-writing and reporting is somewhere between the extremes exemplified by Germany and France. In Italy, for instance, the Court of Cassation writes rather elaborate opinions, which ordinarily disclose the facts as well as the various steps in the reasoning of the court. As a rule, however, these full opinions are not published. The published report consists only of a so-called *massima* which "may be roughly described as a rule or head-note.... In many cases it contains very abstract and general propositions, often including mere *obiter dicta*. This increases the difficulty of understanding the real significance of a *massima*."[46] The lawyers representing the parties in the case receive copies of the complete opinion of the court. Other lawyers and legal scholars also can obtain such copies from the clerk of the court by paying a moderate fee. Thus, it is not quite impossible for one engaged in legal research to inform himself fully and authentically concerning the true holding of a decision of the Court of Cassation; but the method is cumbersome, and in practice Italian lawyers ordinarily limit their study of the case law to the published *massime*.[47]

The age of a code is another factor affecting the significance of case law. With the years, the judicial and doctrinal gloss growing around a code and filling its gaps becomes as much a part of the legal tradition of a nation as the terms of the code itself. As new social and technological conditions arise which were unknown to the codifiers' generation, the text of the code may become inadequate, and in the absence of legislative revision the courts must fashion answers to the new questions as best they can.[48] The importance of this factor varies from country to country, depending on the age of each country's codes, and the speed of social developments.

Another element of variety in the civil-law systems' attitude toward case law stems from express provisions in the codes themselves. Almost all of the civil codes, with the notable exception of Germany (see *supra* sec. 1), contain express directions to the judges as to (i) what may be considered proper sources of law, and (ii) what may not be so considered.[49] These provisions, some of which are reprinted immediately following this Note, range all the way from the express *prohibition* of case law in the Code Napoleon to emphatic *recognition of* the possibility of deriving guidance from precedents.

1993 (18,569). Rapport de Cour de la Cassation 1993, Table B at 446.

46. G. Gorla, Some Comments on the Italian Legal System, With Particular Reference to the Law of Contracts, in 1 Formation of Contracts—A Study of the Common Core of Legal Systems 297, 298 (R. Schlesinger ed., 1968), where further references can be found.

The "scanty, abstract" nature of the *massime* was the subject of comment by an American court in Instituto Per Lo Sviluppo Economico v. Sperti Products, Inc., 323 F.Supp. 630, 636 (S.D.N.Y.1971).

47. For severe and detailed criticism of the system, see G. Gorla, Lo studio interno e comparativo della giurisprudenza, 1964 Foro Italiano, Part V, pp. 73 ff.

48. The reader will recall that the significance of a code's age was commented on, also, by the German Constitutional Court in the *Soraya* case.

49. For collections of code provisions of this kind, see Cheng, General Principles of Law As Applied by International Courts and Tribunals 400–08 (1953).

PART THREE

A Topical Approach to Law in Global Societies

CHAPTER 7

LEGAL EDUCATION AND THE PROFESSION

The materials in this chapter deal with legal training and with the structure and organization of the legal profession. There are marked differences in both general education and legal education between the United States and the rest of the world, since basic legal education is a graduate program only in the U.S. Although some countries, most notably Japan, are moving toward the U.S. model by postponing basic legal education until the graduate level, students almost everywhere in the world (including England) begin their academic legal education immediately after secondary school.[1]

Different models of legal education and professional organization cannot be captured fully by the common law/civil law opposition. As we have already mentioned, historically only a limited number of the legal traditions of the world have included a professionalized dispute resolution system. Thus, the degree of professionalization in dispute resolution provides a useful point of comparison as we study different systems.

The literature on legal education in civil-law countries—even considering only the writings in English—is voluminous.[2] The most cursory examination of this literature shows that the models of legal training in the civil-law countries are not uniform. Nevertheless, common historical roots and the strong influence exerted by some leading systems have produced certain features which can be called typical.[3]

1. For a broad-based comparative study, though now not completely up-to-date, see Q. Johnstone & D. Hopson, Lawyers and Their Work—An Analysis of the Legal Profession in the United States and England (1967). A very interesting discussion (unfortunately in French) of what occurs when lawyers from a common-law system and those from a civil law system must interact on a ongoing basis in connection with a long-term project; see J.-F. Guillemin, Le Tunnel sous la Manche: Confrontation et Fusion Permanentes de deux Cultures Juridiques Réputées Antagonistes, in Centre Français de Droit Comparé, L'entreprise et le droit comparé 107 (1995). The author of the item was head counsel of one of the large French construction companies involved in the Channel Tunnel project and as such working very closely with counsel for the British firms participating in the same project. For an interesting comparative discussion of American legal education through the eyes of a French law teacher, see L. Lorvellec, L'*Alma mater au prétoire. Les responsabilitiés des facultés de droit aux États Unis*, 5 Justices 97 (January–March 1997).

2. Every year, the Journal of Legal Education and other periodicals add numerous new items to the bulk of this literature, as a brief look at the standard bibliographical sources will reveal.

3. Cf. generally R. Goebel, Professional Qualifications and Educational Requirements for Law Practice in a Foreign Country: Bridging the Cultural Gap, 63 Tul.L.Rev. 444 (1989).

Perhaps the most typical and universally shared feature of civilian legal education is the monopoly of the University. In order to become a member of the legal profession in a civil-law country, one must receive all, or at least a substantial part of one's training at a University. By way of contrast, in the United States a significant number of law schools are not University-affiliated (whatever the meaning of University affiliation of a law school might be), and in some States—though their number is diminishing—it is still possible to prepare for the bar examination by "reading" the law in a law office. A *caveat* is in order, however. For the last thirty years at least, universities in general have been subject to reforms in many countries and, in addition, concerns about the adequacy of legal education have led to significant reforms designed to improve the relation between theoretical training and practical experience—a concern frequently voiced in the United States as well. Further changes must thus be expected and are to some extent already in the planning stage, especially in Europe, under pressures for harmonization from the market and the European Union.

1.   THE EDUCATION AND QUALIFICATION OF WESTERN LAWYERS IN HISTORICAL PERSPECTIVE

There is one feature of legal education that is common to all civil-law systems: the monopoly position which the University occupies (at least with respect to the first part of a future lawyer's training), such that a University legal education has come to be regarded as a hallmark of the civil law. Nevertheless, we have learned to search the roots of the Western Legal Tradition before "the great divorce" that characterized Europe in the eleventh century. As the reader recalls, the Universities occupied the central role in the Continent, while the Courts at Westminster Hall successfully competed for the dominant role in legal production in England. Beyond the Channel in England, Courts themselves educated legal professionals who would eventually practice and become the future generations of lawyers and judges. The roots of western legal professionalism, however, must be located earlier, when an independent legal profession was born within the technicalities of adjudicatory procedures in Rome.

Universities as now understood, with distinct faculties of law, did not come into being until the twelfth century. (See the article by H. Coing, *supra* p. 331). Thus, professional legal instruction by officially approbated legal experts (*iurisperiti*) can be traced to the fifth century A.D. and perhaps to the fourth century as well, but classical Roman law (approximately 150 B.C.–250 A.D.) developed independently of formal law schools and of formalized academic qualifications.

Classical Rome knew no professional judges. Its leading lawyers were the jurists whose writings shaped the Civil Law and are preserved in Justinian's Digest, and the orators whose forensic performances survive mainly through Cicero's detailed accounts of his own forensic efforts. In the classical period, jurists mainly disdained forensic oratory.[1] Students should keep in mind that this internecine rivalry occurred at the top of the legal profession. Both jurists and orators belonged to the senatorial or (latterly) equestrian classes of society. Litigants could be represented in court by any honest man,[2] including a freedman, acting as a *procurator* (hence "proctor" in admiralty and in ecclesiastical courts more than a millennium later). Notaries as yet were simply the scriveners who wrote instruments known as *tabellae*. As *tabelliones,* they were to mature into a separate profession— although not, in Roman days, into one enjoying *ex officio* the numerous privileges and immunities to which advocates were entitled.[3]

It seems reasonably clear that by the fifth century at the latest, professional instruction in law was obtainable at law schools in Rome, Constantinople and (for a time most prominently) at Beryt (Beyrouth).[4] Advocates became members of the legal profession only upon demonstrating sufficient legal knowledge, acquired from professors at law schools (now law faculties). Both advocates and professors were members of a learned profession, but professors (who teach and examine prospective advocates) were more learned, and they claimed (and usually were accorded) a much higher rank in the social and official hierarchy. The Western Empire spoke Latin, which was the language of the classical Roman law; the Eastern Empire spoke Greek, which was also the language of the New Testament. Academic lawyers in Beirut and Constantinople were of course fluent in Greek, but they taught in Latin from books of authority written by Roman jurists in that language.[5]

One direct consequence of the privileged status of Latin, and of law school taught lawyers at a few administrative centers, was the entrenchment of the division of the forensic legal profession into a "higher" and a "lower" branch: *advocates* at the imperial courts, and *procurators* at the lower ones. The *procurators* (originally the personal agents or representatives of an absent litigant) became pleaders in lower courts, and their

1. This is usually attributed to the Causa Curiana, described in Cicero, Brutus 38–42 & 51–53, where the oratory of Lucius Crassus defeated Quintus Scaevola, a leading jurist.

2. Women could not postulate (appear in court or before public officials) on behalf of others: Dig. 3, 1, 1, 5 (Ulpian). As there narrated, this disability went back to "a shameless woman called Carfania who by brazenly making applications and annoying the magistrate gave rise to (its incorporation into the Praetorian) edict."

3. For detailed discussion of the *tabelliones*, see Hans A. Ankum, Les Tabellions Romains, Ancêtres Directs des Notaires Modernes, in Atlas du Notariat, Le Notariat dans le Monde 5 (1989). *See also* A. H. M. Jones, 1 The Later Roman Empire 515–16 (1964). The combination of "privilege" with "immunity" is apparently traceable to Cod. 2, 7, 7 (439), conferring upon the *togati* of the Illyrian prefecture the same privileges and immunities enjoyed by those of the Oriental prefecture.

4. Paul Collinet, Histoire de l'École de Droit de Beyrouth (1925), is still the definitive account.

5. 2 Jones, *supra*, note 3, at 987–91. The sources used by law students before Justinian's codification are listed in § 1 of his Const. Omnem, of December 16, 533, enacting the Digest. See also Collinet, *supra*, note 4, at 209–23.

inferior status was reinforced by their need to consult *advocates* learned in the (Roman) law (and fluent in Latin) in complicated cases.[6] On the non-litigious side, changes in the law of evidence and in the formal requirements for important transactions (especially donations) combined with the need for documentation by a largely illiterate and monolingual population to enhance the importance of the notary.

Students should be aware that shortly after Justinian's codification (533–563 A.D.), knowledge of learned Roman law based on familiarity with the teachings of classical Roman lawyers became extinct in the Western Empire (mainly today's Italy, France, and Spain). Roman legal forms and the Latin language survived in Italian municipal administration, notarial practice, and especially the Church—although to what extent is still debated.[7] The "second life" of Roman law, starting with the rediscovery of the Digest in the late eleventh century and law teaching at Italian universities in the twelfth found the notarial profession already in place.[8] The "learned" lawyers acquired their legal knowledge, in Latin, in multi-year university courses following Justinian's curriculum but now also including Canon law. It was this latter legal system which provided the first coherent scheme of hierarchical juridical organization and legal procedure.[9]

It is likely that this profession, and ecclesiastical court practice generally, provided the prevailing model for civil lawyers. Surprisingly at least to the uninitiated, it did so even in England, where admiralty lawyers were divided, well into the nineteenth century, into advocates educated in the civil law at Oxford or Cambridge, and proctors (a contraction of procurators) or pleaders of a more humble practical background. This parallel should not be stretched too far, however, because the English notary (although clearly of canon or civil law progeny) was not a major factor in this scheme (or, for that matter, in English law generally).[10]

In Continental civil-law countries, on the other hand, the notarial profession prospered. This was so although (or perhaps because) it became

---

6. 2 Jones, *supra* note 3, at 989.

7. See especially Ugo Gualazzini, L'Insegnamento del Diritto in Italia durante l'Alto Medievo, in Ius Romanum Medii Aevi Part I5b*a a* (1974); Paolo Frezza, L'Influsso del Diritto Romano Giustinianeo nelle Formule e nella Prassi in Italia, id. I, 2, *c e e* (1974) (with discussion of notaries at 99–108); and most recently Charles M. Radding, The Origins of Medieval Jurisprudence, Pavia and Bologna 850–1150 (1988).

8. Heinrich Gehrke, Die privatrechtliche Entscheidungsliteratur Deutschlands 167–213 (1975), lists well over one hundred collections of *consilia* by professors at German universities alone.

9. James A. Brundage, The Rise of Professional Canonists and the Development of

the Ius Commune, 112 ZZS Kan. 26, 42–43 (1995). In 1274, the Second Council of Lyon adopted an oath of office for *advocates* and *procurators* in ecclesiastical tribunals. See also, by the same author, The Medieval Advocate's Profession, 6 Law & Hist. Rev. 493 (1988), and The Profits of the Law: Legal Fees for University–Trained Advocates, 32 Am. J. Legal Hist. 1 (1988), and for further medieval canon law background, James J. Hogan, Judicial Advocates and Procurators, An Historical Synopsis and Commentary 32–51 (Catholic University of America, Canon Law Studies No. 133, 1941). For France, see Jean Pierre Royer, Histoire de la Justice en France 145–53 (1995).

10. For full discussion, see C. W. Brooks, R. H. Helmholz & P. G. Stein, Notaries Public in England Since the Reformation (1991).

divided, functionally but not necessarily personally, into judicial and non-judicial notaries. The former were (and are still today) professionally qualified notaries serving *ad hoc* as clerks of court in ecclesiastical proceedings.[11] The latter became, in effect, quasi-public officials in private practice when the "public instruments" passed by notaries became entitled to *"fides publica"* in the same manner as judicial documents, and when territorial sovereigns entrusted them with the task of serving as repositories of the public instruments recorded in their protocols.[12] Admission as a notary in most civil-law countries was strictly restricted by number, and thus, in effect, conferred of a territorial monopoly or quasi-monopoly.[13] Central to this consolidation of the notarial profession was the position of the notary as a trustworthy recorder of judicial proceedings, and as a skilled and reliable draftsman and keeper of other public instruments.[14]

The *jurisconsult* differed from the advocate not only in his occupation (typically that of a professor of law at a university) but also by his academic formation, which included several years of study beyond the *licenciate* for the attainment of the degree of *doctor utriusque iuris*,[15] made known to the academic world through the publication of a dissertation.

The *iuris consulti* who taught Roman and Canon law at the universities were familiar with the law actually prevailing in their localities. Yet until about the mid-eighteenth century, they did not teach that law to their students. Especially after the consolidation of territorial sovereignty and the proliferation of princely legislation following the Peace of Westphalia (1648), this meant that the law faculties were increasingly teaching dead

11. Codex Iuris Canonici, Can. 1437 (1983) reads as follows: "§ 1 A notary is to be present at every hearing, so much so that the acts are null unless signed by the notary. § 2 Acts drawn up by notaries constitute public proof." This provision is traceable to the Fourth Lateran Council (1215). See Charles J. Duerr, The Judicial Notary (Catholic University of American Canon Law Studies No. 312), ch. 2 (1951). In the Church of England, the office of Judicial Notary fell to be exercised by the diocesan registrar, who held a much sought-after office of profit. See Brooks et al., *supra* note 10, at 30–34.

12. For historical background, see especially Pie Hein Gerver, L'Itali, le Berceau; Peter–Joh. Schuler, Rezeption und Ausbildung des Öffentlichen Notariats in Deutschland und im Deutschen Sprachraum; and José Bono y Huerto, Evolucion Medieval del Notariado en España y Portugal, in Atlas du Notariat, *supra* note 3, at 45, 115, & 59.

13. For the effects of the *droit de présentation* (re-introduced by the Restauration in 1816) on the French notarial profession,

see Ezra N. Suleyman, Private Power and Centralization in France: The Notaires and the State (1987).

14. See, e.g., Gerver, *supra* note 12, at 46–47; Pedro A. Malavet, Counsel for the Situation: The Latin Notary, A Historical and Comparative Model, 19 Hastings Int'l & Comp.L.Rev. 389, 418–19 (1996). The texts of instructions on *ars notariae* used in thirteenth-century Bologna are discussed in Eduardo Bautista Pondé, Orígen y Historia del Notariado, ch. 11 (1967). The "studied" nature of the notarial profession is evidenced by the French term for the notary's bureau (*étude*).

15. In the German parts of the Holy Roman Empire, this degree at one time conferred the privileges of the (lower) nobility. Gerald Strauss, Law, Resistance, and the State, The Opposition to Roman Law in Reformation Germany 4–5 (1986). This privilege receded after the Thirty Years' War (1618–1648), when the aristocracy laid claim to State offices requiring professional qualifications.

secular law in a dead language and—more to the point—that the rulers, the bench, the bar, and the public, could not rely on the legal proficiency of university law graduates.

This basic flaw in the civil-law scheme of legal education escaped massive reaction "from above" until the latter part of the eighteenth century, when many (but not all) rulers at long last directed the university law faculties to teach the law of the land in the vernacular.

On the practitioner's side the scheme of a divided profession emerged in the late Roman Empire, where clients could be (and in places like Roman Egypt of necessity had to be) represented by *procuratores* in the lower courts, while the law school-trained advocates had the right of audience at the higher ones. Later organized professionally in associations called Order, College, and the like, advocates saw themselves as a learned profession free from technical concerns, devoted to the science of the law, and entitled to privilege for that reason (as well as, more directly, by virtue of their social status superior to the procurators).[16]

The system just sketched was contrary to two central notions of the French Revolution: that of *égalité* which was opposed to privilege, and that of popular sovereignty, which was regarded as incompatible with the existence of *corps intermédiaires* (intermediate organizational bodies) between the people and their elected representatives. (In the following, students should keep in mind that the French Revolution *directly* affected much of continental Europe outside of France: Belgium, the Netherlands, Germany west of the Rhine, and parts of Switzerland as well as Italy). Feudalism, and with it, the old judicial order, fell in France on the "Night of August 4" (1789);[17] in September of the year following, the National Assembly decreed that, "The men of law, previously called advocates, who can no longer form any order or corporation, will not have any special costume in their duties." The profession of *procureurs* was abolished three months later, to be followed in January, 1791, with the concomitant creation of that of *avoués,* which performed essentially the same functions but did not enjoy a monopoly of forensic representation, and was open to citizens at large as well as to *"hommes de loi."*[18] On September 15, 1793, finally, the Convention abolished the universities, including their law faculties.[19] Revolutionary France had thus broken with a civil-law tradition traceable at least to the late Roman Empire—or so it seemed before Napoleon assumed power some six years hence.

16. As to France, see, e.g., *id.* 26–28 (advocates), and 38–40 (procurators). For massive documentation on Germany, Italy, and Switzerland, see Hannes Siegrist, Advokat, Bürger und Staat, Sozialgeschichte der Rechtsanwälte in Deutschland, Italien und der Schweiz (18.–20. Jh.), 2 vols. 1996.

17. See Michael P. Fitzsimmons, The Parisian Order of Barristers and the French Revolution, ch. 2 (1987). Bailey Stone, The French Parlements and the Crisis of the Old Regime (1987) provide detailed and well-documented accounts of the French legal profession and the judiciary before the Revolution.

18. Decree of September 2, 1790, quoted in Fitzsimmons, *supra* note 17 at 54.

19. *Id.* at 102–03.

Early in the nineteenth century, legal instruction became available again in two private law schools in Paris.[20] Eight days before the effective date of the Civil Code, on March 13, 1804, the French system of qualification for judicial office and the practice of law, and of legal education in conjunction therewith, was recast along lines familiar to modern civil lawyers. Central to this scheme was the requirement of the study of law, at state-operated schools (later faculties) of law, for a specific period of years depending upon the career chosen, documented by state examinations and degrees. The profession of advocate was recreated. Advocates and *avoués* were required to acquire an academic legal education as thus provided, and their admission to practice was further contingent upon the completion of a probationary period (*stage*).[21] The impact of this State monopolization of legal education, qualification for judicial office, and the practice of law, on the rest of Europe is indicated by the law schools set up in cities outside of Paris, including Brussels, Koblenz, and Turin.[22]

Soon thereafter, the law schools were integrated, as faculties of law, into the French (public) university system as recreated in 1806, and a few years later the "French model" of modern civil law was complete. Civil, criminal, and commercial substantive law, as well as civil and criminal procedure, were codified in the "Cinque Codes," legal education at State university law faculties was mandatory for judges, prosecutors, advocates, and procurators (*avoués*), and the professional competence of advocates and procurators was further assured by the requirement of a probationary period (*stage*) before full qualification. This scheme assured that the State would now teach the new law at its own institutions—and by a new method.[23]

That new method was, in essence, the teaching of the texts of the new law by rote, pursuant to a detailed uniform curriculum prepared by the Ministry of Education.[24] Exposition of the text of the Cinque Codes in the sequence prescribed by the Ministry was quintessentially exegetic, and the dominant French style of legal reasoning until the latter part or the nineteenth century has accordingly been called the "*école de l'exégèse.*"[25] Enforced rigorously throughout the Empire by government inspectors, this

---

20. For the history of these schools (The Academié de Législation and the Université de Jurisprudence), corresponding roughly to the Consulate regime (1799–1804), see *id*. 134–47.

21. Law of 22 Ventôse year XII, summarized id. 150–51. The Law of 27 Ventôse year VIII (March 18, 1800) had re-established the profession of procurators (called avoués), and the Law of 25 Ventôse year XI (March 16, 1803) had regulated the notarial profession.

22. Robert Jones, A History of the French Bar 71* note (h) (Am. ed. 1856). This is a highly informative book for those inter-ested in legal history, as it reproduces pertinent statutes, decrees, legislative materials, and even examination requirements in English translation.

23. See especially Fitzsimmons, *supra* note 17, Chapters 6 and 7.

24. The key sources are quoted and discussed in Adolf Bürge, Das Französische Privatrecht im 19. Jahrhundert 496–520 (1991).

25. The classic study still is Julien Bonnecase, L'Ecole de l'*exégèse* en Droit Civil (1924). Bürge, *supra* note 24, has more recently subjected this characterization to a searching reexamination.

scheme of education all but physically infused the law of the "Cinque Codes" into the minds (and perhaps also the hearts) of generations of French judges, prosecutors, and lawyers. The successful implementation of the continental, bureaucratic model of judicial administration by a university-trained judiciary sitting in multi-layer, multiple-panel, multiple-judge courts would have been all but impossible without this standardized process of mass producing "new" lawyers.

German universities, on the other hand, survived the French Revolution and the Napoleonic period with little interruption. Although courses on Prussian law and French Law were given at Berlin and Heidelberg where they were the "law of the land," by far the most important legal system taught there and throughout Germany was modern Roman law. This applied as such, and was the primary system, only in a small number of States. Thus, German law students were free to "hear" (to attend class) on whatever legal subject whenever taught, but the offering was likely to consist in large part of courses remote from the law then in effect in their home states or law districts. (This is quite similar to what happens today in a national law school in the United States, where the same "law" is taught no matter whether the school is located in Atlanta, San Francisco, New Haven or Houston).

Centralization of power produced the notion that laws student are "seedlings of the State": as judges, prosecutors, higher civil servants, and (last and least by design) as practicing lawyers. The prototype was the career judge. His training (and consequently, that of other candidates for entry into the legal professions) started with study at an approved law faculty for a minimum period of three years, followed by the "first" State law examination. If successful, the candidate then entered State service as a provisional civil servant, receiving practical training and instruction in the judiciary, the prosecutor's office, and in governmental departments. This four-year training was concluded with the "second" (or "great") state examination. Successful candidates could then apply for entry into judicial, prosecutorial, or civil service careers, or the private practice of law.[26]

This scheme is still in effect in Germany today, although the period of apprenticeship (or internship) between the "first" and "second" State examinations has been reduced a number of times. Crucially, both this period of post-university training and the minimum time spent on university law study are prescribed by statute, and both the "first" and the "second" examinations are *State* examinations. Thus, university law study is still required, but its minimal duration is determined by State statute rather than university rules for the attainment of academic degrees. Indeed, German universities generally retained autonomy over the conferral of doctoral degrees and qualification for law faculty appointment, but the *bacallaureus* and the *magister legum* were displaced by certificates denoting the successful completion of State examinations. Nineteenth-

26. Gerhard Dilcher, Die Preussischen Juristen und die Staatsprüfungen Zur Entwicklung der juristischen Professionalisierung im 18. Jahrhundert, in Festshrift Fur Hans Thieme 353 (1986).

century Liberal reform efforts were ultimately successful in abolishing the *numerus clausus* for admission to the practice of law as an advocate, but "free" advocacy was claimed (and ultimately vindicated) by a State-licensed profession.

Study at a University law faculty for the requisite number of years prescribed by law, followed by a successful passing of an examination documented by a license or degree, is now a standard feature of qualification for all branches of the legal profession in virtually every civil-law country. As we have seen, however, that was not always so even for advocates, let alone for procurators and notaries. But with the plentitude of State control over the process comes enhanced public responsibility for the product.

Today, in addition to the State-granted law degree, the status symbol of the transnational lawyer in civil-law countries is now the LL.M. degree, achieved abroad after voluntary additional study. Originally a product mainly of the United States designed in major part for export abroad, this has become, in the last twenty years, all but a standard offering of law faculties in Europe.

Currently, the organizational differences between England and the U.S. are as significant as those between France and Germany, and there is no reason to believe that the countries belonging either to the common law or to the civil law are closer to each other than across the borders of the legal family. Consequently, it is within the notion of the western legal tradition as a family of legal systems sharing some deep structural analogies that our discussion should be carried on.[27]

What we have learned thus far is sufficient to realize how the history and development of the organization of the legal profession are related to a number of classic distinctions between common law and civil law. The common lawyer is practical and pragmatic. He is the product of the practical needs of the bench at Westminster Hall. The civil lawyer is theoretical and abstract. He is the product of law professors in the Universities.[28] The common law judiciary is composed of leaders of the legal profession. The civilian judiciary is a bureaucracy whose members are often much less qualified than the much more prestigious and remunerative practicing bar (let alone academicians).[29] The relationship between the attorney and the judge is consequently much closer in the common law where judges share the attorneys' professional interests.[30] The attorney performs the starring role in the Anglo–American adversary procedural model. His role is much more limited in the civilian model, where discovery

27. Following my previous work I refer to the Western legal tradition as rule of professional law. See Mattei, Three Patterns of Law: Taxonomy and Change in the World's Legal Systems, 45 Am.J.Comp.L. 5 (1997).

28. See Dawson, The Oracles of the Law (1968).

29. See M. Cappelletti, The Judicial Process in Comparative Perspective (1989).

30. On this different comparative institutional posture C.W. Wolfram focuses his comparative Paris paper: C.W. Wolfram, Multi-disciplinary Partnership in the Global and Domestic Law Practice of European and American Lawyers, (Paris, 1997).

as well as all the preparatory activity are considered official business, which is the province of the judge-bureaucrat (see *infra*).[31]

We know from the previous historical discussion of the civil law that these brutal comparative generalizations are not accurate and they are consequently under attack today.[32] On the one hand, the great comparative law scholar Gino Gorla has shown the major role historically played by courts and practitioners on the Continent as well.[33] On the other hand, it is easy to observe that the academic approach to legal thinking known as legal formalism has characterized a great part of American legal culture, and that in (at least) the last two hundred years, academic legal education is the rule everywhere in the common law world, so that the education of the legal profession and its way of thinking may have become less practical.[34]

Each one of the comparative oppositions just mentioned is consequently in need of qualification.[35] For example, in certain civilian jurisdictions, such as Germany, a judicial appointment is a much-coveted and prestigious job.[36] Even the opposition between adversary and non-adversary procedure is likely to have been overestimated, and attorneys play a large and increasing role also in civil law litigation.[37]

2. UNITARY PROFESSION IN THE COMMON LAW: THE UNITED STATES

Lawyers organized themselves professionally in the United States rather recently, around the end of the last century. What remains today from the epic period of frontier lawyering is a somewhat greater informality as well as a radical difference from the English professional organization, and from almost all other epiphanies of common law: the organization of the American legal profession is not based on the dichotomy between barristers and solicitors. While in Canada, Australia, and New Zealand, lawyers have traditionally been called to the bar by one of London's Inns of Court, and solicitors have followed a legal education largely based on the English model, the development of the American legal profession has

---

31. See M. Damaška, The Faces of Justice and State Authority (1986).

32. See, e.g., J. Gordley, Common Law e Civil Law. Una Distinzione che sta scomparendo? in Studi in Onore di R. Sacco (1994).

33. See G. Gorla–L. Moccia, A Revisiting of the Comparison Between Continental Law and English Law (16th–19th century), 2 J. Leg. History 143 (1981).

34. See the brilliant synthesis of G. Gilmore, The Ages of American Law (1979); as usual, the United States is the front-running experience. Most recently, some judges and

members of the practicing bar have complained that American Legal education has ceased being practical and became too academic.

35. See some discussion in U. Mattei, Comparative Law and Economics (1997).

36. See Blankenburg and Shultz, German Advocates: A Highly Regulated Profession, in 2 Lawyers in Society. The Civil Law World (Abel and Lewis eds., 1988) at 124ff.

37. Abel, Lawyers in the Civil Law World, in Abel and Lewis supra, note 36 at 4, as well as many of the papers in Abel Lewis (1989). See, on the evolution in civil law

asserted itself with a different character, accompanying that of the university.[1]

In theory, the authority over the legal profession is exercised by the States, which can decide the matter free from national worries. Because of a number of technical devices, of which the "doctrine of inherent powers" is the most powerful, U.S. lawyers have been able to escape all political controls by legislatures, becoming a "self-regulating" profession to an extent that has no counterpart elsewhere.[2] Nobody has put it in a clearer way than Professor Wolfram, a recognized expert in the field, and the chief Reporter for the Restatement of the Law governing Lawyers, of the American Law Institute:

> "Regulation (of the legal profession), to the extent it exists, is determined by lawyers and their close allies, lawyers who are for the moment judges. Groups of Lawyers in the American Bar Association draft the professional rules in the form of "model" suggestion to the States, where most regulation occurs. In the States other groups of lawyers (typically closely allied with the States Bar Association) review the national model and determine the extent to which they will recommend adoption of or variations from the model ... the result is a fair degree of uniformity in regulation across the country although the theoretical potential for wide variation exists. In almost all States the final determination of the shape of the rules is made by the State's Supreme Court ... quite content to do what the Bar recommends...."[3]

Despite some degree of State diversity, in practice, if compared to any civilian experience, the American Bar Association, a national non-governmental organization with no formal rule making power, has succeeded to become almost a tyrant over professional law in the United States. A rather typical common law attitude, that might explain at least in part the success of the practicing American bar to self-regulate and escape political regulation (the inherent power doctrine), is the degree to which the Bar and the Bench are co-identified in the U.S. Again quoting Professor Wolfram, "In the United States judges *are* lawyers and continue to be such even after appointment or election to the bench." In England, as we will see, the fortunate and privileged position of Barristers has been defeated in Mrs. Thatcher's era. The uniqueness of the U.S. situation, however, would not be understandable without consideration of the attorney's education, itself rather surprising for a civilian observer.

The uniformity standards that the American Bar Association imposes over law schools in order to receive "accreditation" seem even stronger

procedure and on its impact on the role performed by attorneys in litigation, infra Chapter 8 at 707.

1. There is no lack of literature regarding this. A classic example, although dated, is C. Warren, A. History of the American Bar, 1911; A.H. Chroust, The Rise of The Legal Profession in America, 2 vol., 1965.

2. See Wolfram, *Lawyer Turf and Lawyer Regulation—The Role of Inherent Power Doctrine,* 12 U. Ark. Little Rock L. R. 1 (1989).

3. See Wolfram, Multidisciplinary Partnerships in the global and domestic law practice of European and American Lawyers, Paris Paper 23, 24.

than the remarkable U.S. academic creativity. They impose a large amount of black letter law in the curriculum so that "alternative models" of academic legal education not specifically targeted to the training of attorneys are substantially absent. A comparative observation might question whether such an ABA-imposed uniformity can be considered responsible for the trend of lawyers to borrow from other academic disciplines, with the latter simply ignoring lawyers. It would be hard for a civilian lawyer to give lessons of anti-formalism to his U.S. colleague. Still, the fact that a professional organization of practitioners might grant prestige to an academic institution (by accrediting it) rather than the other way around is bewildering for the Civilian observer. But the uniformity of the U.S. "legal brain" that results from these three years of legal education, and the generalized professional character of American legal education, are certainly a major structural difference between the U.S. and elsewhere.[4]

Since its foundation in 1878 (in the core of the Langdell era at Harvard) the American Bar Association has always carried out its own professional project in a relationship (sometimes of collaboration, sometimes of opposition) with the Association of American Law Schools (AALS).

The American lawyer has the formal title of Attorney at Law; one achieves this title today after having passed a relatively selective (though very easy by Japanese standards!) Bar examination administered at the state level. The exam is nevertheless mainly centered on those general principles of the law that are taught at the law schools nationwide. A National Conference of Bar Examiners produces a "multistate exam" that most States adopt at least for part of their test. In a number of States, only graduates from ABA-approved schools can take the Bar exam. In such States, the percentage rate of passing is even higher than in other States, such as California, in which the ABA has not been successful in obtaining this last monopoly, and in which a JD from a non-accredited law school is enough to take the exam. Everywhere, the great majority of students graduating from the major law schools (those acknowledged by the ABA and members of the AALS) will pass the exam, and that selection mostly concerns students from less important law schools, that do not require assiduous attendance. The passage rate in America is incomparably higher than in European civil law jurisdictions, let alone Japan.[5]

Because of this, the selection of the legal profession takes place mostly before the beginning of law school, by the Law School Admission Test, an examination that takes place at the national level. To achieve a high score on this test is a necessary, but still insufficient, prerequisite to be admitted to one of the best law schools. Such graduate schools, when selecting the admission applications, will also take into consideration other varied factors of culture, environment, and personal situation, as well as the prestige of

4. This aspect has been critically discussed by D. Kennedy, Legal Education and the Reproduction of Hierarchy: A Polemic Against the System: A Critical Edition (2004).

5. Comparative data in K. Rokumoto–S. Ota, The Issue of Lawyer Population in Japan, Kahey Rokumoto (Ed.), The Social Role of the Legal Profession (1993).

the undergraduate schools attended (only in the U.S. and in the Philippines is law school a graduate school), and the proficiency of the applicant as an undergraduate student. The entry into a good law school is the true and only guarantee of professional success; from that point to the admittance to the Bar the selection is almost non-existent, since most of the screening has already happened.

An observer from a different legal tradition would be particularly struck by numerous aspects of the modern American legal profession; among these, however, the size of the law firms is undoubtedly the most outstanding.[6] In 1999, the thirty largest law firms in the United States had on average of 734 lawyers, even while just fifteen years before the top twenty had an average of 374.[7] If these are the peaks, one must mention that a law firm of fifty lawyers (that would be the largest in Italy and one of the very largest in Germany or France) is considered a medium-small firm in the United States.

This obviously must not make one forget that, statistically, in America most lawyers still practice in individual offices, or in very small professional associations. These smaller firms traditionally have not had available much of the sophisticated apparatus for legal research that is characteristic of large law firms. Their library is limited to a few dozen volumes of legal encyclopedias, from which they draw the cases to quote in their pleadings.[8] In the last few years, however, a dramatic change from this perspective has been caused by the generalized availability of on-line legal research. No doubt this technological change, dramatically lowering the transaction costs of legal information, already has had a tremendous organizational impact on the American Law firm.

Another aspect that strikes the imagination of the foreign observer is the aggressive advertising that American lawyers are allowed. Looking under the entry "lawyers" in an American Yellow Pages directory is a bewildering experience for the foreign lawyer. Legal services are advertised in variable quality and quantity, just as any other product or service is, from car rentals to dishwasher repairs. The professional self-perception of the average European attorney would be disturbed by this "commodification" of his self-perceived noble service, though matters are slowly changing. Nevertheless, this "Yellow Pages impression" must not be overrated. In fact, the number of lawyers that resort to heavy advertising in the U.S. is under 10%.[9] Resorting to explicit advertising to attract clients has not always been the rule in the United States; it has asserted itself only recently, as an answer to consumers' claims of the need to be informed, along with a generalized policy that is favorable to competition between

6. See, for a critical discussion, J. Flood, Megalawyering in the Global Order: The Cultural, Social and Economic Transformation of Global Legal Practice, 3 Int. J. Legal Profession 169 (1996).

7. Cf. Abel, United States: The Contradictions of Professionalism, in Abel and Lewis, 2 Lawyers in Society. The Common Law World (Abel and Lewis eds., 1988), at 229 for the 1985 figures. The 1999 are published in 21 The American Lawyer, July 1999 (insert).

8. Cf. J.H. Merryman, The Authority of Authority, 6 Stanford L. Rev. 613 (1954).

9. Cf. Abel, in Abel and Lewis *supra* note 7.

economic agents. Advertising for lawyers, as for doctors or other profession-als, just followed naturally (although resistance has not been absent[10]) from the American confidence with market practices, and from the "egalitarian" and informal spirit of American society in comparison to the Old Continent. American professionals simply are not ashamed of being on the market, just as any other provider of services. They are not considered a noble cast, or in general part of a particularly respected elite. Fees are not considered a token of client's gratitude for a noble art, as sometimes they still are in other cultures. Dealing (directly) with money is not considered socially shameful or degrading for a doctor, let alone for or an attorney.

On the other hand, the possibility of resorting to the advertising instrument is in itself unwelcome only to those who encourage a conserva-tive, guild-minded, image of the legal profession.[11] Indeed, we will also find clear signs of the civil law opening up from this perspective. Advertising might present unpleasant features as well because of its focus on personal injury law.[12] Other peculiar features of the U.S. organization of the legal profession are the absolute freedom of contingency fees and the peculiar allocation of the costs of justice. These structural features determined the birth of a plaintiff bar (the one resorting to heavy advertising) as opposed to a defendant bar. Interestingly, no such informal division of the legal profession exists elsewhere.

The civil law jurist is scandalized (and perhaps envious) when he discovers that, not unusually, more than half of the "prize" of a successful litigation ends up in the pockets of the lawyers. He is also surprised when he finds in most newspapers' classified advertisements an entry regarding what he perceives as a "market of rights," in which plaintiffs' attorneys appear to sell rights as commodities, inviting anyone who believes to have suffered a tort or personal injury to show up at the law firm, naturally with no strings attached.

Such a picture is completed by two other institutional aspects that may in no way be underrated: in the first place, the rule by which each party provides for the costs of his own lawyer;[13] secondly, the presence of the public interest firms.[14]

10. See Abel, in Abel and Lewis, *supra* note 7.

11. The prohibition of advertising is modeled on the fiction, arising from the in-quisitorial mentality, according to which the litigant who is right will find a judge that will find him so; it is also founded on the limited negotiability of services of the defense, seen as performed in the interest of justice and not of the client. See *infra*.

12. See S. Sugarman, Doing Away with Personal Injury Law (1989).

13. In many law systems the losing party is responsible for the costs of the law-suit. The American system is also isolated from the rest of the world (with the only exception of the Japanese) when it doesn't include among the costs of the losing party the fees of the lawyers. Naturally there are many variations in the civil law family as well as regards what costs each party should be responsible for, so that the operational comparison from this point of view becomes rather complex. Cf., however, the work of W. Pfenningstorf, *The European Experience with Attorney Fee Shifting*, 47 Law and Contemp. Probl. 37 (1984). Details on the American model are included in other contributions on the issue, included in that same thematic number of the review.

14. For ample details, see M. Cappellet-ti, J. Gordley, E. Johnson, Jr., Toward Equal

Let us briefly dwell on the practical aggregate impact of all of the mentioned peculiar institutional arrangements. At first glance, one notices a remarkable incentive to file lawsuits regarding personal injury and all those cases in which a skilled plaintiff bar can hope to impress the jury: car-accident and product-liability litigation are strongly encouraged, as well as lawsuits regarding emotional damage, including sexual harassment and other culturally hot fields of law in today's United States. The incentives for plaintiffs to litigate these cases go beyond the hope to find a sympathetic jury due to the fact that the possibility of contingent fee shifts the costs of the unsuccessful lawsuit from the plaintiff to the attorney. This rule on the distribution of costs, in fact, allows a plaintiff to settle beforehand with his own attorney the economic implications of whatever result is reached. On the other hand, the attorney who is paid only in case of victory is moved to discourage the lawsuit with no possibility of success, and in this way renders a screening service that is also useful from the social point of view. Moreover, attorney's fees absorb a large percentage of the cake because they reflect the allocated consequences of the risk of losing. Such a screening has not proved effective, so that today there has been an explosion of statutes that, whenever providing for a cause of action, introduce fee shifting provisions that move from the American rule to the looser-pays-all arrangement familiar in the continent. Thus, also from this perspective, differences might be more apparent than real.

As a consequence of this incentive's scheme, it is personal injury litigation that mostly floods the agenda of the United States courts, rousing violent reactions that end up affecting the effective protection of rights. The overcrowded judicial system also gives incentives to the creative development of new professions, such as that of mediators, offering non-confrontational solutions, which represent another trend in modern United States law.[15] Such mediators, although often legally trained, do not need to pass the Bar examination, so that the blooming of this profession ends up meaning some loss of power of the organized bar.

In several cases, moreover, the mentioned incentive mechanisms will not provide sufficient encouragement for an attorney to take cases. The attorney is discouraged from engaging in a lawsuit where the economic value of potential rights remains low, even after accounting for the possibility of the award being inflated by the jury.[16] One can think, to give an example, of family litigation, an area in which, as a consequence to the failure of the described incentive scheme to grant access to justice, a lot of the mediator's business is concentrated. Other areas in which the mentioned incentive scheme fails are property law and general contract law,

Justice: A Comparative Study of Legal Aid in Modern Societies (1975); F.H. Zemans (ed.), Perspectives on Legal Aid: An International Survey (1979).

15. Cf. J. McFarlane (ed.) Rethinking Disputes: The Mediation Alternative (1997).

16. For further detail, see S. Sugarman, Doing Away with Personal Injury Law, *supra* note 12.

where there are no possibilities of large damages awards. In the absence of such possibility, the plaintiff bar will not step in to gamble.

To be sure, in some of these cases the availability of the so-called public interest law firms might provide access to justice. These law firms are financed by several public and private sources. They specialize in public interest issues, such as the environment, the protection of minors or of the handicapped, etc. But even here there are limitations. Public interest law firms, acting most of the time as private attorneys general,[17] are interested in those cases that have innovative potential from the point of view of creating new rights; those cases, in other words, in which the present structure of rights is challenged with the goal of creating a new one. These are the cases by which the firm might acquire visibility and consequently obtain new financing. Paradoxically, the litigant whose ultimate success is more clearly recognized will risk remaining deprived of any protection of his undisputed rights. The demands of these litigants might be assisted by attorneys serving in a pro bono capacity—that is, the free-of-charge activity of some lawyers, encouraged in some cases by the tax structure. These last mentioned aspects of the U.S. way to solve the problem of access to justice outside of any systematic involvement of the State are rather interesting for the civilian observer, particularly nowadays that social budgets tend to shrink everywhere in the West. It has, however, been critically pointed out that this pro bono activity is mostly emphasized by the Bar associations as a way to carry on their guild-minded "professional project." In this view, this is a low cost way for the American attorney to regain a facade of social respectability. Its practical impact on granting access to justice is, however, very low.[18]

3. DIVIDED PROFESSION IN THE COMMON LAW: ENGLAND

In England, the legal profession is traditionally divided into two professional groups. It has been so from medieval times to this day: today's barristers and solicitors are the direct heirs of the sergeants and of the attorneys, respectively.[1]

The division between the two branches of the profession is of a functional type and has traditionally been legally enforced: barristers are specialized in legal representation before the superior courts (Supreme Court of Judicature, House of Lords, and, in a certain way, Crown Court), while solicitors carry out all preliminary tasks of a law suit, other than legal representation. Solicitors, in other words, take care of the business relations with the client, and it is their responsibility to retain a barrister.

---

17. Cf. Cappelletti, Governmental and Private Advocates for the Public Interest in Civil Litigation, 75 Mich. L. Rev. 794 (1975); H. Koetz, A. Homburge, Klagen Privater im oeffenittichen interesse, 1975; Cappelletti, Jolowicz, Public Interest Parties and the Role of the Judge in Civil Litigation, 1975.

18. See Abel, Revisioning Lawyers, in Abel & Lewis (Eds.), Lawyers in Society, abridged and partially updated Edition (1995).

1. See J.H. Baker, An Introduction to English Legal History (3d ed., 1992); Dawson, The Oracles of the Law (1968).

Barristers can, however, be directly retained by foreign lawyers and by individuals residing outside of the U.K. Ordinary people, however, cannot directly contact a barrister whenever it proves necessary to come before a superior court. This last observation is likely to surprise the civilian, as well as the U.S. observer, although in the modern world of professional specialization it is not uncommon for an attorney to hire another one, just as a general doctor hires the specialist. What might surprise the observer is not so much that this happens, but the fact that legal constraints determine that this should be so in England.

Such historical partition of functions has given rise to remarkable diversities, existent to this day (although incrementally disappearing from some sectors of the legal practice) from the point of view of access to the profession, professional organization, and the number of members in each branch of the profession. There are in England about nine thousands barristers today, as opposed to some sixty thousand solicitors. The close relationship, as mentioned before, between bench and bar results in a traditional monopoly of the barristers not only of legal representation before the superior courts, but also of the possibility of becoming a judge. This contributes to the traditionally greater prestige of the barristers in contrast with the cadet branch of the profession—until recently it was the case that only barristers could become, whenever skillful, fortunate and appropriately connected, superior judges.

The clear-cut, functional diversity between barristers and solicitors, as well as the remarkable privileges of the first, was a point that was bound to impress the observer from a different tradition, although possibly not the French lawyer, who is herself acquainted with the deep difference between the *Avoué*, the *Avocat*, and the *Notary*.[2]

The forces of the market proved to be stronger than the legal tradition even in insular England. The growth of the solicitor's profession and its rise in prestige in the last quarter of a century is a fact that cannot be denied. In 1997, two solicitors have even been appointed Q.C. (the very élite of the English bar), something unthinkable only twenty years ago. Quite early, the late Professor Glanville Williams[3] was perceptive of the winds of change, and discouraged the young jurist in the process of taking up the career of the bar. He did so in a bestselling booklet, *Learning the Law*, considered the English counterpart of Karl Llewellyn's *Brumble Bush*. It is interesting to briefly consider the market-driven reasons that were offered in order to perceive the degree and the directions of change (if any) in the last three decades.

First, to become a barrister it is necessary to attend an Inn of Court, the guild-school that since medieval times has taken care of the training and education of the bench and the bar. This schooling, perhaps more than any other factor, suggests the difference between *civil law* and *common law*. Admittance to an Inn today requires a recognized degree (not neces-

---

2. See *infra*.

3. G. Williams, Learning the Law (10th ed. 1978).

sarily in law), and the passing of an exam (part of which is remitted to those possessing a law degree). The non-legally trained applicant has to spend one year attending a course in substantive law. Although admittance to the bar is not itself particularly expensive, every applicant to pass the exam has to attend a year-long Bar Vocational Course at an accredited institution. He has to pay fees for this. Once admitted, one must consume the meals, participate in the didactic activity of the Common Council, and above all exercise for 12 months the activity of pupilage with a barrister before being able to start independent practice. The young lawyer has to face stringent competition to find a barrister who is willing to accept him as a pupil. It might not be true, as it was thirty years ago, that once a barrister, the young lawyer cannot make a living for many years, having to practice as a "floater" meeting solicitors here and there, at the desk of some senior colleague who at that moment will not be using it, before finding permanent chamber space within the Inns of Court.[4] Today, about one third of the active barristers practice outside of this traditional London location. It is, however, still true that the junior barrister has to face stringent competition to find chambers and that remarkable professional expenses (barristers must take on one or more clerks, specialized secretaries that ensure the smooth running of a chamber) make the initial period of the profession very hard, except for the very few able to enter leading chambers, who might be immediately making as much as their solicitor fellows.[5] This long lasting competition creates economic and social discrimination, and maintains the racial and gender structure of the bar profession, despite recent signs of change particularly as far as women are concerned. Regardless, the barrister's profession is still much more traditionally composed than the solicitor's.[6]

The enlarged jurisdiction of the county courts, in which solicitors also have always had *ius postulandi* (right to appear), has of recent greatly reduced the "cake" that barristers may share between themselves, and hence today the prospective mid-term earnings might not appear so very enticing either. Besides, you do not have to be a Barrister to be involved in the extra-judicial legal practice (particularly the international one) that, especially in London, is the wealthiest sector of the legal profession.

To become a solicitor—the sector of the profession that has taken the lead in the large international law firms—it is sufficient to practice, pass an examination run by the Law Society,[7] and obtain a nomination (automatic) from the Master of the Rolls. Almost all solicitors today have a university degree in law (L.L.B.). The Law Society, founded in 1825 and registered in 1831, has exercised since 1888 the monopoly of admission to the roll of solicitors.

---

4. *Id.*

5. *Id.* at 160.

6. See Menkel Meadow, Feminization of the Legal Profession: The Comparative Sociology of Women Lawyers, in 3 Lawyers in Society Comparative Theories (Abel and Lewis eds. (1989)) at 196.

7. Solicitors Act 1974.

The solicitors' main source of income, besides the litigation in which they traditionally perform all tasks that precede the intervention of the barrister, derives from conveyance and from probate, that is, from the drafting of the documents related to the transfer of land and to matters regarding wills. In these areas they have enjoyed a monopoly, which, in turn, has suffered a blow from the antitrust philosophy of recent conservative governments. An early reform granted the power of conveyance to a new profession, the "licensed conveyancers." Further, today, after the Courts and Legal Services Act of 1990, the building societies and the banks may offer this service to their clients.

Nevertheless, it has been the solicitor's profession that has been able to change more in the last 30 years and to seize the opportunities offered by the globalization of the economy, taking the lead not only in the U.K. but all around Europe and possibly worldwide. While the largest barrister's chambers (who are formally, nevertheless, mainly expense sharing arrangements) do not overcome 40 lawyers, solicitor's firms (which until 1969 were restricted by law to a maximum of 20 partners) today rival in number the largest U. S. firms. Clifford Chance counts more than 1400 lawyers worldwide, and a few other are well beyond 500. Despite some resistance, the Law Society is even giving signs of openness towards solicitors' participation in multi-disciplinary partnerships with accountants and other professionals. Solicitors are getting ready for the "super-market" future of the legal profession.

As a consequence, the 30 year-old warning of Professor Glanville Williams to the young and bright lawyer that it might not be worth the effort to undertake the long path to the Bar seems still justified. State-conferred monopolies simply do not matter when the arena of real business is the international practice. As Professor Wolfram has pointed out, self imposed restrictions might be devastating for a professional guild wishing to compete in the global market. The younger generation, having available a ready and interesting professional alternative, might simply go for that. Possibly some of the recent improvements in the comparative attractiveness of the bar (such as the possibility to make a living in the first years and the opening of extra-inns of court chambers) might also be explained as an adaptive, efficient reaction by the barristers to recent institutional changes and to the solicitor's competition.

Amongst barristers (and today also among solicitors) there is a "career": the most established seniors will receive the coveted title of Q.C. that is Queen's Counsel (or K.C. when there is a king). This is an acknowledgment of prestige that distinguishes them from all simple barristers (juniors). The Q.C. will come before the courts accompanied by one or more juniors, whose fees in turn are an expense of the client who wishes to engage a patron of such prestige.[8]

---

8. The prestige of the Q.C., is such that it is usually to them that one goes to for arbitrators.

The Courts and Legal Services Act of 1990 has further jeopardized the true significance of the privileges of the barristers, striking at the roots of some important peculiarities of the English professional organization as it had developed in the courts through the centuries. Until this important reform, the main Inns of Court (Inner Temple, Middle Temple, Lincoln's Inn and Gray's Inn) were the sole trustees of the power to admit the junior barrister to legal representation before the superior courts. Such remarkable power was not established in any statute, but was of customary nature, historically arising from the trust that the bench acknowledged to these centers of legal education.[9]

The 1990 statute swept away this monopoly of the bar, assigning it to a public body, the Lord Chancellor's Advisory Committee on Legal Education, that may grant other bodies besides the Inns of Court (as for example the solicitor's Law Society) the power to select the legal representatives that may obtain rights of audience before superior courts. As the same statute provides that superior judges must be chosen from amongst the latter, one can see that not only may solicitors one day be able to obtain rights of audience in those superior courts of common law, to this day barred to them, but may even become judges (as well as Q.C.) in them.

The underlying philosophy to this statute is the protection of the consumer of the "justice service."[10] It also reflects the fight against any form of monopoly, typical of the conservative government of Mrs. Thatcher. One look at the composition of the Committee (which also is to determine who is authorized to teach law) gives the measure of the triumph of politics over professionalism: the majority of the members within the committee are in fact non-jurists. Along with the lay members there are two judges, one of which (the President) is a Law Lord or a judge of the Supreme Court, and the other a circuit judge or former circuit judge; two barristers; two solicitors; and two academic jurists. The presence of the latter is a significant legislative acknowledgment of the growth of the role of Law faculties in England, closely following the decline of legal education at the Inns of Court.

One final note should be added. The English system of attorneys' fees does not present peculiarities that would strike the imagination of the continental jurist: the contingent fee is looked upon with suspicion, as is aggressive advertising.[11] The loser will bear the costs of both lawyers; as a consequence, the risk in which the potential plaintiff engages is significant, such that a risk-averse person would not be pushed to engage in a lawsuit.[12] While there are differences between the way in which solicitors

9. Today the Inns of Court are no longer divided in their rather impoverished educational function. They are grouped in a Common Council of legal education.

10. The same statute creates a Legal Service Ombudsman, destined to sanction eventual abuse committed by barristers and solicitors.

11. Fees partially based on results (conditional fee agreements) have been however admitted by the Courts and Legal Services Act, C. 41, Sec. 58.

12. On the economical concept of risk aversion, and on some important applications to the juridical phenomena, see R. Cooter and

and barristers are compensated (the former by statutory fees, the latter by *quantum meruit*) such different schemes do not seem to affect the structure of incentives to litigate.

4.   Unitary Profession in the Civil Law: Germany

The first aspect of the organization of the legal profession that strikes the common law observer considering the German model is the high degree of involvement of the State. The role of the government and that of the attorney are traditionally perceived as "in conflict" in common law. One only has to think about the conflict between the common lawyers and the Tudors in England,[1] as well as the impressive role of attorneys against the government in civil rights cases in the U. S.[2] To the contrary as we know in Germany, the attorney's role is historically framed by the need of the modern, absolute State to have available trustworthy functionaries.[3] This aspect of the German model is shared in quite a number of other countries outside of the western legal tradition. It is true in Japan, where the "invention" of the attorney dates back little more than one century,[4] and it is also true in a number of former and current socialist countries.[5]

It is sufficient here to recall that traditionally, the entire process of legal education in Germany functions to educate a unitary jurist. The focus is still mostly to educate judges and prosecutors rather than adversary attorneys.[6] The legal profession is as a consequence highly unitary in Germany, not only in the sense that there are no significant private practitioners beyond attorneys,[7] but also in the sense that the culture of the attorney and that of his counterpart on the bench is rather common. Even the notary is somewhat less blooming as a profession in Germany as compared to other Latin countries, and in certain *Landers* (states), the same individual can operate simultaneously as a *Rechtsanwalt* (Attorney) and as a Notary, something not acceptable for the Latin *Notarile* tradition.[8]

T. Ulen, Law and Economics, pp. 58, 415 (2007).

1. See Baker, An Introduction to English Legal History (2002).

2. See L. Friedman, A History of American Law (1982).

3. See, however, on the degree of independence historically maintained, Blankenburgh, Changes in Political Regimes and Continuity of the Rule of Law in Germany, in H. Jacobs, Courts, Law and Politics in Comparative Perspective 249 (1996).

4. See Rokumoto–Ota, supra p. 639, note 5. See, however, F. Upham, Law and Social Change in Post War Japan (1983).

5. See, as far as Hungary is concerned, A. Sajo, The Role of Legal Profession in Social Change in Hungary in Rokumoto *supra* p. 639, note 5 at 141ff.

6. See Blankenburg and Shultz, German Advocates: A Highly Regulated Profession, in Abel and Lewis, *supra* p. 637, note 36.

7. There are in Germany a number of paralegal professions that might compete in some aspects of the Rechtanwalt. See H. Schack, The Role of the Legal Profession in Germany, in Rokumoto (ed.) *supra* p. 639, note 5 at 109.

8. This possibility, not common in civil law, is open also in Guatemala.

There are almost 70 thousands practicing attorneys in today's Germany,[9] and the attorney's role is highly regulated. Traditionally he was strictly forbidden from advertising. A decision of the Federal Constitutional Court in July 1987, however, has determined that the self-imposed restrictions contained in the Federal Bar Association Rules lack legal authority. Today, some "decent informative advertising is now generally considered as permitted."[10] The attorney is very restricted in his organizational form: attorney partnerships are still limited to the form of associations. The mentioned relaxation of the Federal Bar Association Rules have carried as a consequence in the last few years, the birth of "supra-regional partnerships," which by opening the door to nationwide practice, is the first step for the diffusion of the Wall Street model and even of the multi-disciplinary partnership with accountants and other professionals.[11] Another step in this direction is a 1994 amendment to the Statute of Advocates (following a local and European case law favoring liberalization) which allows advocates to combine with some professionals offering other services (such as patent agents and tax advisers).[12] Despite this evolution, the average German legal practice is still tiny. Less than 10% of the law firms contain more than five lawyers. The largest law firm today (Oppenhof and Radler) has about 200 lawyers, but any firm of 50 lawyers is still considered among the largest.[13]

This high level of involvement from the State has its positive aspects. On the one hand, Germany has earned the admiration of civilized countries as far as its liberal system of access to justice, where the Rechtanwalt acting on behalf of less affluent clients are compensated by the State at the same level as privately hired attorneys.[14] On the other hand, the quality of legal services is guaranteed by the highly qualified educational characteristics of the German attorney due to its length and thoroughness. Also, the most outrageous restrictive practices due to the guild mentality of the Bar in a number of countries are limited. The young lawyer during his training receives a decent salary from the State so that, differently than most English pupils, and French or Italian juniors he will not be exploited by senior members of the profession that too often by pretending to educate him in reality profit from low pay secretarial help.

The German legal profession is incrementally growing in size as well as in the diversity of its components. To be sure, the more the State is involved, the less legal qualifications other than those certified by it are likely to be recognized. The German system (and the Japanese) is today the most challenged and rigid, as far as opening up to the needs of the global profession by allowing foreign lawyers to practice in the national soil.[15]

9. See Blankenburg–Shultz, in Abel and Lewis, *supra* p. 637, note 36 at 106, reporting of 67,562 attorneys in 1993.

10. See Schack, *supra* note 7 at 116.

11. *Id.* at 117.

12. See Blankenburg–Shultz, in Abel and Lewis, *supra* p. 637, note 36 at 106.

13. See Schack, *supra* note 7 at 116.

14. See *id.*

15. See Vlassopoulou V., *Ministerium fur Justiz, Bundes und Europaangelegenheiten, Case C–340/89,* May 7, 1991, 1991 E.C.R. I 2357.

---

5.   DIVIDED PROFESSION IN THE CIVIL LAW: FRANCE

France is traditionally introduced to common law students as the example of a civil law country characterized by a legally enforced divided and specialized legal profession. The French legal evolution can be understood as a three step process. The pre–1971 phase was characterized by a sharp distinction between two kinds of advocates. The *Avoué* was responsible of written pleadings and the *Avocat* was to orally address the Court. The French system was characterized by extreme informality for all activity, in which neither *Avocats* or *Avoué* had monopolies, and where anybody was allowed to advise on legal issues.[1] A number of other practitioners could be seen in action, notably a specialized bar, having monopoly on supreme jurisdictions, and a profession of *Agréé*, practicing in front of commercial courts. A large monopoly of Notaries on a variety of fields mainly within the law of property and successions completes the picture.[2]

In 1971 and in 1990, two statutes attempted to simplify the system. They have been only partially successful in their attempt to limit monopolies. The 1971 reform combined several of the professions formerly involved in litigation into one, that of *Avocat*. While the *Agréés* disappeared, the *Avoués* have been able to survive this reform (as well as the 1990 one) as far as the Court of Appeals is concerned. In that intermediate jurisdiction, the *Avoué* still enjoys a lucrative monopoly. The same 1971 reform for the first time regulated the giving of legal advice in France. The new profession of *Conseil Juridique* was born. During their twenty years of existence, *Conseil Juriques* became quite important as legal advisers for business firms and were often organized in rather large firms. Foreign, in particular American, law firms active in France were invariably organized in that form. Certainly they became powerful enough to obtain a new enactment that in 1990 grandfathered them into the leading profession of *Avocat*. In this way they obtained the right to appear in all Courts except the *Cour de Cassation* and the *Conseil d' Etat*, where a group of 90 attorneys called *Avocats au Conseil d' Etat et à la Court de Cassation* has a monopoly.[3] The profession of *Conseil Juridique* consequently disappeared. Informal legal

---

1. In 2009 there were 444 avoués with monopoly before the intermediate appellate courts. See http://www.chambre-nationale. avoues.fr/ (last visited Jan. 21, 2009).

2. In 2007 there were 8,494 notaires in France (6,268 pursuing their profession as partners in civil partnerships and professional corporations; 1,988 practicing on an individual basis). Only 1,929 notaires are women. The average age is 49. To underline their importance: each year, notaries receive 20 million clients, manage capital transactions worth a total of 790 billion US dollars, draw up more than 4.3 million official deeds and have turnover of 8 billion US dollars. The breakdown of notarial activity based on turnover is the following: real estate, construction, sales, leases (49%), credit-related instruments (14%), family instruments and deeds of succession (26%), real estate negotiation (4%) and company law, consulting, expert appraisal, estate planning (7%). See www. notaires.fr (last visited Jan. 21, 2009).

3. See http://www.ordre-avocats-cassa tion.fr (last visited Jan. 21, 2009).

advice was never banned, but the same 1990 reform requires that as of 1996, even unlicensed legal advisers are required to have legal education.

The 1990 legislation and implementing decree have a number of transitional provisions concerning the status of former *conseils juridiques* who prefer not to immediately become *avocats*, but otherwise, there are no survivals in French law comparable to the surviving impact of the rules on the *avoués* that you mentioned. However, the French rules on the *conseils juridiques* have had a significant impact on the law of some American States, such as New York. The 1971 French statute and regulations reforming the legal profession and creating the *conseils juridiques* threatened to subject any foreign lawyer from a non–European Community country to severe disadvantages unless the country of the lawyer's nationality would, under comparable conditions, grant French lawyers a status similar to that of a *conseil juridique*. Most of the American lawyers and law firms exposed to this threat were from New York, and understandably they launched a massive lobbying offensive in order to have reciprocal legislation enacted in New York.[4] Their efforts were crowned by success. A 1974 New York statute,[5] implemented by Court of Appeals Rules,[6] permits a foreign lawyer to become a Legal Consultant in New York. Such a Legal Consultant may give legal advice to clients and may also prepare legal instruments except those relating to real estate, decedents' estates, and matrimonial relations (i.e., those which in a civil-law country normally would be prepared by a notary). Thus, New York granted foreign lawyers the kind of reciprocity the French had been insisting on. During the first decade of the New York statute's operation, more than seventy foreign lawyers, possessing specialized knowledge of the laws of about thirty different countries, were licensed as foreign legal consultants,[7] and more followed later.

At first, the French Government took the view that so long as French lawyers could practice as legal consultants in New York, a condition of reciprocity existed between France and the United States. As a result, the favorable treatment accorded to New York lawyers was extended by the

---

4. The reader will recall (from our study of the *Shoop* case, *supra* at 178) that a foreign lawyer from a common-law country may, under certain conditions, be admitted in New York as a full-fledged member of the Bar, without having to take the bar examination. Lack of U.S. citizenship, of course, does not disqualify her. Application of Griffiths, 413 U.S. 717, 93 S.Ct. 2851 (1973). Lawyers from civil-law countries, on the other hand, generally have to pass the bar examination in order to become regular members of the New York Bar and may even have to repeat some of their law school education, though credit is ordinarily given to some extent for foreign degrees. For them, the alternative of becoming admitted as legal consultants (which does not hinge on passing an examination) may be particularly attractive. For a detailed listing

concerning the rights of foreign law school graduates to take the bar examination, to be admitted without taking the bar examination, and, on the effect of an American graduate degree on these rights, see American Bar Association Section on Legal Education and Admission to the Bar and National Conference of Bar Examiners, Comprehensive Guide to Bar Admission Requirements, 1993–94, Chart VII.

5. McKinney's N.Y. Judiciary Law § 53(6), as added by L.1974, Ch. 231.

6. Part 521 of the N.Y. Court of Appeals Rules for the Admission of Attorneys, 22 N.Y.C.R.R. Part 521.

7. See N.Y. Law Journal, June 4, 1984, p. 1.

French to lawyers from other states. Thus the other states got a free ride on New York's coattails and initially felt under no pressure to enact "foreign legal consultant" legislation of their own.

The situation, however, quickly changed when in the early 1980s increasing numbers of American law firms, not only in New York but in other jurisdictions as well, developed plans to open branch offices on the Pacific rim, especially in Japan. As part of U.S.–Japanese trade negotiations, protracted discussions took place concerning the "import" and "export" of legal services. In these discussions the Japanese emphasized reciprocity, and, understandably less willing than the French to equate New York with the United States, they insisted on strict state-by-state reciprocity, though the rights eventually granted foreign lawyers were somewhat limited.[8] The pressure thus put on jurisdictions other than New York caused a number of them, including Alaska, California, Connecticut, Florida, Georgia, Hawaii, Michigan, New Jersey, Ohio, Oregon, Texas, Washington, and the District of Columbia to adopt statutes or rules similar to New York's.[9]

But, in the meantime, the situation in France changed radically. There is no longer a separate profession, the *conseils juridiques,* authorized only to give legal advice, because they were merged with the *avocats* by the 1990 legislation. Foreign lawyers who are not from a European Union country may now be admitted as French *avocats* after passing an examination showing a sufficient knowledge of French law without fulfilling any of the educational and training requirements imposed on their French counterparts, but only if reciprocity exists. This presumably means full access to the legal profession, but the matter is not entirely free from doubt. Furthermore, the current French rules make it plain that reciprocity must exist with the "territorial unit" in question—in other words, for the United States, on a State by State basis.[10]

8. As a result of the discussions mentioned in the text, the Japanese Diet on March 23, 1986, promulgated the "Special Measures Law Concerning the Handling of Legal Business by Foreign Lawyers" (Law No. 66 of 1986). Effective April 1, 1987, this statute made it possible for American lawyers under certain conditions to be licensed as foreign legal consultants, subject to state-by-state reciprocity. The Japanese rules impose various restrictions on foreign legal consultants. See R.H. Wohl, S.M. Chemtob and G.S. Fukushima, Practice by Foreign Lawyers in Japan (ABA Section on Int'l Law and Practice 1989); Chin Kim and S. Siemer, Foreign Lawyers in Japan and the United States, 20 Korean J.Comp.L. 67 (1992); McK. Birmingham and Th.R. Radcliffe, Japan invites Lawyers ... sort of, Business Law Today, Jan./Feb. 1994, p. 55; L. Coulter, Japan's Gaiben Law. Economic Protectionism or Cultural Perfectionism, 17 Houston J.Int'l L. 431 (1995).

9. For a complete list see American Bar Association Section on Legal Education and Admissions to the Bar and National Conference of Bar Examiners, Comprehensive Guide to Bar Admission Requirements, 1993–94, Chart X, and American Bar Association, Section on International Law and Practice, Report to the House of Delegates, Model Rule for the Licensing of Legal Consultants (includes text of model rule), 28 Int'l Lawyer 207, 214–15 (1994).

10. The reciprocity rule is contained in art. 11(1) of the 1971 statute, as amended in 1990 and, subsequently in 1993. The statute itself requires reciprocity as to the activity the foreign lawyer proposes to exercise in France. That would suggest that if the foreign lawyer, for instance, proposes to engage

The French legal profession is also much freer than its German counterpart as far as the legal form of its activity. As of 1990, members of all regulated professions (not only lawyers) can operate in forms resembling American partnerships or even corporations. This legal framework was introduced to a profession almost entirely engaged in solo practice: In 1988, out of about 17,000 *Avocats* in France, 13,000 were solo practitioners, 2,300 were merely sharing office space, and fewer than 800 were members of formal partnerships. On the other hand, the merger with the former *Conseil Juridique* changes significantly these figures. Most of the 3,000 that were active in Paris were members of relatively large firms.[11]

The French legal scenario is thus characterized by the traditionally extensive and successful activity of practicing lawyers in promoting their different guilds, accompanied by a rather relaxed attitude of the State towards the needs to regulate the legal profession. The outcome has been competition between different professional groups to secure monopolistic positions or to defeat the monopolies of previous groups. As a consequence, the quality of the legal service provided and the capacity of the practicing bar to face government power has been questioned many times.[12]

While the system has been traditionally open to foreign attorneys as well, the last wave of reform may have cut the other way. While many foreigners registered as *Conseil Juridiques* prior to 1990 are now full-fledged attorneys in France, newcomers are paying the price of this grandfathering, and now must go through the CAPA (bar examination) and all the formal requirements to be admitted.

The trend towards a unitary profession, although made difficult by the defenses of guild-monopolies, also seems to be present in France. Not only has the *Avocat* merged with the *Conseil Juridique* (and with foreign practitioners), but the associate practice is also developing quickly in France, and many firms can now provide many types of legal and paralegal services. A number of French law firms today contain more than 100 lawyers, and the largest one (Fidal) has over one thousand attorneys. These new, large French law firms "have established connections with foreign firms, mostly within the E.U. to make real international groups: it is the

only in giving advice on international business transactions, there might be reciprocity with States having legal consultant rules. But the decree implementing the statute (see art. 100 of Decree 91–1197) and even more so the Regulation (*arrêté*) of the Minister implementing the rules of the statute and decree on the qualifying examination imply that reciprocity means access to the legal profession as such. See the *arrêté* of the Minister of Justice of January 7, 1993, 1993 J.O. 1428. The question will eventually have to be settled by legislation or court decision. See fur-

ther Chapter 3, sec. 4B, *supra*, especially at nn. 37 & 38. On the question of reciprocity generally, see S.M. Cone, The Issue of Reciprocity in Regulating United States Lawyers in the European Community, in American Bar Association (Sections on International Law and Practice and on Litigation), Frontiers of European Litigation: 1992 and Beyond (Course Book, Tab E, 1991).

11. *Id.* at 87.

12. See P. Fouchard, Le Role social de professions Juridiques en France, in Rokumoto, *supra* p. 639, note 5 at 67ff.

multinationalization of the law firm started very recently by French lawyers but at this point well advanced."[13]

NOTES AND QUESTIONS

(1) The academic part of legal education in France, as in most civil law countries, is (to use U.S. expression) undergraduate. This, of course, marks a significant contrast between the U.S. system of legal education and the civil law one. It seems difficult to explain this contrast in terms of differing present day social conditions or of divergent policy objectives. Thus one suspects that the reasons for the contrast can be discerned only by the student of history. Does the history of universities and of other (academic or professional) educational institutions perhaps shed some light on the matter?

(2) In France, as in most countries, a candidate's legal training is divided into an academic and a practical phase. The kind of practical training which candidates receive during that phase depends on which branch of the legal profession they intend to enter. Those that contemplate a judicial or prosecutorial career must try to gain acceptance in the Institute of Judicial Studies, which provides practical and theoretical training to future judges and prosecutors, and, if they finish their training period successfully, practically guarantees an initial position. If their aim is to become an *Avocat*, they must attend the professional training institute, and are then subject to a probationary period. If they aspire to become *Notaires*, the practical training will be of a different specialized nature. This means that under the French system the young legal candidates must select a *particular branch* of the legal profession *before* they enter the practical phase of their training.

Under the French system the *Avocats*, even during the probationary period, are members, though junior members, of the Bar. Thus, they initially obtain such membership, with many of its privileges and responsibilities, at the average age of 24 or 25, and before having acquired much practical experience.

Vlassopoulou v. Ministerium für Justiz, Bundes– und Europaangelegenheiten Baden–Württemberg

Court of Justice of the European Communities, 1991.
[1991] I E.C.R. 2357.

. . . Besides her Greek diplomas, Mrs. Vlassopoulou has a doctorate in law from the University of Tübingen (Germany). Since July 1983 she has been working with a firm of German lawyers at Mannheim and in November 1984 she received permission to deal with foreign legal affairs concerning Greek law and Community law, in accordance with the Rechtsberatungsgesetz (Law on legal advice) (Bundesgesetzblatt III, p. 303). As far as German law is concerned, Mrs. Vlassopoulou practises under the responsibility of one of her German colleagues in the firm.

13. *Id.* at 91.

On 13 May 1988, Mrs. Vlassopoulou applied to the Ministry for admission as a Rechtsanwältin. The Ministry refused her application on the ground that she did not have the qualifications, laid down by Paragraph 4 of the Bundesrechtsanwaltordnung (Federal regulation on the profession of Rechtsanwalt) (Bundesgesetzblatt 1959 I, p. 565), for the holding of judicial office, which are necessary for admission to the profession of Rechtsanwalt. Basically, those qualifications are acquired by studying law at a German university, passing the First State Examination, completing a preparatory training period and then passing the Second State Examination. The Ministry also stated that Article 52 of the EEC Treaty did not give the applicant the right to exercise her profession in the Federal Republic of Germany on the basis of her professional qualification obtained in Greece.

Mrs. Vlassopoulou's appeal against the Ministry's decision was dismissed by the Ehrengerichtshof (Lawyers' Disciplinary Council). She then appealed against the decision of that body to the Bundesgerichtshof (Federal Supreme Court), which, taking the view that the dispute raised a question concerning the interpretation of Article 52 of the EEC Treaty, referred the following question to the Court of Justice for a preliminary ruling:

> Is freedom of establishment within the meaning of Article 52 of the EEC Treaty infringed if a Community national who is already admitted and practising as a lawyer in her country of origin and for five years has been admitted in the host country as a legal adviser (Rechtsbeistand) and also practices in a law firm established there can be admitted as a lawyer in the host country only in accordance with the statutory rules of that country?

* * *

The second paragraph of Article 52 of the EEC Treaty provides that "[f]reedom of establishment shall include the right to take up and pursue activities as self-employed persons ... under the conditions laid down for its own nationals by the law of the country where such establishment is effected ..."

According to the Italian and German Governments, it is clear from that provision that in the absence of Community rules for coordinating conditions of access to, and the pursuit of, self-employed activities as a lawyer and in the absence of directives on the mutual recognition of diplomas a Member State is entitled to make admission to a Bar dependent on the fulfillment of non-discriminatory conditions laid down by national law.

In this regard, it must be stated first of all that in the absence of harmonization of the conditions of access to a particular occupation the Member States are entitled to lay down the knowledge and qualifications needed in order to pursue it and to require the production of a diploma certifying that the holder has the relevant knowledge and qualifications (see the judgment in Case 222/86 *Union Nationale des Entraineurs et*

Cadres Techniques Professionnels du Football (Unectef) v. Heylens and Others [1987] ECR 4097, paragraph 10).

It is established that no measure has yet been adopted under Article 57(2) of the EEC Treaty concerning the harmonization of the conditions of access to a lawyer's activities.*

Furthermore, when Mrs. Vlassopoulou made her application on 13 May 1988, no directive on the mutual recognition of diplomas giving access to the profession of lawyer had been adopted under Article 57(1) of the EEC Treaty.

Directive 89/48/EEC on a general system for the recognition of higher-education diplomas awarded on completion of professional education and training of at least three years' duration (Official Journal 1989 L 19, p. 16), which was adopted by the Council on 21 December 1988 and which the Member States had to implement by 4 January 1991, does not apply to the facts of this case.

However, in laying down that freedom of establishment is to be attained by the end of the transitional period, Article 52 of the Treaty thus imposes an obligation to attain a precise result, the fulfillment of which had to be made easier by, but not made dependent on, the implementation of a programme of progressive measures (see the judgment in Case 11/77 *Patrick v. Ministre des Affaires Culturelles* [1977] ECR 1199, paragraph 10).

Moreover, it is also clear from the judgment in Case 71/76 *Thieffry v. Conseil de l'Ordre des Avocats a la Cour de Paris* [1977] ECR 765, at paragraph 16, that, in so far as Community law makes no special provision, the objectives of the Treaty, and in particular freedom of establishment, may be achieved by measures enacted by the Member States, which, under Article 5 of the Treaty, must take "all appropriate measures, whether general or particular, to ensure fulfilment of the obligations arising out of this Treaty or resulting from action taken by the institutions of the Community" and abstain from "any measure which could jeopardize the attainment of the objectives of this Treaty."

It must be stated in this regard that, even if applied without any discrimination on the basis of nationality, national requirements concerning qualifications may have the effect of hindering nationals of the other Member States in the exercise of their right of establishment guaranteed to them by Article 52 of the EEC Treaty. That could be the case if the national rules in question took no account of the knowledge and qualifications already acquired by the person concerned in another Member State.

Consequently, a Member State which receives a request to admit a person to a profession to which access, under national law, depends upon the possession of a diploma or a professional qualification must take into consideration the diplomas, certificates and other evidence of qualifications which the person concerned has acquired in order to exercise the same

* See, however, the Note following this decision.

profession in another Member State by making a comparison between the specialized knowledge and abilities certified by those diplomas and the knowledge and qualifications required by the national rules.

That examination procedure must enable the authorities of the host Member State to assure themselves, on an objective basis, that the foreign diploma certifies that its holder has knowledge and qualifications which are, if not identical, at least equivalent to those certified by the national diploma. That assessment of the equivalence of the foreign diploma must be carried out exclusively in the light of the level of knowledge and qualifications which its holder can be assumed to possess in the light of that diploma, having regard to the nature and duration of the studies and practical training to which the diploma relates (see the judgment in Case 222/86 *Unectef v. Heylens*, cited above, paragraph 13).

In the course of that examination, a Member State may, however, take into consideration objective differences relating to both the legal framework of the profession in question in the Member State of origin and to its field of activity. In the case of the profession of lawyer, a Member State may therefore carry out a comparative examination of diplomas, taking account of the differences identified between the national legal systems concerned.

If that comparative examination of diplomas results in the finding that the knowledge and qualifications certified by the foreign diploma correspond to those required by the national provisions, the Member State must recognize that diploma as fulfilling the requirements laid down by its national provisions. If, on the other hand, the comparison reveals that the knowledge and qualifications certified by the foreign diploma and those required by the national provisions correspond only partially, the host Member State is entitled to require the person concerned to show that he has acquired the knowledge and qualifications which are lacking.

In this regard, the competent national authorities must assess whether the knowledge acquired in the host Member State, either during a course of study or by way of practical experience, is sufficient in order to prove possession of the knowledge which is lacking.

If completion of a period of preparation or training for entry into the profession is required by the rules applying in the host Member State, those national authorities must determine whether professional experience acquired in the Member State of origin or in the host Member State may be regarded as satisfying that requirement in full or in part.

Finally, it must be pointed out that the examination made to determine whether the knowledge and qualifications certified by the foreign diploma and those required by the legislation of the host Member State correspond must be carried out by the national authorities in accordance with a procedure which is in conformity with the requirements of Community law concerning the effective protection of the fundamental rights conferred by the Treaty on Community subjects. It follows that any decision taken must be capable of being made the subject of judicial proceedings in which its legality under Community law can be reviewed and that the person concerned must be able to ascertain the reasons for the decision taken in his regard (see the Judgment in Case 222/86 *Unectef v. Heylens*, cited above, paragraph 17).

Consequently, the answer to the question submitted by the Bundesgerichtshof must be that Article 52 of the EEC Treaty must be interpreted as requiring the national authorities of a Member State to which an application for admission to the profession of lawyer is made by a Community subject who is already admitted to practise as a lawyer in his country of origin and who practises as a legal adviser in the first-mentioned Member State to examine to what extent the knowledge and qualifications attested by the diploma obtained by the person concerned in his country of origin correspond to those required by the rules of the host State; if those diplomas correspond only partially, the national authorities in question are entitled to require the person concerned to prove that he has acquired the knowledge and qualifications which are lacking.

NOTES

(1) The European Union encourages to work as a lawyer in another member state to facilitate the free movement of legal services.[1]

Each member state regulates its own legal profession. Although there may be natural similarities between them, these regulations vary substantially from country to country because they reflect the continuation of often ancient traditions. Community law does not regulate the conditions for exercising the legal professions. However, two European directives, one from 1988 and the other from 1998, set out the conditions in which a lawyer who has qualified in one member state can exercise his or her profession on a permanent basis in another. The 1998 Directive in particular states that any lawyer may pursue the profession on a permanent basis in any other member state under his home-country professional title. The host member state may also impose certain conditions. In principle, a lawyer who has practiced in the host country under his home-country professional title for three years should be integrated in the same way as a lawyer from that country.

However, they may be required to work in conjunction with a lawyer who practices before the judicial authority in question. For other activities the rules of professional conduct of the home state apply without prejudice to respect for

1. There are three key pieces of legislation that affect the legal profession. The Council Directive 77/249/EEC of March 22, 1977 facilitates the effective exercise by lawyers of freedom to provide services (Official Journal L78, March 26, 1977, p. 17). The Directive 98/5/EC of the European Parliament and of the Council of February 16, 1998 facilitates practice of the profession of lawyer on a permanent basis in a member state other than that in which the qualification was obtained (Official Journal L77, March 14, 1998, p. 36). The Directive 2005/36/EC of the European Parliament and of the Council of September 7, 2005 on the recognition of professional qualifications (Official Journal L255, September 30, 2005, p. 22). See also Directive 2006/123/EC of the European Parliament and of the Council of 12th December 2006 on services in the internal market (Official Journal L376, December 27, 2006, p. 36), dealing with questions other than those relating to professional qualifications, for example professional liability insurance, commercial communications, multidisciplinary activities and administratives implification.

the rules of the host state, most notably confidentiality, advertising, conflicts of interest, relations with other lawyers and activities incompatible with the profession of law.

The practice of law permitted under the Directive includes not only the lawyers' home state law, community law and international law, but also the law of the member state in which they are practicing. However, this entitlement requires that a lawyer wishing to practice on a permanent basis registers with the relevant bar or law society in that State and is subject to the same rules regarding discipline, insurance and professional conduct as domestic lawyers. Once registered, the European lawyer can apply to be admitted to the host state profession after 3 years without being required to pass the usual exams, provided that he or she can provide evidence of effective and regular practice of the host state law over that period.

The new Recognition of Professional Qualifications Directive of 2005 governs re-qualification. The basic rules require a lawyer seeking to re-qualify in another EU/EEA member state or Switzerland to show that he or she has the professional qualifications required for the taking up or pursuit of the profession of lawyer in one member state and is in good standing with his or her home bar. The member state where the lawyer is seeking to re-qualify may require the lawyer to either: complete an adaptation period (a period of supervised practice) not exceeding three years, or take an aptitude test to assess the ability of the applicant to practice as a lawyer of the host member state. This test only covers the essential knowledge needed to exercise the profession in the host member state and it must take account of the fact that the applicant is a qualified professional in the member state of origin.

(2) As the court points out, Dr. Vlassopoulou had already been licensed in 1984 to practice in Germany as a *foreign* lawyer, but as such, she could only deal with legal affairs concerning Greek law and European Communities law. As amended in December, 1989, the German Attorneys' Law (BRAO) authorizes local bar associations to license lawyers from other European Community countries and, on the basis of reciprocity, from non-EC countries (e.g., the United States). The former can give advice on foreign law, international law, and European Communities law; the latter, only on the law of the foreign country in which they are principally admitted.[2] This *general* admission of foreign lawyers to the practice of their own law on the basis of reciprocity is now quite common. In the United States, for instance, some ten states and the District of Columbia now grant the status of "Foreign Legal Consultant" to qualified foreign lawyers under like conditions.[3]

---

2. BRAO, Sections 206(1) and 206(2), as amended by Act of December 13, 1989, 1989 I BGBl 2135. See Rüdiger Zuck, Das Gesetz zur Änderung des Berufsrechts der Rechtsanwälte und der Patentanwälte, 1990 NJW 1025, 1026–27. As pointed out in *id.* 1026–27, n. 32, the latter restriction works especially to the disadvantage of United States lawyers. Reflecting like restrictions in this country, it is surely not unjust. One of its practical effects has been to keep Ameri-can law firms from capturing the lucrative East German privatization business. See "Berlin: Germany's Legal Capital," 11 Int'l Financial L.Rev. (No. 4) at 14, table at 16 and firm listings at 17–19 (April 1992).

3. Roger J. Goebel, Lawyers in the European Community: Progress Towards Community–Wide Rights of Practice, 15 Fordham L.Rev. 556, 557, n. 2 (1992), listing, in addition to the District of Columbia, Alaska, Cali-

Dr. Vlassopoulou was seeking admission in Germany as a *German* lawyer. She was obviously qualified academically, but had taken neither the first nor the second German bar examinations. The court mentions, but does not discuss directly, the European Communities Directive of December 21, 1988, "on a general system for the recognition of higher-education diplomas awarded on completion of professional education and training of at least three years' duration."[4] That directive had to be implemented by Member States by January 4, 1991 (article 12). It defined "diploma" to include certificates showing that the holder "has successfully completed a post-secondary course of at least three years' duration, or of an equivalent duration part-time, at a university or establishment of higher education or another establishment of similar level and, where appropriate that he has successfully completed the professional training required in addition to the post-secondary course," and that he or she "has the professional qualifications required for the taking up or pursuit of a regulated profession in that Member State" (article 1a). Nationals of Member States who hold such diplomas from a Member State and who wish to pursue a "regulated profession in a host Member State" may not be refused permission to do so on the grounds of insufficient qualification (articles 2 & 3). However, for professions requiring "precise knowledge of national law and in respect of which the provision of advice and/or assistance concerning national law is an essential and constant aspect of the professional activity," the host Member State may require either an "adaptation period" or an "aptitude test" (article 4b).

Since the definition of "diploma" covers the qualification achieved by German lawyers on the successful completion of the second bar examination, Germany could, as of 1991, make the admission of academically trained and licensed lawyers from other Community countries *as German lawyers* contingent only on an adaptation period or an aptitude test. The latter of these courses was chosen. Pursuant to federal legislation enacted in July 1990 and implemented by Regulations promulgated in December that year, European Community nationals who are holders of "diplomas" as defined in the above quoted guideline can be admitted to practice as a *German Rechtsanwalt* upon successfully taking an aptitude test.[5] This consists of relatively brief, German language oral and written examinations in German civil law (excluding family law and successions, but including pertinent rules of civil procedure and bankruptcy), and in two of five elective subjects (public law, criminal law, family law and succession, commercial law, or labor law).[6] The examinations test only legal knowledge "relating to the professional practice of a lawyer."[7]

Lawyers from European Community (now Union) countries like Dr. Vlassopoulou, with the requisite knowledge of German law and the German language, can now quite routinely be admitted to practice in Germany *as German lawyers*. (Dr. Vlassopoulou, happy to relate, promptly did so). In 1991, when the

fornia, Connecticut, Hawaii, Michigan, New Jersey, New York, Ohio, Oregon, and Texas.

4. O.J. 1989 L 19, at 16.

5. Act of July 6, 1990, 1990 I BGBl 1349; Regulations of December 18, 1990, 1990 I BGBl 2881. For discussion, see Wilhelm Feuerich, Die Umsetzung der Diplomanerkennungsrichtlinie durch das Eignungsprüfungsgesetz für die Zulassung zur Rechtsanwaltschaft, 1990 N.J.W. 1144.

6. Regulations, *supra* note 5, sec. 6.

7. *Id.* sec. 7(1). It is understood that this was a major concession, sought by the Commission of the European Communities.

system just outlined came into effect, it took a German lawyer some seven to eight years after high school to reach the same professional objective. Foreign competition (and the appearance of "queue-jumping" *German* competitors with "diplomas" from other Community countries) thus made yet another reform of German legal education all but inescapable. This reform reduced the minimum period of apprenticeship or internship between the first and second State examinations to two years.

On September 24, 1996, the Commission of the European Union issued a draft Directive "to facilitate practice of the profession of lawyers on a permanent basis in a Member State other than in which the qualification was obtained." O.J. 1996 C. 355/19. That draft Directive was adopted by the Council in December 1997. Despite its present caption, it seeks to assure a "temporary right to practice" as well. Lawyers qualified to practice law in a country of the European Union are to be entitled to practice in other European Union countries on a *temporary* basis (for up to five years) by mere registration with the appropriate professional body, but only under their un-translated home country professional title. Thus, a German or Austrian lawyer registered for "temporary" practice in, e.g., France or Italy would have to describe himself as *"Rechtsanwalt,"* and not as *Avocat, Avvocato,* or *Procurator Legale.* Significantly, however, such a "temporary" practitioner from another European Union jurisdiction would be entitled, pursuant to article 5(1) of the Directive, to *"inter alia* give advice on the law of his home Member State, on Community law, on international law *and on the law of the host Member State."* (Emphasis supplied). As provided in article 5(2) and (3) such "temporary" ("guest?") lawyers may be denied the right to practice in matters of probate and conveyancing limited by law to local lawyers, as well as in criminal matters reserved to lawyers unless in association with local counsel of record. Otherwise, however, even "guest lawyers" from other European Union countries would be placed in virtually the same position as local lawyers.

Article 10 of the Directive is entitled "Integration as a lawyer of the Home Member State." Its key operative provision reads as follows:

1. A lawyer practicing under his home-country professional title who has effectively pursued regularly for a period of at least three years an activity involving the law of the host Member State including Community law shall, with a view to his gaining admission to the profession of lawyer in the host Member State and practicing there under the professional title corresponding to the profession in that State, be exempted from the conditions set out in article 4(1)(b) of Directive 89/48/EEC.

Thus, "guest lawyers" will in effect be able to be "naturalized" as members of the host country bar upon a showing of regular ("effective") local practice for at least three years, but without the examination presently required. Article 10 goes onto provide the prerequisites for proof of three years' "effective" practice, including, notably, "documentation" of the cases handled, but it takes care to spell out that the local licensing authorities have power only to *consider* applications for "integration" and not to *examine* the applicant. A successful applicant for "integration" would be entitled to practice in the host country using his "home-country professional title, expressed in the official language or one of the official languages of his home country, alongside the professional title used in the host Member State" (article 10(6)).

The Directive will make obsolete, as between lawyers from European Union countries, the increasingly other-worldly disqualification of "guest" lawyers from giving advice on the law of the host country. Indeed, as stated in its Preamble (5), that is one of the chief objectives of the Directive:

> [B]y enabling lawyers to practice temporarily under their home-country professional titles on a permanent basis in a host Member State, it meets the needs of consumers of legal services who, owing to the increasing trade flows resulting from the internal market, seek advice when carrying out cross-border transactions in which international law, Community law and domestic laws often overlap.

(3) With the increased involvement of lawyers in business counseling as well as litigation, something of an informal division of labor seems to take place in many countries in those areas where the law does not strictly assign functions to one profession or the other. For example, notaries are often quite active in areas where their assistance is required by law for the preparation of certain documents, such as real estate transfers, wills, and prenuptial agreements. Thus, they are likely to do a fair amount of counseling and drafting (even when they have no monopoly) in connection with family wealth planning and real estate transactions; lawyers, on the other hand, tend to dominate in connection with business transactions, where notaries, if their participation is mandatory, sometimes intervene only to prepare the required formal notarial instruments, the basic contents of which have already been laid down by the lawyers involved. It should be noted that for some time now in the Netherlands "enterprising attorneys and notaries have formed amalgamated firms, which provide substantially all the services of a large U.S. law firm."[8] But firms composed of lawyers and notaries also exist in some places in Germany.[9] Furthermore, recent legislation in several countries authorizes the creation of firms composed of several types of professionals. We may therefore see an extension of that practice.

Other transformations are due to the fact that large and medium-large law firms set up offices in countries other than that of their home office. As we know, many "foreign" law firms exist in Paris, but other places, such as Brussels (because of the European Union), Tokyo or New York (for European or Japanese firms) are also popular venues. The large British firms of solicitors seem to be especially active in that connection, but they are by no means the only non-American ones. There are today a number of informal arrangements in which firms from several, often numerous, countries participate to assist each other.[10] In Europe, a more formal arrangement is available for collabora-

---

8. E. E. Murphy, Jr., A Guide to Foreign Law Source Materials and Foreign Counsel, 19 Int'l Lawyer 39, at 46 (1985); cf. H. J. Snijders, Independence and Responsability [sic] of Judges and Lawyers in H .J. Snijders & M. Ynzonides (eds.), Role and Organization of Judges and Lawyers in Contemporary Societies (Netherlands National Reports) 31, 62–64 (1992).

9. As already mentioned briefly, in some parts of Germany, lawyers may also be notaries; this facilitates such an arrangement. On the reasons why lawyers may be notaries in some parts of Germany, see G. Rohde, Plaidoyer für das freie Anwaltsnotariat, 24 Zeitschr. für Rechtspolitik 452 (1991).

10. Dutch firms appear to be particularly active in that area, creating ties especially with law firms in the surrounding area (Belgium, France, Germany). See A.W. Jongbloed, Professional Ethics and Procedural

tive efforts by entities that do, however, remain formally separate: the European Economic Interest Grouping (EEIG).[11] That device has been used by law firms from several countries to formalize their cooperative relationship. The Grouping is not substituted for its participating entities. In case of a malpractice claim, the firm directly involved, not the Grouping, would have to be sued.[12]

---

6.   LEGAL EDUCATION AND LEGAL PROFESSION IN EAST ASIA

Setsuo Miyazawa, Kay–Wah Chan, and Ilhyung Lee, The Reform of Legal Education in East Asia

4 Annual. Rev. of Law Soc. Sci. 14.1–14.28 (2008).
(some footnotes omitted other changed and renumbered).

CHINA

Since the founding of the People's Republic of China in 1949, there have been substantial changes in her legal system, corresponding to political, social, and economic development in the country. Changes to China's legal education system followed accordingly.

Initially, a Soviet-style socialist legal system was adopted.[1] Legal education that time was mainly for training general judicial cadres. Later, political movements, including the Cultural Revolution (1966–1976), led China into a state of legal nihilism. Legal education came to a virtual standstill.[2] In the late 1970s, China began to reconstruct her legal system and legal education system. The past three decades have seen dramatic development: From the two law schools that survived the Cultural Revolution, as of the end of 2006 more than 620 institutions offer legal education at the undergraduate level. Although there has not been the substantial structural reform experienced in Japan and Korea, the Chinese legal education system is not static. It has been and still is evolving and developing. New structural and pedagogical elements have been introduced. These are reforms in the broadest sense.

China's professional layer of the legal system has a civil law flavor, and its legal education in principle follows the European Continental model.

Fairness, in H. J. Snijders and M. Ynzonides, *supra* note 8 at 3, 27–28.

11. The EEIG (which finds its origin in a Council Regulation of 1985) is designed to make it easier for companies in different countries to do business together. Its activities must be ancillary to those of its members, and, as with a partnership, any profit or loss it makes is attributed to its members. There are now several thousand EEIG, active in fields as varied as agricultural marketing, research and development, motorcycle preservation, and legal services.

12. See Klabbers & Sellers (Eds.), The Internationalization of Law and Legal Education (2008) and Drolshammer & Pfeifer, The Internationalization of the Practice of Law (2001).

1. Gao L. 2002. What makes a lawyer in China? The Chinese legal education system after China's entry into the WTO. Willamette J. Int. Law Dis. Res. 10:197–237.

2. Wang Z. 2002. Legal education in contemporary China. Int. Law. 36(4):1203–12.

However, most of the newly introduced elements principally originate in the United States. In fact, China has been greatly influenced by American legal education over the past 20 years. . . .

China has seen substantial expansion in both the JM (Juris Master) and the clinical programs. The number of institutions with JM programs has increased from 8 to 50,[3] and clinical programs have expanded from the initial 7 institutions to 51 law schools or departments as of June 2006.[4] A nonprofit academic organization, the Committee of Chinese Clinical Legal Educators, was founded in July 2002 with the mission, among other things, to promote the growth of clinical legal education in China. However, despite this substantial growth, institutions with JM or clinical programs still represent a very small proportion of all the tertiary institutions that offer legal education (more than 620). Institutions with JM programs are also concentrated in the more developed regions of China. There are only five institutions offering the program in the western area of the country. Furthermore, the JM program coexists with other law degree programs (LLB, LLM, and doctorate). There are no clear differences between the four types of programs, and this has resulted in chaos. Graduates from all these formal legal education programs as well as degree holders from other disciplines (who need to have professional legal knowledge) can take the National Judicial Examination ("the Examination"), and they compete with each other in the legal market. In short, there is still a disconnection between formal legal education in China and the pathway to taking the Examination and ultimately practicing law. Numerous literatures have pointed out problems and drawbacks in the adoption of American legal pedagogical features in Asia. Owing to space limitations, this review discusses only a few.

JAPAN

The Japanese government established the Justice System Reform Council (JSRC) under the cabinet on July 27, 1999. Article 2 of the Law Concerning the Establishment of the JSRC stipulated that the goals of the JSRC were clarifying the role to be played by justice in Japanese society in the 21st century and examining and deliberating about fundamental measures necessary for the realization of a justice system that is easy for the people to utilize, participation by the people in the justice system, achievement of a legal profession as it should be and strengthening the functions thereof, and other reforms of the justice system, as well as improvements in the infrastructure of that system.

The JSRC presented its recommendations for a comprehensive reform of the justice system to Prime Minister Jun'ichiro Koizumi on June 12, 2001 (Justice System Reform Council 2001). The recommended reforms included, among other matters, speedier trials, introduction of lay judges in

3. Huo X. 2007. Zhongguo Faxue Jiaoyu Fansi [Re-examining the Legal Education in China]. Beijing: China Renmin Univ. Press.

4. Mao L. 2007. Clinical legal education and the reform of the higher legal education system in China. Fordham Int. Law J. 30:421–34.

serious criminal cases, extension of criminal legal aid from the post-indictment stage to the post-arrest stage, establishment of a national network of staff lawyers who will provide civil and criminal legal aid on a full-time basis, introduction of a system to accredit alternative dispute resolution (ADR) programs, and deregulation of practicing attorneys. To employ these reforms, a larger number of lawyers is required than Japan had at the time, particularly practicing attorneys. Hence, the JSRC prioritized an increase in the number of lawyers, setting a goal to triple the number of new lawyers by 2010 and recommending the establishment of law schools at a postgraduate level by 2004 as a centerpiece of the new system. The introduction of new law schools has been widely discussed internationally. At least four law journals outside Japan published symposium issues on this topic.[5] Policy makers and administrators rarely publish papers in English; it is also rare for native Japanese opponents of the law school system to publish anything in English. . . .

The old system of legal education and training of lawyers in Japan consisted of (a) undergraduate four-year law faculties, (b) the national bar examination administered by the Justice Ministry, and (c) the apprenticeship administered by the Supreme Court. There are nearly 100 undergraduate law faculties, with approximately 200,000 students. Ever since their introduction in the late nineteenth century, though, these undergraduate law faculties have never been considered a part of the process to educate future lawyers.[6] The national law faculties were originally established to educate future government bureaucrats. In postwar Japan, law faculties have functioned as general education programs to produce a workforce in business, government, and other walks of life. Although there are no other places to receive a comprehensive legal education, an undergraduate law degree (LLB) is not required for one to take the national bar examination.

Because completion of formal legal education is not a requirement, a large number of people take the national bar examination. However, the exam has never been purely a qualifying examination in which any number of people who earn a certain score will pass. Rather, there is an artificial quota on the number of bar examination passers, which is determined mainly by the positions available at the Legal Training and Research Institute (LTRI) operated by the Supreme Court. Those who pass the exam have, then, spent two years of apprenticeship (recently reduced to 18 months) as judicial trainees with stipends paid by the government. Schooling is provided at the beginning and end of this period at the LTRI, and trainees receive field experience in between at local courts, local prosecutor's offices, and local law offices in assigned regions all over the country. Faculty members at the LTRI are temporarily assigned practitioners, and

5. (Asian-Pacific Law & Policy Journal in 2000 and 2001, Zeitschrift für Japanisches Recht in 2001, Australian Journal of Asian Law in 2005, and Wisconsin International Law Journal in 2006).

6. Miyazawa S, Otsuka H. 2002. Legal education and the reproduction of the elite in Japan. In Global Prescriptions: The Production, Exportation, and Importation of a New Legal Orthodoxy, ed. Y Dezalay, BG Garth, p. 162.

the LTRI curriculum focuses primarily on doctrines and practical skills either developed or accepted by mainstream judges who control the LTRI. Upon completion of the period of apprenticeship, trainees choose one of the three branches of legal profession (the judiciary, the procuracy, and the bar) for their career. Thus, the quota on exam passers is set by the number of positions at the LTRI and by the judicial budget. Only approximately 500 per year passed until 1990, a passage rate of approximately 2%. Although the number was gradually increased to approximately 1000 by 1999, under pressure from outside the legal profession that passage rate was still only approximately 3% of exam takers. Therefore, passing the bar examination traditionally has been everything for aspiring lawyers, and thus the system was often called "selection of lawyers by a single point."

Although the bar examination has been extremely competitive, its content has been limited to the so-called Six Laws (Constitutional Law, Civil Law, Commercial Law, Criminal Law, Civil Procedure, and Criminal Procedure) and a few electives that fluctuated, and completion of comprehensive legal education has, in fact, been unnecessary. The bar examination has been administered in three disjointed stages: multiple choice, essay, and oral exam.

Because only those who pass an earlier stage can proceed to the next stage, preparation for the multiple choice examinations at the beginning, which requires rote memorization of a vast amount of information, became a predominant concern for applicants. Hence, proprietary cram schools developed into year-round operations overshadowing undergraduate law faculties as institutions to provide legal education to future legal professionals. Although most bar examination passers are actually graduates of undergraduate law faculties, their legal education is largely limited to that provided by cram schools.

The result of the old system is an extremely small number of lawyers, particularly practicing attorneys, for a highly developed country. There were only 15,000 attorneys in the 1990s for a nation with 120 million people. The distribution of attorneys was also highly skewed.

Approximately 60% were in Tokyo and Osaka, and many jurisdictions of branches of district courts—referred to as zero-one districts—had either one or no attorney. Furthermore, because law is taught only at undergraduate law faculties, and legal education of those who pass the bar examination is largely limited to that provided by a cram school, lawyers with backgrounds other than law, particularly in science, are extremely rare.

An early critic of this old system was Hideo Tanaka, an Anglo–American law professor at the University of Tokyo, who also taught at Harvard Law School. Tanaka (1982) characterized the LTRI as an organized apprenticeship that should be distinguished from professional legal education provided by autonomous faculty members in a university setting protected by academic freedom. He called for a transformation of university legal education to professional legal education. Because the LTRI had worked as the major factor in preventing an increase of lawyers and in maintaining an extremely conservative judiciary, Miyazawa (1998), also a former visiting professor at Harvard and other North American law schools, proposed establishing law schools that provide professional legal education at a postgraduate level and replacing the LTRI with clinical programs at law schools.

One proposal for reducing the bottleneck effect of the LTRI was to reduce the number of people who were required to receive training there. For instance, reformers suggested that training at the LTRI be required only for those who want to become an assistant judge or a prosecutor. However, the mandatory unified apprenticeship at the LTRI had been introduced in postwar Japan as part of practicing attorneys' efforts to elevate their professional status to that of judges and prosecutors (Hattori 1963). Thus, most attorneys wanted to keep this system, and they opposed any proposals that would increase their number. The Justice Ministry and the Supreme Court also wanted to keep the LTRI because it was a place where they recruited intelligent and conformist trainees (Kawabata 2002). Therefore, as long as the three branches of the legal profession controlled policymaking on lawyer training, there was no hope for a fundamental change. . . .

Problems started to appear in the fall of their first year, October 2004. The Bar Examination Committee under the Justice Ministry indicated that it had no intention of accelerating efforts to reach the targeted number of 3000 new passing lawyers per year before 2010. The number of passers of the first round of the new bar examination, scheduled to be given in 2006 to the first cohort of the two-year shorter courses, was projected to be much lower than 50%, which, although vastly improved from before, did not reach the 70–80% passage rate expected by the JSRC. The expectation was, of course, that the later passage rate would simply go down to as low as 30%. Deans and faculty members of many law schools, including Miyazawa, aggressively lobbied and campaigned, but they ultimately succeeded in raising the expected passage rates in the immediate years only by a few percentage points.

Although reformers might have anticipated this low passage rate from the beginning because of the lack of coordination between the Education Ministry and the Justice Ministry, it nevertheless had a chilling effect both outside and inside law schools. Interest in law schools dwindled, particularly among those with non-law academic backgrounds or working experience. The larger aptitude test had only approximately 13,000 applicants in 2008, only approximately 40% of the number in 2003; 69% were from undergraduate law faculties, and only 7.6% were from science and medicine. In 2007, only 15 law schools had a majority of entering students described as having "life experience"; only 3 law schools had a majority of entering students coming from non-law undergraduate fields. Faculty members at many law schools lament the decline of student quality. Within the law schools, the pressure from students for better bar examination preparation is rapidly rising. The new examination consists of multiple choice examinations and essay examinations in three broad areas of law (public law, private law, and criminal law) as well as an essay exam in one area of electives. Although applicants take all the examinations at the same time, in May, their essay examinations are not graded unless they obtain certain points in multiple choice examinations. The contents of essay exams have changed significantly from the old bar exam to better reflect law school curricula, but the multiple choice exam has quickly become the predominant concern of applicants, as in the old system.

Furthermore, because reformers assumed that a much higher proportion of applicants would pass the exam, applicants are allowed only three tries within five years of graduation. Naturally, rote memorization of statutes, doctrines, and cases has become a preoccupation of most students; students themselves began demanding changes in curriculum and teaching methods merely to prepare them better for test taking. In the meantime, the passage rate of the first round of the new bar examination in 2006 was 48%, and the rate went down to 40% in the second round in 2007. These rates were slightly higher than predicted because an unexpectedly large number of students postponed taking the exam, although that will simply contribute to further decline of passage rate in the very near future. Thus, law schools have already lost their position as the centerpiece of the training of lawyers through a process to the bar examination. In the 2007 bar examination, only 10 law schools had a passage rate of more than 50%; 24 law schools had a passage rate of less than 25%. If Standard 303(c) of the ABA Accreditation Standards were applied to those law schools, many would fail because their situation might be construed to "inculcate false hope, constitute economic exploitation." A little scandal erupted as a result. In Japan, leading law professors make and grade the bar exam. A professor of Keio Law School, one of the top private law schools, who was a bar examiner, gave hints to his students about relevant cases before the bar exam in 2007. The Justice Ministry did not consider his action to be cheating because, according to the Ministry, the cases he told his students about were among the cases students should have studied anyway. The "winners" in Japan's reform effort have been, of course, the cram schools. The aptitude tests have created a new market for them, and the two-year shorter programs have also created business for them because applicants are tested for their legal knowledge. Now most applicants of the new bar exam take cram school courses or, at least, mock examinations provided by them. There are even rumors that some law schools have entered into arrangements to have their students taught by a cram school during the academic year. One law school failed in the most recent round of accreditation for being too much like a cram school; some other law schools face the same prospect....

The reform of legal education in Japan was initiated by the business community, who wanted a far larger number of better-educated lawyers with broader backgrounds who could better protect and realize business interests. Scholars and practitioners who wanted to change the legal education system because of the perceived deficiencies of the old system joined the reform movement. Their motivation was to rectify Japan's legal system.

The establishment of the JSRC under the Cabinet was the decisive step toward realizing legal education reform. However, reformers fell into two camps: progressives and conservatives.

Progressive reformers wanted to introduce fundamental and pervasive changes, and their ideas for the new system were inspired by the American system. But conservative reformers ultimately controlled the reform: Although they recognized the deficiencies of the old system, they also wanted to maintain many parts of the status quo. Their ideas for the new system were not inspired by the American system as much as those of progressive reformers were.

There were also powerful resisters: The Justice Ministry and the Supreme Court wanted to maintain the highly competitive bar examination and the LTRI. The Justice Ministry and the Education Ministry did not coordinate in the effort to narrow the gap between the number of law school students and the number of people who can pass the bar exam to realize the high passage rate envisioned by the JSRC. The result was a system that looked like it was modeled after the American system in its basic structure but that actually had many differences from the American system, particularly compromises and loopholes to appease resisters and opponents. The 74 new law schools were established, with approximately 5800 students in each class, far exceeding the target 3000 new lawyers expected to be produced in 2010. Although these new law schools produced many tangible results in an extremely short period, both pedagogically and structurally, the low passage rate of the new bar examination from its beginning has already had chilling effects on applicants, expectations from students, and the pedagogical contents of many law schools. Furthermore, by 2008 the Justice Ministry and the JFBA began to change their positions about the "3000 in 2010" target. Moreover, the bypass route that allows people to take the new bar examination without going to a law school will be introduced in 2013. Political leadership at the very top, from the prime minister, is needed but is not likely. While working to maintain the 3000 in 2010 policy, on the one hand, and keeping the bypass as narrow as possible, on the other hand, some law professors, including Miyazawa, have proposed that law schools should radically reduce their student body so that they can assure that a majority of their students will pass the bar examination and that the quality of legal education they were expected to introduce will be maintained. There is no sign that major law schools will take up such a proposal, however. Therefore, at least the pedagogical contents of law schools are facing a real possibility of collapse. As is explained in the next section, the Korean government has carefully monitored the Japanese reforms and has recently decided to introduce a new system that avoids the deficiencies of the Japanese system of law schools and resembles more closely the American system.

KOREA

The Korean legal system is but one example of the still present Japanese influence on Korea's institutions, a result of the colonial occupation in the first half of the twentieth century. Much of legal education in Korea is based on the Japanese model. So when Japan undertook reforms in the education and training of law professionals and implemented a graduate-level law school in 2004, interested counterparts in Korea took note and closely monitored the situation across the East Sea. For years, Korean policy makers have also considered reforms for their own legal education system, under criticism that it is outdated and ill designed to meet the needs of the contemporary setting. In July 2007, after years of debate, delay, and some opposition, Korea's National Assembly enacted legislation paving the way for the implementation of a U.S.-style professional law school.[7] The Act on the Establishment and Management of the Law School was widely seen as the last formal hurdle before the law school in Korea could become a reality. As of this writing, universities that have been awarded a law school are in the midst of hectic preparations to begin operations in March 2009. As explained herein, the establishment of the law school in Korea is the centerpiece of profound reforms in Korean legal education. . . .

Under the current traditional Korean system—which will continue to be in effect at least until 2012—admission to the bar in Korea differs from the U.S. counterpart and is similar to that seen in Japan before it introduced the law school in 2004. The first step to becoming a lawyer in Korea is the national judicial service examination, Korea's equivalent to the state bar exam in the United States. (The examination is administered in three sequential parts; only those applicants who are successful in the first part may advance to the next.) There are few formal qualifications for taking the examination. No college education is required, although in reality many of the successful candidates are graduates of first-tier universities. In practice, many applicants, even those who are full-time university students, spend years in cram schools preparing for the examination. There is a maximum number of candidates who may pass the examination each year, as set by the government (currently 1000), which results in a very low passage rate. In recent years, approximately 5% of applicants have been successful in passing the Korean bar examination. Successful candidates then must attend the Judicial Research and Training Institute (JRTI), under the supervision and authority of the Korean Supreme Court, for a two-year program. Traditionally, the top graduates of the JRTI have become career judges and prosecutors, with the rest going into private practice. . . .

Although many universities have a college of law—the academic department that traditionally attracts the most academically competitive students—the vast majority of students from the undergraduate law department do not enter law practice. They either were unsuccessful in the bar examination or have different plans, often accepting positions in corporations or government. In addition, very few university law professors are admitted to practice. Those who aspire to positions in academia prepare for graduate study (often abroad), instead of the bar examination. As a

---

7. Kim TJ. 2007. Law school to open in 2009. The Korea Times, July 4.

result, there is little exchange between the practicing bar and legal academia. Lastly, although the university professor enjoys a high status in Korean society, the lawyer, judge, or prosecutor likely eclipses the law professor in status, given the low passage rate for the bar examination. In reality, those who are admitted to the bench or bar enjoy a most privileged status in society, often with job security and economic rewards. Or as one commentator observed, "Once you pass the national bar examination, then your privileged lifelong social status of the 'natural aristocracy' in Tocqueville's terms is guaranteed"[8] For years, the system of training and educating lawyers in Korea has been severely criticized. Those who pass the examination are rewarded with enrollment at the JRTI, another target of critics. If the name (Judicial Research and Training Institute) is indicative of its mission, the institute at best prepares candidates for careers as jurists and perhaps prosecutors (positions to which the top graduates go). In short, the legal education process in Korea is composed of a competitive examination testing rote recollection with no educational prerequisites, followed by training geared to career judges and prosecutors. Critics charge that the system does not adequately prepare graduates with the necessary training to be capable members of a legal profession in a society that increasingly demands legal counsel in a wide range of situations. To some commentators, equally troubling as the lack of adequate professional training is the problem of legal ethics. Commentators have raised concerns about unethical practices among prosecutors and judges, including the institutional tendency to protect members and maintain the status quo. They suggest that the system is to blame for the lack of emphasis on ethics and professional responsibility. One commentator brings to light the practice of *junkwan-ye-wu*, or the practice of courts giving favorable treatment to recently retired judges from the same court, judges who then represent parties as private counsel.[9] "In a survey conducted by a Korean newspaper, 45 out of 100 practicing attorneys admitted that they have experienced such preferential treatment. Incumbent judges are expected by custom to help former colleagues in this way" (Kim 2001).

All the criticisms have led to calls for reform of legal education, with some proponents demanding an overhaul of the system. Two former deans of Seoul National University College of Law have urged that change is "desperately needed"[10] and "long overdue."[11] Indeed, there have been serious discussion and debate over reform under every civilian presidential administration. The centerpiece of the reforms, and the most controversial, is the proposal of a graduate-level professional school similar to the law school seen in the United States. As one commentator put it, the new U.S.-

8. Choi DK. 2001. Proposed legal education reform in Korea: Toward professional model. Ritsumeikan Law Rev. 18:93–112.

9. Kim JW. 2001. The ideal and the reality of the Korean legal profession. Asian-Pac. L Policy J. 2:45–68.

10. Song SH. 2001. Legal education in Korea and the Asian region. J. Legal Educ. 51:398–402.

11. Ahn KW. 2006. Law reform in Korea and the agenda of "graduate law school." Wis. Int. Law J. 24:223–42.

type law school in Korea would lead to the training of the legal profession "through education, not through examination."[12]

As discussed above, critics of the current legal education system have urged that reform is necessary for a Korean society that is in rapid transformation. Reformists call for significant change to fix a system that they see as "broke," to quote the American vernacular. It is not clear whether those who urge reform are principally from the same constituency or institution or interest group. It does appear, however, that those who back the proposal for the implementation of a professional law school have received training in, and been influenced by, U.S. legal institutions. Those who oppose the American influence and the U.S.-type law school appear to be more diverse in group identification. In all events, a close examination of those who argue in support of and those in opposition to the proposed reforms provides a revealing window to Korean society and the societal mindset. Some of the most vocal opposition has come from expected quarters—the bench and bar. To many, the judiciary's rejection of the initial proposals for the law school reflected judges' resentment of the idea of abolishing the JRTI and losing control and authority over the only formally approved institution of legal education and training. Likewise, opposition to reforms from practicing lawyers was seen as the bar's negative reaction to the plan of increasing the number of law graduates, which would force current lawyers to share with a larger pool the economic rewards of an exclusive profession.

Members of the bench and bar also reportedly raised concerns that implementing the proposed law school would affect the quality of legal education and training and, consequently, the quality of the legal practice. Perhaps this was a veiled statement, reflecting a deeper mistrust of university law faculty by the old guard of judges, prosecutors, and lawyers. And perhaps the mistrust is understandable in light of the Korean obsession with placement in the societal hierarchy.

There has also been the argument that establishing a professional law school is, to put it bluntly, un-Korean and unfair in that it discriminates against those members of society who do not have the financial means for such an opportunity. As Kyong–Whan Ahn[13] notes, "To the average Korean, [the bar] exam has been a symbol of fairness, equality, and most of all, a decisive opportunity to achieve a Korean dream." Apparently, this argument continues to resonate with some, even though statistically those who pass the bar examination with only a high school education compose only a small portion of the already tiny percentage of successful candidates. Finally, consideration of the U.S.-type law school comes at a time when anti-American sentiment in Korean society is high. For years, opposition to an overhaul of the legal education system (and implementation of the professional law school specifically) was successful in creating delays.

12. Choi DK. 2001. Proposed legal education reform in Korea: Toward professional model. Ritsumeikan Law Rev. 18:93–112.

13. Ahn KW. 2006. Law reform in Korea and the agenda of "graduate law school." Wis. Int. Law J. 24:223–42.

Ultimately, however, advocates of reform prevailed with the National Assembly's dramatic action in the closing minutes of the legislative session in the summer of 2007. . . .

After years of discussion and debate, Korea is poised to implement the professional law school. As Japan opted for the law school format in 2004, Korea too is heading in that direction.

The significant reforms in Korea—structural, pedagogical, and otherwise—represent fundamental changes in the education and training of legal professionals and a departure from the traditional methods. Perhaps reform is all the more urgent to prepare a legal profession to better meet the needs of a society in transformation. Korea observers will monitor the law school and the profession closely, to see their role and development in a rapidly changing society and to see how many U.S. approaches are adopted to meet Korean needs. . . .

Comparison

In China, the reconstruction of the country from the destruction during the Cultural Revolution and the adoption of the socialist market economy created a need for a rapid increase and improvement of the legal profession. Top political leaders became the main reformers of legal education, and they proposed to emulate the American system of legal education. One result is the introduction of JM (Juris Master) programs at a postgraduate level, although pedagogical reforms, particularly clinical programs, have also been introduced. However, graduates of undergraduate law faculties may also take the bar examination, and JM programs still occupy a small fraction of legal education in China. Nonetheless, the prospect of the expansion of American-style legal education appears likely because of commitment from the political leadership.

In Japan, the business community wanted deregulation to revitalize the Japanese economy and wanted a more accessible and effective justice system as an alternative to government agencies to protect their interests. The business community took the initiative in comprehensive justice system reform, which included legal education reform as the first priority to provide the personnel base for the entire reform effort. Political leaders who responded to that initiative created a political opportunity, allowing other reformers to advance their own ideals, and those who wanted fundamental changes chose the American system as the one that would most satisfy their needs. However, resistance and opposition from those who had vested interests in the status quo were so strong that more conservative reformers ultimately led the actual design and implementation of reform, resulting in many compromises and loopholes, and those conservative reformers avoided reference to the American system. Yet, institutionally speaking, reform along the American model is more pervasive in Japan than in China because graduation from law school is required of all applicants to the new bar examination, although undergraduate law faculties still exist. Pedagogical reforms are also more pervasive in Japan than in China mainly because chartering and accreditation standards encourage them. The new law schools have produced various tangible changes in an extremely short period. Nevertheless, a series of obstacles to the stable development of such reform in Japan is apparent.

One obstacle is a wide gap between the number of law students and the number of bar examination passers, which has resulted in a passage rate so low that students now pressure law schools to focus on preparation for the bar examination. Another obstacle is that the Justice Minister and the organized bar are opposed to a rapid increase of bar examination passers. Additionally, beginning in 2012 a bypass route will allow people to take the bar examination without going to a law school. If made too wide, this bypass route could make law schools meaningless. The high-level political leadership that supports reform has disappeared, and the future of new law schools looks quite precarious.

The reform movement in Korea was initiated by reformist law professors who criticized deficiencies in the existing system and who saw the need for an expanded and better-educated cadre of legal professionals. However, the real impetus for reform was provided by the government, particularly the Education Ministry. Strong opposition from the bench and the bar delayed reform, but the government ultimately managed to pass a bill to introduce new professional law schools at a postgraduate level. The new Korean system will look the most like the American system among the three countries: Universities with law schools will close undergraduate law faculties, and the number of law students will be closely synchronized with the expected number of passers of the bar examination. Pedagogical reforms have been introduced even at undergraduate law faculties, but new professional law schools will certainly expand them.

How can we explain the similarities and differences in legal education reform in the three countries? The subject of this review is the introduction of U.S.-style elements of legal education to East Asian countries, which can be considered a part of broader efforts to implement legal change....

The relative strengths of American influence in the three countries differ on the basis of local conditions. The more limited range of reform in China compared with Japan and Korea, despite the strong commitment among top political leadership, may be a result of the lack of institutional capacity to implement a more large-scale reform and the relative strength of those with vested interests vis-à-vis the institutional capacity available to reformers. The difference between Japan and Korea may be explained in terms of the difference in the continuing high-level political support for the American system and in terms of the relative strength of U.S.-oriented reformers, on the one hand, and non-U.S.-oriented reformers, resisters, and opponents, on the other hand.

There is no doubt that legal education in China, Japan, and Korea will continue to change. Differences in the strengths and ways of American influence will continue to provide materials for building and testing theories of legal changes.

* * *

Today, China has a significant class of professionalized lawyers, educated in modern law schools. However, it is not necessarily evident what their role is in contemporary Chinese society. Is it, or should it be, different from lawyers' roles in the U.S., for example? For answers to this question, consider the following excerpt by William Alford.

William P. Alford, *Of Lawyers Lost and Found: Searching for Legal Professionalism in the People's Republic in China*, in Raising the Bar: The Emerging Legal Profession in East Asia

in Raising the Bar: The Emerging Legal Profession in East Asia
287 (William P. Alford ed., 2007).

. . . American scholars and policy-makers concerned with legal development in the People's Republic of China (PRC) share a deep faith in the value of China developing a legal profession that operates as we would like to think our own does. Indeed, this idea is so deeply ingrained that it is rarely broken out for examination, but instead is treated as an obvious good, the attainment of which is essentially a matter of time. Virtually all such observers seem to assume that lawyers, whether out of idealism or self-interest or some blend thereof, will prove to be a principal force leading the PRC toward the rule of law and a market economy, while some go so far as to treat the development of an indigenous legal profession as crucial to the promotion in China of a more liberal polity.

The hidden assumptions regarding the Chinese legal profession found in both U.S. academic writing and policy papers warrant a scrutiny they have yet to receive here or abroad. Lurking not too far underneath the surface of such portrayals are further assumptions about the inexorability of convergence along a common path remarkably (surprise) similar to our own. Unexamined, such assumptions run the risk of leaving us with an impoverished understanding not only of the role that the emerging legal profession is playing in China, but also of both the complexity of legal development there more broadly and the limits of the idea of professionalism in law. This, in turn, may generate unwarranted expectations on our part as to the manner in which change may come in China while reinforcing the arguably inflated sense that too many of us in the American legal world have of our own profession's historic importance. . . .

It would certainly be erroneous to ignore either the exponential growth in the size of the Chinese legal profession over the past twenty-five years or the accompanying changes in its manner of organization, educational attainments, or relationship to officialdom, let alone the very substantial ways in which the Chinese legal system more generally has developed since the end of the Cultural Revolution in the mid–1970s. In little more than a generation, the Chinese bar has expanded from 3,000 members to some 150,000, with officials continuing to make noises about plans for China to have 300,000 lawyers by the year 2010. Whereas the operative legal framework in 1981 spoke of "state legal workers," the current governing national statute describes lawyers as professionals with duties to society as well as to the state (Zhonghua Renmin Gongheguo Lüshi Fa 1996).[1] Nor, it is fair to say, are we dealing only with issues of size and nomenclature here, as the vast bulk, at least in urban areas, of China's law firms, all of which previously were under direct state ownership, are now organized as partnerships or collectives, and there is considerable evidence, at least at the anecdotal level, of lawyers wishing to shield their practice from intensive state scrutiny, if for no other reason than to avoid unlawful exactions.

Even as we recognize such changes in the Chinese profession, however, we would do well not to overstate the impact that they are making. Resort to law and lawyers remains very much the exception in Chinese affairs both large and small. This is so, notwithstanding the inordinate publicity accorded such matters, particularly in the western media (where they have a bit of the dancing bear quality that also greets foreigners in China who manage to utter more than a few garbled phrases in Mandarin). Perhaps most tellingly, the Chinese Communist Party (CCP), which is not only the nation's leading repository of political power but which also continues to be its single most consequential actor economically and in many other respects, remains above the state's law, both as a formal and as a practical matter, as has been borne out all too painfully by those who have sought through the courts to cabin it, even as the CCP remains intimately involved in the selection and oversight of judicial personnel. The same insulation from the state's law holds true for individual members, particularly those of consequence, who have been more likely to be called to task for corruption (whether in their governmental or CCP guises) via the CCP's internal disciplinary processes than through public positive law, save for those unlucky enough to be singled out for exemplary punishment (Luo 1996).

It is not only important cadres or others within the CCP, however, who have yet to acquire a taste for lawyers. Litigation in the PRC rose steadily during the 1990s before leveling off at approximately six million cases per annum (exclusive of actions to enforce judgments which, since 2004, have been added to the overall figures for litigation reported by the Supreme People's Court in its annual work report). But, even before we scrutinize the content of such cases, their number needs to he set in context. To a far greater extent than most outside observers appreciate, China remains fundamentally an administrative state, with administrative recourse (whether for routine civil matters or to address deviance, as through re-education through labor) the norm, rather than the exception, and with respect to which lawyers essentially have a scant role representing clients. Beyond this, lawyers have had little, if any, part to play in vital avenues through which tens of millions of individuals routinely seek redress, includ-

1. Editors' note: The 1996 Lawyers' Law has been recently amended, effective as of June 1, 2008. Although the amended law does not contain exactly the same formulation of lawyers' duties as its predecessor, Article 1 of the amended law still states that one of the law's primary goals is to "enable lawyers to fulfill their roles in the building of the socialist legal system."

ing the letters and visits *(xinfang)* process, extrajudicial mediation, resort to rice roots legal workers *(falü gongzuozhe,* also referred to as *jiceng falü fuwuzhe),* and other yet more informal processes. But we also need to scrutinize litigation itself; if we do, we can see that not more than approximately one out of every ten litigants appears to have been using legal counsel. And, if we press our inquiry further, we may do well to question the simple equation that virtually all observers make between litigation and legality, by asking precisely what it is that lawyers are doing even when present, given the near certainty of conviction in criminal cases (the area in which citizens are, by far, most likely to be represented by counsel), the fact that the judiciary continues to be characterized by a relatively low level of legal training, and the proliferation of accounts of lawyers and judges using litigation as a pretext for bribery.

One might respond to criticisms regarding the frequency with which citizens use lawyers by suggesting that it does not necessarily diminish the core argument of those who have been relatively sanguine about the building of a legal profession in China and its implications, but instead shows simply that the process is more time-consuming than many assumed or perhaps that more resources ought to be devoted to the task than they had initially thought. But as the aforementioned account suggests, rather than presuming that the changes of recent years a fortiori have been a boon for the rule of law, we need more thoroughly to probe what is underway in China. That type of research, in part regarding illicit behavior (some of which may carry severe criminal sanctions, including the death penalty), is not easy to conduct—most especially in a society in which a number of important matters, particularly concerning the administration of criminal justice, remain off-limits, especially for foreigners. There is, however, a growing volume of articles to be found in the Chinese media regarding widespread corruption in legal processes (which lawyers are inclined to blame on judges and judges on lawyers), but questions of the role of the CCP in judicial processes—including the selection and promotion of judicial personnel—remain under-examined.

My own interviews of scores of Chinese and foreign lawyers, judges, legal academics, and businesspeople working in Beijing, Shanghai, and other major cities suggest that the expansion of the Chinese bar has been accompanied by increasing corruption, with lawyers at times a conduit for, if not the instigators of, such behavior. Indeed, although the list of questions I developed for these interviews did not specifically address corruption, each PRC lawyer interviewed brought up this topic him-or herself, with some expressing regret at what they described as the need to engage in such behavior in order to stay competitive and others boastful about what they claimed was their capacity to reach virtually any Chinese judge. My sampling, to be sure, makes no pretense of being broadly representative of the nation's bar as a whole. If anything, however, it drew disproportionately on urbanites with elite legal educations (whether obtained in China or abroad or both) whose predominantly business-oriented law practices and broader life experience generally involve a greater exposure to the sort of international norms typically lauded by those who vest considerable hope in China's developing a domestic counterpart to the bar in this country.

Presumably, without minimizing such problems, some outside analysts may be tempted to view them as likely to abate substantially as increasingly professionalized lawyers (and others) with an interest in the cleaner administration of justice make their presence felt. That may happen, but then again, it may not—for reasons having to do with the degree to which the Chinese legal profession remains interwoven with the party/state. Western, and especially American, observers remain far too quick to read the Communist Party's ebbing enthusiasm for Marxist ideology and economics as encompassing either a concomitant receptivity to competing sources of authority or a naïve ignorance or obliviousness on the part of the CCP's leadership to the potential impact of forces set in motion by the policies of the reform era. We need to guard against underestimating either the CCP's desire to retain power or the self-interest of those who are benefiting from the manner in which power is now held and exercised. . . .

To heed the state's ongoing presence in the affairs of Chinese lawyers is no to suggest that the nature of its involvement is unchanged from the days whet socialism was more than an adjective used to justify whatever economic measures the CCP might wish to promote. Senior partners interested in maximizing revenues may be none too keen to spend time in empty ideological exercise while warnings against representing the Falungong and other activists are, as one of the more outspoken members of Beijing's legal community put it, utterly superfluous. But before we break out the *maotai* (a Chinese liquor quaffed on special occasions) and celebrate the ways in which the profit motive may be sapping the ideological content of the party/state's efforts at political control, we need soberly to consider the possibility that it may be reinforcing the CCP's hold on power and impeding, rather than facilitating, movement toward the rule of law specifically and liberalism more generally.

There are undoubtedly exceptions, but it could be argued that at least some in the Chinese bar, and perhaps most especially elite business practitioners in the capital, have struck a Faustian bargain with the party/state, willingly accepting a good life materially and in terms of prestige and security in return for foregoing certain of the attributes (most notably, a considerable measure of independence from the state) generally associated with legal professionalism in liberal democratic states and for acquiescing in the role the CCP has accorded itself in Chinese political and legal life. This is perhaps most readily apparent in the array of corporatist alliances formed between the party/state and lawyers. At their most extreme, this may include links between officialdom and law firms in which work is directed, foreign study opportunities promoted, authorizations for specialized tasks granted, and permits clients need doled out in return for pecuniary gain. We ought not, for instance, to be any more mesmerized by the proliferating forms of ownership of PRC law firms than we would be by those of industrial enterprises. In both cases, placards suggesting that a firm is non-state may still mask close financial and other ties to pertinent officials, while an ongoing designation as state-owned does not necessarily mean that we can rest assured that all proceeds are, at the end of the day, finding their way into state coffers.

But even if such practices are not as widespread as my interviewing would seem to suggest, there is the arguably more vexing dilemma presented by the ways in which lawyers benefit from the current distribution of power. This is neither to paint all PRC lawyers with a single brush nor to ignore challenges that legal professionals may face worldwide. Rather it is to demand that those of us who consciously target China's lawyers as likely to be a major force in promoting greater liberality, confront such institutional factors and associated collective action problems (e.g., the disincentive, noted by many lawyers I interviewed, to eschew bribery if one wishes to retain clients). These factors surely present a daunting and very concrete set of challenges that noble visions of the place of legal professionals in other societies alone cannot will away.

7.   THE AMERICANIZATION OF THE LEGAL PROFESSION

If there is one thing that strikes the observer of recent transformations of the legal profession most, it is the tremendous influence of the U.S. model. While some are beginning to argue that perhaps the high point of the influence has been already reached, and that American legal education might be embarking on a declining path, there is no question that for the time being, the observations of Professor Wiegand at the beginning of the post-Berlin Wall era is still the case. The excerpt following Professor Wiegand's analysis describes recent educational reforms in East Asia, where Japan, in particular, is moving to a U.S.-influenced model.

Wolfgang Wiegand, The Reception of American Law in Europe

39 Am.J.Comp.L. 229 (1991).

The internationalization of law has become a matter of great significance due to the increasing population mobility and to the growth rate of the world economy. A series of recent events evidences a new dimension of internationalization, both in their form and in their effect. One example is the standardization of law within the European Community. Whereas to a certain extent this arises automatically, owing to the close economic and political relationships between member countries of the EC, it also results from the internationalization and globalization of financial markets. A second development, less spectacular but of more far-reaching consequence, is the subject of this paper: The Reception of American Law in Europe.

* * *

Symptoms and Observations

Studies at an American university today are of comparable value and prestige to studies of the *ius commune* in Italy during the Middle Ages. There is impressive evidence of this fact.

The Situation at the Universities

The (official) Swiss National Fund[1] annually provides so-called *Nachwuchsstipendien* (training funds). Their purpose is to "provide research students, whose ultimate aim is to acquire a teaching or research position, with the possibility of completing their studies, especially overseas." Statistics for law candidates in respect of the countries which they chose for their postgraduate studies during the years 1971–1986 show the following:

Of a total of 171 subsidized students, 88 (51.5%) studied in the U.S. The trend is even clearer when considered for the eighties alone: of 103 stipendiaries, 64 (62.1%) attended an American university for postgraduate studies. Because the selection criteria for the award are purposely elitist, the principal conclusions to be drawn from the statistics are as follows:

Almost two thirds of the state-subsidized elite students in the field of jurisprudence completed their academic studies by way of a postgraduate course in America. Since the primary purpose of these subsidies is to attract the next generation to teaching and research positions, an aim that is to a large extent achieved, then it also can be concluded that 50% or more of the future Swiss law professors will have an American degree.

This will strengthen a development which already is easy to detect. In particular branches (commercial and constitutional law), studies and postgraduate studies in the U.S. will be considered a requirement for a university professor. The transferral in favor of the U.S. can also be proved in a quantitative form: for example, of the 16 members of a faculty at the University of Bern Law School, six have absolved a part of their studies at United States universities, some even having taught there. Most of them also travel regularly to the U.S. for further education.

The Situation in Industry and Law Firms

After passing the examinations, many students, mostly those of above-average ability, come to their professors to request letters of reference. Very often, these are required for an application for postgraduate studies at an American university, which they intend to finance privately. Their answers to the question as to their motives provides a surprisingly illuminating picture. Two points are frequently mentioned in addition to a rather general interest in postgraduate studies:

— that American law is extremely important for a position in private industry or in a bank;

1. I thank the Swiss National Fund ("Schweizerischer Nationalfonds") for the materials; the following observations have been confirmed by my own experience as member of the research commission of the University of Bern, which is responsible for fellowships.

— an American education is imperative for a position in a law firm (some even talk in terms of a precondition to employment).

Without undertaking a much broader investigation of the labor market it is not possible to determine how relevant these assessments are. There are, however, certain indications, such as that which can be derived from the following advertisement: "On behalf of a well-established Notary, we seek a lawyer, available beginning 1st of April 1988, or thereafter by agreement, who possesses a Bernese Notary license and who would assist the Notary in general duties and in preparation of highly interesting mandates. *Initially the assistant will undertake, during one-third of his/her working hours, further studies of American legal language and legislation. Costs thereof will be fully reimbursed. . . .*"[2]

Even though this may be an isolated case, I have been able to determine, during many discussions with ex-students, that those who are engaged in positions in private industry and the major banks could not cope with the demands of their work without a knowledge of American law.

Although these are only personal impressions, the situation in law firms is more easily definable. In order to gain definite indications in this respect, I have researched the situation at the larger law firms in Zurich. Almost all of the firms approached submitted answers. An evaluation of the questionnaires produces the following results:

Total active lawyers: 261

— 129 (49%) have absolved an American postgraduate study, of which

— LL.M.: 52 = 19.9%

— MCL/J: 35 = 13.4%

— other American law studies: 41 = 15.7%

This conclusion requires further amplification on various points. As in other academic fields, the trend is stronger with respect to young lawyers. Whereas an American degree is rather the exception in the case of older interviewed partners, it is almost the rule with respect to the younger ones. In addition, various offices pointed out that they expect an American degree from those of their younger employees who ultimately wish to be integrated into the partnership. Given this fact, an average of 60% of highly qualified younger lawyers have an American degree today, and the tendency is increasing. On the other hand, the result should be qualified to the extent that Zurich is not representative of Switzerland in general. This is not, however, a critical factor; it is, after all, in these densely populated areas where by far the most and the largest legal disputes are processed.

In this respect, the results from Zurich and, to the extent available, from Geneva,[3] Bern, and Basel, are extremely informative; they reveal that,

2. Advertisement in the Swiss newspaper "Bund" of February 20, 1988 (emphasis added).

3. An inquiry in Geneva resulted in a figure of 30.2% of the active lawyers having an American degree.

in the large law firms, those with a predominant influence on the development of the law of the country, the trend is similar to the trend at the universities: A substantial number of the legal practitioners have completed an American education, and amongst the younger generation, the trend is increasing.

NOTES AND QUESTIONS

(1) *Latin America.* The diffusion of the U.S. model implies more reliance on the market than on the State to finance Legal education. Not only U.S. lawyers, but also U.S. law schools are extremely expensive. True, the loan system provides some relief, and some grants and scholarships are available particularly in the top tier schools. But most students graduate law school with severe debt, and the degree of social diversity in U.S. law schools is declining in direct proportion with the surge of costs. The money issue is not a problem unique to the U.S.

Financial problems affect very severely legal education through Latin America. In some countries, such as Chile, in the last 25 years the number of elite private schools has multiplied, creating incentives for the public institutions to improve the quality of their education, but also reinforcing a class-based structure of the legal profession. Elsewhere things are perhaps more difficult. A Peruvian observer puts it quite brutally:

> Throughout Latin America, but specifically in Peru, the legal education is in crisis. The legal system is inefficient and corrupt, the number of lawyers is extraordinary, and the ones that actually exercise their profession are themselves considered inefficient and corrupt.

> For decades politicians have tried to overturn this conception of inefficiency and corruption by modernizing the legal system, buying more computers, making more modern laws, and raising the salaries of judges. As to the problem of the extraordinary number of unemployed, ill prepared and corrupt lawyers, many politicians consider that the answer is to restrict the creation of new law faculties and to fix the curriculum of the existing ones, following the traditional legal education system. This, of course, has generated some resistance because law faculties are the most cost-efficient of a university. Although they require a lower investment compared to other faculties, they generate more revenue because of high enrollment.[1]

In both North and South America, legal education is thus continually challenged by a need for financial resources and better facilities.

> Studies done by Latin American researchers find that many law schools in Latin America need to improve their resources, to provide a better education for students and thereby produce higher quality attorneys. The physical conditions and needs of different schools must be weighed and valued in a case-by case setting, but there are some common problems

---

1. See Ana Cecilia MacLean, Rethinking Legal Education in Latin America, 12 L. & Bus. Rev. of the Americas, 503 (2006).

identified by researchers that seem to interfere with many Latin American law schools including poor physical facilities, limited and obsolete library resources, outdated curricula, weak research communities unable to participate in knowledge production and to confront economic and social problems.

Another major issue identified by studies of Latin American law schools is hiring and retaining full time faculty. With many schools going under-funded or experiencing issues with corruption, teaching salaries cannot match opportunities for employment outside of the field of legal education. This fact leaves many law schools without resources to attract top faculty and leaves current faculty dissatisfied. This problem is already being addressed through governmental and educational reform in some countries.[2]

This state of the art of legal education in Latin America has been the subject of much local and international attention in the form of an early and recurring effort in the domain of "law and development."[3] The deep differences in structural and cultural condition between the Latin America "semi-periphery" and the EU–US "center," where traditionally the wealthy, Latin American legal elite is educated, have been analyzed by the Colombian scholar Diego Lopez Medina who has contributed the opposition between "contexts of production" and "contexts of reception" to the toolkit of comparative law.[4]

(2) The previous materials demonstrate in action a major phenomenon of "North–Americanization" of the global legal culture. Graduate education, traditionally an exclusively US feature is now colonizing important legal cultures and might become synonymous of a "modern" educational system. Interestingly, this process seems to be stronger than the major collapse in U.S. international legal prestige produced by the Bush administration. Can you suggest an explanation?

(3) While the common feature of being an "undergraduate" characterizes the European system of legal education, local variations throughout Europe seem traditionally very acute. In the last few years, educational programs such as "the Erasmus" exchange have involved scores of law students spending one or more semesters abroad and getting their work "recognized" by their school. To facilitate these exchanges, deemed very important for the future development of a "European culture," the so called "Bologna process" has been set in motion and named after a declaration of Rectors of European Universities held in Bologna in 1999.

The Council of Europe and the European region of UNESCO have jointly prepared the Lisbon recognition Convention on recognition of academic qualifications, which has been ratified by the majority of the 29 European countries party to the Bologna process. The program, that most European countries are in the process of implementing, aims at a full compatibility and recognition of

2. See John Mills & Timothy McLendon, Law Schools as Agents of Change and Justice Reform in the Americas, 20 Fla. J. Int'l L. 5 (2008).

3. See Trubeck and Santos, The New Law and Economic Development (2006).

4. See Diego Lopez Medina, Teoria Impura del Derecho: La Transformacion de la Cultura Juridica Latinoamericana (2004).

academic work wherever performed by students in one European academic institution. While many criticisms have been voiced due to a variety of provisions that seem to excessively "privatize" higher education, the impact on legal education has been to divide the academic part of law study in two: an introductory three years degree (Bachelor's degree) followed by a two years more advanced degree (Masters Degree), necessary for admission to the traditional legal professions (attorney, judge, notary). Law students not interested in the traditional legal profession are offered a variety of introductory and specialized degrees allowing more flexibility.

(4) The high variety of legal professionals makes it very difficult a) to employ the traditional civil law v. common law opposition, and b) to generalize in any significant way. Here, the only exception is the notary, a high level legal professional figure in the civil law, and a lay individual performing a relatively modest function of officially checking documents in the common law. Generally speaking, the more recent transformations in the organization of the legal profession, such as the progressive increase in size of firms, are to a great extent determined by market forces more than by changes in the legal regime, so that "specialization" is nearly everywhere dependent on choices made by a professional, rather than imposed by monopolies.

8.   LAWYER'S COMPENSATION. BEGINNING OF A FICTIONAL DIALOGUE CONCERNING A NOT-TOO-FICTIONAL CASE[1]

The following is the transcript of a conference taking place in a big midwestern city in the office of Malcolm Smooth, Esq., General Counsel of the giant International Dulci–Cola Corporation. In addition to Mr. Smooth, the conference participants are Kathleen Edge, Esq., Assistant General Counsel, and Dr. André Comparovich, Professor of Law at a prestigious law school.

Smooth: Thank you Professor Comparovich for having accepted our retainer, and being willing to act as our consultant on difficult problems of foreign law. As you know, our company has branch offices or subsidiaries in almost every country of Europe, Asia, Africa and Latin–America. This produces quite a few legal problems. Recently, both our company and some of our American personnel have become involved in a lot of litigation abroad. Our office receives regular reports concerning such litigation, and we are supposed to provide some overall direction and coordination.

Comparovich: Whenever you have a legal problem abroad, the most important step is the intelligent selection of foreign counsel and the making of appropriate arrangements concerning his or her compensation. This is not only the most important step, but also, as a rule, the first one in point of time. Though frequently involving problems of foreign law (especially

---

1. The case of Haifisch v. International Dulci–Cola Corporation reflects the composite facts of several actual lawsuits that ended in settlements or unreported decisions; but all names, places and dates are purely fictional, and do not point to any existing corpora-

with respect to the foreign lawyer's fees), this first step usually has to be taken by American counsel without the help of a foreign lawyer.

Edge: We learned it the hard way. From among the many foreign lawsuits in which our company has been involved a particularly puzzling one was exactly related to that issue: *Haifisch v. International Dulci–Cola Corporation.*

About five years ago, we contemplated a reorganization of our subsidiary in Ruritania. We contacted Mr. Haifisch (H), a Ruritanian lawyer who then resided in New York, and inquired whether and on what terms he would be willing to do the legal work in connection with the planned reorganization. After some initial correspondence, H flew here from New York at our expense, and we conferred with him for several hours, going over the problems involved in the reorganization and negotiating his fee. No definite agreement was reached, at least not according to our recollection. The reorganization project was subsequently abandoned, and we so informed H. Thereupon, H sent us a bill in the amount of 800,000 Ruritanian Guilders (equivalent to $500,000), allegedly in accordance with the statutory fee schedule of Ruritania, which is said to be based on the amount involved in the lawyer's activity.

(a) Attorneys' Fees

Comparovich: There is no uniform "civil-law system" on compensation of attorneys and on "how much" legal services cost, let alone on "how much" legal professionals "make." Sometimes, there is no uniform system in the lawyer's fees even within one country. The comparative lawyer can only study some general trends.

In France, the fees of *avoués* and notaries are regulated by official tariffs. The honorarium paid to an *avocat*, however, like that of an English barrister, traditionally was thought of as a voluntary and spontaneous token of the client's gratitude. As recently as 1885, the Bâtonnier (President) of the Paris Bar stated in a treatise: "The avocat does not discuss any money question with his client. He requests nothing from him either before or after the case."[1] In the course of the 19th and 20th centuries, it has become recognized that the *avocat*—as the provider of professional services—has a legally enforceable right to compensation, the amount of which, unless fixed by agreement, is determined in accordance with principles similar to the notion of *quantum meruit*, except that, as noted before, for those activities which formerly came within the purview of the *avoués* at the courts of first instance, a fee schedule prevails.[2] Any fee dispute must be settled by a special procedure, which involves submitting it to the

---

tion or to any individual, living or dead. The dialogue resumes at 715.

1. Quoted by Lepaulle, Law Practice in France, 50 Colum.L.Rev. 945, 949–50 (1950). The long history of this tradition, which originated in ancient Rome, is discussed by

Pound, The Lawyer From Antiquity to Modern Times 51–55 (1953).

2. See art. 10 of the French Law No. 71–1130 on the legal profession, as amended by a Law No. 91–647 of July 10, 1991, 1991 J.O. 9170, 1991 D.L. 310, art. 72.

president (called *bâtonnier*) of the local ("integrated") bar, with review by the presiding judge of the court of appeals.[3] Nevertheless, it remains customary for an *avocat* to ask the client to pay at least a portion of the anticipated fee in advance.

Smooth: What about contingent fees? In the US, an attorney may agree to forfeit compensation in case of a loss and may even finance the litigation, advancing all of its costs.

Comparovich: Our colleagues in the civil-law world traditionally use a Latin term when they speak of an agreement made in advance pursuant to which the lawyer's compensation is to be a percentage of the amount recovered: *pactum de quota litis*. The reference to an agreement (*pactum*) that transfers a part (*quota*) of the conflict (*litis*) to the attorney is per se loaded with a negative connotation. The traditional civil-law (and English) rule has always been that it would be both unethical and unlawful for an attorney to enter into an agreement that would give the attorney a personal interest or stake on the litigation. This has always been considered a serious issue of public policy because of fear that the attorney would lose its objective stance and become a party in the proceeding.

Some have argued for a change in order to make access to lawyers easier for people of limited means but not covered by the formal legal aid scheme. The traditional prohibition against fees based solely on the result to be obtained persists in most countries. However, most countries allow an agreement providing, in addition to a fixed fee, for a supplemental payment, an enhancement of the regular fee based on the result to be obtained or the work performed (called "success fee").[4] Some countries, however, as a protection to the client, may impose a limit, and the agreement may not exceed a certain percentage.[5]

The traditional attitude of hostility toward the contingent fee is declining in some civil-law countries. Under pressure from the European Union, which emphasized competition, the policy deeming contingency fees illegal has been mitigated in many places. In France, it has been modified to a limited extent, in Germany, the Constitutional Court in 2007 has held that its complete prohibition is unconstitutional, and in Italy, contingency fees were completely legalized in 2006, provided they are accepted in writing.[6] Some civil-law countries now allow contingent fees.

As a corollary of the traditional rule, American contingent fee agreements or decisions awarding these fees used to be considered contrary to public policy and thus unenforceable in civil law countries, such as Germany. It is an indication of the change in attitudes mentioned that a 1992

---

3. Decree No. 91–1197 of November 27, 1991, arts. 175–179. The *bâtonnier's* decision, once no longer subject to review, can be enforced in the same manner as a judgment. Of course, the *bâtonnier* will normally first attempt to obtain an amicable settlement.

4. See, e.g., the French Law No. 71–1130 on the legal profession (art. 10).

5. In Greece, the success fee may not exceed 20% of the amount in litigation. See the Greek Lawyers Code (arts. 92 and 95); Yessiou–Faltsi, Civil Procedure in Hellas 117 (1995).

6. See Italian Civil Code (art. 2233), as amended in August 11, 2006.

decision of the German Supreme Court declared an American contingent fee decision subject to enforcement in Germany.[7]

The rule against contingent fees, however, is not limited to civil-law countries. This has traditionally been the rule in the United Kingdom (with the exception of Scotland) and also in the countries of the Commonwealth as a corollary of the prohibition against champerty and maintenance (the act of encouraging another person to litigate for one's personal profit). However, since the nineties, there has been a relaxation of that prohibition in the United Kingdom, and now a client may agree to pay a success fee to his or her attorney in addition to the regular fee ("conditional fee agreement"—CFA). As is the rule in the US, they cannot be used in criminal or family matters. Attorneys may now offer a "non win, no fee agreement" to their client with a "success fee" of no more than 25% of the damages and not to exceed 100% of the regular fee, to be deducted from the client's award.[8]

In Germany, however, creative entrepreneurs conceived a device that, in practice, completely circumvents the prohibition against contingent fees. Some firms now finance all the aspects of litigation, including costs and attorneys fees. The client chooses his or her own attorney and the firm only finances the litigation. If the plaintiff loses, the firm will absorb the loss, but, if the plaintiff prevails, the firm will get a percentage of the recovery, usually between 30 and 50 percent. The agreement is not illegal because the firm is not an attorney and is not subject to the legal prohibition against contingency agreements. Moreover, the agreement may not even be against public policy because, although it has all the practical effects of a contingency fee agreement, it really avoids the conflicts of interests since it is the company and not the attorney who buys into the client's claim.[9]

Edge: But if lawyers cannot accept retainers on a contingent basis, how can middle-class litigants of moderate means ever enforce their rights?

Comparovich: To begin with, one should not assume that litigation costs and attorneys fees are as high as in the US. For a number of reasons,[10] the level of such costs traditionally has been modest in most civil-law countries. To begin with, the cost of legal representation is much smaller and more predictable (hourly rates are not as pervasive, especially

7. See the Decision of June 4, 1992, 45 N.J.W. 3096 (1992), translated in part in 32 I.L.M. 1327 (1993), reproduced and discussed in the sixth edition of this book at 955ff.

8. See N. Andrews, English Civil Procedure 796–816 (2003); A. Zuckerman, Zuckerman on Civil Procedure—Principles of Practice 999–1086 (2008). Originally, the CFA was not recoverable from the losing party, since 2000, however, it is. See *infra* Chapter 7, Section 8(b) at 691 (Attorney Fee Shifting).

9. See P. Murray & R. Stürner, German Civil Justice 124–25 (2004).

10. Some of the reasons are set forth by R.B. Schlesinger, The German Alternative: A Legal Aid System of Equal Access to the Private Attorney, 10 Cornell Int'l L.J. 213, at 215–16 (1977). In France, for instance, fees payable to the government as such in connection with court proceedings have been abolished in order to facilitate access to justice. However, parties must pay, for lawyers' court appearances, in addition to the lawyer's honorarium, a fee, called *droit de plaidoirie*, which goes into the official lawyers' retirement fund. See French Social Security Code, art. L 723–3.

in litigation). In addition, the absence of discovery makes it for a much cheaper proceeding.[11] In recent years, there has been a marked increase in litigation costs in civil-law countries but not nearly as explosive as in the U.S.

The cost-risk of a party who is not poor but of moderate means can, however, be quite severe in a civil-law country. This is due not only to the absence of the contingent fee, but also to the fact that, according to the general civil-law rule, the loser is liable for reimbursing the winner's attorneys fees as part of the recoverable "costs."[12]

The prohibition of contingency fee agreements coupled with the English rule on fee shifting means that, in addition to court costs, the loser has to pay the attorneys fees for both sides. Quite often, this can be a ruinous burden, a risk not every person is willing to take, especially if the right to be vindicated is uncertain. This difficulty has a chilling effect on the evolution of the legal system.

In some European countries, however, this problem has been successfully alleviated by commercially marketed legal-expense insurance.[13] There are currently some proposals and ongoing discussion in Europe to make legal expense insurance mandatory in certain situations. Another solution to this problem is legal aid.[14]

The German model is much more restrictive and unique with a comprehensive statute that provides an elaborate schedule with a detailed regulation of attorneys' fees, thus, the name "fee schedule." In about 50 or so pages, it lists and defines in great detail every conceivable litigating or counseling activity. For each such activity, it provides a number of "points" or "fee units." The value of a point or fee unit is variable, depending on the amount involved in the matter or, in case of litigation, the amount in controversy. The higher the amount in controversy, the higher the value of each point, but it will represent a smaller percentage. This reflects the fact that even a case involving a rather limited amount may involve a considerable amount of work but is far from making the fee always commensurate with the actual amount of effort. Therefore, in case of litigation, the fees

---

11. See *infra*, Chapter 8, Section 3(e) at 756.

12. See *infra*, Chapter 8, Section 8(6) at 671 (Attorney Fee Shifting).

13. See M. Kilian, Alternatives to Public Provision: The Role of Legal Expenses Insurance in Broadening Access to Justice: The German Experience, 30 Journal of Law and Society 31 (2003); R. A. Riegert, Empirical Research About Law: The German Picture, 2 Dickinson Int'l L. Annual 1, 38–40 (1983); W. Pfennigstorf & S. L. Kimball, Aspects of Legal Expense Insurance: A Review of Four New Publications, 1983 A.B.F. Research J. 251; W. Pfennigstorf, Legal Expense Insurance: The European Experience in Financing Legal Services (1975). For a book-

length treatment of legal expense insurance in Germany, see W. Harbauer, Rechtsschutzversicherung (4th ed. 1990). To accompany the recent, though limited, availability of contingent fees in England, the organization of solicitors, the Law Society, has made a scheme available under which a client can purchase litigation insurance, even on an *ad hoc* basis, which covers legal fees payable to the other side if the case is lost and the out-of-pocket disbursements of the client's solicitor. This is in addition to the legal expense coverage available commercially and also through labor unions, etc., in advance of litigation.

14. See *infra*, Chapter 7, Section 8(c) at 696 (Legal Aid).

are based on the amount in controversy and the activities performed in the proceeding. In non-litigated matters, the schedule is based on the type of service performed.

If the party loses the case, the amount thus calculated represents what the client must pay to his or her attorney as well as to the winner's attorney. Through a written agreement, client and attorney may contract for a higher amount than the one stated in the statute, but the amount must be reasonable. In the absence of an express agreement, the statutory tariff prevails. Regardless of the agreement between the party and his or her attorney, the losing party will pay only what is provided for in the statute. The statute is so detailed as to include charges for various costs, such as travel time, postage, telephone, photocopy, etc. The law is periodically reviewed, but the amounts are not very high, particularly in comparison with the U.S. legal market.[15]

Consistent with the civil-law tradition, the German law never allowed any type of contingency agreements (either increasing compensation in case of victory or decreasing it in case of loss) nor could the compensation be calculated as a percentage of the recovery (or of the controversy). However, since 2008, contingency fees became allowed under certain conditions. In addition to certain formal requirements, the RVG requires that the client may not have access to court due to his economic circumstances without the contingent fee agreement. The statutory amendment was enacted immediately after the Federal Constitutional Court held that the absolute prohibition of contingent fees violated the German Constitution.[16] This is a major departure from the traditional German practice and legal ethic standards.

The German model of a detailed fee schedule is not particularly common. The general civil-law rule is not so different from the common-law: attorneys' fees are a private agreement between the client and the attorney,[17] but there may be some statutory or ethical limitations to keep them at a reasonable amount.[18] The concept of "reasonable" may be different in different countries. In some countries, statutes or the bar association may prescribe proposed range of fees.

In order to maintain the dignity of the legal profession, some countries may provide for a minimum amount and make it illegal or unethical to

---

15. See the new German attorney's fee statute *Rechtsanwaltsvergütungsgesetz* (RVG), enacted in July, 1st, 2004. The old Bundesrechtsanwaltsordnung (BRAGO), enacted in July 26, 1957, is carefully analyzed in P. Murray & R. Stürner, German Civil Justice 112–115 and 346–48 (2004). See also M. Wendler, B. Buecker & B. Tremml, Key Aspects of German Business Law (2006) (Part V).

16. See RVG, § 4a amended in June 12, 2008 (BGBl. I S. 1000). See the decision of Dec. 12, 2006 (BVerfG NJW 2007, 979).

17. See, e.g., the French Law No. 71–1130 on the legal profession (art. 10).

18. See Rule 1.5 of the U.S. Model Rules of Professional Responsibility (stating that "a lawyer shall not make an agreement for, charge, or collect and unreasonable fee or an unreasonable amount for expenses" and listing the "factors to be considered in determining the reasonableness of a fee").

charge below it. These rules have a strong anticompetitive character and are slowly being challenged.[19]

Contingent fees are becoming more widely permissible than they were in the past. In the countries that authorize them, the fee agreement is thus no longer necessarily for a fixed amount. Furthermore, in France, only that part of the work that relates to the former *avoué* functions is subject to a fee schedule.[20] Other in-court activities (the oral presentations) and the increasingly important and lucrative consulting and drafting work are remunerated according to the agreement made between the lawyer and the client. It is always advisable for both client and attorney to prepare a written attorney fee contract, but, in the absence of such an agreement, the fee must be established on what is basically a *quantum meruit* basis, taking into consideration the amount and complexity of the work, the prestige of the lawyer, and the financial situation of the client.[21] As we have seen before, when there is an agreement, it can provide for a contingent element (success fee) as long as it also includes a fixed fee.[22]

Edge: American lawyers are not necessarily completely unfamiliar with fee schedules. A comprehensive fee schedule once existed in New York and was abolished only at the time of the general overhaul of civil procedure in 1848. Of course, that was in the rather distant past.

Smooth: Am I right in assuming that under the German system, the amount and difficulty of the work actually performed by the lawyer, the lawyer's standing, the client's wealth, and the result achieved are immaterial in setting the fee under the schedule?

Comparovich: Yes, generally that is so, although it is important to understand that the amount and difficulty of the work to be performed is indirectly computed in the fee calculation. The model is not perfect however and may lead to perverse results.

Smooth: We certainly were not familiar with that system when we negotiated with H. He asked us about the value of our Ruritanian subsidiary and we told him it was between 90 and 100 million US dollars.

Comparovich: Well, given a matter of that magnitude, it is not surprising he might have been entitled to a fee of $500,000 under the Ruritanian schedule for just conferring with you. You certainly would have been better off coming to an agreement with him about his fee before discussing anything of substance.[23]

19. In Italy, for example, the minimum amount was abolished under pressure from the Court of Justice of the European Communities. See V. Varano & A. De Luca, Access to Justice in Italy, 7 Global Jurist 5–6 (2007).

20. See Décret n° 80–608, July 30, 1980 (fixing the avoués fees before the courts of appeal).

21. See, e.g., the French Law No. 71–1130 on the legal profession (art. 10).

22. See *supra* at 686ff.

23. Since many civil-law countries have no rule against the splitting of a cause of action (and considering that court costs, attorneys' fees, and fee shifting are likely to be based directly or indirectly on the amount in controversy), it is possible for a plaintiff to reduce costs by suing only for a limited amount (just enough to make it possible for the case to be appealed to the highest court,

(b) Attorney Fee Shifting

Smooth: That advice would have been quite helpful. But in international litigation, the fees of our own lawyers are only part of the total cost risk we must consider when we decide whether to litigate or not.

Comparovich: As we have seen before, the first consideration is that the "cost" of litigating in civil law countries is considerably lower than in the US. Overall, several characteristics of the civil-law procedure tend to make it much cheaper than common-law procedure. For example, neutral experts are much cheaper than the marked-driven party appointed experts. In addition, civil-law countries have virtually no "discovery", so there are no expenses related to depositions or exchange of documents.[1] These expenses are not "taxable costs" in the U.S., i.e., the prevailing party will not be reimbursed for them. The awards are much lower as well, as are the amount of attorneys' fees.

Another consideration is related to the general civil-law rule on attorney fee shifting. It is generally true that, as in the US, the loser will have to pay the winner's "costs and expenses." These are likely to be considerably less than in the US for a variety of reasons, including the lack of depositions and court reporters. However, the cost risk may still be very large because, contrary to what is generally true in the US and in a very small number of countries, such as Japan and China, in most civil and common-law countries, the loser must pay all or part of the winning party's attorneys' fee. The rationale is that the winner must be made whole and reimbursed for the expenses incurred in enforcing his or her right.

This rule is also adopted in most common law countries, including England.[2] The fee-shifting rule is known in the US as the "English rule" as opposed to the "American rule," but it can also be referred to as the "continental rule" or the "civil-law rule".

The "loser pays all" rule is obviously of very great importance in considering whether to litigate abroad, even if you have made a reasonable arrangement for a fee with your own lawyer.[3] However, one should not

---

if such appeals depend on the amount in controversy). See *infra* Chapter 8, Section 3(J) at 817 (Finality of Judgments: Claim Preclusion and Issue Preclusion).

Note that, as in the matter on which H had originally been consulted, the system of fee schedules may result in fairly substantial fees even when no litigation is involved. Transactions for which the use of a notary is mandatory will obviously be even more expensive since the fee of the notary, generally calculated on similar principles (i.e., based on a percentage of the value of the transaction), will be in addition to any lawyer's fee. The ability to negotiate the notary's fee may be quite limited.

1. See *infra*, Chapter 8, Sections 3(e) at 756 (Evidence and Discovery) and 3(h) at 795 (Expert Evidence).

2. See N. Andrews, English Civil Procedure 823–59 (2003); A. Zuckerman, Zuckerman on Civil Procedure—Principles of Practice 999–1086 (2008); B. Cairns, Australian Civil Procedure 505–36 (2005).

3. This is independent of whether there are assets in the place where one litigates. If the foreign party obtains a judgment for attorneys' fees, it is likely to be enforced in the United States. Cf. C.H. Peterson, Foreign Country Judgments and the Second Restatement of Conflict of Laws, 72 Colum.L.Rev. 220, 254 (1972) (collecting cases). Furthermore, if the foreign action was based on foreign law, a suit directly for fees may be successful even in the United States, on the

overstate this point, because attorney fees in most civil law countries are considerably lower than in the U.S. Even in England, where hourly rates are notoriously much higher than in the U.S., the final amount may be much lower because of the absence of discovery and other devices.

More generally, as will be developed below, the U.S. "privatizes" procedure to a great extent so that private attorneys perform most of the activity that in the civil law is performed by judges and other court employees. From the perspective of the common-law observer, in the civil-law tradition, the state "subsidizes" the costs of private litigation.

In some countries, a foreign plaintiff must deposit security for costs and expenses (*cautio judicatum solvi*), and the amount required to be deposited takes the opposing lawyer's prospective fee into consideration. The "security for costs" has become less common, especially because of constitutional rules of access to justice or because some treaties exclude them.

Edge: Isn't it unfair to force the loser to pay the value of an expensive legal team selected by the opponent, including the excessive hours of work that the attorneys, partners, associates, and paralegals devoted to the case?

Comparovich: American observers are always uneasy with the fee-shifting rule because of the peculiarities of their own legal system. However, one must understand the fee-shifting rule in the context of the litigation realities of civil-law countries. First of all, the practice of having several lawyers working on an hourly basis is not at all common. Second, the agreement between the client and his or her attorney is absolutely irrelevant for the court determination of the amount of the fee award, which is done based on criteria established in law.

However, the UK has a curious example that directly contradicts this argument. As we have seen, since the nineties, the UK allows a client to enter into a private agreement with his or her attorney to pay a success fee in addition to the regular fee ("conditional fee agreement"—CFA).[4] Originally, the CFA was not recoverable from the losing party. Since 2000, however, it is.[5] It is indeed a very strange rule.

Smooth: And how is the amount calculated?

Comparovich: The answer varies from country to country. As we have seen before, the German statutory fee schedule applies both to the obligation between the client and his or her attorney (although the client may agree to pay more) as well as to the loser.

The French system is different. In France, the court has a discretionary power to assess some or all of that fee against the losing party whenever it seemed inequitable to leave those fees (or, indeed, other, not normally recoverable expenses) on the shoulders of the winner. The judge

ground that the same law that applies to the substance applies to the attorney's fees.

4. See *supra*, Chapter 7, Section 8(a) at 685 (regarding the English success fees).

5. See the Courts and Legal Services Act of 1990, as amended in April 1, 2000, by section 27 of the Access to Justice Act of 1999.

must asses all or part of the not otherwise recoverable costs (including the lawyer's fee) on the losing side. In determining the amount, the judge will take into consideration the general equities and the financial circumstances of the parties. The judge may even completely refrain from assessing these expenses.[6] In countries where there is no such discretion, and they are in the majority, the cost risk is thus a substantial factor in determining whether to litigate or not, especially when combined with the non-availability of a contingent fee.

The ALI/UNIDROIT Principles of Transnational Civil Procedure adopts the fee shifting rule, and state that the winner should be awarded all or a substantial portion of its reasonable costs. They authorize the court to withhold or limit costs and attorneys' fees in exceptional cases when there is clear justification for doing so. The court may also "limit the award to a proportion that reflects expenditures for matters in genuine dispute and award costs against a winning party who has raised unnecessary issues or been otherwise unreasonably disputatious."[7]

Brazil has a peculiar rule within the civil-law tradition because it openly conditions the fee award to a direct percentage of the amount in controversy in pecuniary claims. The general rule is that the court will determine the award of attorneys' fees between 10 and 20% of the judgment, considering the quality and quantity of the legal work performed. If each party wins part of a claim, the court will allocate the fees proportionally.[8]

Contrary to the civil-law tradition, until 2004, the "American Rule" prevailed in Belgium: the winner would not be able to recover attorney's fees and costs from the loser except for a very small amount (from 30 € to 500€) as "procedural costs" (*indemnité de procédure—IDP*). In 2004, the Belgian Court of Cassation put a time-bomb under this accepted, although sometimes criticized, Belgian rule. It first decided that damages in a breach of contract included attorney's fees and costs "necessary for its enforcement". Two years later, it extended this rule to tort cases.[9] Some lower courts applied the new rule vigorously, while others ignored it, basically stating the attorney's fees and costs were not "necessary". After some time, the Constitutional Court interfered in the debate, applauding the Cassation judgments and summoning the legislature to solve the issue promptly and conclusively.[10] Instead of resolving the problem by encapsulating it in the substantive law (breach of contract or tort), as the Court of Cassation did, the legislature redefined the old concept of the *indemnité de*

---

6. See French Code of Civil Procedure (art. 700).

7. See Principle 25 and Rule 32, ALI/UNIDROIT, Principles of Transnational Civil Procedure (2006)

8. See Brazilian Code of Civil Procedure (arts. 20 and 21).

9. See Judgment of Sept. 4, 2004, Arrêts de la Cour de Cassation 1271 (2004)

(contract case); Judgment of Nov. 16, 2006, Journal des Tribunaux 14 (2007) (tort case).

10. See Judgment of April 19, 2006 (Moniteur Belge, July 7, 2006); Judgment of June 14, 2006 (Moniteur Belge, August 14, 2006) and Judgment of January 17, 2007 (Moniteur Belge, 9 March 2007).

procédure, as a fixed contribution for costs and attorney's fees.[11] Neither does the act provide for a full recovery of costs and attorney's fees nor is it calculated according to the real amount spent. The loser only has to pay a lump sum, based on the amount in controversy and calculated on the basis of the plaintiff's claim (so counterclaims are disregarded). The judge may increase or decrease the IDP within established ranges, taking into account the financial resources of the losing party (used only for a decrease, not for an increase of the IDP), the complexity of the case, the contractually agreed damages for breach of contract, and the fact that the situation is obviously unreasonable (a catch all criterion).[12]

Smooth: Isn't the US coming closer to the English rule as a result of a variety of fee-shifting statutes? It is also widely known that juries inflate awards to reflect the fact that a third of the award will generally be paid to the attorney. This practice operates as a one-way fee shifting. Also, contracts usually have an attorney fee shifting clause in case one of the parties need to employ legal services.

Comparovich: It is true that there are several fee shifting statutes, but they are just limited exceptions to the general American Rule that each party must pay its own attorney's fee. In addition, some fee shifting provisions either expressly provide or are interpreted as applying only to a prevailing plaintiff (not to a prevailing defendant). This is what is called "one-way fee shifting."

On the other hand, the U.S. Supreme Court held that the fee-shifting provision of the Copyright Act must be applied in an evenhanded manner to both parties.[13] However, it rejected an invitation to apply the "English Rule" that the loser automatically pays the winner's attorneys' fees without express statutory provision. Since the "American Rule" of no fee-shifting was still the general principle, and the statute merely said that the court *may* impose lawyers' fees, it would, in the court's view, have been improper to interpret that provision to provide for an automatic, totally nondiscretionary shifting of lawyers' fees to the loser.

In short, then, U.S. courts shift attorneys' fees only in special situations, such as when it is important to encourage individuals to act as a "private attorney general" as in civil rights and some other special cases, or to discourage vexatious behavior in litigation. But in other respects, the American Rule is still very much in force and legislative or judicial attempts to abolish it have not been successful so far. The U.S. Supreme Court reaffirmed the "American rule" and rejected the possibility of judicially created exceptions: only express statutory authorization (or contractual provisions) may overrule the "American rule." There are over one

---

11. See Act of April, 21 2007 (Moniteur Belge, May 31, 2007) (the Act entered into force on January 1, 2008); Belgian Royal Decree of October 26, 2007 (Moniteur Belge, November 9, 2007).

12. See Belgian Code of Civil Procedure (art. 1022).

13. Fogerty v. Fantasy, Inc., 510 U.S. 517, 114 S.Ct. 1023 (1994) (interpreting 17 U.S.C. § 505).

hundred federal statutory provisions authorizing fee shifting, comprising a substantial proportion of federal civil litigation.[14]

The contrast between the "American" and "English" rule has important practical consequences and is a recurring academic topic in comparative civil procedure, raising fascinating issues of social policy. An economic analysis of the issue is extremely complex and depends on the specifics of each type of case and the parties involved.

The American rule, especially when coupled with the contingent fee, reduces the plaintiff's cost risk and thus encourages access to justice, even in instances in which the legal theory asserted is novel or doubtful. One may say that the encouragement is maybe too much, for a party has absolutely nothing to lose even if the claim is not particularly strong.[15] Some of those cases will be won by plaintiffs and will become precedents that will improve the legal system. The English rule, however, discourages unmeritorious litigation and moreover any litigation, except by a party very sure of winning and thus likely to have a case based on well established law. This may explain to some extent why the pace of change of the common law is slower in England than in the United States.[16] It will be interesting to see what effect recent changes in English law, for example, in connection with conditional fees, will have on all of this.

On the other hand, the American rule, especially when coupled with high cost of litigation and high attorney fees in the US, also means that a party with a meritorious claim may not have full access to courts whenever the amount in controversy is relatively too small to justify the unreimbursed expenses with litigation costs and attorney's fees.

The English rule also encourages a party to litigate if it believes it has a meritorious claim or defense; its cost risk is very small in that case. To the contrary, an American party may more be willing to settle, especially if the non-recoverable expenses are likely to be out of proportion with the sum a settlement will cost, even if a meritorious claim seems certain. Nevertheless, some corporations who are frequent defendants, fearing a reputation for easily settling will encourage frivolous and thus, in the end, still very costly suits, have adopted a policy of not settling under any circumstances.

All these differences have a direct consequence on the type of controversy each procedural system is optimal to hear. Common-law procedure is much more expensive, but correspondingly more able to handle complex cases, in which there is a need to conduct extensive discovery, but not access for claims below a certain amount.

---

14. See Alyeska Pipeline Service Co. v. Wilderness Society, 421 U.S. 240, 95 S.Ct. 1612 (1975).

15. Rule 11(b) of the Federal Rules of Civil Procedure states that the party and the attorney may be sanctioned, if the claim or defense is not warranted by existing law or by a nonfrivolous argument for changing existing law or for establishing new law. Rule 11(c)(5)(A), however, states that in this case the sanction may not be monetary.

16. See the detailed study by J.R.S. Pritchard, A Systemic Approach for Comparative Law: The Effect of Cost, Fee and Financing Rules on the Development of Substantive Law, 17 J. Legal Studies 451 (1988).

(c) Legal Aid

Smooth: What about indigent litigants who have no or insufficient means to pay for legal assistance?

Comparovich: To deal with the plight of the litigant or would be litigant of insufficient means, most civil-law countries have long recognized legal aid as a public function to be regulated by law.[1] This is not different from the fact that these same countries consider education and health care a public function.

In some civil-law countries, free legal aid is a constitutional right.[2] In other countries, the right derives from acts of the legislature.[3] Statutory schemes ensure that in civil and criminal cases, a party of insufficient means will be represented by competent counsel. These schemes vary from country to country in their details, scope, and strength. In some countries there are limited legal aid provisions (e.g. Italy). Other countries (e.g. the Netherlands and the Scandinavian countries) have instituted the most comprehensive legal aid systems in terms of coverage, extending eligibility to large segments of society.[4]

Edge: What is necessary for an applicant to get legal aid?

Comparovich: Most civil-law countries have, in addition to nationality requirements, two conditions for receiving legal aid: financial need and a meritorious claim or defense. In the UK, they are called the "means test" and the "merits test."

The "means test" is far more difficult to comply with than the "merits test." Typically, the potential plaintiff merely has to show the claim or defense "has a sufficient prospect of success and is not maliciously assert-

---

1. For comprehensive but now somewhat dated information on legal aid in civil-law and other foreign countries, see Zemans (ed.), Perspectives on Legal Aid: An International Survey (1979); Cappelletti, Gordley & Johnson, Jr., Toward Equal Justice: A Comparative Study of Legal Aid in Modern Societies (1975); [International Legal Center] Committee on Legal Services to the Poor in the Developing Countries, Legal Aid and World Poverty: A Survey of Asia, Africa and Latin America (1974); and the multi-volume work edited by Cappelletti and Garth, Access to Justice (1978–79). For more recent works, see Regan, The Transformation of Legal Aid: Comparative and Historical Studies (1999); Rhode, Access to Justice (2004); Yuille, No One's Perfect (Not Even Close): Reevaluating

Access to Justice in the United States and Western Europe, 42 Colum. J. Transnat'l L. 863 (2004) and the references in note 3.

2. See the Constitutions of Belgium (art. 23, § 3, 2°), Italy (art. 24 as interpreted by the Italian Constitutional Court), the Netherlands (art. 18), Portugal (art. 20), Brazil (art. 5, LXXIV), and Spain (art. 24).

3. See England and Wales (Access to Justice Act 1999), Sweden (Legal Assistance Act 1973), and Norway (Legal Assistance Act 1980).

4. See Yuille, No One's Perfect (Not Even Close): Reevaluating Access to Justice in the United States and Western Europe, 42 Colum. J. Transnat'l L. (2004) 863 (describing these systems in detail and comparing them with the U.S. reality).

ed"[5] or is not manifestly inadmissible or devoid of substance.[6] These two factors are separately analyzed by the court.

Legal aid can be granted for all or part of the proceeding and to assist in coming to a settlement before the action comes to trial. It even can be granted for the purposes of seeking enforcement of a judgment or other enforceable document.

It was argued in Germany that this rule, though quite favorable to the litigant seeking assistance, nevertheless violates the Equal Protection clause of the German Constitution because a wealthy party would be free to initiate even a hopeless action. Nevertheless, the Federal Constitutional Court rejected the argument and upheld the rule though it later ruled that where the applicant's case depends on a doubtful issue of law, the application must be granted, since a wealthy person would certainly be able to have a doubtful question of law resolved by the courts.[7]

The British rules are much stricter. The Legal Services Commission (LSC) will review an application against criteria set out in its Funding Code.[8] The exact nature of this assessment will vary depending on the type of case and the level of help required. For legal representation, the test is designed to measure, taking all the circumstances into account, whether a privately paying client of moderate means would spend his or her own money on taking the case. The Commission must consider, for example, the prospects of success, any alternative sources of funding, and any other circumstances such as wider public interest or overwhelming importance to the applicant. It will also consider the possible benefits of litigation and, where possible, compare them to the likely costs.

Edge: What showing does an applicant have to make concerning the "means test," regarding his or her financial circumstances?

Comparovich: In Germany, until 1980, only a "poor" person was able to obtain legal aid in litigation. But a 1980 amendment of the German Code

---

5. See German Code of Civil Procedure (§ 114). For a description of the German system, as amended in 1980, see Fisch, Recent Developments in West German Civil Procedure, 6 Hastings Int'l & Comp.L.Rev. 221, 272–75 (1983); Herbert A. Hirte, Access to the Courts for Indigent Persons: A Comparative Analysis of the Legal Framework in the United Kingdom, United States and Germany, 40 Int'l & Comp.L.Q. 91 (1991); Blankenburg, Patterns of Legal Culture: The Netherlands Compared to Neighboring Germany, 46 Am. J. Comp. L. 1 (1998); Murray & Stürner, German Civil Justice 116–125 (2004).

6. The French rules on legal aid can be found in Law No. 91–647 of July 10, 1991, 1991 J.O. 9170, 1991 D.L. 310. Detailed rules are found in the (executing) Decree No. 91–1266 of December 19, 1991 J.O. 16609, 1992 D.L. 15. In Belgium the provisions are laid down in the Code of Civil Procedure (arts. 508/1–23).

7. The first case is cited and discussed in Fisch, Recent Reforms in German Civil Procedure: The Constitutional Dimension, 1 Civ.Just. Q. 33, 39–40 (1982). The later judgment is the Decision of March 13, 1990, 44 N.J.W. 413 (1991).

8. The Legal Services Commission was established under the Access to Justice Act (1999). The Legal Services Commission Manual is a required reference tool for publicly funded solicitors in England and Wales. The Manual provides invaluable guidance on the Community Legal Service (CLS) and Criminal Defence Service (CDS), the two schemes run by the Commission. It is available in four volumes. Volume 3 contains the Funding Code, which determines which cases the Commission may fund as part of the Community Legal Service. The Code consists of two parts: Part 1, containing the funding criteria, and Part 2, the procedures.

of Civil Procedure eliminated all references to "poverty" or "poor" litigants. Under the current provision, assistance is to be granted to any party
who in the light of his or her "personal economic circumstances" is wholly
or partly unable to bear the costs of the litigation in question.[9] This means
that a party of moderate means, although not poor, may have court costs
and attorney fees wholly or partially paid out of public funds.[10] However, to
the extent that the applicant has income or assets in excess of certain
specified amounts, such excess may have to be used towards repaying,
perhaps in installments, the public treasury's expenditure. Assistance may
be partial rather than total, and it may take the form of a mere advance,
which eventually must be repaid. Compared to the pre–1980 provisions,
which authorized assistance only to "poor" litigants, this new scheme
considerably expands the group of people who may receive some form of
public assistance with respect to litigation expenses. At least in cases
involving large claims (and correspondingly substantial litigation expenses),
members of the middle class may be among the beneficiaries of the revised
scheme.

The French system is more specific. An applicant will receive legal aid
if the average of his combined resources for the preceding calendar year
(excluding family allowances and certain welfare benefits) does not exceed a
certain threshold set by statute each year. For example, legal aid applications made in 2008 are examined on the basis of resources received in 2007.
From January 1, 2008 the monthly resources limit for a single person was
€885 ($1,162) for full legal aid and €1,328 ($1,744) for partial legal aid. In
both cases, the limit is raised by €159 ($209) for the first two dependents
(mostly children) and by €101 ($133) for the third and subsequent depen-
dents.[11] If the resources of the applicant exceed the limits, he or she may
still be able to receive legal aid if his or her action is particularly worthy of
interest, given its subject matter and likely cost. The resources statement is
not required if the applicant is entitled to benefits from the National
Solidarity Fund or to the Occupational Integration Minimum Income, or if
he or she is entitled to a war veteran's or victim's pension.

Similar rules can be found in other countries. The Italian system is
available only to individuals falling below a legally determined maximum
annual income. In order to satisfy the test, an applicant must produce
evidence of his or her financial situation. All this information, which must
be kept current, is also subject to verification by the fiscal police.[12] The
same is true of England and Wales. Any money or assets which are the
subject of the dispute will be disregarded in the assessment of an applicant's financial resources. However, any income that is currently received
from the asset will be included.

---

9. German Code of Civil Procedure
(§§ 114 and 115).

10. In Germany, public funds are available for that purpose; the same is true in
France. But this is not true of all civil-law
countries.

11. See Law No. 91–647, arts. 4–
6. See http://www.vos-droits.justice.gouv.

fr/index.php?rubrique=10066&ssrubrique=
10067 (last visited on Jan. 21, 2009).

12. Presidential Decree No. 115 of 30
May 2002 (Official Journal No. 126 (15 June
2002)), art. 88.

Sometimes, funding is conditional. In France, legal aid can be withdrawn during or after the proceedings if, in the course of the proceedings, the beneficiary receives such resources that legal aid would not have been given if he had had them at the time of the application; or, as a result of the enforceable judgment, the beneficiary receives such resources that legal aid would not have been given if he had had them at the time of the application.[13] Similar provisions exist in nearly all civil-law countries.

Whilst all civil-law countries have income thresholds to receive legal aid, the amount of those thresholds differ from country to country and depend on the financial resources the government allocates for legal aid. In some countries, like Italy, the majority of the middle class will not have any access to legal aid. However, more than 45% of the Dutch households are eligible for legal aid and 80% of the Swedish people can enjoy general legal aid.

Edge: Suppose an applicant meets all the requirements you mentioned. What is the procedure by which a lawyer is appointed to represent him or her in a civil case?

Comparovich: The answer to this question varies from country to country, but the main features are similar. The person is free to select the attorney of his or her choosing, and the lawyer who accepts the position will generally be paid from public funds. If the person cannot find an attorney, one will be appointed. This system is called "judicare" in a clear reference to the "medicare" system.

In some countries, the application must be made in a certain institution and in others, directly to the court. In Germany and the Netherlands, the party seeking assistance must apply directly to the court. The court hears the case and issues an independent decision in every instance.[14] In France, the allegedly indigent party must apply to a "Legal Aid Bureau" (*bureau d'aide juridictionnelle*) for the area where he or she lives or where the court is situated. This Bureau is an independent commission composed of representatives of the Government, judiciary, and organized Bar.[15] In England and Wales, the application is made to the Legal Services Commission (LSC) who runs the legal aid scheme.

Edge: The reality in the U.S. is completely different. With the exception of some cases that have a quasi-criminal flavor (e.g. paternity actions), there are only limited statutes authorizing the appointment of attorneys for civil litigants.[16]

13. See French Law No. 91–647, art. 50, Belgian Code of Civil Procedure (art. 508/20, § 1).

14. See German Code of Civil Procedure § 121. In the Netherlands, applications must be filed with the Council for Legal Aid (see the Act of Legal Aid of 23 December 1993, in particular, arts. 2–11).

15. See, Law No. 91–647 and the implementing Decree 91–1266.

16. See Mallard v. United States District Court, 490 U.S. 296, 109 S.Ct. 1814 (1989) (holding, over a dissent by four Justices, that the statute which permits federal district courts to request attorneys to represent indigent litigants in civil rights cases does not permit courts to require such representation. On the other hand, it stated: "In a time when the need for legal services among the poor is growing and public funding for

Although in the US the government is the largest provider of legal services to the poor, the model is different from the civil-law "judicare." Instead of private attorneys paid by public funds, the tendency has been towards the use of "staff attorneys" employed by organizations supported by the Legal Services Corporation (LSC). The LSC does not provide legal services directly, but grants to local organizations that represent clients in low-income areas. LSC-funded activities are limited due to their unpredictable funding and substantial restrictions. As a result, some have said that the US is an "underdeveloped country" in its statutory provisions of legal services to the poor.[17]

These restricted governmental services are supplemented by other tools. The contingent fee arrangement is a form of access to justice that may be superior to legal aid in some situations but is not available when there is no substantial monetary award involved.[18] Other important players are the public interest lawyers, sponsored by organizations like the National Association for the Advancement of Colored People (NAACP), the Legal Defense and Education Fund (LDF), the American Civil Liberties Union (ACLU), and the Mexican American Legal Defense and Educational Fund (MALDEF). However, their field of action is mostly restricted to impact litigation cases. Legal services for the poor are also provided by the private bar on a *pro bono* basis by solo practitioners and small, medium, and large law firms. This form of legal aid has become increasingly important in the US.[19] Most American law schools also provide legal aid through clinics. Many advocate that pro bono work must be mandatory for attorneys. Some law schools have made it a requirement of graduation.

Edge: Which model do you favor, the "judicare" or the "staff attorney"?

Comparovich: There is a large amount of literature on the controversy concerning the relative merits of each model.[20]

Staff attorney systems are effective in the pursuit of what one usually calls "law reform" or "public interest" litigation, and we are familiar with the spectacular effects of some of that litigation in the US, particularly in creating important precedents. However, since their numbers are limited, they may not be able to provide assistance in run of the mill litigation to all that need it. Besides, as the controversies surrounding the Legal Services

such services has not kept pace, lawyers' ethical obligation to volunteer their time and skills pro bono publico is manifest.")

17. Justice Earl Johnson, Jr., Equal Access to Justice: Comparing Access to Justice in the United States and Other Industrial Democracies, 24 Fordham Int'l L.J. 83, 98 (2000).

18. See *supra* Chapter 7, Section 8(a) at 685 (discussing contingent fees) .

19. According to the Final Report on the Implications of the Comprehensive Legal Needs Study, 73% of the matters brought to a

lawyer by low-income families in 1992 was handled pro bono. See Cantril, Agenda for Access: The American People and Civil Justice: Final Report on the Implications for the Comprehensive Legal Needs Study 26 (1996).

20. See Cappelletti & Johnson, Jr. Toward Equal Justice Revisited, 2 The Common Law Lawyer No. 6, at 2 ff (1977); Brakel, Styles of Delivery of Legal Services to the Poor: A Review Article, 1977 American Bar Foundation Research J. 217; id., Surrebuttal: Further Comments on Styles of Delivery of Legal Services to the Poor, 3 The Common Law Lawyer No. 1, at 2 ff.

Corporation show, a staff attorney system is probably more exposed to the vagaries of the political process.[21]

The private attorneys in a "judicare" system seem less attracted to "public interest" type litigation, but, in those countries where the compensation provided is adequate, private lawyers appear to do a satisfactory job in representing their clients, even in routine matters such as divorces.[22] Furthermore, they do represent an influential constituency favoring government funding for legal aid to the poor.

The ideal solution would be a system combining elements of both systems.[23]

Edge: Have any foreign countries experimented with such a two-track approach?

Comparovich: Yes. In Sweden and some Canadian provinces, the client has a choice between a "staff attorney" and a private lawyer paid by government funds.[24]

Smooth: The "judicare" System, in which the appointed lawyer receives compensation from public funds, sounds very interesting. Is it available throughout the civil-law system?

Comparovich: It depends on the economic development of the country. Nearly all European legal systems provide for compensation for a lawyer who places himself or herself in the service of legal aid.

Not long ago in some European countries, such as Italy,[25] there was no compensation from public funds at all for the lawyer. As a result, members of the profession were not particularly anxious to obtain such assignments, and in practice, the task of representing the poor was largely left to the younger and less experienced lawyers. The official legal aid scheme thus acquired a well-deserved poor reputation, with the further consequence that little use was made of it, and private organizations, like labor unions, tried to fill the gap.[26] Since 2002, the situation has slightly improved.[27]

---

21. On the attempts to reduce funding, see, e.g., Jost, Legal Initiatives Stall, 82 A.B.A.J. 20 (March 1996) and Houseman, Civil Legal Assistance for Low–Income Persons: Looking Back and Looking Forward, 29 Fordham Urb. L.J. 1213, 1214 (2002).

22. In countries where a "judicare" system is in force, expenses have risen, especially where legal advice has been included, but the cost does not seem to be exorbitant. See Blankenburg, Subventionen für die Rechtsberatung im Rechtsvergleich, 19 Zeitschr. für Rechtspolitik 108 (1986) (giving figures for Germany, the Netherlands, and the United Kingdom).

23. For a similar proposal, see Saltzman, Private Bar Delivery of Civil Legal Services to the Poor: A Design for A Combined Private Attorney and Staffed Office Delivery

System, 34 Hastings L.J. 1165 (1983). See also Yuille, No One's Perfect (Not Even Close): Reevaluating Access to Justice in the United States and Western Europe, 42 Colum. J. Transnat'l L. 863 (part 5).

24. See Lindblom, Procedure, in Strömholm (ed.), An Introduction to Swedish Law 95, 127–29 (1981).

25. See the report by V. Vigoriti, in Zemans, *supra* note 1, at 177ff.

26. The labor unions regarded their position in the legal aid field as a source of power and, for this reason, apparently have failed to support attempts to bring about statutory improvements in Italy's official legal aid scheme. See Vigoriti, *supra* note 25.

27. Presidential Decree No. 115 of 30 May 2002, Official Journal No. 126 (15 June 2002).

In France until 1972, lawyers appointed to represent indigent litigants had to serve without compensation with the result that such cases usually had to be handled by inexperienced *avocats stagiaires*. The 1972 reform legislation created the "judicare" system in France and it was improved by a 1990 statute.[28] Every year the French State allows a state grant to every local Bar. Among other things, the amount of this grant depends on the number of legal aid proceedings the lawyers of the local Bar have carried out. The rates of compensation, periodically increased over the last decades, are still relatively modest though by no means insignificant.[29] Junior attorneys count on this income and are glad to take legal aid cases as a way of getting both additional income and a broad range of experience.

In Germany, on the other hand, a system of compensating court-appointed lawyers out of public funds has been in operation for a long time. On the whole, the system seems to meet with the approval of the general public as well as the Bar.[30] As a result of the 1980 amendment, the German system now benefits not only litigants who are outright poor, but all those who are financially unable to bear the cost of the particular litigation. The rates at which court-appointed attorneys are compensated in legal aid cases are considerably lower than the ordinary statutory fee schedule.[31] In relatively small matters, there is no significant difference between the two schedules. But, as the amounts involved in the litigation become larger, the fees payable by private clients under the ordinary schedule can rise to very substantial amounts, while the progression under the legal aid schedule is much less steep.[32] Thus, in a large case the fee paid to a court-appointed lawyer out of public funds will be considerably less than the fee that would be paid by a private client. Nevertheless, the rates under the legal aid schedule are by no means negligible with the result that court appointments to represent assisted litigants are sought after by many lawyers, including some of the more experienced ones. Only when the financial stakes in the case become high is it less interesting to provide legal aid services.

Edge: Does the lawyer appointed to represent an assisted client remain uncompensated or compensated at lower-than-ordinary rates, even if the lawyer wins the client's case?

28.   See Law No. 91–647, art. 27.

29.   Each activity in a proceeding is worth a certain number of points. The value of each point is adjusted periodically. See Law No. 91–647, art. 27. For the table indicating the "points", see Decree No. 91–1266, art. 90. The same system exists in Belgium. The value of a point for the year 2007–2008 was about €22 ($28.90). A normal civil proceeding before the Court of First Instance (e.g. a tort case or a breach of contract) is worth 15 points, thus about €330 ($433).

However, there is the possibility of additional compensation (i.e. additional points) for, for example, presentation of expert evidence (6 points per meeting), a personal appearance of the parties (3 points), travel, etc.

30.   See Schlesinger, The German Alternative: A Legal Aid System of Equal Access to the Private Attorney, 10 Cornell Int'l L.J. 213 (1977).

31.   See *supra* at Chapter 7, Section 8(b) at 691 (Attorney Fee Shifting).

32.   For details see Fisch, *supra* note 5.

Comparovich: This must be understood in the context of the traditional fee-shifting rule in civil-law countries, under which the winner's attorney fees are paid by the loser. Even if an appointed lawyer under some legal aid program assisted the winning party, such fees will be taxed against the loser at the ordinary statutory rate rather than the legal aid rate.

Therefore, if a German lawyer appointed to represent a party is unsuccessful, he or she is paid at the legal aid rate (from public funds). If successful, he or she recovers statutory fees at the higher regular rate (from the loser).

Edge: Does this not inject a "contingent" element into the compensation of a lawyer appointed to represent an assisted litigant?

Comparovich: Not really. Although the financial outcomes are different in this situation, it remains true that an *agreement* between attorney and client, providing for compensation expressed only in terms of a percentage of the expected recovery, is unethical and void in a majority of civil-law countries.[33]

What happens in the case we are discussing is that, when the indigent litigant—who received legal aid—wins the case, the legal aid system can be put aside with respect to the payment of the lawyer and the normal rules on attorneys' fees will apply. This principle has many practical applications.

In France, when the judgment awards financial benefits to the winning indigent who received legal aid, the appointed lawyer *can* (not *must*) claim normal attorneys' fee after the Legal Aid Bureau has revoked the legal aid decision. The amount of the benefits must be so that, if the indigent had them on the day he applied for legal aid, he would not have received legal aid because he would have failed the "means test."[34] For example, a lawyer represented a client who had been granted legal aid in an automobile accident case and eventually obtained a settlement of $30,700, with a large percentage attributed to pain and suffering. The lawyer demanded a fee of $3,160 on the grounds that the client now had adequate funds. The client argued that since tort damages in France were only compensatory, he really was not any better off than before the accident, and the award just reflected actual, though non-material, losses. The Cour de cassation disagreed, holding the settlement could be taken into consideration. The attorney's fee in this case, now claimed outside the legal aid system, is somewhat less than ten percent of the recovery, still a rather different result than what would have happened in the U.S.[35]

In Belgium, when the winner, who received legal aid and thus free assistance of a lawyer, collects (legally limited) compensation from the loser for attorneys' fees, this compensation is awarded to the lawyer who must deduct this from the compensation he will receive from the state.[36] In some

33. See *supra* at Chapter 7, Section 8(a) at 685 (discussing the *Pactvm De Quota.*

34. See Law No. 91–647, art. 36.

35. See Cass.civ.1st, May 26, 1993, 1994 D.J. 39.

36. See Belgian Code of Civil Procedure (art. 508/19).

cases, the compensation paid by the loser exceeds the State compensation, in which case the lawyer can retain the surplus. This can be a further incentive for (young) lawyers to participate in the legal aid system.

It is important to observe that the civil-law attorney fee shifting (as much as the common law contingent fee) plays an important role in facilitating access to justice.

The loser, even if financially weak, will have to pay the fees to which the winner attorney is entitled in accordance with the ordinary statutory fee schedule. Under German law, the public treasury helps the assisted litigant by paying his or her own attorney (and court costs); but, the legal aid scheme does not protect the loser from having to pay the regular fees of the opponent's attorney. The rule in France is somewhat different. The beneficiary of legal aid who loses must pay the winner's expenses that are part of official costs (*dépenses*), though, for equitable reasons, the court may charge the government with part of them. Independently of whether it is a case of legal aid or not, French courts have a great deal of discretion to take into consideration equitable factors in deciding the amount to be paid or even whether to impose them on the loser or not.[37]

Smooth: From this brief description, it seems that the existing civil-law legal aid is far better than ours. Shouldn't we seek to learn from their superior efforts?

Comparovich: It is difficult to give a definitive answer because things change very rapidly and there are different crosscurrents. Increasing budgetary constraints sometimes exercise a limiting influence. On the other hand, the European Convention on Human Rights, which has been widely accepted, has just the opposite impact at least in Europe.[38] And, of course, the result will be different if we are talking about an affluent European or a developing Latin American country.

In principle, despite differences and difficulties to generalize, the European tradition has proved far better than the U.S. in caring for the poor litigant. In fact, "the American rule" makes any civil litigation different from personal injury, which has with a potential high award and punitive damages, practically unaffordable.

With respect to the European context, one should also mention that on January 27, 2003, the Council of Europe adopted a directive to improve access to justice in cross-border disputes by establishing minimum common rules relating to legal aid for such disputes.[39] It can be considered as the first (European) step in imposing more extensive positive duties upon the member states. The provisions of this directive only apply to "cross-border" civil cases, where the person requesting legal aid does not live in the

---

37. See supra at 692–93. See Law No. 91–647 (arts. 42 and 75); Code of Civil Procedure (arts. 696 and 700).

38. See European Convention on Human Rights (Article VI, § 3(c)), discussed infra.

39. See Council Directive 2002/8/EC of January 27, 2003, Official Journal L26, January 31, 2003, p. 41.

member state in which the case will be heard or the decision enforced. The directive establishes the principle that persons who do not have sufficient resources to defend their rights in law are entitled to receive appropriate legal aid. This directive has been implemented in nearly all European countries.

Smooth: What about the situation in criminal cases?

Comparovich: In criminal cases, the United States is appallingly behind standards of acceptability despite some progress since *Gideon v. Wainwright*.[40] The level of some public defendants in criminal matters, including death row cases, is pathetic and shameful.

In civil law countries the situation is more mixed; some have recently improved their system, but in some others the defendant is still only entitled to a lawyer who receives no compensation.

The Council of Europe recognized legal aid in criminal proceedings as a fundamental right. Article 6 of the European Convention of Human Rights specifies that anyone charged with a criminal offense has the right to defend himself or herself in person, through legal assistance of his own choosing, or, if he or she does not have sufficient means to pay for legal assistance, to be given it free when the interests of justice so require.[41] Although this provision only relates to criminal matters, the European Court of Human Rights has ruled this principle also applies to civil matters.[42] The third paragraph of Article 47 of the Charter of Fundamental Rights of the European Union also provides that legal aid will be made available to those who lack sufficient resources, insofar as such aid is necessary to ensure effective access to justice.

Unlike the European Court of Human Rights, the U.S. Supreme Court is more reluctant in expanding the right to the assistance of counsel for civil litigation.[43]

Smooth: And what about aid for indigent persons who need legal advice or help with the preparation of legal documents (for example debt management, consumer protection, social benefits, housing, etc.)?

Comparovich: The situation is more mixed in Europe. Although in Italy nothing is provided for free and legal information or advice outside of court is not subsidized, other countries may provide a range of tools.

---

40. 372 U.S. 335, 83 S.Ct. 792 (1963).

41. See European Convention on Human Rights (Article VI, § 3(c)). Under the Protocol on the Right of Individual Petition, the matter can be reviewed by the European Commission and the European Court of Human Rights. See Quaranta v. Switzerland, Judgment of 24 May, 1991, 12 Human Rights L.J. 249 (1991).

42. See, e.g., Airey v. Ireland, Judgement of 9 October 1979 (Application No. 6289/73); Del Sol v. France, Judgment of 26 February 2002 (Application No. 46800/99);

Steel and Morris v. United Kingdom, Judgment of 15 February, 2005 (Application No. 68416/01); Sialkowska v. Poland, Judgement of 22 March 2007 (Application No. 8932/05) and Bobrowski v. Poland, Judgement of 17 June 2008 (Application No. 64916/01). These judgments can be consulted on http://cmiskp.echr.coe.int/tkp197/search.asp?skin=hudoc-en (HUDOC database) (last visited on Jan. 21, 2009).

43. See, e.g., Lassiter v. Department of Social Services, 452 U.S. 18, 101 S.Ct. 2153 (1981).

In France, free legal advice has traditionally been provided to some extent by the organized bar on a volunteer basis, the social service departments of municipalities, and the like. This system has been formalized and extended by the 1991 legislation reforming legal aid. This legislation creates in each *département* (analogous to a county) an official Legal Aid Council (*conseil départemental de l'accès au droit*), which must, in essence, provide legal aid in the form of advice, counseling, and the drafting of documents, by contracting with any appropriate individuals, organizations, etc.[86] The same is true in Belgium, where in each department there is a Commission for Legal Aid (*commission d'aide juridique*) that organizes daily or weekly meetings were lawyers voluntarily give legal advice.[87] Once a lawyer has given advice to a person, she cannot—in a later phase—act as a legal representative in a proceeding for that same person.

In countries with a more developed legal aid system, legal advice is provided by coordinating organizations or law centers. In the Netherlands, for example, Legal Aid Bureaus—administered by five Councils for Legal Aid and staffed by government-employed attorneys—give initial advice to indigent clients. These bureaus can take on a limited number of welfare cases and serve as the initial point in the legal aid application process, making referrals to legal aid attorneys. Non-governmental organizations also provide advice and assistance to the poor, such as the law shops (staffed with law students) in the Netherlands and the Citizens' Advice Bureau ("CABx") in the UK. In many civil-law countries, labor unions provide legal help for their members.

Edge: That all sounds like a good idea, but in discussing the problems of indigent litigants I think we are straying from our main purpose of being here.

Comparovich: You may encounter them as opponents, though.

86. See Law No. 91–647, arts. 53—64. Legal assistance of the "advising" kind under the scheme mentioned is usually given in the courthouse or a municipal building. Since this may be discouraging to some people, there are volunteer organizations that provide free legal advice in other accessible locations (free clinics for the homeless, etc.). It appears, and may be worth noting, that the founder of one such organization is a French lawyer who obtained a graduate degree in the United States. La Rue, No. 38, March 1997, p. 20.

87. See Belgian Code of Civil Procedure (art. 508/2–6).

CHAPTER 8

PROCEDURE

1. INTRODUCTION

This chapter focuses on the procedural institutions of Ruritania, a fictional model for a civil-law country. The emphasis will be on institutions and principles that are common to most or several of the civilian systems. Although there will be many illustrative references to the law of particular countries, the principal aim of the discussion will be to build a *model* exhibiting the *typical* features of civil-law procedure. It cannot be doubted that such typical features exist and distinguish civil law procedure from common law (and especially American) procedure. This is due, in addition to other historical factors, to the impact of a few seminal systems, particularly Germany and France, and to the criss-crossing influences exerted by legislation, other legal developments, and scholarly writings in many countries. This complex network of influences has been interestingly surveyed in an article discussing German-inspired elements in the French Code of Civil Procedure of 1975.[1]

Of course, civil law countries share many *problems* with the common-law world and, in particular, with the United States. These include the increase in litigation due to new substantive developments (in consumer law, environmental protection, civil and human rights etc.), a shortage of human and material resources, omnipresent budgetary constraints, and judicial backlog. But the *solutions* to these problems are likely to be quite different, and even similar problems may have a somewhat different complexion. For instance, the United States, delay has been primarily a problem of the first instance courts. In civil-law countries, it is often pervasive throughout the judicial hierarchy and may even be at its worst at its apex.[2]

1. See R. Stürner, Das Deutsche Zivilprozessrecht und seine Ausstrahlung auf andere Rechtsordnungen—von Deutschland aus gesehen, in W.J. Habscheid (ed.), Das Deutsche Zivilprozessrecht und seine Ausstrahlung auf andere Rechtsordnungen 3, 37–39 (1991). Cf. G. Rouhette, L'influence en France de la science allemande du procès civil et du code de procédure civile allemand, id. at 159 ff.

2. See, for instance, on the French Supreme Court (*Cour de cassation*), M. Peyrot, La Cour de cassation a pris du retard dans le traitement des dossiers, Le Monde, May 18,

1994, p. 13. Some figures on that court are given infra, n. 386. On Italy, see O.G. Chase, Civil Litigation Delay in Italy and in the United States, 36 Am.J.Comp.L. 41 (1988). But note that some institutions more typical of the common law have occasionally been introduced in civil law countries, such as the *amicus curiae*, class actions, certiorari, etc.

Some further cross-currents may be bridging the common law—civil law divide. Thus, it is worth noting that a French author recently has suggested that, in view of the increasing concern for fundamental rights in

The reader may find it desirable, along with this study of Ruritanian procedure, to look at the actual procedural system (including the non-typical and purely local features) of a selected civil-law country. Many valuable English-language materials, in the form of succinct surveys, are available. The reader should be warned, though, that civil procedure has often been subjected not only to occasional major overhauls but also to a great deal of minor tinkering. No English-language book or article is therefore likely to stay up-to-date for a long time. Where accurate knowledge of details is essential, recourse must be had to current materials from the country involved on the original language, such as treatises, monographs, annotated editions of codes of civil procedure, and the like. Only a few selected issues can be discussed here.

A reader who is limited to materials in English will encounter serious difficulty in studying the civil procedure of any country. But some monumental works are available, such as Herzog, Civil Procedure in France (1967); Cappelletti & Perillo, Civil Procedure in Italy (1965); Ginsburg & Bruzelius, Civil Procedure in Sweden (1965); Cremades & Cabiedes, Litigation in Spain (1989). The books on Italy and Sweden are seriously outdated but still valid in many parts because the respective codes of civil procedure are still in force. They had a vibrant life but are now slowly dying of dignifying old age. However, the books on France and Spain suffered a premature death a few years after their publication due to the demise of their respective century-old codes of civil procedure: France enacted a new code in 1975 (the previous code was from 1806)[3] and Spain enacted a new one in 2000 (the previous code was from 1881).

There are, however, some recent works, which provide more updated information, such as Yessiou–Faltsi, Civil Procedure in Hellas (1997); Goodman, Justice and Civil Procedure in Japan (2004); Murray & Stürner, German Civil Justice (2004); Taniguchi, Reich & Miyake, Civil Procedure in Japan, looseleaf. Of particular interest is Taelman (ed.) International Encyclopaedia of Laws. Civil Procedure, looseleaf, 5 vols. (2007) (with monographs from Australia, Austria, Bangladesh, Bulgaria, Canada, China, Costa Rica, Czech Republic, Denmark, Egypt, Finland, France, Germany, Greece, Hungary, India, Israel, Italy, Kenya, Lithuania, Morocco, Peru, Romania, South Africa, Spain, Sweden, Uruguay, U.S.A, Venezuela, Zim-

---

the area of civil procedure, the decisions of the United States Supreme Court in the procedural due process field can provide "rich teachings," especially in view of the ideological closeness between the French Declaration of the Rights of Man and the American Bill of Rights. See S. Guinchard, F. Ferrand & C. Chainais, Procédure Civile 60–61 (2008).

3. For more than 30 years, from 1975 to 2007, the official name of the new French Code was the "New Code of Civil Procedure" (le Nouveau Code de procédure civile). An Act of December 20, 2007 finally dropped the word "New".

The enactment of the new Code of Civil Procedure by decree has not received the unanimous applause of the French Bar. The Code was drafted in the Ministry of Justice, mainly by judges on temporary assignment to the Ministry. Legislation would, of course, have had to be approved by Parliament which has many lawyer members (especially on the appropriate committees). The claim has thus been made that the new code reflects more the views of the judiciary than of the bar.

babwe etc). Some codes of civil procedure have been translated into English, like the French in 2007, the Japanese in 1998, and the German in 1990.

Information about European civil procedure can be found on the website of the European Judicial Network in civil and commercial matters, managed by the European Commission and regularly updated. It contains a large quantity of information about the European Member States, Community law, European law, and various aspects of civil and commercial law, including civil procedure.[4] On European civil procedure one also has to refer to van Caenegem, History of European civil procedure (1973); Van Rhee, European Traditions in Civil Procedure (2005); Layton & Mercer, European Civil Practice, 2 vols. (2004); Vogenauer & Hodges, Civil Justice Systems in Europe (2009).

In the last decade, academic interest for Comparative Civil Procedure has increased in the U.S., as can be demonstrated by the publication of several law review articles by prominent proceduralists that, up to that point in their prolific careers, had written exclusively about U.S. civil procedure. The recent appearance of "cases and materials" further validates the point. See Main, Global Issues in Civil Procedure (2006); Chase, Hershkoff, Silberman, Taniguchi, Varano & Zuckerman, Civil Litigation in Comparative Context (2007). See also McClurg, Koyuncu & Sprovieri, Practical Global Tort Litigation (2007) and McCaffrey & Main, Transnational Litigation in Comparative Perspective (2010). The fifth edition of the celebrated treatise James, Hazard & Leubsdorf, Civil Procedure (2001) is pregnant with comparative comments carefully placed throughout the book to put American civil procedure in comparative perspective. See also Hazard & Taruffo, *American Civil Procedure* (1993), a book written by an American and an Italian scholar, presenting a comparative account of American civil procedure for foreigners, and Hazard & Dondi, *Legal Ethics. A Comparative Study* (2004), also written by an American and an Italian scholar.

Generally speaking, the two major civil-law procedural families are the Romanic (derived from Roman law) and the Germanic (derived from the Germanic customs). Historically, all European countries have suffered major influence from both traditions for many centuries, and determining today whether a particular device has Roman or Germanic origins has only academic value. Giuseppe Chiovenda once observed that the then existent Italian procedure was "neither more Roman nor less Germanic than the existing procedure of Germany."[5] Even if hidden in a sea of homogeneity, today there are some clear difference between modern Romanic and Germanic procedure, although the differences are not nearly as striking as the differences between civil-law and common-law procedure.

---

4. http://ec.europa.eu/civiljustice/index_en.htm (last visited Jan. 21, 2009).

5. See Chiovenda, Roman and Germanic Elements in Continental Civil Procedure, in Engelmann, A History of Continental Civil Procedure 875, esp. at 883 and 912 (discussing the odyssey of Romanistic and Germanic influence in France, Italy, and Germany).

The modern Romanic civil procedure has been particularly influential and prevails in France, Italy, Spain, Portugal, Belgium, the Netherlands, Latin America, Africa, and Asia. All countries suffered the influence of Roman law including those of the common law tradition. In the more recent past, in the XIX Century, many countries adopted the (old) French Napoleonic Code of Civil Procedure of 1806 because of either Napoleon's military conquests or its intrinsic intellectual value. Most of its rules had been modelled from an ancient ordinance (the *Ordonnance du Châtelet* or *Ordonnance Louis* of 1667) so that the code was neither modern nor innovative.[6]

The significance of the Napoleonic Code of Civil Procedure cannot be underestimated. Even though it was not the first legal code to be established in a European country, it is considered the first successful codification and strongly influenced the law of many other countries, such as Italy, The Netherlands, Belgium, some German states, Russia, Poland, etc. Thus, the Napoleonic code has had varying influence over the civil-law systems of the countries of modern continental Europe, with the exception of the Scandinavian countries. The French Code, however, was neither adopted nor influential in Spain, who modeled its codes of 1855 and 1881 on the local tradition of the Siete Partidas of the late 1200s. The Siete Partidas was extremely influential in Latin America (and Luisiana) as well.

Modern German civil procedure has also been extremely influential and prevails in Germany, Austria, and Switzerland. When Japan wanted to modernize and westernize, it relied heavily on the German Code of Civil Procedure (of 1877) and enacted a code in 1890 (with some French influence as well). Ever since the American Occupation following World War II, Japan has felt the increasing influence of U.S. civil procedure, yet has not abandoned its Germanic past.[7] In addition, modern German civil procedure has been influential on modern French and Italian procedural scholarship. One American author has suggested German procedure as a model for reform in the United States.[8] At the end of this chapter, the reader may want to ask whether that is a valid argument. The Austrian system of civil procedure (actually consisting of four separate "Codes," one

---

6. See See Holtman, The Napoleonic Revolution (1981); L. Cadiet & G. Canivet, De la Commémoration d'un Code à l'Autre: 200 Ans de Procédure Civile en France (2006) (celebrating the 200 years of the Napoleonic Code of Civil Procedure and its influence in Europe and elsewhere).

7. See Taniguchi, Reich & Miyake, Civil Procedure in Japan 1–33–1–40 (2008); Goodman, Justice and Civil Procedure in Japan 67–71 (2004).

8. See Langbein, The German Advantage in Civil Procedure, 52 U.Chi.L.Rev. 823 (1985). This article has created lively controversy. See, e.g., Gross, The American Advantage. The Value of Inefficient Litigation, 85 Mich. L. Rev. 734 (1987); Allen, Köck, Reichenberg & Rosen. The German Advantage in Civil Procedure: A Plea for More Details and Fewer Generalities in Comparative Scholarship, 82 Nw. U. L. Rev. 705 (1988); Bernstein, Whose Advantage After All, A Comment on the Comparison of Civil Justice Systems, 21 U.C. Davis L.Rev. 587 (1988); Reitz, Why We Probably Cannot Adopt the German Model of Civil Procedure, 75 Iowa L.Rev. 987 (1990); Stiefel & Maxeiner, Civil Justice Reform in the United States—Opportunity for Learning from "Civilized" European Procedure Instead of Continued Isolation?, 42 Am.J.Comp.L. 147 (1994).

dealing with jurisdiction, one with procedure, one with the enforcement of judgments, and another with some special proceedings) has influenced procedural law in many other countries (such as Germany) and is generally acclaimed as an enlightened piece of legislation.

There has always been constant movement of procedural ideas among European countries, and this reality is particularly pressing at a time of European integration. There is also exchange between Latin American countries, and a constant influence of European civil procedure. The same level of exchange of procedural ideas occurs with common-law procedure.

It is also interesting to observe the modest birth of a (uniform) European Civil Procedure. In implementing article 65 of the EC Treaty, the European legislator had to take action with regards to the harmonization of private law and civil procedure. This was done in the autumn of 1999 when the European Council held a special meeting at Tampere, Finland devoted to the establishment of an area of freedom, security, and justice in the European Union. The member states wanted the European Commission to take a number of initiatives to improve access to justice for individuals and corporations in Europe. Since then, a number of council regulations have been enacted.[9]

2. RECENT DEVELOPMENTS

The turn of the century has witnessed a busy couple of decades for civil procedure. Law reforms of near revolutionary proportions were enacted in several countries, modernizing the traditional paradigms. We have seen the recent enactment of several brand new codes of civil procedure, such as Uruguay (1988), The Nederlands (1988 and 2002), China (1991 and 2008), Peru (1992) Portugal (1995), Japan (1996), The Philippines (1997), Luxembourg (1998), Spain (2000). In 2009, a national code will displace all the cantonal codes in Switzerland. In 1998, England enacted an unprecedented "code", placing it one step closer to the civil-law procedure.

Several other countries, such as the United States, Brazil, Germany, Austria, Mexico, Argentina, Italy, France, Belgium, to name just a few, also

---

9. Council regulation (EC) No 1346/2000 of 29 May 2000 on insolvency proceedings; Council regulation (EC) No 1348/2000 of 29 May 2000 on the service in the Member States of judicial and extrajudicial documents in civil or commercial matters; Council Regulation (EC) No 44/2001 of 22 December 2000 on jurisdiction and the recognition and enforcement of judgments in civil and commercial matters; Council Regulation (EC) No 1206/2001 of 28 May 2001 on cooperation between the courts of the Member States in the taking of evidence in civil or commercial matters; Regulation (EC) No 805/2004 of the European Parliament and of the Council of 21 April 2004 creating a European Enforcement Order for uncontested claims; Regulation (EC) No 1896/2006 of the European Parliament and of the Council of 12 December 2006 creating a European order for payment procedure and Regulation (EC) No 861/2007 of the European Parliament and of the Council of 11 July 2007 establishing a European Small Claims Procedure. All these regulations can be consulted on http://eur-lex.europa.eu/en/index.htm.

enacted sweeping procedural reforms, many of them in installments for over two decades. The bulk of the reform movement dealt with inefficiency, expense, and delay. Procedural law reform is a recurrent topic in comparative law. Several books and special issues of law reviews have recently been published about procedural reform worldwide.[1]

The European Union and its courts has also been an important vehicle of procedural reform to such an extent that it is possible to say there is a European Civil Procedure. This adds a layer of complexity in understanding the national procedural laws in European countries. The unification of the different procedural systems in Europe seems inevitable, and the aforementioned European regulations are direct evidence of this evolution.

There have also been several major international initiatives for the unification of civil procedure that will have a profound impact on future generations of scholars and legislators.

The first important international initiative was the creation of a Model Code of Civil Procedure for Ibero–American countries.[2] The project took two decades to complete and was sponsored by the Ibero–American Institute of Procedural Law. Its reporters were Adolfo Gelsi Bidart, Luis Torello, and Enrique Vescovi, all from Uruguay. The objective was to create a model that could guide a unifying and modernizing law reform in the existing procedural codes of Ibero–American countries. The initiative was largely successful: not only did several Ibero–American countries reform their procedural laws in line with the proposals, but at least one country (Uruguay) adopted it almost verbatim.[3]

The second initiative, the Approximation of Judiciary Law in the European Union, was inspired by the success of the Ibero–American Model Code. It was reluctantly sponsored by the European Commission and spearheaded by Marcel Storme (Belgium) and a group of 12 prominent scholars from each of the then 12 Member States of the European Community. The working premise was that differences in domestic procedural law affect the free circulation of judicial decisions therefore creating distortions that may affect the "internal market" of a soon to be integrated Europe. Although the original idea was to create a full-fledged European Code of Civil Procedure modelled after the Ibero–American Code, that overly ambitious project was quickly abandoned in favor of a more modest endeavor: a selection of a dozen or so relevant procedural devices. The objective was to

---

1. See, e.g., 45 Am. J. Comp. L. 649–944 (1997); A. Zuckerman et al. (eds.), Civil Justice in Crisis. Comparative Perspectives of Civil Procedure (1999); Trocker & Varano (eds.), The Reforms of Civil Procedure in Comparative Perspective 255–258 (2005).

2. Ibero-america is a geo-cultural concept, referring to the countries in Latin America, Portugal, and Spain. These countries share a common history and culture but can be further divided into two subgroups of Portuguese (Portugal and Brazil) and Hispanic tradition (Spain and Spanish speaking countries).

3. See Bidart, Torello & Vescovi, Anteproyecto de Código Procesal Civil Modelo para Iberoamerica, Revista de Processo, vols. 51–53 (1988). The same institute later published its Model Code of Criminal Procedure.

study the procedural law of the Member States and propose a model for their approximation.[4]

There are several differences between the EU Approximation Rules and the Ibero-American Model Code. First, the Ibero-American project was supposed to be just a "model" upon which national legislators would be inspired to voluntarily pick and chose what, how, and when to change their own laws. The EU project was supposed to be implemented in each country through EU directives. Second, the EU project was not a full-fledged code, as we have seen. Third, the EU project had to deal with a far more challenging diversity of legal cultures, reconciling not only the Romanic and Germanic, but also the Anglo legal tradition. The Ibero-American Project only needed to deal with the vastly more similar Portuguese and Spanish legal traditions.

The third major international initiative was the proposal of an ambitious Hague Convention on Jurisdiction and Foreign Judgments in Civil and Commercial Matters, a project sponsored by The Hague Conference on Private International Law. The General Reporters were Peter Nygh (Australia) and Fausto Pocar (Italy). The objective was to create a treaty with common rules of jurisdiction and recognition of judgments to which several countries would become signatories, thus introducing the rules in their domestic law. If approved, this convention would facilitate the worldwide enforcement of judgments and provide something akin to full faith and credit to judgments of the signatory countries. It was hoped to be of similar significance as the UN Convention on the Recognition and Enforcement of Foreign Arbitral Awards of 1958 (New York Convention),[5] but the project proved to be much too ambitious at the time and resulted in a much more modest convention limited to choice of court clauses.[6] The failure left an inevitable feeling of "unfinished business," and it is predictable that The Hague Conference will revisit the issue in the near future.

Building upon the experience of these three initiatives, The American Law Institute (ALI) and the Institute for the Unification of Private Law (UNIDROIT) joined forces to propose the Principles and Rules of Transnational Civil Procedure. This ambitious project was headed by Geoffrey C. Hazard Jr. (USA), Michele Taruffo (Italy), Rolf Stürner (Germany), and Antonio Gidi (Brazil) and had the support of hundreds of prominent scholars, judges, and practitioners from all over the world. The project took a decade to complete. The objective was to create procedural principles and

---

4. See Storme (ed.), Approximation of Judiciary Law in the European Union (1994).

5. See the Preliminary Draft, Prel. Doc. No 11 (2000), which has the most complete proposal. The ALI proposed rules to implement the Hague Convention in the U.S., regardless of whether the U.S. was to become a signatory party. Since the Convention failed, they instead proposed an independent draft for a federal statute that would impose uniform standards for recognition and enforce-

ment of foreign judgments in the U.S. See ALI, Recognition and Enforcement of Foreign Judgments: Analysis and Proposed Federal Statute (2006). The Reporters were Andreas Lowenfeld and Linda Silberman, with the participation of dozens of people.

6. See the Hague Convention on Choice of Court Agreements (Concluded 30 June 2005).

rules that would transcend domestic procedural norms and be uniformly applied in international commercial litigation throughout the world. Such a uniform approach to international litigation would minimize the natural hesitation of litigating in a foreign country and hopefully foster the creation of a truly international litigation bar with lawyers confidently litigating in any jurisdiction. Since it also acknowledges internationally recognized standards of fair and efficient procedure, it also had the indirect effect of becoming a model for domestic law reform and international arbitration.[7]

The ALI/UNIDROIT project was broader and more limited than the EU initiative. It was broader to the extent that it potentially involved all countries in the world because it was not limited to a culturally connected and limited geographical location, such as Europe. Dealing with the exceptionalism of the U.S. procedural system made the challenge virtually impossible. On the other hand, the ALI/UNIDROIT Project was more limited because it was restricted to international commercial litigation.

The last three initiatives (EU, ALI/UNIDROIT, and The Hague) have failed to a large extent because they had to bridge apparently insurmountable gaps between civil-law and common-law procedure. It would have been much easier to create uniformity among solely civil-law or common-law countries, but it would also be a pretty useless and empty enterprise because they are already similar enough. The real obstacle was that these projects attempted to not only obtain uniformity within these legal traditions, but also among them. However, the experience left the fundamental seeds of curiosity and possibility in the minds of all involved. Perhaps their most relevant contribution was to spur discourse and educate the participants. Those that were skeptical in the beginning of the process became believers and supporters with time. The road now is paved for future experimentations.

Another element connecting these initiatives is that, for the first time, international organizations demonstrated a serious commitment to working with harmonization, uniformization, or approximation of procedural rules. The European Union has had a lasting and profound impact on the domestic laws of its members. Procedural law is not an exception and is directly influenced by Regulations and Directives and indirectly influenced by decisions from the Court of Justice of the European Communities and the European Court of Human Rights.[8]

---

7. See ALI/UNIDROIT, Principles of Transnational Civil Procedure (2006), also available at http://www.unidroit.org/english/principles/civilprocedure/main.htm. Several books and articles have been published about that initiative. See, e.g., Fouchard (ed.), Vers un Procès Civil Universel? (2001) [France]; Andenas, Andrews, Nazzini (eds.), The Future of Transnational Civil Litigation (2004) [England]; Ferrand (ed.), La Procédure Civile Mondiale Modélisée (2004) [France]. See also

the special issues of 33 Texas Int'l L. J. (1998) [USA]; Derecho PUC (1999) [Peru]; 6 Revue de Droit Uniforme (2001) [Italy]; 33 NYU J. Int'l L. and Pol. (2001); 11 Tribunales de Justicia (2002) [Spain].

8. See A. Biondi, Minimum, Adequate or Excessive Protection? The Impact of EC Law on National Procedural Law, in N. Trocker & V. Varano, The Reforms of Civil

More recently, there has been a proposal for a Model Class Action Code with the objective of implementing a comprehensive class action statute in civil law countries.[9] Thereafter, the Ibero–American Institute of Procedural Law sponsored another model code, limited to class actions in Ibero–American countries. The reporters were Ada Pellegrini Grinover, Kazuo Watanabe, and Antonio Gidi, with active collaboration of a few other scholars.[10] These works led to important class action bills in Brazil and Mexico.[11]

It is also important to mention the work of the International Association of Procedural Law. For decades, it has been a forum for legal experimentation, and its work has been instrumental to the worldwide development (and uniformization) of procedural law.

Procedural law reform and experimentation is in full swing and there is no sign of slowing down in the foreseeable future.

3.   THE COURSE OF A CIVIL LAWSUIT

Dialogue resumes.

[The dialogue, that started on Chapter 7, does not aim at the systematic presentation of the civil procedure of any single country. However, in connection with the discussion of specific issues, some significant aspects of the procedural rules of Germany, France, Italy, Spain, Portugal, Belgium, the Netherlands, Japan, Brazil, Argentina, Mexico, and other European and non-European civil-law countries will be mentioned and contrasted as illustration. The details of minute procedural differences among the several national legislations will ordinarily be neglected, for the purpose of portraying a broad perspective of the civil-law civil procedure.

Comparative civil procedure is dedicated to the study of the systems of dispute resolution that foreign countries employ to decide domestic controversies. Since a foreign attorney is rarely allowed to enter an appearance in a foreign court representing a client in a civil proceeding without hiring local counsel, the subject serves no practical purposes for the practitioner, beyond curiosity, law reform, self-knowledge, and all cultural and spiritual benefits offered by the study of comparative law in general.

Procedure in Comparative Perspective 233–42 (2005).

9. See Gidi, The Class Action Code: A Model for Civil Law Countries, 23 Ariz. J. Int'l & Comp. L. 37 (2005).

10. See Gidi & Ferrer (eds.), La Tutela de los Derechos Difusos, Colectivos e Individuales Homogéneos. Hacia un Código Modelo para Iberoamerica (2004).

11. The original Mexican proposed class action statute, drafted by Benítez, Ferrer and Gidi, can be found in the appendix of Gidi & Ferrer (eds.), Código Modelo de Procesos Colectivos. Un Diálogo Iberoamericano 447–453 (2008). The final product of the Brazilian Class Action Bill No. 5.139/2009, substantially altered by the work of several scholars and practitioners, can be found in the web site of the Brazilian Presidency, http://www.planalto.gov.br/ccivil_03/Projetos/PL/2009/PL/2009/msg238–090413.htm   (last visited May 16, 2009).

However, there is an important practical side to comparative civil procedure, especially when one is involved in international litigation or international arbitration, at home or abroad. Therefore, whenever possible, we will discuss pressing issues of serving a defendant, obtaining evidence, or enforcing a U.S. judgment abroad (as well as doing the same at home, for a foreign client). It is essential to understand how litigation proceeds in foreign countries, not only to avoid looking insensitive or ignorant in the eyes of the client or foreign counsel, but especially for making informed strategic decisions.

Comparing legal systems also involves analyzing their historical evolution. Therefore, it is important to put common-law and civil-law civil procedure in their historical perspective to shed light on the modern legislation.

The overall result is a review of U.S. civil procedure in a comparative context, bringing about unexpected facets of U.S. law].

Comparovich: Every time you enter into a deal or operation which might possibly become the subject of litigation in country X, it is fundamental to have the law of that country in the back of your mind and to procure and preserve the kind of evidence that will stand up in its courts. Even lawyers involved primarily in the drafting of contracts or the negotiation of acquisitions must have some familiarity with the rules of civil procedure and evidence of the countries involved.[1]

Smooth: In addition, our company and Ms. Edge and I as individual lawyers and members of Bar Association committees, are very much interested in procedural reform in our own State, and perhaps we could get a few ideas from the civil-law world. Unfortunately, however, we are quite puzzled by what we see of the jurisdictional and procedural principles which courts in civil-law countries seem to apply. You are known as a great expert on comparative civil procedure, and perhaps you can dispel our ignorance.

(a) Personal Jurisdiction (Territorial Competence)

Smooth: I suggest to follow the case we already started to discuss when Mr. H sued Dulci Cola for his fees. H sued us in the Tribunal of First Instance in Ruritania. How could that court have personal jurisdiction over us? We would have understood if the action was against our Ruritanian subsidiary, but it was against the American parent, Dulci–Cola International, incorporated in Delaware and having its main place of business in this state. H attempted to serve us in the U.S. I can see that it is possible to sue a defendant outside the jurisdiction where the action is pending (long arm jurisdiction) if the defendant has some reasonable connection with that jurisdiction (minimum contacts), but otherwise, service in the State or

---

1. See Y. Huyghé de Mahenge, L'assistance dans la gestion de litiges internationaux, in Centre Français de Droit Comparé, L'Entreprise et le Droit Comparé 167, 169–72 (1995); Fontaine & De Ly, Drafting International Contracts: An Analysis of Contract Clauses (2006).

country where the action is pending is, after all, necessary not only to provide notice but also to give the court jurisdiction.

Comparovich: Let us leave methods of service of process aside for the moment; we will get back to them.[1] The civilians reject the idea that service of process has anything to do with jurisdiction, though formal notice to the defendant is, of course, an essential (even constitutional or due process) requirement in order to be able to proceed. In other words, for the civil-law, if there is jurisdiction, you can (and must) effectuate service, but service as such has no effect on jurisdiction.

Except on the issue of "tag jurisdiction," this is largely true in the U.S. as well, although American lawyers do not see it that way. In the U.S., certainly for historical reasons, service of process is studied together with jurisdiction. Conceptually, however, notice has nothing to do with jurisdiction. The idea that a court asserts jurisdiction through service of process may have been acceptable in the U.S. in the 1800s, when the U.S. Supreme Court decided that states have jurisdiction only over people and things located within its territory, but not over those outside it.[2] However, by now U.S. civil procedure should have been able to separate them into two distinct aspects. The function of the service of process is merely to give notice to the defendant. If a court does not have jurisdiction over a person to begin with, it cannot acquire jurisdiction by service of process alone (unless the service is performed within the territory, which is the case of tag jurisdiction). If the court does not have jurisdiction and the defendant is served with process, he or she will enter a special appearance, challenge jurisdiction, and the case will be dismissed for lack of personal jurisdiction. So, here is an area where U.S. procedure could learn a lot from civil-law procedure.

Quite frankly, Rule 4(k)(1)(A) of the Federal Rules of Civil Procedure is written upside down, when it states that "serving a summons (...) establishes personal jurisdiction over a defendant (...) who is subject to the jurisdiction of a court (...)" A court has jurisdiction over a defendant because there is a state statute establishing jurisdiction over the controversy and the defendant has minimum contacts with the forum, not because the court served the defendant with process.

Parenthetically, as you know, the traditional notion that service of process within the territory can give jurisdiction over the defendant even in the absence of factors that connect the defendant to the forum (tag jurisdiction) has always been attacked by legal writers.[3] In Burnham v.

1. See *infra*, Chapter 8, Section 3(b) at 736.

2. See Pennoyer v. Neff, 95 U.S. 714 (1877) (stating that the basis of jurisdiction was physical presence).

3. See, e.g., A. Ehrenzweig, The Transient Rule of Personal Jurisdiction: The "Power" Myth and Forum Conveniens, 65 Yale L.J. 289 (1956); R. Schlesinger, Methods of Progress in Conflict of Laws, 9 J.Publ.L. 313, esp. at 317–18 (1960); R. Weintraub, An Objective Basis for Rejecting Transient Jurisdiction, 22 Rutgers L.J. 611 (1991); P. Hay, Transient Jurisdiction, Especially Over International Defendants: Critical Comments on Burnham v. Superior Court, 1990 U.Ill.Rev. 593.

Superior Court, the United States Supreme Court missed an opportunity to repudiate the principle, especially after the same Court had disavowed quasi in rem jurisdiction a decade earlier in Shaffer v. Heitner. However, the opinion affirming it on historical tradition was a plurality, and some of the other Justices might have come to a different conclusion if the defendant did not have some actual ties with California where the action had been instituted. Moreover, the composition of the court was essential to the case's outcome.[4]

Another peculiarity is that civil-law procedure does not operate with the concept of "personal jurisdiction," meaning jurisdiction over the person of the defendant. The concept used is "territorial competence," meaning competence to adjudicate a specific controversy between two or more people, something similar to, but different from the U.S. concept of "venue."[5]

Here again, the civil-law standard is more logical than the American. Even in the U.S., unless we are talking about general jurisdiction, a court does not have jurisdiction over a person *tout court*, but merely jurisdiction to adjudicate a specific controversy in which that person is involved. It is said that a person must have "minimum contacts" with the forum, but this concept is misleading because it is not enough for the person to have such contacts: it is essential that these contacts be related to the lawsuit. This is the concept of "relatedness," which is essential in cases of specific jurisdiction.

An example will clarify this point. Although New York would have jurisdiction to adjudicate a conflict arising out of a tort allegedly committed by a Florida domiciliary in New York, it will not have jurisdiction to adjudicate a conflict arising from a car crash allegedly caused by the same person in Illinois. So, the same person may have minimum contacts with a state for a certain controversy, but not for another. This is because it is the controversy and not the person who must have contacts with the state. Therefore the "minimum contacts" test is not very useful. It is true that Florida will always have jurisdiction over the Florida domiciliary concerning any matter that may have happened anywhere in the world, but this is the concept of general jurisdiction, for which "minimum contacts" is not relevant.

Smooth: It is no wonder that personal jurisdiction is so unnecessarily complex in the U.S.

Comparovich: The U.S. is indeed the only country in which issues of personal jurisdiction are so important. Personal jurisdiction, subject matter

---

4. See Burnham v. Superior Court, 495 U.S. 604, 110 S.Ct. 2105 (1990) (tag jurisdiction) and Shaffer v. Heitner, 433 U.S. 186, 97 S.Ct. 2569 (1977) (quasi in rem jurisdiction).

5. Territorial competence must not be confused with "material competence" or "subject matter competence", meaning the competence to adjudicate a specific type of controversy, either because of the subject matter (commercial law, family law, labor law, etc.) or because of the amount in controversy (in some countries, some courts have competence to adjudicate controversies up to a certain amount). See *supra* Chapter 6, Sec-

jurisdiction, and the Erie doctrine account for half the duration of a law school course on civil procedure. However, personal jurisdiction (the constitutional analysis of minimum contacts), subject matter jurisdiction (the division of labor between federal and state courts), and the Erie doctrine (the application of state law by federal courts), are a peculiarity of the complexities of the U.S. federal system and are probably more issues of constitutional law and federalism than of procedure. They have received substantial attention from the U.S. Supreme Court and academics. In civil-law systems, territorial competence and subject matter jurisdiction are technical procedural matters with no particular academic or jurisprudential interest.[6] The Erie doctrine is a non-issue.

Edge: Our company is often involved in litigation abroad and the issue of personal jurisdiction frequently is connected with the issue of recognition and enforcement of judgments.

Comparovich: Indeed questions of jurisdiction may appear twice. First, if you wish to initiate an action, you must be sure that the court has jurisdiction under the terms of its own legal system, or it will dismiss the action. You will also be concerned about the jurisdictional reach of courts in places where you prefer not to be sued.

Second, suppose you have initiated an action against a defendant in an American court and win the case, but the defendant is judgment proof in the U.S. In that case, you will have to enforce the judgment in a foreign country. The foreign courts will not recognize the U.S. judgment, unless they are convinced that the American court had jurisdiction under the foreign court's own notions as to the jurisdiction of foreign courts. The rules they apply in such a case, sometimes referred to as rules of "indirect" jurisdiction (because relating to the jurisdiction of another court), are frequently based on the "mirror image" principle. The foreign court will be considered as having had sufficient jurisdiction to entitle its judgment to recognition or enforcement if the local rules of jurisdiction, applied conversely, would have given it jurisdiction.[7]

In other words, it is a fundamental principle of civil-law as well as common-law thinking that, when an action is brought in F–1 (forum 1), and the F–1 court examines the question of whether it has power to adjudicate the case, the court will determine that question in accordance with F–1 law. If recognition or enforcement of the F–1 judgment is later sought in F–2, the latter court (even assuming that the judgment is valid under F–1 law) will probably refuse to recognize or enforce the F–1

---

tion 3 at 489 (discussing the organization of courts).

6. In civil-law countries, subject matter jurisdiction involves the division of labor between courts (such as family, commercial, civil, criminal, and administrative courts).

7. See, e.g., the Italian statute on Private International Law of May 31, 1995, No. 218, 1995 Gaz. Uff. No. 128, art. 64(a) [here-inafter Italian Private International Law statute] (stating that a foreign judgment will be recognized in Italy if "the foreign judge had jurisdiction according to the principles of the Italian law"); to the same effect, Austrian Law on the Enforcement of Judgments (*Exekutionsordnung*) § 80(1). Cf. F.K. Juenger, The Recognition of Money Judgments in Civil and Commercial Matters, 36 Am.J.Comp.L. 1, 13–19 (1988).

judgment, unless the F–2 court is persuaded the F–1 court had jurisdiction under the jurisdictional rules in F–2. So both countries will use their own domestic jurisdictional rules. This is subject to an important qualification: if there is an applicable treaty, then international or supra-national law may become the rule of decision in both countries.

In some respects more liberal, the French courts are generally satisfied with a reasonable connection between the foreign court and the defendant, but, on the other hand, claim exclusive jurisdiction in cases involving French nationals as defendants and will thus not enforce foreign judgments against such nationals unless there has been a waiver.[8]

In any situation in which litigation with international parties is threatened, or simply a possibility, it is thus quite important to be aware of the jurisdictional rules of all the places where an action might be possible as well as where the resulting judgment might be enforced (or simply recognized). Suppose, for example, you are being sued in a place where you have no assets and you believe the action, though lacking in merit, is not worth defending, e.g., for public relations reasons. You might then well decide to avoid the cost of litigation and let it go by default. But if the resulting judgment will be recognized in some third country where you do have assets, your decision may have to be quite different. And that recognition is, to a large extent, going to depend on the third country's rules of (indirect) jurisdiction.

Edge: To what extent are questions of jurisdiction and the recognition and enforcement of judgments governed by international agreements?

Comparovich: There are great numbers of international agreements. There are many bilateral agreements and also some multilateral ones. These agreements are usually divided into two categories. The first one is the so-called "simple" agreements, which regulate the conditions (including the jurisdictional conditions) a judgment must fulfill to be entitled to recognition or enforcement, but have no effect on its validity where rendered and no impact on cases, unless recognition or enforcement elsewhere is involved.

There are also the so-called "double" agreements, which create binding jurisdictional rules for the participating countries that must be observed, whether or not recognition or enforcement abroad will ever be needed for a particular decision. In addition, they provide for the recognition and enforcement of decisions from other "treaty countries." The most important of the multilateral conventions is probably the 1968 Brussels Convention on Jurisdiction and the Recognition and Enforcement of Judgments in Civil and Commercial Matters among the member countries of the European Union and the almost identical 1988 Lugano Convention between these countries and most members of the European Free Trade Association. The Brussels I Regulation 44/2001 superseded these two conventions, with few differences.[9] Important for Latin America is the 1979 Montevideo Conven-

---

8. See *infra* at 730 the discussion of French Civil Code (arts. 14 and 15).

9. See Council Regulation (EC) No 44/2001 of 22 December 2000 on jurisdiction

tion.[10] There are also a number of multilateral conventions limited to specialized subjects.

Apart from these bilateral or regional agreements, there is no world-wide treaty that would facilitate the international recognition and enforcement of foreign judgments. In the late 1990s, the Hague Conference on Private International Law started an ambitious project but failed.[11] In sharp contrast, international arbitration awards are much easier to enforce than judgments thanks to the New York Convention of 1958.

The United States is not a party to any international agreement on the recognition or enforcement of international judgments. Although there has been a proposal,[12] there is no federal legislation on the matter. It is entirely left to the individual states, which adopt a relatively liberal policy of recognition.[13] The absence of a comprehensive treaty on the subject is one reason why choice-of-forum clauses are so important in international contracts.[14]

Edge: What jurisdictional bases do the civilians approve of?

Comparovich: It is common, particularly in international litigation and comparative civil procedure to distinguish between "ordinary" jurisdictional rules, which are widely accepted and generally considered as fair, and "exorbitant" rules which are peculiar to one or two countries and considered by most other countries as inappropriate.

The "ordinary" rules of personal jurisdiction (or territorial competence) are really not substantially different in common-law and civil-law. It is true, however, that, in the time of *Pennoyer*, before long-arm jurisdiction was recognized in the U.S., the difference between American and civilian notions concerning the proper basis of jurisdiction was much more pronounced.

The civil-law tradition has a rule of "general jurisdiction" and one of "specific jurisdiction." The court with general jurisdiction over a defendant

and the recognition and enforcement of judgments in civil and commercial matters (Council Reg (EC) 44/2001). See, generally, B. Hess, T. Pfeiffer and P. Schlosser, The Brussels I Regulation 44/2001. Application and enforcement in the EU (2008). There is also a Brussels IIbis Regulation: Council Regulation (EC) No 2201/2003 of 27 November 2003 concerning jurisdiction and the recognition and enforcement of judgments in matrimonial matters and the matters of parental responsibility.

10. English version at 18 I.L.M. 1224 (1979).

11. See, The Hague Conference on Private International Law, Draft Convention on Jurisdiction and Foreign Judgments in civil and Commercial Matters, available at www.hcch.net (last visited Jan. 21, 2009).

12. See ALI, Recognition and Enforcement of Foreign Judgments: Analysis and Proposed Federal Statute, 2006 (proposing a draft federal statute that would provide a federal standard for the recognition and enforcement of foreign judgments). This proposal was largely a reaction to the Hague Convention on Jurisdiction and Foreign Judgments in civil and Commercial Matters.

13. Cf. Hilton v. Guyot, 159 U.S. 113, 16 S.Ct. 139 (1895) and the National Conference of Commissioners on Uniform State Laws, The Uniform Foreign Country Money–Judgments Recognition Act (1962).

14. The aforementioned ambitious Hague Convention was ultimately reduced to merely a Convention on Choice of Forum.

is the one located in the domicile of a person or the seat of a corporation. Instead of domicile, some countries may adopt residence or, in international matters, habitual residence. The concept of the "seat" of a corporation varies from country to country but could be loosely defined as its headquarters or principal place of business. At the domicile or seat, the defendant may be sued on any cause of action, regardless of where it happened. This is not different from the U.S. rule.

Another common ground for general jurisdiction is consent, either as a voluntary submission to the jurisdiction of a particular forum or through waiver. The consent may be manifested either in a choice of forum clause or through a general appearance in a proceeding. The choice of forum clause may give jurisdiction to a certain forum that would otherwise not have it and that jurisdiction may even be exclusive. However, some more progressive civil-law countries have placed some exceptions in consent jurisdiction either through the courts or through statutes. For example, choice of forum clauses in consumer contracts are void. However, when business entities, in a freely negotiated contract, have agreed through a choice of forum agreement on the exclusive jurisdiction of the courts of a certain country, most other countries will enforce that clause and will not entertain the litigation, unless the clause is considered oppressive or unreasonable, particularly in contracts of adhesion.

Regarding forum selection clause, it is interesting to observe the convergence between civil-law and common-law countries. The majority of the civil-law systems started with the rule that country B, although otherwise with jurisdiction, is deprived of it by the parties' agreement conferring exclusive jurisdiction to the courts of A. In time, however, it was found necessary to qualify this rule in order to protect parties of inferior bargaining power from unreasonable and oppressive clauses. American courts, in sharp contrast to the majority of civilians, started out by holding that the parties have no power by their agreement to "oust" a court of jurisdiction. In time, however, not too long ago,[15] it became recognized that the "ousted" court, even though it was not deprived of jurisdiction, might still refuse to exercise its jurisdiction. This way might, and indeed should, give effect to the parties' agreement, provided such agreement is not unreasonable or oppressive. Thus, although coming from the opposite starting point, U.S. courts ultimately have reached a position quite similar to the approach presently prevailing in the majority of civil-law systems.

Edge: What about long-arm jurisdiction of civil-law countries?

Comparovich: In the civil-law world, the long-arm notion is much older than in the U.S.

In addition to the courts with "general jurisdiction" over the defendant, there are also several alternative options for "specific jurisdiction." For example, in contracts disputes, the place of performance and, in torts

---

15. The matter was finally settled in M/S Bremen v. Zapata Off–Shore Co., 407 U.S. 1, 92 S.Ct. 1907 (1972). See F. K. Juen-ger, Supreme Court Validation of Forum Selection Clauses, 19 Wayne L. Rev. 49 (1972).

disputes, the place where the harmful act occurred. This is not different from the current U.S. rules, at least after *International Shoe* (and the minimum contacts standard) replaced *Pennoyer* (and the physical presence standard).

In general, in civil-law countries there is concurrent competence between the courts of general and specific jurisdiction so the plaintiff may choose between suing the defendant in his or her domicile or seat or in the alternative venue. Sometimes, however, the alternative venue has exclusive competence.

Most civil-law countries also have exclusive competence to decide matters of real property within its territories and more liberal rules benefitting the creditor of alimony and consumers, who may sue in their own domicile.

By comparing the French rules of territorial competence with a U.S. state statute on personal jurisdiction, one can easily see the similarities but have an appreciation for the different approaches.[16] There are some technical differences, such as, e.g., the absence of tag jurisdiction in civil-law countries. However, the major difference is that civil-law countries do not need to perform the constitutional control that must happen in the U.S. through the "minimum contacts" analysis, but this has to do with constitutional law and the federal system, not exactly with procedure.

The issue of personal jurisdiction is further complicated in the U.S. because some states do not adopt a laundry list of situations in which they exercise jurisdiction. Rather, they adopt the California approach, according to which "a court of this state may exercise jurisdiction on any basis not inconsistent with the Constitution of this state or of the United States." By conflating the constitutional and procedural analysis, these states bring the "minimum contacts" approach, with all its problems, to the procedural law.

Michigan Statutes on Personal Jurisdiction
Chapter 7. Bases of Jurisdiction
600.701. Individuals; general personal jurisdiction

Sec. 701. The existence of any of the following relationships between an individual and the state shall constitute a sufficient basis of jurisdiction to enable the courts of record of this state to exercise general personal jurisdiction over the individual or his representative and to enable such courts to render personal judgments against the individual or representative.

(1) Presence in the state at the time when process is served.

(2) Domicile in the state at the time when process is served.

(3) Consent, to the extent authorized by the consent and subject to the limitations provided in section 745.

---

16. For a detailed account of German rules of territorial competence, see Murray & Stürner, German Civil Justice 138–49 (2004).

600.705. Limited personal jurisdiction over individuals

Sec. 705. The existence of any of the following relationships between an individual or his agent and the state shall constitute a sufficient basis of jurisdiction to enable a court of record of this state to exercise limited personal jurisdiction over the individual and to enable the court to render personal judgments against the individual or his representative arising out of an act which creates any of the following relationships:

(1) The transaction of any business within the state.

(2) The doing or causing an act to be done, or consequences to occur, in the state resulting in an action for tort.

(3) The ownership, use, or possession of real or tangible personal property situated within the state.

(4) Contracting to insure a person, property, or risk located within this state at the time of contracting.

(5) Entering into a contract for services to be rendered or for materials to be furnished in the state by the defendant.

(6) Acting as a director, manager, trustee, or other officer of a corporation incorporated under the laws of, or having its principal place of business within this state.

(7) Maintaining a domicile in this state while subject to a marital or family relationship which is the basis of the claim for divorce, alimony, separate maintenance, property settlement, child support, or child custody.

600.711. Corporations; general personal jurisdiction

Sec. 711. The existence of any of the following relationships between a corporation and the state shall constitute a sufficient basis of jurisdiction to enable the courts of record of this state to exercise general personal jurisdiction over the corporation and to enable such courts to render personal judgments against the corporation.

(1) Incorporation under the laws of this state.

(2) Consent, to the extent authorized by the consent and subject to the limitations provided in section 745.

(3) The carrying on of a continuous and systematic part of its general business within the state.

600.715. Corporations; limited personal jurisdiction

Sec. 715. The existence of any of the following relationships between a corporation or its agent and the state shall constitute a sufficient basis of jurisdiction to enable the courts of record of this state to exercise limited personal jurisdiction over such corporation and to enable such courts to render personal judgments against such corporation arising out of the act or acts which create any of the following relationships:

(1) The transaction of any business within the state.

(2) The doing or causing any act to be done, or consequences to occur, in the state resulting in an action for tort.

(3) The ownership, use, or possession of any real or tangible personal property situated within the state.

(4) Contracting to insure any person, property, or risk located within this state at the time of contracting.

(5) Entering into a contract for services to be performed or for materials to be furnished in the state by the defendant.

600.751. Jurisdiction over land irrespective of ownership

Sec. 751. The courts of record of this state shall have jurisdiction over land situated within the state whether or not the persons owning or claiming interests therein are subject to the jurisdiction of the courts of this state.

French Code of Civil Procedure
Chapter II: Territorial Jurisdiction[17]

Article 42

The territorially competent court is the one of the place where the defendant lives, unless otherwise provided.

If there are several defendants, the plaintiff may, at his or her choosing, file the case before the court of the place where any of them lives.

If the defendant's domicile or residence is unknown, the plaintiff may bring his case before the court of the place where he or she is found or before the court of his choice if he or she lives abroad.

Article 43

The place where the defendant lives means:

— in relation to a natural person, the place of his or her domicile or, in default, his or her residence,

— in relation to a corporation, the place where it is established.

Article 44

In real estate matters, the court of the place where the property is located has exclusive jurisdiction, to the exclusion of any other.

Article 45

In matters of wills (succession), the following actions will be brought before the court of the place where the succession is opened, until distribution has been completed:

— actions among heirs;

— actions brought by the deceased creditors;

— actions related to the implementation of the dispositions causa mortis.

---

17. Unofficial translation by the authors.

Article 46

The plaintiff may file a case, at his or her choosing, either in the courts of the place where the defendant lives or:

— in contractual matters, before the court of the place of the delivery of the goods or the place of performance of the service;

— in tort matters, before the court of the place of the event or the place where the damage was suffered;

— in mixed matters, before the court of the place where real property is situated;

— in matters of alimony, the court of the place where the creditor lives.

Article 47

When a judge or a court officer is a party to litigation within the jurisdiction of the court in which he or she works, the plaintiff may bring the case before a court in an adjacent district.

Article 48

Any contractual clause that departs, directly or indirectly, from the rules of territorial jurisdiction is deemed non-existent, unless it has been agreed between merchants and that it has been specified clearly (. . .).

Edge: We have a fair amount of products liability litigation. Where can we be sued in such a case?

Comparovich: This would depend. Under the Brussels I Regulation (art. 60.1(a)) companies are considered to be domiciled at their "seat," that is, where their effective headquarters is located. If there is a suit against Duci–Cola International, headquartered in the U.S., it will thus be considered as domiciled in the United States. Art. 4.1 of the Brussels I Regulation provides that the rules of jurisdiction do not apply to defendants domiciled outside the Convention territory; the Member States may apply their own national rules to such defendants, including those that are considered exorbitant. Of course, if you have a subsidiary there and the action is against it, the Regulation rules would apply since it would be a separate legal entity domiciled in the Convention territory.[18]

---

18. Note that in most civil law countries, except when "exorbitant" rules apply, the location of an establishment such as an (unincorporated) branch provides jurisdiction over the main company only as to matters related to the branch but will not make possible a "general" exercise of jurisdiction as to the main entity, contrary to what is true in the United States. See Helicopteros Nacionales de Colombia v. Hall, 466 U.S. 408, 104 S.Ct. 1868 (1984). This is what is called "doing business jurisdiction" as a source of general jurisdiction. See the Michigan statute above (600.711(3)). But see Lloyd's Register of Shipping v. Societe Campenon Bernard, Case No. C–439/93, April 6, 1995, 1995 E.C.R. 961, holding that there was jurisdiction over a British company in France where the French branch of that company had concluded a contract in France with plaintiff

Smooth: How does the civil-law deal with a situation in which the defendant acts in one country, but causes an injury in another? Suppose a product made by our Danish subsidiary caused an injury in Germany. Under art. 2.1 of the Brussels I Regulation it could, of course, be sued at its domicile, which is its headquarters in Denmark, since the place of incorporation and actual headquarters coincide. But art. 5.3 seems to indicate it could also be sued where the injury occurred. Is that correct?

Comparovich: You are right, and there is a twist to that. A French potash mining company polluted the Rhine River, and this caused harm downstream to a Dutch tree nursery that used Rhine water for irrigation. The tree nursery sued the French company in the Netherlands on the basis of art. 5.3 of the old Brussels Convention. The French company argued the "harmful event" to which that provision referred had occurred in France when they dumped their effluent into the Rhine. The Court of Justice of the European Communities took a broader view. It said, "harmful event" means both the event that had precipitated the harm, as well as the actual harm itself. Where the two occurred in different places, the plaintiff could bring the action in either.[19]

Edge: I once read a case that thoroughly confused me. A Swiss Bank sued two defendants in a French court. One of the defendants was a French corporation; the other was an individual U.S. citizen domiciled in New York. To my utter amazement, the French court apparently exercised personal jurisdiction over both defendants, although admittedly there was no long-arm or other basis of jurisdiction over the American defendant, who had no contact whatsoever with France. If the American party had been the sole defendant, the action would have failed on jurisdictional grounds; the French court conceded that. Nevertheless, it was held that the French court's undoubted jurisdiction over the French defendant in some way extended to the American co-defendant. This is a puzzling case. Are we to infer from it that a civil-law court, once it obtains proper jurisdiction

---

French firm, even though the contract had to be performed in Spain and was actually performed by the Spanish branch. A principle similar to the civil law rule may also apply in some countries influenced by the common law. See G. Bamodu, Jurisdiction and Applicable Law in Transnational Dispute Resolution before the Nigerian Courts, 29 Int'l Lawyer 555 (1995).

19. See Handelswekerij G.J. Bier BV v. Mines de Potasse d'Alsace, Case No. 21/76, November 30, 1976, 1976 E.C.R. 1735. But the Court of Justice limited that holding somewhat in a case in which a British national, temporarily working in France, felt she had been libelled by a French newspaper article mentioning her in passing in connection with a report on money-laundering allegedly engaged in by her employer. She subsequently returned to England. The offending newspaper had its main circulation in France, but a limited number of copies were also sold in the United Kingdom and other European countries. The Court of Justice interpreted art. 5.3 of the Convention to mean that the newspaper could be sued in France for the entire damage but in any of the other Member States only for the damage caused there, as determined by local law. Shevill v. Presse Alliance SA, Case No. C–68/93, March 7, 1995 E.C.R I–415. The opinion and the—exceptionally two—submissions by the Advocates General are also interesting to read because of their discussion of differences in libel law between France, other civil law countries, and England, where the law resembles that in the United States before the United States Supreme Court started applying freedom of the press principles to it.

over one of the defendants, will automatically assert jurisdiction over all co-defendants, regardless of whether or not there is any valid basis of jurisdiction as against each one of them?

Comparovich: Concerning this question, which is important in practice, particularly in international litigation, the civil-law systems do not speak with a single voice. In a number of civil-law countries, of which Germany was typical, the answer is essentially the same as under U.S. law: the issue of personal jurisdiction must be separately and independently examined with respect to each defendant. In other civil-law countries, however, of which France is typical, when one party is subject to jurisdiction, the court will have jurisdiction over any other person properly joined, even if the court otherwise would not have jurisdiction over them. The requirement that the joinder be proper means that there must be some connection between the claims against both defendants.[20]

Edge: This is an odd rule. It makes jurisdiction dependent on whether the joinder was proper.

Comparovich: This rule is interesting from the point of view of judicial efficiency but has been criticized as unfair. The relative merits of the French rule of "jurisdiction by joinder" and of the opposite German rule were intensively debated. However, the French model prevailed on the Brussels Convention, but the Court of Justice of the European Communities interpreted the need for a connection between the claims against the original and additional party fairly strictly.

The same rule was maintained on the Brussels I Regulation. Art. 6.1 states that "a person domiciled in a Member State may also be sued (...) where he is one of a number of defendants, in the courts for the place where any one of them is domiciled, provided the claims are so closely connected that it is expedient to hear and determine them together to avoid the risk of irreconcilable judgments resulting from separate proceedings". To the extent the Brussels I Regulation rules are applicable, i.e., in litigation involving persons domiciled in the European Union, these prevail over national law, so this type of "jurisdiction by joinder" now is part of German law as well. So, the "jurisdiction by joinder" is exercised only towards domiciliaries of the European Union and not against other foreigners (including U.S. parties).

Smooth: You told us the jurisdictional rules of the Brussels I Regulation apply only to defendants who are domiciliaries of a signatory country, and national rules, including so-called "exorbitant" rules, apply to non-domiciliary defendants. Since Dulci–Cola International is domiciled in the

---

20. See French Code of Civil Procedure (art. 42.2) (quoted above, stating that "if there are several defendants, the plaintiff may, at his or her choosing, file the case before the court of the place where any of them lives"). Note that in France, arts. 14 and 15 of the Civil Code, discussed later, deal explicitly with the jurisdiction of the French courts in international situations. But where these articles are not relevant, the international jurisdiction of the French courts must (as in the situation mentioned here) be derived from the French rules indicating, for internal cases, which court in France has jurisdiction. This is true in a number of other countries as well.

United States as far as the Regulation is concerned, that principle concerns us a great deal. It seems discriminatory to us.[21]

Comparovich: You are certainly correct on that point, although at least the rule is based on domicile, not nationality. A non-national of a signatory country must be treated like a national, as long as its domicile is in that country. Therefore, there is no discrimination based on "nationality". In addition, there is a treaty and reciprocity between countries that aspire to harmonize their legal systems, and this can hardly be called discriminatory. Moreover, the "discrimination" can also be reversed. Some "exorbitant" rules of the Brussels I Regulation, like the above mentioned "jurisdiction by joinder," may be exercised towards domiciliaries of the European Union, but not against other foreigners.

However, in other respects the situation is even worse than you suggest, for the Regulation also has a sort of "full faith and credit" provision which requires the Member States to recognize and enforce each other's judgments to the extent they are covered by the Regulation. What is more, except where the jurisdiction of the original court is based on the rules concerning "exclusive" jurisdiction (as in the case of immovable property), the second court may not even reexamine the jurisdiction of the original court; it may only review, in the case of a default judgment, whether the defendant received adequate notice.[22] That goes even beyond the full faith and credit provisions of the United States Constitution.

21. On the discriminatory aspects of the Brussels Convention, see, e.g., K. Nadelmann, The Common Market Judgments Convention and a Hague Conference Recommendation: What Steps Next? 82 Harv.L.Rev. 1282 (1969); B.M. Carl, The Common Market Judgments Convention—Its Threat and Challenge to Americans, 8 Int'l Lawyer 446 (1974). On United States efforts concerning a judgments convention, see generally E. Scoles & P. Hay, Conflict of Laws §§ 24.38, 24.39 (2d ed. 1992 and Supp. 1994). Note that the new Italian Private International Law statute art. 3(2), in a liberal spirit, states that the jurisdictional rules of the Brussels Convention also apply to non-domiciliaries of contracting States.

22. See arts. 33, 34ff. of the Brussels I Regulation. The rule that jurisdiction may not normally be reviewed in the second forum was evidently based on the notion that, under the Regulation, the jurisdictional rules are the same in both fora, and the defendant could have raised the objection in the first forum. It is thus dangerous to let a case go by default where the Convention applies.

On the duty of the court in the second forum to determine whether due notice was given if there was a default judgment, see Lancray SA v. Peters & Sickert KG, Case C–305/88, July 3, 1990, 1990 E.C.R. 2726, holding that the court must verify the defendant received notice in sufficient time and the notice was correct as to form under the law of the place where the proceedings had been initiated. The same principle is frequently found in national laws on the recognition of foreign judgments. See, e.g., Italian Private International Law statute art. 64(b) & (c) (no violation of essential procedural rights and summons brought to knowledge of defendant); Austrian Law on the Enforcement of Judgments (*Exekutionsordnung*) § 80(2) (in hand service of summons required).

In addition to lack of due notice, under art. 27 violation of public policy is also grounds for failure to recognize or enforce a foreign judgment, but that concept must be used very sparingly under the Convention. Another ground for refusing recognition or enforcement will be discussed *infra*, on the effect of the pendency of another action. See *infra* Chapter 8, Section 3(c) at 742 (discussing "parallel proceedings" or "lis pendens").

Note that in a purely internal situation too, in civil law countries, once a judgment

Edge: What are the "exorbitant" bases of jurisdiction?

Comparovich: Both common-law as well as civil-law countries have several examples of "exorbitant jurisdiction." By definition, they are not widely accepted. Each example is the result of peculiarities and historical accidents of individual legal systems. Many of them are listed in Annex I of the Brussels I Regulation (see also arts. 3.2 and 4.2), which makes them inapplicable against EU domiciliaries. Other examples can be found in the draft of the failed Hague Convention on Jurisdiction and Foreign Judgments.

Nationality of the parties is one example, if not narrowly limited. It will be exorbitant whether it is the nationality of the plaintiff or the defendant, although the nationality of the plaintiff is clearly more oppressive of foreigners. A good example is contained in Articles 14 and 15 of the French Civil Code.

Article 14. An alien, even if not residing in France may be summoned before the French courts for the fulfillment of obligations contracted by him in France with a French person; he may be summoned before the courts in France for obligations contracted by him in a foreign country with French persons.

Article 15. A French national may be called before a French court for obligations contracted by him in a foreign country, even with an alien.

Article 14 has been interpreted more broadly than its language requires. Thus it is applicable to actions not related to the law of obligations, such as divorce proceedings. No connection with France, except the French nationality of the plaintiff, is required, though it does not apply in real estate matters where the land is located outside France.[23] Perhaps even more significant, Article 15 has been interpreted as meaning that it "... states a jurisdictional rule which, unless its beneficiary has waived it, excludes any concurrent jurisdiction by a foreign court ..." and further that it is waived only if the defendant has "... clearly and unequivocally, manifested his intent to waive the privilege [granted French nationals by Article 15] to be sued only in France ..."[24] These rules, as interpreted by

has been rendered and all available means provided in the laws on civil procedure to obtain its reopening or review have either been unsuccessful or are no longer available because of lapse of time, no further attack on the judgment is possible for lack of jurisdiction, even if it is a default judgment. Civil procedure codes do, however, provide a procedure for reopening cases where a judgment has been rendered by default, but it has strict time limits. See, e.g., French Code of Civil Procedure art. 571 (reopening must be demanded within one month from the time of formal service of the judgment, but with additional time available for parties abroad. See ibid. arts. 528, 538. A failure to act timely may be excused for a sufficient reason; ibid. art. 540).

23. Note that one French intermediate appellate court has held that it would be a "fraud on the law," and therefore not permissible, for a non-French national to assign a claim against another non-French national to a French national in order to provide a basis for jurisdiction in France. This could obviously have particularly oppressive results. See Garret Corp. c. Soc. E.A.S., Cour d'appel Montpellier, May 2, 1985, 76 Rev.cr. d.i.p. 108 (1987).

24. The quoted passage is from Mme. X. v. Y., Cass.civ.1st, May 18, 1994, 1995 D.J.

the courts, "confer to the French nationals a true privilege of having jurisdiction based on nationality."[25]

Another example is the ownership of property in a country leading to *in personam* jurisdiction whenever the property is unrelated to the litigation. This device is known in the U.S. as *"quasi in rem* jurisdiction." A provision to that effect is Section 23 of the German Code of Civil Procedure. Contrary to the U.S. counterpart, no "attachment" of the property in Germany is necessary for its use nor is jurisdiction limited to the value of the property. But a similar provision in Austria[26] was amended in 1983, to provide that the statute in question could not be used if the value of the Austrian property was disproportionately low in relation to the amount in controversy in the intended action. Then the German Supreme Court held in 1991, that Section 23 must be interpreted to mean that property in Germany is a basis for jurisdiction of the German courts only if there is a reasonable connection between the facts of the case and Germany, for instance because plaintiff is domiciled in Germany.[27] The rule thus seems to becoming less "exorbitant."[28]

Another "exorbitant" basis of jurisdiction occasionally found is the domicile of the plaintiff (not to be confused with the universally accepted basis, domicile of the defendant).

Another example is the assertion of jurisdiction based solely on the location in which the contract from which the dispute arises was signed. That is to be distinguished from the universally accepted basis of the place where the contract was to be performed.

Some examples that are considered exorbitant assertions of jurisdiction in most countries are widely accepted in the United States. One is general jurisdiction based exclusively on activity carried out by the defendant on the forum unrelated to the dispute ("doing business jurisdiction").[29] Naturally, if the activity carried out in the forum is related to the dispute, the jurisdiction is universally accepted. The problem is the assertion of general

---

20. The French Supreme Court (*Cour de cassation*) also held that the participation by the French defendant in the case on the merits, though objecting to jurisdiction on the basis of art. 15, and his failure to renew that objection before the intermediate appellate court in the country rendering the judgment could properly be considered as not amounting to a waiver by the court below, so the foreign judgment had no effect in France. Because of cases like these, clear and precise choice of forum clauses (preferable specifying explicitly that the French party waives any reliance on arts. 14 and 15) are particularly important in transactions involving French parties.

25. See Y. Loussouarn & P. Bourel, Droit International Privé 551 (1999).

26. Law on the Jurisdiction of the Regular Courts in Civil Matters [*Jurisdiktionsnorm*] § 99(1).

27. Decision of July 2, 1991, 33 N.J.W. 3092 (1992). See also Shaffer v. Heitner, 433 U.S. 186, 97 S.Ct. 2569 (1977) (requiring minimum contacts even in *quasi in rem* jurisdiction cases).

28. See generally, F.K. Juenger, Forum Shopping, Domestic and International, 63 Tulane L.Rev. 553, 566 (1989).

29. See Helicopteros Nacionales de Colombia, S.A. v. Hall, 466 U.S. 408, 104 S.Ct. 1868 (1984) (general jurisdiction over the defendant based on substantial, as opposed to minimum contacts). See the Michigan statute above (600.711(3)).

jurisdiction over the defendant based exclusively on substantial business conducted in the forum that is unrelated to the litigation.

As we have already seen, another example of jurisdiction widely accepted in the United States, but regarded as "exorbitant" elsewhere, is the assertion of jurisdiction based exclusively on service of process within the territory of the state (tag jurisdiction).[30] Tag jurisdiction, however, is a common although controversial basis of jurisdiction in cases of human rights violation, war crimes, genocide, torture, or crimes against humanity. Some countries go further and assert "universal jurisdiction".

Smooth: The situation seems ripe for an international convention in which the U.S. would give up tag and doing business jurisdiction, and the civil-law countries would abandon their exorbitant assertions of jurisdiction.

Comparovich: The European Union strengthened its bargaining position by entering into a convention among its member states (now the Brussels I Regulation). Under the terms of that Regulation, the European countries (a) forego the use of exorbitant bases of jurisdiction as against defendants domiciled within the EU, but (b) strengthen exorbitant jurisdiction as against all other non-resident defendants (including those in the U.S.) by agreeing that they will recognize and enforce each other's judgments. The proposed Hague Convention on Jurisdiction and Judgments may have failed because of this power imbalance between the U.S. and the European Union.

Edge: If I understand you correctly, this means that in civil and commercial matters each of the EU countries has two separate sets of jurisdictional rules. One set of rules is embodied in the Regulation, for cases in which the defendant is a EU domiciliary. The other one, entirely different, including exorbitant rules, is derived from the national law and applied to defendants that are not EU domiciliaries.

Comparovich: On the one hand, the situation is not so different in the U.S. A judgment from one state, even if its jurisdiction is based on an exorbitant assertion of jurisdiction (like tag or doing business), will be enforced in any other state through the Full Faith and Credit Clause of the U.S. Constitution. So, the U.S. too spread the effect of an exorbitantly obtained judgment over the whole country. On the other hand, however, the U.S. does not practice the kind of discrimination against defendants domiciled outside the U.S. which marks the EU Regulation.

Edge: Do you perhaps have an actual case that would show how the Brussels Convention can affect American parties? This might bring its impact home to us more forcefully.

Comparovich: The following case was decided under the original Brussels Convention. In reading the case, you should bear in mind that the Convention does not cover all types of litigation. It does not cover administrative law proceedings, for example. In the area of private law, it is

---

30. See Burnham v. Superior Court, 495 U.S. 604, 110 S.Ct. 2105 (1990).

inapplicable in cases involving divorce, separation, or annulment (though it applies in support cases) and also does not apply in succession matters or in bankruptcy cases.

FONDATION SOLOMON R. GUGGENHEIM
v. CONSORTS HELION–RUMNEY

Cour d'appel Paris (1st ch.), 17 nov 1993, 83 Rev. cr. d.i.p. 115 (1994) (with an annotation by Prof. H. Gaudemet–Tallon). [Peggy Guggenheim had given her Venice mansion and the art collection it contained to the Solomon R. Guggenheim Foundation, expressing the wish that the interior arrangement not be modified; three of her descendants (or their spouses) later sued the Guggenheim Foundation in Paris on the ground that her wish had not been respected. The plaintiffs appear to have been French and British citizens living in Paris. They based jurisdiction on Article 14 of the French Civil Code and on the Brussels Convention. The Guggenheim Foundation objected to the jurisdiction of the Paris courts. The court's opinion follows:]

Grounds of the decision:

On the nature of the claim: Under Article 1 of the Brussels Convention, matters relating to wills and succession are not covered by that Convention. In the present case, [the Venice Building] and the collection which it contains were the object of gifts with the donor reserving to herself the usufruct of [life estate in] the building and imposing an obligation concerning the custody and preservation of the collection [upon the donee]. The transfer of ownership of the properties in question thus took place during the lifetime of Peggy Guggenheim so that the present litigation does not concern estate matters ... and is thus covered by the Brussels Convention.

On the domicile of the Solomon R. Guggenheim Foundation: The Foundation argues that it is domiciled in Italy as it is registered [in the commercial register] in Venice, having its secondary seat there; if that argument is correct, then the Foundation must be considered as domiciled in the territory of a State party to the Brussels Convention and could rely on the legal rules of the State of its domicile as well as on Article 3 of the Convention, according to which Article 14 of the [French] Civil Code, which grants jurisdiction to the French courts [in cases involving French plaintiffs] cannot be used [against a party domiciled in a signatory State].

Under Article 53 of the Brussels Convention, the domicile of a corporate entity depends on the location of its "seat."

Article 5(5) of the Convention provides that a defendant domiciled in a contracting State may be sued in another contracting State when the litigation involves the operation of a branch, agency or other like establishment and the suit is brought at the court of the place of that establishment.

It results from these provisions that the secondary seat of a corporate entity cannot be considered as its domicile and that the applicability of Article 5(5) depends on the fact that the seat of the defendant is located in a signatory State.

It follows that since the seat of the Solomon R. Guggenheim Foundation is in New York, the Foundation must be considered as having its domicile in that city, the registration in Italy having no importance. As the interpretation of Article 5(5) is clear, there is no need to refer the matter to the Court of Justice of the European Communities.

On the applicability of Article 16(1) of the Brussels Convention: According to the Court of Justice of the European Communities (Decision of January 10, 1990, *Reichert v. Dresdner Bank*) Article 16(1) of the Brussels Convention must be interpreted as meaning that the provision on the exclusive jurisdiction, for litigation concerning real property, of the courts of the contracting State where that real property is located relates not to all actions involving rights relating to real property but only to those concerning rights which, on one hand, fall within the ambit of the Brussels Convention and on the other relate either to the size, nature, ownership or possession of some real property or to the existence of other rights *in rem* concerning such property and which are intended to give to the holders of such rights the [legal] protection of the prerogatives attached to their rights.

However, the action intended by the [plaintiffs] mainly seeks a return of the premises to their original condition, in conformity with the wishes of the donor, and the award of compensation for the "moral" damage inflicted; the plaintiffs further seek a court investigation into the continued presence of the (original) items and concerning the feasibility of a complete restoration of the original condition of the property.

An action of this kind is founded on the law of personal rights, and the existence, extent or makeup of rights *in rem* relating to real property is not involved.

As a consequence, the present suit does not come within the purview of Article 16(1) of the Brussels Convention; in this connection, a reference to the Court of Justice of the European Communities does not appear necessary since that court, in the case mentioned above, has already defined the field of application of the Article.

It follows that, based on the provisions of Articles 3 and 4 of the Brussels Convention, taken together with Article 14 of the French Civil Code, the plaintiffs, who are domiciled in Paris, could validly bring this suit before the *tribunal de grande instance* of such city.

That court was thus correct in ruling that it had jurisdiction. Therefore, the request to dismiss for lack of jurisdiction must be rejected.

Concerning Article 700 of the New Code of Civil Procedure: The Solomon R. Guggenheim Foundation is liable for expenses and must pay the plaintiffs the amount of FF 10,000 by virtue of Article 700 of the New Code of Civil Procedure.

For these reasons:-the Court rejects the request to dismiss for lack of jurisdiction and remands the case and the parties before the *Tribunal de grande instance* in Paris.

Comparovich: The decision of the Paris intermediate appellate court was affirmed in a brief opinion by the French Supreme Court (*Cour de cassation*) which expressly noted its approval of the intermediate appellate court's reasoning.[31] As noted above, the Brussels Convention (as the Brussels I Regulation) did not apply to cases involving divorce, the validity of a marriage, and some other matters, but does normally apply in support cases. Because this results in occasional difficulties, some suggested the conclusion of a Convention which would cover these excluded matters.

Smooth: Suppose one of our delivery trucks hits and injures a French banker living in New York while working for the New York branch of a French bank. If I understand what you have told us correctly, the French national could sue us in France on the basis of Article 14 of the French Civil Code based on his or her nationality alone, regardless of the fact that the case would have no real connection with France. The Brussels I Regulation would not help us either, since Dulci–Cola International is not domiciled in the Community. However, since a proceeding in France about a conflict that occurred in New York would be extremely inconvenient for all involved, could we ask the French court to dismiss the case on the basis of *forum non conveniens*?

Comparovich: You are certainly correct in your assessment of Article 14 and of the Regulation.[32] The Paris court of appeals, which sometimes shows an innovative and independent spirit, indicated some time ago that a French court should not take jurisdiction under Article 14 if the case really had no substantial connection with France—making, in essence, a *forum non conveniens* argument. But the French *Cour de cassation* left no doubt that there is nothing discretionary about Article 14; if it is applicable, the French court must exercise its jurisdiction.[33] The idea that a court that has jurisdiction *must* exercise it appears quite firmly rooted in civil law countries in spite of some voices to the contrary. The English courts, following the Scottish lead, have adopted the doctrine of forum non conveniens.[34] However, the doctrine cannot be applied now that the UK is constrained by the jurisdictional rules of the Brussels Regulation.

31. See *Fondation Solomon R. Guggenheim v. Consorts Hélion*, Cass. civ. 1st, July 3, 1996, 86 Rev.cr.dr.int.pr. 97 (1997) (with an annotation by Prof. Gaudemet–Tallon).

32. But suppose in Brussels, Belgium, a French banker living there were to be hit by a truck belonging to the Belgian incorporated subsidiary of Dulci–Cola, which also has its management headquarters in Belgium. In that case, art. 3.2 of the Brussels I Regulation would prevent that French banker from suing the Belgian subsidiary in France on the basis of art. 14.

33. See, e.g., X v. Mme. Y, Cass. civ.1st, Jan. 27, 1993, 1993 D.J. 602. (French courts must hear divorce case brought in France by French husband of couple living in Belgium, though case closely connected with Belgium; the husband had in fact started a divorce action in Belgium, but the court ruled that did not amount to a waiver of art. 14, since he had later discontinued it. The Brussels Convention does not apply in divorce cases and thus was not relevant). Cf. Soc. Intercomi v. Soc. Corepsen, Cass.civ.1st., December 18, 1990, 80 Rev.cr.d.i.p. 759 (1991).

34. E.g. Spiliada Maritime Corp. v. Cansulex Ltd., [1986] 3 All E.L.R. 843, [1987] A.C. 460.

(b) Service of Process

Smooth: I now understand how H could claim the Ruritania courts had jurisdiction as to Dulci–Cola International and that the question of jurisdiction is not related to service of process. In fact, H did try to serve us, but how he did it confused me quite a bit.

Comparovich: The rules on service of process are, of course, of great importance in international litigation. You know from our discussion of the Brussels I Regulation that, in the absence of proper service, a default judgment cannot be recognized or enforced in another Member State of that Regulation,[1] and national rules tend to be analogous.[2] How did H try to serve you?

Smooth: First they sent "letters rogatory" to the State Superior Court asking it to effectuate service. I was not sure what these were, but the Superior Court rejected them in any event, citing an old case involving Mexico.[3]

Comparovich: Letters rogatory are requests made by a court in one country (or even State) to a court in another country (or State) to provide the first court with some form of assistance in connection with litigation, something we usually refer to as international judicial assistance or international judicial cooperation. Letters rogatory (also called letters of request) can be used for various purposes, such as to obtain evidence located elsewhere, to obtain depositions of witnesses or, as in your case, to effectuate service. For the latter purpose they are particularly popular in Latin American countries. They are not the only way in which courts can provide each other with international judicial assistance. Until after the end of World War II, the United States was somewhat aloof about such assistance, but many foreign countries had both treaties and statutes on the topic.[4] For several decades, however, that situation has been quite different. The federal statutes on civil procedure and the Federal Rules have been substantially improved, and the same has been true in many States. The Federal courts would have had authority to comply with H's request, and so would a number of State courts. These rules provide, however, that assistance with service does not mean the recognition of jurisdiction. In fact, I am puzzled that, given these changes, your Superior Court still relied on the old case you cited.

Edge: Well, it is good that H did not think of requesting assistance from the federal courts. However, some time later we got an envelope from

---

1. See *supra* p. 729 and note 22.

2. See, e.g., Austrian Law on the Enforcement of Judgments (*Exekutionsordnung*) § 80(2); Italian Private International Law statute, art. 64(1)(b) & (c).

3. In re Letters Rogatory out of First Civil Court of Mexico, 261 Fed. 652 (S.D.N.Y. 1919).

4. See H. L. Jones, International Judicial Assistance, 62 Yale L.J. 515 (1953). For a detailed, but somewhat dated, description of procedures used in international judicial assistance, see B. A. Ristau, International Judicial Assistance (1986–1990). This useful work covers international judicial assistance generally (not just service of process), in criminal and civil matters.

the local Ruritanian consulate[5] containing a summons to appear before the Ruritanian court, with a stamped notation that it had been served upon an official of the Ruritanian Ministry of Justice several weeks before. We found that notation very confusing.

Comparovich: Undoubtedly, Ruritania still follows the traditional (now largely modified) practice of *signification au parquet* [service of process through the public prosecutor]. Under this procedure, the document to be served abroad was transmitted to the local prosecutor's office or a superior office[6] who then attempted to have it delivered to the addressee, usually through diplomatic or consular channels, which are typically slow. Service normally was deemed to have been completed by the delivery to the prosecutor, so that the time to appear began to run at that time. The procedure was thus very likely to lead to default judgments and, since the same method was applied to the notification of judgments, it also meant that the time to request a reopening or to appeal had elapsed before the defendant knew of the judgment. As we mentioned earlier, the resulting judgment was not subject to collateral attack where rendered and could be enforced there.

This practice is not completely unfamiliar to the U.S. tradition. It was once commonly used in cases of automobile accidents involving out of state motorists or litigation involving out of state corporations. As we have seen before, during the time of *Pennoyer* and before *International Shoe*, the basis of jurisdiction was physical presence, not minimum contacts. States had jurisdiction only of people and corporations located within its territory. The appearance of cars and big corporations changed the society in ways that put severe stress on the jurisdictional standards of the time. For example, cars made people much more mobile, making it easy for a person to enter a state, cause an accident and return to his or her home state immune from jurisdiction in the state of the accident. Because of that, some states enacted statutes providing that, by entering the state and using the privilege of operating a car in the state, a non-resident motorist was appointing a certain public officer to receive service of process on his or her behalf. The officer would then mail the notice to the person.[7] This practice only ended after World War II, with *International Shoe*. Out of state corporations also had, and still have, to appoint a local agent to receive service of process.

5. The United States does not object to foreign consulates transmitting official papers, but United States consular officials abroad normally should not serve "legal process." See 22 C.F.R. § 92.85.

6. Hence the name of *signification au parquet*. *Parquet* was the name originally given in France to the prosecutor's office because the prosecutor, like the defendant's lawyer, argued from a stand on the wooden floor (*parquet*) of the courtroom, while the judges were sitting on a raised platform. In current French practice, the prosecutor also sits on a (separate) dais on the same level as the judges.

For a discussion of some aspects of *signification au parquet* in English, see Volkswagenwerk A.G. v. Schlunk, 486 U.S. 694, 108 S.Ct. 2104 (1988).

7. See, e.g., Hess v. Pawloski, 274 U.S. 352, 47 S.Ct. 632 (1927) (appointment was implicit); Kane v. New Jersey, 242 U.S. 160, 37 S.Ct. 30 (1916) (motorists had to stop and sign a document).

Edge: Has there been some international reaction against that practice?

Comparovich: There have been a number of international agreements intended to deal with service of process in a more rational way, but the U.S. originally did not participate. A change came in 1964, when the U.S. joined the Hague Conference on Private International Law, an intergovernmental organization that drafts treaties intended to improve international relations affecting private parties. Some of its work has dealt with substantive law matters but it has also done much in the field of international judicial cooperation.[8]

That matter is of particular interest to the U.S. because the United States regards civil actions as an essentially private affair, and it allows foreign litigants to effectuate service or to attempt to obtain the deposition of a witness in some informal way. In many civil-law countries, where the judge, in other words a public official, plays a much more active role, all aspects of a suit are considered as in some way affected by national sovereignty. Hence these countries may require that process be served in their territory only through the use of local public officials, that depositions of witnesses for litigation elsewhere be taken only in front of local judges, etc., with the formalities, bureaucracy, complications, and delays you can imagine. Furthermore, some countries will not enforce American judgments against their residents, unless service has been effectuated in the manner prescribed by their law.[9]

But the frustration was mutual. American notions on international judicial cooperation sometimes also frustrated civil law countries. They considered it essential under their law that American public officials be involved in proceedings in the United States in connection with actions pending in their home countries, but that form of American assistance was not forthcoming.

Smooth: Has the Hague Conference done something about service of process?

Comparovich: In 1965, the Hague Conference adopted the Hague Convention on the Service Abroad of Judicial and Extra–Judicial Documents in Civil and Commercial Matters.[10] It is currently in effect among around 60 countries, including most of the United States' major trading

---

8. In addition to the Hague Service Convention and the Hague Evidence Convention, which are discussed in this chapter, some other Hague Conventions to which the United States is a party are of considerable interest for American lawyers. These include the Hague Convention for the Elimination of the Requirement of Legalization, which replaces the need for the cumbersome "chain" authentications of documents often needed when documents are to be used abroad by one "Apostille," and the Hague Convention on the Civil Aspects of International Child Abduction, which seeks to prevent such abductions and to facilitate the recognition of custody decisions, somewhat along the lines of the Federal Child Kidnapping Prevention Act.

9. On these problems, see H. L. Jones, *supra* note 4.

10. Opened for signature November 15, 1965, 20 [1] U.S.T. 361, T.I.A.S. No. 6638, entered into effect for the United States February 10, 1969.

partners. It provides for the transmittal of documents to be served abroad to a "Central Authority" (in the U.S., the central authority is the U. S. Department of Justice Office of International Judicial Assistance; in other countries, it may be the Ministry of Justice or some equivalent body), which must make sure that they are served properly. Although better than nothing, it is still a bureaucratic and slow process, and practitioners try to avoid it whenever possible. Service by mail is also permissible under the Hague Convention (and often the cheapest and most expeditious way), but signatory countries may prohibit it.[11]

Smooth: What happened to the *signification au parquet* after the Hague Convention?

Comparovich: The Convention attempts to prevent the "due process" problems that the service *au parquet* may create. A default judgment may not be entered in a Hague Convention country against a defendant in another signatory country, unless actual receipt of notice has been reasonably demonstrated by one of the several methods of proof of service provided by the Convention.[12] Similar changes have often been made in domestic law. In France (but applicable in all instances, not only when defendants in the Hague Convention countries are involved), the process server must, immediately after serving the *prosecutor*, send a certified copy of the summons by registered mail to the defendant return receipt requested. Service is void if the registered letter is not sent. If the court where the action is pending is not convinced that the defendant received timely notice, it may order any additional steps that may be useful to inform the defendant.[13]

Smooth: You said that the Hague Convention is applicable in "civil and commercial matters". This expression has no meaning to me. Was it intended to include or exclude anything in particular?

Comparovich: This expression is commonly used in civil-law countries, although it may have a slightly different meaning in each of them. It is frequently used in international treaties, such as the Brussels Convention and Brussels I Regulation. Administrative and criminal matters, for example, are certainly not included. Many countries have separate conventions dealing with a variety of problems related to these (e.g. conventions dealing with cooperation in antitrust matters, in securities regulation, etc). This limitation may have unexpected consequences. A German "Central Author-

---

11. Note that Germany objects to service by mail. Japan does not, but some courts in the United States have limited its usefulness, arguing that in connection with the use of the mails, the Convention speaks of "sending" while in other contexts it uses the expression "serving". From this, they drew the conclusion that use of the mail was not possible where formal service was necessary, only where a less formal notification was involved. See, e.g., Cooper v. Makita, U.S.A., Inc., 117 F.R.D. 16 (D.Me.1987).

12. Hague Convention, arts. 15, 16. See generally, G. B. Raley, A Comparative Analysis: Notice Requirements in Germany, Japan, Spain, the United Kingdom and the United States, 10 Ariz.J.Int'l & Comp.L. 301 (1993).

13. See French Code of Civil Procedure (arts. 686, 687, and 693). See *supra* p. 729, note 2 as to the need for a court enforcing a foreign default judgment to make sure notice was given in due time.

ity" relied on the aforementioned exclusion of criminal matters to refuse service in connection with American lawsuits in which punitive damages were demanded. This position has been rejected by the German courts, which have held quite consistently that the proceedings were civil in nature, not criminal, since involving only private parties, and any problem with German public policy could be raised if an attempt were made to enforce the American judgment later in Germany.[14]

Smooth: The U.S. Supreme Court has had occasion to deal with service of process abroad and the Hague Convention. Would it affect us when we are concerned with international litigation?

Comparovich: Definitely. In that case an action was brought in Illinois against Volkswagen of America, Inc., the American subsidiary of the German carmaker Volkswagen AG, by serving the agent for the receipt of process in Illinois (whom Volkswagen, Inc. had appointed in conformity with Illinois law in order to be authorized to do business there). Subsequently, the plaintiff decided to include Volkswagen AG in the suit and again effected service on the same agent. Volkswagen AG did not object to the jurisdiction of Illinois, but argued that, as it was located in Germany, a party to the Hague Convention, service upon it could be effectuated only by the means specified in the Convention. In Volkswagenwerk AG v. Schlunk,[15] the U.S. Supreme Court recognized in an earlier case it has stated the use of the Convention was mandatory[16] but held that, according to the very terms of Article 1 of the Convention, it applied only where service had to be effectuated abroad. The Court held service abroad was not necessary in the case, since under Illinois law the service on the subsidiary's agent (located in the U.S.) was sufficient.

The majority was aware this reference to the law of the forum to determine whether the service was to be made in the U.S. or abroad would fuel the bad features of *notification au parquet*, which the Hague Convention attempted to eliminate. Moreover, the decision would encourage other countries to use the device, but, it discounted that danger.[17]

Smooth: Do the Federal Rules of Civil Procedure address the matter?

---

14. In one instance the issue even reached the Federal Constitutional Court. See the Constitutional Court Decision of December 7, 1994, 34 I.L.M. 975 (1995). See also OLG Munich, May 9, 1989, 10 IPrax 175 (1990). On the attitude of the German courts when a judgment for punitive damages must be enforced in Germany, see the decision of the German Federal Supreme Court of June 4, 1992.

15. See *supra* note 6.

16. Société Nationale Industrielle Aérospatiale v. U.S. District Court, 482 U.S. 522, 107 S.Ct. 2542 (1987), discussed *infra* at 814ff.

17. The case seems to be an example of a situation where easy cases make bad law. In *Schlunk*, there was obviously very little danger that Volkswagen AG's American subsidiary would fail to inform the German parent of the initiation of litigation: the subsidiary was 100% owned by the German parent and largely shared the top management. But in other instances that may not be so. For a critical comment, see H. Koch, Haager Zustellungsübereinkommen oder "Zustellungsdurchgriff" auf Muttergesellschaften? 9 Iprax 313 (1989).

Comparovich: Only in part. An amendment to Rule 4, effective 1993, now formally recognizes the Hague Service Convention. Under Rule 4(f) as amended, service in a foreign country may be made by any internationally agreed means reasonably calculated to give notice, such as the Hague Convention; or, when permissible under a convention, by means of the foreign country authorities, if reasonably calculated to give notice, or as directed by foreign authority in response to letters rogatory or, unless prohibited by the law of the foreign country, by personal delivery of summons and complaint or any form of mail requiring a signed receipt, dispatched by the Clerk to the party, or any other means as directed by the court not prohibited by international agreement. Of course, the above provisions also cover situations where an agreement other than the Hague Service Convention applies, such as the Inter–American Convention on Letters Rogatory,[18] or there is no international agreement in point. But while the Rule clearly indicates that, when service must be made abroad and a convention is applicable the convention must be used if calculated to give notice, it does not address the point in *Schlunk* that it is a matter for the law of the forum whether service abroad is necessary in the first place.[19]

In 2000 and 2007, the European Union adopted Regulations establishing procedural rules to facilitate transmission of documents from one Member State to another.[20] To streamline the process, the Regulation establishes "transmitting agencies" and "receiving agencies" in charge of serving documents in the Member State where the receiving party resides. Depending on the Member State, these "agencies" may be courts, bailiffs, or other authorities. The Regulation provides for a standard form to be used and provides a manual listing the receiving agencies in each Member State. The Regulation also provides that documents can be sent direct to the addressee by mail (registered letters with acknowledgement of receipt or equivalent).

18. OAS Treaty Series No. 43, 14 I.L.M. 339 (1975), effective for the United States in relations with several Latin–American countries since 1988. Its service provisions too have been interpreted somewhat restrictively. See generally R. G. Anderson, Transnational Litigation Involving Mexican Parties, 25 St. Mary's L.J. 1059 (1994); A. J. Levitt, An Illinois Lawyer's Guide to Service of Process in Mexico, 82 Ill.B.J. 434 (1994).

19. Note that Rule 4(f) is applicable in the Federal courts but State courts as well are bound by the United States Supreme Court's interpretation of the Service Convention in *Schlunk* in view of the Supremacy Clause.

For some articles on service of process after *Schlunk*, see, e.g., Chin Kim & E.Z. Sisneros, Comparative Overview of Process: United States, Japan and Attempts at International Unity, 23 Vand.J.Transn.L. 405 (1990); J. E. Spiret, The Foreign Defendant: Overview of Principles Governing Jurisdiction, Venue, Service of Process and Extraterritorial Discovery in U.S. Courts, 28 Tort & Ins.L.J. 553 (1993).

20. See Regulation (EC) No 1393/2007 of the European Parliament and of the Council of November 13, 2007 on the service in the Member States of judicial and extrajudicial documents in civil or commercial matters (service of documents), and repealing Council Regulation (EC) No 1348/2000 (Official Journal L324, December 10, 2007, p. 79).

(c) **Parallel Proceedings (Lis Pendens)**

Comparovich: In transnational litigation, both parties prefer to have the litigation conducted in a forum favorable to them, either because it is closer to home or because of other procedural advantages. This leads to "forum shopping," and it often happens that each party initiates litigation concerning the dispute between them in a different country. This situation, called in civil-law countries lis pendens (Latin for "pending litigation"), leads to difficult problems.[1]

Smooth: In the U.S., if an action is filed in a court and subsequently another action involving the same parties, the same cause of action, and the same claim is filed in another court in the same jurisdiction, each court has the discretionary power to stay its own proceedings if the other court is more appropriate. The identity between the lawsuits must be such that any judgment in one would amount to *res judicata* in the other. Is that also true if the second action is instituted in a different country?

Comparovich: The issue here is whether to give deference to a lawsuit previously instituted in a foreign country, foregoing the country's own interest in adjudicating matters within its jurisdiction in the name of procedural economy, comity, and fairness. Some countries will dismiss or stay their own proceedings, but, according to the traditional rule, other countries will ignore the foreign action and both lawsuits will simultaneously proceed for a determination of the merits.

Both rules have advantages and disadvantages. Under the rule that the second court will not dismiss or stay its proceedings, each party will seek to expedite the action in the forum it considers more favorable. The first party that obtains a final judgment will then try to use that judgment as res judicata in the other forum. Thus you get what one might describe as a "race to judgment." The other rule, however, encourages a "race to the courthouse" at the very beginning of the litigation process. It is not uncommon, therefore, for a potential defendant to bring a lawsuit to declare that he or she is not liable (seeking, therefore, a negative declaratory judgment) in country A, to preempt the lawsuit for damages in country B.

The considerations are closely related to the recognition of foreign judgments, as it pertains to the level of deference to give to foreign courts. However, the level of deference demanded here is more acute because there is concurrent jurisdiction to decide the matter, and the court must dismiss a proceeding already instituted under its own procedural laws. Countries do not offer uniform solutions to these problems, but this is an area of constant evolution.

In the U.S., the rules are different depending on whether the parallel proceedings are within the same state, in different states, within the Federal system, or between federal and state courts. When an action is

---

1. For an interesting comparative analysis, see M. A. Lupoi, Conflitti Transnazionali di Giurisdizioni (2002).

instituted in a federal court after a similar action had been instituted in a foreign country, the federal court has a discretionary power to stay or dismiss, which is generally influenced by factors similar to those concerning *forum non conveniens*.[2]

Edge: What about civil law countries?

Comparovich: Civil law countries do not usually treat the issue as a discretionary one. The law will either mandate to dismiss or will mandate to proceed. The German courts will dismiss an action if it had been instituted earlier in a foreign court and a judgment rendered in that action would be entitled to recognition in Germany.[3] Article 9 of the 1987 Swiss Conflict of Law statute likewise provides the Swiss action must be dismissed if it is to be anticipated that the first-seized foreign court will, within a reasonable time, render a judgment entitled to recognition in Switzerland.[4]

Italy and France originally explicitly rejected the notion that the pendency of another action abroad could have any impact on their courts' jurisdiction. Italian law now requires a mandatory stay, so that the action may resume if the foreign proceeding is dismissed. French courts now have a discretionary power to dismiss. Both countries also require that the foreign judgment be entitled to recognition.[5]

2. Cf. G.A. Bermann, The Use of Anti-suit Injunctions in International Litigation, 28 Colum.J.Transnat.L. 509 (1990); T.C. Hartley, Comity and the Use of Anti-suit Injunctions in International Litigation, 35 Am.J.Comp.L. 487 (1987). But see Neuchatel Swiss General Ins. Co. v. Lufthansa Airlines, 925 F.2d 1193 (9th Cir.1991), citing Ingersoll v. Granger, 833 F.2d 680 (7th Cir.1987), seeming to hold that a federal court normally should exercise its jurisdiction and grant a dismissal or stay on account of the pendency of another action abroad only in exceptional circumstances. Some of the cases requiring "exceptional circumstances" rely on precedents dealing with issues of federalism, a matter irrelevant for the present problem. See L.E. Teitz, Taking Multiple Bites of the Apple: A Proposal to Resolve Conflicts of Jurisdiction and Multiple Proceedings, 26 Int'l Lawyer 21 (1992), referring to a model act adopted in Connecticut. On State law see also Klein v. Superior Court, 198 Cal.App.3d 894, 244 Cal.Rptr. 226 (6th Dist.Ct.App. 1988), discussed in more detail *infra* p. 856, note 2. See also ALI, Recognition and Enforcement of Foreign Judgments: Analysis and Proposed Federal Statute (2006).

3. See Decision of the Bundesgerichtshof of March 18, 1987, 40 N.J.W. 3083

(1983) (also holding that the law of the place where the action was instituted determines the date of its institution).

4. See the translation of the statute by J.C. Coran, S. Hankins & S. Symeonides in 37 Am.J.Comp.L. 193 (1989), and another translation at 29 I.L.M. 1244 (1990). Cf. I. Schwander, Ausländische Rechtshängigkeit nach IPR–Gesetz und Lugano-Übereinkommen, Vogel Festschrift 395 (1991).

5. See Italian Code of Civil Procedure (art. 3) revoked in 1995 by the Italian Private International Law statute (art. 7.1) (modelled to some extent on the equivalent rules of the old Brussels and Lugano Conventions). See Carpi & Taruffo, Commentario Breve al Codice di Procedura Civile 13–7 (2002).

Cass.civ.1st., November 26, 1974 JDI 1975, 108 and Rev.crit.DIP 1975, 491; Cass. civ.2e, November 17, 1993 JCP 1994 II, 22346, Cass.soc, May 7, 1996 Rev.crit.DIP 1997, 77, Cass.civ.1st., January 21, 1992 JCP 1992 IV, 838 and Cass.civ.1st., June 17, 1997 Rev.crit.DIP 1998, 452. See also L. Cadiet & E. Jeuland, Droit judiciaire privé 177–79 (2006); Y. Loussouarn & P. Bourel, Droit International Privé 548–49 (1999); P. Mayer & V. Heuzé, Droit International Privé 313–17 (2004).

Some countries, however, still follow the old rule that a proceeding filed abroad has no lis pendens effect, and both lawsuits must proceed concurrently.[6]

The Brussels I Regulation also covers the subject and supercedes domestic law in the circumstances where it applies (i.e. litigation within the European Union). Article 27 provides that where proceedings involving the same cause of action between the same parties are brought in courts of different Member States, any court other than the court "first seized" shall, on its own motion, stay its proceedings until such time as the jurisdiction of the court first seized is "established."[7] If the jurisdiction of the first court is "established," any court other than the court first seized shall decline jurisdiction in favor of that court.[8] Though the jurisdictional rules of the Regulation apply only to domiciliaries of signatory countries, according to the Court of Justice of the European Communities the old (identical) art. 21 of the Convention applied, regardless of the domicile of the parties, whenever the two actions took place in member countries, since its purpose is the avoidance of irreconcilable judgments within the Convention territory. The provision can thus also benefit an American party to litigate in a Convention country.[9] The expression "cause of action" in art. 27, which is a translation from the text in the original languages, cannot, for that reason, be read in its common law pleading sense. The Court of Justice interprets the requirement rather liberally; the Court seems to consider it satisfied when the same legal relationship is the basis for both proceedings.[10]

6. See Brazilian Code of Civil Procedure (art. 90).

7. The Court of Justice has ruled that a court was "seized" of an action under the (old) Convention when it was definitely pending there, but that had to be decided under national law. Zelger v. Salinitri, Case No. 129/83, June 7, 1984, 1984 E.C.R. 2397. Accord (under German national law) that the law of the place where a case has been instituted defines when it starts being pending there, Bundesgerichtshof, Decision of March 18, 1987, 40 N.J.W. 3083 (1987).

8. For a more detailed discussion of the old Convention provisions on the effect of another action pending, see P. Herzog, Brussels and Lugano, Should You Race to the Courthouse or Race for a Judgment?, 43 Am. J.Comp.L. 379 (1995). Note that most of the national rules on the subject state the local action will be stayed (or dismissed) if the judgment resulting from the foreign action is likely to be recognized locally. There is no such provision in art. 27, presumably because judgments rendered in one of the Member States must be, with very minor exceptions, recognized in every other such country.

9. Cf. Overseas Union Ins. Ltd. v. New Hampshire Ins. Co., Case C–351/89, June 27, 1991, 1991 E.C.R. I–3317. But the enforcement provisions of the Convention clearly do not apply to a judgment rendered in a country that is not a party to the convention. Owens Bank, Ltd. v. Bracco, Case No. C–129/92, January 20, 1994, 1994 E.C.R. I–117.

10. E.g., applicability of art. 21 of the old Convention (which had the same language as art. 27 of the current Brussels I Regulation) if one action for payment of the purchase price of goods, the other to have the contract of sale declared void or discharged: Gubisch Maschinenfabrik KG v. Palumbo, Case 144/86, December 8, 1987, 1987 E.C.R. 4861; or action for damages to freight carried by ship and action for limitation of liability for that same damage: The Tatry, Case C–406/92, December 6, 1994, 1994 E.C.R. I–5439. The actual equivalent of the words same "cause of action" in the French text of the Convention is same *objet et cause*. The translator preparing the English text of the Gubisch case, *supra*, for the official Court of Justice Reports noted (at 1987 E.C.R. 4863) a better translation for that term than simply

When actions pending in two Member States are "related" rather than identical, under art. 28 of the Regulation, an automatic dismissal (after jurisdiction in the first court has been established) is not necessary. Where these actions are pending at first instance, the second court may also, on the application of one of the parties, decline jurisdiction if the court first seized has jurisdiction over the actions in question, and its law permits the consolidation thereof. Two actions are considered related if they are so closely connected that it is expedient to hear and determine them together to avoid the risk of irreconcilable judgments resulting from separate proceedings.[11]

Article 29 of the Brussels I Regulation finally states where actions come within the "exclusive" jurisdiction of several courts, any court other than the court first seized shall decline jurisdiction in favor of that court.

Articles 27 to 29 of the Brussels I Regulation and the analogous national rules mentioned thus encourage a "race to the courthouse." The effects of the "race to the courthouse" under the (old) Brussels Convention and the new Brussels I Regulation are amplified by the rule already mentioned, requiring the almost automatic recognition of judgments from other signatories. The Regulation does, however, have a provision dealing with the situation where there may still be irreconcilable judgments in two Member States. Under Article 34.3, a Member State judgment irreconcilable with a local judgment is not to be recognized. Apparently, there is no requirement that the local judgment have been rendered before the one from the other State.[12] Similar rules are also quite common in national legislation.[13] Furthermore, Article 34.4 provides that a judgment from

the "same cause of action" might have been the "same subject matter and cause of action."

11. The Court of Justice has held that the old identical provision of the Convention must be interpreted in light of the purpose of improving the administration of Justice in the Community by coordinating legal proceedings in several Member States. See The Tatry, *supra* note 10. (Actions by certain owners of cargo damaged on ship related to action by owners of ship to obtain exoneration from (or limitation of) liability for damage to other cargo owned by other shippers, but damaged during the same voyage.)

12. In other words, one party gains no advantage over the other party by "racing" forward with its litigation to obtain a judgment first if it does not then also race to have it enforced in the State where the other action is pending before a judgment is rendered in that action.

13. But national rules often require the domestic judgment to have been rendered earlier. As a result some defendants, when sued outside their home country, bring proceedings in their home country involving the same matter (e.g., by suing for a declaration that the foreign proceedings are without merit), which they try to bring to a conclusion before the foreign proceedings. In that way, enforcement of the judgment rendered in the foreign proceedings can be blocked. On this practice in Japan, see Y. Takaishi, O. Hirakawa & F. Tomatsu, Securities–Related Disputes in Japan, 14 Hastings Int'l & Comp. L.Rev. 423, 427–30 (1991). A similar tactic, but under the Convention, was involved in the Union Insurance Co. case, *supra* note 9.

A potential defendant, faced with the prospect of being sued in a country with an efficient judiciary, may bring first, in a country with a slower proceeding, a negative declaratory lawsuit (seeking a declaration that the conduct of the potential defendant, now plaintiff, is not illegal and that there is no liability). Since the court first seized must hear the case to the exclusion of any others, the potential plaintiff (now defendant) is stuck in a country with a slower proceeding and is more vulnerable to settlement proposals.

another Member State need not be recognized if it is irreconcilable with a judgment rendered in a third country, provided that the earlier judgment fulfils the conditions necessary for its recognition in the Member State addressed.

Edge: All this discussion begs the question: when is a lawsuit considered instituted for purposes of lis pendens? This information is important to determine which proceeding was "previously instituted." According to Rule 3 of the U.S. Federal Rules of Civil Procedure, "a civil action is commenced by filing a complaint with the court." Is this a standard rule?

Comparovich: Each country determines when a lawsuit is instituted, and local laws differ greatly. In some countries, like in the United States, the lawsuit commences when the complaint is filed with the court; in others, when the defendant is formally served with process; other countries have still different guidelines, depending on the peculiarities of their proceedings.

(d) Pleadings and Formation of Issues

Comparovich: What happened next in Mr. H's action?

Edge: We authorized L, a Ruritanian lawyer, to appear for the defendant. He filed an answer, which, like the complaint, contained some discussion of legal points as well as a prayer for relief and, of course, factual denials and allegations. In essence, the answer raised the following issues:

(1) Although realizing that this was a weak point, we denied the jurisdictional facts alleged by H, and expressly objected to the court's jurisdiction.

(2) Concerning the merits, we

(a) denied that a definite contract had been made;

(b) argued as a matter of law that H's fee, even if the alleged contract had been made, would not be governed by Ruritanian law;

(c) pointed out that, according to H's own assertions the alleged oral contract was made in New York, and that according to the law of this State the contract is illegal because H engaged in the unauthorized practice of law.[1]

Smooth: You will note that point (2)(b) raises a question of law. The complaint was expressly and exclusively based on the Ruritanian statutory tariff. Hence the complaint was bad on its face if under the applicable choice of law rule that retainer was not governed by Ruritanian law. I pointed this out to L and asked him to move to dismiss for failure to state a claim upon which relief can be granted (12(b)(6) motion), but from L's reply to my letter I gathered that he simply did not get my point.

Comparovich: You seem to assume that under Ruritanian procedure the plaintiff, having invoked a certain theory of law in the pleading, may not recover on any other theory. Although this used to be the prevailing

---

1. Cf. In re Roel, 3 N.Y.2d 224, 165 N.Y.S.2d 31, 144 N.E.2d 24 (1957).

view in the United States, it is not anymore.[2] In civilian procedure, the traditional rule, in keeping with the generally more active role of the judge, is the court is not confined to the legal theories espoused by the parties.[3] This is supported by two legal principles expressed in Latin: *iura novit curia* (the judge knows the law [so one does not need to plead it]) and *da mihi factum, dabo tibi ius* (give the judge the facts and the judge will give the law). Even though this is the current rule in all civil-law countries, in the past they were not always unanimous concerning this question.[4]

Moreover, demurrers and their modern counterparts (12(b)(6) motion), like many of the U.S. pre-trial motions, serve the purpose of neatly separating issues of law from issues of fact so that in the end a few clearly formulated material issues of fact can be submitted to the jury.[5] In civil-law countries, where no jury participates in the decision of civil cases, such early separation of factual and legal issues is unnecessary. Hence no demurrers or motions to dismiss for insufficiency, and no other motions addressed to the pleadings exist.

Smooth: Without such motions, how do civilians narrow and formulate the issues?

Comparovich: The Romano–Canonistic system, which dominated procedural thinking on the continent from the 13th to the 18th century, had two outstanding characteristics: First, the proceedings, including the examination of witnesses, were largely conducted *in secret*. Second, the task of hearing the parties, the witnesses, and even the lawyers was often left to subordinate officials who had to reduce everything to *writing*; the judges then based their decisions exclusively on the written record.[6] The modern procedural codes of the civilians reflect a violent reaction, and indeed a revolt, against this medieval system.[7] They stress that all proceedings shall

---

2. See Clark on Code Pleading, Sec. 43 (1947).

3. See the Codes of Civil Procedure of Germany (§§ 130, 132, 253), France (art. 12), Italy (art. 113).

4. See, e.g., Millar, The Formative Principles of Civil Procedure, 18 Ill.L.Rev. 1, 94, at 113 (1923); id., Civil Pleading in Scotland, 30 Mich.L.Rev. 545, at 562, 736 (1931).

5. In non-jury cases, this rationale does not hold; but the procedural merger of law and equity is thought to compel us to employ the same procedural devices in both kinds of cases.

6. See Engelmann–Millar, A History of Continental Civil Procedure 457–8 (1927); Cappelletti and Perillo, Civil Procedure in Italy 36 (1965). For the fundamental differences between this "Romano–Canonistic" system, which was developed during the middle ages, and classical Roman procedure, see id., at 26–31. But note that French civil pro-

cedure always left more room for orality, in particular in connection with the presentations of the lawyers.

7. The statement in the text is true of most civil-law systems; but there are differences among them as to (a) the exact time of that revolt, (b) its abruptness or gradualness, and (c) the thoroughness with which the Romano–Canonistic features were eliminated. In Spain, and even more in Latin America, the process of reforming the Romano–Canonistic features of civil procedure has been more timid and slow—so much so that the discussion which follows is frequently subject to some qualification as applied to Latin-American countries. The reader who is interested in civil procedure in those countries is referred to 16 International Encyclopedia of Comparative Law (Civil Procedure, M. Cappelletti, ed.), ch. 6, pt. VI (by E. Vescovi) (1984), and, for information reflecting some more recent changes, to K. S. Rosenn, Civil

be *oral* and *public* throughout. Consequently, they de-emphasize the written pleadings[8] and treat them as merely preparatory to a hearing in open court, at which the attorneys orally present their clients' allegations, arguments and prayers for relief (*plaidoire*).

This, at least, is the theory. In practice, the presiding judge of a busy court sometimes will cut the hearing so short that the attorneys "oral" presentation may amount to little more than a reference to their "preparatory" pleadings previously filed. There are differences in this respect from country to country, and in fact from locality to locality, depending on the workload of each court and the temperament of the presiding judge. Furthermore, this traditional system has, in some places, been modified in order to speed up proceedings.

These oral presentations are really not so important, because everything is written down in the written pleadings (*la citation*) and briefs (*les conclusions*). Those are the main source of information for the judge. The emphasis is on the written documents and the evidence, not on *les plaidoiries*.

In some countries it is possible, however, that during the oral presentation the lawyer will propose an amendment or new arguments. In that case, the proceedings will be suspended, so that the lawyer may present a written amendment and the opponent may reply (*conclusions*).

In some countries, the judge may propose the parties to substitute the oral presentation by an interactive debate between them.[9] The ALI/Unidroit Principles and Rules of Civil Procedure adopts a similar rule, by allowing the court to allow the lawyers to "engage with each other and with the court in an oral discussion concerning the main issues of the case".[10]

At the same time, or subsequently at an adjourned hearing, the attorneys make offers of proof concerning disputed issues of fact.

In many civil-law countries, the presiding judge is under a duty, if necessary, to make the parties clarify their demands, allegations and offers of proof. Section 139 of the German Code of Civil Procedure, for instance, provides as follows:

> (1) The court will discuss with the parties the relevant facts and issues in dispute from a factual and legal perspective to the extent reasonable and to raise questions. The court will make the parties to declare, in a timely and complete manner, their positions concerning

Procedure in Brazil, 34 Am.J.Comp.L. 487 (1986); R. B. Capalli, Comparative South American Civil Procedure, A Chilean Perspective, 21 U. Miami Inter–Am.L.Rev. 239–310 (1989/90); and R. G. Vaughn, Proposals for Judicial Reform in Chile, 16 Fordham Int'l.L.J. 577 (1992–93).

8. See Millar, Some Comparative Aspects of Civil Pleading Under Anglo–American and Continental Systems, 12 A.B.A.J. 401 (1926).

9. See Code of Civil Procedure of Belgium (art. 756ter, as amended in 2007).

10. See Rule 31.1; ALI/UNIDROIT, Principles of Transnational Civil Procedure (2006).

all material facts, especially to supplement insufficient references to the relevant facts, to designate the means of proof, and to set forth claims based on the facts asserted.

(2) The court may base its decision on a claim, other than a minor secondary claim, on a point of fact or law which a party has apparently overlooked or considered insignificant only if the court has called the parties's attention to the point and given opportunity for comment on it. The same provision applies if the court's understanding of a point of fact or law differs from the understanding of both parties.[11]

Such rule is but a summary of the duty of a German judge to give hints and feedback to the parties, through a dialogue with their attorneys. Such duty, which has existed in German law for more than a century, is now pervasive throughout the proceeding, and is valid during the evidentiary and appeals phases. Failure to observe such principle is an error of law, ultimately reviewable by the German Supreme Court. If a court decides the case on a point not previously discussed with the parties, this is also a constitutional error, violation of the "due process" provision of the German Constitution, which opens access to the Constitutional Court.[12]

Smooth: This seems to make it possible for the court to inject new legal and factual issues into the case, and thus, in effect, to help an unprepared or incompetent attorney who did not think of those issues.

Comparovich: Quite so. But it seems that you have pointed to a virtue rather than a vice of the German and French provisions. Lawsuits should be decided on their merits and not necessarily in favor of the party who can find (and afford) the shrewdest lawyer.[13]

Section 139 of the German Code has been called the Magna Carta of fair procedure for the very reason that it effectively reduces (although it cannot eliminate) the impact of the relative ability of counsel upon the outcome of litigation and increases the probability of an ultimate decision that is legally and factually correct. On the other hand, the rule is not as paternalistic as one might think and the judge will not substitute the work of the attorney. The rule is neither a violation of the principle of adversarial process nor does it compromise the court's impartiality. However, the court must find a proper balance: as stated by a commentator, a judge who oversteps the boundaries of this rule will appear partial, but a judge that is too passive is violating the rule and the "German concept of the state's social responsibility to provide substantial justice" (...) "The right road undoubtedly lies somewhere in the middle".[14]

---

11. See P. Murray & R. Stürner, German Civil Justice 166–77 (2004) (discussing the principle and also providing a more complete translation of the rule).

12. See the Constitutional Court Decision of May 29, 1991, 44 N.J.W. 2823 (1991).

13. See also the arguments in J.H. Langbein, The German Advantage in Civil Procedure, 52 U. Chi. L. Rev. 823 (1985) and

E.C. Stiefel & J.R. Maxeiner, Civil Justice Reform in the United States—Opportunity for Learning From "Civilized" European Procedure Instead of Continued Isolation? 42 Am. J. Comp. L. 147 (1994).

14. See P. Murray & R. Stürner, German Civil Justice 166–77 (2004) (citing Franz Klein: "the truly neutral judge is the one whose activity results in material justice between the parties").

Let me illustrate this with the following example:

Plaintiff, who was injured in a traffic accident, first sued the individual tortfeasor T, and obtained a judgment against him; but T apparently failed to satisfy the judgment. In the present action, based on the German "direct action" statute, plaintiff seeks to recover from T's liability insurer. Under the German statute, plaintiff can recover from the insurance company only if he or she alleges and proves facts giving rise to liability on the part of the insured (T). Plaintiff in this case alleged no such facts, but merely asserted that he had obtained a *judgment* against T holding the latter liable for a certain amount of damages.

The court of first instance dismissed the action against the insurance company, pointing out that the latter had not been a party to plaintiff's prior action against T, and hence was not bound by the judgment against T.[15] Under these circumstances, the court of first instance held, the plaintiff's reference to the judgment was not a proper substitute for the necessary allegation of facts creating liability on the part of T. The court of first instance thus ruled the complaint to be insufficient.

On plaintiff's appeal, the intermediate appellate court reversed and remanded. In the higher court's view, the court of first instance should have noticed that plaintiff's lawyer was mistaken in believing that defendant insurance company was bound by the judgment in the prior action. By asking proper questions pursuant to § 139 of the Code of Civil Procedure, the lower court should have called the lawyer's attention to this mistake, and thus should have made it clear to the lawyer that it was necessary to allege, and offer to prove, the facts underlying T's liability. This failure of the lower court to comply with the mandate of § 139 was held to be reversible error.[16] In reversing, the appellate court criticized the lower court for having sacrificed justice to speed.

Edge: Suppose the facts of a case suggest the possibility that the defendant might win on the basis of an affirmative defense, but the defendant's lawyer has failed to raise such defense. For instance, the facts show that plaintiff's claim is stale, but defendant has not invoked the statute of limitations. Does a German court, in order to comply with § 139, have to educate the defendant's lawyer in such a situation?

Comparovich: A big controversy rages concerning this question among German courts and writers. According to the view which until recently was the prevailing one, a distinction must be drawn. If defendant's lawyer, though not explicitly invoking the statute of limitations, in some way has

---

15. The reader should assume that under German law the court of first instance was correct with respect to this res judicata point. Under U.S. law, the result might be different if the insurance company financed and controlled T's conduct of the prior action. See Restatement Second, Judgments, § 39 (1982).

16. OLG Düsseldorf, Decision of July 25, 1974, DRZ 1974, 327. For a similar holding, in a slightly more complicated factual setting, see OLG München, Decision of July 14, 1973, OLGZ 1973, 362.

pointed to the staleness of plaintiff's claim or to the difficulty of defending the action after years of inaction on plaintiff's part, § 139 clearly requires the court to seek clarification of the defendant's opaque hints, and such clarification can be attained only by asking whether or not the defendant wishes to assert the statute of limitations defense. Where, on the other hand, the defendant has totally failed to assert, or even to hint, that the action is time-barred, the court under this view was not compelled, and not even authorized, to alert the defendant (and especially a defendant represented by counsel) to the availability of an affirmative defense such as the statute of limitations. According to most of the courts and writers holding this view, it follows that a judge who in the latter case nevertheless asks a question alerting the defendant can be forced by the plaintiff to recuse himself.[17]

The contrary view, which appears to be in the ascendancy among lower courts as well as legal authors, is to the effect that even a defendant who is represented by counsel and who has totally neglected to assert an affirmative defense such as the statute of limitations must be alerted by a question asked pursuant to § 139, if the circumstances of the case suggest the possible availability of such a defense.[18]

Edge: With respect to affirmative defenses that serve the cause of justice, this may be a sound view. But the statute of limitations defense does not serve that cause. Therefore, the policy behind § 139 does not seem to apply in this instance.

Comparovich: A German legal writer has expressed a similar argument.[19] It is true that the statute of limitations serves peace rather than justice; but *quaere* whether in our scale of values the postulate of peace should be treated as inferior to that of justice.

Smooth: Whichever way this controversy regarding affirmative defenses is ultimately resolved, it is plain that § 139 modifies the adversary nature of the procedure and gives the court broad powers, not only to influence the formulation of the issues, but even to inject into the lawsuit important issues not brought up by the parties. Have other civil-law countries adopted provisions similar to the Germans' § 139?

Comparovich: Yes. The trend in the more advanced civil-law systems clearly goes in that direction. To mention but two examples: The old Japanese Code of Civil Procedure has followed in the footsteps of German § 139 and the same rule prevailed in the new code.[20] France has also

---

17. For references, see E. Peters, Richterliche Hinweispflichten und Beweisinitiativen im Zivilprozess 89–90, 99–100, 135–38 (1983); E. Schneider, Richterlicher Hinweis auf Verjährungsablauf, 39 N.J.W. 1316 (1986); V. Hermisson, Richterlicher Hinweis auf Einrede-und Gestaltungsmöglichkeiten, 38 N.J.W. 2558 (1985). The reasons given for the formerly prevailing view usually were derived from the "principle of adversariness" or the "nature of an affirmative defense." But these are question-begging arguments.

18. See ibid.

19. See Hermisson, *supra* note 17 at 2561.

20. See the current Japanese Code of Civil Procedure (arts. 137, 138, 149, and 151). See Goodman, Justice and Civil Procedure in Japan 205–11 (2004).

adopted similar rules. According to the French system, the judge *may* invite the parties to provide factual or legal explanations that he or she deems necessary for the resolution of the dispute or to clarify matters otherwise obscure. The court cannot support its decision on a point of law not mentioned by the parties, unless they have been given a chance to present their views.[21]

There is one important difference between the German provision and its Japanese and French counterparts. The German Code casts the rule in mandatory terms, with the result that it is clearly reversible error for the court not to ask a clarifying question when such a question is indicated. Under the French and Japanese provisions, the court "may" ask clarifying questions. In a long line of vacillating and often criticized decisions, the Japanese Supreme Court has struggled with the question under what circumstances the lower courts' failure to ask questions should be treated as reversible error.[22]

The French provisions also are not entirely free from ambiguity. The Code of Civil Procedure makes it clear that a discretionary power is involved, not normally an obligation. Furthermore, under art. 12, the court may not raise a new issue where both parties clearly intend to limit the controversy to certain matters. The judge does, however, appear to have an obligation to apply the correct rule of substantive law (when no new factual assessment is involved) to the facts alleged by the parties, but this does not imply an obligation to raise factual issues or procedural defenses.[23] In fact, lack of jurisdiction may generally be raised on the court's own motion only if public policy is involved or where the defendant has defaulted.[24]

Smooth: It appears from our discussion that a provision of this kind, whether cast in mandatory or in permissive terms, greatly adds to the court's power to direct the course and to influence the outcome of the litigation. But these provisions also deprive the court of the power (a power that appears to exist under U.S. law) to dream up a new legal theory not presented by either party, and to decide the case on that theory without having given the parties an opportunity to discuss it.

Comparovich: You are absolutely right. Both the German and the French Codes make this crystal-clear. Keep in mind, moreover, that this prohibition—against deciding a case on a point not previously discussed with the parties—is clear-cut and nondiscretionary in France as well as in Germany, and may result in a void judgment. This is an important element of the modern civil-law adversarial process. A similar rule has been adopted in Portugal and Italy.[25]

---

21. See the French Council of State Decision of October 12, 1979 mentioned *supra* p. 530, note 20 and French Code of Civil Procedure (arts. 8, 13, 16, and 442).

22. See T. Hattori & D.F. Henderson, Civil Procedure in Japan, § 7.02[10] (1985) (discussing the provisions of the old code).

23. See e.g. Cass.civ.2d, February 14, 1985, 1985 Gaz.Pal 2. 640.

24. See French Code of Civil Procedure (arts. 92 and 93).

25. See Codes of Civil Procedure of Germany (§ 139) and France (Art. 16). See also the Council of State decision of October 12, 1979, concerning art. 12 of the Code of

Edge: Contrast this rule with the situation in the US and other civil and common-law countries, where trial as well as appellate courts may decide cases on legal theories thought up by the judges and never discussed with the parties. The Supreme Court of the United States sets a bad example in this respect. When deciding a case on the basis of a "plain error" not briefed by the parties but noticed by the Court ex officio under its Rule 24.1(a), the Justices ordinarily announce their decision without first inviting the parties to submit comments or observations.

Smooth: On *Diemer v. Diemer*, 8 N.Y.2d 206 (1960), the husband sued for a legal separation on the ground of ruel and inhuman treatment arguing that his wife refused to have sexual relations. She admitted the factual allegation but argued that it did not constitute cruelty as a matter of law. The Court of Appeals held that he was entitled to a separation, but on the ground of "abandonment." In rejecting the dissenters' objection that the abandonment theory had not been pleaded or argued below, the majority noted that there was no dispute on the facts and the pleading for a separation was sufficient. The case is a proceduralist's dream in teaching pleading law but is rarely cited or followed by subsequent cases.

This makes the words "due process" ring hollow.

Comparovich: Your point is well taken. Indeed, this rule exists exactly because of the right to be heard (principle of contradictory) of the due process of law, which includes the right to participate not only in the decisions of fact, but in the decisions of law as well. Therefore, this provision reflects a constitutional mandate.

When courts commit abuses of this kind too patently and too frequently, their power to render such surprise decisions may at least in part be curtailed by the legislature. This is also true in the U.S. In California "before the Supreme Court, a court of appeal, or the appellate division of a superior court renders a decision in a proceeding other than a summary denial of a petition for an extraordinary writ, based upon an issue which was not proposed or briefed by any party to the proceeding, the court shall afford the parties an opportunity to present their views on the matter through supplemental briefing. If the court fails to afford that opportunity, a rehearing shall be ordered upon timely petition of any party."[26] As a matter of fact, even in the absence of a specific provision, in practice, it is not uncommon for US courts to invite attorneys to submit briefs on relevant issues that were not raised below.

Smooth: To come back to the normal course of a lawsuit in a civil-law country: What happens after the parties have presented their allegations and offers of proof and have responded to such clarifying questions as the court may have put to them?

Civil Procedure, mentioned *supra* p. 530, note 20 and the text relating to it. See also the Codes of Civil Procedure of Portugal (art. 3, as amended in 1995 and 1996), Italy (art. 183).

26. See Cal. Government Code § 68081, added by L. 1986, Ch. 1098.

Comparovich: The next step is a decision by the court. In some instances, that decision will be a final judgment. In other cases, the decision will take the form of an *interlocutory order for the taking of evidence*. On the basis of the parties' offers of proof, but in the words of the court,[27] that order will specify the precise propositions on which evidence is to be taken and also the means of proof, e.g., the names of the witnesses to be examined. In some civil-law countries, the order does not name the witnesses, but directs the party who has made the offer of proof to furnish the witnesses' names and addresses at a stated time, i.e. at a time well in advance of the actual examination of such witnesses by the court.

If the court is composed of three judges, the order may provide that during the proof-taking stage of the litigation the three-judge panel be represented by one of its members or even another judge that did not participate in the first ruling.

Civil-law procedural codes specify the various means of proof that the court may order, such as, obviously, the examination of witnesses, documents, the appointment of court experts, etc., which we will discuss shortly.

Smooth: Do you mean to say that under civil-law procedure I could not introduce a witness unless his or her name and the propositions to be proved by the testimony have been previously notified to my opponent, and have been incorporated into an interlocutory order of the court?

Comparovich: This is precisely what I mean. There is no such thing as a surprise witness under that system, except in proceedings involving temporary injunctions or other provisional remedies, and rare other instances in which there is no time for interlocutory orders.[28]

U.S. civil procedure has evolved considerably on this matter in the past decades and the possibility of any sort of surprise at trial has been sharply curtailed in the past decades, particularly with the development of judicial case management and the pre-trial conferences of Federal Rule of Civil Procedure 16(e).

Smooth: However, it is widely known that civil-law attorneys cannot interview or "coach" a witness before the judge interrogates him or her. How could an attorney know what the testimony will be about? Isn't this an invitation to tamper with the witnesses?

Comparovich: The civilian lawyer usually regards it as his client's job to investigate the facts.[29] The lawyer rarely engages in factual investigation. The lawyer's role is only to present the facts and argue the legal arguments and remedy. Normally, he or she will not have much contact

---

27. In most civil-law countries, orders, and judgments are formulated by the court, and not by the attorneys.

28. See also the somewhat broader French rule in the French Code of Civil Procedure art. 231 (so-called *enquête sur-le-champ*) under which the court may immediately hear any witness whose testimony may

be useful and who happens to be there during some other measure of proof (e.g., when the court, as it is authorized to do, visits the premises involved in the litigation).

29. During the course of the proceeding, the investigation of fact is reserved for the judge, not the attorney.

with witnesses outside of the courtroom; thus, there is little opportunity for coaching witnesses or for "tampering" with them. In some continental countries, moreover, there are canons of ethics prohibiting an attorney from discussing the facts of a case with a prospective witness.[30]

This limitation undoubtedly makes it more difficult for an attorney to perform his or her duties in civil-law countries. It is not uncommon for a witness to be called upon to a hearing only to reveal that he or she has no relevant first hand knowledge of the facts of the case. Because of that, and because of the increasing need to present a summary of the witness statements, Principle 16.3 of the Principles of Transnational Civil Procedure provides "[t]o facilitate access to information, a lawyer for a party may conduct a voluntary interview with a potential nonparty witness."[31]

This is evidence that differences in standards of professional responsibility that exist between common and civil law procedure stem not only from the differences in the law itself, but also from the differences on the roles of the lawyers and courts.

Edge: This is an important limitation, which we shall have to keep in mind in our dealings with local counsel abroad.

Comparovich: In Becker v. Webster, 171 F.2d 762, 765 (2d Cir.1949), Judge L. Hand remarked that the custom of interviewing witnesses before trial and reducing their proposed testimony to writing is "universal," and it would be a "fantastic extreme" to consider such custom unprofessional for an attorney in any country. This strikingly erroneous remark of the eminent jurist proves the hazards inherent in uncritically assuming that one's own domestic practices are "universal."

The difference of rules may put attorneys involved in international litigation in some very difficult situations. According to U.S. law, not interviewing a witness (i.e. not taking deposition) may be considered a violation of professional ethics. In other countries, doing so would be considered illegal or unethical. Incidents have been reported of American lawyers who attempted to interview witnesses in foreign countries in connection with litigation pending in the U.S. being accused of subornation of perjury and having to settle such litigation to obtain dismissal of the charges.

An interesting recent development in civil law countries is the gradual acceptance of the *amicus curiae*. Inspired in the American experience, and emboldened in the practice on the European Court of Human Rights,[32]

---

30. See, e.g., von Büren, Zur Praxis der Zürcherischen Aufsichtskommission über die Rechtsanwälte, 45 Schweizerische Juristen–Zeitung 102 (1949). In Germany, the prohibition was dropped in the 1963 revision of the Canons of Ethics (Richtlinien für die Ausübung des Rechtsanwaltberufs, §§ 4 and 58); but it is still in force in other civil-law countries. See 16 Int'l Ency.Comp. L., ch. 6, § 446 (1984). The Dutch Rules of Conduct for Lawyers (rule 16) stipulate that a lawyer cannot interview the opponent's witnesses outside the court but apparently this prohibition does not apply to "persons with a special relationship with the client".

31. See ALI/UNIDROIT, Principles of Transnational Civil Procedure (2006).

32. The device is expressly provided for in the Rules of Procedure of the European Court of Human Rights, art. 37(2).

some civil-law courts are going beyond the literal text of the civil procedure codes and allowing the participation of nonparties who are not witnesses. The idea seems to be getting broad international acceptance, particularly, but not only, in cases involving controversies of public interest. It has even been adopted in Principle 13 and Rule 6, of the ALI/UNIDROIT, Principles and Rules of Transnational Civil Procedure.[33]

The Paris intermediate Court of Appeal may have been the pioneer in a civil law country, when it invited the *bâtonnier* (presiding officer) of the Paris bar to inform it on certain rules governing the legal profession and when, in a later case brought by a victim of AIDS contaminated blood against the compensation fund for such victims, invited the famous AIDS researcher Prof. Luc Montagnier to enlighten it on certain factual points.[34] Subsequently, the French *Cour de cassation* also employed the *amicus curiae* device in a case involving surrogate mothers.[35] However, many received the practice with criticism and perplexity. Contrary to the practice in the U.S., however, the *amicus curiae* is understood to be a true friend of the court and not of one of the parties. A civil-law lawyer can easily confuse the role of the *amicus* with that of the court-appointed expert, particularly when the *amicus* is invited by the court itself.[36]

(e) Evidence and Discovery[1]

Smooth: To come back to our case, the court in fact issued an interlocutory order of the kind we are talking about (*interlocutory order for the taking of evidence*).[2] That order had several features that baffled me. For example, it did not contain a single word concerning the documentary

33. See ALI/UNIDROIT, Principles of Transnational Civil Procedure (2006).

34. See the decisions of June 21 and July 6, 1988, 1989 D.J. 341, on professional rules, and the decision on AIDS, X. v. Fonds d'indemnisation des transfusés et hémophiles contaminés, October 16, 1992, 1993 D.J. 172 (with note by Y. Laurin).

35. See Cass. Civ. 1ère, 31 mai 1991. Another example was Ass. Plén. 29 juin 2001, JCP 2001, p. 1709. See V. Y Laurin, La consécration de l'amicus curiae devant la cour de cassation, Gaz. Pal. 15 juin 1991, Doct.; J.C.P. 1992.I.3603; Dix années de mise ne oeuvre de l'amicus curiae, Petites Affiches, 24 déc. 1997, p. 17.

36. See generally Silvestri. L'amicus curiae: uno strumento per la tutela degli interessi nom rappresentati, Riv. Trim. Dir. Proc. Civ. 679 (1997); Bueno, Amicus Curiae no Processo Civil Brasileiro. Um Terceiro Enigmático (2006).

1. In a number of civil-law countries some parts of what we would call the law of evidence are contained in civil codes, which of course interact with the provisions of the civil procedure codes. This is probably a historical accident. For example in the Netherlands, the evidence provisions of the Civil Code were, on the occasion of its revision, removed from that Code and integrated in revised form with the Code of Civil Procedure. For a translation with comment, see J. M. Hebly, The Netherlands Civil Evidence Act 1988 (1992).

For comprehensive discussions of the manner in which facts are proved in civil cases under German and French law, see J. H. Langbein, The German Advantage in Civil Procedure, 52 U.Chi.L.Rev. 823 (1985), but see J. C. Reitz, Why We Probably Cannot Adopt the German Advantage in Civil Procedure, 75 Iowa L.Rev. 987 (1990); J. Beardsley, Proof of Fact in French Civil Procedure, 34 Am.J.Comp.L. 459 (1986).

2. For the form of such an order, see 2 E. J. Cohn, Manual of German Law 193–94 (2d ed. 1971).

evidence, especially the correspondence we had with H both before and after his visit here.

Comparovich: I assume the correspondence had been attached to the pleadings or had been placed in some other way into the court's case file, often referred to by its French designation *dossier*?

Smooth: Yes, but wasn't it still necessary to introduce the documents into evidence? In the U.S., documents need to be introduced as evidence through "authentication," a proceeding through which the person who signed the document attests to orally having done so, a witness swears to have seen the person sign it, or an expert witness attests to the signature.

Comparovich: The arcane U.S. practice you just described is much more time-consuming, expensive, and cumbersome than that of the civil-law countries.[3] The civilian view is that a document proves its own existence, unless the opponent specifically challenges its authenticity, and[4] it is unnecessary to waste time by formally introducing it in evidence. Hence, a party is permitted to submit documents in his possession[5] in an

---

3. For a critical discussion of the rule traditionally prevailing in the U.S., see J. W. Strong, Liberalizing the Authentication of Private Writings, 52 Cornell L.Q. 284 (1967) and Broun, Authentication and contents of writings, 1969 Law & Soc. Ord. 611. More recently, however, there are several opportunities to bypass the "authentication procedure," such as "requests for admission" of the genuineness of documents (Rule 36), pre-trial conference (Rule 16), some self-authentication rules (Evidence Rule 902, UCC § 1–202), and even some statutes and rules that provide that the genuiness of a writing would be deemend admitted unless a sworn denial is included in the answer. See Christopher B. Mueller and Laird C. Kirkpatrick, Evidence. Practice under the Rules, 2nd edition, 1999, p. 1406 and Strong et al., McCormick on Evidence, 5th edition, 1999, pp. 357–359.

4. Such challenge is rendered particularly difficult in the case of notarial protocols and other "public" or "official documents," which are those prepared by a public official in the course of a public duty. It has long been considered that such public officials are vested with "public faith" and therefore the documents they draft carry a strong presumption that they are conclusive evidence of their contents. See Schlesinger, The Notary and the Formal Contract in Civil Law, 1941 Report of the New York Law Revision Commission 403, 413 and German Code of Civil Procedure, §§ 415–418. In France, the party who is unsuccessful in contesting the authenticity of a notarial or similar "public" document (for which a special procedure called *inscription de faux* must be used) is subject to a civil fine ranging from 15 to 1,500 euro and may be liable for damages. French Code of Civil Procedure (art. 305). A similar provision exists in Belgium, but limited to damages. See Belgian Code of Civil Procedure, art. 905. The U.S. law may reach a very similar result when there is a request for admission of the genuineness of a document in the discovery phase (Rule 36) and the opponent fails to admit. If the genuineness is ultimately proved, the party that made the original request may be awarded costs and attorney's fees (Rule 37(c)(2)). See Strong *et al.*, McCormick on Evidence 358 (1999).

5. As to documents in the possession of the opponent or of a third party, see the discussion of discovery, infra. One important point, however, should be noted immediately: specific documents as well as entire files of documents in the possession of some public office—including another court—normally can be sent for, and attached to the court's *dossier* without much formality. This practice (*Aktenbeiziehung* in German terminology) is of particular importance in personal injury litigation, where the entire record of an earlier criminal action (or, if there was no criminal action at least, police reports and the like) thus can be globally incorporated into the *dossier* of the court dealing with a subsequent civil suit.

informal way, provided he notifies the opponent and gives him a copy and an opportunity to inspect and reply.[6]

Smooth: But in this way the court's *dossier* will be cluttered with irrelevant documents.

Comparovich: As a matter of self-interest, the parties will not provoke the judges' anger by submitting totally irrelevant stuff, and the court, sitting without a jury, will be able to appraise the evidentiary value of each document.

Smooth: But the documents may contain hearsay or opinion.[7]

Comparovich: So what? Except for matters of privilege and of personal incompetence to testify (based on reasons such as kinship, tender age, or prior felony convictions),[8] civilian codes contain *no exclusionary rules of evidence,*[9] and particularly no hearsay or opinion rule.[10]

Most of the grounds which under U.S. law serve to preclude the admission of evidence, according to the civilians merely affect its weight.[11] They consider the weight accorded to each item of documentary or other evidence to be a matter for the court's *free evaluation.*

The existence of exclusionary rules of evidence in the United States appears related to the use of jury trials in civil cases.[12] Common-law

---

6. On the duty to make documents available to the other side for inspection before handing them to the court, see, e.g., French Code of Civil Procedure (arts. 132–136). This is a corollary of the adversarial principle that governs civil procedure in civil-law systems.

7. The reader will note that even under U.S. law, a document executed by a party normally can be introduced against such party; third-party documents frequently will be admissible under one of the many exceptions to the hearsay rule.

8. As to competence to testify and to take an oath, the rules in civil-law countries often contain more restrictions than one finds in U.S. law. See H. Silving, The Oath, 68 Yale L.J. 1329, 1527, at 1543–51 (1959). Regarding testimonial privileges, see M. Pieck, Privilege Against Self–Incrimination in The Civil Law, 5 Villanova L.Rev. 375 (1960); cf. Otto BV v. Postbank, NV, Case No. C–60/92, Nov. 10, 1993, 1993 E.C.R. I–5683. Of course, there are the obvious rules against the disclosure of confidential information by doctors, lawyers, etc.

9. Although modern civil-law systems generally reject exclusionary rules of evidence, some exclude evidence obtained in violation of the right of privacy. The European Court of Human Rights, for example, has stated that this violates the right to a fair proceeding as well as art. 8 of the European Convention ("Everyone has the right to respect for his private and family life, his home and his correspondence"). This rule applies in civil as well as criminal actions and is irrespective of whether the evidence was obtained by police officers or private individuals.

10. A witness may, of course, be asked to state the source of his or her knowledge. If a witness or a document points to a named individual as such source, the court may call that individual as a witness or direct the parties to call him or her. See Hammelmann, Hearsay Evidence—A Comparison, 67 L.Q.Rev. 67 (1951).

11. Civilians sometimes refuse to understand or to comply with, U.S. technical rules regarding admissibility of evidence. A striking example is reported by F. H. Thomann, Recent Developments in Swiss International Law, 14 Int'l Lawyer 525, 527 (1980).

12. See Herzog, The Probative Value of Testimony in Private Law, 42 Am.J.Comp. L.Supp. 275, 276 (1994), and Wigmore, Evidence in Trials at Common Law § 7.3: "... as a practical matter, the use of a jury, for whatever reason, ordinarily results in the use of rules of evidence." (Tiller's Revision 1983).

countries that have abandoned the jury trial in civil cases have also abandoned the hearsay rule and several other exclusionary rules of evidence. A case in point is England, which weakened the hearsay rule in 1938 and 1968 and then completely abolished it in 1995, "because it was perceived to be anachronistic".[13]

The "exclusion" of all hearsay seems to be a drastic rule that prevents consideration of relevant evidence; it can only be justified by the lack of trust that jurors can arrive at a reasonable decision with exposure to less-than-perfect evidence. After all, it is not a secret that evidentiary rules are considered an important method of "jury control," along with summary judgment, jury instructions, voir dire, new trial, mistrial, special verdicts etc.

On the one hand, one is hardpressed to conclude that evidentiary rules, rather than assure reliability of evidence, in practice, tie the hands of the trier of fact. On the other, it must be recognized that only a system that provides such broad discovery can have the luxury of excluding relevant evidence, merely because it may have some perceived imperfection.

In civil law countries, it is expected that a professional judge, as opposed to amateur jurors, will be able to accord different probative value (weight) to second-hand and first-hand testimony. It is undeniable that relevant hearsay evidence helps the court better understand the totality of the facts of the case, which is why the hearsay rule has so many exceptions in U.S. law. The result is that the civil-law trier of fact has at her disposal a wider range of relevant evidence.

Edge: By a process of gradual erosion of the hearsay rule, U.S. law is moving toward the civil-law approach. Would it not simplify and improve U.S. law if the hearsay and opinion rules were thrown out altogether?

Comparovich: There is no doubt that such a reform would simplify U.S. law, reduce the content of Evidence books by one third, and bring cheer to the hearts of future bar examination candidates. Whether total elimination of the exclusionary rules of evidence would improve the fact-finding process is less certain. Perhaps one should draw a distinction between jury and non-jury cases. With respect to the latter, the arguments in favor of adopting the civilian approach are strong, but even on this point the experts are divided.[14] However, the practice in non-jury cases, such as administrative proceedings and bench trials, in which there is a professional judge serving as finder of fact instead of lay jurors, is that the rules of evidence are much more relaxed.

Edge: You mentioned the expression "free evaluation". This expression often comes up in our dealings with international litigators. Does it have a special meaning?

13. See Andrews, English Civil Procedure 725 (2003).

14. See J. Weinstein, Probative Force of Hearsay, 46 Iowa L.Rev. 331 (1961); F. E. Booker and R. Morton, The Hearsay Rule, The St. George Plays and The Road to the Year Twenty–Fifty, 44 Notre Dame Law. 7 (1968); Damaška, Of Hearsay and its Analogues, 76 Minn. L. Rev. 425 (1992).

Comparovich: None that you should be concerned with, but it is important to understand it because common law observers are usually unnecessarily baffled with this expression. Although frequently used by civil-lawyers, it has no special or complex meaning. It can only be understood on the historical perspective of the concept of "legal proof".

In Romano–Canonistic procedure there existed a complex system of mechanical rules precisely determining the number and quality of witnesses necessary to prove an event or to overcome other evidence. According to the old principle of "legal proof", when the law prescribed a specific form, no other evidence is allowed to prove a fact, regardless of how convincing it might be. The old principle of "legal proof" would give mathematical value to each piece of evidence, requiring, e.g., at least two witness to prove a fact in court. If the party presented only one witness, the party presented half proof (one witness is the same as no witness: *testis unus, testis nullus*).

The principle of "free evaluation of proof" is simply a modern repudiation of the old system of "legal proof". Instead of being bound by mathematical formulas previously established by the legislature, the judge is free to evaluate the evidence and to reach the most appropriate conclusion.[15] Civilians regard this principle—coupled with the absence of exclusionary rules—as the cornerstone of their treatment of evidentiary problems.

Still today, however, there are some rare but important examples of "legal proof", i.e., facts that can only be proved in court with a specific type of evidence as prescribed by law, and no other evidence would be admissible either to prove or disprove it. The most notable examples are facts that can only be proven by an official document prepared by a notary public and facts that can only be proven by written evidence. Some contracts, like mortgage, purchase of real property, marriage must be performed by a notary. These public documents may in some respects have a conclusive effect, which cannot be overcome, or can be overcome only by a very complex procedure. No other evidence is allowed. Most contracts above a small amount must by performed in writing. Another example is the ancient relic of the "decisory oath."[16] Chile still seems to be bound by many of the mechanical rules of the Romano–Canonistic procedure.[17]

Smooth: Let us come back to the interlocutory order for the taking of evidence. The first paragraph of the order called for the personal appearance of H before the court so that he could be questioned about the conversations we had with him during his visit here. This puzzled me for a number of reasons. First of all, it seemed to me that before H testified in

---

15. See Codes of Civil Procedure of Japan (art. 247), Italy (art. 116), Brazil (art. 131), Argentina (art. 386), Mexico (arts. 197–218), Spain (arts. 348, 376, 382.3 and 348.3). See also Rule 28.2 of the Transnational Rules of Civil Procedure. See also ALI/UNIDROIT, Principles of Transnational Civil Procedure (2006).

16. See *infra* at 774–77 (discussing the decisory oath).

17. See R. B. Cappalli, Comparative South American Civil Procedure: A Chilean Perspective, 21 U. Miami Inter–Am. L. Rev.

court, we should have been given an opportunity for a pre-trial examination.

Comparovich: The jury is composed of a number of lay citizens that must be assembled together to hear all the evidence in a case and decide controverted issues of fact. Because it would be extremely difficult to reconcile the schedules of 12 people for an extended period of time, the presentation of evidence must be held in the shortest amount of time possible, preferably concentrated in a single continuous session. Because due process requires the parties to have an opportunity to challenge the opponent's evidence, and because the only time to do that is the concentrated trial, it follows that all evidence must be discovered before the jury trial commences.[18]

Working without a jury, the civil-law judge is a permanent official that may adjourn court sessions and recommence it in a later date, as is convenient for the parties.[19] Therefore, the civilians do not have to divide a civil lawsuit into (a) the pretrial phase and (b) the "trial." A "trial," in the sense of a single, dramatic, concentrated and uninterrupted presentation of everything that bears on the dispute, is unknown to them.[20] Their traditional practice is to develop a case through a series of successive hearings[21] of which evidence is taken at some.[22] In the absence of a need of a "trial,"

239, 274 (1989–1990) (also discussing some other Latin American countries).

18. See Geoffrey C. Hazard, Jr., Discovery and the Role of the Judge in Civil Law Jurisdictions, 73 Notre Dame L. Rev. 1017, 1020 (1998).

19. See Geoffrey C. Hazard, Jr., Discovery and the Role of the Judge in Civil Law Jurisdictions, 73 Notre Dame L. Rev. 1017, 1021 (1998) (observing that the logic of inquiry in the civil-law framework is "to subdivide a case issue by issue, or by clusters of issues, considering both facts and law as to each issue. Concerning any such issue or cluster of issues, law and facts can be considered together because there is no jury to share in the decisional process (. . .) In contrast, the logic of a jury trial is to subdivide the case into issues of law, regardless of the relationship of legal issues to each other, and issues of fact.")

20. The statement in the text refers to civil procedure. In criminal matters, whether or not heard by a jury, the civilians do require a "trial," (more or less) in the sense in which we understand the term. See infra sec. 2C.

Concerning recent attempts of German (and to some extent other) reformers to introduce the notion of a single, concentrated "final" or "main" hearing, which thus has features of a trial, into *civil* procedure, see

the discussion of the "Stuttgart Model," *infra* at 788ff.

The absence of a "trial" in the American sense in civil law civil procedure has led some foreign lawyers and officials, not knowing that the "trial" was but a part of the total lawsuit, to misunderstand the word "pretrial" in connection with discovery. They believed it was a private investigative procedure intended to find out, before any suit was ever brought, whether the plaintiff might have a claim against someone. See, e.g., the French Senate Report justifying the French so-called "blocking statute" cited in V. Mercier and D.D. McKenney, Obtaining Evidence in France for Use in United States Litigation, 2 Tulane J.Int'l & Comp.L. 91, at 101 n. 70 (1994).

21. Clearly, this is an important difference between civil-law and common-law procedure. For an attempt to explain this difference, and to put it into the context of a broader comparison of the two systems in terms of political history, see Damaška, The Faces of Justice and State Authority 51–52 (1986).

22. In non-jury cases, piecemeal trials are not entirely unknown in the United States, although we regard them as unusual. In the Philippines, where an American-de-

there is no room for a "pretrial" examination. Note, also, that in your case H's testimony was taken primarily to give him an opportunity to tell the court his side of the story. Any use you might make of his examination for *discovery* purposes would be merely incidental and probably ineffective.

Edge: Is there then no discovery in civil-law procedure?

Comparovich: In most civil-law countries, discovery is almost nonexistent. Even in those countries in which it exists—a relatively new phenomenon—discovery is considerably more limited than in the U.S.[23] The devices civilians use to extract information or documents from an unwilling opponent or third party are correspondingly weaker than those in the U.S. The absence of sweeping contempt powers in civil-law countries is also an important factor explaining the difficult expansion in this area.

It is important to underline the principle of the autonomy of the parties in a civil-law proceeding. This means that parties autonomously set the limits of the dispute brought before court. The parties involved, the object and the cause of action and the factual arguments relied on by the plaintiff to support his claim offer a first delimitation of the claim. It is within these limits—that can be widened by the defendant (e.g. by way of a counterclaim)—that the judge will have to render judgment. This principle also affects the evidence rules in that way that only the parties decide which evidence they will use in the proceedings. It is a general rule that a party cannot–directly or through the judge—demand his opponent for evidence.

There are cultural factors, such as concerns for privacy, that limit discovery in civil-law countries. The traditional principle has always been, and in most countries still is, that a party in a civil proceeding cannot be compelled to produce evidence against its interest or to help the opponent in proving his or her case. The only known exceptions were when the party being requested mentioned the document in one of the papers filed with the court or when the requesting party had a substantive law right to obtain the document, such as commercial books, medical records, contracts, receipts, etc (*actio ad exhibendum*). Indeed, this is still the rule in most civil-law countries.[24] It is as if the "privilege against self incrimination" had application beyond the realm of criminal procedure. Therefore, the parties traditionally have the burden of gathering all evidence necessary to prevail in a case before bringing the lawsuit and have no expectations of "help" from the opponent. There has never been a right to request production of a document from an opponent (or third party) simply because the evidence was relevant to prove a fact in a civil proceeding. Such a tradition does not

rived system of civil procedure (but without a jury) has long prevailed, piecemeal trials seem to be the rule rather than the exception. See G.W. Pugh, Aspects of the Administration of Justice in the Philippines, 26 La. L.Rev. 1, at 21–22 (1965).

23. Before the enactment of the Federal Rules of Civil Procedure, in 1938, discovery in the U.S. was also extremely limited. Discovery was not available at Common Law, only Equity.

24. See, e.g., Brazilian Code of Civil Procedure (art. 339–41 and 355–63).

die overnight; it continues to influence the exercise of judicial discretion, even in those countries in which legislative changes have been made.[25]

There is a relatively new, but firm trend in civil-law countries to adopt a limited form of document discovery as a corollary to the duty to cooperate with the court in the fact-finding process.[26] It might also be argued that the constitutional guarantee of access to justice includes a guarantee to access to relevant evidence.[27] Incidentally, there has always been a duty to cooperate with the court (always) and with each other (sometimes) in public international litigation before international tribunals.[28]

Civil-law countries have evolved at a different pace, but there is a clear trend in allowing a very limited form of discovery of documents.[29] These changes represent a critical deviation from the civil-law tradition and are considered by some almost revolutionary; there is some indication that it would never come close to the American practice. Some notable examples are France, The Netherlands, Luxembourg, Germany, Spain, and Japan.[30]

25. See Herzog, Civil Procedure in France 233–34, 239 (1967); Beardsley, Proof of Fact in French Civil Procedure, 34 Am. J.Comp.L. 459 (1986); Millar, The Mechanism of Fact Discovery: A Study in Comparative Civil Procedure, 32 Ill.L.Rev. 261 et seq., 424 et seq. (1937); Homburger, Functions of Orality in Austrian and American Law, 20 Buff.L.Rev. 9, 19–32 (1970); D. Gerber, Extraterritorial Discovery and the Conflict of Procedural Systems, 34 Am.J.Comp.L. 745, 757–67 (1986); L. Cadiet & E. Jeuland, *Droit judiciaire privé*, 365–66 (2006); P. Murray & R. Stürner, German Civil Justice 277 (2004); Comoglio, Ferri & Taruffo, 1 Lezioni sul Processo Civile 485–87 (2006).

26. See, e.g., French Civil Code art. 10, as amended in 1972 (stating that every person must cooperate with the administration of justice's pursuit of the truth and that unjustified refusal may be coerced and sanctioned). See also Brazilian Code of Civil Procedure (art. 339); Portuguese Code of Civil Procedure (arts. 266 and 519).

27. See the Spanish Constitution, art. 118 (stating that all must cooperate with courts requests in a proceeding).

28. See Amerasinghe, Evidence in International Litigation 96–146 (2005).

29. See Freitas, La Preuve dans l'Union Eurepéenne: Différences et Similitutes, in Freitas (ed.), The Law of Evidence in the European Union 22 (2004); Trocker & Varano, Concluding remarks, in Trocker & Varano, The Reforms of Civil Procedure in Comparative Perspective 255–258 (2005).

30. See the Codes of Civil Procedure of France (arts. 11 and 138–142), the Netherlands (arts. 19–a, 22 and 833–843b, as amended in 1988, 1989, and 2002); Luxembourg (arts. 279–288), Germany (§§ 138, 142, 144, 421–429, as amended in 2002), Japan (arts. 132–2–132–4, 163 and 219–25, enacted in 1996 and amended in 2001 and 2003), Spain (arts. 328–332, enacted in 2000).

See Mercier and McKenney, *supra* note 20 at 95; L. Cadiet & E. Jeuland, Droit Judiciaire Privé 365–67 (2006); S. Guinchard, F. Ferrand & C. Chainais, Procédure Civile 932–35 (2008); Hebly, the Netherlands Civil Evidence Act 1988 4, 16–18 (1992); Otto BV v. Postbank, NV, Case No. C–60/92, Nov. 10, 1993, 1993 E.C.R. I–5683 (in English); Murray and Stürner, German Civil Justice 277–78 (2004); Walter, The German Civil Procedure Reform Act 2002: Much Ado About Nothing?, in Trocker & Varano, The Reforms of Civil Procedure in Comparative Perspective 76 (2005) (considering the 2002 innovation in Germany "close to revolutionary"); Oliva & Diez–Picazo, Derecho Procesal Civil. El Proceso de Declaración 341–45 (2000); Taniguchi, Reich & Miyake, Civil Procedure in Japan 7–124 to 7–130 (2008); Huang, Introducing Discovery into Civil Law 157–217 (2003); Kojima, Japanese Civil Procedure in Comparative Law Perspective, 46 U. Kan. L. Rev. 687 (1998); Goodman, Justice and Civil Procedure in Japan 331–51 (2004); Taniguchi, The 1996 Code of Civil Procedure of Japan—A Procedure for the Coming Century?, 45 Am. J. Comp. L. 767 (1997) (observing that some academics and lawyers advocated

Some countries, like Italy, Greece, Portugal, and Belgium, have had this limited form of document discovery for decades.[31] In countries where this device has existed for a long time, it may be less effective in terms of scope and enforcement than in those that were consciously emulating common-law discovery.

From these influential countries, adoption in other civil law countries is almost certain in the near future. A limited form of discovery (between the U.S. and the civil-law models) has also been adopted in the ALI/UNIDROIT's Principles and Rules of Transnational Civil Procedure.[32]

There are some variations in the procedure and scope of discovery in each country, but it is possible to offer a broad outline of "civil-law discovery." If a party needs a relevant document that is in the possession of the opposing party or a third person, he or she must make a request to the court, identifying the document and its contents with reasonable specificity. Some legal systems recognize the difficulty of identifying a document that the party has probably never seen. In Japan, the party may describe the document broadly and shift the burden of identifying it to the document holder. The party must also prove that the document exists and is in the possession of the person.

The document holder must either produce the document or give a legitimate reason for refusal, such as irrelevance, privilege, self-incrimination, personal embarrassment, trade or state secret, etc. Some countries may have further exceptions, but the mere fact that the document is against the holder's interest is not a legitimate reason for refusal.

Japanese law allows the court to hold an *in camera* examination (i.e. without the presence of the opposing party) to determine whether the document is discoverable, but, since there is no jury and the judge is the fact finder, the mere fact that the judge could see a document that is not discoverable would defeat the purpose of a privilege.

If the refusal is unjustified, the court will issue an order for the production of the document or part of it. In some countries, but not all, the court may impose a coercive daily fine (*astreinte*) similar to but weaker than a coercive contempt in the U.S. to encourage production by a party or third person. Because in most civil-law countries the fines may not be high,

an American-type of discovery during the drafting of the new Japanese Code, but it was strongly opposed by the industry and the government, and adoption of a general discovery rule was abandoned at an early stage).

31. See the Codes of Civil Procedure of Italy (arts. 210–12), Greece (art. 451), Portugal (arts. 266, 519 and 528–39), and Belgium (arts. 877–882). See Carpi & Taruffo, Commentario Breve al Codice di Procedura Civile 665–73 (2002); F. P. Luiso, II Diritto Processuale Civile 120–124 (2007); Yessiou–Faltsi, Civil Procedure in Hellas 361–362 (1995);

Freitas *et al.*, 2 Código de Processo Civil Anotado 438–73 (2008).

32. See Principle 16 and Rules 21–23, ALI/UNIDROIT, Principles of Transnational Civil Procedure (2006); Huang, Introducing Discovery into Civil Law 381–87 (2003) (with a proposal of rules of disclosure and discovery for civil-law countries). A much more limited, cumbersome, and ambiguous discovery proceeding was adopted in art. 4 of the EC Project. See Storme (ed.), Approximation of Judiciary Law in the European Union (1994).

the strongest form of enforcement is the drawing of adverse inferences from a party's noncompliance with discovery requests. So to be able to fully benefit from this sanction, the requesting party must describe the contents of the document or, at least, the facts to be proved with it.

The situation is more difficult if the document is in the possession of a third-person. In that situation, the courts cannot draw adverse inference against the party, and the party that requested the document may never have access to essential documents to prove her claim. Most civil-law countries have no effective way of coercing a non-party to produce relevant documents through coercive fines. Some civil-law countries may punish a non party criminally for disobedience of a court order, but this is a rare occurrence, and many civil-law countries may not be able to punish the non-party at all.

Although the expense for compliance of such a limited discovery request is minimal, in Italy, it is expressly provided that the party requesting a document must pay for any expense incurred by the document holder to discharge him or her of his or her obligation to produce the document in court. In sharp contrast, the party complying with discovery requests in the U.S. must bear its costs.

There must be a party request: the court ordinarily cannot order the production of documents *sua sponte*, unless the parties made reference to a document on their pleadings, or they are mentioned in any papers filed in the court record. This is a corollary to the adversarial principle of the autonomy of the parties.

For decades, in most civil-law countries, there has been a right to ask public agencies and public companies for the production of relevant documents. This is not considered a violation of the principle of separation of powers.[33]

Smooth: What about deposition of witnesses? Is it available in civil-law countries?

Comparovich: Despite being one of the most common discovery devices in U.S. practice, and one that American litigators have come to take for granted, deposition of witnesses is infrequently used in the United Kingdom and in most other common-law countries. Discovery in the United Kingdom and in most common-law countries is generally much less invasive than in the U.S. and is usually restricted to documents.[34] As a matter

---

33. For example, in actions seeking money damages French courts may request the tax authorities to produce tax documents that might be useful. More generally, in spite of the traditional rule that administrative matters must go to the administrative courts, the regular courts may ask administrative agencies to produce documents that may be useful in cases pending before them. See, e.g., Decision of July 21, 1987, Cass.civ.1st., 1987 Bull.Civ.I, No. 248 at 181.

34. See Andrews, English Civil Procedure 595ff (2003); Hartley, Comity and the Use of Anti–Suit Injunctions in International Litigation, 35 Am. J. Comp. L. 487, 502–06 (1987), noting also the very limited use of the civil jury and the existence of stricter pleading rules in England. Indeed, both factors may be relevant for the relative weakness of discovery devices in that country. More precise pleading will help define the issues and lessen the need for discovery to achieve that

of fact, depositions had an extremely limited role in the U.S., before the enactment of the Federal Rules of Civil Procedure in 1938, similar to the current tradition in other common-law and in civil-law countries. Therefore, to some extent, this is not an entirely civil—law common—law distinction, but a distinction between the U.S. and the rest of the world.

The mere idea of "deposing" a witness is problematic in civil-law procedure. Since the proceeding is not structurally divided into pretrial and trial and since the gathering of evidence and its production into the official record are done simultaneously by the court (not by the parties), "pretrial" deposition as a preparatory investigation for the "trial" is of limited usefulness.

Naturally, when a witness may not be available in the future, due to travel or impending death, a party may request the court to take his or her interrogation in advance. This practice is called deposition *de bene esse* in the U.S. and *ad perpetuam rei memoriam* in civil-law countries. It is not a deposition in the American sense because it is not taken by the attorneys but by the court itself. It is considered a provisional measure to perpetuate the evidence for future use, especially before a lawsuit is brought.

Edge: But I imagine that a civil-law attorney certainly would want to "interview" a witness in advance of the court hearing, either to explain the situation to her or to find out in advance what she will say in court.

Comparovich: This is not usually done for two reasons. The first reason is that judges would look with extreme suspicion on a witness that was previously interviewed by an attorney. Not only will the witness's credibility be impaired (in some civil-law systems, this would be a violation of rules or ethical standards, not so in Germany or Japan), but there is also an economic disincentive to conduct such an interview.[35] The parties, however, may interview witnesses and report their findings to the attorneys.

It is not unheard of that a court interrogation of a witness would end abruptly, because the witness was professing his or her ignorance about the facts of the case.

In Japan, however, a party may serve the opponent written interrogatories directly (i.e., without court intervention) during or even before the commencement of the lawsuit ("interparty interrogatories"). The future of this experimentation is uncertain, however, because there is no sanction for noncompliance.[36]

Smooth: It is interesting to see that civil-law countries are completely unaffected by one of the most contentious debates in U.S. civil procedure

---

purpose; if a surprise piece of evidence is presented, the absence of a jury makes it more feasible to adjourn a trial to a later date and makes it unnecessary to "leave no stone unturned" before a one-time, unrepeatable trial.

35. See Murray and Stürner, German Civil Justice 293–97 (2004) (observing that, in Germany, attorney's fees are based on lump sums, not hourly rates and lawyers generally will not be paid for discovery efforts.)

36. See Japanese Code of Civil Procedure (art. 163).

for the past several decades: the broad scope of discovery with its high cost and potential for abuse.

Comparovich: Most of these problems are specific to U.S. civil procedure, although other common law countries complain about them as well.

It is clear from the above description that the civil-law discovery does not permit what is known pejoratively as "fishing expeditions." This is an extensive, time-consuming, intrusive, and expensive exploratory investigation conducted without court supervision and goes beyond the strict limits of the object of a proceeding with the only objective of finding damaging evidence against the opponent. Countries have different perceptions of the term. In civil-law countries, everything beyond the limited scope of civil-law discovery will be considered impermissible "fishing expedition," even a very limited request under U.S. law. However, there are several levels of "fishing expeditions," and one should not throw away the baby with the bath water. There is in principle nothing wrong with conducting a limited amount of discovery to find out necessary information.[37]

In addition to cultural differences in approach, the civil-law discovery also has some important technical differences that further limit discovery. To begin with, while American discovery may involve a broad description of categories of documents, civil-law discovery is limited to documents reasonably identified. In addition, because of the time and energy wasted in this bureaucratic process, it is possible a party will not request, and the court will not order, production of a document so long as the facts may be proven with other evidence.

Another difference is that common-law discovery is conducted privately in the lawyers' offices without court participation. The attorneys issue a subpoena to parties and third persons for the production of documents, and they must comply under penalty of severe sanctions. The court only becomes involved to enforce production or if the parties cannot agree on the appropriateness of a request. For a civil-law observer, this proceeding gives an appearance that the discovery is an extrajudicial affair and this leads to some misunderstanding about the nature of the discovery process.[38]

In contrast, civil-law discovery requires a party's motion, hearing the document holder, a court decision over the document discoverability, and a court order. This cumbersome practice is not much different from the U.S. document discovery in force before the 1970s amendments to the Federal Rules of Civil Procedure. According to the then in force Rule 34, a party had to make a motion and show good cause, and the court would then issue

37. See, e.g., Chase *et al.*, Civil Litigation in Comparative Context 224 (2007) (referring to a rare case in which the German Federal Supreme Court, while formally upholding the prohibition against "fishing expedition," authorized a medical student to inspect hospital research records to find information about her infection.)

38. Indeed, although discovery is an integral part of a judicial proceeding, this would not be such a far fetched observation. The Advisory Committee's Note to the 1970 amendments to Rule 34 stated that its objective was to have the rule on discovery of documents operate "extrajudicially," not by court order.

a court order. The need for a court order was limited to document discovery; depositions could be taken simply by giving notice to the other parties. The 1970 amendments shifted the operation of document discovery from the hands of judges, and the device took today's extrajudicial shape.[39]

One may predict, however, an evolution similar to what happened in the U.S. (culminating in the 1970 amendment). With time, as civil-law lawyers and courts get accustomed to the requirements and scope of discovery, parties may simply bypass this bureaucratic process and simply start requesting each other for the production of documents. At first, they may start doing this informally, but this will soon be the norm. If there is a conflict regarding the propriety of the discovery request, the legal system may impose the burden either on the party requesting discovery or the party resisting it to seek court intervention. It is also possible to imagine that with time, the law will require the parties to comply with reasonable requests automatically or be sanctioned later. On the one hand, this is a much more streamlined procedure because it frees the court's time. On the other, this straightforwardness may make civil-law discovery as out of control as U.S. discovery. The Spanish law seems to have already started this new trend by using language that implies a party may directly request documents from each other.

Another difference is that, in U.S. practice, discovered evidence need not be produced at trial. Sometimes, they cannot be produced at all because they are inadmissible due to exclusionary rules of evidence.[40] There is a clear difference between what is discoverable and what is admissible at trial.[41] Other times, the party has no interest in producing at trial some of the evidence obtained through discovery, either because they are repetitive or not strictly relevant to the controversial issues to be proven, or for other strategic reasons. The scope of discovery is much broader than what is strictly necessary to be presented to the fact finder. The scope of discovery, therefore, is vast: every document that is remotely relevant to the claim or defense may be discovered. For good cause, the court may even broaden the search to any document remotely relevant to the subject matter involved in the action.[42] In most cases, a party will present at trial only a miniscule percentage of the documents obtained through discovery.

The civil-law practice is completely different and has profound consequences on the scope of discovery. Because of the absence of a structural division between pretrial (conducted by the parties outside of court direct supervision) and trial (conducted in court under direct court supervision) in civil-law countries, the process of gathering evidence is not segregated from

---

39. The Advisory Committee on Civil Rules had tried to make discovery extrajudicial in 1955, but the proposal was not approved. See Fleming James, Jr., Civil Procedure 195 (1965). It is interesting to observe that after 1970 most amendments related to discovery in the U.S. had the objective of curtailing discovery and fighting discovery abuse.

40. Also because of specific procedural provisions such as FRCP 32.

41. FRCP 26(b)(1), for example, states that inadmissible evidence may be discovered, if it may lead to admissible evidence.

42. FRCP 26(b)(1).

the process of officially introducing evidence into the court record. When a civil-law judge orders a person to produce a certain document, it is usually for immediate incorporation into the record.[43] This represents a further limitation on the scope of civil-law discovery because it considerably raises the stakes of the concept of "relevance." Instead of just "relevant to the claim" or "relevant to the subject matter of the dispute," a civil-law judge will only order production of documents that are admissible and necessary to prove some specific fact of a claim specifically made.

This limited scope excludes several important categories of documents that are discoverable in the U.S. but may be considered inappropriate "fishing expedition" in civil-law countries, such as (a) documents that are only indirectly relevant, but may lead to another relevant document or witness, (b) categories of documents loosely described (all internal memos related to the litigation within a certain date), (c) documents the party does not know exist, (d) documents the party does not know the contents of, etc.

Another limitation to civil-law discovery, closely related to the one above is the following. In U.S. procedure, because the jury is the trier of fact, in principle, the parties are free to present all evidence it wants at trial, with little judicial control. In civil-law systems, because the judge is the trier of fact, a judge must approve the introduction of any evidence into the record. Because a judge closely controls the relevance of evidence, and will only accept production of evidence that it considers necessary for his opinion, this is a further limitation to civil-law discovery.

The court's power to reject the production of evidence often baffles common law observers. However, although broad, the court's power is not arbitrary. The court can only reject production of evidence, when the requirement is in some way irrelevant, such as when the evidence sought is irrelevant, unnecessary, repetitive, burdensome, etc.

An indirect limitation for the civil-law discovery is the fee-shifting rule. Contrary to what happens in the U.S., in civil-law countries (as well as most common-law countries) the loser pays the winner's attorney's fees.[44] This makes it economically risky for a party to state a claim in the hopes of obtaining evidence during the discovery process. If one cannot obtain by informal means the necessary evidence to prove one's case before commencement of the lawsuit, that person has an economic disincentive to bring the lawsuit.

The scope of civil-law discovery, therefore, is much narrower than U.S. discovery (or the discovery that may be obtained in any common-law country). Each country is still developing its own scope of discovery and

---

43. See, e.g., French Code of Civil Procedure art. 138, permitting only the discovery of a document that a party proposes to use in a pending case. Tocker and Varano have identified a trend of permitting discovery before the commencement of a lawsuit in order to assist the parties in deciding whether to settle or whether to start a lawsuit in the first place. See Trocker & Varano, Concluding remarks, in Trocker & Varano, The Reforms of Civil Procedure in Comparative Perspective 256–258 (2005) (discussing France, Japan and England).

44. See *supra* Chapter 7, Section 8(b) at 691 (discussing attorney fee shifting).

forms of enforcement. In civil-law countries, discovery is a rather new innovation of the end of the 21st century and beginning of the XXI century, and case law is still being developed. However, a common ground among civil-law countries is bound to emerge in the future.

Discovery of electronically stored information, with its attendant problems of volume and costs, further complicates the issues and will abruptly end the age of innocence of civil-law discovery.

Edge: This lack of discovery devices in civil-law countries is surprising for an American observer.

Comparovich: An extensive system of broad access to evidence may be essential for accuracy of results, and the access to evidence may even be considered an integral part of the constitutional guarantee of access to justice. However, as Americans have very early realized, it comes with a high cost and is in direct conflict with the ideal of an inexpensive and efficient access to justice.

While it is true that some claims that are common in U.S. courts may never be brought in civil-law countries because they are ill equipped to discover the truth, it is also a fact that some claims that are common in civil-law countries may never be brought in U.S. courts because the cost of litigating them is prohibitive.

Although inapplicable to the reality of U.S. litigation, the civil-law discovery may be on its way to achieving a balance between the high cost of U.S.-style discovery and the societal cost of not having an effective device to discover otherwise unavailable evidence. Once the cat is out of the bag, however, i.e., once civil-law countries start accepting discovery, it will be difficult to stop, and the scope of discovery, just like it happened in the U.S., might start to grow uncontrollably.

Smooth: How is it then, that civil-law litigants obtain the evidence they need to prove the facts of their case?

Comparovich: Sometimes, parties simply don't obtain the necessary evidence, and the court must make a final decision with the imperfect information available on the record. One of the ways to make this decision is to apply the general rule of burden of proof.[45]

Much to the surprise of American observers, the civil-law procedure survives well without discovery for a number of reasons. Oral testimony is not considered essential in some civil-law countries in the first place, so the focus is placed on written evidence. This reduces the importance of depositions.

The traditional civil-law procedure, however, is not completely insensitive to the difficulties of obtaining documents. As we have seen before,

---

45. Each party must prove the facts it alleges. The party who invokes a right must prove it, and the party who invokes a release from an obligation must prove it was dis- charged. See the Civil Codes of France (art. 1315), Belgium (art. 1315), Italy (2697). See the Codes of Civil Procedure of Brazil (art. 333), Belgium (art. 870).

substantive law has always entitled litigants to obtain certain important documents from parties, third persons, and public officials.

Some legal systems may also provide for strict liability and shifting the burden of proof in situations in which evidence is particularly difficult to obtain, such as medical malpractice, employment, consumer, or product liability litigation. These devices circumvent a more pressing need for discovery in situations in which one would expect that only one of the parties has the evidence.[46]

The absence of exclusionary rules of evidence in civil-law countries, as we have seen, means the civil-law trier of fact will be exposed to a larger amount of evidence than its American counterpart. This further offsets the lack of discovery.

Another issue that makes the lack of discovery less problematic in civil-law countries is the absence of claims in which the "intent" of a person is relevant. For example, in civil-law countries there are no punitive damages. But this begs the question: civil-law countries cannot develop the concept of punitive damages exactly because they have no discovery.

The court-appointed expert is invested with the power to demand the parties and third persons to produce any information or documents necessary for the investigation and may draw adverse inferences from noncompliance.[47]

In addition, as will be discussed below, in many civil law countries it is possible, and in some quite usual, for a private plaintiff to join in a criminal prosecution of a tort that is also a criminal act (such as negligent driving) and to demand damages directly from the criminal court. In such cases, the victim benefits from the evidence put forward by the prosecution, and the police investigation eliminates the need for the party to engage in detailed factual inquiries.[48]

It is true, however, that many rights in civil-law countries have no judicial remedy. Some lawsuits are frequently lost and others not even brought to justice because of the absence of an effective device for gathering evidence. In addition to that, many substantive law situations are not legally protected because the legal system is unable to obtain the necessary evidence (the absence of punitive damages in civil-law is just one example). This situation is unacceptable and civil-law countries would do well to create or improve their procedural devices in order to facilitate a party's right to obtain all evidence necessary to prove a claim. One may predict with some certainty that this will happen in the near future; however,

---

46. For example, art. 6 of the Brazilian Consumer Code authorizes the court to shift the burden of proof. See Gidi, Aspectos da Inversão do Ônus da Prova no Código do Consumidor, 3 Rev. Dir. Proc. Civ. (1996). Similar provisions can be found in several European Consumer Codes.

47. See, e.g., French Code of Civil Procedure, art. 275. See *infra* Chapter 8, Section 3(h) at 795 (Expert Evidence).

48. See *infra* Chapter 8, Section 5 at 855 (Procedural Treatment of Concurrent Criminal and Civil Liability).

there will be strong opposition, particularly from large corporations and other actors with evidence and information to hide.

It is interesting to observe that U.S. pretrial discovery is directly traceable to Roman and especially to Canon law.[49]

Edge: These relative weaknesses of "discovery" in the civil-law systems must play a large role in the strategic planning of lawyers who are contemplating transnational litigation and find they have a choice between a forum in the United States and a civil-law forum.[50]

Comparovich: There are many factors that influence a lawyer's choice of forum in international litigation, such as differences in substantive law and choice-of-law rules, location of assets and witnesses, efficiency and reliability of the legal system, ease of enforcement, potential amount of the award, availability of punitive damages, standard of proof, ease in proving facts, amount and recoverability of costs and attorney's fees, and many others.[51] But my experience has been that the availability of discovery looms larger than all the other factors.

Sometimes, a plaintiff engaged or intending to engage in litigation in a civil-law country will go so far as to institute a second action in the U.S. without ever intending to bring the case to trial, merely for the purpose of obtaining the advantage of American-style discovery. Since a litigant may do whatever it pleases with the material obtained through discovery (unless there is a protective order or party agreement), he or she is free to use it in litigation in a foreign court.

If, in such a case, the defendant moves to dismiss or stay the American action on forum non conveniens grounds, and the court concludes the case could more conveniently be tried abroad, the court can relegate the plaintiff to a trial in the foreign tribunal, yet let him have the benefit of American-style discovery. Several techniques are available to accomplish this. The court may (a) defer a ruling on the forum non conveniens motion until after discovery is completed,[52] or (b) "dismiss subject to the condition that defendant corporations agree to provide the records relevant to the plaintiff's claims."[53]

49. See Millar, The Mechanism of Fact Discovery: A Study in Comparative Civil Procedure, 32 Ill.L.Rev. 261, 424 (1937).

50. American courts have taken cognizance of the relative weakness of discovery in civil-law countries. See, e.g., Pain v. United Technologies Corp., 637 F.2d 775, 789 (D.C.Cir.1980), cert. denied, 454 U.S. 1128, 102 S.Ct. 980 (1981).

If the allegedly more convenient alternative forum is a civil-law jurisdiction, such weakness may be a factor militating against forum non conveniens dismissal of an action brought in an American court. See, e.g., Mobil Tankers Co., S.A. v. Mene Grande Oil Co.,

363 F.2d 611 (3d Cir.1966); cf. Forum Non Conveniens in Products Liability Cases, 76 A.L.R.4th 22 (1990).

51. Some of the factors determining the choice between a civil-law and a common-law forum are interestingly discussed in the Court's opinion in Piper Aircraft Co. v. Reyno, 454 U.S. 235, 102 S.Ct. 252, 263–64, especially note 18 (1981), citing an earlier edition of this book.

52. See Omnium Lyonnais v. Dow Chemical Co., 73 F.R.D. 114 (C.D.Cal.1977).

53. See Piper Aircraft Co. v. Reyno, *supra* note 51, note 25. But see In re Union Carbide Corp. Gas Plant Disaster, 809 F.2d

In a recent case, a party in France used a different approach. After a suit in the commercial court in Paris had been appealed to the intermediate appellate court, where the proceedings were to be *de novo*, one of the parties sought to take depositions in the United States under the rules concerning assistance to foreign courts. It does not appear that the Paris court had actually asked for any assistance. The Second Circuit granted the request, holding that it was for the French courts to decide whether to accept the evidence so produced.[54]

(f) Party and Witness Statements

Smooth: To come back to our case, there was a second reason for my confusion regarding the court's order calling for the personal appearance of H in court. I had always thought that in civil-law countries the parties were incompetent to testify.[1]

Comparovich: There is a vast misunderstanding in this area. The civilians hold to the idea that a party cannot be a "witness" in the traditional sense. There are some reasons for this. First, it is considered that a party does not need to testify in her favor because anything she has to say about the facts of the case will be said on her behalf by her own attorney in the complaint and in the briefs exchanged afterwards. Second, a party's testimony is considered untrustworthy anyway. Moreover, the parties' contentions are mere allegations, not really evidence. Also, historically, when the oath had some religious significance, it was thought to be unfair to put a party in a position to have to choose between winning a case or burning in hell. Therefore, a party should never be forced to testify under oath.

However, there are several reasons why a court needs to hear what a party has to say, not only because she is most knowledgeable about the facts, but also because sometimes, she is the only person with knowledge about some facts.

There is great variation on the way civil-law countries regulate the party statement in open court, but it is possible to make some very general comments.[2]

195, 205–06 (2d Cir.1987), cert. denied, 484 U.S. 871, 108 S.Ct. 199 (1987), holding that the court cannot, as a condition for dismissing the suit to be tried in India, impose a requirement that the American party (which had sought the dismissal) must agree to discovery in the United States under American rules in the Indian action because, once the case is dismissed, the court has no power to enforce an equivalent condition against the Indian party.

54. See Euromepa S.A. v. R. Esmerian, Inc., 51 F.3d 1095 (2d Cir.1995).

1. At common law—at least since the 16th century—parties were not competent to testify as witnesses. But throughout the common-law world, this rule has been changed by statutes enacted since the middle of the 19th century.

2. See, *e.g.*, the Codes of Civil Procedure of Italy (arts. 116–17 and 228–231), Germany (§§ 445–55), Spain (arts. 300–16), France (arts. 184–198), Portugal (arts. 552–67), Brazil (arts. 342–48), Belgium (art. 992–1004) the Netherlands (art. 164), Japan (149, 151, and 207–11). See van Rhee (ed.), European Traditions in Civil Procedure 187–89 and 235–65 (2005).

In some countries, the court may order the parties to make an oral statement to clarify the facts of the case. In other countries, although a party can never call herself to the witness stand, she can call the opponent (or a co-party) to extract adverse statements or confessions. In Germany, a party that wishes to make an oral statement may request the opponent's consent or a court waiver, if there is no consent.

The questioning of the party proceeds in the same way as the questioning of witnesses, including questions from the opponent, except that the party is never put under oath. Therefore, contrary to what happens with witnesses, the consequences of a lie are merely procedural and not criminal. As we will see below, traditionally, witnesses are questioned by the judge, not by the parties directly as is the rule in common-law countries. Whenever a party wants to ask a question, it must do so through the judge.[3]

Some countries allow only adverse statements to have any evidentiary effect. In other countries, even when the interrogated party makes only self-serving statements, the effect of such statements is governed by the principle of free evaluation.[4]

In some countries, the court may draw adverse inferences from the party's refusal to participate, to answer a specific question, or to present evasive answers, unless there is a legitimate reason for refusal, such as irrelevance, privilege, self incrimination, personal embarrassment, trade or state secret, etc. In other countries, the refusal to participate or to answer is considered an outright confession. In some countries, courts are hesitant to rely solely on an uncorroborated testimony of a party, but normally, there will be corroborating evidence in the record, because of the absence of exclusionary rules of evidence.

These civilian methods also tend to influence the practice of international arbitration tribunals, whenever the arbitrators, or a majority of them, have been brought up in the civil law.[5]

Edge: Yet, I have heard of cases in which, a party may be put under oath in civil-law countries.[6]

Comparovich: You are probably referring to the "decisory oath," an archaic device still in use in some countries like France, Belgium, Italy, and Luxembourg.[7]

---

3. See *supra* at 781.

4. The German Code of Civil Procedure (§ 453) is explicit on this point. Art. 198 of the French Code of Civil Procedure is similar in its effect.

5. See, e.g., M. Straus, The Practice of the Iran–U.S. Claims Tribunal in Receiving Evidence from Parties and from Experts, 3 J.Int. Arbitration 57 (1986).

6. See in the Matter of Rutherfurd's Estate, 182 Misc. 1019, 46 N.Y.S.2d 871 (1944).

7. See French Civil Code, arts. 1357–1369 and Code of Civil Procedure, arts. 317–22; Italian Civil Code, arts. 2736–39, 2960 and Code of Civil Procedure, arts. 233–43; Belgian Civil Code, art. 1358–69; Luxembourgian Civil Code, arts. 1358–65. The Spanish Civil Code, arts. 1236–38, also provided for the decisory oath, but these provisions were revoked by the Code of Civil Procedure enacted in 2000. See Merryman & Pérez-Perdomo, The Civil Law Tradition. An Introduction to the Legal Systems of Europe and Latin America (third edition) 119–120 (2007).

The gist of it is that a party, being unable to prove a disputed fact (let us call it fact X) in any other way, may "defer an oath" to an opponent, provided it is within his or her personal knowledge, and the matter involved rights the party may freely dispose of (thus, e.g., not the existence of a marriage).

This is done by asking the opponent to affirm, under oath, the proposition that X is true. The court then fixes a time and place for the hearing in which the oath will be taken. If the party does not take the oath, the truth of fact X is deemed conclusively established in favor of the opponent who demanded the oath. If, on the other hand, the party takes the oath, this is treated as conclusive proof of fact X for the purposes of the proceeding. In either case, there is no issue of credibility for the court to determine, and judgment will be entered accordingly.

If, subsequently, fact X, although affirmed in a decisory oath, should turn out to be untrue, the judgment entered cannot be set aside. The only remedies are a criminal prosecution for perjury and damages.

To add a complicated twist to this already confusing device, the person may "refer" the oath back to the party who originally "deferred" it, thus asking the latter to affirm, under oath, that X is untrue. The procedure is the same above, except that the roles of the parties are reversed.

Some civil-law systems have also preserved a variant of the decisory oath called "supplemental oath." The latter is not "deferred" by a party but ordered by the court on its own motion. The name derives from the fact that it is supposed to supplement the incomplete evidence available in the record, as when there is some evidence tending to prove fact Y, but it is not quite sufficient. In such a case the court may order the party asserting Y to affirm by a supplemental oath. The supplemental oath cannot be "referred back" to an opponent, as with the decisory oath. There is disagreement as to whether the supplemental oath has the same conclusive effect as the decisory oath.

The history of the decisory oath dates back to Roman Law.[8] Whether or not stemming from the same original source as the Roman decisory oath, there is a similar device in Islamic and in Jewish law.[9]

For a 21st Century observer, only a naive person would put herself in the position of losing a case by putting the outcome of the lawsuit exclusively in the hands of the opponent. However, to fully understand this device, it is important to observe that a party will normally only use the decisory oath as a last resort, i.e., if she does not have any other means of discharging her burden of proof. So the party would lose the case any way. The case may even be on appeal. Also, historically speaking, for a God

8. See Millar, The Formative Principles of Civil Procedure, 18 Ill. L. Rev. 94 (1923); Silving, The Oath, 68 Yale L.J. 1329, 1338–40 (1959).

9. See Hellman v. Wolbrom, 31 A.D.2d 477, 479, 298 N.Y.S.2d 540 (1st Dept.1969);

Liebesny, Comparative Legal History: Its Role in the Analysis of Islamic and Modern Near Eastern Legal Institutions, 20 Am. J.Comp.L. 38, 46–51 (1972).

fearing individual, the risk of eternal damnation was a significant deterrent.

The use of the decisory oath seems quite unrealistic in our society, and the historical interest of the decisory oath is greater than its present-day practical significance. Insofar as Western legal systems are concerned, even where codes have preserved the decisory oath, it is not frequently used. The unsworn interrogation of parties, introduced in modern times and mentioned above is, where available, much more frequent.

Edge: When we were engaged in our litigation with Mr. H, it occurred to me that it might embarrass H if he were forced to affirm his mendacious allegations under oath. We, therefore, wrote to our lawyer in Ruritania and asked him to consider whether a decisory oath should be deferred to H. The lawyer answered that Ruritania had abolished the decisory oath almost half a century ago.

Comparovich: Indeed, the decisory oath existed in most countries, but they started abolishing it about a century ago.

Some civil-law countries, nowadays, like Germany, follow a device first developed in Austria. Adapting certain aspects of the old supplemental oath and combining them with some features consciously borrowed from the deposition procedure developed in English Chancery practice,[10] the Austrian reformers have created a system under which the court has broad discretionary power to order the personal appearance of the parties and to interrogate them. As we saw above, no oath is administered to a party *before* the interrogation; but *after* it, the court, acting in the light of the parties' demeanor and in light of all the other evidence in the record, may in its discretion give one of them an opportunity to affirm its testimony by an oath. This device is used when the court is not sufficiently convinced by the unsworn testimony, but feels the testimony should be believed if reaffirmed under oath.[11]

The court is prevented from putting both parties under oath so as to avoid the spectacle of conflicting partisan oaths.

In some countries, this policy is extended, and a similar rule of selective admission to the oath is applied, to interested witnesses.

This oath is not conclusive, but subject to free evaluation of the affiant's credibility. However, since the party admitted to the oath normally will be the one whose version of the facts appeared more plausible to the

10. See E. J. Cohn, New Regulations in the German Code of Civil Procedure, 17 J.Comp.Leg. & Int'l L. (3d ser.) 73, 79–80 (1935); Pekelis, Legal Techniques and Political Ideologies: A Comparative Study, 41 Mich.L.Rev. 665, 679 (1943). The wheel thus turned full cycle. The chancery practice of party interrogation had in turn been borrowed from continental, Romano–Canonistic procedure. See Hickman v. Taylor, 329 U.S. 495, 515, 67 S.Ct. 385, 395 (1947); (concurring opinion by Jackson, J.); Ragland, Discovery Before Trial 13–16 (1932); Coing, English Equity and the Denunciatio Evangelica of the Canon Law, 71 L.Q.Rev. 223, at 237–38 (1955).

11. See, e.g., German Code of Civil Procedure (art. 452).

court in the first place, chances are that in practice, the party oath thus administered will determine the outcome of the case.

Theoretically, it would seem that countries that still have the supplemental oath have the same power as a German court: to end the interrogation of the parties by permitting one of them to affirm its version of the facts by an oath. This result could be accomplished by first interrogating the parties as described above and then administering a "supplemental oath" to one of them. But it appears that the courts in practice hardly ever make use of this possibility.

Smooth: I am beginning to understand the civilian methods of examining parties. Yet, there is another point that puzzles me in connection with the court's order directing the examination of H. Doesn't the civil law require a writing for every contract involving more than a trifling sum?

Comparovich: You are correct. Some civil-law countries provide that contracts involving matters above a certain amount must be celebrated in writing (or through a notary). Except when authorized by law, one cannot prove the matters in a contract subjected to this rule using witnesses exclusively. Witness may be used, however, to supplement a beginning of written proof.[12]

There are certain exceptions to these formalistic rules. Common exceptions are when the person, through no fault of his own, loses the document, or when he was not in a position to request a written document. The Italian Civil Code, while in principle adhering to the French rule, grants the court discretionary power to admit testimonial evidence of contracts "having regard to the character of the parties, the nature of the contract and any other circumstances." Therefore the judge may accept proof by witnesses exclusively, when the type of transaction is customarily made orally (trade usage), when the person is illiterate[13] etc.

These restrictions are usually applicable only to "civil" and not "commercial" transactions. The Commercial Code, therefore, may establish the "principle of freedom of proof" and authorize oral testimony for the proof of commercial transactions.[14]

12. See the Civil Codes of France (arts. 1341–48), Italy (arts. 2721–26), Belgium (art. 1341), Luxembourg (art. 1341–48), Brazil (arts. 227), Argentina (art. 1193). Countries that have recently updated their rules on the amount may provide for an amount equivalent of about U.S.$1,000.00 (France and Brazil) or U.S.$3,000.00 (Luxembourg and Argentina). The Italian Civil Code, however, still specifies an amount equivalent of U.S.$4 and the Belgian Code, U.S.$500.

13. Today, the problem of illiteracy is no longer a significant one in Italy; but it plays an important role in developing countries, many of which have a legal system based on, or modeled after, the French codes. Some of them have found it necessary to modify the requirement of written and notarial form for the transactions of illiterates, because notarial services are not easily available in their rural areas. See, e.g., Farnsworth, Law Reform in a Developing Country: A New Code of Obligations for Senegal, 8 J.Afr.L. 6 (1964).

14. See, e.g., the Commercial Codes of France (article L 110–3), Belgium (section 25). This illustrates the importance of the distinction between civil and commercial

Such general restrictions exist mainly in countries with a predominantly French influence. They do not exist in countries of Germanic influence, like Germany, Switzerland, and Austria.[15]

These restrictions are but one example of the low esteem that oral evidence traditionally has in the civil-law tradition. We discussed this matter above, when we were discussing the oral deposition of witnesses and a party's statements in court.[16] In 1975, however, the French Civil Code was amended to provide that the declarations made by a party at her personal appearance in court [informal interrogation] as well as her refusal to answer or failure to appear at the interrogation may be considered by the court as the equivalent of a beginning of written proof.

In addition to the restrictions above, certain types of transactions are subject to special provisions requiring notarial form.

Smooth: Apparently, Ruritania had no such restrictions or, at least, they were not applicable to us.

Comparovich: If the Ruritanian code contained similar provisions, the court would have been faced with an interesting conflict of laws question. The French courts in a celebrated case enforced an oral contract made in England which, had it been made in France, would not have been enforceable.[17]

The same result would probably follow today, under the terms of the Convention on the Law Applicable to Contractual Obligations, done at Rome, on June 19, 1980. Article 9.1 provides (except in the case of consumer contracts) that a contract concluded by persons in the same country is valid if it satisfies either the form requirements of the place where it has been concluded or those of the place the law of which regulates the contract's substance. An analogous result would seem to follow in Germany even apart from the convention under the very similar Article 11 of the Introductory Law for the German Civil Code.

In the United States, the tendency has been to disregard the question of whether requirements of form for contracts are matters of substance or procedure and instead focus on an approach based on the closest connection or the "dominant interests." This would undoubtedly be applied in the majority of States to the converse question of whether an oral contract made in France in disregard of Article 1341 could be enforced in a jurisdiction not having similar legislation.[18]

Edge: Even assuming that Ruritania had adopted the same requirements of written contract, and further assuming that the Ruritanian court

---

courts. See *supra* Chapter 6, Section 3(b) at 494 (discussing commercial courts).

15. For an interesting comparative discussion of form requirements, see J. M. Perillo, The Statute of Frauds in the Light of the Functions and Dysfunctions of Form, 43 Fordham L.Rev. 39 (1974).

16. See *supra* this section.

17. See Benton v. Horeau, decided by the French Cour de Cassation on August 24, 1880, Dalloz 1880. 1. 447, discussed by Judge Coleman in Mandelbaum v. Silberfeld, 77 N.Y.S.2d 465, 469 (City Ct.1944), and by Lorenzen, The Statute of Frauds and the Conflict of Laws, 32 Yale L.J. 311, 318–20 (1923).

18. Auten v. Auten, 308 N.Y. 155, 124 N.E.2d 99 (1954).

would apply these provisions to a contract made and performable in the United States, this might not have helped us. After all, the correspondence showed there were serious negotiations looking toward a contract. Didn't this constitute "a beginning of written proof"?

Comparovich: Perhaps. Whether the correspondence "makes the alleged fact probable" is a question of fact.[19] However, all this is purely academic because Ruritania has not adopted any general restriction on oral proof of contracts. Of course, Ruritania, like all civil-law countries, subjects certain *types* of transactions to the requirement of a simple writing or of a notarial document; but it does not have a sweeping, *general* rule comparable to the French Law tradition.

Note, however, that these restrictions are not totally foreign to the common law tradition. One only needs to remember the 300 year old English Statute of Frauds (requiring certain contracts to be signed and in writing)[20] and the parole evidence rule (barring a party to a written contract from presenting evidence against its content). Although virtually abolished in England in 1954, such restrictions are still common in the U.S., although they have a much more limited scope than in civil-law countries. The irony is that, in the U.S., the restrictions apply generally to commercial contracts, not to contracts among private parties, whereas in civil-law countries, the restrictions apply only to contracts among private parties, not to commercial contracts.

Smooth: The interlocutory order further provided that Ms. Edge and I should testify concerning our conversation with H.

Comparovich: Aren't you officers of the defendant corporation?

Smooth: I am a Vice–President, but Ms. Edge is not a corporate officer. I suppose this was the reason why the order designated only Ms. Edge as a witness. With respect to me, it directed that "defendant corporation appear personally by its legal representative, Mr. Malcolm Smooth," and be examined in the same manner as the plaintiff.

Comparovich: This is merely a logical application of the civilian view that the two concepts, "party" and "witness," are mutually exclusive. Was your testimony taken here, by way of letters rogatory?[21]

---

19. See Planiol–Ripert, Treatise on the Civil Law (11th ed. 1939), Translation by the Louisiana State Law Institute, Vol. 2, Part 1, Sec. 1124 (1959). For a reaffirmation by the French *Cour de cassation* of the principle that what suffices as a beginning of written proof is a matter essentially within the discretion of the courts below see, Epx Aubriet v. Cts. Collet, Cass.civ.1st, June 27, 1995, 1996 D.J. 133.

20. See, e.g., Restatement Second of Contracts, § 111; U.C.C. § 2–201 ("Formal Requirements; Statute of Frauds. (1) Except as otherwise provided in this section a contract for the sale of goods for the price of $500 or more is not enforceable by way of action or defense unless there is some writing sufficient to indicate that a contract for sale has been made between the parties and signed by the party against whom enforcement is sought or by his authorized agent or broker.")

21. Cf. 28 U.S.C.A. § 1782.

Smooth: No. We did not object to being examined in Ruritania, because we had some other business to which we had to attend in that part of the world.

Edge: What struck us, however, was that, under the terms of the interlocutory order, the examination of Mr. Smooth and myself was to take place, not in the presence of the whole three-judge court, but before a single member of that court.

Comparovich: Such is the practice in many civil-law countries.

In some civil-law countries, the single judge charged with preparing the case for the court's final decision has the power to issue and execute the interlocutory orders for the taking of evidence. Once the case is ripe for a final decision, i.e., when all evidence is taken and put in the file, it goes back to the full three-judge chamber. This, at least, is the practice prevailing in civil-law countries that still have three judge panels, and, in some of them, it is required that there be a final hearing before the full chamber. We have already discussed the more radical innovation recently adopted in Germany and France, which makes it possible to transfer a case to a single member of the chamber for proof-taking *and final determination.*[22]

Smooth: That means that factual issues ultimately must be decided by three judges, only one of whom has seen and heard the witnesses.

Comparovich: Quite so. This is the feature of present-day continental procedure that has been most arduously criticized.[23] It violates the "principle of immediacy" advocated by most leading scholars and especially by Franz Klein, the famous Austrian proceduralist of the late 19th century.[24] On the other hand, there is a practical problem of economy and of limited judicial resources, even though in most civil-law countries the number of judges is greater than in the U.S. For these reasons, in Germany, where the principle of "immediacy" is considered particularly important, the use of the single judge for hearing witnesses in a three-judge court was expanded in the 1990s. Since the 2002 reforms, the general rule has been that one member of the panel hears and decides the case as a single judge, unless one of the legal exceptions applies or the case proves to be complex or significant.[25]

Edge: When we travelled to Ruritania, we looked forward to being confronted with H and to seeing him squirm under our vigorous cross-examination.

---

22. See *supra* at 493ff.

23. See, e.g., 1 Cappelletti, La testimonianza della parte nel sistema dell'oralitá 149 ff. (1962).

24. See Lenhoff, The Law of Evidence: A Comparative Study Based Essentially on Austrian and New York Law, 3 Am. J.Comp.L. 313, 318 (1954).

U.S. law has many comparable examples of procedural arrangements under which is-

sues of fact may be determined by a judge who has never personally seen or heard the witnesses. See, e.g., FRCP 53(c)(1)(C). Due Process attacks on such arrangements, which in civil-law parlance violate the "principle of immediacy," have been rejected. See Razatos v. The Colorado Supreme Court, 549 F.Supp. 798 (D.Colo.1982), and cases there cited.

25. Murray & Stürner, German Civil Justice 53–54 and 210–212 (2004)

Comparovich: I am sure you were doubly disappointed. The presiding judge does not have to hear all of the witnesses (or parties) at the same time. Also, there is really no "cross-examination" of witnesses. But the judge usually has the discretionary power to confront witnesses with each other (or parties), and witnesses normally must be heard in the presence of the parties and their lawyers.[26]

Edge: We discovered that. As H had a professional engagement on the day set for our examination, the judge interrogated us but adjourned H's examination to a date two weeks later. As to cross-examination, we learned that it simply does not exist.

Comparovich: The interrogation of witnesses varies from country to country and also depends on the peculiarities of each case and the personalities of each judge.[27] Traditionally in civil-law countries, all the questioning is done by the judge, not by the parties, as is the rule in the common law. After administering the oath, the judge starts by summarizing the general subject of the examination, and then asks the witness to give a narrative of her version of the facts on her own words. After this open examination, the judge may ask more specific questions to clarify or supplement the witness statements or to probe into the witness's credibility.

Every witness is heard individually, in the absence of other witnesses who have not testified yet. The court on its own initiative of at the request of one of the parties may confront witnesses face to face with each other and with the parties, especially in case of conflicting testimonies.

If the court is composed of a panel of three judges, one of them will be appointed as the presiding judge to take the evidence and do the report. If there is more than one judge, the presiding judge must allow every member of the court to ask questions.

After the court's interrogation, the parties have the right to request the court to ask further questions, but it is ultimately the judge who asks these questions, and not necessarily in the exact form proposed by the attorneys.[28] A judge will not ask a question that is irrelevant, repetitive, leading, privileged or with intent to harass the witness, and may rephrase a question improperly asked. In some civil-law countries, parties have a more limited role in questioning witnesses: all a party may do is to pose questions through the court, never directly to the witness. In other countries, the court may permit counsel to address questions directly to the witnesses, usually after the court's interrogation.[29] But anything resembling a U.S. cross-examination is rare.[30]

---

26. See, e.g., the Codes of Civil Procedure of France (arts. 208–215), Belgium (arts. 933–944).

27. See, e.g., the Codes of Civil Procedure of Germany (arts. 373–400), France (arts. 204–31), Japan (art. 190–206).

28. See, e.g., the Codes of Civil Procedure of France (art. 214) and Belgium (art. 936), both providing that the parties may

neither interrupt, nor address, or seek to influence the witnesses when they testify. All questioning must be conducted by the court.

29. In Germany, such permission must be granted upon counsel's express demand if the question is admissible. See German Code of Civil Procedure (§ 397).

30. But see Murray & Stürner, German Civil Justice 53–54 and 296–97 (2004) (ob-

These rules are consistent with the absence of a jury. Since the judge is the trier of fact, he is the one who ultimately must be convinced of the facts, and he is the most appropriate person to conduct the questioning. This task also keeps judges "awake" during boring sessions and explains somewhat the overriding position of the judge in civil-law litigation. However, the parties, who have more knowledge of the facts and more interest in ascertaining the truth, are precluded from participating in the process of taking evidence.

A consequence of these rules is that civil-law attorneys do not have a refined skill of questioning and cross examining witnesses, and may be at a disadvantage in international arbitrations conducted under common law rules.

Some countries provide that a court may question more than one witness at the same time and confront them. Even in countries that do not have this provision, a judge may do so under the broad powers of evidence taking.

In most civil-law countries, moreover, a witness testimony is not taken *verbatim*, and the judge dictates a summary of the testimony to the clerk. Thus, only the summary of the answers becomes part of the record. There is the constant danger that, in formulating the summary, the judge will unintentionally alter its meaning. Attentive lawyers may try to correct the court, but one may only intervene so many times before irritating the judge. In some countries, the court reporter himself is in charge of summarizing the testimony.[31]

In Sweden, unless the court directs otherwise, witnesses are questioned in a proceeding very similar to the one used in the U.S. This practice has been in effect for several decades. The parties' attorneys ask questions directly to the witnesses. The party who called the witness starts the "principal examination," and then the opponent may cross-examine the witness through leading questions. In some circumstances, such as if there is antagonism between the witness and the party, if a party is not represented by counsel, or if the witness is nervous, the court may conduct the examination.[32] This flexibility is possible only in a system with no jury.

Since World War II in Japan, at least in principle, the examination of witnesses proceeds in a fashion similar to the U.S., and the lawyers now conduct the questioning, a role formerly reserved to the judge in the pre-occupation period. The general rule is that a witness will be examined first

serving that in Germany the party may challenge the credibility and probe the witness in ways resembling a "more restrained and less dramatic" cross-examination).

31. This was the rule in Japan, but now, the courts record the hearing and transcribe the tapes. See Japanese Rules of Civil Procedure, art. 68. See Taniguchi, Reich & Miyake, Civil Procedure in Japan 7–101 (2008).

32. See Lindell, Civil Procedure in Sweden 181–84 (2004); Swedish Code of Civil Procedure, art. 36:17; Ginsburg and Bruzelius, Civil Procedure in Sweden 288 (1965).

by the party who called her (direct examination), then by the opponent (cross examination), and only then by the court. Because there is no jury, the judge may interrupt at any time.[33] However, the court may change this order and ask questions first.[34] Some commentators have expressed a skeptical view of whether the U.S.-style is really working in Japan.[35]

Smooth: The traditional civil-law system of interrogation seems an invitation to mendacity. I was trained to believe, with John Henry Wigmore, that cross-examination is "the greatest legal engine ever invented for the discovery of truth".

Comparovich: You have a point to a certain extent. Civilians, on the other hand, may argue that the spontaneous narrative of an uncoached[36] witness is preferable to an artificial and (so far as direct examination is concerned) often pre-arranged series of questions and answers. And, naturally, the power of cross-examination may also contribute to distort the facts, especially by discrediting otherwise honest witnesses. Of course, civilians are not unaware of the problem of lying witnesses, but often believe this is an inherent problem of oral testimony. Countries with a French influence in particular often use written evidence in situations in which this would not be possible in the United States. The practice started in an informal way under the Old Code of Civil Procedure. The courts freely admitted written statements and affidavits by persons having knowledge of the facts in lieu of oral testimony given in court.

Lawyers would also sometimes ask a process server (*huissier de justice*) to go to a certain place and then describe the event or place observed. The record of that observation is considered evidence at trial. Since a process server is a semi-public officer, much like a notary, such a statement (*constatation*) has a high degree of effectiveness.[37]

The French Code of Civil Procedure has formalized the use of written sworn statements as proof of fact, called *attestation*.[38] It considers such affidavits as the equivalent of oral testimony and admissible whenever oral testimony is admissible. Such statements must be handwritten and contain

---

33. See art. 113(3) of the Japanese Rules of Civil Procedure

34. See art. 202 of the Japanese Code of Civil Procedure.

35. See Goodman, Justice and Civil Procedure in Japan 358–63 (2004) (commenting on the awkward difficulty of Japanese lawyers to master the arts of examination and cross-examination after the American Occupation [insensitively] imposed such proceedings in Japan and stressing their incompatibility with a system that does not follow the adversary model. The author also observes that although all aspects of the U.S. trial are present, the Japanese trial is completely different).

36. See *supra* p. 755, note 30 and related text.

37. Before French divorce law was liberalized, such statements were often used in divorce cases as proof of adultery (so-called *constat d'adultère*). Of course, the presence of the process-server at a place bespeaking adultery, such as the exit from a hotel in the morning, where the future defendant with the "other woman" or "other man" just happened to be, was frequently pre-arranged by both parties to bypass the limitations of the law.

38. See French Code of Civil Procedure arts. 199–203, enacted in 1975.

a statement that the author is aware that false statements may lead to criminal prosecution.[39]

Although the law expressly requires that the affiant must have personal knowledge of the facts, in France there is no prohibition against production of hearsay evidence. Therefore, it is for the court to decide to what extent testimony is to be discounted or even disregarded because of its indirect character. Letters, for instance, are frequently used as proof of the facts therein recited or to show a state of mind etc.[40]

No particular procedure is necessary for them to be introduced into the record, except that they must be submitted to the opponent for review as a corollary of the adversary system. The parties will generally obtain them on their own and attach them to the pleadings after having made them available to the opposing side, as is the case with other documents. The court may also order its production *sua sponte*.

There is no question that the procedure of filing witnesses' affidavits on the court record is a much more efficient and cheaper way to produce evidence than the time and energy-consuming personal interrogation of each witness. However, it is also much less reliable. Therefore, if necessary, the judge may request that a person providing a written statement appear in person in a hearing for oral interrogation. In practice, however, this rarely happens, and French proceedings are frequently decided on an exclusively written record of documents and affidavits.

The French Code enacted in 1975 has continued, in modified form, the practice of *constatation*. The Court may charge any person (but in practice it is usually a process server, i.e., a *huissier*) to observe a place, event, etc and report to the court. The report is normally written but may be oral, in which case it must be taken down by the clerk and filed in the *dossier*. The report (*constatation*) must relate facts only and may not contain any opinions.[41]

The use of affidavits may be considered a new trend in comparative civil procedure, a trend that goes directly against the sacred cow of the 20th Century, the principle of orality. Because of its strong commitment to the principle of orality, in German civil procedure, the use of writings has long been much more restricted than in France. In an attempt to streamline procedures, their use was expanded in 1990. The innovation, modeled on the French procedure, has not been as widely used as it is in France.[42] The German rule was thereafter further transplanted into Japanese law: if the parties do not object, a Japanese court may submit the questions proposed

---

39. See French Criminal Code, art. 441–7 (providing for prison term up to three years and a fine of up to 45,000 Euros, for both the person making as well as the person using a false affidavit).

40. See generally, Bruckner, The Taking of Evidence in France, 5 Transnat'l Lawyer 759 (1992).

41. See the French Code of Civil Procedure (arts. 249–55).

42. See German Code of Civil Procedure § 377(3), as amended in 1990.

by the parties in writing to the witness and accept the answers in a memorandum.[43]

The device was embraced also by the ALI/Unidroit, Principles and Rules of Transnational Civil Procedure because it would be more efficient and cheaper to obtain testimony. The Reporters observed that affidavits might be of particular value when related to facts that are not in serious dispute, but demonstrated certain skepticism of the practice, especially if another party challenges the statements in the affidavit.[44]

However, the trend has had some opposition. The Zurich Court of Appeals rendered a judgment in 2003 in which it explicitly said that written witness statements are not valid testimony in Swiss court proceedings and the court cannot take it into account as evidence when rendering the judgment. The Court also held that if a written witness statement has been provided with the assistance of counsel, this witness is not uninfluenced and thus may lack credibility, even if he or she confirms the written statement at on oral hearing conducted by the judge.[45]

Smooth: The argument about the advantages of "spontaneous," as opposed to "guided," witness testimony leaves me cold, and the use of written statements instead or oral testimony even more so.

Comparovich: Personally, and speaking on the basis of practical experience under both systems, I share your belief that the U.S. method of examining witnesses results in a more vigorous and, as a rule, a more effective search for truth.[46] But the point is highly controversial, and even the admirers of the U.S. method must recognize that the common-law system of examination by counsel contributes to the inordinate cost of litigation in this country and in England,[47] a condition which is further aggravated by the fact that in so many cases in the U.S., attorneys go over the same ground twice, first in pre-trial depositions and then again at trial.

Edge: Apart from the merits and demerits of the two systems, it seems that the differences between civil-law and common-law methods of examin-

---

43. See Japanese Code of Civil Procedure, art. 205 and 278 and Rules of Civil Procedure, art. 124 (both enacted in 1996). The device exists in exceptional circumstances in Sweden, including whenever there are "special reasons" with respect to costs or inconvenience. See Lindell, Civil Procedure in Sweden 184–86 (2004).

44. See Rule 23.4 and Comment R–23F; ALI/UNIDROIT, Principles of Transnational Civil Procedure (2006).

45. Judgment of Zurich Court of Appeal of 24 October 2003, ZR 106 (2007) 65.

46. The remark in the text is limited to civil proceedings. In a criminal case, where the presiding judge of a civil-law court, in interrogating the defendant and the witnesses, has the benefit of a thorough official investigation conducted prior to the trial, the situation is quite different. See *infra* Chapter 8, Section 4 at 828 (Criminal Procedure).

47. Amos, A Day in Court at Home and Abroad, 2 Camb.L.J. 340, 348–49 (1926) (stating that "A foreigner would be likely to say that in the pursuit of technical perfection we have thrown too great a share of the task of bringing out the truth upon the parties themselves or their professional advisers and representatives. The day in court puts a great premium upon forensic skill; and its necessary corollary, an adequate system of preparation, makes considerable demands upon the judgment and experience of solicitors and counsel. . . .")

ing witnesses may lead to practical problems in litigation pending before our own courts. If in such a case the deposition of a witness has been taken in a civil-law country and in accordance with civil-law methods, the question may arise whether such deposition will be admissible at a U.S. trial.[48]

Comparovich: For the federal courts, this troublesome question has been largely resolved by FRCP 28(b)(4) through language added in 1963: "Evidence obtained in response to a letter of request need not be excluded merely because it is not a verbatim transcript, because the testimony was not taken under oath, or because of any similar departure from the requirements for depositions taken within the United States."[49]

Edge: It is also interesting to consider the converse situation. What if the Ruritanian court, in an action pending there, addresses a letter rogatory to an American court, requesting that the testimony of a witness residing here be taken in accordance with Ruritanian methods of interrogation?

Comparovich: The U.S. District Courts are expressly authorized to comply with such a request. 28 U.S.C. § 1782 provides that a district court may take the testimony of a person using the procedure of the foreign country.[50] Thus it may happen that the civil-law methods of interrogation are practiced in an American courtroom. In practice, however, this task is apt to be performed by a magistrate rather than a district judge (28 U.S.C. § 636).

(g) The "trial" (Evidentiary Hearings)

Smooth: Let us come back to our case. The examination of Ms. Edge and of myself and the examination of H, two weeks later, produced no surprises. Each side stuck to its guns. After these hearings, our lawyer L asked us whether we had any further evidence to offer. This amazed me. I thought the trial was over.

Comparovich: As I said before, there is no such thing as a "trial" in continental civil procedure. Unless the court suspects you of dilatory tactics, you may always offer new evidence after some evidence has been taken. Sometimes, it is only through the examination of one witness that a new witness or document is discovered, or a new field of inquiry is opened up.

The court will hold a series of conference-like evidentiary hearings that will proceed at irregular intervals, taking evidence and preparing the record of the case (*dossier*) for a final decision.[1]

---

48. See H. Smit, International Aspects of Federal Court Procedure, 61 Colum.L.Rev. 1031, 1058–59 (1961).

49. The principle has been made applicable in criminal cases as well. See United States v. Salim, 664 F.Supp. 682 (E.D.N.Y. 1987), aff'd 855 F.2d 944 (2d Cir.1988).

50. See also the discussion of the Evidence Convention, *infra* Chapter 8, Section 3(i) at 809 (Discovery and Gathering of Evidence Abroad).

1. See a more detailed description in M. Taruffo, Civil Procedure and the Path of a Civil Case, in J. Lena & U. Mattei, Introduction to Italian Law 158, 163–64 (2002).

Smooth: Is this not a piecemeal method of trying cases?

Comparovich: Indeed it is, but such a method has certain advantages. The testimony of a witness can always take an unexpected turn.[2] In that event, the piecemeal system gives the parties a chance to study such testimony, to conduct new investigations, and then, in light of such investigations (and of what the witness has said), to make further offers of proof.

Moreover, in a system without jury trial, in which the court not the parties is in charge of fact finding, this method seems to the the natural one to follow.

Edge: Under our system, a similar function is served by discovery, which lets the parties take an advance look at what the witness is likely to say at the trial.

Comparovich: True, but note that the U.S. system is much more wasteful in that, at least in theory, almost every witness has to testify twice, first by way of pretrial examination and a second time at trial. This is obviously only a theoretical possibility. In practice, most cases end either by settlement, summary judgment, or other types of dismissal without a trial. Only a small percentage of the cases, between 3 and 15% depending on the court, goes to trial. This reality makes the two systems similar to each other because discovery also is conducted piecemeal.

Under the civil-law system, each witness normally testifies only once, unless it is necessary to call the witness again. It is also possible that, if the case is tried *de novo* before the intermediate appellate court,[3] the same witness will be interrogated again; but in practice this is rare. Through the piecemeal system, the civilians thus manage, as a rule, to interrogate each witness only once, but nevertheless afford the parties an opportunity to meet the witness's (perhaps unexpected and possibly untrue) testimony by suitable counter-evidence.

The critics of the piecemeal system tend to emphasize its potential for delay. The efficiency with which a case is steered through a smaller or larger number of successive hearings varies not only from country to country, but even within a single country, from one court to another. Much depends on the personality of the presiding judge, and, of course, the caseload in the particular jurisdiction.

The hearing is the most complex aspect of civil-law proceeding, and the most difficult to make comparative generalizations, because it involves all aspects of what is known as pretrial and trial in the common-law procedure. There are so many variables that make it extremely complex, almost impossible, the task of outlining a "civil-law" hearing. Situated between the quick pleading phase and the furtive final decision, the hearing involves

---

2. The danger of such surprise developments is, of course, enhanced by the civilian rules and practices discouraging lawyers from interviewing witnesses in advance. See *supra* Chapter 8, Section 3(d) at 746 (Pleadings and Formation of Issues).

3. See the discussion of appeals, *infra* Chapter 6, Section 3(c) at 496 (Intermediate Court of Appeals).

almost everything in a proceeding. It involves a series of procedural acts, like making evidentiary decisions, taking all sorts of evidence (documents, experts, witnesses, and parties), meeting with parties and attorneys, etc. Therefore, more than a device or a moment in the proceeding, it is considered a phase: the preparatory phase (preparatory to a final judgment that it).

The proceeding of the preparatory phase will further depend on a miriad of other factors, such as the peculiarities of fact or law, the type of court, the behavior of the parties, the rules and practice, the personalities of the judge.

One particularly efficient German judge, sitting in Stuttgart in the late 1960s and early 1970s, persuaded his local colleagues to experiment with a novel calendar practice, which has become known as the "Stuttgart Model."The essence of this experiment is described as follows: "[Upon receipt of the complaint and the answer] the court deliberates on the measures to be taken in preparation for the trial. These may consist in demanding from the parties supplementation of the factual allegations contained in the pleadings, outlining the court's prima facie attitude to the legal problems involved and inviting comments thereon, requiring the submission of documents, etc. When the parties have complied with this order the case is set down for an oral hearing to which the personal appearance of the parties and all witnesses whose testimony appears relevant is ordered. At the oral hearing, which—in complete distinction from the habits of most German courts—is conceived as the one and only hearing, the court discusses the matter with the attorneys and parties and then examines the witnesses, after complying with the rules of the Code by making the prescribed 'order for evidence.' "[4] When the taking of evidence is completed, the court retires and deliberates and then announces its tentative conclusions to the parties and their counsel. This is followed by the final arguments of counsel, which naturally will focus on the crucial points revealed by the court's previous statement of its tentative conclusions. The final decision of the court is rendered within a week after the hearing.[5]

This experimental system was tried out not only at Stuttgart, but in some other localities as well. It is claimed that on average about 85–90% of civil proceedings employing the Stuttgart Model were disposed of—whether by settlement or judgment—in one hearing. Thus, the use of the piecemeal method remained necessary only in 10 to 15% of the cases (probably the more complicated ones).

Smooth: In this way, for the majority of cases there is a real "trial" in the common law sense of the term. Sounds like a good idea to me.

Comparovich: The German legislators were of the same opinion. In 1976, after the Stuttgart Model experiment had gone on for almost 10

---

4. See Cohn, Manual of German Law 201–02 (2d ed. 1971).

5. For a comprehensive description and discussion of the Stuttgart Model experiment by the judge who initiated it, see R. Bender, The Stuttgart Model, in Vol. II, Book 2, of M. Cappelletti (ed.), Access to Justice, at 431–75 (1979).

years, a statute was passed which strongly encouraged all German courts to adopt some of the Stuttgart Model practices.[6] The key provision of this important statutory reform is Section 272 of the Code of Civil Procedure, which, as amended by the 1976 statute, now postulates that, "As a rule, the case should be disposed of in a single, comprehensively prepared oral hearing (main hearing)."

The words "as a rule," which qualify the mandate of Section 272, still vest much discretion in the presiding judge of each court. Judges accustomed to the formerly prevailing system of piecemeal proof taking in successive hearings sometimes used that discretionary power to "fall back into the old trot."[7] On the whole, however, it appears the 1976 reform has had a measure of success in expediting civil litigation.[8]

Smooth: Assuming the majority of German courts attempt to comply with Section 272 and to dispose of a large percentage of their cases in a single trial, how do they implement the mandate of that provision that such trial must be "comprehensively prepared"?

Comparovich: The court does not conduct an investigation *sua sponte*. It is a basic principle of civil-law civil procedure that the parties and not the court determine the parameters of the litigation by their allegations. Equally fundamental, though subject to some limited exceptions,[9] is the principle that the court, in determining what evidence should be heard, is limited to such evidence as has been offered by the parties. These basic principles have not been altered by the German reform of 1976. Thus, in directing the court to prepare the "trial," the draftsmen of Section 272 were principally interested in ensuring that well before its date, the court will elicit all proper allegations and offers of proof *from the parties*.

Civil law countries have devised over the decades a complex balance between the autonomy of the parties and the active role of the judge in civil proceedings. This balance is not really well-understood and varies from country to country, from time to time, from court to court. However, it is a crucial element for understanding the civil-law procedure.

The autonomy of the parties is revered as a fundamental principle with several practical consequences in civil procedure. It is called *disposition-maxime* in German and *le principe dispositif* in French or the principle of

---

6. This was done by the "Simplification Amendment" (*Vereinfachungsnovelle*) to the Code of Civil Procedure, BGBl. 1976 I 3281. For a discussion, see Gottwald, Simplified Civil Procedure in West Germany, 31 Am. J.Comp.L. 687 (1983), and Fisch, Recent Developments in West German Civil Procedure, 6 Hastings Int'l & Comp.L.Rev. 221 (1983). For subsequent changes, see *supra* p. 780ff.

7. Baumbach–Lauterbach–Albers–Hartmann, Zivilprozessordnung, Anno. 4 preceding § 272 (45th ed., 1987).

8. See Gottwald, Simplified Civil Procedure in West Germany, 31 Am.J.Comp.L. 687, 700 (1983).

9. Pursuant to § 273 of the German Code of Civil Procedure, the court may ex officio procure certain types of evidence. For instance, the court may obtain public records, order the personal appearance of the parties, and appoint experts, all this without waiting for any offer of proof coming from the parties. Note, however, that the court cannot *sua sponte* subpoena non-expert witnesses who have not been named by the parties.

the adversarial proceeding in English. The parties must have full control of the proceeding. Civil Procedure in civil-law countries is an "adversarial" proceeding, not, as many common-law observers wrongly think, "inquisitorial." The common and civil-law procedures are "adversarial" in their own way: there is a common-law adversarial process and a civil-law adversarial process. It is the same thing, just different.

In common-law, "adversarial proceeding" has a connotation connected to the competitive nature of the proceeding, while this ideology does not exist in civil-law countries.

In contrast, by "adversarial proceedings", civil-law attorneys refer to the fact that the court is limited by the parties's claims, allegations of facts, and presentation of evidence. This does not mean, however, that the judge is a passive bystander or a mere umpire, as the traditional common-law judge. Although limited in the merits of the proceeding, the civil-law judge plays an active role with respect to the procedure. Among other things, the judge supervises the orderly evolution of the proceedings and compliance with procedural rules, making decisions within a reasonable time. This active role also implies that, in some civil-law countries, if the parties do not succeed in producing sufficient evidence, the judge may request *sua sponte* the production of any admissible evidence, whenever necessary for a decision on the merits (the scope of such power depends from country to country).[10] For example, the judge may order a complementary inquiry, including, the submission of certain documents, the hearing of witnesses, an official inspection, the personal appearance of the parties in court, the appointment of an expert.[11] However, the judge must at all times respect the right of the parties to be heard and give them an opportunity to give their points of view.[12]

A good example of how the French structures this balance is the fact that the judge may "invite" the parties to bring into the proceeding all interested parties whose presence appears necessary for the resolution of the dispute. However, the initiative of effectively bringing them into the proceeding rests with the parties.[13]

The worldwide trend in civil-law countries favors giving more power to the judge. Even in common law countries, the tendency is to stress the power of the "managerial judge", as the recent law reforms in the U.S. and England can easily demonstrate. There is a minority of civil-law scholars, however, who, fearful of abuse, see this as a very dangerous development and would favor a more passive judge, destitute of any initiative and power.

---

10. See the French Code of Civil Procedure (arts. 10 and 143).

11. See the French Code of Civil Procedure (arts. 179, 180, and 184).

12. See French Code of Civil Procedure (art. 16). See L. Cadiet & E. Jeuland, Droit Judiciaire privé 328–50, esp. 328–29 and 342– 44 (2006) (also observing that the tendency to give more power to the judges is compensated by a tendency to reinforce the right to be heard).

13. See French Code of Civil Procedure (art. 768–1).

Edge: This fits in with the issue (clarifying functions and duties of a German court) which we touched upon in discussing Section 139 of the Code.[14]

Comparovich: You are absolutely right.

Smooth: It seems clear from what you have told us that the German Code requires the court, before trial, to exchange communications—probably repeated communications—with the parties or their lawyers. Is this done in writing or by way of a preliminary hearing?

Comparovich: It is within the discretion of the presiding judge, and either method may be used.

Regardless of which method of communication is chosen, the real problem is to force the parties, and especially the defendant, to submit all their allegations and offers of proof speedily enough so that the decisive hearing can be held within a few months after the filing of the complaint with no further subsequent hearings necessary. Addressing this problem, the Code authorizes the court to fix deadlines for the submission of allegations and offers of proof. If a party delays the proceeding by failing to meet such a deadline, the sanction is drastic: a belatedly submitted allegation or offer of proof will be rejected, unless the lateness is "sufficiently excused."[15] Moreover, even if no deadline has been set, the parties are under a duty to submit all their allegations and offers of proof expeditiously, and, if a party causes delay by violating that duty in a grossly negligent manner, such party will be hit by the same drastic sanction: preclusion of the assertions dilatorily presented.

Smooth: Do the German courts make frequent use of this formidable power to preclude?

Comparovich: An affirmative answer to your question seems to be indicated by the large number of reported cases involving such preclusion.

Edge: This large number of reported cases also reveals something else: that judges and lawyers spend much of their time on fights over the preclusion issue rather than on the resolution of the parties' substantive disputes.

Comparovich: You have put your finger on the neuralgic spot of the 1976 reform. The intensity and duration of squabbles over preclusion of allegedly belated submissions are enhanced by the fact that an unjustified order of preclusion violates not only the Code of Civil Procedure, but at least in the more serious instances, also violates the precluded party's constitutional (due process) rights. Frequently therefore, such squabbles go through two successive appeals in the hierarchy of ordinary courts and in addition have to be dealt with by the already overburdened Constitutional Court.[16]

---

14. See *supra* Chapter 8, Section 3(d) at 746 Sp. p. 748ff.

15. German Code of Civil Procedure, § 296. For a more detailed description of the German courts' power to preclude belated or dilatory assertions of the parties, see Fisch, Recent Developments in West German Civil Procedure, 6 Hastings Int'l & Comp.L.Rev. 221, 243–54 (1983).

16. See the decision of the Constitutional Court dated April 14, 1987, reported in

The German legislature addressed this problem in 2004 by enacting an extraordinary claim for the right to be heard. That means that the parties are not allowed to file directly a claim to the Constitutional Court after the final appeal is dismissed. Rather they have to file a motion with the court below. If that motion is dismissed, of course, the party may still go to the Constitutional Court. However, the work of the Constitutional Court is substantially reduced.[17]

Nevertheless, as I have mentioned already, the reform has succeeded in reducing the average duration of lawsuits. Although some judges have been criticized as "hyper-active" and "hyper-speedy,"[18] the majority of observers seem to feel that the reform has expedited the litigation process without unduly sacrificing substantive justice.[19] In any event, there is no doubt that the Stuttgart Model and the subsequent German reform legislation have injected some new ideas into the traditional civilian approach to the handling of civil litigation.

Edge: Have other countries taken notice of this bold German experiment?

Comparovich: It has received a great deal of attention and in some places, has been adopted in modified form. In France, when a case is first brought,[20] the presiding judge of the panel to which it is assigned must confer with the lawyers for both parties to see how it can be terminated quickly. If at that hearing the pleadings and evidence presented show this is possible (e.g., if the case involves only questions of law or questions of fact based only on unchallenged documents already attached to the pleadings), the presiding judge determines a day for the final hearing. If the hearing, pleadings, and evidence presented demonstrate that a final decision is possible (e.g., whenever the case involves only questions of law or questions of fact based only on unchallenged documents already attached to the pleadings), the presiding judge will schedule a day for the final hearing within a reasonable time. In the final hearing, the lawyers will present their closing speeches to the full panel with their views on the law and facts.

If, however, an immediate final hearing does not appear possible, the case is assigned to a single judge, who is a member of the 3–judge panel and called *juge de la mise en état*. That judge plays a key role in preparing the

40 N.J.W. 2003 (1987), where references to many of the earlier decisions in point can be found and the further decision of the Constitutional Court of May 5, 1987, 40 N.J.W. 2733 (1987). For a collection of cases, see K. G. Deubner, Das unbewältigte Gesetz, Entscheidungen zur Zurückweisung verspäteten Vorbringens, 40 N.J.W. 1583 (1987).

17. See German Code of Civil Procedure, § 321a.

18. See H.-J. Birk, Wer führt den Zivilprozess—der Anwalt oder der Richter?, 38 N.J.W. 1489 (1985).

19. See the articles by Gottwald and Fisch, *supra* notes 8 and 15, and (with some reservations) Baumbach–Lauterbach–Albers–Hartmann, Zivilprozessordnung, Anno. 4 preceeding § 272 (45th Ed., 1987) where further references can be found.

20. See French Code of Civil Procedure (arts. 755–87). We only discuss the adversarial proceedings before the Court of First Instance (*Tribunal de Grande Instance*), not the *tribunal d'instance*, the *jurisdiction de proximité*, the *tribunal de commerce*, the *procedure gracieuse*, or other specialized courts.

case for the final hearing and judgment of the 3–judge panel. She will "supervise the loyal conduct of the procedure," deal with any preliminary and procedural matters, and collect all necessary evidence. To do so, she has at her disposal an exhaustive range of tools: she may hear the parties and their attorneys and bring their attention to relevant issues, invite the attorneys to provide factual and legal explanations necessary for the resolution of the dispute, encourage settlement, make procedural decisions regarding joinder of claims and parties, etc. One of her tasks is to fix time-limits necessary for the examination of the matter according to the nature, urgency, and complexity of the case. She will impose deadlines in which the parties have to exchange their written arguments. The *juge de la mise en état* also plays an important role in gathering evidence. She will hear the parties (even *sua sponte*), order the transmission, delivery, and production of certain documents, appoint an expert, conduct a judicial inspection, etc. She not only orders these measures, but also oversees their implementation. These orders are not ordinarily subject to immediate appeal, but rather, are appealable with the final judgment. When the case is ready for decision, the judge declares this phase closed and sets a date for the final hearing before the three-judge court.

It is a very common misconception to translate the *juge de la mise en état* as "pretrial judge." One can find such a mistake on the official website of the French Government in the English version of the French codes.[21] This demonstrates both the difficulty of legal translation as well as a misunderstanding of the dichotomy between trial and pretrial in common-law civil procedure. Of course, it all depends on the concept of "trial." In common law, "trial" is the presentation of the evidence to the trier of fact (judge or jury), whereas "pretrial" is everything before trial, but it mainly refers to the discovery phase. Discovery is comprised basically of exchange of documents and deposition of witness, and is entirely conducted in the lawyers' offices without court participation (only indirect court supervision). By definition, the trier of fact does not take any evidence during the pretrial phase.

When one calls the *juge de la mise en état* a pretrial judge, the meaning of the words "trial" and "pretrial" are completely different and may lead to great confusion. "Trial" here is the final hearing, what in the U.S. would be called the "closing statements," the opportunity for the parties to make their final oral presentation of the issues of fact and law to the fact-finder. Therefore, "pretrial" is the phase where the presiding judge takes the evidence into the record. It is the phase in which the court will take documents, appoint an expert, take the written expert report, question the expert if necessary, question witnesses, etc.[22]

The above proceeding assumes the case will be decided by a panel of three judges, as was traditionally the case in most European civil-law

21. See www.legifrance.gouv.fr (last visited Jan. 21, 2009).

22. An analogous procedure prevails on the occasion of the hearing *de novo* before the intermediate court of appeals, but, as the judges before these courts have the title *conseiller*, one speaks there of a *conseiller de la mise en état*.

countries. Of course, the final hearing takes place before a single judge in those instances where the single judge replaces the panel. In that case, the same judge that prepares the case will make the final decision.[23]

After a 1981 amendment, the presiding judge may even, if the existence of the claim does not appear to be seriously in doubt, grant the plaintiff, if necessary subject to giving security, a "provisional advance" on the final judgment including an interim payment to the creditor. This advance is usually the minimum amount likely to be awarded. It appears a significant number of cases terminate that way because the plaintiff, having obtained a substantial amount, is content not to pursue the matter further and the defendant, with an idea of how the panel member closest to the case is thinking, does not wish to risk what most likely could only be an increase in damages and greater costs.[24]

There exists an even speedier method for terminating certain disputes. Traditionally, the presiding judge may, after notice and a hearing held quickly, grant provisional remedies, for instance, to prevent irreparable harm, protect assets, etc. This is a traditional provisional measure that exists in all countries. However, as amended in 1985 and 1987, the French Code of Civil Procedure authorizes the presiding judge to grant a plaintiff an "interim payment" as long the existence of the claim is, again, not seriously in doubt.[25] There is no requirement that a liquidated claim be involved; the procedure can be used in automobile accidents, construction contracts, etc. Normally, the advance will be the minimum amount of damages that appears certain. This procedure is also used a great deal, and litigation often is not continued once the "advance" has been awarded. The decision is subject to enforcement in the same way as a judgment.[26] In Brazil, a judge may also summarily grant a total or partial advance of the final judgment.[27]

---

23. See *supra* Chapter 6, Section 3(a) at 490 (Courts of First Instance).

24. See French Code of Civil Procedure art. 771(3).

25. The procedure is applicable before the court of general jurisdiction (*tribunal de grande instance*), French Code of Civil Procedure art. 809(2), and before the Commercial Court, ibid. art. 873.

26. See W. R. Baker & P. F. Fontbressin, The French Référé Procedure, A Legal Miracle, 2 U. Miami Y.B. Int'l L. 1 (1992/93). The article discusses the French provisional remedy (*référé*) procedure in general in some detail as well as the specific use of that procedure to obtain an advance (which frequently is final) on a future (and actually often no longer sought) judgment, a procedure known as *référé-provision*. For a further discussion of the *référé* procedure as well as

of the *juge de la mise en état*, which notes that often the latter is the only one who actually hears the case, see J.-F. Burgelin, J.-M. Coulon & M.-A. Frison–Roche, Le juge des référés au regard des principes procéduraux, 1995 D. Chr. 67.

There are accelerated procedures in Germany in certain, but more limited, instances, such as claims resulting from negotiable instruments, see German Code of Civil Procedure (arts. 592–605a) and certain other liquidated claims, (arts. 688–703d).

27. See Brazilian Code of Civil Procedure (art. 273). See L. G. Marinoni, Antecipação da Tutela (2006). For a comparative analysis, see A. P. Grinover, Procedimientos Preliminares o Sumarios: Alcance e Importancia, in M. Storme & C. Gómez Lara (eds.) I XII Congreso Mundial de Derecho Procesal 163 (2005).

In Italy, apparently under French and German influence, 1990 amendments to the Code of Civil Procedure seek to expedite proceedings by having a single judge handle most litigation and by compelling parties to proffer their evidence in the initial phase of the proceedings.[28] In many other civil law countries, however, the piecemeal system still prevails, though sometimes somewhat ameliorated.[29] Also, when necessary, even in countries such as France or Germany, multiple hearings before the court are not excluded.

Smooth: How does a lawsuit ever end under that system?

Comparovich: Although conducted piecemeal, one should resist the temptation of considering the traditional civil-law proceeding anarchical, without beginning or end. The parties usually present all the documentary evidence in their possession in the pleading phase. If necessary, the court will hear witnesses and order the production of further documents. Evidence that could and should have been offered in the first round may be rejected if offered later on. Hence, the later offers ordinarily deal with new points suggested by the evidence previously taken, or by colloquy between court and counsel. After two or three rounds of this, new points are not likely to arise. In this connection one must also remember that at every stage of the proceeding the court (or the single judge) may have taken an active part in clarifying the issues and in asking the parties to offer evidence on the crucial points.[30] Although ordinarily it is for the parties to allege and prove the facts, there are certain types of evidence, especially expert opinions, which the court may even obtain on its own motion.[31]

(h) Expert Evidence

Smooth: This is what happened in our case. After H and we had been interrogated, a new interlocutory order was entered, advising the parties that the court would ask the Ruritanian Institute of Comparative Law for an opinion on the following question: "Assuming H was retained by the defendant for legal work in connection with the reorganization of defendant's subsidiary, and assuming further that the question of H's compensa-

---

28. Law No. 353 of November 26, 1990, discussed in M. Barazzutti, The Reform of the Italian Code of Civil Procedure, 5 International Law (State Bar of California, International Law Newsletter) No. 1, 7 (1992).

29. It seems to be in effect in Japan but the total volume of litigation is relatively low there. See M. Kato, The Role of Law and Lawyers in Japan and the United States, 1987 Brigham Young U.L.Rev. 627, 632 (1988); it is in use in Latin America but more recent changes often provide that successive evidentiary hearings must take place within a brief time span (ordinarily no more than thirty days) specified in the Code of Civil Procedure or set by the judge. See R. B. Cappalli, Comparative South American Civil Proce-

dure: A Chilean Perspective, 21 U. Miami Inter–Am. L.Rev. 239, 270–72 (1989–1990).

30. During the last half-century, most civil-law countries have amended their procedure codes so as to strengthen the power of the court (or the single judge) to expedite the litigation. To what extent these reforms have been successful is a matter of considerable debate. For comparative discussions, see W. J. Habscheid, Richtermacht oder Parteifreiheit, 81 ZZP 175 (1968); J. Jacob, Accelerating the Process of Law, in M. Storme & H. Casman (eds.), Towards a Justice with a Human Face 303 ff. (1978).

31. More liberally, French Code of Civil Procedure art. 143 authorizes the court to order any proof measure on its own motion.

tion is governed by American law, what statutory tariff or other rule would determine the amount of such compensation?''

Comparovich: It is interesting to observe that H had predicated his complaint exclusively on Ruritanian law and had not pleaded any foreign law. Nevertheless, once the court decided that foreign law governed the retainer, it had the duty to ascertain the applicable rule in the United States. This means that in Ruritania foreign law is treated as an issue of law and not fact, and the court has a duty to ascertain it.

Edge: Is it common for civil-law courts to consult with Institutes of Comparative Law regarding the law of foreign countries?

Comparovich: This method is not the only one used in civil law countries, but, where it is available (as, e.g., in Germany), the courts usually prefer it to all other methods.

It is no accident that use of an academic institute as an expert is particularly widespread in Germany, where the judicial practice of asking the law faculty of a university for advice on how to decide a pending case retained its great practical importance well into the 19th century.[1] Another factor may be the existence of institutes of considerable reputation able to provide such information, such as the Max Planck Institute.

Another method, usually used in France, is to obtain a statement of foreign law (*certificat de coutume*) from a lawyer practicing in the foreign country, from a knowledgeable local person, such as a law professor, or from the country involved's local consulate or embassy, if it is willing to do this.[2]

Under the European Convention on Information on Foreign Law (London, June 7, 1968), the member states must supply information concerning their law and procedure in civil and commercial matters as well as on their judicial system to foreign courts when problems of foreign law arise in the course of legal proceedings.[3] Under the terms of the Convention, each member must set up two bodies: a "receiving agency" to receive requests for information from another member and to take action on its request, and a "transmitting agency" to receive requests for information from its judicial authorities and to transmit them to the competent foreign receiving agency. Nearly all the European countries have ratified this

---

1. See Zajtay, Le traitement du droit étranger dans le procès civil, 1968 Riv.Dir.Intern.Pri. e Proc. 233, 253.

2. See the interesting case X ... v. Mme. Y, Cour d'appel Paris, June 14, 1995, 1996 D.J. 156, involving the validity and effect on their French assets of a marriage concluded in Lebanon between a Polish national and a Lebanese national originally of the Greek Orthodox religion who had first married another Greek Orthodox Lebanese national and had contracted the (second) marriage with the Polish national without previously obtaining a divorce, but after converting to Islam and marrying the second time in accordance with Islamic law, which permits polygamy. The case involved the use of a variety of the proof procedures mentioned in the preceding pages, in addition to a *certificat de coutume* issued by the Polish consulate in Paris concerning Polish law.

3. European Treaty Series No. 62. Additional protocol, Strasbourg, 15 March 1978 (European Treaty Series No. 97).

convention as the U.S. Belarus (1997), Costa Rica (1976), and Mexico (2003).

In the U.S., there is a ready supply of foreign-trained attorneys, many with an LLM degree from a U.S. law school, who master not only the English language, but also the U.S. legal system. Although many of them are authorized to practice law in the U.S., this is not necessary for an expert, because this is not "practice of law."

Edge: This practice worked well in our case. After about a month, the institute rendered its opinion, saying that in dealing with "American" contract law, it is necessary to consult state law rather than federal law; that under applicable state law there is no tariff for attorney fees;[4] and that in the absence of express agreement, the attorney is entitled to a "fair and reasonable" fee. They added that in the United States the question of what is "fair and reasonable" would be determined by a jury, and that in any event, it was not a question of law. They refused, therefore, to express an opinion on the amount of the fee, and suggested that an expert familiar with the actual practice in the United States should determine such amount.

Comparovich: Sounds like a sensible opinion.

Smooth: We thought so too. We informed L that we had hired the President of our local Bar Association to testify as our expert on the amount of the fee but L wrote back that the court would appoint somebody from its permanent official list of experts. It turned out that no expert on U.S. attorney fees was on their permanent list. Therefore, the court wrote to the Ruritanian Bar Association and on its recommendation, appointed an elderly, retired lawyer from Cleveland who had settled down in sunny Ruritania as the expert.

Comparovich: Theoretically, you could have offered the testimony of your own expert in addition to that of the court-appointed expert.

Smooth: In our case, the continental system worked well. The expert testified that $5,000 would be a fair and reasonable fee for the work H alleged to have done.

Edge: Notice the subtle humor? That was exactly 1% of what H demanded.

Smooth: While we are happy now, I have to confess that we were very uncomfortable with this procedure. Is this the standard procedure civil-law countries use to deal with issues of expert evidence in general?

Comparovich: This is the general practice in civil-law countries. Courts all over the world are frequently faced with complex issues of fact that require special technical or scientific knowledge. Courts must receive the necessary knowledge in order to reach a decision. This is a problem that must be managed by every procedural system. However, civil-law systems and common-law systems do it in a different way.

---

4. See *supra* Chapter 7, Section 8 at 684 (Lawyer's Compensation).

Ordinarily, in the common-law tradition, each party presents its own expert, and each pays their fees. This cost is not recoverable from the loser.[5] Experts are considered a witness and are even called "expert witnesses." An expert may not have witnessed the disputed fact itself, but witnesses the available evidence and offers a reasonable rendition of the facts. For example, although the expert did not witness the defendant signing the contract, conceiving a baby, or causing a car accident, through scientific analysis, the expert may explain what happened with an acceptable degree of certainty. Under that perspective the expert is indeed a witness.

This common-law practice of party-appointed expert is being slowly abandoned in England, where, since the enactment of the new procedural rules in 1998, the tendency is to adopt a system of "single joint expert," strikingly similar to the civil-law tradition.[6]

Edge: What is the practice in the civil-law tradition?

Comparovich: Expert evidence is reasonably uniform in civil-law countries. The codes of civil procedure regulate the matter with extreme detail. There are small technical differences among legal systems, but the civil-law expert evidence is virtually standard.[7]

Whenever scientific or technical knowledge is necessary to ascertain a certain fact, the parties will request the court to appoint one or if necessary, more experts. Most countries allow the court to appoint an expert on his or her own initiative, and only a few countries do not.[8]

Because the taking of expert evidence involves time and money, a party may have an incentive to use it as a procedural weapon against its

---

5. The fees of court-appointed experts, however, are considered recoverable costs. See 28 U.S.C. § 1920(6).

6. See Civil Procedure Rules, Part 35; Andrews, English Civil Procedure 737–62 (2003).

7. See the Codes of Civil Procedure of France (arts. 232—284–1), Italy (arts. 61–64, 191–201, and 441), Brazil (arts. 145–147 and 420–439), Belgium (art. 962–990, as amended in 2007), the Netherlands (arts. 194–200), Portugal (arts. 568–591), Spain (arts. 335–352), Germany (§§ 402–414), Japan (arts. 212–218 of the code and 129–136 of the Rules of Civil Procedure), Greece (arts. 368–90), Argentina (arts. 183, 333, 385, 457–78, and 773).

See Freitas (ed.), The Law of Evidence in the European Union (2004); Murray and Stürner, German Civil Justice 280–90 (2004); Oliva & Diez–Picazo, Derecho Procesal Civil. El Proceso de Declaración 351–65 (2000); Taniguchi, Reich & Miyake, Civil Procedure in Japan 7–107—7–111 (2008); Goodman, Justice and Civil Procedure in Japan 363–67 (2004); Carpi & Taruffo, Commentario Breve al Codice di Procedura Civile 186–96 and 628–48 (2002); F. P. Luiso, II Diritto Processuale Civile 92–93 (2007); Comoglio, Ferri & Taruffo, 1 Lezioni sul Processo Civile 488–91 (2006); Yessiou–Faltsi, Civil Procedure in Hellas 328–32 (1995); L. Cadiet & E. Jeuland, Droit Judiciaire Privé 390–400 (2006); S. Guinchard, F. Ferrand & C. Chainais, Procédure Civile 981–98 (2008); Vincent et al., Institutions Judiciaires 636–46 (1999); Freitas et al., 2 Código de Processo Civil Anotado 522–57 (2008); H. Theodoro Júnior, I Curso de Direito Processual Civil 512–24 (2005); E. Falcón, II Tratado de Derecho Procesal Civil y Comercial 1095–1193 (2006).

8. For example, in Spain, the court may appoint an expert on its own motion only in a very limited number of cases involving higher societal interests, such as paternity claims. See Spanish Code of Civil Procedure (art. 339(5)).

opponent. Therefore, the court may reject a party request if the expert evidence is not necessary because either the issue does not require special knowledge or is evident in light of other evidence on the record. This principle of "subsidiarity" also means that only when there are no faster and cheaper methods of inquiry can the court appoint an expert.[9]

In addition to a court-appointed expert, civil-law judges can personally inspect a place, event, etc, if necessary, in the presence of a court-appointed expert.[10]

Smooth: If the court has the duty to appoint the expert, the judge must choose one. How can a judge do that?

Comparovich: There are some variations among legal systems and judges. But the general rule is simple: the court will appoint an expert of his or her own choosing, generally, a professional in private practice or a public official. The expert must not only have the required knowledge, but he or she must also comply with the requirements of the respective profession.

In some countries, the court will choose an expert from a registry of thousands of names available in the courtroom. In some countries, this list is compiled by each professional category. Some countries are more restrictive than others regarding the court's discretion to appoint a professional not listed in the official registry. The existence of such a registry is essential to the judge's task of finding an expert. However, it is very difficult to compose such a registry, as illustrated by the Belgian experience. The Belgian Code of Civil Procedure always provided for a registry of experts, but the government never compiled it. When the expert provisions were amended in 2007, the government tried to implement it, but there was no consensus on how to compile the registry. The whole idea of registry was temporarily abandoned.

In some countries, the court may also appoint a research center, an institute, a university, a consulting firm, or a governmental institution to submit the name of a specific person to conduct the investigation. The court-appointed expert also may contact other experts to counsel him or her in other areas of expertise.

The court does not interview candidates or make an informed selection among several prospective candidates. Therefore, sometimes, the court does not have a clear idea of the real extent of the expert knowledge, and the appointment may be done haphazardly. In some countries, the appointment is done through a lottery and in others it is totally at the discretion of the court. It is possible that judges will simply appoint experts who worked well with them in previous cases.

In simple everyday cases involving traffic accidents, biology, chemistry, accounting, medicine, architecture, engineering, forensic, patent, handwrit-

9. See Belgian Code of Civil Procedure (art. 875bis).

10. See Codes of Civil Procedure of France (arts. 179–83), Brazil (§§ 440–43), Germany (§§ 371–372a), Italy (art. 258–62), Belgium (arts. 1007–1016 and 986).

ing, etc, it makes no difference who the expert is. Any person with minimal knowledge on the subject matter will do. In more complex issues, however, or in those involving more specialized or cutting edge knowledge, the parties maybe in a much better position to identify a person who is truly knowledgeable on the subject matter. Therefore, in some civil-law countries, the court may request the parties to suggest names of potential experts. A problem arises, however, when there may be conflicting "schools of thought" on a subject, and the mere selection of an expert implies the selection of the result.

In some countries, the choice of a specific expert is the court's prerogative, and, depending on the country's sensitivity to issues of due process and party participation, the court may or may not hear the parties' opinion on the matter. The rule that courts must hear the parties before making a decision seems much more enlightened and reflects the current trend. In other countries, if the parties agree on the name of a specific expert, the court must respect that decision, unless there is reason not to. In Belgium before the 2007 amendments, parties could mutually agree on a certain expert, and the court was bound by their choice. Now, the parties can suggest names, but the Court makes the ultimate decision.

Some countries expressly provide that a court may not appoint more than one expert to investigate the same matter, unless it requires multidisciplinary knowledge or for some other reason. Other countries authorize appointment of more than one expert if necessary. For example, in Portugal, the court or the parties may require that the investigation be conducted by three experts, two appointed by each party and a third one by the judge. However, the principle of procedural economy dictates that judges should not appoint more than one expert, unless strictly necessary.

Experts are not considered a "witness" and are not treated as such. Civil-law attorneys would even object to the common-law denomination "expert witness", because they did not "witness" any fact, but instead merely aid the court in understanding complex issues. They are simply referred to as "experts." It is interesting to observe, however, that German law differentiates "experts" from "expert witnesses". Expert witnesses are people with special knowledge who actually witness a fact related to their knowledge, like a doctor who was on an accident scene and witnessed malpractice of the ambulance crew. Expert witnesses are treated like normal witnesses.[11]

The court-appointed expert is a neutral, impartial, non-partisan, and objective technical assistant to the court. He or she is a kind of an *ad hoc* officer of the court, a delegate. This does not mean the expert is a public employee. The court-appointed expert can be a person in private practice that may be called sporadically to help the court system and will receive a fee for such services from the parties.[12]

11. See German Code of Civil Procedure (§ 414).

12. Because of the specialization of law firms in some common law countries, some experts are maintained on retainer by the attorneys, and there may be a professionalization of the role of experts.

In some countries, the expert performs the investigative duties under oath, and in most countries, experts may pay damages caused to a party or suffer criminal sanctions whenever appropriate.

Civil-law courts must take the expert's competence, impartiality, and objectivity very seriously because it is the foundation under which the whole structure of expert evidence is built. Therefore, the expert must excuse himself or herself and the parties may challenge the selection of an expert for several reasons with the court ruling on such challenge. In some countries, the grounds for challenging an expert's impartiality are equated to the ones used to challenge a judge's impartiality. The codes simply remand to the article related to recusal or disqualification of a judge. In other countries, the grounds for challenging an expert are equated with the ones to challenge a witness. The reasons themselves are very similar either way and generally relate to conflicts of interest, such as a personal stake in the case, a family or friendship relationship with the parties, etc. What is important here is the symbolism in some countries of equating the expert with the judge.

In some countries, the expert has a duty to accept the appointment, particularly in those in which the professional's name is part of a court registry. However, the professional may be excused from the duty for good reason.

In the discharge of its functions, the court-appointed expert is invested with the power to demand the parties and third persons to produce any information or documents necessary for the investigation. The court may assist the expert in this regard and may draw adverse inferences from a party's noncompliance.

Edge: The parties seem to be entirely at the disposal of the court-appointed expert. I do not feel comfortable with this situation at all. I would feel powerless.

Comparovich: The parties may privately hire "assessors" of their own choosing in order to understand and control the court-appointed expert's investigation. Due process considerations (principle of contradiction) require these assessors (or the parties themselves if no assessor is engaged) to have a reasonable opportunity to participate in the court-appointed expert's investigation. Party assessors must exercise the opportunity to actively participate in all phases of the investigation, pointing to facts, evidence, information, scientific techniques, etc. Once the court-appointed expert comes to a conclusion, it will be an uphill battle to convince him or her otherwise.

It would be a grave misunderstanding, however, to equate the party assessors to the common-law practice of party-appointed expert because the party assessor's partisanship is kept in check by the presence of the court's expert.

Even if the judge has the required technical or scientific knowledge, the need for the parties to participate in the investigative process, requires the court to appoint an expert. Since the judge does not offer a written report of the evidentiary issue but rather makes a decision at the end, a party will not have an opportunity to challenge the court's assessment of the facts. Contrary to what happens with legal issues, it would not be acceptable for the court to come to its own conclusions of fact without party participation.

In some countries, the appointment of a neutral expert may not be necessary when the parties hired private assessors, conducted their own investigation, and filed a written report with the court. The court may consider the information available in record enough. The new Spanish code encourages such practice and almost makes the appointment of a neutral expert an exception. This is a major departure from traditional civil-law practice, and, considering the new developments in England, it may be going on the wrong side of the historical evolution. However, the Spanish rule, although an interesting blend of common-law and civil-law practices, may lead to unintended consequences because of its rigid rules. The rules encourage the parties to present the assessor's report and require the appointment of a court expert in their pleadings, or the parties waive their right to do so. Since the plaintiff will not have another opportunity to present an expert report, the plaintiff will be hard-pressed to file one with the complaint, just in case the defendant wants to do the same. Once the plaintiff presents a report, the defendant will have a practical requirement to do the same. The rule seems to create the wrong incentives, unnecessarily raising the stakes, tensions, and expenses.

The expert investigation is conducted under court control and must be open to party participation at all times. Party participation is a corollary of the adversarial principle that dominates civil-law procedure.

The court submits to the expert a list of questions to be answered and sets a deadline. The way these questions are produced may vary from country to country. Either court compiles the list of questions with consultation from the parties, or the judge will submit his or her own questions, and the parties may formulate supplemental ones, or the parties will submit their questions and the judge will formulate supplemental ones. While the investigation is being conducted, the court or the parties may submit further questions and even broaden or limit the scope of investigation. Questions submitted by the parties are subject to control by the court, which will not approve them if they are inappropriate in any way.

During the investigation process, parties and their party assessors have the possibility to formulate remarks on provisional or interim reports of the expert, which can be answered by the expert. In other words, there is a real debate between the expert and the parties and their party assessors.

If problems arise during the investigation, the expert or the parties can go back to the court that appointed the expert to solve these problems (e.g. when the expert is no longer impartial, when he or she must be replaced because of sickness, when new questions have to be answered by the expert, etc.).

The expert will then submit a final written report to the court with copies for each party. On the report, the expert will describe the investigation and the methods employed and answer all questions with a reasoned explanation. The party assessors may also file a written report, which must be taken into consideration in the court's decision. Some countries encourage the expert and the assessors to file a joint report if all are in agreement. In some countries, the party assessors' reports are presented as an annex to the expert's final report.

Smooth: It seems that the expert works closely with the party assessors. This joint work may lead to the development of common grounds, and their differences may be narrowed down to the most important issues. In the U.S., the experts work entirely independently from each other, and their reports are only exchanged after they are finished and only if the party decides it will use it at trial.[13]

Comparovich: You can appreciate the subtleties of the civil-law expert evidence. This is a real possibility, but does not exist in many systems. In practice, each one performs his or her own investigation independently. This should be an improvement in some civil-law systems and was recently seriously considered in the English procedural reform.[14]

If there remains any ambiguity, omission, or contradiction after the expert presents the written report, the court and the parties may submit further questions in writing or even request further investigation. If the report is complete or all remaining questions are adequately answered, the expert evidence is concluded. If necessary, however, the court and the parties may ask the expert to appear at a court hearing for further oral questioning. The interrogation, for lack of a better way, proceeds in the same way as a witness interrogation. If more than one expert was appointed, they may be questioned at the same time.

The court may allow the court-appointed expert to participate in the questioning of parties, witnesses, and party assessors, and even put questions to them.

The party assessors have an important role in helping the party that hired them to challenge the results or methodology of the court-appointed expert. The assessors may also be interrogated by the court.

If the expert report is still insufficient after all clarifications, the court on its own initiative or on motion of any party, may appoint another expert to conduct a second investigation of the same facts.

Edge: The presentation of a "written report" is a major departure from U.S. practice in which experts are supposed to orally present their findings at a court hearing.

---

13. See FRCP 26(a)(2)(B) and (b)(4).

14. See Lord Woolf, Access to Justice. Final Report 147–49 (1996).

Comparovich: The difference may be much less significant than you initially might think. In U.S. practice, the parties will exchange their experts' written reports during the pretrial phase.[15]

In any event, the U.S. practice of oral expert presentation may make sense in a system divided into pretrial and trial phases, particularly because the jury will not be able to sit at a desk and read the expert report. Sitting without a jury, a professional judge has the luxury of reading the report and only uses the more cumbersome device of interviewing the expert if necessary.

In addition, since 1998 in England, "expert evidence is to be given in a written report unless the court directs otherwise."[16]

Smooth: It seems to me that the civil-law expert evidence only works if the science is straightforward or if there is no substantial challenge to the court-appointed expert's report. But what if there are different schools of thought regarding the matter investigated? Or what if there are substantial discrepancies between the analysis presented by the court-appointed expert and the party assessors or between the first and second investigation?

Comparovich: The court is the ultimate trier of fact and is not bound by the opinion of its expert. Rather, the report is merely advisory and the court is free to grant it the appropriate credence in light of the credibility and qualifications of the expert, the strength and internal consistency of its own reasoning, and of all other evidence available in the record (principle of "free evaluation of proof").[17] The party assessor dissatisfied with the expert report will certainly provide the judge with critical information to better evaluate it.

In some countries, if the party assessor successfully challenges the court appointed-expert, the court must appoint another expert. In other countries, the judge is free to choose between the expert and the assessor's opinion or even to arrive at his or her own conclusions. If the court orders a second investigation, the second expert report does not invalidate the first, even when they are inconsistent. The court will then have two neutral reports in addition to the assessors' reports. In Germany, the court may appoint a "super expert" that will help the court make a more educated choice between all expert evidence available. In other countries, it is possible for the court to appoint three experts for the second investigation instead of one. In any event, the judge must give a reasoned explanation of his or her decision. By the end of the proceeding, it is expected that the experts will have sufficiently educated the court on the subject matter, and the court can make a decision.

As the ultimate fact finder, the court has the duty to ascertain the facts of the case and issue a decision on the merits. Regardless of how complex the facts, this is a burden that the court may not escape. If the

---

15. See FRCP 26(a)(2)(B).

16. See Civil Procedure Rules, Part 35.5(1); Lord Woolf, Access to Justice. Final Report 140 (1996).

17. See *supra* Chapter 8, Section 3(e) at 756 (Evidence and Discovery), Esp. pp. 758–60.

court is not fully convinced even after all the safety guards provided for by the legal system (court expert, party assessors, further questions in writing and orally, second court expert), the court must reach a decision based on the burden of proof.

Edge: But once a court-appointed expert is in place, how realistic is it to expect that a court will not follow the advice of its own "neutral" expert and instead follow the advice of the "partisan" expert?

Comparovich: You certainly have a point. A system of court-appointed experts may quickly transform into one of "court-anointed expert." In practice, courts generally rely on the expert's opinion, especially because to challenge it would demand knowledge, time, and energy that courts do not have.[18] Empirical research shows that judges follow the court-appointed expert in 90 or 95% of the cases.[19]

One way of seeing these statistics is to think that judges are following the safest path, in detriment of the best evidence. Another way of seeing it, however, is to assume that the neutral expert is indeed playing its intended role and providing reliable information. It would indeed be awkward if judges were not following the court-appointed expert. The pessimist approach also misses the point that judges do not follow the court-appointed expert in 5 to 10% of the cases, a clear sign of independence in appropriate circumstances.

In any event, the question is not whether the civil-law expert evidence is perfect because it clearly is not. The issue is whether it is better overall than the American party-driven practice. As we have seen, some common-law commentators have answered this question in the affirmative.

Smooth: In the U.S. and other common law countries, each party pays for the expert they appoint. But who pays for the court-appointed expert in civil-law countries?

Comparovich: The court-appointed expert must be paid for his or her services, regardless of the outcome of the report or of the case. The party who requested the expert evidence will anticipate the expert's fees and expenses, unless that person is a beneficiary of some legal aid scheme. If both parties made the request, the judge may allocate the expense accordingly. If the court ordered the expert on its own initiative, it will decide which party will anticipate the fees, but generally the burden will fall on the party with the burden of proof or the party who has the most interest in the outcome of the investigation. The party never pays the expert

18. See Beardsley Proof of fact in French Civil Procedure, 34 Am. J. Comp. L. 459, 484–85 (1986); Murray and Stürner, German Civil Justice 289–290 (2004).

19. See L. Cadiet & E. Jeuland, Droit Judiciaire Privé 390–92 and note 299 (2006) (citing Contis, Penvern & Triomphe, Incidence des Expertises sur le Dénouement des Litiges et Suites Effectivement Donnés aux Expertises Judiciaires (1998), for the proposition that French judges follow the expert 90% of the times). In Germany, empirical studies have shown that the number is 95%. See Sendler, Richter und Sachverständige, 39 N.J.W. 2907, esp. at 2909 (1986) (where this heavy judicial dependence on the official expert is critically discussed). See Hammelmann, Expert Evidence, 10 Mod.L.Rev. 32, 38 (1947).

directly and instead, deposits the money into court. The court will pay the expert after he or she has completed the work, although the experts may receive a retainer and costs immediately. If the depositing party prevails in the end, these costs will be recovered from the losing party.

Because this is largely an official enterprise, not subjected to the vagaries of the "free market," the cost of expert evidence is generally much lower in civil-law countries than in the common law.[20] A cynic might even say it is more expensive to purchase a partisan expert than it is to pay a reasonable fee to a neutral expert.[21] However, these costs may still represent a relatively significant sum because the amount in controversy in civil-law litigation is usually much smaller than in common-law litigation.

Edge: The idea of a "neutral" expert is nothing short of revolutionary from a U.S. perspective.

Comparovich: It is less iconoclastic than you might think. As we have seen before, since 1998, the general rule in England is the neutral court-appointed expert. The English rule has a striking similarity to the "civil-law expert evidence."[22] From England, this rule will quickly spread into other common-law countries, and in a decade or so no one will consider it "revolutionary" or based on a foreign tradition.

The ALI/UNIDROIT, Principles and Rules of Transnational Civil Procedure also adopted the civil-law tradition of a neutral court-appointed expert.[23]

Although clearly not the practice in the U.S., a court-appointed expert is not incompatible with the U.S. legal system. U.S. courts may appoint a neutral expert on its own initiative or on motion of any party. The court may select the expert agreed on by the parties or appoint one of its own selection. The expert is entitled to compensation paid by the parties and as directed by the court. The loser will reimburse the winner of any costs related to the court-appointed expert.[24]

It is true, however, that courts do not exercise this prerogative often, particularly in jury trials. The main hesitation, it seems, is the appearance that a "neutral" expert might have in the eyes of the jurors. Jurors may place an exaggerated reliance on the neutral expert to the detriment of the party-appointed experts.

Smooth: However, considering the reliance that professional judges apply to court-appointed experts, one may argue whether there is any difference at all. And maybe that is the way it should be in the first place.

---

20. See Lord Woolf, Access to Justice. Final Report 137–52 (1996) (considering expert evidence one of the two major causes of unnecessary cost in England, the other being uncontrolled discovery).

21. The high cost may not be due only to the amount of the fees, but also to an incentive to present several experts to the jury. A RAND research found that experts testified in 86% of cases and the average was 3.3 experts per trial. See Gross, Expert Evidence, 1991 Wis. L. Rev. 1113.

22. See Civil Procedure Rules, Part 35.

23. See Rule 26; ALI/UNIDROIT, Principles of Transnational Civil Procedure (2006).

24. See, e.g., FRE 706. This power has existed for centuries.

Comparovich: You certainly have a point there. It is surprising that the U.S. would maintain the jury trial yet be so skeptical of in the jury's ability to discern the proper credibility of less-than-perfect evidence. The institution of the jury receives paternalistic treatment and does not have an opportunity to receive relevant evidence like hearsay, neutral expert, etc.

In a blatant display of distrust of juries, the Supreme Court recognized that judges are a "gatekeeper" and must not admit expert evidence that is not scientifically reliable.[25] Implicit in that decision is the recognition that juries cannot distinguish junk science from scientific evidence. Instead of proposing the use of court-appointed experts to present evidence at trial, however, some commentators suggested the use of court-appointed experts merely to assist the court in making the determination on the admissibility of the expert evidence. The jury would still have the task of choosing between two party-appointed experts. This technique was suggested both by Blackmun in *Daubert* as well as by Breyer in his concurrence of *Joiner*. Their lead has been blindly followed by many.

The U.S. could go a step further even if it does not accept the neutral expert. The rules could encourage the parties to submit a list of several experts and voluntarily agree on one name, or at least exchange the names and reports of every expert they hired and disclose whether they will use them at trial or not.

The practice of appointing a Special Master may come close to the concept of civil-law expert evidence. The Special Master is nonpartisan, neutral, appointed by the court, and paid through the court.[26]

There is nothing "revolutionary" in law when you are open to revisit old myths.

Smooth: I could live with a system of court-appointed experts. This is one feature of their system that I admire. It avoids the battle of partisan experts, which has become such a sorry part of our practice.

Comparovich: Your enthusiasm for the court-appointed expert is shared by many eminent scholars and reformers in this country.[27] For more than a century, its use has been suggested by hundreds of commentators[28] with no success.[29] Lawyers have always been strongly opposed to it.[30]

---

25. See Daubert v. Merrell Dow Pharmaceuticals, Inc., 509 U.S. 579 (1993); General Electric Co. v. Joiner, 522 U.S. 136, 118 S.Ct. 512 (1997); Kumho Tire Co. Carmichael, 526 U.S. 137, 119 S.Ct. 1167 (1999).

26. See FRCP 53.

27. The efforts of those who favor the official expert and the inroads these efforts have made upon U.S. traditional practice are discussed in the Advisory Committee's Note accompanying Rule 706 of the Federal Rules of Evidence, where further references can be found. For a discussion of English and American practice with respect to court-appointed experts, see Basten, The Court Expert in Civil Trials—A Comparative Appraisal, 40 Mod.L.Rev. 174 (1977).

28. See, e.g., Gross, Expert Evidence, 1991 Wis. L. Rev. 1113, 1187–1207 (also commenting on the first editions of Wigmore's treatise on Evidence, of 1903, 1923 and 1940); Langbein, The German Advantage in Civil Procedure, 52 U.Chi.L.Rev. 823, 835–41 (1985); Strong *et al.* McCormick on Evidence 30–32 (1999).

29. See Cecil & Willging, Accepting Daubert's Invitation: Defining a Role for Court–Appointed Experts in Assessing Scien-

It is clear that the U.S. debate would greatly benefit from the knowledge of comparative law.

However, one must be mindful that the court-appointed expert may also have its flaws. It is common to say that since there is no neutral science, there are no neutral experts either. In addition, there is always a risk that the court-appointed expert owes his or her appointment to "connections," at least in countries in which they are not selected through a lottery.[31] The expert may also be incompetent, or corrupt.[32] However, corruption in the legal system depends more on societal standards than any type of technique employed.

The effect of the expert's incompetence or corruption is even more deleterious than that of similar weaknesses on the part of a judge who, under the civil-law system, may be only one of three members of a panel. Moreover, judicial error can be corrected on appeal while the expert's erroneous or corrupt opinion will poison the lower and the appellate court's record. It is true that in many civil law countries new evidence can be produced on appeal, and a party dissatisfied with an expert's conclusions may be able to have another expert appointed for the appellate proceedings and maybe even in the first instance, but this will not remove the original expert's report from the record.

Smooth: But the party-appointed expert is not devoid of problems either.

Comparovich: Most people accept the "battle of experts" as a natural result of adversary procedure, but, as we have seen, it is not inevitable.

It is commonplace even within the common law to doubt the neutrality and impartiality of the party-appointed expert. A cynic may even consider it an oxymoron. The reality is that party-appointed experts are under terrible pressures and have an incentive to be partisan. Lord Woolf lamented that "experts sometimes take on the role of partisan advocates instead of neutral fact finders or opinion givers".[33]

There is an implicit bias in how the system of party-appointed experts operates. To begin with, the mere fact that the party selects the expert raises suspicions. A party may contact a dozen experts and hire only the

tific Validity, 43 Emory L.J. 995 (1994); Cecil & Willging, Court–Appointed Experts: Defining the Role of Experts Appointed Under Federal Rule of Evidence 706 (Federal Jud. Ctr. 1993) (describing a broad research on the use of court-appointed experts in Federal Courts).

30. Lord Woolf attributes a resistance against neutral experts to attorneys "who are reluctant to give up their adversarial weapons." See Lord Woolf, Access to Justice. Final Report 140 (1996).

31. See Ploscowe, The Expert Witness in Criminal Cases in France, Germany and Italy, 2 Law & Contemp.Probs. 504, 508–09 (1935).

32. See, e.g., Jacobson v. Frachon, 138 L.T.R., N.S., 386 (C.A.1927); Pause, Der "unabhängige" Sachverständige, 38 N.J.W. 2576, 2577 (1985).

33. See Lord Woolf, Access to Justice. Final Report 137–52 (1996). The Final Report presents a critical X–Ray of the problems with party-appointed experts in England and is not shy on its criticism of experts exaggerated partisanship. The Final Report suggested the adoption of court-appointed expert in England.

ones who will be sympathetic to their positions, no matter how marginal the professed opinion actually is in the scientific community. Parties tend not to use experts who are not favorable to their cause. In the U.S., the name of the expert and the written report are not even disclosed to the opponent, unless it will be used at trial.[34] The party-appointed expert also receives all the information and instructions from the parties and is paid by the parties. If an expert disagrees with the positions of the parties, his or her services will be abruptly terminated. The conflict of interest and economic incentives are obvious and operate in favor of rendering a favorable opinion.[35]

In addition, a system of party-appointed expert sends the wrong signal to the expert who sees his or her role not so much as an officer of the court or a "neutral" advisor, but rather as a "hired gun." That is why the new English Rules make it clear that the party-appointed expert is supposed to help the court and that "this duty overrides any obligation to the person from whom he has received instructions or by whom he is paid."[36]

(i) Discovery and Gathering of Evidence Abroad

Comparovich: As we have seen, while U.S. procedure regards the entire pre-decision course of a lawsuit, including the collection and presentation of evidence, as an essentially private matter to be handled by the parties and their attorneys, the civil-law tradition has stamped the word "official" on these matters. The result is that, although offers of proof ordinarily have to come from the parties, the process of proof-taking is dominated by the court.[1] This basic difference between civil-law and common-law attitudes can lead to thorny problems whenever an action is brought in one country but a relevant item of evidence is located in another.

Smooth: We frequently face problems of this kind, especially when, for purposes of litigation in U.S. courts, we try to obtain evidence located abroad and we needed what is called international judicial assistance or international judicial cooperation. A number of years ago in a U.S. case, we needed the testimony of two witnesses who lived in a civil-law country. When we tried to take the witnesses' depositions in the foreign country in accordance with U.S. procedure, we discovered that the country did not permit such a procedure, and that nobody, except a judge duly appointed, may examine a witness within the territory of that country.

Comparovich: This rule, which prevails in the majority of civil-law countries, is the logical consequence of their fundamental notion that the taking of evidence in a lawsuit is not a private matter, but a function of the state, and may be performed only by judges or other officials deriving their

---

34. FRCP 26(a)(2)(A).

35. See Langbein, The German Advantage in Civil Procedure, 52 U.Chi.L.Rev. 823, 835 (1985) (referring to the "subtle pressures to join the team-to shade one's views, to conceal doubt, to overstate nuance, to downplay weak aspects of the case that one has been hired to bolster. Nobody likes to disap-

point a patron" and concluding that "the more measured and impartial an expert is, the less likely he is to be used by either side").

36. See English Civil Procedure Rules, Part 35.3.

1. See *supra* Chapter 8, Section 3(e) at 756 (Evidence and Discovery).

authority from the local sovereign (such as police officers or certain public servants in tax matters). Naturally, a lawyer will present to the court documents that are in the possession of the client and the names or written statements (affidavits) of friendly witnesses.[2]

Edge: Is this not an archaic notion?

Comparovich: It is neither archaic nor modern, just different. Some policy arguments can be adduced in its favor. Where judges, rather than aggressive party representatives, are in charge of evidence-taking, the privacy and other interests of witnesses are apt to be better protected. Of course, from the standpoint of the American party involved in international litigation, the civil-law approach has its drawbacks because it forces them to use the more cumbersome, expensive, slow, and formalistic method of letters rogatory (also known as letters of request), a request directed to a foreign court to take the deposition of a witness (or obtain documents).

Smooth: A letter rogatory for the depositions of the two witnesses was indeed issued. One witness voluntarily appeared and testified before a court in the foreign country. She was interrogated by the judge himself under the local rules of interrogation of witnesses. Her testimony was not recorded verbatim. The judge dictated to the clerk a summary of her testimony. When at trial in the U.S., we tried to introduce that summary into evidence, but our opponent objected to it as hearsay, and there ensued quite a squabble over its admissibility. But this was a long time ago, and this problem has been much ameliorated because of actions taken in the United States and in some civil-law countries.

Comparovich: You are quite right. A major breakthrough in that area was the Hague Evidence Convention.[3] Almost 50 countries are currently parties, including most of the United States' trading partners, such as France, China, India, Mexico, Russia, Spain, Germany, UK, Italy, Netherlands, and Switzerland.

Letters rogatory are processed according to the local procedure. However, the Hague convention requires that whenever possible, the local court should accommodate special requests from the foreign court regarding the method or procedure for the taking of the evidence, even if it departs from the local rules and traditions. The execution of letters rogatory may not be refused simply because the country claims exclusive jurisdiction over the subject matter, or its legal system does not provide for the claim or relief sought.[4]

The Hague Evidence Convention was incorporated as domestic law in a number of civil-law countries. In France, for example, the Code of Civil Procedure specifically provides that questions and answers may be transcribed or recorded verbatim (as opposed to a summary), and the parties

---

2. We discussed witnesses' written statement at 783ff.

3. Convention on the Taking of Evidence Abroad in Civil and Commercial Matters, done at The Hague, March 18, 1970; entered into force for the United States October 7, 1972, TIAS 7444, available at http://www.hcch.net.

4. Arts. 9 and 12 of the Hague Convention.

and their counsel may ask questions to the witness as long as all communications are stated or translated into French. The foreign judge may also assist the interrogatory.[5]

To make the admission of such testimony possible in U.S. litigation in spite of the hearsay rule, the Federal Rules of Civil Procedure provide in Rule 28(b)(4) that "evidence obtained in response to a letter of request need not be excluded merely because it is not a verbatim transcript, because the testimony was not taken under oath, or because of any similar departure from the requirements for depositions taken within the United States."

The rule in the U.S. is the same as in France. The testimony will be taken according to the Federal Rules of Civil Procedure, unless the U.S. court prescribes a different procedure, "which may be in whole or part the practice and procedure of the foreign country."[6]

Note that neither 28 U.S.C. § 1782, nor Rule 28(b)(4), nor the French Code of Civil Procedure require that the letters rogatory be issued under the terms of a treaty dealing with international judicial assistance. Therefore, they have broad application, including in cases related to countries that are not signatories of The Hague convention.

Some countries may also have bilateral conventions, making it even easier to obtain evidence abroad. A number of Latin American countries are not parties to the Hague Evidence Convention, but there is a separate Inter–American Convention on the Taking of Evidence Abroad and Letters Rogatory under the Organization of American States that covers this issue.[7]

The European Union has its own internal regulation on the matter, which streamlined the taking of evidence between member states and introduce a simple and expeditious court-to-court transmission.[8] The regulation requires each member state to appoint specific courts in charge of complying with such requests and to comply with them within 90 days. The regulation also provides for the possibility of direct taking of evidence by the requesting court in another member state. This regulation prevails over any bilateral or multilateral agreements or arrangements concluded be-

---

5. See French Code of Civil Procedure, arts. 736–48, esp. 739–41. The reference to exclusive French jurisdiction refers mainly to arts. 14 and 15 of the Civil Code; see *supra* p. 730ff. See also the German Law Implementing the Hague Evidence Convention.

6. See 28 U.S.C. § 1782. A more controversial issue is whether the evidence request is discoverable under U.S. law or foreign law. Some U.S. courts have held that discoverability of the evidence requested under U.S. law is not necessary for the use of section 1782 by foreign litigants. See In re Letter Rogatory From First Court of First Instance in Civil

Matters, Caracas, Venezuela, 42 F.3d 308 (5th Cir.1995); Note, International Judicial Assistance: Does 28 U.S.C. § 1782 Contain a Discoverability Requirement? 18 Fordham Int'l L.J. 332 (1994).

7. See OAS Treaty Series No. 65, 24 I.L.M. 472 (1985).

8. See the Council Regulation (EC) No 1206/2001 of 28 May 2001 on cooperation between the courts of the Member States in the taking of evidence in civil or commercial matters (Official Journal L174, 27th June 2001), in force since January 2004.

tween member states and in particular the aforementioned Hague Convention. So, if evidence in a French proceeding has to be obtained in Spain, this Regulation applies; if the evidence has to be obtained in the U.S., then the Hague Convention applies. A recent study on its application, done in March 2007, has concluded that most requests are complied within the 90 days period as imposed by the regulation.

Smooth: However, the second witness, although duly notified, failed to appear before the court in the foreign country. When we petitioned the foreign court to compel the witness' to appear and testify, our petition was rejected on the ground that there was no judicial cooperation treaty between that country and the United States. In the absence of such a treaty, the court stated it had no authority under its law to compel a witness to appear and testify for purposes of litigation pending in another country.

Comparovich: Whenever the production is voluntary, there is no problem. A country has no obligation to give assistance to other countries in litigation but may do so out of deference to other nations, expecting a similar behavior when the situation is reversed (comity).

However, the Hague Evidence Convention explicitly provides that a court executing a Letter of Request "shall apply the appropriate measures of compulsion to the same extent as are provided by its internal law for the execution of orders issued by the authorities of its own country" against the witness.[9]

Many of the problems that formerly plagued international litigants, as a result of the divergences between civil and common law, have been resolved or alleviated by the Hague Evidence Convention. However, an obvious point should be kept in mind: The Convention applies only between countries that are parties to it; but, as we have seen, a number of countries have amended their rules concerning international judicial assistance to be in conformity with the Convention, but have not necessarily specified that these amended rules apply only in relations with other Convention countries.

Edge: Can the Hague Evidence Convention be used to obtain documentary evidence located abroad? Can we get document discovery?

Comparovich: In principle, yes. But some of the signatories fear that the Convention's mechanism might be used for American-style "fishing expeditions" led to the inclusion of the following language in the Convention:

Art. 23. A Contracting State may at the time of signature, ratification or accession, declare that it will not execute Letters of Request issued for the purpose of obtaining pre-trial discovery of documents as known in Common Law countries.

---

9. See art. 10 of the Hague Evidence Convention. For the U.S. rule, see 28 U.S.C. § 1782.

Almost all nations that are parties to the Convention made declarations under Article 23 including other common-law countries like the UK and Australia.[10] As a matter of fact, the article was proposed by the UK.[11] The Convention did, however, have one beneficial effect. The national officials mainly involved in its operation meet occasionally to review its operation, and these meetings have provided an occasion for explaining the significance and actual operation of discovery in the United States. As a result, a number of countries that made a declaration under Article 23 have subsequently amended them to the effect that they will permit discovery of clearly specified and directly relevant documents needed in pending litigation, but this is clearly not enough for an American litigant.[12]

Smooth: This is a testament to the huge gap between civil law and common-law procedure regarding discovery.[13] In addition, the fact that Art 23 was inserted in the Convention in the first place indicates many countries resent American-style discovery when used by litigants (including the U.S. Government as a litigant) for extraterritorial information-gathering, especially the notorious "fishing expeditions."

Comparovich: In civil-law countries, contrary to U.S. practice, the taking of evidence is monopolized by judges and can neither be conducted by foreign attorneys nor foreign courts.[14] The unilateral imposition of extraterritorial discovery rules has been perceived for several decades by both civil and common-law countries as a violation of their sovereignty.

As it was recognized in the Restatement (Third) of Foreign Relations Law, "no aspect of the extension of the American legal system beyond the territorial frontier of the United States has given rise to so much friction as the requests for documents in investigation and litigation in the United States."[15]

This resentment is intensified when American litigants (including the U.S. Government) seek to extract information from foreign nationals and domiciliaries who have been brought into U.S. courts by expansive and perhaps exorbitant theories of jurisdiction.[16]

Motivated by such resentment, several countries, including some of the U.S. closest friends and allies, like France, The Netherlands, Sweden, Switzerland, and even common-law countries like the UK, Canada, and Australia, have adopted so-called "blocking statutes," prohibiting compli-

10. The Inter–American Evidence Convention contains, in its art. 9, a provision similar to art. 23 of the Hague Convention.

11. See Born & Rutledge, International Civil Litigation in United States Courts 967 (2007). The authors also state that English courts have been the most receptive to U.S. discovery requests, but that "it is well settled that English courts will only order discovery of particular documents or narrow, specifically defined categories of documents, that were already known to exist, that were intended to be used as evidence, and that are directly relevant to disputed issues." p. 989.

12. This is the gist of civil-law discovery in those countries where it is available. See *supra* Chapter 8, Section 3(e) at 756 (Evidence and Discovery).

13. See *id.*

14. The same is true regarding the service of process and other judicial activity. See *supra* Chapter 8, Section 3(b) at 736 (Service of Process).

15. See Restatement (third) of Foreign Relations Law, § 442, Reporters' Note 1 (1987).

16. See *supra* at 730ff.

ance with discovery orders of American courts. Such legislation has been brought about by American attempts at extraterritorial discovery in antitrust cases; others had a more general purpose.

France has gone so far as to make it a criminal offense, punishable by fines and imprisonment, to request, investigate, or transmit abroad any "documents or information of an economic, commercial, industrial, financial or technical nature that may constitute proof intended for legal or administrative proceedings in another country" (except pursuant to international agreement).[17]

Blocking statutes, however, are as much about a violation of a country's sovereignty as they are about protecting local industry against U.S. discovery. So much so that some blocking statutes are limited to certain industries, such as banking, uranium, shipping, etc. It also has to do with the fact that this is a unilateral situation: since civil-law countries do not have broad discovery, only common-law countries make such "invasions."

In sharp contrast, neither U.S. law nor U.S. judicial philosophy shows any indication that the taking of evidence in U.S. territory for use in judicial proceedings abroad would be considered a violation of U.S. sovereignty.

Edge: Litigants and witnesses caught in the cross-fire of American discovery orders and such foreign "blocking" legislation are not to be envied. If the litigant complies with the U.S. discovery request, he or she will violate the foreign law; if the litigant refuses, he or she may suffer discovery sanctions, such as adverse inferences, default, contempt, etc.

Edge: But a request under the Hague Convention is still a very formalistic and cumbersome proceeding, and it may take months or years to be completed. A court must send a request to a "central authority" in the foreign country (Ministry of Justice or State Department), which will then forward the request to the appropriate court. After the request is complied with, the court will send the evidence collected to the central authority who will then forward it to the foreign court. In addition, most countries made the declaration of art. 23 of The Hague Evidence Convention and will not comply with discovery requests. This exasperates American litigants, and they try to bypass the Hague Convention whenever possible.

Comparovich: Indeed. You may have heard of the *Aérospatiale* case.[18] Defendant, a French government-owned aircraft manufacturer, was sued in

---

17. Law No. 80–538 of July 18, 1980. See also Council Regulation (EC) No 2271/96 of 22 November 1996, protecting against the effects of the extra-territorial application of legislation adopted by a third country, and actions based thereon or resulting therefrom. The Council of the European Union adopted a framework regulation and agreed to joint action to "protect" the interests of the European Union and its citizens against the extraterritorial application of legislation by non-member states. These measures were adopted in response to the extraterritorial application of certain measures by the United States, concerning trade with and investment in Cuba, as well as investment in Iran and Libya.

18. See Société Nationale Industrielle Aérospatiale v. United States District Court, 482 U.S. 522, 107 S.Ct. 2542 (1987).

a federal district court in Iowa for personal injury after one of its aircrafts was involved in an accident in Iowa. Invoking Rules 26 to 37 of the Federal Rules of Civil Procedure, plaintiffs sought discovery by way of interrogatories, requests for admission, and requests for production of documents. Most of the documents and other items of information requested were in the custody of the defendants in France. The District Court ordered defendants to comply with plaintiffs' discovery requests. The Court of Appeals for the Eighth Circuit granted review by mandamus in view of the novelty of the questions presented, but let the discovery order stand.[19] Defendants, supported by the U.S. Government and a number of foreign governments as amici curiae,[20] sought further review in the U.S. Supreme Court. Their arguments were predicated on (a) the Hague Evidence Convention, (b) the French "blocking" statute, and (c) general notions of international comity.

Edge: The first question would appear to be whether the Evidence Convention applied at all to the facts of this case. If the documents and other items of information requested were in the hands of a non-party residing in France, resort to the Convention would be necessary to force such non-party to produce the information. But in this case, the information was in the custody of a party to the action, a party over whom the American court had personal jurisdiction. That party can be compelled to produce the information *in Iowa*. No judicial assistance by any French court is needed. Thus, it seems to me, the Evidence Convention was not applicable at all.

Comparovich: That was the position taken by the lower courts, not only in this case, but in a number of similar cases as well. Under this interpretation, the effect of the Evidence Convention would be limited to information in the hands of persons who are not parties to the action.

Smooth: Alternatively, one could argue the plaintiffs could have elected to seek the information *either* through Convention channels *or* in accordance with the Federal Rules of Civil Procedure.

Comparovich: That was one of the plaintiff's arguments: the Hague Evidence Convention is not the exclusive or mandatory method of obtaining evidence abroad.[21] Even if this argument is accepted, however, the question remains whether principles of international comity should not impel an American court, either as a rule or under the circumstances of a particular case, to try to obtain the information through Convention channels *before* resorting to the more drastic unilateral methods provided by its own discovery provisions.

The U.S. Supreme Court basically took the view espoused by Mr. Smooth. It held that the Convention *could* be applied to information in the hands of parties to the litigation over which the court had jurisdiction; but,

19. In re Société Nationale Industrielle Aérospatiale, 782 F.2d 120 (8th Cir.1986). and Switzerland (reprinted in 25 I. L. M. 1475–1586 (1986)).

20. Amicus curiae briefs urging reversal were filed by the UK, France, Germany, **21.** Art. 27 of the Convention appears to support the argument for non-exclusivity.

since such parties had an obligation to obey orders of the court, use of the Convention was not mandatory as to them: they could simply be ordered to comply with discovery requests or suffer the sanctions provided for in Rule 37 of the Federal Rules, such as dismissal, default, contempt of court, drawing adverse inferences, etc. In the interests of comity, however, in making such an order an American court should weigh all the factors in the case, including hardship for the foreign party, problems of sovereignty, etc. With regard to the French "blocking" statute, the Court decided the defendants had made no showing that they would be put in a situation where they risked problems with their own government if they complied with the discovery order because they had not made any request to the French government for permission to waive the French statute. Thus, comity did not mandate the issuance of a protective order on that ground.

Needless to say, the Supreme Court's decision caused great frustration and diplomatic embarrassment in Europe.[22] This is only a brief summary of the decision, which generated a vast literature in the U.S. and abroad.[23]

In 1993, thus after *Aérospatiale*, there was an amendment to Rule 28(b) of the Federal Rules of Civil Procedure, which now provides that "a deposition may be taken in a foreign country (A) under an applicable treaty or convention; (B) under a letter of request (...); (C) on notice, before a person authorized to administer oaths either by federal law or by the law in the place of examination; or (D) before a person commissioned by the court (...) A letter of request (...) may be issued (...) (B) without a showing that taking the deposition in another manner is impracticable or inconvenient.".The Rule appears to indicate a preference for discovery in conformity with the Hague Evidence Convention (or any other applicable international instrument) where testimony must be taken in a foreign country. However, the Rule is not inconsistent with *Aérospatiale*, which covered discovery of documents from a party but indicated in a more general way that the Evidence Convention was not an exclusive remedy. The Advisory Committee stated that, "This revision is intended to make effective use of the Hague Convention (...) and of any similar treaties that the United States may enter that provide procedures for the taking of depositions abroad. The party taking the deposition is ordinarily obliged to conform to an

22. See Baumgartner, Is Transnational Litigation Different?, 25 U. Pa. J. Int'l Econ. L. 1297 (2004) (analyzing the historical evolution, before and after *Aérospatiale*, of what became known as the "judicial conflict" or "judicial war" between the U.S. and Germany).

23. E.g., G.B. Born & S. Hoing, Comity and the Lower Courts: Post Aérospatiale Applications of the Hague Evidence Convention, 24 Int'l Lawyer 393 (1990), noting, at 407, a judgment by a lower court in Germany refusing to enforce an American judgment on the ground the American court had not complied with the Evidence Convention; D. J. Gerber, International Discovery after Aérospatiale: The Quest for an Analytical Framework, 82 Am.J.Int'l L. 521 (1988); J.P. Griffin & M. N. Bravin, Beyond Aérospatiale: A Commentary on the Foreign Discovery Provisions of the Restatement (Third) and the Proposed Amendments to the Federal Rules of Civil Procedure, 25 Int'l Lawyer 331 (1991). For a helpful discussion on obtaining evidence in France after the Aérospatiale case, see V. Mercier & D. D. McKenney, Obtaining Evidence in France for Use in United States Litigation, 2 Tulane J.Int'l & Comp.L. 91 (1994).

applicable treaty (. . .) if an effective deposition can be taken by such internationally approved means. (. . .) For a discussion of the impact of such treaties upon the discovery process and of the application of principles of comity upon discovery in countries not signatories to a convention, see *Société Nationale Industrielle Aérospatiale v. United States District Court*, 482 U.S. 522, 107 S.Ct. 2542 (1987).''

(j) Finality of Judgments: Claim Preclusion and Issue Preclusion

Comparovich: But let us come back to our case. What was said in the decision of the Ruritanian Tribunal of First Instance?

Smooth: The decision was disappointing in one aspect. Concerning the facts, the court completely swallowed H's story, which they found to be corroborated by the correspondence. They even believed H's assertion that the contract, by its express terms, was performable in Ruritania. On that basis, the opinion overruled our objection to the court's jurisdiction. This is what a U.S. lawyer would call long-arm jurisdiction.

Following the factual finding that we had retained H, the opinion rejected our defense of illegality, and then proceeded to discuss the choice of law question whether the retainer, and H's compensation under it, should be governed by the law of the place of performance, or the law of the place where the contract was made. The opinion espoused the latter view as being in accordance with the presumed intention of the parties.[1] Referring to the opinions of the Institute and of the expert, the court further found that under the law of the place where the contract was made, H was entitled to a fee of $5,000.

At the end of the opinion, it was explained that H, having recovered only a minute fraction of his demand, must in effect be treated as the losing party. The ordering part of the judgment, therefore, after directing the defendant to pay $5,000 to the plaintiff, further provided that the plaintiff should bear all costs and should reimburse the defendant for the latter's attorneys' fees. Our bill of costs (including attorneys' fees) was substantial, because the amount involved in the litigation ($500,000) was relatively high. At any rate, it came to more than $5,000, so that on balance Mr. H owed us money. This outcome greatly increased my respect for the Ruritanian courts.[2]

Edge: H appealed, but suppose he had not. In that event, would Ruritanian law have precluded him from bringing a new action for his fee against the same defendant?

Comparovich: Yes.

Edge: Does this mean the civil-law systems recognize the same rules of res judicata that we apply in the U.S.?

Comparovich: It has been said that, ''the doctrine of res judicata is a principle of universal jurisprudence forming part of the legal systems of all

---

1. See the 6th edition of this book, Chapter VIII at 933, for a detailed discussion of choice of law issues.

2. See *supra* Chapter 7, Section 8(b) at 691 (Attorney Fee Shifting).

civilized nations.''[3] This, however, is true only insofar as the basic principle is concerned. With regard to the detailed rules of res judicata, there is considerable diversity among legal systems.[4]

Smooth: Don't all legal systems, or virtually all of them, agree that once an action has been judicially determined on the merits, a second action between the same parties is precluded if it involves the same cause of action?

Comparovich: They do, but this is an instance of what I have called ''mere acoustic agreement'' among legal systems: all of them utter identical or similar sounds, but they do not have the same meaning. Although the objective is the same (finality and procedural economy), there is no agreement concerning the definition and the dimensions of a ''cause of action.'' Terms such as ''claim,'' ''demand,'' or ''subject matter,'' sometimes are used in civil-law countries, instead of ''cause of action.''

To summarize it, ''the concept of claim preclusion is broader in common law than in civil law systems. In the civil law tradition, only the claims formally raised in an earlier proceeding are barred from being relitigated. Claims not raised in a previous action may be the object of a subsequent proceeding. The common law tradition, however, precludes not only claims actually raised, but also those that could potentially have been raised but were not. Therefore, all claims that *can* be raised in a proceeding, arising from the same conflict (i.e., transaction) between the parties, *must* be raised under penalty of being precluded in a future action.''[5] Give example for non Americans.

Most civil-law countries do not have a rule against splitting a cause of action. This can be explained with two examples: (A) A plaintiff, although claiming that defendant owes $500,000, asks in the complaint for a judgment in the amount of only $20,000. (B) A plaintiff, who suffered personal and property damage, claims only the property damages. While the first example of claim-splitting is allowed in German and Portuguese law, it is not allowed in most civil-law countries.[6] The second example is widely accepted.

In civil-law countries, a plaintiff may be prompted by cost-saving considerations to sue for less than the full amount of his or her claim, since

3. Gates v. Mortgage Loan & Ins. Agency, 200 Ark. 276, 284, 139 S.W.2d 19, 23 (1940).

4. See W. J. Habscheid, Rechtsvergleichende Bemerkungen zum Problem der materiellen Rechtskraft des Zivilurteils, published as a separate reprint from Offerings in Honor of C. N. Fragistas (Thessaloniki 1967); A. Zeuner, Rechtsvergleichende Bemerkungen zur objektiven Begrenzung der Rechtskraft im Zivilprozess, in H. Bernstein, U. Drobnig & H. Kötz, Festschrift für Konrad Zweigert 603 (1981).

5. See Gidi, Class Actions in Brazil: A Model for Civil Law Countries, 51 Am. J. Comp. L. 311, 384–86 (2003).

6. Compare Murray & Stürner, German Civil Justice 357–8 (2004) and Freitas, A Acção Declarativa Comum 112 (2000) with Oliva & Diez–Picazo, Derecho Procesal Civil. El Proceso de Declaración 505 (2000) and L. Cadiet & E. Jeuland, Droit Judiciaire Privé 465–66 (2006).

court costs, attorneys' fees, and the fee shifting are likely to be based directly or indirectly on the amount in controversy.[7] A judgment in the first action, whether in plaintiff's or defendant's favor, under the majority civil-law rule will have no claim-preclusion effect with respect to the $480,000 balance of plaintiff's claim or the personal damage but may settle the matter.

If the plaintiff prevails in the first lawsuit, he or she may be encouraged to bring a second lawsuit. If the plaintiff loses, she will probably never claim the remaining money. Even in the absence of an applicable rule of claim (or issue) preclusion, the parties generally will expect that the second court will reach the same conclusions as the first. In exceptional situations (e.g., discovery of previously unknown evidence, or a new turn in the decisions of the highest court), it may occasionally be promising to relitigate the matter. With respect to the first claim (of $20,000 or property damage), claim preclusion will prevent relitigation in any legal system.

The traditional formulation of the civil-law rule is well represented by art. 1351 of the French Civil Code: "the preclusive effect of a judgment is limited to the subject matter of the action. The thing claimed must be the same, the claims must be based on the same grounds, and between the same parties."[8] The operative word here is "claim." It is the claim that must be the same, not what is known in the U.S. as "cause of action," which is interpreted as "all claims arising out of the same transaction or occurrence."[9]

Smooth: This is claim preclusion. What about issue preclusion?

Comparovich: As we move from claim preclusion (also known as res judicata or doctrine of bar and merger) to issue preclusion (usually referred to as collateral estoppel), the disagreement between common-law and civil-law procedure becomes even more intense. With respect to issue preclusion, there is not even acoustic agreement among legal systems.[10]

7. See *supra* Chapter 7, Section 8(a) and (b) at 685 (discussing attorneys' fees and fee shifting).

8. See Codes of Civil Procedure of Brazil (art. 301.2), Portugal (arts. 497–98), Spain (arts. 42.2, 216 and 222.2), Germany (§ 322.1), Japan (art. 114.1), Belgium (art. 23).

9. See Gidi, Class Actions in Brazil: A Model for Civil Law Countries, 51 Am. J. Comp. L. 311, 384–86 (2003) (arguing that the expression "cause of action" has a much broader meaning in common law systems, referring to the whole controversy between the parties. *Res judicata*, correspondingly, has a much broader scope in common-law than in civil-law systems).

See also Restatement (Second) of Judgments § 24(1) (1982) ("When a valid and final judgment rendered in an action extinguishes the plaintiff's claim (...) the claim extinguished includes all rights of the plaintiff to remedies against the defendant with respect to all or any part of the transaction, or series of connected transactions, out of which the action arose"). A broad and pragmatic definition of "transaction" is given in § 24(2) of the Restatement. See also Fleming James, Jr., Geoffrey C. Hazard, Jr. & John Leubsdorf, Civil Procedure §§ 11.8 and 11.9 (2001); Jack Friedenthal, Mary Kay Kane & Arthur Miller, Civil Procedure 639–48 (1999).

10. See Millar, The Premises of the Judgment as Res Judicata in Continental and Anglo–American Law, 39 Mich.L.Rev. 1 ff., 238 ff. (1940); Taruffo, " 'Collateral Estoppel' e Giudicato Sulle Questioni (I) and (II)," Riv. Dir. Proc. 651 and 272 (1971 and 1972).

According to the common-law doctrine of issue preclusion, an "issue" that was a necessary step to the decision in one lawsuit cannot be relitigated in a second lawsuit ("preclusion"). For example, if a court enforces a contract clause in the first lawsuit, no party may challenge the validity of the contract in a second lawsuit because it was a "necessary step" to the enforceability of the clause. In order to avoid surprises, the issue must have been contested and fully litigated in the first lawsuit, and it must have been predictable that the issue would come up again in a future proceeding.

Civil-law countries do not have a uniform rule regarding issue preclusion, but, as a general proposition, it does not exist. After all, the motives of a final judgment are not binding.[11] Civil-law countries accept that a contract can be considered valid for the enforcement of a clause and be considered invalid in another proceeding for the purpose of enforcing another clause. This is a blind deference to a formality: the parties are the masters of the proceedings, and they establish the subject matter of the controversy strictly through their pleadings.

Issue preclusion exists, however, in Portugal and Greece.[12] According to some commentators, issue preclusion exists in Spain, but others do not share this novel position.[13]

In France, it seems that case law accepted that the logical steps necessary for the final judgment may be object of preclusion. However, case law is still ambiguous.[14] Thus, on March 28, 1995, the 1st civil chamber of the French *Cour de cassation* ruled that a judgment ordering a surety to pay a certain sum prevents that same surety from later claiming that the suretyship agreement was void. However, the same panel ruled on April 11, 1995, that a decision holding that a lease was terminated due to the landlord's failure to repair did not imply a finding that the lease was initially valid, and the lessee could subsequently raise the issue of invalidity of the lease.[15]

---

11. See Taniguchi, Reich & Miyake, Civil Procedure in Japan 7–157—7–158 (2008); Goodman, Justice and Civil Procedure in Japan 273, note 98, 420–21, 503 (2004); Murray & Stürner, German Civil Justice 358–9 (2004). See Brazilian Code of Civil Procedure (arts. 468–69).

12. In Portugal, it is a creation of case law, whereas in Greece, it is expressly provided for in art. 331 of the Greek Code of Civil Procedure. See Freitas *et al.*, 2 Código de Processo Civil Anotado 350–52 (2008); Yessiou–Faltsi, Civil Procedure in Hellas 241–42 (1995).

13. Compare Oliva & Diez–Picazo, Derecho Procesal Civil. El Proceso de Declaración 505–511 (2000) with M. Ortells Ramos, Derecho Procesal Civil 565–66 (2005).

14. See S. Guinchard, F. Ferrand & C. Chainais, Procédure Civile 256–64 (2008); L. Cadiet & E. Jeuland, Droit Judiciaire Privé 464–65 (2006) (citing contradictory precedents).

15. See Epx. Leclerc v. Sté. AGIP; Maison de Santé de l'Orangerie v. Centre de radiologie etc. de l'Orangerie, both 1996 D.J. 121 with a note by A. Bénabent discussing other cases and noting the relation between the problem raised by these cases, and the question of whether all issues concerning a contract must be raised at the same time.

See also the decision of the Court's *Assemblée plénière* of June 3, 1994, summarized by the Court in its Annual Report for 1994 (at 373–76) and thus, presumably recommended to the particular attention of the bench and bar, ruling that a decision holding

In any event, even in those countries in which issue preclusion exists, it may be controversial and have a more restrictive scope than in common-law countries. None of them will go as far as U.S. law does in extending the doctrine of collateral estoppel. Most of them will limit it severely, e.g., by applying it only to the "overriding issue" of fact or law determined in the first action.[16]

Recent developments on this matter are conflicting. While the Court of Justice of the European Communities may be on its way to accepting issue preclusion for international litigation within the European Union,[17] the ALI/UNIDROIT Principles and Rules of Transnational Civil Procedure counsel against giving issue preclusion to foreign judgments.[18]

However, it seems the trend in civil-law countries is towards slowly abandoning the formalistic approach of requiring a direct relationship between the pleadings and res judicata and accepting issue preclusion. Civil-law countries, however, would greatly benefit from studying the common-law practice, particularly the requirements that the issue be fully litigated, and that its recurrence be predictable.

This discussion has important consequences for international litigation, especially for the recognition of a foreign judgment. Which law should apply when the countries accord different scopes of res judicata (either claim or issue preclusion): the law of the country who issued the judgment or the law of the country recognizing it?[19] The Restatement (Third) of Foreign Relations states that the rule to be applied is the same as in the recognition of judgments between sister states within the U.S.: "a judgment of a foreign country ordinarily has no greater effect in the United

that a defendant had to complete the necessary notarial documents for a real estate transaction, in spite of defendant's argument that there was no consent (and thus no contract) did not prevent a subsequent judgment for the former defendant, now plaintiff in a separate action to have the contract declared void because in violation of the Civil Code rules on the minimum price in real estate transactions.

For a case that turned on the precise limits of the doctrine of collateral estoppel under Dutch law, and on the non-recognition of the doctrine in Swiss law, see Bata v. Bata, 39 Del.Ch. 258, 163 A.2d 493, especially at 502–11 (1960). The relevant Swiss rule is even more extensively discussed, and Swiss authorities are quoted, in In re Zietz' Estate, 207 Misc. 22, 135 N.Y.S.2d 573, 578–9 (Sur. Ct.1954), aff'd 285 App.Div. 1147, 143 N.Y.S.2d 602 (1st Dept.1955), motion for leave to appeal dismissed, 1 N.Y.2d 748, 152 N.Y.S.2d 295, 135 N.E.2d 49 (1956).

16. See the authorities cited *supra* note 15, especially the discussion of Dutch law in

the Bata decision and the article by Casad, at 62–70.

17. See Murray & Stürner, German Civil Justice 365–6 (2004).

18. See Principle 28 (stating that a court should only give issue preclusion effect to a foreign judgment "to prevent substantial injustice."). On Comment P–28C, it explains that "substantial injustice" would occur when a "party has justifiably relied in its conduct on a determination of an issue of law or fact in a previous proceeding." This is corollary of the principle of good faith, which also prohibits a party from taking a position contradictory to the one taken in a previous proceeding (*venire contra factum proprium*).

19. For discussions of the inherent conflicts issues, see R. C. Casad, Issue Preclusion and Foreign Country Judgments; Whose Law?, 70 Iowa L.Rev. 53 (1984); C. H. Peterson, Foreign Country Judgments and the Second Restatement of Conflict of Laws, 72 Colum.L.Rev. 220, 263 (1972); Bermann, Transnational Litigation 356–57 (2003).

States than in the country where the judgment was rendered." However, there are decisions on the opposite direction.[20]

Edge: Might this stem from a feeling on the part of the civilians that in their systems—due to the absence of effective discovery devices and to the relatively weak role played by counsel in the unearthing and presenting of evidence—the fact-finding process in the first action is intrinsically unreliable?[21]

Comparovich: It is, of course, true that where the decision in the first action is the result of slipshod fact-finding, the injustice thus inflicted on the loser grows in direct proportion to the expansion of the preclusionary effect upon claims and issues which a legal system accords to that decision. I doubt, however, that the civilians' relative caution in dealing with res judicata and especially with issue preclusion is due to any conscious lack of confidence in their own fact-finding processes.

Moreover, one might say the opposite is true: because U.S. law is so confident in the effectiveness of its discovery devices, coupled with extremely lenient pleading rules (notice pleading), liberal amendments, the possibility for the judge to decide beyond the parties' claims, and a very expensive proceeding, it provides for a much more restrictive preclusive effect to its judgments.[22] The civilian approach, however, is logical and consistent with a restrictive view of the principle of the adversarial process. Since the parties are the masters of the proceeding, only they can determine its precise scope. If they chose a more limited scope than the full conflict, their choice must be honored. The U.S. approach, however, is also oriented to protecting the interests of the court system.

Edge: What, then, is the reason for that cautious attitude in civil-law countries?

Comparovich: For a civil-law court, it is usually possible to make effective use of the findings made in a previous action, even though the doctrine of collateral estoppel may be non-existent in the particular legal system or inapplicable to the case at hand. This is so because the absence of exclusionary rules of evidence[23] enables a civil-law court simply to send for the file of the prior proceeding and to use its contents, including the decision and the findings recorded therein, as evidence in the new action. Under U.S. law, the former judgment is treated as hearsay. Thus, as a rule (though subject to exceptions) it is not admissible evidence in later litigation.[24] Therefore, the civilians are not faced with the hard choice an

---

20. ALI, The Restatement (Third) of Foreign Relations, § 481, comment c.

21. A somewhat similar thought has been suggested in the interesting article by Toyohisa Isobe, Civil Procedure, in 15 Japan Annual of Law and Politics 77, 81 (1967), referring to a paper by Tecoichireco Kikawa.

22. See James, Hazard & Leubsdorf, Civil Procedure § 11.2 (2001) (noting that "[a]s the rules of procedure have expanded the scope of the initial opportunity to litigate, they have invited a corresponding expansion of the extent to which that opportunity forecloses a subsequent opportunity").

23. See *supra* at 758–759.

24. For a thorough and critical discussion of the rule and the exceptions, see H. Motomura, Using Judgments as Evidence, 70 Minn.L.Rev. 979 (1986).

American court normally must make in cases of this kind: either treat the findings made in the prior case as binding (which often leads to harsh results), or completely disregard those findings and exclude them as evidence (which may be unrealistic and wasteful). This all-or-nothing approach of the common law has been criticized by Bentham and others.[25] The civilians, by rejecting or restricting the doctrine of collateral estoppel while simultaneously treating the earlier findings as evidence, in effect have adopted the intermediate view advocated by these critics.

Therefore, as much as some procedural devices in a foreign country may look unreasonable at first glance, once we know more about it, we discover there is internal consistency within the legal system.

Moreover, it is not entirely true that there is no issue preclusion in civil-law countries. There may be some exceptions.

For example, there are situations where a party finds it particularly important to have an issue of fact or law judicially determined in such a way that the determination will be binding in future litigation between the same parties. Some civil-law systems, therefore, provide a special form of declaratory judgment action for this purpose, but it must be specifically required by one party. The claim is treated as an incidental declaratory action within the main proceeding. This device, however, is not frequently used.[26] Furthermore, in Germany, Japan, Portugal, and Spain issue preclusion is specifically allowed in case of set-off (compensation of mutual debts between persons indebted to each other).[27] However, a set-off may be understood also as a counterclaim.

NOTES AND QUESTIONS

(1) What are the basic similarities between common-law and civil-law procedure? What accounts for these similarities? How far do they reflect "universal procedural policies?"[1] How far, for instance, do they reflect agreement on the values underlying, and inherent in, the rule of law? How far do they represent adherence by both systems to the fundamental principles of rationality, objectivity, and impartiality?[2] How far do they go beyond these fundamentals?

(2) What are the essential differences between common-law and civil-law procedure? What accounts for these differences? To what extent are particular procedural practices the product of a particular governmental structure or

---

25. See 7 Works of Jeremy Bentham 171 (Bowring ed., 1843).

26. See Millar, *supra* note 15; the Codes of Civil Procedure of Japan (art. 145), Germany (§ 256.2), Brazil (art. 5, 325, 470).

27. See the Codes of Civil Procedure of Germany (§ 322.2), Japan (art. 114.2), Portugal (art. 274.2.b), Spain (arts. 222.2 and 408). See Murray & Stürner, German Civil Justice 358–9 (2004); Oliva & Diez–Picazo, Derecho Procesal Civil. El Proceso de Declaración

509–11 (2000); Freitas, A Acção Declarativa Comum 108–13 (2000).

1. See A. T. von Mehren, The Importance of Structures and Ideologies for the Administration of Justice, 97 Yale L.J. 341, 347 (1987).

2. For one effort to identify the principles which rational persons would expect courts to use, see Michael Bayles, Principles for Legal Procedure, 5 Law & Phil. 33 (1986).

political or economy ideology?[3] Would it be true to say that all of these differences can ultimately be traced to the different *roles* played by the various actors in the drama of litigation? Consider, in this connection, that common law and civil law clearly differ as to the distribution of functions (a) between professional and lay adjudicators; (b) between parties and their lawyers (especially during the investigative phase of litigation); and (c) between court and counsel.[4]

What are the historical roots of the essential differences between common-law and civil-law procedure?

Do these differences, even though rooted in tradition, indicate any basic schism between the common-law and civil-law orbits concerning relevant moral, political, or social values?[5] This question is important; to the extent that it is answered in the negative, it would follow that these differences have been produced by historical factors that are accidental and irrelevant in terms of the problems and values moving us today. It would further follow that there is no intrinsic virtue in keeping the civil law "pure" from common-law influences or in the U.S. continuing refusal even to experiment with procedural institutions of a civilian bent.[6] The 2000 English civil procedure rules are an example of such successful experimentation.

(3) If we attempt not only to compare but also to evaluate procedural institutions, what standards and criteria should we use? At the outset, can we agree that the aim of a sound system of procedure is "the just, speedy and inexpen-

3. For an influential analysis of procedural systems—both civil and criminal—in terms of different patterns of distribution of authority and different views about proper functions of government in the administration of justice, see Damaška, The Faces of Justice and State Authority (1986).

4. For a comparative discussion of the peculiar features of common-law fact-finding, focusing on the significance of the divided tribunal, concentrated proceedings, and adversary presentation of evidence, see Damaška, Evidence Law Adrift (1997).

5. Is it true that the U.S. procedural arrangements and institutions reflect its antipathy to governmental intervention, while the civilian attitude is more "etatist?" Compare J. B. Board, Jr., Legal Culture and the Environmental Protection Issue, 37 Albany L.Rev. 603, 609–10 (1973), with Pekelis, Legal Techniques and Political Ideologies: A Comparative Study, 41 Mich.L.Rev. 665 (1943), reprinted in Law and Social Action: Selected Essays of Alexander H. Pekelis (M. Konvitz ed. 1950).

6. It is true, of course, that in some respects (e.g., jurisdiction over non-resident defendants, prevention of surprise), the U.S. law has moved in the direction of civil-law

solutions. But this has come about haphazardly and not as the result of a systematic effort to learn from the experience of others.

For suggestions (and counter-suggestions) concerning the use and limits of the comparative method for purposes of procedural reform, R. B. Schlesinger, Comparative Criminal Procedure: A Plea for Utilizing Foreign Experience, 26 Buff.L.Rev. 361, 382–85 (1977); J. H. Langbein, The German Advantage in Civil Procedure, 52 U.Chi.L.Rev. 823 (1985); J. C. Reitz, Why We Probably Cannot Adopt the German Advantage in Civil Procedure, 75 Iowa L.Rev. 987 (1990); Gross, The American Advantage: The Value of Inefficient Litigation, 85 Mich.L.Rev. 735 (1987); Allen, Köck, Reichenberg & Rosen, The German Advantage in Civil Procedure: A Plea for More Details and Fewer Generalities in Comparative Scholarship, 82 Nw.U.L.Rev. 708 (1988), with Langbein's Reply, id. 763, and a rebuttal, id. 785; Ernst C. Stiefel & James R. Maxeiner, Civil Justice Reform in the United States—Opportunity for Learning from "Civilized" European Procedure Instead of Continued Isolation?, 42 Am.J.Comp.L. 147 (1994); John H. Langbein, The Influence of Comparative Procedure in the United States, 43 Am.J.Comp.L. 545 (1995).

sive determination" of every justiciable dispute?[7] The goal of many of the most recent procedural reforms indeed seems to have been a search for a balance between justice, delay, and cost.

Assuming that we find common-law procedure superior in some respects, and civil-law procedure in others, to what extent is it possible to combine the best features of both? To what extent are the features of each procedural system so interdependent that not one can be changed without altering the nature of the whole system?[8]

An example of a superior common-law rule (mostly American, since it still does not exist in England) influencing the civil-law tradition is the adoption of class action legislation in several civil-law countries. It is just a matter of time before class actions exist in every single country.

An important first systematic effort to draft rules of procedure for transnational litigation that combine the most attractive features of both systems was the one sponsored by The American Law Institute (ALI) and the Institute for the Unification of Private Law (UNIDROIT).[9]

The European Union is also a good example of civil procedure unification, bringing civil-law and common-law traditions closer to each other.

One may also consider the Swedish Code of Judicial Procedure, promulgated in 1942 and in force since 1948, which reflects an interesting combination of continental and Anglo–American features.[10] An interesting feature is the flexibility in allowing the witness examination to be left to the parties or to the judge, according to the specific situation.[11]

(4) At the outset, the reformer who seeks to utilize foreign experience will meet the challenging question of how far rules of procedure that seem to work well in one country can be transplanted into another country governed by a different legal system. At first blush, it will seem that provincialism, which is particularly entrenched in procedural subjects, should be overcome and common-law lawyers as well as civilians should profit from each other's ideas and experiences. Further analysis shows, however, that the matter is more complicated. The numerous differences in procedural concepts and techniques that exist between the common-law and the civil-law worlds cannot be reduced to a common denominator because these differences fall into two distinct categories.

---

7. See FRCP 1.

8. For a broad attack on procedural traditionalism, with special emphasis on legal aid, class actions, and alternatives to traditional forms of civil litigation, see the multivolume comparative study by M. Cappelletti (ed.), Access to Justice (1978–79), especially the General Report (by Cappelletti & Garth) at the beginning of the first volume.

9. See ALI/UNIDROIT, Principles of Transnational Civil Procedure (2006). See *supra* at 713–14.

10. For an English translation of the code, see The Swedish Code of Judicial Procedure (1998). A thorough and incisive commentary can be found in Ginsburg & Bruzelius, Civil Procedure in Sweden (1965). For concise discussions, see Lindblom, Procedure, in 1 An Introduction to Swedish Law 95 (1981); Orfield, The Growth of Scandinavian Law 284–90 (1953); Ekelöf, Das schwedische Untergerichtsverfahren in Zivil- und Strafsachen, vol. 82 of the Schriftenreihe der Juristischen Studiengesellschaft Karlsruhe (1967); Lindell, Civil Procedure in Sweden (2004).

11. See *supra* at 782.

On the one hand, we observe differences that, however accidental their historical origin may be, relate to matters of genuine popular interest and feeling; matters, moreover, that under the U.S. system may be insulated from easy legislative reform by constitutional provisions. The question of lay participation in the administration of justice is the prime example, but not the only one. The elevated status of judges in common-law countries and the corresponding paucity of judicial manpower, as distinguished from the usual civil-law system of a more numerous civil service judiciary,[12] constitutes another tradition of such long standing that it may be beyond the reformer's reach. It follows that continental practices which are inconsistent with (a) the jury system or (b) the traditional status and organization of the common law judiciary, could not be duplicated in common law countries in the foreseeable future, even were the legal profession desirous of doing so. So long as the civil jury remains with the rule in the U.S., it will always be necessary to introduce all the evidence in *one* concentrated trial that then becomes the focus of the whole proceeding, as distinguished from the successive hearings and *enquêtes*, which in civil-law procedure serve to build up the all-important dossier.[13] The U.S. extreme economy in the number of judicial positions compels us to preserve the somewhat lopsided division of labor between Bench and Bar, which burdens counsel with many of the chores that the civil law imposes upon the court.

On the other hand, there are large areas of the law of procedure where the existing institutions are not so strongly underpinned by cherished traditions and hence are less resistant to change. It is in these areas that the reformer is most likely to derive practical benefit from comparison.[14] As a prime example, one might mention the litigation problems of the poor and of parties of limited means. Further examples are furnished by procedural problems that typically arise in environmental and consumer protection lawsuits, as well as in litigation involving a multiplicity of parties and issues. In such cases, American

12. In 1998, Germany had almost 21,-000 judges or one judge per 4,000 people, the U.S. had about 10,500 judges or one judge per 27,000 people. In 2001, the the UK had about 2,500 judges or one judge per 21,500 people. These are extreme examples, because Germany is the country with more judges in the world, both in absolute numbers as well as per capita. See Murray & Stürner, German Civil Justice 38 (2004).

P. Calamandrei, with his usual insight (although perhaps a trifle hyperbolically), makes a similar point in Procedure and Democracy 83 (1956): "The same judicial function that some 6000 career judges are unable to perform effectively in Italy is accomplished successfully and with considerably greater rapidity in England by not more than 100 judges!"

Richard A. Posner, Law and Legal Theory in the UK and USA 21–30 (1996), through an interesting exercise in slight-of-hand, has challenged the conventional wisdom about the fewness of English judges by treating barristers (who sometimes perform certain quasi-judicial functions) as if they were judges.

13. On the other hand, it should be kept in mind that in criminal cases civilian as well as common-law systems utilize lay adjudicators and espouse the idea of a single concentrated trial. With respect to criminal procedure, therefore, it has been thought that the U.S. might be able to benefit from civil-law experience without having to change any cherished institutional arrangements. See *infra*, Chapter 8, Section 4 at 828 (Criminal Procedure).

14. For some interesting remarks concerning the extent to which a study of civil-law procedure can bear fruit for purposes of procedural reform in a common-law country, see Going to Law—A Critique of English Civil Procedure—A Justice Report 28–29 (1974).

judges, at least in the federal system, feel an increasing need to assert greater control in the pretrial process and to play a more "managerial role". Continental experience in dealing with the same problems can be a useful source of inspiration for reformers.[15] Today, there is a feeling among American lawyers that in the past we unforgivably neglected the problems of the impecunious litigant, and that further progress needs to be made, especially with respect to civil litigation. Yet in the U.S. frantic rush to right old wrongs, they have paid too little attention to the large store of relevant experience accumulated in foreign countries, including those of the civil-law orbit.[16]

Foreign experience can be utilized even more easily when we deal with matters that are non-political and generally conceded to be of a technical nature, such as the question of whether issues should be formulated by formal written pleadings or orally in open court, and the related question whether and to what extent the court should be able to influence such formulation. Modern pretrial procedure, as exemplified by Rule 16 of the Federal Rules of Civil Procedure, shows that with respect to this question the U.S. is slowly (perhaps too slowly) moving toward continental ideas. The same is true with respect to the question of whether a party should be permitted to keep its evidence from the other side until the moment when such evidence is actually produced. The civilians, on the other hand, might profitably study, for instance, the benefits and costs of the common law more efficient discovery procedures (originally of civilian provenance), and the potentialities, in the search for truth, of vigorous examination and cross-examination by counsel, instead of by the court, the writ of certiorari, the power of the Supreme Court, instead of the Legislature, to enact rules of procedure. In summary, while the common-law procedure would greatly benefit from a more active judge, the civil-law procedure would benefit from more active parties.

Of particular interest is a comparative look at the law of evidence.[17] To continental lawyers it is a cause of pride that they have essentially freed their courts from the fetters of artificial restrictions on the admission of relevant evidence. In common-law countries, on the other hand, many of these restrictions have survived to this day, although there is controversy concerning their basis in history, policy, and logic. Some scholars assert that our rules of evidence are a by-product of the jury system and are necessary for a proper functioning of that system.[18] If that is the true and only justification for exclusionary rules of evidence, then the U.S. should follow the example of their civilian brethren and (much more radically than they have done heretofore) discard such rules in all non-jury proceedings.

Other scholars, however, have attempted to justify the hearsay rule[19] on the ground that the testimony of a witness not having first-hand knowledge is

15. See M. Cappelletti & B. Garth, A Comparative Conclusion, in 16 Int'l Ency. Comp.L. (Civil Procedure), ch. 6 (Ordinary Proceedings in First Instance) (1984).

16. See *supra* Chapter 7, Section 8(c) at 696 (Legal Aid).

17. The point we are about to make was later further developed in Damaška, *supra* note 4.

18. This is the well-known Thayer thesis. J. B. Thayer, A Preliminary Treatise on Evidence at the Common Law 266 (1898). More recently, this widely accepted thesis has been subject to criticism. See, e.g., J. H. Langbein, The Criminal Trial Before the Lawyers, 45 U.Chi.L.Rev. 263, 306 (1978).

19. Similar arguments might conceivably be made in support of other exclusionary rules.

inherently unreliable and hence dangerous to the integrity of the fact-finding process, no matter who may be the trier of fact.[20] The soundness of this view, which would tend to preserve at least some of the present exclusionary rules in non-jury as well as jury cases, is hotly disputed.[21] Thorough scrutiny of the civilians' experience may well be the most promising step toward resolving the dispute.[22]

A comparative approach to matters of procedure becomes an immediate practical necessity in the ever-growing number of cases in which litigation cuts across national boundaries. Many of the problems arising in such litigation can be resolved only by international judicial cooperation.[23] Bringing about such cooperation is one of the objectives of intelligent procedural reform. In the United States, this specific subject of reform was badly neglected until the late 1950s; since then, however, rapid progress has been made, first by a highly successful program of unilateral revision of American procedures for providing and obtaining international judicial assistance,[24] and, since 1964, by active participation in the treaty-writing work of the Hague Conference on Private International Law. Thus, as has been shown in the preceding materials, some of the difficulties caused by differences between civil-law and common-law procedure have been overcome or mitigated during the last five decades. The task, however, is far from complete.[25]

4.   Criminal Procedure

All U.S. lawyers should be interested in the subject of comparative criminal procedure. Indeed the U.S. system of criminal justice has been so

---

20.   See F. E. Booker & R. Morton, The Hearsay Rule, The St. George Plays and the Road to the Year Twenty–Fifty, 44 Notre Dame Law. 7 (1968).

21.   See McCormick on Evidence §§ 60, 327 (J. W. Strong ed., 4th ed. 1992); A. L. Levin & H. K. Cohen, The Exclusionary Rules in Nonjury Criminal Cases, 119 U.Pa. L.Rev. 905 (1971). For a particularly effective presentation of the case against the present state of the law, see J. B. Weinstein, Probative Force of Hearsay, 46 Iowa L.Rev. 331 (1961).

22.   Cf. Weinstein, *supra* note 21, at 347.

An interesting comparative discussion of the hearsay rule appears in Damaška, Of Hearsay and Its Analogues, 76 Minn.L.Rev. 425 (1992), as part of a symposium on hearsay rule reform (id. 363–889). Damaška points out that, while continental law does not categorically exclude hearsay, it does impose limitations on the use of second-hand evidence, especially in criminal cases; more-

over, these limitations are buttressed by safeguards (such as the requirement that the trier of fact justify reliance on such evidence in a reasoned opinion, and the reviewability of the grounds given on appeal) that would be hard to duplicate in a common law system. Thus the civil law protects against the dangers of reliance on hearsay in ways that the common law does not, and this may suggest that proposals to abandon the common law hearsay rule ought to be approached with caution.

23.   See *supra* Chapter 8, Sections 3(b) and (i) at 736 and 809 (discussing service of process and discovery abroad).

24.   See Fourth Annual Report of the Commission on International Rules of Judicial Procedure (1963) (the Commission and its Advisory Committee were created by Congress in 1958, 72 Stat. 1743); International Cooperation in Litigation: Europe 1–15, 409–64 (H. Smit ed., 1965).

25.   This is shown most dramatically by the continuing imbroglio regarding the use of American-style discovery in transnational liti-

signally unsuccessful that every attempt should be made to study and learn from the relevant experience of other nations. This is especially true in more recent years when, within the so called "war on terror" more than one stronghold of due process of law has been assaulted. Comparative criminal justice, as a field of legal scholarship has been on the rise not only because systems learn from each-other (on the good as well as on the bad), but also because many fundamental systemic and cultural differences between legal traditions appear quite resistant thus transforming the criminal process into a formidable laboratory of comparative research.[1]

For reasons different than the need to restore a certain degree of internationally acceptable legal standards, there is another practical reason for prospective American lawyers to be familiar with models of criminal procedure different from the U.S. one. In fact, under traditional rules of international law and under the terms of Status of Forces Agreements, U.S. military people (and their dependents) who commit crimes abroad can be subject to prosecution by "receiving states," most of which belong to the civil-law orbit.[2] The U.S. Senate's consent to the ratification of the first and most important of these treaties, the NATO Status of Force Agreement,[3] was coupled with a statement of "the sense of the Senate"[4] which, among other things, directed the armed forces to study the criminal procedure of countries where U.S. troops are stationed[5] and to observe and report on the adequacy and fairness of trials of U.S. military personnel in the courts of those countries.[6]

gation. See *supra* Chapter 8, Section 3(i) at 809.

1. See P. Roberts, *On Method: The Ascent of Comparative Criminal Justice* in 22 Oxford J of Legal Studies, 539 (2002).

2. See S. Lazareff, Status of Military Forces Under Current International Law (1971); J. M. Snee & K. A. Pye, Status of Forces Agreements and Criminal Jurisdiction (1957). The constitutional problems arising in this context were highlighted in Holmes v. Laird, 459 F.2d 1211 (D.C.Cir.1972), cert. denied, 409 U.S. 869, 93 S.Ct. 197 (1972). The number of such prosecutions has been declining because of a policy of seeking waivers of foreign jurisdiction whenever possible. Compare, e.g., the figures quoted in S. Riesenfeld, Book Review, 67 Am.J.Int'l L. 377 (1973), with those in Report of the Judge Advocate General of the Army, October 1, 1994, to September 30, 1995, in 44 Mil. Just.Rptr., at cxiii, cxvi-cxvii (West 1997).

At least in capital cases, however, the policy of seeking waivers of foreign jurisdiction has run up against current European reluctance, on human rights grounds, to surrender defendants who face charges punishable by death under U.S. law. See Steven J. Lepper, Short v. The Kingdom of the Nether-

lands: Is It Time to Renegotiate the NATO Status of Forces Agreement?, 24 Vand.J.Transnat'l L. 867 (1991); John E. Parkerson & Steven J. Lepper, Jurisdiction—NATO Status of Forces Agreement—U.S. Servicemen Charged with Criminal Offenses Overseas—European Convention on Human Rights, 85 Am.J.Int'l L. 698 (1991); John E. Parkerson, Jr. & Carolyn S. Stoehr, The U.S. Military Death Penalty in Europe: Recent Threats from Recent European Human Rights Developments, 129 Mil.L.Rev. 41 (1990).

3. 4 U.S.T. 1792, TIAS. No. 2846, 199 U.N.T.S. 67 (1953).

4. 4 U.S.T. 1828–29.

5. This legislative request has been called "the first instance of the study of comparative law being required by a legislative body of the United States." Schwenk, Highlights of a Comparative Study of the Common and Civil Law Systems, 33 N.C.L.Rev. 382, 397–98 (1955).

6. See J. H. Williams, An American's Trial in a Foreign Court: The Role of the Military's Trial Observer, 34 Mil.L.Rev. 1 (1966).

Even a cursory look to the most important reforms of criminal procedure worldwide[7] shows very clearly that the U.S. model became hegemonic in the aftermath of World War II. This hegemony has inspired important reforms in many civil law countries attracted by the U.S. adversary "arms lengths" model of procedure.[8] The phenomenon was certainly originated by a widely diffused perception that the U.S. criminal justice system, despite the repulsion generated in many quarters by the death penalty issue, could be considered highly desirable from the perspective of due process of law. This perception has certainly been encouraged by the spectacular successes the Warren Court usually emphasized by domestic students of criminal procedure.

In the following Article, adapted and updated for the purpose of this edition, the first Author of this casebook takes a very interestingly critical view.

R. B. Schlesinger, Comparative Criminal Procedure: A Plea for Utilizing Foreign Experience

26 Buffalo L. Rev. 361 (1977).[1]

. . .

(a) Outline of the Course of a Criminal Proceeding in a Continental Country

In the civilian systems,[2] as in our own, the policeman normally is the first public official to arrive at the scene of an alleged crime, or to receive a

---

7. See R. Vogler, A World View of Criminal Justice (2005).

8. See the classic study by Mirjan Damaška, The Faces of Justice and State Authority (1986).

1. What follows is an excerpt from the printed version of the 1976 James McCormick Mitchell Lecture presented by Prof. Schlesinger to the Faculty of Law and Jurisprudence, State University of New York at Buffalo, on October 14, 1976, followed by a supplementary note on recent developments in continental criminal procedure and on recent suggestions about how foreign experience can be utilized in reforming American law on the subject. Despite being more than thirty years old, the description offered in Schlesinger's article is still fundamentally accurate. For this edition, while we kept the text unchanged, we have modified and updated footnotes where necessary and we have renumbered its sections.

2. On French criminal procedure in particular, see A. V. Sheehan, Criminal Procedure in Scotland and France (1972); Richard S. Frase, "Introduction" to The French Code of Criminal Procedure 1–40 (29 Ameri-can Series of Foreign Penal Codes, G. L. Kock & R. S. Frase trans., rev. ed. 1988); R. S. Frase, Comparative Criminal Justice as Guide to American Law Reform: How Do the French Do It, How Can We Find Out, and Why Should We Care? 78 Calif. L. Rev. 542 (1990); Bron McKillop, Anatomy of a French Murder Case, 45 Am.J.Comp.L. 527 (1997); G. W. Pugh, Administration of Criminal Justice in France: An Introductory Analysis, 23 La.L.Rev. 1 (1962); Edward A. Tomlinson, The Saga of Wiretapping in France: What It Tells Us About the French Criminal Justice System, 53 La.L.Rev. 109 (1993); Edward A. Tomlinson, Nonadversarial Justice: The French Experience, 42 Md.L.Rev. 131 (1983); Most recently J. Hodgson, French Criminal Justice. A Comparative Account of the Investigation and Prosecution of Crimes in France (2006).

On criminal procedure in Germany, see J. H. Langbein, Comparative Criminal Procedure: Germany (1977); The Criminal Justice System of the Federal Republic of Germany (Association Internationale de Droit Pénal, 1981); J. Herrmann, The Federal Republic of Germany, in Major Criminal Justice Systems:

report concerning it.³ He may conduct an informal investigation; but his power to arrest the suspect without judicial warrant, or to proceed to warrantless searches and seizures, is seriously limited. Thus, whenever measures are contemplated by the police that affect the freedom of the suspect, it becomes necessary at a very early stage of the investigation to involve the prosecutor and the court.

There is no grand jury. The official phase of the pretrial investigation is in the hands of a judge—whom the French call juge d'instruction (investigating judge)—or of the prosecutor.⁴ Both the judge and the prosecutor are essentially civil servants. The judge enjoys the usual guarantees of judicial independence. The prosecutor typically does not; he may be a link in a hierarchical chain of command, often leading up to the Minister of Justice. Nevertheless, except perhaps in cases having strong political overtones, the civil-servant prosecutor operating in a continental system can be expected to be reasonably impartial. He does not have to run for re-election; and his promotion within the civil service hierarchy may depend as much on his efficiency in sorting out and dropping investigations mistakenly commenced against innocent suspects as it does on his record of procuring convictions of the guilty.⁵

The magistrate or prosecutor conducting the investigation will build up an impressive dossier by interrogating all available witnesses, including

A Comparative Survey 106 (G. F. Cole, S. J. Frankowski & M. G. Gertz eds., 2d ed. 1987); M. Dubber, American Plea Bargains, German Lay Judges, and the Crisis of Criminal Procedure, 49 Stan.L.Rev. 547 (1997); R. S. Frase & T. Weigend, German Criminal Justice as a Guide to American Law Reform: Similar Problems, Better Solutions? 18 B.C. Int'l & Comp.L.Rev. 317 (1995).

For detailed analysis and comparison of criminal procedure in France, Germany, and England, see Comparative Criminal Procedure (J. Hatchard, B. Huber & R. Vogler eds., 1996). See also the relevant chapters in Criminal Procedure Systems in the European Community (C. van den Wyngaert ed., 1993). For a comparative introduction of the systems of Belgium, France, Germany, England and Italy, see European Criminal Procedures (J. Spencer & M. Delmas–Marty eds. 2002).

On the historical antecedents of criminal procedure in civil-law countries, see Esmein, History of Continental Criminal Procedure (1913); Ploscowe, The Development of Present–Day Criminal Procedures in Europe and America, 48 Harv.L.Rev. 433 (1935); J. H. Langbein, Torture and the Law of Proof (1976).

3.   It is important not to equate French or German police officers with their Ameri-

can counterparts. In the more advanced continental countries, police officers engaged in criminal investigation tend to be highly professionalized members of a tightly-knit non-local organization and are subject to internal institutional constraints which are probably more effective than those operative in the United States in assuring adherence to the legal rules circumscribing police powers.

4.   According to formal statements of the law, informal police inquiries should proceed only to the point necessary to avoid the disappearance of evidence. In practice, however, the police usually conduct extensive inquiries prior to forwarding the findings to the prosecutor or the judge.

5.   An excellent discussion of these problems can be found in C. Guarnieri, Pubblico Ministero e Sistema Politico (1984). Observe also that in many continental systems the discretionary powers of the prosecutor are more narrowly circumscribed than in this country. See, e.g., Herrmann, The Rule of Compulsory Prosecution and the Scope of Prosecutorial Discretion in Germany, 41 U.Chi.L.Rev. 468 (1974). Concerning prosecutorial discretion *not* to prosecute, see Damaška, The Reality of Prosecutorial Discretion, 29 Am.J.Comp.L. 119 (1981). Highly instructive comparative chapters devoted to the prosecutor and the police can be found in J. Spencer & M. Delmas–Marty, *supra* note 2.

those named by the suspect, and collecting other relevant evidence. The suspect himself will be interrogated, and in most continental countries such interrogation will take place in the presence of his counsel. In many civil law countries the law expressly provides that the suspect has a right to remain silent and that he must be informed of this right. Of course, there is no physical compulsion to make him talk. Experience in continental countries shows, nevertheless, that in the preliminary investigation as well as at the trial itself the defendant usually does talk. The reasons for this will be explored below.

At the conclusion of the official investigation, the prosecutor (or, in some countries, the investigating magistrate) must decide whether in his judgment the evidence is strong enough to warrant the bringing of formal charges against the suspect. If charges are brought, the accused still does not necessarily have to stand trial. Under the traditional civil-law practice, the dossier now goes to a three-judge panel—on a higher level of the judicial hierarchy. Only if this panel, having studied the dossier and having given defense counsel an opportunity to submit arguments and to suggest the taking of additional evidence, determines that there exists what we would call "reasonable cause," will the accused have to stand trial. (It should be noted here how misleading it can be to call the continental procedure "inquisitorial" and to contrast it with our allegedly "adversary" process. Under continental procedure, the accused has a two-fold opportunity to be heard—first in the course of the preliminary investigation, and again when the three-judge panel examines the dossier—before any decision is made whether he has to stand trial. This should be compared with the completely nonadversary grand jury proceeding by which in the overwhelming majority of American jurisdictions a prosecutor can obtain an indictment.)

In every civil-law country, counsel for the accused has the absolute right to inspect the whole dossier. This will be discussed later.

At the trial, the bench normally (though not uniformly) will consist of one or three professional judges and a number of lay assessors. The jury system, which was introduced in continental Europe in the wake of the French Revolution, more recently was replaced in most continental countries by the system of the mixed bench.[6] Under this system, the profession-

---

6. See Damaška, Structures of Authority and Comparative Criminal Procedure, 84 Yale L.J. 480, 492–93 (1975). For a thorough study of the system of the mixed bench, see Casper & Zeisel, Lay Judges in the German Criminal Courts, 1 J.Legal Stud. 135 (1972). On the mixed *cour d'assises* in France, see Roderick Munday, Jury Trial, Continental Style, 13 Legal Stud. 204 (1993).

On the recent reintroduction of jury trial in Russia, where it existed between 1864 and 1917, see Stephen Thaman. The Resurrection of Trial by Jury in Russia, 31 Stan.J.Int'l L.

61 (1995). See also James W. Diehm, The Introduction of Jury Trials and Adversarial Elements into the former Soviet Union and Other Inquisitorial Countries, 11 J. Transnat'l L. & Pol'y 1 (2001). Spain was committed by art. 125 of its 1978 Constitution to reinstitute jury trial and did so in 1995. For comparison between the two models Stephen C. Thaman, Europe's New Jury Systems, in World Jury Systems (Neil Vidmar ed. 2000), 322. There have been proposals to revive trial by jury in Japan, where it existed in limited form from 1928 to 1943. See Meryll Dean, Trial by Jury: A Force for Change in Japan,

al judges and the lay assessors together form the court, which as a single body passes on issues of law as well as fact, and determines both guilt and sentence. Thus, the trial does not have to be bifurcated into a first hearing devoted solely to the issue of guilt, and a subsequent second hearing dealing with the sentence.[7] The issue of guilt and the measure of punishment are determined simultaneously and by the same body of adjudicators.

The dossier, reflecting the pretrial investigation, plays a role during the trial as well. Three of the dramatis personae at this point are thoroughly conversant with its contents: the prosecutor, the defendant's counsel, and the Presiding Justice. The Presiding Justice has the dossier in front of him during the trial. On the other hand, the lay judges, and often the professional judges other than the Presiding Justice of the court, are unfamiliar with the dossier. Consequently, only the evidence received in open court (as distinguished from the contents of the dossier) may be considered in reaching a decision.

After a reading of the charges, the Presiding Justice normally will call upon the defendant to give his name and occupation and to make a statement concerning his general background. Then, after a warning that he has the right, at his option, to remain silent concerning the charges against him, the defendant will be asked what (if anything) he wishes to say about the charges.[8] The defendant, who is not put under oath, at this point has the opportunity to tell his side of the story by way of a coherent statement. This will be followed by questions addressed to the defendant. In practice most of the questioning will be done by the Presiding Justice, who is well prepared for this task by previous study of the dossier in his hands. Prosecution and defense counsel may suggest, or be permitted to ask, additional questions.

Frequently, the defendant's response to such questioning will be a confession. But regardless of whether he confesses before or during the trial, trial proceedings must go on, and the court must satisfy itself of the defendant's guilt by means of evidence corroborating his confession. In other words, the defendant cannot waive his right to trial by "pleading guilty" (or nolo contendere).

44 Int'l & Comp.L.Q., 379 (1995); see also Richard Lempert, A Jury for Japan? 40 Am. J.Comp.L. 37 (1992). Lester W. Kiss, Reviving the Criminal Jury in Japan, in Vidmar cit. at 354. The law finally passed on May 28, 2004 ended up creating mixed panels requiring selected citizens to take part in criminal court trials of certain severe crimes and make decisions together with professional judges both on guilt and on the sentence. These citizens are called "Saiban-in" (lay judge). The panel should be made of six Saiban-in and three professional judges. According to the law the system must be implemented by May 2009.

7. The participation of lay judges has the further effect that the trial has to be a continuous session without substantial interruptions or adjournments. Thus, in contrast to the successive, chopped-up hearings that characterize civilian *civil* proceedings, a *criminal* trial under their system has the quality of a single, concentrated, and dramatic event; it is truly a "trial" in our sense of the word.

8. The trial described in this and the following three paragraphs of the text reflects the applicable code provisions. In practice, many of the steps outlined in the text can be omitted or condensed in cases where a confession has been obtained, that is, in the great majority of routine cases.

After this interrogation of the defendant, the witnesses will be examined in similar fashion. Normally, the witnesses will be the same individuals whose preliminary testimony is recorded in the dossier; but additional witnesses, not discovered in the course of the pretrial investigation, may be subpoenaed by the defense or may appear voluntarily at the trial. Non testimonial evidence, especially physical evidence, also may be produced, and the court may inspect the place of the crime.

Rules leading to the exclusion of relevant evidence are less numerous than in this country, and much less capable of impeding the fact-finding process.[9] Counterparts to our "exclusionary rule" exist in few civil law countries; even where they exist (as in Germany), their practical impact is much less significant than here.[10]

After closing arguments by prosecution and defense, and after the defendant has been accorded the last word, the court retires to deliberate. The lay judges, whose vote in most (but not all) continental countries carries the same weight as that of their professional colleagues, may outnumber the latter.[11] In the great majority of civil-law countries, the judgment does not have to be unanimous; and the fact that it is not unanimous will not be disclosed. Unless the judgment is one of acquittal, it will pronounce conviction and sentence. It will say, for example, that defendant is found guilty of armed robbery and for such crime is sentenced to four years in the reformatory.

9. That exclusionary rules are unique of the common law tradition is now commonly considered a gross exaggeration. Exclusion of illegally obtained evidence is the average rule. See for a standard civilian experience, D Giannoulopoulus, The Exclusion of Improperly Obtained Evidence in Greece: Putting Constitutional Rights First, 11 International J of Evidence and Proof, 181 (2007).

10. Reasons for the weak practical implementation of existing exclusionary rules in the civil-law systems are discussed in Damaška, Evidentiary Barriers to Conviction and Two Models of Criminal Procedure: A Comparative Study, 121 U.Pa.L.Rev. 506 (1973) at 523–24. See also C. M. Bradley, The Exclusionary Rule in Germany, 96 Harv. L.Rev. 1032, 1063 (1983). See more recently P. Roberts, Faces of justice adrift? Damaška's Comparative Method and the Future of Common Law Evidence in Crime, Procedure and Evidence in a Comparative and International Context. Essays in Honour of Professor Mirjan Damaška, 261 (J. Jackson, M. Langer & P. Tillers eds. 2008) (hereinafter Festshrift Damaška)

11. It has been argued, however, that the purposes of lay participation—to keep the professional judges from performing their tasks too routinely, and to increase popular confidence in the administration of justice—can be attained without having the lay members of the panel outnumber (and conceivably outvote) the professional judges. This argument, coupled with the further consideration that, historically, the inclusion of a lay element in criminal tribunals is only a surviving remnant of the 19th-century transplantation of the English jury trial into the continental systems, led (West) Germany in 1974 to change from a system in which the trial court dealing with the gravest crimes consisted of three professional judges and six lay assessors to one in which the number of lay assessors was reduced to two. The 1974 amendment is embodied in the Gerichtsverfassungsgesetz [GVG] § 76, as re-promulgated by Law of May 9, 1975, [1975] BGBl I 1077. See 1 Löwe-Rosenberg, Die Strafprozessordnung und das Gerichtsverfassungsgesetz, Introduction, ch. 15, annos. 6–9 (23d ed. 1976). The statement in the text is still correct with respect to other continental countries.

As a rule, the judgment of the court of first instance is subject to an appeal on both the law and the facts.[12] New evidence may be presented to the appellate court, and the proceedings before that court, which has power to review the sentence as well as the determination of guilt or innocence, may amount to a trial de novo. The decision of the appellate court normally can be attacked by a second appeal to a court of last resort, but in this last court only questions of law will be reviewed. The right to appeal is given not only to the defendant but to the prosecutor as well.[13]

In concluding this brief overview, I should like to stress that it is too highly abbreviated to be totally accurate, and that it does not make sufficient allowance for the considerable differences that exist among the various civil-law systems of criminal procedure. My hope is that despite such over-generalization I have been able to highlight some of the important features that are common to a number of the civil-law systems and set them apart from our procedure.

(b) Arrest and Pretrial Detention in Civil–Law Countries

With the above comments as a background, let me now turn to a discussion of some of the procedural devices and arrangements to be found in civil-law countries that might provide American reformers with food for thought.

The first two items—treated together because they are so closely connected—are arrest and pretrial detention.

In this country, it is still the general rule that criminal proceedings routinely "start with the harsh, and in itself degrading, measure of physical arrest."[14] In the federal courts, and in less than one-half of the states, this brutal and (as a rule) unnecessary routine has been modified by statutory provisions that in certain situations authorize the issuance of a summons in lieu of arrest. But these modifications are halfhearted; frequently they are limited to cases of minor violations, and most of the relevant provisions leave it to the discretion of the police or the prosecutor whether a summons should take the place of physical arrest.

The civil-law countries, on the other hand, unanimously recognize that the initiation of a judicial proceeding, whether civil or criminal, never

---

12. In some continental countries, there are exceptions to this rule: the decisions of the courts dealing with the gravest crimes sometimes are subject to an appeal only on points of law. See G. O. W. Mueller & F. Le Poole–Griffiths, Comparative Criminal Procedure 210 (1969). These presently illogical exceptions can be explained only on historical grounds. They date back to the 19th-century period when an English-style system of jury trials (which of course precluded appellate review of the jury's express or implied factual findings) prevailed on the continent.

13. The reader will recall that Justice Cardozo called attention to this civil-law practice in Palko v. Connecticut, 302 U.S. 319, 58 S.Ct. 149 (1937). See *supra* at 64. On the history of criminal appeal in England and Wales, R. Patterden, English Criminal appeals 1844–1994 (1996).

14. S. A. Cohn, "Criminal Records"—A Comparative Approach, 4 Ga.J.Int.Comp.L. 116 (1974). Cf. Richard A. Posner, Overcoming Law 484 (1995): "the arrest of Joseph K in the first chapter of [Kafka's] *The Trial* is immensely more *civilized* than any arrest would be likely to be in the land of freedom at the threshold of the twenty-first century."

requires the defendant's physical arrest. It follows, according to civilian thinking, that the necessary notification of the defendant is to be effected by a summons, in criminal as well as civil proceedings, and that it is unthinkable to use physical arrest as a routine measure against a suspect who has not yet been tried and who, consequently, must be presumed innocent.

The question whether a suspect should be detained pending trial is, in the civilians' view, completely separate and distinct from the routine of initiating the proceeding. Except in carefully defined emergency situations, a judicial order is required to detain the suspect before trial. The requirements for the issuance of such an order are strict. In West Germany, for instance, it can be issued only if the court, by definite findings of fact, determines that the following three elements exist: First, there must be strong reasons for believing that the suspect has committed the crime.[15] Second, the evidence before the court must show a specific, rational ground for pretrial detention, such as danger of flight or danger of tampering with the evidence.[16] Third, such detention must meet the requirement of proportionality; that is, it will not be ordered if the hardship caused by it is disproportionate to the gravity of the offense.[17] The order, which must state the grounds on which each of these requirements is thought to be met, is subject to immediate appeal.[18]

Compare this rational design of pretrial detention with our traditional law of arrest and bail. Probable cause that the suspect has committed the crime, a ground merely supporting the initiation of prosecution, suffices for arrest. Once arrested, the suspect's release depends on his capacity to post bail. Under procedures still prevailing in many states, an indigent defendant can thus be kept in jail despite the absence of any rational justification for detaining him, while the wealthy suspect may be released even though he is likely to flee or to intimidate witnesses. It is true that recently, through the Federal Bail Reform Act and similar legislation in a minority of states, we made progress in this area. But note that the provisions of the federal Act as well as those of state statutes authorizing so-called "Own Recognizance" (O.R.) releases become operative only after the suspect has been subjected to the (frequently unnecessary) indignity of the initial arrest. There is a further contrast to continental practice: in many states (but not under the federal Act) an application for "O.R." release may be denied without any statement of reasons, and in some jurisdictions the burden is upon the arrestee to show good cause why he should be released. It follows, I submit, that even in our most liberal jurisdictions something

---

15. Strictly speaking, this is a ground supporting the initiation of proceedings, rather than justifying detention as such.

16. In homicide cases, this requirement is eliminated. In cases involving certain other types of very serious crimes the requirement can be met by a finding that the suspect would be likely to commit similar offenses if released.

17. Moreover, pretrial detention is precluded in most of the cases in which the maximum sentence does not exceed six months.

18. The detainee also has the right at any time to demand a judicial inquiry regarding the continuing existence of all the requirements for detention.

might yet be gained by comparative study of the subject of arrest and pretrial detention.[19]

The two remaining topics I should like to discuss have one feature in common: both of them bear, directly and importantly, upon the central function of the criminal process, the ascertainment of truth.[20]

(c) Discovery

The first of these two related topics comes under the heading of "discovery." The continental systems invariably provide that at an early stage of the proceedings, and in any event well before the trial, the defendant and his counsel acquire an absolute and unlimited right to inspect the entire dossier, that is, all of the evidence collected by the prosecution and the investigating magistrate.[21] Thus it is simply impossible to obtain a conviction by a strategy of surprise.[22] It must be remembered, moreover, that in most cases there can be a trial de novo on appeal, which, of course, acts as a second barrier against the successful use of surprise evidence.

To facilitate inspection of the dossier by defense counsel, German law provides that upon his request he should normally be allowed to take the dossier to his office or home for thorough and unhurried study.

Concerning this latter point, and generally concerning details of inspection procedure, other continental systems may not go quite so far as the German Code. But defense counsel's basic right to timely inspection of the entire dossier has become an article of faith throughout the civil law world—and, indeed, in the socialist orbit as well. This is well illustrated by an incident that occurred during World War II, when representatives of the United States, Great Britain, France, and Soviet Russia met in London to prepare the Charter of the International Tribunal which later tried the principal war criminals at Nuremberg. Among other issues of procedure, the question of discovery came up for discussion. Mr. Justice Jackson, who attended the meeting as the representative of the United States, later reported that at that point the Soviet Delegation objected to our practice on the ground that it is not fair to defendants. Under the Soviet system when

19. For a case showing that (with respect to pretrial detention) even the most liberal American jurisdictions still do not accord the defendant the same legal safeguards normally applicable in the more enlightened civil-law countries, see Van Atta v. Scott, 27 Cal.3d 424, 166 Cal.Rptr. 149, 613 P.2d 210 (1980).

20. See for a broad comparative discussion critically touching on a variety of key comparative juxtapositions, E. Grande, Dances of Criminal Justice: Thoughts on Systemic Differences and the Search for the Truth, in Festshrift Damaška, 145.

21. See Damaška, Barriers, *supra* note 10, at 533–34. A good example of a code

provision spelling out the details of this right of inspection is § 147 of the German Code of Criminal Procedure (*Strafprozessordnung*).

The prosecutor must include in the dossier every document that contains any information relating to the investigation; nothing except purely internal instructions and communications among members of the prosecutorial staff may be kept from the defendant. See 1 Löwe-Rosenberg, Die Strafprozessordnung und das Gerichtsverfassungsgesetz § 147, anno. 2 (22d ed. 1973).

22. See, e.g., Murray, A Survey of Criminal Procedure in Spain and Some Comparisons with Criminal Procedure in the United States, 40 N.D.L.Rev. 7, 9, 13 (1964).

an indictment is filed every document and the statement of every witness which is expected to be used against the defendant must be filed with the court and made known to the defense. It was objected that under our system the accused does not know the statements of accusing witnesses nor the documents that may be used against him, that such evidence is first made known to him at the trial, too late to prepare a defense, and that this tends to make the trial something of a game instead of a real inquest into guilt. It must be admitted that there is a great deal of truth in the criticism.[23]

So far as the Nuremberg trial was concerned, the problem was overcome by a compromise between the common-law and civil-law positions. What seems significant beyond the immediate context, however, is the fact that Mr. Justice Jackson had to listen to, and did not have much of an answer for, this lecture on due process delivered by his Soviet counterpart.[24]

In its aversion to unlimited pretrial discovery in criminal proceedings, the American legal system today stands virtually alone. In England, the older common law tradition of trial by surprise has long been abandoned, and present English practice, by a combination of procedural devices and informal arrangements, permits defense counsel, well before the trial, to become fully familiar with every element of the facts known to the prosecution.

In this country, although we are ahead of the rest of the world with respect to discovery in civil procedure, we have been remarkably slow in taking the blindfolds from the eyes of the criminal defendant. Many states have not even begun to devise effective tools for criminal discovery.[25]

The hope that broad criminal discovery would be forced on the states by the Supreme Court has not been fulfilled. The contours of the limited constitutional right recognized in cases such as Brady v. Maryland[26] are

23. Quoted by Bull, Nuremberg Trial, 7 F.R.D. 175, 178 (1948).

24. However, as we shall soon see, fair comparison requires that the problems of criminal discovery be placed in a larger context. The continental defendant acquires an unlimited right to discovery only *after* pretrial investigators had ample opportunity to "discover" information from him. This opportunity is unparalleled in American criminal prosecutions.

25. The preliminary hearing, in its American (as distinguished from English) form is not an effective discovery device. See Goldstein, The State and the Accused: Balance of Advantage in Criminal Procedure, 69 Yale L.J. 1149, 1183 (1960); cf. Adams v. Illinois, 405 U.S. 278, 282, 92 S.Ct. 916 (1972), id. at 292 (Douglas, J., dissenting). Moreover, in most of those American jurisdictions that have not abolished grand juries,

the prosecutor can cut off the defendant's right to a preliminary hearing by securing an indictment. See A.L.I., A Model Code of Pre-Arraignment Procedure 592 (1975), and authorities cited therein. Hawkins v. Superior Court, 22 Cal.3d 584, 150 Cal.Rptr. 435, 586 P.2d 916 (1978), recognized the defendant's right to a preliminary hearing even in cases in which the prosecution had obtained a grand jury indictment; but this was eliminated in 1990 by Proposition 115. See *infra* note 29.

Nor is the motion to inspect grand-jury minutes a viable discovery tool. See, e.g., Proskin v. County Court of Albany County, 30 N.Y.2d 15, 330 N.Y.S.2d 44, 280 N.E.2d 875 (1972).

26. 373 U.S. 83, 83 S.Ct. 1194 (1963). See also Brown v. Chaney, 469 U.S. 1090, 105 S.Ct. 601 (1984) (Burger, C.J., & White &

quite indistinct, with the result that this constitutional doctrine supplies reliable guidelines only in cases of outrageously suppressive tactics employed by the prosecution.

A few jurisdictions, including the federal courts,[27] have progressed beyond the Neanderthal stage.[28] But under the Federal Rules the defendant is still precluded from getting a pretrial look at the most vital materials—the statements made by government witnesses or prospective government witnesses. With very few exceptions,[29] state discovery practice in the so-called liberal states is subject to similar limitations, and in many American jurisdictions, including the federal system, even the names of the People's witnesses cannot be obtained as of right before trial.[30]

In no American jurisdiction does the defendant have a right to continental-style inspection, to discovery routinely obtained and unlimited in scope.[31]

I submit that experience gained under the continental systems could be exceedingly useful in dealing with the classical anti-discovery arguments that continue to mold the attitude of our courts and legislators. Let us look, first of all, at the "abuse" argument, which is born of the fear that the defendant, once he is apprised of the State's evidence, will be enabled to prepare perjured testimony and to bribe or intimidate, or perhaps even eliminate, the witnesses for the prosecution. It must be conceded that in many situations, and especially in cases involving organized crime, this danger is real. American advocates of discovery have replied that the danger can be minimized by giving the court discretionary power to issue protective orders.[32] Quaere, however, whether it is a satisfactory solution to leave everything to the court's discretion. The civil law has a better answer to the "abuse" argument. Under the continental systems—and I shall soon

Rehnquist, JJ. dissenting from denial of cert.); United States v. Agurs, 427 U.S. 97, 96 S.Ct. 2392 (1976). It must be emphasized that Brady and cognate cases usually do no more than require disclosure at trial, when disclosure is of limited usefulness.

27. See Fed.R.Crim.Proc. 16.

28. For a current review of the state of U.S. law, see Wayne R. LaFave & Jerold H. Israel, Criminal Procedure §§ 20.1–20.7 (2d ed. 1992 & Supps.).

29. Until recently, the most notable exception was California, which allowed the defense fairly wide discovery in criminal cases. However, Proposition 115 (the "Crime Victims Justice Reform Act"), eff. June 6, 1990, restricted defense discovery, while expanding discovery for the prosecution, in order to eliminate the "one-way street" and make discovery more "reciprocal." Its provisions are summarized in Raven v. Deukmejian, 52 Cal.3d 336, 342–46, 276 Cal.Rptr. 326,

329–32, 801 P.2d 1077, 1080–83 (1990). See also Proposal 115: The Crime Victims Justice Reform Act, 22 Pac.L.J. 1010 (1991); Victims Rights Symposium, 23 Pac.L.J. 815 (1992). The constitutionality of its discovery provisions was upheld, against sharp challenge, in Izazaga v. Superior Court, 54 Cal.3d 356, 285 Cal.Rptr. 231, 815 P.2d 304 (1991).

30. Note, however, that the absence of broad discovery rights is sometimes compensated by informal discovery arrangements: in many jurisdictions prosecutors have an "open file" policy for most cases. Strict formal rules are applied only where reasons exist to fear for the safety of a witness or the security of evidence. See 2 Encyclopedia of Crime and Justice 619 (S. H. Kadish ed., 1984).

31. See Damaška, Barriers, *supra* note 10, at 534.

32. The Federal Rules already authorize such protective orders. See Fed.R.Crim. Proc. 16(d)(1).

explain this more thoroughly—the defendant normally will have stated his own version of the facts in considerable detail at a very early stage of the proceedings. Thus, at the time when he or his counsel inspects the dossier, his position has assumed a sufficiently firm shape so that it can no longer be effectively improved by fabrications.[33] The further danger, that prosecution witnesses might be bribed or intimidated, usually is neutralized in the civil-law systems by the sensible rule that if at the trial the witness suddenly suffers a loss of memory or seeks to contradict his prior statements, his previous testimony can be used not only to assist his power of recall but even as substantive evidence. A slight modernization of our antediluvian rules of evidence (including the rule against impeaching one's own witness) would permit our courts to reach the same result.[34]

To kill or incapacitate a prosecution witness before the trial, again will not help the defendant at all in a civil-law country; the previous testimony of the witness is recorded in the dossier, and if the witness in the meantime has become unavailable, this particular portion of the dossier may be read at the trial.

In the U.S. system, the problem of utilizing pretrial depositions is somewhat more difficult because of the constitutional confrontation requirement. But the Supreme Court's 1970 decision in California v. Green[35] makes it clear that, subject to certain safeguards, the deposition of an unavailable witness may be used at the trial even under our system. In some situations such use now is authorized by the Federal Rules.[36]

33. It must be remembered that at trial in a continental country the presiding judge has the dossier at hand and is thoroughly familiar with its contents. Thus, if the defendant should present a recently fabricated story at trial, the presiding judge may ask about any contradictions between that story and the defendant's previous testimony, or inquire why the defendant failed to mention the point when previously questioned by investigating officials. Should the defendant deny the accuracy or completeness of the portions of the dossier to which the presiding judge refers, the officials who recorded the previous statements of the accused may be called as witnesses. See Löwe-Rosenberg, *supra* note 21, § 254, anno. 6. Thus, any attempt to change the defendant's original story may well hurt rather than help the defense, unless the change is satisfactorily explained. Where the change is a fabrication, it is unlikely that such an explanation can be presented.

34. Under the Federal and Revised Uniform Rules of Evidence the prior inconsistent statement can be used for impeachment purposes (Rule 607); but, under Rule 801(d)(1), as a House–Senate Conference Committee phrased it after long and bitter controversy, it is admissible as substantive evidence only if originally made under oath. Thus a prior inconsistent statement, contained in unsworn testimony given to the police by a witness (before he was intimidated or bribed), cannot be used as substantive evidence under the Federal and Revised Uniform Rules of Evidence.

The state courts are split on whether the witness' prior inconsistent statement can be used as substantive evidence. The view that it can be so used is gaining ground, but may still be the minority position. See Annotation, 30 A.L.R.4th 414 (1984); McCormick on Evidence §§ 36, 37, 38, 251 (J. W. Strong ed., 4th ed. 1992).

35. 399 U.S. 149, 90 S.Ct. 1930 (1970).

36. Fed.R.Crim.Proc. 15(e). Note, however, that this rule, although liberal by comparison with our traditional approach, is more restrictive than the practice in continental countries, where even unsworn statements made by the witness to the police or the prosecutor can be read at the trial if the witness in the meantime has died or if for other reasons his testimony has become difficult to obtain.

It follows, I submit, that the answers by which the civilians have neutralized the "abuse" argument against effective discovery are relevant in our system as well.

The only other respectable argument against unlimited discovery is that of prosecutors crying "one-way-street." Even if one is free from prosecutorial bias, one must wonder why, in an allegedly adversary system, one party should have to play with completely open cards, while the other party—the party who presumably has the most intimate knowledge of the facts—has the right to sit back and in effect to limit his utterances to two taunting words: "Prove it." Some writers have attempted to answer this question within the framework of our system, but their answers have largely failed to persuade our courts and legislators. As a practical matter, it does not seem likely that unlimited discovery—the hallmark of civilized criminal procedure—will be widely and effectively introduced into our system unless the "one-way-street" argument can be laid to rest.[37] To do that, one must take a fresh look, aided by comparison, at the whole problem of the defendant's contribution to the ascertainment of the true facts. This brings me to the final topic of the present discussion.

(d) The Accused as a Source of Information

The role of the accused as a source of information in the truthfinding process is an important and thorny topic in any system of criminal procedure. It is also the topic concerning which—upon superficial inspection—the gap between common law and civil law appears most unbridgeable.

Closer analysis, however, shows that the rock-bottom principle that is the foundation of all specific rules in this area of the law today is shared by virtually all civilized legal systems: no physical compulsion may be used to make the suspect talk. In this sense, almost all civilized legal systems give the suspect, even before he becomes the defendant, the right to remain

The restrictions built into Rule 15(e) reflect the Supreme Court's interpretation of the due process and confrontation clauses. See California v. Green, cited *supra* note 35. Keeping in mind, however, the need for the protection of witnesses who are willing to testify against powerful and ruthless criminals, a strong argument can be made in favor of the less restrictive German rule.

37. The basis of the argument against "one-way-street" discovery is plain enough. If a criminal proceeding is regarded as essentially a sporting contest between opposing counsel, it follows that no greater burden of making pretrial disclosures should be imposed on the prosecution than is imposed on the defense. If, on the other hand, the ascertainment of truth is perceived as the major and essential objective of such a proceeding,

then it is clear that defendant's silence is at least as inimical to the attainment of that objective as lack of discovery, because "[m]any offenses are of such a character that the only persons capable of giving useful testimony are those implicated in the crime." Kastigar v. United States, 406 U.S. 441, 92 S.Ct. 1653 (1972), quoted with approval in United States v. Mandujano, 425 U.S. 564, 96 S.Ct. 1768 (1976). For a contribution to the critique based on the argument of the exceedingly stronger position of the prosecutor as opposed to the suspect, Elisabetta Grande, Dances of Criminal Justice, *supra* note 20; For a broad critique of the common law attitude to evidence, P. Roberts, Faces of Justice Adrift? Damaška's Comparative Method and the Future of Common Law Evidence, in Festshrift Damaška, 295.

silent.[38] The more enlightened legal systems, whether of the common-law or the civil-law variety, also are in agreement today on the principle that from the very beginning of the investigation the accused is entitled to the assistance of counsel. It follows that when the suspect, at any stage of the proceedings, is called upon to exercise his all-important option—to talk or not to talk—at least the more enlightened legal systems will make it possible for him to be guided by counsel's advice.

Up to this point, I repeat, there is a large measure of agreement among civilized and enlightened legal systems, regardless of whether they belong to the common-law or the civil-law orbit. Crucial differences, however, come to light when we ask the next question: Which course will counsel advise the defendant to take? Under our system, "any lawyer worth his salt will tell the suspect in no uncertain terms to make no statement to police under any circumstances."[39] Quite often, counsel will keep his client equally silent at the trial; indeed, in the many cases where the client has a criminal record, our majority rule permitting the prosecution to unearth such record on cross-examination makes it almost impossible for counsel to let the defendant take the stand. In its perverse striving to keep the defendant silent, our law, furthermore, seeks to assure the defendant and his counsel that legal rules can repeal the laws of logic, and that by legal rules the jury can be induced not to draw the natural inferences from defendant's silence. In Griffin v. California[40] the Warren Court—over a powerful dissent by Mr. Justice Stewart—held that no state may permit any judicial comment (no matter how fair and reasonable) upon defendant's failure to testify.[41]

In thus encouraging the accused to remain silent, our legal system stands virtually alone. In England, defendants rarely opt for silence, because English law differs from ours in two crucial respects. If the accused takes the stand, the English rule is to the effect that he cannot by reason of that alone be cross-examined as to previous convictions. And if he remains silent, the judge is authorized by English law to suggest to the jury that it draw an adverse inference from the defendant's failure to explain away the evidence against him.[42]

38. See Pieck, The Accused's Privilege Against Self–Incrimination in the Civil Law, 11 Am.J.Comp.L. 585 (1962).

39. Watts v. Indiana, 338 U.S. 49, 59 (1949) (Jackson, J., concurring & dissenting). Note that the prosecution cannot impeach a defendant's testimony at trial by pointing to his post-arrest silence. This prohibition extends to remarks in a prosecutor's closing argument. See Doyle v. Ohio, 426 U.S. 610, 96 S.Ct. 2240 (1976); Cleveland v. Pulley, 551 F.Supp. 476, 478 (N.D.Cal.1982).

40. 380 U.S. 609, 85 S.Ct. 1229 (1965). The arguments against this holding are cogently stated in Justice Stewart's dissent, id. at 617, and even more elaborately in Chief Justice Traynor's opinion in People v. Modes-to, 62 Cal.2d 436, 42 Cal.Rptr. 417, 398 P.2d 753 (1965). For an exchange on the Griffin rule, see D. B. Ayer, The Fifth Amendment and the Inference of Guilt from Silence: Griffin v. California after Fifteen Years, 78 Mich. L.Rev. 841 (1980); C. M. Bradley, Griffin v. California: Still Viable After All These Years, 79 Mich.L.Rev. 1290 (1981).

41. After Griffin, the Supreme Court created yet another incentive for defendants to stay off the stand at trial: if they testify, they can be impeached by an otherwise inadmissible confession. See Harris v. New York, 401 U.S. 222, 91 S.Ct. 643 (1971).

42. D. Karlen, G. Sawyer & E. M. Wise, Anglo–American Criminal Justice 184 (1967); see also M. H. Graham, Tightening the Reins

Implementing a similar policy by partly different techniques, the continental systems likewise discourage the accused from standing mute. In many (though not all) of those systems the defendant's silence may serve as corroborating evidence of guilt. Even where, as in West Germany, this traditional rule has been modified, a defendant generally is not well advised to remain silent. At the very outset of the trial, he has to stand in front of the judges, to be questioned by the Presiding Justice of the court. True, he may refuse to answer any questions relating to the charges against him; but he must announce such refusal in open court and cannot simply, as he might under a common law system, remove himself from the questioning process by deciding not to take the stand.[43] Moreover, only in the event of a total refusal by the defendant to answer any questions relating to the charges does German law prohibit the drawing of inferences from his silence. If he answers any of such questions, but then refuses to answer others, the court may draw logical inferences from his refusal. Thus, selective silence is strongly discouraged. Total silence of the defendant (although in theory under the present German rule it does not support adverse inferences) will occur only rarely in a German court because it carries with it a grave disadvantage for the defendant: since there will be no separate hearing regarding the sentence,[44] a totally silent defendant may forfeit the opportunity to present facts tending to mitigate his punishment.[45]

of Justice in America: A Comparative Analysis of the Criminal Jury Trial in England and the United States (1984); G. Van Kessel, The Suspect as a Source of Testimonial Evidence: A Comparison of the English and American Approaches, 38 Hastings L.J. 1 (1986). Under the Criminal Justice and Public Order Act, 1994, suspects questioned by the police are now warned that silence may count against them at trial; and adverse inferences are permitted to be drawn from failure to answer questions or explain actions either to the police or at trial.

43. See Damaška, Barriers, *supra* note 10, at 527–30.

44. See *supra*, pt. I. A strong argument to take into consideration the structure of sentencing for purposes of comparative criminal law scholarship is recently made by R.S. Frase, Sentencing and Comparative Law Theory, in Festshrift Damaška, 351; See also for discussions including Japan and China, respectively J. Dignan, Penal Systems: A Comparative Perspective, (2006); and C. Tata & N. Hutton, Sentencing and Society. International Perspective (2002).

As to whether a unitary system of guilt-determination and sentencing would be constitutionally permissible under our law, the authorities appear to be in conflict. See D. B. Ayer, *supra* note 40, at 859.

45. Under German law the questioning of the defendant at trial is divided into two phases. The first deals with the defendant's personal history and general circumstances, while the second phase centers on the specific charges. The right to remain silent comes into play only when the second phase is reached. It follows that mitigating facts relating to defendant's personal history and general circumstances (for example, poverty or lack of education) can always be mentioned by the defendant during the first phase. But mitigating facts connected with the crime itself (e.g., that the defendant was only a minor participant, or tried to persuade accomplices not to hurt the victim, or is remorseful) cannot be brought out by the testimony of a defendant who decides to remain completely silent during the second phase of the questioning, the phase dealing with the specific charges.

The disadvantage thus suffered by a silent defendant is further accentuated if a confession in itself is treated as a mitigating circumstance. Under German law a confession should lead to mitigation only if it is indicative of sincere repentance; but many

The continental systems, moreover, reject our dysfunctional rule that previous convictions of the defendant can be proved if, but only if, he takes the stand. The rules developed in those systems regarding admissibility of previous convictions are neither simple nor uniform, but they exhibit unanimity on the crucial point: the admissibility of previous convictions never hinges on whether or not the defendant testifies.[46] Thus he will never be dissuaded from testifying by the fear that his decision to do so will open the door to evidence of his criminal record.

Nor does a defendant who decides to testify before a continental court have to dread that a prosecution for perjury might arise out of such testimony. What he says in his defense is not under oath.[47]

Thus the inducement to speak, and not to stand mute, is very strong in the civil-law systems. Experience shows that "almost all continental defendants choose to testify" at the trial.[48] This being so, the accused normally has little to lose and much to gain by presenting his side of the story not only at the trial, but also in the earlier phases of the proceeding.[49] If the accused is innocent, this may lead to an early dismissal of the charges. In any event, the combination of a talking defendant and unlimited discovery will clarify the issues well before trial and make the trial both shorter and more informative—much to the benefit of an innocent defendant.

In cases where the accused is clearly guilty, the same combination of factors will prove equally potent. Through active colloquies between the accused and the investigator, combined with inspection of the dossier, such an accused and his counsel are apt to become persuaded that a denial of

courts nevertheless tend to accord a confession an automatic mitigating effect. See H. H. Jescheck, Lehrbuch des Strafrechts 714 (3d ed. 1978); Damaška, Barriers, *supra* note 10, at 528 n. 44. In the Far East the role of a confession as a mitigating circumstance is especially pronounced. See the Japanese Criminal Code § 42; Korean Criminal Code § 52.

46. See Damaška, Barriers, *supra* note 10, at 518. The Federal Rules of Evidence now provide for some limitations on the use of prior convictions to impeach the defendant who takes the stand. See McCormick, *supra* note 34, § 42.

47. In their free evaluation of the evidence the triers of the facts must weigh the accused's statement along with all other items of proof; and no adverse inference can be drawn from the fact that the statement is unsworn, because the accused is not eligible to be put under oath.

There is a fine comparative discussion of the point in an appendix forming part of the late Judge Jerome Frank's dissenting opinion in United States v. Grunewald, 233 F.2d 556, 587–92 (2d Cir.1956). Judge Frank's dissent ultimately prevailed: the decision of the majority of the court of appeals was unanimously reversed by the Supreme Court, 353 U.S. 391, 77 S.Ct. 963 (1957).

48. Damaška, Barriers, *supra* note 10, at 527.

49. It should be remembered that in some continental countries the pretrial investigation is conducted by a judge, and that the same judge may have the power to determine whether the accused should be detained (and remain detained) pending trial. The accused may find it unwise, therefore, to incur the judge's displeasure by a stubborn refusal to help in clearing up the facts. The investigating judge is apt to be quite impartial, in the sense of being indifferent to whether the facts unearthed ultimately will show guilt or innocence. But the judge does have a personal and professional interest in clearing up the case as expeditiously as possible and may become irritated when the investigation is obstructed by lack of cooperation.

guilt simply will not stand up. The usual result is a confession, followed by an attempt to present evidence of mitigating circumstances.

Thus, by combining unlimited discovery for the benefit of the defense with rules making it advantageous for the accused to talk, the continental systems have fashioned a highly efficient vehicle for the ascertainment of truth. If the accused is in fact innocent, unlimited pretrial discovery will give him the best possible chance—a much better chance than he would have under a system of trial by surprise—to meet whatever evidence there may be against him. And if he is guilty, the unavailability of silence as a viable strategy will make his conviction more probable and less time-consuming.

NOTES AND QUESTIONS

(**1**) The last part of Professor Schlesinger's article, not reproduced here, deals with "The Teachings of Foreign Experience," that is, with the lessons that reformers of the U.S. system of criminal procedure might derive from a study of comparable civil-law institutions. It does not contemplate wholesale imitation of foreign models, but rather suggests that American criminal justice might be made marginally more efficient and just if, like continental systems, it placed greater emphasis on principles favoring discovery and disfavoring the accused's silence in criminal cases.

Other scholars have proposed more radical reforms that would incorporate other features of civil-law systems such as the investigation of criminal charges by a judicial official, the absence of guilty pleas and therefore of plea-bargaining, more strictly controlled prosecutorial discretion and streamlined trial before a mixed bench of professional judges and lay jurors.[1] These proposals have been criticized in turn.[2] One ground of criticism is that continental

---

1. See, e.g., K. Davis, Discretionary Justice: A Preliminary Inquiry 191–95, 224–25 (1969); L. L. Weinreb, Denial of Justice (1977); J. H. Langbein, Controlling Prosecutorial Discretion in Germany, 41 U.Chi. L.Rev. 439 (1974); id., Land Without Plea Bargaining: How the Germans Do It, 78 Mich.L.Rev. 204 (1979); id., Mixed Court and Jury Court: Could the Continental Alternative Fill the American Need?, 1981 Am. B.Found.Res.J. 195; J. H. Langbein & L. L. Weinreb, Continental Criminal Procedure: "Myth" and Reality, 87 Yale L.J. 1549 (1978); G. W. Pugh, Ruminations Re Reform of American Criminal Justice (Especially Our Guilty Plea System): Reflections Derived from a Study of the French System, 36 La. L.Rev. 947 (1976).

See also Craig M. Bradley, Reforming the Criminal Trial, 68 Ind.L.J. 659 (1993). In another vein, Prof. Bradley, in light of foreign experience in both common and civil law

countries, has proposed national enactment of a comprehensive code of police practices for the United States. See Craig M. Bradley, The Failure of the Criminal Procedure Revolution (1993), especially ch. 5 ("What Other Countries Are Doing"), at 95–143.

2. See, e.g., J. Darby, Lessons of Comparative Criminal Procedure: France and the United States, 19 San Diego L.Rev. 277 (1982); Marcus Dirk Dubber, American Plea Bargains, German Lay Judges, and the Crisis of Criminal Procedure, 49 Stan.L.Rev. 547 (1997); A. S. Goldstein & M. Marcus, The Myth of Judicial Supervision in Three "Inquisitorial" Systems: France, Italy, and Germany, 87 Yale L.J. 240 (1977); id., Comment on Continental Criminal Procedure, 87 Yale L.J. 1570 (1978); T. Weigend, Continental Cures for American Ailments: European Criminal Procedure as a Model for Law Reform, 2 Crime & Just. 381 (1980); William T. Pizzi, Understanding Prosecutorial Discre-

procedure actually comes closer in practice to our own system of prosecutor-dominated bargained-justice than seems to be recognized by those who favor importing continental methods as a cure for the ills of American criminal justice. In fact, under very similar economic pressures, often originated by strong special interests of multinational corporations active in the "security industry" booming within the logic of the war on terror, criminal procedure systems seem to be abandoning quite substantially early worries about due process fairness. Consequently, plea bargaining responsible as it is to a large extent of the phenomenon of massive incarceration in the U.S. (more than two million inmates up ten times since the late nineteenth seventies) has been transplanted worldwide even in jurisdictions such as Germany traditionally opposed to the logic of bargained criminal justice.[3]

Recent contributions to this debate generally take it for granted that wholesale adoption of major elements of a non-adversary system is unlikely to occur in the United States. Even so, considerable differences of opinion remain about what reforms, based on continental models might be feasible. Professor Frase,[4] for instance, cautiously concludes that the most feasible reforms are likely to relate to peripheral rather than central differences between common law and civil law systems; in his view, civil law restrictions on the use of arrest and pretrial detention, or controls on prosecutorial discretion, provide a more likely model for American reform than rules allowing full discovery for the defense or disfavoring the accused's silence. Professor Van Kessel,[5] on the other hand, concludes that foreign systems provide useful examples of ways in which the extreme lengths to which the adversary system has been taken in the United States might be moderated, without abandoning its essentially adversary character, and includes full discovery of the prosecution's case and encouraging the accused to testify among the reforms he regards as feasible. More recently some leading comparative criminal procedure scholars, within a major re-thinking of the "accusatorial" vs. "inquisitorial" opposition now broadly considered "comparatively sterile"[6] have argued that the adversarial ideal might actually be only rhetoric in the U.S. criminal procedure. Its comparative harshness must be put at the center of the stage,[7] understood within old and new systemic oppositions,[8] and explained from the perspective of a power ratio that, with the exception of trials involving very rich defendants, is incommensurably in favor of the prosecution.

tion in the United States: The Limits of Comparative Criminal Procedure as an Instrument of Reform, 24 Ohio St.L.J. 1325 (1993).

3. See T. Weigend, The Decay of the Inquisitorial Ideal: Plea Bargaining Invades German Criminal Procedure, in Festshrift Damaška, at 39.

4. Richard S. Frase, Comparative Criminal Justice as a Guide to American Law Reform: How Do the French Do It, How Can We Find Out, and Why Should We Care?, 78 Calif.L.Rev. 542 (1990). See also Richard S. Frase & Thomas Weigend, German Criminal Justice as a Guide to American Law Reform:

Similar Problems, Better Solutions?, 18 B.C.Int'l & Comp.L.Rev. 317 (1995).

5. Gordon Van Kessel, Adversary Excesses in the American Criminal Trial, 67 Notre Dame L.Rev. 403 (1992).

6. See E. Grande, in Festshrift Damaška, *supra* note 20 at 146.

7. See J.Q. Whitman, Harsh Justice. Criminal Punishment and the Widening Divide between America and Europe (2005).

8. See W.T. Pizzi, Sentencing in the U.S: An Inquisitorial Soul in an Adversarial Body? In Festshrift Damaška, at 65.

On the whole, notwithstanding the scholarly debate, there has been remarkably little public agitation for a major overhaul of criminal procedure in the United States during the past few decades. In the absence of a public debate "informal procedures" have been able to develop within the War on Terror often producing major international scandals such as in the case of "renditions" and "secret imprisonments". By contrast, other countries seem to have been going through a phase of heightened concern with procedural reform in criminal cases. This is true, of course, in Eastern Europe, where, along with other changes, a massive reconstruction of criminal procedure has been underway.[9] But it is true of Western Europe as well, where (in large part as a result of experience with the European Convention on Human Rights) one concern of reformers also has been to devise better safeguards for the rights of the accused.[10] Even beyond the European Convention such issues have emerged, often critically as it should be the case in front of any model of justice of the winners, at the level of the so-called transnational justice where different attempts have been made to build common standards beyond national boundaries.[11] Among peripheral countries whose legal system has been visited by Western inspired ideas of due process through super-national systems of criminal justice one finds such diverse countries as Sierra Leone, east Timor, Kosovo and Cambodia.[12] While scholars now observe that, perhaps also because

9. See, e.g., the Symposium on The Protection of Human Rights in the Administration of Criminal Justice in Central and Eastern Europe and the Former Soviet Union, 63 Rev.Int.Droit Pénal 501–1023 (1992). See also Joachim Herrmann, Models for the Reform of Criminal Procedure in Eastern Europe: Comparative Remarks on Changes in Trial Systems and European Alternatives to Plea Bargaining, in Criminal Science in a Global Society: Essays in Honor of Gerhard O. W. Mueller 61 (E. M. Wise ed. 1994). Most recently, Steven C. Thaman, The Two Faces of Justice in the Post–Soviet Legal Sphere: Adversarial Procedure, Jury Trial, Plea Bargaining and the Inquisitorial Legacy, in Festshrift Damaška at 99; and Davor Krapac, Some Trends in Continental Criminal Procedure in Transition Countries of South–Eastern Europe in Festshrift Damaška at 119.

10. See The Criminal Process and Human Rights: Towards a European Consciousness (Mireille Delmas–Marty ed., 1995). This activism in criminal justice reform is not limited to the civil law. Criminal procedure rates a section to itself in The Gradual Convergence: Foreign Ideas, Foreign Influences, and English Law on the Eve of the 21st Century 33–63 (Basil Markesinis ed., 1994). See also Craig M. Bradley, The Convergence of the Continental and the Common Law Model of Criminal Procedure, 7 Crim.L.F. 471 (1996). The latter is a review of Criminal Justice in Europe: A Comparative Study

(Christopher Harding, Phil Fennell, Nico Jörg & Bert Swart eds., 1995), which mainly compares Dutch and English criminal justice, although it contains some excellent general chapters on the effect of European Community and human rights law on criminal justice, including an essay (at 41–56) by Nico Jörg, Steward Field & Chrisje Brants on the question: "Are Inquisitorial and Adversarial Systems Converging?" See also the colloquium on the theme Inquisitoire–Accusatoire: un écroulement des dogmes en procédure pénale?, 68 Rev.Int.Droit Pénal 17–229 (1997). Most recently, M. Delmas–Marty, Reflections on the Hybridization of Criminal Procedure, in Festshrift Damaška, at 251.

11. See John Jackson, Transnational Faces of Justice: Two attempts to build Common Standards Beyond national Boundaries, in Festshrift Damaška, at 221 fascinatingly discussing issues of due process in what he calls the "international system of criminal justice" which includes the Special Tribunal for former Yugoslavia, for Rwanda and the International Criminal Court. See also on possible risks, M. Cherif Bassiouni, Extraterritorial Jurisdiction: Application to "Terrorism" in Festshrift Damaška, p. 201.

12. See International Criminal Courts: Sierra Leone, East Timor, Kossovo and Cambodia (C.P.R. Romano, A. Nollkaemper, J.K. Kleffner eds. 2004).

of the remarkable absence of the U.S. from the worry of building international legality, elements of the inquisitorial model have penetrated transnational justice[13] (e.g. the non elected prosecutor must seek exculpatory evidence and the objective truth), even a cursory look of the English model shows that the excesses of the adversary ideal have been erased from the system.[14]

While the criminal judge's power to "sum up" made for a traditionally more activist position of the English criminal bench as compared to the U.S. counterpart, the right to remain silent, as we have already mentioned, has been abolished in 1994.[15] One should also mention that the Crown Prosecution Service, rather than elected prosecutors are in charge of prosecution in England. Their professionalism rather than political accountability may produce incentives to more objectivity in the result of trials not making the prosecution "score", like in the U.S., only when capable of gaining as hard a conviction as possible.[16] Moreover, the Criminal Justice Act of 2003 has introduced full both ways disclosure in the English criminal process though its effective functioning at the moment is under scrutiny. The same Act has obliterated the jury in certain cases where there is risk of tampering with it or which are deemed excessively complex. Finally, since 2005 the Lord Chief Justice has produced a protocol ordering criminal judges to use significant case management tools to avoid delays in jury trials and a thorough debate on getting completely rid of it perhaps substituting it with mixed panels in ongoing. Police practices were thoroughly revised in the Police and Criminal Evidence Act 1984, but even that major reform seemed insufficient in light of a number of well-publicized cases involving convictions based on unreliable confessions. As a result, in 1991 a Royal Commission on Criminal Justice (known as the Runciman Commission) was appointed and originated a large debate on revamping the whole system but thus far no coherent reform followed.[17] Nevertheless while its most bold proposal to give an "investigative role" to criminal judges was not adopted, because of this input the Criminal Appeal Act of 1995 instituted a Criminal Cases Review Commission granting to it significant power to review miscarriages of justice and re-open processes. The Act even granted to the Court of Appeals the unheard of power to seek out new evidence and information by requiring the Commission's intervention thus introducing into the system significant aspect of the inquisitorial search for the truth.[18] In 1998, the Human Rights Act has structurally incorporated the European Convention on Human Rights into the English legal system, and the impact of its many

---

13. See M. Langer, The Rise of Managerial Judging in International Criminal Law, 53 Am J. Comp. Law 835 (2005).

14. See the excellent detailed and updated discussion in Catherine Elliot & Frances Queen, English Legal System, (8th ed. 2007).

15. Ivi at 377.

16. This discussion is echoed in many of the papers contained in The Judicial Role in Criminal Proceedings (S. Doran & J.D. Jackson eds. 2000).

17. Report of the Royal Commission on Criminal Justice, Cm. 2263 (HMSO 1993).

For a summary of the Commission's recommendations, see 1993 Crim.L.Rev. 637. The Commission was headed by Lord Runciman and is commonly referred to as the Runciman Commission. One of the research studies prepared for the Commission is a very valuable work by Leonard H. Leigh & Lucia Zedner, A Report on the Administration of Criminal Justice in the Pre–Trial Phase in France and Germany (The Royal Commission on Criminal Justice, Research Study No. 1, HMSO 1992).

18. See Elliott & Queen, *supra* note 14 at 534, 544.

provisions related to the criminal procedure will certainly have a large impact and likely produce more convergence with the civil law tradition.

About the same time that the British legal systems was moving its significant steps away from the extremes of the adversary model a French Commission on Criminal Justice and Human Rights proposed abolishing the investigative responsibility of the *juge d'instruction*[19]—an inversion of traditional positions that led a character in a contemporary detective novel to remark: "Just as the Brits are begging for a judge of instruction, the French are doing their best to get rid of him . . ."[20] In fact, the French system has progressively abolished the position of the investigative magistrate and has given a more active role to the defense. Despite recommendations, the Judge d' Instruction was not abolished but its use is however restricted to a small minority of the most serious cases. Data of the Ministry of Justice show that in 2005 of about one million new criminal cases only about thirty-thousands have seen him or her involved. The vast majority is investigated by the police or the parquet. A Law of June 15, 2000 has instituted a check by a "Judge of Freedom", while a system of "guilty pleas" yielding to the fascination of negotiated justice was introduced in France with a law of March 9, 2004.[21]

(2) It has been said more generally that "the inquisitorial systems of continental Europe are gradually taking on more characteristics of Anglo–Saxon procedure . . ."[22] The main developments that can be cited to support this proposition are (i) decreased use or abolition of the *juge d'instruction*, (ii) increased use of analogues to plea bargaining that allow for consensual disposition of criminal cases, and (iii) adoption of adversary forms of trial, most notably in Italy (where a new Code of Criminal Procedure enacted in 1988 combined all three developments).[23] We will consider each of them in turn.

---

19. Commission Justice pénale et Droits de l'Homme, La mise en état des affaires pénales (La Documentation Française 1991). The Commission was headed by Prof. Mireille Delmas–Marty and is commonly referred to as the Delmas–Marty Commission.

20. Nicholas Freeling, Flanders Sky 11 (1992). An earlier Freeling story, The Bugles Blowing (1975), contains a very informative, albeit fictional, exposition of the relationship between the *police judiciare* and the *juge d'instruction*.

21. Extensive amendments to the French Code of Criminal Procedure were contained in Law No. 92–1336 of Dec. 16, 1992 (which was tied to the adoption of a new Penal Code to replace the French Penal Code of 1810) and in Law. No. 93–2 of Jan. 4, 1993, which was based in part on the recommendations of the Delmas–Marty Commission. The law of Jan. 4, 1993, was enacted two months before the elections of March 1993 in which the Socialists lost their legislative majority. A subsequent Law No. 93–1013

of Aug. 24, 1993, reversed some, but not all, of the changes which had been adopted eight months before. The current situation is discussed in D. Charvet, Reflexions autour du plaider coupable (2004) Dalloz Chr 2517. The debate (very harsh) on criminal justice reform is unfolding again in France under the Presidency of Mr. Sarkozy.

For accounts of these reforms in English, see Helen Trouille, A Look at French Criminal Procedure, 1994 Crim.L.Rev. 735; Stewart Field & Andrew West, A Tale of Two Reforms: French Defense Rights and Police Powers in Transition, 6 Crim.L.F. 473 (1995). See also Hodgson, French Criminal Justice. A Comparative Account of the Investigation and Prospection of Crimes in France (2006) and the review by Jacqueline Ross, 55 Am J. Comp. Law 370 (2007).

22. Stephen Thaman, General Report, 63 Rev.Int.Droit Pénal 505, 528 (1992).

23. Also in point, perhaps, is the fascination with jury trial that has cropped up in unlikely places. See *supra* p. 832, note 5.

(i) As indicated above, the official pretrial investigation is conducted in some countries by a judge (the French *juge d'instruction*), in others by the prosecutor. The French system of an investigating judge is traditional on the continent. Germany has completely substituted investigation by the prosecutor. Other countries seem to be moving toward the German model.[24] In the German system, the prosecutor still has to obtain the approval of a judge for certain measures that interfere with personal liberty, but there is not, as in France, direct judicial control of the preliminary investigation.

Even in France, the *juge d'instruction* increasingly has become a marginal figure.[25] As mentioned, investigation supervised by a judge takes place only in connection with the most serious crimes; the percentage of cases in which it occurs has been decreasing; and where it occurs it has been a subject of great criticism.[26] Decisions regarding pre-trial detention are now checked by the Freedom judge, thus posing remedy to some of the worries of having the *juge d'instruction* involved in that decision.

(ii) There can be no plea bargaining in the strict sense of the term so long as the defendant is never asked to plead. Yet forms of plea bargaining can be found in the Criminal procedure Codes of core civil law countries including Italy, France, Spain, Poland and many Latin American jurisdictions.[27] In the face of mounting criminal caseloads, there seems to be increasing use in continental as well as in common law countries of devices for consensual disposition that avoid or foreshorten a trial.[28]

In Germany, there has been considerable controversy about such "bargaining."[29] Even the extent to which it occurs has been controversial, although it now seems to be a not uncommon practice and is estimated to figure in twenty to thirty percent of all criminal cases (although not in cases involving crimes of violence) which is still an irrelevant figure when compared to the ninety-plus% in the U.S. There are three principal types of "bargain."

The first occurs in the context of the prosecutor's power under § 153a of the Code of Criminal Procedure to drop the charges in "misdemeanor" (Vergehen)[30] cases if the accused agrees to "contribute" a certain sum of money to a

24. See Barbara Huber, The Office of the State Prosecutor in Europe: An Overview, 63 Rev.Int.Droit Pénal 557, 569–75 (1992).

25. See René Lévy, Police and the Judiciary in France Since the Nineteenth Century: The Decline of the Examining Magistrate, 33 Brit.J.Crim. 167 (1993).

26. See R. S. Frase, *supra* note 4, at 667.

27. See arts. 444 ff Codice de procedura penale (Italy); 495–7ff Code de procédure penale (France); Arts. 652, 688, 694 Ley de ejuiciamento criminal (Spain); arts. 335, 343, 387 Kodeks postepowania karnego (Poland). M. Langer, *Evolution in Latin American Criminal Procedure*, 55 Am. J. Comp. Law 617 (2007). Recent data from many jurisdic-

tions can be found in S. Thaman, Plea Bargaining, Negotiating Confessions and Consensual Resolution of Criminal Cases, in General Reports of the XVII Congress of the International Academy of Comparative Law (K. Boele–Woelki & S. Van Erp, eds. 2007).

28. On analogues to plea bargaining in France, see R. S. Frase, *supra* note 4, at 626–47.

29. See M. Dubber, *supra* note 2; Joachim Herrmann, Bargaining Justice—A Bargain for German Criminal Justice?, 53 U.Pitt. L.Rev. 755 (1992).

30. "Misdemeanors" (*Vergehen*) are crimes carrying a minimum statutory penalty of a fine or less than a year in prison. In German law, this category covers a number of quite serious offenses that would be re-

charitable organization or to the state. The court must consent to this sort of arrangement, but such consent is practically never withheld.

The second type of "bargain" occurs in connection with the procedure under § 407 of the Code of Criminal Procedure by which the prosecutor may apply to the court for a "summary penal order" (Strafbefehl) imposing a specific fine without a hearing. Such orders tend to be granted as a matter of course. If the defendant objects within two weeks, a hearing must be held; but, if the defendant accepts the order, it acquires the force of a conviction and sentence. While formerly only fines could be imposed through a "summary penal order," since 1993 it has been possible to use the Strafbefehl procedure to impose a suspended prison sentence of up to one year, provided the defendant is represented by counsel.

The third type of "bargain", which proved to be the most controversial, involves the accused's agreement to make an in-court confession (which will reduce the amount of evidence that has to be heard and so considerably shorten the trial, but not, as with our plea bargaining, abort it entirely). The agreement may be the result of negotiations between defense counsel and the prosecutor, and given in exchange for the prosecutor's agreement to drop collateral charges or to ask for a lenient sentence. The agreement can also be the result of negotiations between defense counsel and the judge: the judge, without making a definite commitment, may indicate the possibility of a sentencing concession if the defendant will save everyone time by making a full confession in open court.[31] Where once it would generally have been condemned out of hand, in recent years the legality and desirability of this type of "bargaining" has been the subject of sharp and heated debate.

While the practice appeared in the early eighties, it reached the Supreme Court[32] only in 1997 when a defendant brought an appeal although he had received exactly the sentence he had bargained for, claiming that the procedure violated basic principles of criminal procedure law. Very interestingly for a civil law systems reluctant to recognize case law (particularly in areas as sensitive as criminal matters governed as they are by ideas of strict legality, see *supra* Chapter 6 at 477) the Court ruled that negotiations (understandings) before or during trial were not illegal per se but stated some ground rules that must be observed for the procedure not to violate principles of fairness. Among those: "that the negotiations (but not their exact content) be made public at the time of the trial and their result be put on the trial record; that any agreement needed the consent of the prosecutor, lay judges and the defendant (but that it was sufficient to inform them after a provisional agreement had been reached between defense counsel and the presiding judge); that the Court could not promise a fixed sentence but was limited to indicating a sentence cap in case the defendant made confessions; that no undue pressure must be exerted upon the defendant to come forward with a confession; that the sentence must reflect the seriousness of the offence and the defendant's guilt (but the fact of the confession could be taken into account as a mitigating factor); and that the

garded as felonies in the United States, e.g., larceny, nearly all white-collar crimes, and most drug offenses.

31. See M. Dubber, *supra* note 2, at 764–65.

32. See *Bundesverfassungsgericht*, Judgment of 28 August 1997, 43 *Entscheidungen des Bundesgerichtshofes in Strafsachen* 195.

defendant or his lawyer must not, in the course of negotiations, be induced or even asked to promise not to file an appeal against the judgment".[33] Such guidelines proved effective with the only exception of the last issue (waiver of appeal) on which different panels diverged in interpretation. But also this last point was put to rest by a Grand Panel in criminal matters (*Großer Strafsenat*) which in 2005 confirmed the legality of negotiated justice and the need to protect the defendant from coercion to wave in advance the right to appeal.[34] Because this acceleration of case law towards negotiated justice has created some embarrassment for the traditional theory of the sources of law and quite harsh scholarly complaint, the Federal Minister of Justice is currently exploring the possibility to introduce a new article (par. 257c) to the Code of Criminal Procedure practically reflective the case law development.

Interestingly in the same year 2005 the plea bargaining that, like in Germany, lived in the English legal system a semi-clandestine life refused in public but applied in practice, dramatically emerged. In Regina v. Goodyear the Court of Appeals held that a party can request to the judge to put in writing the maximum sentence it would get in case of guilty plea before trial. The English judge is subsequently bound by his indication. However he cannot disclose the maximum he would have been inclined to give in case of full fledged trial to avoid undue pressure on the defendant.[35]

(iii) Over the past century and a half, elements of the adversary trial have been adopted in Spain, Norway, Denmark, Sweden, and Japan and many more including such leading jurisdictions such as France and Germany.

The pivotal experience of this "Americanization process" has been Italy with a reform dating back to 1988. At one stroke, the new Italian Code of Criminal Procedure, which took effect on October 24, 1989, abolished the investigating magistrate, authorized various analogues to plea bargaining, and replaced the old judge-dominated trial with a more clearly adversarial procedure.[36] Colombia seems to have done the same in 1991, although with consider-

33. See Thomas Weigend, The Decay of the Inquisitorial Ideal: Plea Bargaining Invades German Criminal Procedure, in Festshrift Damaška, at 49.

34. Bundesgerichtshof Judgment March 3, 2005, 50 Entsheidungen des Bundesgherichtshofes in Strafsahen 40.

35. See C. Elliott & F. Queen, cit. *supra* note 14 at 395.

36. For information in English on the new Italian code, which has attracted considerable attention, see Mario Chiavario, The Criminal Process in Italy, in The Criminal Process and Human Rights, *supra* note 9, at 33; Ennio Amodio & Eugenio Selvaggi, An Accusatorial System in a Civil Law Country: The 1988 Italian Code of Criminal Procedure, 62 Temp.L.Q. 1211 (1989); Louis F. Del Duca, An Historic Convergence of Civil and Common Law Systems—Italy's New "Adver-

sarial" Criminal Procedure System, 10 Dick. J.Int'l L. 73 (1991); Lawrence J. Fassler, The Italian Penal Procedure Code: An Adversarial System of Criminal Procedure in Continental Europe, 29 Colum.J.Transnat'l L. 245 (1991); Stephen P. Freccero, An Introduction to the New Italian Criminal Procedure, 21 Am. J.Crim.L. 345 (1994); Vittorio Grevi, The New Italian Code of Criminal Procedure: A Concise Overview, in 2 Italian Studies in Law 145 (Alessandro Pizzorusso ed. 1994); William T. Pizzi & Luca Marafioti, The New Italian Code of Criminal Procedure: The Difficulties of Building an Adversarial Trial System on a Civil Law Foundation, 17 Yale J. Int'l L. 1 (1992); Jeffrey J. Miller, Note, Plea Bargaining and Its Analogues Under the New Italian Criminal Procedure Code and in the United States: Towards a New Understanding of Comparative Criminal Procedure, 22 N.Y.U.J.Int'l L. & Pol. 215 (1990).

ably greater powers being vested in the public prosecutor during the pretrial investigation.[37] The Italian performance as a "good pupil" of the American hegemonic model has been rewarded by the "donors" community gathered in Bonn to organized reconstruction of war-torn Afghanistan. Italians have thus been entrusted of drafting the new Afghani criminal procedure, thus serving as a middleman in exporting the U.S. model (and ideology) even there.[38]

Under the new Italian code, the pretrial investigation is conducted by the public prosecutor (or by the police acting under the prosecutor's direction). Defense counsel is entitled to be present during crucial stages of the investigation. Statements taken from the accused without counsel being present generally are inadmissible at trial. The full dossier (or "prosecutor's file") containing the evidence accumulated during the pretrial investigation is no longer made available to the trial court, although it is available to defense counsel in advance of the preliminary hearing which closes the pretrial phase: in this respect, the defense has a right to unlimited discovery of all information in the prosecution's hands. A "preliminary investigation judge" (*giudice per le indagini preliminari*, often abbreviated "g.i.p.") must approve certain measures taken by the prosecutor such as arrests, searches, and wiretaps. The pretrial judge may hold a special "evidentiary hearing" (*incidente probatorio*) to record for use at trial testimony which is likely to become unavailable, and ultimately holds a "preliminary hearing" (*udienza preliminare*)—mainly a review of the dossier—to determine whether charges are warranted.[39]

The code provides for a number of "special proceedings" by which the preliminary hearing can be skipped and a case brought immediately or directly to trial, or by which a full trial can be avoided. The latter include (1) the "proceeding by penal decree" in which the defendant agrees to pay half the usual fine for a minor offense; (2) "application of punishment on request of the parties" in which a defendant can bargain to have the normal sentence reduced by up to one-third, so long as the negotiated period of imprisonment does not exceed two years; and (3) "abbreviated trial" in which the defendant agrees to summary adjudication at the preliminary hearing in exchange for a sentence reduced by one-third in the event of a finding of guilty.

At the trial itself, the prosecution and then the defense present their own evidence and engage in direct examination and cross-examination of witnesses. Out-of-court statements generally are inadmissible (at least under the code as it was originally enacted). The judge, however, is not supposed to be entirely passive, and may suggest new lines of inquiry or take over the questioning of a witness once the parties have completed their examination.

---

37. See Michael R. Pahl, Wanted: Criminal Justice—Colombia's Adoption of a Prosecutorial System of Criminal Procedure, 16 Fordham Int'l L.J. 608 (1992–93).

38. See F. Ahmed, Judicial Reform in Afghanistan: A Case Study in the New Criminal Procedure Code, 29 Hastings Int. and Comp. Law Rev. 93 (2005).

39. After the first wave of literature, some more recent comparative work has pointed out a variety of phenomena of "resistance" when typical civilian attitude to the search of the truth have prevailed (particularly the search for exculpatory evidence). See E. Grande, Italian Criminal Justice. Borrowing and Resistance, 48 Am. J. Comp. Law 227 (2000) and an updated version E. Grande, Italian Criminal Justice. The Resistance of a Mentalité, in J. Lena & U. Mattei (eds.) Introduction to Italian Law (2002).

Amendments enacted in the face of a plague of Mafia criminality during the early 1990s, as well as a long string of decisions by the Italian Constitutional Court altering or annulling particular provisions have modified the system established by the original code thus making the "resistance" produced by a variety of institutional factors thoroughly examined in the literature eventually prevail.[40] The "new" criminal procedure has been amended many times[41] and its evolution has been an important laboratory in the study of the hybridization between the different models of procedure.

(4) Despite the mentioned elements of convergence, the atmosphere in criminal trial courtrooms in most civil law countries is very different from that in an American courtroom.[42] Particularly striking for the U.S. observer is the fact that the examination of the accused and of the witnesses is primarily conducted by the presiding judge.[43] This feature of the procedure, abandoned in Italy, lends itself to abuse if the president of the court is a "hanging judge"; but the effect, under the U.S. system, of clever and unfair cross-examination by a skillful prosecutor may be worse, because the accused who takes the stand is subjected to the additional psychological torture of having to testify under oath.[44] On the basis of what we have discussed thus far, if you were an accused would you rather be tried under the common-law or under a civil-law system?

In order to answer such a tricky question one should control many factors, some highly variable through civil law jurisdictions and possibly even through the criminal justice systems of the different States of the U.S.[45] A synthesis was

---

40. See Grande, note 39.

41. The most recent updated black letter discussion in the English language is L. Marafioti, Italian Criminal Procedure. A System Caught Between Two Traditions, in Festshrift Damaška, 81.

42. For comparative descriptions, by a sensitive non-lawyer, of the atmosphere in the criminal courts of various nations, see Sybille Bedford, The Faces of Justice (1961). With emphasis on the difference between Soviet-style trials and those in non-socialist countries, atmospheric elements are also interestingly discussed by J. N. Hazard, Furniture Arrangement as a Symbol of Judicial Roles, 19 ETC.: Review of General Semantics 181 (1962).

43. As we have seen, nothing may be used against the defendant that is not brought out in open court during the trial. The *dossier* compiled during the preliminary investigation is not evidence. The presiding judge, however, is thoroughly familiar with its contents and usually has it at hand during the trial. Interrogation of the accused and of witnesses by the presiding judge thus becomes thorough and searching. From this, uninformed observers occasionally have inferred that there is no presumption of innocence in civil-law countries.

The inference is, of course, nonsensical. See Esmein, History of Continental Criminal Procedure (1913), at 46; Schwenk, Comparative Study of the Law of Criminal Procedure in NATO Countries, 35 N.C.L.Rev. 358, 373–74 (1957); Mirelli v. Switzerland, European Court of Human Rights, Judgment of March 25, 1983, 4 Hum.Rts.L.J. 215 (1983).

Reasons for civilian reluctance to abandon "unilateral examination" by an impartial official are discussed in Damaška, Presentation of Evidence and Factfinding Precision, 123 U.Pa.L.Rev. 1083, 1093 (1975).

44. An argument has been made that the accused's interrogation under oath is a *tortura spiritualis*. See H. Silving, The Oath, 68 Yale L.J. 1329, 1527 passim (1959). In practice, however, the fear of an independent perjury prosecution does not loom too large among the factors that make the accused's decision to testify a difficult one.

45. For example, incriminating evidence (of various degrees of strength) may point to guilt, even though in fact the accused is innocent. The accused's preference for one or the other of the two systems of prosecution could be affected by this factor. For some other considerations, see the suggestions in J. H. Langbein, Comparative Criminal Procedure: Germany 150 (1977).

attempted by the late Professor Schlesinger that deserves being kept here and which is likely still true despite the discussed decline in many systems of the "inquisitorial model" with its attempt to have the truth prevail over the needs of a more efficient system of adjudication: If I were guilty—explained the great Master of comparative law—I would prefer a system under which I can obtain sentencing and other concessions in exchange for a plea of guilty, and under which, if my case came to trial, I can stand mute, and effectively object to incriminating evidence on technical grounds. But if I were innocent, I would prefer a system under which I have a right to discover all of the incriminating evidence, and to challenge it, before it is decided whether I have to stand trial. And if there is a trial, then (as an innocent defendant) I would much rather be tried under a system that makes it impossible for the prosecution to spring surprises at the trial; which enables me to present evidence without regard to technicalities, and to utilize all of the exculpating evidence unearthed by the official investigation; and which does not subject me to the difficult choice between standing silent and testifying under oath. Moreover, if acquitted, I would prefer a system that makes the state pay my counsel's fee.[46]

(4) On the light of the complex transformations described above what do you think it is today the significant of the opposition "inquisitorial" v. "adversary"? Do you think it still carries some meaning? At a practical level? At a symbolic one? You should by now be familiar with the idea of legal transplants and of the many nuances in the global phenomenon of the diffusion of law. Please think at the "adversary" v. "inquisitorial" metaphor within that framework and think about its legitimacy or usefulness.[47]

5.   PROCEDURAL TREATMENT OF CONCURRENT CRIMINAL AND CIVIL LIABILITY

In practice we often encounter cases in which one and the same wrongful act entails both criminal and civil liability. In such a situation, many civil-law jurisdictions give the injured party a right of election: he or she may bring an independent civil action, or may intervene in the criminal action and become a co-plaintiff together with the public prosecutor. If the victim chooses the latter method, which often will be speedier and less

---

46.   In contrast to our system, most other countries have adopted indemnity schemes under which the accused, if acquitted, is reimbursed for his counsel's fee. For Germany, see Code of Criminal Procedure § 467(I). Thus an innocent defendant, even though not eligible for legal aid, does not have to fear that a successful defense will involve a crushing financial burden. Compare this with the situation in the United States, where an innocent defendant sometimes is forced to plead guilty (perhaps to a lesser charge) in order to avoid the prohibitive expense of a trial. One should however consider that this very civilized feature of German law is not shared by most civil law countries. See U. Mattei, Access to Justice. A Renewed Global Issue? in General Reports of the XVII Congress of the International Academy of Comparative Law (K. Boele–Woelki & S. Van Erp eds. 2007).

47.   See on these questions Elisabeta Grande, Imitazione e diritto (2000). See also, M. Langer, From Legal Transplants to Legal Translations: The Globalization of Plea bargaining and the Americanization Thesis in Criminal Processes, 45 Harvard International L.J. 1 (2004).

expensive, the criminal court has jurisdiction to include in the sentence a provision for damages to be paid by the defendant to the injured plaintiff,[1] who is referred to as the "partie civile."[2]

The practical significance of this procedure is enhanced by the fact that in many civil-law countries it is a crime negligently to cause bodily injury to another; this has the effect that automobile accidents frequently are followed by criminal prosecution, even when there was no violation of traffic regulations or of other penal statutes specifically dealing with the operation of automobiles.[3] However intervention (in the criminal proceed-

1. In the U.S., statutes often provide for restitution as a condition of probation. See, e.g., N.Y. Penal Law § 65.10, subd. 2(g). This, however, provides the victim with weaker protection than the civilian procedure, since restitution as a condition of probation is an informal adjunct to sentencing rather than a civil remedy obtainable in a criminal proceeding. The victim has no procedural rights (e.g., no right to appeal, and no right to enforce the order providing for restitution). See also Pennsylvania Dep't of Public Welfare v. Davenport, 495 U.S. 552, 558, 110 S.Ct. 2126, 2131 (1990). The broadly based victims' movement of recent years led to the adoption of the Federal Victim and Witness Protection Act of 1982. Pub.L. No. 97–291, 96 Stat. 1248. Under sec. 5(a), restitution need no longer be a condition of probation, but can be *ordered* in addition to, or in lieu of, any other penalty. See 18 U.S.C. § 3579(a)(1). The federal act has served as a model for similar state legislation, and has transformed restitution from a discretionary condition of probation into an independent measure of relief for the victim. There are still, however, fairly severe limits on the victim's participation in the (criminal) trial itself.

2. For details, see Larguier, The Civil Action for Damages in French Criminal Procedure, 39 Tul.L.Rev. 687 (1965); P. Campbell, A Comparative Study of Victim Compensation Procedures in France and in the United States: A Modest Proposal, 3 Hastings Int'l & Comp.L.Rev. 321 (1980); A. V. Sheehan, Criminal Procedure in Scotland and France 20–23 (1975); E. Lobedanz, Schadensausgleich bei Straftaten in Spanien und Lateinamerika (1972), reviewed by J. G. Fleming in 21 Am.J.Comp.L. 615 (1973). For a broad comparative discussion of the subject, see J. A. Jolowicz, Civil Remedies in Criminal Courts, in 11 Int'l Ency.Comp.L., ch. 13, especially at 4–15 (1972). The "partie civile" procedure in the context of mass inju-

ries and mass claims is discussed in W. B. Fisch, European Analogues to the Class Action: Group Action in France and Germany, 27 Am.J.Comp.L. 51, 60–68, 71–74 (1979). On the treatment of the victim in European criminal procedure generally, see M. Joutsen, The Role of the Victim of Crime in European Criminal Justice Systems (HEUNI Publications Ser. No. 11, 1987). See also Matti Joutsen, Victim Participation in Proceedings and Sentencing in Europe, 3 Int'l Rev.Victimology 57 (1994); William T. Pizzi & Walter Perron, Crime Victims in German Courtrooms: A Comparative Perspective on American Problems, 32 Stan.J.Int'l L. 37 (1996). S. Walter, Victims' Rights in the German Court System, 19 Federal Sentencing Reporter, 2006.

For an American judicial opinion describing the status of the *partie civile* in a Swiss criminal proceedings, see Klein v. Superior Court, 198 Cal.App.3d 894, 244 Cal.Rptr. 226 (6th Dist.Ct.App. 1988). In this case, the California action was stayed, mainly because the plaintiff had asserted the same tort claim against the same defendant in a criminal proceeding previously commenced in Geneva. The court held that, for purposes of the doctrine of abatement and forum non conveniens, it makes no difference whether the prior proceeding in which the same claim has been asserted is technically a civil or a criminal one. The important point is that a plaintiff should not ordinarily be permitted to pursue a single claim simultaneously in two different courts.

3. The *partie civile* procedure can be of significance also in defamation cases, because in France (and many other civil-law countries) defamation constitutes a crime as well as a tort. See B. S. Markesinis, The Not So Dissimilar Tort and Delict, 93 L.Q.Rev. 78, 103–07 (1977).

ing) by the partie civile is of great practical importance in some civil-law countries, but not in others. In theory, most civil-law countries provide for some form of such intervention. As a practical matter, it seems that in France and Italy[4] many victims of traffic accidents prosecute their damage claims in this way; but in Germany the victims rarely seek to recover their damages in the criminal proceeding, in part because of jurisdictional and procedural restrictions which until recently rendered it unattractive from the standpoint of the injured person to proceed in this manner.[5]

Where possible, if the injured person prefers to pursue his claim for damages by way of an independent civil action, the criminal proceeding normally will end before the civil one, and the whole criminal dossier— including the pre-trial investigation, the evidence introduced at the trial, and the decision of the court—can be used as evidence in the civil action.[6]

4. The new Italian Code of Criminal Procedure of 1989, while introducing an adversarial system, left intact the tradition of permitting victim participation in the trial. See, especially, arts. 410, 493, 496 & 523.

5. The German Victim Protection Law (Opferschutzgesetz, BGBl I 1986, 2496) enacted in 1986 was aimed at extending the rights of the victim in criminal procedure; among other things, it abolished limitations on the amount recoverable, as well as several other restrictions on the intervenor's claim. See the new §§ 403 subs. I, 404 subs. V, and 406 subs. I of the Code of Criminal Procedure. But subsequent studies suggest the persistence of old attitudes that view the victim as "an alien body" in the criminal process, whose presence retards the expeditious handling of criminal cases. See B. Markesinis, Comparative Law—A Subject in Search of an Audience, 50 Mod.L.Rev. 1, 16 (1990); Helmut Kury, Michael Kaiser & Raymond Teske, Jr., The Position of the Victim in German Criminal Procedure—Results of a Germany Study, 3 Int'l Rev.Victimology 69 (1994). Thus, with the significant exception of sexual assault cases where victim participation has become quite common, victim participation in German criminal trials still seems to be relatively infrequent. See Pizzi & Perron, *supra* note 2, at 55 and 59.

6. Under rules of evidence prevailing in common-law countries, many obstacles would stand in the way of an attempt globally to introduce the criminal "dossier" as evidence in a subsequent civil action.

As to police reports, see Annotation, 31 A.L.R.4th 913 (1984). If an officer was under a duty to make the report, the officer's own observations in the report usually are admissible under the official records exception to the hearsay rule; but statements of other witnesses, even though recorded by the officer on the scene, normally are excluded. Likewise, the testimony of witnesses is generally inadmissible as hearsay. See Healy v. Rennert, 9 N.Y.2d 202, 213 N.Y.S.2d 44, 173 N.E.2d 777 (1961) (witness' sworn testimony given at prior criminal trial only exceptionally admissible in subsequent civil action). Even in modern jurisdictions, such hearsay would be admissible only under the extraordinary circumstances envisaged, e.g., by Fed. R.Evid. 804(b)(1) or 803(24).

As to the admissibility of the criminal judgment itself, there is much controversy in the common-law world. Even in jurisdictions which are not totally opposed to the admissibility of such a judgment, fine distinctions have been drawn depending on (a) whether the judgment is one of conviction or of acquittal; (b) whether it was entered after trial or upon a plea of guilty or nolo contendere; and (c) whether the criminal proceeding involved a real crime or a mere traffic violation. See McCormick on Evidence § 298 (J. W. Strong ed., 4th ed. 1992). Compare Fed. R.Evid. 803(22) and Cal.Evid.Code § 1300, with Wheelock v. Eyl, 393 Mich. 74, 223 N.W.2d 276 (1974). Even where a statute seemingly authorizes the admission of a criminal judgment in a subsequent civil case, the trial court may have discretionary power to reject it. See, e.g., Clemmer v. Hartford Ins. Co., 22 Cal.3d 865, 879, 151 Cal.Rptr. 285, 292, 587 P.2d 1098, 1105 (1978).

The injured person's lawyer (who may have looked at the police report as part of his or her own investigation) normally will be

Thus, whichever method the injured person chooses for the assertion of the damage claim, one thing is certain: the fact-finding process involved in the determination of that claim is greatly strengthened by the parties' ability to utilize the dossier of the criminal proceeding, i.e., of a proceeding in which as a rule much more vigorous discovery methods have been used than would be permitted under continental civil procedure.[7] The civil law thus strengthens the position of the victim which is by no means deprived of the advantages that stem from a criminal proceeding even in the case in which the prosecutor (where constitutionally possible)[8] decides not to prosecute; but the precise nature of the recourse available against an idle prosecutor varies from country to country.

In one group of civil-law countries, led by France, it is provided that, where the prosecutor refuses to bring charges, the victim may act directly to initiate a criminal proceeding. Details of this procedure depend on whether more or less serious offenses are involved. While the prosecutor remains technically responsible for such victim-initiated proceedings, in practice it normally is left to the victim to conduct the case. The victim's procedural rights are substantially (though not in every detail) the same as those of the public prosecutor.[9]

In Germany and in countries following its example, the approach is somewhat different. Under the German doctrine, known as the "legality principle," the prosecutor has no discretionary power to forego prosecution of a serious offense; if there is reasonable cause to believe that such an offense has been committed, and that D is the perpetrator, the prosecutor must bring charges against D. If the prosecutor refuses, the victim can appeal to the intermediate appellate court; and, if that court, after studying

able, under American law, to take depositions of persons who testified in the previous criminal proceeding, and to call them as witnesses at the civil trial. But this will consume much more time and effort than the civil-law methods mentioned in the text. Moreover, where the criminal record consists of grand jury testimony followed by a plea, the plaintiff in a subsequent civil action may have difficulty in gaining access to such testimony. See R. M. Buxbaum, Public Participation in the Enforcement of the Antitrust Laws, 59 Calif.L.Rev. 1113, 1140 (1971).

7. American readers will note that the reverse problem arises under their legal system, which liberally grants discovery in civil actions but puts severe restrictions upon fact-gathering in criminal proceedings. In the United States the parties to a criminal proceeding often attempt to use (or abuse) the discovery devices available in a civil suit in order to obtain information or evidence that is wanted mainly for purposes of a concurrent criminal proceeding, but could not be

secured under rules governing a proceeding of the latter kind. Cf. United States v. Kordel, 397 U.S. 1, 90 S.Ct. 763 (1970). See also the 1977 decision of the House of Lords in In re Westinghouse El. Corp. Uranium Contract Litigation, [1978] 2 W.L.R. 81, 17 Int'l Legal Materials 38 (1978).

8. In Italy, the prosecution has a "constitutional duty" to prosecute. Art. 112 Constitution.

9. See Sheehan, *supra* note 2, at 21–22. Under the French system the victim need not seek damages in order to cause institution of proceedings in cases where the public prosecutor refuses to act. It suffices for the victim to show that he has the right to seek damages "in principle". See R. Merle & A. Vitu, Traité de Droit Criminel, vol. 2 Procédure Pénale 67–68 (2d ed. 1973).

For the Austrian variant of the system, see Foregger & Serini, Die österreichiche Strafprozessordnung, § 48, anno. I (2d ed. 1976).

the dossier and (when indicated) making additional investigations, decides that there is probable cause, it orders the prosecutor to bring charges. Needless to say, this order is binding on the prosecutor.[10]

There are a few exceptions to the German rule just stated. Perhaps the most important exception relates to the crime of negligently causing bodily harm—the crime most frequently committed by careless drivers of motor vehicles. The public prosecutor is required to institute a criminal proceeding involving this particular crime only if official prosecution is determined to be necessary by reason of the public interest. In other words, when dealing with this particular kind of crime, the prosecutor (exceptionally) does have a measure of discretion. But if, in the exercise of that discretion, the prosecutor decides that an official prosecution is not warranted in the case at hand, then the victim, as private prosecutor, can directly initiate a criminal proceeding.

In other words, even though the victim's position under German law is different from what it would be in France, the two systems substantially agree on what the victim of an automobile accident can do if the prosecutor refuses to initiate criminal proceedings against the allegedly guilty driver: in such a case, the victim can institute criminal proceedings despite the prosecutor's decision. But one must keep in mind that in France this result flows directly from a general rule, i.e., a rule applicable to the victim of any crime, while in Germany the same result is reached by virtue of an exception—an exception applicable to victims of the crime of negligently inflicting bodily harm. If a different kind of crime were involved (e.g., robbery or arson), the victim's position under German law would be quite different, as I have explained.

Thus the civilian systems give the victim a much stronger position in criminal proceedings than a victim would have under the law of the United States.[11] It is worth noting, moreover, that this stronger position is accord-

---

10. See German Code of Criminal Procedure §§ 172–175. For details of this *Klageerzwingungsverfahren* (i.e., mandamus proceeding against the prosecutor), see Langbein, Comparative Criminal Procedure: Germany 113–14 (1977).

11. Under U.S. law, mandamus to compel the prosecutor to prosecute does not lie, because the decision to prosecute is generally regarded as discretionary. For arguments in favor of limiting that discretion, see A. Goldstein, The Passive Judiciary: Prosecutorial Discretion and the Guilty Plea 9–11 (1981).

Letting the victim prosecute when the public prosecutor refuses to do so may be equally unworkable. In the United States, the public prosecutor usually has complete control of the decision to file charges. The position in the U.S. differs, in this respect, from that in England, where any person (not solely the victim) is entitled to initiate a criminal prosecution. This right was preserved in section 6 of the Prosecution of Offences Act, 1985, which created for the first time in England a single Crown Prosecution Service. If the Crown Prosecution Service declines to prosecute, a private party can still bring a prosecution. In practice, however, the right is rarely exercised; moreover, in order to provide a check on capricious private prosecution, the Director of Public Prosecutions has power to take over the case and seek leave of the court to drop the charges.

Notwithstanding the general American rule giving the public prosecutor complete control of the decision to prosecute, a handful of states purport to allow private individuals to initiate criminal cases; statutes in others permit individuals to seek a court order directing the prosecutor to proceed or appoint-

ed not solely to victims who seek damages in the criminal proceeding.[12] In contrast to the U.S., where the public prosecutor enjoys a monopoly of prosecution, many civilian jurisdictions allow initiation of prosecution by the victim, either generally (as in France) or at least exceptionally in certain important instances of frequently committed misdemeanors.[13] In addition, victims are often entitled to intervene in a criminal proceeding brought by the public prosecutor, even though they do not seek to recover damages in that proceeding. Until recently, this right of intervention was somewhat restricted in Germany; it existed primarily in cases where the public prosecutor had been judicially compelled to prosecute. In 1986, however, amendments to the Code of Criminal Procedure greatly expanded the victim's right to intervene, and today that right no longer depends on whether the prosecutor was judicially compelled to act.[14] Moreover, in many other European countries the victim's right of intervention exists in every criminal case, even when the public prosecutor has instituted the proceeding. As intervenor, the victim has important procedural rights: for example, to call witnesses, to ask questions of them, to make closing arguments, and (in some countries) to recover attorney's fees from a convicted defendant. These rights reflect recognition of the fact that the victim has a strong interest in the outcome of the criminal process.

Also in the U.S. the influence of the victim on the course of the criminal proceeding is increasing under a wave of reforms. In many states, victims are now entitled to be heard before the sentencing court or the

ing a special prosecutor. But some of these statutes have been held unconstitutional: considerations both of separation of powers and of due process have led the courts to postulate (perhaps erroneously, see A. Goldstein, *infra* note 15) that no criminal proceeding can be commenced without the participation, or at least approval, of the public prosecutor. See, e.g., People v. Municipal Court (Pellegrino), 27 Cal.App.3d 193, 103 Cal.Rptr. 645 (1972). For further references, see Stuart P. Green, Note, Private Challenges to Prosecutorial Inaction: A Model Declaratory Judgment Statute, 97 Yale L.J. 488 (1988). Cf. United States v. Cox, 342 F.2d 167 (5th Cir.1965) (upholding the requirement of Fed. R.Crim.Proc. 7(c)(1) that the U.S. attorney sign the indictment, and holding that he may, in his discretion, abort a prosecution by failing to sign).

For further (and in part conflicting) authority on this point, see Annotation, 24 A.L.R.4th 316 (1983).

12. Note, however, that while civil law systems more readily permit victims to pursue private claims in criminal proceedings, civilians generally draw a much sharper distinction than common lawyers between civil and criminal remedies. One consequence is that civil law systems are virtually unanimous in rejecting the notion of punitive damages recoverable by the victim (as distinguished from fines paid to the state as punishment). See, e.g., Harvey McGregor, Personal Injury and Death, 11 Int'l Ency.Comp. L., Torts, ch. 9, sec. 6 (1983). The civilian aversion to punitive damages is such that courts in civil law countries have refused to recognize and enforce American judgments insofar as they award punitive damages. See, e.g., the decision of the German Federal Supreme Court of June 4, 1992, reproduced and discussed in the sixth edition of this book at 955ff.

13. German law allows private prosecution for several misdemeanors apart from negligently causing bodily harm; in some European countries, a narrow class of misdemeanors can be prosecuted *only* by the victim.

14. The right of intervention is now conferred upon the victims of all those offences that attack "highly personal values" (e.g., sex offences, offences against freedom or honor, and most offences against life and limb.) See § 395 subs. I of the Code of Criminal Procedure, in effect since April 1, 1987.

parole board makes a decision. Recent federal legislation requires public prosecutors to consult with victims at critical stages of the proceeding, and "victim impact statements" must sometimes be prepared.[15] Yet, even the most dramatic reforms stop short of enabling the victim to participate as of right in the entire criminal process, and especially in its trial phase.[16]

The interaction between the criminal proceeding and the victim's civil claim gives rise to the question of the consistency problem between the civil and criminal judgment in cases where the victim chooses to bring an independent civil action. However, the criminal dossier being admissible as evidence in the civil action, an inconsistency between the results reached in the two proceedings will not occur too frequently. In what is probably a majority of civil-law systems, this slight danger of inconsistent results is regarded with equanimity.[17]

A minority group led by France, however, has adopted the principle that a criminal judgment is absolutely conclusive and binds the whole world (including, of course, the injured party).[18] This absolute res judicata

---

15. See Victim and Witness Protection Act, *supra* note 1. The victims' movement and its effects on criminal justice reform are perceptively discussed in A. Goldstein, Defining the Role of the Victim in Criminal Prosecution, 52 Miss.L.J. 515 (1982). For the most updated state of the art in the U.S. see E. Blondel, Victim's Rights in an Adversary System, 58 Duke L.J. 237 (2008)

16. See Dix v. Superior Court, 53 Cal.3d 442, 279 Cal.Rptr. 834, 807 P.2d 1063 (1991), for a strong statement limiting victims to the specific rights spelled out in the "Victims' Bill of Rights" (added to the California Constitution in 1982), and emphatically rejecting, despite constitutional and statutory provisions broadening victims' rights, any idea of allowing a crime victim or other member of the public standing to intervene as a co-prosecutor in a criminal proceeding against another person.

In State v. Berg, 236 Kan. 562, 694 P.2d 427 (1985), a statute permitting counsel for the complaining witness to assist the public prosecutor, and allowing such "associate counsel" to seek a court hearing on the public prosecutor's decision to drop the charges, was held *not* to confer a right to appeal the trial court's order dismissing the complaint.

17. In some of the majority countries, e.g., The Netherlands, the danger of inconsistency is further reduced by the rule that the civil court must treat the criminal judgment as presumptively correct; the presumption, however, is rebuttable. See E. L. Johnson, *infra* note 18.

In most American jurisdictions, on the other hand, the consistency problem would be taken seriously and treated under the heading of collateral estoppel. See *supra*, Chapter 8, Section 3(J) at 817 (Finality of Judgments). An acquittal in the criminal proceeding would have no collateral estoppel effect in the subsequent civil action. Whether a criminal judgment of conviction after trial has such an effect depends largely on the attitude which a particular jurisdiction adopts concerning the question of "mutuality." See R. C. Casad, Res Judicata in a Nutshell § 5–73 (1976).

18. See the brief but interesting discussion by E. L. Johnson, Res Judicata: A Comparative Study of the Effect of Convictions and Acquittals in Subsequent Civil Proceedings, 18 Current Legal Problems 81 (1965).

There is, however, an important exception to the French rule that a criminal judgment is res judicata as against the whole world. As the reader will recall (see *supra* Chapter 8, Section 4 at 828 (Criminal Procedure), in 1972 the French adopted the German *Strafbefehl* (summary penal order) procedure. See Law No. 72–5 of Jan. 3, 1972 (Rec.Dalloz Hebd. 1972, at 58). If the defendant does not file a timely objection, such a penal order acquires the force of a judgment convicting and sentencing the defendant. However, art. 528–1 of the French Code of Criminal Procedure, as amended by the above-mentioned law of 1972, expressly provides that the penal order, even if it acquires the force of a judgment, shall not have any res judicata effect in a subsequent civil action

effect is accorded not only to judgments of conviction, but to acquittals as well. In practice, the rule is rendered tolerable only by limiting the conclusive effect of the criminal judgment to what we would call the court's precise "holding." The cases seeking to stake out a line of demarcation between binding holdings and non-binding dicta—especially with respect to acquittals in traffic accident cases—are numerous and often difficult to reconcile. One important rule, however, seems to be well established: when it is possible for the victim of an automobile accident to recover from the driver or owner of the car on a theory of absolute or quasi-absolute liability, the victim may be successful in the civil action even though the driver has been acquitted of a charge of criminal negligence.[19]

that might be brought against the defendant for damages caused by the infraction. Thus, in the case of a petty offense, the res judicata effect of a French criminal judgment will depend on whether the criminal proceeding was instituted in the regular manner or by way of the penal order procedure.

19. See P. Herzog, Civil Procedure in France 138 (1967), and authorities there cited.

It should be remembered, also, that in the criminal proceeding the driver usually is charged with a specific negligent act, such as speeding, going through a red light, or the like. Acquittal of that specific charge does not prevent the civil court from imposing liability on the basis of some other (actual or presumed) act of negligence.

CHAPTER 9

SELECTED ISSUES IN PRIVATE LAW

Legal techniques or modes of thought diffused through a given professional legal community, particularly in the domain of private law, on their face are politically colorless.[1] The Code, for example, has been used by democratically elected parliaments as well as by autocrats such as Napoleon and Hitler. The rules embodied in a code may be liberal, paternalistic, or socialistic, or may represent any other brand or mixture of political and economic views. In each instance, these views are the product of a particular time and a particular place.

Illuminating issues are how the value judgments of the legislator or legislators are reflected in the positive provisions of a code, and how code provisions, although their language may remain unaltered, change their meaning with the rise of new regimes and new political and social philosophies. The code provisions and other materials of which the examples will consist, are in part of recent vintage; but others go back more than 200 years. This calls for a caveat concerning their comparability. It will be found that the social changes which took place in the wake of the French Revolution are clearly and dramatically spelled out in the Code Napoleon. That code, as we know, legalized the demise of feudalism and ratified the triumph of the *tiers état*. It did so, mainly, by the use of two concepts: *freedom of contract* and a redefinition of *ownership* in terms of an absolute right, unfettered by entailment, freely alienable, and strongly, almost fiercely, protected against any public or private interference.[2] These two

---

1. See E. Patterson and R. B. Schlesinger, Problems of Codification of Commercial Law, N.Y.Leg.Doc. (1955) No. 65A, at 50–51, 57–61, 1955 Report of the New York Law Revision Commission at 80–81, 87–91; R. Cotterrell, Comparative Law and Legal Culture, in Oxford Handbook of Comparative Law 709–737 (M. Reimann & R. Zimmermann eds., 2006).

It has been argued, however, that the "spontaneous order" of a common law system is more favorable to political liberty than codification. See 1 F. A. Hayek, Law, Legislation and Liberty (1973). From the point of view of economic analysis, it likewise has been suggested that, on the whole, "judge-made rules tend to be efficiency-promoting while those made by legislators tend to be efficiency-reducing." R. A. Posner, Economic

Analysis of Law 560 (7th ed. 2008); see also R. A. Posner, Judicial Behavior and Performance: An Economic Approach, 32 Fla.St. U.L.Rev. 1259 (2006); N. Gennaioli and A. Shleifer, The Evolution of Common Law, 115 J.Pol.Ec. 43 (2007). But cf. U. Mattei, Comparative Law and Economics 207–10 (1997).

2. It has been said, and often repeated, that the French Civil Code of 1804 is "the code of the employer, of the creditor and of the property owner." J. Charmont, Le droit et l'esprit démocratique 54 (1908). See G. Ripert, Le régime démocratique et le droit civil moderne 17–18 (1948); R. Pound, The French Civil Code and the Spirit of 19th Century Law, 35 B.U.L.Rev. 77 (1955); J. Gordley, Myths of the French Civil Code, 42 Am.J.Comp.L. 459 (1994).

concepts, revolutionary as they were 200 years ago, belong to the sphere of *private law*, and, consequently, appear clearly on the face of the *Code civil*. The economic and social changes which have taken place during the present century, on the other hand, mostly are reflected in the growth of such *public law* fields as administrative law, labor law, social security, taxation, nationalization, and public corporations.[3] Many of these changes, therefore, are only faintly reflected on the face of the modern private law codes.[4] While the moral, political, and social spirit of the early 19th century is unmistakably imprinted upon the provisions of the Code Napoleon, we must often dig more deeply, and draw subtler inferences, if we seek to find indications of 20th and 21st century social developments in private law codes and private law decisions of the last two generations.[5] No account of the transformation from a model of economic *laissez faire* into a system of "social private law" fundamentally limiting such freedom also in private law is richer than the one offered by Duncan Kennedy. In his important study Kennedy describes a global legal intellectual climate that he calls classical legal theory CLT, dominant through the nineteenth century and securely imbedded in bourgeois ideas of contractual freedom and absolute ownership, followed by the development of a twentieth century "social" intellectual climate.

Duncan Kennedy, Two Globalizations of Law and Legal Theory

36 Suffolk L.R. 631, 648 (2003).

[footnotes omitted. Text partially edited for sake of contextualization]

The initial innovators of The Social were German-speaking, including Jhering, Gierke, and Ehrlich, but the main globalizers were French-speaking, Saleilles, Geny, Duguit, Lambert, Josserand, Gounod, and Gurvitch. Like the Marxists (the other significant early twentieth century

---

3. Despite the enormous growth of public law, private law is far from having atrophied. On the contrary, constant increase in the mobility of persons, goods, and ideas, and in the total volume and frequency of business transactions, has further enhanced the importance of private law; the modern institutions of public law have rather added a new dimension of complexity to a vigorously surviving system of private law. In communist systems, private law to some extent was displaced by public law; the experience of former communist countries (see *supra* Chapter 3, Section 3, at 214, p. 214ff) illustrates the great mass of public as well as private law legislation required to develop and sustain a contemporary market or mixed economy.

4. The statement in the text is subject to at least one qualification: the changed status of women does appear on the face of many of the civil codes.

5. See F. Wieacker, Das Sozialmodell der klassischen Privatrechtsgesetzbücher und die Entwicklung der modernen Gesellschaft (Heft 3 der Schriftenreihe der Juristischen Studiengesellschaft Karlsruhe, 1953), and the three-volume work by J. Savatier, Les métamorphoses économiques et sociales du droit civil d'aujourd'hui, especially the first volume entitled Panorama des mutations (3d ed. 1964); see also David Kennedy, Laws and Developments, in Law and Development: Facing Complexity in the 21st Century. Essays in honour of Peter Slinn 17, 21–23 (J. Hatchard and A. Perry–Kessaris eds., 2003); A. Riles, Comparative Law and Socio–Legal Studies, in Oxford Handbook, *supra* note 1, 775–812.

school critical of Classical Legal Theory), they interpreted the actual regime of the will theory (freedom of contract) as an epiphenomenon in relation to a "base"-in the case of the Marxists, the capitalist economy and in the case of The Social, "society" conceived as an organism. The idea of both was that the will theory in some sense "suited" the socio-economic conditions of the first half of the nineteenth century. But The Social people were anti-Marxist, just as much as they were anti-laissez faire. Their goal was to save liberalism from itself.

Their basic idea was that the conditions of late nineteenth century life represented a social transformation, consisting of urbanization, industrialization, organizational society, globalization of markets, all summarized in the idea of interdependence. Because the will theory was individualist, it ignored interdependence, and endorsed particular legal rules that permitted anti-social behavior of many kinds. The crises of the modern factory (industrial accidents, pauperization) and the urban slum, and later the crisis of the financial markets and the Great Depression, all derived from the failure of coherently individualist law to respond to the coherently social needs of modern conditions of interdependence.... From this "is" analysis, they derived the "ought" of a reform program, one that was astonishingly successful. There was labor legislation, the regulation of urban areas through landlord/tenant, sanitary and zoning regimes, the regulation of financial markets, and the development of new institutions of international law. The is-to-ought move appealed to a very wide range of legitimating rhetorics. These traversed the left/right spectrum, leaving out only Marxist collectivism at one extreme and pure Manchesterism at the other.

The Social, then, could be based on socialist or social democratic ideology (perhaps Durkheimian), on the social Christianity of Protestant sects, on neo-Kantian "situational natural law," on Comtean positivism, on Catholic natural law, on Bismark/Disraeli social conservatism, or on fascist ideology. In other words, The Social, like CLT, was initially a consciousness (though always in an embattled relationship with CLT, rather than straightforwardly hegemonic in the way CLT had been in the brief period between about 1850 and 1890) within which it was possible to develop different and conflicting ideological projects. Regardless of which it was, the slogans included organicism, purpose, function, reproduction, welfare, instrumentalism (law is a means to an end)-and so anti-deduction, because a legal rule is just a means to accomplishment of social purposes.

A crucial part of the social critique of Classical Legal Theory was the claim that it maintained an appearance of objectivity in legal interpretation only through the abuse of deduction. According to The Social people, CLT people understood themselves to operate as interpreters (judges, administrators, law professors) according to a system of induction and deduction premised on the coherence, or internal logical consistency, of the system of enacted legal norms. One mode was to locate the applicable enacted rule; a second was to develop a rule to fill a gap by a chain of deductions from a more abstract enacted rule or principle; a third, the method of "constructions," was to determine what un-enacted principle must be part of "the system," given the various enacted elements in it, if we were to regard it as internally coherent, and then derive a gap filling rule from the construction. . . .

One juristic response to social legislation was to assimilate it to the Classical positivist model by adding new legal topics corresponding to new statutes, without modifying the premises or the methods of doctrinal analysis in any way. The advent of The Social added norms and provided new fields for legal science. In every country that has a Western system of legal education, it seems that some part of instruction proceeds in this way, with classical fields coherent in a classical way, and social fields coherent in a social way.

The social jurists themselves were more ambitious. Their notion was that the reform effort to make law adapt to society required a thorough revamping of the juristic universe. In civil procedure, for example, the adversary system was obviously mal-adapted to a modern, interdependent, flexible, complex industrial system. We needed many new types of procedures that would get us out of the typical individualist battle model. In criminal law, we needed to individualize punishment but also to make it socially effective by identifying the types of criminals and the social causes of crime. Even contract law, the core of the core, needed revision, in the direction, for example, of pre-contractual duties, liberalization of excuses, functional rather than formalist interpretation of formalities.

We needed new types of courts-labor courts, merchant courts, juvenile courts and family courts, as well as new types of procedure. Commercial law needed to be reformed to meet the requirements of the new style of enterprise, particularly the fact that most transactions were between very large companies, or between large enterprises and individual actors with no bargaining power at all. Corporate law needed to be revamped because of the radical separation of ownership and control.

It was not just a matter of reconceptualizing and then reforming the maladaptive, ideologically individualist doctrinal substance that had emerged in the late nineteenth century. The anti-formalist strand in The Social current emphasized gaps, conflicts and ambiguities in the corpus of positive law, and consequently the role of the judge, either as an abuser of deduction or as a rational law maker. In the United States, stare decisis was discredited as abuse of deduction par excellence, and layers of socially-oriented early case law were discovered in order to multiply conflicts and open the space for reform.

The civilian dispute about what counted as a "source of law" was resolved in favor of the legitimacy of *jurisprudence* (judge-made law), whatever the "official portrait" might continue to be. Moreover, all law interpreters, in the social vision, including professors and administrators, and lawyers when they draft contracts, lawyers when they choose litigation and settlement strategies, lawyers when they give advice on liability, are engaged in law-making. What the enterprise does will be affected at every stage by interpretations made by the lawyers, and those interpretations will be contestable. . . .

As I have already said, this was not about politics. It might be true that their version of social justice could be characterized politically as more corporatist, communitarian, anti-formalist, and pluralist than the thought of their enemies in the liberal traditions of the center and right. But they did not think that the mere commitment to social justice in the is-to-ought mode of The Social put them in danger of eroding the distinction between law and politics. . . .

The second globalization followed the channels established by the first. Students from all over Europe went to France and Germany to study law. From the middle of the nineteenth century up to the 1930's, students from the part of the rest of the world under Western influence flocked to Europe. From the colonies, they went to their respective "metropoles," the Senegalese to Paris, the Indonesians to Amsterdam, and so forth. If they had a choice, they went to the European capital with the most prestige in their part of the periphery (Latin Americans to Paris, Unitedstateseans to Germany).

First Germany and later France were the fountains of The Social, but it developed simultaneously in many places, even though most of those places imported elements from Germany and France and had relatively little or no influence back. In Italy it was first moderately left, and then fascist. In Spain (Franco), Portugal (Salazar) and Greece (Metaxas), it was fascist; in the Netherlands and (Fabian) Britain, moderately left. The Unitedstatesean sociological jurisprudes (Pound, Cardozo, and Brandeis were the most important) developed a version that was first moderately left and then moderately right. They drew extensively on the French and Germans, but were also strongly influenced by Holmes, who developed, before Geny, a peculiarly American variant of the "abuse of deduction" thesis. . . .

As The Social established itself in the West, students from Eastern Europe, Latin America, South, East and Southeast Asia, the Arab world, and Africa appropriated it and took it home. A crucial dimension of the spread of The Social was nationalism, but in at least three modes, rather than as a unitary phenomenon. First, nationalism, as irredentism and as the drive for ethnic purity, was understood by the progressive European social people to be, along with class conflict, the scourge that might well destroy European civilization.

Theorists of The Social undertook a deep rethinking of public international law in an effort to contain and shape nationalism understood as a life creating and also life destroying irrational force. . . . At the very same time, The Social was one of the key slogans of nationalism itself, in its fascist form, but also in authoritarian right wing variants in many parts of the world, including the new states carved out of the Ottoman and Austro–Hungarian Empires, and Latin American countries such as Argentina (Peron) and Brazil (Vargas). This meant that, during the interwar period, progressive or revolutionary left wing reformers in countries like Colombia and Mexico, and their right wing enemies, employed virtually identical social, corporatist, anti-capitalist, anti-liberal rhetorics. The Mexican federal labor laws of the 1930s, a famous accomplishment of the revival of the Mexican left under Cardenas, closely resembled, if they were not actually modeled on, Mussolini's *Carta di Lavoro*.

Finally, in the colonies, nationalism meant national independence, and was the call of the people as a whole to arms against the colonial master. The colonial powers recruited natives to staff the lower levels of their administrations, and elements from pre-colonial elites survived, and pursued success in the new order through European education. . . .

There was a pattern, identified for the Egyptian case by Amr Shalakany, to the process by which a part of the legal elite of one country after another made The Social its own. In case after case, the importing elite found something in the national culture that would make The Social, as opposed to the formalist individualism imputed to CLT, *uniquely appropriate to the nation in question*.

In Europe, the Catholic South (Portugal, Spain, Italy, along with Hungary) could emphasize that The Social was the philosophy of the Church enunciated in *Rerum Novarum* (1897), which means "of new things," and the "new things" were industrialization, urbanization, interdependence and the rest of The Social. In the 1930s the Vatican struck its infamous deal with fascism, memorialized in the social rhetoric of *Quadrigessimo Anno* (the encyclical of 1937 marking the fortieth anniversary of *Rerum Novarum*). In the Protestant North, the Dutch were able to interpret The Social as particularly appropriate to the interdependent culture of dike-based land reclamation. In Russia, there was the famous peasant village community, or *mir*.

In a striking essay published in the *Harvard Law Review* in January 1917, Roscoe Pound laid the ills of modern Unitedstatesean society at the door of the "Romanization" of Unitedstatesean law during the second half of the nineteenth century. He presented CLT as an "alien" mode of legal thought, whose formalist individualism had displaced the "organic" common law mode based on the notion of "relation" (husband and wife, master and servant, landlord and tenant). The rediscovery of common law medieval tradition was to be the basis for bringing Unitedstatesean law into harmony with twentieth century conditions of social interdependence. Citations to the German and French civilian originators of the program he proposed were few and far between (though plentiful in his later works, representing The Social as the consensus of advanced European legal thought).

In Latin America, the right wing authoritarians appealed to *Hispanidad*, whose social essence was Catholic but also uniquely American. In Mexico, land reform and the *ejido* system of state regulated and subsidized cooperative peasant agriculture was supposedly a return to pre-Colombian modes of social organization. In Egypt, Sanhouri's eclectic, socially oriented civil code, later adopted or adapted in many other Arab countries, was indigenous and eminently traditional, as well as ultra-modern, because Islamic law was and had always been social.

In Africa, there was Senghor's *negritude*, Kenyatta's African idea of property, and Nyerere's African socialism or *Ujaama*. Sun Yat Sen and then Chiang Kai-shek in China developed the nationalist ideology of the Kuomintang, the main opponent of Chinese communism, as a complex and subtle blend of Confucian, "social" and liberal elements. After World War II, Chiang hired Roscoe Pound as a consultant on the construction of the legal regime of the Republic of China on Taiwan.

The Social could be the public law ideology of a disempowered sub-group in a British colonial structure (the Quebecois in Canada, or the Afrikaaners in South Africa, for example) with civilian private law retaining the formalism of the minority's metropole as a symbol of resistance to the common law of the colonial power. In Palestine, jurists influenced by Savigny and Ehrlich developed a secular "Hebrew law" that was first supposed to be individualist and then social, and then went out of fashion, at the moment when the State of Israel began to develop a highly social regime of public law.

Savigny's formalist derivation of all private law from right and will gave way to Savigny's insistence that national legal orders did and should represent the particular normative order of the people involved. But we are left with the question of why, at the moment of discovering national particularity, *each nation discovered the same thing*? A facile, but initially plausible interpretation would be that The Social was a tool of elites facing precisely the absence of The Social. That is, of elites put in charge of governing territories torn apart by class conflict, or containing wildly heterogeneous tribal, cultural, racial and religious groups, first assembled as colonies according to the interests of the Empires and Great Powers, and then re-parceled at the moment of national independence according to the interests of the Great Powers and of the local elites who were to take their place. The ideology of The Social was (perhaps) not a reflection of national particularity, but an instrument in the "imagining" of presently non-existent national communities. . . .

The welfare state figures heavily in the social and political history of the period of The Social, but as I hope is already clear, it would be wrong to treat it as the "essence" or, from the point of view of law, as the central development. The legal concepts that seem most important are those of social insurance (unemployment, accidents, health, and old age pensions) and entitlements based on need, conceptualized as rehabilitative, with an administration that does the need assessment and delivers services (social work) that are supposed to reintegrate the recipient into the presumably normal universe of the labor market.

These are typical manifestations of The Social, with Bismarkian German origins, adopted throughout the capitalist West. There is an easy transition to the notion of social rights, understood as "third generation" (after private law and political rights), occupying a position of juristic ambiguity typical of the innovations of the period. Social rights were both legal, and even constitutional (first in Mexico, 1917), but non-justiciable as to the level of benefits provided, although justiciable as entitlements, once legislatively established within the administrative law regime of the country in question.

Of course, the welfare state could globalize only to a limited extent, because it presupposed a particular kind of economic, social and administrative development, a measure of political autonomy (i.e., something other than colonial status), and a political configuration. I would characterize the political configuration as one in which a significant measure of redistribution from the middle to the lower-middle and working-class strata, and a significant measure of paternalist control of the spending decisions of those strata (that is, compelling them to insure), could be made plausible, as protection of the social whole, to an electoral majority. . . .

If the Depression and World War II simultaneously stimulated and snuffed out institutional innovations, they made possible, through the sheer intensity of disaster, combined with the defeat of fascism and the containment of communism, a whole collection of institutional triumphs of the progressive version of The Social. . . .

If Jhering is the undisputed grandfather of The Social, John Maynard Keynes was perhaps its genius, even though he thought the save-it-from-itself strategy should operate at the state and international levels, leaving the CLT structure of private property and free contract intact. The Bretton Woods system that the Western industrial powers established for their intra-bloc relations during the Cold War eventually became the world financial regulatory system. As initially conceived, it was a typical example of The Social at work.

First of all, the International Monetary Fund (IMF) was premised on the idea of the interdependence of financial and currency markets, with the danger being runs on national currencies producing chain reaction downward spirals. The way to stop runs was to "nip them in the bud," from a position outside and above any single national strategic actor. There was a shared "public interest" in this kind of intervention, so long as it was carefully limited so as not to interfere with national sovereignty in monetary and fiscal policy.

Of course, macroeconomic monetary and fiscal policy were exactly what the CLT model of free trade, gold standard, and private international law were designed to eliminate. Keynes's contribution in this area was to show that fiscal and monetary policy could function rationally as "counter-cyclical," counteracting through strategic action from the center the individualist capitalist logic of boom followed by bust, and so benefiting everyone in the society. But fiscal and monetary policy also meant deficit spending in periods of economic contraction, and, therefore, opened the possibility of financing the whole program of The Social reformers in the very periods when historically they had been forced to close up shop. . . .

The Bretton Woods institutions gradually expanded to include the whole non-communist world. Between 1945 and the mid–1960s, decolonization brought into existence a world order of independent "nation" states. The old and new national elites of the periphery were free of direct, that is, jurisdictional, control. And without the gold standard, they were free to manipulate their currencies and national budgets for whatever sovereign purposes. They soon discovered, however, that they needed, for whatever purposes, access to world capital markets. This meant that they had to join the Bretton Woods system-either join this game strictly on the terms proposed, that is, within the structure of legal rules already in place, or starve in the dark.

Within The Social, these trends produced, after World War II, a "third worldist" or Bandung reaction (Nehru, Nasser, Sukarno), and a school of progressive public international law. It deployed the social critique of the individualism of classical private law against the post-World War II supposedly reformed and post-colonial international law regime. The formal liberation and enfranchisement of unfree labor in Europe simply shifted the mechanism of exploitation from the transparency of feudalism to the mystification of capitalism. The formal grant of national independence to colonized peoples likewise shifted the transparency of imperial rule to the mystification of neo-colonialism. In place of the exploitative wage bargain, the modern international order worked through the unequal exchange of primary products from the third world for industrial products from the First. This seems to me to have been the last strictly analytic accomplishment of the social consciousness.

It seems useful to distinguish two phases here. The first occurred immediately after the War when the Allies forcefully and systematically transformed the Japanese, German, and Italian systems from a fascist to a progressive version of The Social, and imposed a similar transformation on the South Korean and Taiwanese social and economic systems as the price of protection from the Chinese communists. In Japan, South Korea and Taiwan, land reform was an important part of the transformation, along with at least paper rights for labor unions, at least a paper antitrust regime, and at least paper regulation of the financial system. Germany and Italy were incorporated into the Social Democratic/Christian Democratic model propounded by the progressive social people in the United States, Britain and France (and by German and Italian social democrats before the War).

The second phase was the extension of the import substitution industrialization (ISI) strategy across Latin America and to the newly independent third world, first to very large economies such as those of India, Egypt, Turkey, Iran, and Indonesia, and, after 1960, to the very small economies of newly independent African states. The ISI strategy, which relied heavily on public law and government intervention, was strongly supported by the various United Nations bodies, by the World Bank, and by the United States Agency for International Development (USAID), and it was the initial economic strategy of Taiwan and South Korea (as well as Singapore) before they gradually shifted to export-led growth. It was a product of Keynesian liberalism as much as of democratic socialism, just as strongly anti-communist as it was against laissez-faire.

ISI typically involved the exploitation of the countryside, supposedly for the sake of industrial capital formation in the cities, through tariffs and through the marketing boards that the social people had pioneered in the 1930s. Aside from South Korea and Taiwan, at the moment of maximum communist threat and maximum liberal influence in Washington, only a very few progressive regimes (for example, Egypt, Bolivia) actually broke up large estates. The refusal to join the Soviet bloc was more than a matter of diplomacy. Reforming third-world elites adopted the economic institutions of the social current rather than those of communism.

1.   Freedom of Contract

(a) The Parties' Freedom to Shape Their Contracts and Other Transactions

FRENCH CIVIL CODE

Art. 1134. Contracts lawfully entered into have the force of law for those who have made them.

They can be rescinded only by mutual consent or for causes allowed by law.

They must be performed in good faith.[1]

SWISS CODE OF OBLIGATIONS

Art. 19. Within the limits of the law, the parties may determine the terms of their contract as they please.

Contract terms at variance with provisions of law are permissible unless they are inconsistent with a cogent provision,[2] contra bonos mores or violative of the public order or the right of personality.[3]

SWISS CIVIL CODE[4]

Art. 11. Every man is capable of rights. For all men, therefore, within the bounds of the law's regulation the same capacity exists to have rights and duties.

Art. 27.... No one can renounce his freedom or restrict himself in its use in a degree offensive to law or morality.

1. The reader will recall that the historical roots of the sweeping principle announced in Art. 1134 have been traced in an earlier part of this book (see *supra* Chapter 4 at 343ff).

2. Concerning the distinction between *ius cogens* and *ius dispositivum*, see *infra* pp. 873 and 903.

3. The meaning of the expression "right of personality," as used in the Swiss Code of Obligations, will become clearer by reading Art. 27 of the Civil Code, *infra*.

4. Transl. by R. P. Shick, and reprinted by permission of the American Bar Association.

FEDERAL CIVIL CODE OF MEXICO[5]

Art. 6. The will of private persons cannot exempt from the observance of the law, nor alter it nor modify it. Private rights which do not directly affect the public interest may be waived only when the waiver does not impair rights of third parties.

Art. 7. The waiver authorized in the foregoing article produces no effect if it is not made in clear and precise terms, so that there is no doubt as to the right which is waived.[6]

NOTES AND QUESTIONS

(1) In civilian terminology, a distinction is drawn between mandatory rules (*ius cogens*), which cannot be abrogated by the parties and render all contrary agreements null and void, and default rules (*ius dispositivum*), which are subject to the autonomy of the parties in the sense that the parties have the power to make agreements contrary to the rule.[1] A rule of the latter type is mere gap-filling law; it comes into play only to the extent that the parties have failed to cover the point in their agreement or other transaction.[2] Yielding rules

5. These provisions are modeled after the text of Articles 6 and 7 of the former Civil Code for the Federal District of Mexico enacted in 1928.

6. The Mexican Constitution, the Civil Code, and other statutes contain elaborate provisions for the protection of employees, rural tenants, and other classes of persons thought to be in need of protection. See, e.g., J. A. Vargas, Introduction to Mexico's Legal System, San Diego Legal Studies, Paper no. 08–007, 12–13, 20–22 (2008), available at http://papers.ssrn.com/sol3/papers.cfm?abstract_id=1085000. Consider the effect of Arts. 6 and 7 upon the waivability of the rights of such persons.

1. See A. Lenhoff, Optional Terms (Ius Dispositivum) and Required Terms (Ius Cogens) in the Law of Contracts, 45 Mich.L.Rev. 39 (1946); E. A. Farnsworth, Comparative Contract Law, in Oxford Handbook of Comparative Law 899, 918–20 (M. Reimann & R. Zimmermann Eds., 2006); M. E. Storme, Freedom of Contract: Mandatory and Non–Mandatory Rules in European Contract Law, 15 Eur.Priv.L. 235 (2007). In French law, the same distinction is sometimes made by referring to some rules which involve public policy, as opposed to those that do not. See French Civil Code Art. 6: One cannot, by private agreements, derogate from laws which concern public policy (*ordre public*) or good morals.

Lawyers brought up in the common law, while familiar with the distinction between *ius cogens* and *ius dispositivum* in the law of contracts, use somewhat different terminology. In referring to those rules which the civilians characterize as *ius dispositivum*, the UCC uses the term "subject to agreement otherwise."

2. In dealing with particular types of contracts, the civil and commercial codes of civil-law countries tend to lay down many rules of *ius dispositivum*. Specifics with which the parties (intentionally or otherwise) have not dealt in the terms of the contract, thus are supplied by the code.

It has been observed that the civilians' frequent use of non-cogent *rules* of contract law marks a contrast to the common-law habit of attempting "to derive all the consequences of a contract from the will of those who made it (or at least ostensibly to do so . . .)." See B. Nicholas, Rules and Terms—Civil Law and Common Law, 48 Tul.L.Rev. 946, 948 (1974). Professor Nicholas interestingly explains the historical reasons for this difference between the two systems. In recent times, however, this contrast has become less pronounced. As common-law countries subject more and more types of contracts (e.g., contracts for sale, transportation, insurance, etc.) to statutory regulation, they become increasingly civilian in their use of constructive terms which are derived, no longer from judicial analysis of the particular contract before the court, but from legislative imposition of

are an important essence of freedom of contracts and one expects more of those in commercial codes rather than in the civil codes.

Mandatory rules are the exception in commercial matters and the Commercial Codes go out of heir way to point them out as exceptions. For example, former Section 67, subdiv. 4, of the German Commercial Code, *supra*, expressly provides that any agreement contrary to the rule of subdiv. 1 (as construed by the courts) would be "null and void." To a German lawyer the provision of subdiv. 4 will appear unnecessary and repetitious, because subdiv. 1 already provides that the notice period to terminate a labor contract period "must" be the same for both parties. The draftsmen of the German codes aimed at accuracy and consistency in the use of terms. Those construing the codes, therefore, have to take the words "must" and "cannot" as conclusive indication of the cogent nature of a code provision, while the terms "may" and "shall" are held to characterize default rules.[3]

This rigorous, systematic use of terminological technique is peculiar to the German Code. The Civil Codes of France and Switzerland do not employ this method, and thus leave more room for judicial interpretation when a question arises concerning the cogent or yielding nature of a code provision.[4]

(2) As we have seen, some of the civilian codes provide that an offer, though not supported by any consideration,[5] normally is irrevocable for the period

rules (albeit rules subject to agreement otherwise) upon certain types of contracts. See H. Beale, A. Hartkamp, H. Kötz, D. Tallon, Contract Law 571–589 (2002).

3. See E. J. Schuster, The Principles of German Civil Law 9–10 (1907).

4. See J. J. Morrison, Legislative Technique and the Problem of Suppletive and Constructive Laws, 9 Tul.L.Rev. 544 (1935). For a comparison between the French and the German approach, see M.W. Hesselink, Non–Mandatory Rules in European Contract Law, 1 Eur.Rev.Contr.L. 44 (2005).

The problem whether and in what way the cogent or yielding nature of code provisions should be made clear in the code itself must be faced by the draftsman of every code dealing with transactional subjects. Compare the German technique with the method employed in former Sec. 1–102(3) and (4) (nowadays Sec. 1–103) of the Uniform Commercial Code.

5. The doctrine of consideration is peculiar to the common law and is not recognized in the civil-law systems, which use different criteria in order to determine whether an agreement should be enforced as a contract. See, e.g., H. Beale, A. Hartkamp, H. Kötz, D. Tallon, *supra* note 2, 127–153; M. Bussani and U. Mattei, The Common Core Approach to European Law, 3 Co-

lum.J.Eur.L. 339, 345 (1997/1998); B. S. Markesinis, Cause and Consideration: A Study in Parallel, in Foreign Law and Comparative Methodology: A Subject and a Thesis 47 f. (B. S. Markesinis ed., 1997); A. G. Chloros, The Doctrine of Consideration and the Reform of the Law of Contract, 17 Int'l & Comp.L.Q. 137 (1968); M. S. Mason, The Utility of Consideration, 41 Colum.L.Rev. 825 (1941); E. G. Lorenzen, Causa and Consideration in the Law of Contracts, 28 Yale L.J. 621 (1919). Even an agreement by which one party promises to make an outright gift to the other is enforceable as a contract in most civil-law countries, provided that it is made in proper notarial form. See, e.g., J. Gordley, The Enforceability of Promises in European Contract Law 24–65 (2001). In France and in a few countries following the French example, even the requirement of notarization can be avoided if the promise is made in the form—though it may be a mere simulation—of an exchange contract. See European Contract Law 27–29 (B. Fauvarque–Cosson and D. Mazeaud eds., 2008); J. Gordley, Enforcing Promises, 82 Cal.L.Rev. 547, 557–558 (1995); J. P. Dawson, Gifts and Promises 74–83 (1980).

Inasmuch as a *contract* does not require consideration in the civil-law systems, it stands to reason that the revocability of an

specified in the offer itself, or for a reasonable period. In this way the principle of transactional autonomy of private parties is carried a step beyond freedom of "contract"; even the mere offer, a unilateral jural act, is made binding. It is mainly in the more modern codes (e.g., the German and Swiss) that this extension of the principle of the parties' transactional autonomy can be observed.[6]

(3) On the whole, however, the tendency of the modern codes is to restrict the scope of the parties' transactional freedom more severely than was thought desirable at the beginning of the 19th century. To be sure, even the Code Napoleon invalidates contracts that are illegal or immoral.[7] But the notion of *lésion*, although well known in pre-code civil law, was consciously rejected by the draftsmen of that Code as a general principle; only in certain instances of well-defined particular transactions (e.g, a sale of immovables where the seller has been victimized) will the French Civil Code authorize the setting aside of a transaction on the ground of a gross disproportion between value given and value received.[8] By way of contrast, we have observed that, under the heading of "lésion" or "usury," some of the more modern codes provide the courts with potent weapons for invalidating one-sided bargains concluded by parties of flagrantly unequal mental or economic strength.[9]

(4) If the principle of freedom of contract embodied in Art. 19 of the Swiss Code of Obligations were carried to its ultimate logical consequence, individuals would be free to make themselves unfree by entering into a contract to that effect. Art. 27 of the Swiss Civil Code makes it clear, however, that the principle of freedom of the personality is of a higher order than the principle of freedom of contract. Contracts which go too far in restricting an individual's personal or economic freedom are declared invalid. The question of exactly where the line should be drawn is left to the courts by one of those "general clauses" which are typical of modern civil-law codes. Many different types of contracts may be affected by the provision.

offer does not depend on the presence or absence of consideration. But an offer inviting a contract for which the law prescribes written or notarial form normally will have to comply with such form requirement.

6. For an extensive comparative treatment of the problem of revocability or irrevocability of offers, see 1 Formation of Contracts—A Study of the Common Core of Legal Systems 109–11, 745–91 (R. B. Schlesinger ed., 1968).

7. See Arts. 1131 & 1133.

8. See J. Gordley, A. T. von Mehren, An Introduction to the Comparative Study of Private Law 464, 481 (2006); H. Dyson, French Property and Inheritance Law 34–35 (2003); B. Nicholas, The French Law of Contract 137–41 (2d ed. 1992); Amos & Walton's

Introduction to French Law 163–64 (F. H. Lawson, A. E. Anton & L. N. Brown eds., 3d ed. 1967).

9. The reader will recall that we have previously studied the relevant provisions in the Civil Codes of Germany and Mexico (see Chapter 5, Section 6 at 433. The differences *inter sese* of the German and Mexican solutions are not without interest. The Mexican Code, although described as a "socialist" one, provides considerably less protection for the weaker party than the older German Code, which was originally drafted during the unquestionably "capitalist" era of Bismarck's Reich. The point may not be of earth-shaking significance; it is important only insofar as it underscores the necessity for caution in the use of (and reliance upon) generalizing labels.

A promise to change or not to change one's religion, or to become or remain a member of a certain religious or political association, clearly would be considered an illicit restriction of the promisor's personal freedom.[10] The same would be true of a clause (as is sometimes found in the employment contract of an airline hostess) amounting to a promise not to marry during a period of substantial duration.[11]

Even contracts which are predominantly business bargains sometimes are struck down as unduly interfering with the personal freedom of one of the parties. Thus Art. 27 would invalidate a promise not to compete, made by the seller of a business, if such promise were so broad in its terms as to preclude the promisor from any future use of his or her skills and experience.[12] An assignment of future wage claims was deemed to violate Art. 27, at least insofar as the wages were necessary to provide a livelihood for the assignor and his or her family.[13]

(5) Do the provisions of the Mexican Civil Code, reproduced above, limit or enhance freedom of contract? Do they, standing by themselves, tend to support the statement—made with regard to the 1928 Code, whose text has been substantially transposed in the 2000 Federal Civil Code of Mexico—that "The ... Code reflects the agrarian and socialistic tendencies of the revolutionary leaders, their desire to subordinate the interests of the individual to those of the community, while leaving him the fullest freedom of action consistent with such subordination ..."?[14]

10. See J. M. Grossen in 2 M. Gutzwiller et al. (eds.), Schweizerisches Privatrecht 297–98 (1967), and authorities there cited; see also F. Dessemontet, T. Ansay, Introduction to Swiss Law 52 (3d ed. 2004).

11. J. M. Grossen, *supra* note 10, 297–98.

12. See F. Dessemontet, T. Ansay, *supra* note 10; see also the comparative study by A. Kuttler, Vertragliche Konkurrenzverbote 47 ff. (1955). Promises not to compete which are contained in employment contracts are governed, not by the "general clause" of Art. 27 of the Civil Code, but by specific (and stricter) provisions of the Code of Obligations.

13. Bundesgericht, Decision of Jan. 21, 1959, BGE 85 I 17, at 30–31 (see art. 325, Swiss Code of Obligations, as amended by the federal law of Dec. 14, 1990, setting limits to the assignment of future wages). Along the same lines, it was held that a management contract under the terms of which a young singer places his entire career in the hands of a manager for a period that the manager can extend indefinitely is an excessive restriction on the personal freedom of the singer, contrary to article 27 of the Civil Code (Bundesgericht, Decision of May 23, 1978, BGE 104 II 108).

In several of the fact situations covered by the Swiss Code provision, our courts might reach the same result on grounds of "public policy"; but in U.S. law. the result in each case would depend on much narrower considerations peculiar to the particular type of contract involved in the case. Even when we use statutes to deal with problems of this kind, we draft them in narrow, specific terms. Cf. Cal. Labor Code § 2855, a provision of great significance for the entertainment industry.

14. O. Schoenrich, The Civil Code of Mexico, at vii (1950). See also *supra* note 9.

(b) Enforcement of Contracts[1]

Vàzquez v. Superior Court (San Miguel y Cía., Intervenor)

Supreme Court of Puerto Rico, 1955.
78 P.R.R. 707.

[Some of court's footnotes omitted; others renumbered.]

■ MR. CHIEF JUSTICE SNYDER delivered the opinion of the Court.

San Miguel & Cía., Inc., and Julián Vázquez Olmedo executed a contract whereby they agreed to organize a corporation in which each of them would own $100,000 worth of stock and of which Vázquez would be General Manager. San Miguel & Cía., Inc., sued Vázquez for performance of the contract and damages. We granted certiorari to review the order of the Superior Court denying the defendant's motion to strike the paragraph of the prayer asking for performance of the contract....

The contract, which is made part of the complaint, provides that the parties have agreed to organize a domestic corporation to engage in commerce in electrical, fluid gas, and refrigeration products, with the principal office in San Juan. The contract contains [elaborate details concerning the manner in which the corporation is to be organized]....

By his motion to strike a portion of the prayer ... the defendant sought a ruling that the plaintiff is not entitled to the remedy of performance of the contract, as distinguished from damages.[1] Rule 12(*f*) of the Rules of Civil Procedure provides that only " ... redundant, immaterial, impertinent, or scandalous matter ..." may be stricken from a pleading. Motions to strike are not favored. Matter will not be stricken "... unless it is clear that it can have no possible bearing upon the subject matter of the litigation. If there is any doubt as to whether under any contingency the matter may raise an issue, the motion should be denied." [Citations.]

We therefore turn to the question of whether the allegations of the complaint, including the prayer, could by any possible contingency entitle the plaintiff to performance of the contract. Under the civil law—contrary to the common law—the fact that a plaintiff who alleges a breach of contract has an adequate remedy by way of damages does not bar him from seeking performance of the contract. The plaintiff "... may choose be-

---

1. For an excellent book-length comparative treatment of the problems connected with enforcement of contracts, see G. H. Treitel, Remedies for Breach of Contract: A Comparative Account (1988), reviewed by P. Winship in 24 Int'l Law. 851 (1990); see also H. Beale, A. Hartkamp, H. Kötz, D. Tallon, *supra* p. 874, note 2, 659–878; G.H. Jones and P. Schlechtriem, Breach of Contract (Deficiencies in a Party's Performance), in 7 Int'l Ency.Comp.L. ch. 17 (1999).

1. We put to one side the contention of the plaintiff that the motion to strike a por-

tion of the prayer should have been denied without further ado, in view of the fact that the prayer is not generally considered as part of the complaint. We assume we would make an exception in this case in view of the brief and general allegations of the body of the complaint. Cf. People v. Henneman, 60 P.R.R. 58, 66. [It should be noted that while the *substantive* private law of Puerto Rico is based on the Spanish-derived Civil Code, the *procedural* Rules of the Commonwealth are patterned after the Federal Rules of Civil Procedure. Eds.]

tween exacting the fulfilment of the obligation or its rescission, with indemnity for damages ...". Section 1077, Civil Code, 1930 ed., 31 L.P.R.A. § 3052; § 1340 of the Civil Code, 31 L.P.R.A. § 3747; Szladits, The Concept of Specific Performance in Civil Law, IV Am.J.Comp.L. 208; Jackson, Specific Performance of Contracts in Louisiana, 24 Tulane L.Rev. 400. But although the adequacy of the remedy of damages plays no role under our law, §§ 1077 and 1340 of the Civil Code do not create an automatic and absolute right to performance of a contract in all cases. For example, this remedy does not lie where the contract is impossible to perform or with rare exceptions where personal services are required. See Szladits, supra; Nuñez v. Soto Nussa, District Judge, 14 P.R.R. 190; Annotation, 135 A.L.R. 279; 5 Williston on Contracts, Rev.Ed., § 1422, p. 3973; id., § 1423A, p. 3983. In the same way, in view of the special nature of a corporation and of some of the provisions of our Corporation Law—Act No. 30, Laws of Puerto Rico, 1911, as amended, 14 L.P.R.A. §§ 52 et seq.—there may be factors and circumstances involved in a particular contract to organize a corporation which would prevent our courts from ordering performance of the contract.

Section 6 of our Corporation Act—14 L.P.R.A. § 81—provides for three or more incorporators. The defendant and three other persons are named in the contract as incorporators. Since the three other persons did not sign the contract, they are not obliged to act as incorporators. The defendant therefore argues that it is impossible for the trial court to compel performance of the contract in view of the possibility that two of these three other persons might refuse to serve as incorporators.

The plaintiff might perhaps argue that the identity of the incorporators is a somewhat formal matter and that new incorporators may be readily secured to replace those who refuse to serve. But incorporators—in addition to subscribing to stock of the proposed corporation—perform important functions in connection with the organization of a corporation. See paragraph 7 of § 7 of the Corporation Act, 14 L.P.R.A. § 82, par. 7. There is therefore considerable force in the contention of the defendant that the failure to obtain three incorporators from the list of four found in the contract would defeat the right of the plaintiff to performance of the contract. However, the case is not ripe for the determination of this question. The willingness of three incorporators to serve is a matter for proof by way of affidavits on a motion for summary judgment or of testimony at the trial, and not for speculation in passing on a motion to strike. For the same reason we can not speculate, as the defendant asks us to do, that it might not be possible to obtain acceptance from three of the persons listed in the Sixth clause of the contract to serve as directors as required by § 9 of the Corporation Act, 14 L.P.R.A. § 85. All these matters may be raised by the defendant at a later stage of the case. We cannot pass on them on a motion to strike.[2]

The President of a corporation must be selected from among the directors, who must be bona fide stockholders. Section 11 of the Corpora-

---

2. The defendant cannot be compelled to serve as a director or as Vice–President and General Manager. *Nuñez v. Soto Nussa, District Judge, supra. Quaere,* whether this

tion Act, 14 L.P.R.A. § 87. The contract provides that Marcelino San Miguel shall be a director and President, but no provision is made for him to be a stockholder. The defendant therefore argues that this will prevent performance of the contract. Here again we cannot assume in considering a motion to strike that the plaintiff will not be able to show that San Miguel is in a position to obtain a qualifying share from the plaintiff corporation. Once more consideration of this matter must be postponed until definite information is before the court on it. . . .

. . . We cannot say on the record before us—a complaint and a motion to strike—that there is no possible contingency on which the plaintiff would be entitled to performance of the contract. The trial court therefore did not err in denying the motion to strike.[3]

NOTES AND QUESTIONS

(1) The "civil law" doctrine stated by the court in the principal case is not peculiar to Spanish-derived codes such as the Puerto Rican one. The principle that obligations, especially contractual obligations, as a rule can be specifically enforced, and that ordinarily it is for the obligee and not for the court to choose between specific performance and a non-specific remedy, has been adopted in the overwhelming majority of civil-law systems.[1] The German Civil Code in § 241 tersely announces the principle: "On the strength of the obligation, the

plus other factors would prevent a judgment for performance of the contract since it is impossible to order performance of all the terms of the contract. . . .

3. [To similar effect, see Redbrick Partners, LP v. Gautier, 552 F.Supp.2d 183, (D.Puerto Rico, 2007). Eds.]

1. In addition to the authorities cited by the court in the principal case, see J. P. Dawson, Specific Performance in France and Germany, 57 Mich.L.Rev. 495 (1959), where the historic development as well as the modern shape of the civil-law doctrine is discussed; K. Zweigert & H. Kötz, An Introduction to Comparative Law 470 f. (Tony Weir trans., 3d rev. ed. 1998); R. Bejesky, The Evolution in and International Convergence of the Doctrine of Specific Performance in Three Types of States, 13 Ind.Int'l Comp. L.Rev. 353 (2003); J. Smits, D. Haas, G. Hesen, Specific Performance in Contract Law: National and Other Perspectives (2008).

The principle that contractual obligations can be specifically enforced was adopted also in socialist legal systems, although somewhat different rules evolved for contracts concluded between state enterpris-

es and those falling outside the sphere of the national economic plan. See O. Ioffe & P. Maggs, Soviet Law in Theory and Practice 210–12 (1983).

A voluminous literature has appeared in recent years on the question of whether specific performance or a non-specific remedy is more desirable in terms of economic efficiency, i.e., the effort to ensure that resources be allocated to their best use. It has been argued that—subject to the existence of special circumstances—non-specific relief better advances efficient resource allocation (at least in the setting of a market economy). See A. Kronman, Specific Performance 45 U.Chi. L.Rev. 351 (1978); T.S. Ulen, The Efficiency of Specific Performance: Toward a Unified Theory of Contract Remedies, 83 Mich.L.Rev. 341 (1984). But cf. A. Schwartz, The Case for Specific Performance, 89 Yale L.J. 271, 279 (1979); S. Shavell, Specific Performance Versus Damages for Breach of Contract: An Economic Analysis, 84 Tex.L.Rev. 831 (2006).

A thoughtful treatment of the economic perspective on contract law can be found in A. T. von Mehren, A General View of Contract, in 7 Int'l Ency.Comp.L., ch. 1 (Contracts in General), at 88 & 104 (1982).

obligee is entitled to demand that the obligor render the performance owed.'' Other codes, especially the Code Napoleon, on their face express themselves less clearly;[2] but this has not prevented the French and other civilian courts from adhering to the same principle.

(2) As the principal case shows, the civilians' recognition of the obligee's right to specific performance (so long as such performance is not shown to be actually impossible) stands in marked contrast to the common law's preference for non-specific remedies. This divergence between civil law and common law would not exist if the civil-law systems had adopted the old Roman rule which was similar to the common-law rule providing for money damages as the primary remedy for breach of contract.[3] Virtually all of the modern civilian codes, however, have rejected this Roman rule and have adopted the opposite principle stated above in Note (31).[4]

(3) The essence of the modern civilian doctrine is that mere unexcused failure to perform at the proper time (i.e., a "breach" in our sense of the word) ordinarily gives rise only to a claim *for performance.*[5] An action for damages,[6] rescission, or restitution will lie only if the obligor is in "default."[7] In the absence of a contract term which expressly makes time of the essence, "de-

2. The French Civil Code and, following it, the codes of many other civil-law countries distinguish between obligations "to give" and obligations "to do" or "not to do." Although the Code Napoleon contains a provision which tends to create some doubt with respect to the obligee's right to demand specific performance of obligations "to do" or "not to do," much of the doubt has been cleared up by the courts. For references, see *supra* note 1; M. Torsello, Remedies for breach of contract, in Elgar Ency.Comp.L. 610, 618–619 (2006); 2 S. Litvinoff, Obligations § 162 (1975).

3. This was the rule during the classical period of Roman law. See W. W. Buckland & A. D. McNair, Roman Law and Common Law 412–13 (F. H. Lawson ed., 2d ed. 1952); R. W. Lee, An Introduction to Roman–Dutch Law 265–66 (5th ed. 1953); R. Zimmermann, The Law of Obligations 96 (1992); P. Stein, Roman Law in European History 10, 87 (1999); H. L. MacQueen, R. Zimmermann, European Contract Law: Scots and South African Perspectives 250 f. (2006). It seems that toward the end of that period the Roman Praetor, like the English Chancellor many centuries later, granted specific performance in certain situations. See T. H. Jackson, Specific Performance of Contracts in Louisiana, 24 Tul. L.Rev. 401, 410–12 (1950).

Modern notions of specific performance, in the civil law as well as the common law, in part are traceable to canon law influence. See H. Coing, English Equity and the Denuncia-

tio Evangelica of the Canon Law, 71 L.Q.Rev. 223 (1955).

4. See C. Szladits, The Concept of Specific Performance in Civil Law, 4 Am. J.Comp.L. 208 (1955); G. H. Treitel, Remedies for Breach of Contract, in 7 Int'l Ency. Comp.L. ch. 16, at 8–17, 22 (1975); and Treitel, *supra* p. 877, note 1, Chapter 3; K. Zweigert & H. Kötz, *supra* n. 31, 470 f.; R. Bejesky, *supra* n. 31, 365–367; M. Torsello, *supra* note 2, 610 f.

5. See, e.g., Sections 241, 242, 280, 320 ff. of the German Civil Code. Pertinent provisions of the codes of other civil-law countries are referred to, and in part quoted (in English translation), in the article by C. Szladits, Discharge of Contract by Breach in Civil Law, 2 Am.J.Comp.L. 334 (1953), in C. Szladits, *supra* note 1 and in H. Beale, A. Hartkamp, H. Kötz, D. Tallon, *supra* p. 874, note 2.

6. The statement in the text refers to damages for non-performance, which must be distinguished from damages for delayed performance. Damages of the latter kind (sometimes consisting merely of legal interest) may be recovered in addition to the performance itself, while specific performance and damages for non-performance are mutually exclusive remedies, at least in the simple case of an indivisible performance.

7. For a thorough discussion of the civil-law doctrine, especially as it applies to the more complex case of a bilateral contract that is still executory on both sides, see M. Torsel-

fault" (in the civilian sense) does not occur automatically as a result of the obligor's failure to render due and timely performance, even though such failure is unexcused; it further requires a "putting in default," i.e., a warning or admonition to perform, to be given to the obligor by the obligee, unless the obligor, by express refusal or prevention of performance, has made it clear that such putting in default would be a futile gesture.

An action for performance, moreover, will lie in every case of unexcused non-performance (unless the contract provides otherwise), while the availability of the other remedies may depend on the gravity of the breach and on additional factors. The result is that, contrary to common-law notions, a judgment ordering specific performance, i.e., performance in accordance with the terms of the contract, is the normal, primary remedy for non-performance in most civil-law countries.[8]

The idea that *performance* of a contract in accordance with its terms is the desirable solution, and that damages, rescission, and restitution constitute at best a second-class substitutes for performance, strongly prevails in modern civil-law systems; so strongly, indeed, that even after being "put in default," and even during the pendency of an action seeking restitution or damages for non-performance, the obligor ordinarily may defeat such action by tendering performance, together with interest (or other damages for the delay) and costs.[9]

(4) On the basis of the rule stated in the principal case, civil-law courts tend to grant *decrees* of specific performance more readily than common-law courts. It is clear, however, that the obligee who has obtained such a decree has won a hollow victory unless the decree can actually be enforced. Therefore, before we can judge the effectiveness of the remedy of specific performance in civil-law systems, we must take a look at the post-judgment procedures available under those systems. This is the purpose of the materials which follow.

GERMAN CODE OF CIVIL PROCEDURE[10]

Sec. 883. If the judgment debtor has to deliver a chattel or a number of specified chattels, the sheriff shall take them and hand them to the judgment creditor.

---

lo, *supra* note 2, 617–618, where further authorities are cited.

In French law, the requirement that the obligor be put in default has given rise to some difficulties and doubts; in principle, however, the requirement appears to be recognized by the prevailing view. See Y.-M. Laithier, Comparative Reflections on the French Law of Remedies for Breach of Contract, in Comparative Remedies for Breach of Contract 103 ff. (N. Cohen & E. McKendrick eds., 2004); S. Litvinoff, *supra* note 2, §§ 212–15, 274–76; P. Bonassies, Cours de Droit Civil 154–58 (mim. 1967).

8. See *supra* note 4.

9. Concerning the French rule, see Y.M. Laithier, *supra* note 7, at 121–122. The Italian rule is discussed in the interesting case of Transamerica General Corp. v. Zunino, 82 N.Y.S.2d 595, 605 (Sup.Ct.N.Y.Co. 1948). See also R. B. Schlesinger, Book Review, 3 Utah L.Rev. 147, 151–2 (1952); M. Torsello, *supra* note 2, 613–614. In the case of reciprocal promises, the rule is subject to additional qualifications. See *supra* notes 4 & 7.

10. The provisions set forth hereunder appear in the Code's 8th Book, entitled "Execution."

The substance of these provisions has remained unchanged for a long time; but the

If the chattel to be delivered is not found, then the judgment debtor, upon motion of the judgment creditor, must affirm under oath that he does not have the chattel in his possession and that he does not know where it is.

The court can change the wording of the affirmation so as to adapt it to the circumstances of the case.

. . .

Sec. 884. If the judgment debtor has to deliver a definite quantity of fungible chattels or securities, the provisions of the first paragraph of § 883 are applicable.

Sec. 885. If the judgment debtor has to turn over, surrender or vacate a parcel of immovable property . . ., the sheriff has to dispossess him and give possession to the judgment creditor.[11]

Sec. 887. If the judgment debtor fails to perform an obligation to do an act which could be performed by a third person, then the court of first instance shall authorize the judgment creditor, upon the latter's motion, to have the act done at the expense of the judgment debtor.

The judgment creditor may at the same time move that the court order the judgment debtor to advance the expenses [of such substituted performance], without prejudice to the judgment creditor's right to demand payment of the balance in case the doing of the act occasions expenses in an amount exceeding the advance payment. . . .

Sec. 888. If an act cannot be performed by a third party, and if such act depends exclusively upon the will of the judgment debtor, then the court of first instance, upon motion, shall order that the judgment debtor be compelled to perform the act. For the purpose of such compulsion, the court may impose either (a) monetary fines, and imprisonment in case such fines are not collectible, or (b) imprisonment. A single monetary fine may not exceed 25,000 Euro. [By way of a cross-reference to another section, the maximum duration of imprisonment under this section is fixed at six months.] . . .

This provision is inapplicable where the judgment orders the judgment debtor to enter into a marriage, to resume marital relations, or to perform services pursuant to a contract for services.[12]

limitations upon the amount of fines that can be imposed under §§ 888 and 890 were introduced by amendments of 1970 and 1974. Prior to those amendments, the Code did not put a ceiling upon the amount of such fines. The 1974 amendment also reduced the maximum duration of imprisonment that can be imposed pursuant to § 888.

For references to cases applying these provisions, see the articles cited in the preceding Notes.

11. This section enables the judgment creditor to obtain *possession* of the premises. If under the terms of the judgment, the judgment debtor has to transfer *title* to the judgment creditor, § 894 (see *infra*) is applicable. Under § 894, the judgment replaces the deed as well as the transferor's consent which normally would be necessary in order to bring about the registration of the transfer in the land register. (Such registration is required in order to bring about a change in

Sec. 890. If the judgment debtor violates a duty to refrain from doing, or to tolerate, a certain act, then upon motion of the judgment creditor the court of first instance shall impose upon the judgment debtor either (a) a monetary fine, and imprisonment in case such fine is not collectible, or (b) imprisonment of up to six months [for each contravention]. A single monetary fine may not exceed 250,000 Euro. The total maximum duration of imprisonment [for all contraventions] is two years.

[The second and third paragraphs of this section provide that the judgment debtor must receive an appropriate warning before he can be condemned to a fine or imprisonment, and that upon the judgment creditor's motion the debtor may be forced to give security for any damage that may arise from further violations on his part.]

Sec. 892. [This section specifies the methods by which the authorities must break any resistance of the judgment debtor against enforcement measures taken pursuant to §§ 887 and 890.]

Sec. 894. If the judgment directs the judgment debtor to make a declaration of intention, such declaration is deemed to have been made as soon as the judgment has become res judicata.[13]

NOTES

(1) Until recently, French law contained no statutory provisions comparable to the foregoing sections of the German Code of Civil Procedure. Thus, on the face of the French codes, the obligee who obtained a decree of specific performance appeared to be in a difficult position. During the past century, however, the French courts, without the help of a written text, developed a remedy: the so-called *astreinte*.[1] In essence, the *astreinte* is an order of the court threatening the judgment debtor with the imposition of a monetary penalty for failure to comply with the judgment. Should the threat fail to produce compliance, then

title. See *infra* Chapter 9, Section 2(a) at 872.)

12. The exception stated in the second paragraph is not as broad as the rule of the first paragraph. For instance, cases in which the defendant has been directed to render an account, to supply certain information, to issue a specified document (e.g., a letter of reference) needed by the plaintiff, normally would be covered by the rule of the first paragraph without coming under the exception.

13. This section of the German Code of Civil Procedure will remind the reader of a somewhat similar institution of U.S. law.: the power of a court of equity to enforce the promise of a vendor of real property by ordering that a document in the nature of a sheriff's deed be delivered to the purchaser. Note,

however, that the German provision is not limited to the enforcement of contracts for the sale of real property; it covers every case in which the defendant has been ordered to execute a document or in some other way to effect a transfer or transaction of any kind.

1. The development of the *astreinte* is instructively discussed by J. Beardsley, Compelling Contract Performance in France, 1 Hastings Int'l & Comp.L.Rev. 93, 95–102 (1977). See also P. Herzog, Civil Procedure in France 560–64 (1967); Amos & Walton, *supra* p. 875, note 8, at 180–82; B. Nicholas, *supra* p. 875, note 8, at 221–24; H. Beale, A. Hartkamp, H. Kötz, D. Tallon, *supra* note 2, 680–681; J. Gordley & A. T. von Mehren, *supra* n. 19, at 532–533; C. Calleros, Punitive Damages, Liquidated Damages, and Clauses Pénales in Contract Actions: A Comparative Analysis of the American Common Law and

the court (perhaps after having modified the amount) authorizes the obligee to collect the penalty. Until about forty years ago, the effectiveness of the *astreinte* was questionable, and indeed was questioned by many legal writers inside and outside of France, because ordinarily the penalty was fixed at the approximate amount of the plaintiff's damages, or was reduced to that amount before it became due to be collected. Thus a recalcitrant defendant could, in effect, force the plaintiff to accept damages in lieu of specific performance. Subsequently, however, the *Cour de Cassation* changed its position and developed the rule that, depending on all the circumstances of the case and especially on the gravity and obstinacy of the defendant's refusal to perform, the penalty may be fixed *and collected* in an amount exceeding the plaintiff's actual damages.[2] This rendered the *astreinte* considerably more effective, especially since in many cases the courts have been willing to fix the penalty in terms of a certain amount for each day of non-performance or for each act of disobedience.[3]

The solution worked out by the French courts (which acquired a statutory basis in 1972)[4] thus has become more similar to the German scheme; but there are still some notable differences:

(a) In cases in which enforcement of the judgment requires pressure "in personam," the French courts utilize only monetary penalties, while the German provisions make it possible, in addition, to resort to imprisonment of the recalcitrant defendant.[5]

(b) Under German law, a fine imposed on the defendant is payable to the State; it flows into the public treasury. In France, on the other hand, a monetary penalty exacted from the judgment debtor is payable to, and may be kept by, the judgment creditor. Where the penalty has been fixed in an amount exceeding the damages suffered by the latter, this may lead to a

the French Civil Code, 32 Brooklyn J.Int'l L. 67, 99 (2006).

2. The 1959 decision of the *Cour de Cassation* which brought about this change can be found, in English translation, in B. Rudden, Courts and Codes in England, France and Soviet Russia, 48 Tul.L.Rev. 1010, 1025 (1974).

3. By Law No. 80–539 of July 16, 1980 (see now Articles L911–6 and following of the Code of Administrative Procedure), the *astreinte* procedure was made available, also, for the enforcement, by the Conseil d'Etat, of administrative court decisions against a governmental unit. Prior to the enactment of that Law, it happened with some frequency that governmental units simply ignored adverse decisions of administrative courts, and this had become something of a scandal. The 1980 statute, enacted in response to that scandal, provides not only for *astreintes* against units of government, but also for fines to be imposed on, and to be paid personally by, recalcitrant officials.

4. The *astreinte* received legislative approval in Law No. 72–676 of July 5, 1972; the

rules regarding the *astreinte* were further revised in 1991 as part of the revision of French rules on the enforcement of judgments. See *supra* ch. IV.

5. The historical and socio-political reasons for the reluctance of French courts (as well as the courts in some other "Latin" countries) to enforce private obligations vigorously are discussed in a fascinating article by A. H. Pekelis, Legal Techniques and Legal Ideologies, 41 Mich.L.Rev. 665 (1943), reprinted in A. H. Pekelis, Law and Social Action 42 (M. R. Konvitz ed., 1950); see also M. Chesterman, Contempt: in the Common Law, but not the Civil Law, 46 Int'l & Comp. L.Q. 521 (1997). However, the stark contrast between the potency of common-law and the weakness of civil-law enforcement mechanisms which was emphasized by Pekelis over sixty years ago has been attenuated in recent years. See A. Blomeyer, Types of Relief Available, in 16 Int'l Ency.Comp.L. (Civil Procedure), ch. 4, at 32–33 (1982); H. Beale, A. Hartkamp, H. Kötz, D. Tallon, *supra* p. 874, note 2, 680–682.

windfall; but if one considers that the real loss suffered by the obligee as a result of the obligor's non-performance may be much higher than the "damages" that are legally recoverable and provable, it becomes clear that at least in some situations such a "windfall" may well serve the ends of justice.

(2) There are some civil-law systems which have adopted French-influenced codes but have not imported the *astreinte* procedure fashioned by the French courts. Under such a system there may be serious difficulties in enforcing a decree of specific performance.

Even in a legal system where there are highly developed provisions for the rendition and enforcement of decrees of specific performance, situations can arise in which this remedy lacks practical usefulness. The complexity or the personal (and perhaps artistic or otherwise creative) nature of the promised acts of performance may make it impractical for a court to formulate and enforce an appropriate decree of specific performance. Moreover, in the many cases in which the promisee is vitally interested in receiving *timely* performance, specific performance often is a useless remedy for the reason that it is impossible to obtain a judicial decree before the date for which the performance has been promised.

A promisee who is vitally interested in obtaining actual and timely performance, and who at the negotiating stage foresees the possibility that for legal or practical reasons the projected contract may not be specifically enforceable, will wish to know whether under the law governing the contract performance can be guaranteed by the insertion of a drastic penalty clause into the contract itself.

(c) Penalty Clauses

Imagine the following monologue by a father afflicted by a severe attack of nerves.

"My daughter's wedding is scheduled for next month, May 15. I'm in deep trouble. She has expressed a strong desire to hold the party in our old country house. A long time ago, I promised her that I would organize the party there. But then I forgot to make arrangements with the builders. A lot of work needs doing to the house, at the very least all the internal walls need painting. There's no way she can hold the party there without the work being done. All the invitations have already been sent. If I don't get things sorted out my daughter will never speak to me again. Yesterday I rushed around looking for a building contractor. None of them promised me that they'd finish the work on time. None of them ruled it out, of course, since they didn't want to lose a customer. But they made no promises. I can't take the risk. It would ruin my relationship with my daughter. I'd pay any money for the certainty."

This situation of the absent minded father, late in organizing his daughter's wedding, is a typical one in which penalty clauses would be very helpful. He may eventually find a builder willing to rush the work, and willing to promise to have the job finished by the date of the wedding, but in return for a high extra price (say 900 dollars extra). But how can the father be sure that the contractor is not making the promise to attract a customer, charging 900 dollars more than the usual price and then finding an excuse for not meeting the deadline? Of course, if this happens the father can sue the builder for damages. It is equally obvious, however, that he will regard damages as a completely unsatisfactory solution. Moreover, how can the wrath of a disgruntled daughter be quantified in dollars and cents?

The father's best option is to include a severe penalty in the contract to cover the eventuality of the contractor failing to complete the work in time. He may frame this clause in such a way that the work falls due on May 12 (three days before the wedding). If the house is not painted by that date, every day (or hour) of delay will cost the contractor 500 dollars. An economist will say that the extra 900 dollars is the premium that the risk averse father is willing to pay in consideration of the insurance offered to him by the contractor. However, the father's mind will not be set at rest merely by buying insurance from an insurance company. Apart from the transaction costs and inefficiencies involved in stipulating two contracts rather than only one, he is not interested in collecting money from the insurance, only in avoiding the anger of his beloved daughter. His sole concern is to have the house ready for her wedding. The builder is in the best position to evaluate the probability that he will complete the work in time, and therefore whether or not he can offer insurance for an event that he can condition by his own behaviour. If the penalty is severe enough he will be given an efficient incentive to perform correctly. He can invest extra money to ensure that he meets the deadline (for example by postponing another job not covered by a penalty clause, but with the consequent risk of losing another client; or by hiring an extra worker to do to job faster). If the extra effort is worth less than dollars 900 minus the risk of having to pay the penalty to the contractor, an efficient contract will be stipulated. This contract consists of two parts: one is the contracted work itself (painting the country house); the other is the insurance on punctual completion of the work. Moreover, since in this situation the contractor is likely to be risk-neutral, while the father is averse or very averse to risk, this shift of risk is efficient.[1]

There are many individuals who find themselves in the same position as the father in our example; people, that is, who set high value on performance and who are willing to enter into this kind of contract. . . .

One could imagine that all modern legal systems would regard as highly beneficial a legal institution which: (i) allows individuals to pursue a legitimate interest such as that of insuring themselves against non-satisfactory contractual performance, (ii) allows other individuals to signal their reliability in the marketplace, (iii) works as an effective enforcement of the natural law maxim of ethics *pacta sunt servanda*, (iv) may perform the beneficial role of avoiding litigation in the overcrowded courts of today.

This, however, is far from being the case. Common law does not allow penalty clauses in contracts. The law in the books is clear and straight

---

1.   See R. Cooter and T. Ulen, Law and Economics, 288 (5th ed. 2008).

forward on the matter. The coherence of penalty clauses ban with the underlying philosophy of freedom of contract is questionable, and the issue is frequently raised both in judicial opinion and in the academic literature.[2]

The ban on penalty clauses stems from the equitable jurisdiction of the Chancellor and is therefore an accident of legal history.[3] The Chancellor intervened on an ad hoc basis in order to eliminate abuses by means of *in personam* orders. A typical ground for intervention was the potential hardship arising from the strict, formalistic enforcement of contractual obligations. One need only consider the treatment meted out to Shylock to understand why penalty clauses constituted a typical situation of intervention by the Chancellor. The terminology itself used by the equity courts was revealing in this regard. Penalties were conceived as bargains "in terrorem", and therefore as null and void.

Of course, it would be unacceptable for any legal system to offer a pound of flesh as insurance on proper performance. The evolution of common law, however, has led to much more than this obvious consequence: all penalties have come to be considered in terrorem. The law set out in the books of common law offers us one extreme historical model....

The anxious father of our example would be entirely unable to relieve his anxiety....

* * *

FRENCH CIVIL CODE (PRE–1975)

Art. 1226. A penalty is a clause by which a person, in order to insure the performance of an agreement, promises something in case such agreement is not performed [by him or her].[4]

---

2. See the case law discussed in the Annotation 12 ALR 4th 891 (1982). See also D. D. Friedman, Law's Order: What Economics Has to Do with Law and Why It Matters 145 f. (2001); M. A. Eisenberg, The Emergence of Dynamic Contract Law, 88 Cal. L.Rev. 1779–1794 (2000); K. W. Clarkson, R. L. R. Miller and T. J. Muris, Liquidated Damages v. Penalties. Sense or Nonsense, 78 Wisconsin L.Rev. 351 (1978); Comment, A Critique of the Penalty Limitation on Liquidated Damages, 50 Southern Cal. L.Rev. 1055 (1977). Some shy steps in the direction of reform have been taken in California: see Sec. 1671 of the California Civil Code and Public Contract Code 10226. See J. Sweet, Liquidated Damages in California, 60 Cal. L.R. 84 (1972); D. A. Jensen, J. W. Craig, Testing the Validity of Liquidated Damages Clauses: Measuring the Application Preference and Consistency of the Intent Test as Applied by the United States Court System, 16 Const. Manag. & Ec. 269 (1998).

3. See W. Holdsworth, 5 History of English Law 292 ff (1924); L. M. Friedman, A History of American Law 244 (1973).

4. Depending on the terms of the contract, the penalty may be forfeited in case of (a) non-performance, or (b) delayed performance (e.g., $500 for each day of delay.) The penalty for delay may be recovered together with specific performance. But as between specific performance and a penalty for non-performance, the obligee must elect (Art. 1228), and may not recover damages for non-performance in excess of the stipulated penalty (Art. 1229).

Although the Code does not say so, it seems to be recognized that the promisor does not have to pay the penalty if non-performance was not due to any fault on his or her part. But this is subject to agreement otherwise; even an entirely faultless non-performing promisor is liable for the penalty if non-performance is due to an event, even a

Art. 1152. When an agreement provides that the party who fails to perform it shall pay a certain amount as damages, no larger or smaller amount may be awarded to the other party.

Art. 1231. The penalty can be modified by the Judge if the principal obligation has been partially performed. [This provision must be read together with Art. 1244 which states that ordinarily the obligor cannot compel the obligee to accept part performance. Moreover, prior to 1975, the French courts held that the protection of Art. 1231 could be stipulated away by the obligor.]

FRENCH CIVIL CODE (1975 REVISION)[5]

By Law No. 75–597 of July 9, 1975, as further amended by Law No. 85–1097 of October 11, 1985,[6] the following second paragraph was added to Art. 1152:

> Nevertheless, the Judge may, even of his or her own accord, reduce or increase the agreed-upon penalty if it is manifestly excessive or ridiculously small. Any contrary stipulation will be considered not written.

Art. 1231 was also amended to read as follows:

> When the engagement has been performed in part, the agreed-upon penalty may be diminished by the Judge, even of his or her own accord, in proportion to what the creditor obtained through the partial performance, without prejudice to the application of Article 1152. Any contrary stipulation will be considered not written.

* * *

GERMAN CIVIL CODE

Sec. 339. If the obligor promises to pay a sum of money as a penalty in the event that he should fail to perform his obligation, or that he should not perform it in a proper manner, such penalty shall be forfeited upon the obligor's default.[7] If the obligation to be performed consists of an omission

---

wholly fortuitous event, the risk of which was assumed. See M. Planiol's Treatise on the Civil Law, vol. 2, pt. 1, sec. 255 (English transl. by Louisiana State Law Institute 1959); C. Calleros, *supra* p. 883, note 1, 99–108.

5. For an interesting discussion of the developments which led to this revision of the Code, see J. Beardsley, Compelling Contract Performance in France, 1 Hastings Int'l & Comp.L.Rev. 93, 103–07 (1977). On the broader movement in French law to permit judges to modify contracts, see P. Legrand, The Case for Judicial Revision of Contracts in French Law (and Beyond), 34 McGill L.J. 909 (1989); H. Beale, A. Hartkamp, H. Kötz, D. Tallon, *supra* p. 874, note 2, 627–629;

European Contract Law, *supra* p. 874, note 5, 236–237; D. Mazeaud, Le juge et le contrat. Variations optimistes sur un couple "illégitime", in Mélanges offerts à J.-L. Aubert 235 (2005).

6. Law No. 85–1097 of Oct. 11, 1985, added the words: "even of his or her own accord" (*même d'office*) which were not contained in the law as originally enacted in 1975.

7. "Default" is a technical term. See text *supra* at p. 880, note 7. Ordinarily, the obligor will be in default only if (a) he or she has received an express warning or admonition to perform, and (b) non-performance is not excused. It would be excused, for instance, by impossibility not due to the obli-

[i.e., a duty to refrain from doing certain acts], then the forfeiture takes place as soon as an act contravening the obligation is committed.[8]

Sec. 340.... If the obligee is entitled to damages for nonperformance, he shall receive the forfeited penalty as the minimum amount of damages. The recovery of further damages is not excluded.[9]

Sec. 343. If a forfeited penalty is disproportionately high, the court may upon the obligor's request[10] reduce it to an appropriate amount. In determining the question of what is appropriate, every rightful interest of the obligee, not only his monetary interest, has to be considered....

GERMAN COMMERCIAL CODE

Sec. 348. A contractual penalty promised by a merchant in the course of his business cannot be reduced under the provisions of § 343 of the Civil Code.

SWISS CODE OF OBLIGATIONS

Art. 161. The forfeited penalty may be recovered even though the obligee has suffered no damage.[11]

If the damage suffered exceeds the amount of the penalty, the obligee may recover the excess only in so far as he proves fault [i.e., a fault of the obligor which caused the non-performance].

Art. 163. The amount of the contractual penalty can be fixed by the parties as they please.

gor's fault, or, in the case of a bilateral contract, by the obligee's own default. See Secs. 275 to 285, 320 to 326 of the Civil Code. (Note the drafting technique typical for this Code: the single word "default" is in effect a cross-reference to a whole galaxy of other interacting provisions.)

The requirement of "default" is subject to agreement otherwise. Thus by express agreement the parties can provide (as under French law) that the penalty is payable even though the promisor's non-performance is due to a fortuitous event. See O. Palandt, Bürgerliches Gesertzbuch § 339, Anno. 2 RdNr. 3 (63rd ed. 2004).

8. I.e., in this case no "default" is necessary, but only a simple breach of the obligation, roughly in the sense in which we understand the latter term. The courts have held, however, that this sentence is *ius dispositivum*, so that the parties, even in the case of a duty not to do, may agree that the penalty shall not be forfeited if the promisor is faultless.

9. Compare this with Art. 1152 of the French Civil Code.

10. Such request may be made by action, or by interposing an affirmative defense in the obligee's action for recovery of the penalty.

11. No action can be brought, however, to recover a penalty stipulated to secure the performance of a promise to marry. Swiss Civil Code, Art. 91. To the same effect see German Civil Code, Sec. 1297.

The penalty cannot be recovered if it is intended to secure the performance of an unlawful or immoral promise.[12] Unless the parties agree otherwise, the penalty cannot be recovered if performance has become impossible due to no fault of the obligor.[13]

An excessively high penalty has to be reduced by the court, according to its discretion.

NOTES AND QUESTIONS

(1) By giving the court the power to *reduce* an excessive penalty, and by providing that this judicial power can never be stipulated away, the French legislators of 1975 modified the original codifiers' fanatical adherence to the principle of freedom of contract. The 1975 revision is in line with the position of most of the modern Codes. This rapprochement between French law and the law of other major civil-law countries no doubt was welcomed by the scholars in charge of the Council of Europe study aimed at harmonizing the member states' laws on the subject of penalty clauses. The outcome of that study was a resolution adopted by the Committee of Ministers of the Council of Europe recommending that courts of the member states be empowered to reduce the sum stipulated in penal clauses where such sum is "manifestly excessive." See Resolution on Penal Clauses in Civil Law (78)3 of January 20, 1978, art. 7. It should be noted that the revised French provisions apply regardless of whether the promisor is a merchant. This is in line with Swiss law, but different from German law. Whether in the future this difference between French and German law will be eliminated as a result of the harmonizing efforts of the Council of Europe remains to be seen.

(2) By authorizing the court to *increase* the amount of a ridiculously low penalty, the French legislator has adopted a rule which at first blush seems to diverge sharply from German and Swiss law, and indeed to be quite novel.

One must remember, however, that under German and Swiss law the obligee can recover damages in excess of the agreed-upon penalty if the obligor is responsible for his failure to perform. This obviates the need for judicial augmentation of the penalty. All the obligee has to do in such a case, is to prove that he has suffered damages in excess of the amount of the penalty. Under German or Swiss law, he can then recover the excess. In contrast, the French Civil Code in Article 1152 provides that when the contract contains a clause fixing a penalty, "no larger or smaller amount can be awarded" as damages. Depending on which side has superior bargaining power, this provision can be used and misused by the obligor as well as the obligee. In drafting construction contracts, for instance, it was customary in France until 1975 to provide for a minimal penalty to be forfeited in case of the obligor's (contractor's) non-performance or delayed performance. Such a contract clause, in conjunction with Article 1152 of the Code Civil, deprived the other party of any right to

---

12. Concerning the point covered in this first sentence of the paragraph, French and German law would be to the same effect.

13. In its substance, the Swiss rule stated in the second sentence of this paragraph is similar to both French and German law. But note the strikingly different stylistic manner in which each of the three codes expresses (or implies) the rule.

substantial damages. The 1975 revision, while adding the above-quoted second paragraph, did not change the original language of Article 1152 which precludes the recovery of damages in excess of the penalty; but when the penalty is "ridiculously small," the court is now authorized by the new second paragraph to increase the amount and in this way, one may assume, to bring it more closely into line with the damages actually suffered by the obligee.

Compared to the German and Swiss provisions, the new French solution may appear complicated. Note, however, that the French court's power to increase an inadequate penalty cannot be stipulated away by the parties. On the other hand, the German–Swiss rule—that excess damages, if proved, can be recovered as such—appears to be subject to agreement otherwise. See O. Palandt, Bürgerliches Gesetzbuch, Section 340, Anno. 3, RdNr. 7 (63th ed., 2004). An obligee who is in an inferior bargaining position thus is more effectively protected by the new French provisions than by the German–Swiss rule.

(3) Experience gathered under the new French provisions has shown that reduction of contractual penalties is sought much more frequently than augmentation. In the exceedingly numerous cases in which judicial reduction of a penalty is asked for, the 1975 revision of the French Code confronts the French courts with many of the questions which the German and Swiss courts have faced for almost a century. One might expect, therefore, that the French courts and commentators would try to benefit from the wealth of experience gathered by the German and Swiss courts in applying their older but rather similar provisions for the reduction of excessive penalties. But such is not the case. French textbooks and articles in legal periodicals have devoted many hundreds of pages to discussing the numerous issues raised by the 1975 amendment; but the French readers are never told that—perhaps only a few kilometers away— the German and Swiss courts have struggled with the same issues for nearly 100 years, and perhaps have reached some arguably sound solutions.

For one who is interested in the broader aspects of comparative law, it is not without interest to observe this extreme example of what in an earlier chapter of this book has been referred to as "the intellectual isolation of each national system which resulted from the codifications."[1]

Suppose the legislature of one of the United States were to enact a new statute similar to one which for a long time has been on the books, and frequently applied by the courts, in a sister state or in some other common-law country. Would our courts and commentators, when wrestling with problems created by the new statute, likewise ignore the relevant experience—including, of course, the judicial decisions—accumulated in the other jurisdiction?

(4) What we have witnessed in the decline of the Napoleonic model is a profound revolution in the approach to contract law: namely, the substitution of one scheme of social organization (the contract) with another one (government by judges).[2]

---

1. See *supra* at 443.

2. P. Legrand, *supra* p. 888, note 5, at 911, quoting M. Kelman, A Guide to the Critical Legal Studies (1987), calls this phe-

nomenon "The development of a contradictory paradigm to the traditional rule of contractual sanctity." On the shift mentioned in the text, see also C. Jauffret–Spinosi, Theorie

This model of judicial law-making was inconceivable when the Napoleonic code was promulgated, since much of the ideology of the French Revolution was directed against the judges.[3] Indeed, in the Napoleonic code, contract law was a necessary and sufficient instrument assigned to the parties so that they could plan their relationship within an assumption of formal equality. The parties to the contract were empowered to act on their own behalf, and they were unable to use the legal system to replace the terms of their agreement. They were given the means to bargain in the shadow of the law, in the sense that they could rely on the enforcing mechanism of the state to preclude opportunistic behaviour by the counterpart. The economic justification for contract law in this model was that it provided protection for the party performing first against opportunistic behavior by the one supposed to perform later. Without contract law the latter would have no incentive to perform.[4] Contract law was a private instrument of regulation. The courts had no entitlement to regulate behavior.

In all the intermediate models between the common law (total ban) and the Napoleonic (always valid) extremes, there has been a dramatic change in the role of the courts and in the entire nature of contract law, a clear passage between the "classic" and the "social" models. The courts, and not private parties, have become the regulators of behavior. The parties do not merely seek agreement among themselves; they must also seek the agreement of the court. This agreement, however, because of the nature of the judicial process, can only come *ex post*; and, moreover, it is highly uncertain. As a consequence, negotiation costs increase because the parties must invest in predicting the behaviour of the courts should the penalty be legally challenged. Hence the system provides a powerful incentive to litigation, since the party seeking to evade the agreed-upon penalty may challenge it in court, hoping that the predicted agreement of the court on the clause will prove to be poorly substantiated. This change in the nature of contracts—from a private enterprise to a joint mixed private/public enterprise of the parties and the courts—calls for an explanation of contract law different from that usually furnished by traditional legal and economic scholarship. Now that the courts are involved in the content of contracts, it seems clear that their role is not merely that of preventing opportunistic behaviour: they act as policy-makers introducing "social" value-judgments to substitute for private ones. This phenomenon of increasingly restricted freedom of contract is apparent, of course, in many areas of the law, and it has been noted by traditional legal scholarship as well as by some of the most outstanding contributions to the law and economics literature.[5] In the

et pratique de la clause générale en droit français et dans les autres systèmes juridiques romanistes, in General Clauses and Standards in European Contract Law 23, 33 ff. (S. Grundmann & D. Mazeaud eds., 2005). For some broader reflections, see F. Cabrillo, The Rise and Fall of Freedom of Contract in Western Economies: A Common Experience, in Internationalisierung des Rechts und seine ökonomische Analyse. Festschrift für Hans–Bernd Schäfer zum 65. Geburtstag 253 f. (T. Eger, J. Bigus, C. Ott, G. von Wangenheim eds., 2008).

3. J. P. Dawson, The Oracles of the Law (1968).

4. This is still the established explanation of contract law in the Law and Economics literature, see R. Cooter & T. Ulen, *supra* p. 886, note 1 at 208.

5. See M. Trebilcock, The Limits of Freedom of Contract (1993); A. Schwartz & R. E. Scott, Contract Theory and the Limits of Contract Law, 113 Yale L.J. 541 (2003).

area of penalty clauses, however, the phenomenon goes much deeper, for it involves such an inherently subjective decision as that concerning price.

Of course, no considerations of efficiency can justify such intervention—which prompts the question of whether this intervention by the state through its courts can be considered the triumph of justice over efficiency. One should consider that whenever the legal system wishes to react against unconscionable contracts (*e.g.* a pound of flesh as a guarantee), it is already equipped with numerous other tools of contract law endorsed by efficiency as well as by equity.[6] The fundamental maxim that resources should not be wasted instructs the judge how to react against Shylock.[7]

In the case of penalty clauses intervention by the Courts constitutes a major project of redistribution, one similar to a rent control ordinance which enables the judge to intervene ex post in the amount of rent agreed upon by the parties. A decision to reduce the amount of rent may be justified by assuming that tenant had no alternative solution to his housing problem in a very tight market. This is not the case of penalties, though, unless we hypothesize that they are imposed on consumers in a standard contract. Here too, however, there is nothing exceptional in the nature of penalty clauses that allows for a harsher regime than exists in the case of other abusive clauses.

Code provisions and case law on penalty clauses introduce an emergency approach (such as rent control ordinances) within the physiology of the system. By so doing they deprive individuals of a tool with which to avoid intervention by the courts.

(5) A undertakes to deliver to B in a year's time 100 tons of a certain commodity at $1,000 per ton. The penalty for non-delivery is to be $200 per ton. A fails to deliver 50 tons; but by the time the year has expired the market price of the commodity has fallen to $500 per ton so that B has in fact saved $500 per ton on the 50 tons which A has failed to deliver. Under pre–1975 French law it seems clear that B can recover the penalty of €50 $200 or $10,000.[8] As revised in 1975, the French provisions authorize judicial reduction in such a case; and, as noted above, while the letter of the law only allows a court to reduce, not to annul, the penalty, a reduction to zero might well be left standing by the Court of Cassation. In German law, if A is a merchant he may have to pay the $10,000 unless it can be said that insistence on payment would be contra bonos mores, or contrary to principles of good faith.[9] Any other party

---

6. See *supra*.

7. See R. Cooter, The Best Right Laws. Value Foundations of The Economic Analysis of Law, 64 Notre Dame L.Rev. 817 (1989).

8. At first blush, this conclusion may seem doubtful, because A has performed in part. But the court's power to apportion the penalty pursuant to old Art. 1231 does not exist if the parties have agreed otherwise; hence that power cannot come into play where, as here, the parties themselves have specified the precise amount of penalty ($200 *per ton*) payable in case of partial non-performance. In a case involving the current Art.

1231, the Court of Cassation has ruled that the article is inapplicable if the contract itself stipulates the amount by which the penalty is to be reduced in the event of part performance. Sàrl Fisson et fils v. Locano, Cass. com., Nov. 19, 1991, 1993 D.J. 56. The appended note indicates that this is consistent with the pre–1975 cases, but probably correct only if the contract stipulates a proportional reduction.

9. See §§ 138 & 242 of the German Civil Code, quoted *supra* (at 565 note 4 and 571 note 20).

Section 138 of the German Civil Code does not authorize reduction of a contractual

in German law might apply to the Court to reduce the penalty on the ground that it was excessive in relation to the actual loss incurred; indeed it would seem that no loss has been incurred and therefore there might be no penalty at all.[10] In English law, on the other hand, the question would turn on whether, when the contract was made, $200 per ton was a reasonable bona fide pre-estimate by the parties of the loss which would be incurred a year ahead on failure to deliver the commodity. If it was such a reasonable pre-estimate, the $10,000 would be recoverable; otherwise it would be a penalty in the strict sense and not recoverable.[11]

(6) The highest court of Switzerland, in its decision of February 25, 1915, BGE 41 II 138, had to deal with the following facts: The defendant, a Swiss inventor, and the plaintiff, a German businessman, had concluded a contract for the joint exploitation of an invention made by the defendant. Under the terms of the contract, the proceeds of patent licensing agreements and of options were to be divided fifty-fifty; to secure this division, all such proceeds were to be deposited with a named Notary in Berlin. A party violating this latter provision was to incur a penalty in the amount of M 10,000. In fact, very substantial amounts were received from patent licensees, and were deposited with the Notary in accordance with the contract. Only in one instance, when the relatively small amount of M 1,000 was received by him from a Japanese optionee on June 23, 1913, defendant inadvertently forgot to deposit the money with the Notary. A short time later, however, defendant informed plaintiff of the receipt of the M 1,000. In November, 1913, defendant actually remitted frs.500 to the Notary for the account of the plaintiff. Apparently the defendant had intended to remit M 500; but through a mistake of his office personnel the remittance was in the amount of frs.500, which at that time was the equivalent of about M 410.

Plaintiff sued for the full amount of the penalty, i.e., frs.12,380 (the equivalent of M 10,000). The lower court reduced the penalty to frs.1,000, and the plaintiff appealed. The court of last resort assumed that under German law

penalty; but in an extreme case, i.e., where the penalty clause of the contract is "immoral," it would invalidate such clause. The German courts appeared to be very reluctant to use the sharp weapon of § 138 to invalidate *a merchant's* promise of a penalty. Recent case law, however, widened the control over penalties even in commercial transactions; see, e.g., BGH May 7, 1997, WM 1997, 1491. The same attitude has been exhibited by the Japanese courts, operating under similar, German-derived code provisions. From a "light" approach towards penalty clauses, Japanese courts shifted to a more intense supervision over them (see Y. Fujita, Procedural Fairness to Foreign Litigants As Stressed by Japanese Courts, 12 Int'l Law. 795 (1978); see also I. Yoshida, Comparison of Awarding Interest on Damages in Scotland, England, Japan and Russia, 17 J.Int'l Arb. 41, 60 (2000)).

10. The matter rests in the discretion of the court. All of the circumstances of the case (as of the time when the court is requested to reduce the penalty) have to be considered. See A. Pinto Monteiro, Clause Pénale/Penalty Clause/Vertragsstrafe, 9 Eur. Rev.Priv.L. 149, 152–153 (2001).

11. For a historical explanation of such a rule, J. Biancalana, Contractual Penalties in the King's Court, 64 Cam.L.J. 212 (2005). A similar disfavor for penalties is shown by Australian courts: see E. Peden & J. Carter, Agreed Damage Clause—Back to the Future? 22 J.Contract L. 189 (2006). For the American rule, see U.C.C. § 2–718(1). For an analysis of American law on the subject, see I. R. Macneil, Power of Contract and Agreed Remedies, 47 Cornell L.Q. 495 (1962); E. A. Farnsworth, Contracts § 12.18, at 811–820 (3d ed. 1999); L. A. DiMatteo, A Theory of Efficient Penalty: Eliminating the Law of Liquidated Damages, 38 Am.Bus.L.J. 633 (2001). See also the Notes following these Illustrations.

(§ 348 of the German Commercial Code) the penalty could not be reduced, and that, consequently, the decision of the case hinged on whether Swiss or German law was to be applied. Turning to the conflict-of-laws question thus raised, the court said that under ordinary rules of private international law the contract would be governed by German law since it was made and performable in Germany; but, in the view of the court, the Swiss rule authorizing reduction of the penalty was so clearly based upon fundamental principles of morality underlying the Swiss social order that to apply a contrary foreign rule would be inconsistent with the Swiss *ordre public*.[12] For this reason, the highest court affirmed the lower court decision by which the penalty had been reduced in accordance with Swiss law.

Was the court correct in assuming that, as applied to the facts of the case, German law differed from Swiss law and that under German law the penalty could not be reduced?[13]

(7) Staccato is a dachshund whose market value is only $75, but whose owner, Professor P, is extremely devoted to him. P, leaving town to attend a meeting of the Association of American Law Schools, entrusts custody of Staccato to D, the owner of a kennel, for 5 days at the rate of $29.00 per day. P and D agree that Staccato is to have a daily portion of one-half pound of Filet Mignon, and D promises a penalty of $1,000 for every day on which Staccato should fail to receive the stipulated food. Thinking that P will never find out, D gives Staccato nothing but scraps; but a disgruntled employee of D informs P, who sues D for $5,000. What result under former French law? Under present French law? Under German law? Under Swiss law? Under English or U.S. law?

Which legal system offers the most desirable solution? In this connection, it should be remembered that dog-lovers are not the only persons who enter into contracts for the purpose of protecting non-monetary interests, or interests which are difficult to evaluate in terms of provable damages. Esthetic and environmental interests, for instance, often are sought to be protected by contractual stipulations involving a penalty. These stipulations reflect the subjective value placed by one party on performance by the other. Under U.S. law, such stipulations normally are unenforceable, even when the promisee is a governmental agency.[14] The promisee thus is relegated to seeking either specific performance or damages. Neither remedy provides reliable protection for environmental or other non-pecuniary interests. The equitable remedy of specific performance is uncertain because of its discretionary nature, and the assessment of damages for injuries to environmental and other non-pecuniary

12. Concerning this conflict of laws point, see the 6th edition of this book, Chapter VIII at 933.

13. Who bears the burden of proof, under German law, as to the existence of the facts upon which the applicability of § 348 of the German Commercial Code depends? In this connection, it should be noted that— except for the bare statement that defendant was an inventor—the opinion of the Swiss court contains no information whatever concerning defendant's occupation.

14. See, e.g. Carrothers Const. Co., L.L.C. v. City of South Hutchinson, 39 Kan. App.2d 703, 184 P.3d 943 (2008); Creative Waste Management, Inc. v. Capitol Environmental Services, Inc., 495 F.Supp.2d 353 (S.D.N.Y.2007); Carr–Gottstein Properties, Ltd. Partnership v. Benedict, 72 P.3d 308 (Alaska 2003). See also the Notes immediately following these Illustrations.

interests has proved to be extremely difficult.[15] Under these circumstances, does the solution offered by the modern civilian codes not appear to be preferable?[16]

(8) In comparing civil-law and common-law approaches to the legal devices by which actual performance of a contract can be secured, one is tempted to formulate some broad conclusions. Would it be correct, for instance, to say that the principle of freedom of contract is carried further by the civilian codes than in common-law systems? Or that the civil-law systems tend to let *the parties* decide whether the promisor should be forced to perform the contract in accordance with its terms, while the common law always gives *the court* the power to make an ultimate—and often discretionary—decision on this point?

(9) In the United States, one encounters increasing skepticism concerning the soundness of the common-law (and U.C.C.) rule invalidating all contractual penalties which do not qualify as liquidated damages. The subtle distinction between penalties and liquidated damages makes for very uncertain results.[17] Law and economics scholars generally have favored enforcing stipulated penalty provisions;[18] and, while Judge Posner once complained that American legislatures and courts seemed "untroubled by academic skepticism of the wisdom of refusing to enforce penalty clauses against sophisticated promisors,"[19] other

---

15. See Note, Assessment of Civil Monetary Penalties for Water Pollution, 30 Hastings L.J. 651 (1979).

16. See also the Notes which immediately follow these Illustrations.

17. See, among others, L. A. DiMatteo, *supra* note 11.

Note that both systems, civil law and common law, inject an element of uncertainty into the calculations of a promisor who considers the probable cost of a contemplated breach. In a common-law jurisdiction, such a promisor often will not know in advance whether the contractual clause ultimately will be treated by the court as valid or invalid. In the majority of modern civil-law jurisdictions, the promisor in such a situation will wonder whether and to what extent the court will reduce the stipulated amount. Yet there is a real difference between the two systems. Under the common-law rule the promisor, although often he cannot be sure, may well hope to have the contract clause declared a penalty, and thus to defeat it completely. In a civil-law country, he knows that at best he can obtain only a *reduction* of the stipulated amount of penalty. The difference between the common-law and the civil-law approaches will make itself felt especially in cases where the stipulated amount is high and clearly intended to pressure the promisor into rendering actual and timely performance. In many cases of this kind a promisor acting

under the common-law rule will be encouraged to breach, because his lawyer will tell him that, if it comes to litigation, the contractual clause probably will be held invalid. Under modern civil law, on the other hand, a promisor contemplating breach will be informed by his lawyer that it is uncertain whether and by how much the court will reduce the stipulated penalty, and that in any event—if the promisor decides to breach—he will probably have to pay more, and perhaps substantially more, than provable damages. Thus the two systems differ considerably in their impact on the promisor's decision to breach or not to breach.

18. See C. J. Goetz & R. E. Scott, Liquidated Damages, Penalties and the Just Compensation Principle: Some Notes on an Enforcement Model and a Theory of Efficient Breach, 77 Colum.L.Rev. 554 (1977); J. F. Brodley & C.-t. A. Ma, Contract Penalties, Monopolizing Strategies, and Antitrust Policy, 45 Stan.L.Rev. 1161, 1177–82 (1993); A. S. Edlin, A. Schwartz, Optimal Penalties in Contracts, 78 Chi.-K.L.Rev. 33 (2003); C. G. Veljanovski, Economic Principles of Law 159–161 (2007). But cf. K. W. Clarkson, R. L. Miller & T. J. Muris, Liquidated Damages v. Penalties: Sense or Nonsense?, 1978 Wis. L.Rev. 351.

19. Lake River Corp. v. Carborundum Co., 769 F.2d 1284 (7th Cir.1985).

observers have noted a trend "to favor freedom of contract by enforcing such clauses as long as they do not clearly disregard the principle of compensation."[20]

In 1977, California undertook a statutory revision of its rules relating to liquidated damages.[21] Although far from radical in their departures from the traditional common-law approach, the California provisions somewhat enlarge the parties' freedom to determine the consequences of a breach, and thus take a hesitant (although still rather timid) step in the direction of civil-law solutions.

At the same time, there are indications of a long-term shift in civil-law thinking toward concern with the relationship between the stipulated penalty and actual loss or injury. This is most clearly illustrated by the post–1975 French developments discussed *supra*. Indeed, it has been suggested that, insofar as they give judges discretion to modify the terms of the contract, all legal systems are tending to "converge" toward "inefficiency" or at least toward an "intermediate position" in which the courts have the ultimate say about whether to enforce stipulated "penalty" provisions.[22]

(10) Specific performance and the penalty clause are functionally related devices. Their possible interaction should be kept in mind. A legal system which discards or excessively weakens either of the two devices thereby will become more dependent on the other.[23] Conversely, it might be argued that the more a legal system strengthens one of the two devices, e.g., specific performance, the less need there will be for rigorous application of the other.

It should be kept in mind, however, that the two devices, although related, are not interchangeable. As was pointed out earlier in this section, there are many situations where no legal system can resort to specific enforcement of a promise, and where actual and timely performance can be assured, if at all, only by a penalty clause. On the other hand, it is obvious (at least in a free-enterprise system) that the device of the penalty clause can be used only when the negotiating situation is such that both parties are willing to assent to such a clause. Thus it makes sense for a legal system to employ both devices, making

20. Farnsworth, *supra* note 11 at 811.

21. See Cal. Civil Code § 1671 and Cal. Public Contract Code § 10226. This statutory revision was based on a recommendation of the California Law Revision Commission. See 13 Cal.L.Rev.Comm'n Reports 2139 (1976). That recommendation, in turn, relied heavily on the study by J. Sweet, Liquidated Damages in California, 60 Cal.L.Rev. 84 (1972), reprinted in 11 Cal.L.Rev.Comm'n Reports 1229 (1973).

22. See U. Mattei, The Comparative Law and Economics of Penalty Clauses in Contracts, 43 Am.J.Comp.L. 427 (1995), reprinted in Mattei, *supra* p. 863, note 1, at 179–99, who nonetheless concludes that the differences between common law and civil law approaches to penalty clauses remain significant. See also P. Winship, As the World

Turns: Revisiting Rudolf Schlesinger's Study of the Uniform Commercial Code "In the Light of Comparative Law", 29 Loy. L.A.L.Rev. 1143, 1150 (1996); A. N. Hatzis, Civil Contract Law and Economic Reasoning: An Unlikely Pair?, in The Architecture of European Codes and Contract Law 159, 176 (S. Grundmann & M. Schauer eds., 2006). With regard to the English side, see L. Miller, Penalty Clauses in England and France: A Comparative Study, 106 Int'l & Comp.L.Q. 53 (2004).

23. The point made in the text is illustrated by the Palestinian case of The Syndics in the Bankruptcy of Khoury v. Slavousky, 5 P.L.R. 378; 1938, 1 A.L.R. 387. The case is interestingly discussed by U. Yadin, Reception and Rejection of English Law in Israel, 11 Int'l & Comp.L.Q. 59, 63–65 (1962).

sure at the same time that neither of them will be used in an oppressive manner.

(d) Freedom of Contract and Disclaimer Clauses in Standardized Contracts

Courts and legislators throughout the world are confronted with problems created by unilaterally drafted, standardized contract conditions. These problems become particularly acute when the standardized contract contains one-sided clauses grossly favoring the side that drafted the document. The materials which follow illustrate the treatment which some of these problems have received in Germany and in other civil-law systems. The interest of a comparative examination of the topic is enhanced, in this instance, by the fact that the most important development in the American law on the subject (U.C.C. § 2–302) may well be regarded as German-inspired.[1]

The discussion which follows will center on the question of the *validity* of standardized disclaimer clauses. The reader should realize, however, that cases involving standard contracts, and especially adhesion contracts, also may raise other issues. These issues, which frequently have to be determined before one even reaches the question of the validity of a particular clause, cannot be examined here in detail; but three of them should be briefly mentioned:

The first of these issues comes under the heading of Formation of Contracts. How does the printed standard form of an enterprise, e.g., of a carrier, bank, or insurance company, become part of a particular contract which the enterprise concludes with a customer, especially in cases in which the enterprise is the offeree?[2] The German courts have held that, even though the offer contains no reference to the standard form, the terms embodied in the form must be read into the contract if the customer (i) knows or should know of the existence of the standard form used by the enterprise, or (ii) knows or should know as a matter of general experience that an enterprise such as the one with which he is dealing normally does business only on the basis of its own standard conditions.[3]

How are standard contracts to be interpreted? In some legal systems there is a tendency to interpret ambiguous provisions of such a contract

---

1. See *infra* at 907ff.

2. For comparative discussions of this question, see O. Lando, Standard Contracts—A Proposal and a Perspective, 10 Scandinavian Studies in Law 127, at 130–33 (1966); 2 Formation of Contracts—A Study of the Common Core of Legal Systems 953–1001 (R. B. Schlesinger ed., 1968); K. Zweigert & H. Kötz, *supra* p. 879, note 1, 347f.

3. A more protective rule applies to consumer transactions; but for contracts among merchants, the rules stated in the text, *supra*, are still in force.

For a comparative discussion of the special problems which arise when offeror and offeree both seek to incorporate their own standardized conditions into the contract, see P. H. Schlechtriem, The Battle of the Forms Under German Law, 23 Bus.Law. 655 (1968); from an economic point of view, see O. Ben-Shahar, An Ex–Ante View of the Battle of Forms: Inducing Parties to Draft Reasonable Terms, 25 Int'l Rev.L. & Econ. 350 (2005).

contra proferentem, i.e., against the party responsible for their formulation.[4] The Italian Civil Code (Art. 1370) explicitly adopted this approach as a rule of interpretation. (The materials which follow, however, deal with situations where the validity rather than the interpretation of a particular clause was at issue.)

The third remark arises from the fact that in some legal systems different rules apply to standardized contracts according to whether both the parties are merchants, or one of them is a consumer. For example, in the European Community a special set of rules applies to the standard contract between a merchant and a consumer, while standard contracts between two consumers or two merchants are subject to the ordinary rules set forth by civil and commercial codes. This duality of regimes compels the question as to the parties' qualities. Who is a merchant? For instance, how shall the law treat an entrepreneur who enters with another businessman into a standardized sales agreement for the purchase of the furniture of his office?

Opinion of the German Reichsgericht in the Matter of G., Defendant–Appellant v. St., Plaintiff–Respondent

1st Civil Division, October 26, 1921, RGZ 103, 82.

[Plaintiff's agent at Mannheim delivered 17 cases of cigars to defendant, a forwarder and carrier, requesting defendant to send them to plaintiff by express freight. Only 16 cases were delivered to plaintiff by defendant, and plaintiff sues for M 5,166, the value of the missing case. Defendant demands that the complaint be dismissed, on the ground that its liability as a forwarder is limited to M 60. By previous public announcements, all Mannheim forwarders had limited their liability to a maximum of M 60 for each shipment.]

The court of first instance granted the relief prayed for by the plaintiff. The intermediate Appellate Court affirmed. Upon the further appeal taken by the defendant, the Reichsgericht affirmed the decisions below.

Reasons: The intermediate Appellate Court holds that the general Announcements of the Mannheim Forwarders became part of the contract between the parties, because the agent of the plaintiff was a merchant residing at Mannheim, who presumably took notice of such announcements in the daily press. The intermediate Appellate Court further points out that contractual exemption from liability is not necessarily contra bonos mores, even though the exemption may cover cases of negligence on the part of employees of the forwarder. But, the court below further says, it is improper and immoral for *all* the Mannheim forwarders to exploit their monopolistic position for the purpose of exempting themselves from liabili-

---

4. See V. Bolgár, The Contract of Adhesion: A Comparison of Theory and Practice, 20 Am.J.Comp.L. 53, 76–77 (1972); K. Zwei-gert & H. Kötz, *supra* p. 879, note 1, 336–342; H. Beale, A. Hartkamp, H. Kötz, D. Tallon, *supra* p. 874, note 2, 568–571.

ty for their own negligence.[1] The court below found that in the case at bar there was negligence on the part of defendant itself, in that on October 16, 1919, the day on which the missing merchandise was stolen, defendant failed to send a second man along with its driver [the idea apparently being that a second man was necessary in order to keep an eye on the trailer while the driver was in his cab].

Appellant argues that under the provisions of Section 276, Subdivision 2 of the Civil Code[2] contractual exemption from liability is improper only in so far as liability for intentional acts is concerned. Therefore, appellant argues, a clause exempting the forwarder from liability for its own negligence is quite proper; it is further said that there cannot be any question of immoral exploitation, inasmuch as the shipper can take out transportation insurance.

These views of the appellant cannot be approved. . . .

. . . The concerted action of all carriers and forwarders residing at Mannheim constituted an immoral exploitation of their actual monopoly, in so far as they attempted to exempt themselves from liability even in case of the forwarder's own negligence. . . . Section 276, Subdivision 2 of the Civil Code does not prohibit the contractual exemption from, or limitation of, liability for any case of negligence. Nevertheless such an agreement is a rare exception in business life, especially where its coverage is intended to be so broad that one of the parties is thereby exempted from liability for its own negligence. The statutory scheme concerning the legal position of commission merchants, forwarders, warehouses and carriers is that in principle such firms are liable for lost or damaged goods and that they can avoid such liability only by proving that the exercise of due care could not have averted the damage (Commercial Code, Sections 390, 407, 417, 429). This state of the law, which was intended by the legislature and is generally regarded as equitable, is completely reversed if the forwarder or carrier exempts himself from liability even for its own fault. If such exemption comes about other than by way of a completely free agreement, and if a whole group of entrepreneurs within a certain district by exploiting their actual monopoly forces such exemption upon those who are dependent upon the services of forwarders and carriers, then such conduct is grossly violative of the moral standards of those people whose thinking is just and

1. At the time of this case, agreements in restraint of trade, as such, were not illegal in Germany. See I. E. Schwartz, Antitrust Legislation and Policy in Germany, 105 U.Pa. L.Rev. 617, 625–41 (1957). After World War II, the Occupation Authorities introduced antitrust laws, which were replaced by the Law Against Restraint of Competition of July 27, 1957 (BGBl 1957 I 1081), as amended, whose § 1 states that "agreements between undertakings, decisions by associations of undertakings and concerted practices, which have as their object or effect the prevention, restriction or distortion of competition, shall be prohibited". On the German competition law, see T. Moellers and A. Heinemann, The Enforcement of Competition Law in Europe (2007).

2. (Now Section 276, subdivision 3): "An obligor cannot be exempted in advance from liability for intentional acts" [i.e., from liability for intentional violation of his duty to perform the obligation in good faith].

equitable. Thus it is contra bonos mores within the meaning of Section 138 of the Civil Code. . . .

* * *

Opinion of the German Reichsgericht in the Matter of Suedd. Transp. Vers. A.G., Plaintiff–Appellant v. W., Defendant–Respondent

1st Civil Division, March 21, 1923, RGZ 106, 386.

[Plaintiff as assignee of the shipper sues defendant forwarder for the full value of goods stolen while in defendant's custody. Plaintiff's assignor had apparently signed defendant's "General Terms and Conditions of Forwarders," a form drafted by the Association of Berlin Forwarders and used by all members of the Association. Section 8 of the form contract provided: "If the value of the goods is stated in the accompanying papers, then the forwarder will insure such goods against local risks for the account of the shipper, at premium rates to be fixed from time to time by the Association of Berlin Forwarders. If no value is stated, or no insurance is desired, then the liability of the forwarder is limited to a maximum of M 1.20[1] for each kilogram gross weight."]

The intermediate appellate court has assumed . . . that the interests of the shipper are fully protected by the willingness of the forwarder to take out insurance if the value of the goods is stated. . . . The court below reasons that inasmuch as the insurance premium would be small in relation to the protection gained, the clause [Section 8] amounts ultimately to nothing but an increase in the freight rate. Therefore, it is said, there is here no immoral exploitation of a monopolistic position.

Plaintiff-appellant [who had lost in both courts below] argues that this reasoning is inconsistent with the decisions of this Court, and especially with RGZ 103, 82.[2] This argument must be regarded as justified.

. . . In most cases the interests of the shipper are not really protected if he is relegated to a money claim against an insurer, and can no longer dispose of the goods. As a rule he is interested in the goods, and not in a cause of action for damages. Therefore he is entitled to insist that the forwarder take the measures required by the circumstances in order to protect the goods from damage or loss. It is the duty of the forwarder so to proceed. From such duty he cannot exempt either himself or his executive employees, by offering to take out insurance. This fundamental principle of law cannot be shaken by the consideration that the shipper, in case the forwarder has violated his duty, is again relegated to a money claim for damages against the latter. In the first place, this claim may be considerably broader than a claim against the insurer.[3] Furthermore, although it

---

1. In view of the inflation then prevailing in Germany, this was tantamount to zero.

2. See the preceding case.

3. Although not citing any specific provision in support of this statement, the Court probably refers to the principle of restitution

may be true that as a rule a claim for damages will be a money claim, it does not follow that the forwarder should have an option to substitute a claim against an insurance company for the performance of his duty of due care—a duty imposed by fundamental and generally recognized principles of law.

* * *

Opinion of the German Bundesgerichtshof in the Matter of E. Gu. (Defendant) v. K. B. (Plaintiff)

2nd Civil Division, February 7, 1964, BGHZ 41, 151.

The defendant had stored furniture and household effects in plaintiff's warehouse. In this action, plaintiff sued for the balance of the storage fees allegedly owed by defendant. The latter ... counterclaimed for damages, asserting that some of the stored articles had been damaged, and that others had been stolen. In the intermediate appellate court, plaintiff's action was successful and defendant's counterclaim was dismissed. Upon defendant's further appeal, the judgment below is reversed and the case remanded.

Reasons: ... It is true that pursuant to § 1 of the Storage Conditions the owner of the warehouse is liable only if he or one of his agents is chargeable with fault. Thus, contrary to the provisions of § 417 par. 1 and § 390 par. 1 of the Commercial Code[1] ..., the burden of proof is placed upon the bailor in all those cases in which the property is lost or damaged in storage. Such a clause, if contained in standardized contract conditions,[2] is irreconcilable with the principles of good faith (Civil Code § 242).[3]

[The court points out that the above-cited provisions of the Commercial Code expressly deal with the question of the burden of proof in cases in which an article of personal property is lost or damaged during storage in a warehouse. The Code provisions make it clear that in such a case the warehouseman can avoid liability only if *he* proves that the loss or damage

---

in kind. That principle, which is embodied in § 249 of the German Civil Code (quoted *supra* at 598), assumes special importance in a period of inflation.

Even when the lost article cannot be returned in specie, the principle of restitution in kind asserts itself, because it follows from the principle that the value of the article must be determined as of the time of the court's decision rather than the (possibly much earlier) time of the loss. See O. Palandt, Bürgerliches Gesetzbuch, Comments preceding § 249, Anno. 9 RdNr. 174 (63rd ed. 2004), and cases there cited. The majority U.S. rule calls for either the market value or a reasonable value at the time of conversion or loss, plus interest. See cases collected in

8A Am.Jur.2d, Bailments, §§ 259 and 260 (1997 & Supps.).

1. The substance of these code provisions is stated in the last paragraph of the decision of Oct. 26, 1921, RGZ 103, 82, reproduced *supra*.

2. The opinion obviously implies that the "Storage Conditions" involved in this case constituted standardized contract conditions or standard terms (allgemeine Geschäftsbedingungen).

3. For an English translation of § 242 of the German Civil Code, see note 20 to the Opinion of the Reichsgericht in the Matter of S. S. v. M. K. Corp., *supra* at 571.

resulted from circumstances which could not have been averted by the exercise of due care.] It is true that these provisions of the Commercial Code constitute *ius dispositivum*[4] ...; thus these provisions yield to a contrary agreement of the parties.... [The court then points out that although in principle the parties have the power to modify the Commercial Code's rule as to the burden of proof, the question remains whether the particular contract clause here in question must be recognized as valid.] With respect to individually negotiated contracts one can say that in general—unless examination of the particular circumstances of a case dictates a different result—there is no objection against contractual terms which allocate the burden of proof in a manner differing from the dispositive provisions of the written law.[5] A different rule, however, applies to standardized contract conditions, which are intended to perform a function similar to that of statutes in affecting the legal process. When one party imposes standard conditions upon the other, true freedom of contract does not exist; standardized contract conditions thus derive their effectiveness, not from the parties' private autonomy, but only from the submission of the other party. Therefore, recognition must be denied to those terms of such standard conditions which for an indefinite number of future cases establish a rule inconsistent with the principles of good faith.

Insofar as dispositive provisions of law were enacted, not for reasons of expediency, but in response to a plain postulate of justice, the effect of such provisions may be modified by standardized contract conditions only if there are sufficient reasons justifying such modification. To be sufficient, the reasons must throw doubt on the postulate of justice underlying the rule of dispositive law, and must indicate that the modified solution [i.e. the solution adopted in the standard conditions] is consistent with justice and equity. The elements of justice which are inherent in the provisions of dispositive law enacted by the legislator are not always of the same strength. The stronger they are, the stricter must be the standard of good faith to which any modification (by way of a clause in a form contract) of such provisions of dispositive law must be held.

[The court refers to a previous case, in which these principles were applied to a warranty disclaimer in a contract of sale.]

A provision in a standard contract which in effect changes the legal rule with respect to the burden of proof cannot be regarded as equitable if the party who submits to the standardized conditions thereby is made to bear the burden of proof as to circumstances that lie within the sphere of responsibility of the party imposing such conditions. The outcome of many lawsuits of this kind depends on the burden of proof. The bailor whose

---

4. See *supra* 360ff.

5. The expression "dispositive provision" (admittedly a teutonism) is a literal translation of the German term "dispositive Vorschrift" or "Dispositivnorm." The term, which is a term of art, is derived from the Latin *ius dispositivum*, which is the opposite of *ius cogens*. Freely translated, the German term could be rendered as "provision of a code or other statute which is subject to agreement otherwise." For the sake of brevity, however, the literal rather than the free translation is used wherever the term appears in this opinion.

goods have been damaged often would be remediless if, having proved the delivery of the goods to the bailee, he had to show, in addition, what the circumstances were under which the stored goods were damaged ..., and had to prove furthermore that these circumstances involved some fault on the part of the bailee. Standard contract conditions, if they are to remain consistent with the requirements of honest dealing in business, cannot change the rule that the risk of failure to ascertain the cause of the damage must be borne by the bailee who has taken undamaged goods into his custody, and that even when the cause has been ascertained, he must prove lack of fault on his part. It is unfair, by subjecting the bailor to standardized contract conditions, to place upon him the burden of proof as to circumstances which are outside of his sphere of influence and which lie within the bailee's area of responsibility. [The court refers to some of its own previous decisions, and to the fact that in the General Contract Conditions of German Freight Forwarders—a standard contract form drafted with the cooperation of trade associations representing shippers as well as freight forwarders and carriers—the burden of proof question was resolved more favorably to the bailor than in the standard contract involved in the instant case.] It follows that § 1 of the Storage Conditions involved in this case is ineffective insofar as it places upon the bailor the entire burden of proving that a fault of the bailee caused the damage to, or the loss of, the stored property. The provisions of §§ 390 and 417 of the Commercial Code must be applied in lieu of the invalid terms of the Storage Conditions.

[Apparently there was some indication that in part the damage was caused by an attempt forcibly to open a cupboard, a desk and other stored articles belonging to the defendant. Thus pilferage was suspected. In this connection, the court refers to § 3 of the Storage Conditions, pursuant to which the warehouseman is not liable for losses caused by burglary or robbery. The court seems to assume that § 3 is valid, but points out that the burden of proving burglary or robbery rests on plaintiff. The damaged articles, and the nature of the damage, must be specified by the defendant (who, if necessary, may inspect the damaged articles which are still in plaintiff's custody); but the burden of explaining and proving the cause of the damage must be borne by plaintiff. Since the lower court erroneously imposed the burden on the defendant bailor, and dismissed his counterclaim when he was unable to meet the burden, the decision below is reversed, and the case remanded for further proceedings not inconsistent with the opinion of the highest court.]

* * *

Opinion of the European Court of Justice in the Matter of Cape Snc et al. (Plaintiff) v. Idealservice Srl (Defendant)

Joined Cases C–541/99 and C–542/99, 3rd Chamber, November 22, 2001, Eur. Court Reports, 2001, I–9049.

Idealservice MN RE Sas and Idealservice Srl (hereinafter "Idealservice") concluded with OMAI and Cape, on 14 September 1990 and 26

January 1996 respectively, two contracts for the supply to them of automatic drink dispensers which were installed on the premises of those companies and were intended to be used solely by their staff. In relation to the performance of those contracts, Cape and OMAI instituted proceedings contesting a payment order, maintaining that the clause granting jurisdiction contained in the contracts was unfair within the meaning of Article 1469a, paragraph 19, of the Italian Civil Code and could not therefore be enforced against the parties to the contracts by virtue of Article 1469d of that code [Art. 1469a and ff of the Civil Code (now repealed and replaced by Art. 33 and ff of the Consumer Code) were adopted to implement the Council Directive 93/13/EEC. Eds.]. The national court takes the view that its jurisdiction to hear the two cases brought before it depends on the construction of those provisions of the Civil Code, which constitute a "servile transposition" of the Directive. In particular, the terms "seller or supplier" and "consumer" used in article 1469a of the Civil Code are a literal transcription of the definitions contained in Article 2 of the Directive. In both cases, Idealservice contends that Cape and OMAI cannot be regarded as consumers for the purposes of applying the Directive. In addition to the fact that they are companies and not natural persons, Cape and OMAI signed the contracts at issue before the national court in the course of their business activity. Considering that the outcome of the two actions before it depended on the construction of the Directive, the Giudice di pace di Viadana stayed proceedings and referred to the Court the following two [sic] questions, which are identical in both cases: " '(1) Is it possible to regard as a consumer an undertaking which, by a contract with another undertaking using a form produced by the latter in so far as the contract falls within the scope of its normal business activity, acquires a service or merchandise for the sole benefit of its employees, which is wholly unconnected with and remote from its normal trade and business? Can it be said in such circumstances that that party acted for purposes which do not relate to the undertaking? (2) If the foregoing question is answered in the affirmative, is it possible to regard any party or entity as a consumer when it is acting for purposes not relating or conducive to its normal trade or business, or does the term consumer relate only to natural persons, to the exclusion of any other? (3) Can a company be regarded as a consumer?' " By its second and third questions, which it is appropriate to consider first, the national court seeks essentially to ascertain whether the term 'consumer' as defined in Article 2(b) of the Directive must be interpreted as referring solely to natural persons. [The judges then examine the reasons of the parties and those of the member States' representatives intervened before the Court] It must be observed that Article 2(b) of the Directive defines a consumer as "any natural person" who fulfils the conditions laid down by that provision, whereas article 2(c) of the Directive, in defining the term "supplier or seller", refers to both natural and legal persons. It is thus clear from the wording of Article 2 of the Directive that a person other than a natural person who concludes a contract with a seller or supplier cannot be regarded as a consumer within the meaning of that provision. Accordingly, the answer to the second and third questions must be that the term "consumer", as defined in Article 2(b) of the Directive, must be interpreted as referring solely to natural persons. In view of the answer given to the second and third questions, it is unnecessary to answer the first.

NOTES AND QUESTIONS

(1) In analyzing the first three preceding cases, it is interesting to compare the two older decisions with the most recent one. Has there been a shift between the 1920s and the 1960s (a) as to the Code provision cited by the court as the basis for its decision, and (b) more importantly, as to the substance of the rule?

(2) The traditional German approach to the whole problem of one-sided standard contracts is characterized by the sweeping nature of the rules which the German courts have developed.[1] Since these rules are based on Code provisions of utmost generality, they can be employed to strike down *any* one-sided clause in a standard contract which the court considers objectionable, regardless of the type of contract, or the type of business, in which it is used.[2]

U.S. statutes and decisions, on the other hand, traditionally deal in casuistic manner with specific types of clauses in specific types of contracts.[3] As to the validity of disclaimer clauses, separate and often unconnected bodies of law, both statutory and decisional, have grown up for public service corporations, railroads, housing authorities, banks, landlords, bailees, building contractors, innkeepers, and other types of business enterprises.[4]

With respect to disclaimer clauses in contracts for the transportation of goods, the casuistic bent of our method is particularly extreme. We start with the general proposition that a common carrier may not exempt itself from liability for its own or its servants' negligence and that a contractual limitation on the amount of the carrier's liability is valid only if a choice of rates is offered.[5] But the rule is subject to qualification by numerous provisions of the

---

1. The German courts' use of the general provisions of their Civil Code for the purpose of invalidating oppressive contracts and contract clauses is enlighteningly discussed by J. P. Dawson, Unconscionable Coercion: The German Version, 89 Harv. L.Rev. 1041 (1976) (note, however, that this article was written before the adoption of the 1976 German statute mentioned below in the text); B. S. Markesinis, H. Unberath & A. Johnston, The German Law of Contract 23–24, 177–178 (2d ed. 2006).

2. It is true that in German law one can find also some specific statutory provisions invalidating certain contract clauses, especially disclaimer clauses, in particular types of contracts. However, in view of the sweeping—and often stricter—rules derived by the courts from the general provisions of the Civil Code, these specific enactments have lost some of their practical importance with respect to those disclaimer clauses

which are contained in standardized contract conditions.

3. See R. B. Schlesinger, The Uniform Commercial Code in the Light of Comparative Law, 1 Inter–Am.L.Rev. 11, 32–33 (1959).

4. See the cases collected in Anno., 175 A.L.R. 8 (1948). For further examples illustrating the extreme casuistry of our decisional and statutory rules dealing with standardized contracts, see J. Sweet, Liquidated Damages in California, 60 Calif.L.Rev. 84, 85–86 (1972), and the collections of specific rules for liability of parking lot operators at 13 A.L.R.4th 362 (1982), photo developers at 6 A.L.R.4th 934 (1981), and astrologers at 91 A.L.R. 3d 766 (1979).

5. See 15 Corbin On Contracts § 85:18 (1993 & Supps.). The essence of this rule has been taken over into U.C.C. § 7–309.

Interstate Commerce Act, the Carriage of Goods by Sea Act, and other federal and state statutes.[6] These statutes have the effect that one and the same limitation of value clause is sometimes valid and sometimes invalid, depending on whether the transportation takes place by railroad, truck, boat, or airplane, and whether it is in international, interstate, or intrastate commerce.[7]

The Uniform Commercial Code has used a variety of techniques in dealing with one-sided contract terms, especially disclaimer clauses. Some of the relevant sections are fairly specific in their language and apply only to particular types of contracts;[8] but the Code also contains a provision of almost civilian sweep, applicable to all transactions governed by the Code, which broadly announces that "the obligations of good faith, diligence, reasonableness, and care prescribed by this Act may not be disclaimed by agreement. The parties, by agreement, may determine the standards by which the performance of those obligations is to be measured if those standards are not manifestly unreasonable."[9]

Even more civilian in style is § 2–302, which deals with "unconscionable" contracts and contract clauses.[10] By virtue of its extraordinary breadth and elasticity,[11] this provision is quite reminiscent of §§ 138 and 242 of the German Civil Code.[12] It must be remembered, however, that in contrast to the German

6. See U.C.C. § 7–103.

7. See 19 Williston On Contracts § 53:13 (R.A. Lord. ed., 4th ed. 2001).

8. See, e.g., §§ 4–103, 7–204, 7–309.

9. Sec. 1–302(b).

10. See, e.g., R. S. Summers, "Good Faith" in General Contract Law and the Sales Provisions of the Uniform Commercial Code, 54 Va.L.Rev. 195, 230–32 (1968); A. A. Leff, Unconscionability and the Code—The Emperor's New Clause, 115 U.Pa.L.Rev. 485 (1967); M. P. Ellinghaus, In Defense of Unconscionability, 78 Yale L.J. 757 (1969); S. Deutch, Unfair Contracts: The Doctrine of Unconscionability (1977); H. Beale, A. Hartkamp, H. Kötz, D. Tallon, *supra* p. 874, note 2, 483; E. A. Farnsworth, *supra* p. 873, note 1, 913–914. For a partly comparative discussion of § 2–302, see Comment, 109 U.Pa. L.Rev. 401 (1961).

For a provision similar to U.C.C. § 2–302, but not limited to sales of goods and, therefore, broader in coverage, see Cal.Civil Code § 1670.5, added by L.1979, ch. 819.

11. The possible argument that a provision of such breadth would give too much uncontrollable leeway to the jury, and therefore could not work satisfactorily in the context of the American legal system, was neatly side-stepped by the drafters, who made it clear that § 2–302 becomes operative only "if the court as a matter of law finds the contract or any clause of the contract to have

been unconscionable." It is further provided in subs. (2) that the parties may submit evidence bearing on the unconscionability of a contract or contract clause; but such evidence, as is pointed out in Official Comment 3, "is for the court's consideration, not the jury's."

12. The drafters of the U.C.C. seem to have thought in terms of the *older* German rule, i.e., the rule applied in the Reichsgericht opinions reproduced *supra.* Apparently they considered the much more far-reaching approach subsequently adopted by the German Bundesgerichtshof, but rejected it. See Section 2–302, Official Comment 1, where the following statement appears: "The principle is one of the prevention of oppression and unfair surprise . . . and not of disturbance of allocation of risks because of superior bargaining power."

Many illustrations of the use of Section 2–302 to invalidate warranty and damages limitation clauses can be found in Anno., 38 A.L.R.4th 25 (1985).

With the 1964 German case reproduced above one might compare A & M Produce Co. v. FMC Corp., 135 Cal.App.3d 473, 186 Cal. Rptr. 114 (1982), striking down as "unconscionable" a warranty disclaimer and consequential damages exclusion clause in a sales contract. At one point (n. 14 at 126) the California court comes close to the reasoning

provisions, which are applicable to all "jural acts" or all "obligations," § 2–302 in terms applies only to contracts for the sale of goods. Whether in this country (in states other then California)[13] § 2–302 will play a pervasive role comparable to that of the "general clauses" of the civilian codes thus depends on the extent to which our courts will be inclined to resort to analogy and to extend the sweep of the section to other types of transactions.

The traditional German method of dealing with disclaimer clauses and other one-sided terms in standardized contracts was evolved by the courts' imaginative and innovative use of some of the Civil Code's very general provisions. What are the advantages and disadvantages of that method as compared to ours? Which of the two methods can more truly be called a case law method?

(3) Despite the boldness which the German courts had displayed in dealing with standardized contracts,[14] there was considerable agitation a few decades ago for a broad legislative attack on the problem. The end result of that agitation, and of a great deal of solid preparatory work, was the *Gesetz zur Regelung des Rechts der allgemeinen Geschäftsbedingungen* (Standard Terms Act) of December 9, 1976, which went into effect on April 1, 1977 (the statute has been repealed with effect of January 1, 2002, and replaced with minor discrepancies by §§ 305 and following BGB).[15] Although legislation on this topic has been passed in many countries during recent years, it is fair to say that the German statute constituted the most thorough treatment of the subject. What follows is a highly condensed outline of the substantive and procedural safeguards which German law provides with regard to standardized contracts.

On the substantive side, there is a lengthy catalogue of forbidden clauses, i.e., clauses which, while permissible in individually negotiated contracts, are no longer tolerated in standardized consumer contracts (§ 309 BGB). In connection with the BGH decision of Feb. 7, 1964, reproduced *supra*, it is worth noting that clauses changing the burden of proof are listed in this catalogue. § 308 BGB lists another series of terms which the court may set aside if they cause an unreasonable detriment to the consumer. These catalogues are supplemented by a catch-all provision of sweeping breadth. The latter provision, which is not limited to consumer transactions but applies to all preformulated standardized contracts of adhesion, invalidates any terms in such contracts which in violation of the dictates of good faith put the other party at an unfair disadvantage (see § 307(1) BGB). Inspired by previous judicial decisions of

---

of the German court. But, in general, the approach of the former is much more cumbersome; it lays down a rule that makes for less predictability of results and creates many more issues of fact than the German rule. Cf. Perdue v. Crocker Nat. Bk., 141 Cal.App.3d 200, 190 Cal.Rptr. 204 (1983).

13. As to California, see *supra* note 10, 122.

14. P. Schlechtriem, A. Ludwigs, The Functions of General Clauses, Exemplified by Regarding Germanic Laws and Dutch Law, in General Clauses and Standards in European Contract Law, *supra* p. 892, note 2, 41f. For

some comparative observations concerning the boldness of judicial law-making in Germany and the United States, see R. B. Schlesinger, Book Review, 15 Am.J.Comp.L. 576, 577–78 (1967).

15. BGBl 1976 I 3317. For an extensive interesting discussion of the statute, see O. Sandrock, The Standard Terms Act 1976 of West Germany, 26 Am.J.Comp.L. 551 (1978); E.M. Holmes & D. Thürman, A New and Old Theory for Adjudicating Standardized Contracts, 17 Ga.J.Int'l & Comp.L. 323, 341–64 (1987).

which the 1964 decision of is typical, the catch-all section further provides that a clause in a preformulated adhesion contract is always invalid if it is inconsistent with the essential policy thrust of a statutory rule, or if it limits essential rights or duties inherent in the nature of the contract to such an extent that attainment of the purpose of the contract is jeopardised.

As to procedure, consumer organizations as well as trade associations may sue to enjoin the use of standardized contracts or contract clauses which are substantively unlawful.[16] An injunction obtained in such an action can be enforced in accordance with Section 890 of the German Code of Civil Procedure (see *supra* sec. A(2)). If in spite of such an injunction the use of the enjoined contract or clause is continued, the injunction decree can be invoked as binding (res judicata) by a private party such as a consumer in subsequent litigation.[17] Thus the danger of conflicting court decisions concerning the effectiveness of the same clause is considerably diminished, and the individual customer no longer bears the main burden of attacking objectionable form contracts or clauses.[18]

(4) Not only Germany and Sweden, but also many other countries have attempted in recent years to find legislative solutions to the problems created by one-sided clauses in standardized contracts.[19] Further, since 1993, "unfair terms in consumer contracts" have been the subject of a European Community Directive (see *infra*, pt. (5) of this Note). Some of the innovative ideas reflected in the solutions adopted in these other countries differ considerably from the German and U.S. approach.[20]

16. See § 1 of the Act on Injunctive Relief (Unterlassungsklagengesetz or UKlaG). § 2 UKlaG (which implements the European Directive 98/27/EC on injunctions for the protection of consumers' interests) establishes the right to seek injunctive relief against any violations of whatever provision protecting consumer interests.

17. UKlaG § 11.

18. A. Stadler, Collective Action as an Efficient Means for the Enforcement of European Competition Law, in Private Enforcement of EC Competition Law 195, 202–203 (J. Basedow ed., 2007). It is worthy comparing the German solution with the Swedish one, which provides for the office of Consumer Ombudsman; the official holding that post, either upon his or her own motion or acting on an outside suggestion, can apply to the Market Court for an order enjoining the use of terms in a standard form contract that are thought unfair to consumers. See J. E. Sheldon, Consumer Protection and Standard Contracts: The Swedish Experiment in Administrative Control, 22 Am.J.Comp.L. 17 (1974); J. J. Boddewin, The Swedish Consumer Ombudsman System and Advertising Self–Regulation, 19 J.Cons.Aff. 140 (2005); J. M. Smits,

Nordic Law in a European Context: Some Comparative Observations, in Nordic Law Between Tradition and Dynamism 55 f. (J. Husa, K. Nuotio, H. Pihlajamäki eds., 2007).

19. A legislative solution of less recent vintage, but of continuing interest, is offered by Art. 1341 of the Italian Civil Code, which enumerates certain types of one-sided clauses (including disclaimer clauses) and provides that if such a clause appears in a standardized contract, it has no effect unless it is "specifically approved in writing." See G. Gorla, Standard Conditions and Form Contracts in Italian Law, 11 Am.J.Comp.L. 1 (1962); see also C. Cicoria, The Protection of the Weak Contractual Party in Italy vs. United States Doctrine of Unconscionability. A Comparative Analysis, 3 Global Jurist (2003), issue 3, article 2. The effect of Art. 1341 is that although the customer may have signed the contract as a whole, the one-sided clause is not effective unless he has indicated his approval of the clause by a separate, additional signature. Compare U.C.C. §§ 2–205 (last half-sentence), 2–209(2), 2–316(2).

20. See M. Ebers, Unfair Contract Terms Directive, in Consumer Law Compendium 341–437 (H. Schulte–Nölke ed., 2008).

In 1964, Israel was the first country to adopt a statute on standard contract terms. It established a voluntary system for approval of such terms by the Board of Restrictive Trade Practices. In 1982, Israel enacted a new Standard Contracts Law, creating a Standard Contracts Tribunal. The tribunal is authorized, at the request of a consumer or supplier, to approve or annul a term contained in a standard contract. The validity a term not approved by the tribunal may still become an issue in litigation before an ordinary court.[21]

(5) As part of the effort to facilitate establishment of a single European market, the European Community adopted in 1993 a Directive on Unfair Terms in Consumer Contracts.[22]

The Directive covers only terms in consumer contracts which have not been individually negotiated.[23] According to Article 3(1) of the Directive, "[a] contractual term which has not been individually negotiated shall be regarded as unfair if, contrary to the requirements of good faith, it causes a significant imbalance in the parties' rights and obligations arising under the contract, to the detriment of the consumer." An Annex of the Directive sets out "an indicative and non-exhaustive list of the terms which may be regarded as unfair" (art. 3(3)). As to procedure, Article 7(1) of the Directive requires member states to ensure that "adequate and effective means exist to prevent the continued use of unfair terms in contracts concluded with consumers by sellers or suppliers." Article 7(2) specifies that "[t]he means referred to in paragraph 1 shall include provisions whereby persons or organizations, having a legitimate interest in protecting consumers, may take action according to the national law concerned before the courts or before competent administrative bodies for a decision as to whether contractual terms drawn up for general use are unfair, so that they can apply appropriate and effective means to prevent the continued use of such terms."

A basic requirement for the application of the regime set forth by the Directive is that the transaction be between a consumer and a party who is

---

21. On the 1982 legislation, see S. Deutch, Controlling Standard Contracts—The Israeli Version, 30 McGill L.J. 458 (1985); V. Lusthaus, Standard Contracts in Israel—New Developments, 54 Rabels Z. 555 (1990); more recently, J. Drexl, Consumer Protection Law under the Israeli Draft Civil Code: A Response from a European and German Perspective, in The Draft Civil Code for Israel in Comparative Perspective 39–50 (K. Siehr & R. Zimmermann eds., 2008).

22. Council Directive 93/13 on Unfair Terms in Consumer Contracts, April 5, 1993, O.J. 1993, No. L95, at 29. On the Directive generally, see R. Brownsword, G. Howells & T. Wilhelmsson, The EC Unfair Contract Terms Directive and Welfarism, in Welfarism in Contract Law 275 (R. Brownsword, G. Howells & T. Wilhelmsson eds., 1994); H.

Beale, A. Hartkamp, H. Kötz, D. Tallon, *supra* p. 874, note 2, 21–23, 521–555.

23. It is nevertheless true that standard terms are capable of endangering not only the consumer, but any contractual partner against whom they are used. This is why the protection afforded by monitoring of terms in Germany extends not only to business-to-consumer transactions, but to business-to-business and consumer-to-consumer transactions as well (see § 307(1) BGB). In other countries, such as France, the protection granted to consumers does not only cover standard terms, but all clauses, be they pre-formulated or individually negotiated. Also in Denmark, Finland and Sweden, according to the general clause (Contract Acts, Art. 36), it is possible for the judge to review individually negotiated standard terms of business-to-business contracts. (see M. Ebers, *supra* note 20, 351–352).

acting for purposes within his or her trade or profession.[24] Thus, the transfer of ownership over immoveables between private persons is not covered by consumer protection rules.[25] The issue of the parties' quality, however, is far from being settled. Should the directive apply when a consumer enters into a contract with a merchant, who does not know (nor should have known) that s/he is contracting with a consumer? Are small businessmen dealing with standard contracts prepared by big corporations to be deemed as professionals or as consumers? Can the Directive apply to the standard contract entered into by a businessman for the supply of goods (maybe similar to those s/he is usually concerned with, but) for private purposes? As we have seen in the fourth case above, the European Court of Justice has answered negatively to the latter question,[26] while in some European jurisdiction national courts extend the consumers' regime to the entrepreneur, at least when the transaction involved is alien to his/her trade.[27]

Drawing a line between consumers and businessmen, however, may be less crucial than it might appear at first glance. Sometimes the high level of protection afforded by law against standard contracts with consumers drives courts to raise the threshold of protection as to include also business-to-business transactions. Reference is, for example, to the German courts' practice of according a special "Reflexwirkung" (reflected effect) to the black lists set forth by §§ 308, and 309 BGB, when applying § 307 BGB to business-to-business contracts.[28]

24. According to Art. 2(b) of the Directive, " 'consumer' means any natural person who, in contracts covered by this Directive, is acting for purposes which are outside his trade, business or profession," while " 'seller or supplier' means any natural or legal person who, in contracts covered by this Directive, is acting for purposes relating to his trade, business or profession, whether publicly owned or privately owned" (Art. 2(c)).

25. E. H. Hondius, The Notion of Consumer: European Union vs. Member States, 5 Sydney L.Rev. 89 (2006).

26. See the decision of the European Court of Justice Cape S.n.c. et al. (Plaintiff) v. Idealservice (Defendant), *supra*. See also European Court of Justice, Jan. 20, 2005, Case C–464/01, Gruber v. Bay. Mr. Gruber was an Austrian farmer who purchased from a German company (BayWa AG) some tiles for the roof of his farmhouse, in part of which he lived with his family, the remaining part being used as a pigsty. Since the tiles were founded to be defective, Mr. Gruber sued BayWa AG before an Austrian Court, relying on the fact that the Court would have applied Art. 13 ff. of the Brussels Convention, which state that a consumer may bring pro-

ceedings against the other party before the courts of the state in which s/he is domiciled. The first instance court took jurisdiction, which was subsequently denied by the appeal court. The Oberster Gerichtshof (Austrian Supreme Court) referred the question to the ECJ, and the latter ruled that "a person who concludes a contract for goods intended for purposes which are in part within and in part outside his trade or profession may not rely on the special rules of jurisdiction laid down in Articles 13 to 15 of the Convention, unless the trade or professional purpose is so limited as to be negligible in the overall context of the supply, the fact that the private element is predominant being irrelevant in that respect."

27. See the Italian and French case-law quoted by E. H. Hondius, *supra* note 25, 89ff; see also O. Lando, Should Business Enterprises Benefit from Consumer Protection, in Festschrift für Peter Schlechtriem zum 70. Geburtstag 577ff (I. Schwenzer, P. Schlechtriem, G. Hager eds., 2003).

28. "According to the case law of the BGH, the black list especially (CC § 309) has an indicative effect of whether the relevant rule leads to a disproportionate imbalance to the detriment of the business." M. Ebers, *supra* note 20, 376.

(e) Contract in a Planned Economy

Although we tend to associate the very idea of "contract" with freedom, it is noteworthy that contracts can have a role to play even in a planned economy. Immediately after the establishment of the People's Republic of China, the emphasis was on ensuring the functioning of the government and public order. Even though bourgeois private law notion such as "property" and "contract" lost their prior significance, it did not mean that they became wholly irrelevant. Rather, as the following excerpt suggests, they were re-signified and their functions altered.

Lucie Cheng & Arthur Rosett, Contract with a Chinese Face: Socially Embedded Factors in the Transformation from Hierarchy to Market, 1978–1989

5 *Journal of Chinese Law* 143 (1991), pp. 168–70

Contract in the Service of Planning

The leadership of the PRC in the 1950s needed a technique to make planning decisions concrete and specific. The aim of the system was to make allocative decisions and distribute goods by plan, not by price. Yet, inevitably, planning was not expected to be perfect and all-encompassing. It was anticipated that some minor routine purchases would be made outside the plan and in emergencies some exchanges would have to be made while the plan was being adjusted to reflect the new circumstances. In practice, it appears that these off-plan transactions remained substantial, although the official view was that they were relatively insignificant. Within the scope of the plan, the assumption was that the planning and the supervising agencies would allocate the materials necessary to enable the enterprise to fulfill its production quota. Planning directives ordered suppliers to provide materials; similar directives dictated where the enterprise was to deliver its production. Procurement outside the planning mechanism when there was input-output planning effect was viewed as serious deviance and was severely punished.

To make planning decisions concrete and specific, the planners drew upon the Soviet experience and created a kind of contract law in the service of the plan. Under this system, ministries and supervising agencies sponsored periodic meetings, sometimes referred to as "goods-ordering conferences," to which were invited all those who were to produce and deliver products under the plan. At these meetings, suppliers for materials would be matched with consumers of those materials, and specific delivery plans would be negotiated. The results of these meetings were embodied in written documents that were referred to as contracts, but which essentially were written planning orders to the enterprises. "Dancing partners" were assigned by the relevant ministry to ensure that there was a supplier for every requirement and an outlet for every product. The terms of these contracts were determined by the orders of the supervising agencies, not by the negotiations of the parties to the transactions.

Most significantly, these contracts were understood to create obligations in the parties who signed them, but few meaningful rights. If the goods that were subject to the contract failed to arrive or were below grade, the problem would be adjusted by the buyer's manager, who would ask the supervising agency to complain to the breaching party's superior in an effort to require performance. Since the supervising agency is likely to be unable to achieve this result, the consequence of the failure to deliver is that the disappointed enterprise's plan will have to be adjusted to reflect its inability to produce and deliver the product planned.

(f) Freedom of Contract and Interest in Islamic Law

The issue of freedom of contract has arisen also in Islamic law in certain specific contexts. As the following excerpt illustrates, the traditional prohibition of interest or usury has been of particular concern for the modern banking industry, where it has been handled in various creative ways.[1]

Abdullah Saeed, *Studies in Islamic Law and Society: Islamic Banking and Interest*

(1996), pp. 1, 16, 39–42, 48–51, 74–76, 108–109, 130–31.

"Islamic banking" is now a widely-known term in both the Muslim world and the West. It denotes a form of banking and finance which attempts to provide services to clients free from "interest." The proponents of Islamic banking argue that interest is *riba* and, as such, is prohibited under Islamic law. This attitude towards interest has led several Muslim scholars and financiers to find ways and means of developing an alternative banking system which would comply with the injunctions of Islamic law, in particular, the rulings related to the prohibition of *riba* . . .

Since the 1960s, the prohibition of *riba* (interest or usury) has been one of the most discussed issues amongst Muslims. This is a consequence of both the perception that bank interest is *riba,* and the prevailing nature of interest in the present world banking system. There are two predominant views concerning *riba*. Many Muslims would contend that the interpretation of *riba* as provided in *fiqh* (Islamic law) is the proper interpretation and so must be followed. This interpretation implies that any increase charged in a loan transaction over and above the principal is *riba*. For others, the prohibition of *riba* is understood as relating to the exploitation of the economically disadvantaged in the community by the relatively affluent. This element of exploitation mayor may not actually exist in modem bank interest. These Muslims would argue that the interpretation of *riba* in the *fiqh* literature is inadequate and does not take into consideration the moral intent of the prohibition as expounded in, or inferred from, the Qur'ān and *sunna* . . . .

---

1. For the role of shari'a in another modern commercial context, see Faisal Kutty, "The Shari'a Factor in International Commercial Arbitration," 28 Loy. L.A. Int'l & Comp. L. Rev. 565 (2006). [Cite book on Interest?]

The Qur'ān, from the very beginning of the Prophet's mission, was concerned with the lower socio-economic groups. It attempted to protect these strata of society by demanding that they not be exploited by the rich and affluent. In this context, the Qur'ān blamed the institution of *riba* and prohibited it, as it was essentially the imposition of an increase on a needy debtor who was having problems in repaying a debt, thus increasing the misery and the debtor's burden, which was compounded as time passed. Again and again, the Qur'ān insisted that such people should be helped, not exploited. It also demanded that the affluent should give money to provide for the needy and disadvantaged. If such debtors could not repay their debts on time, they should be given an extension without any added burden. The economy of Mecca and Medina at the time of the Prophet was more or less a subsistence economy, and large scale lending and borrowing for non-humanitarian purposes did not seem to be widely practiced. Debt in that society appears to have been generally a means of meeting a pressing need on the part of the economically disadvantaged.

This is the moral framework within which the Qur'ān dealt with both the issue of debt and the increases imposed on hard-pressed debtors by their creditors. The context of the *riba*related verses again and again indicated that the Qur'ān was dealing with the issue of *riba* from a moral perspective not a legal one. The *sunna* also dealt with the issue of *riba* from this moral standpoint. However, in Islamic law, in determining what is *riba* and what is not, Muslim jurists focused mainly on whether a particular loan transaction had an element of increase over and above the principal, or whether certain qualities existed in a particular commodity likely to be identified with *riba*. In both cases, the jurists almost totally ignored the nature and circumstances of the transaction, the parties to the transaction, the prevailing economic environment within which it took place, and its purpose. Thus, the issue of *riba* in Islamic law became merely a "legal" issue concerned with the outward "form," having no place whatsoever for the moral framework within which the Qur'ān and *sunna* appear to have dealt with the issue. The point to be made here is that unless the moral importance attached to the prohibition of *riba* is emphasized, which is hardly the case in the current debate, there is a danger that the whole discussion may become a meaningless exercise and a quibble over semantics (as is demonstrated by the case of the use) of hiyal. . . .

Contemporary Muslim scholars have differed as to whether the *riba* prohibited in the Qur'ān applies to modem bank interest. These differences appear to stem from one basic issue: should the emphasis be on the rationale for the prohibition of *riba*, that is, injustice, or should it be on the legal form in which *riba* came to be formally conceptualized in Islamic law. . . .

Modernists like Fazlur Rahman (1964), Muhammad Asad (1984), Sa 'īd al-Najjār (1989) and 'Abd al-Mun'im al-Namir (1989) tend to emphasize the moral aspect of the prohibition of *riba*, and relegate the "legal form" of *riba*, as interpreted in Islamic law to a secondary position. They argue that the *raison d'être* for the prohibition is injustice, as formulated in the

Qur'ānic statement, *"lā tazlimūna wa-lā tuzlamūn"* (Do not commit injustice and no injustice will be committed against you). Modernists also find some support for their views in the works of early scholars, like Rāzi, Ibn Qayyim and Ibn Taymiyya. Rāzi, a commentator on the Qur'ān, in his enumeration of reasons for the prohibition of *riba,* said: "The fourth reason is that the lender mostly would be rich, and the borrower poor. Allowing the contract of *riba* involves enabling the rich to exact an extra amount from the weak poor." The Hanbali scholar, Ibn Qayyim, also linked the prohibition to its moral aspect. Referring to the pre-Islamic *riba,* he says that in most cases the debtor was destitute with no choice but to defer the payment of the debt. It is this reason, according to the Modernists, which makes the prohibition morally sustainable in a changing socio-economic environment. According to the modem commentator on the Qur'ān, Muhammad Asad:

> Roughly speaking, the opprobrium of *riba* (in the sense in which this term is used in the Qur'ān and in many sayings of the Prophet) attaches to profits obtained through interest-bearing loans involving an *exploitation of the economically weak by the strong and resourceful ...* With this definition in mind, we realise that the question as to what kinds of financial transactions fall within the category of *riba* is, in the last resort, a moral one, closely connected with the socio-economic motivation under lying the mutual relationship of borrower and lender.[1]

... The Pakistani scholar, Fazlur Rahman, remarked on the attitude of many Muslims towards interest:

> Many well-meaning Muslims with very virtuous consciences sincerely believe that the Qur'ān has banned all bank interest for all times, in woeful disregard of what *riba* was historically, why the Qur'ān denounced it as a gross and cruel form of exploitation and banned it, and what the function of bank interest [is] today.[2]

For these scholars, it appears that what is prohibited is the exploitation of the needy, rather than the concept of the interest rate itself. It is the type of lending that attempts to profit from the misery of others. Many writers of this trend attempt to differentiate between various forms of interest practiced under the traditional banking system, advocating the lawfulness of some, while rejecting others. The rejection is generally based on a perceived injustice in a particular form of interest....

[T]he Modernists so far have failed to have much impact on the debate on *riba.* Their views, and the "exceptions" to the *riba* prohibition they have advocated, have been met by neoRevivalist critics with both economic and scriptural counter arguments, and their position has been weakened. One of the leading Islamic banking theorists, M.N. Siddiqi, says:

1. Asad, The Message of the Qur'ān 633 (1984).

2. Rahman, "Islam: Challenges and Opportunities," in Welch & Cachia (Eds.), Islam: Past Influence and Present Challenge (1979) at 326.

Efforts of some pseudo-jurists to distinguish between *riba* and bank interest and to legitimise the latter [have] met with almost universal rejection and contempt. Despite the fact that circumstances force many people to deal with interest-based financial institutions, the notion of its essential illegitimacy has always remained.[3]

The position of the Modernists is further undermined by two factors: their inability to present a consistent theory of *riba* on the basis of the rationale of prohibition which is specified in the Qur'ān, and the rise of Islamic banking institutions inspired by neo-Revivalist thinking on the issue of *riba*, which have adopted the view that "any interest is *riba*, and as such is prohibited." . . .

The neo-Revivalist view is the dominant one in the contemporary debate. This view emphasizes the legal form of *riba* as expressed in Islamic law, and insists that the words specified in the Qur'ān should be taken at their literal meaning, regardless of what was practiced in the pre-Islamic period. According to this view, since the Qur'ān has stated that only the principal should be taken, there is no alternative but to interpret *riba* according to that wording. Therefore, the existence or otherwise of injustice in a loan transaction is irrelevant. Whatever the circumstances are, the lender has no right to receive any increase over and above the principal.

Although several leading neo-Revivalists like Mawdūdi and Sayyid Qutb have discussed to some extent the issue of injustice in *riba*, they have generally refrained from stating that it is injustice which is the *raison d'être* of the prohibition. According to Mawdūdi, "the contention that *zulm* (injustice) is the reason why interest on loans has been disallowed and hence all such interest transactions as do not entail cruelty are permissible, remains yet to be substantiated."[4]

Following this line of thinking, neo-Revivalist writers have interpreted *riba* in a way which would not allow any increase in a loan. Mawdūdi defines *riba* as "the amount that a lender receives from a borrower at a fixed rate of interest." Perhaps one of the most important documents on Islamic banking, the CII (Council of Islamic Ideology) Report is more explicit: "There is complete unanimity among all schools of thought in Islam that the term *riba* stands for interest in all its types and forms."[5] Chapra states that "*riba* has the same meaning and import as interest."[6] For these scholars, the prohibition of *riba*, interpreted as interest, is axiomatic. Mohammad Uzair, an Islamic banking theorist, asserts that interest in all its forms is synonymous with *riba*, and claims the existence of consensus on the issue:

By this time, there is a complete consensus of all five schools of *Fiqh* . . . and among Islamic economists, that interest in all forms, of all

3. Siddiqi, Issues in Silamic Banking: Selected Papers 9–10 (1983)

4. Mawdūdi, "Prohibition of Interest in Islam," Al–Islam, June 1986 at 7.

5. CII (Council of Islamic Ideology). Consolidated Recommendations on the Islamic Economic System 7 (1983).

6. Chapra, Towards a Just Monetary System 57 (1985).

kinds, and for all purposes is completely prohibited in Islam. Gone are the days when people were apologetic about Islam, and contended that the interest for commercial and business purposes, as presently charged by banks, was not prohibited by Islam.[7]

But the question remains, "Is this interpretation of *riba* justified?" We do not contend that "any increase over and above the principal" is *riba* irrespective of the circumstances of the loan or debt.... Whatever the value of the neo-Revivalist interpretation of *riba*, it is this interpretation which is the basis of current Islamic banking theory as well as practice....

Islamic banking theorists envisioned that the investment activities of the Islamic bank would be based on the two legal concepts of *mudāraba* and *mushāraka*, alternatively known as Profit and Loss Sharing (PLS). These theorists contended that the Islamic bank would provide its extensive financial resources to the borrowers on a risk sharing basis, unlike the interest-based financing in which the borrower assumes all risks. However, in practice, Islamic banks generally have come to realize that PLS, as envisaged by the theorists, cannot be utilized extensively in Islamic banking due to the risks it imposes on the bank. This realization has led Islamic banks to find ways by which they can limit the flexibility of these two concepts of PLS and transform them almost to risk-free financing mechanisms. This chapter examines how the two concepts of *mudāraba* and *mushāraka* developed in Islamic law and how they are utilized in Islamic banking....

Mudāraba as developed in the *fiqh* literature is a contract where a skilled person may utilise his skill with the money of the investor in order to realise a profit. It does not rest on any explicit *sharī'a* text but it has been practiced from the earliest period of Islamic history. *Mudāraba* as developed in *fiqh* was a contract where the *mudārib* had the necessary freedom to conduct the *mudāraba* in order to realize a profit. Since the *mudārib* was the weaker party in the contract who, by definition, provided his skill as capital to the *mudāraba*, the jurists did not allow the demanding of any guarantee from the *mudārib*. Under Islamic banking, *mudāraba* came to be used in commercial ventures of a very short term nature, where there is no transfer of funds to the *mudārib*. There is no freedom to act, since all the minute details of how the *mudāraba* should be managed are set out in the contract. The role of the *mudārib* is restricted to enforcing the terms of the contract. By means of these terms, and by demanding various forms of guarantee, the bank is able to determine the outcome of the venture so as to ensure that it recovers its capital as well as return on that capital. The general concept of *mudāraba*, that it is a form of venture capital financing or provision of credit to those who lack funds but have the skill to conduct trade or business on an uncertain return which mayor may not be realized, does not appear to be prominent or significantly evident in the Islamic banking *mudārabas*.

7. Uzair, "Impact of Interest–Free Banking," *Journal of Islamic Banking and Finance*, Autumn 1984 at 40.

Mushāraka is justified on the basis of several texts of the *sharī'a* albeit rather arbitrarily. Islamic banks have utilized one form of *mushāraka* that is *'inān* finance partnership. In *fiqh,* it appears that the *mushāraka* is utilised in a venture whose outcome is uncertain, that is, in the sense of a real business venture. In *fiqh,* the partner is given reasonable freedom to act in pursuit of profit. Since the partner is regarded as a trustworthy person, no guarantees are permitted. In profit sharing, the early jurists allowed the parties to share in the profits as agreed upon in the contract, though there was no agreement on the issue. In loss sharing there was no flexibility, as the jurists insisted that it should be according to the capital contribution ratio.

Under Islamic banking, although *mushāraka* is used in several forms, it is the commercial form which has become prominent, where the contract is closely related to the purchase and sale of certain specified goods. The commercial *mushāraka* enables the bank to recover its capital, plus return, without much uncertainty. The partner is restricted in his actions by the detailed terms of the contract which do not leave much freedom to the partner to conduct a *mushāraka* in the real sense of the term as it was developed in *fiqh.* From the terms of the contracts of Islamic banks, it appears that the partner is more like an agent of the bank where the agent's function is to sell the goods involved at the price specified by the bank in order to realize the return the bank is aiming at. The bank's share of capital and its return thereon is well protected by various forms of guarantees and terms of the contract. The partner also appears to be a symbolic figure who has no say in setting out the *mushāraka* contracts, since it is the bank that dictates the *mushāraka* terms.

It is important to note that the utilization of these two concepts purely as PLS is extremely limited in Islamic banking, allowing little optimism regarding its wider use....

Islamic banking theorists argue that Islamic banking should be based on Profit and Loss Sharing (PLS) rather than interest. Islamic banks in practice, however, have found from the very beginning that PLS-based banking is difficult to implement as it is risk-laden and uncertain. The practical problems associated with this financing have led to its gradual decline in Islamic banking, and to a steady increase in the utilization of "interest-like" financing mechanisms. One such mechanism is termed *murābaha.*

Murābaha, a form of deferred payment sale, and a purely commercial contract, although not based on any text of the or the *sunna,* has been allowed in Islamic law. Islamic banks have utilized the *murābaha* contract in their financing activities where goods are involved, and have expanded the scope and extent of its use. Such financing now comprises more than seventy-five percent of Islamic banks' financing by virtue of its having a predetermined return on the banks' investments, much like the predetermined return of interest-based banks.

Murābaha finance and the higher credit price involved therein has clearly shown that there is a value of time in *murābaha* based finance, which leads, albeit indirectly, to the acceptance of the time value of money. It has been conveniently ignored that accepting the time value of money logically leads to the acceptance of interest. Accepting time value in *murābaha* transactions (which is scarcely any different from a purely monetary transaction) and then rejecting the same in monetary transactions appears to be inconsistent and illogical. If Islamic law can allow *murābaha* financing as it is practiced under Islamic banking then the question is, "Is there any moral basis for not allowing fixed interest on loans and advances?"

Religious Supervisory Boards and Islamic Banking

The most widely used approach to ensuring the islamicity of Islamic banking at private sector level, particularly in the Middle East, is that of the Religious Supervisory Board (RSB). Islamic banks employ scholars of Islamic law in a consultancy and advisory capacity to examine their contracts, dealings and transactions. This is to ensure that the day-to-day activities of the Islamic bank in the areas of resource mobilization and allocation are in line with the *sharī'a.*

The Religious Supervisory Board (RSB) Method

The existence of Religious Supervisory Boards (RSBs) in almost all private sector Islamic banks operating in the Middle East in UAE, Kuwait, Bahrain, Jordan, Egypt and Sudan points, *inter alia,* to the religious character of these banks. In some banks, like the Jordan Islamic Bank, there is only one religious consultant, whereas in other banks such as the Faisal Islamic Bank of Egypt (FIBE), the board consists of five members at most, who are scholars of Islamic law and believe in the idea of "Islamic banking." They are given wide powers and authority to examine any contract, method, or activity relating to the conduct of their banks. According to the Articles of Association of FIBE, the RSB would have at their disposal all the means which are available to the auditors, in order to perform their functions. In their banks' annual reports the RSBs certify that the activities of their institutions are according to the *sharī'a,* just as independent auditors certify that the financial position of the bank is fair.

The procedure followed by these Islamic banks to ensure that islamicity of their banking and financial operations could be briefly stated as follows: the management of the bank, when it faces a banking and finance problem which needs to be looked at by the RSB, analyses the problem to some extent, suggests a solution that could be adopted in contemporary banking and finance, explains the constituent elements of the suggested solution, gives an example for clarity, and seeks the opinion of the Religious Supervisory Board on its proposed solution. The Board considers it, and if, in its opinion, there is no objection to that solution from the *sharī'a* viewpoint, endorses it. If there are any objections to the solution or any of its constituent elements, the Board expresses its opinion on the matter, and recommends further modification to the unacceptable elements....

*Views expressed by early jurists cannot answer all modern banking and
finance problems.*

Commercial institutions and contracts developed in the traditional *fiqh*
cannot provide answers for all contemporary highly complex banking and
financial matters. This is due to the large gap between the commercial
institutions and contracts discussed in the traditional *fiqh,* and those which
have been developed and are being developed in the modem period. The
most creative period of the development of *fiqh* goes back to the first four
centuries of Islam, after which a gradual stagnation of the creative process
of *ijtihād* began to take place. From the fifth and sixth centuries AH
onwards, the doctrine of closure of the "gate of *ijtihād*" was accepted by
many jurists. Hence the creativity of many jurists became restricted to the
explanation and limited interpretation of earlier jurists' views. The emphasis on fresh *ijtihād* which was so characteristic of the formative period *of
fiqh* was replaced by *taqlīd,* hindering the development of law in line with
the developments in society.

Ever changing commercial and economic institutions have brought
innumerable and totally novel problems to which answers are not available
in the traditional *fiqh.* For this very reason, one might be justified in
accepting the need for exercising fresh *ijtihād,* on the basis of the principles
and explicit rulings of the Qur'ān and *sunna,* in order to find Islamic
solutions to the emerging problems, rater than attempting to find a view of
an early jurist on an issue which appears to be similar to a modern
financial transaction. Since the ever developing banking and finance methods ale by definition new, and, hence, did not exist in the time of the
revelation, such transactions need constantly to be looked at from the
points of view of broad *sharī'a* principles of justice, equity, fairness, and
compassion.

2. SECURITY OF TRANSACTIONS

(a) The Principle of Publicity in the Transfer of Land

I

The Code Napoleon and all the other 19th century codes in varying
degrees reflect the desire to break the power and privileges of the landed
aristocracy, and to make land as freely marketable as possible, "the result
expected being that every piece of land would always be in the ablest and
fittest hands."[1]

To carry out these aims, the concept of private property was divorced
from the owner's status and public office. Under the influence of the theory
that property was a natural right, not granted by the sovereign but at most

---

1. M. Rheinstein, Some Fundamental
Differences in Real Property Ideas of the
"Civil Law" and the Common Law Systems,
3 U.Chi.L.Rev. 624, 625 (1936); see also F.
Parisi, The Fall and Rise of Functional Property, George Mason Law & Economics Research Paper no. 05–38, 15 ff. (2005), available at SSRN: http://ssrn.com/abstract=
850565.

limited by him, the right of ownership was redefined in absolute terms, negating any idea of an overlord's reversionary interest.[2] Most forms of future interests, being of feudal origin, were radically abolished. In general, the codes of the civil-law world make it possible for several persons to own a piece of realty in common or jointly, and modern legislation in many civil law countries also authorizes horizontal division of buildings and separate ownership of apartments.[3] Subject to limited and carefully defined exceptions, however, the right of ownership cannot be split into successive estates, and of course not into "legal" and "equitable" interests.[4]

All other rights in rem (i.e., rights other than full ownership) are thought of as mere restrictions or encumbrances upon the title of the owner. In many civil-law countries, the principle of the so-called *numerus clausus* of rights in rem has been adopted. This means that the code contains an exhaustive catalogue of permissible restrictions and encumbrances and that other rights in rem cannot validly be created.[5] Hypothecas

---

2. Cf. French Civil Code, Article 544: "Ownership is the right to enjoy and dispose of things in the most absolute manner, provided they are not used in a way prohibited by law or regulations."

Article 545: "No one can be compelled to give up his property, except for public use and against a just compensation payable in advance."

3. For comparative discussions of the subject, which is of tremendous practical importance in today's urbanized world, see 1 A. Ferrer and K. Stecher, Law of Condominium 14–127 (1967); A. N. Yiannopoulos, Property 315–18 (vol. 2 of Louisiana Civil Law Treatise, 3d ed. 1991); J. Leyser, The Ownership of Flats—A Comparative Study, 7 Int'l & Comp.L.Q. 31 (1958); C. van der Merwe, A Comparative Study of the Distribution of Ownership Rights in Property in an Apartment or Condominium Scheme in Common Law, Civil Law and Mixed Law Systems, 31 Ga.J.Int'l & Comp.L. 101 (2002).

It is interesting to note that the first American jurisdiction to pass legislation authorizing "condominium" ownership of apartments was Puerto Rico in 1958 (Horizontal Property Act No. 104, 1958 P.R. Laws 243). How this civilian institution spread from Puerto Rico to most of the States, is interestingly explained by W. K. Kerr, Condominium—Statutory Implementation, 38 St. John's L.Rev. 1 (1963). See also C. J. Berger, Condominium: Shelter on a Statutory Foun-

dation, 63 Colum.L.Rev. 987 (1963). For a comparative and economic analysis, see G. Coloma, An economic analysis of horizontal property, 21 Int'l Rev.L. & Econ. 343 (2001).

4. Under the heading of "usufruct," most civil-law systems make it possible, by inter vivos transaction or by testament, to create an interest in rem which is limited in time. See A. N. Yiannopoulos, Personal Servitudes 9–297, with numerous comparative references (vol. 3 of Louisiana Civil Law Treatise, 3d ed. 1989); J. H. Merryman, Ownership and Estate (Variations on a Theme by Lawson), 48 Tul.L.Rev. 916, 930–32 (1974). The practical significance of this institution varies from country to country, partly as a result of differences in tax laws. In some countries, usufruct arrangements are frequent, while in other civil-law systems the elaborate code provisions dealing with usufruct are virtually a dead letter.

Apart from the usufruct device, it is possible in some (but not all) civil-law countries to create certain forms of future interests in a decedent's entire estate (as distinguished from future interests in individual pieces of property). See Merryman, *id.* at 932–34; Rheinstein, *supra* note 1. For a case in which an American court had to deal with such a civil-law-type future interest, see Hedwig Zietz, 34 T.C. 351 (1960), discussed by O. C. Sommerich & B. Busch, The German First Heir: Owner or Life Tenant?, 11 Am. J.Comp.L. 92 (1962).

5. In civil law countries the *numerus clausus* principle enjoyed tremendous success

(roughly equivalent to mortgages) and servitudes (similar to easements) usually are the most important of the rights so catalogued.[6]

The resulting simplicity of the substantive law of real property greatly contributes to the speed and security of land transactions. In some civil-law countries, notably in Germany, Switzerland and Austria, the marketability of real property is further enhanced by a highly efficient registration system.[7] The materials which follow deal with some aspects of that system.

GERMAN CIVIL CODE

Sec. 873. For any transfer [meaning transfer by transaction inter vivos] of title to land, for the creation of any right in rem encumbering the owner's title, and also for transferring or encumbering such a right in rem, it is necessary, except as otherwise provided by law, that the proper parties agree on the change to be effected, and that the same be registered in the land register.

Sec. 891. If in the land register a right has been registered in the name of a person, it is presumed that the right exists and belongs to such person. [This presumption is rebuttable.]

If a registered right has been canceled in the land register, it is presumed that the right does not exist. [This presumption is rebuttable.]

Sec. 892. For the benefit of a person who by a jural act [i.e., his own jural act, as distinguished from an acquisition by inheritance or by operation of law] acquires an in rem right with respect to a parcel of land, or an in rem right with respect to such right, the entries in the land register are

---

since the enactment of the French civil code 1804: U. Mattei, Basic Principles of Property Law 14 (2000). Many legal systems, not only those belonging to the civil law tradition, codified the *numerus clausus* principle: e.g., Japanese C.C. (Act No. 89 of 1896), Art. 175; Argentine C.C. of 1869 (Law 340), Art. 2502; Louisiana C.C. of 1808, Art. 476–478; Thai Civil and Commercial Code of 1928, Art. 1298; Israeli Land Law No. 5729 of 1969, sec. 2–5. The existence of a similar idea in common law has gained special attention only recently, when economic theories developed to explain the rationale behind that rule. For in-depth analysis, see B. Rudden, Economic Theory v. Property Law: The *Numerus Clausus* Problem, in J. Eekelaar & J. Bell (eds.), Oxford Essays in Jurisprudence 239 (Third Series, (1987)); M. Heller, The Boundaries of Private Property, 108, Yale L.J. 1163, 1177 (1999); T. W. Merrill & H. E. Smith, Optimal Standardization in the Law of Property: The Numerus Clausus Principle, 110 Yale L.J. 1 (2000); F. Parisi, Entropy in Property, 50 Am.J.Comp.L. 595 (2002); H. Hansmann & R. Kraakman, Property, Contract and Verifi-

cation: The Numerus Clausus Problem and the Verification of Property Rights, Harvard Law School, Public Law Research Paper no. 37 (2002), available at SSRN: http://ssrn.com/abstract=323301.

6. For the catalogue of rights in rem permitted by German law, see J. Kohler, Property Law (Sachenrecht), in Introduction to German Law 239–244 (M. Reimann & J. Zekoll eds., 2005). Leases are not mentioned in the catalogue. In Germany, as in the majority of civil-law countries, a lease constitutes a mere contract, and as a rule does not create rights in rem.

7. For a detailed comparative discussion of land registration systems in continental countries (with emphasis on the law of Denmark) see the second volume of F. V. Kruse, The Right of Property (David Philipp trans., 1953). More recently, for a historical and comparative overview of the cadastral and land registration systems also beyond the civilian borders, see G. Larsson, Land Registration and Cadastral Systems: Tools of Land Information and Management (2001).

deemed to be correct, unless an objection against the correctness [of a particular entry] has been registered, or unless the incorrectness [of the entry] is known to the acquirer. If the [registered] holder of a right registered in the land register is subject to a restriction of his power to dispose of such right, and if such restriction exists for the benefit of a particular person,[8] the restriction is not effective as against the acquirer unless it appears in the land register or is known to the acquirer....

SWISS CIVIL CODE

Art. 656. For the acquisition of title to immovable property, an entry [of the transfer] in the land register is necessary.[9]

When, however, title is acquired by ... inheritance, expropriation, execution or judicial decree, the purchaser becomes the owner already before he is registered as such; but he can dispose of the property only when the registration has occurred.

Art. 973. Whoever in good faith has relied upon an entry in the land register, and thereby acquired property or other real rights, is to be protected in such acquisition.[10]

E. J. Cohn (Assisted by W. Zdzieblo): Manual of German Law*

2d Ed. 1968, Vol. 1, Pp. 186–89.

Dispositions regarding immovable property are valid only if the effect which the disposition purports to have is noted in the land register (*Grundbuch*) either by way of an entry or by a cancellation of an existing entry. In addition to the entry or cancellation the parties must conclude an agreement to the effect that the disposition is to come into force. This agreement may be replaced by some other fact such as, e.g., a judgment of a court of law, prescription etc.

No entry is required where rights are transferred by law as, e.g., in case of succession.

Example: A, the owner of Redacre, dies. B is his successor. In this case B becomes owner of Redacre at the time of A's death, even though this

---

8. *Example*: During bankruptcy, the bankrupt is restricted in his power to dispose of assets. This restriction exists "for the benefit" of a particular person, to wit, the trustee in bankruptcy. Suppose X, the owner of Blackacre, goes into bankruptcy. Thereafter, but before the fact of bankruptcy is registered in the land register, X sells and transfers Blackacre to bona fide purchaser Y. Pursuant to the second sentence of § 892 quoted in the text, *supra*, Y acquires good title.

9. ... tapu sicilinde kayit arttir (Turkish Civil Code, sec. 633). Did that make sense

in Turkey in 1926, and does it now? (Tapu sicili = land register; there was none in 1926.)

10. The careful reader will have noticed that these two articles of the Swiss Code in substance lay down the same rules as are contained in §§ 873 and 892 of the German Code, *supra*. But note the striking difference in style!

* Reprinted by permission of The British Institute of International and Comparative Law. Footnotes added.

has not been entered in the *Grundbuch*. The contents of the *Grundbuch* have therefore become inaccurate and B may apply for a correction.

Only dispositions, i.e., the creation, transfer, encumbrance and cancellation of absolute rights in respect of immovable property, require registration and are capable of it. Contractual rights cannot and must not be registered.[1]

> *Example:* (*a*) A sells Redacre to B. This is merely a contract. As such it cannot be registered.

> (*b*) A complies with his obligations under the contract of sale and transfers Redacre to B. This can and must be registered. Without registration the transfer is not valid.

The *Grundbuch* is not a register of deeds. It is a register of titles showing the legal situation of the immovable property to which it refers. . . .

If a right has been registered in the *Grundbuch* in the name of any person, it is presumed that the right exists and belongs to that person. Similarly if a right registered in the *Grundbuch* has been cancelled, it is presumed that the right does not exist (see section 891 *BGB*). These presumptions are rebuttable.

> *Example:* If A, who is registered as owner of Redacre in the *Grundbuch*, sues B, the possessor of Redacre, in order to obtain a judgment of eviction, he need not prove that he is the owner, but B may prove that A is not the owner.

In favour of a person who acquires a right in respect of immovable property by way of a transaction *inter vivos*, the entries in the *Grundbuch* are deemed to be correct, unless the transferee knows of their incorrectness. Sec. 892 *BGB*. This is often referred to as the rule of public faith (*öffentlicher Glaube*) of the *Grundbuch*. It should, however, be noted that it does not require any reliance on the part of the transferee upon the contents of the *Grundbuch*. The transferee is protected in any case in which he did not positively know that the contents of the *Grundbuch* were incorrect. It does not matter whether his ignorance was due to lack of care. It does not even matter whether he ever consulted the *Grundbuch*. Even if he did not know the actual contents of the *Grundbuch* the latter are treated as if they were correct.

> *Example:* A, who is registered as owner of Redacre sells and transfers Redacre to B who is not aware of the fact that C is the true owner of Redacre, A having been registered by a clerical mistake as owner of Redacre, instead of as owner of Slumhouse, which adjoins Redacre. B acquires the ownership of Redacre in consequence of the transfer. C

---

1. It should be noted, however, that a *Vormerkung* (preliminary notation) can be registered for the purpose of securing the future performance of a registree's promise to grant, transfer, alter or cancel a registrable right (§ 883 BGB). See 1 Cohn, Manual of German Law 198 (2d ed. 1968).

loses it and has only a claim against A on the ground of delict or unjust enrichment, sections 892, 823(1), 816 *BGB*, or against the official at the land register office or the state employing him for damages ...

NOTES AND QUESTIONS

(1) *A*, the registered owner of Greenacre, executed a notarial agreement with *B* by which Greenacre was to be sold and transferred to *B*. The notary before whom this agreement was made normally would see to it that without delay *B* will be registered as the new owner. In the instant case, however, one of the parties to the notarial agreement, being unable to appear in person before the notary, was represented by an attorney-in-fact, and the latter's power of attorney had not been executed in proper form; therefore, before submitting the documents for registration, the notary had to wait for a properly executed power of attorney. In the meantime, while the registration of the transfer to *B* is thus delayed, *A* is approached by *C* who offers to purchase Greenacre from *A*. The facts of the pending transaction between *A* and *B* are known to *C*; but *C*, who is anxious to acquire Greenacre and also has a grudge against *B*, by the offer of a higher price and of immediate cash payment persuades *A* to "forget about *B*." In order to carry out their scheme, *A* and *C* go to a different notary (i.e., a notary other than the one who recorded the transaction between *A* and *B*) and tell him that *A* wishes to sell and transfer Greenacre to *C*. The notary routinely checks the register and finds that *A* is registered as the owner; the register, at this point, does not indicate anything concerning the transaction between *A* and *B*. Thus the notary will not hesitate to record the contract between *A* and *C* and the transfer from *A* to *C*. These documents then are promptly submitted to the registration office, and *C* is registered as the new owner.

What are *B's* rights and remedies under German law?

At first blush, *B* appears to be in a difficult position. The plain language of § 873 of the German Civil Code indicates that *C*, since he was the first to obtain registration, obtained good title to Greenacre, regardless of whether he acted in good or bad faith. Thus, on the face of the Code provision, one might conclude that *B* has lost his chance of acquiring Greenacre, and that he is relegated to an action seeking to recover damages for breach of contract from *A* (who may be judgment-proof, if he has managed quickly to dispose of the cash payment received from *C*).

A German court, however, would be able to reach a more equitable result by resorting to one of the "general clauses" of the Civil Code. Sec. 826 of that Code provides that

> One who intentionally damages another in a manner which is contra bonos mores, is liable to the other for restoration of the damage thus caused.

A German court probably would have no difficulty in finding that *C* as well as *A* is liable under this section, since grudge and collusion are involved,[1] but there

---

1. See O. Palandt, Bürgerliches Gesetzbuch § 826, Anno. 8 q RdNr. 52 (63th ed. 2004) and the decisions cited *infra* note 2.

remains the question whether *B* can recover the property itself, as distinguished from money damages. Sec. 826 appears in that part of the Code which deals with torts, and a lawyer brought up in the common law might think that it permits only the recovery of money damages. A reader familiar with the earlier parts of this book, however, will recall another code provision which must be considered at this point: the restitution-in-kind rule embodied in § 249. As the reader knows, that section (which appears in the first part of the Second Book and thus deals with all "obligations," whether based on contract, quasi-contract or tort) provides as follows:

> He who is liable in damages, has to bring about the condition which would exist if the circumstances making him liable had not occurred. If the liability exists for injury to a person or damage to tangible property, then the obligee [at his election] may demand, instead of restitution in kind, the sum of money necessary to effect such restitution.

Under this provision it is possible for *B*, in a tort action, to obtain a judgment against *C* for the recovery of Greenacre.[2] The result thus reached derives additional strength from the doctrine of abuse of rights (see *infra* sec. 3C).

It is interesting to compare the German treatment of this rather common problem with the U.S. approach. The common-law rule gave priority to the first transferee, regardless of the good or bad faith of the later transferee.[3] This rule proved to be a serious obstacle to real estate transactions, because no purchaser could ever be quite sure that his vendor had not executed an effective prior conveyance. To overcome this defect of the law, a recording system was necessary, and such a system could be introduced only by legislation. In England and in some of the American colonies, recording statutes were enacted at an early date. Today, recording or registration acts exist in virtually all common-law jurisdictions. In the United States, the predominant type of recording statute, exemplified by § 291 of the New York Real Property Law, is the so-called "notice-race-statute."[4] Under such a statute, the later transferee prevails if he is the first to have his purchase duly recorded, and if he has acquired his interest in good faith and for a valuable consideration.

Contrast this with the German system. Under that system, the basic rule is that among multiple transferees the one first registered will prevail.[5] In other words, the German rule is the exact opposite of the common-law rule. But just as the common-law rule had to be altered in favor of a subsequent *bona fide* transferee who is the first to record, the seemingly unqualified command of § 873 of the German Civil Code has to be modified so as to withhold the

---

2. See Decision of the Reichsgericht of Dec. 9, 1905, RGZ 62, 137, followed by BGH, decision of June 2, 1981, 1981 N.J.W. 2180. As reiterated in BGH decision of November 19, 1993, 1994 N.J.W. 128, 129, however, § 826 BGB applies in such cases "only if there are grave violations of moral sentiment . . . i.e., conduct of the third party which is incompatible with the basic requirements of loyal legal instinct."

3. See 14 Powell on Real Property, § 82.02 (M.A. Wolf ed. 2000 & Supps.).

4. See *ibid.*

5. In the United States, a similar result is reached in the very few states having a "race-type" recording statute. See *ibid.*

benefits of the section from a later transferee who becomes the first to be registered but who has acted *in bad faith.*

This is a fine example of the phenomenon of convergence so often observed in comparative law. Although the starting points of the two systems—i.e., of the common-law system, on the one hand, and the system of the German and German-inspired codes, on the other—were diametrically opposed to each other, rather similar solutions have emerged in the end. Today it seems to be the law, both under an American recording statute of the predominant type and under the German and German-influenced codes, that in cases of multiple transfers the transferee first recorded or registered as a rule will prevail, provided he did not act with knowledge of a prior (though as yet unrecorded or unregistered) transfer.

Thus, by a process of convergence, a large area of agreement among seemingly diverse legal systems has come into existence. Yet, the agreement is not complete. The remaining differences in the starting point or in theory are apt to make themselves felt on occasion, especially in somewhat exceptional fact situations, such as that presented in the next Illustration.

(2) In proper notarial form, *X* (the registered owner) has sold and deeded Redacre first to *Y*, a purchaser for value, and later to *Z*. The latter is a donee, i.e., he has neither promised nor paid value; but he does not know, and has no reason to know, of the previous transaction between *X* and *Y*. If in this case *Z* is the one who first obtains recordation or registration, he will acquire title and prevail over *Y* under § 873 of the German Civil Code; *Y* will be relegated to an action for damages against *X*, and will have no cause of action against *Z*, who acted in perfectly good faith and whose conduct, consequently, was not tortious.[6] Under most of the American recording statutes, on the other hand, it would seem that *Y* prevails over *Z* in this case, because *Z* is not a purchaser for value.[7] In such a situation, *Z* is not protected by the statute, and *Y*'s common-law priority thus becomes decisive under U.S. law.

(3) *A*, the registered owner of Blackacre, is judicially declared incompetent because of insanity. Without the consent of his committee, he sells and transfers Blackacre to *B*. As *A* succeeds in concealing his incompetency from *B*, from the officiating notary, and from the land register official, the transaction is registered, and *B* is entered as the new owner. Upon discovering the transaction, *A*'s committee sues *B* for retransfer of the property to *A*.

Under German law, *B* loses. If *A* had been declared bankrupt, his power to dispose of Blackacre would have become restricted, and within the meaning of § 892 such restriction would have existed "for the benefit" of a particular person, i.e., the trustee in bankruptcy. Such a limitation is registrable, and in the absence of an appropriate entry in the register, *B* would be protected in his

6. A German lawyer representing *Y* would examine the question whether his client might have a cause of action against *Z* on the theory of unjust enrichment (Civil Code §§ 812 ff., especially 816, 822); but since *X*, from whom *Z* acquired his title, at the time of the transfer to *Z* was not only registered as owner, but actually *was the owner*, the theory of unjust enrichment prob-ably would be no more successful than the tort theory.

7. The term "purchaser" implies this requirement in U.S. law. See Powell, *supra* at § 82.02. Moreover, some statutes, such as McKinney's N.Y. Real Property Law § 291, contain express language spelling out the re-quirement.

bona fide belief that *A* is not bankrupt. But lack of capacity due to incompetency is a different matter; it need not, and indeed cannot, be registered in the land register,[8] because a person's lack of capacity is not a restriction (upon his power of disposal) which exists "for the benefit of a particular person." Therefore, Sec. 892 does not apply by its terms. It is true that one who relies on an entry in the Grundbuch, or the lack of an entry therein, is protected by the principle of "public faith"; but this does not apply to non-registrable matters such as lack of capacity.

(4) Same facts as above; but before being sued by *A*'s committee, *B* sells and transfers Blackacre to *C*. *A*'s committee now sues *C*.

C wins. He acquired the property from a person who, though not the owner, was registered as such. Therefore, *A* has lost his title to *C*, unless *A*'s committee can prove that *C* actually knew of *B*'s lack of title.

C would be equally protected if the transfer from *A* to *B* (or any previous transfer of the same property) had suffered from any other kind of defect. It follows that *C*, before purchasing Blackacre, did not have to search the title back to Charlemagne or Friedrich Barbarossa; all he or his legal adviser had to do was to inspect the land register—a task which, except in unusually complicated cases, will not take more than five or ten minutes of an experienced person's time.[9]

C has not only saved time; but his title, also, is much more secure than under a system which subjects his rights to virtually undiscoverable hazards, such as the title of an adverse possessor, or the many types of conditions, limitations, defects and equities that may lurk somewhere in the chain of deeds upon which his own title depends.[10]

(5) In a case decided by the West German Supreme Court on July 11, 1952, BGHZ 7, 64, the facts were as follows: Plaintiff *P* was the owner, and registered as the owner, of a stately villa in Berlin. At the end of April, 1945, Berlin was

---

8. See F. Baur, Sachenrecht § 15 IV RdNr 29–34 (17th ed. 1999). The only interests and limitations which are permanently registrable are the following: (a) the title of the owner or owners; (b) any rights of other persons (within the catalogue established by the Code) which encumber or restrict the owner's title, especially mortgages and servitudes; (c) transfers of, or encumbrances upon, the rights listed under (b), such as an assignment or pledge of a mortgage; and (d) restrictions upon the power of alienation of a person who has a right registered pursuant to (a), (b) or (c), provided that the restriction operates "for the benefit of a particular person."

9. Tax liens and other encumbrances created by public law are not registrable under the German system. Such liens and encumbrances, therefore, are not covered by § 892, and can be asserted even against a purchaser who had no knowledge of their existence. The notary recording the transaction, however, is under a duty to warn the purchaser of the possible existence of tax liens and the like; and since the public agencies and authorities who conceivably might be the lienees of such liens are known and not too numerous, the purchaser or his attorney usually can make the necessary inquiries within a short time, even if he is not satisfied with the receipts or other documents submitted to him by the vendor. Moreover, in practice, the problem often is solved by an escrow arrangement; the notary, serving as escrow agent, will hold a certain part of the purchase price and pay it over to the vendor only after he has convinced himself that certain tax liens or other public-law encumbrances are non-existent or have been removed. See F. Baur, *supra* note 8, § 15 IV RdNr. 40.

10. E.g., forgeries, matters of heirship, reversionary interests, marriage and divorce, infancy, insanity, etc.

conquered by the Russian army, and a Russian colonel by the name of *S* became military commandant of the part of the city where the villa was situated. In June, 1945, *S* decided to donate the villa to Mrs. *K*, a local resident who had no connection with *P*, but presumably had managed to endear herself to *S*. There was no sale or transfer from *P* to Mrs. *K*; but *S* and Mrs. *K* "persuaded" the German mayor to issue an official document certifying that *S* had "donated" the villa to Mrs. *K*. Through an attorney, Mrs. *K* submitted this document to the officials in charge of the land register, and asked to be registered as the new owner. As the document on its face was most irregular, the officials at first hesitated to register the transfer of title from *P* to Mrs. *K*; but they were told that unless such transfer were registered within 24 hours, they would be summarily executed or sent to Siberia. Under the circumstances then prevailing in Berlin, the credibility of this threat could not reasonably be doubted, and the officials—with the blessing of their superiors, who had been hurriedly consulted—registered Mrs. *K* as owner. In November, 1945, Mrs. *K* by notarial document sold and transferred the villa to defendant *D*, who paid a substantial price, and on Dec. 1, 1945, *D* was registered as owner.

Subsequently, *P* brought an action against *D* for the recovery of the villa. As *P* was unable to offer any evidence of bad faith on the part of *D*, the latter had to be treated as a bona fide purchaser. Pointing this out, and applying § 892 of the Civil Code, the court of first instance dismissed *P*'s action. The intermediate appellate court and the Supreme Court, however, held in favor of *P*. The reasoning of the highest court can be summarized as follows: As a matter of international law as well as German law, it is clear that Mrs. *K* never acquired title. Nevertheless, since *D* was not shown to have had any knowledge of Mrs. *K*'s lack of title, the plain language of § 892 would mandate a decision in *D*'s favor were it not for the unprecedented circumstances under which Mrs. *K* became registered as owner. The registration system is a facility organized and operated by the State. Ordinarily every entry in the land register is an official act, and it is this official quality of the entry upon which its "public faith"—ordained by § 892—is necessarily based. An entry, however, that has been brought about by physical threats against the officials in charge of the register cannot be recognized as an official act.[11] Thus the essential reason for giving the entry its normal effect, as provided in § 892, is lacking here.

The German Supreme Court probably was right in feeling that there is a limit beyond which the principle of the register's "public faith" should not be carried, and that this limit is reached when under the impact of war-connected events the very foundation of the registration system—the independent power and responsibility of the officials in charge—has broken down. It is important to note, however, that the fact situation which gave rise to this decision was most extraordinary and indeed unique in the annals of the German land registration system. On the whole, it must be said that in spite of repeated

---

11. In this context, the court referred to the elaborate body of principles which has been developed by German scholars and administrative courts concerning "*fehlerhafte Staatsakte*" (defective official acts). Such acts may be either "voidable," i.e., susceptible of being set aside through appeals or other reg- ular remedies, or absolutely void. In the principal case, the entry in the land register concerning the transfer to Mrs. *K* was held to be void. See W. Jellinek, Der fehlerhafte Staatsakt und seine Wirkungen. Eine verwaltungs- und prozessrechtliche Studie (1908; 2d repr. 1st ed. 1974).

political and economic upheavals that system has operated smoothly and efficiently since the beginning of the present century.

(6) As the preceding notes have shown, the proper working of a German-style land registration system depends on the competence and incorruptibility of the notaries and registrars who operate the system.

Little imagination is required to conjure up fact situations involving the following elements: (a) Goldacre is owned by X, and X is properly registered as owner. (b) Y, a crook, in some way—due to negligence or corruption on the part of notary or registrar—manages to have a transfer of Goldacre from X to Y registered in the land register. (c) This transfer was never consented to by X; indeed until much later X knows nothing of the whole transaction, which has been brought about by criminal methods (e.g., by forging X's signature, or by a co-conspirator of Y impersonating X). (d) As soon as he is registered as owner, Y sells and transfers Goldacre to Z, and absconds with the proceeds. Z is a bona fide purchaser, i.e., a person whose bad faith cannot be proved. In a situation like this, it is clear that under a provision such as § 892 of the German Civil Code poor X has lost Goldacre, i.e., his title to that property.

In Germany, where notaries and land register officials are apt to be highly competent and incorruptible, situations of this kind arise infrequently. When they do arise, it is possible for the victim to invoke the State's liability for negligent or intentional wrongdoing of its officials,[12] or to recover from the notary who always carries liability insurance.

It goes without saying, however, that it may be dangerous to export the German land registration system to a country—e.g., a developing country—where competence and incorruptibility of notaries and registrars are not as assured as in Germany. If the principle of "public faith" is applied in such a country, large numbers of owners might lose their properties as the result of crooked machinations. In order to avoid these dire consequences, the courts in such a country perhaps will modify the system, e.g., by holding that a purchaser who fails carefully to examine the vendor's whole chain of title is not acting in good faith.[13] Such a holding, however, although it may protect innocent victims of corrupt schemes, destroys the efficiency of the system as a cheap and expeditious mechanism for land transfers.[14]

(7) Many common-law jurisdictions have adopted the so-called Torrens system of registration of title, as distinguished from mere recordation of muniments of title. Although historically independent of the continental system, the Torrens method is similar in its practical effect.[15] In the United States, it has been

---

12. Pursuant to constitutional and statutory provisions, the State is liable for the registrar's negligence. Insofar as notaries are concerned, a specific enactment (§ 19 of the Bundesnotarordnung) provides, by way of an exception to the general rule of state liability for the wrongdoing of officials, that the notary himself must respond for his torts, and that there is no state liability. From the standpoint of the victim, however, this does not make too much difference; in effect he can still sue a "deep pocket," because the notary's liability is always covered by insurance.

13. Apparently, this is what has happened in Mexico. See the exceedingly interesting article by B. Kozolchyk, The Mexican Land Registry: A Critical Evaluation, 12 Ariz. L.Rev. 308 (1970), where the Mexican case law is analyzed.

14. See *ibid*.

15. For a brief description of the operation of the Torrens system, see United States

adopted in a minority of jurisdictions; but even in those jurisdictions it is generally optional with the owner whether he wishes to register his title. It seems that, except in a few communities, registration has been sought for only a small fraction of all titles.[16]

The question whether title registration should be made compulsory, as it is in Germany and Switzerland, is highly controversial in the United States. Up to now the proponents of compulsory registration have been beaten in every state; but the controversy is not yet settled. The following questions, therefore, are not wholly academic:

Do we subscribe to the basic policy considerations which underlie the German and Swiss provisions quoted above? Do the tendencies of the modern welfare state, especially in matters of urban development, make the unimpeded marketability of real estate less important, or more important, as compared to the days of 19th century laissez faire?

Does recording of deeds, in combination with title insurance, afford the purchaser or mortgagee the same degree of protection which he enjoys in Germany or Switzerland, or under the Torrens system?

Does the necessity of title search and title insurance slow down transfers, and add to their cost? On the other hand, how expensive is the initial setting up of a registration system?[17]

v. Ryan, 124 F.Supp. 1 (D.Minn., 3d Div. 1954). For more extensive treatment, see B. C. Schick & I. H. Plotkin, Torrens in the United States (1978); P. O'Connor, Land Registration: Registration of Title in England and Australia: A Theoretical and Comparative Analysis, in Modern Studies in Property Law II, 81 (E. Cooke ed., 2003).

With respect to the underlying theory, American registration statutes differ from the German system. Under our statutes, unregistered interests are eliminated by the combined operation of the doctrines of "jurisdiction in rem" and "res judicata." Therefore, a judicial proceeding is indispensable; but upon successful completion of the proceeding the title of the first registered owner (and not only that of bona fide transferees purchasing from him) becomes indefeasible. The German system, on the other hand, is based on the principle of protecting the bona fide purchaser; under that system, an indefeasible title is acquired, not by the first person to be registered as owner, but only by his first bona fide transferee. The initial registration was effected in Germany by way of a simpler and less expensive judicial proceeding than under our registration statutes.

Concerning a third possible theory justifying the elimination of unrecorded interests (time limitation), see text *infra* at note 22.

16. In England, on the other hand, there were nearly sixteen million registered land titles in 1996, corresponding to three quarters of the total number of titles—with the "real prospect that, within a few years, unregistered conveyancing will be largely a thing of the past." The Law Commission, Thirty–First Annual Report 1996, at 34. Common lands and village greens, too, have now been registered. See A. Samuels, Common Land and Rights of Common: How the Commons Registration Act 1965 has Worked Out, 49 Conv. & Prop. Lawyer 24 (1985). The Land Registration Act 2002, in force since October 13, 2003 (and its implementing legislation recently completed by the Land Registration (Amendments) Rules 2008) is the last stage of the slow legislative process of adopting compulsory land registration in England and Wales, and, at the same time, of fostering the development of fully electronic conveyancing. See, e.g., C. Harpum & J. Bignell, Registered Land. Law and Practice under the Land Registration Act 2002 (2004).

17. A study conducted by an economist has shown that—even allowing for the cost of the initial registration procedure—a registration system is considerably less expensive, and thus less of a burden on real estate transfers, than our traditional recording system. See J. T. Janczyk, An Economic Analysis of the Land Title Systems for Transfer-

In Germany and Switzerland (and in Puerto Rico)[18] the public servants in charge of the land register are judges or other well-qualified officials. In addition, most of the documents necessary for registration must be prepared by, or executed before, a highly trained Notary (see *supra* ch. I, sec. 1B). Are continental United States institutions equally suitable for the efficient operation of a registration system?

Can a compulsory registration system work efficiently in a jurisdiction where the substantive law of real property is complex, and where the number of registrable transactions presumably would be swelled (as compared to Germany) by the inclusion of leases, at least of long-term leases?

The German system has been used, and occasionally abused, for fiscal and regulatory purposes. The system makes it easy to decree that certain transactions may not be registered unless payment of transfer taxes is proved, or unless some administrative permit is obtained and exhibited to the registrar. Can a system of recording deeds be used or abused in the same way?

The compulsory registration system has been adopted in some civilian code jurisdictions and in some common-law jurisdictions. It has been rejected or long delayed both in civil-law[19] and common-law jurisdictions. Thus, as usual in difficult matters, we do not deal with a simple civil-law—common-law dichotomy. What are the forces which bring about, or successfully oppose, the adoption of the system? Is it a question of weighing opposing arguments? Of initial expense vs. continuing social cost? Of rationality vs. tradition? Of title insurance companies and other vested interests vs. the one group which is rarely aided by lobbyists: the general public?

If as a matter of practical politics we must conclude that in this country a workable compulsory registration system is presently unobtainable, can we secure some of the benefits of such a system by other methods, such as Marketable Title Acts or similar attempts to use time limitations for the purpose of extinguishing old interests lurking in the chain of title?[20]

---

ring Real Property, 6 J.Leg.Stud. 213 (1977). This is also the conclusion reached by C. Dent Bostick, Land Title Registration: An English Solution to an American Problem, 63 Ind.L.J. 55 (1988).

18. The Puerto Rican registration system, which follows the Spanish model, is described by H. M. Brau del Toro, Apuntes para un curso sobre el estado del Derecho Inmobiliario Registral Puertorriqueño, bajo la Ley Hipotecaria de 1893, 48 Rev.Jur. U.P.R. 111–495 (1979), and by E. Vazquez Bote, 15 Tratado Teorico, Practico y Critico de Derecho Privado Puertorriqueño: Derecho Inmobiliario Registral (II) (1992); L. R. Rivera Rivera, Derecho Inmobiliario Registral Puertorriqueño (2d ed. 2002).

19. The French system, reformed in 1955, in its essential features is more similar to an American recording statute than to the German Grundbuch. See 2 M. Ferid & H. J.

Sonnenberger, Das französische Zivilrecht 599–600 (2d ed. 1986). For a comparison of the French and German systems, see F. Sturm, Bringt die französische Bodenregisterreform eine Annäherung an das deutsche Grundbuchrecht?, in M. Ferid (ed.), Festschrift für Hans G. Ficker 459 (1967); J. Zevenbergen, Registration of property rights; a systems approach—Similar tasks, but different roles, Notarius International 125, 133 ff. (2003). A fertile field of comparison has been Alsace–Lorraine after 1918, where some (but not all) features of the German system survived under French rule.

20. For references see Powell, *supra,* at § 82.04; P. E. Basye, Clearing Land Titles §§ 171–189 (2d ed. 1970 & 1985 Supp.). The relevant constitutional issues are highlighted by Board of Education of Central School Dist. No. 1 v. Miles, 15 N.Y.2d 364, 259 N.Y.S.2d 129, 207 N.E.2d 181 (1965).

As between the sharply conflicting answers which have been given to each of these questions[21] the reader will have to make his or her own choice, keeping in mind that technological advances in the storage and retrieval of data are rapidly adding a new dimension to the old controversies.[22]

(b) The Principle of Publicity in Transactions Not Relating to Land

One brought up in the common law, even one who favors the Torrens system, is apt to think of it purely in terms of the problem at hand, i.e., of improving the method by which real property is conveyed. To the civilian lawyer, whose tradition tends to encourage broader, more abstractly formulated propositions, the *Grundbuch* is merely one application of a pervasive principle: the *principle of publicity*.[1] The essence of this principle is that all rights and legal relations which may harm or trap an innocent purchaser, or otherwise interfere with the reasonable expectations of persons entering into ordinary every-day transactions, must be made public in some form recognizable to purchasers and other participants in such transactions. With respect to chattels, the principle leads to the postulate that ownership should be publicized by possession; the innocent purchaser may assume that the possessor is the owner, and one who purchases from the possessor will ordinarily acquire good title, even though it turns out that the possessor was a faithless bailee.[2]

There are, however, many types of rights and legal relations which cannot be adequately publicized by possession. In those instances, the principle of publicity usually leads to a requirement of registration in a public register. The land register is one example. Another type of register which is in use in some civil-law countries is the register of matrimonial property rights, designed to publicize the restrictions upon the capacity and the power of alienation of married women, or of their husbands, due to community property or other matrimonial arrangements.[3]

In a typical civil-law country, one encounters a number of public registers thus devoted to the implementation of the principle of publicity.[4]

---

21. For references, see the writings cited *supra* note 169.

22. In England the Land Registration Act 2002 (see above fn. 171) introduced a fully electronic conveyancing system. The automation of the *Grundbuch* in the German *Länder* is a process initiated on the basis of the *Registerverfahrensbeschleunigungsgesetz* of 20 December 1993 (BGBl. I, 2182) and which has been completed in numerous *Länder*.

1. See, for all, F. Baur, *supra* note 8, § 4 RdNr. 9ff.

2. This is the rule in the majority of civil-law systems. Normally the bona fide purchaser is not protected, however, if the possessor turns out to be a thief who has acquired possession without the owner's consent (e.g. see art. 2276 para 2 French civil code). See also *supra* at 392ff.

3. See., e.g., § 1412 BGB, according to which changes to the matrimonial property status contractually agreed by the spouses are effective as against third parties only if they are registered in the matrimonial property register (Güterrechtsregister), or otherwise known to the third party.

4. The reader may be surprised to learn, however, that a public register of non-possessory security interests in movable property—i.e., the kind of public record

In connection with business and commercial activity, the most important of these is the Register of Commerce, already familiar to the reader (see the Note on "Civil" and "Commercial" Law, *supra* sec. 1).[5] The way in which it implements the principle of publicity is shown by the code provisions which follow.[6]

GERMAN COMMERCIAL CODE

Sec. 5. Once a firm[7] is registered in the Register of Commerce, it is not permissible to deny, as against a party invoking the registration, that the business conducted by such firm is a commercial business.

which Art. 9 of the U.C.C. has so successfully established in U.S. law—does *not yet* exist in civil-law countries. The result is that in some of those countries, such as Germany, one encounters unpublicized non-possessory security interests. These are hard to reconcile with the principle of publicity, and often constitute a trap for unwary creditors; but the German courts have recognized their validity. See N. Horn, H. Kötz & H. G. Leser, German Private and Commercial Law: An Introduction 185–88 (T. Weir trans., 1982); 1 E. J. Cohn, *supra* n. 154, §§ 256 & 354. In other civil-law countries, legislators and courts have taken the opposite view: that in the absence of a register in which non-possessory security interests could be recorded, security interests in personal property as a rule cannot be created without delivery of possession. This has been the traditional approach of French law as well as of all other civil law countries, which based their secured transactions laws on the French model: see, e.g., M. Bussani, Le droit civil des sûretés réelles. Le modèle italien, 6 Eur.Rev.Priv.L. 23 ff. (1998). However, the 2006 French reform of the law of secured transactions (ordonnance of March 23, 2006, no. 2006–346) modernized the law by introducing a new registered pledge. In this new system publicity is a necessary requirement for the effectiveness of the security as against third parties (be they subsequent purchasers of the collateral or other creditors) in the debtor's insolvency (see new Arts. 2333 and 2337 French c.c.).

In a number of civil-law countries, Art. 9 has been, and is being, carefully studied with a view to the eventual adoption of a similar solution. The U.C.C. pattern has also been the basis of the Model Law on Secured Transactions elaborated by the European Bank of Reconstructions and Development of 1994 (see J.-H. Röver, Vergleichenden Prinzipien dinglicher Sicherheiten (1999)).

On the different civil law regimes with respect to security interests in movable property, see Report of the Secretary–General: Study on Security Interests (A/CN.9/131), prepared by Ulrich Drobnig, in 8 UNCITRAL Yearbook 171 (1977); E.–M. Kieninger, (ed.), Security Rights in Movable Property in European Private Law (2004). On the European law-making process in this field see The Future of Secured Credit in Europe (H. Eidenmüller & E.-M. Kieninger eds., 2008).

5. The entries made in the Register of Commerce and the documents filed with the Registrar's office are public records. The general rule is that every member of the public has a right to inspect and copy those records. See, e.g., German Commercial Code § 9. The Register of Commerce is run electronically as from January 1, 2007, when Gesetz über elektronische Handelsregister und Genossenschaftsregister sowie das Unternehmensregister of November 10, 2006 (BGBl. I, S. 2553) entered into force.

6. In both France and Germany, the substance of these provisions has been on the books for a long time. However, both countries amended certain details of those provisions in the recent past in order to comply with the compulsory disclosure requirements contained in the First Directive on Company Law Harmonisation issued by the EEC Council of Ministers on March 9, 1968. The code provisions which follow in the text reflect these amendments, which exemplify the way in which Community law increasingly tends to infiltrate the legal systems and affect every-day legal practice in EU member countries.

7. German Commercial Code Sec. 17: "The firm of a merchant is the name under which he conducts his business and signs business documents. A merchant may sue and be sued under his firm name."

. . .

Sec. 15. If a fact which ought to be registered in the Register of Commerce[8] is not registered and published, the person concerning whose affairs the fact should have been registered cannot avail himself of such fact as against a third party, unless such party was aware of the fact.

If the fact has been registered and published, such fact can be relied upon as against a third party. This rule [i.e., the rule stated in the preceding sentence] does not apply to transactions taking place within fifteen days after publication, if the third party proves that he neither knew nor reasonably should have known such fact. . . .

If a registrable fact has been incorrectly published, in that event a third party can avail himself of such fact as published, against the person concerning whose affairs the fact was to be registered, unless the third party was aware of the incorrectness. . . .

* * *

NEW FRENCH COMMERCIAL CODE

Ordonnance no. 2000–912 of September 18, 2000,
O.J. of September 21, 2000 (at 14783).[9]

Art. 64. Entry of a natural person into the Register creates the presumption that he has the quality [i.e., status] of a merchant. Nevertheless, this presumption is inoperative as against third [private] parties and governmental agencies who submit proof to the contrary. Third parties and administrative agencies cannot avail themselves of the presumption if they knew that the person registered was not a merchant.[10]

Art. 65. A person who is required to be registered and has not requested registration within fifteen days from the beginning of his commercial activity cannot avail himself of [the advantages of] his quality of being a merchant until registration, neither with respect to third parties nor with respect to governmental agencies. Nevertheless, he may not

---

8. Among other things, the following must be registered: the legal form under which a business is conducted; all facts pertaining to its ownership; appointment and removal of agents exercising managerial functions, as well as limitations upon, and revocation of, their powers; in the case of a partnership, the names of the general partners, and the names and liability limits of limited partners; in the case of a corporation, the amount of its capital as well as appointment and removal of officers, and limitations upon, and revocation of, their powers.

9. The articles of the new French commercial code reprinted here substitute the Decree No. 84–406 of May 30, 1984, which, however, still regulates some aspects not integrated in the legislative part of the 2000 commercial code. Observe that Art. L123–7 of the commercial code deals solely with individuals (natural persons) rather than with juridical persons. However, entry of corporations and other juridical persons in the Register produces essentially the same effects as the entry of individuals. See J. P. LeGall, Droit Commercial, 64–65, 91 (10th ed. 1985). In addition, the entry of corporations determines legal personality and capacity of these entities (art. 1842 c.c.). See J. Mestre et M.-E. Pancrazi, Droit commercial 189 ff. (25th ed. 2001).

10. Compare this with the even stricter rule of the German Commercial Code § 5. See *infra*, Illus. (5).

invoke his failure to register for the purpose of avoiding responsibilities and obligations inherent in such quality. . . .

Art. 66. In pursuing his activity, the person required to be registered cannot, as against third parties or governmental agencies, avail himself of registrable facts and acts which have not been published in the Register; but such third parties and governmental agencies may nevertheless avail themselves of such facts and acts [against the person who failed to have them registered]. . . .[11]

. . . The provisions in the preceding paragraphs are applicable to facts and acts required to be registered [in the Register of Commerce], even if they have been made public pursuant to some other legal requirement of publicity. These provisions cannot be invoked by third persons and governmental agencies who had personal knowledge of the relevant facts and acts.[12]

NOTES AND QUESTIONS

(1) M, who is a merchant, and is registered as such, appoints X as general manager of his jewelry store and causes this appointment to be registered. On September 15, M fires X and revokes his authority. This latter fact is registered on September 28. On September 26, X, purporting to act for M, purchases jewelry from S, the purchase price of $100,000 to be payable on October 1. S, who did not know that X had been fired, delivered the jewelry to X on September 26. X promptly absconded, taking the jewelry with him. On October 2, S sues M for $100,000. What result under German law? Under French law?[1]

(2) Same facts, except that M is a corporation, and that X was appointed, and later removed, as a corporate officer. Same result?

11. Former Art. 64 of the Commercial Code of 1807, subsequently replaced by Art. 66 of the Decree No. 84–406 of May 30, 1984 and now codified in Art. L123–9 of the new Commercial Code, contained an elaborate enumeration of the facts and acts covered by the provision quoted in the text. Among the facts and acts so covered were, inter alia, "[t]he cessation or revocation of the powers of any person who has been authorized to enter into engagements on behalf of a merchant, a partnership, a corporation, or a public enterprise." In the present version of the relevant provisions, this enumeration has been omitted as unnecessary. There is no doubt, however, that the cessation or revocation of the powers of individuals authorized to act on behalf of a commercial firm continue to be treated as "acts or facts" required to be registered.

12. For details about how the Register is kept in France (there are actually two registers: a local Register and a Duplicate National Register), see the *arrêté* of Feb. 9, 1988, 1998 O.J. 2044, 1988 D.L. 158. In the French Register, individuals who are "merchants" are registered but, since it also is a company register, certain entities which are entities under "civil" law, such as partnerships under "civil" law, also are registered there. Their registration does not imply that they are, technically, merchants.

The existence of a national register facilities statistical studies on numbers and kinds of businesses. On this topic at the European Community level, see Council Regulation 2186/93 of July 22, 1993, 1993 O.J. No. L 196, at 1, on Community coordination in drawing upon business registers for statistical purposes.

1. In comparing the French and German solutions with our own law, the reader should ask under what system it is more likely that disputed and possibly difficult issues of fact will arise.

(3) In 1960, A, B, and C formed and registered a partnership, under the firm name of A & Co. In 1972, C withdrew from the partnership, but his withdrawal was never registered. In April 1979, A & Co. (now consisting of A and B) bought, on credit, merchandise from S at the agreed price of $25,000. In June 1979, A & Co. became insolvent. Shortly thereafter, S sued C for $25,000. What result in France? In Germany?[2]

(4) A is a merchant, but he is not registered. His business friend X buys merchandise priced at $75,000 from Y, on credit; A *orally* promises Y that he (A) will satisfy X's obligation in case X should default. X defaults. Y sues A.

Y wins under German as well as French law. This result flows, not from the principle of publicity, but simply from the fact that A *is* a merchant. As we know, the oral guarantee of a merchant is enforceable in Germany and in France. See *supra* sec. 1. The fact that A is not registered may prevent him from enjoying the advantages of his status; but it does not protect him from the disadvantages. The latter point is explicitly spelled out in the French provisions, while in German law it is taken for granted.

(5) B, who operates as a theatrical manager, but who is not a merchant, on the erroneous advice of his lawyer applied for registration in the Register of Commerce, and was registered as a merchant. His friend X, a television entertainer, hired Y, a famous star, for five appearances on X's show, Y's fee of $40,000 to be payable after the last appearance. B *orally* guaranteed X's obligation to pay Y's fee. Y duly performed, but X defaulted. Y sues B for $40,000. What result under German law? Under French law?

(6) B, the same person as in Illustration 5, has made a contract with P, and under the terms of that contract has forfeited a contractual penalty in the amount of $500,000. The actual damages suffered by P amount to $750, and B feels that the penalty is excessive. Would a German court have power to reduce the penalty?[3]

(7) X Bank agrees to loan $5,000,000 to Y Corp. (a New York corporation) and to Z AG (a German corporation), upon a note on which Y and Z will be jointly and severally liable. Before consummating the transaction, the Bank naturally has to be convinced, by reliable documentary evidence, that the individuals who will sign the note on behalf of Y and Z, respectively, have power to bind the debtor corporations. How much trouble is it to produce such evidence (a) for Y, and (b) for Z?[4]

---

2. Compare § 35 of the Uniform Partnership Act, discussed in J. A. Crane & A. R. Bromberg, Partnership § 81 (1968), as well as §§ 34–35 and 112–128 of the English Companies Act.

3. As to the rules of German law concerning reduction of penalties, see *supra* Chapter 9, Section 1(b) at 933. The penalty promised by B cannot be reduced. The wording of § 5 makes it clear that the merchant status of a registree is irrebuttable and that (contrary to the rule prevailing in situations coming under § 15) it does not even make a difference whether P knew of the incorrectness of the registration.

4. From the German point of view, the question is discussed by K. Jacob–Steinorth, Die Vertretungsmacht bei den wichtigsten amerikanischen Handels-gesellschaften, 1958 Deutsche Notar–Zeitschrift 361. For further references, see H. H. Schippel & H. Schippel, Lateinisches Notariat, 5 Juristen–Jahrbuch 78, 80 (1964/65).

The individuals purporting to represent Y Corp. will need stacks of documents, certified by the secretary of the corporation, in order to prove that they have been duly appointed and that they have the power to represent the corporation in the transaction

(8) In most civil-law countries it is required that foreign enterprises be registered at the national register of commerce of the country in which they carry out their business (see, e.g., §§ 13d ff. German Commercial Code; Art. L 123–1 no. 3, French Commercial Code). In the case of a company doing business in several countries, this requirement often creates problems for the company's lawyers.

Suppose a company incorporated and having its principal place of business in country A seeks to do business in country B. The laws of the latter country are apt to require that the company observe certain formalities in order to "qualify" (to use our terminology) for the doing of business in B. If B is a civil-law country, this process of qualification normally will include registration in B's register of commerce. In cases where A also is a civil-law country, the facts to be registered in B (such as the valid existence and precise legal nature of the registree corporation) normally can be shown quite simply by submitting to the registrar in B a certified copy of the corporation's original registration in A. But if A is a country like the United States, where there is no commercial register, then the facts to be registered in B will have to be proved in other ways, and it will be more difficult to satisfy the official in charge of the register in B, with the result that the whole process of obtaining registration (and thus "qualifying") in B will require considerably more time and effort.[5]

---

3.   The Idea of Justice Boni Mores, Bona Fides and Abus Des Droits—No Separation of Law and Equity

Opinion of the German Reichsgericht in the Matter of G., Plaintiff–Appellant v. F., Defendant–Respondent

3rd Civil Division, October 20, 1933, RGZ 142, 70.

[Plaintiff, an attorney, sues the defendant, his former client, upon a contract providing for contingent remuneration.[1]

Defendant was the lessee of a large hotel property in Berlin. The lease, entered into in 1928, provided for an annual rental of RM 240,000. During the ensuing depression defendant became unable to meet the stipulated rent payments, and around the beginning of 1931 he retained the plaintiff for the purpose of seeking a reduction of rent.

at hand. If these documents raise the faintest doubt concerning an issue of law, the bank probably will, in addition, require an opinion letter to be issued by a law firm. This, of course, adds to the costs of the transaction. It has been observed by experienced international practitioners that in this country the absence of a commercial register often creates a need for lawyers' opinion letters in situations where no such need would exist in a civil-law country. See K. H. Jander & R. Du Mesnil de Rochemont, Die Legal Opinion im Rechtsverkehr mit den USA, 6 Recht der Internationalen Wirtschaft 332, 333 (1976). See also M. Gruson, S. Hutter & M. Kutschera, Legal Opinions in International Transactions: Foreign Lawyers' Response to U.S. Opinion Requests (2d ed. 1989).

5. See E. C. Stiefel, "As They See Us": Typische Rechtsprobleme bei amerikanischen Investitionen in Deutschland, in Festschrift fuer Reimer Schmidt 237, 243 (1976).

1. For background information concerning attorneys' fees in Germany and other civil-law countries, see *supra* Chapter 7, Section 8 at 684.

From the beginning of 1931 the defendant paid to his lessor only one half of the monthly rent installments, whereupon the lessor instituted four actions for the recovery of the balance of four rent installments. On the other hand, defendant, represented by the plaintiff, brought an action against the lessor for refund of alleged overpayments. All these actions were settled in December, 1931. This settlement reduced the annual rental payable by defendant to his lessor from RM 240,000 to RM 165,000.

Concerning plaintiff's fees, the parties entered into an agreement which under date of February 16, 1931 was confirmed by plaintiff as follows:

"... in addition to my statutory fees you will pay to me ten percent (10%) of those amounts which for the duration of the lease you will save as compared to the originally stipulated rental. You will make these payments to me regardless of whether or not you obtain these benefits directly or indirectly through my activities ... You will not enter into any settlement without my cooperation."

On the following day this agreement was supplemented by an additional letter agreement which provided that the ten percent should be reduced to five percent (5%) if it should become necessary for defendant to retain another attorney.

Under date of August 5, 1931, the parties entered into a new supplemental agreement which plaintiff confirmed by letter as follows:

"You have recognized that my claim for fees is justified on the basis of the agreement existing between us. You have contended, however, that prior to entering into the said agreement you did not realize what amounts would become payable thereunder. For this reason you have requested that the stipulated fee be reduced. We have agreed that my percentage participation ... be reduced to five percent. You guarantee that I shall receive a minimum of RM 30,000 out of this participation. In all other respects our former agreement remains unchanged. We have expressly agreed that my participation extends over the whole duration of your tenancy."

Defendant concedes that through the settlement which he made with his lessor in December, 1931, he obtained considerable savings of rent, as compared with the previous terms of the lease. Plaintiff claims that his 5% share of these savings, for the period prior to the commencement of the action, amounts to RM 13,000. Plaintiff is suing for this amount plus interest. Defendant denies the validity of the said agreements. He claims that such participation of a lawyer in the benefits obtained by him for his client is not only professionally unethical but contra bonos mores and hence void.

The court of first instance granted the relief prayed for by the plaintiff. The intermediate Appellate Court reversed and dismissed the complaint. Plaintiff's further appeal to the Reichsgericht was unsuccessful.]

Reasons: ... The contract sued upon is characterized by the feature that defendant did not promise a fixed sum payable in case of successful termination of the matter for which plaintiff was retained, but that plaintiff was to participate in the benefits which his activities were to procure for the defendant by way of legal action or settlement. Defendant promised to plaintiff a specified percentage of these benefits. Plaintiff himself calls this a "savings percentage." The stipulation of such a "savings percentage" is, however, contra bonos mores and hence void, especially if one considers the collateral terms of the agreement. The intermediate Appellate Court was rightly guided by the principles which this Division, in accordance with its prior decisions, had developed in the opinion reported in RGZ 115, 141. As is there pointed out, an attorney, being an organ of the administration of justice, may in his capacity as helper and adviser of his client not be guided by any considerations other than those dictated by the nature of the matter entrusted to him. For this purpose he must retain the necessary freedom as against his client. This position is jeopardized and deprecated if the attorney amalgamates the interest which he has in an adequate remuneration, with the interests of his client, by making his remuneration depend upon the success of the action. A lawyer who enters into such an agreement violates the principles of professional ethics. Only exceptionally may a different conclusion be warranted by the special circumstances of the case.

   This court realizes that legal writers have vigorously attacked the foregoing view, and that this view has not been followed by some of the intermediate Appellate Courts. Nevertheless, this view cannot be abandoned. . . . The unethical nature of an agreement by which a lawyer obtains a part of the product of his activities as his remuneration can be denied only by those who think the individual lawyer should enjoy complete freedom with respect to the economic side of his professional life. But in view of the position which the legislature has conferred upon the legal profession, this is impossible. True, the lawyer, as distinguished from the public official, belongs to a free profession. Nevertheless he does not enjoy the freedom of a private individual whose economic activities are limited only by the general laws. The status of the lawyer is ordered by statute. Special privileges have been bestowed upon him. The legal profession has special importance for the administration of justice and for the public life of the nation. From all this it follows that every individual lawyer is subject to special duties. Section 28 of the Lawyers' Code summarizes these duties by providing that every lawyer is bound to use due diligence in the exercise of his profession and by his professional conduct to prove himself worthy of the respect which his profession requires. This diligence in the exercise of the profession, however, is no longer absolutely assured if the lawyer completely allies himself with the economic interests of his client by making the client promise him a part of the benefits which the client hopes to obtain through the work of the lawyer. In such event, the lawyer's own interest in the matter becomes so great that his legally imposed status as protector of the legal order becomes jeopardized. The lawyer who causes such jeopardy will as a rule violate the canons of professional ethics.

   The very case at hand demonstrates that these are not imaginary dangers, but that a lawyer who through a percentage agreement is strongly interested in the outcome of a matter entrusted to him will more easily resort to improper methods than a lawyer not thus personally interested. While the settlement negotiations with the lessor of the hotel were pending, the defendant sought to obtain more favorable terms by painting his financial condition in the drabbest colors. Therefore, on November 12, 1931, he wrote a letter which was addressed to the plaintiff but which, as plaintiff knew, was meant to be forwarded to the adversary. In this letter defendant pointed out that for financial reasons he was not in a position to accept the offers of settlement previously made by the lessor. Plaintiff states in one of his briefs in the present action that this letter as originally drafted by defendant did not seem to him completely suitable for the purpose for which it was written. Therefore, plaintiff improved the letter, had it re-typed and had defendant approve the new version. Then he sent the letter to the attorney for the lessor, as if it were an original letter of the defendant. The plaintiff himself says concerning this incident ... that it was intended by the use of that letter "to bluff the adversary".... That plaintiff's participation in these deceptive machinations of his client constitutes a grave violation of his professional duties is too plain for argument. There is at least some ground for assuming that plaintiff acted that way only for the reason that he was to derive immediate personal benefits from a more favorable settlement. Of course, our conclusion that the fee arrangement between the parties was contra bonos mores is not based upon the subsequent conduct of the plaintiff. Such conduct merely justifies the suspicion that because of the amalgamation of his own interests with those of his client the plaintiff was no longer able to live up to his professional duties....

The views of this Court concerning the participation of an attorney in the economic products of his work are in complete agreement with the views of the National Honor Court for Attorneys.[2] ...

The view opposing the strictness of this Court in matters of this kind is in the last analysis traceable to a different conception of the nature of the legal profession. This conception, which emphasizes the economic factors, does not sufficiently consider the public law character of the legal profession and the professional duties flowing therefrom. This philosophy was favored by certain general tendencies of recent years. Nevertheless, especially in view of the decisions of the National Honor Court for Attorneys, it cannot be said that that philosophy has ever gained controlling influence. To let this philosophy become victorious at this time, is entirely out of the question, since the national resurrection has generally re-established a

---

2. At the time of the principal case, the National Honor Court for Attorneys was the court of last resort in disbarment and other disciplinary proceedings against attorneys. Under the present, somewhat modified system, such disciplinary matters are handled by a three-tiered hierarchy of honor courts. The court of first instance consists of members of the Bar, while the intermediate appellate court and the court of last resort (a special panel of the Bundesgerichtshof) are composed of professional judges and attorneys. For details see Bundesrechtsanwaltsordnung (Federal Law Concerning Attorneys) of August 1, 1959, as amended, §§ 92–161a.

more moral conception of law.[3] One of the characteristics of this conception of law is the emphasis upon duties rather than rights, especially as regards those who are incorporated into the public legal order. The legal sentiment of today more than of any other period commands us not to loosen, but on the contrary to maintain, the rules preventing the selfish exercise of the legal profession. . . .

Even the presently prevailing philosophy does not make it impossible that exceptionally, under special circumstances, an agreement of the said kind between an attorney and his client may not be considered unethical. The present case, however, does not belong to that exceptional category. On the contrary, the intermediate Appellate Court was correct in holding that the details of the arrangement made by the parties reveal particularly objectionable features.

In this connection the intermediate Appellate Court rightly emphasizes the length of the period for which the defendant promised to make payments to the plaintiff. . . . It is absolutely improper for an attorney to stipulate for such payments which his client is to make for an indefinite period, and at least for a period of almost ten years.

It is true that by the supplemental agreement of August 5, 1931, the plaintiff reduced his participation in the savings obtained by defendant from ten percent to five percent. For this concession, however, plaintiff received ample consideration in the form of a guaranteed minimum of RM 30,000. . . .

The agreements of the parties also contain other stipulations which the intermediate Appellate Court rightly considered as factors militating against the contentions of the plaintiff. Plaintiff was to be entitled to the stipulated remuneration regardless of whether and to what extent defendant's benefits were directly or indirectly caused by plaintiff's work. . . . Furthermore, in case it should become necessary for the defendant to retain another lawyer in lieu of the plaintiff, plaintiff was to remain entitled to five percent of the savings. Settlements were not to be entered into without plaintiff's consent and cooperation.[4] Plaintiff believes that all these stipulations can be justified on the ground that their purpose was merely to secure the rightful claim for the so-called savings percentage; plaintiff says it was his purpose to prevent defendant from evading his obligations. It might be that plaintiff had this aim in mind. His argument

---

3. Note that this decision was rendered about eight months after the Nazis had come into power. Yet, the sentence in the text, *supra*, should not lead the reader to exaggerated conclusions as to the judges' espousal of Nazi ideology. The court, it should be remembered, in this decision re-affirms a view which it had consistently held during the days of Bismarck's Reich and the Weimar Republic—a view, in other words, that had nothing whatsoever to do with Nazism. The reference to "the national resurrection," while not exactly an indication of judicial fortitude, thus may have been mere lip service.

4. Note that this particular clause might render the agreement invalid in many jurisdictions in the United States. See F. B. MacKinnon, Contingent Fees for Legal Services 74–77 (1964); 23 Williston on Contracts § 62:9 (R.A. Lord ed., 4th ed. 2002); C. W. Wolfram, Modern Legal Ethics 170 (1986).

overlooks, however, that the contingent fee arrangement as such was highly objectionable and that it became only more objectionable by security measures intended to tie up the client even more firmly. A creditor may be permitted to secure an *unobjectionable* claim in this manner. Where according to the standards of professional ethics and general morals the claim itself is objectionable, such security measures can only lead to even stronger condemnation. . . .

In the above-mentioned decision of this Division, RGZ 115, at 143, certain conditions are stated under which the stipulation of a percentage fee would not violate the standards of professional ethics. It is there said:

> "If the facts were such that defendant *could not* have undertaken the payment of compensation in any other form, . . . then the contingent nature of the promise would not in itself constitute a violation of the lawyer's professional duties."

Appellant relies upon this statement and argues that the present case . . . is covered by the principles there stated. This is incorrect.

In the first place, the intermediate Appellate Court was right in holding that it was irrelevant whether the plaintiff, as he claims, originally demanded a contingent fee in a fixed amount, and that only upon request of the defendant he agreed to a percentage participation. An attorney is himself responsible for his professional honor, and he has to protect his honor particularly as against improper requests of his client. Plaintiff further argues that defendant refused to promise a straight extra-fee; that defendant sought to justify this refusal by pointing out that the current lease would ruin him unless the rentals were reduced, so that he would be unable to pay more than the statutory fee unless he were to obtain considerable relief through the activity of the plaintiff. In such a situation it may perhaps be possible to justify a fee in a fixed amount, contingent upon success; but it does not follow that a percentage participation is permissible. . . .

It is thus clear that in entering into said arrangement the plaintiff has disregarded his professional duties. But to be invalid pursuant to Section 138, Subdivision 1, of the Civil Code,[5] the agreement must be not only professionally unethical but also generally immoral. The intermediate Appellate Court has been correct in so holding, and has correctly analyzed the logical relation between a violation of professional honor and a violation of the precepts of morality. Not every violation of the former is at the same time a violation of the latter. . . .

. . . On the other hand, we decidedly reject the argument that fee arrangements between attorney and client should be subject only to the principles of professional ethics and should be taken out of the reach of Section 138 of the Civil Code. . . .

As in other cases, it is thus necessary in the instant case to examine whether the violation of professional honor, of which the plaintiff has been

---

5. Quoted *supra* at 565.

guilty, is so grave that persons whose views are just and equitable would consider it morally objectionable.[6] This question has been answered in the affirmative by the intermediate Appellate Court, and rightly so. The applicable standard cannot be based upon the philosophy of those persons who think only in economic terms and who have no understanding of the special legal status which the statute provides for attorneys. If this special status is taken into consideration, the conclusion is clear: in making the arrangement with the defendant, the plaintiff did not live up to the moral standard which an attorney should never relinquish. He pursued his personal advantage so unscrupulously that his conduct, far from being in accord with justice and equity, must be characterized as morally objectionable.

NOTES

(1) In 1944, subsequent to the principal case, an express provision outlawing all contingent fees was incorporated into a statute. Decree of April 21, 1944, amending Sec. 93 of the Law Concerning Attorneys' Fees. But when the statute was re-enacted as Sec. 3 of the Federal Law Concerning Attorneys' Fees of July 26, 1957 (BGBl 1957 I 907), the provision expressly prohibiting contingent fees was omitted. The legislative intention behind this omission was to restore the law as it stood at the time of the principal case, i.e., to leave it again to the courts to derive a solution of the contingent fee problem from the broad principle of Sec. 138 of the Civil Code. In several more recent decisions the Bundesgerichtshof accordingly re-established the rule—and the very limited exceptions—stated in the principal case.[1] In 1994 the legislator tackled the issue, stating that contingency fees violate the law (see § 49 b (2) of the Federal Law Concerning Attorneys' Fees).[2] In 2006, the Constitutional Court held that a law barring contingency fees in all cases may be, under certain narrow circumstances, unconstitutional, and requested the legislator to change it as soon as possible.[3] The Parliament therefore enacted in 2008 the "Gesetz zur Neuregelung des Verbotes der Vereinbarung von Erfolgshonoraren", according to which contingency fees agreements are valid only if but for them the client' financial state would have prevented him to pursue her/his rights.[4]

---

6. The same phrase has been used by German courts innumerable times, in an attempt to define the kind of conduct which is contra bonos mores within the meaning of Secs. 138 and 826 of the Civil Code. This definitional point will be taken up later in this section.

1. See, e.g., Decisions of Dec. 15, 1960, BGHZ 34, 64; Feb. 28, 1963, 16 N.J.W. 1147 (1963); Dec. 4, 1986, 40 N.J.W. 3203 (1987).

2. Until recently (see *infra* Chapter 7, Section 8(a) at 685 (Attorney Fees)) German lawyers could either charge a flat fee, according to the Federal Fee Rules for Attorneys (Bundesgebührenordnung für Rechtsanwälte [BRAGO], BGBl. I, 907, 1957), or contract in advance with their client for an hourly rate.

3. BVerfG, December 12, 2006, 1 BvR 2576/04; on this decision, see European Contract Law, *supra* p. 874, note 5, 136. For a general comparison of the regulation of legal ethics in Germany and the U.S., see D. Luban, The Sources of Legal Ethics: A German–American Comparison, 48 Rabels Z. 245 (1984). See also D. Rueschemeyer, Lawyers and Their Society: A Comparative Study of the Legal Profession in Germany and in the United States 123–45 (1973); U. Schultz, Legal Ethics in Germany, 4 Int'l J.Leg.Prof. 55 (1997).

4. Gesetz zur Neuregelung des Verbotes der Vereinbarung von Erfolgshonoraren, June 12, 2008, BGBl. I, 23, 1000, art. 2.

(2) As per the new law, the lawyer who loses the case receives no fees, or (if the parties expressly agreed on this point) a fee equal or less than the statutory one. In the past, German courts ruled that, if the lawyer who has made an invalid contingent fee agreement, loses the case entrusted to him, he cannot even recover the statutory fee. The German courts reached this result by way of the following reasoning: The client was justified in relying on the validity of the agreement, and presumably arranged his affairs accordingly. The lawyer, therefore, would violate the principles of *bona fides* (Civil Code Sec. 242) by sending a bill for the statutory fee; the client, relying on the terms of the agreement, had no reason to expect such a bill.[5] The lawyer who has entered into an invalid contingent fee agreement would have thus found himself in an unenviable position. He was estopped from recovering any amount which was not due under the terms of the (invalid) agreement; and under no circumstances, even if he was entirely successful, would he have recovered more than the statutory fee.[6]

(3) The case brought before the Constitutional Court[7] arose from a lawsuit lodged by a descendant of a German Jewish who sought compensation for the expropriation of an estate made by the German government against her ancestor. She entered into an agreement with a lawyer according to which, should the lawsuit be successful, the lawyer would have obtained the 33% of the awarded amount. The court awarded the woman with DM 312,000, and therefore the lawyer got DM 104,000. According to the Federal Law Concerning Attorneys' Fees, as amended in 1994, the agreement was illegal. The lawyer was fined, and forced to return to the client all but the fee she was allowed by statute to retain. Against such decision the lawyer filed a complaint to the Constitutional Court, alleging that the law infringed both the client's right to access to justice and her right to freely practice the legal profession. The Court stated that none of these rights was infringed in the particular case. However, since the prospect of future violations of these rights was deemed to be substantial, the Court invited the Parliament to amend the law banning contingency fees.

(4) The common law does not speak with a single voice concerning the question of whether contingent fee agreements are lawful. In England, they have been regarded as illegal,[8] although a limited form of contingent fee is now

---

5. Bundesgerichtshof, Decision of Oct. 26, 1955, BGHZ 18, 340, 8 N.J.W. 1921 (1955).

6. Does the common law permit a lawyer who has made an illegal fee agreement to recover in quantum meruit? See 23 Williston on Contracts § 62:8 (R.A. Lord ed., 4th ed. 2002). In Gonzalez y Barredo v. Schenck, 428 F.2d 971 (2d Cir.1970), the court read the New York and other authorities as basically permitting quantum meruit recovery by a lawyer who made a champertous retainer agreement, but left open the possibility that in certain situations the result might be different, especially when the "vitiating element . . . goes to the essence of the service." This

phrase comes from the opinion of Cardozo, C.J., in Matter of Gilman's Administratrix, 251 N.Y. 265, 272, 167 N.E. 437, 440 (1929).

7. See *supra* note 1.

8. See F. B. MacKinnon, Contingent Fees for Legal Services 38 (1964). But where an English court was asked to enjoin a tort victim from suing the tortfeasor in a U.S. court, the House of Lords held that the contingent nature of the compensation payable to the attorneys representing the victim in *the American court* was not a relevant factor in determining whether the injunction should be granted by the English court. Castanho v. Brown and Root (U.K.) Ltd., [1981] 1 All E.R. 143, 152. Generally, concerning the choice-of-

permitted under the Courts and Legal Services Act, 1990.[9] Contingent fee agreements also were once prohibited in the United States and continue to be disapproved or severely restricted in certain branches of law practice, such as divorce matters, criminal cases and, in some states, lobbying.[10] Moreover, courts always have power to strike down a fee arrangement if it contains objectionable terms or if the fee is excessive.[11] In principle, however, "contingent fees are generally allowed in the United States because of their practical value in enabling a poor man with a meritorious cause of action to obtain competent counsel."[12] In some states, the contingent fee tradition is further

law questions that arise in connection with the compensation of attorneys in transnational litigation, see Restatement (Second) Conflict of Laws § 196 (1971); A. Ehrenzweig, Conflict of Laws 532 (1962).

9. See *supra* at 646–47.

10. See, generally, C. W. Wolfram, Modern Legal Ethics 526–42 (1986); P. Bergman, S. Bergman–Barrett, Criminal Law Handbook 166–167 (2007). In criminal cases defense counsel may not accept contingent compensation, supposedly on the ground that legal services in criminal cases do not produce a *res* with which to pay the fee. ABA Code of Professional Responsibility, Ethical Consideration 2–20. In the case of lawyers working for the prosecution, the reason for the rejection of contingent compensation is that they should seek justice rather than a "successful" outcome and should not have a personal interest in the case.

Even in certain types of civil cases— especially those of quasi-criminal nature such as actions for the abatement of a public nuisance—the lawyer representing a governmental unit must be neutral and hence may not accept a contingent fee. See People ex rel. Clancy v. Superior Court (Ebel), 39 Cal.3d 740, 218 Cal.Rptr. 24, 705 P.2d 347 (1985). The same does not hold, however, for outside attorneys assisting a governmental entity. See, e.g., County of Santa Clara v. Superior Court, 74 Cal.Rptr.3d 842 (Cal.App. 6 Dist., 2008). For disapproved contingent fees in other branches of law practice, see also MacKinnon, *supra* note 8 at 45–53.

11. The judicial determination as to whether a particular fee is excessive ordinarily is made in litigation between the parties to the fee agreement. But such determination may be made also in advance of individual litigation and in more general terms; a court having disciplinary power over attorneys may issue Rules indicating that contingent fees in excess of certain stated percentages will not

be tolerated. Gair v. Peck, 6 N.Y.2d 97, 188 N.Y.S.2d 491, 160 N.E.2d 43 (1959), cert. denied, 361 U.S. 374, 80 S.Ct. 401 (1960); American Trial Lawyers Ass'n v. New Jersey Supreme Court, 66 N.J. 258, 330 A.2d 350 (1974). But cf. In the Matter of the Florida Bar, 349 So.2d 630 (Fla.1977); see also L. Brickam, Contingency Fee Abuses, Ethical Mandates, and the Disciplinary System: The Case Against Case–By–Case Enforcement, 53 Wash. & Lee L.Rev. 1339 (1996); D. L. Rhode, Professional Responsibility. Ethics by the Pervasive Method 799–804 (1998); Ead., Ethics in Practice, in Ethics in Practice. Lawyers' Roles, Responsibilities and Regulation 3, 9 (D. L. Rhode ed., 2003); C. Twigg–Flesner, D. Parry, G. Howells, A. Nordhausen, The Yearbook of Consumer Law 320 (2008).

Cal.Bus. & Prof. Code § 6146 limits contingent fees in medical malpractice cases according to a sliding scale that reduces the percentage of the fee as the amount of the recovery increases. Its constitutionality was upheld in a 4–3 decision in Roa v. Lodi Medical Group, 37 Cal.3d 920, 211 Cal.Rptr. 77, 695 P.2d 164 (1985), appeal dismissed, 474 U.S. 990, 106 S.Ct. 421 (1985). A similar result was reached in Bernier v. Burris, 113 Ill.2d 219, 100 Ill.Dec. 585, 497 N.E.2d 763 (1986).

12. Gair v. Peck, *supra* note 11, 6 N.Y.2d at 103, 188 N.Y.S.2d at 494.

The argument based on the client's poverty becomes somewhat questionable in cases in which the client is wealthy enough to pay a non-contingent fee. See Comment, 20 Ohio St.L.J. 329 (1959). For more general criticism of the contingent fee, duplicating some of the arguments used in the civil-law world, see K. M. Clermont & J. D. Currivan, Improving on the Contingent Fee, 63 Cornell L.Rev. 529 (1978); E. Inselbuch, Contingent Fees and Tort Reform: A Reassessment and Reality Check, 64 L. & Contemp.Probs. 175 (2001).

fortified by statute. Sec. 474 of the New York Judiciary Law, for instance, provides that "The compensation of an attorney or counselor for his services is governed by agreement, express or implied, which is not restrained by law, except that" the amount of the fee must be judicially approved where the client is an infant.[13]

Opinion of the Swiss Federal Court in the Matter of Dr. Haass, Defendant–Appellant v. Leopold Wyler, Plaintiff–Respondent

1st Civil Division, July 3, 1915, BGE 41 II 474.

[Defendant's wife was interested in two estates, in both instances as one of several co-legatees. One of the other co-legatees, Gustav Reber, was managing both estates as fiduciary. Defendant, suspecting that Reber had been guilty of improper management, retained plaintiff, an attorney, requesting him to look after the interests of his (defendant's) wife in the matter. Plaintiff thereupon negotiated with Reber, and both sides seemed inclined in principle to accept a settlement by which Reber would buy out the shares of defendant's wife in both estates. There was, however, considerable bargaining concerning the purchase price to be paid by Reber. While this bargaining went on, plaintiff and defendant agreed in writing that, in lieu of statutory fees to which he was entitled as an attorney, the plaintiff should receive a brokerage commission if he succeeded in selling Mrs. Haass' share in the estates to Reber. The amount of the brokerage fee payable to plaintiff in that event was fixed at fifty percent (50%) of the excess of the purchase price over Fr. 300,000. Shortly after this agreement concerning a brokerage fee had been entered into between the parties, plaintiff succeeded in bringing about a settlement with Reber pursuant to which Reber was to purchase Mrs. Haass' share in the two estates for Fr. 409,000. Reber immediately paid Fr. 155,000 on account, and on the same day defendant paid Fr. 30,000 to plaintiff who issued a receipt "on account of brokerage commission." A few months later Reber paid the balance of Fr. 254,000. Plaintiff then demanded the balance of his brokerage commis-

It is arguable, however, that regardless of the client's financial condition both client and lawyer are best served by a system which recognizes the infinite variety of clients' interests and of lawyers' services by leaving them free, within reasonable limits, contractually to determine the conditions and the amount of the fee. In any event, whether persuaded by this or by other arguments, all American jurisdictions are now unanimous in recognizing that as a rule a contingent fee arrangement is valid. In 1964, MacKinnon (*supra* note 8, at 39) stated that "In this country only Maine retains a complete prohibition against contingent fees." A year later the Maine statute containing the prohibition

(17 Rev.Stat.Ann. § 801) was amended so as to bring Maine into line with all other American jurisdictions. See also Wolfram, *supra* note 10, at 527.

13. For a (somewhat dated) multi-national comparative survey concerning the propriety of contingent fees, see W. Kalsbach, Les barreaux dans le monde 156 (1959). See also K. Gromer–Broc, The Legal Profession in the European Union—a Comparative Analysis of Four Member States, 24 Liverpool L.Rev. 109 (2002); H.–J. Hellwig, Challenges to the Legal Profession in Europe, 22 Penn St.Int'l L.Rev. 655 (2004). See also *supra* Chapter 7, Section 8(a) and (b) at 684.

sion in the amount of about Fr. 24,000, but defendant refused payment of this balance.

Plaintiff thereupon sued for Fr. 24,000 plus interest. By way of counterclaim defendant demanded refund of the Fr. 30,000 paid on account, on the ground that the whole "brokerage commission" agreement was invalid.

While the action was pending, there was a disciplinary proceeding against the plaintiff. In the latter proceeding plaintiff was censured for having, as an attorney, illegally stipulated for compensation in excess of the statutory fee.

In the instant (civil) action the tribunal of first instance of the Canton of Berne dismissed the complaint on the ground that the contract sued upon was invalid. The counterclaim also was dismissed, on the ground that the parties were *in pari turpitudine*.[1] Upon defendant's appeal the Federal Court, as court of last resort in civil cases, reversed the judgment below in so far as it dismissed the counterclaim, and granted defendant's prayer for a judgment against the plaintiff in the amount of Fr. 30,000.]

Reasons: The decision appealed from holds that the agreement between the parties is invalid. Plaintiff argues that said agreement is a brokerage contract, and not a contract by which plaintiff as an attorney stipulated for a fee in the form of a commission dependent upon the result of the controversy.... The question arises whether federal or cantonal law governs.... The relationship between the attorney and his client is under Swiss law ordinarily that of a mandate[2] [citing a commentary, a monograph, and a thesis]. Exceptionally it may be an employment contract. In any event it is a contractual relationship, belonging to the sphere of private law and generally covered by the federal Code of Obligations.[3] The attorney promises to perform certain work, whereas the client promises to pay for the work performed. If the performance of the attorney is defective, he may, pursuant to ordinary principles of private law, be sued for damages. On the other hand, he may sue a client for his fee in an ordinary civil

1. Swiss Code of Obligations, Article 62: "He who unjustly obtains a benefit from another, has to make restitution of the enrichment."

"Such obligation exists especially in a case in which a person has obtained something of value without legal causa, or on the basis of an anticipated causa which did not come into existence, or on the basis of a causa which has subsequently ceased to exist."

Article 63: "He who voluntarily pays a non-existing debt, can demand restitution only if he proves that he mistakenly believed in the existence of the debt."

"No claim can be made for restitution, if the payment was made for a debt barred by the Statute of Limitations, or if the payment was made in performance of a moral duty...."

Article 66: "What has been paid or delivered with the intention of producing an illegal or immoral result, cannot be demanded back."

2. The issue of agency was discussed in the 6th edition of this book, Chapter VI at 853.

3. In Switzerland, most subjects belonging to the sphere of private law, including commercial law, are governed by the federal Civil Code and the federal Code of Obligations. Many subjects of public law, on the other hand, are governed by the laws of the cantons.

action [citing cases]. This does not mean, however, that the cantons are precluded from any influence upon that legal relationship. To the extent that they control the administration of justice as a province of public law,[4] they may regulate the affairs of attorneys, especially with respect to fees. In the latter respect, it has been recognized by the consistent practice of this Court that the cantons may provide for official supervision of attorneys' bills [citing cases] and may subject attorneys' fees to a statutory tariff [citing cases]. It follows that the cantons also must have power to determine the *kind* of remuneration to which the attorney is entitled for his services, and especially to prohibit fees measured by the result of such services. . . . Such cantonal regulations are justified by the legal and factual monopoly of the attorneys. There is also the additional consideration that a percentage participation in the result of a dispute involves a speculation, and that the attorney, who due to his knowledge of the law is in a better position to weigh the chances, occupies a superior position in this connection.

It follows further that the cantons must have the power to determine *which acts* of attorneys should, with respect to the question of remuneration, be considered as connected with the *administration of justice*. Of course the cantons may not treat those services as belonging to the administration of justice which are not covered by this term as generally understood. If they did, they would improperly invade the area of private law which governs the contractual relations between attorney and client; that area is completely and absolutely preempted by federal codes, to the exclusion of the public law of the cantons.

[The Court then points out that in the present case the services rendered by plaintiff were not, or at least not exclusively, the services of a broker, and that, consequently, they were services rendered by the plaintiff as an attorney and as an organ of the administration of justice. That being so, the Court concludes that the Canton of Berne had power to regulate the fees to be exacted by plaintiff for such services. The Court then refers to a Berne statute of 1840, pursuant to which a percentage agreement between attorney and client (*pactum de quota litis*) is illegal. Such, at any rate, had been the construction of the Berne statute by the court below, and the

---

4. Many of the civilians think of procedure, including civil procedure, as a *public law* subject, on the theory that procedural law regulates the functioning of the courts, and that the courts are a branch of the *government*.

With the exception of the Federal Court of Lausanne, the Penal Federal Court and the Administrative Federal Court, the ordinary Swiss courts are cantonal courts and, until the federal civil procedure code is adopted (for a survey on the main provisions of the draft, see S. Lukic, J. Haldy, J.–M. Reymond, D. Tappy, Le projet de code de procédure civile fédérale (2008)), their proce-

dure is governed by the Codes of Civil Procedure of the various cantons. Civil cases which have run through the hierarchy of cantonal courts may be appealed to the Federal Court of Lausanne; the latter Court can reverse the decision below only if it is based on a violation or misapplication of federal law. It must be remembered, however, that the Civil Code and the Code of Obligations are federal laws, so that the Federal Court of Lausanne has the last word on most questions of substantive law which arise in private law cases. See T. Fleiner, Swiss Constitutional Law 88–100 (2005).

federal court is bound by the construction which a cantonal court places upon a statute of its own canton. The present agreement is thus illegal as violating a valid Berne statute.]

Federal law, however, determines what should be the *effect of such illegality* of the agreement in question.... Even though the prohibition violated by the agreement is not a federal but a cantonal statute, the question of the effect of such violation is one of federal law.[5] ... [The Court then points out that Article 20 of the Swiss Code of Obligations,[6] in the same way as Section 134 of the German Civil Code,[7] invalidates illegal contracts.]

The invalidity of the contingent fee agreement further leads to the conclusion that the counterclaim is well founded and that defendant is entitled to demand restitution of the amount of Fr. 30,000 paid on account. By paying this sum to the plaintiff in performance of his promise, defendant has voluntarily paid a non-existing debt within the meaning of Article 63 of the Code of Obligations. He was mistaken concerning the existence of his obligation, being of the opinion that he was paying pursuant to the terms of a contract which was binding upon him and did not incorporate illegal provisions. This must be considered proved, because no other motive appears which might have induced the defendant to make the partial payment in question.... Such mistake of law is sufficient to justify restitution pursuant to Article 63 [citing a case] ... The court below erred in holding that the dismissal of the counterclaim could be based upon Article 66 of the Code of Obligations. The defendant did not pay "with the intention of producing an illegal or immoral result." He paid in the mistaken belief that he was performing a valid and legal contract. Moreover, the result of the performance was illegal, and perhaps immoral, only in so far as the person and the mentality of the plaintiff as payee was involved. There was no illegality or immorality on the part of the defendant as payor. On the contrary, it is the client-payor's interest which was sought to be protected by the statute condemning contingent fees. The principle "in pari turpitudine melior est causa possidentis,"[8] applied by the court below in reliance upon the distinguishable case of [citation], is not applicable to the case at bar.[9]

5. In our legal system, where state law generally predominates in the area of private law, the converse question sometimes presents itself: If a transaction is invalidated by a federal statute, are the consequences, including the restitutionary consequences, of such invalidity determined by state or federal law? Cf. Francis v. Southern Pacific Co., 333 U.S. 445, 68 S.Ct. 611 (1948); H. J. Friendly, In Praise of Erie—and of the New Federal Common Law, 19 The Record 64, 88 (1964).

6. Swiss Code of Obligations, Art. 20: "A contract the object of which is impossible, illegal or immoral, is invalid...."

7. Quoted *supra* at 565, note 4.

8. Freely translated, this Roman maxim means that, where both parties are guilty of equal turpitude, the law will not help one against the other. In varying phraseology, most of the modern civil-law codes have incorporated the maxim into their provisions dealing with unjust enrichment. See, e.g., Art. 66 of the Swiss Code of Obligations (*supra*, note 1), which is the basis of the Court's discussion of the point.

9. If German law had been applicable, the plaintiff attorney, having been successful, could have recovered the amount of his statutory fee. See Notes preceding the principal case. The Swiss Federal Court, by directing

NOTE

A rule invalidating contingent fee agreements naturally raises questions concerning the plight of impecunious litigants. The foregoing cases, therefore, should be considered in the light of the materials on *legal aid* in civil-law countries (*supra* Chapter 7, Section 8(c) at 696).

A closely related problem is that of *recovery of counsel fees* from a vanquished opponent (*supra* Chapter 7, Section 8(b) at 691). This may be an appropriate time, therefore, to review the whole subject of litigation expenses previously discussed in this book, and to compare American and civilian approaches to that problem.

* * *

Oberlandesgericht Celle, Opinion of December 5, 1947

Reported in 2 Monatsschrift für Deutsches Recht 174 (1948).

The plaintiff is over fifty years old. She used to be a gardener and formerly lived in East Prussia. In the fall of 1944, the eastern front moved closer to her home town. Because of the threat of Russian invasion the evacuation of that town was ordered, and the plaintiff fled from East Prussia on October 29, 1944. She was permitted to stay in Göttingen with a family whom she had known previously.

[The defendants, husband and wife, are horticulturists residing in Göttingen. Shortly after her arrival at Göttingen, the plaintiff paid a visit to the defendants whom she had met before. Defendants asked the plaintiff about conditions in East Prussia. Plaintiff gave a truthful report of the unfavorable conditions there. She mentioned that fear of the Russians had induced many people there to commit suicide.] In the course of the conversation the plaintiff said: "Nobody in East Prussia believes in Adolf Hitler any more." Both defendants were present when this remark was made.... A few days later the first defendant (the husband) made a written report to the Gestapo concerning the remarks made by the plaintiff. The second defendant (the wife) saw the report after the first defendant had written it. She did not sign the report, but she did not object to its dispatch. A few days later a Gestapo official interrogated both defendants in their apartment ... The second defendant then made a truthful statement of the conversation with the plaintiff. Upon the denunciation of the first defendant the plaintiff was arrested by the Gestapo. After her arrest the Gestapo telephoned to the first defendant and asked him whether he considered the matter very serious. He answered that it was up to the Gestapo to determine that. He did not retract his denunciation. In the meantime a judicial warrant of arrest was issued against the plaintiff, and she was transferred to the jail of the tribunal of first instance in Göttingen. There she experienced two air attacks ..., by which the jail was damaged.

that plaintiff repay the *entire* sum he had received on account, in effect determined that he should obtain no compensation whatever. It is possible, however, that plaintiff—consis- tently with his contention that he had earned a broker's commission rather than a professional fee—had not raised the point concerning his statutory fee.

For reasons of security she and other prisoners were subsequently transferred to the Insane Asylum in Göttingen and a few days later to the jail of
the tribunal of first instance in Hildesheim. There she was discharged on
August [sic[1]] 25, 1945, shortly before the arrival of the Americans.

... The plaintiff contends that as a consequence of her long imprisonment and the mental anguish occasioned thereby, she suffered a serious
impairment of her health. She demands damages from the defendants
pursuant to Section 826 of the Civil Code.[2]

The tribunal of first instance entered an interlocutory judgment determining the issue of liability in favor of plaintiff and against both defendants, and limiting the further proceedings to the issue of the amount of
damages.

Upon defendants' appeal from this interlocutory judgment, the Oberlandesgericht affirmed the judgment against the first defendant, but reversed the judgment against the second defendant and dismissed the
complaint against her.

Reasons: ... The first defendant has intentionally injured the plaintiff
in a manner violating the moral precepts. Therefore he is liable under
Section 826 of the Civil Code. It can be assumed that the report made by
him against the plaintiff was true. But this is immaterial. So long as it can
be anticipated that a person reported to the competent authorities will be
treated in an orderly proceeding, governed by humane principles, such
denunciation would not be contra bonos mores, at least not in the absence
of improper motives. Such orderly proceeding would have been the rule in
former times. There was no Gestapo. There were no Gestapo methods....

But things were entirely different at a time when the most trivial
political denunciation was sufficient to deliver the denounced person to the
whims of so arbitrary an institution as the Gestapo [citing two recent
decisions of the Oberlandesgericht Frankfurt].

The question of immorality is to be determined pursuant to the views
of those persons whose thinking is just and equitable. There is controversy
among text writers and among judicial decisions whether this refers to the
views prevailing at the time of the allegedly tortious act or to the views
prevailing at the time when liability is sought to be enforced by legal
proceedings. It is not necessary to decide this question here. In the fall of
1944, it was already generally known with what arbitrariness the Gestapo
proceeded, and reasonable men could no longer ignore the irresponsibility
with which a government now recognized as criminal continued the hope-
lessly lost war. The course and outcome of the war could not be affected by
the fact that the plaintiff communicated her sad impressions and her
correct conclusions to a larger or smaller circle of persons.... When the
first defendant denounced the plaintiff in order, as he himself expresses it,

---

1. This date seems to be erroneous. The
correct month was probably April 1945.

2. "One who intentionally damages another in a manner which is contra bonos
mores is liable to the other for restoration of
the damage thus caused."

to render her harmless, he made himself a tool of the Gestapo.... The argument that he was motivated by an honest conviction would help the first defendant only if the inhuman consequences of such denunciation had been unknown to him. [The Court then points out that the first defendant admittedly was an ardent reader of National–Socialist newspapers and magazines, which at that time contained frequent references to the drastic punishment meted out to persons criticizing the regime and its acts. Therefore, the Court concludes, the first defendant undoubtedly knew what consequences his denunciation would have for the plaintiff.] It follows that even under the views prevailing at that time the defendant committed an immoral act.

The first defendant tries in vain to deny his responsibility for the consequences of the denunciation on the ground that the injury occurred only after issuance of the judicial warrant of arrest, and that therefore the causal connection was interrupted. Defendant's purpose was to render the plaintiff harmless, that is, to deprive her of her liberty. For this purpose it did not matter whether the imprisonment was imposed by the Gestapo or by the court. It may be true, as the witness B. testifies, that the judicial warrant of arrest was issued only in order to remove the plaintiff from the control of the Gestapo. This Court takes judicial notice of the fact that this was a practice frequently applied.[3] It is thus clear that without the previous arrest by the Gestapo a judicial warrant of arrest would never have been issued. Even if the judicial warrant of arrest was not specifically issued for this purpose, it was in any event a consequence of the denunciation filed with the Gestapo.

It follows that the first defendant is liable for the damages caused by the imprisonment which was brought about by his denunciation.

With respect to the second defendant a different decision is called for ... [The Court points out that the second defendant did not take part in the denunciation written and filed by the first defendant]. The mere fact that the second defendant, when interrogated by the Gestapo, truthfully reported the facts involved in the denunciation, is not a sufficient basis for the imposition of liability.

NOTES AND QUESTIONS

(1) In a subsequent case, which reached the West German Federal Supreme Court,[1] the facts were basically similar. During World War II, plaintiff had made defeatist, anti-Hitler remarks in front of soldiers, and defendant had denounced her to the Gestapo. As compared to the principal case, however, events took a somewhat different turn in that upon her arrest the plaintiff was

---

3. The German Federal Constitutional Court, in a Decision of Feb. 19, 1957, 6 BVerfGE 132, 214–15, also took judicial notice of this practice, citing the instant case. See W. O. Weyrauch, Limits of Perception: Reader Response to *Hitler's Justice*, 40 Am. J.Comp.L. 237, 244 (1992).

1. Bundesgerichtshof, Decision of May 25, 1955, 8 N.J.W. 1274 (1955).

put before the "People's Court,"[2] and was tried for "subversion of the armed services." Plaintiff was convicted and sentenced to three years of hard labor. In this case, therefore, plaintiff's imprisonment was authorized by the judgment of a court.

The Supreme Court held that the denunciation was an act *contra bonos mores*, because "persons whose views are just and equitable would consider it morally objectionable. Sec. 826 of the Civil Code serves to implement a law of higher order and permits the Court to consider the postulates of true justice not dependent on positive laws." Law of such higher order, the Court held, must prevail over any legislative, administrative or judicial act.

In view of the fact, however, that plaintiff's imprisonment had been authorized by a judicial sentence, the Supreme Court further held that plaintiff could recover damages only if it were shown that the judgment convicting and sentencing her was so unjust that it must be treated as a nullity.[3] Such might be the case if the judgment of the People's Court was based

(a) on a Nazi-tinged and unjust law,[4] or

(b) on an unjust interpretation or application of that law by the People's Court, or

(c) on a sentencing practice of that court so brutal as to be inconsistent with law of a higher order.

For clarification of the question whether the judgment of the People's Court suffered from any of the defects mentioned under (b) or (c), the Supreme Court remanded the case.[5]

2. Only rabid Nazis could become members of this court, which was not a part of the regular judicial system. Its sentences—very frequently death sentences—were unappealable. The procedure was summary, but the accused did receive the semblance of a trial, and occasionally a defendant was acquitted. See K. Loewenstein, Justice, in Governing Post–War Germany 236, 249 (E. H. Litchfield ed., 1953); N. S. Marsh, Some Aspects of the German Legal System Under National Socialism, 62 L.Q.Rev. 366, 372 (1946); G. Gribbohm, Der Volksgerichtshof, 1969 JuS 55; D. Schwab, Literaturschau: Die Rechtsentwicklung im Dritten Reich, 1976 JuS 132, 134 (1976).

3. Cf. Brandt v. Winchell, 3 N.Y.2d 628, 170 N.Y.S.2d 828, 148 N.E.2d 160 (1958).

4. The statute under which plaintiff had been convicted by the People's Court was directed against "subversion" of the armed services in wartime. The Supreme Court observed that this statute, although passed by the Nazi government, was similar to laws enacted in other unquestionably civilized countries, and held that the statute was not unjust on its face, not even from the standpoint of a "higher law."

5. The cautious (perhaps overly cautious) attitude of the Supreme Court may have been due to the consideration that *if* the judgment of the People's Court were treated as "unjust" and hence a nullity, the informer might be subject to criminal as well as civil liability. In a case in which an "unjust" death sentence of the People's Court was foreseen by the informer (the victim's brother), whose volunteered testimony was responsible for the conviction, the informer was held guilty of intentional homicide. Bundesgerichtshof, Nov. 6, 1952, 6 N.J.W. 793 (1953). For discussion of similar criminal cases, see W. Friedmann, Legal Theory 350–56 (5th ed. 1967); C. von Bar, The Common Law of Torts I 51 f. (1998); II 91 (2000).

The Supreme Court did not examine whether the notorious People's Court was not, as an institution, so tainted with totalitarian lawlessness that *every* judgment of that "court" must be considered unjust. By a Resolution of Jan. 24, 1985, the Bundestag declared that the so-called "Volksgerichtshof" (People's Court) was not a court in

(2) Note that the *"contra bonos mores"* concept is used in the Code for two purposes: (a) as a restriction on freedom of contract and other transactions, and (b) in the definition of a tort. The concept thus serves both as a shield and as a sword.

(3) By what standard should a court determine whether a given act is *contra bonos mores*? Is the question one of law, with the result that the judges are presumed to know the answer? Or can it be treated as one of fact, as to which the parties may introduce evidence (e.g., experts' testimony on properly tested community attitudes)?[6] Compare the German courts' formula, which is predicated on the supposed feelings of "persons whose views are just and equitable,"[7] with similar attempts of United States courts to determine the meaning of the terms "good moral character" and "moral turpitude" as used in the immigration laws.[8]

(4) In determining whether conduct is *contra bonos mores* within the meaning of § 138 of the Civil Code, the courts are called on, in effect, to derive legal precepts from "community values." It consequently becomes important to delimit the contours of the relevant "community." In certain circumstances, this community may transcend national borders, even though, under applicable choice-of-law rules, German law governs the transaction. For example, in Germany and in several other European countries, the provisions of the

the traditional sense of the word, but "an instrument of terror used to implement the arbitrary policies of the National–Socialist regime." See Editorial, Bericht aus Bonn, 18 Zeitschrift für Rechtspolitik 93, 94 (1985); B. R. Sonnen, Die Beurteilung des "Volksgerichtshofs" und seiner Entscheidungen durch den Deutschen Bundestag, 38 N.J.W. 1065 (1985); R. Wittman, Tainted Law, in Atrocities on Trial. Historical Perspectives on the Politics of Prosecuting War Crimes 221, 226 f. (P. Heberer & J. Matthäus eds., 2008).

As part of the process of absorbing the former GDR (East Germany) into the German Federal Republic, a First Statute for the Correction of East German Communist Party Injustice (Erstes SED–Unrechtsbereinigungsgesetz), Oct. 29, 1992, BGBl. I 1814, was enacted, providing for nullifying those convictions by East German courts which were "inconsistent with the essential principles of a free order based on the rule of law." See P. E. Quint, The Imperfect Union: Constitutional Structures of German Unification 220–24 (1997).

6. Cf. Judge Frank's provocative dissenting opinion in Repouille v. United States, 165 F.2d 152, 154–55 (2d Cir.1947).

7. Except in the case of members of certain professions (e.g., lawyers, physicians) who are held to higher ethical standards, this

formula is thought to refer to the *average* morality of decent people. See 2 Enneccerus–Nipperdey, Allgemeiner Teil des Buergerlichen Rechts, § 191 I 2 (1960); B. S. Markesinis, H. Unberath, The German Law of Torts 890 (4th ed. 2002).

8. Cf. Johnson v. United States, 186 F.2d 588 (2d Cir.1951); Ablett v. Brownell, 240 F.2d 625 (D.C.Cir.1957); Forbes v. Brownell, 149 F.Supp. 848 (D.D.C.1957). Judge Learned Hand's fascinating opinion in the Johnson case deals with the question whether and under what circumstances an adulterer can be regarded as a person of good moral character within the meaning of the naturalization laws. As a matter of legal method, it is interesting to note that, subsequent to the Johnson decision, Congress sought to take this specific question out of the hands of the judiciary and to resolve it by statute. It is doubtful, however, whether the statute (as interpreted by the courts) has changed the standards laid down in the previous case law, especially in the Johnson decision. For a survey of the relevant case law, see M. Shapiro, Morals and the Courts: The Reluctant Crusaders, 45 Minn.L.Rev. 897 (1961), where references to the relevant writings of many other authors can be found; B.C. Harms, Redefining "Crimes of Moral Turpitude": A Proposal to Congress, 15 Geo.Imm.L.J. 259 (2000).

European Convention on Human Rights have been cited by the courts in deciding whether a particular contractual provision violates public order or prevailing principles of morality.[9]

Another example, arising in a situation in which Germany was not a party to a binding international instrument, is provided by the Budesgerichtshof decision of June 22, 1972, BGHZ 59, 82. In that case, the court dealt with an insurance policy issued by a German insurer to a Nigerian exporter. The policy covered a shipment of art objects from Nigeria to Hamburg, Germany. Six of the objects were lost during the voyage. When the defendant insurer refused to pay for these objects, the plaintiff, as assignee of the insured, brought suit in Germany. It apparently was undisputed that all issues in the case were governed by German law—probably in accordance with a choice-of-law clause in the policy. The defendant asserted that the insurance contract was *contra bonos mores*, since the covered voyage, which involved the exportation of African art objects, violated a Nigerian statute prohibiting such exports.

The lower courts held that the contract was valid. They found that a violation of the Nigerian export prohibition did not affect the interests of the German public and that, consequently, the contract could not be said to be "immoral" within the meaning of § 138.

The BGH rejected the narrow view taken by the lower courts. It recognized that the insurance contract, being governed by German law, was not directly invalidated by the Nigerian statute. Nonetheless, in the view of the BGH, the violation of the law of another country may be relevant as an element of immorality, to be taken into consideration in determining the validity of a contract under § 138. The court called attention to UNESCO resolutions and to the proposed UNESCO convention condemning illicit exports of works of art forming part of a nation's cultural heritage. Although the convention had not been ratified by Germany, the BGH nevertheless regarded the actions taken by UNESCO as indicating that "in the community of nations there exist certain fundamental convictions concerning the right of every country to protect its cultural heritage," and that all practices aimed at subverting that right are reprehensible.

The court concluded that, "in the interest of preserving decency in the international art market," no legal protection should be accorded to transactions by which it is sought to remove cultural property from a nation's territory in violation of that nation's laws. The insurance policy covering such illicit removal was therefore *contra bonos mores* and void.[10]

(5) One of the most interesting developments in post-war German law is that by which judicial determination of what is *contra bonos mores* for purposes of

9. For examples and references, see A. Z. Drzemczewski, European Human Rights Convention in Domestic Law 199–218 (1983); R. Blackburn, J. Polakiewicz, Fundamental Rights in Europe: The European Convention of Human Rights and Its Member States, 1950–2000, 103ff (2001); on the role played in the European legal systems by the European Convention on Human Rights, see European Contract Law, *supra* p. 873, note 1, 138–139.

10. For a comparison of German, Swiss and American approaches, see M. Hellner, Private International Enforcement of Competition Law. The Application of Foreign Competition Law, in Yearbook of Private International Law 2002, 257, 287ff (P. Sarcevic, P. Volken eds., 2003).

the Civil Code has come to be affected by value judgments inherent in provisions of the Constitution.[11] This started with the opinion of the Federal Constitutional Court in the Lüth case (Decision of Jan. 15, 1958, BVerfGE 7, 198). The plaintiff in that case was the producer of the 1950 film "Immortal Beloved." The director of that film was an individual of international fame, who had become notorious by lending his unquestioned artistic talents to the production, during the Nazi period, of base antisemitic propaganda. The defendant Lüth, a high official of the State of Hamburg, was concerned that the reputation of post-war Germany and of its film industry would suffer if a film directed by that notorious individual were shown in Germany and other countries. Therefore, he publicly criticized the plaintiff for having chosen such a tainted individual as the director of "Immortal Beloved" (which in itself was an unobjectionable film), and by such public criticism admittedly sought to discourage the owners of film theaters from exhibiting that film. The court of first instance at Hamburg held that this attempt to bring about a boycott of the film violated § 826 of the Civil Code. Upon direct appeal (which in exceptional cases may be permitted) the Federal Constitutional Court reversed the judgment for the plaintiff which the court of first instance had entered. After a painstaking review of the record, the Constitutional Court concluded that if in balancing the public and private interests involved in this case the court of first instance had accorded the proper weight to the protection of defendant's freedom of speech (and especially of political speech), it would not have found defendant guilty of "immoral" conduct within the meaning of § 826 of the Civil Code.[12] The Constitutional Court did not attempt to produce a single verbal formula for the decision of future cases in which constitutional guarantees might affect the application of the Code's tort provisions, and especially of § 826. It merely held that, in applying § 826, the values reflected in constitu-

11. Certain fundamental rights provided by the German Constitution are viewed not only as safeguards against the state but also as "ordering principles" for social life in general. Accordingly, these rights are not only binding on public authority, but can also exercise an effect (*Drittwirkung*) on private-law relationships. This effect of fundamental rights has repeatedly been acknowledged in decisions of the Federal Supreme Court and the Federal Labor Court. See B. S. Markesinis, Privacy, Freedom of Expression and the Horizontal Effect of the Human Rights Bill: Lesson from Germany, 115 L.Q.Rev. 47 (1999); R. Brinktrine, The Horizontal Effect of Human Rights in German Constitutional Law, 6 Eur.H.Rights L.Rev. 421 (2001); U. Preuï, The German Drittwirkung Doctrine and Its Socio–Political Background, in The Constitution in Private Relations. Expanding Constitutionalism 23ff (A. Sajó & R. Uitz eds., 2005). See also the "Die Welt" case, *supra* at 596, and the two cases following these Notes.

12. Note that the Lüth case deals with incitement to boycott rather than with defamation. In defamation cases the German courts seem to have been somewhat slower than the U.S. Supreme Court to recognize the "radiation effect" of constitutional provisions protecting freedom of speech. Until the late seventies, the German law of libel was virtually unaffected by such provisions: liability attached if plaintiff succeeded in proving mere negligence. In 1977, however, the Federal Supreme Court extended the constitutional protection to cover libelous statements concerning questions of political relevance; with respect to such matters liability now attaches only if reckless disregard of standards of "journalistic diligence" can be established. See C. von Bar, The Common European Law of Torts II, 99–100 (2000); B. S. Markesinis & H. Unberath, *supra* note 7, 472–505, where a comparison is drawn between German and American law; H. Rösler, Dignitarian Posthumous Personality Rights—An Analysis of U.S. and German Constitutional and Tort Law, 26 Berk.J.Int'l L. 153 (2008).

tional provisions must be *considered*. The most important consequence of this holding is that, in proper cases, the Federal Constitutional Court can review the question of whether the ordinary courts, in deciding a purely private dispute seemingly governed by a provision of the Civil Code, have given sufficient weight to those postulates and values which have received constitutional recognition.[13]

In subsequent cases, the Constitutional Court emphasized that it was not trying to usurp the function of reviewing the ordinary courts' interpretation and application of the provisions of the Civil Code, and that it would interfere only where the ordinary courts, in applying provisions such as § 826, had given insufficient weight to freedom of speech or other constitutionally protected values. While admitting that the problem of where to draw the line is a disturbing one, the Court indicated that in general it would not overturn a tort judgment for the plaintiff rendered by an ordinary court where defendant's conduct amounted to more than speech,[14] or where the ordinary courts had treated defendant's utterance as tortious on account of its form rather than its substance.[15]

Opinion of the German Federal Constitutional Court

First Panel, October 19, 1993.
47 N.J.W. 36 (1994).

[Two constitutional complaints (*Verfassungsbeschwerden*) involved the question of the extent to which a court has a constitutional obligation to

13. For an excellent comparative study of *Lüth* and other cases dealing with the "radiation effect" that constitutional values can have on private law relationships, see P. E. Quint, Free Speech and Private Law in German Constitutional Theory, 48 Md.L.Rev. 247 (1989). See also K. M. Lewan, The Significance of Constitutional Rights for Private Law: Theory and Practice in West Germany, 17 Int'l & Comp.L.Q. 571 (1968); D. P. Currie, The Constitution of the Federal Republic of Germany 174–243 (1994); B.S. Markesinis & H. Unberath, *supra* note 7, 392–412, where it can be found an English translations of *Lüth* as well as of subsequent cases, along with some helpful notes on the "constitutionalization" of private law.

14. See, e.g., the *Blinkfüer* case, BVerfGE 25, 256 (1969) (defendant, in addition to "speaking," had put economic pressure on its dealers to boycott the plaintiff's publications). An English-language summary of this interesting case appears in the instructive article by H. G. Rupp, The Federal Constitutional Court and the Constitution of the Fed-

eral Republic of Germany, 16 St. Louis U.L.J. 359, 369 (1972).

15. Decision of the Federal Constitutional Court of May 11, 1976, N.J.W. 1976, 1677 (in defendant's publication the plaintiff's publication had been called a "right-radical demagogic muckraking sheet"). In this case the Court held that the form of an utterance enjoys less constitutional protection than its substance. Since the ordinary courts' condemnation of defendant's utterance in this case was based exclusively on its form, the Constitutional Court did not overturn the judgment for the plaintiff. At the same time, the Court indicated that if defendant had expressed the same criticism of plaintiff's publication in a less offensive form, the Constitution would protect defendant from liability in tort. A translation of subsequent decisions of the Federal Constitutional Court on this point appears in "Decisions of the Bundesverfassungsgericht (Federal Constitutional Court) of the Federal Republic of Germany: 2 Freedom of Speech (1958–1995)" (1998). See also W. Brugger, The Treatment of Hate Speech in German Constitutional Law, 3 German L.J. (2002).

protect one who has agreed to become a surety on terms that turn out to be particularly burdensome. In the first case, the 21–year old daughter of a real estate broker and promoter, later also active in shipping, was asked by her father's bank to become a surety for all his past and future debts; this was a condition for the extension of further credit. The daughter had only casual employment and received welfare benefits for her apparently illegitimate child. The bank officer in question seems to have told her that her signature was essentially a formality and that she should not worry about liability. In the second case, a wife was asked to become a surety for a loan, apparently to finance purchases that would be used to improve the furnishings of the family residence; the wife took care of two small children and had no independent income. In both cases, the German Supreme Court (Bundesgerichtshof) refused to declare the suretyship agreement void. Both sureties filed constitutional complaints. The Constitutional Court held that the constitutional complaint was justified in the first case, but not in the second.]

Reasons:

I ... The two constitutional complaints ... do not attack the relevant provisions of the Civil Code ... but rather the interpretation and implementation of those general clause of the Civil Code, in particular §§ 138 and 242, which require the civil courts to review (critically) the content of contracts....

In its provisions on basic rights, the Constitution contains some fundamental principles governing all areas of the law. These principles become operative through the more specific provisions that regulate the field in question. They are significant in particular for the interpretation of the general clauses contained in the rules of private law [citation omitted]. By referring in a very general way to good morals, the usages of (honest) trade, and good faith, §§ 138 and 242 require the court, when giving effect to them in concrete instances, to be guided by value judgments which receive their inspiration primarily from the basic principles of the Constitution. The Constitution thus obligates the civil courts to use the basic rights as guidelines when interpreting the general clauses. If, as a result of a disregard of that principle, they decide against a party to litigation, then they have impaired the basic rights of that party (and thus opened the way for the filing of a constitutional complaint [citation omitted]).

Nevertheless, it is not for the Constitutional Court to review the interpretation and application of the ordinary rules of law [by the regular courts]. Its only duty is to insure the observation of constitutional norms and rules by these courts.... There is a constitutional violation which requires action by the Constitutional Court only if the decision under review appears to be affected by erroneous interpretations which are based on a fundamental mistake concerning the impact of basic constitutional rights, especially as to the scope of the protection they afford....

II. 1) The suretyship agreement [in the first case] was materially different from run of the mill secured transactions. The complainant accepted a very large risk without having any economic interest in the loan for which she acted as surety. She waived nearly all waivable protective provisions of the Civil Code and accepted an individual liability for the business activities of her father to an extent which far exceeded her economic possibilities. It was evident from the beginning, and could easily be established by the bank, that in the event the complaint would become liable, she would not be able, until the end of her life, to free herself [from the burden of that debt].... Given that situation, questions about the reasons for and the background of the agreement should obviously have asked [by the courts], especially as the parties emphasized this ... [But] the Supreme Court did not ask the question of the extent to which both parties were actually free to enter into the agreement and to decide on its contents. This violates the principle of private autonomy, which the Constitution guarantees.

2) (a) According to the consistent decisions of the Constitutional Court, the ability of individuals to arrange their legal relations according to their own will is part of the general freedom of action (of the individual) [citation omitted]. But the autonomy of the individual is necessarily limited and in need of legal implementation.... But that does not mean that the autonomy of the individual is subject to discretionary action by the legislature, for that would render its constitutional protection meaningless. The legislature must leave the individual an adequate sphere for action....

(b) But since all those who participate in legal relations in the sphere of private law are protected by Art. 21 of the Constitution and thus can insist on the protection of their private autonomy as granted by the Constitution, it is not permissible for the stronger party always to have the legal advantage. The various antagonistic constitutional claims must be examined in their interrelationship and limited in such a way that all parties involved have their constitutional claims protected to the greatest extent possible. In the case of contracts, this balancing (normally) is an (automatic) result of the meeting of the minds of the parties. Both parties obligate themselves and, in this way, implement their individual freedom of action. But if one of the parties has such a preponderant power that, practically speaking, that party alone is able to determine the contents of the agreement, then this means for the other party the imposition of another's will [citations omitted]. Of course, the law cannot create special rules for all those situations in which the equilibrium between the parties is more or less impaired. Considerations of legal certainty require that not every contract be subject to questioning or to revision [by the courts]. However, when a typical situation is involved, where one party to the agreement is in a significantly weaker position and the consequences of the agreement are particularly burdensome for the weaker party, then private law must take this into consideration and provide remedies. This is a consequence of the constitutionally guaranteed principle of private autonomy (Constitution, Art. 21) and of the fact that the [Federal Republic is, under the Constitution] a "social state." Constitution, Arts. 20(I), 28(I).

(c) Current contract law is consistent with these principles. It is true that the drafters of the Civil Code, although they created various protective devices for legally weaker parties, basically assumed . . . the formal equality of all the participants in private law transactions. But that point of view already had been abandoned by the Reichsgericht [the old German Supreme Court in existence until 1945]. . . . Today, there is general agreement that freedom of contract is a means for the appropriate balancing of the parties interests only in the event of an approximate equality of the parties and that compensating for a lack of balance of power in contracting is one of the main functions of present-day private law [citation omitted]. Many of the provisions of the Civil Code are relevant in this connection [citation omitted]. The general clauses of the Civil Code are especially significant. [The Court discusses §§ 138(II) and 242 of the Civil Code at some length and notes that there is not complete unanimity as to the extent to which these provisions make it possible for the courts to provide relief to the weaker party to a burdensome contract.] . . . From a constitutional point of view, it is only relevant to note in this connection that the current law does contain provisions that make it possible [for the courts] to act appropriately if the equilibrium between the parties suffers from a structural distortion. . . . How the courts must act in such as case, and what result they must reach, is primarily a question of ordinary private law, to which the Constitution grants a great deal of leeway. But the constitutional principle of private autonomy is violated if the problems of a gross disparity of power are not noticed at all, or if a solution is attempted using inadequate means.

3) The Decision of the Bundesgerichtshof under review is an example of such a constitutional violation. . . . The suretyship agreement was evaluated as if it were a normal contract of equivalent interest for both parties and involved reasonably obvious risks. All arguments by which petitioner sought to show her inferior negotiating position were rejected [by the court below] with the argument that she was of age and had the obligation to investigate what were the risks she accepted. That kind of response is not sufficient. As already noted, the liability she accepted through the suretyship agreement, which was of no personal benefit to her, was extremely large. In addition, its extent was hard to estimate. The amount mentioned in the agreement covered only the principal of the debt for which she became a surety. Interest and fees for the granting of credit were additional obligations and the suretyship agreement contained no indication as to how they were to be calculated. . . . Even experienced business persons would have had difficulties in assessing the significance and extent of the risk undertaken; for the 21 year old petitioner, who, furthermore, had no relevant education, these risks were completely opaque. In the case of such a substantial inferiority of one of the contracting parties, it is particularly important how the agreement came about and, in particular, how the party enjoying the superior power acts. Nevertheless, the court below denied that the bank had a duty of information and explanation. It even held that it was immaterial that the bank employee pressured the petitioner to sign the suretyship agreement, adding "you do not accept any large liability." . . .

This disregards the constitutional guarantee of private autonomy in such a fundamental way that the decision below cannot stand.*

[On the other hand, the Court ruled that no constitutional violation occurred in the second case, in which a wife became the surety for her husband, apparently in connection with credit to be used to purchase household furniture; given the amount and purpose of the credit, no constitutional issue was involved simply because the surety had no independent income or property.]

* * *

Opinion of the German Federal Labor Court

February 16, 1989, 43 N.J.W. 141 (1990).

[Plaintiff worked for the defendant, a florist, who employed about twenty-five people. When plaintiff learned he was infected with the AIDS virus, he attempted suicide; a week later he told his employer that he was so infected. He also submitted a certificate from a doctor which indicated that, as a result of the suicide attempt, the plaintiff would be incapacitated for an indefinite period. The defendant fired him. When this happened, plaintiff had not yet been employed for six months, and thus was not yet entitled to the protection of § 1 of the Law for Protection Against Dismissals (*Kündigungsschutzgesetz*) which provides that dismissals may be voided unless socially justified. The lower courts held for the defendant, and the Federal Labor Court affirmed, holding that, as § 1 of the Law Against Dismissals was not applicable, the only limits to a dismissal would be §§ 134, 138, 242, and 612a of the Civil Code.]

The court below correctly ruled that the dismissal was not *contra bonos mores*. A dismissal is a declaration of intent (*Willenserklärung*) which *per se* has no moral content. Nevertheless, it may be *contra bonos mores* due to the reasons for it or because of its purpose. The legislator has recognized this in § 13 II of the Law Against Dismissals ... but not every dismissal that might have to be considered as not socially justified under § 1 of that law is therefore also *contra bonos mores*. According to the consistent case holdings of the Federal Labor Court, a dismissal is *contra bonos mores* only if it is based on an improper and immoral (*verwerflich*) motive ... such as vengeance or retribution, or if for other reasons it violates the feeling of decency of all just and right-minded persons [citing cases]. The burden of proof on that issue ... rests with the employee.

---

* An identical result was reached on somewhat similar facts (daughter and finance, both with very limited resources, acting as sureties for loans to parents to finance the purchase or construction of a house) in the subsequent Decision of the Constitutional Court of Aug. 5, 1994, 1 BvR 1402/89, 47 N.J.W. 2749 (1994). On these decisions, see O. O. Cherednychenko, Fundamental Rights, Contract Law and the Protection of the Weaker Party. A Comparative Analysis of Constitutionalisation of Contract Law, with Emphasis on Risky Financial Transactions 89–92, 231–238 (2007); C. Mak, The Constitution of a Common Frame of Reference for European Contract Law, Centre for the Study of European Contract Law Working Paper Series no. 2008/06, 5–6 (2008).

... Some authors have argued that there ought to be an "objective" criterion for a violation of *bonos mores*, since otherwise the protection that Civil Code § 138 II provides would depend on whether the employer is clumsy enough to let his motives become apparent ... state of mind should be immaterial if a result has been produced that should not be permitted by the legal order [citing authors].

In the instant case, however, it is not necessary to decide which view ought to be followed, since the dismissal of the employee does not violate the concept of *bonos mores* as used in § 138, whether the concept be given an objective or a subjective meaning.

... The findings of fact which are binding here ... clearly show that the court below did not consider that the dismissal took place for the sole reason that the employee was infected with AIDS, since ... the medical certificate indicated that the employee would be unable to work for an indefinite period as a result of his attempted suicide.... As a result, it is not necessary to decide whether a dismissal is to be considered as violating *bonos mores* if the employer acts exclusively because of an infection with AIDS which, for the time being, has no impact on work performance.... Nor does the dismissal violate the principle of good faith (Civil Code § 242). The rule of § 242 has only a limited applicability where the Law Against Dismissals is applicable. To the extent that the worker's interest in the continued availability of the workplace is involved, that Law has given a concrete and specific content to the principle of good faith and thus has regulated the matter comprehensively.... Facts which would have to be assessed under § 1 of the Law Against Dismissals are thus not to be evaluated under the principle of good faith. A dismissal violates good faith and is thus void under § 242 only if facts are involved which remain outside the scope of the Law Against Dismissals ... The same result must follow if the Law is not applicable because the employment has lasted less than six months; otherwise, dismissals would be unlawful under § 242 which the law has not prohibited.... In the instant case, the plaintiff has asserted facts which, evaluated under § 1 of the Law Against Dismissals, might not be "socially justified," but they do not, for that reason, violate good faith. No facts have been asserted, nor are any apparent, which constitute the typical violations of the principle of good faith, such as inconsistent actions or dismissals in an offensive manner or at a particularly inconvenient time.

Nor is the dismissal ineffective under § 134 of the Civil Code because it violates a statutory prohibition. The dismissal does not violate the prohibition of discrimination contained in Art. 3 III of the Basic Law (Constitution), because illness is not included in the list of factors on account of which discrimination is prohibited.... That list, however, is complete and not subject to enlargement by analogy [citing a text]. Nor does the dismissal violate the anti-retaliation rule of Civil Code § 612a ... The rule is intended to prevent a situation where a worker might fail to exercise a right because of the fear that the exercise of the right would lead to disadvantages ... As the nature of the rule makes clear, the measure—

in this case the dismissal by the employer—must be an immediate reaction to the assertion of a legal right by the worker . . .

* * *

Opinion of the Swiss Federal Court in the Matter of Rogenmoser Against Tiefengrund A.G.

1st Civil Division, October 10, 1933, BGE 59 II 372.

[In May, 1929, the plaintiff as lessee and the defendant as lessor entered into a lease contract involving the Exchange Restaurant at Zurich. Defendant let the space in question to plaintiff for fifteen (15) years beginning July 1, 1930. The annual rentals were to be progressive and were to rise from an initial annual amount of Fr. 150,000 to Fr. 198,000 annually for the last three years of the contract period.

In June, 1931, plaintiff requested that defendant consent to the reduction of the stipulated rentals, on the asserted ground that plaintiff had been hard hit by the depression. When defendant refused to give such consent, plaintiff brought this action.

He demands primarily judicial modification of the lease contract, either by substituting contingent rentals (contingent upon plaintiff's gross receipts) for the stipulated fixed rentals, or by an outright reduction of the fixed rentals. In the alternative, plaintiff asks for a declaration that he is entitled to rescind the contract of lease.

The Commercial Court of the Canton of Zurich dismissed the complaint.

Upon plaintiff's appeal, this judgment was affirmed by the Federal Court.]

Reasons: . . . Pursuant to Articles 254 and 255 of the Code of Obligations, which deal with the contract of lease, a reduction of rentals or a rescission of the lease contract is possible only if the leased property, at the time when the lessee takes possession or subsequently, is in such a condition that it cannot be used in accordance with the contract of lease. This is not the case here, as appears from plaintiff's own contentions. . . .

Thus there remains, as the only possible basis of the action, plaintiff's contention that the lease contract in question contains as an implied condition a clausula rebus sic stantibus.[1] . . .

---

1. Generally speaking, this Latin phrase, as used by the civilians, means that contracts are made upon the tacit assumption that an existing factual situation having an important bearing on the contract will remain basically stable during the life of the contract. A court applying the doctrine will read into the contract a condition subsequent leading to modification or termination of the contract in case of a substantial change of circumstances.

Treaties among nations give rise to analogous problems in international law. See Restatement (Third), Foreign Relations Law of the United States § 336 (1987).

In Romanist doctrine the view was taken that the so-called clausula rebus sic stantibus constitutes a general limitation on the continued existence of a contractual obligation. Like the other modern codifications, the positive law of Switzerland has not adopted this view. Nevertheless, this Court has recognized that a promisor must be discharged if extraordinary and unforeseeable circumstances render his duty to perform the promise so onerous that insistence upon such performance would cause his economic ruin [citing cases]. However, at the outset there arises the question whether the remedy may consist in judicial adjustment of the terms of the contract, or whether the remedy must be limited to complete termination of the contract. Applied to the instant case, this raises the question whether plaintiff's primary demand for reduction of the rentals should not be denied for this reason alone.... The German Reichsgericht declared it permissible for the court to grant the demand of one of the contracting parties, who had already performed, for an increase of the consideration promised by the other party, and thus to adjust the contract to changed conditions which had been brought about by a rise in the price of raw materials (RGZ 100, page 130). Some legal writers have criticized this decision as a "messing around" of the judge in the terms of binding contracts [citing a monograph by Professor Reichel]. From the standpoint of Swiss law, however, there is no decisive objection against permitting judicial modification of a contract in lieu of its termination. It should be pointed out in the first place that, if termination only is permitted, and modification is not, such termination can, in certain cases, be declared only for the future. In such event the termination has no retroactive effect.... Such prospective termination of the contract, having effect only for the future, is in the last analysis equivalent to judicial adjustment of the contract. Furthermore, it should be considered that the law itself (Code of Obligations Article 373, Subdivision 2), dealing with service contracts of independent contractors, provides for judicial modification of contractual duties. The criticism directed against Article 373, Subdivision 2, of the Code of Obligations [again citing Professor Reichel's book] is without importance here because it presents an argument which can only be addressed to the legislature. [The Court then points out that in a previous decision the principle expressed in Art. 373, subd. 2, was analogously applied and an adjustment of the terms of the contract granted, although the case did not involve a contract of the kind covered by the terms of that Article of the Code.] ... If the opponent of the party invoking the clausula rebus sic stantibus should prefer termination of the contract to the adjustment demanded, the court will as a rule decree termination rather than adjustment, in view of the principle contained in Art. 20, subd. 2, of the Code of Obligations.[2] ...

2. The first subdivision of Art. 20 was referred to in Haass v. Wyler, *supra*. The whole Article reads as follows:

A contract the contents of which is impossible, illegal or immoral, is invalid.

If the defect affects only some parts of the contract then only such parts are invalid, unless it appears that without the invalid part the contract would not have been made at all.

[Having determined that adjustment of the terms of the contract would be a proper remedy *if* the clausula rebus sic stantibus applies, the Court now turns to the question under what circumstances the clausula can be invoked.]

. . . At the bottom of the doctrine of the clausula rebus sic stantibus there is the consideration that even the principle imposing the duty to perform one's contractual obligations is limited by the higher principle of good faith. This is indicated by Art. 24, subd. 4, of the Code of Obligations.[3] If a contract may be rescinded in case of a mistake concerning its necessary original basis, then there must be some relief also in case such basis is subsequently changed in an intolerable degree. . . .

In applying the clausula, this Court has repeatedly used the criterion whether the duty of performance has become so onerous for the obligor that insistence upon his performance would be equivalent to his economic ruin. . . . Upon renewed examination, we cannot adhere to this criterion without qualification. If the principle of bona fides[4] is the yardstick for the application of the clausula, then the decision cannot be made to depend solely upon the effect which the change of circumstances has had upon the *obligor's* duty to perform. The effect of the change on the entire legal relationship must be examined. The criterion of the threatened ruin of the obligor would in the last analysis depend upon his subjective ability to perform. . . . [The court points out that this subjective criterion would be inconsistent with the provision of the Code which prescribes that only objective but not subjective impossibility shall excuse performance.]

The disturbance, through change of circumstances, of the balance between performance and counterperformance must be recognized as a ground for termination or adjustment if such disturbance is great, obvious, excessive. . . . There must be an obvious disproportion. Inasmuch as Art. 21 of the Code of Obligations uses this latter term, we may look to that Article for some indication of what is meant.[5] The question of disproportion is to be determined by the objective value of the performances [rendered or promised] as of the time when the issue of the clausula is before the court. [Citing a textbook and a commentary]. . . .

3. Art. 23 declares a contract to be not binding on a party who in entering into such contract was prompted by a material mistake. Art. 24 declares the mistake to be material if . . .

4. It concerned a factual situation which such party regarded as a necessary basis of the contract under the principles of good faith as generally practiced in business.

4. Compare Sec. 242 of the German Civil Code, quoted in note 20 to S. S. v. M. E. Corp., *supra* at 571.

5. Art. 21 is the Swiss "usury" provision of the Swiss Code of Obligations which reads as follows:

If an obvious disproportion between performance and counterperformance results from a contract the conclusion of which one party has induced by exploiting the distress, lightmindedness or inexperience of the other, then the victimized party may declare within a year from the making of the contract that he is not bound by the contract, and may demand restitution of any performance already rendered.

Even such obvious disproportion, however, is not sufficient to justify termination or adjustment of a contract.... There must be, in addition, the subjective factor that the obligee's insistence upon the terms of the contract amounts to an exploitation of the obligor's emergency, in other words that the conduct of the obligee is usurious and predatory.... The decisive question of the instant case, as correctly formulated by the court below, is thus whether defendant's insistence on the original terms of the contract must be characterized as usurious exploitation of an obvious disproportion, caused by the change of conditions, between performance and counterperformance.[6]

It is true that with respect to the making of a contract a predatory intention of one party and an obvious disproportion of performance and counterperformance are not sufficient to give the victim the option to declare the contract not binding. Pursuant to Art. 21 of the Code of Obligations there must be the additional element of distress, lightmindedness or inexperience on the part of the victim.... The question arises whether it is not inconsistent to terminate a contract merely because of subsequent change of circumstances and exploitation of an obvious disproportion, that is, on the basis of factors which, if they had been present at the time of the making of the contract, would under the rule of Art. 21 not have sufficed to vitiate the contract. But in reality there is no inconsistency. The legislator may assume that a party entering into a contract will know the relative values of his own promise or performance, on the one hand, and of the counterpromise or counterperformance, on the other. It is thus understandable that the legislator assists the obligor only if such obligor, at the time the contract was made, was afflicted with a special weakness (distress, lightmindedness, inexperience). The subsequent disproportion, however, results from a change of circumstances which is not caused by either party, and for which the party who has to suffer from such change bears no responsibility—otherwise he is entitled to no relief. Therefore, it is not necessary to insist on a subjective requirement insofar as the victim is concerned [i.e., the requirement of distress, lightmindedness or inexperience]. Moreover, in a case of such subsequent substantial disturbance of the balance between performance and counterperformance, there will always be distress on the part of one party, and the ultimate ground for termination or modification of the contract lies in the very fact that the other party is exploiting such distress....

[The Court then takes up the contention of the plaintiff that during the crisis years 1931 and 1932 the receipts of his restaurant decreased substantially.] ... The contract of lease was entered into for not less than 15 years. This long duration contained a speculative element, at least on the part of the plaintiff. Also the nature and the size of the premises rendered it clear from the beginning that the contractual risk was a substantial one. Contracts of this kind should not be lightly terminated or

---

6. Would this be a workable rule in a jurisdiction where questions of fact are for the jury?

modified. Where a contract is made for a long period of time, each party must count on substantial fluctuations of the general level of prosperity [citing a decision of a Zurich court].... This does not mean that the clausula rebus sic stantibus is never applicable to contracts of lease. But in the case of such slightly speculative contracts it makes no difference whether the subsequent change of conditions was actually foreseen, or whether it was merely foreseeable. Otherwise the clausula would put a premium on rashness and lightmindedness, to the detriment of the other party.... In the instant case, moreover, it was the plaintiff who repeatedly and insistently urged the defendant to enter into the contract, by picturing various advantages. Particularly in his letter of December 9, 1929,[7] plaintiff referred to the income from his other restaurant, the "Paradise," which he put at Fr. 80–90,000 annually, and with respect to which he said: "This financial reserve may be an attraction also from your point of view." The court below rightly inferred from this that plaintiff was conscious of the possibility of bad years, and that he tried to impress the defendant with his ability to cover any losses from the restaurant in the instant premises by the use of his other revenues. Consequently, plaintiff cannot now contend that defendant, by demanding that plaintiff actually use that "financial reserve," is exploiting a disproportion between performance and counterperformance.... Moreover, plaintiff has not even alleged that the objective rental value of the leased premises has fallen since the time when the contract was made, or that similar space in Zurich would today be available for a substantially lesser rental.

Affirmed.

NOTES AND QUESTIONS

(1) After the principal case had been decided by the highest court, the tenant gave notice of termination pursuant to Art. 269 of the Code of Obligations, which at that time provided that a contract of lease, even before it is terminated or terminable by its terms, shall come to an end at the close of any half-year period if either party, "for reasons of weight which make ... the continuation of the lease intolerable for him," gives three months' notice of termination; to be effective, such notice must contain an offer of "full compensation" for the damages which the other party suffers by reason of the premature termination of the lease.

This notice of termination was followed by new litigation, and the matter, again, came before the highest court. On May 29, 1934, the Federal Court held in Rogenmoser v. Tiefengrund A. G., 60 BGE II 205, that the lease was effectively terminated pursuant to Art. 269 of the Code of Obligations, and remanded the case to the lower court for determination of the amount payable by the tenant as "full compensation."

7. This date is possibly a misprint. Although supplementary agreements between the parties were made in 1930, it appears that the principal contract of lease was made on May 10, 1929.

Upon remand, the lower court fixed the amount of damages at sfrs. 400,000. The tenant appealed again, and the Federal Court, in its third decision dealing with this dispute, held on October 29, 1935 (Rogenmoser v. Tiefengrund A. G., 61 BGE II 259) that this amount should be reduced to sfrs. 200,000. The evidence showed that the premises could be re-let by the landlord only for a substantially lesser rental, and that, consequently, the landlord would suffer an annual loss of revenue of sfrs. 100,000 for the remaining term of the lease, that is, for 11 years. The Court reasoned that under these circumstances, if the tenant had been guilty of a *breach* of the lease contract, the damages would amount to sfrs. 1,100,000; but that in case of a *termination* authorized by Art. 269 the amount so computed was subject to a reduction "*ex aequo et bono.*" The Court took the view that the following considerations justified the drastic reduction (from sfrs. 1,100,000 to sfrs. 200,000):

(a) The tenant was not guilty of fraud or negligence.

(b) The economic crisis was foreseeable not only for the tenant but also for the landlord.

(c) The damages were caused in part by the landlord's stubborn insistence upon payment of a rental which was unbearably high.

(d) If the tenant had to pay the amount of sfrs. 400,000 fixed by the lower court, he would be exposed to misery.

(e) A certain discount must be deducted from rentals payable in future years.

(f) A portion of the premises might be used for purposes other than a restaurant.

Are the 1934 and 1935 decisions of the Federal Court consistent with the principal case? Can you explain why the tenant did not invoke Art. 269 in the principal case?

It was recognized in Switzerland that Art. 269 of the Code of Obligations constituted a specific application of the general principle of the clausula rebus sic stantibus to the law of landlord and tenant. See Oser–Schoenenberger, Das Obligationenrecht, Art. 269, Anno. 1 (1936). That being so, could it not be argued that in the law of landlord and tenant the general principle should be invoked only within the limits specified by Art. 269? Is this the view taken by the Court in the principal case? What conclusions can you draw from the principal case concerning the breadth and pervasiveness of general principles and "general clauses," as distinguished from specific provisions of the codes?

(2) Compare the following case, also decided by a Swiss court: In 1930, at which time plaintiff was an officer and director of defendant corporation, the parties entered into an employment contract which contained a provision whereby defendant promised to pay plaintiff 1000 francs per month from his retirement until the end of his life. Subsequently, it was agreed between the parties that plaintiff's retirement should begin in 1934. The promised monthly payments were made until 1945. In the latter year, defendant reduced the monthly payments to 40% of the promised amount, invoking the clausula rebus sic stantibus on the ground that its business had suffered a severe setback due to conditions then prevailing in Europe. Plaintiff sued for the balance of the promised payments, and was successful in the court of first instance. Upon

defendant's appeal to the Appellate Court of the Canton of Basel, affirmed. The risk of a deterioration of its business was assumed by defendant, as shown by the contract as a whole, and especially by a clause therein dealing with plaintiff's rights in case of defendant's liquidation. [No such liquidation had occurred.] Hence, the deterioration of defendant's business was not an unforeseen event, but a contingency which was, at least implicitly, covered by the terms of the contract. Appellationsgericht Basel–Stadt, February 7, 1947, reported in 45 Schweizerische Juristenzeitung 42 (1949).

(3) The Greek Civil Code of 1946, one of the most modern and most carefully drafted civil-law codifications, has recognized the *clausula rebus sic stantibus* doctrine in the text of the Code itself. Its Art. 388 reads as follows:

> If the circumstances in which the parties, having regard to the rules of good faith and to business practice, decided to conclude a synallagmatic contract,[1] subsequently change, for extraordinary reasons which it was impossible to foresee, and if, as a result of this change, fulfillment of the obligations, taking into account the counter-obligations, becomes inordinately burdensome for the obligor, the latter may request the judge to reduce the obligations at his discretion to a suitable extent, or to rescind the whole of the contract or the part not carried out.

In the *Alsing* case, an arbitration proceeding brought by a subsidiary of the Swedish Match Company against the Government of Greece, the plaintiff asked the arbitrator, on the basis of the foregoing provision, to extend the duration of the contract between the parties; but the arbitrator (the then President of the Swiss Federal Tribunal) held that the frustration of the expectations of the parties was not so profound as to merit judicial intervention. He expressed doubt whether, even if the circumstances of the case justified some judicial tampering with the terms of the contract, it would be proper to prolong its agreed-upon duration.[2]

(4) In Germany the rules on change of circumstances have been generally drawn by Courts and scholars from the general principle of good faith (§ 242 BGB), and this represents one of the most famous examples of German judge-made law doctrine.[3] Since the reform of the law of obligations, which took place in Germany in 2002,[4] those rules have found their statutory home in § 313–314 BGB. According to the former,

1. In civil-law terminology, the expression "synallagmatic" refers to contracts in which both parties make mutually dependent promises. Very roughly, one could equate synallagmatic contracts with bilateral contracts; but, with respect to the term "bilateral," there are subtle differences between common-law and civil-law terminology. See 1 Formation of Contracts—A Study of the Common Core of Legal Systems 92–93 (R. B. Schlesinger ed., 1968).

2. The important parts of the arbitrator's opinion are set forth in S. M. Schwebel, The Alsing Case, 8 Int'l & Comp.L.Q. 320 (1959). See especially *id.* at 341 ff. On the relevant Greek provisions, see A. N. Hatzis,

Introduction to Greek Contract Law, 1 Global Jurist Topics, issue 1, art. 3, 13, 17 (2001).

3. See H. Smit, Frustration of Contract: A Comparative Attempt at Consolidation, 58 Colum.L.Rev. 287 (1958); P. Hay, Frustration and Its Solution in German Law, 10 Am. J.Comp.L. 345 (1961); J. P. Dawson, Judicial Revision of Frustrated Contracts: Germany, 63 B.U.L.Rev. 1039 (1983); K. Zweigert & H. Kötz, *supra* p. 879, note 1, 516ff, where a wealth of further references can be found; R. Zimmermann & S. Whittaker, Good Faith in European Contract Law 25–26 (2000).

4. On the main features of the reform, see S. Grundmann, Germany and the Schuldrechtsmodernisierung 2002, 1 Eur.Rev.Con-

(1) If circumstances which became the basis of a contract have significantly changed since the contract was entered into and if the parties would not have entered into the contract or would have entered into it with different contents if they had foreseen this change, adaptation of the contract may be demanded to the extent that, taking account of all the circumstances of the specific case, in particular the contractual or statutory distribution of risk, one of the parties cannot reasonably be expected to uphold the contract without alteration. (2) It is equivalent to a change of circumstances if material conceptions that have become the basis of the contract are found to be incorrect. (3) If adaptation of the contract is not possible or one party cannot reasonably be expected to accept it, the disadvantaged party may withdraw from the contract. In the case of continuing obligations, the right to terminate takes the place of the right to withdraw.

§ 314 BGB specifies the general rule with regard to long-term contracts.[5]

We face here another example of the dialogues that typically occur in civil law countries between courts, academy and legislators. On the basis of the Code's "general clauses", and inspired by the seminal work of scholars, judges develop a body of experience, which subsequently—often with new refinements—is converted by legislators into written law.

Common-law courts ordinarily will not use the Latin terms *bona fides* and *clausula rebus sic stantibus*; but by invoking "implied conditions," "impossibility," or "frustration of purpose" they often reach comparable results. See E. W. Patterson, Constructive Conditions in Contracts, 42 Colum.L.Rev. 903, 943 ff. (1942); N. R. Weiskopf, Frustration of Contractual Purpose—Doctrine or a Myth?, 70 St. Johns L.Rev. 239 (1996); E. A. Farnsworth, Contracts 619–648 (3d ed. 1999); D. J. Smythe, Bounded Rationality, The Doctrine of Impracticability, and the Governance of Relational Contracts, 13 S.Cal.Interdis.L.J. 227 (2004).[6]

There remains, however, an important difference between the civil-law and the common-law approach to the problem. This difference is illustrated by the dictum in the principal case, to the effect that if the tenant's factual showing had been sufficiently strong, the Swiss court would have had the power (in lieu of terminating the contract) to let the tenant stay in the rented premises for the balance of the agreed-upon period, but at a judicially reduced rent. Common-law courts—although occasionally they show some boldness in "inter-

tract L. 129, 135 (2005); R. Zimmermann, The New German Law of Obligations: Historical and Comparative Perspectives (2006).

5. For a comment on the new provisions, see B. S. Markesinis, H. Unberath & A. Johnston, p. 907, note 1, 23, 320–325; O. Lando, On Legislative Style and Structure, Juridica International 13ff (2006). See also the German reporter's answers in Unexpected Circumstances in Contract Law (E. H. Hondius & H.–C. Grigoleit eds., forthcoming).

6. Common-law courts, indeed, have been criticized for having adopted too sweep-

ing and too "civilian" an approach in dealing with the problem of frustration of contracts. See H. J. Berman, Excuse for Nonperformance in the Light of Contract Practices in International Trade, 63 Colum.L.Rev. 1413 (1963), where it is argued that our courts should return to the true common-law method of deriving a solution in each case from discriminating analysis of the particular contract or type of contract before the court. See also B. Nicholas, Rules and Terms—Civil Law and Common Law, 48 Tul.L.Rev. 946 (1974); L. E. Trakman, Declaring Force Majeure: Veracity or Sham?, available at: http://works.bepress.com/leon_trakman/4 (2007).

preting" the terms of an agreement—rarely assert such a sweeping power to adjust the terms of a contract to changed circumstances.[7] Perhaps there is more need for the exercise of this broad judicial power in the civil-law systems, where a contract, so long as its performance is physically possible, as a rule can be specifically enforced.[8] In the common-law systems, in which the normal remedy for a breach of contract is an action for damages, the necessary adjustment frequently can be brought about by rules permitting a reasonable determination of the amount of damages (see also *infra*, text at note 11).

Both common law and civil law thus have developed methods of adjustment which can be employed in order to reach equitable results in the cases, or at least in some of the cases, in which the contractual relationship has been disturbed by an unanticipated and radical change of circumstances. The difference between common-law and civil-law methods of adjustment is significant mainly in situations involving a long-term contract. Here the extraordinary (and sparingly exercised) power of the courts of some civil-law countries—to let the contractual relationship continue but to modify the terms of the contract—has hardly any counterpart in the common law.[9]

(5) Note the subtlety displayed by the Swiss Federal Court in the Rogenmoser cases. In the first case, the Court refused to employ the sweeping clausula doctrine for the purpose of modifying the contract or releasing the tenant from his contractual obligations. In the second case, however, the Court held that pursuant to a specific provision of the Code, the tenant had the right to

---

7. Even under the liberal rule of U.C.C. § 2–615, commercial impracticability caused by unforeseen circumstances merely "excuses a seller from timely delivery of goods." Official Comment 1. There is no judicial rewriting of the terms of the contract. But the Restatement Second takes a step in the direction of the civil-law approach: for both impracticability (§ 261) and frustration (§ 265) it gives the court the power "to grant relief on such terms as justice requires," including protection of the parties' reliance interests, if this is necessary to avoid "injustice" (§ 272). However, few courts have engaged in such equitable adjustment of contractual relationships. See E. A. Farnsworth, *supra* p. 894, note 11, 624–634. For an elaborate and judicious discussion of the adjustment problem in American law, see S. W. Halpern, Application of the Doctrine of Commercial Impracticability: Searching for "The Wisdom of Solomon," 135 U.Pa.L.Rev. 1123 (1987); D. J. Smythe, *supra* in the text.

It is interesting to note that in Aluminum Company of America v. Essex Group, 499 F.Supp. 53 (W.D.Pa.1980)—one of the leading cases in which an American court assumed the power of price adjustment in connection with a long-term contract—Judge

Teitlebaum's opinion contains (at 93–94) an appendix giving a summary of the remedies utilized by civil-law courts confronted with contracts no longer deemed "fair" in light of changed circumstances.

8. For discussion of a German case in which the court in effect rewrote the terms of a contract the enforcement of which would have been highly inequitable because of drastically changed circumstances, see E. A. Farnsworth, Disputes Over Omission in Contracts, 68 Colum.L.Rev. 860, 883–84 (1968).

9. For one of the rare cases in which a court tampered with the terms of a long-term contract, see Miller v. Campello Co–op. Bank, 344 Mass. 76, 181 N.E.2d 345 (1962) For a more recent example, see Weil, Gotshal & Manges LLP v. CA–Towers @ Shores Center, L.P., 2007 WL 1200096 (Cal.App. 1 Dist. 2007) (Unpublished case). For recitations of the limited scope of the reformation doctrine, see, e.g., Onvoy, Inc. v. ALLETE, Inc., 736 N.W.2d 611 (Minn. 2007); W.N. McMurry Const. Co. v. Community First Ins., Inc., 160 P.3d 71 (Wyo. 2007). Note, however, that the court in that case failed to discuss the relevant issues of law. Other "aberrational" cases of this kind are discussed by S. W. Halpern, *supra* note 7.

terminate the contract, provided he would hold the landlord harmless.[10] The third decision of the Court fixed a very moderate amount of damages.

With no less subtlety, U.S. courts sometimes manage to refuse application of the frustration doctrine, and yet to avoid a "pound of flesh" result. They do so by (a) equity's discretionary refusal to order specific performance,[11] combined with (b) the law court's reliance on the good sense of a jury which, in fixing the amount of damages in a situation like that presented by the principal case, might well arrive at a practical result similar to that ultimately reached in the Swiss litigation.

The foregoing, however, requires some qualification. In situations in which the creditor can bring a legal action in debt, U.S. law. may be less flexible, and more conducive to "pound of flesh" results, than the civilian codes. Similarly, in a situation in which, as in the principal case, a tenant is forced by economic circumstances to abandon the leased property,[12] an action for the full stipulated amount of rent may lie under U.S. law., and not merely an action for damages.[13]

What is the reason for this occasional inflexibility of U.S. law? Could it be connected with the fact that the *forms of action*, although buried and emphatically "abolished" in most jurisdictions, still rule us from their graves, and that, in particular, the distinction between debt and assumpsit is still with us? Perhaps, we are dealing here with one of the areas in which our courts must

---

10. Modern codes frequently contain provisions authorizing unilateral termination for cause (for "reasons of weight") of long-term agreements, such as leases, partnership agreements, and employment contracts. Such termination for cause is possible before the end of the agreed-upon term, but sometimes it is conditioned upon payment of damages.

Code provisions of this kind ordinarily refer to particular types of contracts. In some civil-law countries, however, the courts have used such code provisions as starting points for analogical reasoning and thus have developed a broad principle to the effect that all long-term contractual relationships may be terminated by either party before the end of the agreed-upon period of the contract, if reasons of weight justifying such premature termination can be shown.

11. See, e.g., Malik Corp. v. Tenacity Group, LLC, 961 A.2d 1057 (D.C. 2008); Fisher v. Applebaum, 947 A.2d 248 (R.I. 2008); O'Connor v. Harger Const., Inc., 145 Idaho 904, 188 P.3d 846 (Idaho 2008).

12. In the landlord-tenant cases, a common-law court encounters the additional difficulty that basically a lease is an estate and not a "contract," and that there is doubt concerning the extent to which contract principles may be applied at all. See Sargent v. Smith, 78 Conn.App. 691, 828 A.2d 620

(2003) (rev'd on clearly erroneous factual findings, Sargent v. Smith, 272 Conn. 722, 865 A.2d 1129 (2005); Wright v. Baumann, 239 Or. 410, 398 P.2d 119, 120–21 (1965). On special problems concerning the application of the doctrine of frustration to lease cases, see E. A. Farnsworth, *supra* p. 894, note 11, at 636ff.

As to the contractual nature of a lease in most civil-law countries, see *supra* sec. B(1). The difference between common-law and civil-law thinking regarding the nature of a lease is discussed at length in Viterbo v. Friedlander, 120 U.S. 707, 7 S.Ct. 962 (1887).

13. In the majority of American jurisdictions it has been held that the landlord, unless he has accepted the tenant's surrender of the leasehold, can sue for rent rather than damages, and that the landlord's claim for rent is not defeated or diminished by virtue of his failure, or even his out-right refusal, to look for another tenant or to take any other steps tending to mitigate damages. See the cases collected in 2 M. Friedman on Leases 1085–87 (4th ed. 1997). The lower courts in New York have drawn a distinction between residential and other leases and impose a mitigation requirement if the lease is of the former kind. See, e.g., Forty Exchange Co. v. Cohen, 125 Misc.2d 475, 479 N.Y.S.2d 628 (Civ.Ct.1984).

slowly, step by step, free themselves of the grip of the forms of action[14]—a problem from which civil-law courts have been saved by the strength of their scholars' systematizing influence and by the codifiers' break with the past.

H. C. Gutteridge, Abuse of Rights

5 Cambridge Law Journal 22, 32–39 (1933).[1]

[Most of the author's footnotes omitted; others renumbered.]

. . . [The] operation of the theory of abuse in practice may be illustrated by reference to three of the leading French cases.

Chronologically the first of these is a decision of the Court of Appeal of Colmar given in the year 1855. The owner of a house erected a tall dummy chimney on his roof for the sole purpose of annoying a neighboring householder by depriving him of the access of light to certain of his rooms. Art. 552 of the Code Civil states that the owner of land can plant or build on it whatever he thinks proper, subject only to certain exceptions which are irrelevant for our present purpose.[2] It was argued that the defendant was merely doing what he had an absolute right to do, and that the motive of his act must be disregarded, but it was held by the Court that this was no answer to the claim. Although the defendant was exercising a right given to him by the law he was acting with spiteful intent, and had no serious and legitimate interest in what he was doing. His act must, therefore, be treated as wrongful.

A year later a decision to the same effect was given by the Court of Appeal of Lyons, only in this case the question turned not on the erection of a structure, but on the excavation of the subsoil, the circumstances being much the same as those in Mayor of Bradford v. Pickles.[3] There was a number of adjacent springs yielding the famous St. Galmier mineral water,

14. Cf. Wright v. Baumann, *supra* note 12 and authorities there cited.

1. Reprinted with the permission of the Cambridge Law Journal. For more recent discussions of abuse of rights, but concentrating mainly on American equivalents of the doctrine, see J. M. Perillo, Abuse of Rights: A Pervasive Legal Concept, 27 Pacific L.J. 37 (1995); M. Byers, Abuse of Rights: An Old Principle, A New Age, 47 McGill L.J. 389 (2002).

2. [Article 552 of the French Civil Code still reads as quoted by Prof. Gutteridge. But it must now be read in conjunction with the limits set forth by the Code de l'Urbanisme and the Code de la Construction et de l'Habitation. Today, the owners of the two "spite" structures mentioned by Prof. Gutteridge would not, presumably, have received a building permit. Eds.]

3. [1895] A.C. 587. [That case is still good law in England; but its effect has been greatly weakened by statute. See R. Megarry & H. W. R. Wade, The Law of Real Property 62, 1155–56 (6th ed. 2000); see also M. Taggart, Private Property and Abuse of Rights in Victorian England. The Story of Edward Pickles and the Bradford Water Supply (2002). In the United States the majority of jurisdictions, rejecting the rule of Mayor of Bradford v. Pickles and adopting the doctrine of reasonable use, have reached a result comparable to that of the French decisions. See 9 Powell on Real Property, § 65.03 (M.A. Wolf ed., 2000); R. Pound, The French Civil Code and the Spirit of 19th Century Law, 35 B.U.L.Rev. 87, 95 (1955). For a case which on its facts is similar to the French St. Galmier case, see Hathorn v. Natural Carbonic Gas Co., 194 N.Y. 326, 87 N.E. 504 (1909). Eds.]

and the proprietor of one of the springs installed a powerful pump with the result that the yield of an adjoining spring belonging to another owner was diminished by two-thirds. There does not seem to have been any direct evidence of spite in this case, but it was inferred that the owner of the pump was inspired solely by a desire to inflict harm because he merely wasted the additional supply of water which he had obtained in this way. Reliance was placed by the defendant on Art. 544 of the Code Civil which states that "ownership is the right of enjoying and disposing of a thing in the most unlimited manner provided that it is not utilized in a manner forbidden by law." It was decided in terms that where an act is done with the sole and deliberate intention of inflicting harm it is wrongful and cannot be justified by pleading a proprietary right.[4]

The third case which is of a curious and interesting description was decided many years later [1917] by the Court of Cassation. It is the most famous of all the decisions which have been given on this question and it is one of the few French cases which is referred to by name, i.e., as the *"affaire Clément–Bayard."* The Clément–Bayard Company were the owners of certain hangars in which they housed airships which were being built to the order of the French Government. Friction arose between the company and the owner of the adjoining site, who was piqued by the failure of negotiations for the purchase by the company of his land at a high valuation. He erected within his own boundaries a number of wooden scaffolds of a considerable height fitted with projections bristling with spikes. The intention was, of course, to bring pressure to bear on the company by making it impossible or difficult to launch the airships, and in fact on one occasion an airship collided with one of these structures and was severely damaged. In an action brought by the Clément–Bayard Company for damages and an order for the removal of the obstructions, it was pleaded by the defendant that he was merely exercising a right given to him by the provisions of the Code Civil which have been just cited. It was held successively by the Civil Tribunal of Compiègne, the Court of Appeal of Amiens and the Court of Cassation that the defendant was liable. The case is important because the defendant was in a sense animated by more than one motive. His primary intention seems to have been to force the Clément–Bayard Company to buy him out, but he also intended, if necessary, to wreck their airships for this purpose. It was held that the dominant motive must be taken to have been the infliction of harm, since the circumstances showed that the defendant hoped to secure his ends by the threat of injury to the airships of the plaintiff company. He could not,

---

4. This decision was reached although the defendant was able to point, not only to the general definition of property rights in Art. 544, but also to the specific language of Art. 641 which then read: "The owner of land on which a spring rises is entitled to make such use of it as he pleases." See M. Amos, The Code Napoléon and the Modern World, 10 J.Comp.Leg. & Int'l L. (Ord. Ser.) 222, 232 (1928). More than 40 years after the St. Galmier case, Art. 641 (renumbered 642) was amended by the addition of the words "within the limits and for the purposes of his property."

therefore, be permitted to shelter himself behind the plea that, whereas one of his motives was the deliberate infliction of harm, the other was not.[5]

It seems to be beyond doubt that the French Courts will invariably repress any spiteful exercise of a proprietary right. But the principle of abuse has also been extended so as to cover a much wider area. . . . Thus it has been held to be abusive for an employer to refuse to employ trade unionists where his motive is to damage the trade union, and likewise for a trade union to blacklist an employer from a vindictive motive.[6] Dramatic criticism of an unfavourable character is abusive if it is prompted solely by a desire to harm the author of a play. The malicious institution of legal proceedings also comes under this heading; in fact an English lawyer will find that many matters which we regard as separate wrongs have been swept up by the French Courts into the net of the abuse of rights. Planiol attributes this to the popularity of the word "abuse" ("l'expression a fait fortune") and he holds the opinion, which is supported by other writers, that the concept has been exaggerated and overworked.

. . . [Turning to German law], Art. 226[7] (the famous *"Schikaneverbot"*) runs as follows: *"The exercise of a right is forbidden if it can have no other purpose than to harm some other person."* . . . A close examination of the words employed in Art. 226 shows that its operation is limited to cases in which it is possible to establish that a right has been exercised *solely* for the purpose of harming some other person. As I have already pointed out, this is a matter which it is extremely difficult to prove in a great many cases. The German courts have realized this, and they have accordingly adopted an objective test of intention by which an *animus vicini nocendi* can be inferred from the circumstances. Even so, the difficulties of proof are often such as to render Art. 226 inoperative.[8] But it has been found to be useful

---

5. [Faced with a fact situation remarkably similar to that presented in the French Clément–Bayard case, an American court reached the same result, but without invoking a theory as pervasive as "abuse of rights." See Commonwealth v. VonBestecki, 30 Pa.D. & C. 137 (1937). Compare also Schork v. Epperson, 74 Wyo. 286, 287 P.2d 467 (1955). Eds.]

6. [For a discussion of the doctrine of abuse of rights in the context of French labor law, see A. Lenhoff, Compulsory Unionism in Europe, 5 Am.J.Comp.L. 18, 37–38 (1956); M. Forde, Liability in Damages for Strikes: A French Counter–Revolution, 33 Am. J.Comp.L. 447 (1985); C. A. Scott, Money Talks: The Influence of Economic Power on the Employment Law and Policies in the United States and France, 7 San D.Int'l L.J. 348ff (2006); O. Kaufmann, Weakening of Dismissal Protection or Strengthening of Employment Policy in France?, 36 Ind.L.J. 267 (2007).

Code du Travail art. L1132–1 now prohibits employers from discriminating against workers on account of their participation in a union. There is thus no more need for employees to rely on the doctrine of abuse of rights in such a case. For an analogous rule under German law, see Betriebsverfassungsgesetz (Law on the Organization of Enterprises) § 75. Eds.]

7. [The reference is to Section 226 of the German Civil Code; see note 18 to the Opinion of the German Reichsgericht in the Matter of S. S. v. M. E. Corp., *supra* at 571. Eds.]

8. It may be observed that this is perhaps due, to some extent, to the fact that the parties to an action do not, normally, give evidence in Germany, and are not cross-examined. [The court may, however, order that a party be examined, usually by a member of the court, and sometimes under oath. Professor Gutteridge is nevertheless right in imply-

in the case of the spiteful exercise of proprietary rights, and the experience of German lawyers is that it has not been accompanied by any undesirable restrictions on the liberties of individuals.... It has been held to be abusive for a father to refuse, for purely personal reasons, to allow his son to visit his mother's tomb, situated on land belonging to the father.[9] It is clear, however, that the tendency is to place a strict interpretation on the provisions of Art. 226, and that the role which it plays in checking abuses of legal rights is correspondingly restricted.

The German law of civil wrongs does not recognize any general duty to refrain from inflicting harm on others, but it is much more supple and adaptable in this respect than our law of torts. This is due to the operation of two of the articles of the Civil Code (Arts. 138[10] and 826[11]) which have as their object the repression of acts which are against *Sittlichkeit* ("boni mores").... The standard of boni mores must obviously vary from tribunal to tribunal, but it is a real and potent force in the development of German law, and it has conferred praetorian powers on the German judges. So far as the theory of abuse is concerned it is difficult to conceive of any case in which the malevolent exercise of a right could not be checked by the application of the principle of *boni mores*.

... Mention must also be made of another concept of German law which plays its part in curbing the abuse of legal rights. Where the enforcement of a business contract is in question the Civil Code by virtue of Arts. 157[12] and 242[13] requires that the parties shall act in accordance with *Treu und Glauben*. This again is a term which defies accurate translation, but it means that the parties must act in accordance with good faith as understood by men of affairs. In such cases as commercial sales, for example, this is a principle which may often be invoked to restrain an abusive exercise of a contractual right....

The Swiss law deals with abuses of rights ... [in] Art. 2 of the Civil Code [, which] provides that *"every person is bound to exercise his rights and to fulfil his obligations according to the principles of good faith. The law does not protect the manifest abuse of a right."* It will be observed that nothing is said about intention to harm one's neighbour; the Code goes

---

ing that in Germany as in most civil-law countries the procedural devices for extracting information from an unwilling adversary are weaker than in common-law jurisdictions. See *supra* Chapter 8.]

9. ... Art. 226 has also been employed as a check to prevent the rejection of goods by a buyer for some trivial fault. [citation], and cf. Jackson v. Rotax Motor Co. [1910], 2 K.B. 937. It is also available as a remedy against the malicious institution of legal proceedings. [citation] [for a survey on the case law applying art. 226 BGB, see C. von Bar, *supra* note 211, 55–57. Eds.]

10. [The reference is to section 138. See note 4 to the Opinion of the German Reichtsgericht in the Matter of S. S. v. M. E. Corp., *supra* at 565. Eds.]

11. [The reference is to section 826. See text *supra* at 925–26. Eds.]

12. "Contracts must be interpreted in accordance with the principles of good faith, with due regard to usage." [Again, the reference is to section 157 of the Code. Eds.]

13. [The reference is to section 242. See note 20 to the Opinion of the German Reichtsgericht in the Matter of S. S. v. M. E. Corp., *supra* at 571. Eds.]

straight to the point and condemns an abuse of rights in so many words without defining the phrase in any way. . . .

This is one of the instances of the policy adopted by the framers of the Swiss Codes in abandoning certain questions entirely to the judges. Art. 4 of the Civil Code states that where the law expressly leaves a question to the discretion of a judge he must base his decision on principles of justice and equity, a provision which is supplementary to Art. 1 of the Code[14] which directs the judge to apply the spirit as well as the letter of the law.
. . .

NOTE

For an understanding of the French doctrine of abus de droit it is important to realize that the doctrine is sometimes used as a basis for a *cause of action,* and sometimes as a basis for a *defense.* Where a cause of action is based on defendant's abuse of a right, it is technically supported by the famous Article 1382 of the French Civil Code (see *supra* at 102) which in broad terms imposes liability upon anybody who "causes damage to another." The counterclaim for damages in the case of Kirsch v. Davoust, *infra,* can be so supported.

In those cases, however, in which abus de droit is interposed as a defense against an action based on a technically well-founded right, many French authors have felt that the tort provision of the Code, broad as it is, cannot be the true basis supporting the defense. Therefore, under the leadership of Josserand,[1] they substitute for the older tort theory of abus de droit the modern theory that every Code article or other statute creating a right must be *interpreted* as limiting the exercise of such right to the object for which it was created.[2] It goes without saying that in the hands of judges holding strong progressive convictions this theory of the relativity of rights could become a potent instrument of social reform. Contrary to the expectations of some theorists, however, the French courts have not attempted to use the doctrine for such a purpose.[3] In France as elsewhere, the modern welfare state has

---

14. [See *supra* p. 428ff, 484, and 573ff. Eds.]

1. L. Josserand, supported by the writings of Duguit, Saleilles and Charmont, wrote the classical treatise on the subject, entitled De l'Abus des Droits (1905, 2d ed. 1927).

2. See F. P. Walton, Motive as an Element in Torts in the Common and in the Civil Law, 22 Harv.L.Rev. 501 (1909). In line with the statement in the text, a more recent French author indicates that the doctrine of abuse of rights may come into play (a) when a right is being exercised by somebody having no legitimate interest in doing so (in other words, either out of sheer malevolence or to obtain an illegitimate—collateral—purpose), and (b) when a right given for a specific purpose (as is the right parents have to con-

trol their children) is used for a purpose different from that for which it was given. See F. Pollaud–Dulian, Abus de droit et droit moral, 1993 D.Chr. 97; see also G. Viney & P. Jourdain, Les conditions de la responsabilité 416–421 (3d ed. 2006). Cf. J. M. Perillo. *supra* p. 974, note 1 at 47: "Three kinds of abusive actions are condemned by the doctrine: (1) the predominant motive for the action is to cause harm; (2) the exercise is totally unreasonable given the lack of any legitimate interest in the exercise of the right and its exercise harms another; and (3) the right is exercised for a purpose other than that for which it exists." The sentence quoted is intended to refer to abuse of rights doctrine generally, not merely in French law.

3. See G. Ripert, Le Régime Démocratique et le Droit Civil Moderne 219 (1948).

largely been instituted by legislative and administrative measures and not by judicial expansion of the concept of *abus de droit*.[4]

The preliminary draft of a revised Civil Code prepared in the 1950s by the Civil Code Reform Commission contained an express provision (Art. 147) dealing with abuse of rights:[5]

> Every act or every fact which, by the intention of its author, by its object or by the circumstances in which it occurred, manifestly exceeds the normal exercise of a right, is not protected by the law and makes its author responsible.

> This provision does not apply to rights which by their nature or by virtue of the law can be exercised in a discretionary manner.

As noted elsewhere,[6] the comprehensive revision of the French Civil Code, contemplated in the years shortly after the end of the Second World War, never came to pass, nor was the Reform Commission's proposal inserted into the Civil Code on the occasion of some of its more limited amendments, perhaps because the formulations of the Reform Commission would not have changed the current situation under which the courts must determine exactly when the "normal exercise" of a right is exceeded and what rights are so discretionary that they can never be abused.[7]

4. Social welfare type statutes or administrative regulations may, however, interact with broader principles in complex ways. An example, although somewhat at the margin of "abuse of rights," is provided by French consumer protection legislation. Article 35 of the so-called *loi Scrivener* on consumer protection of 1978, later incorporated into the Consumer Code, provided that "abusive" clauses in consumer contracts could be prohibited by decrees, adopted upon the suggestion of a special advisory committee. Clauses in violation of these provisions were to be considered as nullities. This clearly implied that only clauses specifically declared to be "abusive" by a decree were void. Only one such Decree, with a limited list of "abusive" clauses, was issued at the time. However, from about 1987 on, the *Cour de cassation* began to indicate, and finally clearly stated, that abusive clauses in consumer contracts could be declared void by the court, whether mentioned in a decree or not. See Lorthioir v. Baucheron, Cass.civ.1st., May 14, 1991, 1991 D.J. 449, and for a discussion of the historical development, the note appended to the case in H. Capitant, Les grands arrêts de la jurisprudence civile 386, 387–95 (10th ed. by F. Terré & Y. Lequette 1994). But that was not the end of developments. When the need arose in 1994 to adapt the French Consumer Code to the European Community Consumer Protection Directive [Directive 93/13 of the Council of April 5, 1993 on unfair terms in consumer contracts, 1993 O.J. L 95 at 29], the French Consumer Code was amended, inter alia, by providing generally and without restriction that abusive clauses (defined broadly as clauses which create a substantial imbalance between the parties) are void. The possibility for the enactment of decrees prohibiting specific clauses has been continued, but, consistent with the *Lorthioir* line of cases, the new provision clearly authorizes the courts to deal with "abusive" clauses themselves, even in the absence of a decree. See French Consumer Code Art. L132–1, as amended by Law No. 95–96 of February 1, 1995. Cf. G. Paisant, Les clauses abusives et la présentation des contrats dans la loi no 95–96 du 1er février 1995, 1995 D.Chr. 99; H. Beale, A. Hartkamp, H. Kötz, D. Tallon, *supra* p. 874, note 2, 23, 525–527; M. Ebers, *supra* p. 909, note 20, 360.

5. See L. Julliot de la Morandière (Dainow trans.), Preliminary Report of the Civil Code Reform Commission of France, 16 La. L.Rev. 1, 27–28 (1955).

6. See *supra* Chapter 5, Section 9 at 455ff.

7. French cases recognize that some rights may be so absolute that their exercise can never be an abuse. But the number of such "absolute" or "discretionary" rights seems to have become more and more limited. See the note appended to the *Clément-*

While the French draft appears to have influenced legislators elsewhere, in particular in Luxembourg and the Netherlands,[8] it did not exercise a comparable sway on French scholars. The recent proposal for a revision of the French Civil Code (the so-called "Projet Catala"[9]) contains no provisions about the abuse of rights, even though, in the compilers' mind, "le projet imprime à la justice dans le contrat tout l'élan compatible avec la sécurité juridique" [the project gives breadth to contractual fairness insofar as predictability of law is guaranteed].[10]

For more extensive discussions of the French doctrine of abuse of rights, see, e.g., P. Catala & J. A. Weir, Delict and Torts: A Study in Parallel, 38 Tul.L.Rev. 221 (1964); A. Mayrand, Abuse of Rights in France and Quebec, 34 La.L.Rev. 993 (1974); V. Bolgar, Abuse of Rights in France, Germany and Switzerland: A Survey of a Recent Chapter in Legal Doctrine, 35 La.L.Rev. 1015 (1975); A. N. Yannopoulos, Civil Liability for Abuse of Rights: Something Old, Something New, 54 La.L.Rev. 1173 (1994).

A particular aspect of the abuse of rights doctrine is exemplified by the following case:

Kirsch v. Davoust

Cass. req., June 21, 1926, 1926 Sirey[1] 1.294.

The Court.... Considering that the spouses Kirsch have sought to have nullified, as lacking in the necessary requirements of form and substance, the holographic testament dated December 20, 1918, by which Mme. Redenbach disinherited her sister, Mme. Kirsch, and made Davoust her universal heir; that after the taking of oral testimony the trial judges decided that the testament was duly made and executed by the testatrix, and dismissed the action of the spouses Kirsch, decreeing that they should pay damages in the amount of Fr. 500[2] in favor of Davoust;

Bayard case in H. Capitant, *supra* n. 253, at 278. Thus the *Cour de cassation* noted in a 1994 decision that while an employer was entitled to dismiss an employee (working under an employment contract for an indeterminate period) only for a substantial reason, an employee need give no reason for leaving an employment under such a contract, but that did not mean that such an action could not be abusive, though the burden of proof was on the employer to show it. See Cass. soc., Decision of June 22, 1994, summarized, and therefore emphasized, in the Court's Annual Report for 1994 (Rapport de la Cour de Cassation 1994), at 286.

8. See *infra* text at p. 990, notes 16 and 17.

9. P. Catala, G. Cornu, P. Delebecque, D. Mazeaud, Avant-projet de réforme du droits des obligations (Articles 1101 à 1386 du Code civil) et du droit de la prescription

(Articles 2234 à 2281 du Code civil) (2006) (the text of the project is also available at the website http://www.lexisnexis.fr/pdf/DO/RAPPORTCATALA.pdf). As to the contents of the project, see B. Fauvarque-Cosson & D. Mazeaud, The "Avant-projet Catala": A Draft Revision of the French Law of Obligations and Limitation Periods, Unif. L. Rev. 103 f. (2006).

10. G. Cornu, Introduction, in Avant-projet, *supra* note 9, 9.

1. Sirey was one of the standard French law reporting services; it eventually merged with the rival Dalloz (standard abbreviation D.) service.

2. The amount seems small, but note that this is pre-World War II money; the current equivalent would be a multiple of that sum.

Considering that according to the contention of the appellants that imposition of damages was unlawful, on the ground that the pursuit of legal remedies cannot constitute a wrong unless accompanied by acts of malice or bad faith, which acts were not found by the court; but

Considering that it appears from the findings of the court below that the spouses Kirsch, who had charged that Mme. Redenbach had made no testament at all, neither on December 20, 1918, nor on any subsequent day until her death, have not produced any evidence at the hearing; that they did not hesitate to assert as true a fact of which they were not sure; that they have attributed sentiments to the deceased which were inconsistent with her real sentiments as proved at the hearing; that they have thus altered the truth for the manifest purpose of influencing the judges in favor of their position; that by the protracted proceedings wantonly initiated and pursued by them they have caused Davoust not only trouble but also expenses over and above taxable costs and fees;

Considering that from these dominant findings the court could infer that the spouses Kirsch did not limit themselves to the legitimate pursuit of their legal remedies, but have committed a tort to the prejudice of Davoust, and that the order [of the court below] is thus found to be legally justified, . . .

Rejects the appeal taken against the order of the court at Bourges dated February 25, 1925.

NOTES

(1) In connection with the above case, the reader should consider the question whether in the United States the mere wanton initiation, or defense, of a civil action can be a wrong. For a discussion, see, e.g., Recommendation of the [New York] Law Revision Commission to the 1984 Legislature Relating to Malicious Prosecution Actions, N.Y. Leg. Doc. (1984) No. 65[G]. While the Commission suggested some changes, it advised against the right to interpose a malicious prosecution claim as a counterclaim, fearing such a counterclaim would then become routine in all suits. Such counterclaims were, in fact, fairly common in France before New Code of Civil Procedure Art. 700 provided an alternative remedy. Cf. Fed.R.Civ.Proc. 11 permitting the imposition of attorneys' fees upon a party in the event of "abusive" procedures. Note that while the provision mentioned, and sometimes the possibility of bringing an action for malicious prosecution may be a remedy for the wrongful initiation of proceedings, malicious prosecution is of no help against abusive defense tactics. Strict application of sanctioning rules, such as Rule 11 may provide some relief. However, when a tort action is sought as a remedy, the inconsistency remains that a frivolous point in a counterclaim may possibly provide a basis for a malicious prosecution action, while the identical point interposed as a affirmative defense will not. The absence of a general principle, such as abuse of rights, is clearly a problem here. Cf. J. K. Van Patten & R. E. Willard, The Limits of Advocacy: A Proposal for the Tort of Malicious Defense in Civil Litigation, 35 Hastings L.J. 891 (1984); B. Glesner Fines, Speculating on the Future of

Attorney Responsibility to Nonclients, 37 S.Tex.L.Rev. 1283, 1301 f. (1996); A. Kedem, Can Attorneys and Clients Conspire?, 114 Yale L.J. 1819 (2005).[1]

(2) The ability to recover damages for groundless proceedings (including a groundless defense) had an importance in France not found in other civil law countries. The reader will recall that in France, originally, the "loser pays all" rule meant that the loser had to pay the winning party's *avoué* but not the winning party's *avocat* fees (nor certain other actual expenses not formally considered as reimbursable). In particularly egregious cases, the action for damages for "abusive" use of legal proceedings was thus a convenient way of obtaining reimbursement for such expenses. The New Code of Civil Procedure changed the situation in several steps. It in essence strengthened the case-created rule on "abusive" proceedings when a new Article 32–1, inserted in 1978, provided that in case of dilatory or abusive proceedings, the court could impose a civil fine up to Euro 3.000, in addition to any damages requested. Furthermore, Article 700 of the new Code of Civil Procedure originally gave the judge a discretionary power to impose some or all of the expenses not normally reimbursable on the losing side when equity so demanded; an amendment in 1991 provided in essence that this should normally be done, but nevertheless left the judge a discretionary power to shift only part of the expenses, or none at all if this seemed equitable in the light of the economic and other conditions of the parties. An "abuse" as such is clearly not required now for Art. 700 to be applicable. It would appear, however, that in case of "abusive" proceedings damages (as in the case above) can still be requested, but Article 700, especially since its amendment in 1991, seems to have removed a substantial incentive for the bringing of proceedings charging "abusive" procedures.

(3) As the preceding discussion has shown, a very general principle, such as that of "abuse of rights," can lose some of its significance in a particular area if a specific regulation comes into being for that area which takes care of some of the problems for which the broad rule provided a solution. In the case of "abusive" procedures, this was done by legislation or quasi-legislation.[2] But such an event can also come to pass by case development, even in a country where no formal rule of stare decisis is recognized. Thus the use of the "abuse of rights" principle has become less significant in cases (such as the *Clément-Bayard* case cited by Professor Gutteridge) involving adjoining landowners because the French courts have developed a special principle, somewhat akin to the "private nuisance" doctrine of American law, according to which a land-owner (or person otherwise in possession or control of land) may not interfere to an unreasonable extent with the use and enjoyment of adjacent land. An example would be, for instance, the construction of a much higher building next to a preexisting older one in such a manner that an interference is created with the preexisting building's chimneys.[3] There is clearly no need to show a

---

1. See however Aranson v. Schroeder, 140 N.H. 359, 671 A.2d 1023, 1027 (1995), discussed in G. C. Christie et al., Cases and Materials on the Law of Torts 1405–06 (4th ed. 2004), in which the Court recognized the existence of the tort of "malicious defense".

2. As the reader knows, the French Code of Civil Procedure, and thus also its Article 700, was adopted by decree, but a rule parallel to the 1991 revision of Article 700 of the Code is also found in the 1991 statute dealing with the enforcement of judgments.

3. See e.g. Brun v. S.C.I. du 10, rue Joseph–Liouville, 1971 J.C.P. II. 16781; see also the rulings quoted by G. Viney & P. Jourdain, *supra* p. 978, note 2, 1214–1216.

wrongful intent, and thus problems of proof are less severe than in an action for "abuse of rights," which, therefore, appears to have become less frequent in that area, although it is, of course, still possible. The great advantage of the "abuse of rights" doctrine is that it provides a remedy in all sorts of novel situations, even situations that have not been thought of before. Suits based on that doctrine are therefore still quite frequent in France. The next case and the notes following it show some of its more recent applications, and possible limitations upon it.

Duval v. Chedot

Cass.civ.1st, June 17, 1969, J.C.P. 1970. II. 16162.

[Plaintiff Chedot, the owner of a garage business, for several years had been a client of defendant Duval, a certified public accountant. The latter did all of the bookkeeping and accounting work that became necessary in plaintiff's business, and prepared plaintiff's tax returns. Apparently dissatisfied with defendant's services, plaintiff discharged him in June 1964, and retained another accounting firm. Defendant sent plaintiff a bill in the amount of frs. 2,200 (appr. $500) for services rendered prior to June 1964; but the bill remained unpaid, apparently for the reason (although this is not entirely clear) that plaintiff believed he had a larger claim against defendant for malpractice. Shortly after June 1964, the tax authorities notified plaintiff that they were about to audit his returns for the years 1961–1963. Most of plaintiff's books, ledgers and other documents that were needed for the audit were still in the possession of defendant, who asserted a "right of retention," i.e., the right to retain these documents until payment of his bill.[1] Plaintiff, therefore, asked defendant to let the tax officials see the documents, pointing out that the returns which were the subject of the audit had been prepared by defendant, and that plaintiff would get into serious difficulties if the tax officials were not given access to the books and documents supporting the returns. The defendant, however, refused to make the books and documents available to the tax officials. The officials, who thus were unable to verify the figures in plaintiffs tax returns, then proceeded to estimate the pertinent figures. On the basis of this estimate, they assessed about frs. 16,000 (appr. $3,200) in additional taxes and frs. 23,000 (appr. $4,400) in penalties against plaintiff.

In early 1965, plaintiff brought this action, seeking to hold defendant liable in damages for the amounts thus assessed. Defendant prayed for dismissal of the action, and counterclaimed (a) for his fees in the amount of frs. 2,200, and (b) for a judicial declaration that he could retain the documents in his possession until payment of such fees. On April 26, 1965 the court of first instance at Caen (i) ordered the taking of evidence

---

1. This is somewhat analogous to the retaining lien of, e.g., an American lawyer, though somewhat broader in concept. On the attorney's retaining lien in the United States, see, e.g., Attorney's Retaining Lien: What Items of Client's Property are not Subject to the Lien?, 70 A.L.R.4th 827; see also J. Leubsdorf, Against Lawyer Retaining Liens, 72 Fordham L.Rev. 849 (2004).

concerning plaintiff's claim, and (ii) on defendant's counterclaim entered judgment in accordance with defendant's prayer for relief.[2] No appeal was taken from this decision. After evidence had been taken, the court of first instance on June 20, 1966 entered a judgment permitting plaintiff to recover damages in the amount of frs. 25,000 from the defendant. Upon appeal from the judgment of June 20, 1966, the Court of Appeal at Caen, as intermediate appellate court, reduced the amount of damages, but otherwise affirmed. It is this judgment of affirmance, dated April 10, 1967, that Duval seeks to have reviewed by the Cour de Cassation.]

The Court. . . . Taking note of the principles governing the right of retention;

Considering that the creditor exercising the right of retention is entitled, absent a contrary statutory provision, until full payment of his claim to refuse giving up possession of the things and documents lawfully retained;

Considering that the findings made below show that garage-owner Chedot confided the keeping of his books to Duval, a certified public accountant; that the latter, as determined in a judicial decision no longer subject to appeal,[3] was entitled to retain the books and documents belonging to Chedot as security for the payment of his fees; that the tax authorities assessed penalties against Chedot after Duval, who had been notified by his former client, had declined to furnish the authorities with data in his possession; that Chedot, believing the additional taxes and penalties to be the consequence of Duval's tortious failure [to furnish such data], demanded payment of damages;

Considering that the Court of Appeal has in part upheld this demand on the theory that Duval "has abused his right of retention"; that in so holding—on the asserted ground that Duval should have made the accounting documents retained by him or the data contained therein available to the tax authorities, since it is incumbent upon the retaining creditor to preserve the property of his debtor—the intermediate appellate court has violated the above-mentioned principles;

For these reasons . . . reverses and annuls the judgment rendered herein on April 10, 1967 by the Court of Appeal at Caen, and remands the case to the Court of Appeal at Rouen.

NOTES AND QUESTIONS

(1) The case just cited is one in which the doctrine of "abuse of rights" was held not to be applicable. Several explanations may be given. In an annotation

---

2. In other words, the court ruled that at that stage of the proceedings it was quite clear that the accountant had a right to be paid for his services and thus granted the counterclaim but felt that further investigation was required to decide whether plaintiff's claim for "abuse" of the right of retention should be granted.

3. This is obviously a reference to the lower court decision on the counterclaim, which, by holding for the accountant, clearly implied that he had a good claim to be paid for his services and that up to that time he had not been paid, thus giving rise to the right of retention.

appended to the report of this case (1970 J.C.P. II. 16162), Professor N. Catala–Franjou expresses approval of the result reached by the Cour de Cassation. She points out that by virtue of the right of retention the creditor has no power to sell his debtor's items, but only to retain it. Therefore, Professor Catala–Franjou argues, the right of retention is exclusively negative in nature, and it is of the very essence of the right to cause the debtor inconvenience and embarrassment. The more urgently the debtor needs the item, the more likely he is to pay his debt in order to regain possession. It follows that a creditor who exerts pressure by invoking his right of retention employs his right in a normal rather than an abusive manner. Once, an American court used a very similar argument in a case involving an attorney's retaining lien. See Bulk Oil Transports, Inc. v. Robins Dry Dock & Repair Co., 277 F. 25, 30–31 (2d Cir.1921), cert. denied, 257 U.S. 657, 42 S.Ct. 184 (1922). Prof. Catala–Franjou apparently considers the right of retention as one which cannot be abused under any circumstances, because their exercise is within the absolute discretion of the party involved. See *supra* n. 256. But query, whether, at least in some instances, the exercise of a right of retention might not be abusive in spite of the argument just given, for instance, if a physician who has not been paid refuses to pass a patient's medical records on to another physician who needs them in a life threatening situation.[1] Note that if the plaintiff in the instant situation felt he had a damage claim for malpractice, he would not have lost that claim by paying the accountant when the tax authorities wanted to begin their audit. Perhaps the court considered that, in a way, the plaintiff was responsible for his own predicament. This may be an alternative "realist" rationale for the decision. Under German law, the garage owner could have defeated the accountant's retaining lien by posting security. German Civil Code § 273 III. Note also that while many "abuse of rights" cases involve property rights, the instant case involves a contract-based right. But there does not appear to be any principle that such rights are absolute and thus not subject to the "abuse of rights doctrine."[2]

(2) In connection with the French doctrine of abuse of rights, it is interesting to note that sometimes problems have been involved which have occurred in the United States as well, but which have received a legislative solution. Thus it has been held that a husband's refusal, after a civil divorce, to provide the document known as *"get"* to his wife, such a document making it possible for the wife eventually to be considered as divorced under Jewish religious law and thus able to remarry in a religious ceremony, can be an "abuse."[3] It will also be

---

1. A lower court in Germany held that, since a patient may need medical records for the purpose of treatment by another doctor, there is no right to retain such records, even if they are actually sought for the purpose of malpractice litigation. District Court Freiburg, December 4, 1989, 43 N.J.W. 770 (1990).

2. See also, discussing a decision of the Supreme Court of Canada based on Quebec law, R. Jukier, *Banque Nationale du Canada v. Houle* (S.C.C.): Implications of an Expanded Doctrine of Abuse of Rights in Civilian Contract Law, 37 McGill L.J.221 (1992); with regard to Scots law and other mixed jurisdictions, E. Reid, The Doctrine of Abuse of Rights: Perspectives from a Mixed Jurisdiction, 8 El.J.Comp.L. (2004).

3. See e.g. Cass.civ. 2d, Nov. 21, 1990, 1991 D.J. 434 (holding in essence that damages for abuse of right are appropriate in such a case, but that an *astreinte* imposing a penalty for each day of non-deliverance of the get would not be; see also the critical appended note by Prof. Agostini). This should be

an "abuse" if a landowner, by actions on his own land, prevents legal construction on adjacent property.[4]

(3) The German scheme for dealing with "abusive" exercise of rights is as comprehensive as the French. The tort provision of Section 826 of the German Civil Code (*supra* sec. B(1), text at 925–26) imposes liability on one who intentionally harms another in a manner violating the precepts of *boni mores*. Sec. 138 (see note 4 to S. S. v. M. E. Corp., *supra* at 565) invalidates contracts and other *transactional acts* which violate that principle. From these provisions, and from Sections 157 and 242 which prescribe that all transactions (or "jural acts") should be construed and carried out in good faith, German theorists and judges inferred the existence of a general principle as broad as that explicitly stated in the famous Art. 2 of the Swiss Civil Code.[5]

(4) An illustrative German case dealt with facts which, in somewhat simplified form, may be stated as follows:[6] Plaintiff's husband and her 19–year-old son had deserted from the German army a few weeks before the final collapse of the Nazi government in 1945; they were kept in hiding by plaintiff. Defendant, as the local deputy of the Reich Defense Commissar, was in charge, locally, of a last-ditch drive against "deserters and defeatists." Having heard, through an informer, of the whereabouts of plaintiff's husband and son, defendant had both of them arrested and summarily killed. The husband was shot to death in plaintiff's presence. The killings were in violation even of the positive "laws" then in existence, which required a trial, however perfunctory, before a drumhead court-martial.

Defendant argued that he had acted as an official of the Reich, in the exercise of a public function, and that pursuant to clear provisions of law only the Reich and not the individual official could be held liable for a tort committed under such circumstances. Technically, this was correct. However, at the time when the plaintiff brought her action, the Reich was defunct, and the new German Federal Republic refused to assume the liabilities of the Reich. Hence, plaintiff's cause of action against the former Reich was, as a practical matter, unenforceable and valueless. Held for plaintiff. On their face, applicable provisions of law support defendant's argument that the liability of the Reich for defendant's tort is exclusive. But defendant is abusing his right to invoke that defense. In cases of torts committed by public officials, the exclusive liability of the public body that employed the official has been established by law for two reasons: (1) to protect officials from the threat of civil action, because such threat might inhibit their initiative, and (2) to assist the victim by enabling him to obtain a judgment against a judgment-debtor of unquestionable solvency. In the case at bar the second reason does not hold, the Reich being defunct; and the first reason cannot apply to an act so bestial as to deserve no encouragement whatever. Therefore, the reasons for the principle of the Reich's

compared with the New York "Get" law, N.Y. Dom.Rel. L. § 253 (McKinney 1986).

4. Compare Cass.civ. 3d, March 20, 1978, 1978 Bull.Civ. III No. 128, with N.Y. Real Prop. Actions & Proc. L. § 881 (McKinney 1979); for further French cases regarding abuses related to the exercise of

property rights, see G. Viney & P. Jourdain, *supra* p. 978, note 2, 1213–1216.

5. Art. 2 of the Swiss Civil Code is quoted by Gutteridge, Abuse of Rights, *supra* at 977.

6. Bundesgerichtshof, July 12, 1951, BGHZ 3, 94.

exclusive liability being absent here, the defendant may not invoke the provisions, however plainly apposite, embodying that principle.

(5) Suppose M, who is unmarried, gives birth to a child C. As co-plaintiffs, M and C's guardian sue D, alleging that he is the father of C. M falsely testifies that she had intercourse with D during the period in question. Her testimony is not under oath, but the court seems inclined to believe her and to put her under oath at the next hearing. Thinking that his case is hopeless, D does not appear at that hearing, and the court enters a default judgment against him (a) in favor of M, for $700 hospital expenses, (b) in favor of C, for support in the amount of $120 per month until C reaches the age of 16. D pays M $700, and pays for C's support for two years. He then finds out that during the last year before C's birth, M lived with a man named X. Blood tests are thereupon taken, which establish with certainty that D is not the father of C. Faced with the true facts, M admits that her former testimony was false. D now sues M for repayment of $700. At the same time, he sues C for repayment of the support paid, and asks for a declaratory judgment declaring that he is not liable for further support. The action is based on Sec. 826 of the German Civil Code.[7]

A German court would have no difficulty whatever in letting D recover from M. Relief against judgments has been granted under the broad provision of Sec. 826 not only in cases in which the judgment was obtained by fraud, but also in other cases in which the following three factors are present: (a) the judgment must be incorrect; (b) such incorrectness must be known to the judgment-creditor at the time when he enforces the judgment; and (c) there must be "special circumstances" (not necessarily amounting to fraud in procuring the judgment) which render such enforcement immoral. In the case at hand, there can be no doubt as to the first two factors, and the third would be found in M's false testimony and the concealment of her relationship with X. The res judicata effect of the former judgment is disregarded on the ground that even though the policy implemented by the rule of res judicata is an important one, the principle of morality and justice reflected in Sec. 826 is of a higher order.[8]

7. There are specific provisions for setting aside a judgment obtained by false testimony. German Code of Civil Procedure § 580. But these provisions are not applicable here because the judgment, being a default judgment, technically was not based on M's testimony.

8. See Bundesgerichtshof, Decision of June 21, 1951, 4 N.J.W. 759 (1951), cited with approval in BGHZ 50, 115, at 117 (1968); for further cases, see B. S. Markesinis & H. Unberath, *supra* p. 955, note 7, 890–892. A similar result was reached by the Japanese Supreme Court, which based its decision (in a very dramatic factual setting) on the express prohibition of "abuse of rights" in § 1 of the Japanese Civil Code, as amended in 1947. See Professor Toru Ikuyo's report on Civil Law, 12 The Japan Annual of Law and Politics 33 (1964); J. O. Haley, The Spirit of Japanese Law 126ff (2006). On the Japanese general clause on good faith see J. O. Haley, *supra*, 164ff; H. Oda, Japanese Law, 10, 51, 134–136 (2d ed. 2001).

The American rule has traditionally distinguished between "extrinsic" and "intrinsic" fraud and thus is considerably more restrictive. See, e.g., R. C. Casad, Res Judicata in A Nutshell 275–76 (1976). There is, however, a more modern view that questions the usefulness of that distinction. This view comes, in its effect, close to the position of the German courts. See the Restatement (Second) Judgments, § 68, especially comment a and § 70, comment c (1982).

As to whether D would prevail against C, the cases are in conflict. It has been held that a party such as C's guardian, who did nothing improper in the prior litigation and was unaware at that time of the falsity of M's testimony, may continue to enforce the judgment even if subsequently he learns of the true facts; but there is authority also for the opposite view: that the element of immorality on the part of C's guardian is supplied by his attempt to exploit, *after* he has acquired full knowledge of the facts, a default judgment which the judgment-debtor permitted to be entered because he was the victim of a fraud.[9]

(6) Numerous other German cases applying the doctrine of abuse of rights rely on the principle of good faith announced in Section 242 of the Civil Code (see note 20 to S. S. v. M. E. Corp. *supra* at 571) rather than on the concept of *boni mores* embodied in Section 138 and in the tort provision of Section 826. It was held, for example, that a party to a contract who had advised the other party that the contract could be validly entered into without any formality was prevented by the principle of good faith from later interposing a defense based on the Statute of Frauds.[10] Similarly, the defense of the Statute of Limitations was disallowed if interposed by one who, by settlement negotiations conducted in bad faith, had caused the plaintiff to refrain from the timely commencement of an action.[11]

It was further held that a party to a contract may not suddenly avail himself of a right of rescission which by the terms of the contract he may exercise in the event of certain contingencies, if in prior similar situations he failed to exercise the right and thus led the other party to believe that he did not insist on rigorous enforcement of the contract clause in question. In numerous other cases it was decided that even before the expiration of the statutory period of limitation the exercise of a right may be violative of the principles of good faith and hence improper, if the plaintiff has been silent during a long period of time, and if defendant has changed his position in reliance upon plaintiff's continued inaction.

(7) Subsequently, German legal authors have gone even further and have postulated that non-performance of a contract should be excused under principles of *bona fides* whenever such non-performance serves interests or values which are of a higher order than those promoted by the contract. The famous singer who at the last minute refuses to honor her engagement because her child suddenly has become gravely ill, and she feels that she must not leave the child's bedside, furnishes a fine textbook example.[12] In 2002 the doctrinal rule was embodied in § 275 (3) BGB, according to which

9. See G. Reinicke, Die Kollision zwischen Rechtsfrieden und Gerechtigkeit, 5 N.J.W. 3 (1952) (the title of this article means "The Conflict between Legal Peace and Justice"); see also B. S. Markesinis & H. Unberath, *supra* p. 955, note 7, 356–372.

10. See the decision of the Bundesgerichtshof reported in 1959 Versicherungsrecht 145, 147, where the German court cited and followed the similar holding of the Swiss Federal Court in BGE 72 II 39 (1946); see also the rulings quoted by H. Beale, A. Hartkamp, H. Kötz, D. Tallon, *supra* p. 874, note 2, 279–284.

11. In U.S. law, the doctrine of equitable estoppel generally leads to similar results.

12. See H. W. Baade, Hoggan's History, 16 Am.J.Comp.L. 391 (1968), where a highly controversial German case involving conscientious scruples about performing a contract is presented and analyzed.

"(3) ... the obligor may refuse performance if he is to render the performance in person and, when the obstacle to the performance of the obligor is weighed against the interest of the obligee in performance, performance cannot be reasonably required of the obligor".

How would an American court deal with problems of this kind? Would it make a difference whether the promisee sues at law or in equity, and whether the plaintiff pursues a performance, reliance, or restitutionary interest?

(a) Notes and Questions on Legislative Provisions on Abuse of Right

In developing the far-reaching doctrines discussed above, the French and German courts did not have the benefit of any code provision expressly phrased in terms of "abuse of rights." Many of the more recent codes, however, influenced by the famous Art. 2 of the Swiss Civil Code (quoted by Gutteridge, *supra* at 977),[13] contain explicit provisions of this kind.

(1) In the, Greek Civil Code of 1946 we find two relevant provisions. Art. 288, which is part of the Second Book ("Obligations"), is practically identical with the *bona fides* provision (§ 242) of the German Code. Its importance, however, has been eclipsed by Art. 281 (in the last chapter of the First Book, the "General Part"), which reads as follows:

> The exercise of a right is improper if it evidently exceeds the limits drawn by bona fides, boni mores, or by the social or economic purpose of such right.

During the early years after the enactment of the 1946 Code, the highest court of Greece approached this provision very cautiously and treated it as inapplicable to the exercise (a) of contractual rights and (b) of rights created by cogent rules of law. The Greek Supreme Court abandoned the first of these restrictions fairly quickly, but remained circumspect in dealing with the second of them.[14]

(2) In the Netherlands, the draft of a new Civil Code contained a somewhat detailed provision on the abuse of rights. Perhaps influenced by it, the Dutch Supreme Court decided in 1970 that where the harm caused by the exercise of a right was so great that under the circumstances the person involved, if reasonable, would not have so acted, there could be an abuse of the right.[15] The

---

13. An illustrative Swiss case, in which Art. 2 as well as Art. 1 of the Civil Code was invoked by the court in support of the result reached, appears *infra* at 995. For a discussion of Art. 2 and of the cases implementing it, see V. Bolgar, Abuse of Rights in France, Germany and Switzerland: A Survey of a Recent Chapter in Legal Doctrine, 35 La. L.Rev. 1015, 1030–36 (1975); F. Dessemontet, T. Ansay, *supra* p. 876, note 10, 11, 173.

14. See, e.g., N. A. Deloukas, Der Rechtsmissbrauch im griechischen Privatrecht, in M. Rotondi, L'Abus de Droit 55, at 62 (1979); A. N. Hatzis, Greek Contract Law, *supra* p. 970, note 2, 17; H. L. McCarthy,

Abuse of Rights—Europe's Legal Elephant, 6 Gray Inn's Tax Chambers Rev. 47, 50 f. (2007). For a translation of Greek Civil Code art. 281, see K. D. Kerameus & Ph. J. Kozyris, Introduction to Greek Law 60 (2d rev. ed. 1993), and see also, *id.* at 61, the discussion of the Greek doctrine, to some extent based on the "abuse of right" provision of the Code, of "deactivation of right," somewhat similar to equitable estoppel or latches.

15. Decision of the Hoge Raad of April 17, 1970, 1971 Ned.Jur. 89, summarized in J. M. J. Chorus, P.–H. M. Gerver, E. H. Hondius, Introduction to Dutch Law 111 (4th ed. 2007).

final version of the new Civil Code of the Netherlands contains an Article 3:13 on abuse of rights, fairly closely modelled on the original draft, which reads as follows:[16]

1. The holder of a right may not exercise it to the extent that it is abused.

2. Instances of the abuse of right are the exercise of a right with the sole intention of harming another or for a purpose other than for which it was granted; or the exercise of a right where its holder could not reasonably have decided to exercise it, given the disproportion between the interest to exercise the right and the harm caused thereby.

3. The nature of the right can be such that it cannot be abused.

(3) In 1987, Luxembourg, which uses the French Civil Code (without, of course, the subsequent amendments adopted in France, and subject to the amendments made by the Luxembourg Legislature), adopted a new Article 6–1 of the Civil Code dealing in briefer form than in the Netherlands with abuse of rights. It reads:

Any deliberate act which manifestly exceeds, by its purpose or by the circumstances in which it is carried out, the normal exercise of a right shall not be protected by the law, shall incur the liability of the person responsible and may constitute grounds for action to restrain him from persisting in said abuse.[17]

(4) In Canada, the Quebec courts did adopt a doctrine of abuse of rights, extending it eventually to contract as well as to property rights.[18] The "abuse of rights" principle was then expressly incorporated into the new Quebec Civil Code of 1994 as Article 7:

No right may be exercised with the intent of injuring another or in an excessive and unreasonable manner which is contrary to the requirement of good faith.

(5) The Louisiana Civil Code, contrary to the French Code, did contain some rules on the unreasonable exercise of rights by landowners affecting neighboring properties, but nothing on abuse of rights generally. Attempts to introduce a general provision on "abuse of rights" during the recent revisions which the Code has undergone encountered fairly strong opposition and were abandoned. The Louisiana courts do, however, recognize the doctrine of abuse of rights, but apply it conservatively.[19]

---

16. As translated in New Netherlands Civil Code Patrimonial Law: Property, Obligations and Special Contracts (P. P. C. Haanappel & E. Mackaay trans., 1990). For a comment on the original draft and the decision mentioned, see J. H. Brunner, Abuse of Rights in Dutch Law, 37 La.L.Rev. 729 (1977); with regard to Art. 3:13 BW, J. M. J. Chorus, P.–H. M. Gerver, E. H. Hondius, *supra* note 15, 111, 244.

17. As quoted by J. M. Perillo, *supra* p. 974, note 1 at 39 n.6.

18. See R. Jukier, *supra* note 2, discussing a case in which the Supreme Court of Canada, applying Quebec law, found abuse in the action of a bank which had extended a line of credit to the plaintiffs but then canceled the line of credit, called in the loan, and realized on its security just when the plaintiffs were engaged in discussions concerning the sale of their business. Prof. Jukier noted that plaintiffs would have had a claim in the common-law provinces of Canada as well, but based on a specific narrow rule, not on abuse of rights.

19. See A. N. Yiannopoulos, Civil Liability for Abuse of Right: Something Old, Something New, 54 La.L.Rev. 1173 (1994)

(6) In some Latin American countries, courts and legal authors, strongly influenced by French writers, especially Josserand, adopted the "abuse of rights" principle.[20] An interesting development took place in Argentina. The Argentine Civil Code initially contained an Article 1071 providing that the exercise of a right or the performance of a legal obligation could not constitute an unlawful act. In 1968, however, as part of a revision of the Code,[21] the sentence was modified to state that the "regular" exercise of a right, etc. could not constitute an unlawful act; furthermore a paragraph was added which provides in essence that the law does not protect an abuse of rights, defining an abuse of rights as an act contrary to the purposes of the law or exceeding the limits imposed by good faith, good customs and morals.

(7) In Japan, the doctrine of abuse of rights, originally developed by the courts under European influence, was expressly incorporated into the Civil Code by a 1947 amendment. But it has been said that "The number of cases wherein the doctrine is applied did not notably increase after incorporation into the Code." K. Sono & Y. Fujioka, The Role of the Abuse of Rights Doctrine in Japan, 35 La.L.Rev. 1037, 1044 (1975). It may be true that its codification did not, by itself, have a great impact on the treatment of the abuse of rights doctrine by the Japanese courts. But, whether under the influence of the 1947 Code amendment or not, the Japanese courts have been remarkably creative in developing this doctrine. Two aspects of Japanese case-law, both discussed in M. K. Young, Judicial Review of Administrative Guidance: Governmental Encouraged Consensual Dispute Resolution in Japan, 84 Colum.L.Rev. 923, 970–73 (1984), are particularly interesting:

> The Japanese courts have, independently, arrived at formulations surprisingly similar to the last clause of subsection (2) of the Dutch provision,

(reproducing, at 1174, the provisions of the Louisiana Civil Code mentioned in the text); *Id.*, Abuse of Rights in Louisiana Civil Law, in Aequitas and Equity in Civil Law and Mixed Jurisdiction 201–216 (A. M. Rabello ed., 1997). See also G. M. Armstrong, Jr. LaMaster, J. C. LaMaster, Retaliatory Eviction as Abuse of Rights: A Civilian Approach to Landlord–Tenant Disputes, 47 La.L.Rev. 1 (1986); G. Moreland Redman, Abuse of Rights: An Overview of the Historical Evolution and the Current Application in Louisiana Contracts, 32 La.L.Rev. 946 (1987); J. D. Morgan, The Louisiana Abuse of Rights Doctrine, 64 Tulane L.Rev. 1295 (1990); E. Reid, *supra* note 269; M. Byers, *supra* p. 974, note 1, 389ff.

20. See, e.g., for Colombia, the cases and legal writers quoted in Codigo Civil 26–28 (J. Ortega Torres ed., 1986); see also E. Rengifo García, Del Abuso del Derecho al Abuso de la Posición dominante (2002). On abuse of rights in Puerto Rico, see L. Muniz Arguelles, El Abuso del Derecho en la Legislación y en la Jurisprudencia Puertorriqueña,

24 Rev.Jur.Univ.Interam. de P.R. 177 (1990); C. Campos Cruz, Consideraciones en Torno a la Aplicación de la Doctrina del Abuso del Derecho en el Ambito de la Propriedad Horizontal, 63 Rev.Jur.Univ. Puerto Rico 887 (1994). A number of other civil-law jurisdictions have followed the French and German examples, and have adopted the abuse of rights doctrine despite the absence from their codes of any express language dealing with the exercise of rights. For comparative discussions, in addition to those previously cited, see J. Cueto–Rua, Abuse of Rights, 35 La.L.Rev. 965 (1975); C.F. Sessarego, Abuso del derecho (1992); E. D. Oteiza, Abuse of Procedural Rights in Latin America, in Abuse of Procedural Rights: Comparative Standards of Procedural Fairness 191, esp. 199–201 (M. Taruffo ed., 1999), and, with specific reference to environmental nuisance litigation, A. N. Yiannopoulos, Violations of the Obligations of Vicinage, 34 La.L.Rev. 475, 504ff (1974).

21. By Law 17711 of 1968.

reproduced above; on the basis of such formulations, they make the success of abuse of rights arguments dependent on a social cost-benefit calculus.

The Japanese courts also have made imaginative use of the abuse of rights doctrine in public-law litigation. Professor Young, in his article, provides this example: The Japanese, as is well known, believe strongly in cooperation between governmental bodies and private business enterprises. Accordingly, the competent governmental bodies often issue some form of "guidance" to private firms, even in the absence of statutory authority. Municipalities, for instance, often use such "guidance" to persuade developers to reach an amicable accord with adjoining property owners concerned with the impact of the proposed project on their enjoyment of sunlight, air, etc. The aim obviously is to have the relative rights of developer and adjoining property owners determined by negotiation, not litigation. This is in conformity with the general Japanese attitude towards law and the legal process (see *supra* ___). While, presumably, negotiations based on official "guidance" are normally successful, litigation ensued in one instance (see Young, *supra*, 84 Colum.L.Rev. at 971) because the municipality involved, feeling that the failure of the negotiations was due to the developer's insufficient compliance with official "guidance," refused to supply water to the building erected by the developer. The latter than sued the municipality, asking the Tokyo District court to compel it, by injunction, to provide water. While the developer technically had a right to have his building connected to the water supply, the court did not grant the injunction as a matter of course but first examined carefully whether the developer had made a reasonable effort to reach an agreement with his neighbors concerning their demands for more access to sunlight and air. Only after it concluded that such an effort had taken place was the injunction issued. The case thus stands for the proposition that though a developer may have a formal right to obtain water from a municipality, he abuses that right, and thus will be defeated in any suit seeking to assert it, if he has failed to negotiate in good faith with his neighbors. The municipality's public-law obligation to supply water is thus qualified by the doctrine of abuse of rights, which enables the court, through the use of a cost-benefit analysis, to determine whether the positions taken by the developer and the efforts made by him in the negotiations with the neighbors, were reasonable. Pressure is thus put on the developer to base his relations with his neighbors on reasonable compromise rather than the vindication of legal rights. And even if, exceptionally, compromise is not attained and litigation ensues, it is determined not on the basis of technical legal rights, but on the basis of the court's assessment of the question whether the developer acted reasonably in his negotiations with his neighbors.[22]

(8) Do you think any of the statutory provisions above are necessary, useful? Which one would seem to be the most helpful one? What would you take into consideration in that context?

(b) Comment on Abuse of Right in the Common Law

With respect to each of the cases from civil law sources reproduced or summarized in the foregoing materials, the reader will ask whether an Ameri-

---

22. Further references in C. F. Goodman, The Rule of Law in Japan: A Compara-   tive Analysis 46, 223–226, 272, 354–358 (2d ed. 2003).

can court would have reached the same result. In many instances, the answer will be in the affirmative.

Note, however, the difference in the methods by which the results, even identical results, are reached. The American or English lawyer cannot point to a recognized general concept of abuse of rights, i.e., to a single doctrine so pervasive that it will serve sometimes as a basis for a cause of action and sometimes as a defense or reply, in cases involving such diverse matters as contracts, judgments, family relations, exercise of property rights, and tortious interference with every conceivable type of interest. Therefore, such a lawyer will have to invoke numerous, seemingly unconnected doctrines in dealing with the vast array of cases which civil law lawyers subsume under *Rechtsmissbrauch, abus de droit,* etc.[23]

In which of the cases mentioned above would an Anglo–American lawyer resort to equitable doctrines, such as estoppel and laches? In which of them would he or she argue for the application of one of our specific, compartmentalized tort doctrines, such as false imprisonment, malicious prosecution, abuse of process, and the like?[24] Which of the cases could, in U.S. law., be brought under the prima facie theory of tort?[25]

The absence from US law of a broad, unifying theory of abuse of rights is particularly apparent in cases of spiteful or otherwise antisocial exercise of proprietary rights. To a common-law court dealing with a spite fence problem, it will not easily occur to look for enlightenment in an earlier case involving percolating waters, even though, judging by results, the same principle seems to govern both situations.[26] Statutes of narrow coverage limited to specific problems further reinforce the casuistic character of our method.[27]

23. But note the recent thesis by Prof. Perillo, to the effect that the notion of an "abuse of rights" underlies many of the American decisions in the areas mentioned, though the principle is not usually expressly cited. He does, however, mention Shiver v. United States, 159 U.S. 491, 497, 16 S.Ct. 54, 56 (1895), where the court speaks of a "... manifest abuse of such right." See Perillo, *supra* p. 974, note 1 at 38–39, & 96.

24. For an exhaustive review of American cases where the abuse of rights principle is relevant, see Perillo, *supra* p. 974, note 1. In spite of the tendency of American law to prefer highly fact-specific rules, there are occasional calls for a broader approach. See P. Ward, The Tort Cause of Action, 42 Cornell L.Q. 28, 38 (1956). Nevertheless, when a new tort rule is recognized by statute or case law, courts and commentators brought up in the common-law method frequently proceed to splinter it into numerous (and more or less traditional) categories. This tendency to create rigid new compartments has been decried by E. J. Bloustein, Privacy as an Aspect of Human Dignity: An Answer to Dean Prosser, 39 N.Y.U.L.Rev. 962 (1964) (discussing Prosser's attempt to break down the tort of viola-

tion of the right of privacy into several subcategories).

25. For an interesting discussion of the origin and purpose of the prima facie tort theory, see Nees v. Hocks, 272 Or. 210, 536 P.2d 512 (1975). Many of our courts apply that theory only in cases in which it was the sole or at least the primary purpose of defendant's act to harm the plaintiff. See, e.g., Reinforce, Inc. v. Birney, 308 N.Y. 164, 124 N.E.2d 104 (1954), and other cases cited by M. D. Forkosch, An Analysis of the "Prima Facie" Tort Cause of Action, 42 Cornell L.Q. 465, 476–80 (1957). See also J. E. Brown, The Rise and Threatened Demise of the Prima Facie Tort Principle, 54 Nw.U.L. Rev. 563 (1959); J. C. P. Goldberg, A. J. Sebok, B. C. Zipursky, Tort Law. Responsibility and Redress, 659 (2004). The prima facie tort thus becomes just another narrow pigeonhole, as has been shown by the case of Drago v. Buonagurio, 46 N.Y.2d 778, 413 N.Y.S.2d 910, 386 N.E.2d 821 (1978).

26. Compare Hathorn v. Natural Carbonic Gas Co., 194 N.Y. 326, 87 N.E. 504 (1909), with Schork v. Epperson, 74 Wyo. 286, 287 P.2d 467 (1955).

In the U.S. law of contracts, also, one can observe the lack of a unifying principle concerning the improper exercise of rights, especially in cases where brutal unilateral termination of a contract or lease, though consistent with the terms of the agreement, causes undue hardship or loss.[28] Should such termination be treated as ineffective at least in those instances in which it can be shown that its true purpose was to intimidate the other party, or to punish him or her for the exercise of an unquestioned statutory or constitutional right? Our courts, unable to invoke an established formula such as "abuse of rights," thus far have failed to agree on a principled answer to this question.[29]

Lest one exaggerate the importance of the difference between civil-law and common-law methods, it is well to keep in mind that the civil-law judge, even though using a general principle as a guide, still has to determine, from case to case, whether and in what way the principle should be applied. In addition, once it has been generally recognized that a particular social problem exists, the case-law solution based on a general principle, such as abuse of rights, may be converted into a more narrow, separate legal category or may eventually be replaced by a specific statutory provision.[30] When that is the case, the temptation is strong to think, henceforth, only in terms of the new regulatory provision, rather than in terms of the broad principle. Nevertheless, broad categories do not lose their significance, because they may furnish the basis for appropriate court action in the novel situations, not yet covered by legislation, that always arise in a changing society.[31] Furthermore, as the fate of the French rules on "abusive" contracts shows,[32] if specific legislation is drawn too narrowly to achieve its aim, a broader concept can then intervene.

27. See, e.g., the statutes cited *supra* at pp. 985–86, notes 3 and 4, and compare with the French cases there cited.

28. Employing the casuistic method which in common-law countries usually permeates the statutory as well as the decisional law, Congress has dealt with a narrow and specific parts of this problem, e.g., in the Automobile Dealer Franchise Act of 1956, 15 U.S.C.A. §§ 1221–1225.

29. In U.S. law., the pertinent rules appear to be enshrined in separate compartments. In one compartment, we find the rules governing retaliatory evictions. See 23 A.L.R.5th 140 (1994). Cases in which an employee, serving under an employment contract terminable at will has been discharged for reprehensible reasons are treated and collected in an entirely different compartment. See 93 A.L.R.5th 269 (2001), 104 A.L.R.5th 1 (2002). See also Mt. Healthy City School Dist. Bd. of Educ. v. Doyle, 429 U.S. 274, 283–84, 97 S.Ct. 568, 574 (1977). The rules developed within these compartments are not remembered when cases arise that involve yet other types of contracts, and the absence of a unifying principle may lead to inconsistent results.

Compare House of Materials, Inc. v. Simplicity Pattern Co., 298 F.2d 867, 871–73 (2d Cir.1962) (no relief for retaliatory termination of supplier-customer relationship), *with* L'Orange v. Medical Protective Co., 394 F.2d 57 (6th Cir.1968) (relief granted in a case of retaliatory termination of medical malpractice insurance). As noted, a comprehensive collection of pertinent cases can be found in Perillo, *supra* p. 974, note 1.

30. See the French rules mentioned *supra* at p. 982, notes 2 and 3.

31. Thus the French courts have created a principle of "abuse of a minority position in a corporation" when minority stockholders, who enjoy a blocking position, refuse to go along with majority proposals deemed to be necessary for the good of the company. Consorts Palthey v. Crepet, Cour d'appel Lyon, December 20, 1984, 1986 D.J. 506 (with a note by Prof. Reinhard); see also M. Tricot, Abus de droit dans la sociétés: abus de majorité et abus de minorité, Rev.Trim.Dr. Com. 716 (1994); F.-X. Lucas, La responsabilité des associés minoritaires, 118 Dr.Patrim. 59 (2003).

32. See the discussion *supra* p. 979, note 4.

The common-law judge, on the other hand, who has no verbalized general concept of abuse of rights as a starting point, and who has to find the pertinent authorities under the most disparate headings, may almost subconsciously sense the existence of the underlying general principle. The fact remains, nevertheless, that the civilian thinks in terms of more abstract, considerably broader categories than a follower of the common-law tradition. This is not without practical significance.[33] When a case arises which does not fit into any of our narrower mental compartments, a common-law court must either refuse relief, or take the difficult, seemingly revolutionary step of expanding or exploding the existing compartments. In the same situation, a civil-law court may find it easier to innovate, because it can rationalize the result as the mere "application" of an established general principle.[34]

Opinion of the Swiss Federal Court in the Matter of Weber, Huber & Cie., Defendant–Appellant, Against "Rimba," Plaintiff–Respondent

1st Civil Division, November 4, 1931, BGE 57 II 528.

On November 4, 1930, the M Corporation and defendant entered into a contract of sale under the terms of which M Corporation bound itself to sell, and defendant bound itself to buy, 200 tons of Polish mineral oil, at a price of Fr. 7.60 per 100 kilograms, payable 14 days after shipment.

On December 22, 1930, M Corporation and J Corporation made an agreement by which the latter took over all of the assets and liabilities of the former, and changed its firm name to Rimba Corporation. The excess of the value of the assets of M Corporation over the amount of its liabilities was Fr. 118,266.42 as of December 31, 1930, and this amount was paid to the shareholders of M Corporation by way of transfer to them of sixty-two (62) fully paid shares of J Corporation [now Rimba Corporation]. The President of M Corporation was elected a member of the Board of Directors of Rimba. On Jan. 7, 1931, the registration of M Corporation in the Register of Commerce was canceled, on the basis of a resolution of the Shareholders' Meeting of December 23, 1930, and of the above-mentioned

---

33. The law of privacy furnishes interesting illustrations of the point. See B. C. Murchison' and R. Wacks' articles collected in New Dimensions in Privacy Law: International and Comparative Perspectives, respectively at 32–59 and 154–183 (A. T. Kenyon, M. Richardson eds. 2006); see also J. K. Weeks, Comparative Law of Privacy, 12 Cleveland Marshall L.Rev. 484, especially at 502–03 (1963). But note that seven years after Professor Weeks' article, the right of privacy received a statutory sanction in France. See French Civil Code art. 9. [Rumor has it that this was done at the insistence of then French President (and former Prime Minister) Pompidou who, already ill with cancer, did not want any prying into the state of his health.]

34. With his usual perceptiveness, the late Judge Jerome Frank in two of his opinions (they are well worth reading) emphasized the great influence which a convenient generalization may have on the development of the law. See Guiseppi v. Walling, 144 F.2d 608, 618–19 (2d Cir.1944); Granz v. Harris, 198 F.2d 585, 590–91 (2d Cir.1952).

agreement of December 22, 1930. About the middle of January 1931, the defendant was advised by a circular letter that the assets and liabilities of M Corporation had been taken over by Rimba. Immediately upon receipt of this letter the defendant answered that it could not consent to the transfer to, or assumption by, Rimba of rights and obligations under the contract of November 4, 1930, and that it regarded said contract as annulled. Rimba thereupon insisted that the contract be carried out.

On May 5, 1931, Rimba brought the present action for a declaratory judgment against the defendant, praying for a declaration to the effect that

(1) The contract of November 4, 1930 was validly taken over by the plaintiff and

(2) The defendant is bound to accept two hundred (200) tons of Polish mineral oil from the plaintiff ... and to pay the purchase price of Fr. 15,184 plus interest....

On July 16, 1931 the Commercial Court of the Canton of St. Gallen entered judgment granting the relief demanded by the plaintiff....

[Upon defendant's appeal, the Federal Court affirmed.]

Reasons: 1. If the transaction entered into by M Corporation and J Corporation had constituted a merger in the technical sense of the term, the defendant would have had no choice but to accept the merged corporation as the new obligor of the obligation to deliver the oil. In other words, the consent of the defendant to such change of the person of the obligor would have been unnecessary in that event. It is just for this reason [because the creditors have no choice] that article 669 of the Code of Obligations provides for certain measures of protection in favor of the creditors of merged corporations.[1] But it is questionable whether in the present case there was a merger in the proper sense of the word.

[The Court then points out that according to the view taken by the more recent commentators, two requirements must be met if a transaction is to be treated as a merger in the technical sense of the word: (a) the shareholders of the dissolved corporation must receive payment in the form of shares of the receiving corporation, and (b) the shares of the receiving corporation thus given to the former shareholders of the dissolved corporation must be simultaneously created by an increase in the capital of the receiving corporation. In the present case the first requirement was met; but the second was not, because the sixty-two shares issued to the former shareholders of M Corporation had previously been in the portfolio of J Corporation (as treasury stock), and were not authorized by way of a capital increase immediately preceding such issuance.

---

1. Article 669 (now repealed by the Federal Law no. 221.301 of 2003 on mergers and acquisitions) of the Swiss Code of Obligations provided that in case of merger the assets of the dissolved company were to be kept separate from the assets of the receiving company until the creditors of the former were satisfied or secured.

The Court holds, however, that the court below was correct in leaving open the question whether or not there was a merger in the technical sense of the word; even if there was no merger, plaintiff must win.

The Court takes as its starting point the general rule that one obligor cannot be substituted for another without the consent of the obligee, and that ordinarily this rule must apply even in cases where a whole business, with all its assets and liabilities, is taken over by a purchaser.]

It must be considered, however, that the obligor [of the obligation to sell and deliver the oil] was a corporation. In view of the constant change of economic conditions ..., a person dealing with a corporation must always contemplate the possibility of a merger or of a sale of the whole business of the corporation. For this reason, and because there may always be shifts in the membership of the corporation and in the personnel of its management, the court below correctly held that dealings with a corporation have an impersonal character.... The more modern school of thought among the writers on commercial law emphasizes the concept of the enterprise and of its continuity. Wieland, Commercial Law, Volume 1, page 295. In accordance with this school of thought we hold that where the obligor is a corporation, and such corporation transfers all of its assets and liabilities, the obligee should ordinarily be compelled to accept the transferee as his new obligor unless he can show that there are weighty reasons in the person of the transferee which would make such a result unjust under the particular circumstances of the case. This rule may not apply to all types of contractual relationships; but it does apply, among others, to the contract of sale, which is essentially impersonal in character. In the case at bar the defendant has not adduced any weighty reasons why the transferee should not be acceptable as new obligor.... It is true that this result cannot be based on Article 181 of the Code of Obligations.[2] That provision does not deal with the problem presented by a case in which [as in the instant case] the joint and several liability which Article 181 prescribes for a period of two years is impossible because the registration of the original obligor in the Register of Commerce has been canceled. [What the Court means is apparently this: Article 181 deals with the assumption of liabilities in case A sells his whole business to B. The article provides that during a two year period A and B shall be jointly and severally liable for the obligations of the business which had been incurred prior to the time of its sale. This provision, of course, presupposes that during such two-year period both A

---

2. Art. 181 of the Swiss Code of Obligations reads as follows:

"He who takes over ... a business including assets and liabilities, becomes automatically obligated to the creditors of debts connected therewith, as soon as he has advised the creditors of such taking over or has made a public announcement thereof.

"The old debtor remains liable, severally and jointly, with the new one, for two years [raised to three years by the Feder-

al Law no. 221.301 of 2003 on mergers and acquisitions. Eds.] ..."

For a comparative study of the rights of creditors in cases of this kind, see S. A. Bayitch, Empresa in Latin American Law: Recent Developments, 4 Lawyer of the Americas 1, 7–12 (1972); G. Hertig & H. Kanda, Creditor Protection, in The Anatomy of Corporate Law: A Comparative and Functional Approach 71–99 (R. Kraakman, P. Davies, H. Hansmann, G. Hertig, K. Hopt, H. Kanda, E. Rock eds., 2004).

and B are in existence as natural or juristic persons. In the present case that is not so, because M Corporation, having divested itself of all of its assets and having caused its registration in the Register of Commerce to be canceled, has ceased to exist.[3] The joint and several liability of transferor and transferee, which is contemplated by Article 181 for a period of two years, is therefore impossible. It follows that Article 181 fails to provide a solution for the problem of the instant case.] Therefore, and because there is also no customary law governing this case, we were faced with a gap in the statutory law which had to be filled pursuant to Article 1 of the Civil Code.[4]

2.   Even if one did not wish to go quite so far [meaning: not quite so far as to create a new rule of law by way of judicial lawmaking pursuant to Article 1 of the Civil Code], the question would present itself whether defendant's refusal to accept the plaintiff as its obligor was not an abuse of rights. As to this point, the defendant has merely denied that the precipitous decline in the price of oil constituted the reason for such refusal; but defendant has not indicated any other reason. [The Court then points out that the principle of Article 2, paragraph 2, of the Civil Code,[5] is broad enough to cover the present case. Normally, where one party to a bilateral contract has sought to transfer his rights and obligations to a third person, the other party has a right of election: he may accept the transferee as the obligor of the promises made to him, or he may refuse to do so and insist that the contract be performed by the one who made it. But in the present case defendant has abused this right of election. Defendant has pointed to no factual reason why Rimba should be a less desirable seller than M Corporation. It would seem, therefore, that defendant objects to the substitution of a new obligor merely for the reason that, marketwise, the contract has turned out to be disadvantageous from defendant's point of view.] . . . .

3. The Court assumes that dissolution plus deregistration results in the complete death of a Swiss stock corporation. The common-law rule was similar. But corporation laws now generally provide that for the purpose of satisfying claims by creditors, a corporation, even if dissolved, remains in existence. In a number of States, however, this continued existence for a limited purpose exists only for a specified time period, such as six months, if a notice has been given to creditors and they have failed to assert their claims within the time period mentioned. See 16A Fletcher, Cyclopedia of the Law of Private Corporations, § 8113 (Permanent ed. 1995). Cf. N.Y. Bus. Corp. Law §§ 1006, 1007, for a statute of that kind. And see F. K. Juenger & S. H. Schulman, Assets Sales and Products Liability, 22 Wayne L.Rev. 39, 41 (1975). Thus a situation analogous to that in the principal case, i.e., a situation in which the original promisor is no longer suable can arise in an American setting.

4. For a translation of Art. 1 of the Swiss Civil Code, see *supra* at 484. Other cases in which the Swiss courts have utilized the broad authorization expressed in Art. 1 are discussed by A. E. von Overbeck, Some Observations on the Role of the Judge Under the Swiss Civil Code, 37 La.L.Rev. 681 (1977); K. Zweigert & H. Kötz, *supra* p. 879, note 1, 167ff.

5. For a translation of this provision, see H. C. Gutteridge, Abuse of Rights, *supra* this section at 974. The present case is somewhat extraordinary in that it brings both Art. 1 and Art. 2 into play. Should the Court not have discussed the applicability of Art. 2 *before* it exercised its subsidiary law-making power under Art. 1?

NOTES AND QUESTIONS

(1) After having read the foregoing opinion, try to retrace the steps in the reasoning of the Court (a) on the theory of Article 1, and (b) on the theory of Article 2 of the Swiss Civil Code. In connection with the facts of the case, note its date and the economic conditions of that period. Note also that the "Polish mineral oil" involved was clearly just a standard commodity.

With respect to Article 2: What was the right which defendant abused? For what purpose was that right given? For what purpose did defendant seek to use the right? As to its actual purpose, does defendant carry the burden of proof? A burden of explanation? For further examples applying Article 2, see F. Dessemontet, T. Ansay, *supra* p. 876, note 10, 11, 173.

(2) How would a common-law court analyze the problem? In British Waggon Co. v. Lea, 5 Q.B.D. 149 (1879), the Parkgate Waggon Co. had agreed to let a number of railway cars to the defendants and to keep them in repair. The Parkgate Co. went into liquidation and assigned its rights and duties under the agreement to the British Waggon Co. The defendants contended that the contract was at an end, and refused to accept the services of the British Waggon Co. In holding for the plaintiff, on the ground that the defendants could not have attached special importance to the repairs being done by the Parkgate Co., the court said: "*So long as the Parkgate Company continues to exist*, and, through the British Company, continues to fulfil its obligation to keep the waggons in repair, the defendants cannot, in our opinion, be heard to say that the former company is not entitled to the performance of the contract by them." (Italics added). What if the Parkgate Co. did *not continue to exist*? See E. A. Farnsworth, *supra* p. 894, note 11, 682–717. Is this case entirely comparable to the "Rimba" case?

(3) If an American court today had to deal with a fact situation like that in the "Rimba" case, would the doubts existing under the common law be resolved by § 2–210 of the Uniform Commercial Code?

*

INDEX

References are to pages

†